THE ONE ESSENTIAL GUIDE FOR COMIC BOOK FANS EVERYWHERE

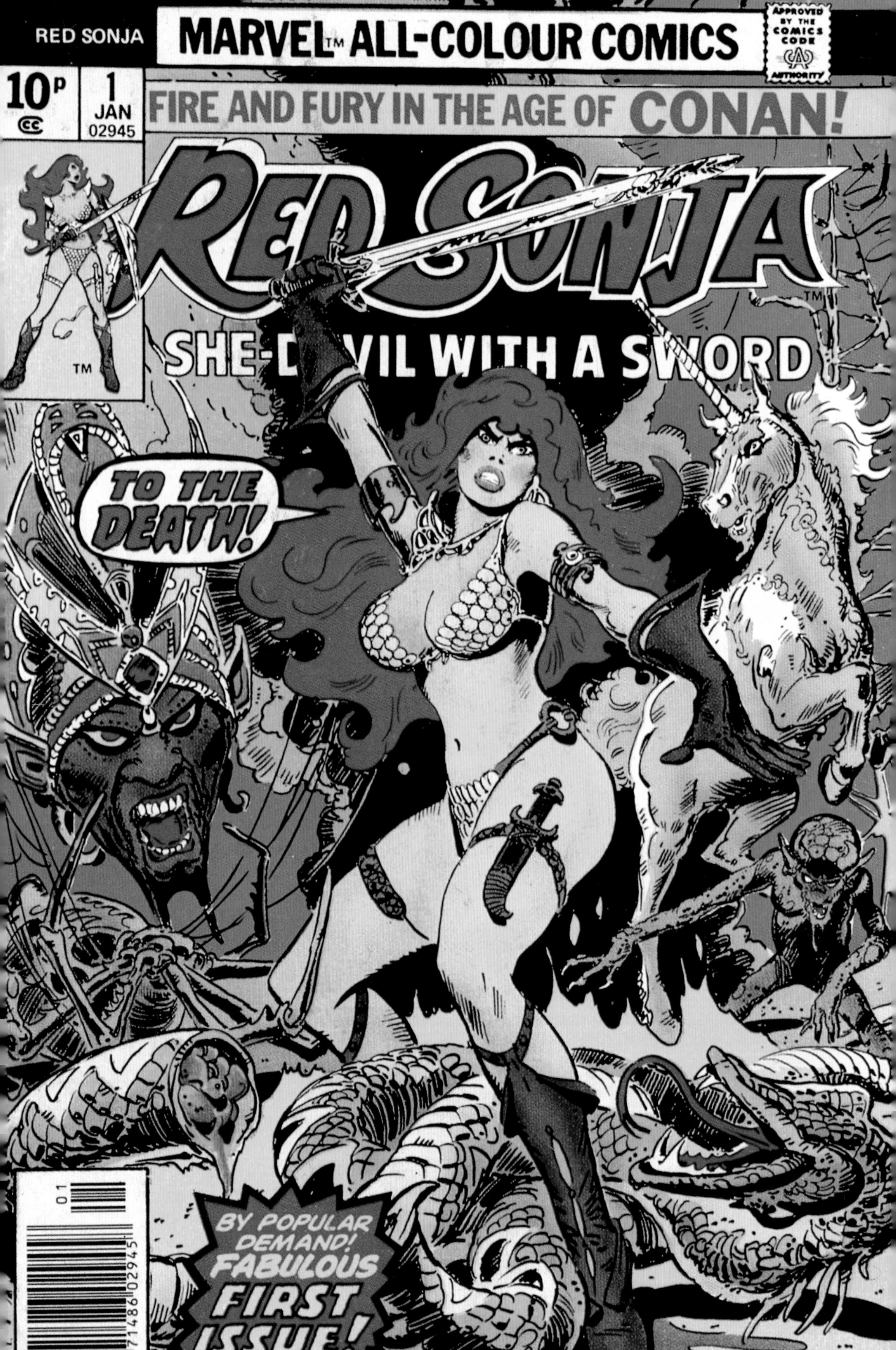

THE COMIC BOOK

THE ONE ESSENTIAL GUIDE FOR COMIC BOOK FANS EVERYWHERE

PAUL SASSIENIE

CHARTWELL
BOOKS, INC.

This book is dedicated to my sons,
Darren Michael Sassienie, and Charles Moss Sassienie,
the next generation of panelologists.

THIS EDITION PUBLISHED BY CHARTWELL BOOKS
A DIVISION OF BOOK SALES INC.
PO BOX 7100
EDISON
NEW JERSEY 08818–7100

1 3 5 7 9 10 8 6 4 2

THIS EDITION PRODUCED FOR BOOK SALES BY EBURY PRESS LIMITED,
20 VAUXHALL BRIDGE ROAD, LONDON SW1V 1SA

EDITED BY MARY REMNANT
DESIGNED BY DAVID FORDHAM
PICTURE RESEARCH BY PAUL SASSIENIE AND NADINE BAZAR

ISBN 1–55521–999–3

PRINTED AND BOUND IN GREAT BRITAIN BY BUTLER AND TANNER LTD, FROME, SOMERSET

CHARTWELL
BOOKS, INC

Opposite title page: RED SONJA No. 1,
January 1977
(™ & Copyright © 1994 Marvel Entertainment Group, Inc.)

Title page: page from DETECTIVE COMICS No. 33,
November 1939, telling in detail for the first time the origin of Batman
(™ & Copyright © DC Comics, Inc.)

CONTENTS

FOREWORD

BY JIM SHOOTER

OU'RE RIDING A SUBWAY TRAIN, THUMBING through a magazine. You come to an ad, done in a comics style. You stop and begin reading it – you almost can't help yourself. The banker next to you, who has been stoically suffering his daily travel ordeal among the hoi polloi with studied aloofness, suddenly begins to read over your shoulder. Further down the car, someone opens his newspaper to the comics page, and straphangers all around manoeuvre for position, craning their necks to read along.

What a powerful medium!

Of course.

Cartoonists have *absolute control* over their message and its presentation. They can take dead aim at an idea and deliver it to readers with great precision. They have the power of the entire English (or other) language working for them, of course, and if that's not enough they can invent **Plasm-speak** or some such. They also can choose any angle, go on location anywhere, and draw anything the human imagination can conjure. Cartoonists are not limited by reality.

They're also not limited by **motion**, as movies are. In the comics, Superman stands tall, proud and powerful – **just so**. He sits erect, dignified and noble – **just so**. In **every single image** his posture conveys his nature and personality. In the movies, inevitably, the camera will catch that awkward protruding-butt moment as the actor sits down. And it is an **actor**, isn't it? You know where to find the **real** Superman, whose cape is always blowing just so.

But you probably knew all that.

What you may not have thought about is the role of the reader. **Your** role, and mine. We're **all** readers.

The comics medium is the only visual medium you take at your own pace – as opposed to its being fed to you at a rate someone else thinks is right.

Straphangers and bankers notwithstanding, the comics medium provides a personal communication between you and the cartoonist, one-on-one. It's an individual experience – and **silent** (unless you're one of those strange types who read them aloud, with or without the dubious excuse of having children around). Jules Feiffer once said, 'radio was too damn public.' Comics are private. You might say intimate. I would.

The best part is that comics are taken in by the **eyes alone**. It's a strictly visual medium, unencumbered by sound. Superman's voice sounds right to you, if you choose to imagine his voice. I never did. The point is that nothing ever sounds wrong, and there are no distractions. No, it isn't the opposite of radio where you're forced to imagine the visual. **It's all their** in comics, but both the audio and the visual are input through your eyes. You choose to 'hear' what you wish, to the extent you wish. Participation, using your mind's ear, is optional.

The ability to set your own pace, combined with the quietness, allow you to concentrate and focus more than is possible, I believe, with two-sense media. Add that fact to the cartoonist's ability to deliver a **pure**, powerful message and it's no wonder comics are uniquely compelling.

The relationship between cartoonist and reader doesn't stop at the initial communication. Comic creators are eminently accessible, much more so than creative types of other media. Spielberg probably won't read your letters, and if you approach him in a public place his bodyguards will probably keep you at bay. However, many – I think **most** – comic creators read their mail eagerly, and if you'd like to tell them what you think face-to-face, you can probably catch them at a convention. Comic readers and creators all come from the same rootstock. We're all readers. We actively pursue contact with one another. Because readers **participate** in the initial, intimate communication by governing, pacing and providing sound, the communication achieved is, in fact, a collaboration between the cartoonist and the reader. There is great joy in this (and any other) creative experience, and so we all want to continue it. We meet and talk, write and read about the medium and each other. Even the most jaded cartoonist cannot help but be influenced by the opinions of readers, or at least by the opinions of other cartoonists – who are readers too, remember. The comics medium is the most collaborative on earth, a grand conspiracy of creativity. God, I love it.

In the beginning was the Word. Soon thereafter came the Light. We can assume that, at that point, you could read the word and see the picture, proving that concept of the comics medium has been around for ever. We're still trying to get it right, but I think we're making progress. What we've got is the most portable, limitless, intense, personal, focused, intimate, compelling, wonderful visual medium in creation.

You're riding the subway. As the stuffy banker objects to your turning the page too quickly, you realize just how powerful this medium called comics truly is. You resolve to learn more about it.

This book is a good place to start.

Jim Shooter

INTRODUCTION

 **Y LOVE AFFAIR WITH COMICS BEGAN AT THE** tail-end of the 1950s when I was seven or eight years old. Every Saturday, my father, an artist who encouraged me to read comics, would buy me *The Dandy, The Beano, The Beezer,* and *The Topper.* Not long after, I graduated to American comics, especially *Superman,* who was and remains a great favourite. However, I found it frustrating to buy *Superman No. 133,* for example, but not have the first 132 issues. I wanted to know what had happened. I wanted to read it from the start!

Once hooked on reading and collecting comics as a hobby, I soon set myself the task of amassing a collection that went back to the beginning. Old comics were difficult to find in London in the early 1960s. Many a weekend, and long bus or train journey ended in disappointment, but it was all worth it when on the odd occasion I would come home with *Superman* or *Batman* comics from the 1940s. I also loved Harvey comics, for the uninitiated, these aren't comics featuring a big white rabbit, but ones published by Harvey Publications that included, *The Friendly Ghost Casper, Sad Sack, Spooky,* and many more. Most Sundays my father took me to London's best known street market, Petticoat Lane, where I usually managed to find missing Harvey issues, in fact more missing issues than my megre pocket-money could stretch to!

By the time I had finished my formal education, which ended with two years at the London College of Printing studying paper, of all things, I had a pretty good comic collection. In the early 1970s, however, comics and I had a brief trial separation. My collection was so big and there were so many new titles being published, that I temporarily stopped buying and reading them. By this time I was in a touring rock band and living away from my parents' home and my comics. Family and friends were not surprised that comics had come to an end in my life, and three or four years went by without my giving them a thought.

One day on a visit to my parents, I re-discovered my treasures. (I would have said re-discovered my youth, but that only leads to old Groucho Marx jokes!) I immediately had a roll-call of all my favourites, they were all still present and correct, and soon after, I transported them from my parents' home to my flat in North London, where I set about re-reading and re-cataloguing every comic. To my amazement I still loved them and nothing had changed!

Now, after more than thirty years, I still get a kick out of Superman fighting for Truth, Justice and the American Way, the Sarge giving the Sad Sack a hard time, Spooky yelling 'Boo!' to anyone in proximity, and Uncle Scrooge swimming in his money-bin. What a great hobby!

Whether you are new to comics or a lapsed panelologist, I hope that this book will serve you both as a source of reference and entertainment.

Paul Sassienie

GOBBLE-GOBBLE GERTIE — SHE GETS HER PIES WITH PERFECT EASE — SHE SHAKES THEM DOWN FROM OUT OF TREES

THE DANDY 2ᴰ

EVERY TUESDAY
No. 657—JUNE 26th, 1954.

KORKY THE CAT

THE HALL IS PACKED, THE SPEAKER SPOUTS—
GOOD JOB HE'S SHORT-SIGHTED!
FOR KORKY SMUGGLED THE AUDIENCE OUT
AND THE AUDIENCE IS DELIGHTED!

HEY! THE TROUT ARE BITING LIKE BILLYO!

HOOKEM ANGLING CLUB

PROFESSOR BOREM WILL LECTURE TO CLUB MEMBERS TO-NIGHT
EVENING DRESS WILL BE WORN

JUST OUR LUCK. WE HAVE TO LISTEN TO THAT OLD BORE SPEAKING.

IS THAT HIM?

YES.

YOU GET YOUR RODS AND BASKETS AND I'LL FIX IT.

ZOO GOODS ENTRANCE

CHEERIO! THEY'LL BE BACK SOON!

OU12

HOOKEM ANGLING CLUB

SMUGGLE 'EM IN ONE AT A TIME, KORKY.

OU12

LATER

HOURS LATER

EXIT

—AND NOW, GENTLEMEN, THAT BRINGS ME TO THE END OF MY TALK — THANK YOU FOR LISTENING SO WELL.

I
History of
Comic Books

PROLOGUE

THE USE OF PICTURES TO TELL A STORY STRETCHES BACK almost to the dawn of man. Palaeolithic art, dating back to the most recent ice age, has been discovered at more than a hundred sites in Western Europe. Cave drawings, depicting the daily lives of cave men, have been found throughout the world, with the oldest known being dated c.14000 BC.

It seems that once our ancestors had found food and shelter, their next task was to draw pictures on cave walls. Drawn with the vitality and elegance of great simplicity, they are our first picture stories and masterpieces of prehistoric art. The painting styles ascribed to Cro-Magnon man embrace a variety of techniques, which include painting with fingers, sticks, pads of fur or moss; daubing; dotting; sketching with coloured material and charcoal; and spray-painting through a hollow bone or by mouth. No one is really sure whether these drawings were used as language, but in most palaeolithic caves, animal figures predominate, suggesting a ritual significance.

▲ CUEVA DE LOS CABALLOS, *prehistoric cave drawing found in Madrid in 1919*

Cave man, believing drawings could magically kill animals, would often paint pictures showing spears being thrown at, or hitting beasts, thus killing them in effigy. Some drawings also ceremoniously praised hunters.

Hundreds of years before they erected the pyramids, the Egyptians had developed hieroglyphics, the first written language. This consisted of 604 different symbols, each with up to three meanings, which were used to form a series of conceptual readable drawings. Inside the pyramids, Egyptian artists drew complex contiguous wall paintings, accompanied by hieroglyphic narration.

Egyptian funerary literature, the Book of the Dead, contained drawings and text consisting of charms, spells and formulas for use by the deceased in the after-world. At first inscriptions, the texts were later papyrus rolls placed inside the mummy case. The earliest collection is from the XVIII dynasty (1554–1350 BC).

▲ *Greek vase showing Theseus killing the Minotaur, sixth century* BC (Michael Holford)

The Greeks often used ornate pictures to decorate their vases and friezes, some commemorating important events or great battles. Artists portrayed Greek heroes such as Achilles and Ajax, and later the Ulysses epic became a recurring theme. Hercules, Hermes, Zeus, and other Greek gods were also great favourites.

◄ THE DANDY No. 657, *26 June 1964* (Copyright © 1994 D.C. Thomson & Company Ltd.)

▲ HOURS OF
MARGUERITE
D'ORLEANS,
a typical illumination incor-
porating the Trinity in the
title letter
(Bibliothèque Nationale, Paris/
Bridgeman Art Library)

After the Romans conquered the Greeks in 300 BC, using Roman names for the gods, artisans continued paying tribute in their drawings and sculptures. Roman art was derivative of the Greek model, although innovations were made such as the decorative wall painting at Pompeii.

The decoration of manuscripts and books with coloured, gilded pictures, decorated initials and ornamental borders is known as illumination. Both ink outline and colour drawings were common, the colour medium usually being tempera.

It is thought that by the second century the papyrus roll was replaced by the parchment codex, a leafed book which produced a compact framework for illuminations. Superb examples of the art of illumination include the seventh- and eighth-century works of the Irish school, with their rich geometric designs and human and animal interlacing, and also Romanesque illumination of the twelfth century with its beautifully decorated initials and stylized figures.

Illuminations were executed largely in monasteries, and were commonly applied to religious books, including gospels, Psalters, and the book of hours. Many are masterpieces; among the greatest is *Très Riches Heures* (c.1415).

As early as the fifth century, stained glass appeared in Christian churches. The use of glass was expanded as the Romanesque wall was eliminated. Integrated with the lofty verticals of Gothic architecture, large windows provided greater illumination that was regarded as symbolic of divine light. Early glaziers followed a full-sized preliminary drawing, known as a cartoon, to cut the glass and fire the painted pieces in a kiln. Examples of twelfth-century stained glass can be found in the windows of such churches as Saint-Denis, in Paris, and Canterbury Cathedral, in England.

The Bayeux tapestry, an embroidery chronicling the Norman conquest of England, is a strip of linen, 230 feet by 20 inches (70 m by 51 cm) in the Bayeux Museum, France. Attributed to William's wife, Queen Matilda, it is a valuable document on the history and costumes of the time, using pictures as language.

The use of the term cartoon to mean a humorous or satirical drawing began in the mid-nineteenth century. The first political cartoons preceded the terminology by some three centuries, appearing in sixteenth-century Germany during the Reformation.

Humans have always used, and continue to use pictures to tell their stories. The space agency NASA recently used drawings, on a deep space exploration vehicle, to show *Homo sapiens* and our position in the universe, should any extraterrestrial being see the craft.

▼ SOLDIERS
ADVANCING TO
HASTINGS, *a detail from*
the Bayeux tapestry,
eleventh century
(Giraudon/Bridgeman Art
Library)

THE COMIC TRADITION IN ART WAS ESTABLISHED IN SEVEN-teenth-century Italy by the 'Carracci'. Caricature, a satirical portrait exaggerating and distorting features, thus making the subject look ridiculous, flourished throughout England in the eighteenth century in the works of Hogarth, Rowlandson and Gillray and became an integral part of the journalism of that time.

▲ *Hogarth's* MARRIAGE À LA MODE *'Death of the Earl', 1745* (Mary Evans Picture Library)

William Hogarth's first real success came in 1732 with a series of six morality pictures, *The Harlot's Progress*, first painted and then engraved. In the series, *Marriage à la Mode*, (1745) considered his masterpiece, he depicts the inane, profligate existence of a fashionable couple with great detail and brilliant characterization. He called them 'modern moral pictures', intended as satirical sermons.

Early British prints, which could be viewed in printers' shop windows, were bought by collectors and often displayed on the walls of coffee houses. The individual prints were sometimes glued into an album to make a book.

The Golden Age of English caricature is considered to be between 1780 and 1830.

A magazine called *The Comick Magazine*, which was wholly text, began publication in England in April 1796. It contained a Hogarth print in every issue.

In 1808 Thomas Rowlandson's prints were published in *The Caricature Magazine*. Both Rowlandson and James Gillray popularized the speech balloon which they incorporated in their cartoons, although Benjamin Franklin, the American statesman, printer, scientist and writer, was the first to use speech balloons in editorial cartoons in his newspaper, *Gazette*.

▲ *Rowlandson's* 'THE HAZARD ROOM' (The Bridgeman Art Library courtesy of the board of trustees of the V&A)

The genre expanded to include cutting political and social satire and finally developed into the cartoon proper.

Punch began publication in 1841 and took a somewhat radical stance, but Victorian respectability and good taste killed a lot of its humour.

The word 'cartoon', as we know it today, was coined in 1843 when *Punch* published drawings by John Leech. *Punch* had previously announced that they would be calling these drawings *Punch's Cartoons*.

A LITTLE TIGHTER.

▲ *Rowlandson's* 'CORSETS, A LITTLE TIGHTER', *1791* (Bettmann Archive)

Cartoons proved to be a most effective method of satirizing or lampooning people, as well as being a way of communicating a message to the many people who were unable to read.

Caricature's popularity spread throughout Europe and to the USA during the nineteenth century, where editorial cartoons became regular features of American newspapers. Thomas Nast is considered to have been one of the most influential artists of his day, with other notables being Daumier, Cruikshank, Tenniel, and Art Young.

One of the most pervasive and striking examples of caricature in literature can be seen in the works of Charles Dickens. Dickens, prior to becoming an author, was a court stenographer and parliamentary reporter, and had his early sketches of London life collected and published as *Sketches by Boz* in 1836.

▲ 'A SCENE AT GREENWICH FAIR', *J. Leech, 1843, published in* Punch

His novel *The Pickwick Papers* started life as a series of connected sketches entitled *The Posthumous Papers of the Pickwick Club* (1836–7; see illustration, page 12). It was the suicide of his artist that forced him to enlarge the text.

The Swiss schoolteacher Randolphe Töpffer drew humorous stories for his pupils, and is considered by some to be the inventor of comics. He wrote on the theory of picture stories in 1845 and went on to influence other pioneers, most notably

Wilhelm Busch, creator of 'Max and Moritz', the two terrible pranksters, who became popular across Europe and America, where they were reinvented years later as 'The Katzenjammer Kids'.

'Dime novels' started selling in America as early as 1860. In the main they were fast-moving thrillers about the American Revolution and the Civil War, and often featured real-life adventurers such as Buffalo Bill and Deadwood Dick and such fictional characters as Nick Carter. These characters were later featured in comic strips which, along with 'pulp magazines',[1] eclipsed dime novels in the 1890s.

Edgar Rice Burroughs was a pulp writer in 1912 when he created a sensation with his story *Tarzan of the Apes* which appeared in the pulp title *The All-Story*, but it was another seventeen years before Tarzan made it to the newspaper strip.

Original PICKWICK CLUB *cover, with Dickens's autograph* (Bettmann Archive)

IN THE BEGINNING

HE DEVELOPMENT OF THE COLOUR PRESS IN THE LATE NINE-teenth century saw humorous non-political cartoons become popular, which soon afterwards evolved into narrative comic strips.

In Britain, Victorian standards considered comic strips and crude drawings to be for the lower classes who enjoyed, for one penny, **Ally Sloper's Half Holiday** No. 1 (3 May 1884). The subheading read: '*Being a selection, side-splitting, sensational and serious for the benefit of old boys, young boys, odd boys generally and even girls*'.

Ally Sloper had, in fact, been around since 1867 in *Judy*, a magazine to rival *Punch*. Ally's creator, Henry Ross, sold the rights to Gilbert Dalziell, who published **Ally Sloper's Half Holiday**, the first comic to feature a regular character.

Comic Cuts was published on 17 May 1890 by Amalgamated press, owned by Alfred Harmsworth, who later became the famous British press baron Lord Northcliffe. There was very little that was fresh about **Comic Cuts** as most of its contents were reprints of previously used cartoons and strips. The only new thing was the price, a mere halfpenny – most of its contemporaries sold for twice that! At first, newsagents refused to stock it, as there was little profit to be had from a halfpenny sale, but its popularity quickly caused them to change their minds.

Harmsworth had previously been an editorial assistant at his rival publisher James Henderson, and Henderson was quick to spot that Harmsworth was stealing his old material, thus being able to produce his half-price comic. Harmsworth, facing a copyright action, possibly the first in comic-book history, immediately began employing his own artists and writers. Issue No. 331 (September 1896) was the first British comic to be printed in full colour. **Comic Cuts**, in various formats, ran for 3,006 issues, until it finally ceased publication in September 1953.

Harmsworth brought out another new title, **Illustrated Chips** No. 1 on 26 July 1890. It was a 16-page half-tabloid comic and only ran for six issues, before it was revamped to an 8-page tabloid and the numbering began again on 6 September 1890.

Illustrated Chips, which was printed on pink newsprint from June 1891 to November 1939[2] when it reverted back to white, ran for more than 3,000 issues until it too ceased publication in September 1953.

In America, colour printing within newspapers began in 1892 in Chicago, and in that year the *Inner Ocean* published a supplement entitled *The Youth's Department* containing various cartoon strips.

By the beginning of the twentieth century the comic strip became established as a syndicated newspaper feature which helped boost circulation. These 'Sunday supplements' proved to be extremely popular with children and parents alike.

The very first comic books were actually compilations of the strips from the Sunday supplements. The first modern American comic strip is acknowledged as being Richard Felton Outcault's 'The Yellow Kid' (16 February 1896), which started life in the supplements and also appeared in arguably the first American comic book recognizable as such, *Hearst's Sunday Journal*, which was published in 1897 and sold for 5 cents.

Between the beginning of the twentieth century and the early 1930s, many publishers wooed the reader with pictorial and cartoon books. Although a great number of the publishers fell by the wayside, many of the characters, such as Little Nemo, Popeye, Little Orphan Annie, Mutt and Jeff and Dick Tracy, survive to this day.

Windsor McCay, Little Nemo's creator, was the first to use colour purely for psychological effect. These brilliantly imaginative strips had Nemo in a dream-world which often defied the laws of physics and allowed for strange and anachronistic backdrops.

In 1910 George Herriman featured in his daily newspaper the strip 'Krazy Kat', one of the first 'funny animals' in comics. By 1916 Krazy Kat was starring in a wacky, surreal Sunday colour strip, moving from his daily home in 'The Family Upstairs' strip.

William Randolph Hearst gave England its first sectionalized Sunday paper in October 1910. Unable to find a British printer capable of printing in four colours, he printed the supplement in the USA and shipped it to England. It went on sale for three halfpence and gave millions of Britons their first taste of Little Nemo, and The Katzenjammer Kids – in full colour!

In 1911, in an effort to boost circulation, the *Chicago American* issued a collection of Bud Fisher's Mutt and Jeff strips in an 18 × 6 inch landscape book, available by sending in six coupons clipped from the newspaper. This first 'comic book' sold a remarkable 45,000 copies. But it wasn't for another eighteen years that the young George Delacorte, working for the pulp publisher New Fiction Company, would hit on the idea again.

In January 1929 Delacorte published **The Funnies** No. 1. It was, until issue No. 5, a weekly publication and the same size as the Sunday supplements which it could easily be mistaken for. The major difference was that the supplements were free with the newspaper and **The Funnies** had a cover price of 10 cents. For this reason it was a failure. Delacorte, from issue No. 25, reduced the price to 5 cents, but **The Funnies** ceased publication with issue No. 36. It is interesting to note that the cover of issue No. 4 was signed with the initials VEP, belonging to Victoria Pazmino, who was the first published female comic-book artist.

In January 1929, 'Tarzan of the Apes' finally graduated from the pulps. Following a test which involved running five panels a day for ten weeks, the readers were hooked. Drawn by the master of the adventure strip, Hal Foster, Tarzan became a regular feature and one of the best-known early strip characters.

Two years after appearing in his first sound cartoon, *Steamboat Willie*, Mickey Mouse made his debut in strip format in January 1930, with the first strips being accredited to Ub Iwerks. Shortly afterwards, Disney artist Floyd Gottfredson took over the strip, which he continued to write and draw for twenty years. He received no credit for his work, as the Walt Disney signature went on all the strips. Gottfredson created the definitive Mickey Mouse, which inspired the many Mickey Mouse artists that followed. In all he was responsible for more than 15,000 strips over a 45-year period.

It was Chicago's gang wars that originally inspired Chester Gould to come up with the Dick Tracy strip. The hard-hitting detective, originally to be called 'Plain-clothes Tracy', was first published in the *Chicago Tribune* in October 1931.

In 1933, Harry Wildenberg of the Eastern Color Printing Co. repackaged some comic strips from the Sunday supplements, reduced the size and published the first comic in a format similar to today's. In order to judge reaction, the first copies of **Funnies on Parade** were given away.

▲ FAMOUS FUNNIES,
SERIES 1,
*February 1934, was the first
10-cent comic book*
(Copyright © 1934 Eastern
Color Printing Company)

Max Charles Gaines, who was a salesman for Eastern Color, persuaded firms like Canada Dry, Procter & Gamble, and Wheatena to use comics as premium giveaways. They were a resounding success and it wasn't long before Gaines tried his own experiment by adding a price tag to the comics. He took a few dozen giveaways and marked them with a 10-cent label. He distributed them to nearby newsstands on Friday. By Monday every copy had sold!

Eastern Color were nervously optimistic about comics with a price tag, but unsure of how best to market them. Remembering George Delacorte's earlier interest, they sold him the entire print run, 35,000 copies, of the 10-cent **Famous Funnies, Series 1**, which Delacorte made available to the public only through chain-stores, as American News, who controlled newsstand distribution, refused to handle it. After its enormous success, American News reconsidered the situation and contracted with Eastern Color for 250,000 comics.

Their next comic, **Famous Funnies** No. 1, became available to a much larger number of people through newsstand distribution. Although it sold well, it took seven issues before the title showed a profit. **Famous Funnies** ran for 218 issues and continued until 1955.

Alex Raymond was working for King Features Syndicate, drawing their answer to Dick Tracy, Secret Agent X-9, which was written by crime novelist Dashiell Hammett, when he came up with the idea for his science-fiction strip. January 1934 saw the first Flash Gordon strips in print.

Raymond also created the globe-trotting adventurer, Jungle Jim, and a year later dropped Secret Agent X-9 to concentrate on his two new strips, which together made up a complete page in the Sunday supplements. Flash Gordon was so popular that a weekly radio show was soon being aired and stores were awash with related merchandise. In 1936 Universal Studios produced a Flash Gordon serial, starring Buster Crabbe, which, at the time, was the most expensive serial ever made.

Alex Raymond was a master of his craft and was considered to be the first in the modern school of comic artists. He was tragically killed in an accident in 1956.

Milton Caniff's Terry and the Pirates made their debut on 19 October 1934 for Captain Paterson's Tribune-News Syndicate. This strip had action, adventure, humour, and the unforgettable Lai Choi San, The Dragon Lady.

▲ FAMOUS FUNNIES
No. 1,
July 1934
(Copyright © 1934 Eastern
Color Printing Company)

In February 1935, ex-cavalry officer and pulp writer, Major Malcolm Wheeler-Nicholson's National Allied Publications, renamed DC Comics, best known today for their Superman and Batman titles, published **New Fun Comics** No. 1.

Rather than reprinting old strips, it featured an anthology of new material, much of it from Wheeler-Nicholson himself. Bearing in mind that other comics were successful because of recognizable Sunday supplement characters, this was a risk. The risk paid off and, later that year, he published his second anthology, **New Comics** No. 1 (December 1935), again featuring new characters. **New Comics**, continuing its numbering, changed its name several times; in 1937 it became **New Adventure Comics** with issue No. 12, and in 1938 with issue No. 32 it became **Adventure Comics**, which ran to issue No. 503 when it ceased publication in 1983.[3]

The year 1936 saw the publication of a number of new titles including, in February, Dell's[4] **Popular Comics** No. 1. This is of particular historical interest as it contained the first comic-book appearances of Dick Tracy, Terry and the Pirates and Little Orphan Annie. In October, Dell resumed publication of their previous failure, **The Funnies**, using the new comic-book format. This time it was a success and continued to run until March 1962 up to issue No. 288.[5]

In April 1936 **King Comics** No. 1 was published by David McKay and contained strips that included Flash Gordon, Mandrake the Magician, and featured the weather-beaten, pipe-chewing sailor, Popeye, on its cover (see illustration, page 16).

In 1937 Wheeler-Nicholson, who was finding it financially difficult to get his third title out, was forced to enter into a partnership with one of his printers, who was

also a creditor, Harry Donenfield. Their new company was called Detective Comics, Inc. and not surprisingly their first comic was **Detective Comics** No. 1 (March 1937). Instead of an assortment of themes, **Detective Comics** concentrated on crime and suspense stories. The initials of the book eventually provided the company with its new corporate name, and the title has the longest uninterrupted run of any comic book, continuing to date.

Despite the success of **Detective Comics**, Wheeler-Nicholson was still in serious financial difficulty. Towards the end of 1937 he sold his publishing interests to Harry Donenfield, who took on accountant friend, Jack Liebowitz, whom he'd been involved with since 1932 in a distribution company, Independent News, as his partner, and they changed the name of the company from Detective Comics, Inc. to National Periodical Publications (referred to as DC from now on).

Although the Depression was raging, Liebowitz had tremendous faith in comics.

Some people viewed comics as just a passing fad. Not me. From the beginning, I felt that comics could be a vital part of the publishing field. They had broad appeal and a great potential for telling stories, I thought that children, in particular, would love the colorful fantasies they presented.

Jack Liebowitz continued working in comics until 1970, and Harry Donenfield remained president of DC until shortly before his death in 1965.

In 1938, comic books experienced their first masked costumed hero, with Lee Falk's The Phantom, who made his comic-book debut in **Ace Comics** No. 11. The Phantom, who first appeared as a strip in February 1936, never became as popular as some of the other costumed heroes, but still crops up from time to time, and his ghost-like persona inspired many similar characters.

BRITAIN'S GOLDEN AGE

RITAIN'S 'GOLDEN AGE' OF COMICS BEGAN EARLY IN THE 1930s when black and white comics were known as 'penny blacks' and comics with colour as 'twopenny coloureds'. Amalgamated Press were still producing numerous titles, including **Comic Cuts**, and **Illustrated Chips**, which hadn't changed much in their 40-year history.

The company's style began to change when artist Roy Wilson was put to work on designing front pages for many of their titles. His excellent work included the Tiddlewink family in **Jingles** (1934), Jack Sprat and Tubby Tadpole in **Jolly** (1935), and George the Jolly Gee Gee in **Radio Fun** (1938).

Readers saw the first British photogravure comic on 8 February 1936 with the publication of Willbank's **Mickey Mouse Weekly** No. 1. The title ran for 920 issues until 28 December 1957.

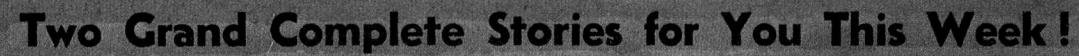

Two Grand Complete Stories for You This Week!

MICKEY MOUSE WEEKLY

Vol. 5, No. 222.   May 4th, 1940

2d EVERY FRIDAY 2d

The Dandy No. 1, the most valuable British comic, began life on 4 December 1937. It was published by the Scottish company, D. C. Thomson and sold for twopence. It came complete with a 'free gift' (an Express Whistler that could make eight engine noises), sported Korky the Cat on its front cover, and was printed in full colour on cheap newsprint.

Delighting three generations and now printed on slightly better quality paper, very little has changed about **The Dandy** in nearly sixty years! Although the strips were very 'British', **The Dandy** was closer than its predecessors to the American style of comics, and was greeted with much enthusiasm.

D. C. Thomson followed their success less than a year later with the publication of **The Beano** No. 1 (30 July 1938). Very similar in style to **The Dandy**, its characters have proved to be popular and enduring. It too offered a 'free gift', a whoopee mask, and also sold for twopence. Today its most popular strips include Dennis the Menace[6] (not to be confused with the American strip of the same name), and the Bash Street Kids. These new comics relied largely on speech balloons as opposed to narration beneath the strips, although there were text stories as well.

Both titles spawned annuals, usually published for Christmas. These hardback books always carried new material and were eagerly awaited by children. The first **Dandy** annual, called *Dandy Monster Comic*,[7] was published in 1939, with *The Beano Book* following a year later.[8]

On seeing the success of Willbank's **Mickey Mouse Weekly**, Amalgamated produced a photogravure comic, **Happy Days** No. 1, on 8 October 1938. **Happy**

Days, in trying to appeal to a wide range of ages, confused the reader, and for that reason the comic failed. After just a few weeks it dropped the expensive photogravure in favour of the more economical letterpress colour process, and eventually disappeared altogether.

Also in October 1938 Amalgamated published **Radio Fun** No. 1, as a sister title to **Film Fun**, which had begun in 1920. Both used cartoon versions of British and American stars of the day in their strips and text stories.

The first *Film Fun Annual* appeared in 1938 and *Radio Fun Annual* followed in 1940.

In March 1939 Amalgamated added **Knockout**[9] to its comic line, and produced a Christmas annual, **The Knockout Fun Book**,[10] starting in 1941. The **Knockout** comic's star was Billy Bunter. Originally created in 1908 by Frank Richards for the story-paper, **The Magnet**, Billy Bunter, known as 'The Fat Owl of the Remove',[11] and his Greyfriars School chums, became firm favourites.

In September 1939 Britain went to war, causing paper shortages which killed off many titles and reduced the size of others. The end of the decade marked the end of Britain's Golden Age.

Remaindered American comic books had been regularly shipped to England, but with the beginning of World War II this soon stopped. The British public were as keen on comics as their American cousins and in February 1940 British publisher Gerald G. Swan, in an effort to fill the gap, published **New Funnies** No. 1. It strongly resembled its American forebears and carried the unprecedented high cover cost of sixpence.

To quench the thirst for superheroes, a lot of publishers encouraged writers and artists to develop some home-grown heroes. Another superhero failure began in D. C. Thomson's **Dandy** No. 272 (5 August 1944). The hero was Len Manners alias The Amazing Mr X, but British readers gave him the thumbs-down and he was dropped fourteen issues later in favour of more traditional humour strips.

In 1945, artist, writer and comic-book historian Dennis Gifford, penned a superhero strip in **Dynamic Comics** entitled 'Mr Muscle … Britain's Superman!', which, by his own admission was, '*Terrible stuff!*'.

British comics, despite numerous brave attempts, really couldn't compete with their American counterparts, especially where superheroes were concerned. When UK distribution of American comics resumed after the war, many British comics disappeared, and any surviving superheroes fell quickly out of vogue.

▲ THE BEANO BOOK,
1954
(Copyright © 1994 D. C.
Thomson & Company)

▲ FILM FUN ANNUAL,
1952
(Copyright © 1952
Amalgamated Press)

2

The Golden Age
1938–45

THE TERM 'GOLDEN AGE' REFERS TO AMERICAN COMICS published between June 1938 and 1945. The comics published around this time were typically 64 pages in length, measured approximately $7\frac{1}{4} \times 10\frac{1}{4}$ inches, and had alluring four-colour covers – in many cases this was deceptive, as the interiors had some pages printed in black and white.

Although many people argue as to when the 'Golden Age' ended (some say as late as 1950), there is no doubt as to when it started. June 1938 saw the publication of the first 'Golden Age' comic book. It was published by DC Comics, and carried the inspired title of **Action Comics** No. 1 (June 1938).

This comic's cover, depicting a man lifting a car above his head in a menacing fashion, caused quite a stir at the time. The man of course was none other than Superman, who without doubt is the most important and influential character in the history of comics.

Superman was the creation of Jerry Siegel and Joe Shuster who were both still at college in Cleveland, Ohio when they began to write and draw comics. They had seen some success with their work as early as 1932 with their own amateur science-fiction publication, **The Advance Guard of Future Civilisation**. Interestingly enough, issue No. 3 of their publication (January 1933) contained a story called, 'The Reign of the Superman'. Sixty years later, DC used the name 'The Reign of the Supermen' as the title for a story-line in their Superman comics following Superman's death and subsequent rebirth.

Superman was written by Jerry and drawn by Joe. Jerry had been intrigued with the concept of a futuristic man who had uncanny powers, the inspiration coming from science-fiction pulps and from one of his favourite books, Philip Wylie's 1930 novel, *Gladiator*, in which the hero finds he can leap 40 feet in the air, has super-strength, with bullets and exploding shells merely bouncing off his chest.

During a hot night in 1933, Siegel, unable to sleep, lay in bed thinking. Bit by bit throughout the long night Superman was conceived. Siegel said:

I hop right out of bed and write this down, and then I go back and think some more for about two hours and get up and write that down. This goes on at two-hour intervals, until in the morning when I have a complete script.'

◄ ACTION COMICS
No. 1,
June 1938, featured the first appearance of Superman, and was the first Golden Age Comic

When dawn broke Jerry raced the twelve blocks to awaken his friend Joe Shuster. Joe became ecstatic when Jerry explained his creation, and without wasting a second, both began developing the strip.

Apart from his other inspirations, Siegel's character was a variation of the pulp hero Doc Savage, who was described in an advertisement for the title as '*Superman Doc Savage – man of Master Mind and Body ...*' The word 'superman' from the German *ubermensch*, was actually coined by the philosopher, Friedrich Nietzsche.

During that year Joe drew a number of Jerry's scripts featuring this, as yet unnamed, character who was originally conceived as a villain who wanted to take over the world.

The scripts were gradually refined until Superman was named and he took on his more recognizable persona. Shuster remembers:

I was inspired, I did the artwork very rapidly. We hit the proper costume for Superman immediately; the first drawing hit the bull's-eye.

They believed that they would be able to sell Superman to newspapers, with a view to syndication, and spent five frustrating years looking for a publisher. As is often the case with something new or different, people were reluctant to try it and all rejected their idea! United Feature's rejection said, '[Superman is], a rather immature piece of work,' and the Bell Syndicate told them, 'We are in the market only for strips likely to have the most extra-ordinary appeal, and we do not feel Superman gets into this category.'

Ironically, by 1941, after Superman had become a popular comic-book hero, more than three hundred newspapers throughout America published him in strip format.[1]

The Superman strip reached Sheldon Mayer, then editor of the McClure Syndicate. '*When the Superman strip first came in,*' recalls Mayer, '*I immediately fell in love with it. I was singing Superman's praises so much that in 1938, Gaines* [Mayer's boss] *finally took the strip to Harry Donenfield ...*'

By chance Harry Donenfield was planning to publish a new anthology title and had contacted Gaines about additional material. Gaines showed him Superman.

DC had already published some of Siegel and Shuster's work, including Dr Occult, Federal Men, and Slam Bradley, so they weren't unknown to Donenfield. He bought the strip and Siegel and Shuster signed a standard release of rights. Donenfield instructed the youngsters to rewrite some of what he had seen. He gave them just three weeks to complete the 13-page story, for which they were paid $10 (£7)[2] a page. Jerry and Joe delivered what became Superman's first appearance.

Donenfield, needing to save space, ordered that the beginning of the work, probably the first week in newspaper-strip terms, be omitted and, on publication in **Action Comics** No. 1, the story seemed to start in the middle. It wasn't until a year later in **Superman** No. 1 that the first story was published in its entirety.

Although Superman was a success, Harry Donenfield dropped him from the covers of **Action Comics** Nos 2–6. The sales of **Action Comics** did, however, continue to grow and soon approached half a million copies per issue, more than double the sales of most other titles. To DC's surprise, a survey showed that people were asking for 'the comic book with Superman in it', and as a direct result he then re-appeared on the covers of 7–10, 13, 15 and 17. With issue No. 19 he became the lead character and has appeared on almost every cover of **Action Comics** since!

At the outset, scant details of his origin were given, merely that this 'star-child' had great powers. He was unable to fly but instead could leap a tall building in a single bound, and outrun a train. He wasn't invulnerable, but bullets merely bounced off his chest. Powers such as X-ray vision appeared later; early on, Superman tore the roof off a house to see inside!

Shuster continued drawing Superman until 1947, but neither he nor Siegel owned any of the rights. From early on they were paid $500 (£333) for each 13-page story and a small percentage of money made from the enormous output of Superman merchandizing. After Shuster quit drawing comics, Siegel began a long and bitter legal battle over the rights to the world's best-known comic-book character. DC eventually acknowledged them as the creators by attaching 'Created by Siegel and Shuster' to the Superman stories, as well as paying them an annual stipend. Joe Shuster died in 1992 and Jerry Siegel lives in semi-retirement in Los Angeles.

The present Superman, who is usually depicted as being approximately 29 years old, would in reality today be more than 80, and although he bears a strong resemblance to the Golden Age Superman, he has gone through many changes of personality, powers, weaknesses, as well as subtle costume changes. Many artists have drawn Superman, including Al Plastino, George Papp, Jack Burnley, Irwin Hasen, Curt Swan, and Wayne Boring. It was Boring who most changed Superman's look, giving him his granite features and muscled body. He also changed the look of the backdrops and soon Metropolis became a streamlined modern city of skyscrapers. Boring's Superman remains the model on which today's Man of Steel is based.

It is impossible to overestimate the significance or importance of Superman. He is indisputably the most imitated character in comics. It is likely that without him we would never have seen the likes of Spiderman, Wonder Woman, X-Men and, more specifically, Batman or, as he was known in 1938, the 'Bat-Man'.

Bob Kane had already conceived the idea of a Bat-Man as early as 1934, but it wasn't until the success of Superman that he took the idea of a costumed superhero seriously. Although Bob was earning as much as $50 (£33) a week, Siegel and Shuster were earning, with money from merchandizing, anything up to $800 (£533) a week each! On hearing of the vast sums that could be earned, he spent an entire weekend creating his new superhero, the Bat-Man. He used drawings of Superman and traced over them to see how he would look in different costumes.

The character was originally inspired through Kane's fascination with Leonardo da Vinci drawings of flying machines, and Kane had in fact made some crude sketches of flying men years before. His names for these flying men had ranged from Bird-Man to Eagle-Man to Hawk-Man, and finally to the Bat-Man. Da Vinci had said: '*Remember that your bird should have no other model than the bat.*' Kane freely admits that his second influence was the movie *The Mark of Zorro* starring Douglas Fairbanks, Sr. Zorro used a mask to conceal his true identity and that gave Kane the idea of giving Bat-Man a secret identity, although it was writer Bill Finger who came up with the character of rich socialite Bruce Wayne. Finger was also responsible for naming Bat-Man's home, Gotham City:

I flipped through the phone book and spotted the name Gotham Jewellers and said 'that's it,' Gotham City. We didn't call it New York because we wanted anybody in any city to identify with it. Of course Gotham City is another name for New York.

The Bat-Man was a self-styled masked vigilante and, after his parents were killed by a mugger, he turned to crime-fighting to bring retribution to all who broke the law: '*I swear by the spirits of my parents to avenge their deaths by spending the rest of my life warring on all criminals.*'

He was a loner and Kane made him more interesting by having him work under the cover of darkness and away from the eyes of the law. His costume conjured up visions of vampires and the supernatural. Kane remembers:

The Batman costume was designed to cloak Bruce Wayne's true identity. I recalled seeing a movie around 1926 called The Bat, *in which the villain wore a bat-like costume which was quite awesome. The main difference being that I changed my character into a hero. I felt that his awesome costume on my hero would throw fear and respect into all the villains that he would encounter.*

The Bat-Man had no super-powers. What made him exciting was the story-lines (which were undoubtedly better plotted than the Superman stories) and the unusual art. Kane was one of the first to use cinematic angles in comics, which gave the reader a new perspective and created a more authentic fantasy world full of dark silhouettes and brimming with atmosphere. This was a world inhabited by dark, sinister villains who, together with the Bat-Man's grim motives for vengeance, made it truly scary. Bill Finger's scripts, reminiscent of detective pulps, complemented Kane's stylized art and brought some of the most bizarre villains to the Batman stories. Most notably The Joker. The white-faced, green-haired, self-styled 'Clown-Prince-of-Crime' was the creation of Kane's young assistant, Jerry Robinson, who got the idea from a playing-card, and Finger knew just how he should look. Kane recalls:

Bill came to me with a photograph of Conrad Veidt from the movie, The Man Who Laughs, *Veidt had this really ghastly smile, and I developed the look of The Joker from that photograph.*

The crime queen Catwoman (originally called The Cat) was also inspired by the movies. In fact she was based on Jean Harlow and given black hair instead of blond to make her more slinky and feline-looking. Both The Joker and Catwoman made their first appearances in **Batman** No. 1 (Spring 1940).

Readers had to wait until December 1941 for the arrival of The Penguin in **Detective Comics** No. 58. Bill Finger recalled:

The Penguin came out of an article in the Saturday Evening Post *on Emperor Penguins. They looked like Englishmen in a fancy club. I decided the character had to have two things, a tuxedo-like costume with a top hat, and an umbrella. I made umbrellas with gimmicks, all weapons which would give him character. I decided to make the villain funny but in a diabolical way.*

'The Case of the Chemical Syndicate' in **Detective Comics** No. 27 (May 1939) marked Batman's first appearance. Although **Action Comics** No. 1 is without doubt the most significant comic book ever, **Detective Comics** No. 27 has in recent years surpassed it as far as prices and market demand are concerned. Kane said in 1985:

You don't always know in the beginning where your creation will go. You hope for the best. I did feel Batman would be a success, but not as big as he wound up being. I'm very proud of him.

During the 1940s many artists and writers worked on Batman, notably Jack Burnley, George Roussos, Fred Ray, Curt Swan, Jerry Robinson, Dick Sprang and Otto Binder.

In the summer of 1939 Superman was given his own title with the publication of **Superman** No. 1. This reprinted stories from **Action Comics** Nos 1–4, with some new pages. Later that year the newsstands were awash with superhero comics, including The Blue Beetle, Amazing Man and the extremely short-lived Wonder Man, who bore a striking resemblance to Superman. DC hit Fox Features Syndicate, the publishers responsible for Wonder Man, with a copyright infringement lawsuit

▲ DETECTIVE COMICS No. 31, *September 1939, had a dark moody Bob Kane cover* (™ & Copyright © 1994 DC Comics, Inc.)

▲ CONRAD VEIDT IN THE MAN WHO LAUGHS, *1927, was the inspiration for the 'look' of The Joker* (The Kobal Collection)

▶ DETECTIVE COMICS No. 27, *May 1939, featured the first appearance of Batman* (™ & Copyright © 1994 DC Comics, Inc.)

▲ SUPERMAN No. 1, *Summer 1939* (™ & Copyright © 1994 DC Comics, Inc.)

No. 27
64 PAGES OF ACTION!
MAY, 1939
Detective COMICS
10¢
STARTING THIS ISSUE: THE AMAZING AND UNIQUE ADVENTURES OF
THE BATMAN!

▶ SPEED COMICS No. 1,
*October 1939, was the first
Harvey comic*
(™ & Copyright © 1994 The
Harvey Entertainment
Company)

◀ MARVEL COMICS
No. 1,
*November 1939, was the first
Marvel comic*
(™ & Copyright © 1994 Marvel
Entertainment Group, Inc.)

as soon as **Wonder Comics** No. 1 (May 1939) appeared on the newsstands. Despite continuing to fight the lawsuit, Fox dropped Wonder Man after the first issue.

Harvey Comics, better known today for their 'funny' titles such as Richie Rich, Little Lotta, Casper the Friendly Ghost and Hot Stuff, began by publishing anthology titles. Harvey Comics was the brainchild of the two Harvey brothers, Leon and Alfred. Their first title was **Speed Comics** No. 1 (October 1939), starring Shock Gibson – The Human Dynamo.

Archie Publications, originally known as MLJ Magazines, from the initials of its founders, Morris Coyne, Louis Silberkleit, and John Goldwater, began publishing in November 1939 with **Blue Ribbon Comics** No. 1, and they followed this with **Top-Notch** No. 1 (December 1939).

Martin Goodman's Timely Comics, (referred to as Marvel from now), entered the arena in October/November 1939[3] with **Marvel Comics**[4] No. 1. This featured two new superheroes. From the pen of Bill Everett came Price Namor the Sub-Mariner,[5] who still continues to play a big part in the 'Marvel Universe', and from Carl Burgos came The Human Torch, a latter-day version of whom is a member of The Fantastic Four.

January 1940 saw the publication of the first science-fiction comic, Fiction House's **Planet Comics** No. 1.

MLJ began 1940 with the publication of the long-surviving **Pep Comics** featuring The Shield – G-Man Extraordinary, who is widely considered to have been the first patriotic hero.

In February, Fawcett's first comic book, **Whiz Comics** No. 2,[6] was published. It featured the first appearance of C. C. Beck's and Bill Parker's Captain Marvel – 'The World's Mightiest Mortal'.

Billy Batson was transformed from a mere mortal to 'The Big Red Cheese', as his enemies called him, by shouting the magic word, 'Shazam!' – this immediately made him ten years older and two feet taller!

After following a stranger into a subway tunnel, the orphan Billy boards a driverless train which takes him to a secret underground hall. There he meets the wizened magician, Shazam, who has battled evil for 3,000 years. Billy is to be his successor and by merely speaking his name he becomes Captain Marvel, the strongest and

▲ BLUE RIBBON
COMICS No. 1,
November 1939
(™ & Copyright © 1994 Archie
Comic Publications, Inc.)

▶ PEP COMICS No.1,
January 1940
(™ & Copyright © 1994 Archie
Comic Publications, Inc.)

mightiest man in the world. On a wall behind the old man an inscription appears explaining the anagram Shazam; 'S' is for Solomon's wisdom, 'H' is for Herclues' strength, 'A' is for Atlas' stamina, 'Z' is for Zeus' power, 'A' is for Achilles' courage and 'M' is for the speed of Mercury.

With more light-hearted, gentle, and generally less violent stories than Superman's, Captain Marvel became the best loved superhero of the 1940s. DC, upset by similarities between Captain Marvel and Superman, soon embarked on a lengthy lawsuit against Fawcett.

The Republic Pictures Corporation[7] serial, *The Adventures of Captain Marvel* (1941),[8] starring Tom Tyler, portrayed Captain Marvel as being totally cold-blooded. He actually commits ruthless murder on several felons and threatens to throw another man to his death unless he talks. The serial was successful and DC added Republic Pictures to its list of those it was suing.

Max Gaines, now working at DC, having beaten Fawcett in securing the title copyright, published **Flash Comics** No. 1, cover dated January 1940 although it hit the newsstands on 20 November 1939. It starred the Flash who was billed as 'The Fastest Man Alive', and also included Hawkman, both of whom continue today.

Will Eisner's comic **The Spirit** began weekly distribution with Sunday newspapers in February 1940. This continued until 1952, although Eisner passed the strip over to other artists, including Lou Fine, Bob Powell and Alex Kotzky, when he went into the army in 1942.

The Spirit was different from other masked comic-book characters in many ways. He had a sense of humour (most other heroes didn't), he was always ready for a

PEP COMICS No.1,
January 1940
(™ & Copyright © 1994 Archie
Comic Publications, Inc.)

▼ WHIZ COMICS
No. 2(1),
*February 1940, featured the
first appearance of Captain
Marvel*
(Copyright © 1940 Fawcett
Publications)

▼ FLASH COMICS
No. 1,
January 1940
(™ & Copyright © 1994 DC
Comics, Inc.)

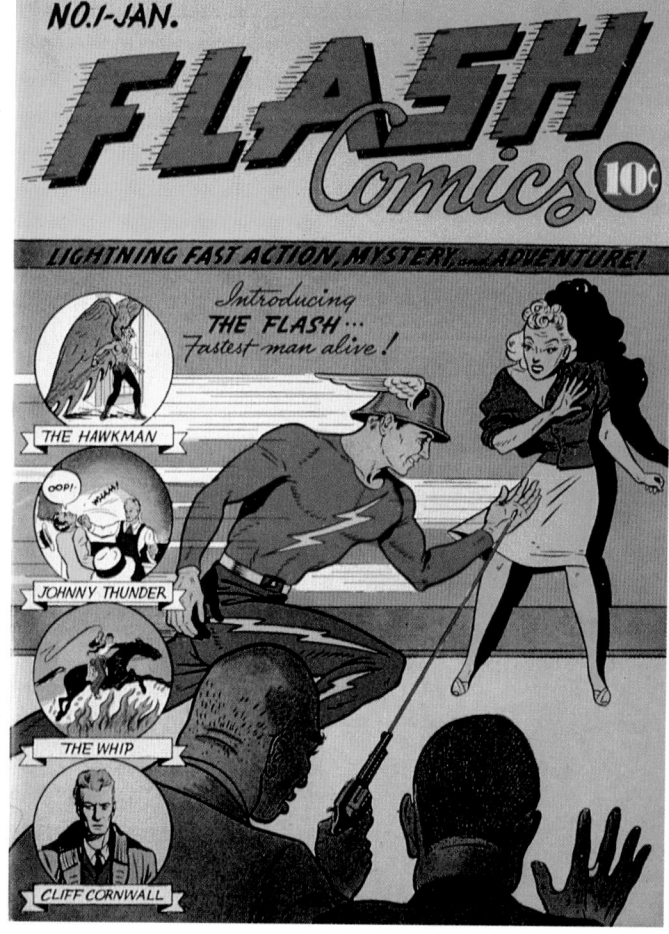

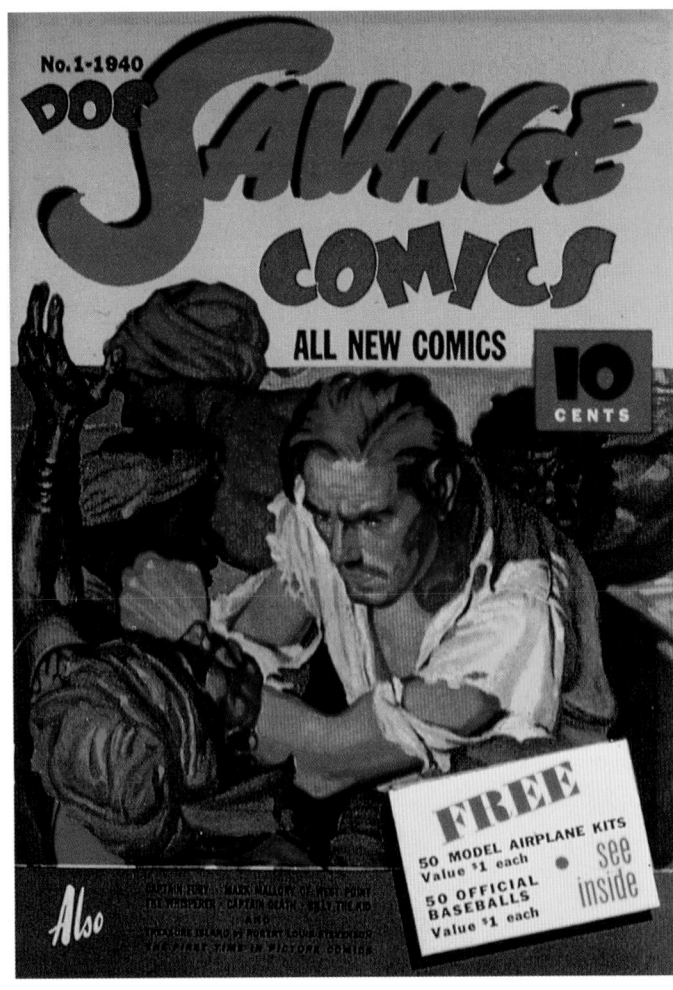

fight and didn't need to put on a pair of tights or sport a cape to have it. He wore a baggy blue business suit, a wide-brimmed hat and an eye-mask which had no visible means of support, for disguise.

In order to reach a more adult audience, Eisner deliberately made The Spirit's world relatively more mature than the world of Superman and Batman and, in so doing, it became more violent. It would take an entire mob to pin The Spirit down. Hoodlums bent pipes over his head, shot at him and slugged him — and The Spirit merely stuck his tongue in his cheek and proceeded to beat the hell out of them.

Pulp publisher Street and Smith took two of their popular 1930s pulp characters and put them into comic books. **Shadow Comics** No. 1 was published in March 1940, followed in May by **Doc Savage Comics** No. 1. For some reason the transition from pulps to comics didn't entirely work, although both characters are still published from time to time today.

Spring was a busy time for DC. They introduced the sinister ghostly Spectre in **More Fun Comics** No. 52[9] (February 1940) and Hourman, a hero whose powers lasted for sixty minutes, in **Adventure Comics** No. 48 (March 1940). They also repeated an exercise from the previous year, issuing a publication filled with all of their main characters, and called **New York World's Fair** (Spring 1940) to coincide with the World's Fair. This was the first time Superman and Batman appeared together on a cover. Like the 1939 edition, it had 100 pages and cardboard covers. It is interesting to note that the 1939 edition originally had a cover price of 25 cents. This was expensive, as almost all other comics sold for 10 cents. The price proved

▲ ADVENTURE
COMICS No. 48,
*March 1940, featured the
first appearance of Hour-
man*
(™ & Copyright © 1994 DC
Comics, Inc.)

prohibitive and the comic didn't do well. DC repriced the remainders and returns
with a 15-cent sticker and sent everyone who had paid 25 cents a free copy of
either **Superman** No. 1 or No. 2 as compensation. The 1940 **New York World's
Fair** was priced at 15 cents – they had learned their lesson.

In spring 1940 the Caped Crusader got his own title in **Batman** No. 1 which
contained the first appearance of The Joker and Catwoman. The cover states: '*ALL
BRAND NEW ADVENTURES OF THE BATMAN AND ROBIN, THE BOY WONDER!*'

Robin had joined Batman in April 1940 in **Detective Comics** No. 38. Bob Kane
had decided to introduce a 'sidekick' for two reasons; firstly it gave Batman a
'Dr Watson' to talk to, and secondly Kane felt that the youngsters reading Batman
would be able to identify with Robin (see illustrations, pages 30, 31):

*I thought that every young boy would want to be like Robin; instead of having to wait to
grow up to become a superhero, they wanted to be one now. A laughing daredevil –
free, no school, no homework, living in a mansion over a Bat Cave, riding in the Bat-
Mobile – he appealed to the imagination of every kid in the world.*[10]

Kane's boss at DC, Jack Liebowitz, didn't like the idea and felt that Batman was
doing well enough by himself. Kane persuaded him to try Robin for one issue and
was proved right. **Detective Comics** No. 38 sold almost twice as many copies as
previous, solo Batman, **Detective Comics** had.

July 1940 saw the publication of DC/All American's[11] **All American Comics** No.
16 (July 1940), which introduced the superhero The Green Lantern – undoubtedly

▲ NEW YORK
WORLD'S FAIR,
1940
(™ & Copyright © 1994 DC
Comics, Inc.)

▶ NEW YORK WORLD'S
FAIR,
1939
(™ & Copyright © 1994 DC
Comics, Inc.)

No 1
SPRING ISSUE
BATMAN
10¢
ALL BRAND NEW
ADVENTURES
OF THE BATMAN
AND ROBIN,
THE BOY WONDER!

◀ DETECTIVE COMICS
No. 38,
April 1940, featured the first appearance and origin of Robin
(™ & Copyright © 1994 DC Comics, Inc.)

◀ ALL AMERICAN
COMICS No. 16,
July 1940, featured the first appearance and origin of The Green Lantern
(™ & Copyright © 1994 DC Comics, Inc.)

▲ HEROIC COMICS
No. 1,
August 1940. Hydroman bears a striking resemblance to The Sub-Mariner, both created by Bill Everett
(Copyright © 1940 Eastern Color Printing Company)

◀ BATMAN No. 1,
Spring 1940
(™ & Copyright © 1994 DC Comics, Inc.)

▼ RED RYDER
COMICS No. 1,
September 1940, was the first comic devoted to a Western theme
(Copyright © 1940 Hawley Publications)

based on Aladdin – who was equipped with a magic ring powered by a magic lantern. His secret identity was Alan Scott, although he was originally going to be called Alan Ladd!

Issue No. 19 of **American Comics** (October 1940) included the first appearance of the pint-sized hero, The Atom. After being mugged in front of his girlfriend, the five-foot Al Pratt is determined to overcome the problems his small stature has given him. He trains and develops tremendous strength, dons a costume and calls himself The Atom.

Timely's **Marvel Mystery Comics** No. 9 (July 1940) was the home to the first 'team-up' of two characters in comic-book history: The Human Torch and The Sub-Mariner appeared together in a 22-page story.

Eastern Color published **Heroic Comics** No. 1 (August 1940), which featured, among others, the costumed hero Hydroman, who bore a striking resemblance to The Sub-Mariner (both were created by Bill Everett).

Later that year DC published **All Star Comics** No. 1 which included the characters The Flash, Hawkman, Sandman and The Spectre, but it wasn't until issue No. 3 that they all appeared together as a team called The Justice Society of America. This was the first of many such 'teams' of superheroes banding together, a tradition that continues to this day. The original team consised of The Flash, The Green Lantern, The Spectre, The Hawkman, Dr Fate, The Hourman, The Sandman, The Atom and Johnny Thunder. Their last appearance in **All Star Comics** was issue No. 57 (February–March 1951).

The first comics totally devoted to a Western theme were published in September 1940. Hawley published **Red Ryder Comics** No. 1 (see illustration, page 32) and Ralstan Purina Co. published **Tom Mix Comics** No. 1.[12] Tom Mix was the first cowboy film star to have his own comic book. Sadly, he was killed in a car crash a month later, although the comic book survived until 1953.

After being one of the most popular characters in its successful **Marvel Mystery Comics**, Marvel gave The Human Torch his own book, **The Human Torch** No. 2[13] (Fall 1940), which also introduced The Human Torch's sidekick, Toro, who had Torch-like powers and, like his mentor, a natural immunity to fire.

One of the most significant publications of 1940 came from Dell in October with their publication of **Walt Disney's Comics and Stories** No. 1, featuring Donald

Duck and Mickey Mouse. The title is still being published and has been in the hands of numerous publishers, including Disney themselves. It is currently being published by Gladstone who now hold the licence for the second time.

This was also the year Superman hit the airwaves on his radio show, where every day on the Mutual Network was heard:

Faster than a speeding bullet!
More powerful than a locomotive!
Able to leap tall buildings at a single bound!
Look! Up in the Sky!
It's a bird!
It's a plane!
IT'S SUPERMAN!

Yes, it's Superman, strange visitor from another planet, who came to Earth with powers and abilities far beyond those of mortal men; Superman, who can change the course of mighty rivers, bend steel in his bare hands; and who, disguised as Clark Kent, mild-mannered reporter for a great metropolitan newspaper, fights a never-ending battle for truth, justice and the American Way!

▲ WALT DISNEY'S
COMICS AND STORIES
No. 1,
October 1940
(Copyright © 1940 Dell
Publishing Company)

Bud Collyer was the voice of Superman. He played Clark Kent as a tenor and dropped his voice, so the audience would know the difference, when he became Superman.

It was the radio show that first came up with Kryptonite, fragments of Superman's exploded world Krypton. Having changed into a radioactive element, Kryptonite weakened natives of Krypton when in close proximity to them. Later it became deadly and the only substance that could kill Superman. However, its rays, like Superman's X-ray vision, could not pass through lead.

Another radio favourite of the era was The Green Hornet, originally played by Al Hodge. He was the creation of radio script-writer Fran Striker, who also created The Lone Ranger and had been involved in his radio success.

Britt (Green Hornet) Reid, grand-nephew of The Lone Ranger, used his inherit-ance, from his great-uncle's silver mine (thus explaining where the silver bullets came from!), to finance his vigilante crime-fighting. Instead of Tonto, The Green Hornet had Kato as his faithful companion. After Pearl Harbor, Kato, originally depicted as Japanese became Filipino.

There were also two 13-part Green Hornet serials, which were shown in movie theatres in weekly instalments. The first serial starred Gordon Jones and the second, Warren Hull who had previously been radio's Mandrake the Magician.

Artist Bert Whitman picked up the rights for the comic book and published **Green Hornet Comics** No. 1 (December 1940) for Helnit Publications. After six issues the title was sold to Harvey Publications who continued the numbering.

In January 1941, Fawcett gave Captain Marvel his own book, **Captain Marvel Adventures** No. 1. He also appeared later in 1941 in Fawcett's anthology title **America's Greatest Comics** No. 1. It seemed that Captain Marvel was growing from strength to strength.

With a cover date of February 1941, DC published a black and white comic, reprinting the cover of **Action Comics** No. 29, to secure the copyright for their new title **World's Best Comics** No. 1 (Spring 1940). The title changed with issue No. 2 to the better known **World's Finest Comics**, the home of Superman and Batman team-ups for more than forty years.

The first comic devoted to war, **War Comics** No. 1, was published by Dell in May 1940. The Second World War was raging in Europe and was just around the

▲ GREEN HORNET
COMICS No. 1,
December 1940
(Copyright © 1940 Helnit
Publications)

▲ AMERICA'S
GREATEST COMICS
No. 1, *Fall 1941*
(Copyright © 1941 Fawcett
Publications)

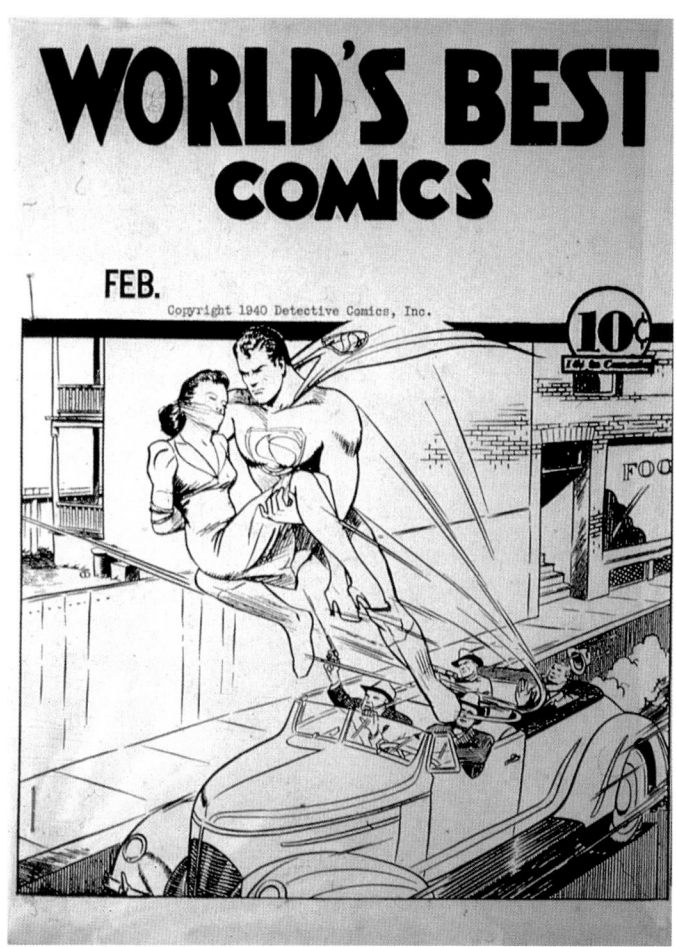

corner for America. During 1941 the Anti-Nazi theme spread like wildfire through comic books.

In March 1941 Captain America, the ultimate patriotic hero, complete with his stars-and-stripes costume was introduced.

The frail and skinny Steve Rogers, deemed unfit for the army, volunteers for a special government experiment to test the effects of a super-serum. The serum builds Rogers' body and brain tissues to an incredible degree, and he is transformed into a fighting avenger. He goes undercover, maintaining his secret identity, as a US army private and soon teams up with the regiment 'mascot', Bucky Barnes, who becomes his young partner and sidekick.

He was the brainchild of Joe Simon and Jack Kirby. The cover of **Captain America** No. 1 shows Hitler taking a beating and Captain America being protected from flying Nazi bullets merely by his shield. No. 1 also saw the introduction of Marvel's first fan club, The Sentinels of Liberty. For 10 cents the lucky member received a metal badge and a membership card. Both are much sought after by collectors today. Captain America was an immediate success and Simon and Kirby employed an assistant to help with the monthly title. The young assistant was publisher Martin Goodman's wife's cousin, a 17-year-old named Stanley Leiber who used the name Stan Lee, and went on to become the most famous writer and editor in the history of comic books. His first published work was seen in **Captain America** No. 3 (May 1941), entitled 'The Traitor's Revenge', a two-part text story. His first comic-book story was published in **Captain America** No. 5 (August 1941).

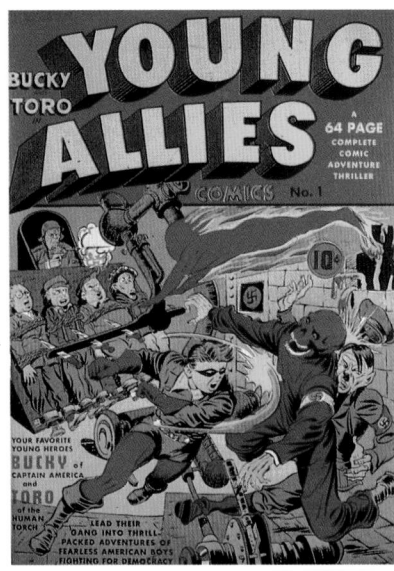

▶ YOUNG ALLIES No. 1,
Summer 1941
(™ & Copyright © 1994 Marvel
Entertainment Group, Inc.)

◀ DAREDEVIL No. 1,
*July 1941, featured Hitler,
the ultimate enemy*
(Copyright © 1941 Lev Gleason)

▲ SUPERMAN No. 17,
July–August 1942
(™ & Copyright © 1994 DC
Comics, Inc.)

Later that year, Captain America joined The Sub-Mariner and The Human Torch in a new title, **All Winners** No. 1 (Summer 1941), where they continued to win the war for America and the Allies.

Marvel continued with their patriotic comics by teaming up Bucky and Toro in their own title, **Young Allies** No. 1 (Summer 1941).

The ultimate enemy of the time was without doubt Hitler, who features in **Daredevil** No. 1 (July 1941). **Superman** No. 17 (July/August 1942) not only featured Hitler but, on its cover, also had Mussolini taking a beating from The Man of Steel.

Quality published their war title **Military Comics** No. 1 in August 1941. It featured half a dozen bomb-blasting heroes, The Blackhawks, who fought not only Nazis but also the Japanese. DC now have the rights to the Blackhawks and continue to publish their adventures from time to time. Quality also published **Police Comics** No. 1 which included Jack Cole's surreal Plastic Man who began featuring on covers from issue No. 5 (November 1941) and got his own title in **Plastic Man** No. 1 (Summer 1943).

September 1941 saw DC formerly instigating legal proceedings, destined to go on for years, against not only Fawcett, but also the artists and writers of Captain Marvel, for copyright infringement of their Superman character.

After listening to expert evidence from artists, writers and editors, although the judge admitted that it was obvious that copying had taken place, he decided to dismiss the case. There was no evidence of unfair competition, or any indication that Fawcett had tried to confuse readers by passing off Captain Marvel as Superman. He further said that DC had lost its copyright when it failed to publish the proper notices on the Superman newspaper strips. DC moved for an appeal, and a new trial began in 1951. It took a further two years before Fawcett settled out of court.

Calling All Girls No. 1 was published in September 1941 by Parents Magazine Institute, and was the first American comic book specifically for girls.

In October 1941, Al Kantor's Gilberton Company began publishing **Classic Comics**,[14] starting with Alexandre Dumas's 'The Three Musketeers' and ending some 28 years later with 'Negro Americans – The Early Years', issue No. 169, (Spring 1969). The title brought adaptations of literature (albeit liberal adaptations in the early issues) to its comic-book pages. So popular were these comics that most of them enjoyed numerous printings, in some cases more than twenty!

▲ PLASTIC MAN,
*Summer 1943, was the first
issue but was not numbered*
(Copyright © 1943 Quality
Comics Group)

In September 1941, Fleischer Studios released the first of seventeen[15] Superman cartoons which used revolutionary techniques, including the rotoscope, a device – invented by Max Fleischer – which enabled animators to trace over live action. To add authenticity, Fleischer used Bud Collyer, the radio voice of Superman, for the first six episodes. These superb cartoons, using the multiplan camera to create a 3-D illusion, resulted in animation rivalling the best Disney cartoons of the day.

After his popularity in The Justice Society of America, DC gave The Green Lantern his own title towards the end of 1941, and introduced two new characters, The Green Arrow, a latter-day Robin Hood, and Aquaman, King of the Sea in **More Fun Comics** No. 73 (November 1941).

December 1941 saw the introduction of one of the most enduring characters of all time, Archie Andrews. MLJ Magazines eventually changed its name to Archie Comics as a result of Archie's success. His first appearance was a back-up feature in **Pep Comics** No. 22, and he made his cover debut in issue No. 36 (February 1943). Archie was the creation of Bob Montana, and was light relief compared to war and superhero comics. Together with Betty, Veronica, Jughead, Reggie and the rest of his teenage gang, he has survived for more than fifty years.

By the end of 1941, it was estimated that more than 50 million people a month were reading comic books, the majority of the audience being male. Max Gaines realized that there was a potentially huge female readership which was not interested in the male-dominated superheroes, and he called in a member of his Editorial Advisory Board, Dr William Moulton Marston, to come up with a superheroine. Marston, using the pen-name Charles Moulton, created the most famous comic-book heroine of all time – Wonder Woman. She made her debut in December 1941 in **All Star Comics** No. 8 and was drawn by Harry Peter. Moulton had drawn heavily on mythology for his character: she was Diana, daughter of Hippolyte, Queen of the Amazons. She moved from her Amazonian home of Paradise Island to live in the guise of Diana Prince, in Washington.

Gaines was proved right – Wonder Woman was an instant success with female readers. Despite the sexual overtones, it is considered that Wonder Woman's exploits are early examples of feminism in print. Her creator was known to have held strong views on the subject of female liberation and equality.

However, Wonder Woman was not the first superheroine. That title belongs to Black Fury (later Miss Fury), who first appeared in April 1941. She was not only the first superheroine, but also the only one to be drawn by a woman, Tarpé Mills.

Dell's **Looney Tunes and Merrie Melodies Comics** No. 1 (1941) saw the first comic-book appearances of Bugs Bunny, Elmer Fudd, Daffy Duck and Porky Pig. Many of the strips were adaptations from then-recent Warner Brothers cartoons. The Bugs Bunny story in issue No. 1 was adapted from the 1940 Merrie Medley cartoon, *A Wild Hare*, directed by Tex Avery, which is widely considered to contain the best origin story of Bugs Bunny. The comic had a cartoon-like feel about it, with Porky Pig bursting through the familiar drum on the front cover, and telling us, '*That's all, folks!*' on the last page.

In December, Fawcett introduced 'Captain Marvel, Jr' in **Whiz Comics** No. 25. He proved popular enough to be given his own book in November 1942.

In January 1942, Wonder Woman starred in **Sensation Comics** No. 1 and was given her own title later that year. **Wonder Woman** ran for 329 issues concluding in February 1986.[16]

Quality began publishing The Spirit in **Police Comics** No. 11 (September 1942) and got his own title, along with his sidekick Ebony – the first regular black comic-book character – in **The Spirit** No. 1 (1944).

▲ CLASSIC COMICS
No. 1,
October 1941, was based on Alexandre Dumas's The Three Musketeers
(Copyright © 1941 Gilberton Publications)

▶ SENSATION COMICS
No. 1,
January 1942
(™ & Copyright © 1994 DC Comics, Inc.)

In December 1942 Fawcett added their heroine, Mary Marvel in **Captain Marvel** No. 18.

Lev Gleason Publications (Comic House) had, up until now, no superheroes in its stable, male or female, and in April 1942 published the first Crimebuster story in **Boy Comics** No. 3.[17]

Gleason's **Silver Streak Comics** changed its title in June 1942 to **Crime Does Not Pay**,[18] inspired by the film of the same name, and was the first all-crime book. In many cases the stories reflected actual criminals' lives. These 'crime' books soon became very popular, despite the initial reluctance of newsstand owners to carry them.

The year 1942 saw the publication of the novel *Superman*[19] by George Lowther, in which a number of subtle changes were made to the legend. Until then, Superman's parents had been Jor-L and Lora; Lowther changed them to Jor-el and Lara, which are still the names used today. He also changed Superman's adopted parents' names from Mary and John Kent to Eban and Sarah Kent and it was explained that Sarah's maiden name was Clark, hence Clark Kent. Eban and Sarah were not kept as names for the Kents, and they later became Martha and Jonathan.

Alongside the superheroes and heroines, the war comics and the crime stories, 'funny animals' were becoming increasingly popular at this time.

In January 1941, Dell published **Animal Comics** No. 1 which included animal photographs as well as strips. One of the most notable strips was 'Bumbazine and Albert' which introduced Walt Kelly's Pogo Possum who at the outset was no more than 'a bit player'. Pogo is unusual in that he started life in a comic book and eventually moved to a newspaper strip.[20] Walt Kelly's work was also seen in **Our Gang Comics** No. 1 (September 1942). Kelly became the editor of *The New York Star* in 1948, where Pogo had become a daily strip the year before.

Kelly was one of a number of animators who sold their work to comic-book publishers. The transition from the screen to the printed page was relatively easy and this freelancing helped boost their income.

George Baker, who had been an animator with the Walt Disney Studio and was now in the army, created The Sad Sack, the unfortunate private soldier. These early strips were published in the army's weekly newspaper *Yank*, and from 1944 the Bell Syndicate distributed them to a number of newspapers.

Marvel's first attempts at humour, **Comedy Comics** No. 9[21] and **Joker Comics** No. 1 (April 1942), featured people rather than animals but it wasn't long before funny animals appeared in Marvel's titles. In October 1942 they published **Terry-Toons** No. 1 featuring Gandy Goose and Sourpuss. Unusual at that time, **Terry-Toons** No. 1 contained a movie-style credits listing for the artists and writers; it even billed publisher Martin Goodman as Executive Producer and Stan Lee as Director.

Kirby and Simon's Newsboy Legion made their first appearance in April 1942 in DC's **Star Spangled Comics** No. 7. They were Tommy, Gabby, Scrapper, and Big Words. After saving the delinquent kids from a spell in reform school, patrolman Jim Harper, who at night became The Guardian, had the kids released to his custody. The Legion didn't know, but often suspected that Harper and The Guardian were one and the same. Kirby and Simon modelled the backdrop on New York, and drew from movie influences for hoods, felons, con-men and killers who appeared regularly in the stories. Kirby said:

I spent all my early life drawing on the sidewalks of the lower East Side. In my kid strips I was only duplicating the atmosphere I knew. The city was my only experience.'

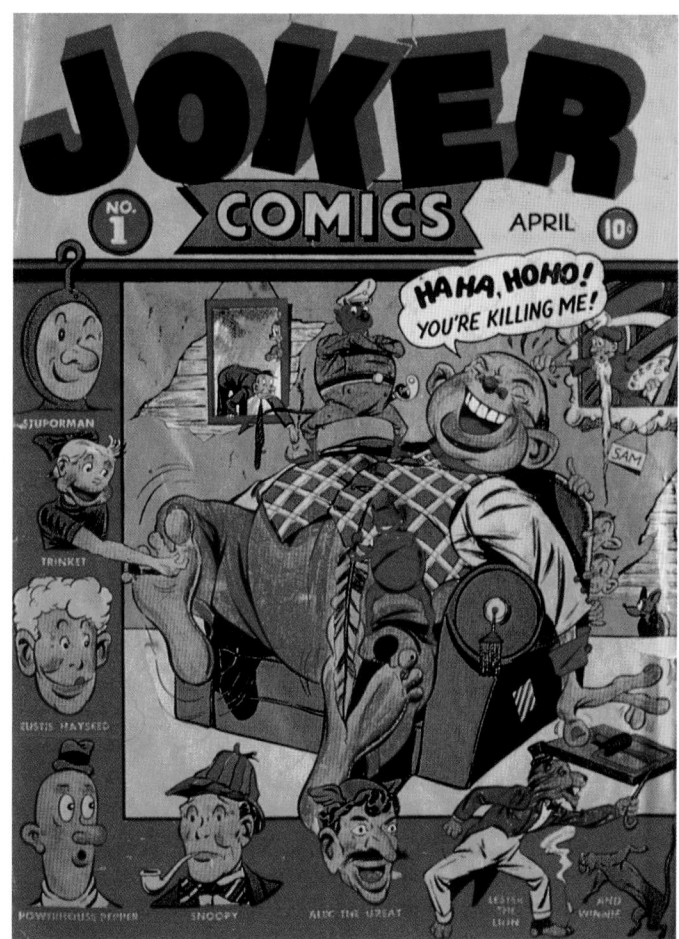

Three months later their second 'kid' team, The Boy Commandos, premiered in **Detective Comics** No. 64 (July 1942). Under Captain Rip Carter, the kids' job was to fight the fascists and free the world. The team was Alfy Twidget from Great Britain, Andre from France, Jan from Holland and Brooklyn from America. They went on to get their own title in **The Boy Commandos** No. 1 (Winter 1942–3), which ran for 36 issues until December 1949, and proved to be the most popular heroes of their genre.

Dell continued to rake in kids' dimes with the publication in July 1942 of one of the first comics to deal with World War II, **War Heroes** No. 1. Also in July, flushed with the success of their cartoon characters in **Looney Tunes and Merrie Melodies Comics**, they revamped and renamed **The Funnies** with issue No. 65. It became **New Funnies** and contained Andy Panda, Oswald Rabbit and Woody Woodpecker strips, all of which had appeared in Walter Lantz's Paramount cartoons.

A month or so later Dell's **Four Color** (Series II) No. 9 (undated), featured 'Donald Duck Finds Pirate Gold', Carl Barks's first comic-book work.

Barks went on to create his most famous character, Uncle Scrooge, five years later and also created Gyro Gearloose, Gladstone Gander, and The Beagle Boys. He drew the 'ducks' anonymously for more than twenty years before receiving well-earned recognition in the early 1970s, when he came to be known as the 'Duck Man'. He retired from drawing at the age of 65 to devote himself to full-time painting. His canvases, depicting Donald & Co. are masterpieces that are sought by collectors and change hands for staggering amounts of money.

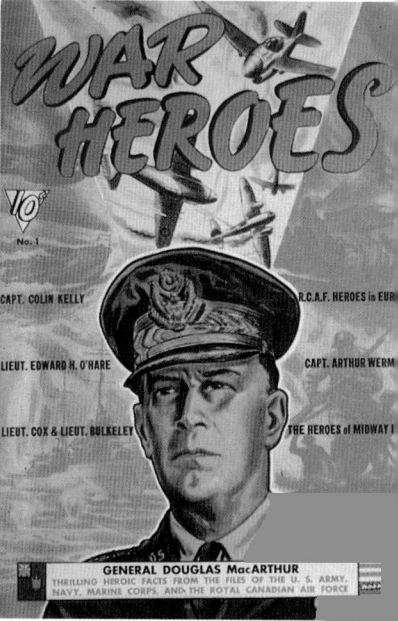

In 1993, at the age of 92, Carl Barks was honoured at Diamond Comics, Inc.'s annual seminar, where lifelong fan and Diamond president Steve Geppi presented him with a special Lifetime Achievement Award.

It was inevitable that there would be a funny animal superhero, and in October 1942 Nedor published **Coo Coo Comics** No. 1, featuring the origin of Super-Mouse, a mouse version of Superman.

Fawcett used Captain Marvel in promoting **Fawcett's Funny Animals** No. 1 (December 1942), in which they introduced one of the first funny animal super-heroes, Hoppy the Marvel Bunny. On the cover, Captain Marvel '*WELCOMES THE NEW ANIMAL HEROES TO FUNNYLAND*'. Hoppy also used the magic word 'Shazam!' to transform into a rabbit version of Captain Marvel.

Towards the end of 1942 MLJ published **Archie Comics** No. 1, plucked from the pages of **Pep**, and setting a trend for the next twenty or so years for 'teenage' characters in comics. Archie has seen off the competition and remained the most popular and enduring teenager in comics.

In 1943, Republic Pictures brought Captain America to the silver screen in a 15-part serial starring Dick Purcell in the title role. The serial seemed to have little in common with the comic: Captain America's alter ego Steve Rogers became Grant Gardner who, instead of being an army private, was a district attorney, and the famous shield was replaced with a gun! Despite these changes, it is considered to be one of the better serials of its type.

The same year, Columbia entered the comic-book serial area with *Batman and Robin*, starring Lewis Wilson as Batman and Douglas Croft as Robin. The dynamic duo do battle against Dr Daka and the slaves of the rising sun.

By 1943, paper shortages caused by the war were hampering the comic-book industry and fewer comics were being produced. Servicemen read comics as light relief and the publishers were quick to give them what they wanted. There were a number of new war titles including Fawcett's **Don Winslow of the Navy** No. 1 (February 1943) and numerous new funny animal and humour titles.

Fawcett, once again, used Captain Marvel to promote their new Western title, **Hopalong Cassidy** No. 1 (February 1943). He is seen in a box on the cover, wearing a cowboy hat, saying: '*HOPALONG'S MY CHOICE FOR ROOTIN' TOOTIN' WILD WEST ACTION*'.

Superhero comics continued to do well and Marvel published another anthology title, **All Select Comics** No. 1 (Fall 1943),[22] starring Captain America, The Sub-Mariner and The Human Torch, while their 'Young Allies' appeared in another new title, **Kid Komics** No. 1 (February 1943).

During the war period, the work of one of Marvel's greatest cover artists, Alex Schomburg, came into its own. In many cases the cover sold the comic and Schomburg's elaborate crowded covers with precise detail and fantastic scenery meant, in some cases, that the cover was better than the interior. Schomburg worked without supervision in his own studio and his classic covers are considered to be the best of their type. More than thirty years later, Schomburg returned to Marvel to draw the cover for **Invaders Annual** No. 1 (1977), where his inimitable style stood out as a brief reminder of his talent.

Marvel continued to push their humorous titles, publishing **All Surprise** No. 1 (Fall 1943), featuring Super Rabbit.

Superman, Batman and Wonder Woman continued to do well for DC Comics, but the only new title they published in 1943 was a humour anthology, **All Funny Comics** No. 1 (December). This contained the first appearance of their teen character Buzzy, styled on Archie.

DON WINSLOW OF THE NAVY
No. 1
FEB. 17
A FAWCETT PUBLICATION
10¢
HI' YA, FRIENDS! MEET COMMANDER DON WINSLOW OF THE NAVY. THIS DYNAMIC STAR OF RADIO AND MOVIES IS HERE TO THRILL YOU IN HIS OWN 68-PAGE COMICS MAGAZINE!

By the end of 1943 it was estimated that comic-book sales were worth $30 million (£20 million) in the US alone, and up to 25 million copies were being sold monthly.

DC continued with humour titles in 1944 with another anthology, **Funny Stuff**[23] No. 1 (Summer 1944), starring The Three Mousketeers, and later with **Buzzy** No. 1 (Winter 1944).

Marvel had also recognized the popularity of teenage comics and published **Tessie the Typist**[24] No. 1 (Summer 1944), and **Junior Miss** (Winter 1944) which featured the life stories of Frank Sinatra and June Allyson. Their title **Miss America Comics**, featuring their superheroine Miss America, lasted only one issue before it changed magazine format to become **Miss America Magazine** (November 1944). It had a photo-cover of a teenage girl in a Miss America costume, the first appearance of the character Patsy Walker, stories and movie reviews as well as features on clothes and makeup. It was well received and ran for fourteen years.

Although not a particularly significant year, 1944 saw an increase in comic-book popularity, with a large number of parents and educators seeing them as being good for children.

One of the big events of 1945 was in January with the first appearance of Superboy in **More Fun Comics** No. 101.[25] DC billed it as: *'The Adventures of Superman when he was a boy.'* The stories were set some fifteen years earlier in Superman's home town of Smallville, somewhere in Kansas. Some of Superman's origin was glossed over and some changed to accommodate Superboy. We had previously seen that after the death of his foster parents, Martha and Jonathan Kent, Superman left Smallville for Metropolis, where the world learned of him for the first time. The Superboy stories tell us that the world already knew about him and that he had been a superhero as a child.

DC began publishing a series of six special edition reprints for the US Navy. They were 52-page, comic-size giveaways and had simplified wording! It seems strange that DC thought of the Navy personnel, who were helping defend America, as being less able to read long words than the children the comics were originally aimed at.

Max Gaines had left DC in 1944 and later that year formed his own company, Educational Comics, which was to change its name to Entertaining Comics, and

today is still referred to as EC Comics. Gaines had always wanted to use comics to educate, and his first few titles included **Picture Stories From American History** No. 1 (1946), **Picture Stories From World History** No. 1 (Spring 1947) and **Picture Stories From Science** (Spring 1947).

With the end of the war in 1945, although superhero comics were still popular, sales began to decline. Soldiers had been buying large quantities of comics made available to them at the camp shops, and were now back in the real world, which meant they were unemployed or in low-paid jobs. Also, the bond between the soldiers and the superheroes, both fighting a common enemy, was now gone.

Although Fawcett published a new superhero title, **Marvel Family** No. 1 (December 1945), featuring Captain Marvel, Captain Marvel, Jr. and Mary Marvel, many publishers began turning their attentions to other genres.

Marvel published a number of new titles aimed at adolescent girls, including **Patsy Walker** No. 1 (Summer 1945) and **Millie the Model** No. 1 (Winter 1945), whose 'innocent' adventures delighted audiences for more than twenty years.

In November 1945, Harvey published **Joe Palooka** No. 1, featuring stories about prize fighting. It had previously had a brief run with the Columbia Comics Group, Nos 1–4 (1942–4). There were also numerous new funny-animal titles.

MLJ's **Archie Comics** continued to be popular and, in June, NBC began airing a radio show based on the character.

MLJ's Katy Keene made her first appearance in **Wilber Comics** No. 5 (Summer 1945) and continues in popularity to this day.

DC's Fox and the Crow made their first appearance in **Real Screen Funnies**[26] No. 1 (Spring 1945).

In Dell's **Four Color** (Series II) No. 74 (June 1945), Marge's Little Lulu made her debut in comics, having previously been a weekly strip in the *Saturday Evening Post* since 1935. Little Lulu's creator, Marjorie Henderson Buell, had nothing to do with creating the comics, although she insisted on approving everything prior to publication, until she sold her rights to Western Publishing in 1977.

No one can say for sure when the Golden Age ended, or what the last Golden Age comic was, but it is widely considered that its ending coincided with the end of the Second World War in Europe in 1945.

It was the end of an era, its like not to be seen again but only imitated and, according to some, improved, with the coming of the Silver Age more than ten years later. The years in between began with what is now called the Post-Golden Age.

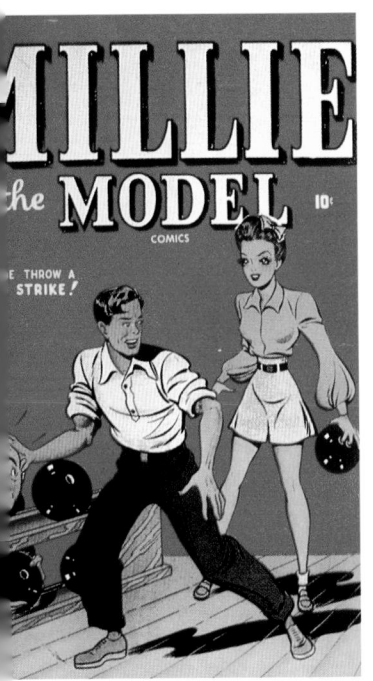

▲ MILLIE THE MODEL No. 1, *Winter 1945* (™ & Copyright © 1994 Marvel Entertainment Group, Inc.)

◀ SPECIAL EDITION U.S. NAVY No. 1, 1945, *was a reprint of* SUPERMAN NO. 34 (™ & Copyright © 1994 DC Comics, Inc.)

▲ PICTURE STORIES FROM AMERICAN HISTORY No. 1, *1946* (Copyright © 1946 EC Comics)

▲ REAL SCREEN FUNNIES No. 1, *Spring 1945* (™ & Copyright © 1994 DC Comics, Inc.)

3

The Post-Golden Age
1945–50

THE WHOLE WORLD MOVED INTO A NEW ERA ON 5 AUGUST 1945 when the city of Hiroshima in Japan was devastated by an atomic bomb. The comic industry was quick to respond with stories and characters with the atomic-bomb and radioactivity themes. The covers of **Atoman** No. 1 (February 1946), drawn by Batman artist Jerry Robinson, and **Science Comics** No. 1 (January 1946) both depict the mushroom cloud of the bomb. **Science Comics** states on its cover, '*The Exciting Story of The Atomic Bomb*', while Atoman, created by Joseph Greene, tells us, '*Atomic power belongs to the whole earth. My Power must be used to help all people, regardless of race or creed or nationality!*' In January 1946, *Picture News* asked the question on its cover: '*Will the Atom Blow the World Apart?*'

There have been numerous 'atom bomb' covers which are sought after by some collectors.

At the San Diego Comic Book Convention in 1991, Jerry Robinson was surprised when I told him I had just paid $200 (£133) for a perfect copy of **Atoman** No. 1:

That's a lot more than I got paid to draw it! In fact I didn't get paid at all for issue two, I was working on issue three when I found out that I wasn't getting paid for issue two, I think the company [Spark Publications], went out of business, so I stopped work on the third issue.

There was no third issue, **Atoman** ceased publication with issue No. 2 (April 1946).

Comics were now a well-established feature of everyday life and with the war over there was no shortage of paper; more comics than ever were being published.

The industry seemed to turn its attention away from superheroes, and in 1946 hardly any new characters emerged, although, in June, Harvey published **Black Cat Comics** No. 1. Black Cat was a Hollywood stunt-girl and early superheroine.

Although comics were originally welcomed by parents and educators as a good thing, by the mid forties social commentators had become uncomfortable with the increasing level of violence portrayed in some comics. Publishers placated critics by publishing comics that educated as well as entertained. DC published **Real Fact** No. 1 (March 1946; see illustration, page 44) and Catholic students were able to read **Treasure Chest Comics** (March 1946), which had a distinct religious flavour.

▲ SCIENCE COMICS
No. 1,
January 1946
(Copyright © 1946 Humor
Publications)

▲ ATOMAN No. 1,
February 1946
(Copyright © 1946 Spark
Publications)

◀ BLACK CAT COMICS
No. 1,
June–July 1946
(™ & Copyright © 1994 The
Harvey Entertainment
Company)

Walt Kelly's Pogo Possum shared his own title with Albert in **Four Color** (Series II) No. 105 (May 1946) and throughout the year funny-animal titles continued to do well, in some cases to the detriment of superhero titles, which by the following year were surpassed in popularity by other genres.

The year 1947 saw the first 'romance' comic, by none other than Captain America's creators, Jack Kirby and Joe Simon, published by Hillman Periodicals and entitled **My Date Comics** (July 1947). It was a resounding flop! It ran for only four issues, after which Simon and Kirby moved their romance idea to the Prize Comics Group where, in September 1947, they published **Young Romance** No. 1, which proved to be a tremendous success. The title ran for 29 years and 208 issues.[1]

The other publishers quickly followed suit by publishing their own romance titles.

Crime, Western, and funny animals also did well in 1947, again to the detriment of superhero titles, although Batman was still in favour and Robin began solo adventures in **Star Spangled Comics** No. 65 (February 1947).

By 1948, Fawcett's Western title **Hopalong Cassidy** was selling more than eight million copies. The other big publishers jumped on the Western stage-coach and began publishing cowboy titles. In January 1948, DC published **Western Comics** No. 1 and in November changed their superhero title, **All American Comics**, to **All American Western**.[2] In September they published **Dale Evans** No. 1, based on the hit television Western series. (See illustrations, pages 46 and 47.)

Marvel's first Western title was **The Two-Gun Kid** No. 1 (March 1948), quickly followed by **Annie Oakley** No. 1 (Spring 1948), **Tex Morgan** No. 1 (August 1948),

ALBERT
The Alligator
and Pogo Possum

by Walt Kelly

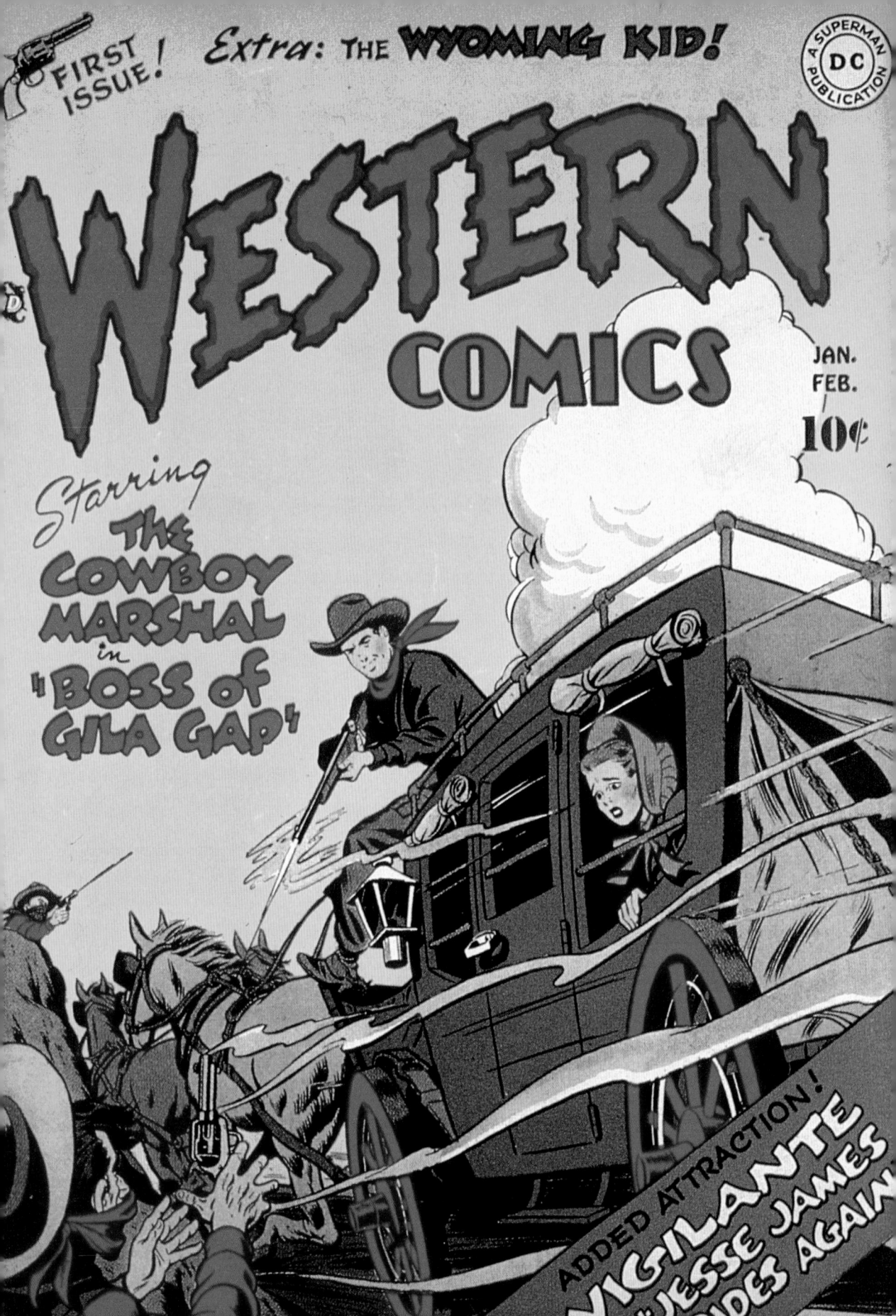

Kid Colt Outlaw No. 1 (August 1948),[3] **Tex Taylor** No. 1 (September 1948) and **Blaze Carson** No. 1 (September 1948). Marvel's publisher, Martin Goodman, was no stranger to the Western, he was merely returning to his pulp publishing beginnings.

Marvel also brought out a string of romance titles, the genre by now being extremely popular. Their first was **My Romance** No. 1 (September 1948).[4] Stan Lee was writing a great number of Marvel's output of both Western and romance titles. He said, '*When we did westerns, I wrote more westerns than anybody; when we did romance I wrote more romances.*'[5]

Despite the popularity of Western and romance titles, the year belonged to crime comics. Their popularity had been steadily growing and in 1948 virtually every publisher was putting at least one crime comic on to the newsstands. Some companies changed existing titles into crime titles. William Gaines, who had taken over EC Comics after the death of his father in a boating accident the previous year, changed the name of **International Comics** to **International Crime Patrol** with issue No. 6 (Spring 1948) and published **War Against Crime** No. 1 (Spring 1948).[6]

In the autumn of 1947, Marvel changed the name of its funny-animal title **Wacky Duck** to **Justice Comics** with issue No. 7[7] and during the next couple of years **Cindy Smith** changed to **Crime Can't Win** with issue No. 41 (September 1950) and **Willie Comics** changed to **Crime Cases Comics** with issue No. 24 (August 1950). **Crimefighters** No. 1 was published in April 1948.[8]

Fox Features Syndicate began publishing **Crimes by Women** in June 1948. The covers usually depicted a seductive-looking woman, and No. 1 featured '*The True Story of Bonnie Parker, Queen of the Gunmolls!*'. St John Publishing's **Crime Reporter** used the same technique for gaining a potential reader's attention, and Ribbage's **Crime Smasher**, with its covers stating '*The Law Always Wins!*' and '*Crime Can't Pay – In Any Way!*', with the exception of issue No. 1 (October 1950) also used images of women, who were mostly helpless and sometimes tied up. Issues Nos 1 and 2 of Fox Features Syndicate's **Murder Incorporated** (January and March 1948), had '*For Adults Only*' printed on the covers, but this certainly didn't stop children buying and reading the comic.

Public opinion against this and other types of comics was growing. A number of crimes perpetrated by youngsters were alleged to be 'copycat' crimes. The senior

psychiatrist for the New York Department of Hospitals, Dr Frederick Wertham, held a conference entitled 'The Psycho-pathology of Comic Books'. He told delegates that comic books were 'abnormally sexually aggressive'. Shortly afterwards, ABC broadcast on the radio a programme called *What's Wrong With Comics?* A number of comic books were banned and teachers, who had once encouraged their pupils to read them, organized the mass burning of comics in schoolyards.

The publishers were concerned by this threat to their companies and, in July 1948, a number of them, including Bill Gaines, formed the Association of Comics Magazine Publishers (ACMP). The ACMP offered publishers a seal of approval if their product met the Association's standard of decency. Qualifying comics would print the Association's seal on their cover. Unfortunately, the industry rejected this form of self-censorship and the Association soon disbanded, but the public continued to blame comics for almost everything wrong with the younger generation.

Despite this anti-comics campaign, more and more new titles were being published. In autumn 1948, the American Comics Group (ACG) published **Adventures into the Unknown** No. 1, which was the first continuous-series horror comic. Issue No. 1 featured an adaptation of Horace Walpole's *Castle of Otranto*.

The public were buying more romance, Western and crime comics than at any other time. However, superhero titles continued to decline, although Superman and Batman sales were given a boost in 1948 by the release of the Columbia serials *Superman*, starring Kirk Alyn in the title role, written by DC's Mort Weisinger, and *The New Adventures of Batman and Robin*, starring Robert Lowery as Batman and Johnny Duncan as Robin.

◄ ADVENTURES INTO
THE UNKNOWN No. 1,
Fall 1948
(Copyright © 1948 American
Comics Group)

▼ SUPERBOY No. 1,
March–April 1949
(™ & Copyright © 1994 DC
Comics, Inc.)

▼ ARCHIE'S PAL
JUGHEAD No. 1,
1949
(™ & Copyright © 1994 Archie
Comic Publications, Inc.)

In March 1949, DC published one of the few new superhero titles that year, **Superboy** No. 1.[9] In fact, superhero titles were selling so badly that Marvel dropped a number of theirs in favour of romance titles. This included **The Human Torch** which became **Love Tales** with No. 36 (May 1949)[10] and **Sub-Mariner**[11] which became **Best Love** with No. 33 (August 1949).

The Western and romance genres were combined in Prize Comics' **Real West Romance** Vol. 1 No. 1, (April/May 1949) featuring *'True-life Ranch Romances'*.

Teen-humour titles were still popular and Archie Comics produced new titles giving already-popular characters their own books. Jughead and Katy Keene got their own titles in **Archie's Pal Jughead** No. 1[12] and, 'by popular demand', **Katy Keene** No. 1.

Harvey published George Baker's hard-done-by soldier, now a civilian, in **Sad Sack Comics** No. 1 (September 1949) and, in March 1950, published **Blondie Comics** No. 16[13] following it up in September 1950 with **Dagwood** No. 1.

The campaign against comics continued with the publication of the findings of a Cincinnati Committee on 'The Evaluation of Comic Books', which stated that *'Seventy percent of all comic books contained objectionable material, from scenes of sadistic torture to suggestive and salacious actions.'* Comics were getting a bad press and continued to be blamed for juvenile delinquency. Some parents and teachers banned comics from their homes and schools, which in a lot of cases merely drove the reading habits of their children underground. Although a 1950 Senate Committee report on the effect of crime comic books upon juvenile delinquency was inconclusive, sales did temporarily fall and a number of states went as far as to legislate against the sale of comics. Nevertheless, where comics continued to be sold, they became even more violent and gory.

SCIENCE
WEIRD SCIENCE
AN ENTERTAINING COMIC
EC
NO. 12
MAY-JUNE
10¢
INTRODUCING A NEW TREND IN MAGAZINES...
SCIENTIFIC SuspenStories WE DARE YOU TO READ!
GOOD LORD, KARL... YOU'RE SHRINKING RAPIDLY... AND THERE'S NOTHING I CAN DO FOR YOU! YOU WILL SOON FIND YOURSELF IN A WORLD THAT NO MAN HAS EVER SEEN... A MICROCOSM OF MOLECULES... ATOMS... ELECTRONS AND PROTONS! AND THEN... YOU WILL CONTINUE TO SHRINK... SHRINK INTO... INTO... WHAT? WHAT WILL YOU FIND, KARL?
FELDSTEIN

4

The Pre-Silver Age
1950–56

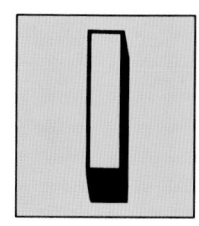

N APRIL 1950, PUBLISHER WILLIAM GAINES AND EDITOR Al Feldstein introduced their New Trend line with the publication of **Vault of Horror** No. 12 (No.1),[1] and **Crypt of Terror** No. 17 (No. 1)[2]. This was quickly followed in May by **Haunt of Fear** No. 15.[3] All three new titles carried the same announcement on their covers: '*Introducing a New Trend in Magazines ... Illustrated Suspenstories We Dare You to Read!*'

Feldstein's Crypt Keeper, Vault Keeper and the Old Witch told the stories in the comics, which even by today's standards are considered, in some cases, if not shocking, certainly gruesome, with bloody decapitations, eyes being ripped out, torture, sadism, gore, axe murders, people buried alive, bondage and cannibalism. Evil triumphed over good regularly – the kids loved them and the parents and teachers hated them.

By now, although keeping the same EC logo, Gaines had changed the meaning of the initials of his company from Educational Comics, his father Max Gaines's laudable title, to Entertaining Comics. EC no longer published comics that 'educated' but instead published comics that 'entertained'. These New Trend comics caused quite a stir and despite complaints from parents and teachers, the publishers made no concessions, and EC's titles became immensely popular.

EC didn't publish only horror titles. In May 1953 the New Trend continued with the launch of two science-fiction titles, **Weird Fantasy** No. 13 (No. 1)[4] and **Weird Science** No. 12.[5] Although the first few issues of these titles had EC's horror style, they later went on to produce some of the best stories and finest art of the genre. They published, initially without his knowledge, a number of Ray Bradbury stories, which they only paid for on being caught. On their covers, these two titles carried the same announcement as the horror titles, with the word 'illustrated' being replaced with 'scientific'. Gaines was reported to have said, '*We at EC are proudest of our Science Fiction.*' Perhaps this was to placate the anti-horror lobby. Both Gaines and Feldstein were avid horror fans.

In 1950, Columbia released their second Superman serial, again written by Weisinger and starring Kirk Alyn, *Superman vs. The Atom Man*, which helped sales of the title.

▲ THE VAULT OF HORROR No. 12, *April–May 1950, was the first issue of this title* (Copyright © 1950 EC Comics)

◀ WEIRD SCIENCE No. 12, *May–June 1950, was the first issue of this title* (Copyright © 1950 EC Comics)

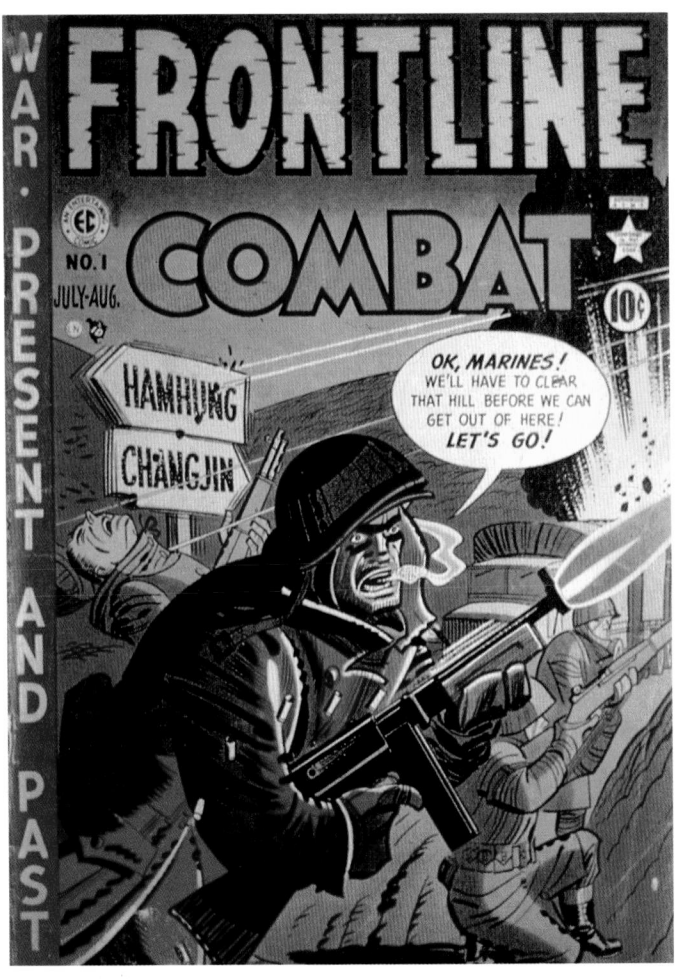

A number of other science-fiction titles began to appear, including DC's **Strange Adventures** No. 1 (August 1950), but in the main new titles were still restricted to Westerns, romance and comics based on real-life film and television personalities, such as DC's **Adventures of Bob Hope** No. 1 (February–March 1950) of which the first four issues sported a photo cover.

During 1951, a great number of publishers emulated the EC horror and science-fiction styles. Harvey Publications went as far as to have hosts similar to the Old Witch and the Vault Keeper in their new titles **Witches Tales** No. 1[6] (January 1951) and **Chamber of Chills** No. 21 (No. 1)[7] (June 1951).

DC published **Mystery in Space** No. 1 (April/May 1951) and in June Marvel, under its Atlas banner, published their horror title **Strange Tales** No. 1,[8] which would later become the home of the Silver Age Human Torch and Doctor Strange. In July ACG added another horror title, **Forbidden Worlds** No. 1.

Also in 1951, EC began its war title, **Frontline Combat** No. 1 (July/August), edited by the superb cartoonist Harvey Kurtzman who wrote and drew some remarkable serious war strips for the book.

By 1952 horror, science-fiction and romance titles had reached their peak and crime titles were declining in popularity. In July DC gave the popular double-act, Martin and Lewis, their own comic with **The Adventures of Dean Martin and Jerry Lewis** No. 1. The title was so popular that it continued after the break-up of the act and it wasn't until November 1957 that it was renamed **The Adventures of Jerry Lewis** with issue No. 41.

▶ WITCHES TALES
No. 1,
January 1951
(™ & Copyright © 1994 The
Harvey Entertainment
Company)

◀ THE ADVENTURES
OF DEAN MARTIN AND
JERRY LEWIS No. 1,
July–August 1952
(™ & Copyright © 1994 DC
Comics, Inc.)

▲ BATTLE No. 1,
March 1951
(™ & Copyright © 1994 Marvel
Entertainment Group, Inc.)

There was an increased circulation in war titles as America was engaged in a 'police action'[9] in Korea and servicemen were, as usual, buying comics. Almost all the publishers were again producing war comics. Marvel's war titles, such as **Battle** No. 1 (March 1951), were full of patriotism and overtly anti-Communist. Many stories not only fought the Korean War but, in the case of DC's **Star Spangled War Stories** No. 131[10] (August 1952) and **Our Army at War** No. 1[11] (August 1952), refought the Second World War. (Marvel successfully refought the Second World War eleven years later in **Sgt. Fury & His Howling Commandos** No. 1 [May 1963].)

Harvey acquired a number of Paramount's animated characters from St John, and in August 1952 published **Little Audrey** No. 25 and, more significant, **Harvey Comics Hits** No. 61 (October 1952) featuring Casper the Friendly Ghost, who was destined to be one of Harvey's mainstays.

Superman titles were still popular, helped by the new TV series which began in 1952 and ran for 104 episodes until 1957. In some episodes, he was given powers which he had nowhere else, including being able to split into two Supermen, and the ability to walk through walls. It starred George Reeves in the title role, who became typecast as Superman and, afterwards unable to get any acting jobs, found work as a wrestler.

Shortly before the TV series there was a movie, *Superman and the Mole Men*. This very low-budget feature, where Superman doesn't even get to fly, also starred Reeves and served as a pilot for the TV series.

George Reeves shot himself in 1959. His fiancée said he had killed himself because *'he was known as Superman to nine million children, but couldn't get a job.'*

One of the most significant publications of 1952 was EC's **Tales Calculated to Drive You Mad** No. 1[12] (October), better known as **Mad**. Early on it was subtitled 'Humour in a Jugular Vein' and was original and fresh. Its creator, and editor for the first 28 issues, was Harvey Kurtzman who said of **Mad**:

We were tired of the war, ragged from science fiction, weary of the horror. Then it hit us! Why not do a complete about-face? A change of pace! A comic-book! Not a serious comic-book … but a comic comic-book! Not a floppity rabbit, giggly girl, anarchist teenage type comic-book … but a comic mag based on the short story type of wild adventures that you seem to like so well.

▲ LITTLE AUDREY
No. 25,
*August 1952, was the first
Harvey issue of this title*
(™ & Copyright © 1994 The
Harvey Entertainment
Company)

▲ THE MARVEL
FAMILY No. 89,
*January 1954, was the last
issue of this title*
(Copyright © 1954 Fawcett
Publications)

▼ THREE DIMENSION
COMICS STARRING
MIGHTY MOUSE No. 1,
*September 1953, was the first
3-D comic*
(Copyright © 1953 St John
Publishing Company)

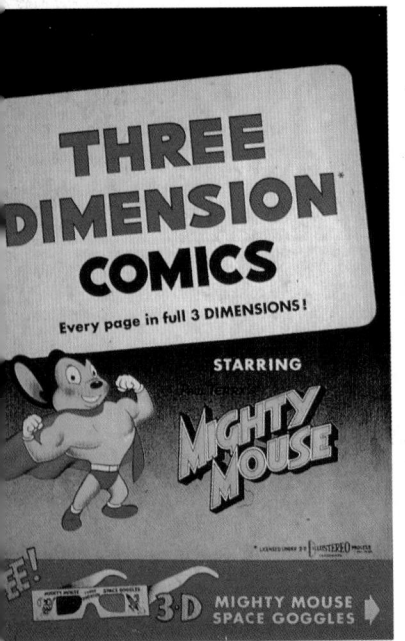

Nothing was sacred. **Mad** made fun of itself and of everything else besides, including comic books: issue No. 4 lampooned Superman with a strip drawn by Wally Wood, in which Superduperman fights his rival Captain Marbles, perhaps as a dig at the DC copyright action against Fawcett; Archie became Starchie – the typical teenager who smoked cigars; Mickey Mouse became Mickey Rodent; and Batman and Robin became Batboy and Rubin; to name but a few.

In 1953, had there been a genre popularity table, superheroes would have been at the bottom. They were now being outsold by almost every other genre, especially horror, romance and Westerns. DC continued to publish the Superman, Batman and Wonder Woman titles, but the other heroes were no more.

DC's twelve-year legal battle against Fawcett, which alleged that Captain Marvel infringed copyright of Superman, came to an end when Fawcett settled out of court. But all too late, in November 1953, **Captain Marvel Adventures** ceased publication with issue No. 150, and The Big Red Cheese said his last '*Shazam*' in **The Marvel Family** No. 89 (January 1954), where the lead story was aptly titled '*And then there were none!*' The Marvel family are seen as silhouettes on the cover where a boy asks the question: '*Holy Moley! What happened to the Marvel Family?*'

Was Captain Marvel merely a copy of Superman? Years later, a new generation of DC employees investigated the trial, and said no. Captain Marvel, and the whole approach of the character, was different from Superman. Of course, they are both variations of the same 'Herculean' theme, but handled in completely different ways.

DC bought the rights to Captain Marvel and in the 1970s began not only publishing new stories but also the stories from the 1940s – the same ones that had been in litigation!

3-D Comics

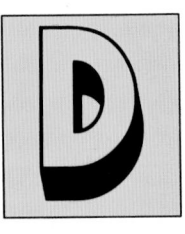

DURING HIS TOUR OF DUTY IN THE ARMY, JOE KUBERT HAD SEEN 3-D photographs in a movie magazine in Germany. The photographs were printed out of register and, when viewed through spectacles in which the left lens was red and the right green, they came together to give a three-dimensional effect. This was nothing new. In fact, the process was patented by Ducros du Hauron in the 1850s. Joe was fascinated by 3-D and, on leaving the army in 1951, set about adapting the process for comics. With his partner, Norman Maurer, fanatical Three Stooges fan and son-in-law of Moe Howard of the Three Stooges,[13] he set up a studio to produce 3-D comics. Their early unpublished attempts included strips using Joe's Tor character and Norman's Three Stooges strips. Finally, on perfecting the process, they converted the artwork for a Mighty Mouse comic for St John Publishing who produced the first 3-D comic in

▶ THREE DIMENSION
BATMAN
ADVENTURES (nn),
1953
(™ & Copyright © 1994 DC
Comics, Inc.)

▲ THREE DIMENSION
ADVENTURES OF
SUPERMAN (nn),
1953
(™ & Copyright © 1994 DC
Comics, Inc.)

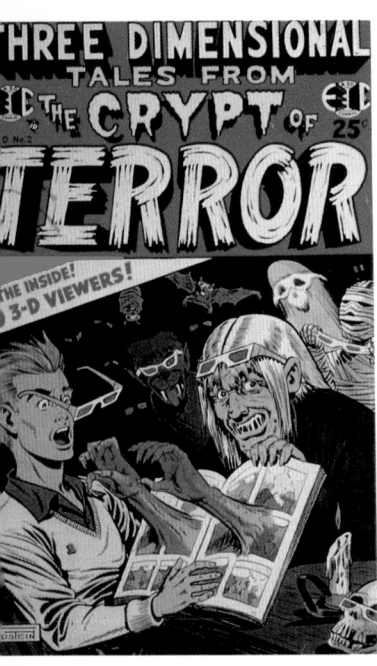

September 1953, **Three Dimension Comics Starring Mighty Mouse** No. 1. Despite the 25-cent price tag, it was a resounding success and went to a second printing the following month. St John quickly followed up with more 3-D titles, including an issue of **Three Dimension Comics** (October 1953) starring the Three Stooges, and **Whack** (October 1953), which was similar to **Mad**. Other publishers quickly followed St John into 3-D and by spring 1954 more than fifty 3-D comics had been published. DC published both Superman and Batman in 3-D, and EC published some of their horror material in the format. There was even an **I Love Lucy** 3-D magazine featuring 'Foto Magic Pictures' and selling at the huge price of 49 cents!

◀ THREE DIMENSIONAL TALES FROM THE CRYPT OF TERROR (nn), *Spring 1954* (Copyright © 1954 EC Comics)

LISTING OF EARLY 3-D COMICS

COMIC TITLE	DATE	PUBLISHER
Mighty Mouse 3-D No. 1	Sep 1953	St John
House of Terror	Oct 1953	St John
Little Eva 3-D No. 1	Oct 1953	St John
Mighty Mouse 3-D No. 1 (reprint)	Oct 1953	St John
Three Stooges 3-D No. 2	Oct 1953	St John
Tor 3-D No. 2	Oct 1953	St John
Tor 3-D No. 2 (reprint)	Oct 1953	St John
Whack 3-D	Oct 1953	St John
3-D-ell No. 1 Rootie Kazootie	Nov 1953	Dell
Adventures in 3-D No. 1	Nov 1953	Harvey
Three Dimension Adventures of Superman	Nov 1953	DC
Abbott and Costello 3-D	Nov 1953	St John
Daring Adventures 3-D	Nov 1953	St John
The Hawk 3-D	Nov 1953	St John
Little Eva 3-D No. 2	Nov 1953	St John
Mighty Mouse 3-D No. 2	Nov 1953	St John
Three Stooges 3-D No 3	Nov 1953	St John
Tor 3-D No. 2	Nov 1953	St John
Katy Keene 3-D	Dec 1953	Archie Comics
Noodnik 3-D	Dec 1953	Comic Media
3-D Funny Movies	Dec 1953	Comic Media
3-D-ell No. 3 Flukey Luke	Dec 1953	Dell
3-D Features Present Jet Pup	Dec 1953	Dimensions
3-D Sheena the Jungle Queen	Dec 1953	Fiction House
Captain 3-D	Dec 1953	Harvey
Funny 3-D	Dec 1953	Harvey
3-D Dolly	Dec 1953	Harvey

COMIC TITLE	DATE	PUBLISHER
True 3-D No. 1	Dec 1953	Harvey
3-D Batman	Dec 1953	DC
Animal Fun 3-D	Dec 1953	Premier
Space Kat-ets 3-D	Dec 1953	Power
The First Christmas 3-D	Dec 1953	Fiction House
3-D Circus	Dec 1953	Fiction House
Indian Warriors 3-D	Dec 1953	Star
Jungle Thrills 3-D	Dec 1953	Star
Super Animals 3-D	Dec 1953	Star
Western Fighters 3-D	Dec 1953	Star
Mighty Mouse 3-D No. 3	Dec 1953	St John
3-D Love	Dec 1953	Sterographic
Super Funnies No. 1 Dopey Duck	Dec 1953	Superior
Felix the Cat 3-D	Dec 1953	Toby Press
I Love Lucy 3-D	1953	Foto Magic(?)
3-D Action	Jan 1954	Atlas
3-D Tales of the West	Jan 1954	Atlas
Adventures in 3-D No. 2	Jan 1954	Harvey
Jiggs and Maggie No. 26 (some 3-D)	Jan 1954	Harvey
Katzenjammer Kids No. 26 (some 3-D)	Jan 1954	Harvey
Sad Sack 3-D Harvey Hits	Jan 1954	Harvey
3-D Romance	Jan 1954	Sterographic
True 3-D No. 2	Feb 1954	Harvey
Peter Cottontail 3-D	Feb 1954	Key
Three Dimensional EC Classics	Spr 1954	EC
3-D Tales from the Crypt	Spr 1954	EC

The craze died as fast as it had caught on and no title continued past a few issues. Within six or so months of the first 3-D comic appearing the phenomenon was forgotten.

What happened next is much more memorable.

NE OF THE MOST SIGNIFICANT FACTORS IN CHANGING publishing habits came about in spring 1954 with the publication of Dr Frederick Wertham's damning book *The Seduction of the Innocent*.[14]

Wertham, who believed comic books to be a major cause of juvenile delinquency, had been a long-time campaigner and critic of them. He first spoke on the subject in 1947. Prior to the publication of *The Seduction of the Innocent*, Wertham had written a number of medical books mostly concerning the brain, including *The Brain as an Organ* (1934), which was used as a textbook in medical schools throughout the world, and *The Catathymic Crisis* (1937) which describes in great detail a new mental disorder.

Wertham had specialized in psychiatry since 1922 and was the psychiatric consultant to the Chief Censor of the United States Treasury Department. As well as teaching psychiatry and psychotherapy, he also lectured at Yale Law School. He was a consultant to the Juvenile Aid Bureau and, between 1948 and 1951, a director of Quaker Emergency Service Readjustment Center, which functioned under the magistrate court in New York.

He had an insatiable desire to 'warn' parents of the evil of comic books, and embarked on a series of public lectures, newspaper and magazine articles and statements that culminated in the publication of his sensationalist anti-comic book which, full of half-truths and convenient statistics, very nearly killed the comic industry.

In *The Seduction of the Innocent*, Wertham devotes 397 pages to his attempt to connect violence in comic books with juvenile crime. He suggests that graphic scenes of sex and violence in comic books would, in many cases, lead otherwise 'normal' children into a horrific world of dark depression and criminal activities.

He viewed comic books as drugs, stating that even children from slum neighbourhoods would find the money to buy them. Their corrupting influence, he writes, would cause children to emulate what they saw on the printed page. In the book he recounts interviews with juvenile delinquents who are quick to agree that comics have influenced their behaviour. He returns to the 'copying' theme over and over.

This factor of copying in action a detail from a comic book had been brought home by the cases where children hanged themselves … A four year old boy in Florida looked through his brother's comic books and his mother found him under a tree stark naked, with a long knife in his hands. Stunned, she asked him why he had undressed himself, and what he was doing. He replied 'The man in the comics did it.' Later he showed her pictures where some 'Mongols' had a white man stripped naked and one of them had a long knife to cut out the American's tongue. In California a very handsome six year old boy on his way home from school one day trudged to the top of a steep cliff. An ardent comic-book reader, he had translated his reading into practice and made for himself a flying cape or magic cloak. Taking a brisk run he jumped off the cliff to fly as his comic-book heroes did. Seriously injured he told his mother, 'Mama, I almost did fly!' A few days later he died from the injuries he had received.

Whether coincidence or not, in a 1954 TV episode of *The Adventures of Superman* entitled 'The Unlucky Number', George (Superman) Reeves warned kids to be careful; 'No one, but no one, can do the things Superman does. And that especially goes for flying!'

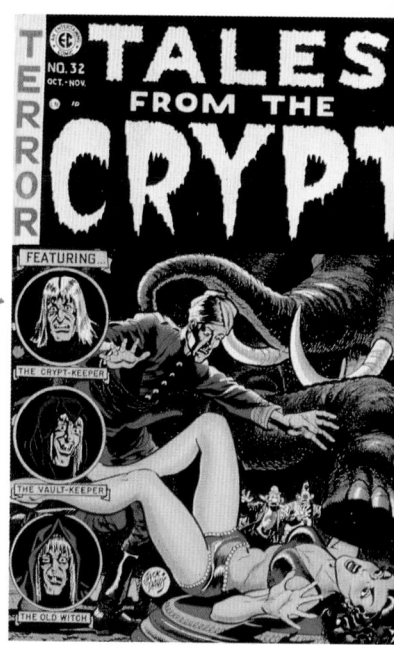

▲ TALES FROM THE CRYPT No. 32, *October–November 1952, was typical of the comics to which Wertham objected* (Copyright © 1952 EC Comics)

Wertham went on:

There is a high correlation between delinquency and reading disorders; that is to say, a disproportionate number of poor or non-readers become delinquents, and a disproportionate number of delinquents have pronounced reading disorders and that reading comics reinforces the disorder. The child frustrated by failure, is made more liable to commit a defiant act. At the same time comics books suggest all kinds of specific defiant acts.

One chapter, entitled 'I Want to be a Sex Maniac', discusses 'comic books and the psycho-sexual development of children'. It leaves the reader with the impression that comic books are the sole reason for any kind of sexual deviation in juveniles. He quotes numerous cases of 'sex delinquents' who seem only too pleased to support his case. A twelve-year-old told him:

In the comic books sometimes the men threaten the girls. They beat them with their hands. They tie them around a chair and then they beat them. When I read such a book I get sexually excited. They don't get me sexually excited all the time, only when they tie them up.

Wertham goes on to say:

The difference between surreptitious pornographic literature for adults and children's comic books is this: in one it is a question of attracting perverts, in the other of making them.

In the passage below, he tries to draw a connection between the increase in homosexuality and comic books.

They [Batman and Robin], constantly rescue each other from violent attacks by an unending number of enemies. The feeling is conveyed that we men must stick together because there are so many villainous creatures who have to be exterminated. They lurk not only under every bed but also behind every star in the sky. Either Batman or his young boy friend are both captured, threatened with every imaginable weapon, almost blown to bits, almost crushed to death, almost annihilated. Sometimes Batman ends up in bed injured and young Robin is shown sitting next to him. At home they lead an idyllic life. They are Bruce Wayne and 'Dick' Grayson. Bruce Wayne is described as a 'socialite' and the official relationship is that Dick is Bruce's ward. They live in sumptuous quarters, with beautiful flowers in large vases, and have a butler, Alfred. Batman is sometimes shown in a dressing gown. As they sit by the fireplace the young boy sometimes worries about his partner: 'Something's wrong with Bruce. He hasn't been himself these past few days.' It is like a wish dream of two homosexuals living together. Sometimes they are shown on a couch, Bruce reclining and Dick sitting next to him, jacket off, collar open, and his hand on his friend's arm. Like the girls in other stories, Robin is sometimes held captive by the villains and Batman has to give in or 'Robin gets killed.'

Robin is a handsome ephetic boy, usually showing his uniform with bare legs. He is buoyant with energy and devoted to nothing on earth or in interplanetary space as much as to Bruce Wayne. He often stands with legs spread, the genital region discreetly evident.

Wertham deliberately, or otherwise, missed the point, that in truth Bruce Wayne and Dick Grayson's relationship was no more than that of father and son.

The US Senate Subcommittee to Investigate Juvenile Delinquency in the United States held public hearings in April 1954 and Wertham gave testimony which damned comics. He told the Chairman, Senator William Langer of South Dakota, that he had a statement of about 20 or 25 minutes, which he was asked to summarize. He told the committee of his credentials and spoke about his publications, including *The Seduction of the Innocents*. He said that his study was the first and only individual large-scale study on the subject of comic books in general. It was his opinion, based on hundreds of cases of all kinds, that without any reasonable doubt and without any reservation comic books were an important contributing factor in many cases of juvenile delinquency, and that it was primarily normal children who were affected.

He went on to mention numerous examples of violence, gore and sex in comics. He implied that the publishers conspired against anyone who threatened them, calling their critics communists. Towards the end of his testimony, answering a question put by Senator Kefauver, best remembered for his subcommittee that set out to put an end to organized crime, Wertham said:

I think Hitler was a beginner compared to the comic book industry. They get the children much younger. They teach them race hatred at the age of 4 before they can read.... This tremendous power is exercised by this group which consists of three parts, the comic book publishers, the printers and last and not least, the big distributors who force these little vendors to sell comic books.... I have a petition from newsdealers that appealed to me to help them so they don't have to sell comic books.... I can tell you of big national magazines, the editors of which would very much like to push the question of comic book problems. They can't do it because they themselves are being distributed by very big distributors who also do comic books, and then they suffer through loss of advertising.

Clearly Wertham believed his own rhetoric and the public, the authorities and finally the publishers all listened, the latter because they had no choice.

The findings of the Senate's report concluded:

This country cannot afford the calculated risk involved in feeding its children, through comic books, a concentrated diet of crime, horror and violence.

The report stated there must be a standard in the form of a code which would eliminate everything in a comic potentially damaging or demoralizing to a youth.

THE COMICS CODE AUTHORITY

 **OLLOWING THE WAVE OF BAD PUBLICITY AFTER THE SENATE** report, the publishers decided to self-regulate their publications. The Comics Magazine Association of America Inc. was set up on 26 October 1954. Their job was to produce a code that members would adhere to. Those doing so would be able to print on the cover of their publication the Authority's logo, thus assuring parents, teachers, distributors, retailers and any comic-book critic that the material contained in the comic met the Authority's high standard. In 1954 the Directors of the Association were: John Goldwater

(President); Jack S. Liebowitz (Vice-President); Martin Goodman (Secretary); Leon Harvey (Treasurer); Mrs Guy Percy Trulock (Code Administrator); Henry Edward Schultz (General Counsel); Leonard Darvin (Executive Secretary). These were the people who were, in the main, responsible, grammatical errors and all, for the 1954 'Code of the Comic Magazine Association of America, Inc.':

CODE FOR EDITORIAL MATTER

GENERAL STANDARDS PART A

1. Crimes shall never be presented in such a way as to create sympathy for the criminal, to promote distrust of the forces of law and justice, or to inspire others with a desire to imitate crimes.
2. No comics shall explicitly present the unique details and methods of a crime.
3. Policemen, judges, government officials and respected institutions shall never be presented in such a way as to create disrespect for established authority.
4. If crime is depicted it shall be as a sordid and unpleasant activity.
5. Criminals shall not be presented so as to be rendered glamorous or to occupy a position which creates desire for emulation.
6. In every instance good shall triumph over evil and the criminal punished for his misdeeds.
7. Scenes of excessive violence shall be prohibited. Scenes of brutal torture, excessive and unnecessary knife and gun play, physical agony, gory and gruesome crime shall be eliminated.
8. No unique or unusual methods of concealing weapons shall be shown.
9. Instances of law enforcement officers dying as a result of a criminal's activities should be discouraged.
10. The crime of kidnapping shall never be portrayed in any detail, nor shall any profit accrue to the abductor or kidnapper. The criminal or kidnapper must be punished in every case.
11. The letters in the word 'crime' on a comics magazine cover shall never be appreciably greater in dimension than the other words contained in the title. The word 'crime' shall never appear alone on the cover.
12. Restraint in the use of the word 'crime' in titles or subtitles shall be exercised.

GENERAL STANDARDS PART B

1. No comics magazine shall use the word horror or terror in its title.
2. All scenes of horror, excessive bloodshed, gory or gruesome crimes, depravity, lust, sadism, masochism shall not be permitted.

3. All lurid, unsavoury, gruesome illustrations shall be eliminated.
4. Inclusion of stories dealing with evil shall be used or shall be published only where the intent is to illustrate a moral issue and in no case shall evil be presented alluringly nor as to injure the sensibilities of the reader.
5. Scenes dealing with, or instruments associated with walking dead, torture, vampires and vampirism, ghouls, cannibalism and werewolfism are prohibited.

GENERAL STANDARDS PART C

1. Ridicule or attack on any religious or racial group is never permissible.

COSTUME

1. Nudity in any form is prohibited, as is indecent or undue exposure.
2. Suggestive and salacious illustrations or suggestive posture is unacceptable.
3. All characters shall be depicted in dress reasonably acceptable to society.
4. Females shall be drawn realistically without exaggeration of any physical qualities.
Note: It should be recognised that all prohibitions dealing with costume, dialogue or artwork apply as specifically to the cover of a comic magazine as they do to the contents.

MARRIAGE AND SEX

1. Divorce shall not be treated humorously nor represented as desirable.
2. Illicit sex relations are neither to be hinted at or portrayed. Violent love scenes as well as sexual abnormalities are unacceptable.
3. Respect for parents, the moral code, and for honourable behaviour shall be fostered. A sympathetic understanding of the problems of love is not a licence for morbid distortion.

4. The treatment of love-romance stories shall emphasise the value of the home and the sanctity of marriage.
5. Passion or romantic interest shall never be treated in such a way as to stimulate the lower and baser emotions.
6. Seduction and rape shall never be shown or suggested.
7. Sex perversion or any inference to same is strictly forbidden.

CODE FOR ADVERTISING MATTER

THESE REGULATIONS are applicable to all magazines published by members of the Comics Magazine Association of America, Inc. Good taste shall be the guiding principle in the acceptance of advertising.

1. Liquor and tobacco advertising is not acceptable.
2. Advertising of sex or sex instruction books are not acceptable.
3. The sale of picture postcards, 'pin-ups', 'art-studies', or any other reproduction of nude or semi-nude figures is prohibited.
4. Advertising for the sale of knives, or realistic gun facsimiles is prohibited.
5. Advertising for the sale of fireworks is prohibited.
6. Advertising dealing with the sale of gambling equipment or printed matter dealing with gambling shall not be accepted.
7. Nudity with meretricious purpose and salacious postures shall not be permitted in the advertising of any product; clothed figures shall never be presented in such a way as to be offensive or contrary to good taste or morals.
8. To the best of his ability, each publisher shall ascertain that all statements made in advertisements conform to fact and avoid misrepresentation.
9. Advertisement of medical, health, or toiletry products of questionable nature are to be rejected. Advertisements for medical, health or toiletry products endorsed by the American Association, shall be deemed acceptable if they conform with other conditions of the Advertising Code.

Wertham scorned self-regulation as misleading; later fans scorned the Code as being the plague that brought death to the comic books that they had loved.

As a result of the Code, publishers, in order to be distributed, were forced to reshape their publications. However, both Gilberton's **Classic Illustrated** and Dell's titles were not submitted for code approval. Their sales were enhanced through their reputations for producing wholesome comics. Dell used their own code, and later printed a pledge to parents, not on the cover but wherever convenient inside.

OST-CODE COMICS ONCE AGAIN BECAME INFANTILE AND bland. Suspense took the place of horror and crime stories, which virtually vanished. Westerns showed fewer shoot-outs and love comics were less explicit. There was also less violence in the seemingly innocent funny-animal comics. And there were casualties. Fiction House Comics went out of business as their comics, often depicting well-endowed women on their covers, could no longer be published under the Code. Within a few months, Eastern Color, United Feature, Star Publications, Toby Press and Sterling Comics had also all gone. Economic pressure also forced many artists out of the industry. Gene Colan and John Buscema went into advertising, while Bill Everett joined a greeting-card company. John Romita, Sr, although staying in the industry, preferred to tell people he was a commercial illustrator rather than admit to being a comic-book artist, with every new job meaning a cut in pay.

EC's publisher William Gaines, having attended the Senate hearing voluntarily and then being put in the difficult position of being asked to give his opinion on whether or not dripping blood from a severed head is suitable reading material for juveniles, was forced to totally rethink his company's entire line which, pre-code, had consisted of mainly horror and crime titles.

In April 1954, Marvel revived **Sub-Mariner Comics**[15] and **The Human Torch**,[16] continuing their numbering from 1949. **The Human Torch** lasted for only three issues and was cancelled with No. 38 in August. Headline produced the first new hero of the 1950s with Joe Simon and Jack Kirby's **Fighting American** No. 1 (April 1954). In May, **Captain America Comics**[17] joined the revival, continuing its numbering from 1950, but this also lasted for only three issues and was cancelled with No. 78 in September.

DC's output was changed to comply with the Code and they also introduced some new titles. They added another Superman title in September 1954 with **Superman's Pal Jimmy Olsen**.[18] This was not so strange, bearing in mind the popularity of the character in the Superman TV series. They also published **My Greatest Adventure** No. 1 (January 1955; see illustration, page 62) and, in August, an anthology title, later to be the first home of The Justice League of America, and

▲ FIGHTING
AMERICAN No. 1,
April–May 1954,
(Copyright © 1954 Prize
Publishing)

▲ CRIME
SUSPENSTORIES
No. 22,
May 1954, was published just before the Senate hearing in April 1954 – comics were normally on the newsstands before the publication date (Copyright © 1954 EC Comics)

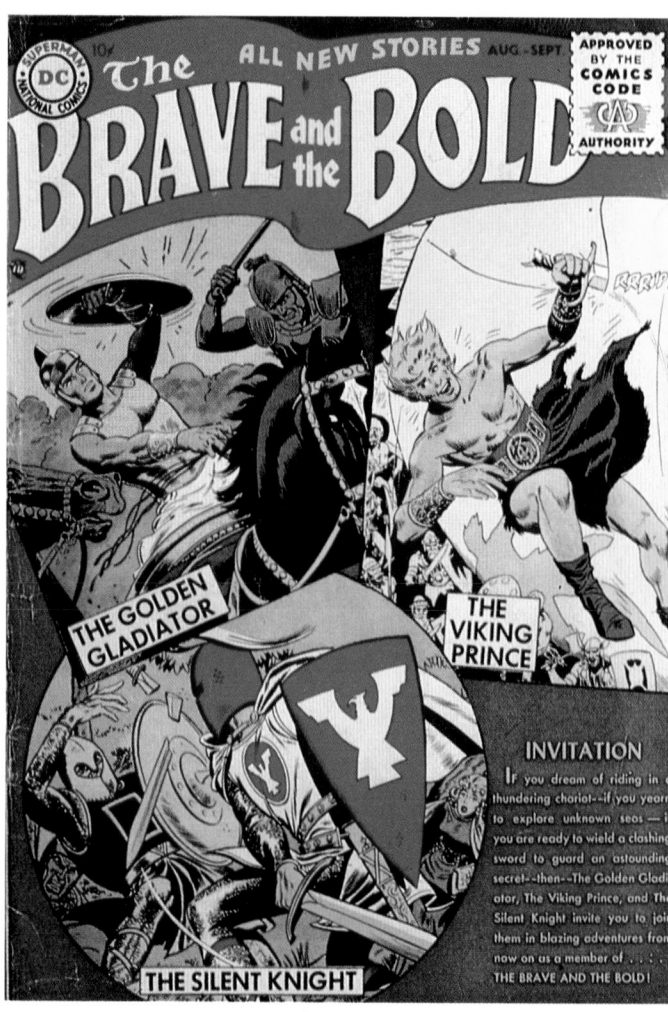

the Silver Age Hawkman, **The Brave and The Bold** No. 1, featuring Kubert's Viking Prince, Silent Knight, and Golden Gladiator. These were adventure rather than superhero stories. DC's Superman, Batman, and Wonder Woman titles were still selling reasonably well, and Superboy was still popular. In March 1955, he was given every boy's dream, a pet dog. **Adventure Comics** No. 210 was the first appearance of the superdog, Krypto, who continued to appear for more than twenty years.

Early in 1955, Gaines replaced his horror titles with comics that adhered to the Code. His 'New Direction' comics included **Piracy** No. 1 (October 1954), **Extra** No. 1 (March 1955), **Valor** No. 1 (March 1955), **Impact** No. 1 (March 1955), **Psychoanalysis** No. 1 (March 1955), **M.D.** No. 1 (April 1955) and **Incredible Science Fiction** No. 30 (July 1955). Gaines, who had only complied with the Code because wholesalers refused to handle product without it, totally denounced it after an anti-racism story in **Incredible Science Fiction**[19] was refused approval. He printed the story anyway and used a false Code Approval logo on the cover. EC's 'New Direction' line never sold as well as the earlier publications and, coupled with further distribution problems, within a year all that remained of EC was **Mad** which ceased being a comic with issue No. 23 and with issue No. 24 became a black and white magazine, which eventually became the biggest selling humour magazine of all time.

Due to the general lack of interest in superhero comics, Marvel's short-lived revival of its flagship heroes came to an end with **Sub-Mariner Comics** No. 42 (October 1955), where '*SUB-MARINER FIGHTS COMMIES AND CROOKS!*'

In November, DC published **Detective Comics** No. 225. The significance of this book is that the back-up feature (Batman always had the lead feature) contained the origin and first appearance of the Martian Manhunter – John Jones (later changed to J'onn J'onzz). This was DC's first new superhero since the end of the Golden Age. Some comic historians suggest that he was the first Silver Age hero, but this is wrong since the Silver Age didn't officially start until the publication of **Showcase** No. 4 (September–October 1956). He was, however, an important stepping-stone towards the Silver Age and was the only original character in The Justice League of America, with the others being existing or revamped heroes.

Science fiction was proving popular in 1956 and in February DC added **Tales of the Unexpected** No. 1 to its suspense/science-fiction stable. Marvel added a number of titles in the same genre, including **World of Suspense** No. 1 (April 1956), **World of Fantasy** No. 1 (May 1956), **World of Mystery** No. 1 (June 1956) and **Mystical Tales** No. 1 (June 1956). From Charlton, there was **Out of this World** No. 1 (August 1956) and **Mysteries of Unexplored Worlds** No. 1 (August 1956).

In March, DC launched **Showcase** No 1 (see illustration, page 64), possibly as a sister title to the fairly successful anthology title **The Brave and the Bold** or, as the title implies, as a try-out for characters who may prove popular enough to get their own titles. **Showcase** No. 1 featured Fireman Farell in three separate stories. On the first page of 'The Story Behind Showcase', we are told that a reader named Larry Blake had written to DC and suggested the idea of a comic devoted to the adventures of firemen. Supposedly other readers had requested books devoted to all manner of subjects, including forest rangers, boy scouts and the career of a TV actress. The editors are seen puzzling over the problem of how to fill all these requests, until …

I've got it – a way to present all *the good ideas sent in by our readers, we'll introduce them one at a time, in a new magazine to be called* Showcase!

The penultimate panel tells the reader:

And so was born Showcase, *the most novel idea in the comic book publishing industry. A magazine inspired by you! For the first issue on the basis of most requests the fire-fighting theme was selected.*

▲ EXTRA! No. 1,
April 1955
(Copyright © 1955 EC Comics)

▲ MAD No. 24,
July 1955, was the first Mad
in magazine format
(Copyright © 1955 EC Comics)

▶ TALES OF THE
UNEXPECTED No. 1,
February–March 1956
(™ & Copyright © 1994 DC
Comics, Inc.)

◀ OUT OF THIS WORLD
No. 1,
October 1956
(Copyright © 1956 Charlton
Comics)

The final panel promises:

There's a big surprise *waiting in the very next issue of* Showcase. *It will introduce a brand new colorful hero suggested by you!*

While it's true to say that **Showcase** No. 2 (May–June 1956), presenting Kings of the Wild, and **Showcase** No. 3 (August 1956), entitled 'The Frogmen', may have been inspired by readers, the invitation to suggest heroes was not extended again, and that was the end of '*the most novel idea in the comic book publishing industry*'.

In June, DC extended their TV-related line with **Jackie Gleason and the Honeymooners** No. 1, which, sadly, ran for only 12 issues, until May 1958. **Detective Comics** No. 233 (July 1956) saw the first appearance of Batwoman, who made occasional appearances across the Batman titles for a number of years.

In September 1956, Harvey Comics published **Baby Huey, The Baby Giant**, No. 1, the crazy baby duck in diapers who was bigger than his parents. Harvey issued two more new titles in November; **Little Lotta** No. 1 and **Spooky, The Tuff Little Ghost** No. 1. Lotta was a fat, strong girl with an enormous appetite, while Spooky was a more mischievous version of Casper, who was forever scaring people by yelling '*BOO!*'.

BRITAIN'S SILVER AGE BEGAN WITH THE PUBLICATION OF Eagle No. 1 on 14 April 1950.

The brainchild of clergyman Marcus Morris and artist Frank Hampson, whose wife thought up the title, **Eagle** was like no other British comic before. Morris, disturbed by the importation of American crime and horror titles, set out to create a wholesome weekly comic for British children. Together with Hampson, he produced a mock-up and eventually sold the idea to the publishers Hulton Press who had little experience in comics and were, at the time, best known for their weekly photo-magazine, *Picture Post*.

They received a handsome budget and, with Hampson as art director and Morris as editor, they set about producing the first issue.

Although not overtly religious in its content, it did adopt a moral Christian policy and initially carried a religious strip called the 'Great Adventurer' on the back page.

Eagle was beautifully produced as a 20-page tabloid photogravure comic with full-colour covers. It dazzled its readers from its first issue.

The comic's biggest claim to fame was its lead feature and cover star, Dan Dare, Pilot of the Future. In his first adventure he is based at the headquarters of the Interplanet Space Fleet. After the disappearance of a number of spaceships, lost in 'the danger zone' on their way to Venus, it isn't long before Dan takes command of the spaceship *Ranger* and sets off[20] on the 'Venusian Expedition of 1996'. Boys all over Britain couldn't wait for the next issue, and letters of approval came pouring in. Very quickly circulation reached a million copies a week, unheard of for any British comic at that time.

Boys of the 1950s looked upon Dan Dare as the pioneer of the space age they were growing up in. Hampson painstakingly researched current space technology to ensure that his stories, which were set in the future, were scientifically as accurate as possible. His artwork improved week by week and he began drawing from models he had built to ensure the lines and angles of his spacecraft and futuristic cities were accurate.

In 1960 Dan Dare was revamped by the much-loved artist Frank Bellamy. Shortly after this Hampson, disillusioned with comics, gave up the strip altogether, went to work for a college as a graphics technician, and became one of comics' forgotten heroes. Some time later he received a Yellow Kid Award from the international jury of the Lucca Festival.

Other early **Eagle** strips included the British radio favourite 'The Adventures of PC 49', a Western strip, 'Seth and Shorty', 'Cowboys' and 'Skippy the Kangaroo', as well as interesting and educational pieces like 'Discovering the Countryside', 'Real Life Mysteries', 'Professor Brittain Explains', and 'Cricket Coaching by Larry Constantine'. There were also text stories, and the editor's page where Revd Morris was able to preach the virtues of Christian ideals – which he managed to do without once mentioning religion. He created the Eagle Club; for one shilling members received an Eagle Badge, a charter of membership and a book of rules. Among other things, they were expected to:

(a) *Enjoy life and help others enjoy life. They will not enjoy life at the expense of others.*

(b) *Make the best of themselves. They will develop themselves in body, mind and spirit. They will tackle things for themselves and not wait for others to do things for them.*

▲ EAGLE No. 1,
14 April 1950, featured the
first appearance of Dan Dare
(Copyright © 1994 Hulton Press)

(c) Work with others for the good of all around them.

(d) Always lend a hand to those in need of help. They will not shirk difficult or dangerous jobs.

Eagle also spawned Christmas annuals, which began publication in 1951. Complete with festive red dust jackets, they boasted '*Great New Strips, Stories, Articles*'.[21]

Eagle ran for 991 issues until 26 April 1969.

The London-based publisher L. Miller had been reprinting Fawcett's Captain Marvel range in black and white. After Fawcett discontinued their entire comic line, Leonard Miller was left stranded. Although his weekly reprint output was big, including numerous Western titles, along with Popeye and Spysmasher, he needed a stopgap superhero.

Artist and creator Mick Anglo remembers:

One day Len [Leonard Miller] phoned and said he wanted to see me urgently. His supply of American material for the Captain Marvel series had suddenly been cut off. Had I any ideas? ... our Gower Street Studio had been drawing new covers for many of the Miller reprints. So I quickly told him I had plenty of ideas, and for my trouble I received a regular supply of work for the next six years.

▲ EAGLE ANNUAL
No. 2,
1952
(Copyright © 1994 Hulton Press)

Anglo took various elements from Captain Marvel and created the 'new' hero, Marvelman.

New? Here's his story. *Daily Bugle* boy reporter Micky Moran is sought out by the recluse astro-scientist, Guntag Bargholt, who is looking for a boy who is honest, studious and with integrity, so that he may share with him the secret key word to' the universe. He treats Micky in a special machine that enables him to use the secret. Just as the scientist is about to die he tells Micky the key word, 'Kimota!' ('Atomic' backwards). When Micky says the word he is transformed into Marvelman, the Mightiest Man in the Universe.

Marvelman made his debut on 3 February 1954 in **Marvelman** No. 25 (the first 24 issues having been **Captain Marvel Adventures**). After other Fawcett-like characters, Young Marvelman and Kid Marvelman, were introduced, it wasn't long before they all got together in the **Marvelman Family** No. 1 (October 1956).

Having resolved their copyright action against Fawcett, DC either ignored Miller's 'new' heroes, or didn't know about them.

In fairness, Marvelman's origins may not have been new but it wasn't long before he became a character in his own right, for his creators took him far away from the traditional world of American superheroes.

Marvelman became the best-loved and best-known British superhero, running for 370 issues over a ten-year period until February 1963. In the British tradition, Christmas annuals were also published from 1954.

The year 1954 also saw the birth of Amalgamated's **The Tiger**, in which began the longest running soccer strip ever, 'Roy of the Rovers'. Over a 22-year period, Roy fell in love, got married and raised a family — all while he continued to score goals for Melchester Rovers!

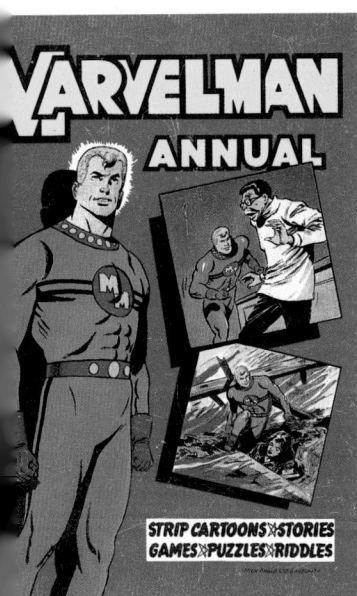

▲ MARVELMAN ANNUAL,
no date,
(Copyright L. Miller Publishing Company [UK])

5

The Silver Age
1956–69

C'S *SHOWCASE NO. 4 (OCTOBER 1956)* WAS THE COMIC that started the Silver Age. It featured '*WHIRLWIND ADVENTURES OF THE FASTEST MAN ALIVE – THE FLASH!*'

The sales of **Showcase** had only been moderate and DC needed a new idea for the book. The editors tossed around ideas until someone mentioned bringing back The Flash. Julius (Julie) Schwartz, who had been with DC since 1944, had worked on the Golden Age Flash and was intrigued with the prospect of reviving him. However, Julie decided not to bring the old Flash out of retirement, but instead to create a new Flash for the 1950s generation of comic readers.

Apart from giving the new Flash the same power of speed, everything else was different. He had a new costume, a new secret identity (Barry Allen), a new origin and a new city to live in.

Schwartz got Robert Kanigher, already writing **Showcase**, to write the book, Carmine Infantino, who was working on some of DC's Western and science-fiction titles, to draw it, and Joe Kubert to ink it. All had worked on the Golden Age Flash.

Infantino recalled, '*I wasn't thrilled – I never liked doing superhero stuff. But I said Okay and we did it.*'

The Flash became the first Silver Age hero, and **Showcase** No. 4 was a tremendous success. DC had managed to combine science fiction with a 'fresh-look' hero, which captured the readers' imagination. Sales reports took time to filter back, and didn't reach DC's offices for months, so it was some time before more tryouts were scheduled. They were planned for: **Showcase** No. 8, **Showcase** No. 13 and **Showcase** No. 14. Before these tryouts, however, Kubert and Kanigher went off to do other things, and were replaced by Gardner Fox and John Broome on the writing front with Joe Giella becoming the principal inker.

Despite the overwhelming demand for more Flash stories, it wasn't until February 1959 that DC gave him his own title with **The Flash** No. 105, continuing the numbering from the Golden Age series. This was somewhat confusing for the young comic fans, many of whom searched for the first 104 issues, believing they contained the adventures of their new hero.

Since the introduction of the Comics Code, Marvel had been experiencing difficulties and these had now become serious. They cancelled 55 titles over the

▲ THE FLASH No. 105, *February–March 1959* (™ & Copyright © 1994 DC Comics, Inc.)

▲ SHOWCASE No. 8, *June 1957, featured the second appearance of the Silver Age Flash* (™ & Copyright © 1994 DC Comics, Inc.)

◄ SHOWCASE No. 4, *October 1956, was the first Silver Age comic* (™ & Copyright © 1994 DC Comics, Inc.)

three-month period from July to September 1957. Almost two-thirds of their titles were gone. Atlas and its famous globe logo were no more. With the demise of Atlas, who had also distributed, Martin Goodman needed a distributor for his few remaining titles, which included **Strange Tales** and **Journey into Mystery** but very little else of any note. He did a deal with one of the largest distributors, American News Company. Unknown to Goodman, American News was also in deep trouble and on the verge of collapse. When the fall came, Marvel was left without a distributor. Things could not have been worse. Goodman told editor-in-chief Stan Lee to let everybody go. Lee remembers:

It was tough letting everybody go, I couldn't even offer free-lance work, I was surprised that Goodman kept me on, but I guess he thought there was a chance.

Goodman struck a deal with DC to have some of his books distributed to the newsstands through their distribution network. With the Atlas trademark gone, the now nameless Marvel limped on, producing dull war, romance and teenage, and a large number of Western titles.

Many more publishers went out of business in 1956, including Ace Magazines, Lev Gleason, Superior Comics and Quality who, prior to its demise, sold its titles (including Blackhawk)[1] to DC. Their demise also saw the disappearance of the last surviving non-DC superhero from the Golden Age, Plastic Man, with issue No. 64 (November 1956).

Meanwhile, Jack Kirby's Challengers of the Unknown had made their first appearance in **Showcase** No. 6 (February 1957), with further appearances in issues 7, 11 and 12. They went on to get their own title in **Challengers of the Unknown** No. 1 (April–May 1958).

The television army series, which gave Phil Silvers undying fame, began its 18-issue comic run in **Sergeant Bilko** No. 1 (May–June 1957) and was followed up a year later with the spin-off title, **Sgt. Bilko's Pvt. Doberman** No. 1 (June–July 1958).

DC editor Mort Weisinger, who had been working on the Superman TV series, suggested giving Superman's girlfriend Lois Lane her own comic book, due to her popularity in the show. She duly got her tryout in **Showcase** No. 9 (July 1957), and **Showcase** No. 10 (September 1957) and was the first tryout to receive its own title, in **Superman's Girl Friend Lois Lane** No. 1 (April 1958).

▲ HARVEY HITS No. 3,
*November 1957, was a tryout
for Richie Rich*
(™ & Copyright © 1994 The
Harvey Entertainment
Company)

◀ ADVENTURE
COMICS No. 247,
*April 1958, featured the first
appearance of The Legion of
Super-Heroes*
(™ & Copyright © 1994 DC
Comics, Inc.)

▶ ADVENTURE
COMICS No. 267,
*December 1959, featured the
second appearance of The
Legion of Super-Heroes*
(™ & Copyright © 1994 DC
Comics, Inc.)

Most funny animals and comics for younger readers had been unaffected by the anti-comics backlash and were still selling well. In May 1957, Dell's **Walt Disney's Comics and Stories** reached its 200th edition and in September Harvey Comics introduced a new tryout title called **Harvey Hits**. In October they gave the baby devil Hot Stuff, wearing Baby Huey-style nappies, his own book, **The Little Devil Hot Stuff** No. 1. Harvey Hits No. 3 (November) was entirely devoted to Richie Rich the Poor Little Rich Boy, who had first appeared along with Little Lotta in **Little Dot** No. 1 way back in September 1953.

By now DC were introducing more and more new characters. A Superboy story in **Adventure Comics** No. 247 (April 1958) saw the first appearance of a group of teen superheroes called The Legion of Super-Heroes from the thirtieth century. It was a simple story: Superboy met up with three super-powered heroes from the future, Cosmic Boy, Lightning Boy (later called Lightning Lad) and Saturn Girl. They tested Superboy and his powers and then admitted him into their club. This story had everything, time travel, costumed heroes and a group of teenagers with cosmic powers. The Legion may possibly have been part of the inspiration for Marvel's Uncanny X-Men some years later. The Legion gained a tremendous fan-following, and more Legion stories were demanded. Their second appearance came 20 issues later in **Adventure Comics** No. 267 (December 1959). There then followed a number of 'crossovers' in other titles which are highly sought after by collectors.

In July, in **Action Comics** No. 242, Superman met the green-skinned villainous Brainiac who travelled space shrinking cities and keeping them in glass bottles. In

▲ LITTLE DOT No. 1,
*September 1953, featured the
1st appearance of Richie Rich*
(™ & Copyright © 1994 The
Harvey Entertainment Co.)

August, The Space Ranger made his debut in **Showcase** No. 15. After his second and final tryout in **Showcase** No. 16 (October 1958), he didn't get his own title but instead was given a regular home in **Tales of the Unexpected**, starting in issue No. 40.

In November, the strange creature Bizarro whose origin was very loosely based on Mary Shelly's Frankenstein, as well as containing elements from the Beauty and the Beast fable, made his first appearance in a book-length story – still unusual in those days – in **Superboy** No. 68.

Issue No. 17 of **Showcase** (December 1958) contained the first appearance of Adam Strange. Like The Space Ranger, he didn't get his own title but, following his second and third appearances in **Showcase** Nos 18 and 19 (February and April 1959), he took over as the lead feature in **Mystery in Space** No. 53 (August 1959).

The year 1958 saw more publishers go out of business, including St John Publishing and Magazine Enterprises. At Marvel, however, things were gradually picking up and Stan Lee was now in a position to start offering work to free lances. He employed some of the greatest names in the industry, including Jack Kirby who had now left DC, Steve Ditko, Al Williamson, Jack Davis, Bill Everett and Don Heck.

In January 1959, Marvel published **Tales of Suspense** No. 1 and **Tales to Astonish** No. 1, both containing science-fiction and monster stories, which Heck described as being full of '*buildings tumbled down all over the place – Japanese monster movie stuff.*'

At DC, The Green Arrow, drawn by Jack Kirby, had his origin retold in a back-up story in **Adventure Comics** No. 256 (January 1959) and, four issues later in May, 'The King of the Sea', Aquaman, made his first Silver Age appearance. Robert Kanigher moved from **Showcase** to revamp Wonder Woman and, in issue No. 105, he did just that by giving her a new origin and modernizing the entire feel of the book. With issue No. 23 (May 1959), **The Brave and the Bold** became more like its sister book **Showcase** and began tryouts. This, and the next issue, were devoted to Kubert's Viking Prince and also told his origin for the first time. Sadly, Viking Prince never got his own title. Neither did the next tryouts, in issue Nos 25–7 and 37–9 (September 1959–January 1960 and September 1961–January 1962). Called Task Force X and codenamed The Suicide Squad, they were a team who battled perils and used unconventional methods of defence.

Also in May, readers were introduced to Superman's cousin Supergirl in **Action Comics** No. 252. Her costume, similar to Superman's, came complete with a miniskirt, years before it became a fashion.

The tryout for a 'supergirl' happened in **Superman** No. 123 (August 1958) in a story called 'The Girl of Steel'.

Supergirl had been born on a fragment of Krypton which had been preserved under a bubble of air when the planet exploded. With the entire city dying from Kryptonite poisoning, her father, Zor-el, who was the brother of Superman's father, Jor-el, sent her to Earth in a rocket. Supergirl was the creation of editor Mort Weisinger and writer Otto Binder who, in 1942, had created Captain Marvel's sister, Mary Marvel.

Archie Comics, seeing the success of DC's superhero revival, employed the talents of Joe Simon and Jack Kirby to update their Golden Age hero The Shield in **The Double Life of Private Strong** No. 1 (June 1959). The title only lasted two issues but, after his appearance in both issues, Archie's most successful Silver Age hero, The Fly, was given his own book in **The Adventures of The Fly** No. 1 (August 1959), which ran for 30 issues until May 1965 and, after a six-month break, returned as **Fly Man** Nos 31–9[2] (May 1965–September 1966).

Showcase No. 20 was a tryout for Rip Hunter Time Master, a scientist with a time machine, which gave artists and writers tremendous scope for settings. He appeared again in Nos 21, 25 and 26, and was given his own book, **Rip Hunter Time Master** No. 1, in March 1961. (See illustrations, pages 76, 77.)

▲ SHOWCASE No. 22, *October 1959, featured the first appearance of the Silver Age Green Lantern.* (™ & Copyright © 1994 DC Comics, Inc.)

In October 1959, DC published **Pat Boone** No. 1, based on the hit singer.[3] It only ran for five issues. DC didn't submit the series to the Comics Code Authority for approval and therefore they don't bear Code stamps on the covers.

After Julie Schwartz's success reviving The Flash, he adopted a similar technique with The Green Lantern in **Showcase** No. 22 (October 1959). Julie recalls:

I have a theory that when you revive a hero, you can base it on the original, but go off on a different track. We decided to come up with expanded activities. I worked out the idea of a whole universe full of Green Lanterns.

Written by Gardner Fox and drawn by Gil Kane, The Green Lantern continued his tryout in **Showcase** Nos 23 and 24 (December 1959 and February 1960), before getting his own title in **Green Lantern** No. 1[4] (July–August 1960).

In January 1960, in **Flash** No. 110, DC introduced Kid Flash, not as a sidekick, but as a character in his own right. Wally 'Kid Flash' West was the nephew of Barry 'Flash' Allen's girlfriend Iris West, and had the same powers as The Flash.

Charlton, through the talent of Steve Ditko, introduced their Silver Age hero Captain Atom in **Space Adventures** No. 33 (March 1960).

Schwartz continued with his revivals and, in March 1960, DC published one of the most significant books of the Silver Age, **The Brave and the Bold** No. 28, which recreated the successful 1940s team, The Justice Society of America. The 1960s version were The Justice League of America, whose original members included Superman, Wonder Woman, Batman, Aquaman, Martian Manhunter and the

▲ SPACE ADVENTURES No. 33, *March 1960, introduced Captain Atom* (Copyright © 1960 Charlton Comics)

▶ THE BRAVE AND THE BOLD No. 28, *March 1960, featured the first appearance of The Justice League of America* (™ & Copyright © 1994 DC Comics, Inc.)

◀ PAT BOONE No. 1, *October 1959* (™ & Copyright © 1994 DC Comics, Inc.)

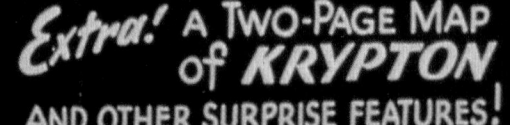

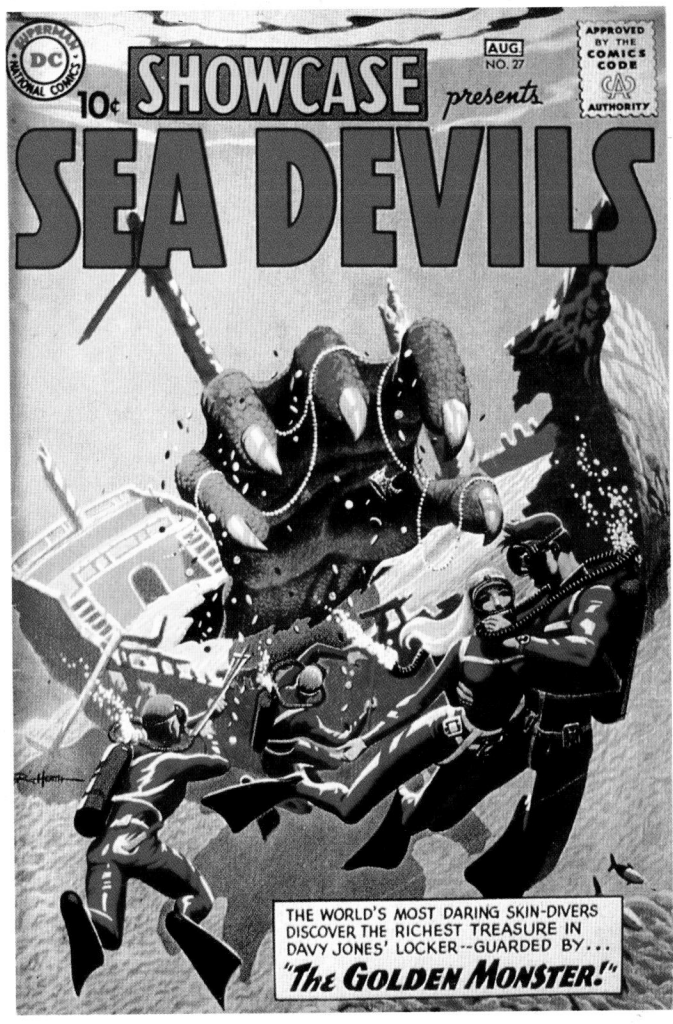

▲ FLASH No. 112,
*May 1960, introduced The
Elongated Man*
(™ & Copyright © 1994 DC
Comics, Inc.)

◀ SUPERMAN ANNUAL
No. 1,
October 1960
(™ & Copyright © 1994 DC
Comics, Inc.)

▶ SEA DEVILS No. 1,
September–October 1961
(™ & Copyright © 1994 DC
Comics, Inc.)

recently revived Flash and Green Lantern. Members continued to join during the Silver Age until it reached the point where, as writer Gardner Fox remembers:

There were so many characters and so little space to devote to each one, the marvel of it is that we could finish the story in the allotted number of pages.

After two further appearances in **The Brave and the Bold** Nos 29 and 30 (May and July 1960), the new team were given their own book in **Justice League of America** No. 1 (October 1960). The series ran for 261 issues until April 1987.

In **Flash** No. 112 (May 1960), DC introduced The Elongated Man, Ralph Dibney, who had the ability to stretch. He had a nose for a mystery and didn't bother with a secret identity. This issue also introduced a readers' letter page, 'Flash Grams', and marked the third appearance of Kid Flash.

In August 1960, **Showcase** No. 27 featured the wonderful work of Russ Heath in the first of three tryouts for The Sea Devils. They appeared again in Nos 28 and 29 (October and December 1960), and won their own title, **Sea Devils** No. 1 (September/October 1961).

DC reprinted stories in the giant-size **Superman Annual** No. 1 (October 1960), with a price tag of 25 cents. The philosophy behind the idea was sound. Firstly, there was a new audience who hadn't read these earlier stories; secondly, it was relatively cheap to produce. Readers were further encouraged to buy the annual by the inclusion of a cover gallery on the back page, as well as a two-page map of Superman's home planet Krypton. The annual proved most successful and DC were

▲ SHOWCASE No. 27,
*August 1960, featured the
first tryout for The Sea Devils*
(™ & Copyright © 1994 DC
Comics, Inc.)

soon producing annuals for many of their titles. The tradition of annuals continues today but, in the main, they no longer carry reprints.

Also in August, Harvey added **Wendy the Good Little Witch** No. 1 to its ghost and spook range. After a number of guest appearances in their other comics, Harvey gave 'The Poor Little Rich Boy' his own title, **Richie Rich** No. 1 (November 1960). Richie Rich, in his many Harvey titles, became the biggest selling character in comics.

DC continued to build on their success with further Golden Age revivals, notably Aquaman who after four tryouts in **Showcase** Nos 30–33 (February–August 1961), got his own title, **Aquaman** No. 1 (January/February 1962).

Another Golden Age hero, Hawkman, had six tryouts in **The Brave and the Bold** Nos 34–6 (March–July 1961) and Nos 42–4 (July–November 1962) before being given his own title, **Hawkman** No. 1 (April–May 1964), and becoming a member of the JLA in **Justice League of America** No. 31 (November 1964).

Marvel published **Amazing Adventures** No. 1 in June 1961, renaming it **Amazing Adult Fantasy** from No. 7 to the end of its run at No. 14 in July 1962. Steve Ditko was the main artist for the last eight issues, with Stan Lee doing most of the writing.

Following on from the success of the first two Supermen annuals, in August 1961 DC published a further three annuals. **Superman Annual** No. 3 reprinted stories featuring 'The Many Faces of Superman', **Batman Annual** Nos 1–1,001, 'Secrets of Batman and Robin', again reprints, and **Secret Origins Annual** No. 1. A DC advertisement for this comic read:

▲ RICHIE RICH No. 1,
November 1960
(™ & Copyright © 1994 The Harvey Entertainment Company)

▲ WENDY THE GOOD LITTLE WITCH No. 1,
August 1960
(™ & Copyright © 1994 The Harvey Entertainment Company)

◀ AQUAMAN No. 1,
January–February 1962
(™ & Copyright © 1994 DC Comics, Inc.)

▶ BATMAN ANNUAL
No. 1,
August 1961
(™ & Copyright © 1994 DC
Comics, Inc.)

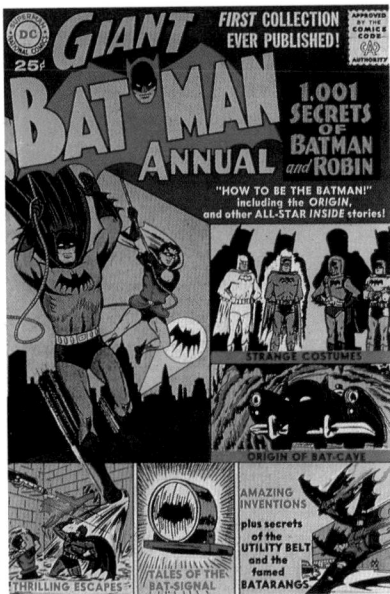

◀ SECRET ORIGINS
ANNUAL No. 1,
August–October 1961
(™ & Copyright © 1994 DC
Comics, Inc.)

At last the giant comic book you've dreamed about is here. A collection of original origin stories of your favourite super stars … The Superman-Batman Team – Wonder Woman – Flash – Green Lantern – J'onn J'onzz – Challengers of the Unknown – Adam Strange – Green Arrow … All together in one magazine! Don't miss this spectacular issue! You'll treasure it all your life!'

In September 1961 Julie Schwartz reintroduced the Golden Age Flash, Jay Garrick, in the masterpiece entitled 'The Flash of Two Worlds', in **Flash** No. 123, where we learn of Earth II, a world where DC's Golden Age heroes live.

The Atom joined the Silver Age in **Showcase** No. 34 (September 1961) and, after appearing in Nos 35 and 36 (December 1961 and February 1962), and got his own book, **The Atom** No. 1 (June 1962).

The Justice League of America may have been the one most important contributing factor in the birth of The Marvel Universe. During a game of golf, DC publisher Jack Liebowitz told Marvel's publisher Martin Goodman of the success he was having with the JLA, which by then was DC's biggest selling title. This gave Goodman the idea for a team of Marvel heroes. He gave the brief to Stan Lee who came up with an outline which Jack Kirby drew. Lee refused to merely copy the competition and insisted on doing something different. And different it was!

Fantastic Four No. 1 (November 1961; see illustration, page 84) pioneered what later became known in comic fandom as 'The Marvel Age of Comics'.

Readers were amazed by the oddball dialogue and the 'real' personalities of The Fantastic Four, which Lee and Kirby concentrated on. They got their powers after being in an experimental rocket that passed through a cosmic ray storm. Their leader, Reed Richards, whom Stan Lee envisaged as '*The world's greatest scientist, who is also a little bit of a bore*', became known as Mr Fantastic and acquired the ability to stretch his body. Richards was engaged to Sue Storm, who became Invisible Girl. Her kid brother, Johnny Storm, was given the name and the powers of Carl Burgos's hero, The Human Torch, who had been created for Marvel's first comic, **Marvel Comics** No. 1 (November 1939). Cosmic rays had turned the fourth member of the team, test pilot Ben Grimm, into a hideous, orange, craggy monster called The Thing. Lee says, '*I wanted something really different and I realized there were no monster, no funny, ugly guy who's a hero.*'

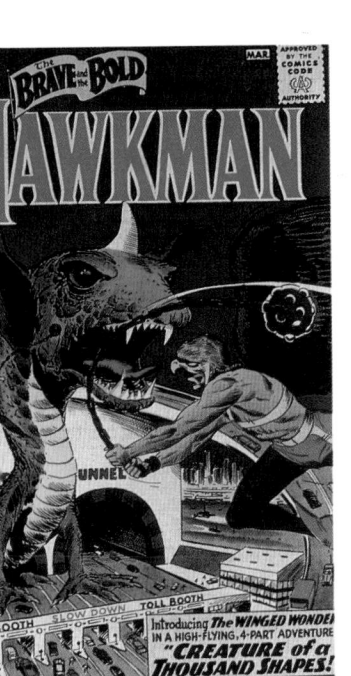

▲ THE BRAVE AND
THE BOLD No. 34,
*March 1961, introduced
Hawkman*
(™ & Copyright © 1994 DC
Comics, Inc.)

▲ SHOWCASE No. 34,
*October 1961, featured the
first appearance of the Silver
Age Atom*
(™ Copyright © 1994 DC
Comics, Inc.)

▶ THE ATOM No. 1,
June–July 1962
(™ & Copyright © 1994 DC
Comics, Inc.)

The readers loved The Fantastic Four and by the third issue Lee was able to run a fan page full of letters of praise.

These heroes broke the mould. They didn't have secret identities and initially didn't have costumes! The concession to costumes came at readers' requests in issue No. 3, when they established their headquarters and were given very simple, basic blue uniforms. From issue No. 4, billed as 'The World's Greatest Comic Magazine', The Fantastic Four became the foundation of the Marvel Universe and continue to date.

The year 1962 saw both Marvel and DC raise their 10-cent cover price to 12 cents. Dell put their 10-cent books up to a hefty 15 cents! However, the price increase did not deter readers – they were buying more comics now than they had for almost a decade.

DC continued tryouts, and **Showcase** No. 37 (April 1962) featured an unusual team of heroes, The Metal Men. They were human-like robots. Their creator, Dr Magnus, seemed to have the task of reassembling them, following their destruction, at the end of every issue. The Metal Men were Gold, Iron, Lead, Mercury, Tin and the shapely female, in love with Dr Magnus, Platinum. As well as having human personalities, they also took on the characteristics of their substances. Mercury was often at boiling point, Tin was weak, Iron was strong, and so on. They became firm favourites with the readers and, after three more **Showcase** appearances, Nos 38–40 (May–October 1962), they got their own title, **Metal Men** No. 1 (April–May 1963).

In May, encouraged by the success of The Fantastic Four, Marvel, without so much as a tryout, unleashed their second Silver Age hero in **Incredible Hulk** No. 1. This time it was gamma rays that transformed Dr Bruce Banner into the menacing, immensely powerful green monster.[5] Initially he was depicted as being quite intelligent, but early on a decision was made to reduce his brain power to contrast with the intellect of his alter ego Bruce Banner. The inspiration for The Hulk came in part from Robert Louis Stevenson's Dr Jekyll and Mr Hyde, and Mary Shelly's Frankenstein.

DC were still distributing Marvel's comics, and restricting them to eight titles a month, so Marvel's third hero, Thor, began life in an existing title, **Journey into Mystery** No. 83 (August 1962). The origin tells of the frail Dr Don Blake discovering Thor's magic hammer in a cave. The hammer enabled him to transform into the mighty god Thor. The character wasn't immediately popular but gained a big following during the mid 1960s. He falls in and out of favour to this day, and has gone through a number of transformations.

Spiderman was to become Marvel's most famous hero, but in 1962 Goodman was reluctant to publish him, believing that people would find a spider-hero distasteful. **Amazing Adult Fantasy** was about to be cancelled. Stan Lee remembers: '*Nobody cares what you put in a book that's going to die, so I threw in Spider-Man*.' The word 'adult' was dropped from the title and **Amazing Fantasy** No. 15 was published in August 1962, including the first appearance and origin of The Amazing Spiderman.[6]

After being bitten by a radioactive spider, high school student Peter Parker gets his arachnidan powers. This hero was like no other before. He was more interested in earning money than saving the world! The readers could easily identify with Parker and his adolescent problems. He was depicted as a wimp and wasn't popular at school; he wore glasses; he was an orphan living with his aunt and uncle; he was broke; he was neurotic; and when he became Spiderman, he was considered to be a criminal! His motivation for fighting crime came from the murder of his Uncle Ben in the first story.

▲ FANTASTIC FOUR
No. 1,
November 1961
(™ & Copyright © 1994 Marvel
Entertainment Group, Inc.)

▶ AMAZING SPIDER-
MAN No. 1,
March 1963
(™ & Copyright © 1994 Marvel
Entertainment Group, Inc.)

▲ JOURNEY INTO
MYSTERY, No. 83,
*August 1961, featured the
first appearance of Thor*
(™ & Copyright © 1994 Marvel
Entertainment Group, Inc.)

◀ AMAZING FANTASY
No. 15,
*August 1962, introduced
Spiderman*
(™ & Copyright © 1994 Marvel
Entertainment Group, Inc.)

Amazing Fantasy No. 15 became one of Marvel's best-selling books and at the bottom of the final page of the story we are told:

Be sure to see the next issue of Amazing Fantasy … For the further Amazing exploits of America's most different new teen-age idol … Spiderman!

The next issue never appeared. Instead Spiderman got his own title, although not until March 1963 (see illustration, page 85).

Meanwhile, back in January 1962, in an adventure story entitled 'The Man in the Ant Hill' in **Tales to Astonish** No. 27, scientist Henry Pym shrank to the size of an ant. Stan Lee decided to bring Pym back and, in September, he became Ant-Man in **Tales to Astonish** No. 35. As well as being able to shrink to their size, he invented a helmet which enabled him to communicate with ants.

Superboy made his final solo appearance in **Adventure Comics** No. 299 (August 1962), which also contained the first appearance of Gold Kryptonite, a substance that could permanently rob Superboy, and later Superman, of their powers. His leaving was to make way for 'Tales of the Legion of Super-Heroes' which, incidentally, still featured Superboy. Due to tremendous demand from fans, DC gave the Legion, now joined by Triplicate Girl, Sun Boy, Chameleon Boy, Bouncing Boy, Shrinking Violet, Invisible Kid and Mon-El, their own series which began in **Adventure Comics** No. 300 (September 1962). The series ran for 80 issues.

Marvel published its first annual, **Strange Tales Annual** No. 1, in September 1962. This reprinted science-fiction stories from pre-superhero Marvel titles.

▲ TALES TO ASTONISH No. 27, *January 1962, introduced Henry Pym who was to become Ant-Man*
(™ & Copyright © 1994 Marvel Entertainment Group, Inc.)

▲ TALES TO ASTONISH No. 35, *September 1962, in which Henry Pym returns as Ant-Man.*
(™ & Copyright © 1994 Marvel Entertainment Group, Inc.)

◀ ADVENTURE COMICS No. 300, *September 1962, begins the Legion of Super-Heroes series*
(™ & Copyright © 1994 DC Comics, Inc.)

In October, thanks to his popularity in The Fantastic Four, The Human Torch began a series in **Strange Tales** No. 101. Also that month, after breaking with Dell, Western Publishing under the banner Gold Key brought out their first book, **Doctor Solar, Man of the Atom**, priced at 12 cents as opposed to Dell's 15-cent tag.

In March 1963, Marvel introduced another hero, Iron Man, in **Tales of Suspense** No. 39 (see illustration, page 88). Industrialist and scientist Tony Stark is injured by a Vietcong booby trap which leaves shrapnel too close to his heart to operate. After being captured by the Communists, he uses their laboratory to invent a device to keep his heart beating after the shrapnel reaches it. The device is built inside body armour, complete with electronically powered arms and air-powered jets. On donning the armour he becomes the powerful, flying, Iron Man.

February 1963 saw the introduction of Gold Key's **Magnus Robot Fighter** No. 1. Set in the distant future, after his training with the robot A-1, Magnus does battle with 'self-thinking' renegade robots. The series ran for 46 issues until January 1977.

DC having acquired a comic adaptation, originally prepared for **Classics Illustrated**, of a James Bond novel by Ian Fleming, which had just been made into a feature film, **Showcase** No. 43 (March/April 1963) featured 007's clash with the infamous Dr No. Unusually, the issue contained no advertisements, in order to accommodate the size of the story.

Thanks to the success of The Justice League of America, The Fantastic Four, and The Legion of Super-Heroes, both Marvel and DC decided to give the fans what

they wanted – more teams! In May 1963, Marvel went back twenty years to refight the Second World War with **Sgt. Fury and his Howling Commandos** No. 1. Nick Fury was a rough, tough, likeable, patriotic soldier and, together with his outfit of ethnically mixed soldiers, including a black man, named Gabe Jones, they continued to beat up Nazis for 167 issues until December 1981.

Also in May, DC's **My Greatest Adventure** No. 80 introduced a team of freaks, The Doom Patrol. They were Larry (Negative Man) Trainor, Cliff (Robot Man) Steele, Rita (Elasti-Girl) Farr, and their leader The Chief, who was a wheelchair-using doctor. **My Greatest Adventure** changed its title to **Doom Patrol** with issue No. 86 (1) in March 1964.

Inspired by the Mutual Network radio show *Cahndu the Magician*, which Stan Lee had enjoyed as a child, Doctor Strange made his first appearance in **Strange Tales** No. 110 (July 1963). After an automobile accident, Doctor Strange, who until then had been a self-centred surgeon, was unable to perform operations due to damaged nerves in his hands. He travelled to the Himalayas where 'The Ancient One' repaired his soul instead of his hands. He studied with his mentor until he was ready to become a protector of humanity. As well as being able to perform magic, he also entered other weird dimensions and worlds, battling wizards. Appealing to the 1960s generation, he became less materialistic, more Bohemian and spiritual, and lived in New York's Greenwich Village. Doctor Strange never became one of Marvel's main characters, but has enjoyed popularity from time to time. It is interesting to note that in **Strange Tales** No. 32 (August 1962), Sazzik the Sorcerer appears and was almost certainly a prototype of Doctor Strange.

Now with more than enough superheroes, Marvel came up with a new super-team in **Avengers** No. 1 (September 1963). The original Avengers were Ant-Man, his female partner The Wasp, Iron Man, Thor and, strangely enough, The Hulk, who left the group in issue No. 2 and came back to fight them, with the recently resurrected Sub-Mariner, in No. 3 (January 1964).

Probably the most significant comic of the year was **The X-Men** No. 1 (September 1963). This was the first team of so-called 'mutants'. Created by Stan Lee and Jack Kirby, they were Slim (Cyclops) Summers, whose eye emitted deadly rays, Warren (The Angel) Worthington III, who had huge feathered wings, Bobby (Iceman) Drake, a reverse of The Human Torch, Jean (Marvel Girl) Grey, who through telekinesis

could move objects, and Hank (The Beast) McCoy, who was huge and had the strength of a gorilla. They were led by Professor Xavier, who like The Chief in The Doom Patrol, was a wheelchair user. In the Marvel vein, these teenage mutants, being different from everyone else, epitomized every youngster's dreams and fears. They were growing up, with their powers still manifesting themselves; they were feared, hated and self-conscious of their unusual gifts. Despite having a lot going for it, **X-Men** was not an immediate hit with the readers. The series didn't really take off until the 1980s. So successful was it then that retailers measured sales of all other comics against sales of **X-Men**! The original series ran for 66 issues before starting to reprint old materials. New stories along with a new X-Men team[7] began again with issue No. 94 (August 1975).

In March 1964, Marvel brought back their Golden Age hero Captain America in a classic Kirby–Lee story in **Avengers** No. 4. Eskimos are worshipping a dark figure in a block of ice when the evil Sub-Mariner throws the block into the sea where it melts. The figure from within is picked up by The Avengers' submarine. It is a bedraggled Captain America who has been in suspended animation for nearly twenty years, thus explaining the fact that he hasn't aged a day. He remembers very little about what happened, except that he had been trying to defuse a flying bomb that his partner Bucky had been clinging to. He had failed and, alas, Bucky had been killed.

Captain America became a sensation for the second time and, according to readers' letters, was the most popular member of The Avengers. When the founding members left, he took over as leader in **Avengers** No. 16 (May 1965). It was fitting that Jack Kirby, the man who had created Captain America, drew his return.

In April, Marvel introduced 'The Man Without Fear' in **Daredevil** No. 1. Matt Murdock, a blind attorney, was initially inspired to crime-fighting after the death of his father, a boxer who lost his life because he refused to throw a fight. Murdock's amazing agility, acrobatic skills and radar sense enabled him to do battle with villains.

Dr No in **Showcase** No. 43 had seen higher sales than normal, so DC decided to create a spy series, which was to premiere in **Showcase** No. 50. The new feature was to be called 'Yankee Doodle Dandy', under the direction of editor Lawrence Nadell, but due to Nadell's untimely death the character was left in the planning stages and was never published. All that remains is the cover art.

Instead, **Showcase** No. 50 (May/June 1964) presented 'I-Spy', which contained little more than reprints, despite the new Infantino and Anderson introduction.

During the 'Second Heroic Age', Batman and Robin had continued more or less the same as they had in the late 1950s. The stories had become far-fetched and distant from Kane and Finger's original Batman. He now regularly fought aliens on other planets, and was himself transformed into various strange creatures. Old villains like The Penguin, The Riddler and The Joker were hardly seen and neither were Batman's original detective skills. It was time for a change of style and pace and Julie Schwartz was the man to bring it about.

As the new editor of **Detective Comics**, Julie Schwartz gave Batman and Robin their new look. He made subtle changes to Batman's costume, giving him a new insignia that resembled the bat-signal. He also gave him a modern Batmobile and put an elevator into the Batcave. And Schwartz brought in new artists and writers, insisting on better plotted stories. The 'new look' Batman was introduced in **Detective Comics** No. 327 (May 1964). The second feature was the first solo adventure of The Elongated Man.

In the following issue, Batman's long-serving, faithful butler Alfred Pennyworth, was killed off. However, he was 'brought back' in No. 356 (October 1966).

▲ THE X-MEN No. 1, *September 1963, introduced the first team of 'mutants'* (™ & Copyright © 1994 Marvel Entertainment Group, Inc.)

'*Make way for the fat fury, Herbie Popnecker.*' After amusing the readers with his magic lollipops and strange powers in ACG's **Forbidden Worlds** and **Unknown Worlds**, 'The Big-Fat Nothing' was given his own title in **Herbie** No. 1 (May 1964) which ran for 23 issues until February 1967.[8]

◀ HERBIE No. 8,
March 1965
(Copyright © 1965 American
Comics Group)

THE LATE SILVER-AGE 1965–69

WHILE DC CONTINUED BRINGING BACK HEROES FROM THE Golden Age (Dr Fate and Hourman in **Showcase** No. 55 [April 1965], Black Cannery in **The Brave and the Bold** No. 61 [July 1965] and The Spectre in **Showcase** No. 60 [January 1966]), and Steve Ditko drew his old superhero for Charlton in **Captain Atom** No. 78[9] (December 1965), most of the other major publishers brought out new superhero comics.

From Archie Publications came **Mighty Comics Presents Mighty Crusaders** No. 1 (November 1965). A new publisher, Tower Comics, emerged, headed up by former Archie editor Harry Shorten, and former Archie artist Sam Schwartz. They proceeded to introduce a range of new superhero, war and teen titles. Their first comic was **T.H.U.N.D.E.R. Agents** No. 1 (November 1965), created by Wally Wood, which ran for 20 issues, and in the same month they published **Tippy Teen** No. 1. The company managed only 81 issues across all titles before their demise in 1970.

In January 1966, after tryouts in both **The Brave and the Bold** and **Showcase**, DC gave their junior 'sidekicks' their own title in **Teen Titans** No. 1.[10] Created by Bob Hanley, they were the junior Justice League of America and proved very popular with readers. The original team were Aqualad, Kid Flash, Robin and Wonder Girl. The Green Arrow's partner, Speedy, after a couple of cameo appearances, joined as a member in issue No. 19 (February 1969).

On 12 January 1966, **Batman** premiered on prime-time American television. Adam West played Batman (although TY (Bronco Lane) Hardin had been first choice) and Burt Ward played Robin, with Alan Napier as Alfred, Neil Hamilton as Commissioner Gordon, and Stafford Repp as Chief O'Hara.

The show, with its one-liners, outrageous clichés and pop-art word sound effects emblazoned across the screen during the fight scenes, became part of the pop-culture of the time. A unique two-nights-in-a-row schedule allowed a terrifying cliff-hanger at the end of the first night's episode, with the conclusion the following night: '*same bat time, same bat channel*'.

Kids started jumping out of windows pretending to be Batman, who they mistakenly thought could fly. Like George Reeves twelve years earlier, The Caped

Crusader made a special announcement warning the youngsters of the danger of playing at being Batman.

An unintended side-effect of portraying Batman in this 'camp' fashion, was the re-emergence of the opinion, originally expressed by Dr Wertham, that Batman and Robin were homosexuals. To help counteract this, producer William Dozier, asked editor Julie Schwartz if a girl could be added to the show. Obligingly, Schwartz created Batgirl whose first appearance was in **Detective Comics** No. 359 (January 1967), and she was written into the TV series. In order to match the continuity of the show, Batman's butler Alfred, killed off two years earlier, was brought back to the comics. However, despite the show's success, Batman creator Bob Kane was not impressed with the parody treatment The Caped Crusader was getting.

Batman was so popular on TV that soon celebrities were lining up to be guest villains on the show. They were each paid $2,500 (£1,667) for their appearance, but many would have done it for free. The list is impressive:

Bat-Villains	Played by	Bat-Villains	Played by
The Archer	Art Carney	The Mad Hatter	David Wayne
The Black Widow	Tallulah Bankhead	Marsha	Carolyn Jones
The Bookworm	Roddy McDowall	Minerva	Zsa Zsa Gabor
Catwoman	Julie Newmar	The Minstrel	Van Johnson
Catwoman	Eartha Kitt	Mr Freeze	George Sanders
The Clock King	Walter Slezak	Mr Freeze	Otto Preminger
Colonel Gumm	Roger C. Carmel	Mr Freeze	Eli Wallach
Dr Cassandra	Ida Lupino	Nora Clavicle	Barbara Rush
Egghead	Vincent Price	The Penguin	Burgess Meredith
False-Face	Malachi Throne	The Puzzler	Maurice Evans
A Gun Mole	Jill St John	The Riddler	Frank Gorshin
Fingers	Liberace	The Riddler	John Astin
The Joker	Cesar Romero	Sandman	Michael Rennie
King Tut	Victor Buono	Shame	Cliff Robertson
Lord Ffogg	Rudy Vallee	The Siren	Joan Collins
Louie the Lilac	Milton Berle	Zelda the Great	Anne Baxter
Ma Parker	Shelley Winters		

▲ *The album of the* BATMAN *television show soundtrack, 1966* (™ & Copyright © 1994 DC Comics, Inc. and 20th Century Fox TV, Inc. and 20th Century Fox Records, Inc.)

Other non-villainous guests also appeared including Van Williams and Edward G. Robinson.

The show, which ended on 14 March 1968, ran for 120 episodes and spawned one motion picture. Reruns continue to be shown all over the world.

Adam West recalls:

When I wore that cape, I really had to believe I was the world's greatest crime fighter, if I didn't believe, the fans wouldn't believe it either.

He continued his association with The Caped Crusader when he became the voice of Batman for Hanna-Barbera's Super Friends animated TV series, with Burt Ward as the voice of Robin.

As a result of the TV show, the entire comic industry saw an enormous increase in sales. Batman, of course, was the most popular, and DC capitalized on this by prominently featuring him wherever they could in other titles.

The year 1966 also saw Superman on Broadway in the musical It's a Bird ... It's a Plane ... It's Superman!, written by David Newman and Robert Benton with music by Charles Strouse and lyrics by Lee Adams. David Newman, with his wife Leslie, went on to script the first three Superman films. After his success in the title role, there were plans to put Bob Holiday in a new Superman TV series, but it never happened.

From February 1966 to July 1967 DC added pop-art go-go checks to the top edge of their books, in order to convey a more 'hip' and 'groovy' image as well as making their books more identifiable on the racks.

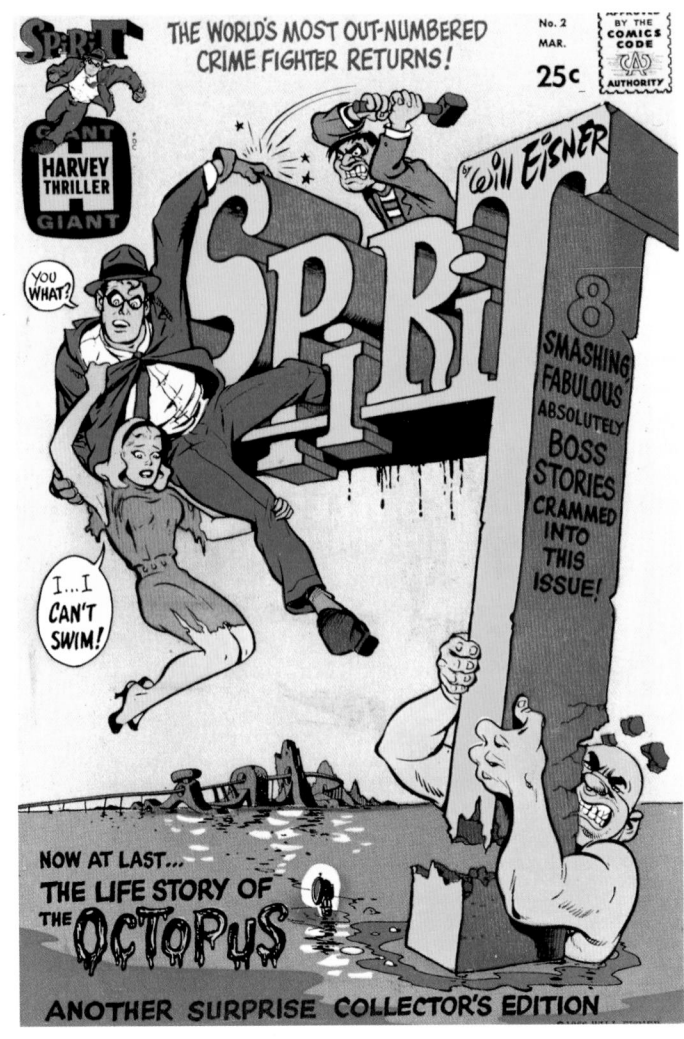

The Silver Surfer made his first appearance in **Fantastic Four** No. 48 (March 1966). He started life as the assistant to the villainous Galactus, but defied his master and became a hero. Later Stan Lee and artist John Buscema gave The Surfer a more detailed background, telling that he was originally Norrin Rodd, who had saved his planet from Galactus. After several guest appearances he won his own title in **Silver Surfer** No. 1 (August 1968) which ran for 18 issues until September 1970. He returned for a one-shot[11] in 1982 and then again in his own title[12] in July 1987, where he still roams the stars on his surfboard and is one of Marvel's most popular characters.

Also in March 1966, Marvel gave Thor his own book in **The Mighty Thor** No. 126, continuing the numbering from **Journey into Mystery.**[13]

In August 1967, Marvel devoted a monthly title, **Not Brand Echh** to parodies of their own heroes. Marie Severin, who worked on the title, became one of the first women to be recognized as a comic-book artist and went on to draw superheroes, including The Hulk. In October, Harvey published a two-issue series reviving Will Eisner's ghostly detective in **The Spirit**. The books contained Eisner reprints as well as some new material.

In November, after the obligatory tryouts,[14] DC launched their last major revival of the decade with **The Spectre** No. 1.

Captain Marvel (a new character, not he of Shazam fame) made his debut in **Marvel Superheroes** No. 12 (1).[15]

Despite the boost to sales following the TV shows, the Silver Age was drawing to a close. One of the signposts pointing to its end was the cancellation, by Archie, Dell and Harvey of their superhero titles. Then, after 25 years, ACG went out of business in the summer of 1967.

By the end of 1968 the superhero had peaked and sales for almost all of the publishers were starting to fall. Marvel, however, continued to grow, taking sales mainly from DC. They were reportedly selling 50 million comics a year and now had the leverage to renegotiate their distribution deal with DC in order to publish more titles. They eventually struck a new deal with Curtis Distributing.

During 1968 and 1969, Captain America, Captain Marvel, Doctor Strange, The Hulk, Iron Man, Nick Fury Agent of S.H.I.E.L.D., The Silver Surfer and The Sub-Mariner all got their own books, or took over existing titles. These were: **Captain America** No. 100 (April 1968), formerly **Tales of Suspense; Captain Marvel** No. 1 (May 1968); **Doctor Strange** No. 169 (June 1968), formerly **Strange Tales; The Incredible Hulk** No. 102 (April 1968), formerly **Tales to Astonish; The Invincible Iron Man** No. 1 (May 1968); **Nick Fury Agent of S.H.I.E.L.D.** No. 1 (June 1968); **Silver Surfer** No. 1 (August 1968); and **The Sub-Mariner** Vol. 2 No 1 (May 1968).

In October 1968, Martin Goodman sold his Marvel companies which he had founded and owned for more than 35 years to Perfect Film and Chemical Corporation. The new company was called Magazine Management. On the surface nothing had changed, with Goodman staying on as president and publisher.

By 1969 the enthusiasm for superhero comics had waned and DC cancelled a number of titles including **The Spectre** and **The Atom & Hawkman**.[16] Most of the other genres were also doing badly and sales slumped generally, not helped by most publishers increasing their prices from 12 cents to 15 cents.

There was a distinct feeling of stagnation, and there seemed to be little direction and no fresh ideas. Even the work of the great artists and writers of the forties and fifties became uninspired. Publishers pumped out lacklustre, bland and boring comics, all too weak and tired to fan the dying embers of an era. It could be argued that the more recent new Marvel titles, which lacked the innovation of that company's earlier output, just fitted into the Silver Age, which was now at an end.

▲ CAPTAIN AMERICA No. 100, *April 1968* (™ & Copyright © 1994 Marvel Entertainment Group, Inc.)

NEW! FIRST TIME IN COMIC-BOOK FORM!
CONAN THE BARBARIAN
15¢
1 OCT
APPROVED BY THE COMICS CODE AUTHORITY
CONAN
THE BARBARIAN
MARVEL COMICS GROUP
TO THE DEATH!
THE COMING OF CONAN!

6

The Post-Silver Age 1970–80

Y 1970 THE DECLINE IN POPULARITY OF SUPERHEROES HAD become an unmistakeable trend. The most popular title of the year was **Archie Comics** which sold more than 500,000 copies per issue.

A great number of the Golden and Silver Age creators had retired or left the industry, although new talents were emerging, such as the excellent artist Neal Adams who, under the editorial guidance of Julie Schwartz, set out to revamp and revitalize Batman. He often teamed up with the talented writer Denny O'Neil and together they attempted to return Batman to his darker, more sinister roots, to shake off the image of the TV show which had trivialized Batman on television and caused a corresponding change in his character in the comics. Adams says, '*We made him a bit more angry than he'd been for a while, a bit more vicious.*'

Adams and O'Neil next turned their attention to The Green Lantern and The Green Arrow. Their work began in **Green Lantern** No. 76 (May 1970). They took a new approach, using the stories to comment on 1970s problems, including ecology, drug abuse and racial prejudice; no subject was taboo.

O'Neil remembers:

I was smart enough to know enormously complex problems couldn't be dissected with a 25-page comic book, and humble enough to know I didn't have solutions anyway. I just hoped the stories might awaken youngsters to the world's dilemmas, giving them an early start so they might find solutions in their maturity.

Although highly acclaimed, and sought after by collectors today, these comics did little to boost DC sales.

Marvel was having the same problems with declining sales and, in October 1970, moved further away from superheroes with a comic-book adaptation of Robert E. Howard's fantasy, **Conan the Barbarian** (see illustration, page 94), which had originally been created in the 1932 pulp story 'The Phoenix on the Sword' in **Weird Tales**, and was seeing some success in paperback reprints. Conan, a soldier of fortune, lives in a prehistoric world populated by demons and wizards and is the epitome of the genre known as sword and sorcery. Roy Thomas wrote the comic and it was drawn by the 21-year-old Barry Windsor-Smith. Thomas said, '*I thought*

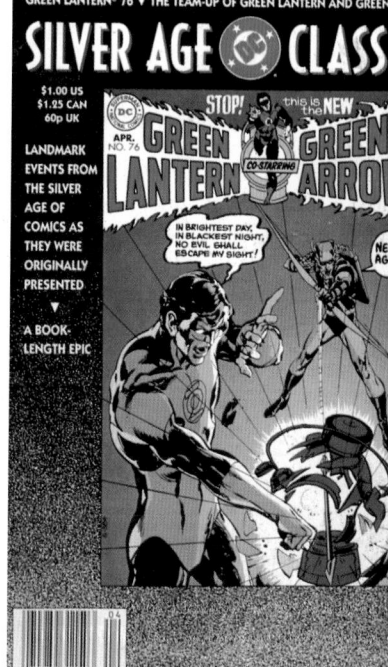

▲ DC SILVER AGE CLASSICS – GREEN LANTERN No. 76, *1992, is a reprint of* GREEN LANTERN No. 76 *from May 1970* (™ & Copyright © 1994 DC Comics, Inc.)

◄ CONAN THE BARBARIAN No. 1, *October 1970* (™ & Copyright © 1994 Marvel Entertainment Group, Inc.)

▲ RED SONJA No. 1,
January 1977
(™ & Copyright © 1994 Marvel
Entertainment Group, Inc.)

▲ AMAZING
SPIDER-MAN No. 97,
*June 1971, was distributed
without the CCA seal of
approval because it contained
an anti-drug story showing
actual drug use*
(™ & Copyright © 1994 Marvel
Entertainment Group, Inc.)

it was a good direction to go in, and to some extent it was a move away from typical comic book material. I wanted to widen the horizon.'

Thomas, who was a former comic fan and had his first work published in 1966 by Charlton in **Son of Vulcan**, gradually based the scripts on his own ideas rather than Howard's. For example, he expanded one of Howard's minor characters, Red Sonja, turning her into Conan's companion. She proved so popular that she was given her own series, **Red Sonja** in January 1977. Thomas's scripts were complemented by Windsor-Smith's art. Thomas remembers, *'He just burst out in a different way than I would have imagined, because I had no idea he was going to work into that art nouveau kind of style.'*

For Marvel, Conan was a gamble that paid off. Despite the fact that the character, being set in the past, had no place in the Marvel Universe, no super-powers and none of the usual Marvel humour, he became immensely popular and continues to this day.

Marvel followed up Conan's success by featuring him in a black and white magazine format, **Savage Tales** No. 1 (May 1971), and in June used another Robert E. Howard character of the same genre in **Kull the Conqueror** No. 1.

Jack Kirby left Marvel and joined DC, who were prepared to give him greater control over the characters he created. He called his three new titles the 'Fourth World' of comics. They were **Forever People** (March 1971), **New Gods** (March 1971) and **Mister Miracle** (April 1971).

Anti-drug propaganda stories featured in DC's **Green Lantern** Nos 85 and 86 (October and November 1971), and issue No. 87 introduced John Stewart who later became the new Green Lantern after Hal Jordan resigned in issue No. 182.

Marvel also published anti-drug stories in **Amazing Spider-Man** Nos 96, 97 and 98 (May, June and July 1971), but as they portrayed actual drug use they were not submitted to the CCA and were distributed without the Comics Code Authority seal of approval. Stan Lee said:

We would do more harm to the country by not running the story than by running it. And I must say that we got a favourable reaction from the press all over the country, and from parents and educators too. Everybody loved what we had done. And because of that, the code was changed.

After 17 years, the Comics Code Authority reviewed its policies and standards in order to allow such stories to gain approval in the future. It also allowed back into coded comics the likes of vampires, zombies and werewolves. The publishers quickly seized this opportunity and the following year newsstands were once again full of horror comics.

In November 1971, both Marvel and DC increased the price of their comics from 15 cents to 25 cents, a bigger price jump than ever before. The reader did, however, get something extra for his money, for both companies increased the page-count from 36 to 52 (including covers). The following month Marvel cut its prices by 5 cents, and reduced the page count, taking it back to 36. This gave them the edge over DC, who continued for another year with their 52-page, 25 cent books.

Stan Lee created Marvel's first comic to take its name from a black hero in **Hero for Hire, Luke Cage** No. 1 (June 1972). Cage, who was an ex-member of a tough street gang, was framed for a crime he didn't commit. In prison he volunteered for an experiment which gave him tremendous strength. He escaped from prison to become a mercenary. From issue No. 17 (February 1974), the title changed to **Luke Cage, Power Man**.[1]

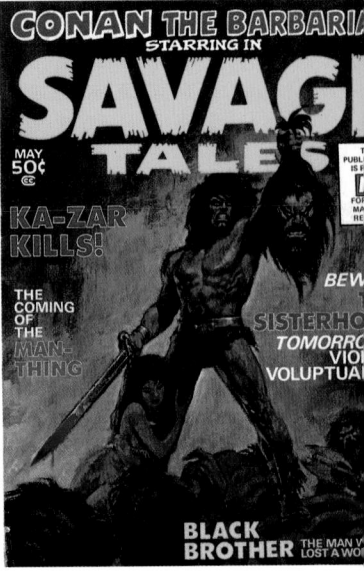

▲ SAVAGE TALES No. 1,
May 1971
(™ & Copyright © 1994 Marvel
Entertainment Group, Inc.)

The changes in the Code allowed Marvel success in the horror genre with 'Werewolf by Night' in **Marvel Spotlight on ...** No. 2 (February 1972), drawn by Gene Colan and written by Marv Wolfman, with a Neal Adams cover. After two more tryouts, in **Marvel Spotlight on ...** Nos 3 and 4 (April and June 1972), he got his own title in September 1972.

Gene Colan and Neal Adams were also responsible for bringing back Bram Stoker's classic character in **Tomb of Dracula** No. 1 (April 1972). Marv Wolfman, who wrote the series from issue No. 7 to the end, is full of admiration for Colan's work on this comic:

Gene Colan's stuff was brilliant. He kept me from doing anything standard, because I had no idea what standard was. We did people oriented stories.

This incarnation of Dracula, which ended with No. 70 in August 1979, became the longest running comic title to feature a villain. In 1973 Jack Palance played the vampire on television – a strange coincidence, as Colan had modelled his Dracula on Palance a year before the show.

DC's contribution to the horror genre came in the form of an anthology title, **Forbidden Tales of Dark Mansion** No. 5 (1)[2] in May 1972, and Berni Wrightson's and Len Wein's **Swamp Thing** No. 1 (November 1972), which told the story of scientist Alec Holland who was transformed into a living plant-like creature at the hands of criminals who murdered his wife while searching for Holland's 'bio-restorative' formula.

Jack Kirby's fascinating variation of the Dr Jekyll and Mr Hyde theme was entitled **The Demon** No. 1 (August 1972), in which demonologist Jason Blood is transformed into the demon Etrigan by reading an inscription on an ancient tomb. Kirby's teenager in a post-nuclear world premiered in his own title in DC's **Kamandi, The Last Boy on Earth** No. 1 (October–November 1972).

On the superhero front, Marvel rounded up a group of loners and put them in a team in **The Defenders** No. 1 (August 1972). First seen in **Marvel Feature** No. 1[3] (December 1971), they included The Hulk, The Sub-Mariner and Doctor Strange.

In November, 13 years after her introduction, 'The Maid of Steel' finally got her own book in **Supergirl** No. 1. It ran for only ten issues until September–October 1974.[4]

During 1973 Marvel continued with monster and horror titles with **The Monster of Frankenstein** No. 1 (January 1973), **Vault of Evil** No. 1 (February 1973), which reprinted stories from the 1950s, and **World's Unknown** No. 1 (May 1973), which only managed eight issues until it was cancelled in August 1974.

Marvel also published some titles in black and white magazine format, aimed at an older audience. These were **Monsters Unleashed** No. 1 (July 1973), **Dracula Lives** No. 1 (no month 1973) and **Tales of the Zombie** No. 1 (August 1973), which revived the 1953 Stan Lee and Bill Everett character. Also on the magazine front, now a separate division of Marvel and headed by Marv Wolfman, 'back by popular demand' came **Savage Tales** No. 2 (October 1973), which continued its numbering from two years earlier.

Dell, comic-book publishers for 37 years, dropped out of the market.

At DC, Captain Marvel saw a revival in **Shazam!** No. 1 (February 1973). DC opted for that title so as not to confuse readers with Marvel's Captain Marvel, who was a completely different character. The front cover of issue No. 1 featured Superman introducing Captain Marvel and, although faithfully recreated by C. C. Beck who had drawn him in the 1940s, the 1970s reincarnation of 'The Big Red Cheese' didn't really work.

▲ MARVEL
SPOTLIGHT ON ...
No. 2,
February 1972
(™ & Copyright © 1994 Marvel
Entertainment Group, Inc.)

▲ AMAZING SPIDER-
MAN No. 129,
February 1974, featured the
first appearance of The Pun-
isher
(™ & Copyright © 1994 Marvel
Entertainment Group, Inc.)

Thanks in part to the Bruce Lee movies, martial arts became popular and Marvel introduced two Kung-Fu titles in April 1974. In comic format there was **Master of Kung-Fu** No. 17,[5] in which the hero was the son of the infamous Dr Fu Manchu, written by Steve Englehart and drawn by Jim Starlin; in black and white magazine format, not needing the CCA Code and therefore more violent, came **The Deadly Hands of Kung-Fu** No. 1. The magazine combined comics with articles and photographs concerning the martial-arts craze, and No. 1 sported a Neal Adams cover.

Marvel's most successful black and white magazine, **The Savage Sword of Conan** No. 1, which continues today, began publication in February 1974.

Two of Marvel's most enduring creations of the 1970s began life in 1974. The Punisher, who made his debut in **Amazing Spider-Man** No. 129 (February 1974), was the idea of Gerry Conway. He had taken over the writing of Spiderman from Stan Lee, and was looking for a new adversary for Spidey. He said:

I wanted to do a dark, street-tough kind of opponent for Spider-Man. I came up with the character, took it to Roy [Thomas], and we decided to do it. John Romita [Marvel's art director], developed the costume. My original sketch was of a guy in a black jumpsuit with a little white skull on his chest, and John did a wonderful thing where he took the skull, made it huge, and made the teeth of the skull form a cartridge belt. It looked terrific.

The Punisher, Frank Castle, started out as a mercenary and relished killing. This 'killer for hire' idea was quickly dropped in favour of his becoming a revenge-seeking crusader. Tortured by the deaths of his wife and children, who were murdered after witnessing a gangland killing, he resolved to track down the murderers and all other law-breakers.

The second of the enduring duo was Len Wein's Wolverine, who made his first appearance on the last page of **The Incredible Hulk** No. 180 (October 1974), where he was portrayed as an unstable agent for the Canadian Government, known as Weapon X. He made his first full appearance the following month in **The Incredible Hulk** No. 181. Wolverine, who's alter ego is Logan, is a mutant, found dying by James (Guardian) McDonald, who nursed him back to health. He possesses the power to heal most wounds to his body and he ages more slowly than normal humans. His skeleton is reinforced with adamantium, the same substance his six unbreakable claws, three under the skin along the back of each forearm, are made from. He is quarrelsome and cocky and sometimes has trouble in containing his rage.

DC continued its regular superhero lines (Superman, Batman, Wonder Woman, etc.) but did very little to inspire new readers. The die-hard DC fan stayed loyal, while many others drifted to Marvel, which by this time had the lion's share of the market.

In a series called **Famous First Edition** (1974–9),[6] DC reprinted various important issues including **Action Comics** No. 1 and **Detective Comics** No. 27. These 'oversized' comics have in some cases been passed off as the originals and, though almost identical, are easily identified by their $10 \times 13\frac{1}{2}$ inch size.

The most significant title to be published in 1975 was **Giant Size X-Men** No. 1 (Summer). After limping along as one of Marvel's minor titles, it was decided to revamp X-Men's line-up. The original members were there, along with several new ones created by Len Wein and Dave Cockrum. These included Nightcrawler, Storm, Colossus and Thunderbird. The new team continued in **X-Men** No. 94 (August 1975), where all of the old members except Cyclops resigned, and the new characters introduced in **Giant Size X-Men** No. 1, along with Wolverine and Banshee, joined. Wein was now editor-in-chief, and due to time constraints was forced to abandon the writing of the new X-Men. From the fourth issue he passed it over to Chris Claremont who had been helping with the scripting from the second issue, so he was no stranger to the new team. Claremont, who as a child had read and enjoyed the original X-Men, had no intention of pursuing a career in comics. His first love was the theatre. After graduating in 1972, in order to pay the bills while looking for acting jobs, he had sold some stories to Marvel. In the spring of 1974 he was offered the job of Marv Wolfman's assistant editor on the magazine line. He agreed to do it for six months to build up some cash but, after Roy Thomas quit as editor-in-chief and Len Wein took over, he was given **X-Men** to work on. As Claremont says, 'The rest is history!' He worked on the title for 17 years until issue No. 279. He remembers:

We had no idea of where we were going or what we were doing. For the first couple of years Dave Cockrum and I were making it up as we went along, and our interests meshed. Len Wein's original ideas were modified in the process. Wolverine, who was conceived as a smart-mouthed teenager, became older and more experienced. Nightcrawler was going to be bitter, twisted and tormented, but we took the approach that Nightcrawler thought it was incredibly cool to be blue and furry. The book took on a totally new direction. The trick with X-Men *was that you couldn't read one issue, something about it would be so interesting that you'd want to come back for the next one.*

Claremont remembers his early days in the Marvel bullpen with great affection:

It really wasn't very big, we all worked together, Stan [Lee] had his own office, and everything else was in one area. It was fun! Everybody was dedicated, I remember calling Stan up at home late one night, he answered the phone and I said it was me, he immediately came back with 'Hello true-believer!' That'll give you some idea.

Marvel added another two superhero teams in **Invaders** No. 1 (August 1975) and **The Champions** No. 1 (October 1975). The Invaders were made up of some of Marvel's heroes from the 1940s who had first got together, without a name, in **Avengers** No. 71 (December 1969). They included Captain America and Bucky, The Human Torch and Toro, and The Sub-Mariner.

The Champions, who were founded to 'help the common man', were Angel, Black Widow, Ghost Rider, Iceman, Hercules and Darkstar. The title lasted 17 issues until January 1978.

In January 1976, DC joined the sword and sorcery market with **Warlord** No. 1,[7] and in the same month revived the Golden Age team The Justice Society of America in **All Star Comics** No. 58, continuing the numbering from 1951 when the title had changed to **All Star Western** after issue No. 57.

After a few guest appearances in other books,[8] the cigar-smoking duck, 'trapped in a world he never made!', got his own series in Marvel's **Howard the Duck** No. 1 (January 1976). Writer Steve Gerber remembers, 'Howard was created totally as a joke and totally on the spur of the moment. It was something completely different.' The story told of Howard being 'zapped' from another dimension to Earth, which he referred to as 'a world of hairless talking apes'.

Howard was dragged into all sorts of adventures and confronted everything from a vampire cow to a giant gingerbread man. The readers loved it! The following year he had a brief run as a newspaper strip, drawn by Gene Colan. Sadly, a dispute arose between Gerber and Marvel, other writers took over, and the book went

▲ AVENGERS No. 71,
December 1969
(™ & Copyright © 1994 Marvel
Entertainment Group, Inc.)

▲ INVADERS ANNUAL
No. 1,
1977, has a typical Schom-burg cover
(™ & Copyright © 1994 Marvel
Entertainment Group, Inc.)

▲ HOWARD THE DUCK
No. 2,
March 1976
(™ & Copyright © 1994 Marvel
Entertainment Group, Inc.)

downhill. It was finally cancelled with issue No. 31 in May 1979. It was briefly revived for two issues, Nos 32 and 33, in January and September 1986 and, in the same year, spawned a misguided movie in which Frank Brunner's and Steve Gerber's creation was unwisely turned into a live-action character. It was executive produced but disowned by George Lucas.

On television, ABC began airing *The New Original Wonder Woman*,[9] set in the 1940s and starring former Miss USA Lynda Carter in the title role. Carter recalls, *'From the start Wonder Woman wasn't just another TV character – I was living out a fantasy.'* She embarked on a strict diet and an intense fitness programme to prepare for the role. One of her fitness instructors remembers Carter's dedication: *'She didn't want to* play *Wonder Woman, she wanted to* be *Wonder Woman.'* In 1977 the action was updated to the 1970s when it moved to CBS where it continued until 1979.

Jack Kirby, who had left DC to return to Marvel, there embarked on a new venture in the **Eternals** No. 1 (July 1976).

In a collaboration, following their joint production in 1975 of a comic-book adaptation of MGM's *Wizard of Oz*, Marvel and DC published **Superman versus the Amazing Spider-Man** (1976). This 92-page oversized comic also had a special printing of 5,000 numbered copies, signed by Stan Lee and Carmine Infantino, which were sold through the mail. The idea came originally from literary agent David Obst, who among others had represented Carl Bernstein and Bob Woodward. Gerry Conway was given the job of writing this epic story:

Because I was one of the only three people at the time who's actually written for both characters, I got the assignment to script the story; for similar reasons, Ross Andru and Dick Giordano were assigned to the art; and Roy Thomas was brought in as creative consultant.

Despite purists complaining that the story did not explain how Superman and Spiderman were together in the same comic-book universe, this was a fan's dream come true. 'The Battle of the Century' was a huge success and paved the way for more Marvel and DC joint ventures, most notably **Batman Vs The Incredible Hulk** (1981) and **Marvel and DC Present The Uncanny X-Men and The New Teen Titans** (1982).

In December 1976, Marvel gave Spiderman his second title in **Peter Parker, The Spectacular Spider-Man** No. 1, where his origin was retold.

On 3 January 1977, Spiderman began a successful run as a syndicated newspaper strip, which was written by Stan Lee and drawn by John Romita.

Three months prior to the release of the movie, on 25 May 1977, Marvel published a six-part adaptation of **Star Wars**,[10] written by Roy Thomas, with art by Howard Chaykin. All six parts were so popular, with more and more fans buying them as the film took off, that they went to as many as seven printings. **Star Wars** became the first comic since the Golden Age to sell more than a million copies per issue.

Marvel's sales were further helped by The Hulk's appearance on television. Beginning in a two-hour pilot on prime-time TV on 4 November 1977, *The Incredible Hulk* starred Bill Bixby and Lou Ferrigno. A second movie, *The Return of The Hulk*, followed three weeks later, and the regular one-hour series began on 10 March 1978. Bixby played Banner, whose name was curiously changed in the TV series from Bruce to David,[11] with bodybuilder and former Mr Universe Ferrigno playing his alter ego. Stan Lee acted as consultant to Universal who produced 80 episodes. The Hulk has been the most successful TV adaptation of a comic-book character

▲ MARVEL AND DC
PRESENT THE
UNCANNY X-MEN AND
THE NEW TEEN
TITANS,
1982
(™ & Copyright © 1994 Marvel
Entertainment Group, Inc. and
DC Comics, Inc.)

to date, and it encouraged other, lower quality television and film projects, including the TV movies *Doctor Strange* (1978), starring Peter Hooten, and *The Amazing Spider-Man* starring Nicholas Hammond. In 1979 there were two Captain America TV movies starring Reb Brown in the title role. Although these did not lead to a regular series, they did help increase sales of the comic book.

By now there were very few comic publishers left. Apart from the big two, Marvel and DC, the rest of the market consisted mainly of Archie, Harvey and Gold Key, plus one or two minor companies.

In December 1977, with a run of just 2,000 poorly printed black and white copies, Dave Sim's Aardvark-Vanaheim self-published **Cerebus the Aardvark** No. 1 (December 1977).[12] It by-passed the normal channels and was independently distributed. **Cerebus**, which has a cult following and continues to this day, was important inasmuch as it was the first successful comic from a small independent publisher.

The year 1977 was an important one for British comics. On 26 February, IPC/Fleetway published its black and white anthology, **2000 AD** No. 1, complete with a 'free gift' – a space spinner. (Issue No. 2's free gift was a set of stickers.) Far more significant was the first appearance of 'Judge Dredd' by Dave McMahon. A violent but well-plotted and well-written strip, it tells the story of civilization after World War III, which began in 2070. Government power has been diminished by the Declaration of Judgement. Judges, who are the law, have almost unlimited authority in keeping the peace, as well as the weapons to uphold the law. Training to become a judge takes fifteen years, and suitable athletic and intelligent children are drafted into the Academy of Law at the age of five. Dredd, who entered the academy in 2071, is now 35 and lives in Mega-City One in North America.

Judge Dredd has appeared with Batman in **Judgement on Gotham** (1991) and **Vendetta in Gotham** (1994), and is now the subject of a forthcoming film starring Sylvester Stallone.

At the beginning of 1978, Jim Shooter took over as editor-in-chief at Marvel. Shooter, born in 1951, had become a comic-book writer at the tender age of 14, two years after he had resolved to make a career in comics. Shooter said, '*I spent a year trying to figure out how Marvel did it. My family needed money, and when you're thirteen years old what can you do? Nobody will give you a job.*' His first work was for DC where he sold three Superboy stories and gained national publicity. But he always wanted to work for Marvel, so in 1969, aged 18, Shooter arranged a meeting with Stan Lee who immediately gave him a job as a staff writer. It lasted only three weeks before he returned to Pittsburgh to take an advertising job. In 1976, he received offers from both DC and Marvel, and took a job with the latter as an associate editor. There he wrote 'Daredevil', 'Ghost Rider', and 'The Avengers', as well as supervising scripts and plots. A sometimes controversial figure, Jim Shooter was the longest serving editor-in-chief Marvel ever had, apart from Stan Lee. Shooter took an active interest in the business affairs of Marvel and was particularly keen on improving writers' and artists' conditions:

The first thing I wanted to do was to get the rates up. We actually doubled the page rates, and then doubled them again. We also made sure everybody had medical coverage. And I established an incentive program that rewarded the talent for staying with a series, which helped avoid continuity problems.

Shooter stayed at the job for nine years and was responsible for some of Marvel's best ideas and innovations. By their own admission, he was a significant factor in creating the Marvel of today.

Warner Communications, with whom DC had merged in 1968, was concerned about declining sales, and so cut back on the number of titles being published. In June 1978, they completely revamped their distribution process.

Sales were helped when Superman burst on to the silver screen in December 1978. With DC maintaining total control, it was produced by the father-and-son team Alexander and Ilya Salkind, and starred Christopher Reeve in the title role. A number of other actors had been considered for the part, including Robert Redford and Warren Beatty. The elder Salkind took it upon himself to give Superman credibility. Concentrating on the script, Ilya recalls:

High on my father's list was Mario Puzo, Mario is an excellent writer who has a great sense of public taste and mores. We made him an offer he couldn't refuse.

The next day was casting:

My father believed that Marlon Brando as Superman's father was essential. He was the only actor who could play a mythical character of the stature we needed.

The film was an entertaining saga of The Man of Steel, and included most of the Superman mythos. It traced his life from Krypton to Smallville to Metropolis, and mixed equal parts of sincerity, special effects (which earned a special Oscar) and send-up. The network TV version added footage of out-takes – including cameos by Noel Neill, who played Lois Lane in the Superman TV series, and Kirk Alyn, who played Superman in the earlier movies, as Lois Lane's parents.

The animated version of *The Fantastic Four* premiered on NBC TV in 1978. Because rights were tied up pending a movie, The Human Torch was replaced by a robot named Herbie. The film was produced by DePatie-Freleng Enterprises, who had been responsible for a number of Looney Tunes cartoons as well as the Pink Panther series. Stan Lee and Roy Thomas wrote some of the scripts along with other top writers. Following the closure of the DePatie-Freleng studio, in 1980 Marvel formed its own animation company, Marvel Productions Ltd., which was headed up by David DePatie. Stan Lee, who had been commuting between the East and West coasts, decided to stay in California, devoting his time to writing, film and TV projects.

In 1979, Marvel published two comics based on popular toys, **Micronauts** No. 1 (January 1979) and **Shogun Warriors** No. 1 (February 1979). There was an obvious benefit to both the comic and the toys, and following the success of the two titles they published **Rom** No. 1 (December 1979), based on the Parker Brothers toy of the same name. **Shogun Warriors** only lasted 20 issues until September 1980, but the **Micronauts** had a respectable 59-issue run until August 1984. **Rom** notched up 75 issues until February 1986. Both **Micronauts** and **Rom** survived long after the toys had fallen out of vogue.

In May 1979, the artist and writer Frank Miller began drawing **Daredevil**, starting with issue No. 158. The character had waned in popularity over the years and was a perfect candidate for Miller's particular talent:

I wanted to use a style where the reader had to do a great deal of the work, where a pair of squiggles and a black shadow became an expressive face in the reader's mind.

Sales of **Daredevil** immediately picked up. He pencilled Nos 158–61, 163–84 and, with issue No. 168, Miller took over the writing. He told tales of violent urban crime, where Daredevil came up against such villains as the overweight gang boss Kingpin and the female assassin, Elektra. Miller took the reader into the minds of the characters, adding an element of realism to the fantasy world of comics:

▲ DAREDEVIL No. 168, *January 1981, featured the first appearance of Elektra* (™ & Copyright © 1994 Marvel Entertainment Group, Inc.)

▲ MICRONAUTS No. 1, *January 1979* (™ & Copyright © 1994 Marvel Entertainment Group, Inc.)

It's not a normal pursuit [being a vigilante] for a human being to follow. In the case of Daredevil, you've got a blind character whose passions are so deep that he takes ridiculous chances.

The mini-series, a new concept introduced by DC in 1979, has since been adopted by almost every other publisher. The first mini-series ran for three issues and was entitled the **World of Krypton** (July–September 1979). Issue No. 1 told the story of the marriage of Superman's parents, Jor-El and Lara. In No. 2, Kal-El (Superman) is sent to Earth. Finally, in No. 3, Krypton explodes. Each mini-series was self-contained and almost completely readable without needing to refer to an on-going title. From the publishers' point of view, this became a good way of trying out ideas, creators and characters before committing too far ahead.

X-Men had been gaining in popularity, thanks partly to John Byrne's excellent art, which had begun with issue No. 108 (December 1977), and Chris Claremont's increasingly complicated and well-plotted story-lines. In No. 120 (April 1979), a new team, Alpha Flight, was introduced, in response to the general surge of popularity of teenage mutant heroes. Alpha Flight made various guest appearances before getting their own title in August 1983.

DC picked up on the popularity of teenage heroes and in January 1980 published **The Legion of Super-Heroes** No. 259 (1),[13] in which Superboy leaves the Legion. Later that year they revived their 1960s team in **The New Teen Titans** No. 1 (November 1980), where new members The Changeling, Raven, Cyborg and Starfire joined existing members Kid Flash, Robin and Wonder Girl. Written by Marv Wolfman and drawn by George Perez, inspiration for the team no doubt came from the X-Men and, although extremely popular, quickly becoming DC's best-selling title, The New Teen Titans never came close to the success of Marvel's mutants.

By the early eighties, more and more newsstands were closing and giving way to chain-stores, many of which did not bother to stock comics. Inflation was running high and the publishers were having distribution problems. Fortunately, this coincided with the opening of a number of specialist comic stores across America. These were being supplied by comic-book distributors on a firm-sale basis rather than the traditional newsstand distribution method of sale-or-return. But it was too late for some publishers. In 1980, unable to suffer the burden of ever-increasing distributor returns, Gold Key stopped supplying newsstand distributors and instead con-centrated their efforts on putting their product into department stores, with a special '3 in a bag' comic package. In 1981, they changed their logo to Whitman, and continued to struggle until 1984 when, after 22 years, they finally ceased publication of comics.

Harvey had also been suffering and, by 1981, were only publishing Hot Stuff and Richie Rich titles. In 1982, they suspended publication altogether, and did not put out another book until 1986. In 1985, in an attempt to fill the 'kiddie-comic' gap that Harvey left, Marvel, under its Star Comic banner, put out a number of titles, including **Heathcliff**, **Muppet Babies**, **Top Dog** and **Fraggle Rock**.

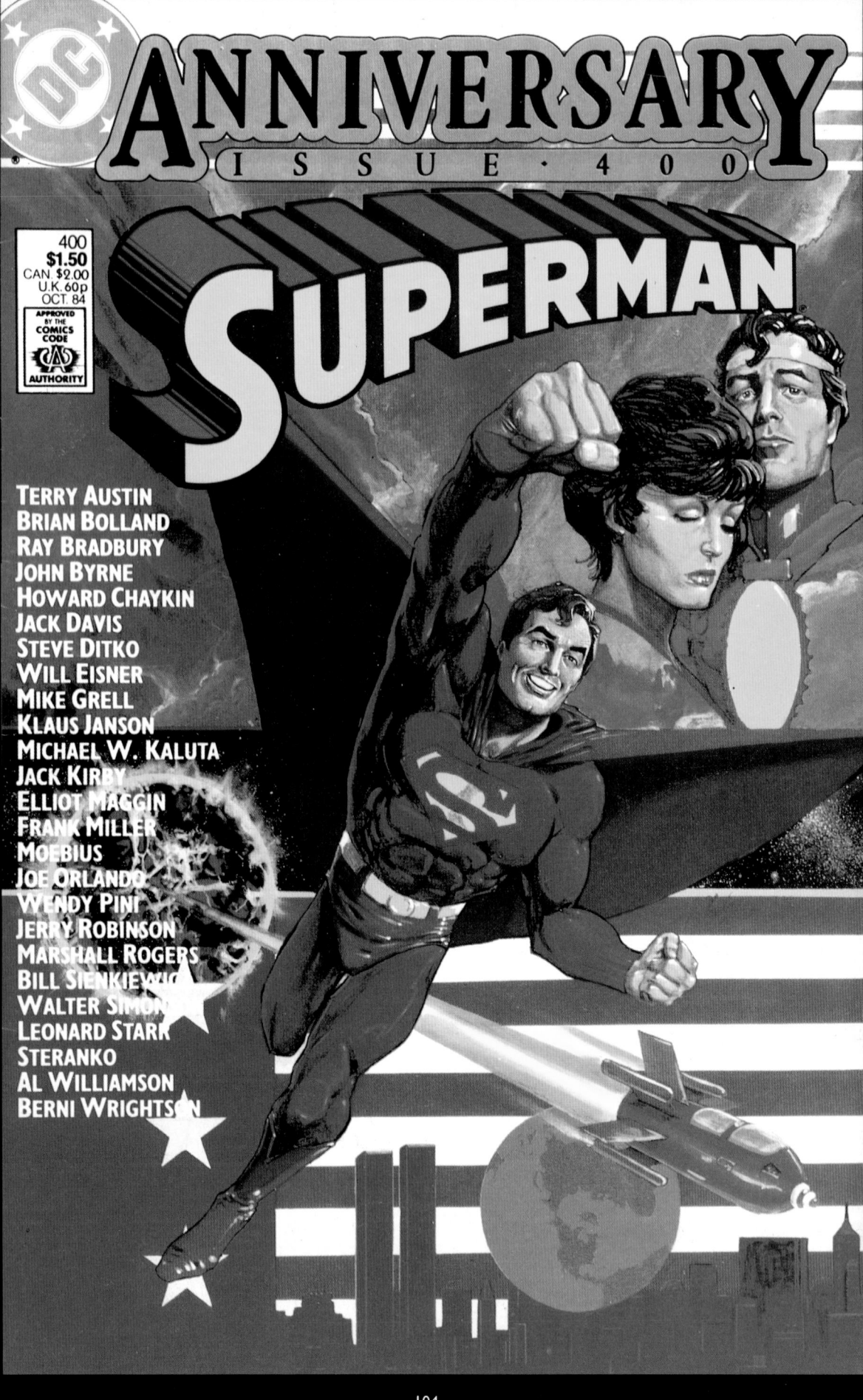

7

A New Era
1981–89

HE SPECIALIST COMIC STORES HAD CREATED A NEW MARKET to nurture and, in order to test it, Marvel supplied issue No. 1 of **Dazzler** (March 1981), only to specialist comic stores. To their surprise and delight they nearly doubled the average sale of their other titles. **Dazzler** No. 1 sold more than 400,000 copies! Perhaps some of these copies were bought in bulk by speculative collectors in the belief that this first 'direct market' comic would become a collector's item and increase in value. Sadly, it did not, but its success did make the publishers realize that, as one door, represented by the shrinking newsstand distribution market, was closing, another bigger, brighter door was opening, in the guise of direct distribution and specialist shops which quickly began appearing all over the country and then throughout the world. The new era had begun.

The new direct market helped small, independent publishers to distribute their products. The first major independent was Pacific Comics which supplied only the direct market and offered royalties based on sales to creators. In November 1981, they published Jack Kirby's **Captain Victory and the Galactic Rangers** No. 1. During its 13-issue run, creators including Steve Ditko and Neal Adams worked on the series.

The movie *Superman II* was released in 1981. Again starring Christopher Reeve in the title role, it was directed by Richard Lester. The film, which defied logic and the Superman legend, tells the hopelessly contrived story of three villains from Krypton, with powers just like Superman's, who threaten the Earth – while Lois Lane and The Man of Steel fall in love. It was full of great effects and was entertainingly played, but lacked the sense of awe and wonder of the original film.

During 1982, more comic stores sprang up, along with more independent publishers. A new company, Comico, put out their first comic, **Primer** No. 1 (October 1982). The second issue heralded the first appearance of Grendel, destined to become immensely popular, and No. 4 saw Sam Kieth's first art in comics. Eclipse Comics, which had sporadically published for the collectors' market, began its first ongoing series with **Sabre** No. 1 (September 1982). The independents had much smaller sales than the big publishers, but enough support to justify their efforts.

▲ DAZZLER No. 1,
*March 1981, was the first
'direct market' only comic*
(™ & Copyright © 1994 Marvel
Entertainment Group, Inc.)

◀ SUPERMAN No. 400,
*October 1984. Following the
third movie, Superman celebrated its 400th issue with a
galaxy of creators con-
tributing*
(™ & Copyright © 1994 DC
Comics, Inc.)

▲ MIRACLEMAN No. 1,
August 1985
(Copyright © 1994 Eclipse)

In the UK, Marvelman[1] was revived in Quality Communication's excellent black and white anthology, **Warrior** No. 1 (March 1982). The revival was written by Alan Moore and drawn by Garry Leach. In 1985, Eclipse began reprinting the work, as a prelude to a new series, in **Miracleman** No. 1 (August 1985).

Warrior No. 1[2] also carried the strip 'V for Vendetta', by Alan Moore and David Lloyd, telling of a hellish future Britain. The series was later reprinted by DC in **V for Vendetta** Nos 1–10 (September 1988–April 1989).[3]

Marvel's answer to DC's mini-series came in September 1982, when X-Men's most popular character began a solo career and starred in a four-issue 'limited series', **Wolverine**. It was written by Chris Claremont and drawn by Frank Miller. Claremont said, '*Until then everybody had thought of him [Wolverine], as a berserk killer, and what we did was to reveal the man inside.*' The four-issue series was very popular with fans and paved the way, thanks to the direct market, for other similar projects.

At the end of the year, Marvel set up a programme that offered creators additional rewards based on sales of their work. Vice-President Michael Hobson said that they had only done it because DC had started a similar programme in November 1982, back-dated to July 1981. However, it cost Marvel a great deal more money than it cost DC, because the incentives did not begin operating until a comic sold more than 100,000 copies. At that time hardly any of DC's titles qualified, whereas almost all of Marvel's did. Jim Shooter said, '*It cost Marvel hundreds of thousands of dollars, but it didn't matter because we kept the good people we had, we attracted other good people, and the plan paid for itself quickly.*'

Another way Marvel encouraged creators was by launching a new line of comics under the Epic banner, beginning with **Dreadstar** No. 1 (November 1982). Under the direction of Archie Goodwin, Epic Comics became a separate division of Marvel, where it published mature material, with creators retaining the copyright in their work.

The year 1982 also saw the birth of the graphic novel when Marvel published **The Death of Captain Marvel** by Jim Starlin. It sold more than 100,000 copies, retailing for $5.95 (£3.95), and went to three printings. Jim Shooter believed that, if comic stores had been included in surveys, it would have made the bestseller list.

Outside the direct market, Marvel published **G.I. Joe, A Real American Hero** No. 1 (June 1982), to tie in with the Hasbro toy and an animated TV show of the same name. The first issue was printed on high-quality Baxter paper, and the series continues to date.

In June 1982, DC capitalized on the popularity of The New Teen Titans and published a four-issue mini-series, **Tales of the New Teen Titans**. DC further exploited the limited-series concept by creating a bigger version, the maxi-series. Published in December 1982, **Camelot 3000** ran for 12 issues. It introduced The Knights of New Camelot and, with Brian Bolland art, was favourably received by fans.

In 1983, there were more publishers in the market than there had been for almost forty years. As well as the two majors, DC and Marvel, Whitman, Charlton and Archie still had limited output. The other publishers, who relied mostly on the direct-sales market, included Eagle, Red Circle,[4] Kitchen Sink, Pacific, Comico, First Comics and Capital, who together with Americomics joined Eclipse.

In March 1983, Marvel published **New Mutants** No. 1, which was actually the second appearance of the new team. They had first appeared in Marvel's fourth graphic novel in 1982. Editor and creator Louise Simonson[5] explained: '*We did a story that we thought was going to be the first issue, but there was a gap in the graphic*

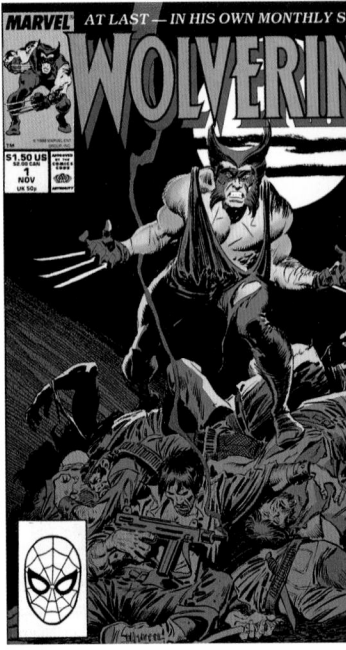

▲ WOLVERINE No. 1,
November 1988
(™ & Copyright © 1994 Marvel
Entertainment Group, Inc.)

novel schedule.' The gap was in fact caused by her husband, Walter Simonson, running late on his **Starslammers** book. **New Mutants** was written by Chris Claremont, with initial input from both Louis Simonson and Jim Shooter, and was drawn by Bob McLeod. It told the story of a new group of teenage mutants who were being trained by Professor Xavier. The title quickly became one of Marvel's best sellers, and with its ever-changing group ran for 100 issues until April 1991. Louise Simonson eventually took over the writing and, when the series ended, its most popular characters formed a new mutant group with their own title, **X-Force** No. 1 (August 1991).

The third Superman movie, again with Christopher Reeve in the title role and directed by Richard Lester, was released in 1983. This appalling sequel trashed everything that Superman is all about for the sake of cheap laughs and a co-starring role for Richard Pryor, as a computer operator who unwittingly gives villainous Robert Vaughn a chance to conquer The Man of Steel. Director Lester's opening slapstick ballet is a funny set piece, but doesn't belong in this film. American interviewer and showbiz gossip columnist Rex Reed said of the film:

Of all the summer trash we're drawing in, Superman III *is the stupidest and trashiest. Superman has run out of diesel and is now flying on cheap muscatel … the sections of the film never blend into any cohesive entity.*

In 1983, something strange was happening in Gotham City. Robin was getting older, while Batman stayed the same age! Dick (Robin) Grayson went off to college, dropped out and joined The New Teen Titans. He got a new costume and changed his name to Nightwing. A new Robin, Jason Todd, was introduced in **Batman** No. 358 (April 1983).[6] Villain Killer Croc, so named because he has the strength and skin of a crocodile, murders husband and wife circus performers, who are Jason's parents. Unaware of his parents' deaths, Jason helps in the capture of Killer Croc and ends up becoming the new Robin. Inexplicably, DC later completely changed Jason Todd's origin, turning him into an entirely different character, with Batman rescuing him from the streets and a life of crime, as told in **Batman** No. 408 (July 1987).

The independents were fighting for market share, producing work ranging from the superb to the abysmal. Some of the better work included First Comics' **American Flagg** No. 1 (October 1983) by Howard Chaykin, and Kitchen Sink's **The Spirit**, which introduced Will Eisner's character to a new generation.

Mirage Studios began what would turn into one of the decade's most successful merchandising phenomena when it published **Teenage Mutant Ninja Turtles** No. 1 (1984). Kevin Eastman and Peter Laird's unlikely heroes fascinated the world and spawned everything from clothing to toys, films and an animated television series. The initial print run for the first issue was just 3,000 copies.[7] By 1988, it had been reprinted five times.

DC published a mini-series by Frank Miller, printed on high-quality paper and entitled **Ronin** Nos 1–6 (July 1983–April 1984),[8] which showed that comics could go beyond being merely light entertainment. It was a story about a decaying future society, mixing Japanese legends with modern technology and man. Miller said:

It changed the rules. It showed me that comics have endless possibilities. I had to adapt my writing and drawing styles for the improved format. The primary difference was, that on the better paper the coloring became a vital part of the story.

Miller is able to tell a story in images and not captions, with his compositions creating a drama that goes beyond words. He uses a revolutionary cinematic style which is

▲ AMERICAN FLAGG
No. 1,
October 1983
(Copyright © 1994 First Comics)

▼ RONIN No. 1,
July 1983
(™ & Copyright © 1994 DC Comics, Inc.)

perfectly suited for the medium of comics. His contribution is unique which is why he remains a powerful influence in the progression of the art form.

In May 1984, Marvel launched the first issue of a 12-part series, **Marvel Super Heroes Secret Wars**. Written by Jim Shooter, pencils by Mike Zeck and inks by John Beatty, it was soon selling 750,000 copies per issue, not surprising considering it featured most of Marvel's heroes, including Spiderman, The Hulk, Iron Man, Thor, Captain America, The Avengers, The X-Men, Wolverine and The Fantastic Four. The heroes, along with a good number of Marvel villains, Dr Doom, Galactus and the like, were transported into outer space where a powerful being, The Beyonder, made them do battle to satisfy his curiosity about earthlings.

In issue No. 8 Spiderman was transported to an alien world. In the course of a battle to save the earth, he obtained a new outfit known as 'the alien costume'. It was solid black with a white spider on the chest and back, and had a white patch on each hand. The costume, which was biologically alive, materialized and vanished at his will. So popular was Spiderman, new costume and all, that Marvel gave him his third title in April 1985 with **Web of the Spider-Man** No. 1.

The inevitable follow-up to **Marvel Super Heroes Secret Wars**, **Secret Wars II** Nos 1–9 (July 1985–March 1986), was not as successful as the previous series, despite the talents of Al Milgrom and Steve Leialoha, but it further helped to put the Marvel Universe into perspective.

In January 1986, Marvel unleashed The Punisher, written by Steven Grant, pencilled by Mike Zeck and inked by Carl Potts, in a five-issue limited series,[9] which resulted in tremendous sales, and the following month they added yet another 'mutant' title with **X-Factor** No. 1, in which the original X-Men regrouped.

March 1986 saw the publication of one of the most influential stories of the decade. It was Frank Miller's four-part series, **Batman: The Dark Knight Returns**. It was an unprecedented success, greeted with much enthusiasm by fans and media alike. The story, set in the near future, sees Batman in his later years when he is a heavy drinker and retired from crime-fighting. He comes out of retirement to do battle with The Joker and various mutants who have overrun the city.

Miller's powerful vignettes, showing Gotham City out of control, in a state of chaos and under siege, are extremely disturbing. Almost everything of the Batman mythos is still there, including Robin, albeit a female version (Carrie Kelly), the Batmobile, Batcave and the utility belt, yet Miller somehow makes it all seem completely different from anything we've seen before. The reader applauds when The Joker dies in the third part, and feels tears welling up when Batman's faithful butler dies in the last book.

Miller manages to bridge the gap between the different personalities of Bruce Wayne and Batman, to the point where they merge to become something more than they were individually. Everything about the character is suddenly completely believable, and the grim settings add to the realism of the story. The book remained in the *New York Times* bestseller list for 38 weeks and Miller's characterization of Batman contributed largely to the way he was portrayed in the 1989 movie.

At the time DC celebrated its fiftieth anniversary in 1985, its universe of characters and situations was in a mess and in need of tidying up and reorganizing. New readers needed to be able to understand what was going on, and to this end DC embarked on a 12-issue maxi-series which was designed to do the job.

Crisis on Infinite Earths Nos 1–12 (April 1985–March 1986) pulled the entire DC Universe together and attempted to explain a number of anomalies. Issue No. 7 saw the death of Supergirl. In issue No. 12 a host of characters were killed off, including The Flash, Lori Lemaris, the Golden Age Robin, The Huntress and Dove.

▶ BATMAN: THE DARK KNIGHT RETURNS No. 1, *March 1986* (™ & Copyright © 1994 DC Comics, Inc.)

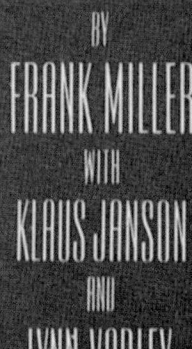

Wally West (Kid Flash), became the new Flash. Critics say it didn't go far enough to resolve continuity problems, but it was the start of a revamping process which continued for the next few years. Having picked up a number of licences from Charlton after they stopped publishing, DC took the opportunity in the series of relaunching some of the old heroes, including Blue Beetle, Captain Atom, Ghost and Banshee.

Following **Crisis on Infinite Earths**, DC updated and revised the Superman legend, starting in a six-part mini-series by John Byrne, **The Man of Steel**, beginning in June 1986. It received a mixed reception, but the fans generally approved of the changes. Some of the ridiculous aspects were dropped and both Superman and Clark Kent became more believable. Clark no longer pretended to be a wimp and Superman became more vulnerable. His arch enemy, Lex Luthor changed from being the crazy scientist to becoming a multi-millionaire businessman, hiding his criminal activities behind a cloak of respectability and obsessed with destroying Superman. Superboy was totally excluded from the continuity. As explained in **Crisis on Infinite Earths**, Earth-2 was where Superman started off as Superboy, while here, on Earth-1, the legend follows the story-line where Clark becomes a superhero for the first time when he's an adult. The Superboy we had seen, it was revealed a year later,[10] was never the boyhood self of Superman, but merely someone from another time-loop created by The Legion of Super-Heroes' arch enemy, The Time Trapper.

In July 1986, Dark Horse began publishing its black and white anthology title **Dark Horse Presents**, where Paul Chadwick's superb 'gentle giant', Concrete, made his debut, getting his own title in March the following year. Born in 1957, Paul Chadwick had his first work published in Marvel's **Dazzler** in 1985. He described Concrete, whom he began developing in 1983, as 'a labour of love'. He has worked on many other comics and also contributed to the design of the attractions at Disney's EPCOT Centre and to the 1986 World's Fair in Vancouver.

In September 1986, DC began publishing the excellent 12-part series **Watchmen**, which examined what superheroes would be like living in the real world. This complex series, later published as a trade paperback, was written by Alan Moore with art by Dave Gibbons, and is one of the finest examples of writing and drawing meshing together to produce one of the best works of the 1980s.

Alan Moore began writing comics in 1980 when he contributed to Britain's **Doctor Who Weekly** and **2000 AD**. He won the British Eagle Award for Best Comic Writer of 1982 and 1983 for his thriller **V for Vendetta**. He won further Eagle Awards, as well as two Jack Kirby Comics Industry Awards, for his work on **Swamp Thing**, which he began writing in 1983, and he won another Jack Kirby Award for **Watchmen**.

Dave Gibbons, who began his comics career in 1973, has illustrated strips for **2000 AD**, including **Rogue Trooper** and **Dan Dare**. In 1982, he worked on the **Green Lantern** series for DC, and in 1987 his work on **Watchmen** won a Jack Kirby Comics Industry Best Artist/Writer Combination Award. He pencilled **Give Me Liberty**, written by Frank Miller, and has also worked on numerous other projects and characters, including Superman, Batman and She-Hulk. More recently, he was responsible for the artwork in the Virgin computer game *Beneath a Steel Sky*, which comes complete with a mini graphic novel. *Beneath a Steel Sky* is the closest thing to a comic book without being one, and possibly the first of many such projects.

Superman's major revision continued with the 'old' Superman waving farewell in an excellent two-part 'imaginary' story in **Action Comics** No. 583 and **Superman** No. 423 (September 1986). Written by Alan Moore, with art by George Perez, and set in 1997, it brought back all of Superman's old villains and friends in a powerful story. The climax comes when, despite vowing never to take a life, Superman kills Mr Mxyzptlk, who turns out to be an evil demonic villain as opposed to the lovable mischievous imp from another dimension. As a result of the killing, Superman exposes himself to Gold Kryptonite, the one substance that permanently removes his powers. He then changes his name, taking his father's initials, to Jordan Elliot, and puts Superman behind him. He is married to Lois Lane and, complete with their baby son, they live happily ever after.

In December 1986, Marvel presented a soldier's view of the Vietnam War, beginning in **The Nam** No. 1. Gritty and true to life, it was written by Vietnam veteran, Doug Murray, with pencils by Michael Golden and continued to 1993.

In January 1987, DC continued the numbering from **Superman** on a new series, **The Adventures of Superman** No 424, and in the same month published **Superman** Vol. 2[11] No. 1, in which most of the old characters were gradually reintroduced in revised form.

The following month, DC's Amazon goddess began a new series, complete with an updated origin in **Wonder Woman** Vol. 2[12] No. 1. It was written by Greg Potter and George Perez, with art by George Perez and Bruce Patterson.

April 1987 saw the publication of the last issue (No. 261) of **Justice League of America**. It made way for a new series, which began the following month, **Justice League** No. 1.[13] The original members were Batman, Guy (Green Lantern) Gardner, Blue Beetle, Mr Miracle, Captain Marvel and Martian Manhunter, who had made their first appearance as a team in **Legends** No. 6 (April 1987).

First Publishing obtained the rights to publish a translated edition of the Japanese comic **Lone Wolf and Cub**, which it began, complete with a Frank Miller cover, in May 1987. Further translations of 'manga' comics began to appear, including Eclipse's biweekly **Mai the Psychic Girl** No. 1 (May 1987).

Spiderman's bachelor days were coming to an end. Stan Lee said, '*I felt we had to marry off Peter Parker someday, because it would give us a whole new angle for stories.*' He also felt that it would be good for the newspaper strip, making it more adult and realistic. So, in **Amazing Spider-Man Annual** No. 21 (1987), Spiderman married his girlfriend Mary Jane Watson. Although the newspaper strip ran different story-lines from the comics, the wedding occurred simultaneously in both mediums.

◀ WATCHMEN No. 1,
September 1986
(™ & Copyright © 1994 DC
Comics, Inc.)

Thanks to the success of the limited series, Marvel gave the 'one man war against crime' his own book in **The Punisher** No. 1 (July 1987), this time written by Mike Baron, with art by Klaus Janson, and Carl Potts editing.

The year 1987 saw the release of the fourth Superman movie, *Superman IV: The Quest for Peace*, directed by Sidney J. Furie. It once again starred Christopher Reeve in the title role. He also received co-story writing and second-unit directing credits.

The film is a disappointing fantasy adventure in which Superman does his bit for world peace by ridding the globe of nuclear weapons – which inspires Lex Luthor to become a black-market arms profiteer. He also challenges Superman by creating Nuclear Man. Although an improvement over *Superman III*, and despite sincere performances, it has second-rate special effects and is very ordinary. In fact, in New York newspapers, it did not receive a single favourable review.

The year 1988 saw the fiftieth anniversary of Superman's first appearance in **Action Comics** No. 1 (June 1938). There was a CBS TV special aired in February, and Superman became the first comic-book character to appear on the front cover of *Time* magazine in March. Further celebrations included an international exposition in Siegel and Shuster's home town, Cleveland, in June.

On 24 May 1988, starting with issue No. 601, **Action Comics** went weekly.[14] This bold attempt proved a failure for DC when the anticipated additional sales didn't materialize. After just 42 issues it went back to a monthly schedule.

Artist Todd McFarlane had quickly shot to fame in the comic-book world following his superb work on **Incredible Hulk** No. 340 (February 1988), in which Wolverine battled The Hulk. In June, beginning with issue No. 298, he took over the art on **The Amazing Spider-Man**. That issue also saw the first appearance, albeit a cameo and without costume, of Venom, the character that McFarlane had co-created with writer David Michelinie. McFarlane had not been a fan of Spiderman's black costume. In fact, he said, '*before I took the book, I knew they were going back to the old one. Otherwise I wouldn't have done it.*' Spidey got his old red costume back in issue No. 300 (August 1988), which was the same issue in which McFarlane began inking his own pencils. This new art style, combined with the return of the red costume, pleased fans enormously, and sales shot up. McFarlane said, '*I think most people liked the traditional costume anyway. But I didn't go back to the same look they were used to – I threw in big eyes and the different webbing and everything else. It was a new look for the old look.*' McFarlane continued to draw Spiderman, with the exceptions of issues Nos 326 and 327, until No. 328, after which Erik Larsen took over.

In September 1988, Epic began publishing a 'manga' title, with **Akira** No. 1, written by Katsuhiro Otomo, who also assisted with new layouts and English translation. In 1983, one of his previous works, **Domu**, a 230-page comic centring around the conflict between an old man and a young girl, both with psychic powers and living in a high-rise apartment complex, won Otomo Japan's science-fiction grand prix, which had previously only been awarded to novels.

Traditionally, in Japan a comic series appears in bi-weekly or weekly magazines and when enough material has been published it is collected together in book format. When the first 25 pages of **Akira** appeared in Japan's *Young Magazine*, the response from readers was overwhelming and circulation increased. **Akira**, which tells the story of the world 38 years after the Third World War began in 1992, was an immediate success for Epic, and continued until 1993.

In 1988, DC published the adult graphic novel, **Batman: The Killing Joke**, written by Alan Moore and drawn by Brian Bolland, which finally discloses The Joker's origin. He was a third-rate stand-up comedian who struggled to earn enough money to feed himself and his pregnant wife. After his wife is electrocuted in a tragic accident,

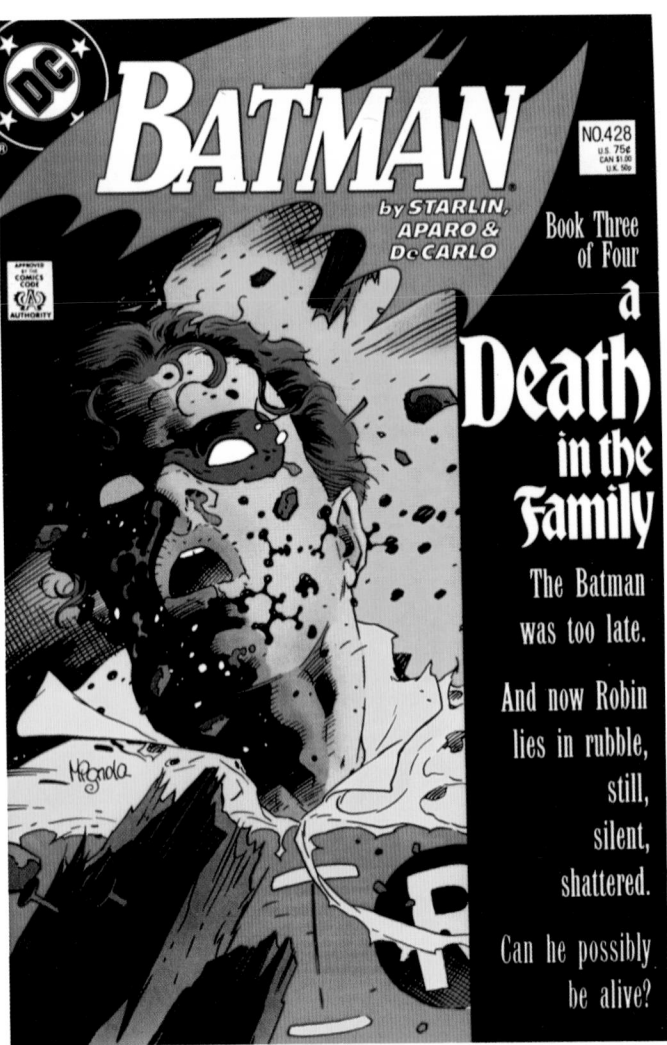

▲ In BATMAN No. 428, *February 1989, Jason (Robin) Todd dies* (™ & Copyright © 1994 DC Comics, Inc.)

he is persuaded by criminals to guide them through the chemical plant where he used to work. Batman wrongly believes him to be the leader of the gang, and in order to escape The Joker plunges into a vat of deadly chemicals that give him a chalk-white face, bright red lips and green hair. **The Killing Joke** was so popular that it went to eight printings.

In December 1988, starting in **Batman** No. 426 and ending in No. 429, DC published a story entitled 'A Death in the Family', in which Jason (Robin) Todd is killed off.[15] Readers voted whether he should live or die. The final count was 5,343 to 5,271 in favour of killing him. Although DC gained tremendous publicity out of this stunt, it was really rather pointless, as the original Robin, Dick Grayson, remained alive and kicking and, in issue No. 457, there appeared yet another Robin. This time it was Timothy Drake, who made his first appearance in issue No. 436, just eight months after the death of Jason Todd.[16]

Despite its futility, the 'Death in the Family' story-line, coupled with advance news of the forthcoming Batman film, nevertheless gave cause for another bout of Bat-mania.

The film was released in June 1989, just after the fiftieth anniversary of Batman's first appearance in **Detective Comics** No. 27 (May 1939). It was directed by Tim Burton and starred Michael Keaton as Batman/Bruce Wayne, and Jack Nicholson as The Joker, with Kim Basinger as Vicki Vale.

Other actors were considered for the title role, including Charlie Sheen, Mel Gibson, Pierce Brosnan and Bill Murray. Fans were outraged when comedian Michael

▲ DETECTIVE COMICS No. 29, *July 1939,* (™ & Copyright © 1994 DC Comics, Inc.)

Keaton, whom Burton had previously directed in *Beetlejuice* (1988), was given the part. Comic stores organized petitions, with many fans threatening a boycott. They soon changed their minds when they saw the movie!

It was Bob Kane who wanted Nicholson as The Joker, without doubt the perfect choice, as was Jack Palance for the role of Grissom, the gang-boss. Veteran British actor Michael Gough was just right in the role of Alfred, and Kim Basinger was convincing as Batman's girlfriend.

Burton was pleased that DC had killed off Robin, as he definitely didn't want him in the movie. A nice twist was The Joker being the murderer of Bruce Wayne's parents,[17] which, once he found out, gave an extra motivation to Batman, although Burton undercapitalized on this. The movie is deliberately dark and grim, with the true feeling of Bob Kane's original Batman coming through, despite inconsistencies with the comics.

Keaton did a good job in playing both parts, though some criticized him for being too laid back. One of the big problems with the film is that, thanks to Nicholson's outstanding performance, the psychotic villainous Joker is so much more potent than the hero Batman.

While 'dark', there's also razzle-dazzle in the movie, with much to grab the attention, including Anton Furst's Oscar-winning production design and Danny Elfman's haunting score. Prince also contributed several songs. It was the top grossing picture of the year, earning more than $240 million (£160 million) and was responsible for 1989 being dubbed 'The Year of the Bat'.

As the decade drew to a close, in November 1989 Marvel celebrated the fiftieth anniversary of their first comic, **Marvel Comics** No. 1 (November 1939), in which, among others, the Sub-Mariner, The Human Torch and Kazar the Great appeared.

After leaving Marvel in 1987, Jim Shooter worked as a free lance until 1989, when he set up Voyager Communications Inc., which began publishing, under its Valiant imprint, characters licensed from the Japanese computer-game giant Nintendo. However, Valiant's real success was to lie in the expansion of its range into superhero comics, which in the early 1990s would make them a cult publisher among fans.

8
The 1990s

 **ESPITE THE FACT THAT THE BATMAN BOOM SOON DIED, AND A** lukewarm reception was given to the computer-generated graphic novel **Batman: Digital Justice** (1990), by Pepe Morenom, the film did more to boost sales of superhero comics than any marketing campaign had ever achieved.

In February 1990, First and Berkley began publishing a new series of **Classics Illustrated**. Despite a great deal of media attention and work by some of the industry's top creators, the series was cancelled after 27 issues.

In April, Gladstone launched its line of EC reprints, which until then were only available through Russ Cochran's deluxe reprint box-sets.

DC compiled **Sandman** Nos 1–8 (January–August 1989), 'Preludes and Nocturnes', into the first of a number of Sandman trade paperbacks, thanks to the increased popularity of Neil Gaiman's 'Dream' character. The thought-provoking stories which often have philosophical, literary, historical and mythological content, revolve around 'The Endless', who are Destiny (the oldest), Death, Desire, Despair, Delirium and the lead character Dream himself, Morpheus – Lord of the dream world. The series continues under DC's Vertigo imprint and has won numerous awards.

The big comic of 1990, which couldn't fail, thanks to Marvel's marketing department, was **Spider-Man** No 1 (August). Written and drawn by Todd McFarlane, it came in a variety of different coloured covers and had an initial print run of 2.35 million copies. More printings followed and it became the biggest selling American comic ever.

McFarlane, relying more on visuals than plot, broke with recent tradition and, using his inimitable artistic talent, brought back old-fashioned story-telling to comics.

In November, **Superman** Vol. 2 No. 50 announced the engagement of Clark Kent and Lois Lane. It gained much media attention, and caught retailers on the hop, with the book selling out within hours of its arrival. DC quickly obliged with a second printing to satisfy the demand.

The year 1990 also saw the release of the live-action movie *Teenage Mutant Ninja Turtles*, with a tremendous pre-teen following that could be counted on to fill cinemas.

◀ SANDMAN No. 1, *January 1989* (™ & Copyright © 1994 DC Comics, Inc.)

▲ SPIDER-MAN No. 1, *August 1990* (™ & Copyright © 1994 Marvel Entertainment Group, Inc.)

The story tells of New York being terrorized by a series of crimes perpetrated by the youthful members of a ninja gang called The Foot. Their awesome leader, Shredder, whose face is concealed behind a mask, is played by James Saito. What no one knows is that New York's citizens include four rather unusual individuals who aren't afraid to take on the teenage shadow warriors on their own ground. They are Michelangelo (played by Michelan Sisti), Donatello (Leif Tildon), Leonardo (David Forman) and Raphael (Josh Pais), who together are the smart-talking, sewer-dwelling, pizza-eating Teenage Mutant Ninja Turtles. With the help of their martial-arts master, a one-eared rat named Splinter (voiced by Kevin Clash), and the childlike vigilante Casey Jones (Elias Koteas), the Turtles team up with Hoag to get to the bottom of matters.

Brought to life by state-of-the-art special effects, techniques that combine performers in full-body suits with radio-controlled animation, the Turtles and their mentor emerge as genuine characters, rather than larger-than-life advertising come-ons. In addition, the relationships that motivate Splinter, the Turtles and the movie's human characters are positive without being cloying.

One conspicuous flaw in the Teenage Mutant Ninja Turtle universe, however, is the film's uniformly dark cinematography. *Film noir* aesthetics notwithstanding, this imagery often becomes distracting. The flashback to the genesis of the Turtles, who were little green pet-store terrapins exposed to radioactive waste, and their meeting with Splinter, once the pet of a ninja master, is so under-lit that without the rat's voice-over narration it would be difficult to follow.

The movie boosted comic sales even further than the overwhelming mass of merchandise had.

The other comic-book character to get the movie treatment that year was Dick Tracy. With wild changes in tone and pace, and set in a strikingly stylized comic-book city of the thirties, Disney's Dick Tracy tells the story of the soulless detective's search for justice, family and identity.

Although it looked good and was impeccably edited, this exceedingly well-made film lacks life and dimension; it seems to search for a tone and personality while the audience is left unable to identify with or care about the characters. Warren Beatty plays Tracy and does a good job; other notables are Al Pacino as Big Boy Caprice, Paul Sorvino as Lips Manlis, a cameo from Dustin Hoffman as Mumbles, and Madonna, whose album *I'm Breathless* came out to coincide with the movie's release, as Breathless Mahoney.

Batman was the most publicized film of 1989, with merchandise such as T-shirts, bed sheets, mugs and bumper stickers bearing the Batman logo, everywhere. One year later, it was the Dick Tracy logo which appeared everywhere. Coffee cups and hats were dedicated to the selling of the film, but to add to the merchandising, and in lieu of Batman's built-in audience, Dick Tracy had the always controversial and mysterious Warren Beatty as its star.

Comic-book *aficionados* could hardly wait; Beatty fans were excited; and Disney executives, unsure of the outcome, held their breath. Although the merchandising and publicity were relatively tame compared with the Batman onslaught, with the exception of one ingenious nation-wide publicity stunt that required patrons to purchase a Dick Tracy T-shirt in order to be admitted to a sneak preview of the film (a great example of killing two birds with one stone), Dick Tracy remained the most highly touted, eagerly awaited movie of 1990.

The hype and press surrounding the release of the film was absolutely necessary, considering the content of the movie itself, for although it is visually breathtaking, it is never thrilling, suspenseful or exciting and has a disturbingly hollow feel. In fact,

◂ MAGNUS ROBOT
FIGHTER No. 0,
*1992, was published between
issues Nos 8 and 9*
(™ & Copyright © 1994 Voyager
Communications, Inc.)

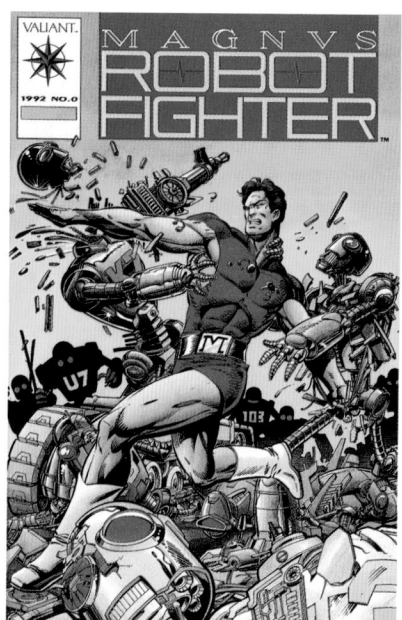

◂ SOLAR, MAN OF THE
ATOM No. 1,
September 1991
(™ & Copyright © 1994 Voyager
Communications, Inc.)

despite its mass-culture origins, this weirdly personal film plays more like a character study than a comic-book adventure.

The true star of this film is Pacino, who provides the only true 'entertainment' in the movie with his wildly over-the-top performance as Big Boy. In many ways he out-Jokers Jack Nicholson's Joker in Batman. Ranting and raving like a lunatic, he creates a thoroughly fascinating villain. His excellent performance earned him a Best Supporting Actor Oscar nomination.

On 16 May 1991 one of the first American comics to appear in Russia was published. The 200,000-copy print run of **Mickey Mouse** sold out within hours.

Also in May, DC comics introduced a new cross-over concept with **Armageddon 2001** No. 1. It featured most of DC's heroes and introduced a new character, Waverider. During the next few months the rest of the story continued in some of DC's other titles, before concluding in **Armageddon 2001** No. 2 (October 1991).

Jim Shooter's and Steve Massarsky's Valiant, having obtained licences from Western Publishing for Gold Key characters Magnus, Doctor Solar and Turok, published its first superhero comic in May 1991, **Magnus Robot Fighter** No. 1.[1] Their next new book brought back Doctor Solar as the most powerful being in the Valiant Universe, in **Solar, Man of the Atom** No. 1 (September 1991). From this base, Shooter, with the gradual introduction of new characters, the first being Rai,[2] successfully created a completely new cohesive universe. He was quick to employ the talents of some of the best creators in the industry, including Barry Windsor-Smith, Bob Layton and Don Perlin. Most early Valiant titles had extremely small print runs and quickly escalated in price, with demand outstripping supply.

In June, another comic broke the 'best seller of all time' record when Marvel shipped 3.5 million copies of **X-Force** No. 1. Included with the comic were five different trading cards, one bagged in each issue, and clever marketing meant that collectors, who were completists, had to buy five issues of the same comic in order to get all the cards. The comic was good enough to go to a second printing, minus the cards, within a matter of weeks.

One of the most refreshing comics of the 1990s is Cartoon Books' **Bone** by Jeff Smith. Bone is a cartoon character set in a fantasy world inhabited by humans as well as non-humans. The clean lines and humour are reminiscent of Walt Kelly's Pogo, who Smith freely admits was an influence.

▾ BONE No. 1,
July 1991
(Copyright © 1994 Cartoon
Books)

▶ X-MEN Vol. 2, No. 1,
October 1991, cover 'A'
(™ & Copyright © 1994 Marvel
Entertainment Group, Inc.)

◀ SILVER SURFER Vol. 3,
No. 50,
June 1991
(™ & Copyright © 1994 Marvel
Entertainment Group, Inc.)

Issue No. 1 (July 1991), now in its sixth printing, was Smith's first published work. He had originally drawn Bone as a strip in his college newspaper, the *Ohio State Lantern*, between 1982 and 1986, although he says he conceived the character years before at the age of five! At the 1993 San Diego Convention, he won both the Eisner Award and the Russ Manning Newcomers award for his work.

On 22 July 1991, Marvel Comics became a publicly owned corporation when it was launched on the New York Stock Exchange. At the end of the first quarter, revenues for the period were $38,300,000 (£25,533,000) with a net income of $6,700,000 (£4,467,000). The stock value was two and a half times what it had been at the initial offering.

Marvel continued its innovative marketing ploys, which almost all other publishers quickly followed, with publication of **Silver Surfer** No. 50, which had a cardboard cover that was deeply embossed and finished with silver foil. It was an instant sell-out, immediately going to a second printing, which caused escalating prices for the first printing. This was followed by **Ghost Rider** No. 15, which had a glow-in-the-dark cover, and **Wolverine** No. 50, which sported a die-cut cover.

The biggest gimmick of the year came in October with the publication of **X-Men** Vol. 2[3] No. 1. This time the same comic had five different covers, which were published weekly, resulting in sales to distributors and retailers of 8.2 million copies. However, sales to consumers were disappointing and many speculators lost a lot of money – just a few months later copies could be bought at half cover price. Some retailers are still stuck with thousands of copies.

DC joined the gimmick market with the mini-series **Robin II**. The first issue had four different covers, each with a Robin hologram, and a lower priced fifth version with no hologram. Issue No. 2 had three different covers with Batman holograms, and a fourth non-hologram version. Issue No. 3 had two different covers, both with a Joker hologram, and a third non-hologram cover. Finally, issue No. 4 merely had two covers, one with a bat-signal hologram and one without.

DC's new Impact line, catering for a younger audience, revived a number of Archie Comics' Golden Age heroes, including The Fly, Jaguar, The Shield and The Black Hood. By the end of 1992 all of the titles had been cancelled.

The creators behind the best-selling comics of all time, Todd McFarlane, Jim Lee and Rob Liefield, all felt they weren't getting a good enough deal with Marvel and

▲ YOUNGBLOOD
No. 1,
April 1992, was in flip-book format
(™ & Copyright © 1994 Rob Liefeld)

in March 1992 they left to form Image Comics. Their first publication, Liefield's **Youngblood** No. 1 (April 1992), complete with its flip-over format and trading cards, broke the record for the best-selling ever independent comic. The record was again broken by McFarlane's **Spawn** No. 1 (May 1992), and then again in August with Lee's **WildC.A.T.S.** No. 1.

Image became so successful that it wasn't long before they were joined by other creators such as Jim Valentino, Erik Larsen, Whilce Portacio and Marc Silvestri.

The new company produced some excellent comics with the now usual gimmicks, such as trading cards and foil covers. The only thing that held it back from becoming the major force it should have been in 1992 was its inability to keep on schedule with its publications.

Meanwhile, at Valiant more new characters emerged and got their own titles: **Harbinger** No. 1 (January 1992); **X-O Manowar** No. 1 (February 1992; see illustration, page 122); **Rai** No. 1 (March 1991); **Shadowman** No. 1 (May 1992); **Archer and Armstrong** No. 0 (July 1992)[4]; and **Eternal Warrior** No. 1 (August 1992). In August, Valiant gave away **Unity** No. 0 which was the prequel to an 18-part story that crossed over in all their titles, with an epilogue, published later that year in **Unity** No. 1, which was also free.

▶ SPAWN No. 4,
September 1992
(™ & Copyright © 1994 Todd McFarlane)

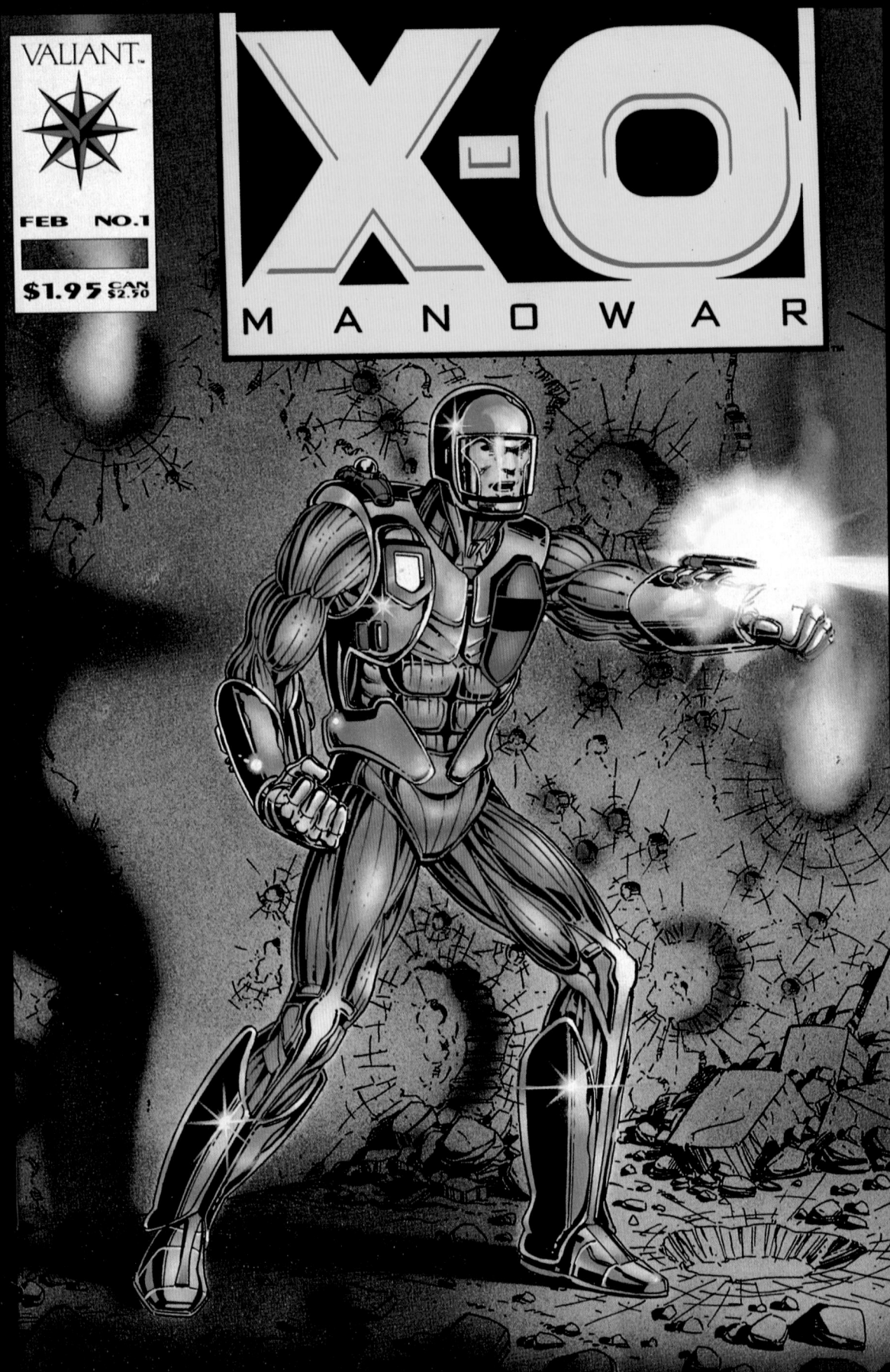

◀ X-O MANOWAR No. 1, *February 1992* (™ & Copyright © 1994 Voyager Communications, Inc.)

Jim Shooter left Valiant in the summer of 1992, after disputes regarding the company's future.

The movie *Batman Returns* opened to mixed reviews in the summer of 1992. Directed by Tim Burton, with Michael Keaton once more in the title role, doing battle with The Penguin played by Danny DeVito, and Catwoman played by Michelle Pfeiffer.

There is a definite contrast between this and the first film, where Gotham City, although dark and oppressive, was still imposing. This time there is a feel of decay pervading the city, and it is hellish and hostile. DeVito plays the Penguin as a sinister homicidal maniac on one level, and on another successfully portrays him as a lonely frustrated outcast, unable to live a normal life due to his grotesque appearance.

Pfeiffer is slinky and sexy in the role of Catwoman, who, like The Penguin, is not an unsympathetic character. She has genuine grievances with her boss Max Shreck, who is the epitome of a male chauvinist pig, and whose only redeeming quality is his love for his son. Naturally enough, there is a romance between Catwoman and Batman.

Keaton is still too laid back as Batman but seems more comfortable as Bruce Wayne.

This much anticipated sequel, although successful – the usual box-office records were broken with the film bringing in more than $46 million (£31 million), was not as good as the first film. *Batman III* is now in production with Robin Williams as The Riddler.

In the autumn of 1992 *Batman: The Animated Series* was premiered on Fox TV. Aimed at children, the series also appealed to adults, and is reminiscent of the Fleischer Superman cartoons of the 1940s, with dark, moody scenes, using shadow and contours to create a gothic aura.

The show has proved very popular and in 1993 won an Emmy Award for Outstanding Animation. A feature-length film, *Mask of Phantasm, Batman the Animated Movie*, was released at the end of 1993 and received favourable reviews.

Man of Steel No. 18 was the first chapter of DC's Doomsday story-line. Many thought that the forthcoming double-sized **Superman** No. 75 might be the issue where Clark and Lois finally tie the knot. How wrong they were. The issue was the culmination of the story-line and ended with the death of Superman.

Doomsday,[5] created by Dan Jurgens, is a mysterious, awesome, powerful warrior, who kills and wrecks for pure pleasure. All we know about him is that he has been imprisoned in a secure cell which is buried in the USA. We don't know why he's there, who put him there, or how long he's been there. He escapes and causes mass destruction on his unstoppable path to Metropolis. After Doomsday has battled with various members of The Justice League,[6] Superman, the only force strong enough to resist him, steps in. Superman stops Doomsday, but it costs him his life.

Dan Jurgens says of Doomsday:

We want to keep his origin a mystery because it gives us something to work with for a good, long time. I actually want to do a Doomsday mini-series where I can explore a lot of things. In my mind, Doomsday had been around for an incredibly long time. I mean incredibly long. I hypothesize, for example, that when his cell was placed here on earth it was long, long ago and that Doomsday, if we would travel throughout the universe, is an almost legendary sort of murderous villain. For example, if someone said to Darkseid, 'Doomsday is coming', even Darkseid would fear Doomsday. Even the Guardians would fear Doomsday. Those are the themes I want to explore in a mini-series.

▼ THE DEATH OF SUPERMAN, *1993, a trade paperback* (™ & Copyright © 1994 DC Comics, Inc.)

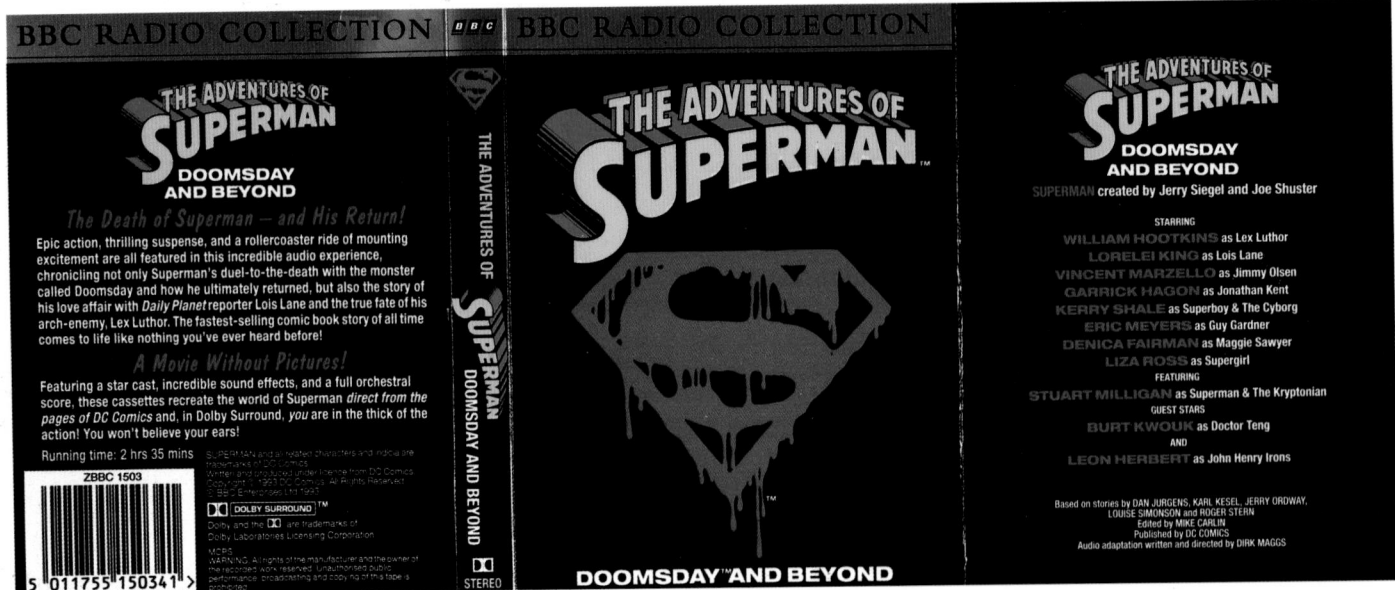

▲ *The audio cassette of the radio serial, ADVEN-TURES OF SUPER-MAN, DOOMSDAY AND BEYOND, 1993*
(™ & Copyright © 1994 DC Comics, Inc. and Copyright © 1994 BBC Enterprises)

Superman No. 75 (January 1993) came complete with a memorial arm-band and a newspaper clipping from the *Daily Planet*. DC's heroes went into mourning in a crossover story-line, 'Funeral for a Friend', after which Superman titles were temporarily suspended until **Adventures of Superman** No. 500 (June 1993), which began the story-line 'Reign of the Supermen', where four pretenders claim to be Superman. Eventually, in **Superman** No. 82 (October 1993), the Last Son of Krypton is 'back for good'.

The amount of publicity surrounding the death and return of Superman ensured DC good sales throughout the period. Apart from the hype, the story-lines were very good and have helped to make all of the Superman titles extremely enjoyable. An excellent novel by Roger Stern followed, as did a superb radio adaptation by Dirk Maggs, which was later released as a BBC double cassette.

Although Doomsday has gone, hurled into space by Hank (Cyborg) Henshaw, Superman, still consumed by the memories of his death, lets his obsessive nature get the better of him. On 12 April 1994, in one of the most eagerly awaited rematches in comics, DC published No. 1 of a three-part mini-series by Dan Jurgens and Brett Breeding, **Superman/Doomsday: Hunter/Prey**.

In January 1993, the one-shot, **Batman: Vengeance of Bane**, acted as a prelude for the forthcoming 16-part 'Knightfall' story-line, which crossed-over in **Batman**, **Detective Comics** and **Showcase '93**.

Bane is a mentally and physically tortured refugee from a Caribbean prison island. He has heard of Batman while in custody and, for his own reasons, vows to destroy him. He comes to Gotham City and manages to release a number of Batman's arch-enemies, including The Joker and The Riddler, from Arkham Asylum, where they are being held.

During a confrontation in **Batman** No. 497 (July 1993), the powerful Bane breaks Batman's back, leaving Bruce Wayne in a wheelchair, and the stage is set for a new Batman to take over.

Jean Paul Valley (Azrael), became the new Caped Crusader in **Batman** No. 500 (October 1993; see illustration, page 126). He was previously seen in the 1992 mini-series **Batman: Sword of Azrael**, where it is disclosed that he is a descendant of a holy order of assassins, who abandons murdering after rescuing Batman. After the 'Knightfall' story-line came to an end, a new story, 'Knightquest: The Search',

▲ SUPERMAN Vol. 2, No. 75, *January 1993*
(™ & Copyright © 1994 DC Comics, Inc.)

▶ NEWSTIME, *May 1993. A special magazine published by DC Comics covering the story of the death of Superman*
(™ & Copyright © 1994 DC Comics, Inc.)

▶ *This 'Funeral for a Friend' poster came with* SUPER-MAN *Vol. 2, No. 75, January 1993*
(™ & Copyright © 1994 DC Comics, Inc.)

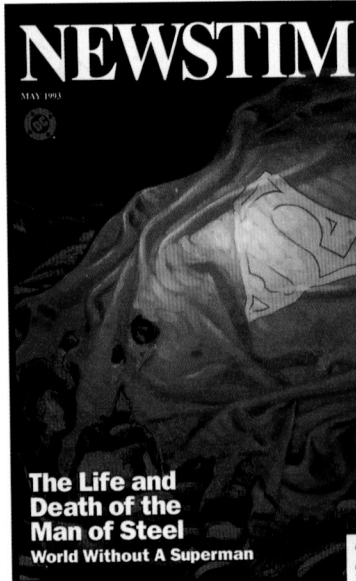

NEWSTIME
MAY 1993

The Life and Death of the Man of Steel
World Without A Superman

THE DEATH OF SUPERMAN

DOOMSDAY

SUPERMAN: THE MAN OF STEEL #18
JUSTICE LEAGUE AMERICA #69
SUPERMAN #74
ADVENTURES OF SUPERMAN #497
ACTION COMICS #684
SUPERMAN: THE MAN OF STEEL #19
SUPERMAN #75

FUNERAL FOR A FRIEND

JUSTICE LEAGUE AMERICA #70
ADVENTURES OF SUPERMAN #498
ACTION COMICS #685
SUPERMAN: THE MAN OF STEEL #20
SUPERMAN #76
ADVENTURES OF SUPERMAN #499
ACTION COMICS #686
SUPERMAN: THE MAN OF STEEL #21
SUPERMAN #77

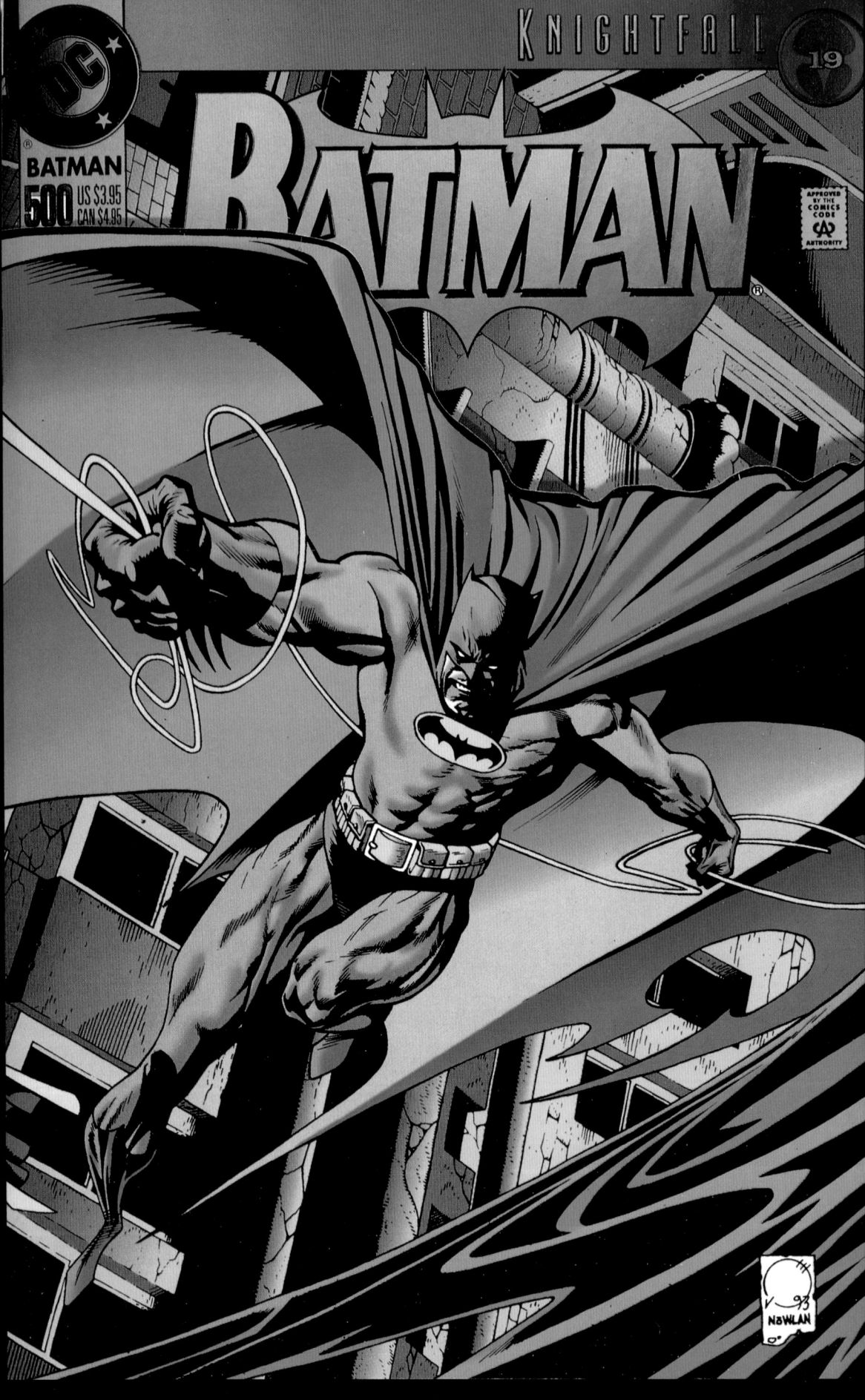

▲ DEATH: THE HIGH
COST OF LIVING,
March 1993
(™ & Copyright © 1994 DC
Comics, Inc.)

◀ BATMAN No. 500,
October 1993
(™ & Copyright © 1994 DC
Comics, Inc.)

▶ ANIMAL MAN No. 1,
September 1988
(™ & Copyright © 1994 DC
Comics, Inc.)

involving Bruce Wayne and Alfred, began in **Justice League Task Force** No. 5 (October 1993), and 'Knightquest: The Crusade' began in **Batman** No. 501 (November 1993), which continued the adventures of the new Batman.

The two 'Knightfall' stories converged and concluded in **Robin** No. 7, and were followed by 'Knightend', where we find out who is going to wear the Bat-suit next. It is rumoured that the original Robin (Nightwing), will take over from Azrael.

In March 1993, DC unified a number of its 'horror and mystery' titles under its new Vertigo imprint, with Karen Berger as Group Editor. These were all aimed at mature readers. The titles included **Sandman**, **Hellblazer**, **Swamp Thing**, **Animal Man**, **Shade the Changing Man** and **Doom Patrol**. New titles quickly followed, notably the three-issue mini-series **Death: The High Cost of Living**[7] (March–May 1993), in which Sandman's older sister Death becomes mortal for a day, and the ongoing title, Matt Wagner's **Sandman Mystery Theatre** No. 1 (April 1993), which is set in sleek 1930s New York and features Wesley Dodds, the gas-masked Golden Age Sandman.

After the change to Vertigo, the titles became more adult and soon the entire line took on its own identity. **Hellblazer**, which had begun telling the story of John Constantine's dealings with the occult in issue No. 1 (January 1988), had always dealt with real-life issues, but now became more gritty and, in some cases, more terrifying.

Buddy (Animal Man) Baxter had gone through numerous changes since **Animal Man** No. 1 (September 1988), including coming back from the dead. The change

▲ HELLBLAZER No. 3,
March 1988
(™ & Copyright © 1994 DC
Comics, Inc.)

▲ THE NIGHT MAN
No.1,
*October 1993, was part of
Malibu's Ultraverse*
(™ & Copyright © 1994 Malibu
Comics Entertainment, Inc.)

to Vertigo gave Jamie Delano and Steve Pugh the opportunity to revitalize and explore the character and his family, which they did superbly.

Vertigo produces some of the finest comics available today, and has certainly been one of DC's major success stories of the 1990s.

In June 1993, Malibu launched their 'Ultraverse' with the publication of **Prime** No. 1. The Ultraverse idea had come about in 1989 when Malibu's editor-in-chief, Chris Ulm suggested a 'writers-based', superhero universe along the lines of the popular 'Thieves World' shared-fantasy universe. Scott Rosenberg, President of Malibu Comics, said:

The idea persisted and after the success of Image (with which Malibu was proud to be associated),[8] it quickly became apparent that the monopoly long held by Marvel and DC had ceased to exist. The field was wide open for a high-quality line of superhero stories told against a consistent and innovative background. Thus the Ultraverse was born!

More titles and characters followed, including Night Man, Freex, Firearm, Sludge and Hardcase, and Ultraverse quickly became a favourite with fans.

Also in June 1993, Dark Horse began publication of a new line of connected superhero titles under the banner 'Comics Greatest World', utilizing the talents of creators such as Frank Miller and Walt Simonson. The good news was that the 16-book weekly series sold for $1 (£0.65) each; the bad news was they contained only 16 pages!

After leaving Valiant, Jim Shooter set up Defiant, and quickly attracted the talents of Chris Claremont, George Perez, Steve Ditko, Mike Barr, David Lapham and others to help create the Defiant Universe.

Defiant's first offering, **Plasm** No. 0, was in fact not a comic book but a set of trading cards that made up the comic, and served as a prequel. Shooter said:

The group that provided the funding included several people who are trading card moguls. Literally on the same day we signed the trading card licence, one of the first questions they asked me was do we have to wait until the comics come out in August [1993] to do the trading cards? I thought, no, why couldn't it be the Defiant preview?

Of the 150-card set, 117 tell the story, while the other 33 cards introduce the characters who populate Plasm.

Shooter's new universe Plasm is a world separated from Earth by a 'nanoseconds-thin reality veil'. The mega-empire known as Plasm dominates the continuum.

Warriors of Plasm No. 1 (August 1993), was written by Shooter and drawn by David Lapham. It was followed by **Dark Dominion** No. 1 (October 1993), **The Good Guys** No. 1 (November 1993) and **War Dancer** No. 1 (February 1994). In August 1993, Marvel filed a lawsuit against Defiant, alleging that the name **Warriors of Plasm** infringed on Marvel's Trademarked name 'Plasmer'. A New York court ruling on 30 September 1993 denied the action. In November, Marvel UK published **Plasmer** No. 1 as the first part of a four-issue mini-series.

Clark and Lois, the New Adventures of Superman premiered on ABC TV on 9 September 1993, and was quickly hailed a tremendous success. With Dean Cain playing a likeable Clark (Superman) Kent, Teri Hatcher as Lois Lane, Michael Landes as Jimmy Olsen, and John Shea as Lex Luthor, the plots are faithful to the comics. It soon began beating Spielberg's *Sea Quest DSV* in the ratings and, at the end of October, a further 22 episodes were commissioned. Jack Larson, who played Jimmy Olsen in the 1950s TV show, is likely to feature as Jimmy's grandfather in a future episode. The producers are also looking for a part for Adam West to play.

▶ EXILES No. 1,
1993, was part of Malibu's Ultraverse
(™ & Copyright © 1994 Malibu Comics Entertainment, Inc.)

▼ WARRIORS OF PLASM No. 1,
August 1993
(™ & Copyright © 1994 Defiant)

In October 1993, minus the hype, without newspaper banner headlines and almost without warning, Marvel killed off Reed Richards (Mr Fantastic), and the villainous Dr Doom in **Fantastic Four** No. 381. Fantastic Four writer Tom DeFalco said, '*After the death of Superman, we could take out the entire Marvel line and nobody's gonna notice.*'

Will they come back? Marvel say no, but only time will tell. Anything can happen in comic books.

In 1993, more and more comics were transferring to other media, and vice versa, than at any time before. Towards the end of the year Hanna-Barbera announced that some of its most famous characters, like Yogi Bear and Huckleberry Hound, would once again be seen in comics. It was Harvey that picked up the licences for publication beginning in 1994.

Dark Horse, who over the years have published a number of successful titles with their origins in film, such as **Aliens, Predator, Robocop, Indiana Jones** and **Star Wars**, have licensed their characters to other media. **The Mask** has been made into a film starring Jim Carrey, due for release in the summer of 1994, and there is also talk of the **Aliens Versus Predator** comic being made into a movie.

Bongo Comics entered the arena at the end of 1993 with the publication of **Simpson's Comics** No. 1, which was received with great enthusiasm and has made the transition from TV to the printed page exceptionally well. Other titles based on the hit Fox TV show quickly followed. **Bartman, Radioactive Man** and Bart's favourite cartoon characters **Itchy and Scratchy** also made it as comics.

DC's parent company, Warner Brothers, having seen the success of the Batman movies, bought back the film rights for Superman.

Marvel continued to see success with the animated TV show *The X-Men*, and Fox TV ordered a daily Spiderman cartoon for summer 1994, as well as showing interest in an animated Avengers series. Universal are looking seriously at a live-action Incredible Hulk movie, while Fox are working on a live action X-men movie. Other Marvel characters that might make it to the silver screen in the near future are Ghost Rider, Doctor Strange, Elektra: Assassin and Cage. It is also possible that the long-awaited Spiderman movie may finally be made during 1994 as once again Hollywood renews its interest in this James Cameron project. On the TV-to-comic front, Marvel, having published **The Ren and Stimpy Show** comic in December 1992, followed it in early 1994 with **Beavis and Butt-Head**, based on MTV's cartoon favourites. With its interest in the toy-giant, Toy-Biz, Marvel's long tentacles continue to stretch across almost the entire entertainment industry.

Malibu's new computer compact disk line, 'Romix', contains complete comic books and uses high resolution graphics, with actors' voices, music and sound effects. Comic books are not so intertwined with other aspects of entertainment that the media are beginning to blur.

Another company with TV connections was Innovation (publisher of such titles as **Quantum Leap, The Vampire Lestat** and **Lost in Space**), which ceased publishing operations on 31 December 1993 after five years in the business.

In January 1994, Malibu launched another new line of creator-owned comics entitled Bravura. The founder creators of Bravura are Dan Brereton, Howard Chaykin, Steven Grant, Dan Jurgens, Gil Kane, Walter Simonson and Jim Starlin, while Barry Windsor-Smith teamed up with writer Chris Ulm for a new Ultraverse title, **Rune** No. 1 (February 1994).

Marvels No. 1 (January 1994), being the first part of a four-issue mini-series painted by Alex Ross and written by Kurt Busiek, is a joy to read and one of the freshest ideas in comics in a long time.

The hero of **Marvels** is photo-journalist Phil Sheldon, and at the beginning in 1939 there isn't a superhero in sight. Dr Phineas Horton unveils his new android creation, The Human Torch, soon after The Sub-Mariner, Prince Namor of Atlantis, makes his first appearance on Earth. The Human Torch and The Sub-Mariner battle it out. Phil takes the photographs and his wonder and awe at seeing superheroes for the first time is superbly conveyed to the reader. Soon other heroes emerge, including Captain America and, when World War II breaks out, a band of new heroes called 'The Invaders' is formed.

Busiek and Ross do not attempt to tell Marvel's history year by year and therefore are able to skip twenty years between issues 1 and 2, with the second part beginning around 1964. Phil is now a successful journalist and is married with two children – a comic-book anomaly means that he's actually aged 20 years! The story opens with The Avengers fighting The Masters of Evil in Manhattan. Reed Richards (Mr Fantastic) marries Sue Storm (Invisible Girl) and, to add realism, Ross even manages to work the Beatles into cameo appearances, along with Dick Van Dyke and Mary Tyler Moore. Then the X-Men arrive on the scene which causes a great deal of speculation as to the safety of the public with these 'mutants' around. Phil comes home to find a mutant baby hiding in his own house, and is forced to re-examine his feelings about these creatures, especially with the mutant-hunting Sentinels on the prowl. In issue No. 3, The Avengers are accused of being super-villains and Tony Stark is being investigated by Congress for refusing to reveal Iron Man's true identity. Phil, who is now working for J.J. Jameson's newspaper, hasn't the benefit of knowing that Tony Stark is Iron Man, therefore he goes along with the view that Stark and his company are up to no good. Enter Galactus, who is going to destroy the world. The 'Marvels', especially The Fantastic Four, save the day, but the public reaction is that it couldn't have been that difficult. Phil's attitude now changes and he gets mad when people criticize the heroes. In the final issue, The Avengers are cleared of criminal charges and are fighting the Kree-Skrull war in outer space. Phil tries to help the heroes' collective reputation by clearing Spiderman of the charge of murdering Captain George Stacey (father of Gwen Stacey, Peter Parker's fiancée). He is about to interview Gwen when she is kidnapped by The Green Goblin. Phil is sure that Spiderman will save her but, as fans know, he fails and she dies at the hand of The Green Goblin, as told in **Amazing Spider-Man** No. 121 (June 1973).

The entire series, with its breathtaking painted pages and thought-provoking script, recreates some of Marvel's most famous scenes and presents them from a different perspective. It is a comic-book masterpiece that is destined to become a classic. A second series is planned in which Kurt Busiek will collaborate with artist Tristan Shayne and tell the story of the Marvel Universe as viewed through the eyes of a policeman and his brother.

DC's prestigious hard-cover graphic novel **The Power of Shazam** (January 1994), written and illustrated by Jerry Ordway, retells the origin of Captain Marvel. Ordway, who worked on the book for two years, successfully recaptures the original flavour of The Big Red Cheese, bringing his adventures to a new generation in an exciting, well-told and superbly illustrated story. A monthly series is planned to follow.

DC's **Zero Hour: Crisis in Time**, due for publication later in 1994, is planned to be a five issue-mini series and will result in major restructuring of the DC Universe. Written by Dan Jurgens, it is designed to deal with inconsistencies which occurred following **Crisis on Infinite Earths** which tidied up the DC Universe in 1985–6.

▶ THE POWER OF SHAZAM, *January 1994* (™ & Copyright © 1994 DC Comics, Inc.)

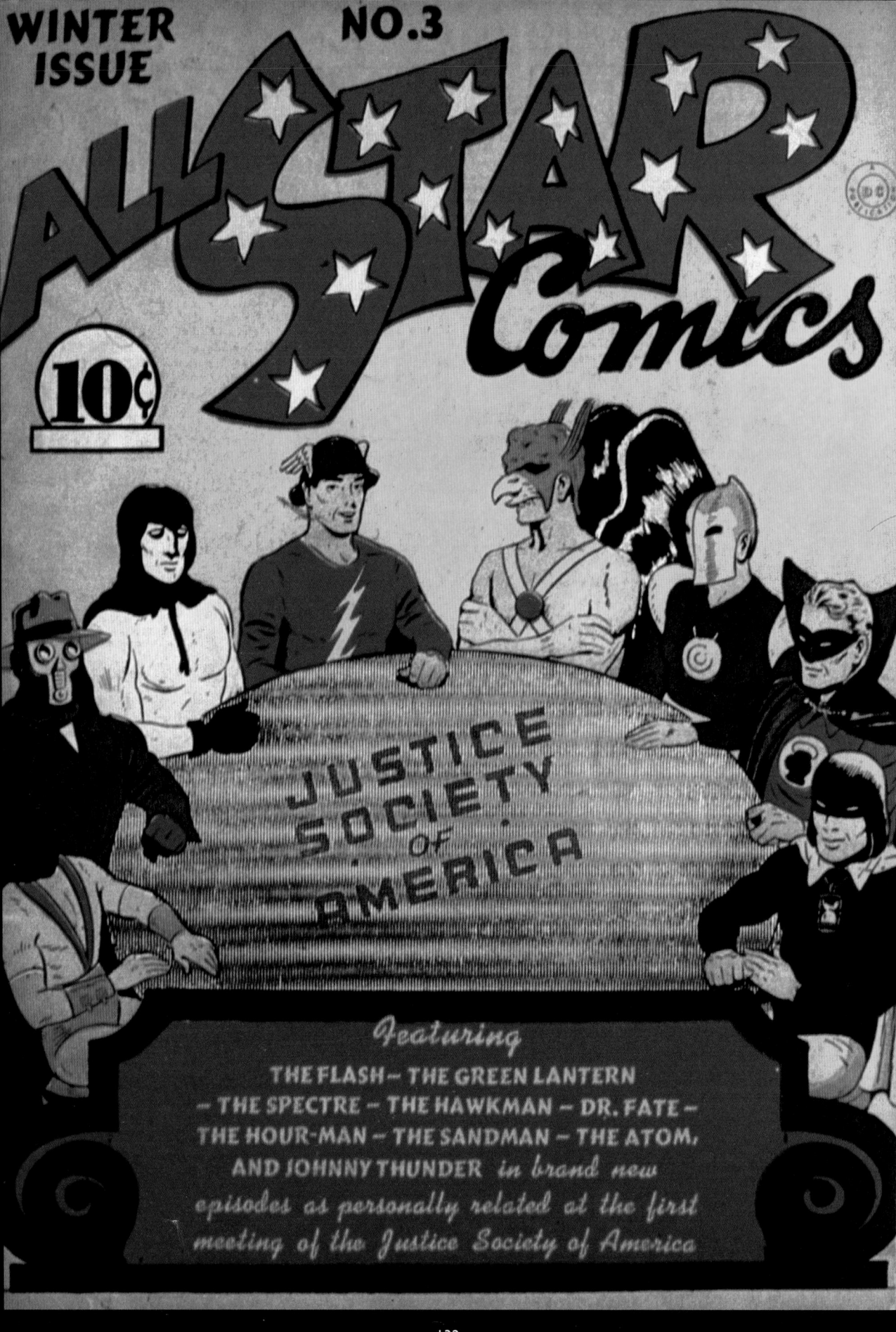

WINTER ISSUE

NO.3

ALL STAR Comics

10¢

JUSTICE SOCIETY OF AMERICA

Featuring

THE FLASH — THE GREEN LANTERN
— THE SPECTRE — THE HAWKMAN — DR. FATE —
THE HOUR-MAN — THE SANDMAN — THE ATOM,
AND JOHNNY THUNDER *in brand new*
episodes as personally related at the first
meeting of the Justice Society of America

9

Grading, Assessing and Collecting

PAPER

URING THE EARLY 1970s, I STUDIED PAPER for two years at the London College of Printing. While this would be largely unnecessary for the average collector, it is important to have a basic understanding of the subject in order to know how best to store and lengthen the life of a comic book.

Most comics are produced using the weakest paper available and were originally designed to be a form of disposable entertainment, rather than collected and kept for many years.

Being an organic compound, from the moment it is manufactured paper begins to decompose. The collector has the ongoing job of slowing down this natural process. Before we can do that we need to know what paper is and how it is made.

Paper was probably invented c. AD 105 in China, where it was made from a mixture of bark and hemp. The basic paper-making process exploits the ability of plant-cell fibres to bond together when a pulp made from the fibres is spread on a screen and dried.

Today, paper is made principally from wood pulp combined with pulps from waste paper or, for fine grades of paper, with fibres from cotton rags.

For newsprint and other inexpensive papers, used for comics, the pulp is prepared mechanically by grinding the wood. Chemical pulp is made by boiling a mixture of wood chips with either soda, sulphite or sulphate, a process that removes much of the lignin, the chief non-carbohydrate constituent of wood, which functions as a natural binder and support for the cellulose fibres. The pulp is then poured on to a wire screen where the water drains away and the fibres begin to mat. The paper layer then passes through a series of rollers that dry, press and smooth it and add various finishes.

Lignin is highly reactive to the acid which remains after the paper-making process, and once acid decomposition begins it contributes to the weakening and breakdown of the cellulose fibres. Ultimately, after losing their strength, these are unable to bend or flex without breaking, thus causing the paper to become brittle. When the lignin breaks down it changes colour, going from off-white to yellow to tan and finally turning brown. The higher the acid content, the faster this will occur.

When oxidation, the chemical breakdown occurring in the presence of oxygen, takes place, the process is speeded up by the oxygen reacting with the acid to hydrolyse the paper. Hydrolysis, which is drastically accelerated by increased temperatures, causes the length of the cellulose fibres to shrink, again weakening the paper.

If properly looked after, comics can retain most of their original attributes for many years or even many generations. Too few collectors give this most important subject enough attention, and it is common to see comics only a few years old, that weren't cared for, prematurely faded and brown, while others, 40 or 50 years old, that were cared for, remaining in excellent condition.

Preservation is not a matter of luck and can only be achieved by carefully following the correct procedures.

◀ ALL STAR COMICS No. 3,
Winter 1940
(™ & Copyright © 1994 DC Comics, Inc.)

PRESERVATION AND STORAGE

Here is a ten-point list for proper storage and care of paper collectables.

1. Store comics at a very low, consistent temperature.
2. Keep comics away from all humid areas, and if possible install an air-conditioner in the storage area.
3. Keep comics away from all pollutants, including the dreaded sulphur dioxide found in the air, as it will react with moisture and produce sulphuric acid inside your comics!
4. Keep comics away from oxygen. The ideal storage place would be a vacuum, which is totally unrealistic. The alternative is an air-tight, inert-gas environment, such as a Mylar™ bag, which *must* be tightly sealed.
5. Keep comics away from direct sunlight. They will only take a day or so to turn noticeably yellow if exposed to strong sunlight.
6. Keep comics away from bright fluorescent lights. They will begin to discolour after just a few days' exposure.
7. When examining or reading a comic, ensure that your hands are dry and that the light source is a conventional low-wattage bulb.
8. Pack comics upright, tight in boxes with lids. It is usual to see comics going brown from the outer edges in, therefore the tighter they are packed the less chance there is of dangerous gases being able to penetrate. If storing the comics in a Mylar™ or similar bag, you don't need backing boards in every bag. However, they are useful to avoid spine roll, and should be inserted as
stiffeners every five to ten comics. If the comics are stored in thin bags, use an acid-free backing board in every bag.
9. Polypropylene bags, so called acid-free or otherwise, are very bad news for comics. They do protect comics from accidental spills, moisture and vermin, but the decomposing chemicals in the bag will migrate to the paper and accelerate the ageing process. If you must keep comics in plastic bags, change them regularly, once a year or so, but, when not in transit, comics are better stored naked than in plastic bags.
10. If you intend to display your comics in a den or a study, ensure that they are protected under, but not in contact with, ultra-violet protective glass or plastic.

ASSESSING CONDITION

ENERALLY SPEAKING, COLLECTORS PREFER whatever they collect to be in as close to original condition as possible.

Obviously, there are exceptions to this with some collectors not minding the condition of the comic as long as it is complete, and others setting a standard of condition as dictated by finance, as prices of vintage comics are dramatically affected by their condition.

It is also fair to say that the number of surviving 'High Grade' copies are far fewer than the number of surviving 'Low Grade' copies, thus, sometimes, leaving the collector with no choice but to buy a lower than ideal grade.

What do we mean by the terms 'High Grade' and 'Low Grade'?

In the early days of comic collecting as a hobby, dealers would often run mail-order advertisements stating, 'All comics offered for sale are in Good or better condition'. By the mid 1950s, coin-collecting terms started to be used to describe the condition of comics, and a five-point grading system became widely accepted. It ran from 'Mint' at the top to 'Poor' at the bottom, with 'Fine', 'Good' and 'Fair' in between. This was expanded by the late 1950s to include 'Very Fine', and 'Very Good', and in the early 1960s,

with the addition of 'Near Mint', it became the basis for the system in use today.

Later, the scale was further extended by the addition of 'Plus' and 'Minus', following the grades, indicating a better or worse copy.

Despite the introduction of a system, dealers in the early days still used a broad brush in advertising, and it was common to see, 'All comics are in Good to Mint condition, unless otherwise stated', which is a bit like a store saying, 'All of the clothes we sell will fit you or not!'

Clearly, this was unacceptable and, with collectors demanding more and detailed descriptions, the dealers gradually responded. Unlike today, at that time there was very little difference between the price of a Mint copy and a Good copy.

So during the last 30 years a less-than-perfect system has come to be used by dealers and collectors to describe the condition of a comic. It is possible to visualize the condition of a book merely by being told its grade, along with any other relevant details, assuming that the person describing the book is able to accurately perform the operation of grading.

You will quickly learn which collectors and dealers are able to do this very difficult job. Only when you finally see the comic itself will you know if the description you were given was correct.

**AKE TIME TO LEARN HOW TO 'GRADE'. IT** will pay dividends in the future, especially when buying or selling books through the mail.

One of the most important things to remember when grading a comic is that its age is irrelevant. A 50-year-old comic *must* be graded the same way as a brand new comic! Unfortunately, far too many people do take age into account. I cannot count the number of times that I have heard, '… well, considering how old it is!'

If someone describes a 30-year-old comic book as being Mint, and you are not familiar with the way they grade, it is a good idea to ask them to compare it to a new comic book published this week. That very often brings the retort, 'well, considering how old it is …'

It will initially be difficult for the novice to accurately grade a comic within the industry-required tight parameters. Therefore, the best way to get started is to use some non-grading terms and put three comics into very broad categories. 'like new', 'average' and 'weak'.

We are going to use a brand new unread comic as our yardstick to which to compare all other comics.

Pick one up and hold it at arm's length. What is your first impression? The cover should have full gloss and no blemishes or creases. While it is true to say that you can't judge a book by its cover, it is a very good start. Slowly bring the comic closer and confirm your first impression.

Now lay the book flat in the palm of one hand and gently curl it very slightly upwards. Slowly open the cover until it is about two-thirds open.

Examine the inside front cover for any damage, and look at the first page for any signs of creasing. Observe the top and bottom of the pages, seeing if they are all approximately the same size. It is common for the cover to be marginally bigger than the interior. Bring the comic to your nose and smell the first page, which should smell of printer's ink and nothing else.

Now, still cupping the comic in the palm of your hand, carefully open it to the centrefold, where the staples are, and check that they are both there and have been accurately placed in the fold, with the staple legs being almost, if not completely, flat.

Close the comic and observe the back cover and last page, checking for blemishes and creases. Place the comic flat on a table and, supporting the front cover with your left hand, slowly turn the pages with your right, allowing the pages to fall open into your left hand. Check for any defects and notice the page colour, which should be consistently creamy white. Now pick up the comic and hold it at the centre of the spine with the longest open side facing down, and very gently shake it from side to side. It should bring a

crisp rattle to your ears. Hold the comic vertically, with the spine facing you, and check that the staple bars on the outer spine are centred and neatly placed. Finally, hold it at arm's length once again to confirm your original opinion.

We will assume that your comic was brand new and unread and that you are satisfied that it doesn't have any faults. Put the comic to one side for the moment. We are going to grade it 'like new'.

Now compare an older comic that has been read a number of times to the 'like new'. Hold it at arm's length and confirm that it does not have the same eye appeal as the 'like new'.

After selecting a suitable candidate, it would now be useful to quickly read the descriptions for the grades 'Fine' (page 137) and 'Very Good' (page 138). Having done this, perform the same grading operations as with the 'like new' comic, keeping in mind what you've read about Fine and Very Good, and confirm that what you are looking for falls roughly into the category of a read copy with some faults, which we'll call for the purposes of this exercise 'average'.

Now find a comic that is obviously in bad condition. If you don't have one, go to your local comic store and ask for an inexpensive, lowish-grade comic from the last twenty or so years. Don't spend a lot of money on it.

Read the descriptions of the grades 'Good' and 'Fair' (page 138). Performing the grading operation, confirm that the comic falls roughly into one of these categories, being overall an inferior copy when compared to the copy you have just graded as 'average'. We'll call this comic 'weak'.

You now have three comics in distinctly different conditions.

The next job is not a quick one, and it is a good idea to do it when you have plenty of time and you are not tired. It is essential for the novice to do this in one sitting. Take at least 150 to 200 non-new comics, all with covers, and carefully and slowly ascertain which of the three categories each comic comes closest to. Don't worry if they have different faults, just put them into the group they fit best.

At the end of this, it would be useful to have fairly even stacks. If you don't, continue grading more comics until there are at least 30 to 40 comics in each stack. Now briefly review each comic one by one in all three stacks, putting them into one of the other stacks if necessary. Then read the descriptions of Mint, Near Mint and Very Fine (page 137), familiarizing yourself with the allowable faults in each grade. It will be useful to make notes of the allowable faults, to help reinforce what you have read.

Pick up the comics in the stack that are approximately 'like new' and regrade each one, looking for the allowable faults in Near Mint and Very Fine. With a bit of luck you should now be able to break the stack into three. Don't worry if you can't, and you still find that all of the books stay in the 'like new' stack. It either means they really are Near Mint to Mint or you aren't being critical enough.

In this case, reread the descriptions and go through them again. If you end up with only two stacks, i.e., Mint and Near Mint, and you are certain that none of the books have allowable faults in the grade Very Fine, don't worry for now. It is possible some of the books in the 'average' stack will gain a rank on regrading.

Now reread your notes on Very Fine and make further notes after reading the allowable faults in Fine and Very Good.

Take the comics in the 'average' stack, regrade them and look for allowable faults in Very Fine, Fine and Very Good. You should now have five stacks, in order from left to right, Mint, Near Mint, Very Fine, Fine and Very Good. The comics in each stack should be in similar condition to each other. Recheck all stacks, making adjustments where necessary.

Reread your notes on Very Good and make further notes after reading the allowable faults for Good and Fair. Don't worry about Poor at this stage.

Take the comics from the 'weak' stack and regrade them, looking for the allowable faults in Very Good, Good and Fair. You should have now added another two stacks, Good and Fair.

Read the description of Poor (page 138), and check the comics in the Fair stack to see if any of them fall into the category of Poor. If so, start a new stack.

Carefully put the comics away, keeping them in their stacks. Come back to them in a day or two, after further familiarizing yourself with the grades listed on pages 137–8, and review your grading. By learning some of the terms contained in the glossary you may find that you are able to further categorize the stacks. For example, you might find that a comic you have graded as Very Fine has particularly white pages, making it reasonable to describe this book as either 'Very Fine, with white pages' or possibly 'Very Fine Plus'.

Since grading is subjective, with dozens of factors to take into consideration, it is surprising that most experienced dealers and collectors arrive at the same or very close to the same grade when assessing a book.

Experience will allow you to fine-tune your grading to the point where you are able to easily add a plus or a minus to the overall grade. There is no substitute for practice. Keep regrading your collection. Today's Mint in a few months time may only appear to be Very Fine. Ask for advice on your grading skills at your local comic store. As long as they have the time, most will be pleased to help and advise you.

A word of warning; do not grade thousands of books in one sitting, as you will become blind to the faults. Do not grade in a hurry and, most importantly, never grade when you are tired.

The Grades

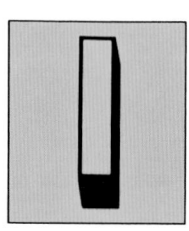

DON'T THINK THAT THE OCCASIONALLY USED grade Pristine Mint exists, as one is always able to find faults no matter how small. I have therefore excluded it. I have also excluded the sometimes used grade Near Mint Plus (NM+), as I believe a Plus at that level is irrelevant. Double Plus (for example, Fine Plus Plus [FN + +]) is occasionally used to describe a book, but in

my experience, this term is a waste of time, and either the comic is good enough to go up into the next grade or one Plus should be removed. Most dealers would agree with this sentiment.

The list begins with Mint and ends with Poor, the lowest recognizable grade. Coverless is also included — while not a recognized grade, it is worthy of a mention.

What follows is a full listing of all the grades currently being used, accompanied by a description and advice on the grade.

Ranks and Abbreviations

1	MINT	M	7	FINE PLUS	FN+	13	GOOD PLUS	G+
2	NEAR MINT	NM	8	FINE	FN	14	GOOD	G
3	NEAR MINT MINUS	NM−	9	FINE MINUS	FN−	15	GOOD MINUS	G−
4	VERY FINE PLUS	VFN+	10	VERY GOOD PLUS	VG+	16	FAIR	FR
5	VERY FINE	VFN	11	VERY GOOD	VG	17	POOR	PR
6	VERY FINE MINUS	VFN−	12	VERY GOOD MINUS	VG−	18	COVERLESS	

THE GRADES IN DETAIL

A PERFECT, FLAWLESS COPY WITH absolutely no faults visual to the naked eye. Printing defects, or bad cutting after printing, are not acceptable. The comic must be cut square and be completely flat. The cover must have all of its original gloss and the pages must not have discoloured from their original slightly creamy white colour. The spine must be tight and show no signs of any cracking. The staples must show no sign of ageing whatsoever and must be centred and in line with each other. If the comic is held up by the spine and shaken lightly a crisp sound should be heard. The pages should not smell of any damp, mustiness or acidity. An arrival date, that is written in pencil, generally will not detract from this grade providing that the pencil date is quite light and does not show through to the inside front cover. An ink arrival date is not allowed in this grade.

ADVICE ON MINT

FOR
- Post-1975 comics easy to find.
- Will never need upgrading.
- Will never be as inexpensive again.
- The best investment grade.
- Easy to sell or trade.
- Pride of ownership.

AGAINST
- Pre-1965 comics are very difficult to find.
- Generally priced above price-guide prices.
- Requires delicate handling.
- Requires the ultimate in storage conditions.
- Should not be read or regularly handled.

PRICES
- Anything up to two or three times price-guide price.
- Up to four times price-guide price for key issues.
- Up to eight times price-guide price for pedigree copies.

CONCLUSION
- Whenever possible, buy this grade above all others.
- If you are new to grading, or at all unsure, get a second or third opinion from a reputable dealer or experienced collector.
- Some less reputable or inexperienced dealers and collectors often describe Near Mint comics as Mint. Caution is advised.
- Remember to examine your new comic carefully before buying it, as not all brand new comics are Mint. Quite often a new comic can be badly cut or marked in some way.

THIS IS THE MOST COMMON grade to describe a near-perfect copy with most conditions of Mint still applying. A great number of reputable dealers and collectors use this as their top grade, as Mint comics are virtually non-existent. Some minor blemishes are allowed: very slight colour fading on the cover, a minute colour flake, a tiny stress mark at a staple or very slight wear at a corner. A tiny spine split at the top or the bottom, caused during the binding process is allowed. It doesn't quite have the beauty of a Mint copy, but is still a very attractive high-grade copy.

ADVICE ON NEAR MINT

FOR
- Post-1975 comics easy to find.
- Can only be upgraded to Mint.
- Will never be as inexpensive again.
- An excellent investment grade.
- Easy to sell or trade.
- Pride of ownership.

AGAINST
- Pre-1965 comics are difficult to find.
- Generally priced above price-guide prices.
- Not very much cheaper than a Mint copy.
- Requires delicate handling.
- Requires excellent storage conditions.
- Regular reading or handling is not recommended.

PRICES
- Anything up to double price-guide price.
- Up to four times price-guide price for key issues.
- Anything up to eight times price-guide price for pedigree copies.

CONCLUSION
- If you cannot find a Mint copy, buy this grade.
- If you are new to grading, or at all unsure, get a second or third opinion from a reputable dealer or experienced collector.
- This is the grade that some of the more reputable dealers are now using as their top grade. If you are buying regularly from such a dealer and once in a while he tells you that he has a Mint copy of something, then it is probably going to be the case.

STILL A SUPERB COPY THAT is instantly recognizable as being of an extremely high grade. The comic is completely flat and most of the cover gloss has been retained. The colours on both front and back covers are very bright and sharp. No further colour fading is allowed in this grade. The pages are still creamy white, although some yellowing, providing it is consistent across the page, is allowed. Some wear could be starting to show, possibly there are tiny creases and stress marks around the staples, where the comic has been opened a number of times. Tears, major creases or even slight browning are not allowed in this high grade. However, one or two *tiny* colour flakes or colour flecks are permitted.

ADVICE ON VERY FINE

FOR
- Post-1975 comics easy to find.
- Can only be upgraded to Mint, Near Mint, Nea Mint Minus or Very Fine Plus.

- Will never be as inexpensive again.
- A very good investment grade.
- Easy to sell or trade.
- Pride of ownership.

AGAINST
- Pre-1965 comics are often difficult to find.
- Generally priced above price-guide prices.
- Requires delicate handling.
- Requires excellent storage conditions.
- Regular reading or handling is not recommended.

PRICES
- Anything up to double price-guide price.
- Up to four times price-guide price for key issues.
- Anything up to eight times price-guide price for pedigree copies.

CONCLUSION
- If you cannot find a higher grade, buy this grade.
- If you are new to grading, or at all unsure, get a second or third opinion from a reputable dealer or experienced collector.

AN ATTRACTIVE, BETTER THAN AVERAGE copy, which has survived well. Still relatively flat and mostly clean. Up to half the cover gloss could be gone, and the corners of the book are starting to show signs of slight wear, as is the spine. The staples are in place but might show slight signs of rusting. Off-centred printing is acceptable, as are other small printing or folding defects. The pages may be starting to yellow or brown around the edges, as could the inside front and back covers. Colour flaking is evident, along with the possibility of one, or two at the most, minor tears or chips. There must be no major creases, although a number of minor creases are acceptable. There should be no stains or writing on the cover, except for a pencil arrival date, which is permitted. This is usually the minimum grade for the serious collector.

ADVICE ON FINE

FOR
- Pre-1965 comics relatively easy to find.
- A reasonable investment grade.
- Could be upgraded.
- Usually priced at price-guide price or only marginally higher.

AGAINST
- Not as easy to sell or trade as the higher grades.
- Not as attractive to look at as the higher grades.
- Will need upgrading for the more serious collector.

PRICES
- Usually around or slightly above price-guide price.
- Up to double price-guide price for key issues
- Anything up to three times price-guide price for pedigree copies.

CONCLUSION
- Try to buy a higher grade.

VERY GOOD (VG)

THIS IS THE GRADE THAT is most commonly offered for sale, and it is not what it sounds! Very Good describes a low-grade, well-worn copy. It has been well read and could have a number of creases including a subscription crease. The centrefold may be loose or detached, with the cover showing significant signs of wear, and could possibly be loose around the staples. There could be a spine roll, and the pages are browning but not brittle. There is still some cover gloss, but the colours could look dull and faded. There may be store stamps, other stamps or writing on the cover.

Tears and chips are present, although no large pieces should be missing from either the cover or the interior. There may be minor tape repairs.

ADVICE ON VERY GOOD

FOR
- Pre-1965 comics relatively easy to find.
- Could be upgraded.
- A way of buying key books cheaply.
- Usually priced at price-guide price.
- Sometimes the best candidates for restoration.

AGAINST
- Not as easy to sell or trade as the higher grades.
- Not a good investment grade.
- Not as attractive to look at as the higher grades.
- Will definitely need upgrading for the more serious collector.

PRICES
- Usually around price-guide price.
- Slightly above price-guide price for key issues.

CONCLUSION
- Try to buy a higher grade, unless you want to collect particularly expensive issues and are unable to afford them in higher grades.
- If you do not mind restored comics, then this can be a good grade to buy for restoration purposes, depending on the comic's faults.

GOOD (G)

AGAIN, NOT WHAT IT SOUNDS. Good is one of the lowest grades. Almost all faults are acceptable. There is almost no cover gloss and a great number of creases. It is generally worn beyond being collectable. It could be very brown inside, with the pages having lost most of their original colour. However, the pages must not be brittle. There could be chunks out of the front and/or back covers. Soiling of one form or another is acceptable. The book is, however, complete in terms of pages. There could be a coupon or advertisement cut out, as long as the story is not affected. Tape, glue and other forms of repair are acceptable.

ADVICE ON GOOD

FOR
- Pre-1965 comics easy to find.

- Could be upgraded.
- A way of buying key books cheaply.
- Almost always priced at price-guide price.
- Sometimes good candidates for restoration.

AGAINST
- Not easy to sell or trade.
- Not a good investment grade.
- Not attractive to look at.
- Will definitely need upgrading for the more serious collector.

PRICES
- Almost always price-guide price.
- Sometimes slightly above price-guide price for key issues.

CONCLUSION
- Try not to buy this grade, unless you do not care about condition or want to collect particularly expensive issues and cannot afford them in a higher grade.
- If you do not mind restored comics, then this can sometimes be a good grade to buy for restoration purposes, depending on the comic's faults.

FAIR (FR)

FAIR IS HEAVILY WORN AND POSSIBLY badly soiled, with very little of its original beauty remaining. With multiple faults, it is generally not desirable to collectors. It still must be readable, although non-story pages could be missing. It could have large pieces out of its covers, which may be detached from the staples. The edges may be ragged and the pages may show signs of becoming brittle. The spine could be split and one or both staples may be rusted or missing. There are likely to be tears, and there could be multiple repairs.

ADVICE ON FAIR

FOR
- Pre-1965 comics are common.
- Could be upgraded.
- Inexpensive.
- Almost always priced at price-guide price.
- Make good reading or research copies.

AGAINST
- Difficult to sell or trade.
- A bad investment grade.
- Unattractive to look at.
- Will definitely need upgrading for almost all collectors.
- Brittle comics can literally fall to pieces when examined.

PRICES
- Almost always price-guide price.
- Occasionally slightly above price-guide price for key issues.

CONCLUSION
- Try not to buy this grade, unless you really do not care about condition or want a reading copy.
- If you do not mind restored comics, then this can occasionally be suitable for restoration purposes, depending on the comic's faults.

POOR (PR)

THIS IS THE LOWEST GRADE TO describe a book that still has its cover, or at least most of it. Poor is a worse example of Fair, the differences being: Poor may be brittle, or have story pages missing. There could be mildew, or insect holes, severe staining, and water soaking. It is not thought of as a collectable grade.

ADVICE ON POOR

FOR
- Priced at a tiny fraction of Mint.
- Might make good reading or research copies.

AGAINST
- Almost impossible to sell or trade.
- No real investment value.
- Unattractive to look at.
- Almost never good candidates for restoration.
- Not collectable.
- Brittle comics can literally fall to pieces when examined.

PRICES
- Prices vary, but are almost always cheap, as dealers and collectors normally cannot wait to sell or trade.

CONCLUSION
- Don't buy this grade.

COVERLESS

THIS IS NOT SO MUCH A grade, but more of a major fault. The interior of a coverless copy could be in any of the grades described.

ADVICE ON COVERLESS

FOR
- Priced at a tiny fraction of Mint.
- Makes a good reading or research copy.

AGAINST
- Very difficult to sell or trade.
- No investment value, unless being used for restoration purposes.
- Not collectable.

PRICES
- Prices vary, but are almost always cheap.
- Key issues in really high grade can still be expensive.

CONCLUSION
- Do not buy coverless comics unless you already have, or think you can get, a cover.
- They are sometimes useful for reading, research or restoration purposes.

NLIKE RESTORATION OF FINE ART, comic-book restoration, although now accepted, is still frowned upon by many dealers and collectors, and it continues to get negative publicity. At the moment, restored comics sell at considerably lower prices than I believe they will in years to come. With a diminishing supply of vintage comics, professionally restored books are bound to become more and more acceptable in the future.

Many collectors believe an unrestored Fine is preferable to a restored Near Mint. That is a matter of opinion, and also depends on what work has been done to the restored book. Personally, if the work is good and has been carried out by a professional restorer, I will take the Near Mint restored every time.

The main reasons for restoring a book are to improve its appearance, stop further deterioration and, lastly, to capitalize on an investment.

If you are a collector who is only interested in appearance, then restoration could be a good way of building a collection of books that appear to be high grade. Make no mistake about it, a Near Mint restored comic is not a Near Mint book, it merely appears to be.

Some comics will literally fall to pieces unless they have some work done to them. This is a matter of weighing up the cost involved, as professional restoration, which is the only kind I would recommend, is not cheap. Rates, even for simple work, can be as high as $75 (£50) per hour. As a rule of thumb, the comic should be worth at least $200 (£133) in its present condition before you should consider spending any money on restoring it. Of course, there are exceptions to that, and professional restorers will be pleased to advise on individual books.

Restoring for profit is becoming more common. Collectors will often seek out a 'low grade' bargain, have it restored and then sell it for a profit. There is nothing wrong with this, but you really need to know what to look for when buying, and also have a rough idea of the restoration costs involved, and what the eventual restored grade is likely to be. I would suggest that this practice is not for the novice.

There are many techniques used in restoring paper collectables. Here is a list of the more common ones.

- Bleaching – A process involving the use of bleaches to whiten the cover and/or pages, this often leaves a distinctive smell.
- Solvent cleaning – The use of solvents to remove stains.
- Water cleaning – The use of water to remove stains, which is not as effective as solvent cleaning.
- Colour touching – A process involving the retouching of areas of missing colour. Restorers commonly use acrylic, which is water based prior to application, but not water soluble after it dries, and printer's ink, which is oil based.

- Re-glossing – A fixative is sprayed on to the cover to re-gloss it.
- De-acidification – The use of chemicals to reduce the acid content of a comic's pages.
- Mending – A general term covering the mending of holes, tears or splits in the comic or its spine. Sometimes rice paper is used for mending purposes.
- Piece replacement – The replacement of missing pieces from the cover, pages or the spine. Rice paper is often used for this procedure. A number of comics with 'Marvel chipping' have been treated in this way.
- Pressing – A process that flattens a comic. If done professionally, it is widely considered not to be restoration, although it should be included when describing the grade.

- Spine roll removal – A process involving the removal of a spine roll, this is often difficult to detect.
- Staple(s) reinforcement – The reinforcement of one or both staple holes at the centrefold and/or the cover, using materials such as rice paper.
- Staple(s) replacement – The removal of the original staple(s) and replacement with another, which, wherever possible, should come from a comic of the same period.
- Tape removal – The removal of sticky tape with the use of chemicals.

I don't believe in the term 'let the buyer beware'. Restoration must be disclosed when buying and selling comics. Some restorers will certificate their work, and this should always be included with the comic.

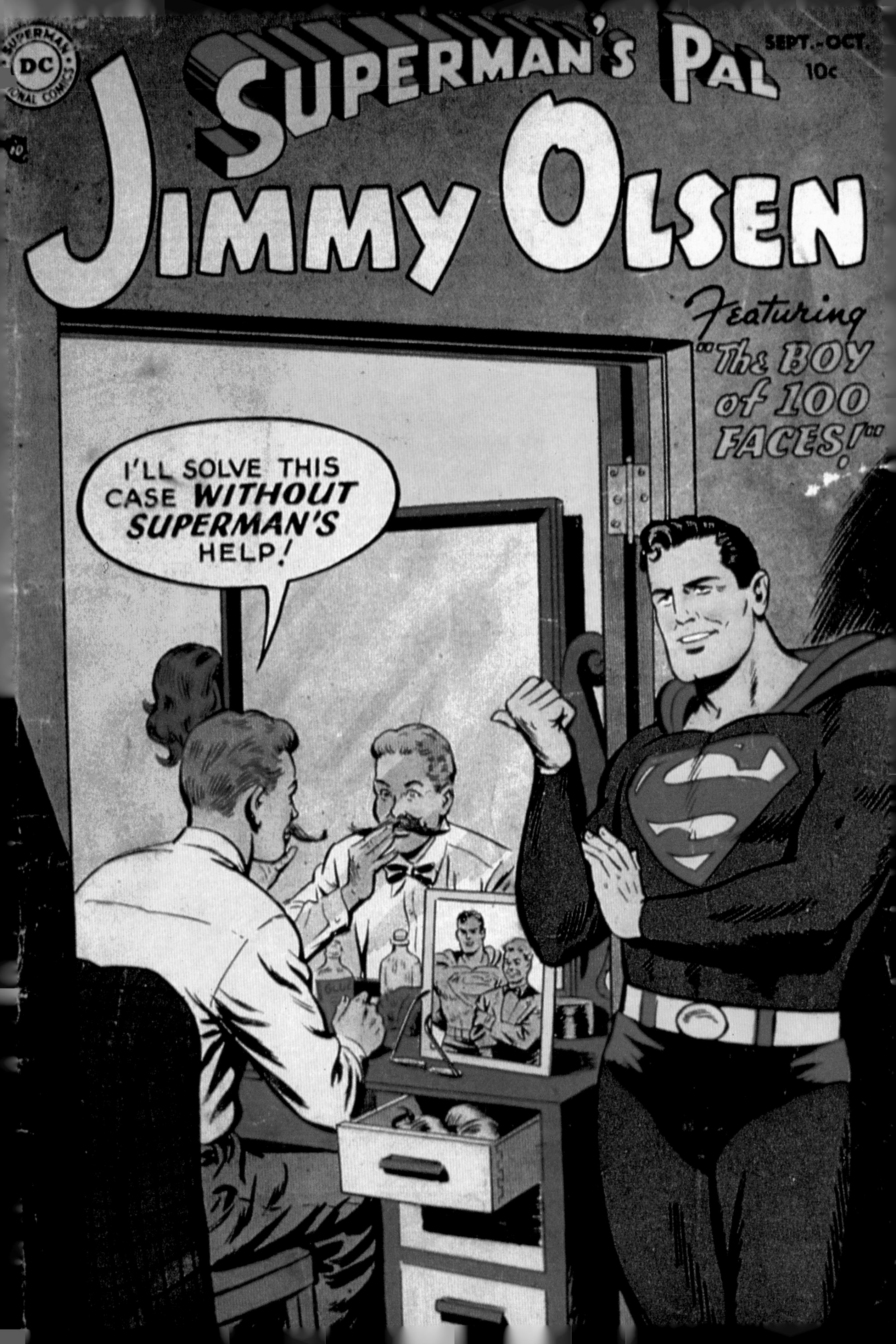

SUPERMAN NATIONAL COMICS DC
SUPERMAN'S PAL
SEPT.-OCT.
10¢
JIMMY OLSEN
Featuring "The BOY of 100 FACES!"
I'LL SOLVE THIS CASE WITHOUT SUPERMAN'S HELP!

Collecting

**HEN COMIC BOOKS WERE FIRST PUBLISHED** in the 1930s, no one would have guessed that 60 years later anyone would be interested in them, let alone pay thousands of dollars for a comic originally costing 10 cents.

Like newspapers, comics were designed to be disposable, which is why they were printed on cheap paper which would deteriorate relatively quickly. People did not keep comics for any particular reason. Of course, there were those who bundled them up and put them in the attic, just as some people did with newspapers. But in the main, the majority of comics bought in the early years were, one way or another, destroyed.

As comics became more popular, it was common for children to keep them to reread or trade with their friends. Condition was never a factor; as long as a comic could be read — which was all it was designed for — it was a tradable item among children.

Those children wanting to buy old comics were limited to jumble sales and second-hand bookshops for a source of supply, although most bookshops did not bother to keep comics.

It was common for comics to be donated to paper-drives, children's homes and hospitals, or generally discarded.

During the 1930s and 1940s, a tradition grew up among science-fiction fans, who were generally older than the children reading comics, to save their magazines.

At this time a small number of amateur fan magazines began to be circulated to enthusiasts, where small-ads appeared either offering magazines for sale or asking for particular issues.

The fan-magazine, latterly called a fanzine, continued into the 1950s, when a number were produced devoted to the EC line of comics, but with the demise of EC the fanzines disappeared too.

In 1960, at the World Science Fiction Convention, fans Pat and Dick Lupoff gave away copies of the first issue of their fanzine, *zero*. It had a section called 'All in Color for a Dime', devoted to comics from the 1940s. Fanzines totally devoted to comics started appearing, and gradually a network of enthusiasts formed. Meeting informally to exchange and discuss comics, these fans were no longer children, and many sought the comics they had read years before. The publishers' attitude to fans, who were now becoming collectors, was one of bewilderment. The letter column in **Superman** No. 135 (February 1960), carried the following request and DC's answer:

Dear Editor

Inasmuch as your office can't supply back-numbers of your various SUPERMAN magazines, would it be possible for you to print my address so that readers who have old issues can swop or sell them to me?

Jack Darrell, Chicago, ILL.

(Sorry, but old issues of used magazines are known disease-carriers, so we can't encourage such swapping. – Ed.)

DC editor Julie Schwartz began printing readers' full addresses in the letter columns, which led to fans communicating with each other. Two such fans were Roy Thomas and Jerry Balis, and their communication led to the publication of what was probably the first real comic fanzine, *Alter Ego* (March 1961) which, together with CBG's Don and Maggie Thompson's fanzine, *Comic Art*, was influential in bringing even more fans together.

◀ SUPERMAN'S PAL JIMMY OLSEN No. 1,
September–October 1954
(™ & Copyright © 1994 DC Comics, Inc.)

Many more fanzines followed, some only running for one or two issues, but by now the fans were in touch with each other across the USA and collecting was starting to take off.

Comic conventions began in 1964, when hobbyists bought, sold and traded back issues – in the main, not for profit but merely to improve their collections. Not long after the first conventions, some bookshops began devoting a section to old comics.

Condition became more important but still was not the crucial factor. In the bullpen page across Marvel's range in August 1967, the following appeared (Stan Lee speaks first):

Item – We just received a letter that may be of interest to all you Believers who like to save your Marvel mags – so we'll pass it along to you right now –

Dear Stan,
I have trouble with pages that come loose from too much handling, and have found a way to correct this. Just open the staples and put a piece of transparent tape on the outside cover and exact centre of the book. Then close the staples again. It preserves the magazine no matter how many times it is read. No more loose pages! Sincerely, Bud Cavadini, Cashton, Wisc. 54619.

In 1970, Robert M. Overstreet published his first comic-book price guide, which helped to add a certain respectability to collecting, bringing comics into the realms of other collectables such as coins and stamps. It also brought home to many fans the economic aspect of their hobby, with **Action Comics** No. 1 listed in the guide at a massive $300 (£200), an increase of 3,000 per cent on its original price of 10 cents 32 years earlier. (In the 1993 edition of

The Official Overstreet Comic Book Price Guide, **Action Comics** No. 1 was listed at $75,000 [£50,000].)

In 1973, fandom was still small, but that year Phil Seuling persuaded less enthusiastic publishers, like DC, to sell him comics on a non-returnable basis, which he in turn sold to shops. This was the beginning of direct distribution, which had come about because fans demanded a better, more reliable way of buying new comics than the newsstands were able to offer.

Before long a small number of specialist comic shops began to appear, with enthusiastic collectors travelling miles to buy new comics. Old comics also had a place in these stores, but it was the expanding convention circuit that really fuelled the fire of the back-issue market.

Comic collecting has grown tremendously since those early days and, now, all but the smallest towns in the USA have at least one, if not more, specialist comic store.

The specialist store no longer looks like a dusty old bookshop, but is bright and airy, carrying a complete range of comics for all ages, as well as back issues, collectables, archival supplies and other related merchandise, which, in some stores, includes watches, T-shirts, baseball caps, trading cards, etc.

The creators, many of whom are fans themselves, along with the publishers and distributors, are very much part of fandom today, and are regularly seen at conventions, promoting their products or just talking to fans.

There is an increasing number of older people coming back to comics – whether this is due to a desire to recapture their youth or otherwise, comic collecting continues to grow. If you are new to the hobby, welcome, you are among friends.

STARTING AND MAINTAINING A COLLECTION

**HE FIRST THING A COLLECTOR NEEDS TO** establish is what comics he wants to collect – is it a particular genre, character, title or perhaps publisher that interests him? Who knows how your taste will alter and how your collection will change and grow? It is important, however, to start small. It could be that you already have some comics. If not, buy some new ones – it is the best way to start! With more than a thousand titles published each month you will need to be selective. If you are at

all unsure, ask for advice at your local comic store, or from a mail-order service. They'll be pleased to give you details of current titles.

For reasons of nostalgia, many collectors coming back to comics try to find the issues they remember from their childhood. Depending on when your childhood was, there is a chance that these back issues could be expensive. Buy a price guide which will enable you to ascertain roughly the cost of collecting, for example, a complete run of **Spider-Man** from 1963 to date, or all of the issues of **Superman** from 1960 to date. Decide what your minimum requirement regarding condition is, and then set about tracking them down. A good way to start is to visit your nearest specialist store and browse through their back issues, or call a mail-order service and ask them for a catalogue.

Check the listings of conventions or shows in *The Comic Buyers Guide* or *Comics International*, and go along to see what's on offer. Do not be too eager to spend your money, it's worth checking all the dealers before making a purchase.

It's also worth asking dealers who stock the type of material you're collecting if they run a 'wants list' service. If they do, give them a list of what you are looking for, detailing titles, issue numbers and a range of acceptable conditions. If they find a match from your list, they will contact you and offer the item. Whether you buy it or not is up to you – there is no obligation involved in giving a dealer, mail-order service or store such a list. All they require is that you keep them updated on any changes to your 'wants'.

Be sensible when compiling a wants list. Even if you ultimately want to collect every issue of **Batman**, only list those you feel you will be able to buy immediately. You can always add to the list as time goes by.

Some of the bigger dealers use bespoke computer software, which can take some of the pain out of compiling a list. For example, you may want to collect every appearance of a particular character, or all of the work of a creator. Just tell the company; there is a good chance that they will have this information and can compile the list for you, sending you a copy for your records.

When buying back issues you will find variations in prices for what seem to be different examples of the same comic. Check a current price guide or update, but keep in mind that all guides are retrospective and their contents are only an indication as to what you might pay, not the definitive price for a comic. Having said that, and allowing for market movements, they do give you a very good idea of price, unless you are dealing with a pedigree or particularly high-grade copy, which one would expect to pay over the guide price for.

Another thing to bear in mind is that one dealer's Very Fine is another dealer's Near Mint. It is most important to establish how a dealer grades his comics or you may find you have paid what you thought was one dealer's lower price for his Near Mint copy only to discover that you have actually overpaid for what in reality is only a Very Fine copy. Beware of dealers at shows or conventions who do not price their books, and also beware of dealers who refuse to grade their comics, asking you what grade you think it is. This is very dangerous, especially for the novice grader.

Most dealers are honest, but there are some who deal in stolen comics. If you buy a stolen comic, knowingly or unknowingly, and the original owner can prove it is his, you will be forced by law to give it back, despite the fact that you have paid for it. Always ask for a receipt; reputable dealers will have no problem with this and many issue them as a matter of course.

When you are buying back issues, check to see if the company offers an unconditional money-back guarantee. This is particularly important when buying through the mail, where you have not seen the comic. Most reputable stores and mail-order services will offer this facility. When responding to advertisements, try to establish whether the advertiser is a collector or a dealer, and be careful when sending money to advertisers. There have been cases where the sender has received nothing in return.

Do not accept long delivery dates for back issues – 7–14 days is acceptable; anything more than that, for whatever reason, is not.

There are a few disreputable dealers who specialize in selling the same comic a number of times. You could find that all you get for your money is a credit note. These credit notes are fine if you intend to do further business with that company, but ensure that the credit note is redeemable, at any time, for your money back. Ask this question at the outset; if the answer is no, find another dealer.

Paying by credit card could give you some additional protection. At least if the company takes credit cards it is an indication, but not proof, that they are fairly well established.

'Alternatives' are bad news in most cases. Some mail-order services will ask you to list alternatives in the event of your selection not being available. I would suggest you avoid those companies that insist on this. Tell others that merely request it that, in the event of your selection not being available, they should either send you a credit note or your money back. This should be less of a problem when paying by credit card, as the company should not take any money until they are dispatching your order. Be careful though – some companies take the money immediately they receive the order. Tell them not to.

Check with dealers what their policy is on upgrading. It could be that you will settle for a lower grade now in order to have the comic in your collection, and want to buy a higher grade when finances allow or it becomes available. Reputable dealers, if selling you an upgrade, should be prepared to offer you very close to what you originally paid them for the first comic. If a lot of time has elapsed, you may even show a profit, although by the same token your upgrade will also cost you more.

Find out from mail-order services how they will mail your order to you. The comics should at least be packed in comic bags, with more expensive items being packed in a Mylar™ or equivalent. Some services have custom-made mailing-boxes, which usually offer good protection to the comics. Expensive comics should be sent either by a service like Federal Express or the United Parcel Service, where a signature is required on delivery. The alternative is a type of mailing which also requires a signature.

Ordinary post is generally acceptable for lower valued comics, although it is worth asking about postal insurance, as once the package is mailed the responsibility becomes yours.

To maintain a collection of new comics, the best thing to do is to set up a standing order for the titles at a comic store or, if this is inconvenient, take out a subscription with a mail-order service.

The difference between the two is that, in most cases, you will pay for the standing order on collection, whereas a subscription is normally paid for in advance. Either way, you will be guaranteed not to miss an issue.

Good subscription services will supply you with a monthly order form detailing the titles on offer, for publication two to three months in advance. They will also supply a useful free newsletter giving more detailed information about advance products. Some services offer regular subscribers discounts or bonuses for regular business, and there are also various discount clubs that can save you money and ensure the company of your loyal patronage.

One such club in the UK offers rising discounts off back issues and new comics, as well as other bonuses such as free price guides, a free copy of *Previews*, *Comics International* and other publications. They also give club members priority on their computerized wants list service, and mail out all club members' back issues in comic bags with protective backing boards.

Discount clubs are useful and worth investigating. There is normally an initial charge as well as an annual fee. Take into account the bonuses and calculate whether or not the discounts will cover the cost of membership.

Auctions are another source of back issues, and the larger auction houses spend a great deal of time ensuring that the lots are accurately graded. If you are considering buying from an auction, it is important to keep a level head. It is easy to be caught up in the fervour of the bidding going on around you. Set a maximum price that you are prepared to pay for an item and go no further, bearing in mind that, in addition to your successful bid price, you will also have to pay a commission, plus the appropriate sales tax.

Auctions by mail, which are run by dealers, are another matter entirely. There are some auction-by-mail dealers who are entirely honest. However, there are an increasing number who prey on unsuspecting collectors through various deceptive means. Use only those that come recommended to you either by a reputable store, non-auction-by-mail dealer, or fellow collector.

First and foremost, comics are for enjoying and reading. Do not be afraid to handle and read new comics. They will, of course, need careful storage after you have read them. As your collection grows, it will be necessary to develop a cataloguing system. This will allow you easily to find a particular comic, and also ensure that you do not buy the same comic twice (this is easily done). Your catalogue, which is best stored on a computer database, but can be hand-written, should include the title, the issue number, the grade, and the location of each comic.

Collectors store their comics alphabetically, by publisher, artist, date, character, or a combination of these. There is no right or wrong way and you will soon find a system that suits you best.

Familiarize yourself with the storage techniques described on page 134, and ensure that you have always got an adequate supply of archival materials on hand. These can be purchased from stores or through the mail.

SELLING AND TRADING

HERE COMES A POINT WHEN MOST COL- lectors re-evaluate their collections. Sometimes storage space becomes a problem, or your collecting tastes change. Either way, it is useful to know how best to sell comics individually or in bulk.

Selling high-grade key issues is never a problem as collectors are always looking for these and dealers are usually keen to have them in stock and will pay a decent percentage of guide or retail price to acquire them. Each dealer will vary, but you can expect to get anywhere between 50 per cent and 80 per cent – more, if you are prepared to accept trade instead of cash. Advertising in trade newspapers can also be a good way of selling individual issues, but take care when sending comics through the mail, especially to complete strangers.

Selling nondescript runs of recent or non-key issues is more

▶ DETECTIVE COMICS No. 33,
November 1939, is a safe investment. This key issue, retelling Batman's origin,
continues to show a high rate of return
(™ & Copyright © 1994 DC Comics, Inc.)

difficult and can cause frustration and disappointment. Dealers usually have more than enough stock of this type and will probably not be particularly interested, unless you are prepared to sell them very cheaply. If you are, then there is no problem. However, there are ways of getting a better price.

Firstly, complete runs of a title may be worth advertising in a trade newspaper. List the title, the numbers and their condition, together with a price, and your telephone number. You could get lucky. But, if you split a run, selling only the key or hot issues, you are likely to get stuck with the rest.

Secondly, if you are selling to a dealer, make it easy for the dealer to buy everything. Make the package as attractive as possible by the inclusion of some key or hot issues. Of course, I am not suggesting that you break up your collection to do this, but you do stand a far better chance of selling everything if there are at least a few desirable books included.

Telephone the dealer to first ascertain an initial interest, then send as detailed a list as possible, ensuring that you keep a copy. It may be that you have a price in mind, in which case let the dealer know, as you could save each other a lot of time. If you do not want cash, or all cash, you can almost always do a better deal accepting trade or part-trade, whereby all or part of your payment will be in the form of other comics or a trade voucher which can be used at a later date. It is not uncommon to be able to achieve a sticker-for-sticker trade, which means that you will get the full retail price on your comics in exchange for comics from the dealer at his full retail price. It should be noted that normally any discount you may be entitled to will be ignored in such transactions. It is very unlikely that you will be able to get sticker-for-sticker if the items you are selling are not comparable to what you are buying. Dealers will not take large numbers of recent issues in a sticker-for-sticker trade against key books.

A dealer will definitely need to confirm your grades before buying, so be prepared to send or take the books for appraisal. When sending books to a dealer who is unknown to you, it can be useful to obtain a reference; legitimate dealers will be happy to comply.

There may be big differences in the offers you get, so shop around. Generally, the larger dealers have more funds available for buying and a better range of stock for trading.

BUYING BACK ISSUES AS AN INVESTMENT

OMEONE ONCE SAID, 'THERE WILL NEVER *ever be any more old [Golden Age and Silver Age] comics, only more people wanting to collect them.'*

Old comics are a diminishing commodity. Most collectors will not part with their collections and, in some cases, once a comic is in a collection, it is never seen again.

There are more and more people coming into the hobby and a finite supply of comics useful for investment purposes. As a result, the prices keep going up.

What is a good investment? When talking about back issues, it is probably easier to say what is not a good investment.

Once collecting became more organized, condition and storage became factors, and collectors started to take better care of their comics. The result is that there are many more surviving high-grade issues from the mid 1970s to the present than there are from the previous four decades. Therefore, it is unlikely that this more recent material is ever going to reach the dizzying heights of the prices of certain Golden Age and Silver Age comics. It is an accepted fact that there are no rare or scarce comic books after 1975.

However, sometimes there can be sharp increases in the prices of this newer material. When a character is revived or reintroduced, there will sometimes be dramatic price jumps in comics containing his earlier appearances as demand for these once-ordinary issues goes up.

◀ JUSTICE LEAGUE OF AMERICA No. 1,
October/November 1960
(™ & Copyright © 1994 DC Comics, Inc.)

▲ MORE FUN COMICS No. 34,
August 1938 – this high-grade non-key Golden Age book shows regular small increases in value
(™ & Copyright © 1994 DC Comics, Inc.)

A good example of this is **Amazing Spider-Man** No. 129 (February 1974), cover price 20 cents, in which The Punisher made his first appearance. In 1976 that comic could be bought for 40 cents or less. When The Punisher became a popular character in his own right, the price rocketed and, by 1989, reached $75 (£50). It peaked at about $300 (£200) in 1992 before dropping back to its now fairly stable price of about $250 (£167). Another similar example is Wolverine, who appeared in his first full story[1] in **The Incredible Hulk** No. 181 (November 1974). Anyone who bought that issue for 25 cents will be delighted to know that it is now worth about $300 (£200) in Near Mint. But for every such case there are literally thousands of comics worth little more than their cover price.

On the whole, comics after the early to mid 1970s are not a good investment. Some could increase in value, but never at the same rate as key Golden and Silver Age books. I do not believe that comics from this period should be considered for investment purposes if there is the option of picking up earlier keys.

Invest in what you know. If you do not know, learn. Find out about trends and get in as early as possible. The prices of back issues of **Batman** and **Detective Comics** went through the roof when the Batman movie came out in 1989. During 1988, many dealers and collectors stockpiled Batman material and made a killing. Of course, once the demand peaked, prices of the more recent material fell back a long way, and people who had bought at the top lost money. But the prices of pre-1970s issues did not fall back very far and still continue to rise. (See illustrations, pages 145, 146.)

The trick is not only knowing what to buy, when to buy and how much to pay for more recent material; it is also knowing when to sell in order to maximize your profit.

The very best investments are key Golden and Silver Age comics – comics from 1938 to 1969 that are significant for some reason. It might be a first appearance of a character or the first work of an artist that creates the demand. Following his death on 8 February 1994, comics containing Jack Kirby's work increased in price; even the non-key issues were in greater demand.

The safe investment money goes into the obvious: **Action Comics** No. 1 – the first appearance of Superman; **Detective Comics** No. 27 – the first appearance of Batman; **Showcase** No. 4 – the first appearance of the Silver Age Flash, and the first Silver Age book. These will continue to show big increases in price and are solid investments. They are also very expensive.

It is possible to buy lesser key books for a fraction of the cost of a major key. For example, **Superman** No. 30 (September/October 1944), containing the first appearance and origin of the devilish imp Mr Mxyzptlk,[2] can be bought for approximately 1 per cent of the cost of an equivalent grade **Action Comics** No. 1, and over the years has shown steady growth. Some of these lesser issues can still be picked up relatively cheaply, and can show the owner a better annual rate of return than just about any other non-comics investment I can think of.

The word 'investment' implies a relatively long time. This is not necessarily so, but the longer you hold on to Golden and Silver Age investments, the more they are going to appreciate. The major keys will continue to rise year after year, with the lesser issues sometimes stagnating for a year or two or only showing modest increases. But, ultimately, they are all considered good investments.

I know an investor who has his entire retirement plan in comic books. He said, after weighing up the options, that historically there is nothing to touch comics for growth, and that instead of investing in a conventional pension he has put his money into comics. By the way, this investor is not a collector and has no interest, outside of a financial one, in the comics.

Is this folly? I do not think so, although everyone knows that investments can go down as well as up, I really cannot see a time when old comics are going to be in less demand than they are today. As a result, prices must continue to rise. Therefore, the best time to invest is now. High-grade vintage comics are never going to be as cheap again.

If you do not have a good understanding of comics, treat the investment as you would any other, and get expert advice. I strongly recommend the larger, more established dealers for this, as they have been doing it a long time and understand the market. You are going to need a dealer who is able to sell as well as buy your investment for you. The larger dealers will generally work on a small commission basis and rely on repeat business. If they are good at what they do, both buyers and sellers will be pleased to give them a reference, so do not be afraid to ask a dealer for testimonials.

There are now dealers who have investment departments and such dealers will often prepare sample portfolios for you, and are always pleased to offer general advice.

You can monitor your investment by buying an annual price guide and price guide updates, as well as checking prices in dealers' ads in the trade newspapers.

Buying New Comics as an Investment

UYING NEW COMICS IS FAR SIMPLER THAN buying back issues for investment purposes. If you do not have a good understanding of the market, don't do it!

There are many speculators buying multiple issues of what they believe are going to be hot comics. They know what they are doing and still get it wrong as many times as they get it right.

You need to be extremely careful about buying 50 or 100 copies of a comic that has just, or recently, been published. Many other people are doing exactly the same thing.

If you must buy multiple copies for investment, make sure that you do not hold on to them for too long, as this market is extremely volatile. Today's hot comics, in most cases, become yesterday's news very quickly.

The things to look out for are new titles, first appearances and new publishers, especially those who produce comics with small print runs. Make sure that every copy you buy is in Near Mint condition and that you follow the storage advice on page 192 in order to keep them that way.

Follow prices regularly by reading the trade newspapers and dealer ads, as well as calling dealers and going to shows or conventions. When the price reaches an acceptable level, sell as fast as you can, as once prices peak they drop very quickly. Worse than that, within a very short time you may find that there is absolutely no demand for what was the hottest new comic for years.

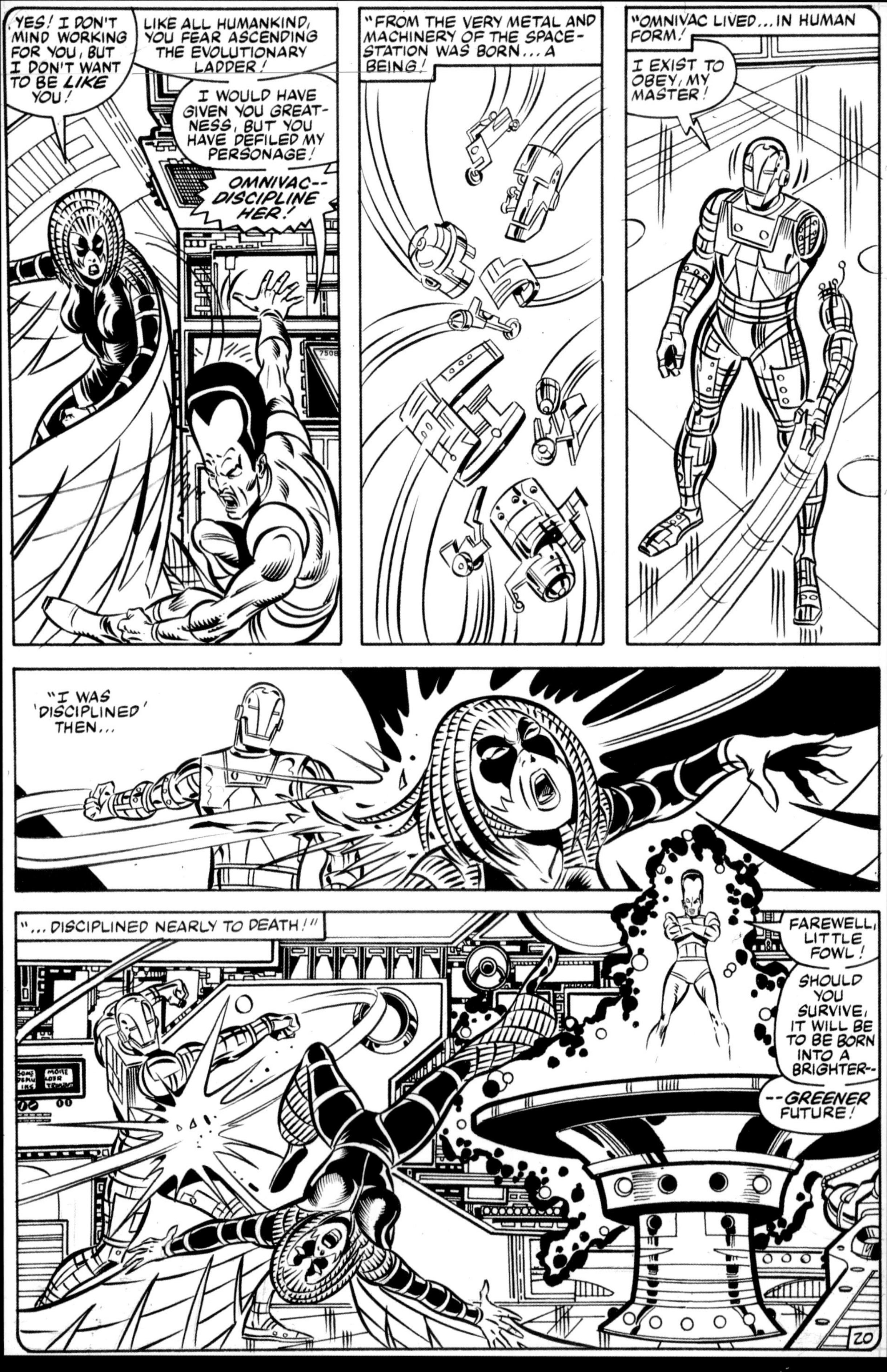

YES! I DON'T MIND WORKING FOR YOU, BUT I DON'T WANT TO BE *LIKE* YOU!

LIKE ALL HUMANKIND, YOU FEAR ASCENDING THE EVOLUTIONARY LADDER!

I WOULD HAVE GIVEN YOU GREATNESS, BUT YOU HAVE DEFILED MY PERSONAGE!

OMNIVAC-- DISCIPLINE HER!

"FROM THE VERY METAL AND MACHINERY OF THE SPACE-STATION WAS BORN... A BEING!

"OMNIVAC LIVED... IN HUMAN FORM!

I EXIST TO OBEY, MY MASTER!

"I WAS 'DISCIPLINED' THEN...

"... DISCIPLINED NEARLY TO DEATH!"

FAREWELL, LITTLE FOWL!

SHOULD YOU SURVIVE, IT WILL BE TO BE BORN INTO A BRIGHTER--

--GREENER FUTURE!

20

11

Original Comic-book Art

NE OF THE BIGGEST ATTRACTIONS IN collecting comic-book artwork is that each piece is a one-off original.

Original art is what the creator hands in to the publisher, who in turn gives it to the printer, who uses it to produce the end product.

Although each artist varies in his or her technique, in making the artwork the usual procedure is for the artist to first outline the page construction and then lightly pencil the panels, which are then drawn in more heavily. Following this, each panel is inked using a pen and India ink, or a brush. Sometimes one artist will do the pencils and another the inks.

From the very beginnings of newspaper strips, comic books and animation, there was always a small number of enthusiasts who collected the original art. However, interest in this aspect of the hobby greatly increased shortly after the end of the Golden Age.

During the mid 1960s, when fandom started to become more organized, each summer Phil Seuling staged a comic convention in New York. One of the main attractions for fans was the number of creators that attended, most of whom were fans themselves.

For the first time, fans and creators met face to face. In many cases, the artists would offer their work for sale and, before long, original comic-book art became a recognized collectable in its own right.

Jerry Weist, author of *Original Comic Art*, said:

The same young artists who had grown up on Harvey Kurtzman and Albert Feldstein's MAD, and produced the early fanzines of the 1950s, *were now part of the 'cultural revolution' that was beginning to evolve all over America.*[1]

At the early shows were many budding artists, including the young Berni Wrightson who, years later, among other great work, drew The Swamp Thing, with the cover art now selling for anything up to $2,500 (£1,667), and interior pages for $1,000 (£667) each!

Many creators were employed on a 'work-for-hire' basis, whereby publishers paid them so much per page and retained the original art. During the early 1970s, many artists began to negotiate better terms with the publishers and, as a result, a number of the larger publishers, including Marvel and DC, started returning creators' work to them, resulting in more and more material being available to the increasingly hungry market. A number of newspapers followed suit, and returned original art from syndicated strips.

One of the most significant occurrences of that period was when Marvel, after a long-running battle, returned to Jack 'King' Kirby all of his artwork they had held on file.

Publishers today automatically return artwork to creators, and it is unthinkable for an artist not to retain, or at least control, his original work.

In the early days, artwork was considered valueless after publication. Despite a great deal of it being destroyed, not only by the publishers but also by the artists themselves, there is still a surprising amount of early work surviving. Some of it can be seen by the public either in permanent exhibitions or in occasional displays. For example, occasional displays are sometimes seen at the Museum of Modern Art in New York City and the Smithsonian in Wash-

◀ Original art from INCREDIBLE HULK No. 283,
May 1983
(™ & Copyright © 1994 Marvel Entertainment Group, Inc.)

▶ Neal Adam's original cover art from X-MEN No. 59,
August 1969, recently sold for $3,000 (£2,000)
(™ & Copyright © 1994 Marvel Entertainment Group, Inc.)

ington DC. Permanent displays can be seen at the National Cartoonists Society in New York City, Ohio State University in Columbus, which houses an exhibition that includes the Milton Caniff collection, and Boston University, with their exhibition including almost the entire run of Harold Gray's *Little Orphan Annie*.

Thanks to Harold Gray insisting on getting his work back from the Chicago Tribune Syndicate after publication, almost all of it survives.

EC Comics publisher Bill Gaines would not throw away original art. Instead, he stored almost everything he had published in the 1950s in a vault. In 1980 he appointed Russ Cochran as his agent and slowly sold the pieces to collectors through a series of quarterly auction catalogues. Cochran put other major pieces, from the likes of Alex Raymond and George Herriman, into the auctions, which further helped widen collectors' interest.

Original art can be costly, although it does not have to be expensive to be collectable. It is still possible to find interior pages of well-known comics or strips for less than $50 (£33).

People buy original art for many reasons, including the character, the artist, the genre, the time-period, or just the fact that they like the look of a particular piece.

Some collectors frame certain pieces and decorate their homes or offices with them, as you would with a painting.

Many collectors prefer to buy covers, splash pages or pages that are particularly significant for some reason. These items are therefore generally more expensive than regular pages. The art from the Carmine Infantino and Murphy Anderson classic cover to **Flash** No. 123 sold at Sotheby's, New York, in 1991 for $16,000 (£10,667).

Neal Adams, who started his comic-book career by drawing Archie in 1959, is another highly sought-after artist. The cover from

X-Men No. 59 (August 1969) was recently sold to a collector for $3,000 (£2,000).

Some artists are more collectable than others. The recent sad death of Jack Kirby has already pushed up prices of his work, which was always in demand, even prior to his death.

The new artists are also in great demand, and recently Sotheby's, New York, sold the complete artwork of **X-Men** (October 1991) by Jim Lee, together with an unpublished cover, for $40,000 (£26,667).

Art from certain newspaper strips is highly collectable. Work from artists such as Hal Foster, Chester Gould, Milton Caniff, George Herriman and Alex Raymond, among others, is always being sought by collectors, and generally sells for top-dollar.

Original art is almost always available at the larger comic shows and conventions. A few retail stores and mail-order services also deal in it. The auction houses Sotheby's and Christie's East now have regular original art auctions which during the last couple of years have proved most successful.

ANIMATION CELS

NIMATION CELS HAVE BECOME VERY COL-lectable during the last ten or so years, with production drawings, backgrounds and the hand-painted cels themselves being collected as an art form in their own right.

A cel is a painting on celluloid of a character or objects, which is based on an animator's original pencil drawing. The cels are placed on background paintings and filmed during production of the movie. Most pre-1960 cels were painted and inked by hand. After this outlines were generally photocopied on to the cel, with interior lines being hand-drawn.

Sotheby's and Christie's East have regular animation cel auctions, with some pieces selling for headline-making prices. Early Walt Disney cels are among the most expensive, with almost anything from *Snow White and the Seven Dwarfs* (1937) always in great demand. In 1991, Sotheby's, New York, sold a matching setup with a pan production background, containing Snow White, The Prince and all Seven Dwarfs, for a staggering $209,000 (£139,333)! But the top price to date is $450,000 (£300,000), which was paid for a rare black and white Disney animation cel with matching

background. It featured Mickey Mouse and Clara Cluck in an opening scene from the 1934 Disney Studios cartoon, *Orphan's Benefit*.

Also in demand are cels from the other Disney classics, such as *Fantasia* and *Pinocchio*, with interest now expanding to other studios, such as Fleischer, Warner Brothers and Hanna-Barbera.

The market is not restricted to early work. Some of the original artwork from 20th Century Fox Features' animated TV series, *The Simpsons*, auctioned in 1991 at Christie's East, fetched high prices. A setup of Bart Simpson playing baseball brought $7,920 (£5,280), while a cel specially created for the occasion, of Bart trying to auction his sister Maggie, sold for $24,000 (£16,000).

There are now some speciality stores that sell animation art, and it can also be purchased at theme parks, such as MGM Studios at Disney World in Florida, Universal Studios in California and Florida, as well as being available at regular auctions.

Some mail-order services selling original comic-book art now have sections of their catalogue devoted to animation cels.

As with comic-book art, the range of prices is enormous, but for less than $100 (£67) it is possible to start a collection.

◄ FOUR COLOR (Series II) No. 74, *June 1945, featured the first appearance of Little Lulu in comics* (Copyright © 1945 Dell Publishing Company)

Trivia Quiz

How much do you know about comic books? The answers to the following questions, which range from easy to obscure, are printed on the next page, but are also contained in the main text.

1. What was the name of the first Golden Age comic book?
2. Who created Superman?
3. What is Superman's secret identity?
4. In which story and comic did Batman make his first appearance?
5. Who created Batman?
6. What is Batman's secret identity?
7. Who played Batman and Robin in the 1966 TV series?
8. Who played Batman and Robin in the 1989 film?
9. Who is sometimes called The Big Red Cheese?
10. Who created The Spirit?
11. Name the first team of superheroes.
12. Who created Captain America?
13. Where did Superboy live?
14. What was the first Silver Age comic?
15. Who made their first appearance in *The Brave and the Bold* No. 28 (March 1960)?
16. Who is Peter Parker?
17. Robert Redford and Warren Beatty were both considered for the movie role that was given to Christopher Reeve. What was it?
18. What was Valiant's first superhero comic book?
19. When did The Silver Surfer make his first appearance?
20. What is acknowledged as being the first modern American comic strip?
21. Which publishing company was founded by George T. Delacorte, Jr?
22. When did The Punisher first appear?
23. When did Robin make his first appearance?
24. Who created Uncle Scrooge?
25. When did Gwen Stacey die?
26. What does DC stand for in that publisher's name?
27. In which year did both Marvel and DC raise the cover price of their comics from 10 cents to 12 cents?
28. Who are Gold, Iron, Lead, Mercury, Tin and Platinum better known as?
29. Who is The Man Without Fear?
30. Which comic from issue No. 4 to date is billed as 'The World's Greatest Comic Magazine'?
31. What is significant about *Amazing Fantasy* No. 15 (August 1962) apart from it being the first and last issue of that title?
32. Who were the original members of The Legion of Super-Heroes?
33. What was the name of the Robin who replaced Dick Grayson?
34. Which character did Edgar Rice Burroughs create in 1912, who first appeared in the pulp title *The All-Story* (1912)?
35. What do the letters in 'Shazam' stand for?
36. Who wrote the book, *The Seduction of the Innocent*?
37. Who killed Superman in January 1993?
38. Which comic-book character got married in the summer of 1987?
39. Which British character appeared with Batman in *Judgement on Gotham* (1991) and *Vendetta in Gotham* (1994)?

40. How was Supergirl related to Superman?
41. Which publisher is best known today for the Richie Rich, Little Lotta, Casper the Friendly Ghost and Hot Stuff titles?
42. In October 1962, which member of The Fantastic Four began a solo series in *Strange Tales* No. 101 (October 1962)?
43. What happened in Russia on 16 May 1991?
44. When was *Superboy* No. 1 published?
45. Where did Wonder Woman make her first appearance?
46. Who created the hard-done-by soldier, The Sad Sack?
47. In *Journey into Mystery* No. 83 (August 1962), who discovered Thor's magic hammer in a cave?
48. Which team were Slim Summers, Warren Worthington III, Bobby Drake, Jean Grey and Hank McCoy all members of?
49. In November 1972, what did scientist Alec Holland become?
50. What was Archie Publications originally called?
51. Who created Price Namor, The Sub-Mariner?
52. Who created The Human Torch?
53. What is the title of the American comic book that has had the longest uninterrupted run?
54. Who is the lead character in the 1994 *Marvels* mini-series?
55. Who created both The Lone Ranger and The Green Hornet?
56. What connection did The Green Hornet have with The Lone Ranger?
57. What did the publisher ACG's initials stand for?
58. In 1972, who created The Demon and Kamandi?
59. When did The Spectre make his first appearance?
60. Which is Marvel's most successful black and white magazine?
61. In 1939, why did Fox Features Syndicate drop Wonder Man after the first issue of *Wonder Comics*?
62. In which comic did The Green Lantern first appear?
63. Who created Mutt and Jeff?
64. In February 1940, why did *Whiz Comics* begin its numbering with 2 instead of 1?
65. What are the characters Destiny, Death, Desire, Despair, Delirium and Morpheus collectively known as?
66. Who is the most powerful being in the Valiant Universe?
67. Who publishes *Simpsons*, *Bartman*, *Radioactive Man* and *Itchy & Scratchy Comics*?
68. Why were *Amazing Spider-Man* Nos 96, 97 and 98 distributed without the Comics Code Authority seal of approval?
69. In October 1993, who became the new Batman in *Batman* No. 500?
70. When was Captain America joined by The Sub-Mariner and The Human Torch in a new title, *All Winners Comics* No. 1?
71. In June 1959, which publisher updated their Golden Age hero The Shield in *The Double Life of Private Strong* No. 1?

72. In September 1986, who did Superman kill in the two-part imaginary story told in *Action Comics* No. 583 and *Superman* No. 423?
73. Which long-running series began publication in October 1941 with an adaptation of Alexandre Dumas's *The Three Musketeers* and ended some 28 years later with 'Negro Americans – The Early Years' in the spring of 1969?
74. Where did Batwoman make her first appearance?
75. Who was responsible for more than 15,000 Mickey Mouse strips over a 45-year period?
76. Where could you find Jeff Smith's first published comic-book work?
77. Who created Little Lulu?
78. Who was the first new DC hero to be created after the end of the Golden Age?
79. In which comic did Superman and Batman first appear together on a cover?
80. The Golden Age Green Lantern's secret identity was Alan Scott. What was he originally going to be called?
81. What was the first comic to be supplied to the direct market only?
82. In which comic was Jason (Robin) Todd killed?
83. In October 1959, which popular singer of the day had a five-issue comic-book series?
84. Which DC mini-series by Frank Miller told the story of a decaying society of the future, mixing Japanese legends with modern technology and man?
85. What was the only issue of DC's *Showcase* to carry no advertisements inside the book?
86. What was the title of Gold Key's first publication?
87. Where did Bugs Bunny, Elmer Fudd, Daffy Duck and Porky Pig all make their first comic-book appearances?
88. Who were Tommy, Gabby, Scrapper and Big Words?
89. What was the title of Marvel's first graphic novel?
90. According to the 1988 DC graphic novel, who started off as a third-rate stand-up comedian?
91. In which strip could you see Lai Choi San, The Dragon Lady?
92. In 1938, who made his comic-book debut in *Ace Comics* No. 11?
93. Which surreal character made his first appearance in Quality's *Police Comics* No. 1 (August 1941)?
94. Who were Task Force X better known as?
95. When did Charlton's Captain Atom make his first appearance?
96. William Gaines changed the meaning of the initials EC from what to what?
97. What was the name of Marvel's first fan club?
98. Where can you find Superduperman fighting his rival Captain Marbles?
99. Where did the first team-up in comic books occur, and who with?
100. Clark (Superman) Kent's adopted parents are Martha and Jonathan, but what did George Lowther call them in his 1942 Superman novel?

ANSWERS TO TRIVIA QUIZ

▶ POLICE COMICS
No. 5
December 1941
(Copyright © 1941 Quality
Comics Group)

1. *Action Comics* No. 1 (June 1938).
2. Jerry Siegel and Joe Shuster.
3. Clark Kent.
4. 'The Case of the Chemical Syndicate' in *Detective Comics* No. 27 (May 1939).
5. Bob Kane.
6. Bruce Wayne.
7. Adam West played Batman and Burt Ward played Robin.
8. Michael Keaton played Batman; there was no Robin in the film.
9. Captain Marvel.
10. Will Eisner.
11. The Justice Society of America, who made their debut in *All Star Comics* No. 3 (Winter 1940).
12. Joe Simon and Jack Kirby.
13. Smallville, Kansas.
14. *Showcase* No. 4 (October 1956). It featured the first appearance of the Silver Age Flash.
15. The Justice League of America.
16. Spiderman.
17. Superman.
18. *Magnus Robot Fighter* No. 1 (May 1991).
19. In March 1966 in *The Fantastic Four* No. 48.
20. Richard Felton Outcault's 'The Yellow Kid' (16 February 1896).
21. The Dell Publishing Company.
22. February 1974 in *Amazing Spider-Man* No. 129.
23. April 1940 in *Detective Comics* No. 38.
24. Carl Barks.
25. Gwen Stacey died at the hand of The Green Goblin in *Amazing Spider-Man* No. 121 (June 1973).
26. Detective Comics.
27. 1962.
28. The Metal Men.
29. Daredevil, who first appeared in April 1964 in Marvel's *Daredevil* No. 1.
30. *The Fantastic Four*.
31. *Amazing Fantasy* No. 15 was home to the first appearance and origin of Marvel's most famous hero, The Amazing Spiderman.
32. Cosmic Boy, Lightning Boy and Saturn Girl, who first appeared in *Adventure Comics* No. 247 (April 1958).
33. Jason Todd, who was introduced in *Batman* No. 358 (April 1983).
34. Tarzan of the Apes.
35. 'S' is for Solomon's wisdom, 'H' is for Hercules' strength, 'A' is for Atlas's stamina, 'Z' is for Zeus's power, 'A' is for Achilles' courage and 'M' is for the speed of Mercury.
36. Dr Frederick Wertham. It was published by Rinehart & Co., Inc. N.Y. in 1954.
37. Doomsday, in *Superman* No. 75.
38. In *Amazing Spider-Man Annual* No. 21 (1987) Spiderman married Mary Jane Watson.
39. The British character Judge Dredd.
40. Supergirl was Superman's cousin. Her father, Zor-el, was the brother of Superman's father, Jor-el.

41. Harvey Comics, the brainchild of brothers Leon and Alfred Harvey. Their first title was *Speed Comics* No. 1 (October 1939).
42. The Human Torch.
43. The publication of one of the first American comics to appear in Russia. The 200,000-copy print run of *Mickey Mouse* sold out within hours.
44. March 1949.
45. *All Star Comics* No. 8 (December 1941).
46. George Baker.
47. Dr Don Blake.
48. The X-Men, who made their first appearance in *X-Men* No. 1 (September 1963).
49. In Berni Wrightson and Len Wein's *Swamp Thing* No. 1 scientist Alec Holland was transformed into the living plant-like creature The Swamp Thing.
50. MLJ Comics, from the initials of its founders Morris Coyne, Louis Silberkleit and John Goldwater. They changed the name following the success of their Archie character.
51. Bill Everett.
52. Carl Burgos.
53. *Detective Comics* No. 1, which was published in March 1937 and continues to date.
54. Photo-journalist Phil Sheldon.
55. Fran Striker.
56. The Lone Ranger was The Green Hornet's great-uncle.
57. American Comics Group.
58. Jack Kirby.
59. February 1940 in *More Fun Comics* No. 52.
60. *The Savage Sword of Conan*, which began publication in February 1974 and continues today.
61. As soon as *Wonder Comics* No. 1 appeared on the newsstands in May 1939, DC issued a lawsuit against publishers Fox Features Syndicate, alleging a copyright infringement of their Superman character. Despite continuing to fight the lawsuit, Fox dropped Wonder Man after the first issue.
62. *American Comics* No. 16 (July 1940).
63. Bud Fisher.
64. No. 1 was originally going to be called *Flash Comics* and was printed in black and white to secure copyright of the title. It was cancelled at the last minute due to DC having already printed *Flash Comics* No. 1.
65. The Endless, characters from Vertigo's *Sandman*.
66. Solar. His first Valiant appearance was in *Solar, Man of the Atom* No. 1 (September 1991).
67. Bongo Comics.
68. They contained anti-drug stories but as they protrayed actual drug use they were not submitted to the CCA, and were distributed without the Comics Code Authority seal of approval.
69. Jean Paul Valley (Azrael).
70. Summer 1941.

71. Archie Comics employed the talents of Joe Simon and Jack Kirby to update their Golden Age hero The Shield.
72. In the two-part imaginary story told in *Action Comics* No. 583 and *Superman* No. 423 (September 1986) written by Alan Moore with art by George Perez, Superman kills Mr Mxyzptlk, who turns out to be an evil demonic villain, as opposed to the lovable mischievous imp from another dimension.
73. In October 1941 Al Kantor's Gilberton Company began publishing *Classic Comics* with an adaptation of Alexandre Dumas's *The Three Musketeers*.
74. *Detective Comics* No. 233 (July 1956).
75. Floyd Gottfredson. He received no credit for his work, as the Walt Disney signature went on all the strips. Gottfredson created the definitive Mickey Mouse, which inspired the many Mickey Mouse artists that followed.
76. In *Bone* No. 1 (July 1991).
77. Marjorie Henderson Buell.
78. In November, DC published *Detective Comics* No. 225. The significance of this book is that the back-up feature contained the origin and first appearance of The Martian Manhunter – John Jones (later changed to J'onn J'onzz). This was DC's first new superhero since the end of the Golden Age.
79. *New York World's Fair* (Spring 1940).
80. Alan Ladd.
81. *Dazzler* No. 1 (March 1981).
82. *Batman* No. 428 (February 1989).
83. Pat Boone.
84. *Ronin* Nos 1–6 (July 1983–April 1984).
85. No. 43 (March/April 1963), featuring Dr No.
86. *Doctor Solar Man of the Atom* No. 1 (October 1962).
87. In Dell's *Looney Tunes and Merrie Melodies Comics* No. 1 (1941).
88. Jack Kirby's and Joe Simon's Newsboy Legion who made their first appearance in April 1942 in DC's *Star Spangled Comics* No. 7.
89. *The Death of Captain Marvel* (1982).
90. The Joker, in *The Killing Joke*, written by Alan Moore and drawn by Brian Bolland.
91. In Milton Caniff's 'Terry and the Pirates'.
92. Lee Falk's The Phantom.
93. Jack Coles's Plastic Man.
94. The Suicide Squad.
95. In *Space Adventures* No. 33 (March 1960).
96. From Educational Comics to Entertaining Comics.
97. The Sentinels of Liberty.
98. In EC's *Mad* No. 4 (April/May 1953).
99. In Timely's *Marvel Mystery Comics* No. 9 (July 1940), Human Torch and Sub-Mariner appeared together.
100. Eban and Sarah Kent. These were not kept as names for the Kents and they later became Martha and Jonathan.

Guide to Identifying

Dandy and *Beano* Annuals

YEAR	*DANDY* BOOK COVER DESCRIPTION	*BEANO* BOOK COVER DESCRIPTION
1939	Korky the Cat is pointing to other *Dandy* characters.	No Annual.
1940	Korky the Cat is hanging upside down from a trapeze.	Pansy Potter is holding a see-saw for other *Beano* characters.
1941	Korky the Cat is leading a musical procession.	*Beano* characters appear from a giant egg.
1942	Desperate Dan is towing *Dandy* characters in a boat.	Lord Snooty is playing the bagpipes.
1943	Korky the Cat is leading other *Dandy* characters on bicycles, while Desperate Dan rides a steamroller.	Three-legged race.
1944	Korky the Cat is on a ball, kicked by Desperate Dan.	Pillow-fight.
1945	Korky the Cat is on skis, while Desperate Dan is on a pair of tree-trunks.	Ostrich-drawn cart.
1946	*Dandy* characters in star-shapes.	Leap frog.
1947	Korky the Cat being tossed in a blanket.	Big Eggo is swallowing a cricket ball.
1948	Korky the Cat uses other Dandy characters as puppets.	Big Eggo and other *Beano* characters are playing musical instruments.
1949	Korky the Cat with a cigar and top-hat; Desperate Dan is carrying his case.	Biffo the Bear and other *Beano* characters around a taxi.
1950	Korky the Cat is pouring hot water into the sea.	Biffo the Bear is painting a portrait.
1951	Korky the Cat as a circus ringmaster.	Biffo the Bear is riding a mechanical horse, rodeo scene.
1952	Korky the Cat's toy shop. *Dandy* characters are clockwork toys.	Biffo the Bear is nailing up pictures of *Beano* characters.
1953	Korky the Cat tricks mice with parcels.	Jack Flash carries Biffo the Bear.
1954	Korky the Cat hides fish under top-hat.	Biffo the Bear on a desert island, with Dennis the Menace holding a crab.
1955	Korky the Cat using his tail to fish.	Policeman is stopping Dennis the Menace and Biffo the Bear from fishing.
1956	Korky the Cat's joke shop sign painting.	Biffo the Bear controls toy *Beano* characters, General Jumbo style.
1957	Korky the Cat is on a train luggage rack, stealing fish.	Football match.
1958	Korky the Cat catches fish using a magnet.	Biffo the Bear juggling, Dennis the Menace and Minnie the Minx releasing bees from a hive.
1959	Korky the Cat first sails in a canoe and then an umbrella.	Little Plum is leap-frogging over Dennis the Menace and being chased by a goat.
1960	Korky the Cat uses a letter-box as a pantry.	Biffo the Bear is doing a jigsaw puzzle of The Bash Street Kids.
1961	Korky the Cat is balancing an egg on his nose.	Red cover with pictures of *Beano* characters on the top and bottom.
1962	Korky the Cat is under a lamppost, frying bacon and eggs.	Jonah is dancing on the mast of a sinking ship.
1963	Korky the Cat is looking through port-holes.	The Bash Street Kids on a swing.
1964	Korky the Cat is sitting in a deck-chair, eating a pie.	Biffo the Bear is holding a barbell and being tickled.
1965	Korky the Cat is pouring itching powder on a pantomime horse.	Little Plum and Minnie the Minx are blowing up a Biffo the Bear head balloon.

Index of Creators

This is not intended to be a definitive index of creators but is a starting point for the new collector. Dates of birth have been included where available, but this information is not always forthcoming from creators or their families.

CREATOR	Date of Birth	BEST-KNOWN WORK
Abnett, Dan	(1965)	Death's Head II, Punisher, Knights of Pendragon
Acerno, Jerry	(1961)	Power Man and Iron Fist, Secret Origins, All Star Squadron, Superman, Batman
Adams, Art	(1963)	Co-creator of Longshot, Asgarian Wars in X-Men and New Mutants
Adams, Greg	(1958)	Nomad, Deathlok, Morbius Revisited, Daredevil, Marvel Comics Presents, Avengers
Adams, Neal	(1961)	Batman, Green Arrow, Green Lantern, X-Men, and Ms Mystic
Addams, Charles	(1912)	Addams Family
Adkins, Danny Lee	(1937)	Superman, Ka-Zar, Doctor Strange, Sub-Mariner, X-Men
Adlard, Charlie	(1966)	Judge Dredd Megazine
Albert, Andrea	(1967)	Twilight Zone, Ghostbusters, Green Hornet, Tales of the Green Hornet, Kato II
Albrecht, Jeff	(1957)	Namor, Robocop: Prime Suspect, New Warriors, Barbie, Iron Fist, Daffy Duck
Allred, Michael		Madman
Almond, Bob	(1967)	Warlock and the Infinity Watch, Guardians of the Galaxy Annual
Amaro, Gary		Sandman
Anderson, Brad	(1924)	Marmaduke
Anderson, Brent Eric	(1955)	Co-created Somerset Holmes
Anderson, Jeff	(1957)	Judge Dredd, Transformers, Thundercats, Knights of Pendragon
Anderson, Murphy	(1926)	Batman, Flash, Spectre. Created Adam Strange, and The Atomic Knights
Andru, Ross		Wonder Woman, Metal Men, Flash
Anglo, Mick		Marvelman
Aparo, Jim	(1932)	Batman, Brave and the Bold. Co-creator of The Outsiders
Apthorp, Brian	(1955)	Captain Power, Bucky O'Hare, 3-D Rocketeer movie adaptation book

CREATOR	Date of Birth	BEST-KNOWN WORK
Aragones, Sergio	(1937)	Mad, Groo
Ator, Robin	(1954)	Kyra, Terminator
Augustyn, Brian		Gotham by Gaslight
Austen, Chuck	(1960)	Zot!, Badger, Trouble with Girls
Austin, Terry		Excalibur, Camelot 3000, Superman, Legends of the Dark Knight
Avery, Tex	(1908)	Bugs Bunny, Porky Pig, Daffy Duck
Ayers, Dick	(1924)	Sgt Fury, Jonah Hex, S.H.I.E.L.D., Phantom Rider
Bachalo, Chris	(1965)	Death: the High Cost of Living, Sandman, Shade the Changing Man
Badger, Mark	(1958)	Gargoyle, Martian Manhunter, Batman: Run Riddler Run
Bagley, Mark	(1957)	Amazing Spider-Man, New Warriors
Baker, George	(1915)	The Sad Sack
Baker, Matt		Phantom Lady
Balis, Jerry		Co-editor (with Roy Thomas), of Alter-Ego (fanzine)
Barber, Whitney	(1975)	Dark Knight, Killing Joke, Batman: Year One, Digital Justice
Barbera, Joseph	(1911)	Yogi Bear, Flintstones, Jetsons, Huckleberry Hound, Tom and Jerry
Barbour, David	(1961)	Spring Heel Jack: A Mystery of Mysteries and Zero Tolerance
Barker, Clive	(1952)	Night Breed, Hellraiser
Barker, Gary	(1957)	Incredible Hulk, Morbius Revisited
Barks, Carl	(1901)	Donald Duck, Uncle Scrooge
Baron, Mike	(1949)	Nexus, Badger, Punisher, Flash, Archer and Armstrong
Barr, Mike	(1952)	Camelot 3000, Batman: Son of the Demon, Star Trek, Maze Agency, Detective Comics
Barreiro, Mike	(1955)	Hellblazer, Superman: Man of Steel annual
Barry, Dan	(1923)	Johnny Quick, Vigilante, Gang Busters
Baxendale, Leo		The Bash Street Kids

INDEX OF CREATORS

160

INDEX OF CREATORS

CREATOR	Date of Birth	BEST-KNOWN WORK
Chen, Steve		Rai, Harbinger
Cherkas, Michael	(1954)	New Frontier, Suburban Nightmares, Silent Invasion
Chichester, D. G.	(1964)	Doctor Zero, Powerline, Hellraiser, Nightbreed, Punisher/Black Widow, Wolverine, S.H.I.E.L.D.
Chrislip, Bruce	(1954)	Cerebus bi-weekly, Cerebus High Society, Cerebus Church and State
Claremont, Chris	(1950)	X-Men, Wolverine, Aliens Vs Predator
Clark, Randy	(1963)	Nexus, Badger, Dreadstar, Muppet Babies
Clopper, Brian	(1967)	Crow's Nest – CBG, Amazing Heroes Swimsuit, Look and Find Spiderman
Clowes, Dan		Eightball, Lloyd Llewellyn
Cochran, John	(1943)	Creepy, Eerie, Vampirella, Green Tales, Comics Journal
Cockrum, David	(1943)	Legion of Superheroes, Avengers, New X-Men
Colan, Eugene	(1926)	Daredevil, Iron Man, Doctor Strange, Dracula, Captain America, Captain Marvel
Cole, Jack	(1918)	Created Plastic Man and Midnight
Collins, Max	(1948)	Dick Tracy, Batman, Wild Dog, Ms Tree
Collins, Nancy A.		Swamp Thing
Collins, Steve	(1954)	Looney Tunes, Tiny Toons Adventures
Collins, Terry	(1967)	Doc Savage, Jughead, Lost in Space, HP Lovecraft's Cthulhu, Quantum Leap, What The?
Conrad, Tim	(1951)	Almuric, Conan, Epic Illustrated
Conway, Gerry	(1952)	Amazing Spider-Man, Punisher, Firestorm, JLA
Cool, Anna-Maria	(1956)	Hook, Barbie, Barbie Fashion
Corben, Richard	(1940)	Rowlf, Creepy, Heavy Metal
Costanza, John		New God, Green Lantern/Green Arrow
Costanza, Pete		Classics Illustrated, Nemesis, Jimmy Olsen
Cowan, Denys	(1961)	Deathlok, Question
Craig, Johnny	(1926)	Crime Suspenstories, Iron Man
Crandall, Reed	(1917)	Doll Man, Blackhawk, Classics Illustrated, The Twilight Zone, Creepy and Eerie
Crane, Roy	(1901)	Captain Easy, Buz Sawyer
Crumb, Robert	(1943)	Underground cartoons
Danko, Dan	(1966)	Warstrike, Man of War, Ultraverse
David, Peter	(1956)	Web of Spiderman, Spectacular Spiderman, Amazing Spider-Man, Star Trek, Dreadstar, X-factor
Davis, Alan	(1956)	Excalibur, Marvelman, Captain Britain
Davis, Dan	(1957)	Flash Annual, Showcase '93, Dark Horse Comics
Davis, Guy		Sandman Mystery Theatre
Davis, Jack	(1926)	Tales from the Crypt, Two-Fisted Tales and Vault of Horror
Davis, Jim	(1945)	Garfield
Davis, Michael	(1958)	Shado, etc.
Davis, Rob	(1954)	Star Trek, Star Trek: Next Generation, Quantum Leap
De Jesus, Robert	(1967)	Ninja High School
DeBeck, Billy	(1890)	Barny Google
De Carlo, Dan		Betty and Veronica
DeFalco, Tom		Marvel Comics
DeFuccio, Jerry	(1925)	Two-Fisted Tales, Frontline Combat, Mad, Cracked
DeMulder, Kim	(1955)	Defenders, Airboy, She-Hulk, Nick Furty, Robocop, Punisher, Superboy, Nam, Hellblazer
DeVries, David	(1966)	Aquaman, Greatest Team-up Stories Ever Told, Dragon Lance, Doctor Fate, Nexus Legends

CREATOR	Date of Birth	BEST-KNOWN WORK
Dechnik, Suzanne		Terminator, Real Ghostbusters, Green Hornet, Twilight Zone, Tales of the Green Hornet
Delano, Jamie		Hellblazer
Delbo, José	(1933)	Billy the Kid, Turok, Wonder Woman, Superman, World's Finest, Transformers, X-O Manowar
Delepone, Michael	(1964)	Sherlock Holmes: Return of the Devil, Alien Nation: The Firstcomers
Dennis, John	(1950)	Caliber Presents, Comet, West Coast Avengers annual, Wonder Woman annual, Tarzan
Dent, Lester		Doc Savage
Deschaine, Scott	(1957)	Vortex, Street Music, Anything Goes, Mr Monster, Knockabout, Mythos
Dillon, Dick		Blackhawk, JLA
Dillon, Steve	(1962)	Hellblazer, Laser Eraser and Pressbutton
Dinehart, Eric	(1952)	Alien Encounters, Tales of Terror, Grave Tales, Splatter, Dark Horse Presents
Dini, Paul		Elvira, Batman Adventures
Dirks, Rudolph	(1877)	The Katzenjammer Kids
Disney, Walter	(1901)	Mickey Mouse, Donald Duck
Ditko, Steve	(1927)	Amazing Spider-Man, Blue Beetle, Doctor Strange, Captain Atom, Speedball
Dixon, Chuck	(1954)	Airboy, Savage Sword of Conan, Detective Comics, Batman, Alien Legion, Green Hornet, Punisher
Doran, Colleen	(1963)	A Distant Soil
Dorkin, Evan	(1965)	Bill and Ted's Excellent Comic, Deadline USA, Predator: Big Game, Flaming Carrot
Dorman, Dave	(1958)	Aliens: Tribe, Indiana Jones: Fate of Atlantis, Star Wars: Dark Empire, Predator: Race War
Dorne, Susan	(1958)	Green Hornet, Married with Children
Dorran, Colleen		Valor
Dorscheid, Les	(1959)	Batman/Dracula: Red Rain, Aliens: Hive, Classics Illustrated, Deadman: Love after Death and Exorcism
Drake, Arnold		Doom Patrol
Drake, Stan	(1921)	Eternal Warrior, Blondie, Solar: Man of the Atom
Draut, Bill		Bee-Man, Jigsaw, Spyman, Jack Frost, Teen Titans
Drucker, Mort	(1929)	Mad Magazine
Duffy, Jo	(1954)	Power Man and Iron Fist, Moon Knight, Star Wars, Wolverine, Punisher, A Distant Soil, X-factor
Dutter, Barry	(1964)	Nightcat, Captain Planet, Marvel Tales, Hellraiser, What The?
Eastman, Kevin	(1962)	Teenage Mutant Ninja Turtles
Echevarria, Felipe	(1959)	Alfred Hitchcock's Psycho, Alien National, Flash, Tomorrow Knights, Barbie, Power Pack Special
Edgington, Ian		Aliens
Eisman, Hy	(1927)	Blondie, Tom and Jerry, Little Lulu, Katy Keene, Archie, Felix the Cat
Eisner, Will	(1917)	Spirit, Sheena, Hawks of the Seas, Yarko, Blackhawk, Doll Man and Uncle Sam
Elder, William	(1922)	Frontline Combat, Two-Fisted Tales, original layout work on Mad
Elias, Lee	(1920)	Black Cat, Green Hornet, Green Arrow, Cave Carson, Tommy Tomorrow
Ellison, Harlan	(1934)	Hulk, Avengers, Twilight Zone, Weird Tales, Detective Comics, Daredevil
Ely, Bill		Mr District Attorney, Gang Busters, Rip Hunter

![Showcase No. 14 cover presenting The Flash](Cover of Showcase No. 14, June, 10¢, DC National Comics, Approved by the Comics Code Authority. "Presenting THE FLASH! Whirlwind adventures of the fastest man alive! Featuring 'Giants of the Time-World!'")

INDEX OF CREATORS

◀ SHOWCASE No. 14,
June 1958, featured the fourth appearance of the Silver Age Flash
(™ & Copyright © 1994 DC Comics, Inc.)

INDEX OF CREATORS

INDEX OF CREATORS

CREATOR	Date of Birth	BEST-KNOWN WORK
Knapp, Bill	(1962)	Green Hornet, Aliens, Flash, American Splendour
Kotzky, Alex		Spirit
Krigstein, Bernard	(1919)	Early EC Horror titles, Marvel Tales, Strange Tales
Kubert, Adam	(1959)	Wolverine 75, X-Men 25, Ghost Rider and Blaze: Spirits of Vengeance
Kubert, Andy	(1962)	Sgt Rock, Adam Strange, Doc Savage, Savage Sword of Conan, Uncanny X-Men, X-Men
Kubert, Joe	(1926)	Viking Prince, Rip Hunter, Sgt Rock, Hawkman, Tarzan
Kudo, Kazuya		Mai the Psychic Girl
Kurtzman, Harvey	(1924)	Co-created Mad Magazine
Lago, Ray	(1958)	Hellraiser, Dark Horse Presents, Dark Horse Comics
Laird, Peter		Teenage Mutant Ninja Turtles
Lansdale, Joe		Jonah Hex: Two Gun Kid, Blood and Shadows
Lantz, Walter	(1900)	Woody Woodpecker
Lapham, David	(1970)	Warriors of Plasm, H.A.R.D. Corps, Harbinger
Larsen, Erik	(1962)	Savage Dragon, Amazing Spider-Man, Spiderman
Larson, Gary	(1950)	The Far Side
Law, Davey		Dennis the Menace (British)
Layton, Bob	(1953)	X-O Manowar, Second Life of Doctor Mirage, Iron Man
Leach, Garry	(1954)	Miracleman, Judge Dredd, Dan Dare
Leach, Gary	(1957)	Carl Barks Library, Little Lulu Library, Micky Mouse in Color, Uncle Scrooge in Color
Lee, Jae	(1972)	WildC.A.T.S. Trilogy, Youngblood, Strikefile, Spiderman
Lee Jim	(1964)	WildC.A.T.S., Stormwatch
Lee, Stan	(1922)	Captain America, Strange Tales, Fantastic Four, Hulk, Amazing Spider-Man, Doctor Strange
Leonardi, Rick	(1957)	Spiderman 2099
Lessman, Linda	(1948)	Man Thing, Tomb of Dracula, Fantastic Four, Amazing Spider-Man, Grimjack, Badger
Levitz, Paul		Legion of Super-Heroes
Lieber, Larry		Rawhide Kid, The Wasp, Spiderman newspaper strip
Liefeld, Rob	(1967)	Deathmate, Darker Image, Brigade, Youngblood, New Mutants, X-Force
Lim, Ron	(1965)	Thanos Quest, Infinity Gauntlet, Infinity War, Infinity Crusade
Lloyd, David	(1950)	V for Vendetta, Dr Who Weekly
Locher, Dick		Dick Tracy
Loeb, Jeff		Challengers of the Unknown mini-series
Lopresti, Aaron	(1964)	Amazing Spider-Man, Spectacular Spiderman, Web of Spiderman annual, New Warriors annual, What If?
Lowther, George		Superman novel.
Lustig, John	(1953)	Donald Duck Adventures, Uncle Scrooge, Ducktales, Daffy Duck
Lyle, Tom	(1953)	Robin (mini series), Comet
MacDonald, Heidi		Comics Journal, Amazing Heroes
Mackie, Howard		Ghost Rider
Mahlstedt, Larry	(1956)	Incredible Hulk, Marvel Age, Marvel Tales, Flash, Legion of Super-Heroes, Dr Fate, Green Arrow
Maneely, Joe		Black Knight, Ringo Kid
Mangels, Andy	(1966)	Child's Play, Freddy's Dead, Nightmare on Elm Street, Quantum Leap
Manley, Michael	(1961)	Quasar, Alpha Flight, Transformers, Doctor Zero, Darkhawk, Sleepwalker, Punisher War Zone
Manning, Russell	(1929)	Magnus Robot Fighter for Gold Key
Marder, Larry		Beanworld
Marks, Bill	(1962)	Mister X, Doc Chaos, Yummy Fur, Bloodlines, Badlands
Marlette, Doug	(1951)	Kudzu
Marsh, Jesse		Tarzan, Gene Autry
Marshall, Charles	(1963)	Planet of the Apes, Quantum Leap, Dread of Night, Fugitive
Marshall, Paul		Firebrand
Martin, Alan		Tank Girl
Martin, Don	(1931)	Mad Magazine
Martin, Gary	(1956)	Nexus: Origin, Captain Crusade, Micky Mouse Adventures, Darkwing Duck, Little Mermaid
Mason, Tom		Dinosaurs for Hire, Ex-Mutants, Robotech II: The Sentinels
Masteoseiro, Rocke		Space Adventures
Mattsson, Steve	(1959)	Black Panther, Boris the Bear, Idol, Shann the She-Devil in Marvel Comics Presents
Maurer, Norman		3-D Comics, Three Stooges
Mayer, Sheldon	(1917)	Superman, Black Orchid, Sugar and Spice
Mazzuccelli, David	(1960)	Daredevil, Batman, Rubber Blanket
McCay, Winsor	(1872)	Little Nemo
McCloud, Scott		Zot!
McDaniel, Walter	(1971)	Earth 4
McDuffie, Dwayne		Damage Control, Deathlok, The Demon, Ultraman
McElroy, Clint	(1955)	Blood is the Harvest, Freejack, Universal Soldier, Green Hornet, Illegal Aliens
McFarlane, Todd	(1961)	Spawn, Amazing Spider-Man
McGregor, Don		Sabre
McKean, Dave		Violent Cases, Arkham Asylum, Sandman, Black Orchid
McKeever, Ted		Plastic Forks
McKenna, Mark	(1957)	Dr Fate, Legion, Doom Patrol, Griffin, Nomad, Doctor Strange, Darkhold, Punisher War Zone
McKie, Angus		The Blue Lily
McLaughlin, Frank		Judomaster, Flash, Aquaman, Atom, Green Lantern, Captain America
McLaurin, Marc	(1964)	Alien Legion, Akira, Moebius, Punisher, Alpha Flight, Hellraiser, Nightbreed, Groo, Spiderman
McLeod, Bob	(1951)	The New Mutants
McMahon, Dave		Judge Dredd
McManua, Shawn		Sandman
McWilliams, Al		Dell comics, Gold Key comics
Medina, Angel	(1964)	Megaton, Dreadstar, Badger, Incredible Hulk, What The?, Soviet Super Soldiers
Menashe, Rachelle	(1961)	Terminator, Predator: Cold War, Aliens, Young Indiana Jones, Robocop Vs Terminator
Meskin, Mort	(1916)	Vigilante, Johnny Quick, Golden-Lad
Messner-Loebs, William	(1949)	Mr Monster, Johnny Quest, Wastelands, Dr Fate, Justice League Europe
Michelinie, David		Spiderman, H.A.R.D. Corps
Mignola, Mike	(1960)	Aliens, Batman: Gotham by Gaslight
Miller, Frank	(1957)	Batman: The Dark Knight Returns, Daredevil, Ronin, Sin City
Milligan, Pete		Animal Man, Enigma, Shade: Changing Man
Mills, Pat	(1949)	Marshal Law, Slaine, Third World War
Mingo, Norman	(1896)	Alfred E. Neuman
Mishkin, Dan	(1953)	Blue Devil, Amethyst, Wonder Woman, DC Comics Presents, Brave and the Bold, Dragons, Dragonlance
Miyazaki, Hayao		Nausicaä of the Valley of Wind
Moldoff, Sheldon	(1920)	Hawkman, Flash, Green Lantern, Kid Eternity, Sea Devils, Batman, Legion of Super-Heroes

INDEX OF CREATORS

▶ CATWOMAN No. 1,
February 1989
(™ & Copyright © 1994 DC Comics, Inc.)

166

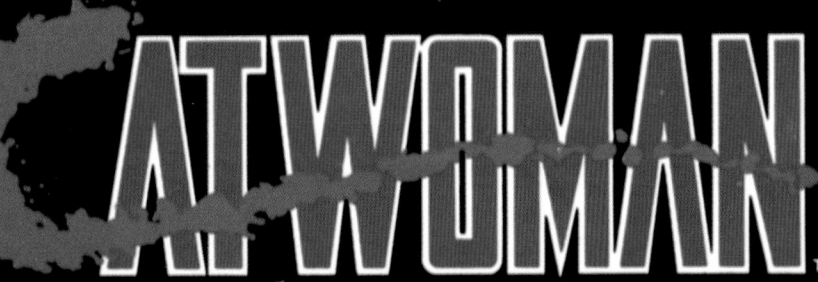

NEW FORMAT
MINI-SERIES

1 OF 4 $1.50
$1.85©
FEB 89 UK 80p

SUGGESTED
FOR MATURE
READERS

TM

In the Ruins
of Innocence,
the BATMAN'S
Enemy is
Born...

A Four Issue
Mini-Series by
Mindy Newell,
J.J. Birch,
& Michael Bair

INDEX OF CREATORS

CREATOR	Date of Birth	BEST-KNOWN WORK
Platt, Stephen		Moon Knight, Prophet
Ploog, Mike	(1940)	Werewolf by Night, Frankenstein, Ghost Rider, Man-Thing, Weird World and Kull
Plunkett, Sandy	(1955)	Ant-Man, Spiderman, Black Panther
Pollack, Rachel		Doom Patrol
Portacio, Whilce		Wetworks, Uncanny X-Men
Potter, Greg		Wonder Woman
Potts, Carl	(1952)	Punisher War Journal, Shadowmasters, Alien Legion, Spellbound, Moon Knight, Doctor Strange
Powell, Bob		Spirit, Green Hornet, Daredevil, Giant-Man
Premiani, Bruno		Doom Patrol
Prosser, Jerry	(1963)	Exquisite Corpse, Aliens: Hive, Cybernetics
Pucket, Kelly		Batman Adventures
Pugh, Steve		Animal Man
Purcell, Gordon	(1959)	Star Trek, Flash, War of the Gods, Wonder Man, Cage, Young Indiana Jones
Purcell, Howard		Mr District Attorney, Gang Busters, Sea Devils, Space Ranger
Quesada, Joe	(1962)	X-O Manowar, Spelljammer, Batman: Sword of Azrael, X-Factor, Ninjak
Raboy, Mac	(1914)	Captain Marvel, Flash Gordon
Ranson, Arthur		Look-In, Danger Mouse, Batman: Legends of the Dark Knight
Ray, Fred		Batman
Raymond, Alex	(1909)	Flash Gordon, Secret Agent X-9, Rip Kirby and Jungle Jim
Reddington, James		House of Mystery, Avengers, Avengers West Coast, Who's Who, Marvel Comics Presents, Sleepwalker
Reed, Daniel	(1960)	What If?, Indiana Jones, Transformers, Incredible Hulk, Marvel Comics Presents, Forgotten Realms
Reid, Ken		Roger the Dodger
Reinhold, Bill	(1955)	Justice Machine, The Badger, Intruder, Hellraiser, Silver Surfer: Homecoming
Reinman, Paul		Might Crusaders, Shadow, Flyman
Rhodes, Fred		Sad Sack, Beetle Bailey
Richards, Frank		Billy Bunter
Richardson, Mike		Dark Horse Comics
Richmond, Tom	(1966)	Married with Children, Mr Lizard 3-D Special
Roach, David	(195?)	Judge Dredd
Roberts, Dave	(1960)	Femforce, Femforce Up-Close, Good Girl Art Quarterly
Robinson, James	(1963)	Terminator: Secondary Objectives, Terminator: One Shot, Terminator: Endgame, Legends of Dark Knight
Robinson, Jerry	(1922)	Batman, Detective Comics, Green Hornet, Black Terror
Rockwell, Scott	(1958)	Hero Alliance, Vampire Lestat, Maze Agency, On a Pale Horse, Ex-Mutants
Rodier, Denis	(1963)	L.E.G.I.O.N. '93, Aliens, Legacy of Superman, Wonder Woman, New Gods, Sleepwalker
Rogers, Marshall		Batman, Doctor Strange
Romita Jr, John	(1956)	Uncanny X-Men, Daredevil: Man without Fear, Punisher War Zone, Iron Man, Spiderman, Cable
Romita Sr, John	(1930)	Captain America, Amazing Spider-Man
Rosema, Scott	(1958)	Amazing Stories, Tiny Toons, Looney Toones, Robotech: The Sentinels, Ex-Mutants
Rosen, Joe		Spiderman, Daredevil, Captain America, Incredible Hulk
Rosenberger, John		Archie, Jughead, Lois Lane
Ross, Alex		Marvels
Ross, Henry		Ally Sloper

CREATOR	Date of Birth	BEST-KNOWN WORK
Roth, Werner		X-Men, Kid Colt Outlaw
Roussos, George		Batman
Rozakis, Bob	(1951)	Superman, Batman, Robin, Batgirl, DC Comics Presents, Hawkman, Teen Titans
Rude, Steve	(1956)	Nexus, World's Finest mini-series
Russell, Craig	(1951)	Sandman
Ryan, Matt		X-Men
Ryder, Tom		X-O Manowar, H.A.R.D. Corps
Saavedra, Scott	(1960)	Chip 'n' Dale Rescue Rangers, Goofy Adventurers, Roger Rabbit's Toontown, Twisted Tales
Sakai, Stan	(1953)	Usagi Yojimbo, Space Usagi
Salicrup, Jim		Spiderman
Sanfelippo, Holly	(1953)	Re-Animator, Monolith, Green Hornet, The Real Ghostbusters, Terminator, Leatherface
Sansom, Art	(1920)	The Born Loser
Santino, Charles	(1955)	Conan the Barbarian, Savage Tales, What The?
Schaffenberge, Kurt	(1920)	Captain Marvel, Superman, Lois Lane, Jimmy Olsen
Schenck, Christophe	(1963)	Miracleman, Tarzan, Robin Hood, Aquaman
Schomburg, Alex		The Fighting Yank, Young Allies, Human Torch
Schultz, Charles	(1922)	Peanuts
Schultz, Mark		Cadillacs and Dinosaurs
Schwartz, Julius	(1915)	All-American Comics, Green Lantern, Flash, Showcase, Brave and the Bold, Mystery in Space
Schwartz, Sam		Archie, Tower Comics
Seagle, Steven	(1964)	Grendel, Grendel Tales
Sears, Bart		Violator
Segar, Elzie C.	(1894)	Popeye
Seidman, David	(1958)	Chip 'n' Dale Rescue Rangers, Donald Duck Adventures, Mickey Mouse Adventures, Roger Rabbit
Sekowsky, Mike		JLA, Human Torch, Captain America, T.H.U.N.D.E.R. Agents, Brave and the Bold
Semeiks, Val	(1955)	Savage Sword of Conan, Conan the Barbarian, Detective Comics Annual, Dr Fate, Aesop's Fables
Seuling, Phil		Father of Direct Distribution
Severin, John	(1921)	Incredible Hulk, Sgt Fury
Severin, Marie		Hulk, Sub-Mariner, Spiderman, Doctor Strange, Strange Tales and Tales to Astonish
Shanower, Eric	(1963)	Showcase, Who's Who, Secret Origins, Action Comics, Nexus, Marvel Comics Presents, Aquaman
Sharp, Liam	(1968)	2000 AD, Death's Head II
Shatner, William	(1931)	Tek World
Shaw, Scott Garlin	(1951)	Little Archie, Betty and Veronica, Teenage Mutant Turtles, Flintstones, Yogi Bear, Donald Duck
Shelton, Gilbert	(1940)	Fabulous Furry Freak Brothers and Fat Freddy's Cat
Shirow, Masamune		Appleseed
Shooter, James C.	(1951)	Marvel Comics, Valiant Comics, Defiant Comics
Shores, Syd		Silver Surfer No. 6 (The Watcher)
Shorten, Harry		Tower Comics
Shuster, Joe	(1914)	Superman
Siegel, Jerry	(1914)	Superman
Sienkiewicz, Bill	(1958)	Moon Knight, The New Mutants
Sikela, Johnny		Action Comics, Superman, Superboy
Silvestri, Marc	(1959)	Uncanny X-Men, Wolverine, Web of Spiderman, Conan the King

INDEX OF CREATORS

INDEX OF CREATORS

CREATOR	Date of Birth	BEST-KNOWN WORK
Velluto, Sal	(1956)	Armor, Megalith, Flash, Justice League of America, Captain America, Double Dragon, Marvel Age
Verheiden, Mark	(1956)	Aliens, Predator, Phantom, Stalkers
Vess, Charles	(1951)	Amazing Spider-Man, Web of Spiderman, Marvel Fanfare, Thor, Rocketeer, Sandman, Concrete
Vincent, Tom	(1956)	Silver Surfer, Speedball, What If?, X-Factor, Marvel Comics Presents, Nick Fury, Defenders
Vozzo, Daniel	(1962)	Dragonlance, Hellblazer, Greatest Batman Stories Ever Told, Greatest Joker Stories Ever Told
Wagner, Geoffrey		Parade of Pleasure
Wagner, John		Judge Dredd, Last American, Judgement on Gotham
Wagner, Matt	(1961)	Grendel, Mage, Batman/Grendel team-up, Sandman Mystery Theatre
Waid, Mark	(1962)	Amazing Heroes, Secret Origins, Legion of Super-Heroes, Batman: Gotham by Gaslight
Wald, Alex	(1949)	Lone Wolf and Cub
Walker, Mort	(1923)	Beetle Bailey
Warner, Chris	(1955)	Dark Horse Comics, Comics' Greatest World
Watkins, Dudley		Lord Snooty, Desperate Dan
Watterson, Bill	(1958)	Calvin and Hobbs
Wayne, Bob		Time Masters
Webb, Kathleen	(1956)	Betty and Veronica, Betty and Me, Little Archie, Jughead, Archie, Barbie Fashion
Wein, Len	(1948)	Superman, Batman, Wonder Woman, Flash, Green Lantern, Swamp Thing, Justice League, Hulk, Thor
Weisinger, Mort		1948 Superman movie, Superman Vs The Atom Man, Superman TV series, Lois Lane, Supergirl
Weisman, Greg	(1963)	Captain Atom, Secret Origins, Teen Titans, Young All-Stars, Justice League of America, Infinity Inc.
Wenzel, David	(1950)	Marvel Team-up, Avengers, Savage Sword of Conan, Iron Fist, The Hobbit
Wheatley, Mark	(1954)	Heavy Metal, Epic, Tales of Terror, Tarzan the Warrior
Wheelan, Ed	(1888)	Fat and Slat, Flash Comics
Wheeler, Doug	(1960)	Doctor Strange, Alien Encounters, Dark Horse Presents, Cheval Noir
Wheeler-Nicholson, Major Malcolm		National Allied Publication, New Fun Comics

CREATOR	Date of Birth	BEST-KNOWN WORK
White, Geoffrey	(1971)	Green Hornet, Twilight Zone, Married with Children, Ralph Snart Adventures, Ghostbusters
Whiting, Jeff	(1964)	The Tick, Paul the Samurai
Whitman, Bert		Green Hornet
Whitney, Ogden		Skyman, Herbie, Nemesis, Magicman, Noman, T.H.U.N.D.E.R. Agents
Wildey, Doug	(1922)	Johnny Quest, The Outlaw Kid, Sgt Rock, Jonah Hex
Wildman, Andrew		X-Men Adventures
Williams, Patrick	(1958)	Sting of the Green Hornet, Real Ghostbusters, Speed Racer, Ralph Snart Adventures, Elementals
Williams, Robert		Zap Comix
Williams, Scott		X-Men
Williamson, Al	(1931)	Weird Fantasy, Weird Science, Flash Gordon
Willis, Damon	(1963)	Aliens: Genocide, Black Hood, Tarzan the Warrior, Blood of Dracula
Wilson, Gahan		The Raven and Other Poems
Wilson, Gavin	(1965)	Doom Patrol, Shade the Changing Man
Wilson, Keith	(1958)	Power of the Atom, What The?, Elementals
Wilson, Roy		Jingles, Radio Fun
Windsor-Smith, Barry	(1949)	Conan, Weapon X, Archer & Armstrong, Eternal Warrior, Rune
Witherby, Mike		Ghost Rider
Woch, Stan	(1959)	Doom Patrol, Black Orchid, World's Finest, Teen Titans, Swamp Thing, Sandman, Hellblazer
Wolfman, Marv	(1946)	Superman, Batman, Mickey Mouse, Duck Tales, Spiderman, Fantastic Four, Daredevil
Wolverton, Basil	(1909)	Creator of Powerhouse Pepper, Target, Joker
Wood, Wallace	(1927)	Weird Science, Weird Fantasy, T.H.U.N.D.E.R. Agents, Daredevil
Wrightson, Berni	(1948)	House of Mystery, House of Secrets, Swamp Thing, Spectre, Heroes for Hope
Wunder, George	(1912)	Terry and the Pirates
Yaco, Link	(1965)	Quantum Leap
Young, Chic	(1901)	Blondie and Dagwood
Yronwode, Cat		Eclipse Comics
Zeck, Mike	(1949)	Secret Wars, Punisher
Zone, Ray	(1947)	Batman 3-D, Disney Comics in 3-D, Roger Rabbit in 3-D, Rocketeer 3D, Ray Bradbury Comics

▶ LOBO No. 1,
November 1990
(™ & Copyright © 1994 DC Comics, Inc.)

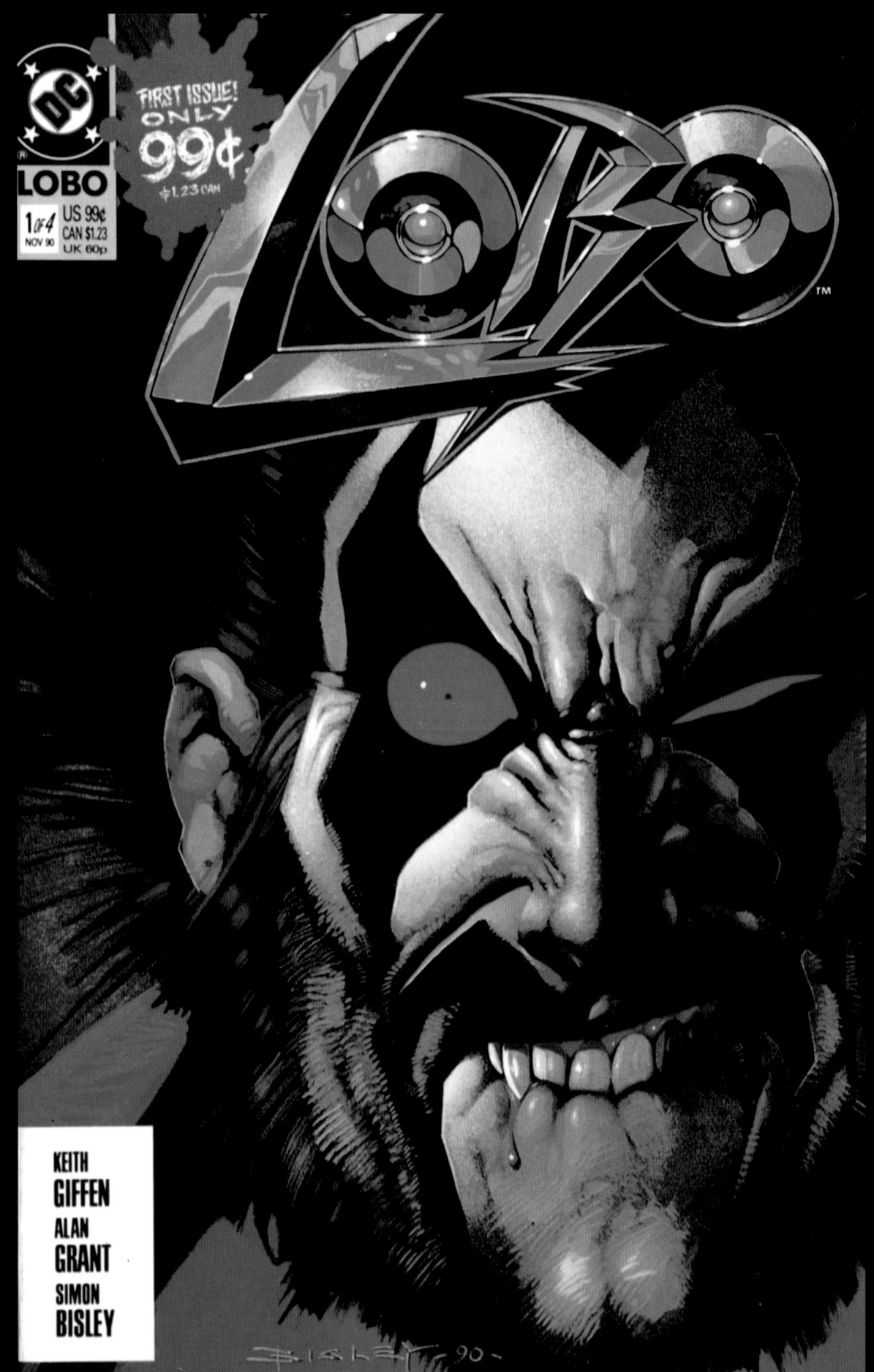

No. 101 Ten Cents OCT. 1946

Action COMICS

IN THIS ISSUE!
SUPERMAN
COVERS ATOM
BOMB TEST!

Glossary of Terms

Where common abbreviations exist, they are printed in brackets after the main term.

advertisement page missing (ad pge out) Advertisement page has been cut or torn out.

Allentown copy (Allentown) Refers to a copy from the collection of 135 Golden Age comics found by James Payette in the late 1980s just outside Allentown, Pennsylvania. They have superb page quality and were generally all high grade.

alter-ego See 'Secret Identity'.

alternatives Some mail-order companies ask customers to list alternative choices when ordering in the event of their original selection previously being sold.

animation cel (cel) Original art from an animated cartoon, painted directly on to the cel.

annual Published once a year.

appearance (app) Indicating the appearance of character(s). For example, 1st Appearance.

archival supplies Materials used to protect and slow-down the ageing process of collectables.

arrival date A date that is either written or stamped on the cover by the wholesaler or retailer. Light pencil 'arrival dates' are not considered a defect.

artist The person(s) responsible for drawing comics.

ashcan Publisher's 'mock-up' for a new title. Sometimes used to procure copyright title. Almost always produced in black and white, sometimes with a colour cover.

atomic-bomb cover (atomic-bomb cvr) Covers depicting atom bombs or their results.

back-cover crease (bk cvr crse) A crease on the back cover.

back cover not printed (bk cvr blank) Printing fault where the back cover is blank.

back-cover stain (bk cvr stn) A stain on the back cover.

back-cover stamp (bk cvr smp) A store or other stamp on the back cover.

back-cover tear (bk cvr tr) A tear in the back cover.

back cover, piece out of (p/o bk cvr) A piece torn or cut out of the back cover.

back cover, missing printing (prnt out bk cvr) Part of the back cover has not been printed.

back cover, no (no bk cvr) Back cover has been torn or cut off.

back cover, tape on (sm tp on bk cvr) Sticky tape on the back cover.

back cover, tape inside (tp insde bk cvr) As above, on the inside back cover.

back cover, writing on (wrt on bk cvr) Writing on the back cover.

back cover, wrong (wrong bk cvr) Another back cover has been substituted.

back issues Comics that are more than a few months old.

back-up A second or third feature in a comic.

backing board (bkg brd) Archival supply which fits inside the comic-bag behind the comic to support it. Acid-free boards are recommended. See 'pH'.

balloon The area where comics' characters' words or thoughts appear. Usually there is a tail pointing to the character in question. Thought balloons have a rounded more irregular pattern to distinguish them from speech.

Baxter paper Trade name for a higher quality paper than newsprint, which publishers have taken to using on some comics.

Bethlehem copy A comic from the extremely high-grade Silver, Pre-Silver and Post-Golden Age collection, originally belonging to Stanley Pachon and found by Phil Weiss and Joe Rainone in the mid 1980s. Many of the books can be identified by the 'E.J. Kery Bethlehem PA' stamp on the back cover.

big little books Small books published in the 1930s and 1940s usually selling for 39 cents. They had a page of text followed by a full-page illustration, and sometimes adapted comic strips.

Bi-monthly Published every other month.

bi-weekly Published every other week.

black and white (b&w) Comics printed in black and white, sometimes with a colour cover.

bleaching (rest, bleach) A restoration process involving the use of bleaches to whiten the cover and/or pages. Often leaves a distinctive smell.

book What the industry calls a comic.

bondage Refers to a story or a cover containing a female in bondage.

boo-boo Used in the 1960s by DC Comics in their letter columns to denote a mistake or an error.

book-case edition Usually, a set of hardbacks that come in a prestigious, high-quality, sometimes leather/leatherette, cardboard case. See 'slip-case edition'.

◀ ACTION COMICS No. 101,
October 1946, atomic-bomb cover
(™ & Copyright © 1994 DC Comics, Inc.)

book-length story A self-contained story running the entire length of the comic.

bookshelf format A name used by Marvel for a special edition of a comic that is not quite a graphic novel but approaches it. See 'prestige format'.

bound volume Comics bound together to make a book. When done professionally, the spines of the comics are trimmed or removed.

breakdowns Artist's rough sketches or layouts, sometimes drawn by one artist and then pencilled by another, with a third inking the drawings.

British copy See 'pence copy'.

brittle A condition of paper which has deteriorated and lost its flexibility, thus causing it to flake and chip easily.

bronze age Refers to the period from 1970 to 1979, which followed the Late Silver Age. It is more commonly referred to as the Post-Silver Age.

bronze edition Denotes a special edition of a comic, usually produced in limited numbers.

browning Caused by an increased level of oxidization of the pages, resulting in a darkening of the paper. This is the stage after 'tanning' and the one before 'brittle'.

bullpen, the Marvel 'Bullpen' originally described a place where prisoners were held and later the area where baseball pitchers warmed up. At Marvel, it is a big room where creators all work together.

cameo A guest appearance of a character.

Canadian copy Comics printed for distribution in Canada, sometimes containing no advertisements.

caption Boxes above or below the panels used to describe the scene.

cartoon Originally a full-size drawing used as a preliminary design for a painting, stained-glass windows, a tapestry, or a mosaic. Latterly, a drawing or sequence of drawings, often with speech, which tell a story or make a humorous point. Also a filmed sequence of drawings using the technique of animation to make a film.

catalogue A collector's listing of his collection.

catalogue, mail-order Catalogues sent to customers from mail-order companies.

centrefold The centre folio of a comic which comprises 4 printed pages.

centrefold, missing (miss cntrfld) The centre folio has fallen or been pulled out.

centrefold, loose (lse cntrfld) The centre folio has either come off of, or is only loosely attached to the staples.

chewed Damage caused by rodents or insects gnawing at the comic.

chip A piece no bigger than 1 square millimetre.

chip out A missing chip (see above).

chip replaced (chip rep) A missing chip has been replaced.

chipping Indicates more than one chip is missing. See 'Marvel chipping'.

Christmas cover (Xmas cvr) Covers depicting Christmas scenes, Santa Claus, Christmas trees, etc. Desirable to a number of collectors.

classic cover (classic cvr) Considered to be important because of its content.

Classics Illustrated (Classics) Comics published by Gilberton between 1941 and 1969. Many were reprinted a number of times, and the way of distinguishing printings is by the use of the highest reorder number (HRN), contained in a list, usually on the back cover.

Classics International America's largest comic-book retailer.

cleaned A comic that has had dirt and dust removed, either from its cover(s), interior or both, not involving the use of solvents or water. If done professionally, it is not usually considered to be restoration. See 'cleaned, solvent' and 'cleaned, water'.

Cleaned and pressed (cln & press) See 'cleaned' and 'pressed'.

cleaned, solvent (rest, sol cln) A restoration process involving the use of solvents to remove strains.

cleaned, water (rest, wtr cln) A restoration process using water to remove stains. Not as effective as solvent cleaning.

coffin box Sometimes called a 'long box'. See 'comic box'.

collector's edition An edition supplied to specialist stores only.

colour flake Where the printed layer of colour has come away thus making visible the white paper underneath. A flake is no larger than 2 square millimetres.

colour fleck A smaller version of a colour flake. A fleck is no larger than 1 square millimetre.

colorist The artist who colours the black and white art.

colour separation The process by which colour printing is achieved, by separating four basic colours (black, magenta, yellow and cyan).

colour touch (clr touch) A restoration process involving the re-touching of areas of missing colour.

comic-bag A polypropylene clear bag used to protect a comic.

Comic Book Price Guide for Great Britain (UK guide, British guide, McAlpine's) British price guide listing both American and British comics. See 'price guides'.

Comic Book Price Guide, Official Overstreet, The (guide, price guide, Overstreet's, Bob's, the Bible) The original price guide for American comics. Used by dealers and collectors, who consider it to be the definitive guide, especially for Golden and Silver Age books. See 'price guides'.

comic boxes (boxes) Heavy cardboard boxes with lids, for storing comics. They usually come flat and need to be assembled.

Comic Buyer's Guide (CBG) A weekly newspaper for the trade and collectors.

comic, piece out of entire (p/o comic) A piece either cut or torn out of the entire comic.

comic, tear through (tr thru comic) A tear through the entire comic.

Comics Code Authority (CCA) The rules and regulations of The Comics Magazine Association, applying a moral standard to the output of their members, denoted by the seal of approval printed on the cover of the comic.

Comics International (CI) A monthly British publication for the trade and collectors.

Comics Magazine Association of America Established in the mid 1950s, following public pressure, this is a body of censorship and approval. It is funded by publishers who wish to submit their material. See 'Comics Code Authority'.

comix See 'underground'.

complete run A sequence of issues, sometimes being the entire run from the first to last issue, or a group of numbers making up a complete story-line or containing every appearance of a character.

completist A collector who aims to collect everything within certain parameters. For example, every No. 1, all appearances of Batman, all Simon and Kirby work, etc.

convention (con) A gathering of fans and professionals to promote, buy and sell comics, and attend 'panels' and talks. Professional promoters normally get sponsorship from publishers and distributors for the larger events. See 'San Diego Comic Art Convention'.

corner damage (crn dam) Damage to one or more of the corners of a comic.

corner impacted (crn impact) A dent on one of the corners, which may be on just the cover, or the whole comic.

Cosmic Aeroplane Collection Sometimes referred to as 'The Salt Lake City Collection', where it was found in 1979. The collection consists of approximately 2,000 comics from the mid 1940s to the mid 1950s, and probably belonged to an art school as there are pencil check marks in the margins, which could have been put there to indicate which panels the teachers wanted the students to draw. The collection is relatively high grade.

costumed hero A non-super-powered hero, who wears a costume.

costumed villain A non-super-powered criminal, who wears a costume.

coupon Usually inviting the reader to cut out and mail to the advertiser.

coupon cut A coupon has been cut from the comic.

coupon out A coupon has been torn from the comic, as opposed to neatly cut.

cover The outer folio, making 4 printed pages, usually printed on slightly better paper than the interior, and normally glossed.

cover chipping (cvr chip) See 'chipping'.

cover crease (cvr crse) A crease on the cover, smaller than 2 inches.

cover crease, heavy (hvy cvr crse) A crease on the cover, larger than 2 inches.

cover detached (cvr det) The cover has become detached from the staples.

cover, double (dble cvr) An error during the binding process, where two covers are stapled to

▶ BATMAN No. 27,
February–March 1945, a typical Christmas cover
(™ & Copyright © 1994 DC Comics, Inc.)

the interior pages. The outer cover often protects the inner, and some collectors find these comics highly desirable.

cover faded (cvr fade) See 'fading'.

cover flake (cvr flake) See 'colour flake'.

cover fleck See 'colour fleck'.

cover, high gloss (hi glos cvr) The cover has particularly good natural gloss.

cover, ink on (ink on cvr) Printer's ink has spilled on to the cover.

cover loose (lse cvr) The cover is loose on the staples.

cover missing, part of (part cvr missing) Part of the cover has been cut or torn off.

cover, piece out of (p/o cvr) A piece has been torn or cut from the cover.

cover re-gloss (rest, cvr re-glos) A restoration process in which the cover is re-glossed.

cover roll (cvr rl) The edge of the cover curls up, while the rest of the comic is flat.

cover stain (cvr stn) A stain on the cover.

cover stamp (cvr stmp) An ink stamp produced with an inking pad, usually containing a store or collector's name.

cover sticker (cvr stkr) Usually a price sticker, which when removed leaves an outline.

cover, tape inside (tp inside cvr) There is a piece of sticky tape on the inside of the cover.

cover, tape pulled off (tp pulled off cvr) Sticky tape has been pulled off of the cover, leaving a mark.

cover tear (cvr tr) A tear in the cover.

cover trimmed (cvr trim) Only the cover had been trimmed, rather than the whole comic. See 'trimmed'.

cover wrinkle (cvr wrkle) Cover is wrinkled, similar to creased.

cover, writing on (sm wrt on cvr) Writing on the cover, which is not a pencil arrival date.

cover, wrong A fault during the binding process, where the cover of one comic is stapled to the interior of another.

coverless A comic that has lost its cover.

credit note Sometimes offered instead of a refund by stores or mail-order companies. More reputable firms will offer money back against these credit notes.

crossover (x-over) A story where one or sometimes more characters will appear in another character's title.

database Dealer's computerized record of stock and/or list of customers.

DC Archives Hardbacked books reprinting some of DC's comics. A good way of reading the stories, whether you have or haven't got the comic. See 'Marvel Masterworks'.

de-acidified (rest, de-acid) A restoration process in which a comic has had the acid reduced from its pages.

dealer A person who makes a living buying, selling and trading comics.

dealer, part-time As above, on a part-time basis.

debut First appearance of a character.

Dell 4-color (4-color) Comics, with numerous different titles produced by the Dell Publishing Company between 1939 and 1962.

Denver copy A comic from the high-grade collection bought at auction, as part of the estate of a lady from Pennsylvania, by a family from Denver, Colorado. They eventually sold the collection, which consisted of 153 Golden Age No. 1s to James Payette in 1984.

Diamond Distributors, Inc. America's largest distributor of new comics.

Diamond UK Limited A distribution company supplying new comics to the UK, owned by Diamond Distributors, Inc.

die-cut A cover that has, for marketing purposes, deliberately had pieces cut out of it during the printing process, using a die.

digest A slim paperback, usually containing reprints, measuring 4 × 6 inches.

direct distribution The distribution of comics to specialist shops, cutting out normal newsstand distributors. Stores order in advance on a non-returnable basis. See 'newsstand edition'.

direct-sales market The market resulting from the above.

distributor A company that buys from publishers and sells to the retailers.

distributor stripes (distrib strips) Coloured stripes, usually sprayed on by a distributor, to enable a stack of comics to be easily identified in a warehouse. Stripes are not a defect.

downgrade Where a collector exchanges or sells his better copy for a lesser copy.

drug story A story which shows the actual taking of drugs.

ducks Has come to mean the entire Disney family of duck characters.

dungeons and dragons (d&d) A role-playing adventure game. See 'role-playing games'.

duo-tone Comics printed in black and white and only one other colour, although the cover was usually printed using four colours. These were common in the 1930s.

dust jacket A removable paper cover used to protect the binding of a book.

dust shadow (dst shad) Usually seen at the edges, these dark shadows are caused by oxidation, where a comic stored in a stack was not completely covered by the ones above, and has been subject to dust, dirt and harmful light.

Eagle Awards Annual British fan awards.

Edgar Church Collection See 'Mile-High copy'.

edge damaged (dam edge) The edge of the comic has become damaged in some way.

elseworlds DC's current version of 'imaginary stories', where characters like Batman are taken from their usual surroundings and set in other times or places. Such stories have no effect on continuity. See 'imaginary stories'.

embossed cover A cover that has been embossed during the printing process, for marketing purposes.

eraser mark The marks left when writing is removed using an eraser. Most noticeable on covers, where in most cases the eraser also removes some of the surface gloss.

Excelsior! Stan Lee's tag line in many articles and in his bullpen page in Marvel's comics. The word was first used in comics by publisher James Henderson to announce the arrival of the British comic *Funny Folk* in December 1874.

eye-appeal The initial look of a comic when held at arm's length.

fading (fade) Due to exposure to ultra violet, from sunlight or fluorescent tubes, the colours have faded.

fan-boy A derogatory term referring to a fan whose entire life revolves around comics.

fandom The world of comics fans.

fanzine A publication for and by fans. A combination of the words 'fan' and 'magazine'.

file copy A copy from the publisher's files. It has come to be assumed that all of these are high grade but that is not always the case.

flashback A sequence showing previous events, either to update the new reader or as part of the current story.

foil cover A special 'heavy-stock' cover with a metallic sheen, produced for marketing purposes.

folio A sheet of paper folded once in the middle to produce 4 pages. A 32-page comic book is made up of 8 folios.

four-colour printing A process involving the use of black, red, yellow and blue inks, to create a full-colour effect.

foxing A dark spotty effect, usually on the edges, caused by mould.

front cover, missing printing (miss prt on frt cvr) Part of the front cover has not been printed.

front cover, no (no frt cvr) The front cover has been cut or torn off.

front cover, piece out of (p/o frt cvr) A piece either cut or torn from the front cover.

front cover, tape inside (tp in frt cvr) There is sticky tape on the inside front cover.

front cover, tape on (tp frt cvr) There is sticky tape on the front cover.

front cover, tear (tr frt cvr) There is a tear in the front cover.

front cover, writing on (wrt frt cvr) There is writing on the front cover.

front cover, wrong Another front cover has been substituted.

◀ IRON MAN No. 300,
March 1993, a typical foil cover
(™ & Copyright © 1994 Marvel Entertainment Group, Inc.)

fumentti A method of telling the story using photographs in the panels, with speech balloons superimposed.

funnies Refers to comics containing humour characters that are not animals, and usually not teenage characters. For example, Richie Rich, Little Lulu, etc.

funny animal Refers to comics containing animal humour characters. For example Bugs Bunny, Daffy Duck, etc.

gatefold cover (gatefld cvr) A cover which folds out.

genre The type or category a comic falls into; for example, superhero, romance, Western.

giveaway A comic given away as a 'premium', rather than being sold.

gold edition See bronze edition.

Golden Age (GA) The period from June 1938 (*Action Comics* No. 1) to 1945.

Golden Age, post (post GA) Period immediately following the Golden Age, from 1945 to 1950.

Golden Age, pre (pre GA) Period immediately before the Golden Age, from 1933 to 1938.

good girl art An offensive term to describe pin-up-style pictures of, usually, well-endowed girls.

grade The condition of a comic.

grading The method of establishing the condition of a comic.

graphic novel Coined by Will Eisner in the late 1970s, it describes a hard- or soft-back comic book of high quality reproduction. It has come to mean new work rather than reprints. See 'trade paperback'.

gravure Intaglio printing process (i.e. where the printing image is recessed into a cylinder and filled with ink which is transferred onto paper). Used for very long print runs since this type of cylinder wears less quickly than letterpress. Also called 'photogravure' when the printing plates are made photographically, which is usually the case these days.

hack A person who is able to produce art or writing to order. A derogatory term, implying a lack of emotion or sensibility.

headlights A slang terms for large, protruding breasts.

highest reorder number (HRN) See 'Classics Illustrated'.

▶ ADVENTURE COMICS No. 103,
April 1946, key issue featuring the first appearance of Superboy
(™ & Copyright © 1994 DC Comics, Inc.)

hologram cover (hologram cvr) A cover that has a hologram printed on it, or attached to it. Holography is a method of reproducing a three-dimensional image of an object by means of light-wave patterns recorded on a photographic plate or film. When the photographic recording is later illuminated with coherent light of the same frequency as that used to form it, a three-dimensional image of the object becomes visible, and the object can be viewed from various angles. No 3-D glasses are required to see the effect.

hot Usually refers to recently published comics that are in great demand. Can also refer to key issues, and certain comics that have not previously been in demand, but suddenly are. See 'sleeper'.

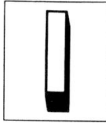

imaginary story A series of stories that appeared in some of DC's titles in the 1960s, most notably Superman titles. These stories were 'imaginary' and had no effect on continuity. For example, Superman's death, Lois Lane marrying Superman, etc. See 'What if?'

imports A UK term referring to this week's new comics imported from the USA.

indentation (indent) Usually caused by excess pressure of a thumb or finger along the edge of the cover.

independents Comics that are not published by the major publishers. They usually have smaller print runs and are aimed at a more specialized audience.

indicia Information regarding the publisher, title, number and date, usually found at the bottom of the first page, but sometimes printed at the bottom of the inside front cover.

infinity cover (infinity cvr) A scene on the cover that repeats into infinity.

ink stained (ink stn) Defect where printing ink has got on to the comic, usually the cover.

ink-stained edge (ink stn edge) See 'ink stain'.

inked Artists' line drawings that are made ready for the final production process by being inked.

inker The artist who does the inking.

inkpot awards Annual awards given at the San Diego Comic Art Convention for services to comics fandom.

introduction (intro) The introduction of a new character.

investor Someone who buys comics purely as an investment.

Isle of Wight copy A copy from the collection found in the Isle of Wight, UK in 1989 by Stateside Comics Plc. It consisted of more than 15,000 comics from the 1940s to the 1970s. What was interesting about this generally high-grade collection was the number of multiple copies of Golden Age books that were previously thought of as scarce.

joined pages (joined pges) A defect occurring during the binding process, where pages are not separated along the right-hand side.

Justice League of America (JLA) DC's Silver Age team of superheroes.

Justice Society of America (JSA) DC's Golden Age team of superheroes.

Kansas City copy A copy from the generally high-grade small collection found in Kansas.

key issue (key) An issue of historical importance to collectors. This might be the introduction or the first, second, etc. appearance of a character, or a creator's first work.

laminated cover (laminated cvr) Early method used by collectors to protect their comics. This process actually destroys any value the comic has, and these copies should be avoided.

Larson copy Copies from the mostly high-grade Lamont Larson collection, found by Joe Tricarchy in Nebraska in the early 1980s. The collection

▶ SUPERMAN No. 149,
November 1961, contains the imaginary story 'The Death of Superman', more than thirty years before DC actually killed him off
(™ & Copyright © 1994 DC Comics, Inc.)

consisted of approximately 2,500 comics from the late 1930s to the late 1940s. Most bear either Larson's first name, last name, or the letter 'L' in pencil on the cover, and some coupons are filled in. The initials, in this case, actually enhances the value, as these comics can easily be identified as coming from a pedigree collection.

letter page (lettercol) A page in comics where fans write to the editor or creator. Sometimes there is a printed response. In the early 1960s the letters mostly pointed out mistakes, (see 'boo-boo'). However, over the years the letter page has become an integral part of many comics, giving both fans and creators a chance to speak.

letterpress A printing process using a raised inked surface.

limited distribution (LD) A UK term referring to post-1970 comics, which had a limited distribution in the UK.

limited edition A comic which is limited to a specific, relatively small, print run. See 'numbered edition'.

limited series A title with a pre-set number of issues in its run, and not planned to be ongoing.

long box Sometimes called a 'coffin box'. See 'comic box'.

magazine box (mag box) A storage box for magazines. See 'comic box'.

magazine format A larger than comic-size publication.

mando paper High quality paper, not as good or as white as Baxter paper but better than newsprint.

manga Japanese comics.

match Where a dealer has found in his inventory a comic on a collector's list. See 'wants list'.

mature readers, for A comic labelled this way is not intended for children.

market share The way publishers measure their sales against other publishers.

Marvel chipping (Marvel chip) A defect during the cutting process, where the instrument became dull, causing tears and/or chips at the top, bottom and/or the right-hand side of the comic. So named because it mostly affected Marvel comics from the late 1950s through to the early 1960s. However, many other companies' comics suffered in the same way. See piece replacement.

Marvel chipping, heavy (hvy Marvel chip) See 'Marvel chipping'.

Marvel chipping, slight (slt Marvel chip) See 'Marvel chipping'.

Marvel Masterworks Hardbacked books reprinting some of Marvel's comics. A good way of reading the stories, whether you have the comic or not. See 'DC Archives'.

Marvelite A fan of Marvel comics.

maverick pages (maverick pges) A printing term used to describe pages that vary in size and/or shape, from the others.

maxi-series See 'limited series'.

mending (rest, mend) A restoration process involving the mending of holes, tears or splits in the comic or its spine.

mega-series See 'limited series'.

Merry Marvel Marching Society (MMMS) A fan club created by Stan Lee in January 1965. For a dollar, each member received a membership card, a letter, stickers, badges and a plastic record, 'The Voices of Marvel', which contained the voices of the bullpen, including Stan Lee and Jack Kirby.

mid spine (mid spn) The area of the spine between the two staples.

Mile High Comics America's largest comic dealer.

Mile High copy (Mile High) A copy from the collection found by Chuck Rozanski in Denver, Colorado in 1977. The collection consisted of approximately 18,000 comics, being some of the best examples of surviving Golden Age comics. They have exceptionally white pages, outstanding eye appeal and a fresh smell. Originally owned by Edgar Church, it is widely considered to be the best pedigree collection found to date.

mini-series See 'limited series'.

miscut A defect caused during binding, where the pages and/or cover are not cut square or to the correct size.

monthly Published monthly.

movie tie-in A comic based on, or tied into, a movie.

multiple copies More than one copy of the same comic.

multiple of guide (multiple) A comic that sells for a multiple of the Price Guide price, usually key issues or pedigree copies.

Mylar™ Uncoated, inert polyester film, used widely for the storage of paper collectables when made into sleeves or bags. Mylar is the trademark of the Dupont Co.

Mylite A thinner version of a Mylar™ bag, ideal for bulk storage.

named copy See 'pedigree copy'.

newsagent UK equivalent of 'newsstand'.

newsprint A cheap paper that most comics are printed on.

newsstand A place where newspapers, magazines and comics are sold.

newsstand edition An edition especially for newsstand distribution. Usually available on a returnable basis, from newsstand distributors. See 'direct market'.

no date Where a comic is not dated either on its cover or interior pages.

no number (NN) Where a comic is not numbered either on its cover or interior pages.

no prize A prize which consisted of a specially printed empty envelope, awarded to fans who spotted a mistake in a Marvel comic. The idea was conceived by Stan Lee in the 1960s.

non-Code Comics which do not carry the CCA seal of approval. See 'Comics Code Authority'.

not distributed (ND) A UK term referring to some pre-1970 comics which had no distribution in the UK.

numbered edition (numbered) A comic which is limited to a specific, relatively small, print run, with each copy being numbered. See 'limited edition'.

one-shot When only one issue of a title is published either by design or otherwise.

ongoing A title with no pre-set number of issues in its run, which is planned to continue for the foreseeable future.

origin (orgn) The story where a character's origin is told.

original art (orig art) The original drawings used by the printers for producing comics.

Overstreet, Robert M. Collector, author, recognized leading authority on comics and related items. His price guide is considered to be the comic's price 'bible' by the majority of dealers and collectors. His first price guide was published in 1970. See 'Comic Book Price Guide, Overstreet's Official, The'.

page, large piece out of (lg p/o pge) A piece, larger than 2 inches, has been cut or torn out of an interior page.

page loose (lse pge) A page, not the centrefold, has become loose.

page missing (miss pge) A page has been cut or torn out.

page, small hole in (sm hle in pge) A hole in the interior pages, which are not perforations.

page, small piece out of (sm p/o pge) A piece, smaller than 2 inches, has been cut or torn from an interior page.

pages, supple (supple pges) The opposite of brittle, where the pages have not deteriorated and are pliable and limber.

page stain (stn pge) Stain on an interior page.

page tear (pg tr) A tear on an interior page.

pages, trimmed (trim pges) See 'trimmed'.

pages, white (wte pges) Pages that are unusually white for the comic's age or known storage conditions.

page, writing on (wrt on pge) There is writing, which is not an arrival date, on a page.

painted cover (paint cvr) A cover produced from a painting as opposed to a drawing.

panel (1) A story panel. (2) A group of people

debating a subject or answering questions at a convention.

panel cut A story panel has been neatly cut out.

panel out A story panel has been torn or ripped out.

panelologist Literally, one who studies panels. However, it has come to mean one who researches comics, or who amasses a collection.

Parade of Pleasure (PoP) A hardback book by Geoffrey Wagner, published by Derric Verschoyle Ltd. in 1954, containing a section devoted to the censorship of American comics. See 'The Seduction of the Innocent' (page 57).

part-trade A transaction where comics are paid for partly with cash and partly with other comics. This can refer to dealings between both collectors and dealers. See 'trade voucher'.

pedigree copy A usually high-grade copy from a known named collection such as Mile High or Allentown.

pence copy Copies printed in the USA for distribution in the UK, with the price being printed in pence rather than cents. Most of these copies were Marvel's from the early 1960s, which also have printed at the bottom of the inside front cover: 'sole distributors in the United Kingdom – Thorpe & Porter Ltd'.

penciller An artist who draws the comic, prior to it being inked for final reproduction.

pencils The drawings made by the penciller.

perfect binding A binding term where the pages are glued to the cover as opposed to being saddle stitched. Also called squarebound.

perforations Small holes sometimes seen down the right-hand side of interior pages. These holes are a result of the printing process and not considered a defect.

pH This stands for p(otential of) h(ydrogen). Developed by Dr Sorenson in 1909, this is a measure of the acidity or alkalinity of a solution, numerically equal to 7 for neutral solutions, the number increasing with increasing alkalinity and decreasing with increasing acidity. Used by dealers, collectors and restorers for determining the amount of acidity in the pages of a comic.

photo cover (photo cvr) A cover with a photograph by itself or accompanied by drawings.

photogravure See 'gravure'.

Photo-Journal, The (*Photo-Journal*, or Gerber's) Devised and compiled by Ernest and Mary Gerber, this is a monumental work spanning four volumes, containing colour photographs of virtually every American Golden Age and a great number of Silver Age comics. It was published in 1990 by Gerber Publishing Company, Inc., which is now owned by Steve Geppi, president and CEO of Diamond Comic Distributors, Inc.

Piece replacement (rest, pce rep) A restoration process involving the replacement of missing pieces from the cover, pages or spine. Rice paper is often used for this procedure. A number of comics with Marvel chipping have been treated in this way.

pinhole (pinhle) A hole in the pages that is not a perforation.

pin-up page A page with a drawing of a character,

sometimes with a message from the artist or character. Popular during the 1960s, but are still seen occasionally now.

pin-up page, missing (pin-up miss) Pin-up page has been cut or torn out.

platinum edition See 'bronze edition'.

poly-bagged A comic that is deliberately pre-bagged by the publisher for marketing purposes. These comics lose a great deal of their value if removed from the sealed bag, thus causing some collectors to buy two copies, one to read and one to keep in its original condition.

poly-bag missing (miss p/bag) See 'poly-bagged'.

post-Code Comics published after February 1955. See 'Comics Code Authority'.

Poughkeepsie copy (Poughkeepsie) A copy from the collection of Dell file copies found at Western Publishing's warehouse in Poughkeepsie, NY.

pre-Code Comics published before February 1955. See 'Comics Code Authority'.

premium Originally the same as giveaway, but more recently has come to describe special limited issues, given to retailers, dealers and sometimes collectors by publishers or distributors. These comics normally have small print runs and can sometimes command high prices.

pressed A comic that has been flattened. If done professionally, it is widely considered not to be restoration.

prestige format A name used by DC for a special edition of a comic that is not quite a graphic novel but approaches it. See 'bookshelf format'.

previews Monthly magazine produced by Diamond Distributors, Inc., used by the trade and fans, listing all the new products two to three months in advance. It also contains interviews, articles and useful advice.

price guides Mostly published annually, a compilation of prices for comics in three or four different grades. The prices are arrived at through observation of the market, experience, survey and the reports of special advisers. While it is true that the prices are retrospective and only intended to be a guide to current prices rather than listing the actual prices, Silver Age and especially Golden Age comics are likely to be less volatile than new material. See 'updates'.

print run The number of copies the publisher decides to print of a particular issue.

printer's ink Ink used in the printing process.

provenance Value is sometimes added to a comic if it is known and can be proved to have originated from a well-known or named collection.

public appearance (pa) The public appearance of a creator, usually for a signing session at a convention or store.

publisher's announcements Announcements, advertising a new title or character, given to retailers, usually via a distributor. These have become collectable in their own right.

pulp A magazine cheaply produced on low-grade wood-pulp paper. Mostly printed in the 1920s and 1930s, these magazines contained mainly adventure stories.

punch hole (pnch hle) Holes made by a hole-punch for the purpose of putting the comics into a two or three-ringed binder. Such comics are almost valueless.

quarterly Published four times a year.

reading copy A low-grade copy, not collectable but suitable for reading or research purposes.

research copy See 'reading copy'.

remainders Comics that were unsold at the news-stand. In some cases a third, a half, or the entire cover was removed prior to the comic being sent back to the distributor for credit.

repaired (rep) A comic that is repaired as opposed to restored. The repair could include glue, and/or tape.

reprint The reprinting of previously published stories, sometimes compiled into a book. See 'trade paperback'.

restoration (rest) A process that, in some way, has restored the comic to a previous better condition. Some of the techniques are described on page 139. Despite their improved appearance, restored comics are never worth as much as an unrestored equivalent copy. Most reputable collectors and dealers will state what has been done to a restored comic. Some professional restorers supply a certificate or letter with their finished work.

Reuben The annual award given by The National Cartoonists Society, named after the late cartoonist Rube Goldberg.

revival A story or comic that reintroduces a character that has not appeared for some time.

rice paper Thin, almost transparent paper often used by restorers. See 'piece replacement'.

rip An uneven tear.

role-playing game (rpg) A game where the players assume the characters of the game. The outcome is determined through a combination of luck, skill and strategy. Although Dungeons and Dragons is the best known, there are a number of rpgs involving comic-book characters.

saddle stitched A binding term, where the pages and cover are stapled together at the centre.

Salt Lake City Collection See 'Cosmic Aeroplane Collection'.

▶ THE BEATLES' LIFE STORY No. 1,
September–November 1964, a typical photo cover
(Copyright © 1964 Dell Publishing Company.)

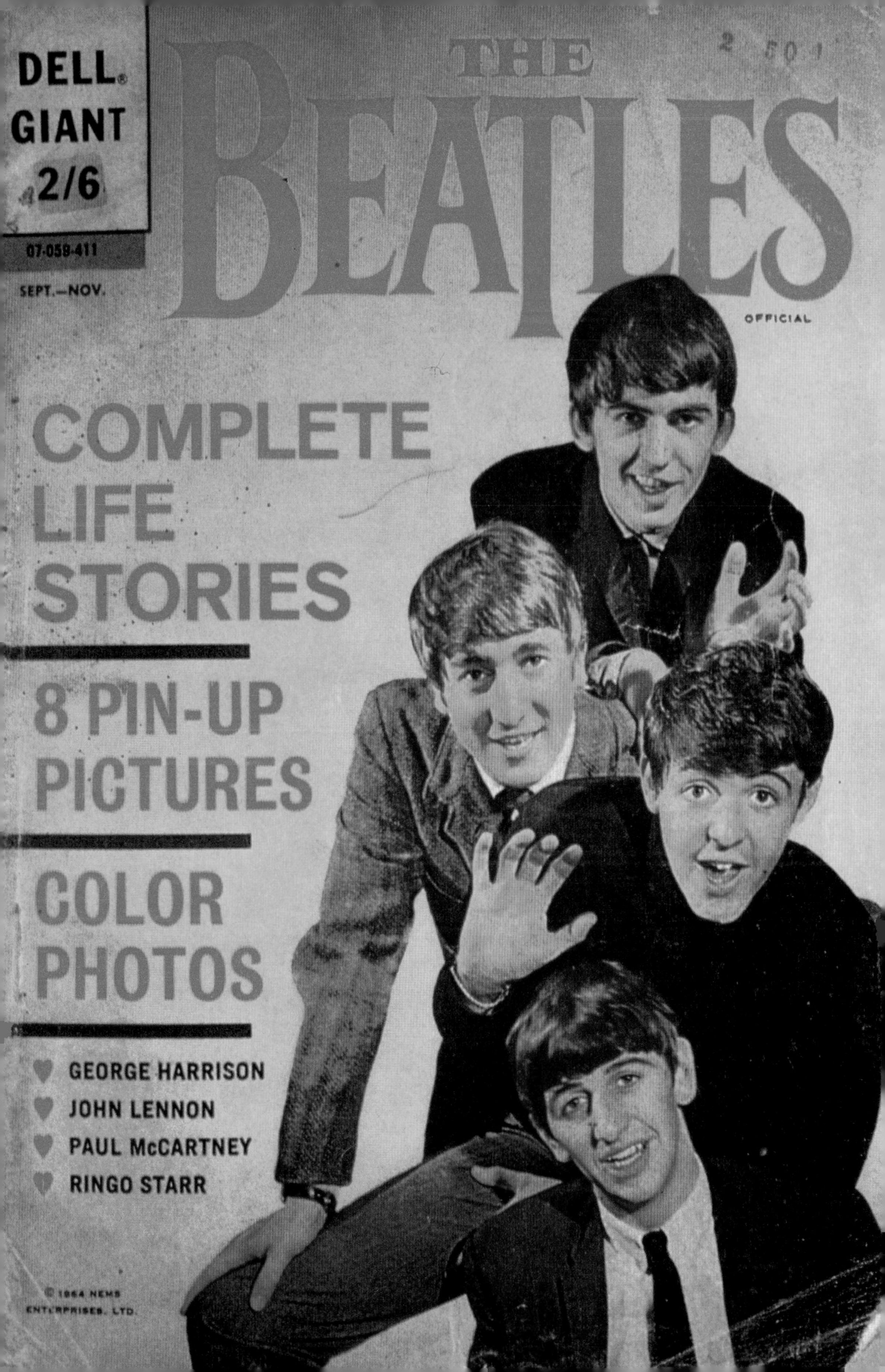
DELL GIANT
2/6
07-058-411
SEPT.—NOV.
THE BEATLES
OFFICIAL
COMPLETE LIFE STORIES
8 PIN-UP PICTURES
COLOR PHOTOS
GEORGE HARRISON
JOHN LENNON
PAUL McCARTNEY
RINGO STARR
© 1964 NEMS ENTERPRISES, LTD.

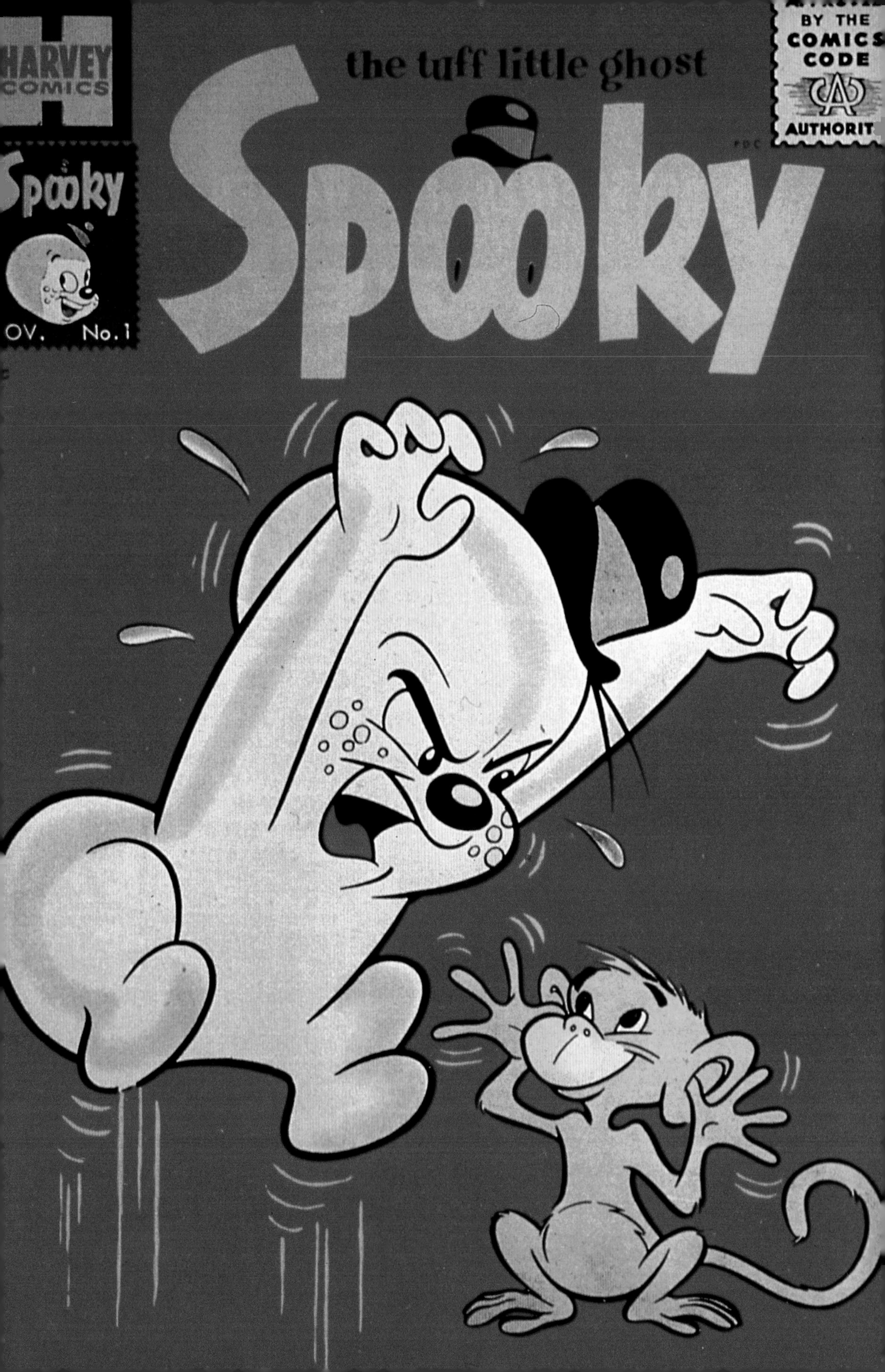

San Diego Comic Arts Convention The world's largest comic convention. Held annually in San Diego CA, it brings together professionals and fans from all over the world. Some of the convention's activities, which include previews, films, talks, panels, games, awards and the now-famous fancy-dress parade, take place on a number of conveniently located sites, all fairly near to the main convention centre. The dealers' and artists' areas cover more than 200,000 square feet! Prior to the four-day convention, there is an Expo Trade Show where publishers promote their new products to retailers. (The trade show is not open to the public.) The year 1994 marked the 25th anniversary of this convention.

San Francisco copy A copy from the San Francisco Collection, found by John Barrett and Bud Plant in 1976. The collection consisted of approximately 2,000 Near Mint and Mint comics from the 1940s. A copy from this collection is identifiable by a small stamp signature, Tom Rielly, who may have been the original owner, on the back cover of most copies.

scarce More copies are in demand than are available, owing to a small print run, a market trend or a combination of both.

script The text of a comic-book story, which sometimes contains directions for the artist.

scripter A person who writes the script for a comic-book story.

scuff A slight abrasion on the cover or page.

secret identity Many comic-book heroes have two identities, the most famous being Clark Kent who is secretly Superman.

Seduction of the Innocent, The (SOTI) A book written by Dr Frederick Wertham and published in 1954 by Rinehart & Co., Inc. It tried to connect juvenile delinquency to the reading of comics. The US Senate hearings, which led to the formation of the Comics Code Authority, used this damning book, and also called Wertham to give testimony. See 'Comics Code Authority' and 'Parade of Pleasure'.

show Similar to a convention, but usually there will not be any guests, panels or talks. A gathering of fans and dealers concentrating on the buying, selling and trading aspects of the hobby.

sidekick The partner of a costumed, masked superhero or other character, usually younger, mostly male, although there are exceptions to both these criteria.

signed and numbered (signed & num) A combination. See 'numbered edition' and 'signed copy'.

signed copy A copy that has been signed by a creator connected with the publication.

signed copy with sketch As 'signed copy' but with a sketch either on a separate piece of paper or on the comic itself, drawn by one of the creators of the publication.

signing A gathering, which could be in a store or elsewhere, for fans to meet a creator and have their comics signed.

Silver Age (SA) The period starting with the publication of *Showcase* No. 4 in September–October 1956, and ending in 1969.

Silver Age, late The period between 1965 and 1969.

Silver Age, post (post SA) The period covering the 1970s, sometimes referred to as the Bronze Age.

Silver Age, pre The period between 1950 and the publication of *Showcase* No. 4 in September–October 1956.

sleeper A comic that was not previously in demand but has now become hot. Such comics may contain a brief (or otherwise) appearance of a character that has been revived or suddenly become popular. It could also have become hot due to the sudden popularity of a particular creator who was previously unknown.

slip-case edition Usually a hardback that comes in a prestigious high-quality, sometimes leather/leatherette, cardboard case. See 'book-case edition'.

small press A small publisher. See 'underground'.

smoke damage (smoke dam) Dark discolouring caused by the comic coming in contact with smoke.

special A special edition published, in some cases, to mark an event.

spine (spn) The hinged back of the comic.

spine chipping (spn chip) Chipping which occurs along the spine. See 'chipping'.

spine damage (dmge spn) Damage that has been caused to the spine.

spine, piece out of (p/o spn) A piece missing, through damage, from the spine.

spine repaired (rep spn) A damaged spine that has been repaired.

spine roll (spn rl) A defect caused by the reader folding back the pages as they were read, resulting in the left edge curling up.

spine roll removal (rest, spn rl rm) A restoration process involving the removal of a spine roll.

spine, split (spn splt) The spine has become split, usually just above and/or below the staples.

spine, taped (tp spn) The spine has been taped for reinforcement.

spine tear (spn tr) A tear in the spine.

spine, weak (wk spn) The spine has become weak, usually through excessive handling or other faults.

splash page A panel taking the space of the entire page. Normally at or near the beginning of a story, it may also include creator credits.

splash panel As above, not taking up the entire page but still larger than other panels.

squarebound See 'perfect binding'.

stain (stn) A stain on the cover and/or the pages, which has been caused by contact with a foreign substance.

stain, rust The cover and/or the pages have come in contact with a rusty object, usually the staples, which leaves a reddish brown rust stain.

stamp, date (dte stmp) See 'cover stamp'.

stamp, name (name stmp) See 'cover stamp'.

standing order A method of reserving comics by placing an advance order with a retailer, ensuring that an issue is not missed.

staple bar The part of the stable visible on the outside of the comic.

staple detached A staple has fallen, or been taken out.

staple, extra (extra stple) A binding fault where more than the normal number (usually two) staples appear in the comic.

staple, indented The staple bar is recessed into the spine, as opposed to resting on top.

staple legs The part of the staple visible only at the centrefold, being the part that has penetrated the paper.

staple, off bottom (off bot stple) Where part of the comic, usually the centrefold, or the cover has come away from the bottom staple.

staple, off top (off top stple) Where part of the comic, usually the centrefold, or the cover has come away from the top staple.

staple reinforced (rest, stple reinfrcd) Restoration process, involving the reinforcement of a staple hole at the centrefold and/or the cover, using additional materials.

staple replaced (rest, stple replced) A restoration process, involving the removal of the original staple and replacement with another staple, which should come from a comic of the same period wherever possible.

staple, rusty (rust stple) Staples which, through coming into contact with excess moisture, have oxidized.

Stateside Comics Plc Europe's largest comic dealer.

sticker damage (stkr dam) Damage caused by the removal of a sticker.

sticker-for-sticker trade Where one or more comics are traded for others at full retail prices. See 'trade' and 'trade vouchers'.

sticker, price Some stores still use price stickers on the cover to label their comics. These comics and stores should be avoided.

strips Strip cartoons that originally appeared in Sunday supplements.

subscription (sub) A mail-order method of buying new comics, by placing an advance order with a retailer or publisher.

subscription crease (sub crse) A definite crease in the centre of the comic running from top to bottom, which can cause the ink to crack. It was caused by the comic being folded prior to being mailed from the publisher to the subscriber. This no longer occurs as comics are now mailed flat.

subscription fold A lighter version of above, usually no cracking is present.

Sunday supplements (supplements) Refers to the section of the supplement containing comic strips.

superhero A hero, usually costumed, with superhuman powers.

superhero, pre Describes early editions of titles prior to their containing superhero stories, for example, *Adventure Comics* Nos 1–39, pre-Sandman, *Journey into Mystery* Nos 1–82, pre-Thor.

super-villain A criminal, usually costumed, with superhuman powers.

◀ SPOOKY, THE TUFF LITTLE GHOST No. 1,
November 1955
(™ & Copyright © 1994 The Harvey Entertainment Company)

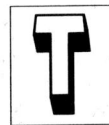

tanning A less severe form of browning.

tape (tp) Sticky tape which has found its way on to the cover and/or pages of a comic.

tape removal (rest, tp rem) A restoration process involving the removal of sticky tape with the use of chemicals.

tax, sales Sales tax is applied to all sales of comics in the USA, the percentage varying from state to state. Customers ordering out-of-state do not pay sales tax. In the UK, sales tax is called Value Added Tax (VAT) and, at this time, comics are zero-rated.

team-up The teaming up of two or more characters in one story.

3-D comic A process using out-of-register drawings, which by the wearing of special glasses enables the reader to see a 3-D effect.

3-D glasses Usually made from cardboard, with the left lens red and the right green.

3-D glasses detached (glasses det) Glasses which were originally sewn in to the comic are still included but have become detached.

3-D, no glasses (misng glasses) The 3-D glasses, originally present, do not accompany the comic.

3-part novel A complete story in three chapters, contained in one comic.

time payments Offered by some dealers as a way of paying for comics over a period of time via regular payments. It is common for the dealer to retain the comics until the final payment has been made. However, that is not always the case.

trade A form of barter, used by dealers and collectors, using comics and/or other collectables.See 'part trade' and 'sticker-for-sticker trade'.

trade paperback A softback book reprinting stories or entire comics. Not to be confused with graphic novels, which contain new material.

trade vouchers Vouchers given by dealers for the exchange of comics. These may be used to 'buy' other comics from the dealer and are not normally exchangeable for cash. Dealers will normally pay a higher price for comics from collectors, if they can pay for them with a trade voucher.

trimmed (trim) A repair process where damaged edges are cut with a sharp blade, scissors or guillotine. Trimming is not a restoration process, and

such comics are considered to be defective and worth considerably less than they would have been in their original state.

true life Comic stories based on real-life characters or events.

TV tie-in A comic based on or tied into a TV programme.

Typo A typographical error.

under guide A comic being advertised or sold for under a price-guide price, usually meaning Overstreet's.

underground Comics produced outside of the main distribution and publishing network. Some are drug or sex related, while others merely would

not justify large print runs. They are, in many cases, self-published and range from excellent to terrible. Sometimes referred to as 'comix' or 'small press'.

updates Periodical updates to annual price-guides. Most useful for new hot comics, which tend to have volatile prices.

upgrade Selling or trading a lower grade for a higher grade copy of the same comic.

value added tax (VAT) UK's sales tax. See 'tax, sales'.

valuation service A service offered for some of the larger dealers, whereby a comic is graded and valued. Usually for insurance purposes.

What if? Marvel's version of the 'imaginary story'.

wants list A list supplied by collectors to dealers containing comics they are looking for. Held on computer by the larger dealers.

washed See 'cleaned'.

water damaged (wtr dam) Damage caused by coming in contact with water or other aqueous liquids, causing wrinkling, rippling and stains.

water ripple (wtr ripl) See 'water damage'.

water soaked (wtr sk) A severe case of water damage.

weekly Published weekly.

Wertham, Dr Frederick See '*Seduction of the Innocent*'.

White Mountain copy A copy from the extremely high-grade collection originating from New England.

▲ WHAT IF? No. 1,
February 1976,
(™ & Copyright © 1994 Marvel Entertainment Group, Inc.)

zines See 'fanzines'.

▶ THE MUNSTERS No. 11,
February 1967, is a typical TV tie-in, with a photo cover
(Copyright © 1967 Gold Key)

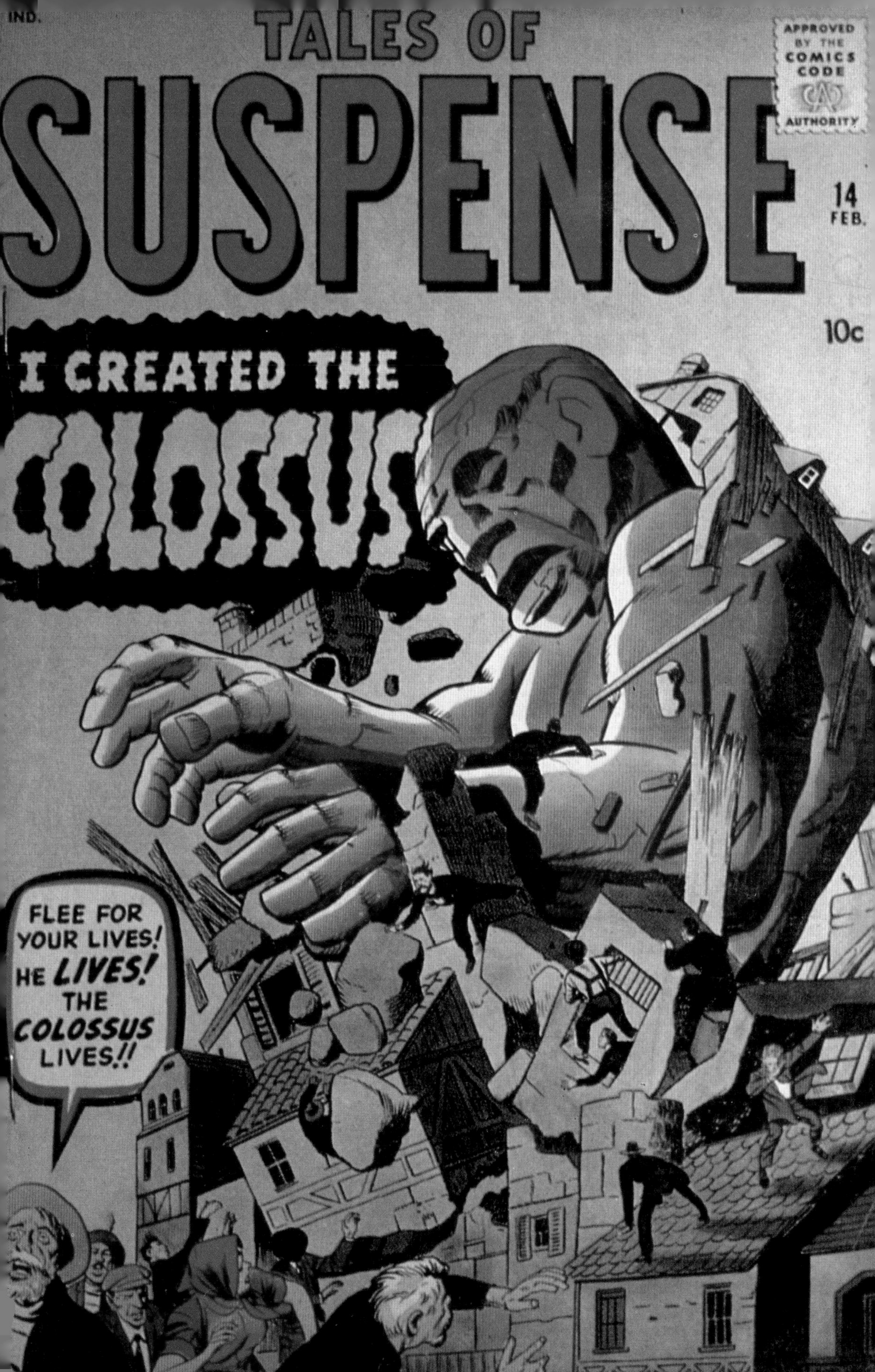

IND.
TALES OF SUSPENSE
APPROVED BY THE COMICS CODE AUTHORITY
14 FEB.
10c
I CREATED THE COLOSSUS
FLEE FOR YOUR LIVES! HE LIVES! THE COLOSSUS LIVES!!

Acknowledgements

Grateful thanks to the following people who have helped me in the writing of this book.:

Nadine Bazar, Duncan McAlpine, Duncan McMillan, Andonis Petrou, Bill Schanes, and Dez Skinn.

Special thanks to my wife Melanie Sassienie for her help with the Creators Index and a million other things.

My mother for her undying encouragement, and for not throwing out my comic books.

Mary Remnant for all of her hard work in editing.

Long-time friend and colleague Martin Gold for his never-ending research and help in compiling the Comics Titles Index.

Life-time friend and collaborator on many comedy scripts, Howard Ricklow, for his legal advice.

My good friend Steve Geppi, a fountain of information and President and CEO of Diamond Distributors, Inc. for many things, including allowing me to photograph items from his personal collection, and giving me access to the negatives from *The Photo-Journal Guide to Comics.*

Everyone at Stateside Comics Plc.

My agent Andrew Sewell whose idea the whole thing was!

Index of Comic Titles

and Their Publishers

A number of publishers are (or were) either owned by a larger company, and sometimes use (or used) a different imprint for certain titles. This index lists a large number of publishers' imprints and subsidiaries. However, there are exceptions. For example, DC's Vertigo imprint titles are still listed as DC as a great number of these titles continued their numbering when the Vertigo imprint was added. DC's Milestone, Piranha Press, and Impact imprints are also listed as DC. Prior to becoming DC Comics, Inc., DC were also known as National Periodical Publications. Another example of this is Marvel's Epic and Star and Marvel (UK) imprints which are listed as Marvel. Avon Periodicals have in some cases been listed as Avon Books. MLJ is always referred to as Archie Comics. In certain cases where another publisher or publisher's subsidiary has taken over a title mid-run and the dates were unclear or unknown, only the first publisher has been listed. Where no start number (Srt No.) is given, this indicates that the first issue (or issues) was not numbered.

A

COMIC TITLE	PUBLISHER	Vol No.	Srt No.	End No.	Str. Year	End Year	COMMENTS
!GAG!	HARRIER		1	7	1984	1989	
'ARRY'S BUDGET	GUY RAYNOR		1	21	1886	1886	
10-4 ACTION	C.B. NEWS		1	6	1981	1982	
100 PAGES OF COMICS	DELL PUBLISHING COMPANY		1	1	1937	1937	
1001 NIGHTS OF BACCHUS	DARK HORSE COMICS		1	1	1992	1992	
101 DALMATIANS MOVIE ADAPTATION	WALT DISNEY		1	1	1991	1991	
101 DALMATIANS: CANINE CLASSICS	WALT DISNEY		1	1	1992	1992	CARTOON TALES
101 OTHER USES FOR CONDOM	APPLE COMICS		1	1	1990	1990	
110 PILLS	CHA CHA COMICS				1990	1990	
12 O'CLOCK HIGH	DELL PUBLISHING COMPANY		1	2	1965	1965	
1941	HEAVY METAL				1981	1981	
1963	IMAGE COMICS		1	6	1993	1993	
1984	WARREN PUBLISHING CO		1	10	1978	1980	
1994	WARREN PUBLISHING CO		11	29	1980	1983	FORMERLY 1984
2-GUN WESTERN	ATLAS	2	4	4	1956	1956	FORMERLY BILLY BUCKSKIN
2000 AD ACTION SPECIAL	FLEETWAY		1992	1992	1992	1992	
2000 AD ANNUAL	FLEETWAY		1978	1993	1978	1993	
2000 AD MONTHLY	EAGLE		1	6	1985	1985	
2000 AD MONTHLY, BEST OF	FLEETWAY		1	80	1985	1992	
2000 AD PRESENTS	QUALITY (FLEETWAY)		1	24	1986	1988	
2000 AD SCI-FI SPECIAL	IPC		1978	1991	1978	1992	PREVIOUSLY 2000 AD SUMMER SPECIAL SUPERCOMIC
2000 AD SHOWCASE	FLEETWAY	1	25	60	1988	1990	FORMERLY 2000 AD PRESENTS
2000 AD SHOWCASE	FLEETWAY	2		10	1992	1993	
2000 AD SUMMER SPECIAL SUPERCOMIC	FLEETWAY		1	1	1977	1977	
2000 AD WEEKLY	FLEETWAY		1	871	1977	NOW	
2000 AD WEEKLY GIVEAWAYS	FLEETWAY				1978	NOW	
2000 AD WINTER SPECIAL	FLEETWAY		1	4	1988	NOW	
2000 AD YEARBOOK	FLEETWAY		1993	1994	1993	1994	
2001 A SPACE ODYSSEY	MARVEL ENTERTAINMENT GROUP		1	10	1976	1977	
2001 NIGHTS	VIZ		1	13	1990	1991	
2010	MARVEL ENTERTAINMENT GROUP		1	2	1985	1985	
2099 UNLIMITED	MARVEL ENTERTAINMENT GROUP		1	3	1993	NOW	
21ST CENTURY VISIONS	PAPER TIGER/DRAGON'S WORLD LTD				1993	1993	
3 FUNMAKERS, THE	STOKES & CO.		1	1	1908	1908	
3 LITTLE PIGS, THE	GOLD KEY		1	2	1964	1968	
3-D ACTION	ATLAS		1	1	1954	1954	
3-D ADVENTURE COMICS	STATS ETC		1	1	1986	1986	
3-D ALIEN TERROR	ECLIPSE		1	1	1986	1986	
3-D CIRCUS	FICTION HOUSE		1	1	1953	1953	
3-D DOLLY	HARVEY PUBLICATIONS		1	1	1953	1953	
3-D DOLLY	UNITED-ANGLO PRODUCTIONS		1	1	1953	1953	HARVEY REPRINTS
3-D FEATURES PRESENT JET PUP	DIMENSIONS PUBLIC		1	1	1953	1953	
3-D FUNNY MOVIES	COMIC MEDIA/ALAN HARDY ASSOCIATE		1	1	1953	1953	
3-D HEROES	BLACKTHORNE		1	1	1986	1986	
3-D LOVE	MIKEROSS PUBLICATIONS		1	1	1953	1953	
3-D MONSTERS	FAIR PUBLISHING		1	1	1964	1964	
3-D ROMANCE	MIKEROSS PUBLICATIONS		1	1	1954	1954	
3-D SHEENA, JUNGLE QUEEN	FICTION HOUSE		1	1	1953	1953	
3-D TALES OF THE WEST	ATLAS		1	1	1954	1954	
3-D TRUE CRIME	3-D COMICS		1	1	1992	1992	
3-D ZONE PRESENTS	3-D ZONE		1	20	1987	NOW	
3-D-ELL	DELL PUBLISHING COMPANY		1	3	1953	1953	FEATURING FLUCKEY LUKE
3-STAR ADVENTURES, THE	R. TURVEY/B.C.M. DEMOB		1	2	1947	1947	
357!	MU PRESS		1	4	1991	1992	
3D EYE	PAPER TIGER/DRAGON'S WORLD LTD				1982	1987	
3X3 EYES	INNOVATION		1	5	1991	1992	
666: MARK OF THE BEAST	FLEETWAY		1	18	1992	1993	

INDEX OF COMIC TITLES AND THEIR PUBLISHERS

COMIC TITLE	PUBLISHER	Vol No.	Srt No.	End No.	Str. Year	End Year	COMMENTS
67 SECONDS	MARVEL ENTERTAINMENT GROUP		1	1	1992	1992	
77 SUNSET STRIP	GOLD KEY		1	2	1962	1962	
77 SUNSET STRIP COMIC ALBUM	WORLD DISTRIBUTORS LTD		1	1	1963	1963	DELL REPRINTS
87TH PRECINCT	TOP SELLERS		1	2	1962	1962	REPRINTS
A CONTRACT WITH GOD	TITAN BOOKS				1989	1989	
A DATE WITH MILLIE	MARVEL ENTERTAINMENT GROUP	1	1	7	1956	1957	
A DATE WITH MILLIE	MARVEL ENTERTAINMENT GROUP	2	1	7	1959	1960	
A DISTANT SOIL	ARIA PRESS		1	2	1993	NOW	
A SCIENCE AFFAIR	ANTARTIC PRESS		1	2	1994	1994	
A SMALL KILLING	MARVEL ENTERTAINMENT GROUP		1	1	1992	1992	
A+	MEGATON COMICS		1	5	1977	1978	
A-OK	ANTARTIC PRESS		1	1	1992	1992	
A-TEAM ANNUAL, THE	WORLD DISTRIBUTORS LTD		1	1	1984	1984	
A-TEAM SPECIAL	MARVEL ENTERTAINMENT GROUP		1	2	1985	1986	
A-TEAM, THE	MARVEL ENTERTAINMENT GROUP		1	3	1984	1984	
A-V IN 3-D	AARDVARK-VANAHEIM		1	1	1984	1984	
A.B.C. WARRIORS	QUALITY (FLEETWAY)		1	8	1990	1991	
A.B.C. WARRIORS	TITAN BOOKS		1	2	1983	1988	
A.B.C. WARRIORS: KHRONICLES OF KHAOS	MANDARIN (2000 AD BOOKS)		1	1	1992	1992	
A.B.C. WARRIORS: KHRONICLES OF KHAOS	QUALITY (FLEETWAY)		1	4	1993	1993	
A.B.C. WARRIORS: THE BLACK HOLE	TITAN BOOKS		1	1	1991	1991	
A.R.M.	ADVENTURE COMICS		1	3	1990	1990	
A1	ATOMEKA		1	6	1989	1992	
A1	MARVEL ENTERTAINMENT GROUP		1	4	1992	1993	
A1 COMIC	D.I. BURNSIDE		1	3	1946	1946	
A1 COMICS	MAGAZINE ENTERPRISES		1	139	1944	1955	
A1 COMICS	P.M. PRODUCTIONS		1	1	1945	1945	
A1 TRUE LIFE BIKINI CONFIDENTIAL, THE	ATOMEKA		1	1	1990	1990	
AARDVARK	AARDVARK PUBLICATIONS		1	1	1974	1974	
AARGH!	MAD LOVE		1	1	1988	1988	
ABBIE AN' SLATS WITH BECKY	UNITED FEATURES SYNDICATE		1	4	1948	1948	
ABBOTT AND COSTELLO	CHARLTON COMICS		1	22	1968	1971	
ABBOTT AND COSTELLO COMICS	ST JOHN PUBLISHING		1	40	1948	1956	
ABBOTT AND COSTELLO IN 3-D	ST JOHN PUBLISHING		1	1	1953	1953	
ABLSOM DAAK: DALEK KILLER	MARVEL ENTERTAINMENT GROUP		1	1	1990	1990	
ABRAHAM LINCOLN LIFE STORY	DELL PUBLISHING COMPANY		1	1	1958	1958	
ABYSS, THE	DARK HORSE COMICS		1	2	1989	1989	
AC ANNUAL	AC COMICS		1	4	1991	NOW	
ACCIDENT MAN	APOCALYPSE		1	1	1991	1991	
ACCIDENT MAN	DARK HORSE COMICS		1	3	1993	1993	
ACE	HAMILTON COMPANY PUBLISHING (UK)		1	1	1947	1947	
ACE	HARRIER		1	1	1987	1987	
ACE ADVENTURE ALBUM, THE	MORING		1	1	1956	1956	
ACE COMIC, THE	VALENTINE & SON		1	1	1948	1948	
ACE COMICS	DAVID MCKAY PUBLICATIONS		1	151	1937	1949	
ACE COMICS PRESENTS	ACE COMICS		1	4	1987	1987	
ACE HIGH WESTERN COMIC	GOULD-LIGHT		1	5	1953	1953	
ACE MALLOY OF THE SPECIAL SQUADRON	ARNOLD BOOK CO.	50	65	1951	1965		
ACE OF COMICS, THE	WILLIAM FOSTER		1	1	1947	1947	
ACE OF FUN COMIC, THE	ESTUARY		1	2	1947	1947	
ACE-HIGH WESTERN COMICS	INTERNATIONAL		1	1	1945	1945	
ACES	ACME PRESS		1	5	1988	1988	
ACES HIGH	EC COMICS		1	5	1955	1955	
ACHILLES STORM AND RAZMATAZ	AJA BLUE COMICS		1	3	1990	1990	
ACK THE BARBARIAN	INNOVATION		1	1	1991	1991	
ACOMIC BOMBSHELL	CARTOON ART		1	1	1947	1947	
ACT OF LOVE	KITCHEN SINK		1	1	1992	1992	
ACTION	TITAN BOOKS		1	1	1990	1990	
ACTION 21	ENGALE		1	10	1988	1989	
ACTION ADVENTURE	GILLMOR MAGAZINES		2	4	1955	1955	FORMERLY REAL ADVENTURE COMICS
ACTION ALBUM	MORING		1	1	1956	1956	
ACTION ANNUAL	IPC	1977	1985	1977	1985		
ACTION COMICS	DC COMICS INC.		1	696	1938	NOW	
ACTION COMICS	L. MILLER PUBLISHING COMPANY (UK)		1	2	1958	1958	REPRINTS
ACTION COMICS (THEATRE GIVEAWAY)	DC COMICS INC.				1947	1947	
ACTION COMICS ANNUAL	DC COMICS INC.		1	5	1987	NOW	
ACTION COMICS REPRINT	DC COMICS INC.		1	1	1976	1988	
ACTION FIGURE DIGEST	ACTION FIGURE NEWS & REVIEW		1	3	1991	NOW	
ACTION FIGURE NEWS	ACTION FIGURE NEWS & REVIEW		1	7	1992	NOW	
ACTION FORCE	MARVEL ENTERTAINMENT GROUP		1	50	1987	1988	
ACTION FORCE MINI COMIC	IPC		1	5	1983	1983	
ACTION FORCE MONTHLY	MARVEL ENTERTAINMENT GROUP		1	15	1988	1989	
ACTION HEROES	STARLOG		1	4	1991	1991	
ACTION PICTURE LIBRARY	IPC		1	30	1969	1970	
ACTION SERIES	L. MILLER PUBLISHING COMPANY (UK)		1	12	1958	1958	
ACTION SERIES	YOUNG WORLD		1	11	1964	1964	
ACTION STREAMLINE COMICS	STREAMLINE		1	1	1950	1950	US REPRINTS
ACTION SUMMER SPECIAL	IPC		1	1	1976	1980	
ACTION WAR PICTURE LIBRARY	FAME PRESS		1	?	1965	?	
ACTION WEEKLY	IPC	1	1	37	1976	1976	
ACTION WEEKLY	IPC	2	1	50	1976	1977	
ACTUAL CONFESSIONS	ATLAS		13	14	1952	1952	FORMERLY LOVE ADVENTURES
ACTUAL ROMANCES	MARVEL ENTERTAINMENT GROUP		1	2	1949	1950	BECOMES TRUE SECRETS #3 ONWARDS
ADAM 12	GOLD KEY		1	10	1973	1976	
ADAM AND EVE A.D.	BAM PRODUCTIONS		1	8	1986	1987	
ADAM STRANGE	DC COMICS INC.		1	3	1990	1990	
ADDAMS FAMILY	GOLD KEY		1	3	1974	1975	
ADDAMS FAMILY EPISODE GUIDE	PERSONALITY COMICS		1	1	1992	1992	
ADDAMS FAMILY OFFICIAL MOVIE MAGAZINE	TRIDENT		1	1	1991	1991	
ADDAMS FAMILY SPECIAL	STARLOG		1	1	1990	1990	

COMIC TITLE	PUBLISHER	Vol No.	Srt No.	End No.	Str. Year	End Year	COMMENTS
ADLAI STEVENSON	DELL PUBLISHING COMPANY		12007612	12007612	1966	1966	
ADOLESCENT RADIOACTIVE BLACKBELT HAMSTERS	ECLIPSE		1	9	1986	1988	
ADOLESCENT RADIOACTIVE BLACKBELT HAMSTERS CLASSICS	PARODY PRESS		1	1	1990	1990	
ADOLESCENT RADIOACTIVE BLACKBELT HAMSTERS IN 3-D	ECLIPSE		1	4	1986	1986	
ADVANCED DUNGEONS AND DRAGONS	DC COMICS INC.		1	36	1986	1991	
ADVANCED DUNGEONS AND DRAGONS ANNUAL	DC COMICS INC.		1	1	1990	1990	
ADVENTURE ALBUM	G.T. LIMITED		1	1	1959	1959	
ADVENTURE ANNUAL, THE	BOARDMAN		1	1	1953	1953	
ADVENTURE COMICS	DC COMICS INC.		32	503	1938	1983	FORMERLY NEW ADVENTURE COMICS
ADVENTURE HERO	SCION		1	1	1952	1952	
ADVENTURE IN DISNEYLAND	WALT DISNEY				1955	1955	
ADVENTURE INTO FEAR	MARVEL ENTERTAINMENT GROUP		1	31	1970	1975	
ADVENTURE INTO MYSTERY	ATLAS		1	8	1956	1957	
ADVENTURE STORY COMIC	ODHAMS		1	1	1951	1951	
ADVENTURE STREAMLINE COMICS	STREAMLINE		1	1	50'S	50'S	US REPRINTS
ADVENTURERS	ADVENTURE COMICS	1	0	10	1986	1987	
ADVENTURERS	ADVENTURE COMICS	2	0	9	1987	1989	
ADVENTURERS	ADVENTURE COMICS	3	1	6	1989	1990	
ADVENTURERS, THE	AIRCEL		1	2	1986	1986	
ADVENTURES	ST JOHN PUBLISHING		1	1	1949	1949	BECOMES SPECTACULAR ADVENTURES WITH ISSUE NO.2
ADVENTURES FOR BOYS	BAILEY ENTERPRISES				1954	1954	
ADVENTURES IN 3-D	HARVEY PUBLICATIONS		1	2	1953	1954	
ADVENTURES IN 3-D	UNITED-ANGLO PRODUCTIONS		1	2	1954	1954	
ADVENTURES IN THE MYSTWOOD	BLACKTHORNE		1	1	1986	1986	
ADVENTURES IN WONDERLAND	L. MILLER PUBLISHING COMPANY (UK)		1	2	1955	1955	
ADVENTURES INTO DARKNESS	BETTER STANDARD PUBLICATIONS/VISUAL EDITIONS		5	14	1952	1954	
ADVENTURES INTO TERROR	ATLAS		1	31	1950	1954	FORMERLY JOKER COMICS
ADVENTURES INTO THE UNKNOWN	A PLUS COMICS		1	4	1990	NOW	
ADVENTURES INTO THE UNKNOWN	AMERICAN COMIC GROUP		1	174	1948	1967	1ST CONTINUOS SERIES HORROR COMIC
ADVENTURES INTO THE UNKNOWN	ARNOLD BOOK CO.		1	6?	1950	195?	
ADVENTURES INTO THE UNKNOWN SPECIAL	A PLUS COMICS		1	1	1991	1991	
ADVENTURES INTO WEIRD WORLDS	ATLAS		1	30	1952	1954	
ADVENTURES INTO WEIRD WORLDS	THORPE AND PORTER		1	21?	1952	????	
ADVENTURES INTO WONDERLAND	LEV GLEASON PUBLICATIONS		1	5	1955	1956	
ADVENTURES OF ALAN LADD, THE	DC COMICS INC.		1	9	1949	1951	
ADVENTURES OF ALICE	CIVIL SERVICE PUBLICATION/PENTAGON PUBLISHING CO.		1	2	1945	1946	
ADVENTURES OF BARON MUNCHAUSEN	NOW		1	4	1989	1989	
ADVENTURES OF BAYOU BILLY, THE	ARCHIE PUBLICATIONS		1	5	1989	1990	
ADVENTURES OF BIGGLES	STRATO		1	9	50'S	50'S	
ADVENTURES OF BLAKE & MORTIMER: THE TIME TRAP	COMCAT COMICS				1989	1989	
ADVENTURES OF BOB HOPE	DC COMICS INC.		1	109	1950	1968	
ADVENTURES OF CAPTAIN AMERICA	MARVEL ENTERTAINMENT GROUP		1	4	1991	1992	
ADVENTURES OF CAPTAIN JACK, THE	FANTAGRAPHICS		1	12	1986	1987	
ADVENTURES OF CAPTAIN NEMO, THE	RIP OFF PRESS		1	1	1992	1992	
ADVENTURES OF CHARLIE CHAN, THE	CHARLTON COMICS		6	9	1955	1956	FORMERLY PUBLISHED BY CRESTWOOD
ADVENTURES OF CHARLIE CHAN, THE	CRESTWOOD PUBLISHING		1	5	1948	1949	PUBLICATION CONTINUED BY CHARLTON
ADVENTURES OF CHRISSIE CLAUS	HERO GRAPHICS		1	6	1991	NOW	
ADVENTURES OF CHUK, THE	WHITE WOLF PUBLISHING		1	3	1986	1987	
ADVENTURES OF CYCLOPS AND PHOENIX	MARVEL ENTERTAINMENT GROUP		1	4	1994	1994	
ADVENTURES OF DEAN MARTIN AND JERRY LEWIS, THE	DC COMICS INC.		1	40	1952	1957	BECOMES ADVENTURES OF JERRY LEWIS WITH NO.41
ADVENTURES OF DR. GRAVES	A PLUS COMICS		1	2	1991	1992	
ADVENTURES OF FORD FAIRLANE, THE	DC COMICS INC.		1	4	1990	1990	
ADVENTURES OF HAWKSHAW	SAALFIELD PUBLISHING COMPANY				1917	1917	
ADVENTURES OF HERCULES	CHARLTON COMICS		1	13	1967	1969	
ADVENTURES OF HOMER COBB, THE	SAY/BART PRODUCTIONS		1	1	1947	1947	
ADVENTURES OF HOMER GHOST	ATLAS		1	2	1957	1957	
ADVENTURES OF JASPER, THE	ILISON		1	1	1940	1940	
ADVENTURES OF JERRY LEWIS, THE	DC COMICS INC.		41	124	1957	1971	FORMERLY ADVENTURES OF DEAN MARTIN AND JERRY LEWIS
ADVENTURES OF KOOL-AID MAN, THE	MARVEL ENTERTAINMENT GROUP		1	1	1983	1983	
ADVENTURES OF MARGARET O'BRIEN, THE	BAMBURY FASHION		1	1	1947	1947	
ADVENTURES OF MIGHTY MOUSE	DELL PUBLISHING COMPANY		144	155	1959	1962	FORMERLY PUBLISHED BY PINES
ADVENTURES OF MIGHTY MOUSE	GOLD KEY		156	160	1962	1963	FORMERLY PUBLISHED BY DELL
ADVENTURES OF MIGHTY MOUSE	PINES		129	144	1956	1959	FORMERLY PUBLISHED BY ST. JOHN PUBLISHING
ADVENTURES OF MIGHTY MOUSE	ST JOHN PUBLISHING	1	2	18	1952	1955	FORMERLY MIGHTY MOUSE ADVENTURES
ADVENTURES OF MIGHTY MOUSE	ST JOHN PUBLISHING	2	126	128	1955	1955	FORMERLY PAUL TERRY'S COMICS
ADVENTURES OF MR. PYRIDINE	FANTAGRAPHICS		1	1	1988	1988	
ADVENTURES OF OZZIE AND HARRIET, THE	DC COMICS INC.		1	5	1949	1950	
ADVENTURES OF PC. FRANK, THE	HEAVY TRIPP ROCK N' ROLL KARTOON KORP		1	2	1969	1969	
ADVENTURES OF PINKY LEE, THE	ATLAS		1	5	1955	1955	
ADVENTURES OF PIONEER PETE	PIONEER		1	1	1978	1978	
ADVENTURES OF PIPSQUEAK, THE	ARCHIE PUBLICATIONS		34	39	1959	1960	FORMERLY PAT THE BRAT
ADVENTURES OF REX THE WONDER DOG, THE	DC COMICS INC.		1	46	1952	1959	
ADVENTURES OF ROBIN HOOD ANNUAL, THE	ADPRINT		1	3	1956	1958	
ADVENTURES OF ROBIN HOOD, THE	GOLD KEY		1	7	1974	1975	
ADVENTURES OF ROBIN HOOD, THE	MAGAZINE ENTERPRISES		7	8	1957	1957	FORMERLY ROBIN HOOD
ADVENTURES OF ROBIN HOOD, THE	PEARSON		1	3	1959	1959	
ADVENTURES OF SLIM AND SPUD, THE	PRAIRIE FARMER PUBLISHING COMPANY				1924	1924	
ADVENTURES OF STUBBY, SANTA'S SMALLEST REINDEER	W.T. GRANT COMPANY				1940	1940	
ADVENTURES OF SUPERMAN	DC COMICS INC.		424	509	1987	NOW	FORMERLY SUPERMAN 1ST VOLUME
ADVENTURES OF SUPERMAN ANNUAL	DC COMICS INC.		1	5	1987	NOW	
ADVENTURES OF SUPERMAN, THE	FLEETWAY		1	18	1993	NOW	
ADVENTURES OF THE BIG BOY	PARAGON PRODUCTIONS		1	1	1959	1959	

INDEX OF COMIC TITLES AND THEIR PUBLISHERS

COMIC TITLE	PUBLISHER	Vol No.	Srt No.	End No.	Str. Year	End Year	COMMENTS
ADVENTURES OF THE BIG BOY	PARAGON PRODUCTIONS		1	50	1976	1984	
ADVENTURES OF THE BIG BOY	TIMELY COMICS		1	417	1956	NOW	JOINT PUBLICATION WITH WEBS ADV. CORPS
ADVENTURES OF THE DETECTIVE	HUMOR PUBLISHING COMPANY				1930	1930	
ADVENTURES OF THE DOVER BOYS	ARCHIE PUBLICATIONS		1	2	1950	1950	
ADVENTURES OF THE FLY	ARCHIE PUBLICATIONS		1	31	1959	1965	
ADVENTURES OF THE FRINGE	FANTAGRAPHICS		1	2	1992	1992	
ADVENTURES OF THE JAGUAR	ARCHIE PUBLICATIONS		1	15	1961	1963	
ADVENTURES OF THE OUTSIDERS, THE	DC COMICS INC.		33	46	1986	1987	FORMERLY BATMAN AND THE OUTSIDERS
ADVENTURES OF THE THING	MARVEL ENTERTAINMENT GROUP		1	4	1992	1992	
ADVENTURES OF VITAL MAN	BUDGIE PRESS		1	5	1992	1992	
ADVENTURES OF WILLIE GREEN, THE	FRANK M. ACTON COMPANY		1	1	1915	1915	
ADVENTURES OF YOUNG DR. MASTERS, THE	ARCHIE PUBLICATIONS		1	2	1964	1964	
ADVENTURES ON THE PLANET OF THE APES	MARVEL ENTERTAINMENT GROUP		1	11	1975	1976	
ADVENTURES WITH SANTA CLAUS	PROMOTIONAL PUBLICATIONS COMPANY				1950	1950	
AEGIS	ARCOMICS		1	4	1993	NOW	
AEON FOCUS	AEON PUBLISHING				1994	NOW	
AESOP'S FABLES	FANTAGRAPHICS		1	4	1991	NOW	
AFRICA	MAGAZINE ENTERPRISES		1	1	1955	1955	
AFTER DARK	STERLING COMICS		6	8	1955	1955	
AFTER IMAGE	MARTIN BEESON		1	6	1987	NOW	
AFTERSHOCK	MIRACLE COMICS				1994	NOW	
AGAINST BLACKSHARD 3-D	SIRIUS COMICS		1	1	1986	1986	
AGE OF DESIRE	ECLIPSE				1994	1994	MATURE READERS
AGE OF REPTILES	DARK HORSE COMICS		1	2	1993	1994	
AGENT 13: ACOLYTES OF DARKNESS	TSR				1989	1989	
AGENT 13: THE MIDNIGHT AVENGER	TSR				1988	1988.	
AGENT LIBERTY SPECIAL	DC COMICS INC.		1	1	1992	1992	
AGENT UNKNOWN	RENEGADE PRESS		1	3	1987	1988	
AGENT, THE: RICK MASON	MARVEL ENTERTAINMENT GROUP		1	1	1989	1989	
AGGIE MACK	FOUR STAR COMICS CORP/SUPERIOR COMICS LTD		1	8	1948	1949	
AIN'T IT A GRAND & GLORIOUS FEELING	WHITMAN				1921	1921	
AIR ACE	STREET AND SMITH PUBLICATIONS	2	1	12	1944	1946	FORMERLY BILL BARNES (VOLUME 1)
AIR ACE	STREET AND SMITH PUBLICATIONS	3	1	7	1946	1947	
AIR ACE PICTURE LIBRARY	IPC		1	545	1960	1970	
AIR ACE PICTURE LIBRARY HOLIDAY SPECIAL	IPC		1969	1979	1969	1979	
AIR FIGHTERS COMICS	HILLMAN PERIODICALS	1	1	12	1941	1943	
AIR FIGHTERS COMICS	HILLMAN PERIODICALS	2	1	10	1943	1945	
AIR POWER	PRUDENTIAL INSURANCE CO. GIVEAWAY				1956	1956	
AIR WAR PICTURE LIBRARY	M.V. FEATURES		1		1965	???	
AIR WAR PICTURE STORIES	PEARSON		1	42	1961	1962	
AIR WAR STORIES	DELL PUBLISHING COMPANY		1	8	1964	1966	
AIRBOY	ECLIPSE		1	50	1986	1989	
AIRBOY AND MR MONSTER SPECIAL	ECLIPSE		1	1	1987	1987	
AIRBOY COMICS	HILLMAN PERIODICALS	2	11	12	1945	1947	
AIRBOY COMICS	HILLMAN PERIODICALS	3	1	12	1946	1947	
AIRBOY COMICS	HILLMAN PERIODICALS	4	1	12	1947	1948	
AIRBOY COMICS	HILLMAN PERIODICALS	5	1	12	1948	1949	
AIRBOY COMICS	HILLMAN PERIODICALS	6	1	12	1949	1949	
AIRBOY COMICS	HILLMAN PERIODICALS	7	1	12	1950	1951	
AIRBOY COMICS	HILLMAN PERIODICALS	8	1	12	1951	1952	
AIRBOY COMICS	HILLMAN PERIODICALS	9	1	12	1952	1953	
AIRBOY COMICS	HILLMAN PERIODICALS	10	1	4	1953	1953	
AIRBOY COMICS	STREAMLINE	1	1	5	1951	1951	
AIRBOY COMICS	THORPE & PORTER	2	1	1	1953	1953	
AIRBOY MEETS PROWLER	ECLIPSE		1	1	1987	1987	
AIRBOY VS THE AIR MAIDENS	ECLIPSE		1	1	1988	1988	
AIRFIGHTERS CLASSICS	ECLIPSE		1	6	1987	1989	
AIRFIGHTERS MEET SGT. STRIKE	ECLIPSE		1	1	1988	1988	
AIRMAIDENS SPECIAL	ECLIPSE		1	1	1987	1987	
AIRMAN	MALIBU COMICS ENTERTAINMENT INC.		1	1	1993	1993	
AIRTIGHT GARAGE	MARVEL ENTERTAINMENT GROUP		1	4	1993	1993	
AIRWAVES	CALIBER PRESS		1	5	1991	NOW	
AKIRA	MARVEL ENTERTAINMENT GROUP		1	10	1991	NOW	
AKIRA	MARVEL ENTERTAINMENT GROUP		1	33	1988	NOW	
AKIRA DELUXE	GRAPHITTI DESIGNS		1	2	1992	NOW	
AL CAPP'S DOGPATCH	TOBY PRESS PUBLICATIONS		2	71	1949	1949	1ST ISSUE IN SERIES IS IDENTIFIED AS NO.71
AL CAPP'S SCHMOO	TOBY PRESS PUBLICATIONS		1	5	1949	1950	
AL CAPP'S WOLF GAL	TOBY PRESS PUBLICATIONS		1	2	1951	1952	
ALADDIN MOVIE ADAPTATION	WALT DISNEY		1	1	1992	1992	
ALADDIN: MORE ARABIAN NIGHTS	WALT DISNEY		1	2	1993	1993	
ALADDIN: MORE ARABIAN NIGHTS 'TOON TALES	WALT DISNEY		1	1	1993	1993	
ALAN DAVIS' CLANDESTINE	MARVEL ENTERTAINMENT GROUP		1	4	1994	1994	MARVEL UK TITLE
ALAN DAVIS' CLANDESTINE PREVIEW	MARVEL ENTERTAINMENT GROUP		1	1	1994	1994	MARVEL UK TITLE
ALAN MOORE'S SHOCKING FUTURES	TITAN BOOKS		1	1	1986	1986	
ALAN MOORE'S TWISTED TIMES	TITAN BOOKS		1	1	1987	1987	
ALARMING ADVENTURES	HARVEY PUBLICATIONS		1	3	1962	1963	
ALARMING TALES	HARVEY PUBLICATIONS		1	6	1957	1958	
ALBEDO	THOUGHT AND IMAGES	1	0	15	1985	1989	
ALBEDO	THOUGHT AND IMAGES	2	2	7	1991	NOW	
ALEC, THE COMPLETE	ACME PRESS		1	1	1990	1990	
ALEC: DOGGIE IN THE WINDOW	ESCAPE		1	1	1986	1986	
ALEC: EPISODES IN THE LIFE OF ALEC MCGARRY	ESCAPE		1	1	1984	1984	
ALEC: LOVE AND BEARGLASSES	ESCAPE		1	1	1985	1985	
ALEX	HEINEMAN		1	5	1987	NOW	
ALF	MARVEL ENTERTAINMENT GROUP		1	1	1990	1990	
ALF	MARVEL ENTERTAINMENT GROUP		1	50	1988	1992	
ALF ANNUAL	MARVEL ENTERTAINMENT GROUP		1	3	1988	1990	

INDEX OF COMIC TITLES AND THEIR PUBLISHERS

COMIC TITLE	PUBLISHER	Vol No.	Srt No.	End No.	Str. Year	End Year	COMMENTS
ALF HOLIDAY SPECIAL	MARVEL ENTERTAINMENT GROUP		I	2	1988	1989	
ALF SPRING SPECIAL	MARVEL ENTERTAINMENT GROUP		I	I	1989	1989	
ALGIE	TIMOR PUBLISHING COMPANY		I	3	1953	1954	
ALI BABA	CALIBER PRESS		I	I	1993	1993	
ALI-BABA: THETA'S REVENGE	CALIBER PRESS		I	I	1993	1993	
ALIAS	NOW		I	5	1990	1990	
ALIAS STORMFRONT	NOW		I	2	1990	NOW	
ALICE IN WONDERLAND	L. MILLER PUBLISHING COMPANY (UK)		I	I	1941	1941	
ALIEN 3 MOVIE ADAPTATION	DARK HORSE COMICS		I	3	1992	1992	
ALIEN 3 MOVIE ADAPTATION (UK)	DARK HORSE COMICS		I	3	1992	1992	REPRINTS
ALIEN ENCOUNTERS	ECLIPSE		I	14	1985	1987	
ALIEN FIRE	KITCHEN SINK		I	4	1987	1987	
ALIEN LEGION	MARVEL ENTERTAINMENT GROUP	I	I	20	1984	1987	
ALIEN LEGION	MARVEL ENTERTAINMENT GROUP	2	I	18	1987	1990	
ALIEN LEGION: BINARY DEEP	MARVEL ENTERTAINMENT GROUP		I	I	1993	1993	
ALIEN LEGION: JUGGER GRIMROD	MARVEL ENTERTAINMENT GROUP		I	I	1992	1992	
ALIEN LEGION: ON THE EDGE	MARVEL ENTERTAINMENT GROUP		I	3	1990	1991	
ALIEN LEGION: ONE PLANET AT A TIME	MARVEL ENTERTAINMENT GROUP		I	3	1993	1993	
ALIEN LEGION: SLAUGHTERWORLD	MARVEL ENTERTAINMENT GROUP		I	I	1991	1991	
ALIEN LEGION: TENANTS OF HELL	MARVEL ENTERTAINMENT GROUP		I	2	1991	1992	
ALIEN NATION MOVIE ADAPTATION	DC COMICS INC.		I	I	1988	1988	
ALIEN NATION: A BREED APART	ADVENTURE COMICS		I	4	1990	1991	
ALIEN NATION: LOST EPISODES	ADVENTURE COMICS		I	I	1992	1992	
ALIEN NATION: PUBLIC ENEMY	ADVENTURE COMICS		I	4	1992	1992	
ALIEN NATION: THE FIRSTCOMERS	ADVENTURE COMICS		I	4	1991	1991	
ALIEN NATION: THE SKIN TRADE	ADVENTURE COMICS		I	4	1991	1991	
ALIEN NATION: THE SPARTANS	ADVENTURE COMICS		I	I	1991	1991	
ALIEN NATION: THE SPARTANS	ADVENTURE COMICS		I	4	1990	1990	
ALIEN SCREENPLAY BOOK	AVON BOOKS		I	I	1979	1979	
ALIEN WORLDS	BLACKTHORNE		I	I	1986	1986	
ALIEN WORLDS	ECLIPSE		I	I	1988	1988	
ALIEN WORLDS	PACIFIC COMICS AND ECLIPSE COMICS		I	14	1982	1985	
ALIEN: THE ILLUSTRATED STORY	HEAVY METAL		I	I	1980	1980	
ALIENS	DARK HORSE COMICS	I	I	6	1988	1989	
ALIENS	DARK HORSE COMICS	2	I	18	1992	NOW	
ALIENS	DARK HORSE COMICS	2	I	4	1989	1990	
ALIENS	TRIDENT	I	I	17	1991	1992	
ALIENS BOOK ONE	DARK HORSE COMICS		I	I	1990	1991	
ALIENS BOOK TWO	DARK HORSE COMICS		I	I	1990	1990	
ALIENS VERSUS PREDATOR	DARK HORSE COMICS		0	4	1990	1990	
ALIENS VERSUS PREDATOR	DARK HORSE COMICS		I	I	1992	1993	
ALIENS VERSUS PREDATOR	DARK HORSE COMICS		I	I	1993	1993	
ALIENS VS PREDATOR: DEADLIEST OF SPECIES	DARK HORSE COMICS		I	3	1993	1995	
ALIENS, THE	GOLD KEY		I	2	1967	1982	FIFTEEN YEAR GAP BETWEEN NO.I & NO.2
ALIENS: COLONIAL MARINES	DARK HORSE COMICS		I	7	1993	1994	
ALIENS: EARTH WAR	DARK HORSE COMICS		I	I	1991	1991	
ALIENS: EARTH WAR	DARK HORSE COMICS		I	I	1992	1992	
ALIENS: EARTH WAR	DARK HORSE COMICS	3	I	4	1990	1990	
ALIENS: GENOCIDE	DARK HORSE COMICS		I	I	1993	1993	
ALIENS: GENOCIDE	DARK HORSE COMICS	4	I	4	1991	1992	
ALIENS: GENOCIDE	TITAN BOOKS		I	I	1993	1993	
ALIENS: HIVE	DARK HORSE COMICS		I	I	1993	1993	
ALIENS: HIVE	DARK HORSE COMICS	5	I	4	1992	1992	
ALIENS: HIVE	TITAN BOOKS		I	I	1993	1993	
ALIENS: LABYRINTH	DARK HORSE COMICS		I	3	1993	1994	
ALIENS: MUSIC OF THE SPEARS	DARK HORSE COMICS		I	4	1994	1994	
ALIENS: NEWTS TALE	DARK HORSE COMICS		I	2	1992	1992	
ALIENS: ROGUE	DARK HORSE COMICS		I	4	1993	1993	
ALIENS: SACRIFICE	DARK HORSE COMICS		I	I	1993	1993	
ALIENS: SALVATION	DARK HORSE COMICS		I	I	1993	1993	
ALIENS: TRIBES	DARK HORSE COMICS		I	I	1992	1992	
ALIENS: TRIBES	DARK HORSE COMICS		I	I	1993	1993	
ALL ACTION COMIC	MORING		I	I	1956	1956	
ALL AMERICAN COMICS	DC COMICS INC.		I	102	1939	1948	BECOMES ALL AMERICAN WESTERN WITH NO.103
ALL AMERICAN MEN OF WAR	DC COMICS INC.		127	117	1952	1966	FORMERLY ALL AMERICAN WESTERN. AFTER ISSUE NO.128, NUMBERING BEGAN AGAIN WITH NO.2 AND CONTINUED UNTIL NO.117
ALL AMERICAN SPORTS	CHARLTON COMICS		I	I	1967	1967	
ALL AMERICAN WESTERN	DC COMICS INC.		103	126	1948	1952	FORMERLY ALL AMERICAN COMICS
ALL FLASH	DC COMICS INC.		6	32	1945	1948	FORMERLY ALL FLASH QUARTERLY
ALL FLASH QUARTERLY	DC COMICS INC.		I	5	1941	1944	BECOMES ALL FLASH WITH NO.6
ALL FUN COMIC	A. SOLOWAY		I	27	1940	1949	
ALL FUNNY COMICS	DC COMICS INC.		I	23	1943	1948	
ALL GOOD	ST JOHN PUBLISHING		I	I	1949	1949	
ALL GOOD COMICS	FOX FEATURES SYNDICATE		I	I	1946	1946	
ALL GREAT	FOX FEATURES SYNDICATE		I	I	1946	1946	
ALL GREAT	WILLIAM H. WISE		I	I	1945	1945	
ALL GREAT COMICS	FOX FEATURES SYNDICATE		13	14	1947	1947	FORMERLY PHANTOM LADY, BECOMES DAGAR, DESERT HAWK
ALL HALLOWS EVE	INNOVATION		I	I	1991	1991	
ALL HERO COMICS	FAWCETT PUBLICATIONS		I	I	1943	1943	
ALL HUMOR COMICS	QUALITY COMICS		I	17	1946	1949	
ALL LOVE	ACE PERIODICALS		26	32	1949	1950	FORMERLY ERNIE COMICS
ALL NEGRO COMICS	ALL NEGRO COMICS		I	I	1947	1947	
ALL NEW COLLECTORS EDITION	DC COMICS INC.		53	62	1978	1979	FORMERLY LIMITED COLLECTORS EDITION
ALL NEW COMICS	HARVEY PUBLICATIONS		I	15	1943	1947	
ALL OUT WAR	DC COMICS INC.		I	6	1979	1980	
ALL PICTURE ADVENTURE MAGAZINE	ST JOHN PUBLISHING		I	2	1952	1952	
ALL PICTURE ALL TRUE LOVE STORY	ST JOHN PUBLISHING		I	I	1952	1952	

COMIC TITLE	PUBLISHER	Vol No.	Srt No.	End No.	Str. Year	End Year	COMMENTS
ALL PICTURE COMEDY CARNIVAL	ST JOHN PUBLISHING		1	1	1952	1952	
ALL PICTURE COMIC, THE	SPHINX		1	1	30'S	30'S	REPRINTS ALL PICTURE COMIC #1 WITH SOME CHANGES
ALL PICTURE COMICS, THE	SPHINX		1	16	1921	1921	FIRST ENTIRELY PICTORIAL BRITISH COMIC
ALL ROMANCES	ACE PERIODICALS		1	6	1949	1950	BECOMES MR RISK
ALL SELECT COMICS	TIMELY COMICS		1	11	1943	1946	
ALL SPORTS COMICS	HILLMAN PERIODICALS		2	3	1948	1949	FORMERLY REAL SPORTS COMICS BECOMES ALL TIME...
ALL STAR ARCHIVES	DC COMICS INC.		1	2	1992	NOW	
ALL STAR COMIC	A. SOLOWAY		1	27	1940	1949	
ALL STAR COMICS	DC COMICS INC.		1	74	1940	1978	BECOMES ALL STAR WESTERN FROM ISSUE 58 AND THEN CONTINUED ITS NUMBERING FROM ISSUE 58 IN 1976
ALL STAR COMICS INDEX	INDEPENDANT COMICS		1	1	1987	1987	
ALL STAR SQUADRON	DC COMICS INC.		1	67	1981	1987	
ALL STAR SQUADRON ANNUAL	DC COMICS INC.		1	3	1982	1984	
ALL STAR STORY OF THE DODGERS, THE	STADIUM COMMUNICATIONS		1	1	1979	1979	
ALL STAR WESTERN	DC COMICS INC.	1	58	119	1951	1961	FORMERLY ALL STAR COMICS
ALL STAR WESTERN	DC COMICS INC.	2	1	11	1970	1972	BECOMES WEIRD WESTERN TALES
ALL SURPRISE	TIMELY COMICS		1	12	1943	1947	BECOMES JEANIE
ALL TEEN	MARVEL ENTERTAINMENT GROUP		20	20	1947	1947	FORMERLY ALL WINNERS, BECOMES ALL WINNERS & TEEN.
ALL THE FUNNY FOLKS	WORLD PRESS TODAY INC.		1	1	1926	1926	
ALL THE TEARS OF HELL	CATALAN COMMUNCATIONS				1990	1990	
ALL TIME SPORTS COMICS	HILLMAN PERIODICALS		4	7	1949	1949	FORMERLY ALL SPORTS COMICS
ALL TOP	WILLIAM H. WISE		1	1	1944	1944	
ALL TOP COMICS	FOX FEATURES SYNDICATE		1	18	1945	1949	BECOMES MY EXPERIENCE
ALL TOP COMICS	STREAMLINE		1	1	1949	1949	REPRINTS
ALL TRUE ALL PICTURE POLICE CASES	ST JOHN PUBLISHING		1	2	1952	1952	
ALL TRUE CRIME	ATLAS		26	52	1948	1952	FORMERLY OFFICIAL TRUE CRIME CASES
ALL TRUE DETECTIVE CASES	AVON BOOKS		1	4	1954	1954	BECOMES KIT CARSON
ALL TRUE ROMANCE	AJAX		23	30	1955	1957	FORMERLY PUBLISHED BY HARWELL
ALL TRUE ROMANCE	ARTFUL PUBLICATION		1	3	1951	1951	PUBLICATION CONTINUED BY HARWELL
ALL TRUE ROMANCE	HARWELL (COMIC MEDIA)		4	21	1952	1955	PUBLICATION CONTINUED BY AJAX
ALL WESTERN WINNERS	MARVEL ENTERTAINMENT GROUP		2	4	1948	1949	FORMERLY ALL WINNERS, BECOMES WESTERN WINNERS
ALL WINNERS COMICS	TIMELY COMICS		1	21	1941	1947	
ALL WORLDS ALBUM	MORING		1	1	1956	1956	
ALL YOUR COMICS	FOX FEATURES SYNDICATE		1	1	1946	1946	
ALL-OUT WAR	DC COMICS INC.		1	6	1979	1980	
ALL-SORTS COMIC	SCION		1	1	1948	1948	
ALLEY CAT	C M PUBLISHING		1	1	1993	NOW	
ALLEY OOP	ARGO PUBLISHING		1	3	1955	1956	
ALLEY OOP	DELL PUBLISHING COMPANY		1	2	1962	1963	
ALLEY OOP	STANDARD COMICS	10	18	1947	1949	
ALLY SLOPER	ALAN CLASS AND CO LTD		1	4	1976	1977	
ALLY SLOPER	D. MCKENZIE		1	1	1948	1948	
ALLY SLOPER	SLOPERIES, THE		1571	1679	1914	1916	FORMERLY ALLY SLOPER'S HALF HOLIDAY
ALLY SLOPER ANNUAL	JUDY OFFICE		1873	1888	1873	1888	
ALLY SLOPER'S CHRISTMAS HOLIDAYS	SLOPERIES, THE		1884	1913	1884	1913	
ALLY SLOPER'S COMIC KALENDER	JUDY OFFICE		1875	1887	1875	1887	
ALLY SLOPER'S COMIC VOLUME	SLOPERIES, THE		1	1	1913	1913	REPRINTS
ALLY SLOPER'S HA'PORTH	GILBERT DALZIEL		1	10	1899	1899	
ALLY SLOPER'S HALF HOLIDAY	ALLY SLOPER PRODUCTIONS		1	1	1949	1949	
ALLY SLOPER'S HALF HOLIDAY	SLOPERIES, THE	1	1	1570	1884	1913	
ALLY SLOPER'S HALF HOLIDAY	SLOPERIES, THE	2	1	23	1922	1923	
ALLY SLOPER'S QUARTERLY	GILBERT DALZIEL		1	12	NN	NN	
ALLY SLOPER'S SUMMER NUMBER	JUDY OFFICE		1880	1887	1880	1887	
ALMURIC	DARK HORSE COMICS				1991	1991	
ALONG THE FIRING LINE WITH ROGER BEAN	CHAS B JACKSON		1	1	1916	1916	
ALPHA FLIGHT	MARVEL ENTERTAINMENT GROUP		1	130	1983	NOW	
ALPHA FLIGHT ANNUAL	MARVEL ENTERTAINMENT GROUP		1	2	1986	NOW	
ALPHA FLIGHT SPECIAL	MARVEL ENTERTAINMENT GROUP		1	1	1992	1992	
ALPHA FLIGHT SPECIAL	MARVEL ENTERTAINMENT GROUP		1	4	1991	1991	
ALPHA OMEGA COLLECTION	ANACOM		1	1	1988	1988	
ALPHA TRACK	FANTAGOR		1	2	1985	1985	
ALPHONSE AND GASTON AND LEON	HEARST'S NEW YORK AMERICAN AND JOURNAL		1	1	1903	1903	
ALTER EGO	FIRST		1	4	1986	1986	
ALVIN	DELL PUBLISHING COMPANY		1	28	1962	1963	
ALVIN AND THE CHIPMUNKS	HARVEY PUBLICATIONS		1	4	1993	NOW	
ALVIN FOR PRESIDENT	DELL PUBLISHING COMPANY		1	1	1964	1964	
AMAZING ADULT FANTASY	MARVEL ENTERTAINMENT GROUP		7	14	1961		FORMERLY AMAZING ADVENTURES, ... FANTASY
AMAZING ADVENTURE FUNNIES	CENTAUR PUBL						
AMAZING ADVENTURES	MARVEL ENTER						
AMAZING ADVENTURES	MARVEL ENTER						
AMAZING ADVENTURES	MARVEL ENTER						
AMAZING ADVENTURES	MARVEL ENTER						
AMAZING ADVENTURES	ZIFF-DAVIS PUBLISHING						
AMAZING CHAN AND THE CHAN CLAN, THE	GOLD KEY			4	1973	1974	
AMAZING COMICS	MODERM FICTION		1	1	1949	1949	
AMAZING COMICS	TIMELY COMICS		1	1	1944	1944	
AMAZING COMICS PREMIERES	AMAZING PUBLISHING COMPANY		1	4	1987	NOW	
AMAZING CYNICAL MAN	ECLIPSE		1	1	1987	1987	
AMAZING DETECTIVE CASES	ATLAS		3	14	1950	1952	FORMERLY SUSPENSE
AMAZING FANTASY	MARVEL ENTERTAINMENT GROUP		15	15	1962	1962	FORMERLY AMAZING ADULT FANTASY
AMAZING GHOST STORIES	ST JOHN PUBLISHING		14	16	1954	1955	FORMERLY NIGHTMARE
AMAZING HEROES	AMAZING HEROES		1	1	1993	NOW	
AMAZING HEROES	FANTAGRAPHICS		1	203	1981	NOW	
AMAZING HEROES INTERVIEWS	FANTAGRAPHICS		1	4	1993	NOW	

COMIC TITLE	PUBLISHER	Vol No.	Srt No.	End No.	Str. Year	End Year	COMMENTS
AMAZING HEROES PREVIEW SPECIAL	FANTAGRAPHICS		1	11	1985	NOW	
AMAZING HEROES SWIMSUIT SPECIAL	AMAZING HEROES		1	1	1993	NOW	FORMERLY PUBLISHED BY FANTAGRAPHICS
AMAZING HEROES SWIMSUIT SPECIAL	FANTAGRAPHICS		1	4	1992	NOW	
AMAZING HIGH ADVENTURE	MARVEL ENTERTAINMENT GROUP		1	5	1984	1987	
AMAZING MAN COMICS	CENTAUR PUBLICATIONS			27	1939	1942	
AMAZING MYSTERIES	MARVEL ENTERTAINMENT GROUP		32	35	1949	1950	FORMERLY SUBMARINER COMICS
AMAZING MYSTERY FUNNIES	CENTAUR PUBLICATIONS	1	1	4	1938	1938	
AMAZING MYSTERY FUNNIES	CENTAUR PUBLICATIONS	2	1	12	1938	1939	
AMAZING MYSTERY FUNNIES	CENTAUR PUBLICATIONS	3	1	24	1940	1940	ISSUES 2-17 DO NOT EXIST
AMAZING SPIDER-MAN	MARVEL ENTERTAINMENT GROUP		1	387	1963	NOW	
AMAZING SPIDER-MAN	MARVEL ENTERTAINMENT GROUP	2	1	4	1993	NOW	
AMAZING SPIDER-MAN (CANADIAN EDITION)	MARVEL ENTERTAINMENT GROUP		1	4	1990	1993	
AMAZING SPIDER-MAN (GIVEAWAY)	MARVEL ENTERTAINMENT GROUP		1979	1980	1979	1980	
AMAZING SPIDER-MAN AIM TOOTHPASTE GIVEAWAY	MARVEL ENTERTAINMENT GROUP				1980	1980	
AMAZING SPIDER-MAN ALL DETERGENT GIVEAWAY	MARVEL ENTERTAINMENT GROUP		1	1	1979	1979	
AMAZING SPIDER-MAN ANNUAL	MARVEL ENTERTAINMENT GROUP		1	27	1964	NOW	
AMAZING SPIDER-MAN GIANT SIZE	MARVEL ENTERTAINMENT GROUP		1	6	1974	1975	
AMAZING SPIDER-MAN, THE OFFICIAL MARVEL INDEX TO	MARVEL ENTERTAINMENT GROUP		1	9	1985	1985	
AMAZING SPIDER-MAN: ASSASSINATION PLOT	MARVEL ENTERTAINMENT GROUP		1	1	1992	1992	
AMAZING SPIDER-MAN: DEATH OF JEAN DEWOLFF	MARVEL ENTERTAINMENT GROUP		1	1	1991	1991	
AMAZING SPIDER-MAN: FEAR ITSELF	MARVEL ENTERTAINMENT GROUP		1	1	1992	1992	
AMAZING SPIDER-MAN: HOOKY	MARVEL ENTERTAINMENT GROUP		1	1	1986	1986	
AMAZING SPIDER-MAN: KRAVENS LAST HUNT	MARVEL ENTERTAINMENT GROUP		1	1	1990	1990	
AMAZING SPIDER-MAN: PARALLEL LIVES	MARVEL ENTERTAINMENT GROUP		1	1	1990	1990	
AMAZING SPIDER-MAN: SOUL OF THE HUNTER	MARVEL ENTERTAINMENT GROUP		1	1	1992	1992	
AMAZING SPIDER-MAN: SPIRITS OF THE EARTH	MARVEL ENTERTAINMENT GROUP		1	1	1992	1992	
AMAZING SPIDER-MAN: THE WEDDING	MARVEL ENTERTAINMENT GROUP		1	1	1991	1991	
AMAZING SPIDER-MAN: TORMENT	MARVEL ENTERTAINMENT GROUP		1	1	1992	1992	
AMAZING STORIES	ALAN CLASS AND CO LTD			11	60'S	60'S	US REPRINTS
AMAZING STORIES OF SUSPENSE	ALAN CLASS AND CO LTD		1	79?	60'S	60'S	US REPRINTS
AMAZING STRIP	ANTARTIC PRESS		1	2	1994	NOW	
AMAZING WAHZOO	SOLSON		1	6	1986	1987	
AMAZING WILLIE MAYS, THE	SOLSON		1	1	1954	1954	
AMAZING WORLD OF DC	DC COMICS INC.		1	17	1974	1978	
AMAZON ATTACKS 3-D	3-D COMICS		1	1	1990	1990	
AMAZON, THE	COMICO		1	3	1989	1989	
AMBUSH BUG	DC COMICS INC.		1	4	1985	1985	
AMBUSH BUG NOTHING SPECIAL	DC COMICS INC.		1	1	1992	1992	
AMBUSH BUG STOCKING STUFFER	DC COMICS INC.		1	1	1986	1986	
AMERICA IN ACTION	DELL PUBLISHING COMPANY		1	1	1942	1942	
AMERICA IN ACTION	MAYFLOWER HOUSE PUBLICATIONS		1	1	1945	1945	
AMERICA MENACED!	VITAL PUBLICATIONS		1	1	1950	1950	
AMERICA VS JUSTICE SOCIETY AMERICA	DC COMICS INC.		1	4	1985	1985	
AMERICA'S BEST COMICS	STANDARD COMICS		1	31	1942	1949	
AMERICA'S BEST TV COMICS	MARVEL ENTERTAINMENT GROUP		1	1	1967	1967	
AMERICA'S BIGGEST COMICS BOOK	WILLIAM H. WISE		1	1	1944	1944	
AMERICA'S FUNNIEST COMICS	WILLIAM H. WISE		1	2	1944	1944	
AMERICA'S GREATEST COMICS	FAWCETT PUBLICATIONS		1	8	1941	1943	
AMERICAN AIRFORCES, THE	MAGAZINE ENTERPRISES	5		12	1951	1954	
AMERICAN AIRFORCES, THE	WILLIAM H. WISE		1	4	1944	1945	PUBLICATION CONTINUED BY MAGAZINE ENTERPRISES
AMERICAN COMIC ANNUAL	L. MILLER PUBLISHING COMPANY (UK)		1	1	1943	1943	US REPRINTS
AMERICAN EAGLE	STRATO		1	1	1954	1954	US REPRINTS
AMERICAN FLAGG	FIRST	1	1	50	1983	1988	
AMERICAN FLAGG	FIRST	2	1	12	1988	1989	
AMERICAN FLAGG SPECIAL	FIRST		1	1	1986	1986	
AMERICAN FREAK: A TALE OF THE UN-MEN	DC COMICS INC.		1	1	1993	1994	
AMERICAN GRAPHICS	HENRY STEWART		1	2	1954	1957	
AMERICAN LIBRARY	DAVID MCKAY PUBLICATIONS	3	6		1944	1944	
AMERICAN SPECIAL	DARK HORSE COMICS		1	1	1990	1990	
AMERICAN SPLENDOR	PEKAR		1	17	1991	NOW	
AMERICAN TAIL: FIEVEL GOES WEST	MARVEL ENTERTAINMENT GROUP		1	3	1992	1992	
AMERICAN, THE	DARK HORSE COMICS		1	2	1990	1990	
AMERICAN, THE	DARK HORSE COMICS		1	8	1987	1989	
AMERICAN: LOST IN AMERICA	DARK HORSE COMICS		1	4	1993	1993	
AMERICAS PRINTMAKERS	CALIBER PRESS		1	1	1991	1991	
AMERICOMICS	AC COMICS		1	6	1983	1984	
AMERICOMICS SPECIAL	AMERICOMICS		1	1	1983	1983	
AMETHYST	DC COMICS INC.		1	16	1985	1986	
AMETHYST	DC COMICS INC.		1	4	1987	1988	
AMETHYST SPECIAL	DC COMICS INC.		1	1	1986	1986	
AMETHYST, PRINCESS OF GEMWOR...	DC COMICS INC.		1	12	1983	1984	
			1	1	1984	1984	
			1	1	1993	1993	
			1	3	1986	1986	
			1	2	1990	1991	
					1988	1988	
ANCHORS ANDREWS			1	4	1953	1953	
ANDERSON PSI DIVISION	FLEE...		1	1	1991	1991	
ANDREW VACHSS' UNDERGROUND	DARK HORSE COMICS		1	1	1993	NOW	
ANDROMEDA	SILVER SNAIL		1	7	1977	1979	
ANDY CAPP	MIRROR PRESS PUBLICATIONS		1	53	1958	1979	
ANDY CAPP, AFTER A FEW	RAVETTE BOOKS		1	1	1992	1992	
ANDY CAPP, DON'T WAIT UP	RAVETTE BOOKS		1	1	1992	1992	
ANDY CAPP, THE CREAM OF	MIRROR PRESS PUBLICATIONS		1	1	1965	1965	
ANDY CAPP, THE WORLD OF	TITAN BOOKS		1	1	1990	1990	
ANDY CAPP, THIS IS YOUR LIFE	MIRROR PRESS PUBLICATIONS		1	1	1986	1986	
ANDY CAPP, YOU'RE A STAR	MIRROR PRESS PUBLICATIONS		1	1	1988	1988	
ANDY COMICS	ACE MAGAZINES		20	21	1948	1948	FORMERLY SCREAM COMICS, BECOMES ERNIE COMICS

INDEX OF COMIC TITLES AND THEIR PUBLISHERS

COMIC TITLE	PUBLISHER	Vol No.	Srt No.	End No.	Str. Year	End Year	COMMENTS
ANDY DEVINE	L. MILLER PUBLISHING COMPANY (UK)		50	51	1950	1950	REPRINTS FAWCETT SERIES
ANDY DEVINE WESTERN	FAWCETT PUBLICATIONS		1	2	1950	1951	
ANDY HARDY COMICS	DELL PUBLISHING COMPANY		5	6	1954	1954	
ANDY HARDY GIVEAWAY	BENDIX WASHING MACHINES		1	1	1952	1952	
ANDY PANDA	DELL PUBLISHING COMPANY		16	56	1943	1962	
ANGEL	DELL PUBLISHING COMPANY		2	16	1952	1962	
ANGEL AND THE APE	DC COMICS INC.		1	4	1991	1991	
ANGEL AND THE APE	DC COMICS INC.		1	6	1968	1969	BECOMES "MEET ANGEL" WITH ISSUE #7 (FINAL ISSUE)
ANGEL LOVE	DC COMICS INC.		1	10	1986	1987	
ANGEL LOVE SPECIAL	DC COMICS INC.		1	1	1987	1987	
ANGEL OF DEATH	INNOVATION		1	4	1991	1991	
ANGELIC ANGELINA	CUPPLES AND LEON CO.		1	1	1909	1909	
ANGELS ANNUAL, THE	CENTURY 21		1	1	1967	1967	
ANGELS STORYBOOK, THE	CENTURY 21		1	1	1968	1968	
ANGRY SHADOWS	INNOVATION		1	2	1989	1989	
ANGRYMAN	CALIBER PRESS		1	3	1993	NOW	
ANIMA	DC COMICS INC.		1	4	1994	NOW	
ANIMAL ADVENTURES	TIMOR PUBLISHING COMPANY		1	3	1953	1954	
ANIMAL ANTICS	DC COMICS INC.		1	23	1946	1949	BECOMES MOVIE TOWN
ANIMAL COMICS	DELL PUBLISHING COMPANY		1	30	1941	1948	
ANIMAL CONFIDENTIAL	DARK HORSE COMICS		1	1	1992	1992	
ANIMAL CRACKERS	FOX FEATURES SYNDICATE		1	1	1959	1959	
ANIMAL CRACKERS	GREEN PUBLISHING COMPANY		1	10	1946	1950	
ANIMAL FABLES	EC COMICS		1	7	1946	1947	
ANIMAL FAIR	FAWCETT PUBLICATIONS		1	11	1946	1947	
ANIMAL FUN	PREMIER MAGAZINES		1	1	1953	1953	
ANIMAL MAN	DC COMICS INC.		1	1	1991	1991	
ANIMAL MAN	DC COMICS INC.		1	68	1988	NOW	
ANIMAL MAN ANNUAL	DC COMICS INC.		1	1	1993	NOW	
ANIMAL WEIRDNESS	H. BUNCH ASSOCIATES		1	1	1974	1974	
ANIMATED COMICS	EC COMICS		1	1	1947	1947	
ANIMATED MOVIE-TUNES	TIMELY COMICS		1	2	1945	1946	BECOMES MOVIE-TUNES
ANIMATION MAGAZINE	ANIMATION MAGAZINE	6	1	6	1992	1993	
ANIMAX	MARVEL ENTERTAINMENT GROUP		1	10	1986	1987	
ANIME SHOWER SPECIAL	NEW ORDER PUBLICATIONS		1	1	1990	1990	
ANIME!	TITAN BOOKS		1	1	1993	1993	
ANIME: A BEGINNER'S GUIDE TO JAPANESE ANIMATION	TITAN BOOKS		1	1	1993	1993	
ANIMERICA	VIZ	0	1	10	1993	1993	
ANNIE OAKLEY	ATLAS		1	11	1948	1956	
ANNIE OAKLEY	L. MILLER PUBLISHING COMPANY (UK)		1	17	1957	1958	US REPRINTS
ANNIE OAKLEY AND TAGG	DELL PUBLISHING COMPANY		4	18	1953	1959	
ANNIE OAKLEY AND TAGG	GOLD KEY		1	1	1965	1965	
ANNIE OAKLEY AND TAGG	WORLD DISTRIBUTORS LTD		1	10	1955	1956	REPRINTS DELL SERIES
ANNIE THE MOVIE	MARVEL ENTERTAINMENT GROUP		1	3	1982	1982	
ANOTHER CHANCE TO GET IT RIGHT	DARK HORSE COMICS		1	1	1993	1993	
ANT BOY	STEEL DRAGON		1	2	1987	1987	
ANTHRO	DC COMICS INC.		1	6	1968	1969	
ANTI HITLER COMICS	NEW COMICS GROUP		1	1	1992	1992	
ANXIETY TIMES	ECLIPSE		1	1	1992	1992	
ANYTHING GOES	FANTAGRAPHICS		1	6	1986	1987	
APACHE	FICTION HOUSE		1	1	1951	1951	
APACHE	I.W. ENTERPRISES		1	1	1950'S	1950'S	
APACHE DICK	ETERNITY		1	4	1990	1990	
APACHE HUNTER	CREATIVE PICTORIALS		1	1	1954	1954	
APACHE KID	ATLAS		11	19	1954	1956	CONTINUED FROM MEDALION SERIES
APACHE KID	MEDALION PUBLISHING CORPORATION		1	10	1950	1952	ISSUE #53 WAS #1
APACHE KID	STREAMLINE		1	10	1951	1951	
APACHE PICTURE AND STORY ALBUM	MELLIFONT		1	1	50'S	50'S	
APACHE TRAIL	STEINWAY/AMERICA'S BEST		1	4	1957	1958	
APE CITY	ADVENTURE COMICS		1	4	1990	1990	
APE NATION	ADVENTURE COMICS		1	4	1991	1991	
APPLESEED	ECLIPSE		1	4	1991	NOW	
APPLESEED	ECLIPSE	1	1	5	1988	1989	
APPLESEED	ECLIPSE	2	1	5	1989	1989	
APPLESEED	ECLIPSE	3	1	5	1989	1990	
APPLESEED	ECLIPSE	4	1	4	1991	1991	
APPLESEED DATABOOK	DARK HORSE COMICS		1	2	1994	1994	
APPROVED COMICS	ST JOHN PUBLISHING		1	12	1954	1954	
APULHEAD LIVES	APULHEAD PRODUCTIONS		1	1	1976	1976	
AQUABLUE	DARK HORSE COMICS				1989	1989	
AQUABLUE: THE BLUE PLANET	DARK HORSE COMICS				1990	1990	
AQUAMAN	DC COMICS INC.	1	1	4	1986	1986	
AQUAMAN	DC COMICS INC.	1	1	63	1962	1971	
AQUAMAN	DC COMICS INC.	2	1	13	1991	1992	
AQUAMAN	DC COMICS INC.	2	1	5	1989	1989	
AQUAMAN SPECIAL	DC COMICS INC.		1	1	1988	1988	
AQUAMAN: TIME & TIDE	DC COMICS INC.		1	2	1993	1994	
ARACHNAPHOBIA MOVIE ADAPTATION	WALT DISNEY		1	1	1990	1990	
ARAK SON OF THUNDER	DC COMICS INC.		1	50	1981	1985	
ARAK SON OF THUNDER ANNUAL	DC COMICS INC.		1	1	1984	1984	
ARBH: LOST TREASURES	PARODY PRESS		1	1	1992	1992	
ARCADE THE COMICS REVUE	PRINT MINT INC		1	4	1974	1974	
ARCANA ANNUAL	DC COMICS INC.		1	1	1993	1993	
ARCANE COMIX	ARCANE BOOKS		1	5	1987	1991	
ARCHER AND ARMSTRONG	VALIANT / VOYAGER COMMUNICATIONS		0	21	1992	NOW	ISSUE 8 WAS A JOINT COMIC WITH ETERNAL WARRIOR 8
ARCHER AND ARMSTRONG/ETERNAL WARRIOR	VALIANT / VOYAGER COMMUNICATIONS		8	8	1992	1992	
ARCHIE	ARCHIE PUBLICATIONS		1	421	1942	NOW	ISSUES 1-157 HAVE ARCHIE COMICS ON THE COVER

INDEX OF COMIC TITLES AND THEIR PUBLISHERS

COMIC TITLE	PUBLISHER	Vol No.	Srt No.	End No.	Str. Year	End Year	COMMENTS
ARCHIE	GERALD SWAN		1	?	1950	1953	REPRINTS OF US ARCHIE STRIPS
ARCHIE 3000	ARCHIE PUBLICATIONS		1	19	1989	1991	
ARCHIE AND FRIENDS	ARCHIE PUBLICATIONS		1	7	1992	NOW	
ARCHIE AND ME	ARCHIE PUBLICATIONS		1	162	1964	1987	
ARCHIE AND MR. WEATHERBEE	SPIRE CHRISTIAN COMICS		1	1	1980	1980	
ARCHIE ANNUAL	ARCHIE PUBLICATIONS		1	26	1950	1975	
ARCHIE AS PUREHEART THE POWERFUL	ARCHIE PUBLICATIONS		1	6	1966	1967	
ARCHIE AT RIVERDALE HIGH	ARCHIE PUBLICATIONS		1	114	1972	1987	
ARCHIE COMICS	THORPE & PORTER		1	?	1953	???	REPRINTS OF US ARCHIE STRIPS
ARCHIE COMICS DIGEST	ARCHIE PUBLICATIONS		1	126	1973	NOW	
ARCHIE DIGEST ANNUAL	ARCHIE PUBLICATIONS		59	62	1975	1993	
ARCHIE DRUG STORE GIVEAWAY	ARCHIE PUBLICATIONS		1	1	1958	1958	
ARCHIE GIANT SERIES MAGAZINE	ARCHIE PUBLICATIONS		1	632	1954	NOW	
ARCHIE OFFICIAL BOY SCOUT OUTFITTER GIVEAWAY	ARCHIE PUBLICATIONS		1	1	1946	1946	
ARCHIE SHOE STORE GIVEAWAY	ARCHIE PUBLICATIONS				1944	1949	
ARCHIE'S ACTIVITY COMICS DIGEST MAGAZINE ANNUAL	ARCHIE PUBLICATIONS		1	4	1985	1985	
ARCHIE'S CHRISTMAS STOCKING	ARCHIE PUBLICATIONS		1	1	1993	1993	
ARCHIE'S DOUBLE DIGEST MAGAZINE	ARCHIE PUBLICATIONS		1	70	1981	NOW	
ARCHIE'S GIRLS BETTY AND VERONICA	ARCHIE PUBLICATIONS		1	347	1950	1987	BECOMES BETTY AND VERONICA
ARCHIE'S GIRLS BETTY AND VERONICA ANNUAL	ARCHIE PUBLICATIONS		1	8	1953	1960	
ARCHIE'S JOKE BOOK MAGAZINE	ARCHIE PUBLICATIONS		1	288	1953	1982	
ARCHIE'S MADHOUSE	ARCHIE PUBLICATIONS		1	66	1959	1969	
ARCHIE'S MADHOUSE ANNUAL	ARCHIE PUBLICATIONS		1	6	1962	1969	
ARCHIE'S MECHANICS	ARCHIE PUBLICATIONS		1	3	1954	1955	
ARCHIE'S PAL, JUGHEAD	ARCHIE PUBLICATIONS		1	126	1949	1965	
ARCHIE'S PAL, JUGHEAD ANNUAL	ARCHIE PUBLICATIONS		1	8	1953	1960	
ARCHIE'S PALS 'N' GALS	ARCHIE PUBLICATIONS		1	231	1952	1992	
ARCHIE'S PALS 'N' GALS DOUBLE DIGEST MAGAZINE	ARCHIE PUBLICATIONS		1	4	1993	NOW	
ARCHIE'S PARABLES	SPIRE CHRISTIAN COMICS				1973	1975	
ARCHIE'S R/C RACERS	ARCHIE PUBLICATIONS		1	10	1989	1991	
ARCHIE'S RIVAL REGGIE	ARCHIE PUBLICATIONS		1	14	1950	1954	
ARCHIE'S STORY AND GAME COMIC DIGEST MAGAZINE	ARCHIE PUBLICATIONS		1	29	1986	NOW	
ARCHIE'S SUPERHERO SPECIAL	ARCHIE PUBLICATIONS		1	2	1979	1979	
ARCHIE'S TV LAUGH OUT	ARCHIE PUBLICATIONS		1	106	1969	1986	
ARCHIE...ARCHIE ANDREWS, WHERE ARE YOU? DIGEST	ARCHIE PUBLICATIONS		1	91	1977	NOW	
AREA 88	ECLIPSE		1	44	1987	1989	
AREA 88	VIZ		1	2	1991	1991	
ARGONAUTS	ETERNITY		1	5	1991	NOW	
ARGOSY	CALIBER PRESS		1	1	1991	1991	
ARIANE AND BLUEBEARD	ECLIPSE		1	1	1989	1989	
ARIEL	WALT DISNEY		1	4	1992	1992	
ARIEL AND SEBASTIAN: SERPENT TEEN	WALT DISNEY		1	1	1992	1992	CARTOON TALES
ARIK KHAN	A PLUS COMICS		1	3	1991	1992	
ARIK KHAN	SILVER SNAIL		1	3	1977	1979	
ARION THE IMMORTAL	DC COMICS INC.		1	6	1992	1992	
ARION, LORD OF ATLANTIS	DC COMICS INC.		1	35	1982	1985	
ARION, LORD OF ATLANTIS SPECIAL	DC COMICS INC.		1	1	1985	1985	
ARISTOCRATIC X-T.T. THIEVES	COMICS INTERVIEW		1	11	1986	1987	
ARISTOCRATIC X-TRATERRESTRIAL T.T. THIEVES SPECIAL	COMICS INTERVIEW		1	1	1986	1986	
ARISTOKITTENS, THE	GOLD KEY		1	9	1971	1975	
ARIZONA KID, THE	ATLAS		1	6	1951	1952	
ARIZONA KID, THE	STREAMLINE		1	1	1952	1952	US REPRINTS
ARMAGEDDON 2001	DC COMICS INC.		1	2	1991	1991	
ARMAGEDDON FACTOR, THE	AC COMICS		1	2	1987	1990	
ARMAGEDDON: ALIEN AGENDA	DC COMICS INC.		1	4	1991	1992	
ARMAGEDDON: INFERNO	DC COMICS INC.		1	4	1992	1992	
ARMITAGE	FLEETWAY		1	2	1993	1993	
ARMOR	CONTINUITY COMICS		1	13	1987	NOW	
ARMOR	CONTINUITY COMICS	2	1	6	1993	NOW	
ARMOR AND SILVER STREAK	CONTINUITY COMICS		1	6	1985	1985	
ARMORINES	VALIANT / VOYAGER COMMUNICATIONS		1	2	1994	NOW	
ARMOURED GIDEON	FLEETWAY				1991	1991	
ARMY AND NAVY COMICS	STREET AND SMITH PUBLICATIONS		1	5	1941	1942	BECOMES SUPERSNIPE
ARMY AT WAR	DC COMICS INC.		1	1	1978	1978	
ARMY ATTACK	CHARLTON COMICS	1	1	4	1964	1965	
ARMY ATTACK	CHARLTON COMICS	2	38	47	1965	1967	
ARMY OF DARKNESS	DARK HORSE COMICS		1	2	1993	1993	
ARMY SURPLUS KOMIKZ FEATURING CUTEY BUNNY	ECLIPSE		1	5	1982	1985	
ARMY WAR HEROES	CHARLTON COMICS		1	38	1963	1970	
ARRGH!	MARVEL ENTERTAINMENT GROUP		1	5	1974	1975	
ARROW, THE	CENTAUR PUBLICATIONS		1	3	1940	1941	
ARROW, THE	MALIBU COMICS ENTERTAINMENT INC.		1	1	1992	1992	
ARROWHEAD	ATLAS		1	4	1954	1954	
ARROWHEAD	STREAMLINE		1	2	1954	1954	US REPRINTS
ART ATTACK	VISUAL RECORDS		1	1	1977	1977	
ART OF HOMAGE STUDIOS	IMAGE COMICS		1	1	1993	1993	
ART OF JOHN BUSCEMA, THE	SAL Q PRODUCTIONS	1	1	1	1978	1978	
ART OF WALT SIMONSON	DC COMICS INC.		1	1	1989	1989	
ARTHUR JERMYN	CALIBER PRESS		1	1	1993	1993	
ARTHUR, KING OF BRITAIN	CALIBER PRESS		1	1	1993	1994	
ASHES	CALIBER PRESS		1	5	1990	1991	
ASPECT	STEVE MOORE		1	2	1969	1970	
ASSASSIN	TSR	1	1	4	1990	1991	
ASSASSIN	TSR	2	1	1	1992	1992	
ASSASSIN FORCE	GREATER MERCURY COMICS		1	2	1992	NOW	
ASSASSINS INC.	SILVERLINE COMICS		1	4	1987	1987	

201

COMIC TITLE	PUBLISHER	Vol No.	Srt No.	End No.	Str. Year	End Year	COMMENTS
ASTERIX	HODDER AND STOUGHTON/DARGUAD		1	32	1969	NOW	
ASTERIX ADVENTURE GAME BOOKS	HODDER AND STOUGHTON/DARGUAD		1	4	1986	1990	
ASTERIX AND THE ROMANS	HODDER AND STOUGHTON/DARGUAD		1	1	1986	1986	
ASTERIX THE BRAVE	HODDER AND STOUGHTON/DARGUAD		1	1	1987	1987	
ASTERIX THE GAUL	HODDER AND STOUGHTON/DARGUAD		1	1	1985	1985	
ASTONISHING	ATLAS		3	63	1951	1957	FORMERLY MARVEL BOY
ASTONISHING STORIES	ALAN CLASS AND CO LTD				60'S	60'S	REPRINTS US STRIPS
ASTONISHING TALES	MARVEL ENTERTAINMENT GROUP		1	36	1970	1976	
ASTOUNDING STORIES	ALAN CLASS AND CO LTD		1	195	1966	1989	REPRINTS US MATERIAL
ASTRO BOY	GOLD KEY		1	1	1965	1965	
ASTRO BOY'S WAVE WARRIORS	NOW		1	1	1987	1987	
ASTRO BOY, THE ORIGINAL	NOW		1	19	1987	1988	
ASTRO COMICS GIVEAWAY	HARVEY PUBLICATIONS		1		1969	1979	AMERICAN AIRLINE GIVEAWAYS
ASYLUM	MILLENIUM		1	2	1993	NOW	
ASYLUM	NEW COMICS GROUP		1	1	1989	NOW	
ATARI FORCE	DC COMICS INC.		1	20	1982	1985	
ATARI FORCE SPECIAL	DC COMICS INC.		1	1	1986	1986	
ATLANTIS CHRONICLES	DC COMICS INC.		1	7	1990	1990	
ATLAS	DARK HORSE COMICS		1	4	1994	1994	
ATLAS TO THE DC UNIVERSE	DC COMICS INC.		1	1	1990	1990	
ATOM AND HAWKMAN	DC COMICS INC.		39	45	1968	1969	
ATOM ANT	GOLD KEY		1	1	1966	1966	
ATOM SPECIAL	DC COMICS INC.		1	1	1993	1993	
ATOM THE CAT	CHARLTON COMICS		9	17	1957	1959	
ATOM, THE	BUCHANON BOOKS		1	1	1947	1947	
ATOM, THE	DC COMICS INC.		1	38	1962	1968	
ATOM-AGE COMBAT	FAGO PUBLICATIONS		1	3	1958	1959	
ATOM-AGE COMBAT	ST JOHN PUBLISHING		1	1	1958	1958	
ATOM-AGE COMBAT	ST JOHN PUBLISHING		1	5	1952	1953	
ATOMAN	SPARK PUBLICATION		1	2	1946	1946	
ATOMIC AGE	MARVEL ENTERTAINMENT GROUP		1	4	1990	1991	
ATOMIC AGE COMIC, THE	ALGAR/L. BURN		1	1	1947	1947	
ATOMIC BOMB	JAY BURTIS PUBLICATIONS		1	1	1945	1945	
ATOMIC BUNNY	CHARLTON COMICS		12	19	1958	1959	FORMERLY ATOMIC RABBIT
ATOMIC COMIC	FUDGE		1	1	1947	1947	
ATOMIC COMICS	DANIELS PUBLICATIONS		1	4	1946	1946	
ATOMIC COMICS	GREEN PUBLISHING COMPANY		1	4	1946	1946	
ATOMIC COMICS	MUTANT ENTERPRISES		1	1	1975	1975	
ATOMIC MAN COMICS	BLACKTHORNE		1	3	1986	1987	
ATOMIC MOUSE	A PLUS COMICS		1	3	1991	NOW	REPRINTS OF CHARLTON SERIES
ATOMIC MOUSE	CHARLTON COMICS	1	1	54	1953	1963	
ATOMIC MOUSE	CHARLTON COMICS	2	1	13	1984	1986	RAN FROM ISSUE 1#, THEN RESTARTED FROM ISSUE 10#
ATOMIC MOUSE	L. MILLER PUBLISHING COMPANY (UK)		1	4	1953	1953	REPRINTS CHARLTON MATERIAL
ATOMIC RABBIT	CHARLTON COMICS		1	11	1955	1958	
ATOMIC SPY CASES	AVON BOOKS		1	1	1950	1950	
ATOMIC SPY RING	HOTSPUR PUBLISHING CO.		6	6	1949	1949	
ATOMIC THUNDERBOLT, THE	REGOR COMPANY		1	1	1946	1946	
ATOMIC WAR!	ACE PERIODICALS		1	4	1952	1953	
ATTACK	CHARLTON COMICS	1	54	60	1954	1960	
ATTACK	CHARLTON COMICS	2	1	3	1962	1964	
ATTACK	CHARLTON COMICS	3	1	48	1971	1984	
ATTACK	CHARLTON COMICS	4	3	5	1966	1967	
ATTACK AT SEA	CHARLTON COMICS	4	5	5	1968	1968	FORMERLY ATTACK!
ATTACK OF THE MUTANT MONSTERS	A PLUS COMICS		1	1	1991	NOW	
ATTACK ON PLANET MARS	AVON BOOKS		1	1	1951	1951	
ATTACK PICTURE LIBRARY HOLIDAY SPECIAL	IPC		1	3	1982	1984	
ATTACK!	FAME PRESS		1	2	1962	1962	REPRINTS ITALIAN MATERIAL
AUDREY AND MELVIN	HARVEY PUBLICATIONS		62	62	1974	1974	FORMERLY LITTLE AUDREY AND MELVIN
AUGIE DOGGIE	GOLD KEY		1	1	1963	1963	
AUGUSTA THE GREAT	BARRIE & JENKINS		1	1	1977	1977	
AUGUSTA, I	BARRIE & JENKINS		1	1	1978	1978	
AUTHENTIC POLICE CASES	R. & L. LOCKER		1	1	1949	1949	REPRINTS OF US MATERIAL
AUTHENTIC POLICE CASES	ST JOHN PUBLISHING		1	38	1948	1955	
AVALON	COMICO	1	1	4	1992	NOW	
AVALON	COMICO	2	1	4	1993	1993	
AVALON	HARRIER		1	14	1986	1988	
AVANT GUARD: HEROES AT THE FUTURE'S EDGE	DAY ONE COMICS				1994	NOW	
AVATAR	DC COMICS INC.		1	3	1991	1991	
AVENGER, THE	I.W. SUPER		9	9	1964	1964	
AVENGER, THE	MAGAZINE ENTERPRISES		1	4	1955	1955	
AVENGERS	MARVEL ENTERTAINMENT GROUP		1	371	1963	NOW	
AVENGERS ANNIVERSARY MAGAZINE	MARVEL ENTERTAINMENT GROUP		1	1	1993	1993	
AVENGERS ANNUAL	MARVEL ENTERTAINMENT GROUP		1	22	1967	NOW	
AVENGERS ANNUAL, THE	SOUVENIR/ATLAS		1967	1969	1967	1969	
AVENGERS ANNUAL, THE	WORLD DISTRIBUTORS LTD		1978	1978	1978	1978	REPRINTS MARVEL MATERIAL
AVENGERS CHRONICLES	FANTACO		1	1	1982	1982	
AVENGERS GIANT SIZE	MARVEL ENTERTAINMENT GROUP		1	5	1974	1975	
AVENGERS LOG	MARVEL ENTERTAINMENT GROUP		1	1	1993	NOW	
AVENGERS SPOTLIGHT	MARVEL ENTERTAINMENT GROUP		1	40	1987	1991	
AVENGERS STRIKE FILE	MARVEL ENTERTAINMENT GROUP		1	1	1993	1993	
AVENGERS TREASURY	MARVEL ENTERTAINMENT GROUP				1982	1982	
AVENGERS WEST COAST	MARVEL ENTERTAINMENT GROUP		1	102	1985	1993	
AVENGERS WEST COAST	MARVEL ENTERTAINMENT GROUP		1	4	1919	1984	
AVENGERS WEST COAST ANNUAL	MARVEL ENTERTAINMENT GROUP		1	8	1986	1993	
AVENGERS WINTER SPECIAL, THE	MARVEL ENTERTAINMENT GROUP		1	1	1982	1982	REPRINTS MARVEL US MATERIAL
AVENGERS, THE	GOLD KEY		1	1	1968	1968	
AVENGERS, THE	THORPE & PORTER		1	1	1966	1966	
AVENGERS, THE (UK)	MARVEL ENTERTAINMENT GROUP		1	147	1973	1976	
AVENGERS, THE OFFICIAL MARVEL INDEX TO	MARVEL ENTERTAINMENT GROUP		1	7	1987	1988	

COMIC TITLE	PUBLISHER	Vol No.	Srt No.	End No.	Str. Year	End Year	COMMENTS
AVENGERS: DEATHTRAP THE VAULT	MARVEL ENTERTAINMENT GROUP		1	1	1991	1991	
AVENGERS: EMPEROR DOOM	MARVEL ENTERTAINMENT GROUP		1	1	1987	1987	
AVENGERS: KREE SKRULL WAR	MARVEL ENTERTAINMENT GROUP		1	2	1983	1983	
AVENGERS: THE KORVAC SAGA	MARVEL ENTERTAINMENT GROUP		1	1	1990	1990	
AVENGERS: THE TERMINATRIX OBJECTIVE	MARVEL ENTERTAINMENT GROUP		1	4	1993	1993	
AVENGING WORLD	ROBIN K SNYDER		1	1	1973	1973	
AVENUE X	INNOVATION		1	1	1992	1992	
AVIATION ADVENTURES AND MODEL BUILDING	PARENTS MAGAZINE INSTITUTE		16	17	1946	1947	FORMERLY TRUE AVIATION ADVENTURES
AVIATION CADETS	STREET AND SMITH PUBLICATIONS		1	1	1943	1943	
AWFUL OSCAR	MARVEL ENTERTAINMENT GROUP		11	12	1949	1949	FORMERLY AND BECOMES OSCAR COMICS
AX	MARVEL ENTERTAINMENT GROUP		1	1	1988	1988	
AXA	ECLIPSE		1	2	1987	1987	
AXA	FIRST AMERICAN EDITION SERIES		1	1	1985	1985	
AXA	FIRST AMERICAN EDITION SERIES		1	9	1983	1988	
AXEL PRESSBUTTON	ECLIPSE		1	6	1984	1985	
AXIS ALPHA	AXIS		1	1	1994	1994	
AXIS BETA	AXIS		1	1	1994	1994	
AZ	COMICO		1	2	1983	1984	
AZTEC ACE	ECLIPSE	1	1	15	1984	1985	
AZTEC ACE	ECLIPSE	2	1	2	1992	NOW	

B

COMIC TITLE	PUBLISHER	Vol No.	Srt No.	End No.	Str. Year	End Year	COMMENTS
BABE	PRIZE/HEADLINE/FEATURE		1	11	1948	1950	
BABE AMAZON OF OZARKS	STANDARD COMICS		5	5	1948	1948	
BABE RUTH SPORTS COMICS	HARVEY PUBLICATIONS		1	11	1949	1951	
BABY BOOMER COLLECTIBLES	BABY BOOMER COLLECTIBLES		1	1	1993	NOW	
BABY HUEY	HARVEY PUBLICATIONS		1	5	1991	NOW	
BABY HUEY AND PAPA	HARVEY PUBLICATIONS		1	33	1962	1968	
BABY HUEY BIG BOOK	HARVEY PUBLICATIONS		1	1	1993	NOW	
BABY HUEY HOLIDAY SPECIAL	HARVEY PUBLICATIONS		1	1	1992	1992	
BABY HUEY IN DUCKLAND	HARVEY PUBLICATIONS		1	15	1962	1966	
BABY HUEY THE BABY GIANT	HARVEY PUBLICATIONS	1	1	100	1956	1990	
BABY HUEY THE BABY GIANT	HARVEY PUBLICATIONS	2	1	8	1992	NOW	
BABY SNOOTS	GOLD KEY		1	22	1970	1975	
BACCHUS	HARRIER		1	2	1988	1988	
BACHELOR FATHER	DELL PUBLISHING COMPANY		2	2	1962	1962	ISSUE 1 IS FOUR COLOUR 1332
BACHELOR'S DIARY	AVON BOOKS		1	1	1949	1949	
BACK TO THE FUTURE	HARVEY PUBLICATIONS		1	4	1991	1992	
BACK TO THE FUTURE: FORWARD TO THE FUTURE	HARVEY PUBLICATIONS		1	3	1992	1993	
BAD BLOOD	ATOMEKA		1	1	1993	1993	
BAD BLOOD	ATOMEKA		1	3	1993	1993	
BAD COMPANY	FLEETWAY		1	17	1988	1990	
BAD COMPANY	FLEETWAY		1	4	1987	1988	
BAD COMPANY	TITAN BOOKS		1	4	1987	1988	
BAD GIRLS GO TO HELL	AIRCEL		1	3	1992	1992	
BAD LUCK	HEROIC PUBLISHING		1	1	1993	NOW	
BAD NEWS	FANTAGRAPHICS		1	3	1988	1988	
BADAXE	ADVENTURE COMICS		1	3	1989	1989	
BADE BIKER & ORSON	MIRAGE STUDIOS		1	5	1986	1987	
BADE BIKER & ORSON COLLECTION	MIRAGE STUDIOS		1	1	1987	1987	
BADGE OF JUSTICE	CHARLTON COMICS	1	22	23	1955	1955	
BADGE OF JUSTICE	CHARLTON COMICS	2	1	4	1955	1955	
BADGER	FIRST		1	70	1983	1991	
BADGER BEDLAM	FIRST		1	1	1991	1991	
BADGER GOES BERSERK	FIRST		1	4	1989	1989	
BADLANDS	DARK HORSE COMICS		1	1	1993	1993	
BADLANDS	DARK HORSE COMICS		1	6	1991	1992	
BADMEN OF THE WEST!	AVON BOOKS		1	1	1951	1951	
BADMEN OF THE WEST!	MAGAZINE ENTERPRISES		1	3	1953	1954	
BADMEN OF TOMBSTONE	AVON BOOKS		1	1	1950	1950	
BAFFLING MYSTERIES	ACE MAGAZINES		5	26	1951	1955	FORMERLY INDIAN BRAVES
BAKER STREET	CALIBER PRESS		1	10	1989	NOW	
BAKER STREET GRAFFITI	CALIBER PRESS		1	1	1991	1991	
BAKER STREET: CHILDREN OF THE NIGHT	CALIBER PRESS		1	1	1991	1991	COLLECTS BAKER STREET #6-10
BAKER STREET: HONOUR AMONG PUNKS	CALIBER PRESS				1990	1990	COLLECTS BAKER STREET #1-5
BALDER THE BRAVE	MARVEL ENTERTAINMENT GROUP		1	4	1985	1986	
BALLOONATIKS	BEST COMICS		1	1	1991	1991	
BALOO & LITTLE BRITCHES	GOLD KEY		1	1	1968	1968	
BALTIMORE COLTS	AMERICAN VISUALS CORPORATION		1	1	1950	1950	
BAMBI	K.K. PUBLICATIONS		1941	1942	1941	1942	
BAMBI	WHITMAN		1	1	1984	1984	
BAMM BAMM & PEBBLES FLINTSTONE	GOLD KEY		1	1	1964	1964	
BANANA OIL	M.S. PUBLISHING		1	1	1924	1924	
BANANA SPLITS, THE	GOLD KEY		1	8	1969	1971	
BANG ON COMIC	PHILIMAR		1	1	1948	1948	
BANG-ON COMIC, THE	FUDGE		1	1	1947	1947	
BANG-UP COMICS	PROGRESSIVE PUBLISHERS		1	3	1941	1942	
BANNER COMICS	ACE MAGAZINES		3	5	1941	1942	
BANTAM COMICS	P.M. PRODUCTIONS		1	1	1944	1944	
BAOH	VIZ		1	10	1990	1990	
BARABBAS	SLAVE LABOR		1	4	1986	1987	
BARBARIANS	ATLAS		1	1	1975	1975	
BARBARIC TALES	PYRAMID COMICS		1	2	1987	1987	
BARBARIENNE	HARRIER		1	8	1987	1988	
BARBIE	MARVEL ENTERTAINMENT GROUP		1	37	1991	NOW	
BARBIE & KEN	DELL PUBLISHING COMPANY		1	5	1962	1964	
BARBIE FASHION	MARVEL ENTERTAINMENT GROUP		1	38	1991	NOW	

COMIC TITLE	PUBLISHER	Vol No.	Srt No.	End No.	Str. Year	End Year	COMMENTS
BAREFOOT GEN	PENGUIN BOOKS		1	2	1989	1989	
BAREFOOTZ	RENEGADE PRESS		1	1	1986	1986	
BARKER, THE	LOCKER		1	1	1949	1949	REPRINTS QUALITY US MATERIAL
BARKER, THE	QUALITY COMICS		1	15	1946	1949	
BARNEY AND BETTY RUBBLE	CHARLTON COMICS		1	23	1973	1976	
BARNEY GOOGLE & SNUFFY SMITH	GOLD KEY		1	1	1964	1964	
BARNEY GOOGLE & SNUFFY SMITH	TOBY PRESS PUBLICATIONS		1	4	1951	1952	
BARNEY GOOGLE AND SNUFFY SMITH	CHARLTON COMICS		1	6	1970	1971	
BARNEY GOOGLE AND SPARK PLUG	CUPPLES AND LEON CO.		1	6	1923	1928	
BARNYARD COMICS	STANDARD COMICS		1	31	1944	1950	
BARRY M. GOLDWATER	DELL PUBLISHING COMPANY		1	1	1965	1965	
BARTMAN	BONGO COMICS		1	1	1993	NOW	
BASEBALL COMICS	KITCHEN SINK		1	1	1991	1991	
BASEBALL COMICS	WILL EISNER		1	1	1949	1949	
BASEBALL GREATS	DARK HORSE COMICS		1	3	1992	NOW	
BASEBALL HEROES	FAWCETT PUBLICATIONS		1	1	1952	1952	
BASEBALL LEGENDS	REVOLUTIONARY COMICS		1	3	1992	1992	
BASEBALL SLUGGERS	PERSONALITY COMICS		1	3	1992	1992	
BASEBALL SUPERSTARS	REVOLUTIONARY COMICS		1	4	1992	NOW	
BASEBALL THRILLS	ZIFF-DAVIS PUBLISHING COMPANY		1	3	1951	1952	
BASEBALL TRIVIA	PERSONALITY COMICS		1	1	1992	1992	
BASEBALL'S GREATEST HEROES	MAGNUM COMICS		1	2	1991	1992	
BASH STREET KIDS BOOK ANNUAL	D.C. THOMSON		1980	1993	1980	1993	
BASIC HISTORY OF AMERICA ILLUSTRATED	PENDULUM PRESS		1	1	1976	1976	
BASICALLY STRANGE	ARCHIE PUBLICATIONS		1	1	1982	1982	
BASIL THE ROYAL CAT	ST JOHN PUBLISHING		1	4	1953	1953	
BASIL WOLVERTONS FANTASTIC FABLES	DARK HORSE COMICS		1	2	1993	1993	
BAT MASTERSON	DELL PUBLISHING COMPANY		2	9	1959	1962	
BAT, THE	ADVENTURE COMICS		1	1	1992	1992	
BAT, THE	APPLE COMICS		1	1	1990	1990	
BAT, THE	CALIBER PRESS		1	1	1991	NOW	
BATCH	DC COMICS INC.		1	1	1988	1988	
BATGIRL SPECIAL	DC COMICS INC.		1	1	1993	1993	
BATHORY: COUNTESS OF BLOOD	BONE YARD PRESS		1	1	1993	1993	
BATLASH	DC COMICS INC.		1	7	1968	1969	
BATMAN	DC COMICS INC.		1	505	1940	NOW	
BATMAN 3-D	DC COMICS INC.	2	1	1	1966	1966	
BATMAN 3-D	DC COMICS INC.	3	1	1	1990	1990	
BATMAN 3-D	TITAN BOOKS		1	1	1990	1990	
BATMAN ADVENTURES IN AMAZING 3-D	DC COMICS INC.	1			1953	1953	
BATMAN ADVENTURES MAGAZINE	DC COMICS INC.		1	2	1993	NOW	
BATMAN ADVENTURES, THE	DC COMICS INC.		1	16	1992	NOW	
BATMAN AND DRACULA: RED RAIN	DC COMICS INC.		1	1	1992	1992	
BATMAN AND GREEN ARROW: POISON TOMORROW	DC COMICS INC.		1	1	1992	1992	
BATMAN AND JUDGE DREDD: JUDGEMENT ON GOTHAM	DC COMICS INC.		1	1	1991	1991	
BATMAN AND JUDGE DREDD: JUDGEMENT ON GOTHAM	FLEETWAY	1		1	1992	1992	
BATMAN AND JUDGE DREDD: JUDGEMENT ON GOTHAM	MANDARIN (2000 AD BOOKS)		1	1	1992	1992	
BATMAN AND JUDGE DREDD: VENDETTA ON GOTHAM	DC COMICS INC.		1	1	1993	1993	
BATMAN AND OTHER DC CLASSICS	DC COMICS INC.		1	1	1989	1989	
BATMAN AND THE OUTSIDERS	DC COMICS INC.		1	32	1983	1986	BECOMES ADVENTURES OF THE OUTSIDERS WITH NO.33
BATMAN AND THE OUTSIDERS ANNUAL	DC COMICS INC.		1	2	1984	1985	
BATMAN ANNUAL	DC COMICS INC.		1	17	1961	NOW	
BATMAN ANNUAL	FLEETWAY		1960	1993	1960	NOW	REPRINTS US MATERIAL
BATMAN ARCHIVES	DC COMICS INC.		1	3	1991	NOW	
BATMAN BOOK AND RECORD	DC COMICS INC.		1	2	1974	1974	
BATMAN DARK KNIGHT ARCHIVES	DC COMICS INC.		1	1	1993	NOW	
BATMAN FAMILY, THE	DC COMICS INC.		1	20	1975	1978	
BATMAN GALLERY, THE	DC COMICS INC.		1	1	1992	1992	
BATMAN MAGAZINE	FLEETWAY		42	56	1991	1993	FORMERLY BATMAN MONTHLY, PUBLISHED BY LONDON EDITIONS
BATMAN MONTHLY	LONDON EDITIONS MAGAZINES		1	41	1990	1991	BECOMES BATMAN MAGAZINE WITH ISSUE NO. 42
BATMAN MONTHLY (UK)	FLEETWAY	2	1	3	1993	NOW	
BATMAN MOVIE ADAPTATION DELUXE	DC COMICS INC.		1	1	1989	1989	
BATMAN MOVIE ADAPTATION REGULAR	DC COMICS INC.		1	1	1989	1989	
BATMAN PIZZA HUT GIVEAWAY	DC COMICS INC.		1	1	1977	1977	
BATMAN PRELL SHAMPOO GIVEAWAY	DC COMICS INC.		1	1	1966	1966	
BATMAN RECORD COMIC	DC COMICS INC.		1	1	1966	1966	
BATMAN RETURNS MAGAZINE	DC COMICS INC.		1	1	1992	1992	
BATMAN RETURNS MOVIE ADAPTATION	DC COMICS INC.		1	1	1992	1992	
BATMAN RETURNS MOVIE ADAPTATION MAGAZINE	DC COMICS INC.		1	1	1992	1992	
BATMAN RETURNS POSTER MAGAZINE	DC COMICS INC.		1	3	1992	1992	
BATMAN SPECIAL	DC COMICS INC.		1	1	1984	1984	
BATMAN SPECIAL EDITION	FLEETWAY		1	2	1993	1993	
BATMAN STORY BOOK ANNUAL	WORLD DISTRIBUTORS LTD		1966	1967	1966	1967	
BATMAN VERSUS GRENDEL	DC COMICS INC.		1	2	1993	1993	
BATMAN VS PREDATOR	DC COMICS INC.		1	1	1993	1993	
BATMAN VS PREDATOR	DC COMICS INC.		1	3	1991	1992	
BATMAN VS THE INCREDIBLE - SEE DC SPECIAL SERIES							
BATMAN WORLD ADVENTURE LIBRARY	WORLD DISTRIBUTORS LTD		1	10	1966	1967	
BATMAN/DRACULA: RED RAIN	DC COMICS INC.		1	1	1992	1992	
BATMAN/DRACULA: RED RAIN	TITAN BOOKS		1	1	1992	1992	
BATMAN/HOUDINI: THE DEVIL'S WORKSHOP	DC COMICS INC.		1	1	1993	1993	
BATMAN/SPAWN: WAR DEVIL	DC COMICS INC.		1	1	1994	1994	
BATMAN: A DEATH IN THE FAMILY	DC COMICS INC.		1	1	1988	1988	
BATMAN: A DEATH IN THE FAMILY	TITAN BOOKS		1	1	1988	1988	
BATMAN: A LONELY PLACE OF DYING	DC COMICS INC.		1	1	1990	1990	

INDEX OF COMIC TITLES AND THEIR PUBLISHERS

COMIC TITLE	PUBLISHER	Vol No.	Srt No.	End No.	Str. Year	End Year	COMMENTS
BATMAN: ARKHAM ASYLUM	DC COMICS INC.		1	1	1989	1989	
BATMAN: ARKHAM ASYLUM	TITAN BOOKS		1	1	1989	1989	
BATMAN: BIRTH OF THE DEMON	DC COMICS INC.		1	1	1993	1993	
BATMAN: BLIND JUSTICE	DC COMICS INC.		1	1	1992	1992	
BATMAN: BRIDE OF THE DEMON	DC COMICS INC.		1	1	1990	1990	
BATMAN: BRIDE OF THE DEMON	DC COMICS INC.		1	1	1991	1991	
BATMAN: CATWOMAN DEFIANT	DC COMICS INC.		1	1	1992	1992	
BATMAN: CHALLENGE OF THE MAN-BAT	DC COMICS INC.		1	1	1989	1989	
BATMAN: CHALLENGE OF THE MAN-BAT	TITAN BOOKS		1	1	1989	1989	
BATMAN: COMPLETE FRANK MILLER	LONGMEADOW PRESS		1	1	1989	1989	
BATMAN: DARK JOKER-THE WILD	DC COMICS INC.		1	1	1993	1993	
BATMAN: DIGITAL JUSTICE	DC COMICS INC.		1	1	1990	1990	
BATMAN: DIGITAL JUSTICE	TITAN BOOKS		1	1	1990	1990	
BATMAN: FULL CIRCLE	DC COMICS INC.		1	1	1991	1991	
BATMAN: GOTHAM BY GASLIGHT	DC COMICS INC.		1	1	1989	1989	
BATMAN: GOTHAM BY GASLIGHT	TITAN BOOKS		1	1	1989	1989	
BATMAN: GOTHAM NIGHTS	DC COMICS INC.		1	4	1992	1992	
BATMAN: GOTHAM NIGHTS	TITAN BOOKS		1	1	1994	1994	
BATMAN: GOTHIC	DC COMICS INC.		1	1	1992	1992	
BATMAN: GOTHIC	TITAN BOOKS		1	1	1991	1991	
BATMAN: HOLY TERROR	DC COMICS INC.		1	1	1991	1991	
BATMAN: IN DARKEST KNIGHT	DC COMICS INC.		1	1	1993	1993	
BATMAN: KNIGHTFALL	DC COMICS INC.		1	2	1993	1993	
BATMAN: KNIGHTFALL	TITAN BOOKS		1	2	1993	1993	
BATMAN: LEGENDS OF THE DARK KNIGHT	DC COMICS INC.		1	57	1989	NOW	
BATMAN: LEGENDS OF THE DARK KNIGHT "FACES"	TITAN BOOKS		1	1	1994	1994	
BATMAN: LEGENDS OF THE DARK KNIGHT ANNUAL	DC COMICS INC.		1	3	1991	NOW	
BATMAN: LEGENDS OF THE DARK KNIGHT COLLECTION	TITAN BOOKS		1	1	1994	1994	
BATMAN: LEGENDS OF THE DARK KNIGHT HALLOWEEN SPEC.	DC COMICS INC.		1	1	1993	1993	
BATMAN: MANY DEATHS OF THE	DC COMICS INC.		1	1	1992	1992	
BATMAN: MASTER OF FUTURE	DC COMICS INC.		1	1	1991	1991	
BATMAN: NIGHT CRIES	DC COMICS INC.		1	1	1993	1993	
BATMAN: OFFICIAL MOVIE SOUVENIR MAGAZINE	TOPPS		1	1	1989	1989	
BATMAN: PENGUIN TRIUMPHANT	DC COMICS INC.		1	1	1992	1992	
BATMAN: PREY	DC COMICS INC.		1	1	1993	1993	
BATMAN: PREY	TITAN BOOKS		1	1	1993	1993	
BATMAN: RED WATER, CRIMSON DEATH	DC COMICS INC.		1	1	1990	1990	
BATMAN: RED WATER, CRIMSON DEATH	TITAN BOOKS		1	1	1990	1990	
BATMAN: RUN RIDDLER RUN	DC COMICS INC.		1	3	1992	1992	
BATMAN: SEDUCTION OF THE GUN	DC COMICS INC.		1	1	1992	1992	
BATMAN: SHADOW OF THE BAT	DC COMICS INC.		1	24	1992	NOW	
BATMAN: SHADOW OF THE BAT ANNUAL	DC COMICS INC.		1	1	1993	NOW	
BATMAN: SHAMAN	DC COMICS INC.		1	1	1993	1993	
BATMAN: SHAMAN	TITAN BOOKS		1	1	1993	1993	
BATMAN: SON OF THE DEMON	DC COMICS INC.		1	1	1987	1987	
BATMAN: SWORD OF AZRAEL	DC COMICS INC.		1	1	1993	1993	
BATMAN: SWORD OF AZRAEL	DC COMICS INC.		1	4	1992	1993	
BATMAN: TALES OF THE DARK KNIGHT	FUTURA PUBLICATIONS		1	1	1989	1989	
BATMAN: TALES OF THE DEMON	DC COMICS INC.		1	1	1991	1991	
BATMAN: THE ANIMATED MOVIE	DC COMICS INC.		1	1	1993	1993	
BATMAN: THE BLUE, THE GREY AND THE BAT	DC COMICS INC.		1	1	1992	1992	
BATMAN: THE COLLECTED ADVENTURES	DC COMICS INC.		1	1	1993	1993	
BATMAN: THE COLLECTED ADVENTURES	TITAN BOOKS		1	1	1993	1993	
BATMAN: THE CULT	DC COMICS INC.		1	1	1991	1991	
BATMAN: THE CULT	DC COMICS INC.		1	4	1988	1988	
BATMAN: THE CULT	TITAN BOOKS		1	1	1991	1991	
BATMAN: THE DAILIES	DC COMICS INC.		1	3	1991	1991	
BATMAN: THE DARK KNIGHT RETURNS	DC COMICS INC.		1	1	1986	1986	
BATMAN: THE DARK KNIGHT RETURNS	DC COMICS INC.		1	4	1986	1986	
BATMAN: THE DARK KNIGHT RETURNS	TITAN BOOKS		1	1	1986	1986	
BATMAN: THE DEMON AWAKES	DC COMICS INC.		1	1	1989	1989	
BATMAN: THE DEMON AWAKES	TITAN BOOKS		1	1	1989	1989	
BATMAN: THE FRIGHTENED CITY	DC COMICS INC.		1	1	1990	1990	
BATMAN: THE FRIGHTENED CITY	TITAN BOOKS		1	1	1990	1990	
BATMAN: THE JOKER'S REVENGE	DC COMICS INC.		1	1	1989	1989	
BATMAN: THE JOKER'S REVENGE	TITAN BOOKS		1	1	1989	1989	
BATMAN: THE KILLING JOKE	DC COMICS INC.		1	1	1988	1988	
BATMAN: THE KILLING JOKE	TITAN BOOKS		1	1	1988	1988	
BATMAN: THE LONELY PLACE OF DYING	DC COMICS INC.		1	1	1990	1990	
BATMAN: THE SUNDAY CLASSICS	DC COMICS INC.		1	1	1991	1991	
BATMAN: TWO FACE STRIKES TWICE	DC COMICS INC.		1	2	1993	1993	
BATMAN: VENGEANCE OF BANE	DC COMICS INC.		1	1	1993	1993	
BATMAN: VENOM	DC COMICS INC.		1	1	1993	1993	
BATMAN: VENOM	TITAN BOOKS		1	1	1993	1993	
BATMAN: VOW FROM THE GRAVE	DC COMICS INC.		1	1	1989	1989	
BATMAN: VOW FROM THE GRAVE	TITAN BOOKS		1	1	1989	1989	
BATMAN: YEAR ONE	DC COMICS INC.		1	1	1988	1988	
BATMAN: YEAR ONE	TITAN BOOKS		1	1	1988	1988	
BATMAN: YEAR TWO	DC COMICS INC.		1	1	1990	1990	
BATMAN: YEAR TWO	TITAN BOOKS		1	1	1989	1989	
BATS, CATS AND CADILLACS	NOW		1	1	1991	NOW	
BATS, CATS AND CADILLACS	NOW		1	6	1990	NOW	
BATTLE	ATLAS		1	62	1951	1959	FOTO PARADE INC. IS SHOWN INSIDE, AN ATLAS COMPANY
BATTLE	MARVEL ENTERTAINMENT GROUP		63	70	1959	1960	
BATTLE	MICK ANGLO/ATLAS		1	9	1960	1961	
BATTLE ACTION	ATLAS		1	30	1952	1957	
BATTLE ACTION COMIC	CARTOON ART		1	1	1952	1952	US REPRINTS

INDEX OF COMIC TITLES AND THEIR PUBLISHERS

COMIC TITLE	PUBLISHER	Vol No.	Srt No.	End No.	Str. Year	End Year	COMMENTS
BATTLE ACTION IN PICTURES	L. MILLER PUBLISHING COMPANY (UK)		1	3	1959	1959	US REPRINTS
BATTLE ANGEL ALITA	VIZ	1	1	9	1992	1992	
BATTLE ANGEL ALITA	VIZ	2	1	7	1993	1993	
BATTLE ANGEL ALITA	VIZ	3	1	2	1993	1994	
BATTLE ANGEL ALITA PT THREE	VIZ		1	13	1994	1994	
BATTLE ARMOR	ETERNITY		1	3	1988	NOW	
BATTLE ATTACK	STANMORE PUBLICATIONS		1	8	1952	1955	
BATTLE ATTACK	STREAMLINE		1	1	1953	1953	REPRINTS US STANMORE MATERIAL
BATTLE BRADY	ATLAS	10	14	1953	1953	FORMERLY MEN IN ACTION
BATTLE CLASSICS	DC COMICS INC.		1	1	1978	1978	
BATTLE CRY	STANMORE PUBLICATIONS		1	20	1952	1955	
BATTLE CRY	STREAMLINE		1	2	1953	1953	REPRINTS US STANMORE MATERIAL
BATTLE FIRE	STANMORE PUBLICATIONS		1	7	1955	1955	
BATTLE FIRE	STREAMLINE		1	1	1955	1955	REPRINTS US STANMORE MATERIAL
BATTLE FOR A 3-D WORLD	3-D COSMIC		1	1	1982	1982	
BATTLE GROUND	ATLAS		1	20	1954	1957	
BATTLE GROUND	L. MILLER PUBLISHING COMPANY (UK)		1	11	1960	1961	REPRINTS US FAWCETT MATERIAL
BATTLE GROUND	STREAMLINE		1	1	1955	1955	REPRINTS US ATLAS MATERIAL
BATTLE HEROES	STANLEY PUBLICATIONS		1	2	1966	1966	
BATTLE OF THE PLANETS	GOLD KEY		1	10	1979	1980	
BATTLE PICTURE LIBRARY	FLEETWAY	1		1706	1961	1984	
BATTLE PICTURE LIBRARY HOLIDAY SPECIAL	FLEETWAY	1964	1982	1964	1982	
BATTLE PICTURE WEEKLY	FLEETWAY		1	673	1975	1988	
BATTLE PICTURE WEEKLY ANNUAL	FLEETWAY	1988	1988	1976	1984	
BATTLE REPORT	AJAX		1	6	1952	1953	
BATTLE SQUADRON	STANMORE PUBLICATIONS		1	5	1955	1955	
BATTLE SQUADRON	STREAMLINE		1	2	1956	1956	REPRINTS US STANMORE MATERIAL
BATTLE STORIES	FAWCETT PUBLICATIONS		1	11	1952	1953	
BATTLE STORIES	L. MILLER PUBLISHING COMPANY (UK)		1	9	1952	1953	US FAWCETT REPRINTS
BATTLE STORIES	SUPER COMICS	10	18	1963	1963	NO #'S 13 OR 14
BATTLECRY PICTURE LIBRARY	FAME PRESS		1	2	1965	???	
BATTLEFIELD	BRUGEDITOR		1	2	1962	???	
BATTLEFIELD ACTION	CHARLTON COMICS	16	89	1957	1984	
BATTLEFORCE	BLACKTHORNE		1	2	1987	1988	
BATTLEFRONT	ATLAS		1	48	1952	1957	
BATTLEFRONT	STANDARD COMICS	5	5	1952	1952	
BATTLEGROUND	FAME PRESS		1	112	1965	???	
BATTLER BRITTON PICTURE LIBRARY HOLIDAY SPECIAL	IPC	1978	1988	1978	1988	
BATTLESTAR GALACTICA	GRAND DREAMS				1978	1978	
BATTLESTAR GALACTICA	MARVEL ENTERTAINMENT GROUP		1	23	1979	1981	
BATTLETECH	BLACKTHORNE		1	12	1987	NOW	
BATTRON	NEW ENGLAND COMICS		1	1	1992	NOW	
BEACH PARTY	ETERNITY		1	1	1989	1989	
BEAGLE BOYS VERSUS UNCLE SCROOGE	GOLD KEY		1	12	1979	1980	
BEAGLE BOYS, THE	GOLD KEY		1	47	1964	1979	
BEANBAGS	ZIFF-DAVIS PUBLISHING COMPANY		1	2	1951	1952	
BEANIE THE MEANIE	FAGO PUBLICATIONS		1	3	1958	1959	
BEANO BOOK, THE	D.C. THOMSON				1940	1942	BECOMES THE MAGIC-BEANO BOOK
BEANO BOOK, THE	D.C. THOMSON				1951	NOW	FORMERLY THE MAGIC-BEANO BOOK
BEANO COMIC LIBRARY	D.C. THOMSON		1	258	1982	1992	
BEANO COMIC, THE	D.C. THOMSON		1	2684	1938	NOW	
BEANO SUMMER SPECIAL, THE	D.C. THOMSON	1964	1992	1964	NOW	
BEANWORLD	ECLIPSE		1	1	1989	1989	
BEANY AND CECIL	DELL PUBLISHING COMPANY		1	5	1962	1963	
BEAST WARRIORS OF SHAOLIN	PIED PIPER		1	1	1988	1988	
BEAST WARRIORS OF SHAOLIN	PIED PIPER		1	5	1987	1988	
BEATLES EXPERIENCE, THE	REVOLUTIONARY COMICS		1	7	1991	1991	
BEATLES, THE (LIFE STORY)	DELL PUBLISHING COMPANY		1	1	1964	1964	
BEATLES, THE	DELL PUBLISHING COMPANY		1	1	1964	1964	
BEAUTIFUL STORIES FOR UGLY CHILDREN	DC COMICS INC.		1	29	1989	NOW	
BEAUTY AND THE BEAST	INNOVATION		1	6	1993	NOW	
BEAUTY AND THE BEAST MOVIE ADAPTATION	WALT DISNEY		1	1	1992	1992	
BEAUTY AND THE BEAST, NEW ADVENTURES OF	WALT DISNEY		1	2	1992	1992	
BEAUTY AND THE BEAST, THE	MARVEL ENTERTAINMENT GROUP		1	4	1985	1985	
BEAUTY AND THE BEAST: A TALE OF ENCHANTMENT	WALT DISNEY		1	1	1992	1992	CARTOON TALES
BEAUTY AND THE BEAST: PORTRAIT OF LOVE	FIRST		1	2	1989	1990	
BEAVIS AND BUTT-HEAD	MARVEL ENTERTAINMENT GROUP		1	1	1994	NOW	
BECK & CAUL	CALIBER PRESS		1	1	1993	1994	
BECKETT BASEBALL	BECKETT PUBLISHING		1	1	1993	NOW	
BECKETT BASKETBALL	BECKETT PUBLISHING		1	1	1993	NOW	
BECKETT FOCUS ON STARS	BECKETT PUBLISHING		1	1	1993	NOW	
BECKETT FOOTBALL	BECKETT PUBLISHING		1	1	1993	NOW	
BECKETT HOCKEY	BECKETT PUBLISHING		1	1	1993	NOW	
BEDLAM	ECLIPSE		1	2	1985	1985	
BEE 29, THE BOMBARDIER	NEIL PUBLICATIONS		1	1	1945	1945	
BEEM	EDDIE CAMPBELL		1	1	1974	1974	
BEEP BEEP THE ROAD RUNNER	DELL PUBLISHING COMPANY	4	14	1960	1962	
BEEP BEEP, THE ROAD RUNNER	GOLD KEY		1	105	1966	1983	
BEETHOVEN	HARVEY PUBLICATIONS		1	1	1993	NOW	
BEETLE BAILEY	CHARLTON COMICS	67	119	1969	1976	
BEETLE BAILEY	DELL PUBLISHING COMPANY	5	38	1956	1980	
BEETLE BAILEY	GOLD KEY	39	131	1962	1980	
BEETLE BAILEY	HARVEY PUBLICATIONS		1	7	1992	NOW	
BEETLE BAILEY	KING FEATURES	54	66	1966	1968	
BEETLE BAILEY	WHITMAN	132	132	1980	1980	
BEETLE BAILEY BIG BOOK	HARVEY PUBLICATIONS		1	2	1993	NOW	
BEETLE BAILEY GIANT SIZE	HARVEY PUBLICATIONS		1	2	1992	NOW	
BEETLEJUICE	HARVEY PUBLICATIONS		1	3	1991	NOW	
BEETLEJUICE HOLIDAY SPECIAL	HARVEY PUBLICATIONS		1	1	1992	1992	
BEETLEJUICE: CRIMEBUSTERS ON THE HAUNT	HARVEY PUBLICATIONS		1	3	1992	1993	

INDEX OF COMIC TITLES AND THEIR PUBLISHERS

COMIC TITLE	PUBLISHER	Vol No.	Srt No.	End No.	Str. Year	End Year	COMMENTS
BEEZER AND TOPPER, THE	D.C. THOMSON						
BEEZER BOOK ANNUAL, THE	D.C. THOMSON		1	119	1990	1992	
BEEZER COMIC, THE	SCOOP BOOKS		1958	1993	1958	1993	
BEEZER SUMMER SPECIAL, THE	D.C. THOMSON		1	1	1946	1946	
BEEZER, THE	D.C. THOMSON		1973	1992	1973	NOW	
BEHIND PRISON BARS	AVON BOOKS		1	1809	1956	1990	
BEHOLD THE HANDMAID	GEORGE PFLAUM		1	1	1952	1952	
BELINDA AND THE BOMB ALLEY BOYS	MIRROR PRESS PUBLICATIONS		1	1	1954	1954	
BELINDA IN SHOOTING STAR	MIRROR PRESS PUBLICATIONS		1	1	1946	1946	
BELLE AND THE BEAST: NEW ADVENTURES	WALT DISNEY		1	1	40'S	40'S	
BEN BOWIE AND HIS MOUNTAIN MEN	DELL PUBLISHING COMPANY		7	17	1952	1959	
BEN BOWIE AND HIS MOUNTAIN MEN	WORLD DISTRIBUTORS LTD		1	8	1955	???	REPRINTS US DELL MATERIAL
BEN CASEY	DELL PUBLISHING COMPANY		1	10	1962	1965	
BEN CASEY FILM STORY	GOLD KEY		1	1	1962	1962	
BENEATH THE PLANET OF THE APES	ADVENTURE COMICS				1991	1991	
BENEATH THE PLANET OF THE APES	GOLD KEY		1	1	1970	1970	
BEOWULF	DC COMICS INC.		1	6	1975	1976	
BERNI WRIGHTSON, MASTER OF THE MACABRE	PACIFIC COMICS AND ECLIPSE COMICS		1	5	1983	1984	
BERRYS, THE	ARGO PUBLISHING		1	1	1956	1956	
BERYL THE PERIL ANNUAL	D.C. THOMSON		1959	1988	1959	1988	NO ISSUES, 1960,1962,1964,1966,1970,1980
BERZERKER	CALIBER PRESS		1	2	1993	NOW	
BERZERKER	GAUNTLET COMICS		1	1	1993	1993	
BEST COMICS	BETTER PUBLICATIONS		1	4	1939	1940	
BEST FROM BOY'S LIFE, THE	GILBERTON PUBLICATIONS		1	5	1957	1958	
BEST LOVE	MARVEL ENTERTAINMENT GROUP		33	36	1949	1950	FORMERLY SUB-MARINER COMICS
BEST OF BILLY'S BOOTS HOLIDAY SPECIAL, THE	FLEETWAY		1990	1991	1990	1991	
BEST OF BUGS BUNNY, THE	GOLD KEY		1	2	1966	1968	
BEST OF DARK HORSE	DARK HORSE COMICS		1	3	1992	NOW	
BEST OF DC, THE	DC COMICS INC.		1	71	1979	1986	BLUE RIBBON DIGEST
BEST OF DENNIS THE MENACE, THE	FAWCETT PUBLICATIONS		1	5	1959	1961	
BEST OF DONALD DUCK & UNCLE SCROOGE, THE	GOLD KEY		1	2	1964	1967	
BEST OF DONALD DUCK, THE	GOLD KEY		1	1	1965	1965	
BEST OF MARMADUKE, THE	CHARLTON COMICS		1	1	1960	1960	
BEST OF SORCERY	MILLENIUM		1	1	1992	1992	
BEST OF STAR TREK	DC COMICS INC.		1	1	1991	1991	
BEST OF THE BRAVE AND THE BOLD, THE	DC COMICS INC.		1	6	1988	1989	
BEST OF THE WEST	CARTOON ART		1	4?	1951	???	REPRINTS US MAGAZINE ENTERPRISES MATERIAL
BEST OF THE WEST	MAGAZINE ENTERPRISES		1	12	1951	1954	
BEST OF UNCLE SCROOGE & DONALD DUCK, THE	GOLD KEY		1	1	1966	1966	
BEST OF WALT DISNEY COMICS, THE	WESTERN PUBLISHING COMPANY		96170	96173	1974	1974	
BEST OF WHAT IF?	MARVEL ENTERTAINMENT GROUP		1	1	1993	1993	
BEST ROMANCE	STANDARD COMICS		5	7	1952	1952	
BEST WESTERN	MARVEL ENTERTAINMENT GROUP		58	59	1949	1949	FORMERLY TERRY TOONS OR MISS AMERICA MAGAZINE
BESTOFALL COMICS	CARTOON ART		1	1	1948	1948	
BETTY	ARCHIE PUBLICATIONS		1	12	1992	NOW	
BETTY & VERONICA ANNUAL DIGEST MAGAZINE	ARCHIE PUBLICATIONS	1	1	10	1989	NOW	
BETTY & VERONICA ANNUAL DIGEST MAGAZINE	ARCHIE PUBLICATIONS	2	1	67	1980	NOW	BETTY & VERONICA DIGEST MAGAZINE WITH 2-4,44 ONWARD
BETTY & VERONICA DOUBLE DIGEST MAGAZINE	ARCHIE PUBLICATIONS		1	43	1987	NOW	
BETTY AND HER STEADY	AVON BOOKS	2	2	1950	1950		FORMERLY GOING STEADY WITH BETTY
BETTY AND ME	ARCHIE PUBLICATIONS		1	200	1965	NOW	
BETTY AND VERONICA	ARCHIE PUBLICATIONS		1	74	1987	NOW	
BETTY AND VERONICA SPECTACULAR	ARCHIE PUBLICATIONS		1	7	1992	NOW	
BETTY BEING BAD	EROS		1	1	1991	1991	
BETTY BOOP IN 3-D	BLACKTHORNE		1	1	1986	1986	
BETTY BOOP'S BIG BREAK	FIRST				1990	1990	
BETTY PAGE: 3-D COMICS	3-D ZONE		1	1	1991	1991	
BETTY'S DIARY	ARCHIE PUBLICATIONS		1	40	1986	1991	
BEVERLEY HILLBILLIES	DELL PUBLISHING COMPANY		1	21	1963	1971	
BEVERLY HILLBILLIES ANNUAL, THE	WORLD DISTRIBUTORS LTD		1964	1966	1964	1966	REPRINTS DELL MATERIAL
BEWARE	MARVEL ENTERTAINMENT GROUP		1	8	1973	1974	BECOMES TOMB OF DARKNESS
BEWARE	MERIT PUBLISHING		5	15	1953	1955	
BEWARE	TROJAN MAGAZINES		13	16	1953	1953	CLASSED AS ISSUES 1-4 OF MERIT PUBL. EDITION
BEWARE	YOUTHFUL MAGAZINES		10	12	1952	1952	FORMERLY FANTASTIC, BECOMES CHILLING TALES
BEWARE TERROR TALES	FAWCETT PUBLICATIONS		1	8	1952	1953	
BEWARE THE CREEPER	DC COMICS INC.		1	6	1968	1969	
BEWITCHED	DELL PUBLISHING COMPANY		1	14	1965	1969	
BEYOND THE GRAVE	CHARLTON COMICS		1	1	1975	1984	
BEYOND, THE	ACE MAGAZINES		1	30	1950	1955	
BIBLE TALES FOR YOUNG FOLK	ATLAS		1	5	1953	1954	ISSUES 3-5 HAVE PEOPLE INSTEAD OF FOLK ON COVER
BIBLE TALES FOR YOUNG PEOPLE	L. MILLER PUBLISHING COMPANY (UK)		1	5	1954	1954	REPRINTS US ATLAS MATERIAL
BIC	OVO COMIC		1	7	1987	1987	
BIG	DARK HORSE COMICS		1	1	1989	1989	
BIG ADVENTURE BOOK	FLEETWAY		1	1	1984	1984	
BIG ALL AMERICAN COMIC BOOK, THE	DC COMICS INC.		1	1	1944	1944	
BIG BABY HUEY	HARVEY PUBLICATIONS		1	1	1991	NOW	
BIG BLACK KISS	VORTEX		1	3	1989	1989	
BIG BOOK OF EVERYTHING	KNOCKABOUT				1983	1983	
BIG BOOK OF FUN COMICS	DC COMICS INC.		1	1	1936	1936	
BIG BOOK ROMANCES	FAWCETT PUBLICATIONS		1	1	1950	1950	
BIG CHIEF WAHOO	EASTERN COLOR PRINTING COMPANY		1	23	1942	1945	
BIG DADDY ROTH	MILLER PUBLISHING (US)		1	4	1964	1965	
BIG EARS	BIG EARS		1	1	1971	1971	
BIG JIM'S P.A.C.K.	MARVEL ENTERTAINMENT GROUP		1	1	NN	NN	
BIG JON & SPARKIE	ZIFF-DAVIS PUBLISHING COMPANY	4	4	1952	1952		FORMERLY SPARKIE, RADIO PIXIE
BIG K	IPC		1	8	1983	1984	

207

INDEX OF COMIC TITLES AND THEIR PUBLISHERS

COMIC TITLE	PUBLISHER	Vol No.	Srt No.	End No.	Str. Year	End Year	COMMENTS
BIG LITTLE COMIC, THE	P.M. PRODUCTIONS		1	1	1945	1945	
BIG NUMBERS	MAD LOVE		1	2	1990	1990	
BIG ONE, THE	FLEETWAY		1	19	1964	1965	
BIG PARADE COMIC	GRANT HUGHES		1	1	1947	1947	
BIG PRIZE, THE	ETERNITY		1	3	1988	1988	
BIG SHOT	STREAMLINE		1	2	1949	1949	REPRINTS COLUMBIA MATERIAL
BIG SHOT COMICS	COLUMBIA COMICS GROUP		1	104	1940	1949	
BIG SIX	APULHEAD PRODUCTIONS		1	1	1976	1976	
BIG SURPRISE COMIC	TOWER PRESS		1	3	1950	1950	
BIG TEX	TOBY PRESS PUBLICATIONS		1	1	1953	1953	
BIG TOP COMIC, THE	MARTIN & REID		1	1	1949	1949	
BIG TOP COMICS, THE	TOBY PRESS PUBLICATIONS		1	2	1951	1951	
BIG TOWN	DC COMICS INC.		1	50	1951	1958	
BIG VALLEY, THE	DELL PUBLISHING COMPANY		1	6	1966	1967	
BIG-3	FOX FEATURES SYNDICATE		1	7	1940	1942	
BIG-TIME! COMIC	APEX PUBLICITY SERVICE		1	1	1947	1947	
BIG...COMIC	SCION				1948	1949	VARIOUSLY TITLED, UNNUMBERED
BIGGLES	HODDER AND STOUGHTON/DARGUAD				1978	1984	
BIGGLES IN THE CRUISE OF THE CONDOR	JUVENILE PRODUCTIONS		1	1	1955	1955	
BIJOU FUNNIES	H. BUNCH ASSOCIATES		1	1	1974	1974	REPRINTS
BIKER MICE FROM MARS	MARVEL ENTERTAINMENT GROUP		1	3	1993	1993	
BILAL: EXTERMINATOR 17	CATALAN COMMUNCATIONS				1986	1986	
BILL AND TED'S BOGUS JOURNEY	MARVEL ENTERTAINMENT GROUP		1	1	1991	1991	
BILL AND TED'S EXCELLENT ADVENTURE	MARVEL ENTERTAINMENT GROUP		1	1	1989	1989	
BILL AND TED'S EXCELLENT COMIC BOOK	MARVEL ENTERTAINMENT GROUP		1	12	1991	1992	
BILL BARNES COMICS	STREET AND SMITH PUBLICATIONS		1	12	1940	1943	AMERICA'S AIR ACE COMICS FROM ISSUE 2 ON COVER
BILL BATTLE, THE ONE MAN ARMY	FAWCETT PUBLICATIONS		1	4	1952	1953	
BILL BLACK'S FUN COMICS	AMERICOMICS		1	4	1982	1983	
BILL BOYD WESTERN	FAWCETT PUBLICATIONS		1	23	1950	1953	
BILL BOYD WESTERN	L. MILLER PUBLISHING COMPANY (UK)		1	50	1950	1955	REPRINTS US FAWCETT MATERIAL
BILL BOYD WESTERN ANNUAL	L. MILLER PUBLISHING COMPANY (UK)		1	5	1956	1960	
BILL CARTER	FOLDES PRESS		1	3	1947	1947	
BILL SIENKIEWICZ: SKETCHBOOK	FANTAGRAPHICS		1	1	1990	1990	
BILL STERN'S SPORTS BOOK	ZIFF-DAVIS PUBLISHING COMPANY	1	1	2	1951	1951	
BILL STERN'S SPORTS BOOK	ZIFF-DAVIS PUBLISHING COMPANY	2	2	2	1952	1952	
BILLI 99	DARK HORSE COMICS		1	4	1991	1992	
BILLY AND BUGGY BEAR	I.W. ENTERPRISES		1	1	1958	1958	
BILLY AND BUGGY BEAR	I.W. SUPER	10	10	1964	1964		
BILLY BUCKSKIN WESTERN	ATLAS		1	3	1955	1956	BECOMES 2-GUN WESTERN
BILLY BUCKSKIN WESTERN	L. MILLER PUBLISHING COMPANY (UK)		1	2	1956	1956	REPRINTS ATLAS MATERIAL
BILLY BUDD, KGB	CATALAN COMMUNCATIONS		1		1991	1991	
BILLY BUNNY	EXCELLENT PUBLICATIONS		1	5	1954	1954	BECOMES BLACK COBRA
BILLY BUNNY'S CHRISTMAS FROLICS	FARREL PUBLICATIONS		1	1	1952	1952	
BILLY NGUYEN PRIVATE EYE	CALIBER PRESS		1	2	1991	1991	
BILLY NGUYEN PRIVATE EYE COLLECTION	CALIBER PRESS		1	1	1991	1991	
BILLY THE KID	CHARLTON COMICS	9		153	1957	1983	FORMERLY THE MASKED RAIDER
BILLY THE KID (MASKED RAIDER PRESENTS...)	L. MILLER PUBLISHING COMPANY (UK)	50		?	1956	1957	REPRINTS CHARLTON MATERIAL
BILLY THE KID ADVENTURE MAGAZINE	TOBY PRESS PUBLICATIONS		1	30	1950	1955	
BILLY THE KID ADVENTURE MAGAZINE	WORLD DISTRIBUTORS LTD		1	76	1953	1959	
BILLY THE KID AND OSCAR	FAWCETT PUBLICATIONS		1	3	1945	1946	
BILLY THE KID BOOK OF PICTURE STORIES ANNUAL	AMALGAMATED PRESS	1958	1959	1958	1959		
BILLY THE KID WESTERN ANNUAL	WORLD DISTRIBUTORS LTD	1954	1958	1954	1958		
BILLY WEST	STANDARD COMICS		1	10	1949	1952	BILL WEST ON COVER OF ISSUES 9,10
BINGO COMICS	HOWARD PUBLISHERS		1	1	1945	1945	
BINGO, THE MONKEY DOODLE BOY	ST JOHN PUBLISHING	1	1	1	1951	1951	
BINGO, THE MONKEY DOODLE BOY	ST JOHN PUBLISHING	2	1	1	1953	1953	
BINKY	DC COMICS INC.		72	82	1970	1977	
BINKY'S BUDDIES	DC COMICS INC.		1	12	1969	1970	
BIO-BOOSTER ARMOR GUYVER	VIZ		1	3	1993	1994	
BIONEERS	MIRAGE STUDIOS		1	1	1993	NOW	
BIONIC WOMAN ANNUAL	GRAND DREAMS	1977	1978	1977	1978		
BIONIC WOMAN ANNUAL, THE	CHARLTON COMICS		1	2	1977	1978	
BIONIC WOMAN, THE	CHARLTON COMICS		1	5	1977	1978	
BIRDLAND	EROS		1	3	1990	1990	
BIRTHDAY BOOK FOR BOYS	FLEETWAY		1	1	1972	1972	
BIRTHRITE	CONGRESS PRESS		1	3	1989	1991	
BISLEY'S SCRAPBOOK	ATOMEKA		1	1	1993	1993	
BIZARRE ADVENTURES	MARVEL ENTERTAINMENT GROUP		25	34	1981	1983	
BIZARRO COMIC	TROLL PUBLICATIONS		1	2	1972	1974	
BIZZARE 3-D ZONE	BLACKTHORNE		1	1	1986	1986	
BLAAM!	TITAN BOOKS		1	1	1990	1990	
BLAAM!	WILLYPRODS		1	3	1988	1989	
BLACK AND WHITE MAGIC	INNOVATION		1	4	1991	1991	
BLACK AXE	MARVEL ENTERTAINMENT GROUP		1	7	1993	NOW	
BLACK BOB BOOK ANNUAL	D.C. THOMSON	1950	1965	1950	1965		
BLACK CANARY	DC COMICS INC.		1	12	1993	NOW	
BLACK CANARY	DC COMICS INC.		1	4	1991	1992	
BLACK CAT COMICS	HARVEY PUBLICATIONS		1	29	1946	1951	BECOMES BLACK CAT MYSTERY, ..WESTERN ON 16-19
BLACK CAT MYSTERY	HARVEY PUBLICATIONS		30	65	1951	1963	FORMERLY BLACK CAT COMICS, BECOMES ..WESTERN MYST.
BLACK CAT WESTERN	STREAMLINE		1	1	1950	1950	REPRINTS US HARVEY MATERIAL
BLACK COBRA	AJAX		1	3	1954	1955	BECOMES BRIDE'S DIARY
BLACK COMMANDO: DARK DYNAMO	AC COMICS		1	1	1993	1993	
BLACK CONDOR	DC COMICS INC.		1	12	1992	NOW	
BLACK CROSS SPECIAL	DARK HORSE COMICS		1	1	1988	1988	
BLACK DIAMOND	AMERICOMICS		1	5	1983	1984	
BLACK DIAMOND WESTERN	LEV GLEASON PUBLICATIONS	9		60	1949	1956	
BLACK DIAMOND WESTERN	PEMBERTON		1	33	1951	1954	REPRINTS US LEV GLEASON MATERIAL

COMIC TITLE	PUBLISHER	Vol No.	Srt No.	End No.	Str. Year	End Year	COMMENTS
BLACK DOG	KNULLER LTD.		1	1	1969	1969	
BLACK DOMINION	ANUBIS PRESS		1	1	1993	NOW	
BLACK DRAGON, THE	MARVEL ENTERTAINMENT GROUP		1	6	1985	1985	
BLACK FURY	CHARLTON COMICS		1	57	1955	1966	
BLACK FURY	L. MILLER PUBLISHING COMPANY (UK)	50		61	1957	1958	REPRINTS US CHARLTON MATERIAL
BLACK FURY	WORLD DISTRIBUTORS LTD		1	8	1955	1956	REPRINTS US CHARLTON MATERIAL
BLACK GOLD	ESSO SERVICE STATION (GIVEAWAY)		1	1	1945	1945	
BLACK GOLIATH	MARVEL ENTERTAINMENT GROUP		1	5	1976	1976	
BLACK HOLE	WHITMAN		1	3	1980	1980	
BLACK HOOD	DC COMICS INC.		1	12	1991	1992	
BLACK HOOD	RED CIRCLE		1	3	1983	1983	
BLACK HOOD ANNUAL	DC COMICS INC.		1	1	1992	1992	
BLACK HOOD COMICS	M.L.J. MAGAZINES		9	19	1943	1946	
BLACK ISLAND, THE	ESCAPE		1	1	1988	1988	
BLACK JACK	CHARLTON COMICS		20	30	1957	1959	FORMERLY JIM BOWIE
BLACK JACK (ROCKY LANE'S...)	L. MILLER PUBLISHING COMPANY (UK)		1	11	1956	1957	REPRINTS US CHARLTON MATERIAL
BLACK KISS	VORTEX		1	12	1988	1989	
BLACK KNIGHT	MARVEL ENTERTAINMENT GROUP		1	4	1990	1990	
BLACK KNIGHT	TOBY PRESS PUBLICATIONS		1	1	1953	1953	
BLACK KNIGHT SUPER REPRINT	TOBY PRESS PUBLICATIONS		11	11	1963	1963	
BLACK KNIGHT, THE	ATLAS		1	5	1955	1956	
BLACK KNIGHT, THE	L. MILLER PUBLISHING COMPANY (UK)		1	5	1956	1956	REPRINTS US ATLAS MATERIAL
BLACK LIGHTNING	DC COMICS INC.		1	11	1977	1978	
BLACK MAGIC	ARNOLD BOOK CO.		1	16	1954	1954	
BLACK MAGIC	CRESTWOOD PUBLISHING	1	1	6	1950	1951	
BLACK MAGIC	CRESTWOOD PUBLISHING	2	1	12	1951	1952	
BLACK MAGIC	CRESTWOOD PUBLISHING	3	1	6	1952	1953	
BLACK MAGIC	CRESTWOOD PUBLISHING	4	1	6	1953	1954	
BLACK MAGIC	CRESTWOOD PUBLISHING	5	1	3	1954	1954	
BLACK MAGIC	CRESTWOOD PUBLISHING	6	1	6	1957	1958	
BLACK MAGIC	CRESTWOOD PUBLISHING	7	1	6	1958	1961	
BLACK MAGIC	CRESTWOOD PUBLISHING	8	1	5	1961	1961	BECOMES COOL CAT
BLACK MAGIC	DC COMICS INC.		1	9	1973	1975	
BLACK MAGIC	ECLIPSE		1	4	1990	1990	
BLACK MAGIC ALBUM	ARNOLD BOOK CO.		1	1	1954	1954	
BLACK MASK	DC COMICS INC.		1	3	1993	NOW	
BLACK ORCHID	DC COMICS INC.		1	1	1991	1991	
BLACK ORCHID	DC COMICS INC.		1	3	1988	1989	
BLACK ORCHID	DC COMICS INC.		1	6	1993	NOW	
BLACK ORCHID ANNUAL	DC COMICS INC.		1	1	1993	NOW	
BLACK PANTHER	MARVEL ENTERTAINMENT GROUP		1	15	1977	1979	
BLACK PANTHER	MARVEL ENTERTAINMENT GROUP		1	4	1988	1988	
BLACK PANTHER: PANTHER'S PREY	MARVEL ENTERTAINMENT GROUP		1	4	1991	1991	
BLACK PHANTOM	AC COMICS		1	3	1989	1990	
BLACK PHANTOM	MAGAZINE ENTERPRISES		1	1	1954	1954	
BLACK RIDER	MARVEL ENTERTAINMENT GROUP		8	27	1950	1955	FORMERLY WESTERN WINNERS
BLACK RIDER (WESTERN TALES OF...)	L. MILLER PUBLISHING COMPANY (UK)		1	4	1955	1956	REPRINTS US ATLAS MATERIAL
BLACK RIDER RIDES AGAIN	ATLAS		1	1	1957	1957	
BLACK SABBATH	ROCK-IT COMIX		1	1	1994	1994	
BLACK SCORPION	SPECIAL STUDIO		1	1	1991	1991	
BLACK SWAN COMICS	M.L.J. MAGAZINES		1	1	1945	1945	
BLACK TERROR	BETTER PUBLICATIONS		1	27	1945	1949	
BLACK TERROR	ECLIPSE		1	1	1991	1991	
BLACK TERROR	ECLIPSE		1	3	1989	1990	
BLACK WIDOW: THE COLDEST WAR	MARVEL ENTERTAINMENT GROUP		1	1	1990	1990	
BLACK ZEPPELIN, GENE DAY'S	RENEGADE PRESS		1	5	1985	1986	
BLACKBALL COMICS	BLACK BALL COMICS		1	2	1994	NOW	
BLACKHAWK	BOARDMAN		1	15	1949	1953	ISSUES NUMBERED ODDLY
BLACKHAWK	DC COMICS INC.		1	3	1988	1988	
BLACKHAWK	DC COMICS INC.	1	108	273	1944	1984	FORMERLY PUBLISHED BY QUALITY
BLACKHAWK	DC COMICS INC.	2	1	16	1989	1990	
BLACKHAWK	QUALITY COMICS		9	107	1944	1956	
BLACKHAWK	STRATO		1	36	1956	1958	
BLACKHAWK ANNUAL	DC COMICS INC.	2	1	1	1989	1989	
BLACKHAWK INDIAN TOMAHAWK WAR, THE	AVON BOOKS				1951	1951	
BLACKHAWK SPECIAL	DC COMICS INC.		1	1	1992	1992	
BLACKMASK	EASTERN COMICS		1	6	1988	NOW	
BLACKMOON	SOLSON		1	8	1985	1986	
BLACKSTONE, MASTER MAGICIAN COMICS	STREET AND SMITH PUBLICATIONS		1	3	1946	1946	
BLACKSTONE, THE MAGICIAN	MARVEL ENTERTAINMENT GROUP		2	4	1948	1948	
BLACKSTONE, THE MAGICIAN DETECTIVE FIGHTS CRIME	EC COMICS		1	1	1947	1947	
BLACKTHORNE 3-D SERIES	BLACKTHORNE		1	75	1985	1989	
BLACKTHORNE 3-IN-1	BLACKTHORNE		1	2	1986	1987	
BLACKWATCH	HEROIC PUBLISHING		1	6	1993	1993	
BLADE OF SHURIKEN	ETERNITY		1	6	1987	NOW	
BLADE OF THE MINSTREL	VIZ				1990	1990	
BLADE RUNNER	MARVEL ENTERTAINMENT GROUP		1	2	1982	1982	
BLADESMAN SUPER SPECIAL	HEROIC PUBLISHING		1	1	1993	1993	
BLAKE THE TRAPPER	L. MILLER PUBLISHING COMPANY (UK)		1	3	50'S	50'S	REPRINTS
BLAKE'S SEVEN	MARVEL ENTERTAINMENT GROUP		1	23	1981	1983	
BLAKE'S SEVEN ANNUAL	WORLD DISTRIBUTORS LTD	1979	1981	1979	1981		
BLAKE'S SEVEN SPECIALS	MARVEL ENTERTAINMENT GROUP	1981	1982	1981	1982		
BLANCHE GOES TO HOLLYWOOD	DARK HORSE COMICS		1	1	1993	1993	
BLANCHE GOES TO NEW YORK	DARK HORSE COMICS		1	1	1992	1992	
BLANDMAN	ECLIPSE		1	1	1992	1992	
BLAST	G & D PUBLICATIONS		1	2	1971	1971	
BLAST OFF THREE ROCKETEERS	HARVEY PUBLICATIONS		1	1	1965	1965	
BLAST!	JOHN BROWN PUBLISHING		1	7	1991	1991	
BLASTERS SPECIAL	DC COMICS INC.		1	1	1989	1989	

INDEX OF COMIC TITLES AND THEIR PUBLISHERS

COMIC TITLE	PUBLISHER	Vol No.	Srt No.	End No.	Str. Year	End Year	COMMENTS
BLAZE	MARVEL ENTERTAINMENT GROUP		1	3	1993	1993	
BLAZE CARSON	MARVEL ENTERTAINMENT GROUP		1	5	1948	1949	BECOMES REX HART
BLAZE THE WONDER COLLIE	MARVEL ENTERTAINMENT GROUP		2	3	1949	1950	FORMERLY MOLLY MANTON'S ROMANCES
BLAZER COMIC, THE	PHILIMAR		1	1	1949	1949	
BLAZING BATTLE TALES	ATLAS		1	1	1975	1975	
BLAZING COMBAT	WARREN PUBLISHING CO		1	4	1965	1966	
BLAZING COMBAT: WORLD WAR I & II	APPLE COMICS		1	1	1993	NOW	
BLAZING COMICS	ENWIL ASSOCIATES		1	6	1944	1955	
BLAZING SIX-GUNS	AVON BOOKS		1	1	1952	1952	
BLAZING SIX-GUNS	I.W. SUPER		1	18	1964	1964	
BLAZING SIX-GUNS	SKYWALD PUBLISHING		1	1	1971	1971	
BLAZING TRAILS	ALAN CLASS AND CO LTD		1	1	60'S	60'S	REPRINTS US CHARLTON MATERIAL
BLAZING WEST	AMERICAN COMIC GROUP		1	22	1948	1952	
BLAZING WEST	STREAMLINE		1	1	1951	1951	REPRINTS US AMERICAN COMIC GROUP MATERIAL
BLAZING WEST/BOY'S RANCH	STREAMLINE		1	1	1951	1951	
BLAZING WESTERN	AC COMICS	1	1	1	1989	1989	
BLAZING WESTERN	TIMOR PUBLISHING COMPANY		1	5	1954	1954	
BLIP AND THE C.C.A.D.S.	AMAZING COMICS		1	2	1987	1987	
BLITZ	NIGHT WYND ENTERPRISES		1	4	1992	1992	
BLITZKRIEG	DC COMICS INC.		1	5	1976	1976	
BLOCKBUSTER	MARVEL ENTERTAINMENT GROUP		1	9	1981	1982	
BLOCKBUSTER WINTER SPECIAL	MARVEL ENTERTAINMENT GROUP		1	1	1980	1980	
BLONDE PHANTOM	MARVEL ENTERTAINMENT GROUP	12	22		1946	1949	FORMERLY ALL SELECT, BECOMES LOVERS
BLONDE, THE	EROS		1	3	1992	1992	
BLONDIE	NEW YORK STATE DEPARTMENT OF MENTAL HEALTH		1950	1961	1950	1961	
BLONDIE & DAGWOOD FAMILY	HARVEY PUBLICATIONS		1	4	1963	1965	
BLONDIE AND DAGWOOD, ADVENTURES OF	ASSOCIATED NEWSPAPERS		1	1	1956	1956	
BLONDIE COMICS	CHARLTON COMICS	177	222		1969	1976	FORMERLY PUBLISHED BY KING COMICS
BLONDIE COMICS	DAVID MCKAY PUBLICATIONS		1	15	1947	1949	PUBLISHED BY HARVEY WITH ISSUE 16
BLONDIE COMICS	HARVEY PUBLICATIONS	16	163		1950	1965	FORMERLY PUBLISHED BY DAVID MCKAY
BLONDIE COMICS	KING FEATURES	164	175		1966	1967	FORMERLY PUBLISHED BY HARVEY
BLOOD	MARVEL ENTERTAINMENT GROUP		1	4	1988	1988	
BLOOD & ROSES: FUTURE PAST TENSE	SKY COMICS		1	1	1993	1993	
BLOOD & ROSES: SEARCH FOR THE TIME STONE	SKY COMICS		1	2	1994	1994	
BLOOD 'N' GUTS	AIRCEL		1	3	1990	1991	
BLOOD AND KISSES	FANTACO		1	1	1993	1994	
BLOOD FEAST MOVIE ADAPTATION	ETERNITY		1	1	1991	1991	
BLOOD HUNTER	BRAINSTORM COMICS		1	1	1993	NOW	
BLOOD IS THE HARVEST	ECLIPSE		1	4	1992	1992	
BLOOD JUNKIES	ETERNITY		1	2	1991	1991	
BLOOD LINES	VORTEX		1	7	1987	1988	
BLOOD OF DRACULA	APPLE COMICS		1	19	1987	1991	
BLOOD OF THE INNOCENT	WARP GRAPHICS		1	4	1986	1986	
BLOOD SEX AND TERROR	BST COMICS		1	2	1977	1977	
BLOOD SWORD	JADEMAN COMICS		1	53	1988	1993	
BLOOD SWORD DYNASTY	JADEMAN COMICS		1	41	1989	1993	
BLOOD SYNDICATE	DC COMICS INC.		1	11	1993	NOW	
BLOOD VOWS	CRY FOR DAWN PUBLICATIONS		1	1	1992	1992	
BLOOD WING	ETERNITY		1	5	1988	1988	
BLOODBATH	DC COMICS INC.		1	2	1993	1993	
BLOODBROTHERS	ETERNITY		1	4	1988	1989	
BLOODFIRE	LIGHTNING COMICS		1	4	1993	NOW	
BLOODLINES: A TALE FROM THE HEART OF AFRICA	MARVEL ENTERTAINMENT GROUP		1	1	1992	1992	
BLOODLORE	BENT NAIL PUBLICATIONS				1988	1988	
BLOODLUST	SLAVE LABOR		1	6	1990	NOW	
BLOODRUSH	MARVEL ENTERTAINMENT GROUP		1	1	1993	1994	
BLOODSCENT	COMICO		1	1	1988	1988	
BLOODSEED	MARVEL ENTERTAINMENT GROUP		1	2	1993	NOW	
BLOODSHOT	VALIANT / VOYAGER COMMUNICATIONS		1	14	1993	NOW	ISSUE 0 WAS PUBLISHED IN MARCH 1994
BLOODSTRIKE	IMAGE COMICS		1	7	1993	NOW	
BLOODYHOT	PARODY PRESS		1	1	1993	1993	
BLOOM COUNTY: 'TOONS FOR OUR TIMES	LITTLE BROWN				1984	1984	
BLUE BEETLE	CHARLTON COMICS	1	1	5	1964	1965	
BLUE BEETLE	CHARLTON COMICS	2	1	5	1967	1968	
BLUE BEETLE	CHARLTON COMICS	3	50	54	1965	1966	
BLUE BEETLE	DC COMICS INC.		1	24	1986	1988	
BLUE BEETLE	FOX FEATURES SYNDICATE	13	13		1939	1950	
BLUE BEETLE	L. MILLER PUBLISHING COMPANY (UK)		1	3	50'S	50'S	REPRINTS US FOX MATERIAL
BLUE BEETLE	STREAMLINE		1	2	1950	1950	REPRINTS US FOX MATERIAL
BLUE BIRD CHILDREN'S MAGAZINES, THE	GRAPHIC INFORMATION SERVICE		2	10	1957	1958	
BLUE BIRD COMICS	CHARLTON COMICS		1959	1965	1959	1965	
BLUE BOLT	FUNNIES INC./NOVELTY PRESS	1	1	12	1940	1941	
BLUE BOLT	FUNNIES INC./NOVELTY PRESS	2	1	12	1941	1942	
BLUE BOLT	FUNNIES INC./NOVELTY PRESS	3	1	12	1942	1943	
BLUE BOLT	FUNNIES INC./NOVELTY PRESS	4	1	12	1943	1944	
BLUE BOLT	FUNNIES INC./NOVELTY PRESS	5	1	8	1944	1945	
BLUE BOLT	FUNNIES INC./NOVELTY PRESS	6	1	10	1945	1946	
BLUE BOLT	FUNNIES INC./NOVELTY PRESS	7	1	12	1947	1948	
BLUE BOLT	FUNNIES INC./NOVELTY PRESS	8	1	12	1948	1949	
BLUE BOLT	FUNNIES INC./NOVELTY PRESS	9	1	9	1949	1950	
BLUE BOLT	FUNNIES INC./NOVELTY PRESS	10	1	2	1950	1951	
BLUE BOLT	STAR PUBLICATIONS		102	119	1949	1953	BECOMES GHOSTLY WEIRD STORIES
BLUE BOLT ADVENTURES	L. MILLER PUBLISHING COMPANY (UK)		1	2	1951	1951	REPRINTS US NOVELTY MATERIAL
BLUE BOLT SERIES	SWAN		1	22	1952	1954	
BLUE BULLETEER, THE	AC COMICS		1	1	1989	1989	
BLUE CIRCLE	STREAMLINE		1	1	1953	1953	

COMIC TITLE	PUBLISHER	Vol No.	Srt No.	End No.	Str. Year	End Year	COMMENTS
BLUE CIRCLE COMICS	ENWIL ASSOCIATES		1	6	1944	1945	
BLUE COLT	L. MILLER PUBLISHING COMPANY (UK)	50		58	1951	1952	REPRINTS FAWCETT MATERIAL
BLUE DEVIL	DC COMICS INC.		1	31	1984	1986	
BLUE DEVIL ANNUAL	DC COMICS INC.		1	1	1985	1985	
BLUE LILY	DARK HORSE COMICS		1	2	1993	NOW	
BLUE PHANTOM, THE	DELL PUBLISHING COMPANY		1	1	1962	1962	
BLUE RIBBON COMICS	ARCHIE PUBLICATIONS		1	14	1983	1984	
BLUE RIBBON COMICS	M.L.J. MAGAZINES		1	22	1939	1942	
BLUE RIBBON COMICS	ST JOHN PUBLISHING		1	6	1949	1949	
BO	CHARLTON COMICS		1	3	1955	1955	
BOB & BETTY & SANTA'S WISHING WELL	SEARS AND ROEBUCK COMPANY		1	1	1941	1941	
BOB COLT	FAWCETT PUBLICATIONS		1	10	1950	1952	
BOB COMIC BOOK	P.M. PRODUCTIONS		1	1	1949	1949	
BOB SCULLY, TWO FISTED HICK DETECTIVE	HUMOR PUBLISHING COMPANY		1	1	1930	1930	
BOB STEELE WESTERN	AC COMICS		1	1	1990	1990	
BOB STEELE WESTERN	FAWCETT PUBLICATIONS		1	10	1950	1952	
BOB SWIFT	FAWCETT PUBLICATIONS		1	5	1951	1952	
BOBBIN' $3000	PARODY PRESS		1	1	1992	1992	
BOBBY BENSON'S B-BAR-B RIDERS	MAGAZINE ENTERPRISES		1	20	1950	1953	
BOBBY BENSON'S B-BAR-B RIDERS	WORLD DISTRIBUTORS LTD		1	12	1950	1951	
BOBBY COMICS	UNIVERSAL PHOENIX FEATURES		1	1	1946	1946	
BOBBY SHELBY COMICS	HARVEY PUBLICATIONS		1	1	1949	1949	
BOBBY SHERMAN	CHARLTON COMICS		1	7	1972	1972	
BOBBY THATCHER & TREASURE CAVE	ALTEMUS COMPANY		1	1	1932	1932	
BOBBY THATCHER'S ROMANCE	ALTEMUS COMPANY		1	1	1931	1931	
BODY COUNT	AIRCEL		1	4	1990	1990	
BODYGUARD	ETERNITY		1	3	1990	1991	
BOG STANDARD KOMIX	BONK & TALBOT		1	1	1977	1977	
BOGEY	VICAR'S RAW BALLS		1	1	1975	1975	
BOGIE	ECLIPSE				1989	1989	
BOGIE MAN, THE	APOCALYPSE		1	1	1991	1991	
BOGIE MAN, THE	FATMAN PRESS		1	4	1989	1990	
BOGIE MAN: CHINATOON	TUNDRA		1	4	1992	1993	
BOGIE MAN: CHINK SYNDICATE	APOCALYPSE		1	1	1991	1991	
BOGIE MAN: MANHATTAN PROJECT	APOCALYPSE		1	1	1992	1992	
BOGIE MAN: THE MANHATTAN PROJECT	TUNDRA				1992	1992	
BOLD ADVENTURES	PACIFIC COMICS		1	3	1983	1984	
BOLD STORIES	KIRBY PUBLISHING COMPANY				1950	1950	
BOLT & STARFORCE SIX	AMERICAN COMIC GROUP		1	1	1984	1984	
BOLT SPECIAL	AMERICAN COMIC GROUP		1	1	1984	1984	
BOMARC	NIGHT WYND ENTERPRISES		1	5	1992	1993	
BOMBA THE JUNGLE BOY	DC COMICS INC.		1	7	1967	1968	
BOMBAST	TOPPS		1	1	1993	1993	
BOMBER COMICS	ELLIOT PUBLISHING COMPANY		1	4	1944	1945	
BONANZA	GOLD KEY		1	37	1962	1970	
BONANZA	TOP SELLERS		1	8	1970	1971	REPRINTS US DELL MATERIAL
BONANZA	WORLD DISTRIBUTORS LTD		1	1	1967	1967	
BONANZA ANNUAL	PURNELL	1964	1968		1964	1968	
BONANZA WORLD ADVENTURE LIBRARY	WORLD DISTRIBUTORS LTD		1	3	1967	1967	
BONE	CARTOON BOOKS		1	13	1991	NOW	
BONE ADVENTURES, THE COMPLETE	CARTOON BOOKS		1	1	1993	1993	
BONES	MALIBU COMICS ENTERTAINMENT INC.		1	4	1987	1987	
BONZA COMIC	W. FORSHAW/ENSIGN		1	4	1947	1947	
BOOK OF ALL COMICS	WILLIAM H. WISE		1	1	1945	1945	
BOOK OF COMICS, THE	WILLIAM H. WISE		1	1	1944	1944	
BOOK OF NIGHT, CHARLES VESS' THE	DARK HORSE COMICS		1	1	1991	1991	
BOOK OF NIGHT, CHARLES VESS' THE	DARK HORSE COMICS		1	3	1987	1987	
BOOK OF THE DAMNED: A HELLRAISER COMPANION	MARVEL ENTERTAINMENT GROUP		1	2	1991	1991	EPIC TITLE
BOOK OF THE DEAD	MARVEL ENTERTAINMENT GROUP		1	3	1993	1994	
BOOKS OF MAGIC	DC COMICS INC.		1	1	1993	1993	
BOOKS OF MAGIC	DC COMICS INC.		1	2	1994	NOW	
BOOKS OF MAGIC	DC COMICS INC.		1	4	1990	1991	
BOOMERANG COMIC	SCION		1	1	1948	1948	
BOOSTER GOLD	DC COMICS INC.		1	25	1986	1988	
BOOTS AND HER BUDDIES	ARGO PUBLISHING		1	3	1955	1956	
BOOTS AND HER BUDDIES	STANDARD COMICS	5		9	1948	1949	
BORDER GUARD	ETERNITY		1	2	1987	1988	
BORDER PATROL	PL PUBLISHING		1	3	1951	1952	
BORDER WORLDS	KITCHEN SINK	1	1	7	1986	1987	
BORDER WORLDS: MAROONED	KITCHEN SINK		1	1	1990	1990	
BORIS ADVENTURE MAGAZINE	NICOTAT		1	1	1988	1988	
BORIS KARLOFF TALES OF MYSTERY	GOLD KEY	3		97	1963	1980	FORMERLY BORIS KARLOFF THRILLER
BORIS KARLOFF THRILLER	GOLD KEY		1	2	1962	1963	BECOMES BORIS KARLOFF TALES OF MYSTERY
BORIS THE BEAR	DARK HORSE COMICS		1	31	1990	NOW	
BORIS THE BEAR INSTANT COLOUR CLASSICS	DARK HORSE COMICS		1	7	1987	1988	
BORN TO BE WILD	ECLIPSE		1	1	1991	1991	
BORN TO KILL	AIRCEL		1	3	1991	NOW	
BOSTON BOMBERS	CALIBER PRESS		1	6	1990	1991	
BOUNCER COMIC	P.M. PRODUCTIONS		1	1	1949	1949	
BOUNCER, THE	FOX FEATURES SYNDICATE	10		14	1944	1945	FORMERLY GREEN MASK
BOUNCERS	VICTOR GOLLANCZ LTD				1991	1991	
BOXING'S BEST COMICS	BOXING BEST COMICS		1	1	1993	1993	
BOY AND HIS BOT	NOW		1	1	1987	1987	
BOY COMICS	L. MILLER PUBLISHING COMPANY (UK)		1	8	1950	1951	REPRINTS US MATERIAL
BOY COMICS	LEV GLEASON PUBLICATIONS		3	119	1942	1956	
BOY COMMANDOS	DC COMICS INC.	1	1	36	1942	1949	
BOY COMMANDOS	DC COMICS INC.	2	1	2	1973	1973	
BOY COWBOY	ZIFF-DAVIS PUBLISHING COMPANY		1	1	1950	1950	

COMIC TITLE	PUBLISHER	Vol No.	Srt No.	End No.	Str. Year	End Year	COMMENTS
BOY DETECTIVE	AVON BOOKS		1	4	1951	1952	
BOY DETECTIVE COMICS	HERMITAGE/THORPE & FOSTER		1	1	1952	1952	
BOY EXPLORERS COMICS	HARVEY PUBLICATIONS		1	2	1946	1946	
BOY LOVES GIRL	LEV GLEASON PUBLICATIONS		25	57	1952	1956	FORMERLY BOY MEETS GIRL
BOY MEETS GIRL	LEV GLEASON PUBLICATIONS		1	24	1950	1952	
BOY'S RANCH	HARVEY PUBLICATIONS		1	6	1950	1951	
BOYS DUX	CARTOON ART		1	1	1948	1948	
BOYS' RANCH	MARVEL ENTERTAINMENT GROUP		1	1	1993	1993	
BOYS' RANCH	STREAMLINE		1	4	1951	???	REPRINTS US HARVEY MATERIAL
BOYS' WORLD	LONGACRE		1	89	1963	1964	
BOYS' WORLD ANNUAL	ODHAMS	1964		1971	1964	1971	
BOZO THE CLOWN	DELL PUBLISHING COMPANY		1	4	1962	1963	
BOZO THE CLOWN	INNOVATION		1	1	1992	1992	
BOZZ CHRONICLES	MARVEL ENTERTAINMENT GROUP		1	6	1985	1986	
BRADLEY'S	FANTAGRAPHICS		1	1	1992	1992	SIGNED & LIMITED
BRADY BUNCH, THE	DELL PUBLISHING COMPANY		1	2	1970	1970	
BRAGADE	PARODY PRESS		1	1	1993	1993	
BRAIN	MAGAZINE ENTERPRISES		1	7	1956	1958	
BRAIN BOY	DELL PUBLISHING COMPANY		2	6	1962	1963	
BRAINSTORM COMIX	ALCHEMY STUDIOS		1	6	1975	1977	
BRAINSTORM!	ALCHEMY STUDIOS		1	1	1982	1982	
BRAM STOKER'S DRACULA	DARK HORSE COMICS		1	10	1993	NOW	
BRAM STOKER'S DRACULA	TOPPS		1	1	1993	1993	
BRAM STOKER'S DRACULA	TOPPS		1	4	1992	1993	
BRANDED PICTURE AND STORY ALBUM	MELLIFONT		1	1	50'S	50'S	
BRATPACK	TUNDRA		1	5	1990	1991	
BRATS BIZARRE	MARVEL ENTERTAINMENT GROUP		1	4	1994	1994	
BRAVE AND THE BOLD	DC COMICS INC.		1	6	1991	1992	
BRAVE AND THE BOLD, THE	DC COMICS INC.		1	200	1955	1983	
BREAK-THRU	MALIBU COMICS ENTERTAINMENT INC.		1	1	1993	1994	ULTRAVERSE TITLE
BREATHTAKER	DC COMICS INC.		1	4	1990	1990	
BREED	MALIBU COMICS ENTERTAINMENT INC.		1	6	1993	1994	
BREED	G & C PRODUCTIONS		1	1	1946	1946	
BREEZY COMIC	P.M. PRODUCTIONS		1	1	1947	1947	
BREEZY COMICS	DELL PUBLISHING COMPANY		1	1	1962	1962	
BRENDA LEE STORY, THE	CHARLTON COMICS		13	15	1955	1955	BECOMES YOUNG LOVERS
BRENDA STARR	FOUR STAR COMICS CORP./SUPERIOR COMICS LTD	1	13	14	1947	1948	
BRENDA STARR	FOUR STAR COMICS CORP./SUPERIOR COMICS LTD	2	3	12	1948	1949	
BRENDA STARR REPORTER	DELL PUBLISHING COMPANY		1	1	1963	1963	
BRER RABBIT "ICE-CREAM FOR THE PARTY"	AMERICAN DAIRY ASSOCIATION		1	1	1955	1955	
BRIAN BOLLAND'S BLACK BOOK	ECLIPSE		1	1	1985	1985	
BRICK BRADFORD	KING FEATURES		5	8	1948	1949	
BRICK BRADFORD	WORLD DISTRIBUTORS LTD		1	6	1959	1959	REPRINTS US MATERIAL
BRICKMAN	HARRIER		1	1	1986	1986	
BRICKMAN	HARRIER		1	6	1986	1987	
BRIDE'S DIARY	AJAX		4	10	1955	1956	
BRIDE'S SECRETS	AJAX		1	19	1954	1958	
BRIDES IN LOVE	CHARLTON COMICS		1	45	1956	1965	
BRIDES ROMANCES	QUALITY COMICS		1	23	1953	1956	
BRIGADE	IMAGE COMICS		1	4	1992	1992	
BRIGADE	IMAGE COMICS	2	0	6	1993	NOW	
BRIGAND DOOM	FLEETWAY		1	4	1993	1993	
BRIGHT AND BREEZY	P.M. PRODUCTIONS		1	1	1948	1948	
BRINGING UP FATHER	CUPPLES AND LEON CO.		1	26	1919	1934	
BRINGING UP FATHER	KING FEATURES		1	1	1917	1917	
BRINGING UP FATHER, THE BIG BOOK	CUPPLES AND LEON CO.		1	2	1926	1929	
BRINGING UP FATHER, THE TROUBLE OF	CUPPLES AND LEON CO.				1921	1921	
BRIT FORCE	C M PUBLISHING		1	2	1993	NOW	
BRITISH HEROES	SPORTING CARTOONS		1	8	1953	1954	
BROADWAY HOLLYWOOD BLACKOUTS	STANHALL		1	3	1954	1954	
BROADWAY ROMANCES	QUALITY COMICS		1	5	1950	1950	
BROID	ETERNITY		1	4	1990	1990	
BRONCHO BILL	STANDARD COMICS		5	16	1948	1950	
BRONCHO BILL	UNITED FEATURES SYNDICATE		1	2	1939	1940	
BRONCO BILL COMIC	DONALD PETERS		1	1	1950	1950	REPRINTS US MATERIAL
BRONCO BILL WESTERN COMIC	DONALD PETERS		1	17	1951	1952	
BRONCO! PICTURE AND STORY ALBUM	MELLIFONT		1	1	50'S	50'S	
BRONIC SADDLER	L. MILLER PUBLISHING COMPANY (UK)		1	2	1959	1959	REPRINTS US MATERIAL
BRONX	ETERNITY		1	3	1991	1991	
BROONS ANNUAL, THE	D.C. THOMSON	1940		1992	1940	1992	
BROTHER POWER THE GEEK	DC COMICS INC.		1	2	1968	1968	
BROTHERS OF THE SPEAR	GOLD KEY		1	17	1972	1976	
BROTHERS OF THE SPEAR	WHITMAN		18	18	1982	1982	
BROVADOS, THE	SKYWALD PUBLISHING		1	1	1971	1971	
BRUCE GENTRY	STANDARD COMICS		1	8	1948	1949	
BRUCE JONES OUTER EDGE	INNOVATION		1	1	1992	1992	
BRUCE JONES RAZOR'S EDGE	INNOVATION		1	1	1992	1992	
BRUTE	ATLAS		1	3	1975	1975	
BRUTE FORCE	MARVEL ENTERTAINMENT GROUP		1	4	1990	1990	
BUBBLEGUM CRISIS: GRAND MAL	DARK HORSE COMICS		1	4	1994	1994	
BUCCANEER	I.W. SUPER		1	8	1963	1963	
BUCCANEERS	POPULAR		1	1	1951	1951	
BUCCANEERS	QUALITY COMICS		19	27	1950	1951	FORMERLY KID ETERNITY
BUCCANEERS, THE	PEARSON		1	2	1959	1959	
BUCK DUCK	ATLAS		1	4	1953	1953	
BUCK GODOT: ZAP GUN FOR HIRE	PALLIARD PRESS		1	1	1993	NOW	
BUCK JONES	DELL PUBLISHING COMPANY		2	8	1951	1952	
BUCK JONES	WORLD DISTRIBUTORS LTD		1	11	1953	1954	

INDEX OF COMIC TITLES AND THEIR PUBLISHERS

COMIC TITLE	PUBLISHER	Vol No.	Srt No.	End No.	Str. Year	End Year	COMMENTS
BUCK JONES ANNUAL	AMALGAMATED PRESS		1957	1958	1957	1958	
BUCK ROGERS	GOLD KEY		1	6	1964	1979	PUBLICATION CONTINUED BY WHITMAN
BUCK ROGERS	HEROIC PUBLISHING		1	6	1940	1943	
BUCK ROGERS	TOBY PRESS PUBLICATIONS		100	101	1951	1951	
BUCK ROGERS	TSR		1	12	1990	1991	
BUCK ROGERS	WHITMAN		7	16	1979	1982	FORMERLY PUBLISHED BY GOLD KEY
BUCK ROGERS ADVENTURE BOOK	COCOMALT		1	1	1933	1933	
BUCK ROGERS IN THE 25TH CENTURY	WHITMAN		7	16	1981	1982	
BUCK RYAN: THE CASE OF THE OBLONG BOX	MIRROR PRESS PUBLICATIONS		1	1	1946	1946	
BUCKAROO BANZAI	MARVEL ENTERTAINMENT GROUP		1	2	1984	1985	
BUCKY O'HARE	CONTINUITY COMICS		1	1	1988	1988	
BUCKY O'HARE	CONTINUITY COMICS	2	1	6	1991	NOW	
BUCKY O'HARE	D.C. THOMSON		1	20	1992	1992	
BUDDHA'S PALM	JADEMAN COMICS		1	56	1988	1992	
BUDDIES IN THE U.S. ARMY	AVON BOOKS		1	2	1952	1953	
BUDDY	D.C. THOMSON		1	130	1981	1983	
BUDDY TUCKER & HIS FRIENDS	CUPPLES AND LEON CO.		1905	1905	1906	1906	
BUFFALO BILL	BOARDMAN		8	43	1948	1951	
BUFFALO BILL	STREAMLINE		1	2	1952	1952	REPRINTS US MATERIAL
BUFFALO BILL	YOUTHFUL MAGAZINES		2	9	1950	1951	
BUFFALO BILL CODY	L. MILLER PUBLISHING COMPANY (UK)		1	19	50'S	50'S	
BUFFALO BILL COMIC	POPULAR		45	49	1953	1955	CONTINUES FROM BOARDMAN SERIES
BUFFALO BILL PICTURE STORIES	STREET AND SMITH PUBLICATIONS		1	1	1909	1909	
BUFFALO BILL WILD WEST ANNUAL	POPULAR		1	13	1949	1961	
BUFFALO BILL, JR.	DELL PUBLISHING COMPANY		1	13	1956	1959	
BUFFALO BILL, JR.	GOLD KEY		1	1	1965	1965	
BUG MOVIES	DELL PUBLISHING COMPANY		1	1	1931	1931	
BUGALOOS	CHARLTON COMICS		1	4	1971	1972	
BUGHOUSE	AJAX		1	4	1954	1954	
BUGHOUSE FABLES	KING FEATURES		1	1	1921	1921	
BUGS BUNNY	DC COMICS INC.		1	3	1990	1990	
BUGS BUNNY	DELL PUBLISHING COMPANY		28	85	1953	1962	
BUGS BUNNY	GOLD KEY		86	218	1962	1981	
BUGS BUNNY	QUAKER OATS GIVEAWAYS		1	1	1949	1949	
BUGS BUNNY	THORPE & PORTER		1	4	1953	1953	REPRINTS US DELL MATERIAL
BUGS BUNNY	TOP SELLERS		1	?	1973	???	REPRINTS DELL MATERIAL
BUGS BUNNY	WHITMAN		219	245	1981	1983	
BUGS BUNNY 3-D	CHEERIOS GIVEAWAY		1	1	1953	1953	
BUGS BUNNY AND PORKY PIG	GOLD KEY		1	1	1965	1965	
BUGS BUNNY CHRISTMAS FUNNIES	DELL PUBLISHING COMPANY		1	9	1950	1958	NO. 6 ENTITLED BUGS BUNNY CHRISTMAS PARTY
BUGS BUNNY HALLOWEEN PARADE	DELL PUBLISHING COMPANY		1	2	1953	1954	BECOMES BUGS BUNNY TRICK 'N' TREAT HALLOWEEN FUN
BUGS BUNNY TRICK 'N' TREAT HALLOWEEN FUN	DELL PUBLISHING COMPANY		3	4	1955	1956	FORMERLY BUGS BUNNY HALLOWEEN PARADE
BUGS BUNNY'S VACATION FUNNIES	DELL PUBLISHING COMPANY		1	9	1951	1959	
BULLDOG BRITTAIN COMMANDO	L. MILLER PUBLISHING COMPANY (UK)		1	3	1952	1952	
BULLET	D.C. THOMSON		1	147	1976	1978	
BULLET CROW, FOWL OF FORTUNE	ECLIPSE		1	2	1987	1987	
BULLET SPORTS SPECIAL	D.C. THOMSON		1	1	1977	1977	
BULLETMAN	ARNOLD BOOK CO.		10	10	1951	1951	REPRINTS FAWCETT MATERIAL
BULLETMAN	FAWCETT PUBLICATIONS		1	16	1941	1946	
BULLS-EYE	CHARLTON COMICS		6	7	1955	1955	FORMERLY PUBLISHED BY MAINLINE
BULLS-EYE	MAINLINE		1	5	1954	1955	BECOMES CODY OF THE PONY EXPRESS
BULLS-EYE COMICS	HARRY A CHESLER		11	11	1944	1944	FORMERLY KOMIK PAGES, BECOMES KAYO
BULLWINKLE	CHARLTON COMICS		1	7	1970	1971	BULLWINKLE AND ROCKY ON COVER FROM ISSUE 2
BULLWINKLE	GOLD KEY		1	25	1962	1980	TITLE BECOMES BULLWINKLE AND ROCKY FROM 20# TO 25#
BULLWINKLE AND ROCKY	MARVEL ENTERTAINMENT GROUP		1	1	1992	1992	
BULLWINKLE AND ROCKY IN 3-D	MARVEL ENTERTAINMENT GROUP		1	9	1987	1989	
BULLWINKLE FOR PRESIDENT IN 3-D	BLACKTHORNE		1	1	1987	1987	
BUMPER SUPER MAG	BLACKTHORNE		1	1	1988	1988	
BUNNY	YOUNG WORLD		1	1	1964	1964	
BUNTY	HARVEY PUBLICATIONS		1	21	1966	1976	
BURGLAR BILL	D.C. THOMSON		1	1824	1958	1992	
BURIED TREASURE	TRIDENT		1	4	1990	1990	
BURKE'S LAW	CALIBER PRESS		1	5	1990	NOW	
BUSHIDO	DELL PUBLISHING COMPANY		1	3	1964	1965	
BUSHIDO: BLADE OF ZATOICHI WALRUS	ETERNITY		1	4	1988	1989	
BUSTER	SOLSON		1	1	1986	1986	
BUSTER ADVENTURE LIBRARY	FLEETWAY	1960	1993	1960		NOW	
BUSTER BEAR	FLEETWAY		1	36	1966	1967	
BUSTER BOOK ANNUAL	QUALITY (FLEETWAY)		1	10	1953	1955	
BUSTER BOOK OF SPOOKY STORIES	FLEETWAY	1962	1993	1962		1993	
BUSTER BOOK OF THRILLS	FLEETWAY	1975	1976	1975		1976	
BUSTER BROWN COMICS	FLEETWAY		1	1	1962	1962	
BUSTER BUNNY	BROWN SHOE COMPANY		1	43	1945	1959	
BUSTER COMIC	STANDARD COMICS		1	16	1949	1953	
BUSTER COMIC	CARTOON ART		1	1	1947	1947	
BUSTER CRABBE	PHILLIP MARX		1	1	1946	1946	REPRINTS
BUSTER CRABBE, THE AMAZING ADVENTURE OF	PHILLIP MARX		1	12	1951	1953	
BUTCH CASSIDY	LEV GLEASON PUBLICATIONS		1	4	1953	1954	
BUTCH CASSIDY AND THE WILD BUNCH	SKYWALD PUBLISHING		1	1	1971	1971	
BUTCHER, THE	AVON BOOKS		1	1	1951	1951	
BUZ SAWYER	DC COMICS INC.		1	5	1990	1990	
BUZZ	STANDARD COMICS		1	3	1948	1949	BECOMES SWEENEY
BUZZY	KITCHEN SINK		1	2	1990	1990	
BY THE TIME I GET TO WAGGA WAGGA	DC COMICS INC.		1	77	1944	1958	
	HARRIER		1	1	1987	1987	

COMIC TITLE	PUBLISHER	Vol No.	Srt No.	End No.	Str. Year	End Year	COMMENTS

C

COMIC TITLE	PUBLISHER	Vol No.	Srt No.	End No.	Str. Year	End Year	COMMENTS
C-M-O COMICS	CENTAUR PUBLICATIONS		I	2	1942	1942	
CABINET OF DR. CALIGARI, THE	MONSTER COMICS		I	3	1992	1992	
CABLE	MARVEL ENTERTAINMENT GROUP		I	I	1992	1992	
CABLE	MARVEL ENTERTAINMENT GROUP		I	8	1993	NOW	
CABLE T.V.	PARODY PRESS		I	I	1993	1993	
CABLE: BLOOD AND METAL	MARVEL ENTERTAINMENT GROUP		I	2	1992	1992	
CADAVERA	MONSTER COMICS		I	2	1991	1991	
CADET GRAY OF WEST POINT	DELL PUBLISHING COMPANY		I	I	1958	1958	
CADILLACS AND DINOSAURS	MARVEL ENTERTAINMENT GROUP		I	6	1990	1991	
CADILLACS AND DINOSAURS	TOPPS		I	3	1994	1994	
CADILLACS AND DINOSAURS IN 3-D	KITCHEN SINK		I	I	1992	1992	
CADILLACS AND DINOSAURS: TIME IN OVERDRIVE	KITCHEN SINK		I	I	1993	1993	
CAGE	MARVEL ENTERTAINMENT GROUP		I	20	1992	NOW	
CAGES	TUNDRA		I	8	1991	NOW	
CAIN	HARRIS COMICS		I	2	1993	NOW	
CAIN'S HUNDRED	DELL PUBLISHING COMPANY		I	2	1962	1962	
CAIN'S HUNDRED	THORPE & PORTER		I	I	1962	1962	REPRINTS DELL MATERIAL AND MR. DISTRICT ATTORNEY
CALCULUS CAT: DEATH TO TELEVISION	KNOCKABOUT		I	I	1987	1987	
CALIBER PRESENTS	CALIBER PRESS		I	23	1989	1991	
CALIBER PRESENTS: SEPULCHER OPUS	CALIBER PRESS		I	I	1993	1993	
CALIBER PRESENTS: SUB-ATOMIC SHOCK	CALIBER PRESS		I	I	1991	1991	
CALIBER SUMMER SPECIAL	CALIBER PRESS		I	I	1991	1991	
CALIFORNIA GIRLS	ECLIPSE		I	8	1987	1988	
CALIFORNIA RAISINS IN 3-D	BLACKTHORNE		I	4	1987	1988	
CALIGARI 2050	MONSTER COMICS		I	I	1992	NOW	
CALIGARI 2050: ANOTHER SLEEPLESS NIGHT	CALIBER PRESS		I	I	1993	1993	
CALL FROM CHRIST	CAETECHETICAL EDUCATIONAL SOCIETY		I	I	1952	1952	
CALLING ALL BOYS	PARENTS MAGAZINE INSTITUTE		I	17	1946	1948	BECOMES TEX GRANGER
CALLING ALL GIRLS	PARENTS MAGAZINE INSTITUTE		I	89	1941	1949	
CALLING ALL KIDS	PARENTS MAGAZINE INSTITUTE		I	26	1945	1949	
CALLING MATT HARDY	FOLDES PRESS		I	I	1947	1947	
CALVIN & HOBBES: THE DAYS ARE JUST PACKED	ANDREWS AND MCMEEL		I	I	1993	1993	
CALVIN AND HOBBES	ANDREWS AND MCMEEL		I	I	1988	1988	
CALVIN AND HOBBES: ATTACK OF THE MUTANT SNOW GOONS	ANDREWS AND MCMEEL		I	I	1992	1992	
CALVIN AND HOBBES: IN THE SHADOW OF THE NIGHT	ANDREWS AND MCMEEL		I	I	1992	1992	
CALVIN AND HOBBES: LAZY SUNDAY BOOK	ANDREWS AND MCMEEL		I	I	1990	1990	
CALVIN AND HOBBES: ONE DAY THE WIND WILL CHANGE	ANDREWS AND MCMEEL		I	I	1992	1992	
CALVIN AND HOBBES: REVENGE OF THE BABY-SAT	ANDREWS AND MCMEEL		I	I	1991	1991	
CALVIN AND HOBBES: SCIENTIFIC PROGRESS GOES BOINK	ANDREWS AND MCMEEL		I	I	1991	1991	
CALVIN AND HOBBES: SOMETHING UNDER THE BED	ANDREWS AND MCMEEL		I	I	1989	1989	
CALVIN AND HOBBES: THE AUTHORITATIVE	ANDREWS AND MCMEEL		I	I	1991	1991	
CALVIN AND HOBBES: THE ESSENTIAL	ANDREWS AND MCMEEL		I	I	1992	1992	
CALVIN AND HOBBES: THEREBY HANGS A TAIL	ANDREWS AND MCMEEL		I	I	1992	1992	
CALVIN AND HOBBES: WEIRDOS FROM ANOTHER PLANET	ANDREWS AND MCMEEL		I	I	1990	1990	
CALVIN AND HOBBES: YUKON HO!	ANDREWS AND MCMEEL		I	I	1989	1989	
CALVIN AND THE COLONEL	DELL PUBLISHING COMPANY		2	2	1962	1962	
CAMELOT 3000	DC COMICS INC.		I	I	1988	1988	
CAMELOT 3000	DC COMICS INC.		I	12	1982	1985	
CAMELOT ETERNAL	CALIBER PRESS		I	7	1990	NOW	
CAMERA COMICS	MAGAZINE ENTERPRISES		I	9	1944	1946	
CAMP CANDY	MARVEL ENTERTAINMENT GROUP		I	5	1990	1990	
CAMP COMICS	DELL PUBLISHING COMPANY		I	3	1942	1942	
CAMP RUNAMUCK	DELL PUBLISHING COMPANY		I	I	1966	1966	
CAMPUS LOVES	QUALITY COMICS		I	5	1949	1950	
CAMPUS ROMANCE	AVON BOOKS		I	3	1949	1950	
CANARDO: A SHABBY DOG STORY	XPRESSO BOOKS, DIVISION OF FLEETWAY				1991	1991	
CANARDO: BLUE ANGEL	XPRESSO BOOKS, DIVISION OF FLEETWAY				1991	1991	
CANCELLED COMIC CAVALCADE	DC COMICS INC.		I	2	1978	1978	
CANDID TALES	KIRBY PUBLISHING COMPANY		I	I	1950	1950	
CANDY	CITY		I	154	1967	1969	
CANDY	QUALITY COMICS		I	64	1947	1956	
CANDY	WILLIAM H. WISE		I	3	1944	1945	
CANDY COMIC	PHILIMAR		I	3	1947	1948	
CANNON	EROS		I	8	1991	1991	
CANNON	HEROES INCORPORATED		I	4	1964	1971	
CANNONBALL COMICS	RURAL HOME PUBLISHING COMPANY		I	2	1945	1945	
CANTEEN KATE	ST JOHN PUBLISHING		I	3	1952	1952	
CAP'N CRUNCH COMICS	QUAKER OATS GIVEAWAYS				1963	1965	
CAP'N QUICK & A FOOZLE	ECLIPSE		I	3	1985	1985	
CAPTAIN 3-D	HARVEY PUBLICATIONS		I	I	1953	1953	
CAPTAIN 3-D	UNITED-ANGLO PRODUCTIONS		I	I	1954	1954	REPRINTS HARVEY DITKO MATERIAL
CAPTAIN ACTION	DC COMICS INC.		I	5	1968	1969	
CAPTAIN ACTION AND ACTION BOY	DC COMICS INC.		I	I	1967	1967	
CAPTAIN AERO COMICS	HOLYOKE PUBLISHING COMPANY	I	I	12	1941	1942	
CAPTAIN AERO COMICS	HOLYOKE PUBLISHING COMPANY	2	I	4	1943	1943	
CAPTAIN AERO COMICS	HOLYOKE PUBLISHING COMPANY	3	9	13	1943	1944	
CAPTAIN AERO COMICS	HOLYOKE PUBLISHING COMPANY	4	2	25	1944	1946	ISSUES 4-20 DO NOT EXIST
CAPTAIN AMERICA	L. MILLER PUBLISHING COMPANY (UK)		I	?	1954	???	REPRINTS
CAPTAIN AMERICA	MARVEL ENTERTAINMENT GROUP		100	434	1968	NOW	FORMERLY TALES OF SUSPENSE
CAPTAIN AMERICA (U.K.)	MARVEL ENTERTAINMENT GROUP		I	59	1981	1982	REPRINTS
CAPTAIN AMERICA AND THE CAMPBELL KIDS	MARVEL ENTERTAINMENT GROUP		I	I	1980	1980	
CAPTAIN AMERICA ANNUAL	MARVEL ENTERTAINMENT GROUP		I	12	1971	NOW	

COMIC TITLE	PUBLISHER	Vol No.	Srt No.	End No.	Str. Year	End Year	COMMENTS
CAPTAIN AMERICA BOOK AND RECORD	MARVEL ENTERTAINMENT GROUP		1	1	1974	1974	
CAPTAIN AMERICA COMICS	TIMELY COMICS		1	78	1941	1954	ISSUES 74,75 TITLED CAPTAIN AMERICA'S WEIRD TALES
CAPTAIN AMERICA GIANT SIZE	MARVEL ENTERTAINMENT GROUP		1	1	1975	1975	
CAPTAIN AMERICA GOES TO WAR AGAINST DRUGS	MARVEL ENTERTAINMENT GROUP		1	1	1990	1990	
CAPTAIN AMERICA MEETS THE ASTHMA MONSTER	MARVEL ENTERTAINMENT GROUP		1	1	1987	1987	
CAPTAIN AMERICA MOVIE ADAPTATION	MARVEL ENTERTAINMENT GROUP		1	1	1992	1992	
CAPTAIN AMERICA SPECIAL EDITION	MARVEL ENTERTAINMENT GROUP		1	2	1984	1984	
CAPTAIN AMERICA SUMMER SPECIAL	MARVEL ENTERTAINMENT GROUP		1	1	1981	1981	REPRINTS
CAPTAIN AMERICA VERSUS THE ASTHMA MONSTER	MARVEL ENTERTAINMENT GROUP		1	1	1990	1990	
CAPTAIN AMERICA: BLOODSTONE HUNT	MARVEL ENTERTAINMENT GROUP		1	1	1993	1993	
CAPTAIN AMERICA: DEATHLOK LIVES	MARVEL ENTERTAINMENT GROUP		1	1	1993	1993	
CAPTAIN AMERICA: THE CLASSIC YEARS	MARVEL ENTERTAINMENT GROUP		1	1	1990	1990	
CAPTAIN AMERICA: WAR AND REMEMBERANCE	MARVEL ENTERTAINMENT GROUP		1	1	1993	1993	
CAPTAIN AND THE KIDS, THE	DELL PUBLISHING COMPANY		1	32	1947	1955	
CAPTAIN AND THE KIDS, THE	UNITED FEATURES SYNDICATE		1	1	1938	1938	
CAPTAIN AND THE KIDS, THE 50TH ANNIVERSARY ISSUE	DELL PUBLISHING COMPANY		1	1	1948	1948	
CAPTAIN AND THE KIDS, THE SPECIAL SUMMER ISSUE	DELL PUBLISHING COMPANY		1	1	1948	1948	
CAPTAIN ATOM	CHARLTON COMICS		78	89	1965	1967	
CAPTAIN ATOM	DC COMICS INC.		1	57	1987	1991	
CAPTAIN ATOM	MODERN COMICS		83	85	1977	1977	
CAPTAIN ATOM	NATIONWIDE PUBLISHERS		1	7	1950	1951	
CAPTAIN ATOM ANNUAL	DC COMICS INC.		1	2	1988	1989	
CAPTAIN ATOM SECRET OF THE COLUMBIAN JUNGLE	NATIONWIDE PUBLISHERS		1	1	1951	1951	
CAPTAIN BATTLE	LEV GLEASON PUBLICATIONS		1	2	1941	1941	BECOMES BOY COMICS
CAPTAIN BATTLE	MAGAZINE PRESS		3	5	1942	1943	
CAPTAIN BATTLE, JR.	LEV GLEASON PUBLICATIONS		1	2	1943	1944	
CAPTAIN BRITAIN	MARVEL ENTERTAINMENT GROUP		1	1	1986	1986	
CAPTAIN BRITAIN	MARVEL ENTERTAINMENT GROUP		1	39	1976	1977	
CAPTAIN BRITAIN ANNUAL	MARVEL ENTERTAINMENT GROUP		1978	1978	1978	1978	
CAPTAIN BRITAIN AUTUMN SPECIAL	MARVEL ENTERTAINMENT GROUP		1	1	1992	1992	
CAPTAIN BRITAIN MONTHLY	MARVEL ENTERTAINMENT GROUP		1	14	1985	1986	
CAPTAIN BRITAIN SUMMER SPECIAL	MARVEL ENTERTAINMENT GROUP		1980	1983	1980	1983	
CAPTAIN CANUCK	COMELY COMICS		1	14	1975	1981	
CAPTAIN CANUCK FIRST SUMMER SPECIAL	COMELY COMICS		1	1	1980	1980	
CAPTAIN CARROT AND HIS AMAZING ZOO CREW	DC COMICS INC.		1	20	1982	1983	
CAPTAIN CARROT OZ-WONDERLAND WARS	DC COMICS INC.		1	3	1986	1986	
CAPTAIN CONFEDERACY	MARVEL ENTERTAINMENT GROUP		1	4	1991	1992	
CAPTAIN CONFEDERACY	STEEL DRAGON		1	12	1986	1987	
CAPTAIN CONFEDERACY SPECIAL	STEEL DRAGON		1	3	1986	1987	
CAPTAIN COURAGEOUS COMICS	ACE MAGAZINES		6	6	1942	1942	
CAPTAIN EASY	ARGO PUBLISHING		1	1	1956	1956	
CAPTAIN EASY	DELL PUBLISHING COMPANY		10	17	1947	1949	
CAPTAIN EASY	HAWLEY		1	1	1939	1939	
CAPTAIN EO IN 3-D	ECLIPSE		1	1	1987	1987	
CAPTAIN FEARLESS COMICS	HOLYOKE PUBLISHING COMPANY		1	2	1941	1941	
CAPTAIN FIGHT	CARTOON ART		1	1	1950	1950	REPRINTS US MATERIAL
CAPTAIN FLASH	L. MILLER PUBLISHING COMPANY (UK)		1	2	1955	1955	REPRINTS
CAPTAIN FLASH	STERLING COMICS		1	4	1954	1955	
CAPTAIN FLEET	ZIFF-DAVIS PUBLISHING COMPANY		1	1	1952	1952	
CAPTAIN FLIGHT COMICS	FOUR STAR COMICS CORP./SUPERIOR COMICS LTD		1	11	1944	1947	
CAPTAIN FORTUNE PRESENTS	VITAL PUBLICATIONS				1955	1959	
CAPTAIN GALLANT	CHARLTON COMICS		1	4	1955	1956	
CAPTAIN GALLANT	L. MILLER PUBLISHING COMPANY (UK)		1	4	1956	1956	REPRINTS CHARLTON SERIES
CAPTAIN GLORY	TOPPS		1	1	1993	1993	
CAPTAIN HARLOCK	ETERNITY		1	13	1989	NOW	
CAPTAIN HARLOCK CHRISTMAS SPECIAL	ETERNITY		1	1	1992	1992	
CAPTAIN HARLOCK RETURNS	MALIBU COMICS ENTERTAINMENT INC.		1	1	1993	NOW	
CAPTAIN HARLOCK: DEATHSHADOW RISING	ETERNITY		1	6	1991	1991	
CAPTAIN HARLOCK: FALL OF THE EMPIRE	ETERNITY		1	4	1992	1992	
CAPTAIN HARLOCK: THE MACHINE PEOPLE	ETERNITY		2	4	1993	1993	
CAPTAIN HERO COMICS DIGEST MAGAZINE	ARCHIE PUBLICATIONS		1	1	1981	1981	
CAPTAIN HOBBY COMICS	EXPORT PUBLICATIONS ENTERTAINMENT INC.		1	1	1948	1948	
CAPTAIN JET	FOUR STAR COMICS CORP./SUPERIOR COMICS LTD		1	6	1952	1953	BECOMES FANTASTIC FEARS
CAPTAIN JUSTICE	MARVEL ENTERTAINMENT GROUP		1	2	1988	1988	
CAPTAIN KIDD	FOX FEATURES SYNDICATE		24	25	1949	1949	FORMERLY DAGAR, BECOMES MY SECRET STORY
CAPTAIN MAGNET	CARTOON ART		1	2	1947	1948	
CAPTAIN MARVEL	MARVEL ENTERTAINMENT GROUP		1	62	1968	1979	
CAPTAIN MARVEL (PRESENTS THE TERRIBLE FIVE)	MF ENTERPRISES		1	5	1967	1967	
CAPTAIN MARVEL ADVENTURES	FAWCETT PUBLICATIONS		1	1	1945	1945	
CAPTAIN MARVEL ADVENTURES	FAWCETT PUBLICATIONS		1	150	1941	1953	
CAPTAIN MARVEL ADVENTURES	L. MILLER PUBLISHING COMPANY (UK)	1	1	24	1953	1954	REPRINTS FAWCETT MATERIAL
CAPTAIN MARVEL ADVENTURES	L. MILLER PUBLISHING COMPANY (UK)	2	50	58	1956	1956	REPRINTS FAWCETT MATERIAL
CAPTAIN MARVEL AND THE GOOD HUMOR MAN	FAWCETT PUBLICATIONS		1	1	1950	1950	
CAPTAIN MARVEL AND THE LTS. OF SAFETY	FAWCETT PUBLICATIONS				1950	1951	
CAPTAIN MARVEL COLOURING BOOK	L. MILLER PUBLISHING COMPANY (UK)		1	1	1948	1948	
CAPTAIN MARVEL GIANT SIZE	MARVEL ENTERTAINMENT GROUP		1	1	1975	1975	
CAPTAIN MARVEL JNR.	L. MILLER PUBLISHING COMPANY (UK)	1	3	83	1950	1956	REPRINTS FAWCETT MATERIAL
CAPTAIN MARVEL JNR.	L. MILLER PUBLISHING COMPANY (UK)	2	1	24	1953	1954	REPRINTS FAWCETT MATERIAL
CAPTAIN MARVEL JUNIOR	FAWCETT PUBLICATIONS		1	119	1942	1953	
CAPTAIN MARVEL PRESENTS THE TERRIBLE FIVE	MF ENTERPRISES		1	1	1966	1966	
CAPTAIN MARVEL SPECIAL	MARVEL ENTERTAINMENT GROUP		1	1	1989	1989	
CAPTAIN MARVEL STORY BOOK	FAWCETT PUBLICATIONS		1	4	1946	1948	
CAPTAIN MARVEL THRILL BOOK	FAWCETT PUBLICATIONS		1	1	1941	1941	
CAPTAIN MARVEL'S FUN BOOK	SAMUEL LOWE COMPANY		1	1	1944	1944	
CAPTAIN MIDNIGHT	FAWCETT PUBLICATIONS		1	67	1942	1948	

INDEX OF COMIC TITLES AND THEIR PUBLISHERS

COMIC TITLE	PUBLISHER	Vol No.	Srt No.	End No.	Str. Year	End Year	COMMENTS
CAPTAIN MIDNIGHT	L. MILLER PUBLISHING COMPANY (UK)		1	54	1946	1963	REPRINTS
CAPTAIN MIRACLE	ANGLO		1	9	1960	1961	
CAPTAIN N: THE GAME MASTER	VALIANT / VOYAGER COMMUNICATIONS		1	6	1990	1991	
CAPTAIN NICE	GOLD KEY		1	1	1967	1967	
CAPTAIN OBLIVION	HARRIER		1	1	1987	1987	
CAPTAIN PARAGON	AC COMICS		1	4	1983	1984	
CAPTAIN PARAGON & SENTINELS OF JUSTICE	AC COMICS		1	6	1985	1986	
CAPTAIN PLANET	MARVEL ENTERTAINMENT GROUP		1	12	1991	1992	
CAPTAIN POWER AND THE SOLDIERS OF THE FUTURE	CONTINUITY COMICS		1	2	1988	1988	
CAPTAIN ROCKET	PL PUBLISHING		1	1	1951	1951	
CAPTAIN SAVAGE AND HIS LEATHERNECK RAIDERS	MARVEL ENTERTAINMENT GROUP		1	19	1968	1970	
CAPTAIN SCARLET AND THE MYSTERONS STORYBOOK	CENTURY 21		1	1	1969	1969	
CAPTAIN SCARLET ANNUAL	CITY	1967	1968	1967	1968		
CAPTAIN SCARLET ANNUAL	GRAND DREAMS	1994	1994	1994	1994		
CAPTAIN SCARLET/THUNDERBIRDS ANNUAL	CITY		1	1	1969	1969	
CAPTAIN SCARLETT	FLEETWAY		1	1	1993	NOW	
CAPTAIN SCIENCE	CARTOON ART		1	1	1951	1951	REPRINTS
CAPTAIN SCIENCE	YOUTHFUL MAGAZINES		1	7	1950	1951	BECOMES FANTASTIC
CAPTAIN STARLITE IN ROBBERY UNDER ARMS	L. MILLER PUBLISHING COMPANY (UK)		1	1	1957	1957	
CAPTAIN STERNN: RUNNING OUT OF TIME	KITCHEN SINK		1	2	1993	1994	
CAPTAIN STEVE SAVAGE	AVON BOOKS	1	1	13	1951	1953	
CAPTAIN STEVE SAVAGE	AVON BOOKS	2	5	13	1954	1956	
CAPTAIN STORM	DC COMICS INC.		1	18	1964	1967	
CAPTAIN THUNDER & BLUE BOLT	HEROIC PUBLISHING	2	1	2	1992	1993	
CAPTAIN THUNDER AND BLUE BOLT	HEROIC PUBLISHING	1	1	11	1987	1988	
CAPTAIN TOOTSIE AND THE SECRET LEGION	TOBY PRESS PUBLICATIONS		1	2	1950	1950	
CAPTAIN TORNADO	S.N.P.I./MUNDIAL		50	91	1952	1955	
CAPTAIN UNIVERSE	ARNOLD BOOK CO.		1	1	1954	1954	
CAPTAIN VENTURE AND THE LAND BENEATH THE SEA	GOLD KEY		1	2	1968	1969	
CAPTAIN VICTORY	PACIFIC COMICS		1	13	1981	1983	
CAPTAIN VICTORY AND THE GALACTIC RANGERS	PACIFIC		1	13	1981	1983	
CAPTAIN VICTORY SPECIAL	PACIFIC COMICS		1	1	1983	1983	
CAPTAIN VIDEO	FAWCETT PUBLICATIONS		1	6	1951	1951	
CAPTAIN VIDEO	L. MILLER PUBLISHING COMPANY (UK)		1	5	1951	1952	REPRINTS FAWCETT MATERIAL
CAPTAIN VIGOUR	SPORTING CARTOONS		1	17	1952	1954	
CAPTAIN WILLIE SCHULTZ	CHARLTON COMICS		76	77	1985	1986	
CAPTAIN ZENITH COMIC	MARTIN & REID		1	1	1950	1950	
CAPTAIN, THE	ALEXANDER HAMILTON	1	1	1	1949	1949	
CAR 54, WHERE ARE YOU?	DELL PUBLISHING COMPANY	1	2	7	1962	1963	
CAR 54, WHERE ARE YOU?	DELL PUBLISHING COMPANY	2	2	4	1964	1965	
CAR WARRIORS	MARVEL ENTERTAINMENT GROUP		1	4	1991	1991	
CARAVAN KIDD	DARK HORSE COMICS		1	10	1992	1993	
CARAVAN KIDD	DARK HORSE COMICS		1	7	1993	1993	
CARAVAN KIDD HOLIDAY SPECIAL	DARK HORSE COMICS		1	1	1993	1993	
CARDINAL MINDSZENTY	CAETECHETICAL EDUCATIONAL SOCIETY		1	1	1949	1949	
CARDS ILLUSTRATED	WARRIOR PUBLISHING	2	2	1	1993	NOW	
CARE BEARS	MARVEL ENTERTAINMENT GROUP		1	20	1985	1989	
CAREER GIRL ROMANCES	CHARLTON COMICS	4	24	78	1964	1973	FORMERLY THREE NURSES
CARL BARKS LIBRARY	WALT DISNEY		1	19	1991	NOW	
CARL BARKS LIBRARY OF 1940'S DONALD DUCK X-MAS	GLADSTONE		1	1	1992	1992	
CARL BARKS LIBRARY OF UNCLE SCROOGE ONE-PAGERS	WALT DISNEY		1	2	1992	1992	
CARNAGE	ETERNITY		1	1	1987	1987	
CARNIVAL OF COMICS	FLEET AIR SHOES		1	1	1954	1954	
CARNIVAL COMIC, THE	MARTIN & REID		1	1	1949	1949	
CARNIVAL COMICS	HARRY A CHESLER		13	13	1945	1945	FORMERLY KAYO, BECOMES RED SEAL COMICS
CARNIVAL OF SOULS	ETERNITY		1	1	1991	1991	
CAROLINE KENNEDY	CHARLTON COMICS		1	1	1961	1961	
CAROUSEL	F.E. HOWARD	8	8	1948	1948		
CARTOON CAPERS COMIC	MARTIN & REID		1	1	1949	1949	
CARTOON KIDS	ATLAS		1	1	1957	1957	
CARTOONS AND SKETCHES	JAMES HENDERSON		571	612	1901	1902	
CARVEL COMICS	CARVEL CORPORATION		1	5	1975	1976	
CARY COLT	L. MILLER PUBLISHING COMPANY (UK)		1	8	1954	1954	
CASANOVA'S LAST STAND	KNOCKABOUT		1	1	1993	1993	
CASE OF THE WASTED WATER, THE	RHEEM WATER HEATING		1	1	1972	1972	
CASE OF THE WINKING BUDDHA, THE	ST JOHN PUBLISHING		1	1	1950	1950	
CASES OF SHERLOCK HOLMES	RENEGADE PRESS		1	20	1986	NOW	
CASEY CRIME PHOTOGRAPHER	MARVEL ENTERTAINMENT GROUP		1	4	1949	1950	BECOMES TWO GUN WESTERN
CASEY RUGGLES COMIC	DONALD PETERS		1	47	1951	1955	REPRINTS US STRIP MATERIAL
CASPER ADVENTURE DIGEST	HARVEY PUBLICATIONS		1	8	1992	NOW	
CASPER AND	HARVEY PUBLICATIONS		1	12	1987	1990	
CASPER AND FRIENDS	HARVEY PUBLICATIONS		1	5	1991	1992	
CASPER AND NIGHTMARE	HARVEY PUBLICATIONS		6	46	1964	1974	FORMERLY NIGHTMARE AND CASPER
CASPER AND SPOOKY	HARVEY PUBLICATIONS		1	7	1972	1973	
CASPER AND THE GHOSTLY TRIO	HARVEY PUBLICATIONS		1	10	1972	1973	
CASPER AND WENDY	HARVEY PUBLICATIONS		1	8	1972	1973	
CASPER BIG BOOK	HARVEY PUBLICATIONS		1	3	1992	NOW	
CASPER CAT	I.W. ENTERPRISES		1	1	1958	1958	
CASPER DIGEST MAGAZINE	HARVEY PUBLICATIONS	1	1	20	1986	1988	
CASPER DIGEST MAGAZINE	HARVEY PUBLICATIONS	2	1	9	1991	NOW	
CASPER DIGEST STORIES	HARVEY PUBLICATIONS		1	4	1980	1980	
CASPER DIGEST WINNERS	HARVEY PUBLICATIONS		1	3	1980	1980	
CASPER ENCHANTED TALES DIGEST	HARVEY PUBLICATIONS		1	7	1992	1992	
CASPER GHOSTLAND	HARVEY PUBLICATIONS		1	1	1992	1992	
CASPER GIANT SIZE	HARVEY PUBLICATIONS		1	4	1992	NOW	
CASPER HALLOWEEN TRICK OR TREAT	HARVEY PUBLICATIONS		1	1	1976	1976	

INDEX OF COMIC TITLES AND THEIR PUBLISHERS

COMIC TITLE	PUBLISHER	Vol No.	Srt No.	End No.	Str. Year	End Year	COMMENTS
CASPER IN SPACE	HARVEY PUBLICATIONS		6	8	1973	1973	FORMERLY CASPER SPACE SPACESHIP
CASPER SPECIAL	HARVEY PUBLICATIONS		1	1	1990	1990	
CASPER STANGE GHOST STORIES	HARVEY PUBLICATIONS		1	14	1974	1977	
CASPER T.V. SHOWTIME	HARVEY PUBLICATIONS		1	5	1980	1980	
CASPER THE FRIENDLY GHOST	HARVEY PUBLICATIONS	1	1	70	1958	1986	
CASPER THE FRIENDLY GHOST	HARVEY PUBLICATIONS	2	1	21	1991	NOW	
CASPER THE FRIENDLY GHOST	ST JOHN PUBLISHING	1	1	3	1949	1950	
CASPER THE FRIENDLY GHOST	ST JOHN PUBLISHING	2	1	5	1950	1951	
CASPER'S GHOSTLAND	HARVEY PUBLICATIONS		1	98	1958	1979	
CASPER'S SPACESHIP	HARVEY PUBLICATIONS		1	5	1972	1973	BECOMES CASPER IN SPACE
CASPER, THE FRIENDLY GHOST	STREAMLINE	1	1	1	1953	1953	REPRINTS US HARVEY MATERIAL
CASPER, THE FRIENDLY GHOST	TOP SELLERS	2	1	?	1973	1974	
CASTLE OF HORROR	PORTMAN		1	20	1978	1980	
CAT & MOUSE COLLECTION, THE	MALIBU COMICS ENTERTAINMENT INC.		1	3	1990	1993	
CAT AND MOUSE	AIRCEL		1	18	1990	1991	
CAT AND MOUSE	SILVERLINE COMICS		1	1	1988	1988	
CAT CLAW	ETERNITY		1	12	1990	1991	
CAT CLAW: CAT SCRATCH FEVER	ETERNITY		1	1	1991	1991	
CAT TALES	ETERNITY		1	1	1989	1989	
CAT, THE	MARVEL ENTERTAINMENT GROUP		1	4	1972	1973	
CATALYST: AGENTS OF CHANGE	DARK HORSE COMICS		1	3	1994	NOW	
CATHOLIC COMICS	CATHOLIC PUBLICATIONS	1	1	13	1946	1947	
CATHOLIC COMICS	CATHOLIC PUBLICATIONS	2	1	10	1947	1948	
CATHOLIC COMICS	CATHOLIC PUBLICATIONS	3	1	10	1948	1949	
CATHOLIC PICTORIAL	CATHOLIC GUILD		1	1	1947	1947	
CATMAN COMICS	HOLYOKE PUBLISHING COMPANY		28	32	1941	1946	
CATSEYE AGENCY	RIP OFF PRESS		1	1	1992	NOW	
CATWOMAN	DC COMICS INC.		1	4	1989	1989	
CATWOMAN	DC COMICS INC.		1	7	1993	NOW	
CATWOMAN ANNUAL	DC COMICS INC.		1	1	1994	NOW	
CATWOMAN: HER SISTERS KEEPER	DC COMICS INC.		1	1	1991	1991	
CAUGHT	ATLAS		1	5	1956	1957	
CAVE GIRL	AC COMICS		1	1	1988	1988	
CAVE GIRL	MAGAZINE ENTERPRISES		11	14	1953	1954	
CAVE KIDS	GOLD KEY		1	16	1963	1967	
CAVE WOMAN	BASEMENT COMICS		1	1	1994	NOW	
CEASEFIRE	KNOCKABOUT		1	1	1991	1991	
CECIL KUNKLE	RENEGADE PRESS		1	1	1986	1986	
CECIL KUNKLE	RENEGADE PRESS		1	2	1987	1988	
CECIL KUNKLE CHRISTMAS SPECIAL	RENEGADE PRESS		1	1	1988	1988	
CELESTIAL MECHANICS	INNOVATION		1	3	1988	1988	
CENTRIFUGAL BUMBLE-PUPPY	FANTAGRAPHICS		1	8	1987	1988	
CENTURIANS	DC COMICS INC.		1	4	1987	1987	
CENTURY OF COMICS	EASTERN COLOR PRINTING COMPANY		1	1	1933	1933	
CEREBUS	AARDVARK-VANAHEIM		1	1	1990	1991	
CEREBUS BI-WEEKLY	AARDVARK-VANAHEIM		1	26	1988	1989	
CEREBUS COMPANION	WIN-MILL PRODUCTIONS		1	1	1993	NOW	
CEREBUS JAM	AARDVARK-VANAHEIM		1	1	1985	1985	
CEREBUS THE AARDVARK	AARDVARK-VANAHEIM		1	178	1977	NOW	ISSUE 0 WAS PUBLISHED IN JUNE 1993
CEREBUS: CHURCH & STATE	AARDVARK-VANAHEIM		1	1	1991	1992	
CEREBUS: CHURCH AND STATE	AARDVARK-VANAHEIM		1	30	1991	1992	
CEREBUS: FLIGHT	AARDVARK-VANAHEIM		1	1	1993	1993	
CEREBUS: HIGH SOCIETY	AARDVARK-VANAHEIM		1	1	1991	1991	
CEREBUS: HIGH SOCIETY	AARDVARK-VANAHEIM		1	27	1990	1991	
CEREBUS: JAKA'S STORY	AARDVARK-VANAHEIM		1	1	1992	1992	
CEREBUS: MELMOTH	AARDVARK-VANAHEIM		1	1	1993	1993	
CEREBUS: MOTHERS & DAUGHTERS	AARDVARK-VANAHEIM		1	1	1993	1993	
CHAIN GANG WAR	DC COMICS INC.		1	8	1993	NOW	
CHAINGANG	NORTHSTAR		1	4	1992	NOW	
CHALLENGE OF THE UNKNOWN	ACE MAGAZINES		6	6	1950	1950	FORMERLY LOVE EXPERIENCES
CHALLENGE TO THE WORLD	CAETECHETICAL EDUCATIONAL SOCIETY		1	1	1951	1951	
CHALLENGER COMIC, THE	P.M. PRODUCTIONS		1	2	1948	1948	
CHALLENGER, THE	INTERFAITH PUBLICATIONS		1	4	1945	1945	PUBLICATION CONTINUED BY T.C. COMICS
CHALLENGER, THE	T.C. COMICS		2	4	1945	1946	FORMERLY PUBLISHED BY INTERFAITH PUBLICATIONS
CHALLENGERS OF THE UNKNOWN	DC COMICS INC.		1	8	1991	1991	
CHALLENGERS OF THE UNKNOWN	DC COMICS INC.		1	87	1958	1973	
CHALLENGERS OF THE UNKNOWN	STRATO		1	4	1960	1960	REPRINTS DC MATERIAL
CHAMBER OF CHILLS	HARVEY PUBLICATIONS		21	24	1951	1951	
CHAMBER OF CHILLS	MARVEL ENTERTAINMENT GROUP		1	25	1972	1976	
CHAMBER OF CHILLS	WITCHES TALES		5	26	1952	1954	
CHAMBER OF CHILLS MAGAZINE	HARVEY PUBLICATIONS	1	21	26	1951	1952	
CHAMBER OF CHILLS MAGAZINE	HARVEY PUBLICATIONS	2	5	24	1952	1954	
CHAMBER OF CLUES	HARVEY PUBLICATIONS		27	28	1955	1955	
CHAMBER OF DARKNESS	MARVEL ENTERTAINMENT GROUP		1	8	1969	1970	
CHAMBER OF DARKNESS SPECIAL	MARVEL ENTERTAINMENT GROUP		1	1	1972	1972	
CHAMP	D.C. THOMSON		1	87	1984	1985	
CHAMP COMICS	HARVEY PUBLICATIONS		11	29	1940	1944	FORMERLY CHAMPION
CHAMPION	FLEETWAY		1	15	1966	1966	
CHAMPION COMIC, THE	THE JOKER		1	106	1894	1896	
CHAMPION COMICS	HARVEY PUBLICATIONS		2	10	1939	1940	FORMERLY CHAMP COMICS
CHAMPION SPORTS	DC COMICS INC.		1	3	1973	1974	
CHAMPIONS	ECLIPSE		6	6	1986	1987	
CHAMPIONS	HEROIC PUBLISHING		1	14	1987	NOW	
CHAMPIONS ADVENTURES	HEROIC PUBLISHING		1	1	1993	NOW	
CHAMPIONS ANNUAL	HEROIC PUBLISHING		1	2	1988	NOW	
CHAMPIONS CLASSICS	HEROIC PUBLISHING		1	5	1992	NOW	
CHAMPIONS, THE	MARVEL ENTERTAINMENT GROUP		1	17	1975	1978	
CHANGE COMMANDER GOKU	ANTARTIC PRESS		1	1	1993	NOW	
CHANNEL 33 1/3 SUMMER SPECIAL	MARVEL ENTERTAINMENT GROUP		1	1	1983	1983	

COMIC TITLE	PUBLISHER	Vol No.	Srt No.	End No.	Str. Year	End Year	COMMENTS
CHANNEL X	CALIBER PRESS		I	I	1993	1993	
CHAOS CITY AIDS AWARENESS COMIC '93	CHAOS COMICS		I	I	1993	1993	
CHARLEMAGNE	DEFIANT		I	2	1994	NOW	
CHARLES RAND	THORPE & PORTER		I	I	1966	1966	
CHARLIE CHAN	DELL PUBLISHING COMPANY		I	3	1965	1966	
CHARLIE CHAN	L. MILLER PUBLISHING COMPANY (UK)	2	I	2	1955	1955	REPRINTS CHARLTON MATERIAL
CHARLIE CHAN	STREAMLINE	I	I	I	1950	1950	REPRINTS CHARLTON MATERIAL
CHARLIE CHAN, NEW ADVENTURES OF	PEARSON		I	6	1958	1959	
CHARLIE CHAPLIN	TOP SELLERS		I	2	1973	1974	
CHARLIE CHAPLIN FUN BOOK	AMALGAMATED PRESS		I	I	1915	1915	
CHARLIE CHICK'S PAPER	F.W. WOOLWORTH			I	1934	1934	
CHARLIE'S ANGELS ANNUAL	STAFFORD PEMBERTON		1978	1981	1978	1981	
CHARLTON BULLSEYE	CHARLTON COMICS	I	I	5	1975	1976	
CHARLTON BULLSEYE	CHARLTON COMICS	2	I	10	1981	1982	
CHARLTON BULLSEYE SPECIAL	CHARLTON COMICS	2	I	12	1986	1987	
CHARLTON CLASSICS	CHARLTON COMICS		I	9	1980	1981	
CHARLTON PREMIERE	CHARLTON COMICS	2	I	4	1967	1968	
CHASER PLATOON	AIRCEL		I	5	1991	1991	
CHECKMATE	DC COMICS INC.		I	33	1988	1990	
CHEEKY SUMMER SPECIAL	IPC		1978	1982	1978	1982	
CHEEKY WEEKLY	IPC		I	120	1977	1980	
CHEERFUL COMIC, THE	C.A. RANSOM		I	28	1928	1929	REPRINTS
CHEERIE COMIC	HOMER MCCRICK		I	I	1946	1946	
CHEERY CHICKS CHUMMY COMIC	AIDA REUBENS		I	12	1947	1948	
CHEERY COMIC	P.M. PRODUCTIONS		I	I	1944	1944	
CHEERY TIME COMIC	PHILIMAR		I	I	1948	1948	
CHEVAL NOIR	DARK HORSE COMICS		I	49	1989	NOW	
CHEYENNE	DELL PUBLISHING COMPANY		I	25	1956	1962	
CHEYENNE A TELEVISION STORY BOOK	NEW TOWN PRINTERS		1961	1962	1961	1962	
CHEYENNE ANNUAL	WORLD DISTRIBUTORS LTD		1960	1961	1960	1961	
CHEYENNE COMIC ALBUM	WORLD DISTRIBUTORS LTD		I	I	1958	1958	
CHEYENNE KID	CHARLTON COMICS	8	I	99	1957	1973	
CHEYENNE KID	L. MILLER PUBLISHING COMPANY (UK)		I	18	1958	1958	REPRINTS CHARLTON MATERIAL
CHEYENNE WESTERN ALBUM	G.T. LIMITED		I	I	1959	1959	
CHICKS' OWN, THE	AMALGAMATED PRESS		I		1920	1957	NO NUMBERS, DATES ONLY. 1605 ISSUES
CHILD'S PLAY 2	INNOVATION		I	3	1991	1991	
CHILD'S PLAY 2 MOVIE ADAPTATION	INNOVATION		I	I	1991	1991	
CHILD'S PLAY 3	INNOVATION		I	I	1992	1992	
CHILD'S PLAY 3	INNOVATION		I	3	1991	1991	
CHILD'S PLAY: THE SERIES	INNOVATION		I	5	1991	1992	
CHILDREN OF FIRE	FANTAGOR		I	3	1988	1988	
CHILDREN OF THE NIGHT	NIGHT WYND ENTERPRISES		I	4	1992	1992	
CHILDREN OF THE VOYAGER	MARVEL ENTERTAINMENT GROUP		I	4	1993	NOW	
CHILDREN'S CRUSADE	DC COMICS INC.		I	I	1993	1994	
CHILDREN'S FAIRY, THE	AMALGAMATED PRESS		I	76	1919	1921	FORMERLY CHILDREN'S SUNDAY FAIRY
CHILDREN'S HAPPY TRAVEL COMIC	ELLIOT SINCLAIR		I	4	1946	1946	
CHILDREN'S HOLIDAY FUN	JOHN LENG		I	4	1937	1940	
CHILDREN'S OWN FAVOURITE	WORLD SERVICE		I	9	1938	1938	
CHILDREN'S OWN SUNDAY PICTORIAL, THE	SUNDAY PICTORIAL		I	27	1933	1934	
CHILDREN'S POCKET BOOK, THE	J.B. ALLEN		I	I	1949	1949	
CHILDREN'S SUNDAY FAIRY, THE	AMALGAMATED PRESS		23	25	1919	1919	FORMERLY THE SUNDAY FAIRY
CHILDSPLAY	ATLAS UK		I	2	1980	1980	REPRINTS DELL MATERIAL
CHILI	MARVEL ENTERTAINMENT GROUP		I	26	1969	1973	
CHILI ANNUAL	MARVEL ENTERTAINMENT GROUP		I	I	1971	1971	
CHILLER	MARVEL ENTERTAINMENT GROUP		I	2	1993	1993	
CHILLER POCKET BOOK	MARVEL ENTERTAINMENT GROUP		I	28	1980	1982	REPRINTS
CHILLERS GIANT SIZE	MARVEL ENTERTAINMENT GROUP	I	I	I	1975	1975	
CHILLERS GIANT SIZE	MARVEL ENTERTAINMENT GROUP	2	I	3	1975	1975	
CHILLING ADVENTURES IN SORCERY	RED CIRCLE		I	5	1972	1974	
CHILLING TALES OF HORROR	PORTMAN		I	4	1979	1980	REPRINTS
CHINA SEA	NIGHT WYND ENTERPRISES		I	4	1991	1992	
CHIP 'N' DALE	DELL PUBLISHING COMPANY	4	30	1955	1962		
CHIP 'N' DALE	GOLD KEY		I	54	1967	1980	
CHIP 'N' DALE	WHITMAN		55	83	1980	1982	
CHIP 'N' DALE RESCUE RANGERS	WALT DISNEY		I	19	1990	1991	
CHIP 'N' DALE RESCUE RANGERS: SECRET CASEBOOK	WALT DISNEY		I	I	1992	1992	
CHIPS & VANILLA	KITCHEN SINK		I	I	1988	1988	
CHIPS ANNUAL	WORLD DISTRIBUTORS LTD		1980	1981	1980	1981	
CHIPS COMIC	IPC		I	21	1983	1983	
CHIPS COMIC BOOK	IPC		I	I	1984	1984	COMES WITH CASSETTE
CHOICES	ANGRY ISIS PRESS			I	1990	1990	
CHOLLY AND FLYTRAP, NEW ADVENTURES OF	MARVEL ENTERTAINMENT GROUP		I	4	1990	1991	
CHOPPER	FLEETWAY		I	I	1990	1990	
CHOPPER: EARTH, WIND & FIRE	FLEETWAY		I	2	1993	1993	
CHRISTMAS COMIC ANNUAL, THE	C.A. PEARSON		1931	1933	1931	1933	
CHRISTMAS HOLIDAY COMIC ANNUAL	C.A. PEARSON		1936	1939	1936	1939	
CHRISTMAS IN DISNEYLAND	DELL PUBLISHING COMPANY		I	I	1957	1957	
CHRISTMAS PARADE	DELL PUBLISHING COMPANY		I	9	1949	1958	
CHRISTMAS STORYTELLER ANNUAL	MARSHALL CAVENDISH		1983	1984	1983	1984	COMES WITH CASSETTE
CHRISTMAS TREASURY	DELL PUBLISHING COMPANY		I	I	1954	1954	
CHRISTMAS WITH THE SUPERHEROES	DC COMICS INC.		I	2	1988	1989	
CHRISTMAS WITH THE SUPERSWINE	FANTAGRAPHICS		I	I	1989	1989	
CHROMA TICK SPECIAL	NEW ENGLAND COMICS		I	8	1992	NOW	
CHROME	HOT		I	3	1986	1987	
CHROMIUM DARK	CONTINUM COMICS		I	3	1992	NOW	
CHROMIUM MAN	TRIUMPHANT COMICS		I	5	1993	NOW	
CHRONIC IDIOCY	CALIBER PRESS		I	3	1991	1992	
CHRONICLES OF CORUM	FIRST		I	12	1987	1988	
CHRONICLES OF GENGHIS GRIMTOAD, THE	MARVEL ENTERTAINMENT GROUP		I	I	1990	1990	REPRINTS
CHRONICLES OF PANDA KHAN	APPLE COMICS		I	2	1987	1987	

COMIC TITLE	PUBLISHER	Vol No.	Srt No.	End No.	Str. Year	End Year	COMMENTS
CHUCK AMUCK	AVON BOOKS				1989	1989	
CHUCKLER	TARGET PUBLICATIONS		1	238	1934	1938	
CHUCKLES	AMALGAMATED PRESS		1	517	1914	1923	
CHUMMY COMIC	H. JEFFREY		1	1	1948	1948	
CHUMMY COMIC	P.M. PRODUCTIONS		1	1	1944	1944	
CINDER AND ASHE	DC COMICS INC.		1	4	1988	1988	
CINDY	TIMELY COMICS		27	40	1947	1950	FORMERLY KRAZY KOMICS. ISSUE NOS.39-40, "CINDY SMITH". BECOMES "CRIME CAN'T WIN" WITH ISSUE NO.41 (SEPTEMBER 1950)
CINDY SMITH - SEE CINDY							
CINEFEX	CINEFEX		46	55	1990	NOW	
CIRCUS COMIC	P.M. PRODUCTIONS		1	1	1945	1945	
CIRCUS COMICS	HOTSPUR PUBLISHING CO.		1	1	1949	1949	
CISCO KID	DELL PUBLISHING COMPANY		1	41	1950	1958	
CISCO KID COMIC ALBUM, THE	WORLD DISTRIBUTORS LTD		1	3	1955	1957	
CISCO KID, THE	WORLD DISTRIBUTORS LTD		1	51	1952	1955	REPRINTS DELL MATERIAL
CITY ON THE EDGE OF FOREVER	BORDERLAND PRESS		1	1	1991	1991	
CITY, THE	PAN/MACMILLAN		1	1	1994	1994	
CITYSCAPE	NC VENTURE		1	2	1990	NOW	
CIVIL WAR	A PLUS COMICS		1	2	1993	1993	
CIVIL WAR	A PLUS COMICS		1	3	1992	1993	
CLASH	DC COMICS INC.		1	3	1991	1992	
CLASH OF THE TITANS	INDEPENDENT TELEVISION		1	1	1981	1981	REPRINTS US STRIP
CLASS WAR COMIX	EPIC PRODUCTIONS		1	1	1974	1974	
CLASSIC ACTION HOLIDAY SPECIAL	FLEETWAY		1	1	1990	1990	
CLASSIC COMICS	HAWK BOOKS		1	10	1990	1990	REPRINTS SPANISH MATERIAL
CLASSIC GIRLS	ETERNITY		1	4	1991	NOW	
CLASSIC IN PICTURES, A	AMEX		1	12	1949	1949	
CLASSICS ILLUSTRATED	FIRST		1	35	1990	1991	
CLASSICS ILLUSTRATED	GILBERTON PUBLICATIONS		1	169	1941	1969	
CLASSICS ILLUSTRATED (U.K.)	GILBERTON PUBLICATIONS		1	163	1951	1963	REPRINTS FROM US MATERIAL; VARIOUS PRINTINGS
CLASSICS ILLUSTRATED JUNIOR	GILBERTON PUBLICATIONS		501	576	1953	1971	
CLASSICS ILLUSTRATED JUNIORS (U.K.)	GILBERTON PUBLICATIONS		501	516	1955	1956	REPRINTS US MATERIAL
CLASSICS ILLUSTRATED PIXI TALES (U.K.)	GILBERTON PUBLICATIONS		1	88	1959	1963	
CLASSICS ILLUSTRATED SPECIAL ISSUE	GILBERTON PUBLICATIONS		135	135	1955	1962	
CLASSICS ILLUSTRATED: WORLD ILLUSTRATED	GILBERTON PUBLICATIONS		1	34	1956	1963	
CLAW THE UNCONQUERED	DC COMICS INC.		1	12	1975	1978	
CLIENT	A PLUS COMICS		1	3	1992	1993	
CLINT	ECLIPSE		1	2	1986	1987	
CLIVE BARKER'S REVELATIONS	ECLIPSE		1	1	1992	1992	
CLIVE BARKERS DREAD	ECLIPSE		1	1	1992	1992	
CLOAK AND DAGGER	MARVEL ENTERTAINMENT GROUP		1	11	1985	1987	
CLOAK AND DAGGER	MARVEL ENTERTAINMENT GROUP		1	4	1983	1984	
CLOAK AND DAGGER, THE MUTANT MISADVENTURES OF	MARVEL ENTERTAINMENT GROUP		1	20	1988	1991	
CLOAK AND DAGGER: PREDATOR AND PREY	MARVEL ENTERTAINMENT GROUP		1	1	1988	1988	
CLONEZONE SPECIAL	DARK HORSE COMICS		1	1	1989	1989	
CLOSE SHAVES OF PAULINE PERIL, THE	GOLD KEY		1	4	1970	1971	
CLOWN	FLEETWAY		1	1	1993	1993	
CLOWN COMICS	HARVEY PUBLICATIONS		1	3	1945	1946	ISSUE #1 TITLED "CLOWN COMIC BOOKS"
CLUB "16"	HARVEY PUBLICATIONS		1	4	1948	1948	
CLUBHOUSE RASCALS	MAGAZINE ENTERPRISES		1	2	1956	1956	ISSUE #1 TITLED "CLUBHOUSE RASCALS PRESENTS..?"
CLUE COMICS	HILLMAN PERIODICALS	1	1	12	1943	1947	
CLUE COMICS	HILLMAN PERIODICALS	2	1	3	1947	1947	BECOMES "REAL CLUE CRIME" FROM ISSUE #4
CLUTCHING HAND, THE	AMERICAN COMIC GROUP		1	1	1954	1954	
CLYDE BEATTY COMICS	COMMODORE PRODUCTIONS AND ARTISTS		1	1	1953	1953	84-PAGES: PHOTO COVER AND FREE GIVEAWAY BOOK
CLYDE CRASHCUP	DELL PUBLISHING COMPANY		1	5	1963	1964	
CO-ED ROMANCES	PL PUBLISHING		1	1	1951	1951	
COBALT 60	TUNDRA		1	1	1992	NOW	
COBALT 60	TUNDRA		1	2	1992	1992	
COBALT BLUE	INNOVATION		1	2	1989	1989	
COBRA	VIZ		1	12	1990	1991	
COCOMALT BIG BOOK OF COMICS	COCOMALT		1	1	1938	1938	
CODA	CODA PUBLISHING		1	4	1986	1987	
CODENAME: DANGER	LODESTONE		1	4	1985	1986	
CODENAME: GENETIX	MARVEL ENTERTAINMENT GROUP		1	4	1993	1993	
CODENAME: NINJA	SOLSON		1	8	1992	1993	
CODENAME: TOMAHAWK	FANTASY GENERAL		1	1	1986	1986	
CODY OF THE PONY EXPRESS	CHARLTON COMICS	2	8	10	1955	1956	FORMERLY BULLS-EYE: OUTLAWS OF THE WEST FROM #11
CODY OF THE PONY EXPRESS	FOX FEATURES SYNDICATE	1	1	3	1950	1951	ACTUALLY ISSUES #3-#5 OF "COLOSSAL FEATURES"
CODY STARBUCK	STAR REACH				1978	1978	
COFFIN BLOOD	MONSTER COMICS		1	1	1992	1992	
COLD BLOODED: THE COLLECTION	NORTHSTAR		1	1	1993	1993	
COLD-BLOODED CHAMELEON COMMANDOS	BLACKTHORNE		1	6	1986	1987	
COLLECTED PURPLE PICTOGRAPHY, THE	EROS				1991	1991	
COLLECTORS DREAM	G & T ENTERPRISES INC		1	3	1977	1977	
COLOMBUS	DARK HORSE COMICS		1	1	1992	1992	
COLONEL PEWTER	PENGUIN BOOKS		1	1	1979	1979	
COLONEL PEWTER IN IRONICUS	PALL MALL		1	1	1957	1957	
COLONEL PEWTER: BOOK OF URIEL	PALL MALL		1	1	1957	1957	
COLONEL PEWTER: SIRIUS DOG STAR	PALL MALL		1	1	1957	1957	
COLORADO KID, THE	L. MILLER PUBLISHING COMPANY (UK)		50	84	1954	1959	
COLORS IN BLACK	DARK HORSE COMICS		1	4	1994	1994	
COLOSSAL FEATURES MAGAZINE	FOX FEATURES SYNDICATE		33	34	1950	1950	FORMERLY I LOVED
COLOSSAL SHOW, THE	GOLD KEY		1	1	1969	1969	
COLOSSUS COMICS	SUN COMICS PUBLISHING		1	1	1940	1940	

INDEX OF COMIC TITLES AND THEIR PUBLISHERS

COMIC TITLE	PUBLISHER	Vol No.	Srt No.	End No.	Str. Year	End Year	COMMENTS
COLOUR OF MAGIC, TERRY PRATCHETT'S	CORGI		1	1	1992	1992	
COLOUR OF MAGIC, THE	CORGI		1	1	1992	1992	
COLOUR OF MAGIC, THE	INNOVATION		1	4	1991	1991	
COLOURED COMIC	TRAPP HOLMES		1	415	1898	1906	1ST WEEKLY COMIC WITH COLOUR COVER
COLOURED STICK FUN	GERALD SWAN		1	88	1945	1951	
COLOURED STICK FUN BUDGET	GERALD SWAN		1	3	1950	1952	
COLT 45	DELL PUBLISHING COMPANY		4	9	1960	1961	CONTINUED FROM 4 COLOUR SERIES
COLT SPECIAL	AC COMICS		1	3	1985	1985	
COLUMBIA COMICS	WILLIAM H. WISE		1	1	1943	1943	
COLUMBUS	DARK HORSE COMICS		1	1	1992	1992	
COLUMBUS: TRIALS OF DISCOVERY	CALIBER PRESS		1	1	1992	1992	
COMBAT	ATLAS		1	11	1952	1953	
COMBAT	DELL PUBLISHING COMPANY		1	40	1961	1973	
COMBAT CASEY	ATLAS		6	34	1953	1957	FORMERLY WAR COMBAT
COMBAT KELLY	ATLAS		1	44	1951	1957	
COMBAT KELLY AND THE DEADLY DOZEN	MARVEL ENTERTAINMENT GROUP		1	9	1972	1973	
COMBAT PICTURE LIBRARY	MICRON/SMITH		1	1212	1959	1985	
COMEDY CARNIVAL	ST JOHN PUBLISHING		1	1	1950	1950	100 PAGES; CONTAINS REBOUND ST. JOHN COMICS
COMEDY COMICS	MARVEL ENTERTAINMENT GROUP	2	1	10	1948	1950	
COMEDY COMICS	TIMELY COMICS	1	9	34	1942	1946	FORMERLY DARING MYSTERY; MARGIE COMICS FROM #35
COMET	RED CIRCLE		1	2	1983	1983	
COMET ANNUAL, THE	DC COMICS INC.		1	1	1992	1992	CONTAIN IMPACT TRADING CARD; IMPACT TITLE
COMET MAN, THE	MARVEL ENTERTAINMENT GROUP		1	6	1987	1987	SIENKIEWICZ COVERS
COMET, THE	AMALGAMATED PRESS	2	1	580	1946	1958	
COMET, THE	C.A. PEARSON		1	14	1909	1909	PREVIOUSLY BIG BUDGET, THE
COMET, THE	DC COMICS INC.		1	18	1991	1992	IMPACT TITLE
COMIC ADVENTURES	A. SOLOWAY		1	27	1940	1949	
COMIC ALBUM	DELL PUBLISHING COMPANY		1	18	1958	1962	
COMIC ALBUM OF FOLLY AND FASHION	JUDY OFFICE		1	1	1870	1870	
COMIC ALMANAC	FORTEY		1	1	1879	1879	
COMIC BITS	UNITY		1	10	1898	1898	
COMIC BOOK	WEATHER BIRD SHOES		1	1	1954	1954	GIVEAWAY; SEVERAL COMBINATIONS OF STORY
COMIC BOOK MAGAZINE	CHICAGO TRIBUNE AND OTHER NEWSPAPERS		1	5	1940	1943	
COMIC BOOK PRICE GUIDE FOR GREAT BRITAIN UPDATE	PRICE GUIDE PUBLICATIONS		1	1	1992	1992	
COMIC BOOK PRICE GUIDE FOR GREAT BRITAIN, THE	PRICE GUIDE PUBLICATIONS	1990	1994	1990	NOW		
COMIC BOOK, THE	EBURY PRESS		1	1	1994	1994	
COMIC BOOKS	METROPOLITAN PRINTING CO.		1	1	1950	1950	FIVE VARIATIONS
COMIC BUYERS GUIDE	KRAUSE PUBLICATIONS	850	1053	1973	NOW		
COMIC BUYERS GUIDE ANNUAL	KRAUSE PUBLICATIONS	1992	1992	1992	NOW		
COMIC BUYERS PRICE GUIDE	KRAUSE PUBLICATIONS		1	11	1993	NOW	
COMIC CAPERS	A. SOLOWAY		1	27	1940	1949	
COMIC CAPERS	RED CIRCLE		1	6	1944	1946	
COMIC CAVALCADE	ALL AMERICAN COMICS		1	63	1942	1954	
COMIC CHUCKLES	MARTIN & REID		1	1	1944	1944	
COMIC COMICS	FAWCETT PUBLICATIONS		1	10	1946	1947	
COMIC COMPANION	ODHAMS		1	20	1908	1909	
COMIC CUTS	AMALGAMATED PRESS	1			1890	1953	NO. 1 DATED 17 MAY 1890, THEN NO NUMBERS, DATES ONLY
COMIC CUTS	CRAWLEY NEWS		1	2	1983	1983	
COMIC CUTS	H.L. BAKER CO. INC.		1	9	1934	1934	PUBLISHED WEEKLY; NEWSSTAND PUBLICATION
COMIC FANDOM'S FORUM	NEW MEDIA PUBLISHING INC	3	3	1982	1982	PREVIOUSLY TITLED LOC	
COMIC FUN	MARTIN & REID		1	1	1948	1948	
COMIC GUIDE FOR ARTISTS	A PLUS COMICS		1	1	1992	1992	
COMIC HOLIDAY ANNUAL	WARD LOCK		1	1	1877	1877	
COMIC HOME JOURNAL, THE	HARMSWORTH		1	488	1895	1904	PREVIOUSLY BOYS HOME JOURNAL, THE
COMIC LAND	FACT & FICTION PUBLICATIONS		1	1	1946	1946	
COMIC LEDGER, THE	MARTIN & REID		1	1	1949	1949	
COMIC LIFE	AMALGAMATED PRESS				1899	1928	PREVIOUSLY PICTORIAL COMIC-LIFE; NO NUMBERS, DATES ONLY
COMIC MONTHLY	EMBEE DISTRIBUTION CO.		1	12	1922	1922	FIRST MONTHLY NEWSSTAND COMIC PUBLICATION
COMIC MOVIES FLICKER BOOKS	BOOKS & PICTURES		1	10	1949	1949	
COMIC PAGES	CENTAUR PUBLICATIONS	3	4	6	1939	1939	FORMERLY FUNNY PICTURE STORIES
COMIC PAINTING AND CRAYONING BOOK	SAALFIELD PUBLISHING COMPANY		1	1	1917	1917	
COMIC PICTORIAL NUGGETS	JAMES HENDERSON		1	29	1892	1892	
COMIC PICTORIAL SHEET	JAMES HENDERSON		1	1601	1891	1904	
COMIC RELIEF	PAGE ONE PUBLISHERS		1	39	1990	NOW	
COMIC RELIEF COMIC, THE	FLEETWAY		1	1	1991	1991	
COMIC SELECTIONS	PARENTS MAGAZINE INSTITUTE		1	5	1944	1946	
COMIC SHOT	JOHN W. FISHER		1	4	1946	1946	
COMIC SPECULATOR NEWS	COMIC SPECULATOR NEWS		1	3	1992	NOW	
COMIC STORY PAINTBOOK	SAMUEL LOWE COMPANY		1	1	1943	1943	
COMIC TIMES: MEDIA SHOWCASE	COMIC TIMES INC		1	6	1980	1981	
COMIC WONDER, THE	PAGET	1	1	7	1948	1949	
COMIC WONDER, THE	PAGET	2	1	1	1949	1949	
COMIC WORLD	ACEVILLE PUBLICATION		1	19	1991	NOW	
COMICAL COMIC, THE	PHILLIP MARX		1	1	1945	1945	
COMICAL CRACKS	ENSIGN/W. FORSHAW		1	4	1947	1947	
COMICAL PRANKS	ENSIGN/W. FORSHAW		1	3	1947	1947	
COMICAL SNIPS	MODERM FICTION		1	1	1947	1947	
COMICO CHRISTMAS SPECIAL	COMICO		1	1	1988	1988	
COMICO COLLECTION	COMICO		1	1	1987	1987	
COMICO ILLUSTRATED	COMICO		1	1	1992	1992	
COMICO PRIMER	COMICO		1	6	1982	1984	
COMICOLOUR	GERALD SWAN	1	1	11	1946	1949	

COMIC TITLE	PUBLISHER	Vol No.	Srt No.	End No.	Str Year	End Year	COMMENTS
COMICOLOUR	GERALD SWAN	2	I	3	1953	1953	
COMICS DIGEST	PARENTS MAGAZINE INSTITUTE		I	I	1942	1943	100 PAGES
COMICS FOR KIDS	PARODY PRESS		I	I	1993	1993	
COMICS FOR KIDS	TIMELY COMICS		I	2	1945	1945	
COMICS INTERNATIONAL	COMICS INTERVIEW		I	15	1990	NOW	
COMICS INTERVIEW	COMICS INTERVIEW		I	126	1983	NOW	
COMICS INTERVIEW SUPER SPECIAL	COMICS INTERVIEW				1993	1993	DARK KNIGHT NO MORE/KNIGHTFALL
COMICS JOURNAL	FANTAGRAPHICS		40	164	1981	NOW	
COMICS LAND	N. BERNAZZALI	0	0	0	1981	1981	
COMICS MAGAZINE, THE	COMICS MAGAZINE CO.		I	5	1936	1936	BECOMES FUNNY PAGES FROM #6
COMICS NOVEL	FAWCETT PUBLICATIONS		I	I	1947	1947	
COMICS ON PARADE	DONALD PETERS	17		18	1950	1950	FORMERLY SPARKLER COMIC BOOK SERIES
COMICS ON PARADE	L. MILLER PUBLISHING COMPANY (UK)		I	13	1941	1944	
COMICS ON PARADE	UNITED FEATURES SYNDICATE		I	104	1938	1955	
COMICS READING LIBRARIES	KING FEATURES		I	16	1973	1979	
COMICS REVUE	COMICS INTERVIEW		I	79	1988	NOW	
COMICS REVUE	ST JOHN PUBLISHING		I	5	1947	1948	
COMICS SCENE	STARLOG		I	40	1990	NOW	
COMICS SCENE YEARBOOK	STARLOG		I	2	1992	NOW	
COMICS TO HOLD YOU SPELLBOUND	THORPE & PORTER		I	2	1953	???	REPRINTS MARVEL MATERIAL
COMICS VALUE MONTHLY	ATTIC BOOKS		I	79	1988	NOW	
COMICS' GREATEST WORLD: ARCADIA	DARK HORSE COMICS		I	4	1993	1993	
COMICS' GREATEST WORLD: CINNABAR FLATS (VORTEX)	DARK HORSE COMICS		I	4	1993	1993	
COMICS' GREATEST WORLD: GOLDEN CITY	DARK HORSE COMICS		I	4	1993	1993	
COMICS' GREATEST WORLD: STEEL HARBOR	DARK HORSE COMICS		I	4	1993	1993	
COMICS, THE	DELL PUBLISHING COMPANY		I	11	1937	1938	
COMICUTE BUDGET	GERALD SWAN		I	2	1951	1952	
COMIX BOOK	MARVEL ENTERTAINMENT GROUP		I	3	1974	1976	
COMIX INTERNATIONAL	WARREN PUBLISHING CO		I	5	1974	1977	
COMMAND REVIEW	THOUGHT AND IMAGES		I	3	1986	NOW	
COMMANDER BATTLE AND THE ATOMIC SUB	AMERICAN COMIC GROUP		I	7	1954	1955	
COMMANDER BATTLE AND THE ATOMIC SUB	STREAMLINE		I	3	1955	1955	
COMMANDER COMIC, THE	ENSIGN/W. FORSHAW		I	2	1947	1947	
COMMANDER EARTH	GULF OIL COMPANY		I	I	1980	1980	
COMMANDMENTS OF GOD	CAETECHETICAL EDUCATIONAL SOCIETY		I	I	1954	1958	300-SAME CONTENTS IN BOTH EDITIONS
COMMANDO ADVENTURES	ATLAS		I	2	1957	1957	
COMMANDO CRAIG	SCION		I	3	1950	1950	
COMMANDO LIBRARY	D.C. THOMSON		I	2626	1961	1992	
COMMITTED COMIX	BIRMINGHAM ARTS LAB		I	I	1977	1977	
COMPLEAT ALIENS LIMITED EDITION	DARK HORSE COMICS		I	I	1993	1993	
COMPLETE BOOK OF COMICS AND FUNNIES	WILLIAM H. WISE		I	I	1944	1944	196-PAGES
COMPLETE BOOK OF TRUE CRIME STORIES	WILLIAM H. WISE		I	I	1945	1945	132-PAGES
COMPLETE COMICS	NEWTON WICKHAM		I	I	1944	1944	
COMPLETE COMICS	TIMELY COMICS	2		2	1944	1945	FORMERLY AMAZING COMICS #1
COMPLETE FANTASTIC FOUR, THE	MARVEL ENTERTAINMENT GROUP		I	53	1977	1979	REPRINTS MARVEL MATERIAL
COMPLETE GERRY ANDERSON GUIDE, THE	TITAN BOOKS				1992	1992	
COMPLETE LOVE MAGAZINE	ACE PERIODICALS	26	2	6	1951	1952	FORMERLY PULP WITH SAME TITLE
COMPLETE LOVE MAGAZINE	ACE PERIODICALS	27	I	6	1952	1953	
COMPLETE LOVE MAGAZINE	ACE PERIODICALS	28	I	2	1953	1953	
COMPLETE LOVE MAGAZINE	ACE PERIODICALS	29	3	6	1953	1953	
COMPLETE LOVE MAGAZINE	ACE PERIODICALS	30	I	6	1954	1955	
COMPLETE LOVE MAGAZINE	ACE PERIODICALS	31	I	6	1955	1956	
COMPLETE LOVE MAGAZINE	ACE PERIODICALS	32	I	4	1956	1956	
COMPLETE MYSTERY	MARVEL ENTERTAINMENT GROUP		I	4	1948	1949	BECOMES TRUE COMPLETE MYSTERY FROM #5
COMPLETE ROMANCE	AVON BOOKS		I	I	1949	1949	REPRINTED AS WOMAN TO LOVE
COMPLETE SPIDER-MAN, THE	MARVEL ENTERTAINMENT GROUP		I	20	1990	1992	REPRINTS MARVEL MATERIAL
COMPLIMENTARY COMICS	SALES PROMOTION PUBLICATIONS		I	I	50'S	50'S	3 STORY GIVEAWAY
CONAN AND THE RAVAGERS OF TIME	MARVEL ENTERTAINMENT GROUP		I	I	1989	1989	
CONAN OF THE ISLES	MARVEL ENTERTAINMENT GROUP		I	I	1988	1988	
CONAN SAGA	MARVEL ENTERTAINMENT GROUP		I	83	1987	NOW	
CONAN THE BARBARIAN	MARVEL ENTERTAINMENT GROUP		I	275	1970	1993	
CONAN THE BARBARIAN ANNUAL	MARVEL ENTERTAINMENT GROUP		I	12	1983	NOW	
CONAN THE BARBARIAN GIANT SIZE	MARVEL ENTERTAINMENT GROUP		I	5	1974	1975	
CONAN THE BARBARIAN MOVIE ADAPTATION	MARVEL ENTERTAINMENT GROUP		I	2	1982	1982	
CONAN THE DESTROYER MOVIE ADAPTATION	MARVEL ENTERTAINMENT GROUP		I	2	1985	1985	
CONAN THE KING	MARVEL ENTERTAINMENT GROUP		20	55	1984	1989	FORMERLY KING CONAN
CONAN THE REAVER	MARVEL ENTERTAINMENT GROUP		I	I	1987	1987	
CONAN THE ROGUE	MARVEL ENTERTAINMENT GROUP		I	I	1991	1991	
CONAN UNIVERSE, THE HANDBOOK OF THE	MARVEL ENTERTAINMENT GROUP		I	2	1985	1985	
CONAN WINTER SPECIAL	MARVEL ENTERTAINMENT GROUP		I	I	1982	1982	
CONAN: SPECIAL EDITION (RED NAILS)	MARVEL ENTERTAINMENT GROUP		I	I	1983	1983	
CONAN: THE SKULL OF SET	MARVEL ENTERTAINMENT GROUP		I	I	1989	1989	
CONCRETE	DARK HORSE COMICS		I	12	1987	1988	
CONCRETE COLOUR SPECIAL	DARK HORSE COMICS		I	I	1989	1989	
CONCRETE: A NEW LIFE	DARK HORSE COMICS		I	2	1989	1989	
CONCRETE: COMPLETE SHORT STORIES 1986-1989	DARK HORSE COMICS		I	I	1993	1993	
CONCRETE: EARTH DAY	DARK HORSE COMICS		I	I	1989	1989	
CONCRETE: ECLECTICA	DARK HORSE COMICS		I	2	1993	1993	
CONCRETE: FRAGILE CREATURE	DARK HORSE COMICS		I	4	1991	1992	
CONCRETE: LAND AND SEA	DARK HORSE COMICS		I	I	1989	1989	
CONCRETE: ODD JOBS	DARK HORSE COMICS		I	I	1990	1990	
CONDORMAN	WHITMAN		I	3	1981	1982	
CONFESSIONS ILLUSTRATED	EC COMICS		I	2	1956	1956	
CONFESSIONS LIBRARY	AMALGAMATED PRESS		I	44	1959	1960	
CONFESSIONS OF JULIUS ANTOINE - LEA	ACME PRESS				1989	1989	
CONFESSIONS OF LOVE	ARTFUL PUBLICATION		I	2	1950	1950	
CONFESSIONS OF LOVE	GERALD SWAN		I	14	1954	1955	
CONFESSIONS OF LOVE	STAR PUBLICATIONS		7	14	1953	1954	FORMERLY STARTLING TERROR TALES

INDEX OF COMIC TITLES AND THEIR PUBLISHERS

COMIC TITLE	PUBLISHER	Vol No.	Srt No.	End No.	Str. Year	End Year	COMMENTS
CONFESSIONS OF THE LOVELORN	AMERICAN COMIC GROUP		52	114	1954	1960	FORMERLY LOVELORN
CONFIDENTIAL DIARY	CHARLTON COMICS		12	17	1962	1963	FORMERLY HIGH SCHOOL CONFIDENTIAL DIARY
CONFIDENTIAL STORIES	L. MILLER PUBLISHING COMPANY (UK)		1	9	1957	1957	US REPRINTS
CONFLICT PICTURE LIBRARY	BROWN WATSON		1	2	1959	1963	
CONGO BILL	DC COMICS INC.		1	7	1954	1955	
CONGORILLA	DC COMICS INC.		1	4	1992	1993	
CONQUEROR	HARRIER		1	9	1984	1985	
CONQUEROR COMIC	SCION		1	1	1952	1952	
CONQUEROR COMICS	ALBRECHT PUBLISHING CO.		1	1	1945	1945	
CONQUEROR OF THE BARREN EARTH	DC COMICS INC.		1	4	1985	1985	
CONQUEROR SPECIAL	HARRIER		1	1	1987	1987	
CONQUEROR UNIVERSE	HARRIER		1	1	1985	1985	
CONQUEST	HARRIER	2	1	1	1955	1955	
CONQUEST	STORE COMICS	1	1	1	1953	1953	
CONSERVATION CORPS	ARCHIE COMICS		1	3	1993	1993	
CONTACT COMICS	AVIATION PRESS		1	12	1944	1946	
CONTEMPORARY BIO-GRAPHICS	REVOLUTIONARY COMICS		1	4	1991	NOW	
CONTEMPORARY MOTIVATORS	PENDULUM PRESS		3002	3096	1977	1978	
CONTEST OF CHAMPIONS, MARVEL SUPER HERO	MARVEL ENTERTAINMENT GROUP		1	3	1982	1982	
CONTINENTAL FILM PHOTO STORIES	C.A. PEARSON		1	2	1960	???	
CONTRACTORS	ECLIPSE		1	1	1987	1987	
COO COO COMICS	NEDOR (BETTER PUBLICATIONS)		1	62	1942	1952	
COOKIE	A PLUS COMICS		1	1	1992	1992	
COOKIE	AMERICOMICS		1	55	1946	1955	
COOL CAT	PRIZE PUBLICATIONS	8	6	6	1962	1962	FORMERLY BLACK MAGIC
COOL CAT	PRIZE PUBLICATIONS	9	1	2	1962	1962	
COOL WORLD	DC COMICS INC.		1	4	1992	1992	
COOL WORLD MOVIE ADAPTATION	DC COMICS INC.		1	1	1992	1992	
COOPER KIDS, THE	PENDOCK PRESS		1	1	1943	1943	
COPS	DC COMICS INC.		1	15	1988	1989	
COPS: THE JOB	MARVEL ENTERTAINMENT GROUP		1	4	1992	1992	
COR!	IPC		1	196	1970	1974	
COR! SUMMER SPECIAL	IPC		1972	1974	1972	1974	
CORBEN SPECIAL	PACIFIC COMICS		1	1	1984	1984	
CORBO	SWORD AND STONE		1	1	1987	1987	
CORKER COMIC	INTERNATIONAL		1	1	1946	1946	
CORKER COMIC, THE	PHILIMAR		1	1	1949	1949	
CORMAC MAC ART	DARK HORSE COMICS		1	4	1990	1990	
CORONATION SPECIAL	SPORTS CARTOON		1	1	1953	1953	
CORUM THE BULL AND SPEAR	FIRST		1	4	1989	1989	
COSMIC BOOK	ACE COMICS		1	1	1987	1987	
COSMIC BOY	DC COMICS INC.		1	4	1986	1987	
COSMIC HEROES	ETERNITY		1	11	1988	NOW	
COSMIC ICONOCLASM	ESCAPE		1	1	1987	1987	
COSMIC ODYSSEY	DC COMICS INC.		1	1	1992	1992	
COSMIC ODYSSEY	DC COMICS INC.		1	4	1988	1988	
COSMIC POWERS	MARVEL ENTERTAINMENT GROUP		1	6	1994	1994	
COSMIC TALES	TITAN BOOKS		1	1	1982	1982	
COSMO	SUN COMICS PUBLISHING		1	1	1992	1992	
COSMO CAT	FOX FEATURES SYNDICATE	1	1	10	1946	1947	BECOMES SUNNY FROM ISSUE #11
COSMO CAT	GREEN PUBLISHING COMPANY	2	2	4	1957	1957	
COSMO CAT	NORLEN MAGAZINES	3	1	4	1959	1959	
COSMO THE MERRY MARTIAN	ARCHIE PUBLICATIONS		1	6	1958	1959	
COTTON CANDY AUTOPSY, A	DC COMICS INC.		1	1	1991	1991	
COUGAR, THE	ATLAS		1	2	1975	1975	
COUNT DUCKULA	MARVEL ENTERTAINMENT GROUP		1	15	1988	1991	
COUNTDOWN	POLYSTYLE		1	58	1971	1972	
COUNTDOWN ANNUAL	POLYSTYLE		1972	1973	1972	1973	
COUNTDOWN HOLIDAY SPECIAL	POLYSTYLE		1	1	1972	1972	
COUPLES	WORKSHOP		1	1	1972	1972	
COURAGE COMICS	J. EDWARD SLAVIN		1	77	1945	1945	
COURTSHIP OF EDDIE'S FATHER	DELL PUBLISHING COMPANY		1	2	1970	1970	
COWBOY ACTION	ATLAS		5	11	1955	1956	FORMERLY WESTERN THRILLERS
COWBOY ACTION	L. MILLER PUBLISHING COMPANY (UK)		1	18	1956	1957	REPRINTS US ATLAS MATERIAL
COWBOY ADVENTURE LIBRARY	MICRON/SMITH		1	1026	1964	1985	
COWBOY COMIC ALBUM ANNUAL	WORLD DISTRIBUTORS LTD		1	4	1955	1958	
COWBOY COMICS	CENTAUR PUBLICATIONS		13	14	1938	1938	FORMERLY STAR RANGER
COWBOY COMICS/COWBOY PICTURE LIBRARY	AMALGAMATED PRESS		1	468	1950	1962	
COWBOY HERO ANNUAL	L. MILLER PUBLISHING COMPANY (UK)		1	4	1957	1960	
COWBOY IN AFRICA	GOLD KEY		1	1	1968	1968	
COWBOY LOVE	FAWCETT PUBLICATIONS	1	1	6	1949	1950	
COWBOY LOVE	FAWCETT PUBLICATIONS	2	7	11	1951	1951	
COWBOY ROMANCES	MAGAZINE ENTERPRISES		1	8	1946	1952	
COWBOY SAHIB	A PLUS COMICS		1	1	1992	1992	
COWBOY WESTERN	CHARLTON COMICS		49	67	1954	1958	FORMERLY HEROES
COWBOY WESTERN COMICS	CHARLTON COMICS		17	39	1948	1952	FORMERLY JACK IN THE BOX
COWBOY WESTERN COMICS	L. MILLER PUBLISHING COMPANY (UK)		1	6	1956	1956	REPRINTS US CHARLTON MATERIAL
COWGIRL ROMANCES	FICTION HOUSE		1	12	1950	1953	
COWGIRL ROMANCES	MARVEL ENTERTAINMENT GROUP		28	28	1950	1950	FORMERLY JEANIE COMICS
COWPUNCHER	AVON BOOKS	1	1	7	1947	1949	
COWPUNCHER	REALISTIC PUBLICATIONS	2	1	1	1953	1953	REPRINTS AVON SERIES #2
COYOTE	MARVEL ENTERTAINMENT GROUP		1	16	1983	1986	
COZMIC COMICS	H. BUNCH ASSOCIATES		1	6	1972	1974	
CRACK ACTION	ARCHER/KING COMICS		1	5	1953	1953	
CRACK COMICS	QUALITY (FLEETWAY)		1	62	1940	1949	
CRACK COMICS	R. & L. LOCKER		1	1	1950	1950	REPRINTS US QUALITY MATERIAL
CRACK SHOTS	JOHN W. FISHER		1	2	1946	1946	
CRACK WESTERN	POPULAR		1	4	1951	1952	
CRACK WESTERN	QUALITY (FLEETWAY)		63	84	1949	1953	FORMERLY CRACK COMICS

INDEX OF COMIC TITLES AND THEIR PUBLISHERS

COMIC TITLE	PUBLISHER	Vol No.	Srt No.	End No.	Str. Year	End Year	COMMENTS
CRACKAJACK FUNNIES	DELL PUBLISHING COMPANY	2	1	43	1938	1942	
CRACKAJACK FUNNIES	MALTO-MEAL	1	1	1	1937	1937	
CRACKED MAGAZINE	MAJOR MAGAZINES INC		137	150	1958	NOW	
CRACKER	D.C. THOMSON		1	87	1975	1987	
CRACKER JACK COMIC	PHILIMAR		1	1	1947	1947	
CRACKER JACK COMIC	RAYBURN PRODUCTIONS		1	1	1948	1948	
CRACKERS	AMALGAMATED PRESS		1	615	1929	1941	PREVIOUSLY LOT-O'-FUN
CRASH COMICS	RAYBURN PRODUCTIONS		1	1	1948	1948	
CRASH COMICS	TEM PUBLISHING CO.		1	5	1940	1940	
CRASH RYAN	MARVEL ENTERTAINMENT GROUP		1	4	1984	1985	
CRASHER COMIC, THE	KAYEBON PRESS		1	10	1946	1947	
CRASHO COMIC	CARDAL/W. DALY		1	1	1947	1947	
CRAZY	ATLAS		1	7	1953	1954	
CRAZY	MARVEL ENTERTAINMENT GROUP		1	3	1973	1973	
CRAZY COMIC, THE	PHILLIP MARX		1	1	1945	1945	
CRAZY MAGAZINE	MARVEL ENTERTAINMENT GROUP		1	94	1973	1983	
CRAZY, MAN, CRAZY	CHARLTON COMICS	2	2	2	1956	1956	
CRAZYMAN	CONTINUITY COMICS	1	1	3	1991	1992	
CRAZYMAN	CONTINUITY COMICS	2	1	4	1992	NOW	
CREATURES GIANT SIZE	MARVEL ENTERTAINMENT GROUP		1	1	1974	1974	
CREATURES OF THE ID	CALIBER PRESS		1	1	1990	1990	
CREATURES ON THE LOOSE	MARVEL ENTERTAINMENT GROUP		10	37	1971	1975	
CREEPHOLES	MONSTER COMICS		1	1	1991	1991	
CREEPSVILLE	GOGO COMICS		1	5	1991	1991	
CREEPY	DARK HORSE COMICS		1	4	1992	1992	
CREEPY	WARREN PUBLISHING CO		1	146	1964	1985	
CREEPY 1993 FEAR BOOK	HARRIS COMICS		1	1	1993	1993	
CREEPY ANNUAL	WARREN PUBLISHING CO		1	5	1968	1972	
CREEPY THINGS	CHARLTON COMICS		1	6	1975	1976	
CREEPY WORLDS	ALAN CLASS AND CO LTD		1	249	1962	1989	REPRINTS US MATERIAL
CRIME AND JUSTICE	CHARLTON COMICS		1	26	1951	1955	
CRIME AND PUNISHMENT	LEV GLEASON PUBLICATIONS		1	74	1948	1955	
CRIME AND PUNISHMENT	PEMBERTON		1	3	1951	1951	REPRINTS LEV GLEASON MATERIAL
CRIME CAN'T WIN	ATLAS		41	43	1950	1951	FORMERLY "CINDY SMITH"
CRIME CAN'T WIN	ATLAS	2	4	12	1951	1953	
CRIME CAN'T WIN	MARVEL ENTERTAINMENT GROUP	1	41	43	1950	1951	FORMERLY CINDY SMITH
CRIME CASES COMIC	ATLAS	2	5	12	1951	1952	
CRIME CASES COMIC	MARVEL ENTERTAINMENT GROUP	1	24	27	1950	1951	FORMERLY WILLIE COMICS
CRIME CLASSICS	ETERNITY		1	13	1988	1989	
CRIME CLINIC	ZIFF-DAVIS PUBLISHING COMPANY		1	5	1951	1952	
CRIME DETECTIVE COMICS	HILLMAN PERIODICALS	1	1	12	1948	1949	
CRIME DETECTIVE COMICS	HILLMAN PERIODICALS	2	1	12	1950	1951	
CRIME DETECTIVE COMICS	HILLMAN PERIODICALS	3	1	8	1952	1953	
CRIME DETECTIVE COMICS	STREAMLINE		1	7	1951	1951	REPRINTS HILLMAN MATERIAL
CRIME DETECTOR	TIMOR PUBLISHING COMPANY		1	5	1954	1954	
CRIME DOES NOT PAY	ARNOLD BOOK CO.		1	2	1950	1950	REPRINTS LEV GLEASON MATERIAL
CRIME DOES NOT PAY	GOLFING	2	1	1	1945	1945	
CRIME DOES NOT PAY	LEV GLEASON PUBLICATIONS	1	22	147	1942	1955	FORMERLY SILVER STREAK COMICS
CRIME DOES NOT PAY	PEMBERTON		1	6	1951	1951	
CRIME DOES NOT PAY ANNUAL, THE BEST OF	LEV GLEASON PUBLICATIONS		1	5	1944	1951	
CRIME EXPOSED	MARVEL ENTERTAINMENT GROUP		1	14	1948	1952	
CRIME FIGHTING DETECTIVE	STAR PUBLICATIONS		11	19	1950	1952	FORMERLY CRIMINALS ON THE RUN
CRIME FILES	CARTOON ART		1	1	1952	1952	
CRIME FILES	STANDARD COMICS		5	6	1952	1952	
CRIME ILLUSTRATED	EC COMICS		1	2	1955	1956	
CRIME INCORPORATED	FOX FEATURES SYNDICATE		2	3	1950	1951	FORMERLY CRIMES INCORPORATED
CRIME MACHINE	SKYWALD PUBLISHING		1	2	1971	1971	
CRIME MUST PAY THE PENALTY	ACE MAGAZINES		1	48	1948	1956	FORMERLY FOUR FAVOURITES
CRIME MUST STOP	HILLMAN PERIODICALS	1	1	1	1952	1952	
CRIME MYSTERIES	RIBAGE PUBLISHING CO.		1	15	1952	1954	
CRIME ON THE WATERFRONT	REALISTIC PUBLICATIONS		4	4	1952	1952	FORMERLY FAMOUS GANGSTERS
CRIME PATROL	ARCHER/KING COMICS		1	5	1953	1953	
CRIME PATROL	EC COMICS		7	16	1948	1950	FORMERLY INTERNATIONAL CRIME PATROL
CRIME REPORTER	ST JOHN PUBLISHING		1	3	1948	1948	
CRIME REPORTER	STREAMLINE		1	1	1954	1954	REPRINTS FOX MATERIAL
CRIME SMASHER	FAWCETT PUBLICATIONS		1	1	1948	1948	
CRIME SMASHERS	RIBAGE PUBLISHING CO.		1	15	1950	1953	
CRIME SUSPENSTORIES	EC COMICS	1	1	27	1950	1955	
CRIME SUSPENSTORIES	RUSS COCHRAN	2	1	6	1992	NOW	
CRIME SYNDICATE, THE	HOTSPUR PUBLISHING CO.		3	3	1948	1948	
CRIMEBUSTER	WORLD DISTRIBUTORS LTD		1	6	1959	1959	
CRIMEFIGHTER COMICS	SCION		1	1	1951	1951	
CRIMEFIGHTERS	MARVEL ENTERTAINMENT GROUP	1	1	10	1948	1949	
CRIMEFIGHTERS (ALWAYS WIN)	ATLAS	2	11	13	1954	1955	
CRIMES BY WOMEN	FOX FEATURES SYNDICATE		1	15	1948	1951	
CRIMES INCORPORATED	FOX FEATURES SYNDICATE		12	12	1950	1950	FORMERLY MY PAST
CRIMINALS ON THE RUN	PREMIUM GROUP	4	1	7	1948	1949	FORMERLY YOUNG KING COLE
CRIMINALS ON THE RUN	PREMIUM GROUP	5	8	10	1949	1950	
CRIMSON AVENGER, THE	DC COMICS INC.		1	4	1988	1988	
CRIMSON COUGAR	GREATER MERCURY COMICS		1	1	1990	1990	
CRISIS	FLEETWAY		1	63	1987	1991	
CRISIS ON INFINITE EARTHS	DC COMICS INC.		1	12	1985	1986	
CRITICAL ERROR	DARK HORSE COMICS		1	1	1992	1992	
CRITICAL MASS	MARVEL ENTERTAINMENT GROUP		1	7	1989	1990	
CRITICS CHOICE FILES MAGAZINE	PSI FI MOVIE PRESS INC		1	2	1987	1988	
CRITTERS	FANTAGRAPHICS		1	50	1986	1990	
CRITTERS SPECIAL	FANTAGRAPHICS		1	1	1988	1988	
CROMWELL STONE	DARK HORSE COMICS		1	1	1992	1992	
CROSSFIRE	ECLIPSE		1	27	1984	1988	
CROSSFIRE AND RAINBOW	ECLIPSE		1	4	1986	1986	

COMIC TITLE	PUBLISHER	Vol No.	Srt No.	End No.	Str. Year	End Year	COMMENTS
CROSSOVER CLASSICS: THE MARVEL/ DC COLLECTION	MARVEL ENTERTAINMENT GROUP		1	1	1992	1992	
CROSSROADS	FIRST		1	5	1988	1988	
CROW	CALIBER PRESS		1	4	1989	1989	
CROW	TUNDRA		1	3	1991	1992	
CROW COLLECTED	KITCHEN SINK		1	1	1993	1993	
CROW OF THE BEAR CLAW	BLACKTHORNE		1	6	1986	1987	
CROWN COMICS	GOLFING		1	19	1944	1949	
CRUCIBLE	DC COMICS INC.		1	6	1993	1993	
CRUNCH, THE	D.C. THOMSON		1	54	1979	1980	
CRUSADER FROM MARS	ZIFF-DAVIS PUBLISHING COMPANY		1	2	1952	1952	
CRUSADERS	GUILD PUBLICATIONS		1	1	1982	1982	BECOMES SOUTHERN KNIGHTS
CRUSADERS, THE	DC COMICS INC.		1	8	1992	1992	IMPACT TITLE
CRY FOR DAWN	CRY FOR DAWN PUBLICATIONS		1	7	1989	NOW	
CRYIN' LION COMICS	WILLIAM H. WISE		1	3	1944	1945	
CRYING FREEMAN	VIZ		1	2	1993	1993	
CRYING FREEMAN	VIZ	1	1	8	1989	1990	
CRYING FREEMAN	VIZ	2	1	11	1990	1991	
CRYING FREEMAN	VIZ	3	1	10	1991	1992	
CRYING FREEMAN	VIZ	4	1	8	1992	1993	
CRYING FREEMAN	VIZ	5	1	6	1993	1993	
CRYPT OF SHADOWS	MARVEL ENTERTAINMENT GROUP		1	21	1973	1975	
CRYPT OF TERROR	EC COMICS	17	19	19	1950	1950	FORMERLY CRIME PATROL
CRYSTAL PALACE EXHIBITION	CRYSTAL PUBLICATIONS	1991	1991	1991	1991	1991	
CRYSTAR THE CRYSTAL WARRIOR, THE SAGA OF	MARVEL ENTERTAINMENT GROUP		1	11	1983	1985	
CUBBY AND THE CHRISTMAS STAR	R. & L. LOCKER		1	1	1946	1946	
CUIRASS	HARRIER		1	1	1988	1988	
CUPID	MARVEL ENTERTAINMENT GROUP		1	2	1949	1950	
CURIO	HARRY A CHESLER		1	1	30'S	30'S	
CURLY KAYOE COMIC	DONALD PETERS		1	2	1950	1950	REPRINTS US MATERIAL
CURLY KAYOE COMICS	UNITED FEATURES SYNDICATE		1	8	1946	1950	
CURLY'S COMIC	B.B. LIMITED	702	702	702	1950	1950	
CURSE OF THE MOLEMEN	KITCHEN SINK		1	1	1991	1991	
CURSE OF THE MOLEMEN	KITCHEN SINK		1	1	1992	1992	
CURSE OF THE WEIRD	MARVEL ENTERTAINMENT GROUP		1	4	1993	1994	
CUSTER'S LAST FIGHT	AVON BOOKS		1	1	1950	1950	PARTIAL REPRINT OF COWPUNCHER #1
CUTE COMIC	PHILLIP MARX		1	1	1945	1945	
CUTE FUN	GERALD SWAN		1	43	1946	1951	
CUTEY BUNNY, ARMY SURPLUS COMICS FEATURING	ARMY SURPLUS		1	7	1982	1986	
CUTIE PIE	LEV GLEASON PUBLICATIONS		1	5	1955	1956	
CYBER 7	ECLIPSE	1	1	7	1989	1990	
CYBER 7	ECLIPSE	2	1	10	1990	NOW	
CYBERANTICS	GEARY PUBLISHING		1	1	1992	1992	
CYBERCRUSH ROBOTS REVOLT	FLEETWAY		1	14	1991	1992	
CYBERFARCE	PARODY PRESS		1	1	1992	1992	
CYBERFEMMES	PERSONALITY COMICS		1	1	1992	1992	
CYBERFORCE	IMAGE COMICS	0	0	0	1992	1993	
CYBERFORCE	IMAGE COMICS		1	1	1993	1993	
CYBERFORCE	IMAGE COMICS		1	2	1993	NOW	
CYBERPUNK	INNOVATION		1	2	1989	1989	
CYBERPUNK: SERAPHIM FILES	INNOVATION		1	2	1990	1990	
CYBERRAD	CONTINUITY COMICS	1	1	7	1991	1992	
CYBERRAD	CONTINUITY COMICS	2	1	1	1991	1992	
CYBERRAD	CONTINUITY COMICS	3	1	2	1992	NOW	
CYBERSPACE 3000	MARVEL ENTERTAINMENT GROUP		1	8	1993	NOW	
CYCLONE COMICS	BILBARA PUBLISHING CO.		1	5	1940	1940	
CYCLONE ILLUSTRATED COMIC, THE	R. & L. LOCKER		1	1	1946	1946	
CYCLOPS	COMICS INTERVIEW		1	3	1988	1988	
CYCLOPS	INNOCENCE AND EXPERIENCE		1	4	1970	1970	
CYNTHIA DOYLE, NURSE IN LOVE	CHARLTON COMICS		66	74	1962	1964	FORMERLY SWEETHEART DIARY

D

COMIC TITLE	PUBLISHER	Vol No.	Srt No.	End No.	Str. Year	End Year	COMMENTS
D-DAY	CHARLTON COMICS		1	6	1963	1968	
D.R. & QUINCH'S TOTALLY AWESOME GUIDE TO LIFE	TITAN BOOKS		1	1	1986	1986	
DAD'S ARMY	PAN/PICCOLO		1	1	1973	1973	
DADAVILLE	CALIBER PRESS		1	1	1991	1991	
DAFFY DUCK	DELL PUBLISHING COMPANY	4	30	30	1956	1962	
DAFFY DUCK	GOLD KEY	31	127	127	1962	1981	
DAFFY DUCK	TOP SELLERS		1	2	1972	???	
DAFFY DUCK	WHITMAN	128	145	145	1981	1983	ISSUES 131 AND 132 WERE NEVER PUBLISHED
DAFFY TUNES COMICS	FOUR STAR COMICS CORP./SUPERIOR COMICS LTD	12	12	12	1947	1947	
DAFFYDILS	CUPPLES AND LEON CO.		1	1	1911	1911	
DAGAR THE INVINCIBLE	GOLD KEY		1	19	1972	1982	
DAGAR, DESERT HAWK	FOX FEATURES SYNDICATE	14	23	23	1948	1949	FORMERLY ALL GREAT
DAGON	CALIBER PRESS		1	1	1993	NOW	
DAGWOOD COMICS	HARVEY PUBLICATIONS		1	140	1950	1965	
DAGWOOD SPLITS THE ATOM	KING FEATURES		1	1	1949	1949	
DAI KAMIKAZE!	NOW		1	12	1987	1988	
DAIKAZU	GROUND ZERO GRAPHICS		1	8	1992	NOW	
DAIKAZU VS GUGURON	GROUND ZERO GRAPHICS		1	3	1991	1991	
DAILY DEEDS OF SAMMY THE SCOUT, THE	READERS LIBRARY			3	1946	1946	
DAILY EXPRESS CHILDREN'S OWN	EXPRESS PUBLICATIONS		1	8	1933	1933	
DAILY MIRROR BOOK FOR BOYS ANNUAL	MIRROR PRESS PUBLICATIONS	1970	1972	1970	1972		
DAILY MIRROR BOOK OF GARTH	IPC	1975	1976	1975	1976		

COMIC TITLE	PUBLISHER	Vol No.	Srt No.	End No.	Str. Year	End Year	COMMENTS
DAILY MIRROR REFLECTIONS	MIRROR PRESS PUBLICATIONS		1	28	1908	1935	
DAILY PLANET: SPECIAL INVASION EDITION	DC COMICS INC.		1	1	1988	1988	
DAISY AND DONALD	GOLD KEY		1	59	1973	1984	
DAISY AND HER PUPS	HARVEY PUBLICATIONS		21	27	1951	1955	
DAISY COMICS	EASTERN COLOR PRINTING COMPANY		1	1	1936	1936	
DAISY HANDBOOK	DAISY MANUFACTURING CO.		1	2	1946	1948	
DAISY LOW OF THE GIRL SCOUTS	GIRL SCOUTS OF AMERICA		1	2	1954	1965	
DAISY'S RED RYDER GUN BOOK	DAISY MANUFACTURING CO.		1	1	1955	1955	POCKET SIZE
DAKOTA NORTH	MARVEL ENTERTAINMENT GROUP		1	5	1986	1987	
DAKOTAS, THE	PURNELL		1	1	1963	1963	
DAKTARI	DELL PUBLISHING COMPANY		1	4	1967	1969	
DAKTARI ANNUAL	WORLD DISTRIBUTORS LTD	1967	1968	1967	1968		
DALE EVANS COMICS	DC COMICS INC.		1	24	1948	1952	
DALE EVANS, QUEEN OF THE WEST	WORLD DISTRIBUTORS LTD		1	12	1955	1955	REPRINTS DELL MATERIAL
DALEK ANNUAL	WORLD DISTRIBUTORS LTD	1976	1979	1976	1979		
DALEK BOOK, THE	SOUVENIR/ATLAS		1	1	1964	1964	
DALEK OUTER SPACE BOOK, THE	SOUVENIR/ATLAS		1	1	1965	1965	
DALEK WORLD, THE	SOUVENIR/ATLAS		1	1	1966	1966	
DALGODA	FANTAGRAPHICS		1	8	1984	1986	
DALTON BOYS, THE	AVON BOOKS		1	1	1951	1951	
DAMAGE	DC COMICS INC.		1	3	1994	NOW	
DAMAGE CONTROL	MARVEL ENTERTAINMENT GROUP	1	1	4	1989	1989	
DAMAGE CONTROL	MARVEL ENTERTAINMENT GROUP	2	1	4	1989	1990	
DAMAGE CONTROL	MARVEL ENTERTAINMENT GROUP	3	1	4	1991	1991	
DAMIEN DARKE: THE LIVING DEAD	ATOMEKA		1	1	1993	1993	
DAMIEN DARKE: TRAPPED IN TIME	ATOMEKA		1	2	1993	1993	
DAMNED CITY	CONTINUITY COMICS		1	2	1994	1994	CURIOUS IMPRINT
DAN CURTIS GIVEAWAYS	WESTERN PUBLISHING COMPANY		1	9	1974	1974	
DAN DARE ANNUAL	FLEETWAY	1974	1991	1974	1991		
DAN DARE HOLIDAY SPECIAL	FLEETWAY		1	1	1990	1990	
DAN DARE POSTER MAGAZINE	IPC		1	1	1977	1977	
DAN DARE SPACE ANNUAL	LONGACRE		1	1	1963	1963	
DAN DARE SPACE BOOK	HULTON PRESS LTD		1	1	1953	1953	
DAN DARE: PILOT OF THE FUTURE	DRAGON'S DREAM		1	1	1979	1982	
DAN DARE: PILOT OF THE FUTURE	DRAGON'S DREAM		1	3	1979	1982	
DAN DARE: PILOT OF THE FUTURE	HAMLYN PUBLISHING GROUP LTD				1981	1981	
DAN DARE: PILOT OF THE FUTURE COLLECTORS EDITION	HAWK BOOKS		1	1	1987	1987	
DAN DARE: PILOT OF THE FUTURE COLLECTORS EDITION	HAWK BOOKS		1	6	1988	1992	
DAN LENO'S COMIC JOURNAL	C.A. PEARSON		1	93	1898	1899	
DAN TURNER: HOMICIDE HUNCH	ETERNITY		1	1	1991	1991	
DAN TURNER: THE STAR CHAMBER	ETERNITY		1	1	1991	1991	
DAN'L BOONE	MAGAZINE ENTERPRISES		1	8	1955	1957	
DANCES WITH DEMONS	MARVEL ENTERTAINMENT GROUP		1	4	1993	NOW	
DANDEE	FOUR STAR COMICS CORP/SUPERIOR COMICS LTD		1	1	1947	1947	
DANDY BOOK, THE	D.C. THOMSON				1953	NOW	FORMERLY THE DANDY MONSTER COMIC
DANDY COMIC LIBRARY	D.C. THOMSON		1	210	1983	1992	
DANDY COMIC, THE	D.C. THOMSON		1	2718	1937	NOW	
DANDY COMICS	EC COMICS		1	7	1947	1948	
DANDY MONSTER COMIC, THE	D.C. THOMSON				1939	1952	BECOMES THE DANDY BOOK
DANDY SUMMER SPECIAL ANNUAL	D.C. THOMSON	1964	1992	1964	1992		
DANDY-BEANO SUMMER SPECIAL	D.C. THOMSON		1	1	1963	1963	
DANGER	CHARLTON COMICS	2	12	14	1955	1955	FORMERLY PUBLISHED BY COMIC MEDIA
DANGER	COMIC MEDIA/ALAN HARDY ASSOCIATE	1		11	1953	1954	
DANGER	SUPER COMICS		10	18	1964	1964	
DANGER AND ADVENTURE	CHARLTON COMICS		22	27	1955	1956	FORMERLY THIS MAGAZINE IS HAUNTED
DANGER AND ADVENTURE	L. MILLER PUBLISHING COMPANY (UK)		1	3	1955	1955	REPRINTS CHARLTON MATERIAL
DANGER IS OUR BUSINESS	I.W. SUPER		9	9	1964	1964	
DANGER IS OUR BUSINESS	TOBY PRESS PUBLICATIONS		1	10	1953	1955	
DANGER MAN	THORPE & PORTER		1	1	1966	1966	
DANGER MAN	YOUNG WORLD		1	2	1965	1965	
DANGER MAN ANNUAL	WORLD DISTRIBUTORS LTD	1964	1966	1964	1966		
DANGER MAN TELEVISION STORY BOOK	PBS		1	1	1965	1965	
DANGER TRAIL	BAIRNS BOOKS		1	1	1946	1946	
DANGER TRAIL	DC COMICS INC.		1	4	1993	1993	
DANGER TRAIL	DC COMICS INC.		1	5	1950	1951	
DANGER UNLIMITED	DARK HORSE COMICS		1	4	1994	1994	
DANIEL BOONE	GOLD KEY		1	15	1965	1969	
DANIEL BOONE	L. MILLER PUBLISHING COMPANY (UK)		1	35	1957	1959	REPRINTS CHARLTON MATERIAL
DANIEL BOONE, EXPLOITS OF	QUALITY (FLEETWAY)		1	6	1955	1956	
DANIELLE	FIRST AMERICAN EDITION SERIES				1984	1984	
DANNY BLAZE	CHARLTON COMICS		1	2	1955	1955	
DANNY KAYE'S BAND FUN BOOK	H. & A. SELMER		1	1	1959	1959	
DANSE	BLACKTHORNE		1	1	1987	1987	
DARE	FLEETWAY				1991	1991	EXPRESSO BOOKS, A PART OF FLEETWAY
DARE	MONSTER COMICS		1	4	1991	1992	
DARE THE IMPOSSIBLE	FLEETWAY		1	14	1991	1992	
DAREDEVIL	L. MILLER PUBLISHING COMPANY (UK)		1	3	1953	1953	REPRINTS LEV GLEASON MATERIAL
DAREDEVIL	MARVEL ENTERTAINMENT GROUP		1	325	1964	NOW	
DAREDEVIL	PEMBERTON		1	7	1952	1952	REPRINTS LEV GLEASON MATERIAL
DAREDEVIL AND THE PUNISHER: CHILD'S PLAY	MARVEL ENTERTAINMENT GROUP		1	1	1988	1988	
DAREDEVIL ANNUAL	MARVEL ENTERTAINMENT GROUP		1	9	1967	NOW	
DAREDEVIL CHRONICLES	FANTACO		1		1982	1982	
DAREDEVIL COMICS	LEV GLEASON PUBLICATIONS		1	134	1941	1956	No.1, "DAREDEVIL BATTLES HITLER"
DAREDEVIL GIANT SIZE	MARVEL ENTERTAINMENT GROUP		1	1	1975	1975	
DAREDEVIL WESTERN COMICS	CARTOON ART		1	1	1949	1949	REPRINTS FICTION HOUSE MATERIAL
DAREDEVIL WINTER SPECIAL	MARVEL ENTERTAINMENT GROUP		1	1	1982	1982	
DAREDEVIL/BLACK WIDOW: ABBATOIR	MARVEL ENTERTAINMENT GROUP		1	1	1993	1993	

COMIC TITLE	PUBLISHER	Vol No.	Srt No.	End No.	Str Year	End Year	COMMENTS
DAREDEVIL: BORN AGAIN	MARVEL ENTERTAINMENT GROUP		1	1	1989	1989	
DAREDEVIL: FALL OF THE KINGPIN	MARVEL ENTERTAINMENT GROUP		1	1	1993	1993	
DAREDEVIL: GANG WAR	MARVEL ENTERTAINMENT GROUP		1	1	1992	1992	
DAREDEVIL: LOVE AND WAR	MARVEL ENTERTAINMENT GROUP		1	1	1986	1986	
DAREDEVIL: MAN WITHOUT FEAR	MARVEL ENTERTAINMENT GROUP		1	5	1993	1993	
DAREDEVIL: MARKED FOR DEATH	MARVEL ENTERTAINMENT GROUP		1	1	1990	1990	
DAREDEVILS, THE	MARVEL ENTERTAINMENT GROUP		1	11	1983	1983	
DARING ADVENTURES	I.W. SUPER		9	18	1963	1964	
DARING ADVENTURES	ST JOHN PUBLISHING		1	1	1953	1953	3-D
DARING COMICS	TIMELY COMICS		9	12	1944	1945	FORMERLY DARING MYSTERY
DARING CONFESSIONS	YOUTHFUL MAGAZINES		4	8	1952	1953	FORMERLY YOUTHFUL HEARTS
DARING HERO COMIC	SCION		1	4	1951	1952	
DARING LOVE	GILLMOR MAGAZINES		1	1	1953	1953	
DARING LOVE	RIBAGE PUBLISHING CO.		15	17	1952	1953	FORMERLY YOUTHFUL ROMANCES
DARING MYSTERY COMICS	TIMELY COMICS		1	8	1940	1942	
DARK	CONTINUM COMICS		1	2	1991	NOW	
DARK ANGEL	MARVEL ENTERTAINMENT GROUP		6	15	1992	NOW	FORMERLY HELL'S ANGEL
DARK CRYSTAL, THE	MARVEL ENTERTAINMENT GROUP		1	2	1983	1983	
DARK DOMINION	DEFIANT		1	3	1993	NOW	
DARK FANTASY	APPLE COMICS		1	1	1992	NOW	
DARK GUARD	MARVEL ENTERTAINMENT GROUP		1	4	1993	NOW	
DARK HORSE CLASSICS	DARK HORSE COMICS		1	1	1992	NOW	
DARK HORSE COMICS	DARK HORSE COMICS		1	16	1992	NOW	
DARK HORSE COMICS COLLECTOR'S PACKS	DARK HORSE COMICS		1	1	1993	1993	
DARK HORSE FUTURES	DARK HORSE COMICS		1991	1991	1991	1991	
DARK HORSE INSIDER	DARK HORSE COMICS		1	14	1990	NOW	
DARK HORSE INSIDER	DARK HORSE COMICS	2	1	2	1992	NOW	
DARK HORSE PRESENTS	DARK HORSE COMICS		1	81	1986	NOW	
DARK HORSE PRESENTS FIFTH ANNIVERSARY SPECIAL	DARK HORSE COMICS		1	1	1991	1991	
DARK HORSE PRESENTS: ALIENS	DARK HORSE COMICS		1	1	1992	1992	
DARK MANSION OF FORBIDDEN LOVE, THE	DC COMICS INC.		1	4	1971	1972	
DARK MYSTERIES	MERIT PUBLISHING		1	25	1951	1955	
DARK PASSION	HEROIC PUBLISHING		1	2	1992	1993	
DARK SHADOWS	AJAX		1	3	1957	1958	
DARK SHADOWS	GOLD KEY		1	35	1969	1976	
DARK SHADOWS	INNOVATION	1	1	4	1992	1992	
DARK SHADOWS	INNOVATION	2	1	4	1993	1993	
DARK SHADOWS	INNOVATION	3	1	1	1993	1993	
DARK SHADOWS EPISODE GUIDEBOOK	INNOVATION		1	1	1992	1992	
DARK SHADOWS: OLD FRIENDS	INNOVATION		1	1	1993	1993	
DARK STAR HEROES	ANTI-MATTER		1	1	1984	1984	
DARK WOLF	ETERNITY		1	12	1988	NOW	
DARK WOLF	MALIBU COMICS ENTERTAINMENT INC.		1	4	1987	1987	
DARKER IMAGE	IMAGE COMICS		1	1	1993	1994	
DARKEWOOD	AIRCEL		1	5	1988	1988	
DARKHAWK	MARVEL ENTERTAINMENT GROUP		1	37	1991	NOW	
DARKHAWK ANNUAL	MARVEL ENTERTAINMENT GROUP		1	2	1992	NOW	
DARKHOLD: PAGES FROM THE BOOK OF SINS	MARVEL ENTERTAINMENT GROUP		1	16	1992	NOW	
DARKLON THE MYSTIC	PACIFIC COMICS		1	1	1983	1983	
DARKMAN	MARVEL ENTERTAINMENT GROUP	1	1	3	1990	1990	
DARKMAN	MARVEL ENTERTAINMENT GROUP	2	1	6	1993	1993	
DARKMAN MOVIE MAGAZINE	MARVEL ENTERTAINMENT GROUP		1	1	1990	1990	
DARKSTARS	DC COMICS INC.		1	16	1992	NOW	
DARKWING DUCK	WALT DISNEY		1	3	1991	1992	
DARKWING DUCK RETURNS: CAPES AND CAPERS	WALT DISNEY		1	1	1992	1992	
DARKWING DUCK: JUST US JUSTICE DUCKS	WALT DISNEY		1	1	1992	1992	CARTOON TALES
DARLING LOVE	ARCHIE PUBLICATIONS		1	11	1949	1952	
DARLING ROMANCE	GERALD SWAN		1	?	1950	???	
DARLING ROMANCE	M.L.J. MAGAZINES		1	7	1949	1951	
DATE WITH DANGER	STANDARD COMICS		5	6	1952	1953	
DATE WITH DEBBI	DC COMICS INC.		1	18	1969	1972	
DATE WITH JUDY	DC COMICS INC.		1	79	1947	1960	
DATE WITH MILLIE, A	MARVEL ENTERTAINMENT GROUP	1	1	7	1956	1957	
DATE WITH MILLIE, A	MARVEL ENTERTAINMENT GROUP	2	1	7	1959	1960	
DATE WITH PATSY, A	ATLAS		1	1	1957	1957	
DAVY CROCKETT, KING OF THE WILD FRONTIER	DELL PUBLISHING COMPANY		1	1	1955	1955	
DAVID CASSIDY	CHARLTON COMICS		1	14	1972	1973	
DAVY CROCKETT	AVON BOOKS		1	1	1951	1951	
DAVY CROCKETT	CHARLTON COMICS		1	8	1955	1957	
DAVY CROCKETT	GOLD KEY		1	2	1963	1969	
DAVY CROCKETT	L. MILLER PUBLISHING COMPANY (UK)		1	50	1956	1960	REPRINTS
DAYS OF DARKNESS	APPLE COMICS		1	6	1992	1993	
DAYS OF WRATH	APPLE COMICS		1	1	1993	1994	
DAZZLE COMIC	INTERNATIONAL		1	5	1946	1948	
DAZZLER	MARVEL ENTERTAINMENT GROUP		1	42	1981	1986	
DAZZLER	TARGET PUBLICATIONS		1	294	1933	1939	
DC 100 PAGE SUPER SPECTACULAR	DC COMICS INC.		4	22	1971	1973	
DC ACTION	LONDON EDITIONS MAGAZINES		1	6	1990	1990	
DC CHALLENGE	DC COMICS INC.		1	12	1985	1986	
DC COMICS PRESENTS	DC COMICS INC.		1	97	1978	1986	
DC COMICS PRESENTS ANNUAL	DC COMICS INC.		1	4	1982	1985	
DC FOCUS	DC COMICS INC.		1	1	1987	1987	
DC GRAPHIC NOVEL	DC COMICS INC.		1	7	1983	1986	
DC SAMPLER	DC COMICS INC.		1	3	1984	1984	
DC SCIENCE FICTION	DC COMICS INC.		1	7	1985	1987	
DC SPECIAL	DC COMICS INC.		1	29	1968	1977	
DC SPECIAL BLUE- RIBBON DIGEST	DC COMICS INC.		1	24	1980	1982	
DC SPECIAL SERIES	DC COMICS INC.		1	27	1977	1981	No.27 IS BATMAN VS THE INCREDIBLE HULK
DC SPOTLIGHT	DC COMICS INC.		1	1	1985	1985	50TH ANNIVERSARY SPECIAL

COMIC TITLE	PUBLISHER	Vol No.	Srt No.	End No.	Str. Year	End Year	COMMENTS
DC SUPERSTARS	DC COMICS INC.		1	18	1976	1978	
DC UNIVERSE: TRINITY	DC COMICS INC.		1	2	1993	1993	
DEAD CLOWN	MALIBU COMICS ENTERTAINMENT INC.		1	2	1993	1993	
DEAD END CRIME STORIES	KIRBY PUBLISHING COMPANY		1	1	1949	1949	52-PAGES
DEAD IN THE WEST	DARK HORSE COMICS		1	1	1993	1993	
DEAD KID	SKY COMICS		1	4	1994	1994	
DEAD MEAT	FLEETWAY		1	3	1993	NOW	
DEAD OF NIGHT	MARVEL ENTERTAINMENT GROUP		1	11	1973	1975	
DEAD WALKERS	AIRCEL		1	4	1991	1991	
DEAD WHO WALK, THE	REALISTIC PUBLICATIONS		1	1	1952	1952	
DEAD-EYE WESTERN	STREAMLINE		1	7	1950	1951	
DEAD-EYE WESTERN COMIC	THORPE & PORTER		1	2	1953	???	
DEAD-EYE WESTERN COMICS	HILLMAN PERIODICALS	1	1	12	1948	1949	
DEAD-EYE WESTERN COMICS	HILLMAN PERIODICALS	2	1	12	1948	1953	
DEAD-EYE WESTERN COMICS	HILLMAN PERIODICALS	3	1	1	1953	1953	
DEADBEATS	ECLIPSE		1	4	1993	1994	
DEADFACE	HARRIER		1	8	1988	1988	
DEADFACE: DOING THE ISLANDS WITH BACCHUS	DARK HORSE COMICS		1	3	1991	1991	
DEADFACE: EARTH, WATER, AIR & FIRE	DARK HORSE COMICS		1	4	1992	1992	
DEADFACE: IMMORTALITY ISN'T FOREVER	DARK HORSE COMICS				1990	1990	
DEADLIEST HEROES OF KUNG FU	MARVEL ENTERTAINMENT GROUP		1	1	1975	1975	
DEADLINE	TOM ASTOR		1	39	1988	NOW	
DEADLINE CHRISTMAS SPECIAL	TOM ASTOR		1	1	1992	1992	
DEADLINE USA	DARK HORSE COMICS		1	8	1992	NOW	
DEADLY FOES OF SPIDER-MAN, THE	MARVEL ENTERTAINMENT GROUP		1	4	1991	1991	
DEADLY HANDS OF KUNG FU, THE	MARVEL ENTERTAINMENT GROUP		1	33	1974	1977	
DEADMAN	DC COMICS INC.		1	4	1986	1986	
DEADMAN	DC COMICS INC.		1	7	1985	1985	
DEADMAN: EXORCISM	DC COMICS INC.		1	2	1992	1992	
DEADMAN: LOVE AFTER DEATH	DC COMICS INC.		1	2	1990	1990	
DEADPOOL	MARVEL ENTERTAINMENT GROUP		1	4	1993	1993	
DEADSHOT	DC COMICS INC.		1	4	1988	1989	
DEADSHOT DICK WESTERN COMIC	FOLDES PRESS		1	1	1948	1948	
DEADTALES : A BODY	CALIBER PRESS		1	1	1991	1991	
DEADTIME STORIES	NEW COMICS GROUP		1	1	1987	1987	
DEADWOOD GULCH	DELL PUBLISHING COMPANY		1	1	1931	1931	
DEADWORLD	CALIBER PRESS	1	1	25	1986	NOW	
DEADWORLD	CALIBER PRESS	2	5	5	1993	NOW	
DEADWORLD ARCHIVES	CALIBER PRESS		1	4	1992	NOW	
DEADWORLD BITS & PIECES	CALIBER PRESS		1	1	1991	1991	
DEADWORLD: TO KILL A KING	CALIBER PRESS		1	3	1992	1993	
DEAN R KOONTZ'S TRAPPED	ECLIPSE		1	1	1993	1993	
DEAN R. KOONTZ'S TRAPPED	ECLIPSE		1	1	1993	1993	
DEAR BEATRICE FAIRFAX	STANDARD COMICS	5	9	1950	1951		
DEAR HEART	AJAX	15	16	1956	1956		FORMERLY LONELY HEART
DEAR LONELY HEART	ARTFUL PUBLICATION	· 1	8	1951	1952		
DEAR LONELY HEARTS	HARWELL (COMIC MEDIA)		1	8	1953	1954	
DEAR NANCY PARKER	GOLD KEY		1	2	1963	1963	
DEARLY BELOVED	ZIFF-DAVIS PUBLISHING COMPANY		1	1	1952	1952	
DEATH & TAXES: THE REAL COST OF LIVING	PARODY PRESS		1	1	1993	1993	
DEATH 3	MARVEL ENTERTAINMENT GROUP		1	4	1993	NOW	
DEATH DREAMS OF DRACULA	APPLE COMICS		1	1	1991	1991	
DEATH GALLERY	DC COMICS INC.		1	1	1993	1993	
DEATH HUNT	ETERNITY		1	2	1987	1987	
DEATH METAL	MARVEL ENTERTAINMENT GROUP		1	2	1993	1994	MARVEL UK TITLE
DEATH METAL VS GENETIX	MARVEL ENTERTAINMENT GROUP		1	2	1993	1993	MARVEL UK TITLE
DEATH OF CAPTAIN MARVEL - SEE MARVEL GRAPHIC NOVEL							
DEATH OF STUPIDMAN	PARODY PRESS		1	1	1993	1993	
DEATH OF SUPERBABE	PERSONALITY COMICS		1	1	1993	1993	
DEATH RATTLE	KITCHEN SINK		1	18	1985	1988	
DEATH TALKS ABOUT LIFE	DC COMICS INC.		1	1	1993	1993	
DEATH VALLEY	CHARLTON COMICS	7	9	1955	1955		CONTINUES FROM COMIC MEDIA SERIES
DEATH VALLEY	COMIC MEDIA/ALAN HARDY ASSOCIATE		1	6	1953	1954	
DEATH WRECK	MARVEL ENTERTAINMENT GROUP		1	2	1993	NOW	MARVEL UK TITLE
DEATH'S HEAD	MARVEL ENTERTAINMENT GROUP		1	11	1988	1989	
DEATH'S HEAD GOLD	MARVEL ENTERTAINMENT GROUP		1	1	1993	NOW	MARVEL UK TITLE
DEATH'S HEAD II	MARVEL ENTERTAINMENT GROUP		1	15	1993	NOW	
DEATH'S HEAD II	MARVEL ENTERTAINMENT GROUP		1	4	1992	1992	
DEATH'S HEAD II & KILLPOWER: BATTLETIDE	MARVEL ENTERTAINMENT GROUP		1	4	1992	1993	
DEATH'S HEAD II/DIE CUT	MARVEL ENTERTAINMENT GROUP		1	2	1993	1993	
DEATH'S HEAD II/KILLPOWER: BATTLETIDE II	MARVEL ENTERTAINMENT GROUP		1	4	1993	1993	
DEATH'S HEAD II/KILLPOWER: BATTLETIDE III	MARVEL ENTERTAINMENT GROUP		1	4	1994	1994	MARVEL UK TITLE
DEATH'S HEAD II/KILLPOWER: BATTLETIDE SPECIAL	MARVEL ENTERTAINMENT GROUP		1	1	1993	1993	
DEATH'S HEAD: THE BODY IN QUESTION	MARVEL ENTERTAINMENT GROUP		1	1	1990	1990	
DEATH'S HEAD: THE LIFE AND TIMES OF	MARVEL ENTERTAINMENT GROUP		1	1	1990	1990	
DEATH: THE HIGH COST OF LIVING	DC COMICS INC.		1	1	1993	1993	
DEATH: THE HIGH COST OF LIVING	DC COMICS INC.		1	3	1993	1993	
DEATH: THE HIGH COST OF LIVING	TITAN BOOKS		1	1	1994	1994	
DEATHBLOW	IMAGE COMICS		1	2	1993	1994	
DEATHDATE	PARODY PRESS		1	1	1993	1993	
DEATHHAWK	ADVENTURE COMICS		1	3	1988	1988	
DEATHLOK	MARVEL ENTERTAINMENT GROUP		1	32	1991	NOW	
DEATHLOK	MARVEL ENTERTAINMENT GROUP		1	4	1990	1990	
DEATHLOK ANNUAL	MARVEL ENTERTAINMENT GROUP		1	2	1992	NOW	
DEATHLOK SPECIAL	MARVEL ENTERTAINMENT GROUP		1	4	1991	1991	
DEATHMATE BLACK	IMAGE COMICS		1	1	1993	1993	
DEATHMATE BLUE	VALIANT / VOYAGER COMMUNICATIONS		1	1	1993	1993	
DEATHMATE EPILOGUE	IMAGE COMICS		1	1	1993	1993	
DEATHMATE PROLOGUE	VALIANT / VOYAGER COMMUNICATIONS		1	1	1993	1993	

INDEX OF COMIC TITLES AND THEIR PUBLISHERS

COMIC TITLE	PUBLISHER	Vol No.	Srt No.	End No.	Str. Year	End Year	COMMENTS
DEATHMATE RED	IMAGE COMICS		1	1	1993	1993	
DEATHMATE YELLOW	VALIANT / VOYAGER COMMUNICATIONS		1	1	1993	1993	
DEATHROW	HEROIC PUBLISHING		1	1	1993	1994	
DEATHSTROKE THE TERMINATOR	DC COMICS INC.		1	33	1991	NOW	
DEATHSTROKE THE TERMINATOR : FULL CIRCLE	DC COMICS INC.		1	1	1992	1992	
DEATHSTROKE THE TERMINATOR ANNUAL	DC COMICS INC.		1	2	1992	NOW	
DEATHWATCH	HARRIER		1	1	1987	1987	
DEATHWATCH	HARRIS COMICS		1	6	1986	1987	
DEATHWATCH 2000 ADVENTURE SUPPLEMENT	CONTINUITY COMICS		1	1	1993	1993	
DEATHWORLD	ADVENTURE COMICS	1	1	4	1990	1991	
DEATHWORLD	ADVENTURE COMICS	2	1	4	1991	1991	
DEATHWORLD	ADVENTURE COMICS	3	1	4	1991	1991	
DEBBI'S DATES	DC COMICS INC.		1	11	1969	1971	
DEBBIE	D.C. THOMSON		1	518	1973	1983	
DEBBIE DEAN, CAREER GIRL	CIVIL SERVICE PUBLICATION/PENTAGON PUBLISHING CO.		1	2	1945	1945	
DEBBIE DOES DALLAS	AIRCEL		1	6	1990	1991	
DEBBIE PICTURE STORY LIBRARY	D.C. THOMSON		1	2	1978	???	
DEEP RED	FANTACO		1	2	1987	1987	
DEEP SPACE NINE	STARLOG		1	5	1993	NOW	
DEEP, THE	MARVEL ENTERTAINMENT GROUP		1	1	1977	1977	
DEEPSEA	SCION		1	1	1952	1952	
DEFENDERS OF DYNATRON CITY	MARVEL ENTERTAINMENT GROUP		1	6	1992	1992	
DEFENDERS OF THE EARTH	MARVEL ENTERTAINMENT GROUP		1	5	1987	1987	
DEFENDERS, THE	MARVEL ENTERTAINMENT GROUP		1	152	1972	1986	
DEFENDERS, THE ANNUAL	MARVEL ENTERTAINMENT GROUP		1	1	1976	1976	
DEFENDERS, THE GIANT SIZE	MARVEL ENTERTAINMENT GROUP		1	5	1974	1975	
DEFENSELESS DEAD, THE	ADVENTURE COMICS		1	3	1991	1991	
DEFIANT: THE ORIGIN OF THE UNIVERSE	DEFIANT		1	1	1994	1994	
DELL GIANT COMICS	DELL PUBLISHING COMPANY		21	55	1959	1961	
DELL JUNIOR TREASURY	DELL PUBLISHING COMPANY		1	10	1955	1957	
DELLA VISION	ATLAS		1	3	1955	1955	
DELUXE ALBUM SERIES	TOP SELLERS		1	12	1973	1974	REPRINTS
DEMOLITION MAN	DC COMICS INC.		1	3	1993	NOW	
DEMON	DC COMICS INC.	2	1	44	1990	NOW	
DEMON	PORTMAN		1	?	1978	???	
DEMON ANNUAL	DC COMICS INC.	2	1	2	1992	NOW	
DEMON DREAMS	PACIFIC COMICS		1	2	1984	1984	
DEMON HUNTER	AIRCEL		1	4	1989	1989	
DEMON HUNTER	ATLAS		1	1	1975	1975	
DEMON KNIGHT	FIRST				1989	1989	
DEMON WARRIOR, THE	EASTERN COMICS		1	14	1987	1988	
DEMON, THE	DC COMICS INC.	1	1	16	1972	1974	
DEMON, THE	DC COMICS INC.	2	1	4	1987	1987	
DEMONIC TOYS	ETERNITY		1	4	1992	1992	
DEMONS TAILS	ADVENTURE COMICS		1	4	1993	1993	
DEMPSEY AND MAKEPIECE ANNUAL	WORLD DISTRIBUTORS LTD		1986	1986	1986	1986	
DEN	FANTAGOR		1	10	1988	1989	
DEN: NEVERWHERE	FANTAGOR		1	1	1991	1991	
DENIZENS OF DEEP CITY	KITCHEN SINK		1	9	1989	1990	
DENNIS SPECIAL	LONDON EDITIONS MAGAZINES		1	2	1988	1988	
DENNIS THE MENACE	MARVEL ENTERTAINMENT GROUP		1	13	1981	1982	
DENNIS THE MENACE	STANDARD COMICS		1	166	1953	1979	
DENNIS THE MENACE & HIS DOG RUFF	FAWCETT PUBLICATIONS		1	1	1961	1961	
DENNIS THE MENACE (GIANTS)	FAWCETT PUBLICATIONS		1	75	1955	1969	
DENNIS THE MENACE AND HIS FRIENDS	FAWCETT PUBLICATIONS		1	46	1961	1961	
DENNIS THE MENACE AND HIS PAL JOEY	FAWCETT PUBLICATIONS		1	1	1961	1961	
DENNIS THE MENACE AND THE BIBLE KIDS	WORD BOOKS		1	10	1977	1977	
DENNIS THE MENACE ANNUAL	D.C. THOMSON		1956	1993	1956	NOW	
DENNIS THE MENACE BIG BONUS SERIES	FAWCETT PUBLICATIONS		10	11	1980	1980	
DENNIS THE MENACE BONUS MAGAZINE	FAWCETT PUBLICATIONS		76	194	1970	1979	FORMERLY DENNIS THE MENACE GIANTS
DENNIS THE MENACE FUN BOOK	FAWCETT PUBLICATIONS		1	1	1960	1960	
DENNIS THE MENACE FUN FEST SERIES	FAWCETT PUBLICATIONS		16	17	1980	1980	
DENNIS THE MENACE POCKET FULL OF FUN!	FAWCETT PUBLICATIONS		1	50	1969	1980	196 PAGES
DENNIS THE MENACE TELEVISION SPECIAL	FAWCETT PUBLICATIONS		1	2	1961	1962	
DENNIS THE MENACE TRIPLE FEATURE	FAWCETT PUBLICATIONS		1	1	1961	1961	
DENNIS THE MENACE, THE VERY BEST OF	FAWCETT PUBLICATIONS	1	1	2	1979	1980	
DENNIS THE MENACE, THE VERY BEST OF	MARVEL ENTERTAINMENT GROUP	2	1	3	1982	1982	
DEPUTY DAWG PRESENTS DINKY DINK AND HASHIMOTO-SAN	GOLD KEY		1	1	1965	1965	
DER COUNTESS	A PLUS COMICS		1	1	1992	1992	
DESERT STORM JOURNAL	APPLE COMICS		1	9	1991	NOW	
DESERT STREAMS	DC COMICS INC.		1	1	1989	1989	
DESIGN FOR SURVIVAL	AMERICAN SECURITY COUNCIL PRESS		1	1	1968	1968	
DESPERADO	LEV GLEASON PUBLICATIONS		1	8	1948	1949	
DESPERATE DAN BOOK	D.C. THOMSON		1954	1991	1954	1991	
DESTROY	ECLIPSE		1	1	1986	1986	
DESTROY 3-D	ECLIPSE		1	1	1986	1986	
DESTROYER DUCK	ECLIPSE		1	6	1975	1975	
DESTROYER, THE	MARVEL ENTERTAINMENT GROUP		1	1	1992	1992	
DESTROYER, THE	MARVEL ENTERTAINMENT GROUP	1	1	9	1989	1990	
DESTROYER, THE	MARVEL ENTERTAINMENT GROUP	2	1	4	1991	1991	
DESTROYER: TERROR	MARVEL ENTERTAINMENT GROUP	3	1	4	1991	1992	
DESTRUCTOR, THE	ATLAS		1	4	1975	1975	
DETECTIVE COMIC	L. MILLER PUBLISHING COMPANY (UK)		1	8	1959	1959	REPRINTS FAWCETT MATERIAL
DETECTIVE COMICS	DC COMICS INC.		1	671	1937	NOW	
DETECTIVE COMICS	KOSMOS INTERNATIONAL AGENCY		1	1	1947	1947	
DETECTIVE COMICS ANNUAL	DC COMICS INC.		1	6	1988	NOW	
DETECTIVE EYE	CENTAUR PUBLICATIONS		1	2	1940	1940	
DETECTIVE HERO COMIC	SCION		1	1	1952	1952	

COMIC TITLE	PUBLISHER	Vol No.	Srt No.	End No.	Str. Year	End Year	COMMENTS
DETECTIVE PICTURE STORIES	COMICS MAGAZINE CO.		1	7	1936	1937	
DETECTIVES INC.	ECLIPSE		1	1	1988	1988	
DETECTIVES INC.	ECLIPSE	1	1	2	1985	1985	
DETECTIVES INC: A TERROR OF DREAMS	ECLIPSE	2	1	3	1987	1987	
DEVIL DINOSAUR	MARVEL ENTERTAINMENT GROUP		1	9	1978	1978	
DEVIL DOGS	STREET AND SMITH PUBLICATIONS		1	1	1942	1942	
DEVIL KIDS STARRING HOT STUFF	HARVEY PUBLICATIONS		1	107	1962	1981	
DEVIL-DOG DUGAN	ATLAS		1	3	1956	1956	
DEVILINA	ATLAS,		1	2	1975	1975	
DEVLIN WAUGH: SWIMMING IN BLOOD	MANDARIN (2000 AD BOOKS)		1	1	1993	1993	
DEXTER COMICS	DEARFIELD PUBLISHING		1	5	1948	1949	
DEXTER THE DEMON	ATLAS	7	7	7	1957	1957	FORMERLY MELVIN THE MONSTER
DIAMOND ADVENTURE COMIC	ATLAS UK		1	31	1960	1963	REPRINTS FICTION HOUSE MATERIAL
DIANA	D.C. THOMSON		1	720	1963	1976	
DIARY CONFESSIONS	STANMORE PUBLICATIONS	9	14	14	1955	1955	FORMERLY IDEAL ROMANCE
DIARY LOVES	QUALITY (FLEETWAY)	2	31	31	1949	1953	FORMERLY LOVE DIARY
DIARY OF A SPACE PERSON	PAPER TIGER/DRAGON'S WORLD LTD		1	1	1990	1991	
DIARY OF HORROR	AVON BOOKS		1	1	1952	1952	
DIARY SECRETS	ST JOHN PUBLISHING	10	30	30	1952	1955	FORMERLY TEEN-AGE DIARY SECRETS
DICE MAN	IPC		1	5	1986	1986	
DICK BARTON SPECIAL AGENT ANNUAL	BROWN WATSON	1978	1978	1978	1978	1978	
DICK BOSS IN TEXAS	LIBRARY PRESS		1	1	1947	1947	
DICK BOSS, THE ADVENTURES OF	LIBRARY PRESS		1	1	1947	1947	
DICK COLE	STAR PUBLICATIONS		1	10	1948	1950	
DICK HERCULES OF ST. MARKHAM'S	SPORTING CARTOONS		1	17	1952	1954	
DICK TRACY	HARVEY PUBLICATIONS		1	145	1950	1961	
DICK TRACY	STREAMLINE		1	?	1953	???	REPRINTS
DICK TRACY & DICK TRACY JR CAUGHT THE RACKETEERS	CUPPLES AND LEON CO.	2	2	2	1933	1933	
DICK TRACY & JR AND HOW THEY CAUGHT STOOGE VILLER	CUPPLES AND LEON CO.		1	1	1933	1933	
DICK TRACY ADVENTURES	GLADSTONE		1	1	1991	1991	
DICK TRACY IN 3-D	BLACKTHORNE		1	1	1986	1986	
DICK TRACY MAGAZINE	GLADSTONE		1	2	1991	1991	
DICK TRACY MONTHLY	BLACKTHORNE		1	26	1986	1988	
DICK TRACY SHEDS LIGHT ON THE MOLE	WESTERN PUBLISHING COMPANY		1	1	1949	1949	
DICK TRACY WEEKLY	BLACKTHORNE	27	112		1988	1989	FORMERLY DICK TRACY MONTHLY
DICK TRACY, EXPLOITS OF	ROSDON BOOKS INC.		1	1	1946	1946	
DICK TRACY: BIG CITY BLUES	FLEETWAY		1	3	1990	1990	
DICK TRACY: BIG CITY BLUES	WALT DISNEY		1	3	1990	1990	
DICK TRACY: THE UNPRINTED STORIES	BLACKTHORNE		1	4	1987	1988	
DICK TURPIN ANNUAL	GRAND DREAMS		1	1	1980	1980	
DICK WINGATE OF THE US NAVY	TOBY PRESS PUBLICATIONS		1	2	1953	1958	
DICKIE DARE	EASTERN COLOR PRINTING COMPANY		1	4	1941	1942	
DIE CUT	MARVEL ENTERTAINMENT GROUP		1	4	1993	1993	
DIE CUT VS G-FORCE	MARVEL ENTERTAINMENT GROUP		1	2	1993	1993	
DIE MONSTER DIE	ETERNITY		1	1	1991	1991	
DIG 'EM	KELLOGGS		1	1	1973	1973	
DIGITEK	MARVEL ENTERTAINMENT GROUP		1	4	1992	1993	
DILLINGER	RIP OFF PRESS		1	1	1991	1991	
DILLY	LEV GLEASON PUBLICATIONS		1	3	1953	1953	
DILTON'S STRANGE SCIENCE	ARCHIE PUBLICATIONS		1	5	1989	1990	
DIME COMICS	NEWSBOOK PUBLISHING CORP.		1	1	1945	1945	
DING DONG	MAGAZINE ENTERPRISES		1	5	1946	1947	
DINGBATS COMIC	PHILIMAR		1	1	1948	1948	
DINGDONGS COMIC	PHILIMAR		1	1	1948	1948	
DINKY DUCK	ST JOHN PUBLISHING		19	1	1951	1958	
DINO (FLINTSTONES)	CHARLTON COMICS		1	20	1973	1977	
DINO ISLAND	MIRAGE STUDIOS		1	2	1993	1993	
DINO RIDERS	MARVEL ENTERTAINMENT GROUP		1	5	1989	1989	
DINOSAUR BOP	MONSTER COMICS		1	2	1991	1991	
DINOSAUR ISLAND	MONSTER COMICS		1	2	1991	1991	
DINOSAUR REX	UPSHOT		1	3	1987	1987	
DINOSAURS	WALT DISNEY		1	1	1992	1992	
DINOSAURS ATTACK	ECLIPSE		1	1	1991	1991	
DINOSAURS FOR HIRE	ETERNITY		1	9	1988	1989	
DINOSAURS FOR HIRE	MALIBU COMICS ENTERTAINMENT INC.		1	11	1993	NOW	
DINOSAURS: A CELEBRATION	MARVEL ENTERTAINMENT GROUP		1	4	1992	1992	
DIPPY DUCK	ATLAS		1	1	1957	1957	
DIRTY PAIR	ECLIPSE	1	1	4	1988	1989	
DIRTY PAIR	ECLIPSE	2	1	5	1989	1990	
DIRTY PAIR	ECLIPSE	3	1	5	1990	1991	
DIRTY PAIR II: DANGEROUS ACQUAINTANCES	ECLIPSE				1991	1991	
DIRTY PAIR: SIM HELL	DARK HORSE COMICS		1	4	1993	1993	
DIRTY PLOTTE	AIRCEL		1	4	1991	1991	
DISCORDIA	LONDON CARTOON CENTRE		1	1	1991	1991	
DISHMAN	ECLIPSE		1	3	1985	1988	1ST PRINTINGS OF ISSUES 1 AND 2 BY MCLEOD
DISNEY ADVENTURES DIGEST	WALT DISNEY	3	1	8	1990	NOW	
DISNEY COLOSSAL COMICS	WALT DISNEY		1	10	1991	NOW	
DISNEY COMICS ALBUM	WALT DISNEY		1	8	1990	1991	
DISNEY COMICS IN 3-D	WALT DISNEY		1	1	1992	1992	
DISNEY HOLIDAY PARADE	WALT DISNEY		1	1	1991	1991	
DISNEY MAGAZINE	FLEETWAY	2	1		1983	1983	
DISNEY MAGAZINE	HOUSE OF GROLIER	1	1	4	1978	1978	
DISNEY MAGAZINE	LONDON EDITIONS MAGAZINES	1	1	12	1982	1983	
DISNEY MIRROR	MIRROR PRESS PUBLICATIONS		1	100	1991	NOW	
DISNEY TIME	IPC		1	21	1977	1977	
DISNEY TIME SPECIAL	IPC		1	3	1977	1977	
DISNEY'S COMICS IN COLOUR	GLADSTONE		1	7	1991	NOW	

COMIC TITLE	PUBLISHER	Vol No.	Srt No.	End No.	Str. Year	End Year	COMMENTS
DISNEYLAND	IPC		1	298	1971	1976	
DISNEYLAND AUTUMN SPECIAL	IPC		1973	1973	1973	1973	
DISNEYLAND BIRTHDAY PARTY	DELL PUBLISHING COMPANY		1	1	1958	1958	
DISNEYLAND BIRTHDAY PARTY	GLADSTONE		1	1	1985	1985	
DISNEYLAND CHRISTMAS SPECIAL	IPC		1971	1976	1971	1976	
DISNEYLAND FUN TIME SPECIAL	IPC		1971	1978	1971	1978	
DISNEYLAND FUN TIME SPRING SPECIAL	IPC		1979	1979	1979	1979	
DISNEYLAND HOLIDAY SPECIAL	IPC		1972	1980	1972	1980	
DISNEYLAND SPRINGTIME SPECIAL	IPC		1972	1978	1972	1978	
DISNEYLAND SUMMER SPECIAL	IPC		1972	1980	1972	1980	
DISNEYLAND'S BIRTHDAY	GRAPHIC STORY SOCIETY		1	1	1985	1985	
DISTANT SOIL	WARP GRAPHICS		1	10	1991	NOW	
DITKO'S WORLD	RENEGADE PRESS		1	3	1986	1986	
DIVA'S	CALIBER PRESS		1	4	1992	NOW	
DIXIE COMIC	ENSIGN/W. FORSHAW		1	1	1947	1947	
DIXIE DUGAN	COLUMBIA COMICS GROUP	1	1	13	1942	1949	
DIXIE DUGAN	PRIZE/HEADLINE/FEATURE	3	1	4	1951	1951	
DIXIE DUGAN	PRIZE/HEADLINE/FEATURE	4	1	4	1954	1954	
DIXIE DUGAN	UNITED-ANGLO PRODUCTIONS		1	2	1950	1951	REPRINTS COLUMBIA MATERIAL
DIXON OF DOCK GREEN	C.A. PEARSON		1	6	1959	1960	
DIZZLING COMIC	CO-ORDINATION PRESS		1	1	1947	1947	
DIZZY DAMES	AMERICAN COMIC GROUP		1	6	1952	1953	
DIZZY DON COMICS	F.E. HOWARD		1	22	1942	1946	
DIZZY DUCK	STANDARD COMICS		32	39	1950	1952	FORMERLY BARNYARD COMICS
DNAGENTS	ECLIPSE		1	24	1983	1985	
DNAGENTS 3-D	ECLIPSE		1	1	1986	1986	
DNAGENTS, THE NEW	ECLIPSE		1	17	1985	1987	
DO YOU BELIEVE IN NIGHTMARES?	ST JOHN PUBLISHING		1	2	1957	1958	
DO-DO	NATIONWIDE PUBLISHERS		1	7	1950	1951	
DOC CARTER VD COMICS	HEALTH PUBLICATIONS INSTITUTE		1	1	1949	1949	
DOC CHAOS	ANTI-MATTER	1	1	4	1984	1985	
DOC CHAOS	ESCAPE	2	1	2	1988	1988	
DOC CHAOS: THE CHERNOBLE EFFECT	HOOLIGAN PRESS		1	1	1988	1988	
DOC SAVAGE	DC COMICS INC.		1	30	1988	1990	
DOC SAVAGE	DC COMICS INC.		1	4	1988	1988	
DOC SAVAGE	GOLD KEY		1	1	1966	1966	
DOC SAVAGE	MARVEL ENTERTAINMENT GROUP		1	8	1972	1974	
DOC SAVAGE	MARVEL ENTERTAINMENT GROUP		1	8	1975	1977	
DOC SAVAGE ANNUAL	DC COMICS INC.		1	1	1989	1989	
DOC SAVAGE COMICS	STREET AND SMITH PUBLICATIONS	1	1	12	1940	1941	
DOC SAVAGE COMICS	STREET AND SMITH PUBLICATIONS	2	1	8	1941	1943	
DOC SAVAGE GIANT SIZE	MARVEL ENTERTAINMENT GROUP		1	1	1975	1975	
DOC SAVAGE: REPEL	MILLENIUM		1	2	1992	1993	
DOC SAVAGE: THE DEVIL THOUGHTS	MILLENIUM		1	3	1992	1992	
DOC SAVAGE: THE MAN OF BRONZE	MILLENIUM		1	4	1991	1991	
DOC SAVAGE: THE MAN OF BRONZE, DOOM DYNASTY	MILLENIUM		1	2	1992	1992	
DOC SAVAGE: THE MANUAL OF BRONZE	MILLENIUM		1	1	1992	1992	
DOCTOR CHAOS	TRIUMPHANT COMICS		1	2	1993	NOW	
DOCTOR DOOLITTLE	TOP SELLERS		1	2	1973	1974	
DOCTOR GIGGLES	DARK HORSE COMICS		1	2	1992	1992	
DOCTOR GORPON	ETERNITY		1	3	1991	1991	
DOCTOR KILDARE ANNUAL	WORLD DISTRIBUTORS LTD		1	1	1962	1962	
DOCTOR SNUGGLES HOLIDAY SPECIAL	POLYSTYLE		1	2	1981	1982	
DOCTOR SOLAR MAN OF THE ATOM	GOLD KEY		1	31	1962	1982	
DOCTOR STRANGE	MARVEL ENTERTAINMENT GROUP	1	169	183	1968	1969	
DOCTOR STRANGE	MARVEL ENTERTAINMENT GROUP	2	1	81	1974	1987	
DOCTOR STRANGE AND GHOST RIDER SPECIAL	MARVEL ENTERTAINMENT GROUP		1	1	1991	1991	
DOCTOR STRANGE ANNUAL	MARVEL ENTERTAINMENT GROUP	2	1	1	1976	1976	
DOCTOR STRANGE ANNUAL	MARVEL ENTERTAINMENT GROUP	3	2	3	1991	NOW	
DOCTOR STRANGE CLASSICS	MARVEL ENTERTAINMENT GROUP		1	4	1984	1984	
DOCTOR STRANGE GIANT SIZE	MARVEL ENTERTAINMENT GROUP	2	1	1	1975	1975	
DOCTOR STRANGE SPECIAL EDITION	MARVEL ENTERTAINMENT GROUP		1	1	1993	1993	
DOCTOR STRANGE VERSUS DRACULA	MARVEL ENTERTAINMENT GROUP		1	1	1994	1994	
DOCTOR STRANGE, SORCERER SUPREME	MARVEL ENTERTAINMENT GROUP	3	1	62	1988	NOW	
DOCTOR STRANGE: SHAMBALLA	MARVEL ENTERTAINMENT GROUP		1	1	1986	1986	
DOCTOR WHO	MARVEL ENTERTAINMENT GROUP		1	23	1984	1986	
DOCTOR WHO 25TH ANNIVERSARY SPECIAL	MARVEL ENTERTAINMENT GROUP		1	1	1988	1988	
DOCTOR WHO 30TH ANNIVERSARY SPECIAL	MARVEL ENTERTAINMENT GROUP		1	1	1994	1994	
DOCTOR WHO AND THE INVASION FROM SPACE	WORLD DISTRIBUTORS LTD		1	1	1965	1965	
DOCTOR WHO ANNUAL/YEARBOOK	WORLD DISTRIBUTORS LTD		1977	1981	1965	1987	
DOCTOR WHO AUTUMN SPECIAL	MARVEL ENTERTAINMENT GROUP		1986	1987	1986	1987	
DOCTOR WHO CLASSIC COMICS	MARVEL ENTERTAINMENT GROUP		1	15	1992	NOW	
DOCTOR WHO HOLIDAY SPECIAL	POLYSTYLE		1	1	1974	1974	
DOCTOR WHO MAGAZINE	MARVEL ENTERTAINMENT GROUP		195	205	1992	NOW	FORMERLY DOCTOR WHO MONTHLY
DOCTOR WHO MONTHLY	MARVEL ENTERTAINMENT GROUP		44	194	1980	1992	FORMERLY DOCTOR WHO WEEKLY
DOCTOR WHO MONTHLY 10TH ANNIVERSARY SPECIAL	MARVEL ENTERTAINMENT GROUP		1	1	1989	1989	
DOCTOR WHO SPECIAL: JOURNEY THROUGH TIME	GALLEY PRESS		1	1	1986	1986	
DOCTOR WHO SUMMER SPECIAL	MARVEL ENTERTAINMENT GROUP		1980	1991	1980	1991	
DOCTOR WHO WEEKLY	MARVEL ENTERTAINMENT GROUP		1	43	1979	1980	BECOMES DOCTOR WHO MONTHLY
DOCTOR WHO WINTER SPECIAL	MARVEL ENTERTAINMENT GROUP		1977	1991	1977	1991	
DOCTOR WHO YEARBOOK	MARVEL ENTERTAINMENT GROUP		1992	1992	1992	1992	
DOCTOR WHO, THE AMAZING WORLD OF	PBS		1	1	1976	1976	REPRINTS
DOCTOR WHO, THE VERY BEST OF	MARVEL ENTERTAINMENT GROUP		1	1	1981	1981	ALL REPRINTS
DOCTOR WHO: IT'S LARGER ON THE INSIDE SPECIAL	MARVEL ENTERTAINMENT GROUP		1	1	1988	1988	
DOCTOR WHO: THE SIXTIES	VIRGIN				1993	1993	
DOCTOR WHO: VOYAGER	MARVEL ENTERTAINMENT GROUP		1	1	1989	1989	
DOCTOR ZERO	MARVEL ENTERTAINMENT GROUP		1	9	1988	1989	
DODO AND THE FROG, THE	DC COMICS INC.		80	92	1954	1957	FORMERLY FUNNY STUFF

COMIC TITLE	PUBLISHER	Vol No.	Srt No.	End No.	Str. Year	End Year	COMMENTS
DOG BOY	FANTAGRAPHICS		1	10	1987	1988	
DOGFACE DOOLEY	MAGAZINE ENTERPRISES		1	5	1951	1953	
DOLL	RIP OFF PRESS				1989	1989	
DOLL MAN QUARTERLY, THE	QUALITY (FLEETWAY)		1	47	1941	1948	
DOLLMAN	ETERNITY		1	4	1991	1991	
DOLLMAN	POPULAR		1	1	1951	1951	REPRINTS QUALITY MATERIAL
DOLLMAN	R. & L. LOCKER		11	1	1949	1949	REPRINTS QUALITY MATERIAL
DOLLMAN	SUPER COMICS		11	17	1964	1964	
DOLLY	ZIFF-DAVIS PUBLISHING COMPANY		10	10	1951	1951	
DOLLY DILL	MARVEL ENTERTAINMENT GROUP		1	1	1945	1945	
DOLLY DIMPLES AND BOBBY BOONCE'	CUPPLES AND LEON CO.		1	1	1933	1933	
DOMINION	ECLIPSE		1	1	1993	1993	
DOMINION SPECIAL: PHANTOM OF THE AUDIENCE	DARK HORSE COMICS		1	1	1994	1994	
DOMINO CHANCE	CHANCE ENTERTAINMENT		1	9	1982	1985	
DOMINO CHANCE ROACH EXTRAORDINAIRE	AMAZING COMICS		1	3	1987	1987	
DON FORTUNE MAGAZINE	DON FORTUNE PUBLISHING CO.		1	6	1946	1947	
DON MARTIN MAGAZINE	WELSH PUBLICATIONS		1	2	1993	NOW	
DON MARTIN'S DROLL BOOK	DARK HORSE COMICS		1	1	1993	1993	
DON NEWCOMBE	FAWCETT PUBLICATIONS		1	1	1950	1950	
DON WINSLOW OF THE NAVY	FAWCETT PUBLICATIONS		1	73	1943	1955	
DON WINSLOWE OF THE NAVY	L. MILLER PUBLISHING COMPANY (UK)		50	149	1947	1953	REPRINTS FAWCETT MATERIAL
DONALD AND MICKEY	IPC		1	182	1972	1974	
DONALD AND MICKEY (MICKEY AND DONALD)	GLADSTONE		19	20	1993	NOW	
DONALD AND MICKEY CHRISTMAS SPECIAL	IPC		1972	1974	1972	1974	
DONALD AND MICKEY FUN TIME SPECIAL	IPC		1972	1975	1972	1975	
DONALD AND MICKEY HOLIDAY SPECIAL	IPC		1972	1975	1972	1975	
DONALD AND MICKEY IN DISNEYLAND	DELL PUBLISHING COMPANY		1	1	1958	1958	
DONALD AND MICKEY MERRY CHRISTMAS	K.K. PUBLICATIONS		1943	1949	1943	1949	FORMERLY FAMOUS GANG BOOK OF COMICS
DONALD DUCK	DELL PUBLISHING COMPANY		26	84	1952	1962	
DONALD DUCK	GLADSTONE		246	279	1986	NOW	
DONALD DUCK	GOLD KEY		85	216	1962	1982	
DONALD DUCK	IPC		1	18	1975	1976	
DONALD DUCK	WHITMAN		217	245	1981	1984	
DONALD DUCK "PLOTTING PICKNICKERS"	FRITOS GIVEAWAYS		1	1	1962	1962	
DONALD DUCK ADVENTURES	GLADSTONE		1	22	1987	NOW	
DONALD DUCK ADVENTURES	WALT DISNEY		1	37	1990	NOW	
DONALD DUCK ADVENTURES IN COLOUR	GLADSTONE		1	1	1993	NOW	
DONALD DUCK AND THE BOYS	WHITMAN		1	1	1948	1948	
DONALD DUCK AND THE RED FEATHER	RED FEATHER GIVEAWAYS		1	1	1948	1948	
DONALD DUCK BEACH PARTY	DELL PUBLISHING COMPANY		1	6	1954	1959	
DONALD DUCK CHRISTMAS SPECIAL	IPC		1975	1975	1975	1975	
DONALD DUCK COMICS DIGEST	GLADSTONE		1	5	1986	1987	
DONALD DUCK FUN BOOK	DELL PUBLISHING COMPANY		1	2	1953	1954	
DONALD DUCK FUN LIBRARY	PURNELL		1	2	1978	1978	
DONALD DUCK IN "THE LITTERBUG"	KEEP AMERICA BEAUTIFUL		1	1	1963	1963	
DONALD DUCK IN DISNEYLAND	DELL PUBLISHING COMPANY		1	1	1955	1955	
DONALD DUCK'S SURPRISE PARTY	WALT DISNEY		1	1	1948	1948	
DONALD DUCK: 50 YEARS	WALT DISNEY		1	1	1992	1992	
DOOM 2099	MARVEL ENTERTAINMENT GROUP		1	15	1993	NOW	
DOOM FORCE SPECIAL	DC COMICS INC.		1	1	1992	1992	
DOOM PATROL	DC COMICS INC.	1	86	124	1964	1973	FORMERLY MY GREATEST ADVENTURE
DOOM PATROL	DC COMICS INC.	2	1	74	1987	NOW	
DOOM PATROL AND SUICIDE SQUAD SPECIAL	DC COMICS INC.		1	1	1988	1988	
DOOM PATROL ANNUAL	DC COMICS INC.	2	1	2	1988	1988	
DOOM PATROL: CRAWLING FROM THE WRECKAGE	DC COMICS INC.		1	1	1992	1992	
DOOMSDAY +1	CHARLTON COMICS		1	12	1975	1979	
DOOMSDAY SQUAD	FANTAGRAPHICS		1	7	1986	1987	
DOORMAN	CULT PRESS		1	1	1993	NOW	
DOORWAY TO NIGHTMARE	DC COMICS INC.		1	5	1978	1978	
DOPE FIEND FUNNIES	H. BUNCH ASSOCIATES		1	1	1974	1974	
DOPEY DUCK COMICS	TIMELY COMICS		1	2	1945	1945	
DORK HOUSE COMICS	PARODY PRESS		1	1	1992	1992	
DORM GIRLS	CATALAN COMMUNCATIONS				1991	1991	
DOROTHY LAMOUR	FOX FEATURES SYNDICATE		2	3	1950	1950	FORMERLY JUNGLE LIL
DOT AND CARRIE	DAILY NEWS		1	1	1923	1923	
DOT AND CARRIE AND ADOLPHUS	DAILY NEWS		1	1	1924	1924	
DOT AND CARRIE NOT FORGETTING ADOLPHUS	DAILY NEWS		1	1	1925	1925	
DOT AND DASH AND THE LUCKY JINGLE PIGGIE	SEARS AND ROEBUCK COMPANY		1	1	1942	1942	
DOT DOTLAND	HARVEY PUBLICATIONS		62	63	1974	1974	FORMERLY LITTLE DOT DOTLAND
DOTTY (AND HER BOY FRIENDS)	ACE COMICS		35	40	1948	1949	FORMERLY FOUR TEENERS
DOTTY DRIPPLE	HARVEY PUBLICATIONS		1	24	1946	1952	
DOTTY DRIPPLE	MAGAZINE ENTERPRISES		1	24	1946	1952	
DOUBLE ACTION COMICS	DC COMICS INC.		2	2	1940	1940	
DOUBLE COMICS	ELLIOT PUBLISHING COMPANY		1940	1944	1940	1944	132-PAGES
DOUBLE DARE ADVENTURES	HARVEY PUBLICATIONS		1	2	1966	1967	
DOUBLE DRAGON	MARVEL ENTERTAINMENT GROUP		1	6	1991	1991	
DOUBLE LIFE OF PRIVATE STRONG, THE	ARCHIE PUBLICATIONS		1	2	1959	1959	
DOUBLE TALK	FEATURE PUBLICATIONS		1	1	1962	1962	
DOUBLE TROUBLE	ST JOHN PUBLISHING		1	2	1957	1958	
DOUBLE TROUBLE	STAR PUBLICATIONS		1	1	1950	1950	
DOUBLE UP	ELLIOT PUBLISHING COMPANY		1	1	1941	1941	200-PAGES
DOVER THE BIRD	ELLIOT PUBLISHING COMPANY		1	1	1955	1955	
DOWN WITH CRIME	ARNOLD BOOK CO.		50	56	1952	1952	REPRINTS FAWCETT MATERIAL
DOWN WITH CRIME	FAWCETT PUBLICATIONS		1	7	1952	1953	
DOWNSIDE	MACNAMARA & KETLEY		1	6	1988	1991	
DP 7	MARVEL ENTERTAINMENT GROUP		1	32	1986	1989	
DP 7 ANNUAL	MARVEL ENTERTAINMENT GROUP		1	1	1987	1987	
DR. ANTONY KING, HOLLYWOOD LOVE DOCTOR	HARVEY PUBLICATIONS		1	4	1952	1954	
DR. DOOM & DR. STRANGE: TRIUMPH AND TORMENT	MARVEL ENTERTAINMENT GROUP		1	1	1989	1989	

INDEX OF COMIC TITLES AND THEIR PUBLISHERS

COMIC TITLE	PUBLISHER	Vol No.	Srt No.	End No.	Str. Year	End Year	COMMENTS
DR. DOOM & DR. STRANGE: TRIUMPH AND TORMENT	MARVEL ENTERTAINMENT GROUP		9	9	1989	1989	
DR. FATE	DC COMICS INC.		1	4	1987	1987	
DR. FATE	DC COMICS INC.		1	41	1988	1992	
DR. FATE	DC COMICS INC.		1	1	1989	1989	
DR. FATE ANNUAL	DC COMICS INC.		1	1	1982	1982	
DR. FU MANCHU	I.W. ENTERPRISES						
DR. GRAVES	CHARLTON COMICS		73	75	1985	1986	FORMERLY THE MANY GHOSTS OF DR. GRAVES
DR. RADIUM'S BIG BOOK!	SLAVE LABOR				1990	1990	
DR. TOM BRENT, YOUNG INTERN	CHARLTON COMICS		1	5	1963	1963	
DRACULA	DELL PUBLISHING COMPANY		2	8	1966	1973	
DRACULA	ETERNITY		1	4	1990	1990	
DRACULA	NEW ENGLISH LIBRARY		1	1	1974	1974	
DRACULA	NEW ENGLISH LIBRARY		1	12	1972	1973	REPRINTS SPANISH MATERIAL
DRACULA	TOP SELLERS		1	1	1962	1962	REPRINTS DELL MATERIAL
DRACULA	QUALITY (FLEETWAY)		1	1	1974	1974	
DRACULA COMICS SPECIAL	MARVEL ENTERTAINMENT GROUP		2	5	1974	1975	
DRACULA GIANT SIZE	MARVEL ENTERTAINMENT GROUP		1	1	1975	1975	
DRACULA LIVES ANNUAL	WORLD DISTRIBUTORS LTD		1	1	1976	1976	
DRACULA LIVES SPECIAL	MARVEL ENTERTAINMENT GROUP	1	1	87	1974	1976	
DRACULA LIVES!	MARVEL ENTERTAINMENT GROUP	2	1	13	1973	1975	
DRACULA LIVES!	WARREN PUBLISHING CO		1	1	1979	1979	
DRACULA MAGAZINE	TOPPS		1	2	1993	1993	
DRACULA VS ZORRO	WORLD DISTRIBUTORS LTD		1	1	1982	1982	
DRACULA'S SPINECHILLERS ANNUAL	TITAN BOOKS		1	1	1993	1993	
DRACULA, BRAM STOKER'S	DARK HORSE COMICS		1	4	1993	1993	
DRACULA, BRAM STOKER'S MOVIE SPECIAL	NEWMARKET PRESS		1	1	1992	1992	
DRACULA, BRAM STOKER'S: THE FILM AND THE LEGEND	MARVEL ENTERTAINMENT GROUP		1	1	1986	1986	
DRACULA: A SYMPHONY IN MOONLIGHT AND NIGHTMARES	ETERNITY		1	1	1991	1991	
DRACULA: THE LADY IN THE TOMB	ADVENTURE COMICS		1	4	1991	1993	
DRACULA: THE SUICIDE CLUB	TOPPS		1	3	1993	1993	
DRACULA: VLAD THE IMPALER	MARVEL ENTERTAINMENT GROUP		1	1	1988	1988	
DRAFT, THE	MARVEL ENTERTAINMENT GROUP		30	59	1968	1973	
DRAG'N WHEELS	COMICS INTERVIEW		1	3	1988	1988	
DRAGON	ECLIPSE		1	1	1991	1991	
DRAGON CHIANG	MARVEL ENTERTAINMENT GROUP		1	4	1993	1993	
DRAGON LINES	MARVEL ENTERTAINMENT GROUP		1	2	1993	1993	
DRAGON LINES: THE WAY OF THE WARRIOR	MARVEL ENTERTAINMENT GROUP		1	1	1993	1993	
DRAGON STRIKE	MARVEL ENTERTAINMENT GROUP		1	10	1988	1989	
DRAGON'S CLAWS	CALIBER PRESS		1	1	1989	1989	
DRAGON'S STAR	CALIBER PRESS		1	1	1993	1994	
DRAGON'S STAR	NIGHT WYND ENTERPRISES	1	1	4	1992	1992	
DRAGONFIRE	NIGHT WYND ENTERPRISES	2	1	4	1992	1992	
DRAGONFIRE	NIGHT WYND ENTERPRISES		1	4	1992	1992	
DRAGONFIRE: THE CLASSIFIED FILES	NIGHT WYND ENTERPRISES		1	8	1993	1993	
DRAGONFIRE: THE EARLY YEARS	NIGHT WYND ENTERPRISES		1	2	1993	1993	
DRAGONFIRE: THE SAMURAI SWORD	NIGHT WYND ENTERPRISES		1	4	1992	1993	
DRAGONFIRE: UFO WARS	ECLIPSE		1	2	1991	1991	
DRAGONFLIGHT	AC COMICS		1	8	1986	1987	
DRAGONFLY	AIRCEL		1	14	1988	1989	
DRAGONFORCE	AIRCEL		1	4	1990	1991	
DRAGONFORCE CHRONICLES	DC COMICS INC.		1	35	1988	1991	
DRAGONLANCE COMICS	DC COMICS INC.		1	1	1990	1990	
DRAGONLANCE COMICS ANNUAL	DC COMICS INC.		4	5	1990	1991	ISSUES 1-3 PUBLISHED BY TSR
DRAGONLANCE SAGA	TSR		1	3	1988	1989	SERIES CONTINUED BY DC
DRAGONLANCE SAGA	ECLIPSE		1	3	1987	1987	
DRAGONQUEST	AIRCEL	1	1	6	1986	1986	
DRAGONRING	AIRCEL	2	1	15	1987	1988	
DRAGONRING	AIRCEL		1	4	1990	1990	
DRAGONS IN THE MOON	MARVEL ENTERTAINMENT GROUP		1	1	1982	1982	
DRAGONSLAYER	MARVEL ENTERTAINMENT GROUP		1	2	1981	1981	
DRAGONSLAYER	CHARLTON COMICS		1	16	1963	1967	
DRAGSTRIP HOTRODDERS	ACTION TEXT		1	1	1973	1973	224-PAGES
DRAMA OF AMERICA, THE	FANTACO		1	3	1992	NOW	
DREAD	HAMILTON COMICS		1	1	1992	1992	
DREAD OF NIGHT	HAMILTON COMICS		1	1	1992	1992	
DREAD OF NIGHT IN COLOUR	FANTACO		1	1	1992	1992	
DREAD SUMMER SPECIAL	MARVEL ENTERTAINMENT GROUP		1	4	1992	1992	
DREADLANDS	MALIBU COMICS ENTERTAINMENT INC.		1	1	1994	NOW	
DREADSTAR	MARVEL ENTERTAINMENT GROUP		1	64	1982	1986	
DREADSTAR	MARVEL ENTERTAINMENT GROUP		1	6	1985	1985	
DREADSTAR AND CO.	MARVEL ENTERTAINMENT GROUP		1	1	1983	1983	
DREADSTAR ANNUAL	I.W. ENTERPRISES		1	9	1958	1958	
DREAM OF LOVE	I.W. SUPER		1	9	1958	1958	
DREAM OF LOVE	ECLIPSE		1	14	1986	1989	
DREAMERY, THE	DOFFIELD AND CO.		1	1	1905	1905	
DREAMS OF THE RAREBIT FIEND	FLEETWAY		1	1	1993	1993	
DREDD BY BISLEY	DAVID MCKAY PUBLICATIONS		1934	1934	1934	1934	
DRISCOLL'S BOOK OF PIRATES	MARVEL ENTERTAINMENT GROUP		1	8	1986	1987	
DROIDS	DC COMICS INC.		1	1	1990	1990	
DROWNED GIRL, THE	JADEMAN COMICS		1	56	1988	1992	
DRUNKEN FIST	DUCK SOUP		1	3	1979	1979	
DUCK SOUP	WALT DISNEY		1	1	1990	1990	
DUCK TALES THE MOVIE	GLADSTONE		1	13	1988	1990	
DUCK TALES, DISNEY'S	PRIZE PUBLICATIONS		1	3	1949	1950	
DUDLEY	CHARLTON COMICS		1	7	1970	1971	
DUDLEY DO-RIGHT	WEATHER BIRD SHOES		1	1	1941	1941	
DUMBO	WALT DISNEY		1	26	1942	1942	
DUMBO WEEKLY	PARODY PRESS		1	1	1993	1993	
DUMM $2099							

COMIC TITLE	PUBLISHER	Vol No.	Srt No.	End No.	Str. Year	End Year	COMMENTS
DUMMY	NEW MUSICAL EXPRESS			1	1975	1975	
DUNC AND LOO	DELL PUBLISHING COMPANY		1	8	1961	1963	
DUNE	MARVEL ENTERTAINMENT GROUP		1	3	1985	1985	
DURANGO KID	COMPIX	2	1	20	1952	1953	REPRINTS MAGAZINE ENTERPRISES MATERIAL
DURANGO KID	STREAMLINE	1	1	2	1951	1951	REPRINTS MAGAZINE ENTERPRISES MATERIAL
DURANGO KID, THE	MAGAZINE ENTERPRISES		1	41	1949	1955	
DYNABRITE COMICS	WHITMAN		11350	11361	1978	1979	
DYNAMIC	PAGET			1	1949	1949	
DYNAMIC ADVENTURES	I.W. ENTERPRISES		8	9	1964	1964	
DYNAMIC CLASSICS	DC COMICS INC.		1	1	1978	1978	
DYNAMIC COMICS	HARRY A CHESLER		1	25	1941	1948	
DYNAMIC COMICS	I.W. SUPER		1	1	1964	1964	
DYNAMIC COMICS	INTERNATIONAL		1	1	1945	1945	
DYNAMIC THRILLS	GERALD SWAN		1	10	1951	1952	
DYNAMITE	COMIC MEDIA/ALAN HARDY ASSOCIATE		1	9	1953	1954	
DYNAMITE DUNN	L. MILLER PUBLISHING COMPANY (UK)		1	1	1944	1944	REPRINTS UNITED FEATURES MATERIAL
DYNAMO	TOWER COMICS		1	4	1966	1967	
DYNAMO JOE	FIRST		1	15	1986	1988	
DYNAMO JOE SPECIAL	FIRST		1	1	1987	1987	
DYNOMUTT	MARVEL ENTERTAINMENT GROUP		1	1	1977	1978	

E

COMIC TITLE	PUBLISHER	Vol No.	Srt No.	End No.	Str. Year	End Year	COMMENTS
E-MAN	ALPHA PRODUCTIONS		1	1	1993	NOW	
E-MAN	CHARLTON COMICS		1	10	1973	1975	
E-MAN	COMICO		1	1	1989	1989	
E-MAN	COMICO		1	3	1990	1990	
E-MAN	FIRST		1	25	1983	1985	
E-MAN RETURNS	ALPHA PRODUCTIONS		1	1	1994	NOW	
EAGLE	APPLE COMICS		1	26	1986	1989	
EAGLE	CRYSTAL PUBLICATIONS		1	15	1941	1942	
EAGLE	FLEETWAY		1	344	1982	NOW	ISSUES AFTER NO.344 ARE DATED NOT NUMBERED.
EAGLE	RURAL HOME PUBLISHING COMPANY		1	2	1945	1945	
EAGLE ANNUAL	FLEETWAY	1983	1983	1983	1993		
EAGLE ANNUAL	HULTON/LONGACRE/ODHAMS		1	1984	1951	1975	
EAGLE BOOK OF CUTAWAYS, THE	MICHAEL JOSEPH		1	1	1988	1988	
EAGLE BOOK OF MAGIC	HULTON PRESS LTD		1	1	1955	1955	
EAGLE EXTRA	HULTON PRESS LTD		1	10	1953	1953	
EAGLE HOLIDAY SPECIAL	FLEETWAY	1983	1992	1983	1992		
EAGLE HOLIDAY SPECIAL	FLEETWAY	1983	1992	1983	NOW		
EAGLE PICTURE LIBRARY	IPC		1	14	1985	1985	
EAGLE SPECIAL	ODHAMS	1962	1966	1962	1966		
EAGLE WEEKLY	HULTON PRESS LTD.	1	1	52	1950	1951	
EAGLE WEEKLY	HULTON PRESS LTD.	2	1	52	1951	1952	
EAGLE WEEKLY	HULTON PRESS LTD.	3	1	52	1952	1953	
EAGLE WEEKLY	HULTON PRESS LTD.	4	1	38	1953	1954	
EAGLE WEEKLY	HULTON PRESS LTD.	5	1	53	1954	1955	
EAGLE WEEKLY	HULTON PRESS LTD.	6	1	52	1955	1956	
EAGLE WEEKLY	HULTON PRESS LTD.	7	1	52	1956	1957	
EAGLE WEEKLY	HULTON PRESS LTD.	8	1	52	1957	1958	
EAGLE WEEKLY	HULTON PRESS LTD.	9	1	52	1958	1959	
EAGLE WEEKLY	HULTON PRESS LTD.	10	1	45	1959	1960	
EAGLE WEEKLY	HULTON PRESS LTD.	11	1	53	1960	1961	
EAGLE WEEKLY	LONGACRE	12	1	52	1961	1962	
EAGLE WEEKLY	LONGACRE	13	1	52	1962	1963	
EAGLE WEEKLY	LONGACRE	14	1	52	1963	1964	
EAGLE WEEKLY	ODHAMS	15	1	52	1964	1965	
EAGLE WEEKLY	ODHAMS	16	1	52	1965	1966	
EAGLE WEEKLY	ODHAMS	17	1	53	1966	1967	
EAGLE WEEKLY	ODHAMS	18	1	52	1967	1968	
EAGLE WEEKLY	ODHAMS	19	1	52	1968	1969	
EAGLE WEEKLY	ODHAMS	20	1	17	1969	1969	
EAGLE, THE	FOX FEATURES SYNDICATE		1	4	1941	1942	
EAGLE, THE BEST OF	MICHAEL JOSEPH		1	1	1977	1977	
EARTH 4	CONTINUITY COMICS	1	1	3	1993	NOW	
EARTH 4	CONTINUITY COMICS	2	1	1	1993	NOW	
EARTH MAN ON VENUS	AVON BOOKS		1	1	1951	1951	
EASTER STORY	MARVEL ENTERTAINMENT GROUP		1	1	1993	1993	
EAT RIGHT TO WORK AND WIN	SWIFT AND CO.		1	1	1942	1942	
EB'NN	NOW	3	10	1986	1987		SERIES FORMERLY PUBLISHED BY CROWQUILL (1 AND 2)
EB'NN THE RAVEN	CROWQUILL		1	2	1985	1985	SERIES CONTINUED BY NOW COMICS FROM ISSUE #3
EC CLASSIC REPRINTS	EAST COAST COMIX CO.		1	12	1973	1976	
EC CLASSICS	RUSS COCHRAN		1	12	1985	1986	
ECHO CHILDREN'S CHRISTMAS SUPPLEMENT	LIVERPOOL ECHO		1	1	1957	1957	
ECHO OF FUTUREPAST	CONTINUITY COMICS		1	9	1984	1986	
ECLIPSE GRAPHIC ALBUM SERIES	ECLIPSE		1	31	1978	NOW	
ECLIPSE MAGAZINE	ECLIPSE		1	20	1981	1983	
ECLIPSE MONTHLY	ECLIPSE		1	10	1983	1984	
ECLIPSO	DC COMICS INC.		1	16	1992	NOW	
ECLIPSO ANNUAL	DC COMICS INC.		1	1	1993	1993	
ECLIPSO: THE DARKNESS WITHIN	DC COMICS INC.		1	2	1992	1992	
ECTOKID	MARVEL ENTERTAINMENT GROUP		1	6	1993	NOW	
EDDIE STANKY	FAWCETT PUBLICATIONS		1	1	1951	1951	
EDDY CURRENT	MAD DOG		1	12	1987	1988	

COMIC TITLE	PUBLISHER	Vol No.	Srt No.	End No.	Str. Year	End Year	COMMENTS
EDGAR ALLAN POE	CATALAN COMMUNCATIONS				1985	1985	
EDGE	GREATER MERCURY COMICS		1	2	1989	1989	
EDGE OF BRITISH HORROR, THE	MILLENIUM		1	1	1994	1994	
EDGE OF CHAOS	PACIFIC COMICS		1	3	1983	1983	
EDWARD'S HEAVE COMICS	H. BUNCH ASSOCIATES		1	1	1973	1973	
EDWARD'S SHOES GIVEAWAY	EDWARD'S SHOE STORE		1	1	1954	1954	
EERIE	AVON BOOKS		1	17	1947	1954	
EERIE	GOLD STAR PUBLICATIONS LTD		1	4	1972	1972	
EERIE	I.W. ENTERPRISES		1	9	1964	1964	
EERIE	WARREN PUBLISHING CO		1	139	1965	1983	
EERIE ADVENTURES	ZIFF-DAVIS PUBLISHING COMPANY		1	1	1951	1951	
EERIE COMICS	THORPE & PORTER		1	2	1951	1952	
EERIE TALES	ALAN CLASS AND CO LTD		1	2	1962	???	
EERIE TALES	HASTINGS ASSOCIATES		1	1	1959	1959	
EERIE TALES	I.W. SUPER	10		10	1964	1964	
EERIE TALES	SUPER COMICS	10		18	1963	1964	
EERIE YEARBOOK	WARREN PUBLISHING CO		1	3	1970	1972	
EGBERT	QUALITY (FLEETWAY)		1	20	1946	1950	
EH!	CHARLTON COMICS		1	7	1953	1954	
EHLISSA	HIGH LAND GRAPHICS		1	7	1992	NOW	
EIGHTBALL	FANTAGRAPHICS		1	10	1990	NOW	
EIGHTY PAGE GIANT	DC COMICS INC.		1	15	1964	1971	
EL BOMBO COMICS	STANDARD COMICS		1	1	1946	1946	
EL DIABLO	DC COMICS INC.		1	25	1989	1990	
EL SALVADOR A HOUSE DIVIDED	ECLIPSE		1	1	1989	1989	
ELECTRIC BALLET	CALIBER PRESS		1	3	1992	1993	
ELECTRIC UNDERTOW	MARVEL ENTERTAINMENT GROUP		1	5	1989	1990	
ELECTRIC WARRIOR	DC COMICS INC.		1	18	1986	1987	
ELECTROMAN COMICS	SCION		1	6	1951	1952	
ELECTRONIC GAMING MONTHLY	SENDAI PUBLICATIONS	31		54	1989	NOW	
ELEKTRA LIVES AGAIN	MARVEL ENTERTAINMENT GROUP		1	1	1990	1990	
ELEKTRA SAGA, THE	MARVEL ENTERTAINMENT GROUP		1	4	1984	1984	
ELEKTRA: ASSASSIN	MARVEL ENTERTAINMENT GROUP		1	8	1986	1987	
ELEMENTALS OBLIVION WAR	COMICO		1	2	1992	1992	
ELEMENTALS SEX SPECIAL	COMICO		1	2	1991	NOW	
ELEMENTALS SEXY LINGERIE SPECIAL	COMICO		1	1	1992	1992	
ELEMENTALS SPECIAL	COMICO		1	2	1986	1989	
ELEMENTALS THE NATURAL ORDER	COMICO		1	1	1991	1991	
ELEMENTALS, THE	COMICO	1	1	29	1984	1988	
ELEMENTALS, THE	COMICO	2	1	26	1989	NOW	
ELEMENTALS: SEX, LIES, SANS VIDEOTAPE SPECIAL	COMICO		1	1	1991	1991	
ELEMENTALS: STRIKE FORCE LEGACY	COMICO		1	1	1993	1993	
ELEMENTALS: THE ROAD TO OBLIVION	COMICO		1	1	1993	1993	
ELF-THING	ECLIPSE		1	1	1987	1987	
ELF-WARRIOR	ADVENTURE COMICS		1	4	1987	1988	
ELFHEIM	NIGHT WYND ENTERPRISES	1	1	4	1991	1992	
ELFHEIM	NIGHT WYND ENTERPRISES	2	1	4	1992	1992	
ELFHEIM	NIGHT WYND ENTERPRISES	3	1	4	1992	1992	
ELFHEIM	NIGHT WYND ENTERPRISES	4	1	4	1992	1992	
ELFHEIM: DRAGON'S DREAMS	NIGHT WYND ENTERPRISES		1	4	1993	1993	
ELFHEIM: SHADE WARS	NIGHT WYND ENTERPRISES		1	1	1993	1994	
ELFHEIM: TIME OF THE WOLF	NIGHT WYND ENTERPRISES		1	4	1993	1993	
ELFLORD	AIRCEL	1	1	6	1986	1986	
ELFLORD	AIRCEL	2	1	31	1987	1989	
ELFLORD CHRONICLES	AIRCEL		1	7	1990	1993	
ELFLORD: DRAGON'S EYE	NIGHT WYND ENTERPRISES		1	4	1993	1993	
ELFLORD: SHADOW SPELL	NIGHT WYND ENTERPRISES		1	1	1993	1994	
ELFLORD: SUMMERS MAGIC	NIGHT WYND ENTERPRISES		1	1	1993	1993	
ELFLORD: THE RETURN OF THE KING	NIGHT WYND ENTERPRISES		1	2	1992	1993	
ELFLORE	NIGHT WYND ENTERPRISES	1	1	4	1992	1992	
ELFLORE	NIGHT WYND ENTERPRISES	2	1	4	1992	1992	
ELFLORE	NIGHT WYND ENTERPRISES	3	1	2	1992	1992	
ELFLORE: FIRE MOUNTAIN	NIGHT WYND ENTERPRISES		1	1	1993	1994	
ELFLORE: HIGH SEAS	NIGHT WYND ENTERPRISES		1	4	1993	1993	
ELFLORE: LAND OF DREAMS	NIGHT WYND ENTERPRISES		1	4	1993	1993	
ELFQUEST	MARVEL ENTERTAINMENT GROUP		1	32	1985	1988	
ELFQUEST	WARP GRAPHICS		1	21	1978	1985	
ELFQUEST	WARP GRAPHICS		1	8	1989	1992	
ELFQUEST: BLOOD OF TEN CHIEFS	WARP GRAPHICS		1	3	1993	NOW	
ELFQUEST: KINGS OF THE BROKEN WHEEL	WARP GRAPHICS		1	9	1990	1992	
ELFQUEST: NEW BLOOD	WARP GRAPHICS		1	12	1992	NOW	
ELFQUEST: NEW BLOOD SUMMER SPECIAL	WARP GRAPHICS		1	1	1993	1993	
ELFQUEST: SIEGE AT BLUE MOUNTAIN	APPLE COMICS		1	8	1987	1988	
ELFQUEST: THE HIDDEN YEARS	WARP GRAPHICS		1	10	1992	1993	
ELFQUEST: THE HIDDEN YEARS	WARP GRAPHICS		1	9	1993	1993	
ELFQUEST: WAVEDANCERS	WARP GRAPHICS		1	1	1993	1994	
ELIMINATOR	ETERNITY		1	3	1992	1992	
ELIMINATOR SPECIAL	ETERNITY		1	1	1991	1991	
ELLA CINDERS	L. MILLER PUBLISHING COMPANY (UK)		1	1	1942	1942	REPRINTS US STRIP
ELLA CINDERS	UNITED FEATURES SYNDICATE	2	1	5	1948	1949	
ELLERY QUEEN	SUPERIOR COMICS	1	1	4	1949	1949	
ELLERY QUEEN	ZIFF-DAVIS PUBLISHING COMPANY	2	1	2	1952	1952	
ELMO COMICS	ST JOHN PUBLISHING		1	1	1948	1948	
ELMO THE LION, THE ADVENTURES OF	KINGSBURY		1	1	1942	1942	
ELMO, THE FURTHER ADVENTURES OF	KINGSBURY		1	1	1943	1943	
ELONGATED MAN	DC COMICS INC.		1	4	1992	1992	
ELRIC OF MELNIBONE	PACIFIC COMICS		1	6	1983	1984	
ELRIC: SAILOR ON THE SEAS OF FATE	FIRST		1	7	1985	1986	
ELRIC: THE BANE OF THE BLACK SWORD	FIRST		1	6	1988	1989	
ELRIC: THE VANISHING TOWER	FIRST		1	6	1987	1988	

INDEX OF COMIC TITLES AND THEIR PUBLISHERS

COMIC TITLE	PUBLISHER	Vol No.	Srt No.	End No.	Str. Year	End Year	COMMENTS
ELRIC: WEIRD OF THE WHITE WOLF	FIRST		1	5	1986	1987	
ELSEWHERE PRINCE, THE	MARVEL ENTERTAINMENT GROUP		1	6	1990	1990	
ELSON'S PRESENTS	DC COMICS INC.		1	6	1981	1981	
ELVIRA	ECLIPSE		1	8	1993	NOW	
ELVIRA'S HAUNTED HOLIDAY	DC COMICS INC.		1	1	1986	1986	
ELVIRA'S HOUSE OF MYSTERY	DC COMICS INC.		1	12	1986	1986	
ELVIS MANDIBLE, THE	DC COMICS INC.		1	1	1990	1990	
EMERALDAS	ETERNITY		1	4	1991	1991	
EMERGENCY	CHARLTON COMICS	1	1	4	1976	1977	
EMERGENCY	CHARLTON COMICS	2	1	4	1976	1976	
EMERGENCY DOCTOR	CHARLTON COMICS		1	1	1963	1963	
EMERGENCY WARD 10	C.A. PEARSON		1	21	1958	1960	
EMPIRE	ETERNITY		1	4	1988	1988	
EMPIRE LANES	COMICO	1	1	1	1989	1989	
EMPIRE LANES	COMICO	2	1	1	1990	1990	
ENCHANTER	ECLIPSE	1	1	3	1987	1987	
ENCHANTER	PARODY PRESS	2	1	4	1992	1993	
ENCHANTER: PRELUDE TO APOCALYPSE	EXPRESS PUBLICATIONS	1	1	4	1993	NOW	
ENCHANTING LOVE	KIRBY PUBLISHING COMPANY		1	6	1949	1950	
ENCHANTING VISUALETTES	WORLD DISTRIBUTORS LTD		1	5	1949	1950	
ENEMY ACE SPECIAL	DC COMICS INC.		1	1	1990	1990	
ENEMY ACE: WAR IDYLL	DC COMICS INC.		1	1	1991	1991	
ENIGMA	DC COMICS INC.		1	8	1993	1993	
ENSIGN COMIC	ENSIGN/W. FORSHAW		1	4	1947	1947	
ENSIGN O'TOOLE	DELL PUBLISHING COMPANY		1	2	1963	1964	
EO	REBEL STUDIOS		1	2	1992	NOW	
EPIC	MARVEL ENTERTAINMENT GROUP		1	4	1992	1992	
EPIC ILLUSTRATED	MARVEL ENTERTAINMENT GROUP		1	34	1980	1986	
EPIC LITE	MARVEL ENTERTAINMENT GROUP		1	1	1991	1991	
EPICURUS THE SAGE	DC COMICS INC.		1	2	1991	1991	
EQUINOX CHRONICLES	INNOVATION		1	2	1991	1991	
EQUINOX CHRONICLES: BLIND FAITH	CALIBER PRESS		1	3	1993	1993	
EQUINOX CHRONICLES: SPECIAL EDITION	CALIBER PRESS		1	1	1991	1991	
ERADICATORS, THE	SILVERWOLF		1	8	1986	1987	
ERNIE	KITCHEN SINK		1	1	1992	1992	
ERNIE COMICS	ACE PERIODICALS		22	25	1948	1949	FORMERLY ANDY COMICS
ESCAPE	ESCAPE		1	17	1983	1990	
ESCAPE FROM DEVIL'S ISLAND	AVON BOOKS		1	1	1952	1952	
ESCAPE FROM FEAR	PLANNED PARENTHOOD OF AMERICA		1956	1969	1956	1969	
ESCAPE TO THE STARS	SOLSON		1	7	1987	1988	
ESPERS	ECLIPSE		1	5	1985	1987	
ESPIONAGE	BRUGEDITOR		1	8	1967	1967	
ESPIONAGE	DELL PUBLISHING COMPANY		1	2	1964	1964	
ESSENTIAL SHOWCASE	DC COMICS INC.		1	1	1993	NOW	
ETC	DC COMICS INC.		1	5	1989	1990	
ETERNAL BIBLE, THE	AUTHENTIC PUBLICATIONS		1	1	1946	1946	
ETERNAL WARRIOR	VALIANT / VOYAGER COMMUNICATIONS		1	20	1992	NOW	
ETERNAL WARRIOR YEARBOOK	VALIANT / VOYAGER COMMUNICATIONS		1	1	1993	1993	
ETERNALS ANNUAL, THE	MARVEL ENTERTAINMENT GROUP		1	1	1977	1977	
ETERNALS, THE	MARVEL ENTERTAINMENT GROUP		1	12	1985	1986	
ETERNALS, THE	MARVEL ENTERTAINMENT GROUP		1	19	1976	1978	
ETERNALS: THE HEROD FACTOR	MARVEL ENTERTAINMENT GROUP		1	1	1991	1991	
ETERNITY SMITH	HEROIC PUBLISHING		1	10	1987	1988	
ETERNITY SMITH	RENEGADE PRESS		1	5	1986	1987	
ETERNITY TRIPLE ACTION	ETERNITY		1	4	1993	NOW	
ETTA KETT	KING FEATURES		11	14	1948	1949	
EUDAEMON	DARK HORSE COMICS		1	3	1993	NOW	
EUREKA	RON TINER		1	1	1972	1972	
EVA THE IMP	RED TOP/DECKER		1	2	1957	1957	
EVANGELINE	COMICO		1	2	1984	1984	
EVANGELINE	FIRST		1	12	1987	1989	
EVEL KNIEVEL	MARVEL ENTERTAINMENT GROUP		1	1	1974	1974	
EVERYDAY NOVELS AND COMICS	POPULAR FICTION		1	1	1940	1940	
EVERYMAN, THE	MARVEL ENTERTAINMENT GROUP		1	1	1991	1991	
EVERYTHING HAPPENS TO HARVEY	DC COMICS INC.		1	7	1953	1954	
EVERYTHING'S ARCHIE	ARCHIE PUBLICATIONS		1	160	1969	1991	
EVIL ERNIE	ETERNITY		1	5	1991	1992	
EVIL ERNIE: NEW YEAR'S EVIL	CHAOS COMICS		0	0	1993	1993	
EVIL ERNIE: THE RESURRECTION	CHAOS COMICS		1	4	1993	1994	
EVIL ERNIE: YOUTH GONE WILD	CHAOS COMICS		1	1	1993	1993	
EVIL EYE THRILLER, THE	BERNARD KAY/ART PUBLICITY		1	2	1947	1947	
EWOKS	MARVEL ENTERTAINMENT GROUP		1	15	1985	1987	
EX LIBRIS EROTICIS	CHA CHA COMICS				1990	1990	
EX-MUTANTS	ETERNITY		1	15	1988	1991	
EX-MUTANTS	MALIBU COMICS ENTERTAINMENT INC.		1	15	1992	NOW	
EX-MUTANTS ANNUAL	ETERNITY		1	1	1990	1990	
EX-MUTANTS PIN-UP BOOK	ETERNITY		1	1	1988	1988	
EX-MUTANTS SPECIAL EDITION	ETERNITY		1	2	1987	1987	
EX-MUTANTS VIDEO GAME EDITION	MALIBU COMICS ENTERTAINMENT INC.		1	1	1992	1992	
EX-MUTANTS: GOD OR MEN	ETERNITY				1988	1988	
EX-MUTANTS: THE SHATTERED EARTH CHRONICLES	ETERNITY		1	15	1988	1989	
EXCALIBUR	MARVEL ENTERTAINMENT GROUP		1	74	1988	NOW	
EXCALIBUR ANNUAL	MARVEL ENTERTAINMENT GROUP		1	1	1988	1988	
EXCALIBUR SPECIAL	MARVEL ENTERTAINMENT GROUP		1	1	1991	1991	
EXCALIBUR SPECIAL EDITION	MARVEL ENTERTAINMENT GROUP		1	3	1987	1989	
EXCALIBUR: WEIRD WAR III	MARVEL ENTERTAINMENT GROUP		1	1	1990	1990	
EXCALIBUR: XX CROSSING	MARVEL ENTERTAINMENT GROUP		1	1	1992	1992	
EXCITING COMICS	STANDARD COMICS		1	69	1940	1949	
EXCITING ROMANCES	FAWCETT PUBLICATIONS		1	14	1949	1953	

235

COMIC TITLE	PUBLISHER	Vol No.	Srt No.	End No.	Str. Year	End Year	COMMENTS
EXCITING ROMANCES	WORLD DISTRIBUTORS LTD		1	2	1952	1952	
EXCITING WAR	CARTOON ART		1	1	1952	1952	REPRINTS STANDARD MATERIAL
EXCITING WAR	STANDARD COMICS		5	9	1952	1953	
EXILES	MALIBU COMICS ENTERTAINMENT INC.		1	4	1993	NOW	
EXOSQUAD	TOPPS		1	3	1994	1994	
EXOSQUAD	TOPPS		1	3	1994	NOW	
EXOTIC FANTASY	EROS		1	1	1992	1992	
EXOTIC ROMANCES	QUALITY (FLEETWAY)		22	31	1955	1956	FORMERLY TRUE WAR ROMANCES
EXPLOITS OF SPIDER-MAN, THE	MARVEL ENTERTAINMENT GROUP		1	11	1992	NOW	
EXPLORER JOE	ZIFF-DAVIS PUBLISHING COMPANY		1	2	1951	1952	
EXPLORERS OF THE UNKNOWN	ARCHIE PUBLICATIONS		1	6	1990	1991	
EXPOSED (TRUE CRIME CASES)	D.S. PUBLISHING CO.		1	9	1948	1949	
EXPRESS ANNUAL	BEAVERBROOK		1956	1960	1956	1960	
EXPRESS THRILLER COMIC	WILLIAM FOSTER		1	1	1946	1946	
EXPRESS WEEKLY	BEAVERBROOK		39	285	1955	1960	
EXQUISITE CORPSE	DARK HORSE COMICS				1990	1990	
EXTINCT	NEW ENGLAND COMICS		1	2	1992	NOW	
EXTRA COMICS	MAGAZINE ENTERPRISES		1	1	1948	1948	
EXTRA FUN	GERALD SWAN	1	1	4	1940	1940	
EXTRA FUN	GERALD SWAN	2	1	2	1952	1952	
EXTRA!	EC COMICS		1	5	1955	1955	
EXTREME	IMAGE COMICS		1	1	1993	NOW	
EXTREME STUDIOS TOUR '93	IMAGE COMICS		1	1	1993	1993	
EXTREMELY SERIOUS GUIDE TO CLASS, THE	COLUMBUS BOOKS				1988	1988	
EXTREMIST	DC COMICS INC.		1	4	1993	1993	
EYEBALL KID, THE	DARK HORSE COMICS		1	3	1991	1991	

F

COMIC TITLE	PUBLISHER	Vol No.	Srt No.	End No.	Str. Year	End Year	COMMENTS
F-TROOP	DELL PUBLISHING COMPANY		1	7	1966	1967	
F.B.I. COMIC	STREAMLINE		1	2	1951	1951	
F.B.I., THE	DELL PUBLISHING COMPANY		1	1	1965	1965	
FACE, THE	COLUMBIA COMICS GROUP		1	2	1941	1941	
FACULTY FUNNIES	ARCHIE PUBLICATIONS		1	5	1989	1990	
FAFHRD & THE GRAY MOUSER	MARVEL ENTERTAINMENT GROUP		1	4	1990	1991	
FAILED UNIVERSE	BLACKTHORNE		1	1	1986	1986	
FAIRY FUN COMIC	P.M. PRODUCTIONS		1	1	1948	1948	
FAIRY TALE PARADE	DELL PUBLISHING COMPANY		1	9	1942	1946	
FAIRY TALES	ZIFF-DAVIS PUBLISHING COMPANY		10	11	1951	1951	
FAIRY TIME COMIC	DAVID JONES		1	1	1948	1948	
FAITHFUL	MARVEL ENTERTAINMENT GROUP		1	2	1949	1950	
FALCON	MARVEL ENTERTAINMENT GROUP		1	4	1983	1984	
FALL	CALIBER PRESS		1	1	1992	1992	
FALL GUY ANNUAL, THE	GRAND DREAMS		1981	1983	1981	1983	
FALLEN ANGELS	MARVEL ENTERTAINMENT GROUP		1	8	1987	1987	
FALLING IN LOVE	ARLEIGH PUBLICATION CO.		1	143	1955	1973	
FALLING IN LOVE	TRENT		1	8	1955	1955	
FALLS THE GOTHAM RAIN	COMICO		1	1	1991	1991	
FALLS THE GOTHAM RAIN	COMICO		1	2	1992	1992	
FAMILY AFFAIR	GOLD KEY		1	4	1970	1970	
FAMILY FAVOURITES COMIC WEEKLY	L. MILLER PUBLISHING COMPANY (UK)		1	34	1954	1954	
FAMILY FUNNIES	HARVEY PUBLICATIONS		1	8	1950	1951	
FAMILY FUNNIES	PARENTS MAGAZINE INSTITUTE		9	9	1946	1946	
FAMOUS COMICS	UNITED FEATURES SYNDICATE		1	1	30'S	30'S	MID 1930'S, REPRINTS NEWSPAPER STRIPS, 9 VERSIONS
FAMOUS COMICS	WHITMAN		1	3	1934	1934	
FAMOUS COMICS CARTOON BOOKS	WHITMAN		1200	1204	1934	1934	DAILY STRIP REPRINTS
FAMOUS CRIMES	FOX FEATURES SYNDICATE		1	20	1948	1950	
FAMOUS CRIMES	STREAMLINE		1	2	1951	1951	REPRINTS FOX MATERIAL
FAMOUS FAIRY TALES	K.K. PUBLICATIONS		1	2	1943	1944	
FAMOUS FEATURE STORIES	DELL PUBLISHING COMPANY		1	1	1938	1938	
FAMOUS FIRST EDITION	DC COMICS INC.		4	61	1974	1979	
FAMOUS FUNNIES	EASTERN COLOR PRINTING COMPANY		1	218	1933	1955	
FAMOUS FUNNIES	SUPER COMICS		15	18	1964	1964	REPRINTS
FAMOUS GANG BOOK OF COMICS	AVON BOOKS		1	1	1942	1942	
FAMOUS GANGSTERS	AVON BOOKS		1	3	1951	1952	
FAMOUS MONSTERS OF FILMLAND	BROOK STREET COMICS		1	160	1962	1980	
FAMOUS MONSTERS OF FILMLAND	DYNACOM PUBLICATIONS		1	1	1993	NOW	
FAMOUS MONSTERS OF FILMLAND YEARBOOK	WARREN PUBLISHING CO		1963	1971	1963	1971	
FAMOUS ROMANCE LIBRARY	AMALGAMATED PRESS		1	2	1958	???	
FAMOUS STARS	ZIFF-DAVIS PUBLISHING COMPANY		1	6	1950	1952	
FAMOUS STORIES	DELL PUBLISHING COMPANY	2	1	2	1942	1942	
FAMOUS STORIES IN PICTURES	BAIRNS BOOKS		1	12	1955	1955	
FAMOUS TV FUNDAY FUNNIES	HARVEY PUBLICATIONS		1	1	1961	1961	
FAMOUS WESTERN BADMEN	YOUTHFUL MAGAZINES		13	15	1952	1953	FORMERLY REDSKIN
FANCY FREE	SCION		1	1	1951	1951	
FANG	TANGRAM PUBLISHING		1	1	1992	NOW	
FANGORIA	STARLOG		1	130	1981	NOW	
FANGORIA HORROR SPECTACULAR ANNUAL	STARLOG		1	9	1984	NOW	
FANGORIA'S BEST HORROR FILMS	RANDOM HOUSE PRESS		1	1	1994	1994	
FANTACO CHRONICLES SERIES ANNUAL	FANTACO		1	1	1982	1982	
FANTASCI	APPLE COMICS		1	9	1986	1988	
FANTASTIC	ODHAMS		1	89	1967	1968	REPRINTS MARVEL MATERIAL
FANTASTIC	YOUTHFUL MAGAZINES		8	9	1952	1952	FORMERLY CAPTAIN SCIENCE
FANTASTIC ADVENTURES	ACE COMICS		1	1	1987	1987	
FANTASTIC ADVENTURES	SUPER COMICS		9	18	1963	1964	
FANTASTIC ANNUAL	ODHAMS		1968	1970	1968	1970	
FANTASTIC COMICS	AJAX		10	11	1954	1955	FORMERLY FANTASTIC FEARS

COMIC TITLE	PUBLISHER	Vol No.	Srt No.	End No.	Str Year	End Year	COMMENTS
FANTASTIC COMICS	FOX FEATURES SYNDICATE		1	23	1939	1941	
FANTASTIC FABLES	SILVERWOLF		1	1	1987	1987	
FANTASTIC FEARS	AJAX		1	8	1953	1954	FORMERLY CAPTAIN JET
FANTASTIC FOUR	MARVEL ENTERTAINMENT GROUP		1	385	1961	NOW	
FANTASTIC FOUR (U.K.)	MARVEL ENTERTAINMENT GROUP		1	29	1982	1983	
FANTASTIC FOUR ANNUAL	GRAND DREAMS		1	1	1980	1980	
FANTASTIC FOUR ANNUAL	MARVEL ENTERTAINMENT GROUP		1	26	1963	NOW	
FANTASTIC FOUR BOOK AND RECORD	MARVEL ENTERTAINMENT GROUP		1	1	1974	1974	
FANTASTIC FOUR CHRONICLES	FANTACO		1	1	1982	1982	
FANTASTIC FOUR GIANT SIZE	MARVEL ENTERTAINMENT GROUP		2	6	1974	1975	
FANTASTIC FOUR POCKET BOOK	MARVEL ENTERTAINMENT GROUP		1	28	1980	1982	
FANTASTIC FOUR ROAST	MARVEL ENTERTAINMENT GROUP		1	1	1982	1982	
FANTASTIC FOUR SPECIAL	MARVEL ENTERTAINMENT GROUP		1	1	1984	1984	
FANTASTIC FOUR SPECIALS	MARVEL ENTERTAINMENT GROUP		1981	1983	1981	1983	
FANTASTIC FOUR UNLIMITED	MARVEL ENTERTAINMENT GROUP		1	4	1993	NOW	
FANTASTIC FOUR VERSUS THE X-MEN	MARVEL ENTERTAINMENT GROUP		1	4	1987	1987	
FANTASTIC FOUR, THE OFFICIAL MARVEL INDEX TO	MARVEL ENTERTAINMENT GROUP		1	12	1985	1987	
FANTASTIC FOUR: MONSTERS UNLEASHED	MARVEL ENTERTAINMENT GROUP		1	1	1992	1992	
FANTASTIC FOUR: THE TRIAL OF GALACTUS	MARVEL ENTERTAINMENT GROUP		1	1	1989	1989	
FANTASTIC GIANTS	CHARLTON COMICS		24	24	1966	1966	
FANTASTIC SERIES/STUPENDOUS STORIES	FLEETWAY		1	26	1967	1968	
FANTASTIC SUMMER SPECIAL	ODHAMS		1	1	1968	1968	
FANTASTIC TALES	TOP SELLERS		1	20	1963	1963	
FANTASTIC VOYAGE	GOLD KEY		1	2	1969	1969	
FANTASTIC VOYAGES OF SINBAD, THE	GOLD KEY		1	2	1969	1969	
FANTASTIC WORLDS	CARTOON ART		1	1	1952	1952	REPRINTS STANDARD MATERIAL
FANTASTIC WORLDS	STANDARD COMICS		5	7	1952	1953	
FANTASY MASTERPIECES	MARVEL ENTERTAINMENT GROUP	1	1	11	1966	1967	
FANTASY MASTERPIECES	MARVEL ENTERTAINMENT GROUP	2	1	14	1979	1981	
FANTASY QUARTERLY	IPC		1	1	1978	1978	
FANTASY STORIES	JOHN SPENCER		1	6	1967	1967	
FANTOMAN	CENTAUR PUBLICATIONS		2	4	1940	1940	FORMERLY AMAZING ADVENTURE FUNNIES
FAR SIDE GALLERY	ANDREWS AND MCMEEL		1	4	1989	NOW	
FAREWELL TO WEAPONS	MARVEL ENTERTAINMENT GROUP		1	1	1992	1992	
FARGO KID	PRIZE PUBLICATIONS		1	5	1958	1958	FORMERLY JUSTICE TRAPS THE GUILTY
FARGO KID	STRATO		1	1	1959	1959	REPRINTS PRIZE PUBLICATIONS MATERIAL
FARMER'S DAUGHTER, THE	STANHALL		1	4	1954	1954	
FASHION IN ACTION SUMMER SPECIAL	ECLIPSE		1	1	1986	1986	
FASHION IN ACTION WINTER SPECIAL	ECLIPSE		1	1	1987	1987	
FAST FICTION	SEABOARD PUBLISHING/FAMOUS AUTHORS		1	5	1949	1950	
FAST FORWARD: PHOBIAS	DC COMICS INC.		1	3	1992	1992	
FAST ONE	NO EXIT PRESS				1991	1991	
FAST WILLIE JACKSON	FITZGERALD PUBLICATIONS		1	7	1976	1977	
FAT ALBERT & THE COSBY KIDS	GOLD KEY		1	29	1974	1979	
FAT AND SLAT	EC COMICS		1	4	1947	1948	
FAT AND SLAT JOKEBOOK	ALL AMERICAN		1	1	1944	1944	
FAT CAT	EXPRESS PUBLICATIONS		1	1	1979	1979	
FAT FREDDY'S CAT	KNOCKABOUT		1	1	1984	1984	
FAT FREDDY'S CAT, THE ADVENTURES OF	HASSLE FREE PRESS		1	5	1978	1979	REPRINTS
FAT FREDDY'S CAT, THE COLLECTED ADVENTURES OF	KNOCKABOUT		1	1	1975	1975	
FAT NINJA	SILVERWOLF		1	8	1986	1987	
FATHER OF CHARITY	CAETECHETICAL EDUCATIONAL SOCIETY		1	1	???	???	NO DATE
FATHOM	COMICO	1	1	3	1987	1987	
FATHOM	COMICO	2	1	3	1993	1993	
FATIMA...CHALLENGE TO THE WORLD	CAETECHETICAL EDUCATIONAL SOCIETY		1	1	1951	1951	
FATMAN THE HUMAN FLYING SAUCER	A PLUS COMICS		1	3	1992	1993	
FATMAN, THE HUMAN FLYING SAUCER	LIGHTNING COMICS		1	3	1967	1967	
FAUNA REBELLION, THE	FANTAGRAPHICS		1	3	1990	1990	
FAUNTLEROY COMICS	ARCHIE PUBLICATIONS		1	3	1950	1952	
FAUST	NORTHSTAR		1	9	1989	NOW	
FAVOURITE COMIC, THE	AMALGAMATED PRESS		1	324	1911	1917	
FAVOURITE COMICS	GROCERY STORE GIVEAWAYS/DIFF. CORP.		1	3	1934	1934	
FAWCETT MINIATURES	FAWCETT PUBLICATIONS		1	4	1946	1946	FOUR VERSIONS
FAWCETT MOVIE COMIC	FAWCETT PUBLICATIONS		1	20	1949	1952	
FAWCETT MOVIE COMIC	L. MILLER PUBLISHING COMPANY (UK)		50	62	1951	1952	
FAWCETT'S FUNNY ANIMALS	FAWCETT PUBLICATIONS		1	91	1942	1956	
FAZE ONE FAZERS	AC COMICS		1	4	1986	1986	
FEAR BOOK	ECLIPSE		1	1	1986	1986	
FEATURE BOOKS	DAVID MCKAY PUBLICATIONS		42	42	1937	1948	TWO VARIATIONS FOR ISSUES #3, #4
FEATURE COMICS	QUALITY (FLEETWAY)		21	144	1939	1950	FORMERLY FEATURE FUNNIES
FEATURE COMICS	T.V. BOARDMAN		29	33	1940	1941	
FEATURE FILMS	DC COMICS INC.		1	4	1950	1950	
FEATURE FUNNIES	HARRY A CHESLER		1	20	1937	1939	
FEATURE PRESENTATION, A	FOX FEATURES SYNDICATE		5	5	1950	1950	FORMERLY WOMEN IN LOVE
FEATURE PRESENTATIONS MAGAZINE	FOX FEATURES SYNDICATE		6	6	1950	1950	FORMERLY A FEATURE PRESENTATION
FEATURE STORIES MAGAZINE	STREAMLINE		1	1	1951	1951	
FEDERAL MEN COMICS	DC COMICS INC.		2	2	1945	1945	DC REPRINTS FROM 1930'S
FELIX BIG BOOK	HARVEY PUBLICATIONS		1	1	1992	1992	
FELIX THE CAT	DELL PUBLISHING COMPANY		1	19	1948	1951	
FELIX THE CAT	HARVEY PUBLICATIONS	1	62	118	1955	1961	
FELIX THE CAT	HARVEY PUBLICATIONS	2	1	7	1991	NOW	
FELIX THE CAT	MCLOUGHLIN BROS.		1	1	1931	1931	
FELIX THE CAT	PALADIN		1	9	1953	1953	REPRINTS TOBY PRESS MATERIAL
FELIX THE CAT	S.G. BRUCE		1	5	1949	1949	
FELIX THE CAT	TOBY PRESS PUBLICATIONS		20	61	1952	1955	
FELIX THE CAT & HIS FRIENDS	TOBY PRESS PUBLICATIONS		1	3	1953	1954	

COMIC TITLE	PUBLISHER	Vol No.	Srt No.	End No.	Str. Year	End Year	COMMENTS
FELIX THE CAT 3-D COMIC BOOK	TOBY PRESS PUBLICATIONS		1	1	1953	1953	
FELIX THE CAT AND FRIENDS	FELIX COMICS INC.		1	1	1992	1992	
FELIX THE CAT CHRISTMAS BOOK	S.G. BRUCE		1	1	1949	1949	
FELIX THE CAT DIGEST MAGAZINE	HARVEY PUBLICATIONS		1	1	1992	1992	
FELIX THE CAT LITTLE PICTURE BOOKS	S.G. BRUCE		1	6	1948	1948	
FELIX THE CAT SUMMER ANNUAL	DELL PUBLISHING COMPANY		1	3	1952	1954	
FELIX THE CAT WINTER ANNUAL	DELL PUBLISHING COMPANY		1	1	1954	1954	
FELIX THE CAT, THE NINE LIVES OF	HARVEY PUBLICATIONS		1	3	1991	1992	
FELIX'S NEPHEWS INKY & DINKY	HARVEY PUBLICATIONS		1	7	1957	1958	
FEM FANTASTIQUE	AC COMICS		1	1	1988	1988	
FEMFORCE	AC COMICS		1	67	1985	NOW	
FEMFORCE COLLECTORS BONUS PACK	AC COMICS		1	1	1992	1992	
FEMFORCE FRIGHTBOOK	AC COMICS		1	1	1992	1992	
FEMFORCE IN THE HOUSE OF HORROR	AC COMICS		1	1	1989	1989	
FEMFORCE NIGHT OF THE DEMON	AC COMICS		1	1	1990	1990	
FEMFORCE OUT OF THE ASYLUM	AC COMICS		1	1	1987	1987	
FEMFORCE PIN UP PORTFOLIO	AC COMICS		1	1	1987	1987	
FEMFORCE SPECIAL	AC COMICS		1	1	1984	1984	
FEMFORCE UP CLOSE	AC COMICS		1	7	1992	NOW	
FEMINA	CALIBER PRESS		1	1	1992	1992	
FEMME FATALES	C.F.W.	2	1	1	1993	NOW	
FEMME MACABRE	LONDON NIGHT STUDIO		1	1	1993	NOW	
FERDINAND THE BULL	DELL PUBLISHING COMPANY		1	1	1938	1938	
FERRET	MALIBU COMICS ENTERTAINMENT INC.		1	1	1992	1992	
FERRET	MALIBU COMICS ENTERTAINMENT INC.		1	8	1993	NOW	
FEUD	MARVEL ENTERTAINMENT GROUP		1	4	1993	NOW	
FIDO	HOTSPUR PUBLISHING CO.		1	4	1950	1950	
FIESTA COMIC STRIP	GALAXY PUBLICATIONS		1	3	1989	1991	
FIFTIES TERROR	ETERNITY		1	6	1988	1989	
FIFTY WHO MADE DC GREAT	DC COMICS INC.		1	1	1985	1985	
FIGHT AGAINST CRIME	STORY COMICS		1	21	1951	1954	
FIGHT AGAINST THE GUILTY	STORY COMICS		22	23	1954	1955	FORMERLY FIGHT AGAINST CRIME
FIGHT COMICS	CARTOON ART		1	1	1950	1950	
FIGHT COMICS	FICTION HOUSE		1	86	1940	1954	
FIGHT COMICS	STREAMLINE		1	1	1949	1949	
FIGHT COMICS	TRENT		1	2	1960	1960	
FIGHT COMICS ATTACK	CARTOON ART		1	1	1951	1951	
FIGHT FOR FREEDOM	NATIONAL ASSOCIATION OF MFGRS		1949	1951	1949	1951	
FIGHT FOR LOVE	UNITED FEATURES SYNDICATE		1	1	1952	1952	
FIGHT MAN	MARVEL ENTERTAINMENT GROUP		1	1	1993	1993	
FIGHT THE ENEMY	TOWER COMICS		1	3	1966	1967	
FIGHTIN' 5	CHARLTON COMICS		28	49	1964	1982	
FIGHTIN' AIR FORCE	CHARLTON COMICS	1	3	53	1956	1966	
FIGHTIN' AIR FORCE	L. MILLER PUBLISHING COMPANY (UK)		1	3	1956	1956	REPRINTS CHARLTON MATERIAL
FIGHTIN' ARMY	CHARLTON COMICS		16	172	1956	1984	
FIGHTIN' MARINES	CHARLTON COMICS		1	176	1951	1984	FORMERLY THE TEXAN
FIGHTIN' NAVY	CHARLTON COMICS		74	133	1956	1984	FORMERLY DON WINSLOW
FIGHTIN' NAVY	L. MILLER PUBLISHING COMPANY (UK)		1	3	1956	1956	REPRINTS CHARLTON MATERIAL
FIGHTIN' TEXAN	ST JOHN PUBLISHING		16	17	1952	1952	FORMERLY THE TEXAN
FIGHTING AMERICAN	DC COMICS INC.		1	1	1993	NOW	
FIGHTING AMERICAN	HARVEY PUBLICATIONS		1	1	1966	1966	
FIGHTING AMERICAN	PRIZE/HEADLINE/FEATURE		1	7	1954	1955	
FIGHTING BRIT, THE	CARTOON ART		1	1	1948	1948	
FIGHTING DANIEL BOONE	AVON BOOKS		1	1	1953	1953	
FIGHTING DAVY CROCKETT	AVON BOOKS		9	9	1955	1955	
FIGHTING FRONTS	HARVEY PUBLICATIONS		1	5	1952	1953	
FIGHTING INDIANS OF THE WILD WEST!	AVON BOOKS		1	2	1952	1952	
FIGHTING LEATHERNECKS	TOBY PRESS PUBLICATIONS		1	6	1952	1952	
FIGHTING MAN ANNUAL, THE	AJAX		1	1	1952	1952	
FIGHTING MAN, THE	AJAX		1	8	1952	1953	
FIGHTING OUTLAWS	STREAMLINE		1	10	1950	1950	
FIGHTING UNDERSEA COMMANDOS	AVON BOOKS		1	5	1952	1953	
FIGHTING WAR STORIES	STORY COMICS		1	5	1952	1953	
FIGHTING YANK	STANDARD COMICS		1	29	1942	1949	
FILES MAGAZINE: SPOTLIGHT ON ROBOTECH	PSI FI MOVIE PRESS INC				1986	1986	
FILM FUN	AMALGAMATED PRESS		1	2225	1920	1962	
FILM FUN ANNUAL	AMALGAMATED PRESS		1938	1961	1938	1961	
FILM FUNNIES	MARVEL ENTERTAINMENT GROUP		1	2	1949	1950	
FILM PICTURE LIBRARY	C.A. PEARSON		1	3	1959	1959	
FILM PICTURE STORIES	AMALGAMATED PRESS		1	30	1934	1935	
FILM SHOTS	D. MCKENZIE		1	1	1948	1948	
FILM STARS ROMANCES	STAR PUBLICATIONS		1	3	1950	1950	
FINAL FANTASY	WALT DISNEY		1	2	1992	1992	
FINN	FLEETWAY		1	4	1993	NOW	
FIRE	CALIBER PRESS		1	1	1993	1993	
FIRE AND BLAST	NATIONAL FIRE PROTECTION ASSOCIATION		1	1	1952	1952	
FIRE CHIEF AND THE SAFE OL' FIREFLY, THE	NATIONAL BOARD OF FIRE UNDERWRITERS		1	1	1952	1952	
FIREARM	MALIBU COMICS ENTERTAINMENT INC.		1	3	1993	NOW	
FIREBALL XL5 ANNUAL	CENTURY 21		1963	1966	1963	1966	
FIREBALL XL5: A LITTLE GOLDEN BOOK	GOLDEN PRESS		1	1	1963	1963	
FIREFLY, THE	AMALGAMATED PRESS	1	1	51	1914	1915	
FIREFLY, THE NEW	AMALGAMATED PRESS	2	1	111	1915	1917	
FIREHAIR COMICS	FICTION HOUSE		1	11	1948	1952	
FIREHAIR COMICS	I.W. SUPER		8	8	???	???	
FIREHAIR COMICS	STREAMLINE		1	1	1950	1950	REPRINTS FICTION HOUSE MATERIAL
FIRESTAR	MARVEL ENTERTAINMENT GROUP		1	4	1986	1986	
FIRESTORM	DC COMICS INC.	1	1	5	1978	1978	
FIRESTORM	DC COMICS INC.	2	1	100	1982	1990	

INDEX OF COMIC TITLES AND THEIR PUBLISHERS

COMIC TITLE	PUBLISHER	Vol No.	Srt No.	End No.	Str. Year	End Year	COMMENTS
FIRESTORM ANNUAL	DC COMICS INC.	2	1	5	1982	1987	
FIRETEAM	AIRCEL		1	6	1990	1991	
FIRKIN	KNOCKABOUT		1	6	1989	NOW	
FIRKIN	VIRGIN		1	1	1985	1985	
FIRST	INTERSTELLAR RAT		1	1	1981	1981	
FIRST ADVENTURES	FIRST		1	5	1985	1986	
FIRST CHRISTMAS IN 3-D, THE	FICTION HOUSE		1	1	1953	1953	
FIRST COMICS GRAPHIC NOVEL	FIRST		1	20	1984	1984	
FIRST FOLIO	PACIFIC COMICS		1	1	1984	1984	
FIRST ISSUE SPECIAL	DC COMICS INC.		1	13	1975	1976	
FIRST KINGDOM, THE	COMICS AND COMIX CO		1	24	1974	1977	
FIRST KISS	CHARLTON COMICS		1	40	1957	1965	
FIRST LOVE	STRATO		1	18	1961	???	REPRINTS HARVEY MATERIAL
FIRST LOVE	VIRAGO UPSTARTS		1	1	1988	1988	
FIRST LOVE ILLUSTRATED	HARVEY PUBLICATIONS		1	90	1949	1963	
FIRST ROMANCE MAGAZINE	HARVEY PUBLICATIONS		1	52	1949	1958	
FIRST SIX-PACK	FIRST		1	2	1987	1987	
FISH POLICE	APPLE COMICS		18	26	1989	1990	
FISH POLICE	COMICO	2	5	17	1988	1989	
FISH POLICE	FISHWRAP	1	1	11	1985	1987	
FISH POLICE	MARVEL ENTERTAINMENT GROUP		1	6	1992	1992	
FISH POLICE SPECIAL	COMICO		1	1	1987	1987	
FISH POLICE: INSPECTOR GILL OF THE FISH POLICE	APPLE PRESS		1	1	1991	1991	
FISH SHTICKS	APPLE COMICS		1	5	1991	NOW	
FIST OF GOD	ETERNITY		1	4	1988	1988	
FIST OF THE NORTH STAR, THE	VIZ		1	8	1989	1989	
FITS	C. MORRIS BOOKS		1	1	1946	1946	
FIVE STAR WESTERN	SCION		1	8	1951	1952	
FIZZ	MODERM FICTION		1	1	1949	1949	
FIZZER	CORONA SOFT DRINKS		1	2	1978	1978	
FIZZER CHRISTMAS SPECIAL	CORONA SOFT DRINKS		1	1	1979	1979	
FIZZER HOLIDAY SPECIAL	CORONA SOFT DRINKS		1	1	1979	1979	
FIZZER SPRING SPECIAL	CORONA SOFT DRINKS		1	1	1981	1981	
FLAG COMIC	REYNARD PRESS		1	1	1946	1946	
FLAME, THE	FOX FEATURES SYNDICATE		1	8	1940	1942	
FLAMING CARROT	AARDVARK-VANAHEIM		1	17	1984	1985	
FLAMING CARROT	DARK HORSE COMICS		1	30	1984	NOW	CONTINUES FROM THE AARDVARK-VANAHEIM SERIES
FLAMING CARROT COMICS	KILLIAN BARRACKS		1	1	1981	1981	
FLAMING LOVE	QUALITY (FLEETWAY)		1	6	1949	1950	
FLAMING WESTERN ROMANCES	STAR PUBLICATIONS		3	3	1950	1950	FORMERLY TARGET WESTERN ROMANCES
FLARE	HEROIC PUBLISHING	1	1	4	1985	1986	
FLARE	HEROIC PUBLISHING	2	1	14	1988	NOW	
FLARE ADVENTURES	HEROIC PUBLISHING		1	12	1992	NOW	
FLARE ANNUAL	HEROIC PUBLISHING	2	1	1	1992	1992	
FLARE FIRST EDITION	HEROIC PUBLISHING		1	11	1992	NOW	
FLARE VS THE TIGRESS	HEROIC PUBLISHING		1	2	1992	1992	
FLASH	AMEX		1	11	1948	1949	
FLASH	DC COMICS INC.	1	105	350	1959	1985	FORMERLY FLASH COMICS
FLASH	DC COMICS INC.	2	1	87	1987	NOW	
FLASH ANNUAL	DC COMICS INC.	1	1	1	1963	1963	
FLASH ANNUAL	DC COMICS INC.	2	1	6	1987	NOW	
FLASH COMICS	CAMDEN MAGAZINE		1	16	1940	1941	
FLASH COMICS	DC COMICS INC.		1	104	1940	1949	
FLASH COMICS	FAWCETT PUBLICATIONS		1	1	1940	1940	NOT DISTRIBUTED
FLASH FILSTRUP	ARROW/HUTCHINSON		1	1	1981	1981	
FLASH GORDON	CHARLTON COMICS		12	18	1969	1970	CONTINUES FROM KING FEATURES SERIES
FLASH GORDON	DC COMICS INC.		1	9	1988	1989	
FLASH GORDON	DELL PUBLISHING COMPANY		1	1	1943	1943	
FLASH GORDON	GOLD KEY		1	1	1965	1965	
FLASH GORDON	GOLD KEY		19	27	1978	1980	
FLASH GORDON	HARVEY PUBLICATIONS		1	2	1951	1951	
FLASH GORDON	HARVEY PUBLICATIONS		1	5	1950	1951	
FLASH GORDON	KING FEATURES		1	11	1966	1967	
FLASH GORDON	L. MILLER PUBLISHING COMPANY (UK)		1	5	1962	1962	REPRINTS US NEWSPAPER MATERIAL
FLASH GORDON	WHITMAN		28	37	1980	1982	
FLASH GORDON	WORLD DISTRIBUTORS LTD	1	1	6	1953	1953	US REPRINTS
FLASH GORDON	WORLD DISTRIBUTORS LTD	2	1	3	1959	1959	
FLASH GORDON ANNUAL	WORLD DISTRIBUTORS LTD		1967	1980	1967	1980	
FLASH GORDON THE MOVIE	WESTERN PUBLISHING COMPANY		1	1	1980	1980	2 VERSIONS
FLASH GORDON WORLD ADVENTURE LIBRARY	WORLD DISTRIBUTORS LTD		1	8	1967	1967	
FLASH MULTI-PACK	DC COMICS INC.		1	1	1993	1993	
FLASH SPECIAL	DC COMICS INC.		1	1	1990	1990	
FLASH STREAMLINE COMICS	STREAMLINE		1	1	1951	1951	
FLASH TV SPECIAL	DC COMICS INC.		1	1	1991	1991	
FLASH, THE	TOP SELLERS		1	5	1962	1962	REPRINTS DC MATERIAL
FLASH-BANG COMICS ADVENTURE	CARTOON ART		1	1	1948	1948	
FLASHER GORDON	TABOR PUBLICATIONS		1	1	1974	1974	
FLAT TOP	HARVEY PUBLICATIONS		1	6	1953	1955	
FLAXEN	DARK HORSE COMICS		1	1	1992	1992	
FLESH: THE LEGEND OF SHAMANA	FLEETWAY		1	3	1993	NOW	
FLICKER FUN	PHILMAN		1	1	1948	1948	
FLINT ARMBUSTER	ALCHEMY STUDIOS		1	1	1990	1990	
FLINT ARMBUSTER JR SPECIAL	ALCHEMY STUDIOS		1	1	1990	1990	
FLINTSTONE KIDS, THE	MARVEL ENTERTAINMENT GROUP		1	12	1987	1989	
FLINTSTONES	CHARLTON COMICS		1	50	1970	1977	
FLINTSTONES	GOLD KEY		7	60	1962	1970	
FLINTSTONES	HARVEY PUBLICATIONS		1	11	1992	NOW	
FLINTSTONES AT NEW YORK WORLDS FAIR	GOLD KEY		1	2	1964	1965	

COMIC TITLE	PUBLISHER	Vol No.	Srt No.	End No.	Str. Year	End Year	COMMENTS
FLINTSTONES BIG BOOK	HARVEY PUBLICATIONS			2	1992	NOW	
FLINTSTONES BIGGER AND BOULDER	GOLD KEY		1	2	1962	1966	
FLINTSTONES GIANT SIZE	HARVEY PUBLICATIONS		1	3	1992	NOW	
FLINTSTONES IN 3-D	BLACKTHORNE		1	4	1987	1988	
FLINTSTONES MINI COMIC	CITY		1	1	1965	1965	
FLINTSTONES WITH PEBBLES AND BAMM BAMM	GOLD KEY		1	1	1965	1965	
FLINTSTONES, THE	DELL PUBLISHING COMPANY		2	6	1961	1962	
FLINTSTONES, THE	MARVEL ENTERTAINMENT GROUP		1	9	1977	1979	
FLIP	HARVEY PUBLICATIONS		1	2	1954	1954	
FLIPPER	GOLD KEY		1	3	1966	1967	
FLIPPITY AND FLOP	DC COMICS INC.		1	47	1952	1960	
FLOATERS	DARK HORSE COMICS		1	4	1993	1994	
FLOYD FARLAND, CITIZEN OF THE FUTURE	ECLIPSE		1	1	1987	1987	
FLY ANNUAL, THE	DC COMICS INC.		1	1	1992	1992	
FLY BOY	ZIFF-DAVIS PUBLISHING COMPANY		1	4	1952	1953	
FLY MAN	ARCHIE PUBLICATIONS		32	39	1965	1966	
FLY, THE	DC COMICS INC.		1	17	1991	1992	
FLY, THE	RED CIRCLE		1	9	1983	1984	
FLYING A'S RANGE RIDER	DELL PUBLISHING COMPANY		2	24	1953	1959	
FLYING A'S RANGE RIDER	WORLD DISTRIBUTORS LTD		1	16	1954	1955	REPRINTS DELL MATERIAL
FLYING ACES	KEY PUBLICATIONS		1	5	1955	1956	
FLYING ACES	STREAMLINE		1	2	1956	1956	
FLYING CADET	FLYING CADET PUBLISHING	1	1	9	1943	1944	
FLYING CADET	FLYING CADET PUBLISHING	2	1	8	1946	1947	
FLYING MODELS	HEALTH PUBLICATIONS INSTITUTE	61	3	3	1954	1954	
FLYING NUN	DELL PUBLISHING COMPANY		1	4	1968	1968	
FLYING SAUCERS	AVON BOOKS		1	1	1950	1953	3 EDITIONS
FLYING SAUCERS	DELL PUBLISHING COMPANY		1	5	1967	1969	
FOLLOW THE SUN	DELL PUBLISHING COMPANY		1280207	12280211	1962	1962	
FOLLYFOOT ANNUAL	WORLD DISTRIBUTORS LTD		1	1	1973	1973	
FOOD FOR THOUGHT	FLYING PIG		1	1	1985	1985	
FOODINI	CONTINENTAL PUBLICATIONS		1	5	1950	1950	
FOOEY	SCOFF PUBLICATIONS		1	4	1961	1961	
FOOFUR	MARVEL ENTERTAINMENT GROUP		1	6	1987	1988	
FOOLKILLER	MARVEL ENTERTAINMENT GROUP		1	10	1990	1991	
FOOM	MARVEL ENTERTAINMENT GROUP		1	22	1973	1978	
FOOTBALL COMIC, THE	SPORTS CARTOON		1	11	1953	1953	
FOOTBALL FUN BOOK	D.C. THOMSON		1	1	1934	1934	
FOOTBALL THRILLS	ZIFF-DAVIS PUBLISHING COMPANY		1	2	1951	1952	
FOR A FEW TROUBLES MORE	FLEETWAY		1	1	1990	1990	
FOR A NIGHT OF LOVE	AVON BOOKS		1	1	1951	1951	
FOR GIRLS ONLY	BERNARD BAILEY		1	1	1953	1953	
FOR LOVERS ONLY	CHARLTON COMICS		60	86	1971	1976	FORMERLY HOLLYWOOD ROMANCES
FORBIDDEN KINGDOM	EASTERN COMICS		1	11	1988	1989	
FORBIDDEN LOVE	QUALITY (FLEETWAY)		1	4	1950	1950	
FORBIDDEN PLANET	INNOVATION		1	4	1992	1992	
FORBIDDEN PLANET: SAGA OF THE KRELL	INNOVATION		1	1	1993	1993	
FORBIDDEN TALES OF DARK MANSION	DC COMICS INC.		5	15	1972	1974	FORMERLY DARK MANSION OF FORBIDDEN LOVE
FORBIDDEN WORLDS	A PLUS COMICS		1	1	1991	NOW	
FORBIDDEN WORLDS	AMERICAN COMIC GROUP		1	145	1951	1967	
FORBIDDEN WORLDS	STRATO		1	145	50'S	60'S	
FORCE WORKS	MARVEL ENTERTAINMENT GROUP		1	4	1994	NOW	
FORCES IN COMBAT	MARVEL ENTERTAINMENT GROUP		1	37	1980	1981	
FOREIGN INTRIGUES	CHARLTON COMICS		13	15	1956	1956	FORMERLY JOHNNY DYNAMITE
FOREIGN INTRIGUES	L. MILLER PUBLISHING COMPANY (UK)		1	2	1956	1956	REPRINTS CHARLTON MATERIAL
FOREST FIRE	AMERICAN FORESTRY ASSOCIATION		1	1	1949	1949	
FOREVER PEOPLE	DC COMICS INC.		1	11	1971	1972	
FOREVER PEOPLE	DC COMICS INC.		1	6	1988	1988	
FOREVER WAR, THE	NBM PUBLISHING		1	3	1990	1990	
FORGERS, THE	HOTSPUR PUBLISHING CO.		1	1	1948	1948	
FORGOTTEN REALMS	DC COMICS INC.		1	25	1989	1991	
FORGOTTEN REALMS ANNUAL	DC COMICS INC.		1	1	1991	1991	
FORTY-EIGHT FAMOUS AMERICANS	J.C.PENNEY CO.		1	1	1947	1947	
FOSDYKE SAGA, THE	MIRROR PRESS PUBLICATIONS		1	1	1972	1972	
FOUR ACES	NEWTON/WICKHAM		1	1	1945	1945	
FOUR ACES COMIC	L. MILLER PUBLISHING COMPANY (UK)		1	6	1954	1954	
FOUR COLOUR	DELL PUBLISHING COMPANY	1	1	25	1939	1942	
FOUR COLOUR	DELL PUBLISHING COMPANY	2	1	1354	1942	1962	
FOUR DEUCES COMICS	TRANSATLANTIC		1	1	1947	1947	
FOUR FAVOURITES	ACE MAGAZINES		1	32	1941	1947	
FOUR FEATHER FALLS ANNUAL	COLLINS		1960	1962	1960	1962	
FOUR JOLLY MILLER COMIC STRIPS FOR CHILDREN	L. MILLER PUBLISHING COMPANY (UK)		1	4	1943	1943	
FOUR STAR BATTLE TALES	DC COMICS INC.		1	5	1973	1973	
FOUR STAR SPECTACULAR	DC COMICS INC.		1	6	1976	1977	
FOUR TEENERS	A.A.WYN PUBLICATIONS		34	34	1948	1948	FORMERLY CRIME MUST PAY THE PENALTY
FOURMOST	NOVELTY PUBLICATIONS	1	1	36	1941	1949	
FOURMOST	STAR PUBLICATIONS	2	37	40	1949	1950	
FOX AND CROW	TOP SELLERS		1	?	1970	???	REPRINTS DC MATERIAL
FOX AND THE CROW	DC COMICS INC.		1	108	1951	1968	
FOX AND THE HOUND	WHITMAN		1	3	1981	1981	
FOX GIANTS	FOX FEATURES SYNDICATE				1944	1950	NO ISSUE NUMBERS ON COMICS - LISTED BY TITLE
FOX HOLE	CHARLTON COMICS		5	7	1955	1956	
FOXFIRE	NIGHT WYND ENTERPRISES		1	3	1992	1992	
FOXHOLE	MAINLINE COMICS		1	4	1954	1955	CHARLTON FROM #5
FOXY FAGAN COMICS	DEARFIELD PUBLISHING		1	7	1946	1948	
FOXY GRANDPA	N.Y. HERALD		1901	1916	1901	1916	
FOXY GRANDPA SPARKLETS	M.A. DONAHUE CO.		1	8	1908	1908	

COMIC TITLE	PUBLISHER	Vol No.	Srt No.	End No.	Str. Year	End Year	COMMENTS
FRACTURED FAIRY TALES	GOLD KEY		1	1	1962	1962	
FRAGGLE ROCK	MARVEL ENTERTAINMENT GROUP	1	1	8	1985	1986	
FRAGGLE ROCK	MARVEL ENTERTAINMENT GROUP	2	1	6	1988	1988	
FRANCIS, BROTHER OF THE UNIVERSE	MARVEL ENTERTAINMENT GROUP		1	1	1980	1980	
FRANK	NEMESIS COMICS		1	4	1993	1994	
FRANK BUCK	FOX FEATURES SYNDICATE		70	71	1950	1950	FORMERLY MY TRUE LOVE
FRANK BUCK	STREAMLINE		1	1	1950	1950	
FRANK FAZAKERLY	PRESTON SF GROUP		1	1	1991	1991	
FRANK LUTHER SILLY PILLY COMICS	CHILDRENS COMICS		1	1	1950	1950	
FRANK MERRYWELL AT YALE	CHARLTON COMICS		1	4	1955	1956	
FRANKENSTEIN	DELL PUBLISHING COMPANY	1	12283305		1964	1967	
FRANKENSTEIN	TOP SELLERS		1	1	1963	1963	REPRINTS DELL MATERIAL
FRANKENSTEIN COMICS	PRIZE/HEADLINE/FEATURE		1	33	1945	1954	
FRANKENSTEIN JUNIOR	GOLD KEY		1	1	1967	1967	
FRANKENSTEIN, THE MONSTER OF	ARNOLD BOOK CO.		1	5	1953	1954	
FRANKENSTEIN, THE MONSTER OF	MARVEL ENTERTAINMENT GROUP		1	18	1973	1975	
FRANKIE COMICS	MARVEL ENTERTAINMENT GROUP		4	15	1946	1949	FORMERLY MOVIE TUNES
FRANKIE FUDDLE	MARVEL ENTERTAINMENT GROUP		16	17	1949	1949	FORMERLY FRANKIE AND LANA
FRANKIE STEIN'S MINI-MONSTER COMIC BOOK	IPC		1	4	1974	1974	
FRANTIC	MARVEL ENTERTAINMENT GROUP		1	18	1980	1981	
FRANTIC	PIERCE PUBLISHING CO.	1	1	2	1958	1958	
FRANTIC	PIERCE PUBLISHING CO.	2	1	2	1959	1959	
FRANTIC SUMMER SPECIAL	MARVEL ENTERTAINMENT GROUP		1	1	1979	1979	
FRANTIC WINTER SPECIAL	MARVEL ENTERTAINMENT GROUP		1	1	1979	1979	
FRASER OF AFRICA	HAWK BOOKS		1	1	1990	1990	
FREAK BROTHERS, THE FABULOUS FURRY	KNOCKABOUT	0	12		1976	1992	
FREAK FORCE	IMAGE COMICS		1	1	1993	NOW	
FREAKS	MONSTER COMICS		1	3	1992	1992	
FREAKY FABLES	SPHERE BOOKS		1	1	1979	1979	
FRECKLES AND HIS FRIENDS	STANDARD COMICS	5	12		1947	1955	
FRED BASSETT	ASSOCIATED NEWSPAPERS		1	42	1966	NOW	
FRED HEMBECK DESTROYS MARVEL UNIVERSE	MARVEL ENTERTAINMENT GROUP		1	1	1989	1989	
FRED HEMBECK SELLS MARVEL UNIVERSE	MARVEL ENTERTAINMENT GROUP		1	1	1990	1990	
FRED LESLIE'S JOURNAL COMIC BUDGET	CHARLES STRONG		1	7	1902	1902	
FREDDY	CHARLTON COMICS		12	47	1958	1965	FORMERLY MY LITTLE MARGIES BOYFRIENDS
FREDDY KRUEGER'S NIGHTMARES	TRIDENT		1	2	1992	1992	
FREDDY'S DEAD IN 3-D	INNOVATION		1	1	1992	1992	
FREDDY'S DEAD: THE FINAL NIGHTMARE	INNOVATION		1	1	1992	1992	
FREDDY'S DEAD: THE FINAL NIGHTMARE	INNOVATION		1	3	1992	1992	
FREEDOM AGENT	GOLD KEY		1	1	1963	1963	
FREEDOM FIGHTERS	DC COMICS INC.		1	15	1976	1978	
FREEDOM TRAIN	STREET AND SMITH PUBLICATIONS		1	1	1948	1948	
FREEJACK	NOW		1	3	1992	1992	
FREEX	MALIBU COMICS ENTERTAINMENT INC.		1	6	1993	NOW	
FRENCH ICE	RENEGADE PRESS		1	14	1987	1988	
FRENCH TICKLERS	KITCHEN SINK		1	3	1989	1990	
FRENZY	PICTURE MAGAZINES		1	6	1958	1959	
FRESH FUN	GERALD SWAN		1	32	1940	1951	
FRESH FUN DOUBLE SPECIAL	GERALD SWAN		1	1	1941	1941	
FRESH FUN WINTER SPECIAL	GERALD SWAN		1	1	1942	1942	
FRIDAY FOSTER	DELL PUBLISHING COMPANY		1	1	1972	1972	
FRIENDLY GHOST, CASPER, THE	HARVEY PUBLICATIONS		1	260	1958	1989	
FRIENDS	RENEGADE PRESS		1	3	1987	1987	
FRIGHT	ATLAS		1	1	1975	1975	
FRIGHT	ETERNITY		1	13	1988	NOW	
FRIGHT NIGHT 3-D SPECIAL	NOW		1	1	1992	1992	
FRIGHT NIGHT 3-D SUMMER SPECIAL	NOW		1	1	1993	1993	
FRIGHT NIGHT 3-D WINTER SPECIAL	NOW		1	1	1993	1993	
FRIGHT NIGHT ANNUAL	NOW		1	1	1993	1993	
FRIGHT NIGHT I	NOW		1	22	1988	NOW	
FRIGHT NIGHT II	NOW		1	1	1989	1989	
FRINGE	CALIBER PRESS		1	8	1990	NOW	
FRISKY ANIMALS	STAR PUBLICATIONS		44	55	1951	1953	FORMERLY FRISKY FABLES
FRISKY ANIMALS ON PARADE	AJAX		1	3	1957	1957	FORMERLY PARADE COMICS
FRISKY FABLES	NOVELTY PUBLICATIONS		1	44	1945	1949	
FRISKY FROLICS	RENEGADE PRESS		1	1	1986	1986	
FRITZ THE CAT	HEAVY DUTY COMICS		1	2	1972	1973	
FRITZI RITZ	DELL PUBLISHING COMPANY		56	59	1957	1958	
FRITZY RITZ	ST JOHN PUBLISHING		1	59	1948	1955	
FROGMAN COMICS	HILLMAN PERIODICALS		1	5	1952	1953	
FROGMAN COMICS	THORPE & PORTER		1	4	1949	1949	
FROGMEN, THE	DELL PUBLISHING COMPANY		2	11	1962	1965	
FROLIX	A.J. BARTON		1	46	1928	1930	
FROM BEYOND THE UNKNOWN	DC COMICS INC.		1	25	1969	1973	
FROM HELL	TUNDRA		1	3	1991	NOW	
FROM HERE TO INSANITY	CHARLTON COMICS	2	8	12	1955	1956	
FROM HERE TO INSANITY	CHARLTON COMICS	3	1	1	1956	1956	
FROM THE DARKNESS	ADVENTURE COMICS		1	4	1991	1991	
FROM THE DARKNESS BOOK II: BLOOD VOWS	ADVENTURE COMICS		1	2	1992	NOW	
FROM THE VOID	GRAPHIC STORY SOCIETY		1	1	1982	1982	
FRONT LINE	FLEETWAY		1	26	1967	1968	
FRONT LINE COMBAT	L. MILLER PUBLISHING COMPANY (UK)		1	4	1959	1959	
FRONT PAGE COMICS BOOK	HARVEY PUBLICATIONS		1	1	1945	1945	
FRONTEERS	ARCOMICS		1	1	1993	NOW	
FRONTIER CIRCUS	PURNELL		1	1	1962	1962	
FRONTIER DAYS	ROBIN HOOD SHOE STORE		1	1	1956	1956	
FRONTIER FIGHTERS	DC COMICS INC.		1	8	1955	1956	
FRONTIER ROMANCES	AVON BOOKS		1	2	1949	1949	
FRONTIER ROMANCES	I.W. SUPER		1	9	60'S	60'S	

INDEX OF COMIC TITLES AND THEIR PUBLISHERS

COMIC TITLE	PUBLISHER	Vol No.	Srt No.	End No.	Str. Year	End Year	COMMENTS
FRONTIER SCOUT DANIEL BOONE	CHARLTON COMICS	I	10	13	1956	1956	
FRONTIER SCOUT DANIEL BOONE	CHARLTON COMICS	2	14	14	1965	1965	
FRONTIER TRAIL	AJAX		6	6	1958	1958	
FRONTIER TRAIL	L. MILLER PUBLISHING COMPANY (UK)		50	51	1958	???	
FRONTIER WESTERN	ATLAS		I	10	1956	1957	
FRONTIER WESTERN	L. MILLER PUBLISHING COMPANY (UK)		I	13	1956	1957	REPRINTS ATLAS MATERIAL
FRONTLINE COMBAT	EC COMICS		I	5	1951	1954	
FROST	CALIBER PRESS		I	I	1990	1990	
FROST, THE DYING BREED	CALIBER PRESS		I	4	1991	1992	
FRUITMAN SPECIAL	HARVEY PUBLICATIONS		I	I	1969	1969	
FUDGE COMIC, THE	FUDGE		I	I	1947	1947	
FUGITIVES FROM JUSTICE	ST JOHN PUBLISHING		I	5	1952	1952	
FUGITOID	MIRAGE STUDIOS		I	I	1985	1985	
FULL COLOUR COMICS	FOX FEATURES SYNDICATE		I	I	1946	1946	
FULL O'FUN	PHILIMAR		I	3	1949	1949	
FULL OF FUN	I.W. ENTERPRISES		I	8	1957	1964	
FUN AND FROLIC	INTERNATIONAL		I	I	1945	1945	
FUN AND GAMES MAGAZINE	MARVEL ENTERTAINMENT GROUP		I	8	1978	1980	
FUN COMICS	SPIDER	9	12	1953	1953		
FUN FAIR COMIC	PHILIMAR		I	I	1948	1948	
FUN FARE	MARTIN & REID		I	I	1946	1946	
FUN FOR THE FAMILY	ASSOCIATED SCOTTISH NEWSPAPERS		I	38	1940	1941	
FUN PARADE	HOTSPUR PUBLISHING CO.		I	I	1949	1949	
FUN TIME	ACE PERIODICALS		I	4	1953	1953	
FUN TIME	WILLIAMS PUBLISHING		I	13	1972	1973	
FUN WITH REID FLEMING	ECLIPSE				1991	1991	
FUN'S FUNNY SCRAPBOOK	FUN OFFICE		I	2	1892	1892	
FUN-IN	GOLD KEY		I	15	1970	1974	
FUN-IN	WILLIAMS PUBLISHING		I	26	1973	1974	
FUNBEAM	P.M. PRODUCTIONS		I	I	1949	1949	
FUNFAIR	MCKENZIE/VINCENT		I	I	1948	1948	
FUNFAIR COMIC	PHILLIP MARX		I	I	1946	1946	
FUNFAIR COMIC, THE	MARTIN & REID		I	I	1949	1949	
FUNKY PHANTOM, THE	GOLD KEY		I	13	1972	1975	
FUNLAND	ZIFF-DAVIS PUBLISHING COMPANY		I	I	???	???	NO DATE
FUNLAND COMICS	CROYDON PUBLISHERS		I	I	1945	1945	
FUNNIES ANNUAL, THE	AVON BOOKS		I	I	1959	1959	
FUNNIES BUDGET	GERALD SWAN		I	I	1950	1950	
FUNNIES ON PARADE	EASTERN COLOR PRINTING COMPANY		I	I	1933	1933	
FUNNIES, THE	DELL PUBLISHING COMPANY		I	23	1929	1930	
FUNNIES, THE	DELL PUBLISHING COMPANY		I	64	1936	1942	
FUNNY 3-D	HARVEY PUBLICATIONS		I	I	1953	1953	
FUNNY 3-D	UNITED-ANGLO PRODUCTIONS		I	I	1954	1954	
FUNNY ANIMALS	CHARLTON COMICS		I	2	1984	1984	
FUNNY ANIMALS	L. MILLER PUBLISHING COMPANY (UK)		nn	56	1945	1952	REPRINTS FAWCETT MATERIAL
FUNNY BOOK	PARENTS MAGAZINE INSTITUTE		I	9	1942	1946	
FUNNY COMIC	P.M. PRODUCTIONS		I	2	1948	1949	
FUNNY COMICS	A. HALLE		I	I	1948	1948	
FUNNY COMICS	MODERN STORE PUBLISHING		I	I	1955	1955	
FUNNY CUTS	PAGET		I	2	1948	1948	
FUNNY CUTS	TRAPP HOLMES		I	958	1890	1908	
FUNNY CUTS AND BOYS COMPANION	TRAPP HOLMES		I	608	1908	1920	
FUNNY FABLES	AMERICAN COMIC GROUP	I	I	I	1957	1957	
FUNNY FABLES	AMERICAN COMIC GROUP	2	I	2	1957	1957	
FUNNY FEATURES	MARTIN & REID		I	I	1944	1944	
FUNNY FILMS	AMERICAN COMIC GROUP		I	29	1949	1954	
FUNNY FOLK	HAMILTON COMICS		I	I	1947	1947	
FUNNY FOLKS	DC COMICS INC.		I	26	1946	1950	
FUNNY FROLICS	TIMELY COMICS		I	5	1945	1946	
FUNNY FUNNIES	NEDOR (BETTER PUBLICATIONS)		I	I	1943	1943	
FUNNY MAN	MAGAZINE ENTERPRISES		I	6	1947	1948	
FUNNY PAGES	CENTAUR PUBLICATIONS		I	42	1936	1940	
FUNNY PICTURE STORIES	CENTAUR PUBLICATIONS	3	I	3	1938	1938	
FUNNY PICTURE STORIES	COMICS MAGAZINE CO.	I	I	9	1936	1937	
FUNNY PICTURE STORIES	COMICS MAGAZINE CO.	2	I	II	1937	1938	
FUNNY PIPS	C.A. PEARSON		I	16	1903	1903	
FUNNY STUFF	ALL AMERICAN		I	6	1944	1945	
FUNNY STUFF	DC COMICS INC.		7	79	1945	1954	
FUNNY STUFF	HOLLAND PRESS		I	I	1947	1947	
FUNNY STUFF STOCKING STUFFER	DC COMICS INC.		I	I	1985	1985	
FUNNY TUNES	AVON BOOKS		I	3	1953	1954	
FUNNY TUNES	TIMELY COMICS		16	23	1944	1946	
FUNNY TUPENNY	JOHN MATTHEW		I	4	1947	1947	
FUNNY WONDER, THE	AMALGAMATED PRESS		40	1443	1914	1942	FORMERLY THE HALFPENNY WONDER
FUNNY WONDER, THE	HARMSWORTH	I	I	325	1893	1899	
FUNNY WONDER, THE	HARMSWORTH	2	I	109	1899	1899	
FUNNY WORLD	MARBAK PRESS		I	3	1947	1948	
FUNNYLAND COMICS	MARTIN & REID		I	I	1948	1948	
FUNSTAR COMIC, THE	MARTIN & REID		I	I	1949	1949	
FUNTASTIC WORLD OF HANNA BARBERA, THE	MARVEL ENTERTAINMENT GROUP		I	3	1977	1978	
FUNTOWN	MODERM FICTION		I	I	1948	1948	
FURTHER ADVENTURES OF ROBINSON CRUSOE, THE	GROSVENOR ASSOCIATES		I	I	1971	1971	
FURY	MARVEL ENTERTAINMENT GROUP		I	I	1994	1994	
FURY	MARVEL ENTERTAINMENT GROUP		I	25	1977	1977	REPRINTS MARVEL MATERIAL
FUSION	ECLIPSE		I	17	1987	1989	
FUTURE COMICS	DAVID MCKAY PUBLICATIONS		I	4	1940	1940	
FUTURE TENSE	MARVEL ENTERTAINMENT GROUP		I	41	1980	1982	
FUTURE WORLD COMICS	GEORGE W. DOUGHERTY		I	2	1946	1946	
FUTURE WORLD COMIX	WARREN PUBLISHING CO		I	I	1978	1978	

COMIC TITLE	PUBLISHER	Vol No.	Srt No.	End No.	Str. Year	End Year	COMMENTS

G

COMIC TITLE	PUBLISHER	Vol No.	Srt No.	End No.	Str. Year	End Year	COMMENTS
G-8 AND HIS BATTLE ACES	BLAZING COMICS		1	1	1991	1991	
G-8 AND HIS BATTLE ACES	GOLD KEY	1	1	1	1966	1966	
G-BOY COMICS	FUNNIBOOK CO.		1	1	1947	1947	
G-I IN BATTLE	AJAX		1	9	1952	1953	
G-I IN BATTLE ANNUAL	AJAX		1	6	1957	1958	
G-MEN	CALIBER PRESS		1	1	1991	NOW	
G.I. COMBAT	DC COMICS INC.		44	288	1957	1987	
G.I. COMBAT	QUALITY COMICS		1	43	1952	1956	
G.I. JANE	STANHALL		1	11	1953	1955	
G.I. JOE	CUSTOM PIC		1	1	1967	1967	
G.I. JOE	MARVEL ENTERTAINMENT GROUP		1	145	1982	NOW	
G.I. JOE AND THE TRANSFORMERS	MARVEL ENTERTAINMENT GROUP		1	4	1987	1987	
G.I. JOE AND TRANSFORMERS BOOKSHELF EDITION	MARVEL ENTERTAINMENT GROUP		1	1	1993	1993	
G.I. JOE COMICS MAGAZINE	MARVEL ENTERTAINMENT GROUP		1	13	1986	1988	
G.I. JOE EUROPEAN MISSIONS	MARVEL ENTERTAINMENT GROUP		1	15	1988	1989	
G.I. JOE ORDER OF BATTLE	MARVEL ENTERTAINMENT GROUP		1	4	1986	1987	
G.I. JOE SPECIAL MISSIONS	MARVEL ENTERTAINMENT GROUP		1	28	1986	1989	
G.I. JOE YEAR BOOK	MARVEL ENTERTAINMENT GROUP		1	4	1985	1988	
G.I. RAMBOT	WONDER COLOR COMICS		1	1	1987	1987	
G.I. SWEETHEARTS	QUALITY COMICS		32	45	1953	1955	FORMERLY DIARY LOVES, BECOMES GIRLS IN LOVE #46
G.I. TALES	ATLAS		4	6	1957	1957	FORMERLY SGT. BARNEY BARKER
G.I. WAR BRIDES	SUPERIOR COMICS		1	8	1954	1955	
G.I. WAR TALES	DC COMICS INC.		1	4	1973	1973	
G.R.I.P., THE	ECLIPSE		1	2	1994	NOW	
GABBY	QUALITY (FLEETWAY)		1	9	1953	1954	FORMERLY KEN SHANNON
GABBY HAYES ADVENTURE COMICS	TOBY PRESS PUBLICATIONS		1	1	1953	1953	
GABBY HAYES WESTERN	FAWCETT PUBLICATIONS		1	59	1948	1957	
GABBY HAYES WESTERN	L. MILLER PUBLISHING COMPANY (UK)		50	111	1951	1955	REPRINTS FAWCETT MATERIAL
GAG-MAG, THE	CARTOON ART		1	1	1946	1946	
GAGS	UNITED FEATURES SYNDICATE	1	1	9	1937	1942	
GAGS	UNITED FEATURES SYNDICATE	3	10	10	1944	1944	
GAIJIN	CALIBER PRESS		1	4	1991	1991	
GALACTIC WARS COMIX	WARREN PUBLISHING CO		1	1	1978	1978	
GALAXINOVELS: AGENT THREE ZERO	GALAXINOVELS		1	1	1993	1993	
GALAXINOVELS: BLACKRAY	GALAXINOVELS		1	1	1993	1993	
GALAXINOVELS: THIRD PLANET	GALAXINOVELS		1	1	1993	1993	
GALAXINOVELS: VIRTUAL REALITY ZONE	GALAXINOVELS		1	1	1993	1993	
GALLAGHER, BOY REPORTER	GOLD KEY		1	1	1965	1965	
GALLANT ADVENTURE COMIC	SCION		1	4	1952	1952	
GALLANT DETECTIVE COMIC	SCION		1	2	1952	1952	
GALLANT MEN, THE	GOLD KEY		1	1	1963	1963	
GALLANT SCIENCE COMIC	SCION		1	2	1952	1952	
GALLANT WESTERN COMIC	SCION		1	3	1953	1953	
GAMBIT	MARVEL ENTERTAINMENT GROUP		1	3	1993	1994	
GAMBOLS, THE	DAILY EXPRESS/BEAVERBROOK		1	40	1952	NOW	
GAMEBOY	VALIANT / VOYAGER COMMUNICATIONS		1	6	1990	1991	
GAMMARAUDERS	DC COMICS INC.		1	10	1989	1989	
GANDY GOOSE	ST JOHN PUBLISHING		1	6	1953	1958	
GANG BUSTERS	DC COMICS INC.		1	67	1947	1959	
GANG WORLD	STANDARD COMICS	5	6	1952	1953		
GANGSTERS AND GUN MOLLS	AVON BOOKS		1	4	1951	1952	
GANGSTERS CAN'T WIN	D.S. PUBLISHING CO.		1	9	1948	1949	
GANNETS	FRANCIS BOYLE/SOUTHWARK DEVELOPMENT		1	1	1981	1981	
GARGOYLE	MARVEL ENTERTAINMENT GROUP		1	4	1985	1985	
GARRISON'S GORILLAS	DELL PUBLISHING COMPANY		1	5	1968	1969	
GARTH	JOHN DAKIN		1	8	1979	1981	
GARTH	TITAN BOOKS		1	2	1985	1985	
GARTH/ROMEO BROWN	MIRROR PRESS PUBLICATIONS		1	1	1958	1958	
GARTH: MAN OF MYSTERY	MIRROR PRESS PUBLICATIONS		1	1	1946	1946	
GASCHAMBER, THE	ANUBIS PRESS	1	1	1	1993	1994	
GASOLINE ALLEY	REILLY AND LEE PUBLISHERS		1	1	1929	1929	
GASOLINE ALLEY	STAR PUBLICATIONS		1	2	1950	1950	
GASP!	AMERICAN COMIC GROUP		1	4	1967	1967	
GATE OF IVREL: CLAIMING RITES	STAR BLAZE GRAPHICS				1987	1987	
GATES OF THE NIGHT, THE	JADEMAN COMICS		1	6	1990	1991	
GAY COMIC, THE	P.M. PRODUCTIONS		1	1	1945	1945	
GAY COMICS	MODERN STORE PUBLISHING		1	1	1955	1955	
GAY COMICS	TIMELY COMICS		1	40	1944	1949	
GAY COMIX	KITCHEN SINK		1	1	1980	1980	
GEE-WHIZ COMIC	INTERNATIONAL		1	1	1948	1948	
GEM COMICS	SPOTLIGHT COMICS		1	1	1945	1945	
GEMINI 2000 PICTURE LIBRARY	FAME PRESS		1	2	1966	???	
GEMINI MAN ANNUAL	GRAND DREAMS		1	1	1977	1977	
GEN 13	IMAGE COMICS		1	1	1993	NOW	
GENE AUTREY ADVENTURES	BIRN BROTHERS LTD.		1	1	1958	1958	
GENE AUTREY AND CHAMPION	WORLD DISTRIBUTORS LTD		1	34	1956	1958	
GENE AUTREY ANNUAL	WORLD DISTRIBUTORS LTD		1	1	1958	1958	
GENE AUTREY COMICS	CARTOON ART	1	1	19	1950	1952	REPRINTS DELL MATERIAL
GENE AUTREY COMICS	STRATO	2	1	2	1952	1952	REPRINTS DELL MATERIAL
GENE AUTREY COMICS	THORPE & PORTER	3	1	14	1953	1954	
GENE AUTREY STORIES	ADPRINT		1	4	1954	1957	
GENE AUTRY AND CHAMPION	DELL PUBLISHING COMPANY		102	121	1955	1959	
GENE AUTRY COMICS	DELL PUBLISHING COMPANY	1	11	12	1943	1943	1–10 PUBLISHED BY FAWCETT
GENE AUTRY COMICS	DELL PUBLISHING COMPANY	2	1	101	1946	1955	
GENE AUTRY COMICS	FAWCETT PUBLICATIONS	1	1	10	1941	1943	

INDEX OF COMIC TITLES AND THEIR PUBLISHERS

COMIC TITLE	PUBLISHER	Vol No.	Srt No.	End No.	Str. Year	End Year	COMMENTS
GENE AUTRY TIM	TIM STORES		1	1	1950	1950	FORMERLY TIM
GENE DOGS	MARVEL ENTERTAINMENT GROUP		1	4	1993	1993	
GENERAL DOUGLAS MACARTHUR	FOX FEATURES SYNDICATE		1	1	1951	1951	
GENERATION ZERO	DC COMICS INC.		1	1	1991	1991	
GENERIC COMIC, THE	MARVEL ENTERTAINMENT GROUP		1	1	1984	1984	
GENESIS	MALIBU COMICS ENTERTAINMENT INC.		1	1	1993	1993	
GENETIX	MARVEL ENTERTAINMENT GROUP		1	5	1993	NOW	
GENOCYBER	VIZ		1	5	1993	NOW	
GENTLE BEN	DELL PUBLISHING COMPANY		1	5	1968	1969	ISSUE #5 REPRINTS ISSUE #1
GEORGE OF THE JUNGLE	GOLD KEY		1	2	1969	1969	
GEORGE PAL'S PUPPETOONS	FAWCETT PUBLICATIONS		1	19	1945	1950	
GEORGIE COMICS	TIMELY COMICS		1	39	1945	1952	
GERALD MCBOING-BOING AND THE NEARSIGHTED MR. MAGOO	DELL PUBLISHING COMPANY		1	5	1952	1953	
GERONIMO	AVON BOOKS		1	4	1950	1952	
GERONIMO JONES	CHARLTON COMICS		1	9	1971	1973	
GET LOST	MIKEROSS PUBLICATIONS		1	3	1954	1954	
GET LOST	NEW COMICS GROUP		1	3	1987	1987	
GET SMART	DELL PUBLISHING COMPANY		1	8	1966	1967	
GETALONG GANG, THE	MARVEL ENTERTAINMENT GROUP		1	4	1985	1986	
GHOST	FICTION HOUSE		1	8	1951	1952	
GHOST BREAKERS	STREET AND SMITH PUBLICATIONS		1	2	1948	1948	
GHOST COMICS	FICTION HOUSE		1	11	1951	1954	
GHOST COMICS	FICTION HOUSE		9	11	1953	1954	FORMERLY GHOST
GHOST MANOR	CHARLTON COMICS	1	1	19	1968	1971	
GHOST MANOR	CHARLTON COMICS	2	1	77	1971	1984	
GHOST RIDER	COMPIX		1	3	1952	1952	REPRINTS WESTERN ENTERPRISES MATERIAL
GHOST RIDER	MAGAZINE ENTERPRISES		1	14	1950	1954	
GHOST RIDER	MARVEL ENTERTAINMENT GROUP	1	1	81	1973	1983	
GHOST RIDER	MARVEL ENTERTAINMENT GROUP	2	1	47	1990	NOW	
GHOST RIDER & SPIDER-MAN: SPIRITS OF VENOM	MARVEL ENTERTAINMENT GROUP		1	1	1993	1993	
GHOST RIDER (WESTERN) M.E	MAGAZINE ENTERPRISES		1	14	1991	1991	
GHOST RIDER 2099	MARVEL ENTERTAINMENT GROUP		1	2	1994	NOW	
GHOST RIDER AND CABLE SPECIAL	MARVEL ENTERTAINMENT GROUP		1	1	1992	1992	
GHOST RIDER AND CAPTAIN AMERICA: FEAR	MARVEL ENTERTAINMENT GROUP		1	1	1992	1992	
GHOST RIDER ANNUAL	MARVEL ENTERTAINMENT GROUP	2	1	1	1993	NOW	
GHOST RIDER, THE (WESTERN)	MARVEL ENTERTAINMENT GROUP		1	7	1967	1967	
GHOST RIDER/BLAZE: SPIRITS OF VENGEANCE	MARVEL ENTERTAINMENT GROUP		1	19	1992	NOW	
GHOST RIDER: RESURRECTED	MARVEL ENTERTAINMENT GROUP		1	1	1991	1991	
GHOST RIDER: RISE OF THE MIDNIGHT SONS	MARVEL ENTERTAINMENT GROUP		1	1	1993	1993	
GHOST SQUADRON COMICS	UNITED-ANGLO PRODUCTIONS		1	1	1950	1950	REPRINTS FICTION HOUSE MATERIAL
GHOSTBUSTERS	FIRST		1	6	1986	1987	
GHOSTLY HAUNTS	CHARLTON COMICS		20	58	1971	1978	FORMERLY GHOST MANOR
GHOSTLY TALES	CHARLTON COMICS		55	169	1966	1984	
GHOSTLY WEIRD STORIES	ARNOLD BOOK CO.		1	1	1953	1953	REPRINTS STAR MATERIAL
GHOSTLY WEIRD STORIES	STAR PUBLICATIONS		120	124	1953	1954	FORMERLY BLUE BOLT WEIRD
GHOSTS	DC COMICS INC.		1	112	1971	1982	
GHOSTS OF DRACULA, THE	ETERNITY		1	5	1991	1992	
GHOUL GALLERY	AC COMICS		1	2	1994	1994	
GHOUL TALES	PORTMAN		1	5	1979	1980	REPRINTS STANLEY MATERIAL
GHOUL TALES	STANLEY PUBLICATIONS		1	5	1970	1971	
GHOULS	ETERNITY		1	4	1989	1989	
GIANT BOY BOOK OF COMICS	NEWSBOOK PUBLISHING CORP.		1	1	1945	1945	240-PAGES
GIANT COMIC	WORLD DISTRIBUTORS LTD		1	20	1956	1957	REPRINTS VARIOUS US MATERIAL
GIANT COMIC ALBUM	KING FEATURES		1	1	1972	1972	
GIANT COMIC EDITION	UNITED FEATURES SYNDICATE		1	2	40'S	40'S	1940'S
GIANT COMICS	CHARLTON COMICS		1	3	1957	1957	
GIANT COMICS EDITION	ST JOHN PUBLISHING		1	17	1947	1950	ISSUE #5 HAS TWO VERSIONS
GIANT HOLIDAY ADVENTURE COMIC ALBUM, THE	HAWK BOOKS		1	1	1990	1990	
GIANT HOLIDAY FANTASY COMIC ALBUM, THE	HAWK BOOKS		1	1	1990	1990	
GIANT SIZE MINI COMICS	ECLIPSE		1	4	1986	1987	
GIANT SIZE SUPER-STARS	MARVEL ENTERTAINMENT GROUP		1	1	1974	1974	
GIANT SIZE SUPERHEROES	MARVEL ENTERTAINMENT GROUP		1	1	1974	1974	
GIANT SUPER MAG	YOUNG WORLD		1	4	1964	1964	REPRINTS GOLD KEY MATERIAL
GIANT WAR PICTURE LIBRARY	FLEETWAY		1	76	1964	1965	
GIDEON	HODDER AND STOUGHTON/DARGUAD		1	1	1979	1979	
GIDEON AND HIS FRIENDS	HODDER AND STOUGHTON/DARGUAD		1	1	1979	1979	
GIDEON ON THE RIVER BANK	HODDER AND STOUGHTON/DARGUAD		1	1	1979	1979	
GIDEON'S HOUSE	HODDER AND STOUGHTON/DARGUAD		1	1	1979	1979	
GIDGET	DELL PUBLISHING COMPANY		1	2	1966	1966	
GIFT COMICS	FAWCETT PUBLICATIONS		1	4	1942	1949	
GIFT COMICS	L. MILLER PUBLISHING COMPANY (UK)		1	2	1952	1953	
GIFT, THE	FIRST		1	1	1991	1991	
GIGGLE	FLEETWAY		1	38	1967	1968	
GIGGLE COMICS	AMERICAN COMIC GROUP		64	99	1952	1955	
GIGGLE COMICS	CRESTON		1	63	1943	1951	
GIL THORP	DELL PUBLISHING COMPANY		1	1	1963	1963	
GILES ANNUAL	EXPRESS PUBLICATIONS		1	43	1946	NOW	
GILES NURSE SPECIAL	EXPRESS PUBLICATIONS		1	1	1975	1975	
GILGAMESH II	DC COMICS INC.		1	4	1989	1989	
GIMBLEY, SOME TALES FROM	HARVEY PUBLICATIONS		1	6	1987	1987	
GINGER	ARCHIE PUBLICATIONS		1	10	1951	1954	
GINGER FOX	COMICO		1	4	1988	1988	
GIRL	HULTON PRESS LTD		1	619	1951	1964	
GIRL ANNUAL	HULTON PRESS LTD		1953	1965	1953	1965	
GIRL COMICS	MARVEL ENTERTAINMENT GROUP		1	12	1949	1952	BECOMES GIRL CONFESSIONS FROM #13
GIRL CONFESSIONS	ATLAS		13	35	1952	1954	FORMERLY GIRL COMICS
GIRL FROM U.N.C.L.E., THE	GOLD KEY		1	5	1967	1967	
GIRL FROM UNCLE ANNUAL, THE	WORLD DISTRIBUTORS LTD		1967	1969	1967	1969	

COMIC TITLE	PUBLISHER	Vol No.	Srt No.	End No.	Str. Year	End Year	COMMENTS
GIRL OF THE ISLANDS, THE	D.C. THOMSON		1	1	1958	1958	
GIRL PICTURE LIBRARY	IPC		1	2	1984	???	
GIRLS DUX	CARTOON ART		1	1	1948	1948	
GIRLS FUN AND FASHION MAGAZINE	PARENTS MAGAZINE INSTITUTE	5	44	47	1950	1950	FORMERLY POLLY PIGTAILS
GIRLS IN LOVE	FAWCETT PUBLICATIONS		1	2	1950	1950	
GIRLS IN LOVE	QUALITY COMICS	46	57	1955	1956		FORMERLY G.I. SWEETHEARTS
GIRLS' LIFE	ATLAS		1	6	1954	1954	
GIRLS' ROMANCES	DC COMICS INC.		1	160	1950	1971	
GIRLS' CRYSTAL	AMALGAMATED PRESS		1	523	1953	1963	CONTINUATION OF STORY PAPER WHICH RAN FOR 899 PARTS
GIRLS' DIARY	FAME PRESS		1	22	1964	1965	REPRINTS ITALIAN MATERIAL
GIRLS' LOVE STORIES	ARLEIGH PUBLICATION CO.		83	117	???	???	PART OF THE DC AND SIGNAL SERIES
GIRLS' LOVE STORIES	DC COMICS INC.		1	180	1949	1973	SIGNAL PUBLISHING ISSUES 9-65, ARLEIGH 83-117
GIVE ME LIBERTY	DARK HORSE COMICS		1	1	1991	1991	
GIVE ME LIBERTY	DARK HORSE COMICS		1	4	1990	1990	
GIVE ME LIBERTY	PENGUIN BOOKS		1	1	1991	1991	
GIZMO	CHANCE ENTERTAINMENT		1	1	1985	1985	
GIZMO	MIRAGE STUDIOS		1	6	1986	1987	
GLADSTONE COMIC ALBUM	GLADSTONE		1	28	1987	1990	
GLADSTONE COMIC ALBUM SPECIAL	GLADSTONE		1	7	1989	1990	
GLAMOROUS ROMANCES	ACE MAGAZINES		41	90	1949	1956	FORMERLY DOTTY
GLEAM, THE	FRANK SHAW/BEDFORD PUBLISHING		1	147	1901	1904	
GLEE COMIC, THE	PHILIMAR		1	1	1948	1948	
GLEE CUB COMIC, THE	GLOBE FICTION		1	1	1946	1946	
GLOOPS CHILDREN'S COMIC CHRISTMAS ANNUAL	W.C.LENG/SHEFFIELD TELEGRAPH/STAR		1	1	1933	1933	
GLOOPS CHILDREN'S COMIC BIRTHDAY NUMBER	W.C.LENG/SHEFFIELD TELEGRAPH/STAR		1938	1940	1938	1940	
GLOOPS CHILDREN'S COMIC XMAS ANNUAL	W.C.LENG/SHEFFIELD TELEGRAPH/STAR		1	1	1938	1938	
GLOOPS CHRISTMAS ANNUAL	W.C.LENG/SHEFFIELD TELEGRAPH/STAR		1932	1939	1932	1939	
GLOOPS CHRISTMAS ANNUAL CHILDREN'S COMIC	W.C.LENG/SHEFFIELD TELEGRAPH/STAR		1	1	1940	1940	
GLOOPS CLUB FIRST ANNIVERSARY	W.C.LENG/SHEFFIELD TELEGRAPH/STAR		1	1	1929	1929	
GLOOPS CLUB SECOND ANNIVERSARY	W.C.LENG/SHEFFIELD TELEGRAPH/STAR		1	1	1930	1930	
GLOOPS CLUB THIRD BIRTHDAY NUMBER	W.C.LENG/SHEFFIELD TELEGRAPH/STAR		1	1	1931	1931	
GLOOPS COMIC CAT BIRTHDAY NUMBER	W.C.LENG/SHEFFIELD TELEGRAPH/STAR		1936	1937	1936	1937	
GLOOPS THE COMIC CAT JUBILEE NUMBER	W.C.LENG/SHEFFIELD TELEGRAPH/STAR		1	1	1935	1935	
GLOOPS THE LAUGHTER CAT BIRTHDAY NUMBER	W.C.LENG/SHEFFIELD TELEGRAPH/STAR		1	1	1934	1934	
GLOOPS THE LAUGHTER CAT XMAS ANNUAL	W.C.LENG/SHEFFIELD TELEGRAPH/STAR		1	1	1934	1934	
GLOOPS, FIFTH BIRTHDAY OF GLOOPS	W.C.LENG/SHEFFIELD TELEGRAPH/STAR		1	1	1933	1933	
GLOOPS, FOURTH BIRTHDAY BOOK OF	W.C.LENG/SHEFFIELD TELEGRAPH/STAR		1	1	1932	1932	
GLOOPS, THE BOOK OF	W.C.LENG/SHEFFIELD TELEGRAPH/STAR		1	1	1928	1928	
GLOOPS, THE CHRISTMAS BOOK OF	W.C.LENG/SHEFFIELD TELEGRAPH/STAR		1	1	1930	1930	
GLOOPS: SECOND GLOOPERS ANNUAL	W.C.LENG/SHEFFIELD TELEGRAPH/STAR		1	1	1931	1931	
GNATRAT: THE DARK RAT RETURNS	PRELUDE		1	1	1986	1986	
GO-GO	CHARLTON COMICS		1	9	1966	1967	
GO-MAN	CALIBER PRESS		1	4	1989	1990	
GO-MAN : ALL RISE	CALIBER PRESS		1	1	1990	1990	
GOBBLEDYGOOK	MIRAGE STUDIOS		1	1	1986	1986	
GOBBLEDYGOOK	MIRAGE STUDIOS		1	2	1984	1984	
GOBLIN, THE	WARREN PUBLISHING CO		1	4	1982	1982	
GOBO AND MR FIERCE	SAMPSON LOW MARSTON		1	1	1953	1953	
GOBO IN LAND OF DREAMS	SAMPSON LOW MARSTON		1	1	1955	1955	
GOD'S HEROES IN AMERICA	CAETECHETICAL EDUCATIONAL SOCIETY		1	1	1956	1956	
GODHEAD	ANUBIS PRESS		1	1	1992	NOW	
GODZILLA	DARK HORSE COMICS		1	1	1990	1990	
GODZILLA	DARK HORSE COMICS		1	6	1988	1988	
GODZILLA	MARVEL ENTERTAINMENT GROUP		1	24	1977	1979	
GODZILLA COLOUR SPECIAL	DARK HORSE COMICS		1	1	1992	1992	
GODZILLA, KING OF THE MONSTERS SPECIAL	DARK HORSE COMICS		1	1	1987	1987	
GOING STEADY	HEADLINE PUBLICATIONS INC	4	1	1	1960	1960	
GOING STEADY	PRIZE/HEADLINE/FEATURE	3	3	6	1960	1960	FORMERLY PERSONAL LOVE
GOING STEADY	PRIZE/HEADLINE/FEATURE	4	1	1	1960	1960	
GOING STEADY	ST JOHN PUBLISHING		10	14	1954	1955	
GOING STEADY WITH BETTY	AVON BOOKS		1	1	1949	1949	
GOLD DIGGER	ANTARTIC PRESS		1	1	1993	NOW	
GOLD DIGGER MAGAZINE SPECIAL	ANTARTIC PRESS		1	1	1994	1994	REPRINTS
GOLD KEY CHAMPION	GOLD KEY		1	2	1978	1978	
GOLD KEY SPOTLIGHT	GOLD KEY		1	11	1976	1978	
GOLD MEDAL COMICS	CAMBRIDGE HOUSE		1	1	1945	1945	
GOLDEN	AMALGAMATED PRESS		1	135	1937	1940	
GOLDEN AGE	DC COMICS INC.		1	4	1993	NOW	
GOLDEN ARROW	FAWCETT PUBLICATIONS		1	6	1942	1947	
GOLDEN ARROW WELL KNOWN COMICS	BESTMAID/SAMUEL LOWE PUBLICATIONS		1	1	1944	1944	
GOLDEN ARROW WESTERN	ARNOLD BOOK CO.		10	13	1951	1951	REPRINTS FAWCETT MATERIAL
GOLDEN COMICS DIGEST	GOLD KEY		1	48	1969	1976	
GOLDEN HEART LOVE STORIES	D.C. THOMSON		1	2	1960	???	
GOLDEN LAD	SPARK PUBLICATION		1	5	1945	1946	
GOLDEN LEGACY	FITZGERALD PUBLICATIONS		1	16	1966	1972	
GOLDEN LOVE STORIES	KIRBY PUBLISHING COMPANY	4	4	1950	1950		FORMERLY GOLDEN WEST LOVE
GOLDEN PENNY COMIC	FLEETWAY		1	276	1922	1928	
GOLDEN PICTURE CLASSIC	SWORD AND STONE		408	408	1956	1957	
GOLDEN PICTURE STORY BOOK	RACINE PRESS		1	4	1961	1961	
GOLDEN WEST LOVE	KIRBY PUBLISHING COMPANY		1	3	1949	1950	
GOLDEN WEST RODEO TREASURY	DELL PUBLISHING COMPANY		1	1	1957	1957	
GOLDILOCKS AND THE THREE BEARS	K.K. PUBLICATIONS		1	1	1943	1943	
GOLLIWOG COMIC	PHILIMAR		1	1	1948	1948	
GOMER PYLE	GOLD KEY		1	3	1966	1967	
GOOD DOG CAESAR	BROCKHAMPTON PRESS		1	1	1953	1953	
GOOD GIRL ART QUARTERLY	AC COMICS		1	13	1991	NOW	
GOOD GIRLS	FANTAGRAPHICS		1	10	1987	1988	
GOOD GUYS	DEFIANT		1	2	1993	NOW	

COMIC TITLE	PUBLISHER	Vol No.	Srt No.	End No.	Str. Year	End Year	COMMENTS
GOOFY	IPC		1	29	1973	1974	
GOOFY ADVENTURES	WALT DISNEY		1	17	1990	1991	
GOOFY COMICS	NEDOR (BETTER PUBLICATIONS)		1	14	1943	1944	COMPANION TO HAPPY COMICS
GOOFY COMICS	STANDARD COMICS		15	48	1944	1953	
GOOSE	FAWCETT PUBLICATIONS		1	3	1976	1976	
GORE SHRIEK	FANTACO		1	1	1990	1990	
GORE SHRIEK	FANTACO	1	1	6	1989	1990	
GORE SHRIEK	FANTACO	2	1	6	1990	NOW	
GOREZONE	STARLOG		1	26	1990	1992	
GORGO	CHARLTON COMICS		1	23	1961	1965	
GORGO'S REVENGE	CHARLTON COMICS		1	1	1962	1962	
GOSPORT COURIER	J.B. ALLEN		1	1	1947	1947	
GOTHIC ROMANCES	ATLAS		1	1	1975	1975	
GOVERNOR AND J.J., THE	GOLD KEY		1	3	1970	1970	
GRAFIK MUZIK	CALIBER PRESS		1	6	1990	NOW	
GRAND ADVENTURE COMIC	MARTIN & REID		1	1	1946	1946	
GRAND PRIX	CHARLTON COMICS		16	31	1967	1970	FORMERLY HOT ROD RACERS
GRANDSTAND COMIC, THE	MARTIN & REID		1	1	1949	1949	
GRAPHIC NONSENSE	GRAPHIC NONSENSE		1	2	1989	1989	
GRAPHIC STORY MONTHLY	FANTAGRAPHICS		1	12	1990	NOW	
GRAPHIXUS	GRAPHIC EYE		1	6	1977	1979	TWO VERSIONS OF ISSUE #5
GRATEFUL DEAD COMIX	KITCHEN SINK		1	6	1991	NOW	
GRAVE TALES	HAMILTON COMICS		1	3	1991	1992	
GRAVE TALES IN COLOR	HAMILTON COMICS		1	1	1992	1992	
GRAVESTONE	MALIBU COMICS ENTERTAINMENT INC.		1	6	1993	NOW	
GREAT ACTION COMICS	I.W. ENTERPRISES		1	9	1958	1958	REPRINTS
GREAT AMERICAN COMICS PRESENTS...THE SECRET VOICE	FOUR STAR COMICS CORP/SUPERIOR COMICS LTD		1	1	1945	1945	
GREAT COMICS	BARREL O'FUN		1	1	1945	1945	
GREAT COMICS	GREAT COMICS PUBLICATIONS	1	1	3	1941	1942	
GREAT COMICS	JUBILEE COMICS		1	1	1945	1945	
GREAT COMICS	NOVACK PUBLISHING		1	1	1945	1945	
GREAT EXPLOITS	DECKER PUBLICATIONS		1	1	1957	1957	
GREAT FUN COMIC	PAGET		1	1	1950	1950	
GREAT GAZOO, THE (FLINTSTONES)	CHARLTON COMICS		1	20	1973	1977	
GREAT GRAPE APE, THE	CHARLTON COMICS		1	2	1976	1976	
GREAT LOVER ROMANCES	TOBY PRESS PUBLICATIONS		1	15	1951	1955	
GREAT MOUSE DETECTIVE, THE	WALT DISNEY		1	1	1991	1991	
GREAT PEOPLE OF GENESIS, THE	DAVID C. COOK PUBLISHING CO.		1	1	???	???	NO DATE
GREAT SACRAMENT, THE	CAETECHETICAL EDUCATIONAL SOCIETY		1	1	1953	1953	
GREAT WEST	M.F. ENTERPRISES	1	1	1	1969	1969	
GREAT WESTERN	I.W. ENTERPRISES	9	9	9	1954	1954	REPRINTS
GREAT WESTERN	MAGAZINE ENTERPRISES	8	10	10	1954	1954	
GREATER MERCURY COMICS ACTION	GREATER MERCURY COMICS		1	8	1989	NOW	
GREATEST 1950S STORIES EVER TOLD	DC COMICS INC.		1	1	1990	1990	
GREATEST 1960S STORIES EVER TOLD	DC COMICS INC.		1	1	1992	1992	
GREATEST BATMAN STORIES EVER TOLD	DC COMICS INC.		1	1	1988	1988	
GREATEST BATMAN STORIES EVER TOLD	DC COMICS INC.		1	2	1988	1992	
GREATEST BATTLES OF THE AVENGERS	MARVEL ENTERTAINMENT GROUP		1	1	1993	1993	
GREATEST FLASH STORIES EVER TOLD	DC COMICS INC.		1	1	1991	1991	
GREATEST GOLDEN AGE STORIES EVER TOLD	DC COMICS INC.		1	1	1990	1990	
GREATEST JOKER STORIES EVER TOLD	DC COMICS INC.		1	1	1988	1988	
GREATEST SUPERMAN STORIES EVER TOLD	DC COMICS INC.		1	1	1988	1988	
GREATEST TEAM-UP STORIES EVER TOLD	DC COMICS INC.		1	1	1990	1990	
GREEN ARROW	DC COMICS INC.		1	4	1983	1983	
GREEN ARROW	DC COMICS INC.		1	83	1988	NOW	
GREEN ARROW ANNUAL	DC COMICS INC.		1	6	1988	NOW	
GREEN ARROW: THE LONGBOW HUNTERS	DC COMICS INC.		1	1	1989	1989	
GREEN ARROW: THE LONGBOW HUNTERS	DC COMICS INC.		1	3	1987	1987	
GREEN ARROW: THE WONDER YEAR	DC COMICS INC.		1	4	1993	1993	
GREEN GIANT COMICS	PELICAN PUBL./FUNNIES INC.		1	1	1940	1940	
GREEN HORNET 3-D SPECIAL	NOW		1	1	1993	1993	
GREEN HORNET ANNIVERSARY SPECIAL	NOW		1	1993	1991	NOW	
GREEN HORNET ANNUAL, THE	NOW	2	1	1	1992	1992	
GREEN HORNET ANNUAL, THE	WORLD DISTRIBUTORS LTD		1966	1967	1966	1967	
GREEN HORNET COMICS	HELNIT PUBLISHING COMPANIES		1	30	1940	1949	
GREEN HORNET LEGACY SPECIAL, THE	NOW		1	1	1992	1992	
GREEN HORNET, THE	GOLD KEY		1	3	1967	1967	
GREEN HORNET, THE	NOW	1	1	15	1989	1991	
GREEN HORNET, THE	NOW	2	1	29	1991	NOW	
GREEN HORNET: DARK TOMORROW, THE	NOW		1	3	1993	1993	
GREEN HORNET: SOLITARY SENTINEL	NOW		1	3	1992	1992	
GREEN LAMA	SPARK PUBLICATION		1	8	1944	1946	
GREEN LANTERN	DC COMICS INC.	1	1	200	1960	1986	
GREEN LANTERN	DC COMICS INC.	2	1	48	1990	NOW	
GREEN LANTERN AND GREEN ARROW	DC COMICS INC.		1	7	1983	1984	
GREEN LANTERN AND GREEN ARROW COLLECTION	DC COMICS INC.		1	2	1992	1993	
GREEN LANTERN ANNUAL	DC COMICS INC.	1	1	3	1985	1987	ISSUE 1# TALES OF GL CORPS, 2 & 3 GL CORPS
GREEN LANTERN ANNUAL	DC COMICS INC.	2	1	2	1992	NOW	
GREEN LANTERN ARCHIVES	DC COMICS INC.		1	1	1993	1993	
GREEN LANTERN COMICS	DC COMICS INC.		1	38	1941	1949	
GREEN LANTERN CORPS	DC COMICS INC.		201	224	1986	1988	
GREEN LANTERN CORPS QUARTERLY	DC COMICS INC.		1	7	1992	NOW	
GREEN LANTERN SPECIAL	DC COMICS INC.		1	2	1988	1988	
GREEN LANTERN: EMERALD DAWN	DC COMICS INC.		1	1	1991	1991	
GREEN LANTERN: EMERALD DAWN	DC COMICS INC.	1	1	6	1989	1990	
GREEN LANTERN: EMERALD DAWN	DC COMICS INC.	2	1	6	1991	1991	
GREEN LANTERN: GANTHET'S TALE	DC COMICS INC.		1	1	1992	1992	
GREEN LANTERN: MOSAIC	DC COMICS INC.		1	18	1992	1993	

COMIC TITLE	PUBLISHER	Vol No.	Srt No.	End No.	Str. Year	End Year	COMMENTS
GREEN LANTERN: THE ROAD BACK	DC COMICS INC.		I	I	1992	1992	
GREEN MASK, THE	FOX FEATURES SYNDICATE	I	I	11	1940	1944	
GREEN MASK, THE	FOX FEATURES SYNDICATE	2	I	6	1945	1946	
GREEN PLANET, THE	CHARLTON COMICS		I	I	1962	1962	
GREEN-GREY SPONGE-SUIT SUSHI TURTLES	MIRAGE STUDIOS		I	I	1990	1990	
GREENHOUSE WARRIORS, THE	TUNDRA		I	I	1992	1992	
GREGORY	DC COMICS INC.		I	I	1989	1989	
GREGORY II	DC COMICS INC.		I	I	1992	1992	
GREGORY III	DC COMICS INC.		I	I	1993	1993	
GREGORY IV: FATBOY	DC COMICS INC.		I	I	1993	1993	
GREMLINS	MARVEL ENTERTAINMENT GROUP				1984	1984	
GRENDEL	COMICO		I	3	1983	1984	
GRENDEL	COMICO		I	40	1986	1991	
GRENDEL TALES	DARK HORSE COMICS		I	5	1993	1994	
GRENDEL TALES: THE DEVIL'S HAMMER	DARK HORSE COMICS		I	3	1994	1994	
GRENDEL: DEVIL BY THE DEED	COMICO		I	I	1986	1986	
GRENDEL: DEVIL BY THE DEED	DARK HORSE COMICS		I	I	1993	1993	
GRENDEL: DEVIL'S LEGACY	COMICO		I	I	1988	1988	
GRENDEL: DEVIL'S VAGARY	COMICO		I	I	1987	1987	PART OF COMICO COLLECTION
GRENDEL: WAR CHILD	DARK HORSE COMICS		I	I	1993	1993	
GRENDEL: WAR CHILD	DARK HORSE COMICS		I	10	1992	1993	
GREY	VIZ		I	9	1988	1989	
GREYLORE	SIRIUS COMICS		I	5	1985	1986	
GRID, THE	DARK HORSE COMICS		I	3	1990	NOW	
GRIFFIN	DC COMICS INC.		I	6	1991	1992	
GRIM GHOST, THE	ATLAS		I	3	1975	1975	
GRIMJACK	FIRST		I	81	1984	1991	
GRIMJACK CASEFILES	FIRST		I	6	1990	NOW	
GRIMM'S FAIRY TALES	ECLIPSE		I	I	1992	1992	
GRIMM'S GHOST STORIES	GOLD KEY		I	54	1972	1981	
GRIMM'S GHOST STORIES	WHITMAN		55	60	1982	1982	
GRIMM'S GHOST STORIES MINI COMICS	GOLD KEY		I	I	1976	1976	
GRIN	APAG HOUSE PUBLICATIONS		I	3	1972	1973	
GRIPS	GREATER MERCURY COMICS	2	I	12	1989	NOW	
GRIPS	SILVERWOLF	I	I	12	1986	1986	SERIES CONTINUED BY GREATER MERCURY COMICS FROM 5#
GRIPS ADVENTURES	GREATER MERCURY COMICS		I	10	1989	NOW	
GRIPS SPECIAL	GREATER MERCURY COMICS		I	I	1992	1992	
GROO	PACIFIC COMICS		I	8	1982	1984	
GROO CHRONICLES, THE	MARVEL ENTERTAINMENT GROUP		I	6	1989	1990	
GROO SPECIAL	ECLIPSE		I	I	1984	1984	
GROO THE WANDERER	MARVEL ENTERTAINMENT GROUP	2	I	108	1985	NOW	
GROO THE WANDERER	PACIFIC COMICS	I	I	8	1982	1984	
GROO: CARNIVAL	MARVEL ENTERTAINMENT GROUP		I	I	1991	1991	
GROO: EXPOSE	MARVEL ENTERTAINMENT GROUP		I	I	1993	1993	
GROO: FESTIVAL	MARVEL ENTERTAINMENT GROUP		I	I	1993	1993	
GROO: GROO DYNASTY	MARVEL ENTERTAINMENT GROUP		I	I	1992	1992	
GROO: THE BAZAAR	MARVEL ENTERTAINMENT GROUP		I	I	1993	1993	
GROO: THE DEATH OF GROO	MARVEL ENTERTAINMENT GROUP				1987	1987	
GROOVY	MARVEL ENTERTAINMENT GROUP		I	3	1968	1968	
GROUND ZERO	ETERNITY		I	4	1991	1991	
GROUP LARUE	INNOVATION		I	2	1989	1989	
GRUN	HARRIER		I	4	1987	1987	
GUADALCANAL DIARY	DAVID MCKAY PUBLICATIONS		I	I	1945	1945	
GUARDIANS OF THE GALAXY	MARVEL ENTERTAINMENT GROUP		I	I	1992	1992	
GUARDIANS OF THE GALAXY	MARVEL ENTERTAINMENT GROUP		I	46	1990	NOW	
GUARDIANS OF THE GALAXY ANNUAL	MARVEL ENTERTAINMENT GROUP		I	3	1991	NOW	
GUERRILLA GROUNDHOG	ECLIPSE		I	2	1987	1987	
GUERRILLA WAR	DELL PUBLISHING COMPANY		12	14	1965	1966	
GUIDE TO COMIC BOOK ARTISTS	ATTIC BOOKS		I	I	1993	1993	
GULF FUNNY WEEKLY	GULF OIL COMPANY		I	422	1933	1941	
GULLIVER'S TRAVELS	DELL PUBLISHING COMPANY		I	3	1965	1966	
GUMBY'S SUMMER FUN SPECIAL	COMICO		I	I	1987	1987	
GUMBY'S WINTER FUN SPECIAL	COMICO		I	I	1988	1988	
GUMPS, THE	CUPPLES AND LEON CO.	2	8	1918	1931		
GUMPS, THE	DELL PUBLISHING COMPANY		I	5	1947	1947	
GUN FURY	AIRCEL		I	10	1988	1988	
GUN FURY RETURNS	AIRCEL		I	4	1990	1990	
GUN RUNNER	MARVEL ENTERTAINMENT GROUP		I	5	1993	1993	
GUN THAT WON THE WEST, THE	WINCHESTER WESTERN DIVISION/OLIN MATHIESON		I	I	1956	1956	
GUNFIGHTER	EC COMICS		5	14	1948	1950	FORMERLY FAT AND SLAT
GUNFIGHTERS, THE	CHARLTON COMICS		51	85	1966	1984	
GUNFIGHTERS, THE	SUPER COMICS		10	18	1963	1964	REPRINTS
GUNFIRE	DC COMICS INC.		I	2	1994	NOW	
GUNFLASH WESTERN	SCION		I	2	1951	1951	
GUNHAWK, THE	MARVEL ENTERTAINMENT GROUP		12	18	1950	1951	FORMERLY WHIP WILSON
GUNHAWK, THE	STREAMLINE		I	2	1951	1951	REPRINTS MARVEL MATERIAL
GUNHAWKS	MARVEL ENTERTAINMENT GROUP		I	7	1972	1973	
GUNHAWKS WESTERN	ANGLO		I	10	1960	1961	
GUNHED	VIZ		I	3	1991	1991	
GUNMASTER	CHARLTON COMICS		I	89	1964	1967	FORMERLY SIX GUN HEROES. NO ISSUES 5-83
GUNS AGAINST GANGSTERS	CURTIS PUBLICATIONS	I	I	6	1948	1948	
GUNS AGAINST GANGSTERS	NOVELTY PUBLICATIONS	2	I	6	1949	1949	
GUNS OF FACT AND FICTION	UNITED-ANGLO PRODUCTIONS		I	I	1951	1951	
GUNS OF SHAR-PEI	CALIBER PRESS		I	3	1992	1992	
GUNSLINGER	MARVEL ENTERTAINMENT GROUP		I	3	1973	1973	FORMERLY TEX DAWSON
GUNSMOKE	DELL PUBLISHING COMPANY		6	27	1956	1961	
GUNSMOKE	GOLD KEY		I	6	1961	1970	

COMIC TITLE	PUBLISHER	Vol No.	Srt No.	End No.	Str. Year	End Year	COMMENTS
GUNSMOKE	GOLD KEY	2	I	6	1969	1970	
GUNSMOKE	TOP SELLERS		I	2	1970	1971	REPRINTS DELL MATERIAL
GUNSMOKE	YOUTHFUL MAGAZINES		I	16	1949	1952	
GUNSMOKE PICTURE AND STORY ALBUM	MELLIFONT		I	I	50'S	50'S	
GUNSMOKE TRAIL	AJAX		I	4	1957	1957	
GUNSMOKE TRAIL	L. MILLER PUBLISHING COMPANY (UK)		I	4	1957	1957	REPRINTS AJAX MATERIAL
GUNSMOKE WESTERN	ATLAS	32		77	1955	1963	FORMERLY WESTERN TALES OF THE BLACK RIDER
GUNSMOKE WESTERN	L. MILLER PUBLISHING COMPANY (UK)		I	23	1955	1956	REPRINTS ATLAS/MARVEL MATERIAL
GUTTER RAT	CALIBER PRESS		I	I	1993	NOW	
GUY GARDNER	DC COMICS INC.		I	16	1992	NOW	
GUY GARDNER REBORN	DC COMICS INC.		I	3	1992	1992	
GYRO GEARLOOSE IN COLOUR	GLADSTONE		I	I	1993	NOW	

H

COMIC TITLE	PUBLISHER	Vol No.	Srt No.	End No.	Str. Year	End Year	COMMENTS
H.A.R.D. CORPS, THE	VALIANT / VOYAGER COMMUNICATIONS		I	16	1992	NOW	
H.R. PUFNSTUF	GOLD KEY		I	8	1970	1972	
HA HA COMICS	AMERICAN COMIC GROUP		81	99	1953	1955	
HA HA COMICS	CRESTON		I	80	1943	1953	
HACKER FILES, THE	DC COMICS INC.		I	12	1992	1993	
HAIR BEAR BUNCH, THE	GOLD KEY		I	9	1972	1974	
HAIRY CROWS	CALIBER PRESS		I	I	1991	1991	
HALCON COMICS	A. HALLE		I	I	1948	1948	
HALF ASSED FUNNIES	H. BUNCH ASSOCIATES		I	I	1973	1973	
HALF-HOLIDAY	SLOPERIES, THE	24		47	1923	1923	PREVIOUSLY ALLY SLOPER'S HALF HOLIDAY
HALFPENNY COMIC, THE	TRAPP HOLMES		I	467	1898	1906	
HALFPENNY WONDER, THE	AMALGAMATED PRESS		I	39	1914	1914	PREVIOUSLY THE WONDER
HALL OF FAME FEATURING THE T.H.U.N.D.E.R. AGENTS	ARCHIE PUBLICATIONS		I	3	1983	1983	
HALLOWEEN HORROR	ECLIPSE		I	I	1987	1987	
HALLOWEEN TERROR	ETERNITY		I	I	1990	1990	
HALLS OF HORROR	GENERAL BOOK DISTRIB	21		30	1978	1984	FORMERLY HOUSE OF HAMMER
HALO JONES, THE BALLAD OF	QUALITY (FLEETWAY)		I	12	1987	1988	
HALO JONES, THE BALLAD OF	TITAN BOOKS		I	3	1986	1986	
HALO JONES, THE COMPLETE	TITAN BOOKS		I	I	1992	1992	
HAMMER OF GOD	FIRST		I	4	1989	1990	
HAMMER OF GOD BUTCH	DARK HORSE COMICS		I	3	1994	1994	
HAMMER OF GOD: SWORD OF JUSTICE	FIRST		I	2	1991	1991	
HAMMERLOCKE	DC COMICS INC.		I	8	1992	1993	
HAMSTER VICE	BLACKTHORNE		I	10	1986	1987	
HAND OF FATE	ACE MAGAZINES	8		26	1951	1955	FORMERLY MEN AGAINST CRIME
HAND OF FATE	ECLIPSE		I	3	1988	1988	
HANDS OF THE DRAGON	ATLAS		I	I	1975	1975	
HANGMAN COMICS	M.L.J. MAGAZINES	2		8	1942	1943	
HANK	PENTAGON PUBLISHING CO.		I	I	1946	1946	
HANNA-BARBERA BAND WAGON	GOLD KEY		I	3	1962	1963	
HANNA-BARBERA BIG BOOK	HARVEY PUBLICATIONS		I	I	1992	NOW	
HANNA-BARBERA GIANT SIZE	HARVEY PUBLICATIONS		I	3	1992	NOW	
HANNA-BARBERA PARADE	CHARLTON COMICS		I	10	1971	1972	
HANNA-BARBERA SUPER TV HEROES	GOLD KEY		I	7	1968	1969	
HANS CHRISTIAN ANDERSON	ZIFF-DAVIS PUBLISHING COMPANY		I	I	1953	1953	
HAP HAZARD COMICS	ACE PUBLISHING		I	24	1944	1949	
HAPPIJACK, THE	SCOTTISH BOOK DISTRIBUTORS		I	I	1945	1945	
HAPPINESS AND HEALING FOR YOU	ORAL ROBERTS		I	I	1955	1955	
HAPPY COMIC, THE	C.A. RANSOM		I	28	1928	1929	
HAPPY COMICS	NEDOR (BETTER PUBLICATIONS)		I	40	1943	1950	
HAPPY DAYS	AMALGAMATED PRESS		I	45	1938	1939	
HAPPY DAYS	GOLD KEY		I	6	1979	1980	
HAPPY FAMILIES	ALFRED BIRD		I	4	1938	1939	
HAPPY GANG	CHILDREN'S PRESS		I	I	1947	1947	
HAPPY HOOLIGAN	HEARST'S NEW YORK AMERICAN AND JOURNAL		I	2	1903	1903	2 VERSIONS
HAPPY HOOLIGAN	MCLOUGHLIN BROS.	281		281	1932	1932	
HAPPY HOULIHANS	EC COMICS		I	2	1947	1948	
HAPPY JACK	DECKER PUBLICATIONS	I		2	1957	1957	
HAPPY JACK HOWARD	DECKER PUBLICATIONS		I	I	1957	1957	
HAPPY MOMENTS	JOHN MATTHEW		I	I	1946	1946	
HAPPY RABBIT	STANDARD COMICS	41		48	1951	1952	FORMERLY HAPPY COMICS
HAPPY THE CLOWN	CALIBER PRESS		I	3	1993	1993	
HAPPY TIMES FAMILY COMIC, THE	ALGAR/L. BURN		I	5	1946	1947	
HAPPY TUPPENY	RAYBURN PRODUCTIONS		I	2	1947	1947	
HAPPY WARRIOR, THE	HULTON PRESS LTD		I	I	1958	1958	
HAPPY WORLD	MARTIN & REID		I	I	1949	1949	
HAPPY YANK	RAYBURN PRODUCTIONS		I	4	1948	1949	
HARBINGER	VALIANT / VOYAGER COMMUNICATIONS		I	I	1992	1992	2 PRINTINGS. ISSUE 0 CAME WITH THIS TRADE PAPERBACK.
HARBINGER	VALIANT / VOYAGER COMMUNICATIONS		I	27	1992	NOW	ISSUE 0 CAME WITH THE 1992 TRADE PAPERBACK REPRINTING THE FIRST FEW ISSUES.
HARD BOILED DEFECTIVE STORIES	DARK HORSE COMICS		I	I	1992	1992	
HARD BOILED DEFECTIVE STORIES	PENGUIN BOOKS		I	I	1990	1990	
HARD LOOKS	DARK HORSE COMICS		I	10	1992	NOW	
HARD TO SWALLOW	KNOCKABOUT		I	I	1988	1988	
HARDBOILED	DARK HORSE COMICS		I	I	1993	1993	
HARDBOILED	DARK HORSE COMICS		I	3	1990	1992	
HARDCASE	MALIBU COMICS ENTERTAINMENT INC.		I	6	1993	NOW	

COMIC TITLE	PUBLISHER	Vol No.	Srt No.	End No.	Str. Year	End Year	COMMENTS
HARDCORE	DC COMICS INC.			1	1	1993	1993	
HARDKORR	AIRCEL		1	1	1991	1991	
HARDWARE	DC COMICS INC.		1	13	1993	NOW	
HARDY BOYS, THE	GOLD KEY		1	4	1970	1971	
HARDY BOYS/NANCY DREW MYSTERIES ANNUAL	GRAND DREAMS		1979	1979	1979	1979	
HARLEM GLOBETROTTERS	GOLD KEY		1	12	1972	1975	
HARLEM HEROES	FLEETWAY		1	6	1993	NOW	
HARLEQUIN	CALIBER PRESS		1	1	1993	1993	
HAROLD HARE'S OWN PAPER	FLEETWAY		1	230	1959	1964	
HAROLD TEEN	CUPPLES AND LEON CO.				1929	1931	
HARRIER PREVIEW	HARRIER		1	1	1988	1988	
HARRIS TWEED	HAWK BOOKS		1	1	1990	1990	
HARROWERS	MARVEL ENTERTAINMENT GROUP		1	4	1993	1994	
HARSH REALM	HARRIS COMICS		1	3	1994	1994	
HARTE OF DARKNESS	ETERNITY		1	4	1991	1992	
HARVEY	MARVEL ENTERTAINMENT GROUP		1	6	1970	1972	
HARVEY 3-D HITS FEATURING SAD SACK	HARVEY PUBLICATIONS		1	1	1954	1954	
HARVEY COLLECTORS COMICS	HARVEY PUBLICATIONS		1	16	1975	1979	
HARVEY COMICS HITS	HARVEY PUBLICATIONS		51	62	1951	1953	
HARVEY COMICS LIBRARY	HARVEY PUBLICATIONS		1	2	1952	1952	
HARVEY COMICS SPOTLIGHT	HARVEY PUBLICATIONS		1	4	1987	1988	
HARVEY HITS	HARVEY PUBLICATIONS		1	122	1957	1967	
HARVEY HITS COMICS	HARVEY PUBLICATIONS		1	6	1986	1987	
HARVEY HITS MAGAZINE	HARVEY PUBLICATIONS		1	122	1957	1967	
HARVEY POP COMICS	HARVEY PUBLICATIONS		1	2	1968	1969	
HARVEY SPOTLITE	HARVEY PUBLICATIONS		1	6	1987	1988	
HARVEY WISEGUYS DIGEST	HARVEY PUBLICATIONS		1	4	1987	1989	
HATE	FANTAGRAPHICS		1	14	1982	NOW	
HAUNT OF FEAR	EC COMICS	1	15	28	1950	1954	FORMERLY GUNFIGHTER
HAUNT OF FEAR	RUSS COCHRAN		1	6	1991	NOW	
HAUNT OF FEAR	STRATO		1	1	1952	1952	REPRINTS EC MATERIAL
HAUNT OF FEAR, THE	GLADSTONE		1	5	1991	1991	
HAUNT OF HORROR, THE	MARVEL ENTERTAINMENT GROUP		1	5	1974	1975	
HAUNTED	CHARLTON COMICS		1	75	1971	1984	
HAUNTED LOVE	CHARLTON COMICS		1	11	1973	1975	
HAUNTED LOVE	MODERN COMICS	2	1	1	1978	1978	
HAUNTED THRILLS	AJAX		1	18	1952	1954	
HAVE GUN, WILL TRAVEL	DELL PUBLISHING COMPANY		4	14	1960	1962	
HAVOC	MARVEL ENTERTAINMENT GROUP		1	9	1991	1991	
HAWAIIAN EYE	GOLD KEY		1	1	1963	1963	
HAWAIIAN ILLUSTRATED LEGENDS SERIES	HOGARTH PRESS		1	3	1975	1975	
HAWK AND DOVE	DC COMICS INC.		1	1	1993	1993	
HAWK AND DOVE	DC COMICS INC.		1	5	1988	1989	
HAWK AND DOVE	DC COMICS INC.	2	1	28	1989	1991	
HAWK AND DOVE ANNUAL	DC COMICS INC.	2	1	2	1990	1991	
HAWK AND DOVE, THE	DC COMICS INC.	1	1	6	1968	1969	
HAWK, THE	ST JOHN PUBLISHING		1	1	1953	1953	3-D
HAWK, THE	ST JOHN PUBLISHING	4		12	1953	1955	
HAWK, THE	ZIFF-DAVIS PUBLISHING COMPANY		1	3	1951	1952	
HAWKEYE	MARVEL ENTERTAINMENT GROUP		1	1	1985	1985	
HAWKEYE	MARVEL ENTERTAINMENT GROUP	1	1	4	1983	1983	
HAWKEYE	MARVEL ENTERTAINMENT GROUP	2	1	3	1993	1993	
HAWKEYE AND THE LAST OF THE MOHICANS	PEARSON		1	6	1958	1959	
HAWKEYE AND THE LAST OF THE MOHICANS ANNUAL	ADPRINT		1	2	1958	1959	
HAWKMAN	DC COMICS INC.		1	1	1989	1989	
HAWKMAN	DC COMICS INC.	1	1	27	1964	1968	
HAWKMAN	DC COMICS INC.	2	1	17	1986	1987	
HAWKMAN	DC COMICS INC.	3	1	6	1993	NOW	
HAWKMAN ANNUAL	DC COMICS INC.		1	1	1993	NOW	
HAWKMAN SPECIAL	DC COMICS INC.		1	1	1986	1986	
HAWKMOON: THE JEWEL IN THE SKULL	FIRST		1	4	1986	1986	
HAWKMOON: THE MAD GOD'S AMULET	FIRST		1	4	1987	1987	
HAWKMOON: THE RUNESTAFF	FIRST		1	4	1988	1988	
HAWKMOON: THE SWORD OF THE DAWN	FIRST		1	4	1987	1988	
HAWKWORLD	DC COMICS INC.		1	1	1991	1991	
HAWKWORLD	DC COMICS INC.		1	3	1989	1989	
HAWKWORLD	DC COMICS INC.		1	32	1990	1993	
HAWKWORLD ANNUAL	DC COMICS INC.		1	3	1990	1992	
HAWTHORN-MELODY FARMS DAIRY COMICS	EVERYBODY'S PUBLISHING CO.		1	1	50'S	50'S	NO DATE
HAYSEEDS	MACMILLAN		1	2	1971	1972	
HAYWIRE	DC COMICS INC.		1	13	1988	1989	
HE-MAN	TOBY PRESS PUBLICATIONS		1	2	1954	1954	
HE-MAN	ZIFF-DAVIS PUBLISHING COMPANY		1	1	1952	1952	
HEAD COMIX	SIMON AND SCHUSTER				1988	1988	
HEADBANGER	PARODY PRESS		1	1	1993	1993	
HEADLINE COMICS	PRIZE/HEADLINE/FEATURE		1	77	1943	1956	
HEADMAN	INNOVATION		1	1	1990	1990	
HEAP, THE	SKYWALD PUBLISHING		1	1	1971	1971	
HEART AND SOUL	MIKEROSS PUBLICATIONS		1	2	1954	1954	
HEART THROBS	DC COMICS INC.		47	146	1957	1972	SERIES INCORPORATES ARLEIGH PUBLISHING ISSUES #48-101
HEART THROBS	FLEETWAY		1	1	1991	1991	
HEART THROBS	QUALITY COMICS		1	46	1949	1957	SERIES CONTINUED BY DC, & ARLEIGH
HEARTBREAK HOTEL	WILLYPRODS		1	6	1988	1988	
HEARTS AND MIND: VIETNAM LOVESTORY	MARVEL ENTERTAINMENT GROUP		1	1	1991	1991	
HEARTS OF DARKNESS	MARVEL ENTERTAINMENT GROUP		1	1	1992	1992	
HEATHCLIFF	MARVEL ENTERTAINMENT GROUP		1	56	1985	1991	
HEATHCLIFF'S FUNHOUSE	MARVEL ENTERTAINMENT GROUP		1	10	1987	1988	
HEAVY HITTERS ANNUAL	MARVEL ENTERTAINMENT GROUP		1	1	1993	NOW	

INDEX OF COMIC TITLES AND THEIR PUBLISHERS

COMIC TITLE	PUBLISHER	Vol No.	Srt No.	End No.	Str. Year	End Year	COMMENTS
HEAVY METAL MAGAZINE	HEAVY METAL	1	13	13	1978	1979	
HEAVY METAL MAGAZINE	HEAVY METAL	2	6	12	1978	1979	
HEAVY METAL MAGAZINE	HEAVY METAL	3	1	12	1979	1980	
HEAVY METAL MAGAZINE	HEAVY METAL	4	1	11	1980	1981	
HEAVY METAL MAGAZINE	HEAVY METAL	5	1	12	1981	1982	
HEAVY METAL MAGAZINE	HEAVY METAL	6	5	9	1982	1983	
HEAVY METAL MAGAZINE	HEAVY METAL	7	1	1	1983	1984	
HEAVY METAL MAGAZINE	HEAVY METAL	9	2	2	1985	1986	
HEAVY METAL MAGAZINE	HEAVY METAL	11	2	4	1987	1988	
HEAVY METAL MAGAZINE	HEAVY METAL	12	1	4	1988	1989	
HEAVY METAL MAGAZINE	HEAVY METAL	13	1	6	1989	1990	
HEAVY METAL MAGAZINE	HEAVY METAL	14	1	5	1990	1991	
HEAVY METAL MAGAZINE	HEAVY METAL	15	1	7	1991	1992	
HEAVY METAL MAGAZINE	HEAVY METAL	16	1	1	1992	1993	
HEAVY METAL MAGAZINE (1977)	HEAVY METAL		1	3	1977	1977	
HEAVY METAL MAGAZINE (1986)	HEAVY METAL		1	2	1986	1986	
HEAVY METAL MAGAZINE, BEST OF THE	HEAVY METAL		2	2	1986	1986	
HEAVY METAL WAR MACHINE	HEAVY METAL		1	1	1993	1993	
HEAVY PERIODS	GRASS ROOTS		1	1	1980	1980	
HECKLE AND JECKLE	DELL PUBLISHING COMPANY	2	1	3	1966	1967	
HECKLE AND JECKLE	GOLD KEY	1	1	4	1962	1963	
HECKLE AND JECKLE	PINES		25	34	1956	1959	
HECKLE AND JECKLE	ST JOHN PUBLISHING		1	24	1951	1955	
HECKLER, THE	DC COMICS INC.		1	6	1992	1993	
HECTOR COMICS	KEY PUBLICATIONS		1	3	1953	1954	
HECTOR HEATHCOTE	GOLD KEY		1	1	1964	1964	
HEDY DEVINE COMICS	MARVEL ENTERTAINMENT GROUP		22	50	1947	1952	FORMERLY ALL WINNERS OR TEEN
HEDY WOLFE	ATLAS		1	1	1957	1957	
HEE HAW	CHARLTON COMICS		1	7	1970	1971	
HELL RIDER	SPIDER		1	2	1971	1971	
HELL'S ANGEL	MARVEL ENTERTAINMENT GROUP		1	7	1992	1993	
HELL-FIRE RAIDERS	ALAN CLASS AND CO LTD		1	1	1966	1966	REPRINTS FAWCETT MATERIAL
HELLBLAZER	DC COMICS INC.		1	74	1988	NOW	
HELLBLAZER	TITAN BOOKS		1	4	1992	1992	
HELLBLAZER ANNUAL	DC COMICS INC.		1	1	1989	1989	
HELLBLAZER SPECIAL	DC COMICS INC.		1	1	1993	1993	
HELLBLAZER: ORIGINAL SINS	DC COMICS INC.		1	1	1991	1991	
HELLBOY: SEED OF DESTRUCTION	DARK HORSE COMICS		1	4	1994	1994	
HELLHOUND	MARVEL ENTERTAINMENT GROUP		1	3	1993	1994	EPIC TITLE
HELLHOUNDS	DARK HORSE COMICS		1	3	1994	NOW	
HELLO PAL COMICS	HARVEY PUBLICATIONS		1	3	1943	1943	
HELLRAISER	MARVEL ENTERTAINMENT GROUP		1	1	1991	1991	
HELLRAISER	MARVEL ENTERTAINMENT GROUP		1	18	1990	NOW	
HELLRAISER III: HELL ON EARTH	MARVEL ENTERTAINMENT GROUP		1	1	1993	1993	
HELLRAISER SUMMER SPECIAL	MARVEL ENTERTAINMENT GROUP		1	1	1992	1992	
HELLRAISER: BOOK OF THE DAMNED	MARVEL ENTERTAINMENT GROUP		1	3	1991	NOW	
HELLRAISER: CHRONICLES	TITAN BOOKS		1	1	1993	1993	
HELLRAISER: DARK HOLIDAY SPECIAL	MARVEL ENTERTAINMENT GROUP		1	1	1993	1993	
HELLSTORM	MARVEL ENTERTAINMENT GROUP		1	11	1993	NOW	
HEMBECK	FANTACO		1	6	1980	1980	
HEMBECK: THE BEST OF DATELINE:G!!?#	ECLIPSE		1	1	1979	1979	
HENRY	DAVID MCKAY PUBLICATIONS		1	1	1935	1935	
HENRY	DELL PUBLISHING COMPANY		1	65	1946	1961	
HENRY ALDRICH COMICS	DELL PUBLISHING COMPANY		1	22	1950	1954	
HENRY BREWSTER	M.F. ENTERPRISES		1	7	1966	1967	
HEPCATS	DOUBLE DIAMOND		1	6	1989	NOW	
HERBIE	A PLUS COMICS		1	7	1990	1991	
HERBIE	AMERICAN COMIC GROUP		1	23	1964	1967	
HERBIE	DARK HORSE COMICS		1	2	1992	1993	
HERCULES PROJECT	MONSTER COMICS		1	2	1991	1991	
HERCULES UNBOUND	DC COMICS INC.		1	12	1975	1977	
HERCULES: PRINCE OF POWER	MARVEL ENTERTAINMENT GROUP		1	1	1993	1993	
HERCULES: PRINCE OF POWER	MARVEL ENTERTAINMENT GROUP	1	1	4	1982	1982	
HERCULES: PRINCE OF POWER	MARVEL ENTERTAINMENT GROUP	2	1	4	1984	1984	
HERE IS SANTA CLAUS	GOLDSMITH PUBLISHING CO.		1	1	30'S	30'S	
HERE'S HOWIE COMICS	DC COMICS INC.		1	18	1952	1954	
HERMAN AND HIS PALS	BAZOOKA JOE/GRAPEROO		1	1	1970	1970	
HERO	MARVEL ENTERTAINMENT GROUP		1	6	1990	1990	
HERO	PREMIER		1	1	1975	1975	
HERO ALLIANCE	INNOVATION		1	18	1989	NOW	
HERO ALLIANCE	INNOVATION	3	1	5	1992	NOW	
HERO ALLIANCE	WONDER COLOR COMICS		1	1	1987	1987	
HERO ALLIANCE QUARTERLY	INNOVATION		1	4	1991	NOW	
HERO ALLIANCE SPECIAL	INNOVATION		1	1	1992	1992	
HERO ALLIANCE VS JUSTICE MACHINE	INNOVATION		1	1	1990	1990	
HERO ALLIANCE: END OF THE GOLDEN AGE	INNOVATION		1	1	1989	1989	
HERO FOR HIRE, LUKE CAGE	MARVEL ENTERTAINMENT GROUP		1	17	1972	1973	
HERO HOTLINE	DC COMICS INC.		1	6	1989	1989	
HERO ILLUSTRATED	WARRIOR PUBLISHING		1	8	1993	NOW	
HERO ILLUSTRATED SPECIAL	WARRIOR PUBLISHING		1	2	1993	NOW	
HEROES	CHARLTON COMICS		46	48	1953	1953	FORMERLY SPACE WESTERN
HEROES & HEROINES RULE GUIDE	IMAGE COMICS		1	1	1993	1993	
HEROES AGAINST HUNGER	DC COMICS INC.		1	1	1986	1986	
HEROES ALL CATHOLIC ACTION ILLUSTRATED	HEROES ALL CO.		1	74	1943	1948	
HEROES FOR HOPE STARRING THE X-MEN	MARVEL ENTERTAINMENT GROUP		1	1	1985	1985	
HEROES LIKE US	MAJESTIC ENTERTAINMENT		1	1	1994	NOW	
HEROES OF THE SKY	G.T. LIMITED		1	1	1959	1959	
HEROES OF THE WEST	L. MILLER PUBLISHING COMPANY (UK)		150	158	1959	1959	REPRINTS FAWCETT MATERIAL
HEROES OF THE WILD FRONTIER	ACE PUBLISHING		1	2	1956	1956	FORMERLY BAFFLING MYSTERIES
HEROES, INC. PRESENTS CANNON	WALLY WOOD COMICS		1	2	1969	1976	

COMIC TITLE	PUBLISHER	Vol No.	Srt No.	End No.	Str Year	End Year	COMMENTS
HEROIC ADVENTURE LIBRARY	C.A. PEARSON			2	1964	???	
HEROIC COMICS	EASTERN COLOR PRINTING COMPANY		1	97	1940	1955	NOS.1-15 "REG'LAR FELLERS HEROIC COMICS", NO.41 ON, "NEW HEROIC COMICS"
HEROINE	BIRMINGHAM ARTS LAB	1		1	1978	1978	
HERU SON OF AUSAR	ANIA PUBLISHING	1		1	1993	NOW	
HEWLIGAN'S HAIRCUT	FLEETWAY	1		1	1991	1991	
HEX	DC COMICS INC.	1		18	1985	1987	
HEXBREAKER	FIRST				1990	1990	
HI AND LOIS	CHARLTON COMICS	1		11	1969	1971	
HI-ADVENTURE HEROES	GOLD KEY	1		2	1969	1969	
HI-HO COMICS	FOUR STAR COMICS CORP/SUPERIOR COMICS LTD	1		3	1946	1946	
HI-JINX	AMERICAN COMIC GROUP			7	1947	1948	
HI-LITE COMICS	E.R. ROSS PUBLISHING CO.	1		1	1945	1945	
HI-SCHOOL ROMANCE	HARVEY PUBLICATIONS	1		75	1949	1958	
HI-SCHOOL ROMANCE DATE BOOK	HARVEY PUBLICATIONS	1		3	1962	1963	
HI-SPOT COMICS	HAWLEY	2		2	1940	1940	FORMERLY RED RYDER
HI-YO SILVER	WORLD DISTRIBUTORS LTD	1		9	1953	1953	REPRINTS DELL MATERIAL
HICKORY	QUALITY (FLEETWAY)	1		6	1949	1950	
HIDING PLACE, THE	DC COMICS INC.	1		1	1990	1990	
HIGH ADVENTURE	RED TOP/DECKER	1		1	1957	1957	
HIGH CHAPARRAL ANNUAL, THE	WORLD DISTRIBUTORS LTD	1969	1969	1969	1969		
HIGH CHAPPARAL	GOLD KEY	1		1	1968	1968	
HIGH COMMAND	DRAGON'S DREAM	1		1	1981	1981	
HIGH JINKS COMICS	HAMILTON COMICS	1		1	1947	1947	
HIGH SCHOOL AGENT	SUN COMICS PUBLISHING	1		1	1992	NOW	
HIGH SCHOOL CONFIDENTIAL DIARY	CHARLTON COMICS	1		11	1960	1962	
HIGH SEAS COMIC	SCION	1		1	1952	1952	
HIGH SHINING BRASS	APPLE COMICS	1		6	1990	1992	
HIGH SPEED COMIC	SCION	1		1	1951	1951	
HIGHWAY PATROL	C.A. PEARSON	1		8	1959	1960	
HILLBILLY COMICS	CHARLTON COMICS	1		4	1955	1956	
HIP HIP HOORAY COMIC, THE	PHILIMAR	1		1	1948	1948	
HIS NAME IS SAVAGE	ADVENTURE HOUSE PRESS	1		1	1968	1968	
HISTORY OF THE DC UNIVERSE	DC COMICS INC.	1		1	1986	1986	
HISTORY OF THE DC UNIVERSE	DC COMICS INC.	1		2	1986	1986	
HIT COMICS	QUALITY COMICS	1		65	1940	1950	
HITCHHIKER'S GUIDE TO THE GALAXY	DC COMICS INC.	1		3	1993	NOW	
HITLER	MORCRIM	1		2	1977	1977	REPRINTS SPANISH MATERIAL
HITOMI 2 AND HER GIRL COMMANDOES	ANTARTIC PRESS	1		1	1993	NOW	
HOBBIT	ECLIPSE	1		3	1990	1990	
HOCUS POCUS	PARENTS MAGAZINE INSTITUTE	9		9	1946	1946	FORMERLY FUNNY BOOK
HOGAN'S HEROES	DELL PUBLISHING COMPANY	1		9	1966	1969	
HOKUM & HEX	MARVEL ENTERTAINMENT GROUP	1		6	1993	NOW	
HOLI-DAY SURPRISE	CHARLTON COMICS	55		55	1967	1967	FORMERLY SUMMER FUN
HOLIDAY COMIC ANNUAL, THE	C.A. PEARSON	1931	1939	1931	1939		
HOLIDAY COMICS	FAWCETT PUBLICATIONS	1		1	1942	1942	
HOLIDAY COMICS	STAR PUBLICATIONS	1		8	1951	1952	
HOLIDAY FOR SCREAMS	MALIBU COMICS ENTERTAINMENT INC.	1		1	1992	1992	
HOLLYWOOD ACES	CARTOON ART	1		1	1950	1950	REPRINTS FICTION HOUSE MATERIAL
HOLLYWOOD COMICS	NEW AGE PUBLISHERS	1		1	1944	1944	
HOLLYWOOD CONFESSIONS	ST JOHN PUBLISHING	1		2	1949	1949	
HOLLYWOOD DETECTIVES, THE	ETERNITY	1		1	1991	1991	
HOLLYWOOD DIARY	QUALITY COMICS	1		5	1949	1950	
HOLLYWOOD FILM STORIES	FEATURE PUBLICATIONS	1		4	1950	1950	
HOLLYWOOD FUNNY FOLKS	DC COMICS INC.	27		60	1950	1954	FORMERLY FUNNY FOLKS
HOLLYWOOD PICTORIAL ROMANCES	ST JOHN PUBLISHING	3		3	1950	1950	
HOLLYWOOD ROMANCES	CHARLTON COMICS	46		59	1966	1971	FORMERLY BRIDES IN LOVE
HOLLYWOOD SECRETS	QUALITY COMICS	1		6	1949	1950	
HOLLYWOOD SECRETS OF ROMANCE	I.W. SUPER	9		9	60'S	60'S	
HOLLYWOOD SECRETS OF ROMANCE	QUALITY COMICS	1		1	1949	1950	
HOLLYWOOD SUPERSTARS	MARVEL ENTERTAINMENT GROUP	1		5	1990	1991	
HOLO BROS	MONSTER COMICS	1		9	1991	1992	
HOLYOKE ONE-SHOT	HOLYOKE PUBLISHING COMPANY	1		10	1944	1945	ALL REPRINTS
HOME, SWEET HOME	M.S. PUBLISHING	1		1	1925	1925	
HOMER HOOPER	ATLAS	1		4	1953	1953	
HOMER THE HAPPY GHOST	L. MILLER PUBLISHING COMPANY (UK)	1		1	1955	1955	REPRINTS ATLAS MATERIAL
HOMER, THE HAPPY GHOST	MARVEL ENTERTAINMENT GROUP	1	1	22	1955	1958	
HOMER, THE HAPPY GHOST	MARVEL ENTERTAINMENT GROUP	2	1	5	1969	1970	
HOMICIDE	DARK HORSE COMICS	1		1	1990	1990	
HONEY WEST	GOLD KEY	1		1	1966	1966	
HONEYBEE BIRDWHISTLE AND HER PET PEPI	NEWSPAPER DISTRIBUTIONS	1		1	1969	1969	
HONEYMOON	MARVEL ENTERTAINMENT GROUP	41		41	1950	1950	FORMERLY GAY COMICS
HONEYMOON ROMANCE	ARTFUL PUBLICATION	1		2	1950	1950	
HONG KONG PHOOEY	CHARLTON COMICS	1		9	1975	1976	
HONK!	FANTAGRAPHICS			5	1986	1987	
HOODED HORSEMAN, THE	AMERICAN COMIC GROUP	1	21	27	1952	1953	
HOODED HORSEMAN, THE	AMERICAN COMIC GROUP	2	18	27	1954	1956	
HOODED HORSEMAN, THE	STREAMLINE	1		2	1953	1953	REPRINTS AMERICAN COMICS GROUP MATERIAL
HOODED MENACE, THE	AVON BOOKS	1		1	1951	1951	
HOODS UP	FRAM CORP. DIST.	1		6	1953	1953	
HOOK	MARVEL ENTERTAINMENT GROUP	1		1	1992	1992	
HOOK	MARVEL ENTERTAINMENT GROUP	1		4	1992	1992	
HOOK BOOKSHELF EDITION	MARVEL ENTERTAINMENT GROUP	1		1	1992	1992	
HOOK NOVELISATION	FAWCETT PUBLICATIONS	1		1	1992	1992	
HOOK STORYBOOK	MARVEL ENTERTAINMENT GROUP	1		1	1992	1992	
HOOK SUPER SPECIAL	MARVEL ENTERTAINMENT GROUP	1		1	1992	1992	
HOOKS DEVLIN	CARTOON ART	1		1	1950	1950	REPRINTS FICTION HOUSE MATERIAL

INDEX OF COMIC TITLES AND THEIR PUBLISHERS

COMIC TITLE	PUBLISHER	Vol No.	Srt No.	End No.	Str. Year	End Year	COMMENTS
HOORAY!	MODERM FICTION		1	1	1949	1949	
HOOT GIBSON	STREAMLINE		1	6	1950	1950	
HOOT GIBSON WESTERN	FOX FEATURES SYNDICATE		1	3	1950	1950	FORMERLY MY LOVE STORY
HOPALONG CASSIDY	DC COMICS INC.	2	86	135	1954	1959	
HOPALONG CASSIDY	FAWCETT PUBLICATIONS	1	1	85	1943	1954	
HOPALONG CASSIDY AND THE MAD BARBER	FAWCETT PUBLICATIONS		1	1	1951	1951	
HOPALONG CASSIDY COMIC	L. MILLER PUBLISHING COMPANY (UK)		5	5	1948	1948	
HOPALONG CASSIDY COMIC	L. MILLER PUBLISHING COMPANY (UK)	1	50	153	1950	1958	REPRINTS FAWCETT MATERIAL
HOPALONG CASSIDY GRAPE NUTS GIVEAWAY	FAWCETT PUBLICATIONS		1	1	1950	1950	
HOPALONG CASSIDY MEETS THE BREND BROTHERS BANDITS	FAWCETT PUBLICATIONS		1	1	1951	1951	
HOPALONG CASSIDY STORIES	PURNELL		1	6	1953	1958	
HOPALONG CASSIDY STRANGE LEGACY	FAWCETT PUBLICATIONS		1	1	1951	1951	
HOPALONG CASSIDY WESTERN COMIC ANNUAL	L. MILLER PUBLISHING COMPANY (UK)		1959	1960	1959	1960	REPRINTS US MATERIAL
HOPALONG CASSIDY WHITE TOWER GIVEAWAY	FAWCETT PUBLICATIONS		1	1	1946	1946	
HOPE SHIP	DELL PUBLISHING COMPANY		1	1	1963	1963	
HOPPY THE FUNNY BUNNY WELL KNOWN COMICS	SAMUEL LOWE COMPANY		1	1	1944	1944	
HOPPY THE MARVEL BUNNY	FAWCETT PUBLICATIONS		1	15	1945	1947	
HORACE AND DOTTY DRIPPLE	HARVEY PUBLICATIONS		25	43	1952	1955	FORMERLY DOTTY DRIPPLE
HORACE AND DOTTY DRIPPLE COMICS	HARVEY PUBLICATIONS		25	43	1952	1955	
HORNET, THE	D.C. THOMSON		1	648	1963	1975	
HOROBI	VIZ	1	1	8	1990	1991	
HOROBI	VIZ	2	1	8	1991	NOW	
HORRIFIC	ARTFUL PUBLICATION		1	13	1952	1953	
HORROR FROM THE TOMB	PREMIER MAGAZINES		1	1	1954	1954	
HORROR IN THE DARK	FANTAGOR		1	5	1991	1991	
HORROR SHOW	PHANTASM PRESS	7	1	2	1989	1989	
HORROR SHOW: TALES OF FEAR AND FANTASY	CALIBER PRESS		1	1	1991	1991	
HORROR TALES	EERIE PUBLICATIONS	1	7	9	1969	1969	
HORROR TALES	EERIE PUBLICATIONS	2	1	6	1970	1970	
HORROR TALES	EERIE PUBLICATIONS	3	1	6	1971	1971	
HORROR TALES	EERIE PUBLICATIONS	4	1	7	1972	1972	
HORROR TALES	EERIE PUBLICATIONS	5	1	6	1973	1973	
HORROR TALES	EERIE PUBLICATIONS	6	1	6	1974	1974	
HORROR TALES	EERIE PUBLICATIONS	7	1	4	1976	1976	
HORROR TALES	EERIE PUBLICATIONS	8	2	5	1977	1977	
HORROR TALES	EERIE PUBLICATIONS	9	3	3	1978	1978	
HORRORS, THE	STAR PUBLICATIONS		11	15	1953	1954	FORMERLY STARTLING TERROR TALES
HORSE FEATHERS COMICS	LEV GLEASON PUBLICATIONS		1	4	1945	1948	
HOSPITAL NURSE PICTURE LIBRARY	C.A. PEARSON		1	2	1964	???	
HOT DOG	MAGAZINE ENTERPRISES		1	3	1954	1955	
HOT NADS	GHURA		1	1	1980	1980	
HOT ROD AND SPEEDWAY COMICS	HILLMAN PERIODICALS		1	5	1952	1953	
HOT ROD AND SPEEDWAY COMICS	UNITED-ANGLO PRODUCTIONS		1	1	1953	1953	REPRINTS HILLMAN MATERIAL
HOT ROD COMICS	ARNOLD BOOK CO.		1	4	1951	1951	REPRINTS FAWCETT MATERIAL
HOT ROD COMICS	FAWCETT PUBLICATIONS		1	7	1951	1953	
HOT ROD KING	ZIFF-DAVIS PUBLISHING COMPANY		1	1	1952	1952	
HOT ROD RACERS	CHARLTON COMICS		1	15	1964	1967	
HOT RODS AND RACING CARS	CHARLTON COMICS		1	120	1951	1973	
HOT RODS AND RACING CARS	L. MILLER PUBLISHING COMPANY (UK)		50	51	1953	1953	REPRINTS CHARLTON MATERIAL
HOT SHOT CHARLIE	HILLMAN PERIODICALS		1	1	1947	1947	
HOT STUFF	HARVEY PUBLICATIONS	1	1	11	1991	NOW	
HOT STUFF	HARVEY PUBLICATIONS	2	1	4	1991	1991	
HOT STUFF BIG BOOK	HARVEY PUBLICATIONS		1	2	1992	NOW	
HOT STUFF CREEPY CAVES	HARVEY PUBLICATIONS		1	7	1974	1975	
HOT STUFF DIGEST	HARVEY PUBLICATIONS		1	5	1992	NOW	
HOT STUFF GIANT SIZE	HARVEY PUBLICATIONS		1	2	1992	1992	
HOT STUFF HOLIDAY SPECIAL	HARVEY PUBLICATIONS		1	1	1993	1993	
HOT STUFF SIZZLERS	HARVEY PUBLICATIONS	1	1	59	1960	1974	
HOT STUFF SIZZLERS	HARVEY PUBLICATIONS	2	1	1	1992	1992	
HOT STUFF, THE LITTLE DEVIL	HARVEY PUBLICATIONS		1	177	1957	1991	
HOT WHEELS	DC COMICS INC.		1	6	1970	1971	
HOTCH-POTCH	JUDY OFFICE		1	1	1872	1872	
HOTEL HARBOUR VIEW	VIZ		1	1	1990	1990	
HOTSPUR	ECLIPSE		1	3	1987	1987	
HOTSPUR CHRISTMAS SPECIAL	D.C. THOMSON		1963	1963	1963	1963	
HOTSPUR, THE	D.C. THOMSON		1	1110	1959	1981	
HOTWIRE	ATOMEKA		1	1	1993	1993	
HOUSE II: THE SECOND STORY	MARVEL ENTERTAINMENT GROUP		1	1	1987	1987	
HOUSE OF HAMMER	GENERAL BOOK DISTRIB		1	20	1976	1978	
HOUSE OF MYSTERY	DC COMICS INC.		1	321	1951	1983	
HOUSE OF SECRETS	DC COMICS INC.		1	154	1956	1978	
HOUSE OF TERROR	ST JOHN PUBLISHING		1	1	1953	1953	
HOUSE OF YANG, THE	CHARLTON COMICS		1	1	1975	1976	
HOUSE OF YANG, THE	MODERN COMICS		1	2	1978	1978	
HOW AMERICA'S CARTOONISTS HELP SELL SAVING'S BONDS	HARVEY PUBLICATIONS		1	1	1950	1950	
HOW BOYS AND GIRLS CAN HELP WIN THE WAR	PARENTS MAGAZINE INSTITUTE		1	1	1942	1942	
HOW STALIN HOPES HE WILL DESTROY AMERICA	JOE LOWE CO/PICTORIAL NEWS		1	1	1951	1951	
HOW T'MAKE IT AS A ROCK STAR	IPC		1	1	1977	1977	
HOW TO DRAW FOR COMICS	STREET AND SMITH PUBLICATIONS		1	1	1942	1942	
HOW TO PICK WINNERS	NORFIL		1	1	1971	1971	
HOWARD THE DUCK	MARVEL ENTERTAINMENT GROUP		1	14	1979	1981	
HOWARD THE DUCK	MARVEL ENTERTAINMENT GROUP		1	33	1976	1986	
HOWARD THE DUCK ANNUAL	MARVEL ENTERTAINMENT GROUP		1	1	1977	1977	
HOWARD THE DUCK: THE MOVIE	MARVEL ENTERTAINMENT GROUP		1	3	1986	1987	
HOWDY DOODY	DELL PUBLISHING COMPANY		1	38	1950	1956	
HP LOVECRAFT'S CTHULHU	MILLENIUM		1	3	1991	1992	

COMIC TITLE	PUBLISHER	Vol No.	Srt No.	End No.	Str. Year	End Year	COMMENTS
HP LOVECRAFT'S CTHULHU: CULT OF CTHULHU	MILLENIUM		1	1	1993	1993	
HP LOVECRAFT'S CTHULHU: FESTIVAL OF DEATH	MILLENIUM		1	1	1993	NOW	
HUBBA-BUBBA COMIC BOOKS	TRANSATLANTIC		1	1	1947	1947	
HUCK AND YOGI JAMBOREE	DELL PUBLISHING COMPANY		1	1	1961	1961	
HUCKLEBERRY HOUND	CHARLTON COMICS		1	8	1970	1972	
HUCKLEBERRY HOUND	GOLD KEY	8	43	1959	1962		
HUCKLEBERRY HOUND & QUICK DRAW MCGRAW	HARVEY PUBLICATIONS		1	1	1993	NOW	
HUCKLEBERRY HOUND AND YOGI BEAR SUMMER EXTRA	CITY		1	1	1963	1963	
HUCKLEBERRY HOUND AND YOGI BEAR WINTER EXTRA	CITY		1	1	1963	1963	
HUCKLEBERRY HOUND MINI-COMIC	CITY		1	1	1965	1965	
HUCKLEBERRY HOUND SUMMER EXTRA	CITY		1	1	1965	1965	
HUCKLEBERRY HOUND WEEKLY	CITY		1	308	1961	1967	
HUCKLEBERRY HOUND WINTER EXTRA	CITY		1	1	1964	1964	
HUEY, DEWEY AND LOUIE JUNIOR WOODCHUCKS	GOLD KEY		1	61	1966	1982	
HUEY, DEWEY AND LOUIE JUNIOR WOODCHUCKS	WHITMAN		62	81	1982	1984	
HUEY, DEWEY AND LOUIE BACK TO SCHOOL	DELL PUBLISHING COMPANY		1	1	1958	1958	
HUGGA BUNCH	MARVEL ENTERTAINMENT GROUP		1	6	1986	1987	
HUGO	FANTAGRAPHICS		1	3	1984	1985	
HULK - SEE INCREDIBLE							
HULK COMIC	MARVEL ENTERTAINMENT GROUP		1	63	1979	1980	
HULK POCKET BOOK	MARVEL ENTERTAINMENT GROUP		1	13	1980	1981	
HULK, THE	MARVEL ENTERTAINMENT GROUP		10	27	1978	1981	FORMERLY THE RAMPAGING HULK
HUMAN FLY	I.W. ENTERPRISES		1	2	1946	1947	REPRINTS
HUMAN FLY, THE	MARVEL ENTERTAINMENT GROUP		1	19	1977	1979	
HUMAN GARGOYLES	ETERNITY		1	4	1988	1988	
HUMAN SOUP COMICS	SZOSTEK		1	3	1981	1983	
HUMAN TARGET SPECIAL, THE	DC COMICS INC.		1	1	1991	1991	
HUMAN TORCH, THE	MARVEL ENTERTAINMENT GROUP		1	8	1974	1975	
HUMAN TORCH, THE	TIMELY COMICS		2	38	1940	1954	
HUMBUG	HUMBUG PUBLICATIONS		1	11	1957	1958	
HUMBUG	HUMBUG PUBLICATIONS		1	2	1959	1959	
HUMDINGER	NOVELTY PUBLICATIONS	1	1	6	1946	1946	
HUMDINGER	NOVELTY PUBLICATIONS	2	1	2	1947	1947	
HUMPHREY COMICS	HARVEY PUBLICATIONS		1	22	1948	1952	JOE PALOOKA'S FRIEND
HUNK	CHARLTON COMICS		1	11	1961	1963	
HUNTED	FOX FEATURES SYNDICATE		1	2	1950	1950	FORMERLY MY LOVE MEMORIES
HUNTRESS, THE	DC COMICS INC.		1	19	1989	1990	
HUP	LAST GASP		1	4	1991	1991	
HURRICANE	CATALAN COMMUNCATIONS				1991	1991	
HURRICANE	FLEETWAY		1	63	1964	1965	
HURRICANE ADVENTURE COMIC, THE	R. & L. LOCKER		1	1	1946	1946	
HURRICANE COMICS	CAMBRIDGE HOUSE		1	1	1945	1945	
HYBRIDS	CONTINUITY COMICS	1	1	1	1992	1992	
HYBRIDS	CONTINUITY COMICS	2	0	3	1993	1994	
HYBRIDS	CONTINUITY COMICS	3	1	1	1993	NOW	
HYBRIDS: THE ORIGIN	CONTINUITY COMICS		2	4	1992	1993	
HYPER MYSTERY COMICS	HYPER PUBLICATIONS		1	2	1940	1940	
HYPERKIND	MARVEL ENTERTAINMENT GROUP		1	7	1993	NOW	

I

COMIC TITLE	PUBLISHER	Vol No.	Srt No.	End No.	Str. Year	End Year	COMMENTS
I AM LEGEND	ECLIPSE		1	4	1991	1991	
I BEFORE E	FANTAGRAPHICS		1	2	1991	1991	
I COME IN PEACE	GREATER MERCURY COMICS		1	2	1991	1992	
I DREAM OF JEANNIE	DELL PUBLISHING COMPANY		1	2	1965	1966	
I LOVE LUCY	ETERNITY		1	6	1990	1990	
I LOVE LUCY	WORLD DISTRIBUTORS LTD		1	16	1954	1954	REPRINTS DELL MATERIAL
I LOVE LUCY 3-D	FOTO MAGIC		1	1	1953	1953	
I LOVE LUCY COMICS	DELL PUBLISHING COMPANY		3	35	1954	1962	
I LOVE LUCY TOO	ETERNITY		1	3	1991	1991	
I LOVE YOU	CHARLTON COMICS		7	130	1955	1980	FORMERLY IN LOVE
I LOVE YOU	FAWCETT PUBLICATIONS		1	1	1950	1950	
I LOVED	FOX FEATURES SYNDICATE		28	32	1949	1950	
I SPY	GOLD KEY		1	6	1966	1968	
I WANT TO BE YOUR DOG	EROS		1	4	1990	1990	
I WANTED BOTH MEN	STREAMLINE		1	1	1950	1950	
I WAS A CHEAT	STREAMLINE		1	1	50'S	50'S	US REPRINTS
I'M A COP	MAGAZINE ENTERPRISES		1	2	1954	1954	
I'M DICKENS - HE'S FENSTER	DELL PUBLISHING COMPANY		1	2	1963	1963	
IBIS THE INVINCIBLE	L. MILLER PUBLISHING COMPANY (UK)		1	1	1950	1950	REPRINTS FAWCETT MATERIAL
IBIS, THE INVINCIBLE	FAWCETT PUBLICATIONS		1	6	1943	1948	
ICARUS	AIRCEL		1	6	1987	1988	
ICEMAN	MARVEL ENTERTAINMENT GROUP		1	4	1984	1985	
ICG SPOTLIGHT	BLUE COMET	0	0	1993	NOW		
ICG SPOTLIGHT	CONQUEST PRESS	0	0	1993	NOW		
ICG SPOTLIGHT	HEROIC PUBLISHING	0	1	1993	NOW		
ICICLE	HEROIC PUBLISHING		1	5	1993	NOW	
ICON	DC COMICS INC.		1	10	1993	NOW	
IDAHO	DELL PUBLISHING COMPANY		1	8	1963	1965	
IDEAL COMICS	TIMELY COMICS	1	1	4	1944	1946	
IDEAL ROMANCE	KEY PUBLICATIONS		3	8	1954	1955	
IDEAL: A CLASSICAL COMIC	TIMELY COMICS		1	5	1948	1949	
IDOL	MARVEL ENTERTAINMENT GROUP		1	3	1992	1992	
IF THE DEVIL COULD TALK	ROMAN CATHOLIC CATECHETICAL GUILD		1950	1958	1950	1958	
ILLEGAL ALIENS	ECLIPSE		1	1	1992	1992	

COMIC TITLE	PUBLISHER	Vol No.	Srt No.	End No.	Str. Year	End Year	COMMENTS
ILLUMINATOR	MARVEL ENTERTAINMENT GROUP		1	2	1993	NOW	
ILLUMINATUS	RIP OFF PRESS		1	1	1990	NOW	
ILLUSTRATED BIBLE TALES	L. MILLER PUBLISHING COMPANY (UK)		1	8	1953	1954	
ILLUSTRATED CHIPS	AMALGAMATED PRESS	2	1	299	1890	1953	
ILLUSTRATED CHIPS	HARMSWORTH	1	1	6	1890	1890	
ILLUSTRATED DINOSAUR MOVIE GUIDE, THE	TITAN BOOKS				1993	1993	
ILLUSTRATED LIBRARY OF GREAT ADVENTURE STORIES	THORPE		1	1	1952	1952	
ILLUSTRATED LIBRARY OF GREAT INDIAN STORIES, THE	THORPE		1	1	1952	1952	
ILLUSTRATED ROMANCE LIBRARY	WORLD DISTRIBUTORS LTD		1	?	60'S	60'S	
ILLUSTRATED STORIES OF THE OPERAS	BAILY PRESS		1	4	1943	1943	4 VERSIONS
ILLUSTRATED VAMPIRE MOVIE GUIDE, THE	TITAN BOOKS				1993	1993	
IMAGE	IMAGE COMICS	0	0	0	1993	NOW	
IMAGE PLUS	IMAGE COMICS		1	1	1993	1993	
IMAGE SWIM-SUIT SPECIAL	IMAGE COMICS		1	1	1993	1993	
IMAGES	ANTI-MATTER		1	1	1984	1984	
IMAGES OF SHADOWHAWK	IMAGE COMICS		1	2	1993	NOW	
IMAGI-MOVIES	C.F.W	2	2	2	1993	NOW	
IMMACULATE DECEPTION - DISSENTING WOMEN	KNOCKABOUT		1	1	1992	1992	
IMMORTAL DR. FATE, THE	DC COMICS INC.		1	3	1985	1985	
IMMORTALIS	MARVEL ENTERTAINMENT GROUP		1	4	1993	NOW	
IMPACT	EC COMICS		1	5	1955	1955	
IMPACT CHRISTMAS SPECIAL	DC COMICS INC.		1	1	1991	1991	
IMPACT COMICS WHO'S WHO	DC COMICS INC.		1	3	1991	1992	
IMPACT COMICS WINTER SPECIAL	DC COMICS INC.		1	1	1992	1992	
IMPOSSIBLE MAN SUMMER VACATION SPECTACULAR	MARVEL ENTERTAINMENT GROUP		1	2	1990	1991	
IMPRESSIONS OF PAPA AND SON	DAILY SKETCH		1	1	1923	1923	
IN LOVE	CHARLTON COMICS	5		6	1954	1955	FORMERLY PUBLISHED BY MAINLINE
IN LOVE	MAINLINE COMICS		1	4	1954	1955	
IN LOVE WITH JESUS	CAETECHETICAL EDUCATIONAL SOCIETY		1	1	1952	1952	
IN THE DAYS OF THE MOB	HAMPSHIRE DISTRIBUTION LTD.		1	1	1971	1971	
INCAL, THE	MARVEL ENTERTAINMENT GROUP		1	3	1988	1989	
INCOMPLETE DEATH'S HEAD	MARVEL ENTERTAINMENT GROUP		1	12	1992	1993	
INCREDIBLE CRASH DUMMIES	HARVEY PUBLICATIONS	2	3		1993	NOW	
INCREDIBLE HULK (U.K.), THE	MARVEL ENTERTAINMENT GROUP		1	27	1982	1982	
INCREDIBLE HULK AND THE THING: BIG CHANGE	MARVEL ENTERTAINMENT GROUP		1	1	1987	1987	
INCREDIBLE HULK AND WOLVERINE SPECIAL	MARVEL ENTERTAINMENT GROUP		1	1	1986	1986	
INCREDIBLE HULK ANNUAL	MARVEL ENTERTAINMENT GROUP		1	19	1968	NOW	
INCREDIBLE HULK ANNUAL (U.K.)	GRAND DREAMS	1980	1980	1980	1980	1980	
INCREDIBLE HULK ANNUAL (U.K.)	MARVEL ENTERTAINMENT GROUP	1979	1979	1979	1979	1979	
INCREDIBLE HULK GIANT SIZE	MARVEL ENTERTAINMENT GROUP		1	1	1975	1975	
INCREDIBLE HULK SUMMER SPECIAL	MARVEL ENTERTAINMENT GROUP		1	1	1982	1982	
INCREDIBLE HULK VERSUS QUASIMODO	MARVEL ENTERTAINMENT GROUP		1	1	1983	1983	
INCREDIBLE HULK WINTER SPECIAL	MARVEL ENTERTAINMENT GROUP		1	1	1982	1982	
INCREDIBLE HULK, THE	MARVEL ENTERTAINMENT GROUP		1	415	1962	NOW	
INCREDIBLE HULK: FUTURE IMPERFECT	MARVEL ENTERTAINMENT GROUP		1	2	1993	1993	
INCREDIBLE HULK: GROUND ZERO	MARVEL ENTERTAINMENT GROUP		1	1	1992	1992	
INCREDIBLE PUNK & THE MIGHTY FORE	PARODY PRESS		1	1	1993	1993	
INCREDIBLE SCIENCE FICTION	EC COMICS	30		33	1955	1956	FORMERLY WEIRD-SCIENCE FANTASY
INDIAN BRAVES	ACE MAGAZINES		1	4	1951	1951	
INDIAN CHIEF	DELL PUBLISHING COMPANY	3		33	1951	1959	FORMERLY THE CHIEF
INDIAN CHIEF	WORLD DISTRIBUTORS LTD		1	31	1953	1954	REPRINTS DELL MATERIAL
INDIAN FIGHTER	STREAMLINE		1	2	1951	1951	REPRINTS YOUTHFUL MAGAZINES MATERIAL
INDIAN FIGHTER	YOUTHFUL MAGAZINES		1	11	1950	1952	
INDIAN WARRIORS	STAR PUBLICATIONS		1	1	1953	1953	3-D
INDIAN WARRIORS	STAR PUBLICATIONS	7		8	1951	1951	FORMERLY WHITE RIDER AND SUPER HORSE
INDIAN WARRIORS	STREAMLINE		1	1	1951	1951	REPRINTS STAR MATERIAL
INDIANA JONES	MARVEL ENTERTAINMENT GROUP		1	11	1984	1985	
INDIANA JONES AND THE ARMS OF GOLD	DARK HORSE COMICS		1	4	1994	1994	
INDIANA JONES AND THE FATE OF ATLANTIS	DARK HORSE COMICS		1	1	1993	1993	
INDIANA JONES AND THE FATE OF ATLANTIS	DARK HORSE COMICS		1	4	1991	1991	
INDIANA JONES AND THE LAST CRUSADE	MARVEL ENTERTAINMENT GROUP		1	4	1989	1989	
INDIANA JONES AND THE TEMPLE OF DOOM	H. BUNCH ASSOCIATES				1984	1984	OFFICIAL COLLECTOR'S EDITION
INDIANA JONES AND THE TEMPLE OF DOOM	MARVEL ENTERTAINMENT GROUP		1	3	1984	1984	
INDIANA JONES WINTER SPECIAL	MARVEL ENTERTAINMENT GROUP		1	1	1984	1984	
INDIANA JONES, FURTHER ADVENTURES OF	MARVEL ENTERTAINMENT GROUP		1	34	1983	1986	
INDIANA JONES: THUNDER IN THE ORIENT	DARK HORSE COMICS		1	4	1993	1994	
INDIANS	CARTOON ART		1	1	1951	1951	REPRINTS FICTION HOUSE MATERIAL
INDIANS	FICTION HOUSE		1	17	1950	1953	
INDIANS	STREAMLINE		1	25	1953	1953	REPRINTS FICTION HOUSE MATERIAL
INDIANS OF THE WEST	I.W. ENTERPRISES	9		9	1958	1958	REPRINTS
INDIANS ON THE WARPATH	ST JOHN PUBLISHING		1	1	50'S	50'S	NO DATES
INFERIOR FIVE, THE	DC COMICS INC.		1	12	1967	1972	
INFERNO	AIRCEL		1	4	1990	1993	
INFINITY CRUSADE	MARVEL ENTERTAINMENT GROUP		1	6	1993	1993	
INFINITY GAUNTLET	MARVEL ENTERTAINMENT GROUP		1	1	1992	1992	
INFINITY GAUNTLET	MARVEL ENTERTAINMENT GROUP		1	6	1991	1991	
INFINITY INC.	DC COMICS INC.		1	53	1984	1988	
INFINITY INC. ANNUAL	DC COMICS INC.		1	2	1985	1986	
INFINITY INC. SPECIAL	DC COMICS INC.		1	1	1987	1987	
INFINITY WAR, THE	MARVEL ENTERTAINMENT GROUP		1	6	1992	1992	
INFORMER, THE	FEATURE TELEVISION PRODUCTIONS		1	5	1954	1954	
INHUMANOIDS	MARVEL ENTERTAINMENT GROUP		1	4	1987	1987	
INHUMANS, THE	MARVEL ENTERTAINMENT GROUP		1	1	1988	1988	
INHUMANS, THE	MARVEL ENTERTAINMENT GROUP		1	12	1975	1977	
INHUMANS: THE UNTOLD SAGA	MARVEL ENTERTAINMENT GROUP		1	1	1990	1990	
INNOVATION SPECTACULAR	INNOVATION		1	2	1991	NOW	

COMIC TITLE	PUBLISHER	Vol No.	Srt No.	End No.	Str. Year	End Year	COMMENTS
INNOVATION'S SUMMER FUN SPECIAL	INNOVATION		1	1	1991	1991	
INSANE	DARK HORSE COMICS		1	2	1988	1988	
INSIDE CRIME	FOX FEATURES SYNDICATE		2	3	1950	1950	FORMERLY MY INTIMATE AFFAIR
INSIDE IMAGE	IMAGE COMICS		1	3	1993	NOW	
INSPECTOR, THE	GOLD KEY		1	19	1974	1978	
INSPECTRE	ARCOMICS		1	1	1993	NOW	
INTERACTIVE COMICS	ADVENTURE COMICS		1	1	1991	1991	
INTERFACE	MARVEL ENTERTAINMENT GROUP		1	10	1990	1991	
INTERNATIONAL COMICS	EC COMICS		1	5	1947	1947	
INTERNATIONAL CRIME PATROL	EC COMICS		6	6	1948	1948	FORMERLY INTERNATIONAL COMICS
INTERSTATE THEATRES' FUN CLUB COMICS	INTERSTATE THEATRES		1	1	40'S	40'S	MID 1940'S
INTERVIEW WITH THE VAMPIRE	INNOVATION		1	11	1992	1994	
INTIMATE	CHARLTON COMICS		1	3	1957	1958	
INTIMATE CONFESSIONS	I.W. ENTERPRISES		1	2	1964	1964	REPRINTS
INTIMATE CONFESSIONS	I.W. SUPER		9	18	1964	1964	
INTIMATE CONFESSIONS	REALISTIC PUBLICATIONS		1	8	1951	1953	
INTIMATE LOVE	STANDARD COMICS		5	28	1950	1954	
INTIMATE LOVE	WORLD DISTRIBUTORS LTD		1	6	1953	1953	REPRINTS STANDARD MATERIAL
INTIMATE SECRETS OF ROMANCE	STAR PUBLICATIONS		1	2	1953	1954	
INTO THE SHADOW OF THE SUN	ACME PRESS & ECLIPSE		1	1	1988	1988	
INTRIGUE	QUALITY COMICS		1	1	1955	1955	
INTRODUCTION TO CHILE	BOLIVAR		1	1	1976	1976	
INVADERS	MARVEL ENTERTAINMENT GROUP		1	4	1993	1993	
INVADERS ANNUAL, THE	MARVEL ENTERTAINMENT GROUP		1	1	1977	1977	
INVADERS FROM HOME	DC COMICS INC.		1	6	1990	1990	
INVADERS FROM MARS	ETERNITY		1	1	1991	1991	
INVADERS FROM MARS II	ETERNITY		1	3	1991	1991	
INVADERS GIANT SIZE, THE	MARVEL ENTERTAINMENT GROUP		1	1	1975	1975	
INVADERS, THE	GOLD KEY		1	4	1967	1968	
INVADERS, THE	MARVEL ENTERTAINMENT GROUP		1	41	1975	1979	
INVASION	DC COMICS INC.		1	3	1988	1989	
INVASION 55	APPLE COMICS		1	3	1990	1990	
INVASION OF TECHNO-MEN	A PLUS COMICS		1	1	1993	1993	
INVISIBLE PEOPLE	KITCHEN SINK		1	1	1993	1993	
INVISIBLE SCARLET O'NEIL	KITCHEN SINK		1	3	1950	1951	
IRON CORPORAL. THE	CHARLTON COMICS		23	25	1985	1986	
IRON FIST	MARVEL ENTERTAINMENT GROUP		1	15	1975	1977	
IRON HORSE	DELL PUBLISHING COMPANY		1	2	1967	1967	
IRON MAN	MARVEL ENTERTAINMENT GROUP		1	301	1968	NOW	
IRON MAN AND SUB MARINER	MARVEL ENTERTAINMENT GROUP		1	1	1968	1968	
IRON MAN ANNUAL	MARVEL ENTERTAINMENT GROUP		1	14	1970	NOW	
IRON MAN GIANT SIZE	MARVEL ENTERTAINMENT GROUP		1	1	1975	1975	
IRON MAN, THE POWER OF	MARVEL ENTERTAINMENT GROUP		1	1	1993	1993	
IRON MAN: ARMOR WARS	MARVEL ENTERTAINMENT GROUP		1	1	1992	1992	
IRON MAN: CRASH	MARVEL ENTERTAINMENT GROUP		1	1	1988	1988	
IRON MAN: MANY ARMORS OF IRON MAN	MARVEL ENTERTAINMENT GROUP		1	1	1993	1993	
IRON MANUAL	MARVEL ENTERTAINMENT GROUP		1	1	1993	1993	
IRON MARSHAL	JADEMAN COMICS		1	32	1990	1992	
IRON SAGA'S ANTHOLOGY	IRON SAGA PRODUCTIONS		1	1	1987	1987	
IRON VIC	ST JOHN PUBLISHING	2	1	3	1947	1947	
IRON VIC	UNITED FEATURES SYNDICATE	1	22	22	1940	1940	
IRONHAND OF ALMURIC	DARK HORSE COMICS		1	4	1991	1992	
IRONJAW	ATLAS		1	4	1975	1975	
IRONWOLF	DC COMICS INC.		1	1	1986	1986	
IRONWOLF: FIRES OF THE REVOLUTION	DC COMICS INC.		1	1	1993	1993	
IRONWOOD	EROS		1	7	1992	NOW	
IRONWOOD COLLECTION	EROS		1	1	1993	1993	
IS THIS ROMANCE?	MYRA HANCOCK		1	1	1983	1983	
IS THIS TOMORROW?	CAETECHETICAL EDUCATIONAL SOCIETY		1	3	1947	1947	3 VERSIONS
ISIS	DC COMICS INC.		1	8	1976	1978	
ISLAND OF DR. MOREAU, THE	MARVEL ENTERTAINMENT GROUP		1	1	1977	1977	
IT HAPPENS IN THE BEST FAMILIES	POWERS PHOTO ENGRAVING CO.		1	2	1920	1920	
IT MUST BE LOVE	A PLUS COMICS		1	1	1993	1993	
IT REALLY HAPPENED	WILLIAM H. WISE		1	11	1944	1947	
IT RHYMES WITH LUST	ST JOHN PUBLISHING		1	1	1950	1950	
IT! THE TERROR FROM BEYOND SPACE	MILLENIUM		1	4	1992	1993	
IT'S A DUCK'S LIFE	MARVEL ENTERTAINMENT GROUP		1	11	1950	1952	
IT'S ABOUT TIME	GOLD KEY		1	1	1967	1967	
IT'S ALL LIES	GEMSANDERS		1	6	1973	1973	
IT'S FUN TO STAY ALIVE	NATIONAL AUTOMOBILE DEALERS ASSOCIATION		1	1	1948	1948	
IT'S GAMETIME	DC COMICS INC.		1	4	1955	1956	
IT'S LOVE, LOVE, LOVE	ST JOHN PUBLISHING		1	2	1957	1958	
IT'S ONLY ROCK & ROLL COMIX	PETAGNO		1	1	1975	1975	
ITCHY & SCRATCHY COMICS	BONGO COMICS		1	1	1993	NOW	
ITCHY PLANET	FANTAGRAPHICS		1	3	1988	1989	
IVANHOE	DELL PUBLISHING COMPANY		1	1	1963	1963	

J

COMIC TITLE	PUBLISHER	Vol No.	Srt No.	End No.	Str. Year	End Year	COMMENTS
J.J. IT'S ONLY MONEY	BEAVERBROOK		1	1	1972	1972	
JACE PEARSON OF THE TEXAS RANGERS	DELL PUBLISHING COMPANY		2	20	1953	1958	
JACE PEARSON OF THE TEXAS RANGERS	WORLD DISTRIBUTORS LTD		1	21	1953	1954	REPRINTS DELL MATERIAL
JACK & JILL VISIT TOYTOWN WITH ELMER THE ELF	BUTLER BROTHERS/TOYTOWN STORES		1	1	1949	1949	
JACK AND JILL	AMALGAMATED PRESS		1	2	1954	1982	
JACK AND JILL SUMMER SPECIAL	FLEETWAY		1961	1973	1961	1973	

INDEX OF COMIC TITLES AND THEIR PUBLISHERS

COMIC TITLE	PUBLISHER	Vol No.	Srt No.	End No.	Str. Year	End Year	COMMENTS
JACK ARMSTRONG	PARENTS MAGAZINE INSTITUTE		1	13	1947	1949	
JACK IN THE BOX	CHARLTON COMICS		11	16	1946	1947	FORMERLY YELLOWJACKET COMICS
JACK KIRBY'S HEROES AND VILLAINS	PURE IMAGINATION		1	1	1994	1994	
JACK OF HEARTS	MARVEL ENTERTAINMENT GROUP		1	4	1984	1984	
JACK THE GIANT KILLER	BIMFORT & CO.		1	1	1953	1953	
JACK THE RIPPER	ETERNITY		1	3	1989	1990	
JACK-POT COMIC, THE	GRANT HUGHES		1	1	1947	1947	
JACKAROO	ETERNITY		1	3	1990	1990	
JACKIE GLEASON	ST JOHN PUBLISHING	1	1	2	1948	1948	
JACKIE GLEASON	ST JOHN PUBLISHING	2	1	4	1955	1955	
JACKIE GLEASON AND THE HONEYMOONERS	DC COMICS INC.		1	12	1956	1958	
JACKIE JOKERS	HARVEY PUBLICATIONS		1	4	1973	1973	
JACKIE ROBINSON, FAMOUS PLAYS OF	FAWCETT PUBLICATIONS		1	6	1950	1952	
JACKPOT	IPC		1	141	1979	1982	
JACKPOT COMICS	M.L.J. MAGAZINES		1	9	1941	1943	
JACKPOT, THE	SWINNERTONS		1	1	1946	1946	
JADEMAN COLLECTION	JADEMAN COMICS		1	2	1989	1992	
JADEMAN KUNG FU SPECIAL	JADEMAN COMICS		1	1	1988	1988	
JAG	FLEETWAY		1	48	1968	1969	
JAG ANNUAL	FLEETWAY		1969	1972	1969	1972	
JAG SOCCER SPECIAL	FLEETWAY		1	1	1970	1970	
JAGUAR ANNUAL, THE	DC COMICS INC.		1	1	1992	1992	
JAGUAR, THE	DC COMICS INC.		1	14	1991	1992	
JAKE THRASH	AIRCEL		1	3	1988	1988	
JAM	COMICO		1	1	1988	1988	
JAM: JAPANESE ANIMATION MOVEMENT	JAM PUBLICATIONS		1	1	1992	NOW	
JAM: URBAN ADVENTURES	DARK HORSE COMICS		6	6	1993	1994	
JAMBOREE	ROUND PUBLISHING		1	3	1946	1946	
JAMES BOND 007: A SILENT ARMAGEDDON	DARK HORSE COMICS		1	2	1993	1993	
JAMES BOND 007: PERMISSION TO DIE	ECLIPSE		1	1	1992	1992	
JAMES BOND 007: THE SERPENT'S TOOTH	DARK HORSE COMICS		1	2	1992	1993	
JAMES BOND JNR.	MARVEL ENTERTAINMENT GROUP		1	12	1992	1992	
JAMES BOND: FOR YOUR EYES ONLY	MARVEL ENTERTAINMENT GROUP		1	2	1981	1981	
JAMES BOND: LICENSE TO KILL	ACME PRESS		1	1	1992	1992	
JAMES BOND: PERMISSION TO DIE	ECLIPSE		1	3	1989	1991	
JANE	PELHAM/RAINBIRD		1	1	1983	1983	
JANE ARDEN	ST JOHN PUBLISHING		1	2	1948	1948	
JANE AT WAR	WOLFE		1	1	1976	1976	
JANE ON SAWDUST TRAIL	MIRROR PRESS PUBLICATIONS		1	1	1947	1947	
JANE'S JOURNAL	RYLEE		1	1	1946	1946	
JANE'S JOURNAL	THOMAS		1	1	1944	1944	
JANE'S SUMMER IDLE	MIRROR PRESS PUBLICATIONS		1	1	1946	1946	
JANE, FAREWELL TO	MIRROR PRESS PUBLICATIONS		1	1	1960	1960	
JANE: ANOTHER JANE'S JOURNAL	THOMAS		1	1	1945	1945	
JANE: ANOTHER JOURNAL	RYLEE		1	2	1948	1950	
JANE: PETT'S ANNUAL	THOMAS		1	1	1944	1944	
JANN OF THE JUNGLE	ATLAS		8	17	1955	1957	FORMERLY JUNGLE TALES
JAPHET BOOK, THE	DAILY NEWS		1924	1925	1924	1925	
JAPHET HOLIDAY BOOK ANNUAL, THE	NEWS CHRONICLE		1936	1940	1936	1940	
JASON AND THE ARGONAUTS	CALIBER PRESS		1	6	1991	NOW	
JASON GOES TO HELL	TOPPS		1	3	1993	1993	
JAZZ AGE CHRONICLES	CALIBER PRESS		1	7	1990	NOW	
JAZZ FUNNIES	KNOCKABOUT		1	1	1986	1986	
JCP FEATURES	JOHN C PRODUCTIONS INC		1	1	1980	1981	
JEANIE COMICS	MARVEL ENTERTAINMENT GROUP		13	27	1947	1949	FORMERLY ALL SURPRISE
JEEP COMICS	R.B. LEFFINGWELL & CO.		1	29	1944	1948	
JEEP COMICS	R.B. LEFFINGWELL & CO.		1	3	1944	1948	
JEFF HAWKE	TITAN BOOKS		1	2	1986	1987	
JEFF JORDAN, U.S. AGENT	D.S. PUBLISHING CO.		1	1	1947	1948	
JEMM, SON OF SATURN	DC COMICS INC.		1	12	1984	1985	
JEREMIAH 13	CATALAN COMMUNCATIONS				1987	1987	
JEREMIAH: A FISTFUL OF SAND	ADVENTURE COMICS		1	2	1991	1991	
JEREMIAH: BIRDS OF PREY	ADVENTURE COMICS		1	2	1991	1991	
JEREMIAH: EYES LIKE BURNING COALS	ADVENTURE COMICS		1	2	1991	1991	
JEREMIAH: THE HEIRS	ADVENTURE COMICS		1	2	1991	1991	
JEREMIAH: THE HUNTERS	ADVENTURE COMICS		1	2	1991	1991	
JERRY DRUMMER	CHARLTON COMICS		10	12	1957	1957	FORMERLY SOLDIER & MARINE
JERRY IGER'S GOLDEN FEATURES	BLACKTHORNE		1	6	1986	1986	
JESSE JAMES	AVON BOOKS		1	29	1950	1956	
JESSE JAMES	REALISTIC PUBLICATIONS		1	1	1953	1953	REPRINTS
JESSE JAMES COMICS	THORPE & PORTER		1	6	1952	1952	REPRINTS AVON MATERIAL
JEST	HARRY A CHESLER		10	11	1944	1944	FORMERLY SNAP
JESTER	HARRY A CHESLER		10	10	1945	1945	
JESTER AND WONDER, THE	AMALGAMATED PRESS		28	506	1902	1912	PREVIOUSLY THE WONDER AND JESTER
JESTER, THE	AMALGAMATED PRESS	1	534	998	1912	1920	PREVIOUSLY THE JESTER AND WONDER
JESTER, THE	AMALGAMATED PRESS	2	1164	2010	1924	1940	FORMERLY THE JOLLY JESTER
JET	IPC		1	22	1971	1971	
JET ACES	FICTION HOUSE		1	4	1952	1953	
JET COMIC, THE	HAMILTON COMICS		1	1	1953	1953	
JET DREAM AND HER STUNTGIRL SUPERSPIES	GOLD KEY		1	1	1968	1968	
JET FIGHTERS	STANDARD COMICS		5	7	1952	1953	
JET PLANE RAIDERS, THE	HOTSPUR PUBLISHING CO.		1	1	1948	1948	
JET POWER	I.W. ENTERPRISES		1	2	1963	1963	
JET POWERS	MAGAZINE ENTERPRISES		1	4	1950	1951	
JETSONS BIG BOOK, THE	HARVEY PUBLICATIONS		1	3	1992	NOW	
JETSONS GIANT SIZE, THE	HARVEY PUBLICATIONS		1	3	1992	NOW	
JETSONS, THE	CHARLTON COMICS		1	20	1970	1973	
JETSONS, THE	GOLD KEY		1	36	1963	1970	
JETSONS, THE	HARVEY PUBLICATIONS	1	1	4	1992	NOW	
JETSONS, THE	HARVEY PUBLICATIONS	2	1	2	1992	NOW	

COMIC TITLE	PUBLISHER	Vol No.	Srt No.	End No.	Str. Year	End Year	COMMENTS
JETTA OF THE 21ST CENTURY	STANDARD COMICS		5	7	1952	1953	
JEWEL IN THE SKULL, THE	BIG O/SAVOY		1	1	80'S	80'S	
JEZEBEL JADE	COMICO		1	3	1988	1988	
JHEREG	MARVEL ENTERTAINMENT GROUP		1	1	1988	1988	
JIGGS & MAGGIE	HARVEY PUBLICATIONS		22	27	1953	1954	
JIGGS & MAGGIE	STANDARD COMICS		11	21	1949	1953	
JIGSAW	HARVEY PUBLICATIONS		1	2	1966	1966	
JIHAD	MARVEL ENTERTAINMENT GROUP		1	2	1991	1992	
JIM	FANTAGRAPHICS		1	3	1988	1989	
JIM	FANTAGRAPHICS	2	1	1	1993	NOW	
JIM BOWIE	CHARLTON COMICS		15	19	1955	1957	FORMERLY DANGER
JIM BOWIE	L. MILLER PUBLISHING COMPANY (UK)		1	24	1957	1959	
JIM DANDY	LEV GLEASON PUBLICATIONS		1	3	1956	1956	
JIM HARDY	UNITED FEATURES SYNDICATE		1	1	1944	1944	
JIM RAY'S AVIATION SKETCH BOOK	MONTGOMERY WARD		1	2	1946	1946	
JIMMY	N.Y. AMERICAN & JOURNAL		1	1	1905	1905	
JIMMY BRINDLE	JIMMY BRINDLE		1	1	1948	1948	
JIMMY DURANTE COMICS	UNITED-ANGLO PRODUCTIONS		1	2	1950	1950	REPRINTS MAGAZINE ENTERPRISES MATERIAL
JIMMY OLSEN - SEE SUPERMAN'S PAL							
JIMMY WAKELY	DC COMICS INC.		1	18	1949	1952	
JING PALS	VICTORY PUBLISHING CORPORATION		1	4	1946	1946	
JINGLE BELLS COMIC	PHILIMAR		1	1	1947	1947	
JINGLE DINGLE CHRISTMAS STOCKING COMICS ANNUAL	STANHALL		1	2	1951	1952	
JINGLE JANGLE COMICS	EASTERN COLOR PRINTING COMPANY		1	42	1942	1949	
JINGLES	AMALGAMATED PRESS		1	741	1934	1954	
JINGO COMIC	ENSIGN/W. FORSHAW				1946	1947	FOUR ISSUES, ONLY THIRD ISSUE WAS NUMBERED
JINNI	HEROIC PUBLISHING		1	1	1993	1993	
JO-JO COMICS	FOX FEATURES SYNDICATE		1	29	1945	1949	
JO-JO CONGO KING	STREAMLINE		1	1	1950	1950	
JO-JOY, THE ADVENTURES OF	W.T. GRANT COMPANY		1945	1953	1945	1953	
JOAN OF ARC	CAETECHETICAL EDUCATIONAL SOCIETY		1	1	???	???	NO DATE
JOE 90 ANNUAL	CITY		1968	1969	1968	1969	
JOE 90 STORYBOOK	CITY		1	4	1968	1969	
JOE 90: TOP SECRET	CITY		1	34	1969	1969	
JOE 90: TOP SECRET COMIC ANNUAL	CITY		1969	1969	1969	1969	
JOE COLLEGE	HILLMAN PERIODICALS		1	2	1949	1950	
JOE KUBERT'S TOR	DC COMICS INC.		1	4	1993	NOW	
JOE LOUIS	FAWCETT PUBLICATIONS		1	2	1950	1950	
JOE LOUIS COMICS	L. MILLER PUBLISHING COMPANY (UK)		1	2	1950	1951	REPRINTS FAWCETT MATERIAL
JOE PALOOKA	COLUMBIA COMICS GROUP	1	1	4	1942	1944	
JOE PALOOKA	CUPPLES AND LEON CO.		1	1	1933	1933	
JOE PALOOKA	HARVEY PUBLICATIONS	2	1	118	1945	1961	
JOE PALOOKA	STREAMLINE		1	2	1953	???	REPRINTS HARVEY MATERIAL
JOE PALOOKA FIGHTS HIS WAY BACK	HARVEY PUBLICATIONS		1	1	1945	1945	
JOE PALOOKA IN "HI THERE!"	HARVEY PUBLICATIONS		1	1	1949	1949	
JOE PALOOKA IN "IT'S ALL IN THE FAMILY"	HARVEY PUBLICATIONS		1	1	1945	1945	
JOE PALOOKA VISITS THE LOST CITY	HARVEY PUBLICATIONS		1	1	1945	1945	
JOE PALOOKA'S BODY BUILDING INSTRUCTION BOOK	HARVEY PUBLICATIONS		1	1	1958	1958	
JOE PALOOKA'S HUMPHREY	UNITED-ANGLO PRODUCTIONS		1	13	1950	1951	REPRINTS HARVEY MATERIAL
JOE R. LANSDALE'S BY BIZARRE HANDS	DARK HORSE COMICS		1	2	1994	1994	
JOE SINN	CALIBER PRESS		1	1	1993	NOW	
JOE YANK	CARTOON ART		1	1	1954	1954	
JOE YANK	STANDARD COMICS		5	16	1952	1954	
JOHN BOLTON HALLS OF HORROR	PACIFIC COMICS		1	2	1985	1985	
JOHN BOLTON'S BACK DOWN THE LINE	ECLIPSE		1	1	1991	1991	
JOHN BYRNE'S 2112	DARK HORSE COMICS		1	1	1992	1992	
JOHN BYRNE'S NEXT MEN	DARK HORSE COMICS		1	1	1993	1993	
JOHN BYRNE'S NEXT MEN	DARK HORSE COMICS		1	18	1992	NOW	ISSUE 0 WAS PUBLISHED IN APRIL 1992
JOHN CARTER ADVENTURE ANNUAL	WORLD DISTRIBUTORS LTD		1953	1959	1953	1959	
JOHN CARTER OF MARS	WORLD DISTRIBUTORS LTD		1	2	1953	1953	DELL REPRINTS
JOHN CARTER, WARLORD OF MARS	GOLD KEY		1	3	1964	1964	
JOHN CARTER, WARLORD OF MARS	HOUSE OF GREYSTOKE		1	1	1970	1970	
JOHN CARTER, WARLORD OF MARS	MARVEL ENTERTAINMENT GROUP		1	28	1977	1979	
JOHN CARTER, WARLORD OF MARS ANNUAL	MARVEL ENTERTAINMENT GROUP		1	3	1977	1979	
JOHN F. KENNEDY, CHAMPION OF FREEDOM	WORDEN & CHILDS		1	1	1964	1964	
JOHN HIX SCRAP BOOK, THE	EASTERN COLOR PRINTING COMPANY		1	2	30'S	30'S	LATE 1930'S
JOHN LAW, DETECTIVE	ECLIPSE		1	1	1981	1981	
JOHN STEELE SECRET AGENT	GOLD KEY		1	1	1964	1964	
JOHN WAYNE ADVENTURE COMICS	TOBY PRESS PUBLICATIONS		1	31	1949	1955	
JOHN WAYNE ADVENTURE COMICS	WORLD DISTRIBUTORS LTD		1	82	1952	1958	
JOHN WESLEY	AMALGAMATED PRESS		1	1	1953	1953	
JOHNNY ATOMIC	ETERNITY		1	3	1991	1992	
JOHNNY COUGAR'S WRESTLING MONTHLY	FLEETWAY				1992	1993	
JOHNNY DANGER	TOBY PRESS PUBLICATIONS		1	1	1950	1950	
JOHNNY DANGER PRIVATE DETECTIVE	TOBY PRESS PUBLICATIONS		1	1	1954	1954	
JOHNNY DYNAMITE	CHARLTON COMICS		10	12	1955	1955	FORMERLY DYNAMITE
JOHNNY HAZARD	L. MILLER PUBLISHING COMPANY (UK)		1	1	1954	1954	
JOHNNY HAZARD	STANDARD COMICS		5	7	1948	1949	
JOHNNY JINGLE'S LUCKY DAY	AMERICAN DAIRY ASSOCIATION		1	1	1956	1956	
JOHNNY LAW, SKY RANGER	LEV GLEASON PUBLICATIONS		1	4	1955	1955	
JOHNNY MACK BROWN	DELL PUBLISHING COMPANY		2	3	1950	1951	
JOHNNY MACK BROWN	WORLD DISTRIBUTORS LTD		1	21	1954	1955	DELL REPRINTS
JOHNNY NEMO	DEADLINE				1989	1989	
JOHNNY NEMO MAGAZINE, THE	ECLIPSE		1	3	1985	1986	
JOHNNY THUNDER	DC COMICS INC.		1	3	1973	1973	
JOKEBOOK COMICS DIGEST ANNUAL	ARCHIE PUBLICATIONS		1	13	1977	1983	
JOKER COMIC	BAIRNS BOOKS		1	1	1946	1946	

COMIC TITLE	PUBLISHER	Vol No.	Srt No.	End No.	Str. Year	End Year	COMMENTS
JOKER COMICS	TIMELY COMICS		1	42	1942	1950	
JOKER SPECIAL	LONDON EDITIONS MAGAZINES		1	1	1990	1990	
JOKER, THE	DC COMICS INC.		1	9	1975	1976	
JOKER, THE	FLEETWAY		1	655	1927	1940	
JOLIDAY COMIC, THE	D. MCKENZIE		1	2	1948	1948	
JOLLY ADVENTURES	MARTIN & REID		1	9	1946	1949	
JOLLY ARROW	JOHN MATTHEW		1	2	1948	1948	
JOLLY CHRISTMAS BOOK	PROMOTIONAL PUBLICATIONS COMPANY		1951	1955	1951	1955	
JOLLY CHUCKLES	MARTIN & REID		1	11	1946	1949	
JOLLY COMIC	P.M. PRODUCTIONS		1	1	1946	1946	
JOLLY COMIC, THE	AMALGAMATED PRESS		1	250	1935	1939	
JOLLY COMICS	FOUR STAR COMICS CORP/SUPERIOR COMICS LTD		1	1	1947	1947	
JOLLY COWBOY	MARTIN & REID		1	1	1948	1948	
JOLLY FUN	MARTIN & REID		1	2	1946	1946	
JOLLY FUN-RAY COMIC, THE	PHILIMAR		1	1	1947	1947	
JOLLY GIANT COMIC, THE	PHILIMAR		1	1	1946	1946	
JOLLY JACK IN THE BOX COMIC	P.M. PRODUCTIONS		1	1	1949	1949	
JOLLY JACK'S WEEKLY	ASSOCIATED NEWSPAPERS		1	70	1933	1934	
JOLLY JESTER COMIC	PHILIMAR		1	2	1948	1948	
JOLLY JESTER, THE	AMALGAMATED PRESS		999	1163	1920	1924	FORMERLY THE JESTER
JOLLY JINGLES	M.L.J. MAGAZINES		10	16	1943	1945	FORMERLY JACKPOT COMICS
JOLLY JINKS	JOHN LENG		1	1	1938	1938	
JOLLY JINKS COMIC	MARTIN & REID		1	1	1944	1944	
JOLLY JUMBO'S CHRISTMAS BOOK, THE	L. MILLER PUBLISHING COMPANY (UK)		1	1	1944	1944	
JOLLY TIMES	L. BURN		1	1	1947	1947	PREVIOUSLY HAPPY TIMES FAMILY COMIC
JOLLY WESTERN	MARTIN & REID		1	9	1947	1949	
JOLLYBOYS AND GIRLS COMICS	PHILIMAR		1	1	1949	1949	
JON JUAN	TOBY PRESS PUBLICATIONS		1	1	1950	1950	
JON SABLE: FREELANCE	FIRST		1	56	1983	1988	
JONAH HEX	DC COMICS INC.		1	92	1977	1985	
JONAH HEX AND OTHER WESTERN TALES	DC COMICS INC.		1	3	1979	1980	
JONAH HEX: TWO GUN MOJO	DC COMICS INC.		1	5	1993	1993	
JONESY	QUALITY COMICS		1	8	1953	1954	FORMERLY CRACK WESTERN
JONNI THUNDER	DC COMICS INC.		1	4	1985	1985	
JONNY QUEST	COMICO		1	31	1986	1988	
JONNY QUEST	GOLD KEY		1	1	1964	1964	
JONNY QUEST CLASSICS	COMICO		1	3	1987	1987	
JONNY QUEST SPECIAL	COMICO		1	2	1988	1988	
JOSIE	ARCHIE PUBLICATIONS		1	106	1963	1982	
JOSIE AND THE PUSSYCATS	ARCHIE PUBLICATIONS		1	1	1993	1993	
JOURNEY	AARDVARK-VANAHEIM		1	27	1983	1986	
JOURNEY	FANTAGRAPHICS		1	2	1987	1987	
JOURNEY INTO DANGER	L. MILLER PUBLISHING COMPANY (UK)		1	8	1957	1957	ATLAS REPRINTS
JOURNEY INTO FEAR	SUPERIOR COMICS		1	21	1951	1954	
JOURNEY INTO MYSTERY	MARVEL ENTERTAINMENT GROUP	1	1	125	1952	1966	
JOURNEY INTO MYSTERY	MARVEL ENTERTAINMENT GROUP	2	1	19	1972	1975	
JOURNEY INTO MYSTERY ANNUAL	MARVEL ENTERTAINMENT GROUP	1	1	1	1965	1965	
JOURNEY INTO UNKNOWN WORLDS	ATLAS	1	36	38	1950	1951	FORMERLY TEEN JOURNEY INTO UNKNOWN WORLDS
JOURNEY INTO UNKNOWN WORLDS	ATLAS	2	4	59	1951	1957	
JOURNEY: WARDRUMS	FANTAGRAPHICS		1	3	1987	1991	
JOY WHEEL, THE	CHILDREN'S PRESS		1	1	1947	1947	
JOYRIDE COMIC, THE	WILLIAM FOSTER		1	5	1946	1946	
JRF PRESENTS	JOHN LAWRENCE/PHILIP HARBOTTLE		1	4	1985	1986	
JUDGE CALIGULA, THE COLLECTED	TITAN BOOKS		1	2	1991	1991	
JUDGE DREDD	EAGLE	1	1	35	1983	1986	
JUDGE DREDD	QUALITY (FLEETWAY)	2	1	77	1986	1992	
JUDGE DREDD ANNUAL	FLEETWAY		1981	1991	1981	1991	
JUDGE DREDD COLLECTION, THE	FLEETWAY		1	5	1985	1989	
JUDGE DREDD CURSED EARTH, THE COMPLETE	TITAN BOOKS		1	1	1994	1994	
JUDGE DREDD MEGA COLLECTION	FLEETWAY		1	1	1990	1990	
JUDGE DREDD MEGA SPECIAL	FLEETWAY		1	10	1988	NOW	
JUDGE DREDD MEGAZINE	FLEETWAY	1	1	20	1992	1993	
JUDGE DREDD MEGAZINE	FLEETWAY	2	1	45	1993	NOW	
JUDGE DREDD MEGAZINE (US EDITION)	FLEETWAY		1	2	1992	1992	
JUDGE DREDD PERP PACK	FLEETWAY		1	1	1993	1993	
JUDGE DREDD RULES!	FLEETWAY		1	19	1992	NOW	
JUDGE DREDD YEARBOOK	FLEETWAY		1992	1994	1992	NOW	
JUDGE DREDD'S CRIME FILE	TITAN BOOKS		1	4	1989	1989	
JUDGE DREDD'S CRIME FILES	EAGLE		1	6	1986	1987	
JUDGE DREDD'S HARDCASE PAPERS	FLEETWAY		1	4	1991	1991	
JUDGE DREDD, LAW OF	QUALITY (FLEETWAY)		1	33	1989	1992	
JUDGE DREDD, THE CHRONICLES OF	FLEETWAY		1	27	1981	1990	
JUDGE DREDD: AMERICA	FLEETWAY		1	1	1991	1991	
JUDGE DREDD: AMERICA	FLEETWAY		1	2	1993	1993	
JUDGE DREDD: BAD SCIENCE	FLEETWAY		1	1	1990	1990	
JUDGE DREDD: CURSE OF THE SPIDER WOMAN	FLEETWAY		1	1	1990	1990	
JUDGE DREDD: DEMOCRACY NOW	MANDARIN (2000 AD BOOKS)		1	1	1993	1993	
JUDGE DREDD: EARLY CASES	EAGLE		1	6	1986	1986	
JUDGE DREDD: EMERALD ISLE	FLEETWAY		1	1	1993	1993	
JUDGE DREDD: FUTURE CRIME	FLEETWAY		1	1	1990	1990	
JUDGE DREDD: HALL OF JUSTICE	FLEETWAY		1	1	1991	1991	
JUDGE DREDD: HEAVY METAL DREDD	MANDARIN (2000 AD BOOKS)		1	1	1993	1993	
JUDGE DREDD: IN OZ, THE COMPLETE	TITAN BOOKS		1	1	1994	1994	
JUDGE DREDD: MECHANISMO	MANDARIN (2000 AD BOOKS)		1	1	1993	1993	
JUDGE DREDD: METAL FATIGUE	FLEETWAY			1	1991	1991	
JUDGE DREDD: RAPTAUR	FLEETWAY		1	1	1993	1993	
JUDGE DREDD: RAPTAUR	MANDARIN (2000 AD BOOKS)		1	1	1993	1993	
JUDGE DREDD: TALE OF THE DEAD MAN	FLEETWAY		1	1	1991	1991	

COMIC TITLE	PUBLISHER	Vol No.	Srt No.	End No.	Str. Year	End Year	COMMENTS
JUDGE DREDD: TALES OF THE DAMNED	MANDARIN (2000 AD BOOKS)		1	1	1993	1993	
JUDGE DREDD: THE EARLY CASES	EAGLE		1	6	1986	1986	
JUDGE DREDD: THE HUNT FOR BLACK WIDOW	FLEETWAY		1	1	1993	1993	
JUDGE DREDD: THE JUDGE CHILD QUEST	EAGLE		1	5	1984	1985	
JUDGE DREDD: THE JUDGE CHILD QUEST	FLEETWAY		1	1	1991	1991	
JUDGE DREDD: TOP DOG	MANDARIN (2000 AD BOOKS)		1	1	1993	1993	
JUDGE PARKER	ARGO PUBLISHING		1	2	1956	1956	
JUDGEMENT DAY	LIGHTNING COMICS		1	1	1993	NOW	
JUDO JOE	JAY-JAY CORP.		1	3	1953	1953	
JUDOMASTER	CHARLTON COMICS		89	98	1966	1967	FORMERLY GUN MASTER
JUDY	D.C. THOMSON		1	500	1960	NOW	
JUDY CANOVA	FOX FEATURES SYNDICATE		1	3	1950	1950	FORMERLY MY EXPERIENCE
JUDY JOINS THE WAVES	JAY-JAY CORP.		1	1	1951	1951	
JUDY PICTURE LIBRARY FOR GIRLS	D.C. THOMSON		1	2	1963	???	
JUGHEAD	ARCHIE PUBLICATIONS	1	127	352	1965	1987	FORMERLY ARCHIE'S PAL JUGHEAD
JUGHEAD	ARCHIE PUBLICATIONS	2	1	54	1987	NOW	
JUGHEAD	THORPE & PORTER		1	2	50'S	50'S	ARCHIE REPRINTS
JUGHEAD AS CAPTAIN HERO	ARCHIE PUBLICATIONS		1	7	1966	1967	
JUGHEAD DOUBLE DIGEST	ARCHIE PUBLICATIONS		1	22	1989	NOW	
JUGHEAD JONES COMIC DIGEST, THE	ARCHIE PUBLICATIONS		1	87	1977	NOW	
JUGHEAD WITH ARCHIE DIGEST	ARCHIE PUBLICATIONS		1	118	1974	NOW	
JUGHEAD'S BABY TALES	ARCHIE PUBLICATIONS		1	1	1994	NOW	
JUGHEAD'S DINER	ARCHIE PUBLICATIONS		1	6	1990	1991	
JUGHEAD'S FANTASY	ARCHIE PUBLICATIONS		1	3	1960	1960	
JUGHEAD'S FOLLY	ARCHIE PUBLICATIONS		1	1	1957	1957	
JUGHEAD'S JOKES	ARCHIE PUBLICATIONS		1	78	1967	1982	
JUGHEAD'S PAL HOT DOG	ARCHIE PUBLICATIONS		1	5	1990	1990	
JUGHEAD'S TIME POLICE	ARCHIE PUBLICATIONS		1	6	1990	1991	
JUKE BOX COMICS	ARCHIE PUBLICATIONS		1	6	1948	1949	
JULIETTE PICTURE LIBRARY	FAME PRESS		1	2	1966	???	
JUMBO COMICS	CARTOON ART		1	2	1950	1950	FICTION HOUSE REPRINTS
JUMBO COMICS	FICTION HOUSE		1	167	1938	1953	
JUMBO COMICS	HOTSPUR PUBLISHING CO.		1	1	1949	1949	
JUMBO COMICS	R. & L. LOCKER		1	2	1951	1951	
JUMBO COMICS	THORPE & PORTER		1	28	1952	1954	FICTION HOUSE REPRINTS
JUMPING JACKS PRESENTS THE WHIZ KIDS	JUMPING JACKS STORES		1	1	1978	1978	
JUNE	FLEETWAY		1	638	1961	1974	
JUNE AND SCHOOLFRIEND PICTURE LIBRARY HOLIDAY	FLEETWAY		1966	1971	1966	1971	
JUNGLE	STREAMLINE		1	1	1950	1950	FOX REPRINTS
JUNGLE ACTION	ATLAS		1	6	1954	1955	
JUNGLE ACTION	MARVEL ENTERTAINMENT GROUP		1	24	1972	1976	
JUNGLE ADVENTURES	I.W. SUPER		10	12	1963	1964	REPRINTS
JUNGLE ADVENTURES	SKYWALD PUBLISHING		1	3	1971	1971	
JUNGLE BOOK MOVIE ADAPTATION	WALT DISNEY		1	1	1990	1990	
JUNGLE COMICS	BLACKTHORNE		1	6	1988	1988	
JUNGLE COMICS	FICTION HOUSE		1	163	1940	1954	
JUNGLE COMICS	STREAMLINE		1	4	1949	1950	FICTION HOUSE REPRINTS
JUNGLE COMICS	THORPE & PORTER		1	2	1952	???	FICTION HOUSE REPRINTS
JUNGLE GIRL	FAWCETT PUBLICATIONS		1	1	1942	1942	
JUNGLE GIRLS	AMERICAN COMIC GROUP		1	16	1992	NOW	
JUNGLE HERO	SCION		1	1	1951	1951	
JUNGLE JIM	CHARLTON COMICS		22	28	1969	1970	FORMERLY JUNGLE JIM (DELL)
JUNGLE JIM	DELL PUBLISHING COMPANY		3	19	1954	1959	
JUNGLE JIM	KING FEATURES		5	5	1967	1967	REPRINT
JUNGLE JIM	STANDARD COMICS		11	20	1949	1951	
JUNGLE JIM	WORLD DISTRIBUTORS LTD		1	10	1955	1955	DELL REPRINTS
JUNGLE JINKS	AMALGAMATED PRESS		1	62	1923	1925	
JUNGLE JO	FOX FEATURES SYNDICATE		1	6	1950	1951	
JUNGLE LIL	FOX FEATURES SYNDICATE		1	1	1950	1950	
JUNGLE LIL	STREAMLINE		1	1	1951	1951	FOX REPRINTS
JUNGLE TALES	ATLAS		1	7	1954	1955	
JUNGLE TALES OF TARZAN	CHARLTON COMICS		1	4	1964	1965	
JUNGLE THRILLS	STAR PUBLICATIONS		1	16	1952	1954	4 ISSUES, WHICH INCLUDE 2 3-D ISSUES
JUNGLE THRILLS	STREAMLINE		1	1	1952	1952	FOX REPRINTS
JUNGLE TRAILS	SCION		1	3	1951	1952	
JUNGLE TWINS, THE	GOLD KEY		1	18	1972	1975	
JUNGLE TWINS, THE	WHITMAN		18	18	1982	1982	
JUNGLE WAR STORIES	DELL PUBLISHING COMPANY		1	11	1962	1965	
JUNIE PROM	DEARFIELD PUBLISHING		1	7	1947	1949	
JUNIOR CARROT PATROL	DARK HORSE COMICS		1	1	1989	1989	
JUNIOR COMICS	FOX FEATURES SYNDICATE		9	16	1947	1948	FORMERLY L'IL PAN
JUNIOR FUNNIES	HARVEY PUBLICATIONS		10	13	1951	1952	FORMERLY TINY TOT FUNNIES
JUNIOR HOP COMICS	STANMORE PUBLICATIONS		1	3	1952	1952	
JUNIOR MEDICS OF AMERICA, THE	E.R. SQUIRE & SONS		1	1	1957	1957	
JUNIOR MIRROR	MIRROR PRESS PUBLICATIONS		1	75	1954	1956	
JUNIOR MISS	TIMELY COMICS		1	39	1944	1950	
JUNIOR PARTNERS	ORAL ROBERTS		1	29	1959	1961	FORMERLY ORAL ROBERTS' TRUE STORIES
JUNIOR SPIDER-MAN SUMMER SPECIAL	MARVEL ENTERTAINMENT GROUP		1	1	1983	1983	
JUNIOR WOODCHUCKS, WALT DISNEY'S	WALT DISNEY		1	4	1991	1991	
JUNIORS' MAGAZINE	G.W. PEARCE		1	1	1947	1947	
JUNKER	FLEETWAY		1	2	1993	1994	
JUPITER ADVENTURE COMIC	SCOOP BOOKS		1	1	1946	1946	
JURASSIC PARK	DARK HORSE COMICS		1	5	1993	NOW	
JURASSIC PARK	TITAN BOOKS				1993	1993	
JURASSIC PARK	TOPPS		1	4	1993	1993	
JURASSIC PARK OFFICIAL MOVIE SOUVENIR MAGAZINE	TITAN BOOKS				1993	1993	
JURASSIC PARK: RAPTOR	TOPPS			2	1993	1993	
JURASSIC PARK: RAPTORS ATTACK!	TOPPS			4	1994	1994	
JURASSIC PARK: THE FILM STORYBOOK	RANDOM HOUSE PUBLISHING GROUP LTD				1993	1993	

COMIC TITLE	PUBLISHER	Vol No.	Srt No.	End No.	Str. Year	End Year	COMMENTS
JUST DENNIS	ALAN CLASS AND CO LTD		1	1	1965	1965	HALLDEN REPRINTS
JUST KIDS	MCLOUGHLIN BROS.		283	283	1932	1932	
JUST MARRIED	CHARLTON COMICS		1	114	1958	1976	
JUSTICE	MARVEL ENTERTAINMENT GROUP		4	52	1986	1989	
JUSTICE COMICS	MARVEL ENTERTAINMENT GROUP		7	52	1947	1955	FORMERLY WACKY DUCK
JUSTICE INC.	DC COMICS INC.	1	1	4	1975	1975	
JUSTICE INC.	DC COMICS INC.	2	1	2	1989	1989	
JUSTICE LEAGUE ARCHIVES	DC COMICS INC.		1	2	1993	NOW	
JUSTICE LEAGUE EUROPE	DC COMICS INC.		1	50	1989	1993	BECOMES JUSTICE LEAGUE INTERNATIONAL FROM NO.51
JUSTICE LEAGUE EUROPE ANNUAL	DC COMICS INC.		1	3	1990	1992	
JUSTICE LEAGUE INTERNATIONAL	DC COMICS INC.		51	65	1993	NOW	FORMERLY JUSTICE LEAGUE EUROPE NOS.1-50
JUSTICE LEAGUE INTERNATIONAL ANNUAL	DC COMICS INC.		4	4	1993	NOW	
JUSTICE LEAGUE INTERNATIONAL SPECIAL	DC COMICS INC.		1	2	1990	1991	
JUSTICE LEAGUE OF AMERICA	DC COMICS INC.	1	1	261	1960	1987	
JUSTICE LEAGUE OF AMERICA	DC COMICS INC.	2	1	89	1987	NOW	ISSUE NOS.1-7 JUSTICE LEAGUE, NOS.7-25 JUSTICE LEAGUE INTERNATIONAL, JUSTICE LEAGUE OF AMERICA FROM ISSUE NO.26 ON.
JUSTICE LEAGUE OF AMERICA ANNUAL	DC COMICS INC.	1	1	3	1983	1985	
JUSTICE LEAGUE OF AMERICA ANNUAL	DC COMICS INC.	2	1	7	1987	NOW	
JUSTICE LEAGUE QUARTERLY	DC COMICS INC.		1	13	1992	NOW	
JUSTICE LEAGUE SPECTACULAR	DC COMICS INC.		1	1	1992	1992	
JUSTICE LEAGUE TASK FORCE	DC COMICS INC.		1	9	1993	NOW	
JUSTICE LEAGUE: A NEW BEGINNING	DC COMICS INC.		1	1	1989	1989	
JUSTICE LEAGUE: GOSPEL OF MAXWELL LORD	DC COMICS INC.		1	1	1992	1992	
JUSTICE MACHINE	COMICO		1	29	1987	1989	
JUSTICE MACHINE	INNOVATION		1	7	1989	NOW	
JUSTICE MACHINE	NOBLE COMICS		1	5	1981	1983	
JUSTICE MACHINE ANNUAL	COMICO		1	1	1989	1989	
JUSTICE MACHINE ANNUAL	TEXAS COMICS	1	1	1	1984	1984	
JUSTICE MACHINE FEATURING THE ELEMENTALS	COMICO		1	4	1986	1986	
JUSTICE MACHINE SUMMER SPECTACULAR	INNOVATION		1	1	1989	1989	
JUSTICE MACHINE: THE CHIMERA CONSPIRACY	MILLENIUM		1	3	1992	1993	
JUSTICE SOCIETY OF AMERICA	DC COMICS INC.		1	10	1992	1993	
JUSTICE SOCIETY OF AMERICA	DC COMICS INC.		1	8	1991	1991	
JUSTICE TRAPS THE GUILTY	ARNOLD BOOK CO.	2	1	43	1951	1954	PRIZE REPRINTS
JUSTICE TRAPS THE GUILTY	PRIZE/HEADLINE/FEATURE	2	1	92	1947	1958	
JUSTICE TRAPS THE GUILTY	TOP SELLERS		1	8	60'S	60'S	PRIZE REPRINTS
JUSTICE TRAPS THE GUILTY	UNITED-ANGLO PRODUCTIONS	1	1	1	1949	1949	PRIZE REPRINTS
JUSTY	VIZ		1	9	1988	1989	

K

COMIC TITLE	PUBLISHER	Vol No.	Srt No.	End No.	Str. Year	End Year	COMMENTS
K-9 ANNUAL	WORLD DISTRIBUTORS LTD		1	1	1983	1983	
K.O. KNOCKOUT	CARTOON ART		1	1	1947	1947	
K.O. PUNCH, THE	EC COMICS		1	1	1948	1948	
KA'A'ANGA COMICS	I.W. ENTERPRISES		1	8	1954	1954	REPRINTS
KA'A'ANGA COMICS JUNGLE KING	FICTION HOUSE		1	20	1949	1954	
KA-POW	PHIL CLARKE/STEVE MOORE		1	3	1967	1968	
KA-ZAR	MARVEL ENTERTAINMENT GROUP	1	1	3	1970	1971	
KA-ZAR	MARVEL ENTERTAINMENT GROUP	2	1	20	1974	1977	
KA-ZAR THE SAVAGE	MARVEL ENTERTAINMENT GROUP	3	1	34	1981	1984	
KA-ZAR: GUNS OF THE SAVAGE LAND	MARVEL ENTERTAINMENT GROUP		1	1	1990	1990	
KAANGA	THORPE & PORTER		1	2	1952	???	FICTION HOUSE REPRINTS
KAFKA	RENEGADE PRESS		1	6	1987	1987	
KALGAN THE GOLDEN	HARRIER		1	1	1988	1988	
KAMANDI, THE LAST BOY ON EARTH	DC COMICS INC.		1	59	1972	1978	
KAMANDI: AT EARTH'S END	DC COMICS INC.		1	6	1993	1993	
KAMUI, LEGEND OF	ECLIPSE		1	38	1987	NOW	
KANE	DANCING ELEPHANT		1	2	1993	NOW	
KANG THE MIGHTY	SCION		1	1	1950	1950	
KARATE KID	DC COMICS INC.		1	15	1976	1978	
KASCO KOMICS	KASKO GRAINFEED		1	2	1945	1949	
KAT KARSON	I.W. ENTERPRISES		1	1	???	???	REPRINTS
KATHY	MARVEL ENTERTAINMENT GROUP		1	27	1959	1964	ZENITH PUBLISHING, A DIVISION OF MARVEL COMICS
KATHY	STANDARD COMICS		1	17	1949	1955	
KATO III	NOW		1	1	1993	1993	
KATO OF THE GREEN HORNET	NOW	1	1	4	1991	1992	
KATO OF THE GREEN HORNET	NOW	2	1	2	1992	1992	
KATY AND KEN VISIT SANTA WITH MISTER WISH	S.S. KRESGE CO.		1	1	1948	1948	
KATY KEENE	ARCHIE PUBLICATIONS		1	62	1949	1961	
KATY KEENE 3D	ARCHIE PUBLICATIONS		1	1	1953	1953	
KATY KEENE ANNUAL	ARCHIE PUBLICATIONS		1	6	1954	1959	
KATY KEENE CHARM	ARCHIE PUBLICATIONS		1	1	1958	1958	
KATY KEENE FASHION BOOK MAGAZINE	ARCHIE PUBLICATIONS		1	23	1955	1959	
KATY KEENE GLAMOUR	ARCHIE PUBLICATIONS		1	1	1957	1957	
KATY KEENE PINUP PARADE	ARCHIE PUBLICATIONS		1	15	1955	1961	
KATY KEENE SPECIAL	ARCHIE PUBLICATIONS	2	1	33	1983	1990	
KATY KEENE SPECTACULAR	ARCHIE PUBLICATIONS		1	1	1956	1956	
KATZENJAMMER KIDS	STANDARD COMICS		12	21	1950	1953	
KATZENJAMMER KIDS, THE	HARVEY PUBLICATIONS		22	27	1953	1954	
KATZENJAMMER KIDS, THE	STANDARD COMICS		1	21	1947	1953	
KAYO	HARRY A CHESLER		12	12	1945	1945	FORMERLY BULLSEYE AND JEST
KAZTENJAMMER KIDS, THE	DAVID MCKAY PUBLICATIONS		30	44	1945	1946	
KEEN COMICS	CENTAUR PUBLICATIONS		1	3	1939	1939	

COMIC TITLE	PUBLISHER	Vol No.	Srt No.	End No.	Str. Year	End Year	COMMENTS
KEEN DETECTIVE FUNNIES	CENTAUR PUBLICATIONS	1	8	11	1938	1938	
KEEN DETECTIVE FUNNIES	CENTAUR PUBLICATIONS	2	1	12	1939	1939	FORMERLY DETECTIVE PICTURE STORIES
KEEN DETECTIVE FUNNIES	CENTAUR PUBLICATIONS	3	1	24	1939	1940	
KEEN TEENS	MAGAZINE PRESS		1	6	1945	1947	
KEEPING UP WITH THE JONES ANNUAL	CUPPLES AND LEON CO.		1	2	1920	1921	
KEGOR, MONSTER OF THE DEEP	A PLUS COMICS		1	1	1991	1991	
KEIF LLAMA XENO-TECH	FANTAGRAPHICS		1	6	1986	1988	
KELLY JONES MONOLITH ERUPTION SET	COMICO		1	1	1993	1993	
KELLYS, THE	MARVEL ENTERTAINMENT GROUP		23	25	1950	1950	
KELTIK KOMIX	ABERDEEN PEOPLE'S PRESS		1	2	1979	1982	
KELVIN MACE	VORTEX		1	2	1986	1987	
KEN MAYNARD WESTERN	FAWCETT PUBLICATIONS		1	8	1950	1952	
KEN MAYNARD WESTERN	L. MILLER PUBLISHING COMPANY (UK)	1	1	8	1950	1951	FAWCETT REPRINTS
KEN MAYNARD WESTERN	L. MILLER PUBLISHING COMPANY (UK)	2	1	3	1959	1959	FAWCETT REPRINTS
KEN SHANNON	QUALITY COMICS		1	10	1951	1953	
KEN STUART	PUBLICATIONS ENTERPRISES		1	1	1949	1949	
KENNEDY	MORCRIM		1	2	1977	1977	
KENT BLAKE OF THE SECRET SERVICE	MARVEL ENTERTAINMENT GROUP		1	14	1951	1953	
KERRY DRAKE	ARGO PUBLISHING		1	2	1956	1956	
KERRY DRAKE DETECTIVE CASES	MAGAZINE ENTERPRISES		1	33	1944	1952	
KERRY DRAKE IN THE CASE OF THE SLEEPING CITY	PUBLISHERS SYNDICATE		1	1	1951	1951	
KEWPIES	WILL EISNER	1		1	1949	1949	
KEY COMICS	CONSOLIDATED MAGAZINES		1	5	1944	1946	
KEY COMICS	KEY CLOTHING CO./PETERSON CLOTHING	1951	1956	1951	1956		VARIOUS VERSIONS BY DIFFERENT PUBLISHERS
KEY RING COMICS	DELL PUBLISHING COMPANY		1	5	1941	1941	HOLES IN SPINE FOR BINDER
KICKERS INC.	MARVEL ENTERTAINMENT GROUP		1	12	1986	1987	
KID 'N PLAY	MARVEL ENTERTAINMENT GROUP		1	12	1992	1993	
KID CANNIBAL	ETERNITY		1	4	1991	1992	
KID CARROTS	ST JOHN PUBLISHING		1	1	1953	1953	
KID COLT GIANT SIZE	MARVEL ENTERTAINMENT GROUP		1	3	1975	1975	
KID COLT OUTLAW	L. MILLER PUBLISHING COMPANY (UK)		50	52	1951	1951	ATLAS REPRINTS
KID COLT OUTLAW	MARVEL ENTERTAINMENT GROUP		1	229	1948	1979	
KID COLT OUTLAW	STRATO		1	58	50'S	50'S	
KID COLT WESTERN COMICS	THORPE & PORTER		1	7	1952	1952	ATLAS REPRINTS
KID COMICS	TIMELY COMICS		1	10	1943	1946	
KID COWBOY	ZIFF-DAVIS PUBLISHING COMPANY		1	14	1950	1954	
KID DYNAMITE WESTERN COMIC/KID DYNAMITE	L. MILLER PUBLISHING COMPANY (UK)		1	65	1954	1960	
KID ETERNITY	DC COMICS INC.		1	10	1993	NOW	
KID ETERNITY	DC COMICS INC.		1	3	1991	1991	
KID ETERNITY	QUALITY COMICS		1	18	1946	1949	
KID ETERNITY	T.V. BOARDMAN		1	3	1949	1949	QUALITY REPRINTS
KID FROM DODGE CITY, THE	ATLAS		1	2	1957	1957	
KID FROM TEXAS, THE	ATLAS		1	2	1957	1957	
KID KOKO	I.W. ENTERPRISES		1	2	1958	1958	REPRINTS
KID KOMICS	TIMELY COMICS		1	10	1943	1946	
KID MONTANA	CHARLTON COMICS	2	9	50	1957	1965	FORMERLY DAVY CROCKETT FRONTIER FIGHTER
KID MONTANA	L. MILLER PUBLISHING COMPANY (UK)		50	59	1959	1959	CHARLTON REPRINTS
KID MOVIE KOMICS	TIMELY COMICS		11	11	1946	1946	FORMERLY KID COMICS
KID SLADE GUNFIGHTER	ATLAS		5	8	1957	1957	FORMERLY MATT SLADE GUNFIGHTER
KID SLADE GUNFIGHTER	STRATO		1	7	1957	1957	ATLAS REPRINTS
KID ZOO COMICS	STREET AND SMITH PUBLICATIONS		1	1	1948	1948	
KIDDIE CARNIVAL	ZIFF-DAVIS PUBLISHING COMPANY		1	1	1952	1952	
KIDDIE KAPERS	DECKER PUBLICATIONS		1945	1957	1945	1957	
KIDDIE KAPERS SUPER REPRINTS	DECKER PUBLICATIONS		7	18	1963	1964	
KIDDYFUN	GERALD SWAN		1	12	1945	1951	
KIKU SAN	AIRCEL		1	6	1988	1989	
KILLER	ECLIPSE		1	1	1985	1985	
KILLERS, THE	MAGAZINE ENTERPRISES		1	2	1947	1948	
KILLING STROKE, THE	ETERNITY		1	4	1991	1991	
KILLING TIME	MANDARIN (2000 AD BOOKS)		1	1	1992	1992	
KILLPOWER: THE EARLY YEARS	MARVEL ENTERTAINMENT GROUP		1	4	1993	1993	
KILROYS, THE	AMERICAN COMIC GROUP		1	54	1947	1955	
KIMURA	NIGHT WYND ENTERPRISES		1	4	1991	1992	
KINDRED	IMAGE COMICS		1	2	1994	1994	
KINEMA COMIC, THE	AMALGAMATED PRESS		1	651	1920	1932	
KING ARTHUR AND THE KNIGHTS OF JUSTICE	MARVEL ENTERTAINMENT GROUP		1	3	1993	1993	
KING CLASSICS	KING FEATURES		1	24	1977	1977	
KING COMIC	ENSIGN/W. FORSHAW		1	4	1947	1947	
KING COMIC	L. MILLER PUBLISHING COMPANY (UK)		1	14	1954	1954	
KING COMICS	DAVID MCKAY PUBLICATIONS		1	159	1936	1952	
KING CONAN	MARVEL ENTERTAINMENT GROUP		1	19	1980	1983	
KING KONG	MONSTER COMICS		1	6	1991	1991	
KING KONG	TOP SELLERS		1	1	1970	1970	WESTERN PUBLISHING REPRINTS
KING LEONARDO & HIS SHORT SUBJECTS	DELL PUBLISHING COMPANY		1	4	1962	1964	
KING LOUIE & MOWGLI	GOLD KEY	1		1	1968	1968	
KING OF DIAMONDS	DELL PUBLISHING COMPANY	1391209	1391209	1962	1962		
KING OF THE BAD MEN OF DEADWOOD	AVON BOOKS		1	1	1950	1950	
KING OF THE ROYAL MOUNTED	DELL PUBLISHING COMPANY	8	28	1952	1958		
KING OF THE ROYAL MOUNTED	L. MILLER PUBLISHING COMPANY (UK)		1	15	1962	1963	
KING OF THE ROYAL MOUNTIES	WORLD DISTRIBUTORS LTD		1	21	1953	1953	DELL REPRINTS
KING SOLOMON'S MINES	AVON BOOKS		1	1	1951	1951	
KINGDOM OF THE DWARFS	COMICO		1	1	1991	1991	
KINGDOM OF THE WICKED	ATOMEKA		1	2	1993	1993	
KINGS IN DISGUISE	KITCHEN SINK			1990	1990		
KINGS IN DISGUISE	KITCHEN SINK		1	6	1988	1988	
KINGS OF THE NIGHT	DARK HORSE COMICS		1	2	1990	1990	

COMIC TITLE	PUBLISHER	Vol No.	Srt No.	End No.	Str. Year	End Year	COMMENTS
KISS OF DEATH	ACME PRESS		1	2	1987	1987	
KISSYFUR	DC COMICS INC.		1	1	1989	1989	
KIT CARSON	AVON BOOKS		1	8	1950	1955	FORMERLY ALL TRUE DETECTIVE CASES
KIT CARSON & THE BLACKFEET WARRIORS	REALISTIC PUBLICATIONS		1	1	1953	1953	
KIT CARSON COMICS	THORPE & PORTER		1	1	1952	1952	AVON REPRINTS
KIT CARSON'S COWBOY ANNUAL	AMALGAMATED PRESS		1954	1959	1954	1959	
KIT CARSON'S COWBOY ANNUAL	FLEETWAY		1960	1960	1960	1960	
KIT CARTER	DELL PUBLISHING COMPANY		1	1	1962	1962	
KIT COWBOY	L. MILLER PUBLISHING COMPANY (UK)		1	10	1957	1958	
KIT MORAIN	MARTIN & REID		1	1	1949	1949	
KITE FUN BOOK ANNUAL	PACIFIC, GAS & ELECTRIC/SOU. CALIFORNIA EDISON		1954	1981	1954	1981	
KITTY	ST JOHN PUBLISHING		1	1	1948	1948	
KITTY PRYDE AND WOLVERINE	MARVEL ENTERTAINMENT GROUP		1	6	1984	1985	
KITZ 'N' KATZ KOMICS	ECLIPSE		1	5	1985	1986	
KLING KLANG KLATCH	VICTOR GOLLANCZ		1	1	1992	1992	
KLOWN SHOCK	NORTHSTAR	1	1	4	1990	1991	
KLOWN SHOCK	NORTHSTAR	2	1	2	1991	1991	
KNIGHT RIDER ANNUAL	GRAND DREAMS		1982	1983	1982	1983	
KNIGHTHAWK, THE PROTECTOR	CONTINUITY COMICS		1	1	1994	NOW	
KNIGHTS OF PENDRAGON, THE	MARVEL ENTERTAINMENT GROUP	1	1	18	1990	1991	
KNIGHTS OF PENDRAGON, THE	MARVEL ENTERTAINMENT GROUP	2	1	15	1992	1993	
KNIGHTS OF THE ROUND TABLE	DELL PUBLISHING COMPANY		1	1	1963	1964	
KNIGHTS OF THE ROUND TABLE	PINES		10	10	1957	1957	
KNOCK KNOCK (...WHO'S THERE?)	WHITMAN		801	801	1936	1936	
KNOCKABOUT COMICS	KNOCKABOUT		1	14	1980	1987	
KNOCKABOUT TRIAL SPECIAL	KNOCKABOUT		1	1	1984	1984	
KNOCKOUT	AMALGAMATED PRESS		1	1231	1939	1963	
KNOCKOUT	IPC	2	1	106	1971	1973	
KNOCKOUT ADVENTURES	FICTION HOUSE		1953	1954	1953	1954	
KNOCKOUT ANNUAL	FLEETWAY		1959	1962	1959	1962	
KNOCKOUT FUN BOOK ANNUAL	AMALGAMATED PRESS		1941	1958	1941	1958	
KNOW YOUR MASS	CAETECHETICAL EDUCATIONAL SOCIETY		303	303	1958	1958	
KNUCKLES THE MALEVOLENT NUN	FANTAGRAPHICS		1	2	1991	1991	
KO KOMICS	GERONA PUBLICATIONS		1	1	1945	1945	
KOBRA	DC COMICS INC.		1	7	1976	1977	
KOKEY KOALA	TOBY PRESS PUBLICATIONS		1	1	1952	1952	
KOKO AND KOLA	MAGAZINE ENTERPRISES		1	6	1946	1950	
KOLA KOMMANDOS	FLEETWAY		1	3	1993	1993	
KOMIC FUN	REYNARD PRESS		1	1	1948	1948	
KOMIC KARTOONS	TIMELY COMICS		1	2	1945	1945	
KOMIC KRACKERS	HAMILTON COMICS		1	1	1949	1949	
KOMIC PAGES	HARRY A CHESLER		1	1	1945	1945	FORMERLY SNAP
KONA, MONARCH OF MONSTER ISLE	DELL PUBLISHING COMPANY		2	23	1960	1965	
KONG THE UNTAMED	DC COMICS INC.		1	5	1975	1976	
KONGA'S REVENGE	CHARLTON COMICS		2	3	1963	1964	
KONGA, RETURN TO	CHARLTON COMICS		1	23	1960	1965	
KOOKIE	DELL PUBLISHING COMPANY		1	2	1962	1962	
KOOSH KINS	ARCHIE PUBLICATIONS		1	3	1991	1992	
KORAK SON OF TARZAN	DC COMICS INC.		46	59	1964	1972	
KORAK, SON OF TARZAN	GOLD KEY		1	45	1972	1975	
KORAK, SON OF TARZAN	WILLIAMS PUBLISHING		1	44	1971	1974	DELL REPRINTS
KORAK, SON OF TARZAN BUMPER ALBUM	TOP SELLERS		1	1	1973	1973	DC REPRINTS
KOREA MY HOME	JOHNSON AND CUSHING		1	1	50'S	50'S	1950'S
KORG: 70,000 B.C.	CHARLTON COMICS		1	9	1975	1976	
KORNER KID COMICS	FOUR STAR COMICS CORP/SUPERIOR COMICS LTD		1	1	1947	1947	
KRACKER COMIC	REYNARD PRESS		1	6	1947	1947	
KRAZY	IPC		1	79	1976	1978	
KRAZY HOLIDAY SPECIAL	IPC		1977	1983	1977	1983	
KRAZY KAT	HOLT		1	1	1946	1946	
KRAZY KAT COMICS	DELL PUBLISHING COMPANY		1	5	1951	1952	
KRAZY KOMICS	MARVEL ENTERTAINMENT GROUP	2	1	2	1948	1948	
KRAZY KOMICS	TIMELY COMICS	1	1	26	1942	1947	BECOMES "CINDY" WITH ISSUE NO.27 (FALL 1947)
KRAZY KROW	I.W. ENTERPRISES		1	2	1957	1958	REPRINTS
KRAZY KROW	MARVEL ENTERTAINMENT GROUP		1	3	1945	1946	
KRAZYLIFE	FOX FEATURES SYNDICATE		1	1	1945	1945	
KREY	CALIBER PRESS		1	3	1992	1993	
KREY SPECIAL	CALIBER PRESS		1	1	1993	1993	
KRIM-KO KOMICS	KIM-KO CHOCOLATE		1	6	1935	1935	
KRIM-KO KOMICS: LOLA, SECRET AGENT	KIM-KO CHOCOLATE		1	184	1936	1939	
KRULL	MARVEL ENTERTAINMENT GROUP		1	2	1983	1983	
KRYPTON CHRONICLES	DC COMICS INC.		1	3	1981	1981	
KULL AND THE BARBARIANS	MARVEL ENTERTAINMENT GROUP		1	3	1975	1975	
KULL IN 3-D	BLACKTHORNE		1	1	1988	1988	
KULL THE CONQUEROR	MARVEL ENTERTAINMENT GROUP	1	1	29	1971	1978	
KULL THE CONQUEROR	MARVEL ENTERTAINMENT GROUP	2	1	2	1982	1982	
KULL THE CONQUEROR	MARVEL ENTERTAINMENT GROUP	3	1	10	1983	1983	
KUNG FU	BROWN WATSON		1	1	1974	1974	
KUNG FU FIGHTER, RICHARD DRAGON	DC COMICS INC.		1	18	1975	1977	

L

COMIC TITLE	PUBLISHER	Vol No.	Srt No.	End No.	Str. Year	End Year	COMMENTS
L'IL KIDS	MARVEL ENTERTAINMENT GROUP		1	12	1970	1973	
LABOR IS A PARTNER	CAETECHETICAL EDUCATIONAL SOCIETY		1	1	1949	1949	
LAD: A DOG	DELL PUBLISHING COMPANY		2	2	1962	1962	

INDEX OF COMIC TITLES AND THEIR PUBLISHERS

COMIC TITLE	PUBLISHER	Vol No.	Srt No.	End No.	Str. Year	End Year	COMMENTS
LADY AND THE TRAMP	DELL PUBLISHING COMPANY		1	1	1955	1955	
LADY AND THE TRAMP IN "BUTTER LATE THAN NEVER"	AMERICAN DAIRY ASSOCIATION		1	1	1955	1955	
LADY ARCANE	HEROIC PUBLISHING		1	1	1992	1992	
LADY ARCANE	HEROIC PUBLISHING		1	4	1992	1993	
LADY BOUNTIFUL	SAALFIELD PUBLISHING COMPANY		1	1	1917	1917	
LADY CHATTERLEY'S LOVER!	KNOCKABOUT		1	1	1986	1986	
LADY CRIME	AC COMICS		1	1	1992	NOW	
LADY DEATH	CHAOS COMICS		1	3	1994	1994	
LADY LUCK	KEN PIERCE		1	1	1980	1980	
LADY LUCK	QUALITY COMICS		86	90	1949	1950	FORMERLY SMASH
LADY PENELOPE	CITY		1	204	1966	1968	
LADY PENELOPE ANNUAL	CITY		1966	1969	1966	1969	
LADY PENELOPE SUMMER EXTRA	CITY		1966	1966	1966	1966	
LAFF-A-LYMPICS	MARVEL ENTERTAINMENT GROUP		1	13	1978	1979	
LAFFY-DAFFY COMICS	RURAL HOME PUBLISHING COMPANY		1	2	1945	1945	
LANA	MARVEL ENTERTAINMENT GROUP		1	7	1948	1949	
LANCE BARNES: POST NUKE DICK	MARVEL ENTERTAINMENT GROUP		1	1	1993	1993	
LANCE O'CASEY	ARNOLD BOOK CO.		1	1	1951	1951	FAWCETT REPRINTS
LANCE O'CASEY	FAWCETT PUBLICATIONS		1	4	1946	1948	
LANCELOT LINK, SECRET CHIMP	GOLD KEY		1	8	1971	1973	
LANCER	GOLD KEY		1	3	1969	1969	
LAND OF THE GIANTS	GOLD KEY		1	5	1968	1969	
LAND OF THE GIANTS ANNUAL	WORLD DISTRIBUTORS LTD		1969	1970	1969	1970	
LAND OF THE GIANTS TELEVISION STORYBOOK	PBS		1	1	1969	1969	
LAND OF THE LOST COMICS	EC COMICS		1	9	1946	1948	
LANN	KEN PIERCE				1986	1986	
LARAMIE ANNUAL/LARAMIE	WORLD DISTRIBUTORS LTD		1961	1963	1961	1963	
LAREDO	GOLD KEY		1	1	1966	1966	
LAREDO CROCKETT, RANGER	DONALD PETERS		1	44	1953	1955	US REPRINTS
LARGE COW COMIX	ARTS LAB PRESS		1	5	1972	1973	
LARGE FEATURE COMIC	DELL PUBLISHING COMPANY	1	1	30	1939	1942	FORMERLY BLACK & WHITE
LARGE FEATURE COMICS	DELL PUBLISHING COMPANY	2	1	13	1942	1943	
LARIAT, THE	MARTIN & REID		1	1	1950	1950	
LARKS	AMALGAMATED PRESS		1	656	1927	1940	
LARKS, LIFE WITH THE	MIRROR PRESS PUBLICATIONS		1	1	1978	1978	
LARRY DOBY, BASEBALL HERO	FAWCETT PUBLICATIONS		1	1	1950	1950	
LARRY HARMON'S LAUREL AND HARDY COMICS	DC COMICS INC.		1	1	1972	1972	
LARS OF MARS	ZIFF-DAVIS PUBLISHING COMPANY		10	11	1951	1951	
LARS OF MARS 3-D	ECLIPSE		1	1	1987	1987	
LASER ERASER & PRESS BUTTON	ECLIPSE		1	6	1985	1986	
LASER ERASER & PRESS BUTTON 3-D	ECLIPSE		1	1	1986	1986	
LASH LARUE WESTERN	AC COMICS		1	1	1991	1991	
LASH LARUE WESTERN	CHARLTON COMICS		47	84	1954	1961	CONTINUED FROM FAWCETT SERIES
LASH LARUE WESTERN	FAWCETT PUBLICATIONS		1	46	1949	1954	
LASH LARUE WESTERN	L. MILLER PUBLISHING COMPANY (UK)		50	125	1950	1959	FAWCETT REPRINTS
LASSIE	DELL PUBLISHING COMPANY		37	58	1957	1962	
LASSIE	GOLD KEY		59	70	1962	1969	
LASSIE (M.G.M.'S)	WORLD DISTRIBUTORS LTD		1	18	1952	1954	DELL REPRINTS
LASSIE, THE ADVENTURES OF	RED HEART DOG FOOD		1	1	1949	1949	1ST APPEARANCE IN COMICS
LAST AMERICAN, THE	MARVEL ENTERTAINMENT GROUP		1	4	1990	1991	
LAST DAYS OF THE JUSTICE SOCIETY	DC COMICS INC.		1	1	1986	1986	
LAST KISS	ACME PRESS		1	1	1989	1989	FORMERLY KISS OF DEATH
LAST KISS	ECLIPSE		1	1	1988	1988	
LAST OF THE COMANCHES	AVON BOOKS		1	1	1953	1953	
LAST OF THE SUMMER WINE	DAILY STAR		1	1	1983	1983	
LAST OF THE VIKING HEROES	GENESIS WEST		1	12	1987	NOW	
LAST OF THE VIKING HEROES SUMMER SPECIAL	GENESIS WEST		1	3	1989	1991	
LAST ONE, THE	DC COMICS INC.		1	6	1993	1993	
LAST STARFIGHTER, THE	MARVEL ENTERTAINMENT GROUP		1	3	1984	1984	
LATEST COMICS	SPOTLIGHT COMICS		1	2	1945	1945	
LATHE	SKY COMICS		1	1	1993	1994	
LATIGO KID	AC COMICS	1	1	1	1988	1988	
LAUGH	ARCHIE PUBLICATIONS	1	20	400	1946	1987	FORMERLY BLACK HOOD
LAUGH	ARCHIE PUBLICATIONS	2	1	30	1987	1991	
LAUGH COMICS DIGEST	ARCHIE PUBLICATIONS		1	112	1974	NOW	
LAUGH COMIX	M.L.J. MAGAZINES		46	48	1944	1945	FORMERLY TOP NOTCH LAUGH
LAUGH FUN BOOK	P.M. PRODUCTIONS		1	1	1947	1947	
LAUGH WITH MURRAY BALL	LEADER ENTERPRISES		1	1	1974	1974	
LAUGH-IN MAGAZINE	LAUFER PUBLISHING CO.		1	12	1968	1969	
LAUNCH	ELSEWHERE		1	1	1987	1987	
LAUNDRYLAND	FANTAGRAPHICS		1	4	1990	1992	
LAUREL AND HARDY	BYBLOS		1	13	1981	1982	REPRINTS
LAUREL AND HARDY	DELL PUBLISHING COMPANY		2	4	1962	1963	
LAUREL AND HARDY	ST JOHN PUBLISHING		1	28	1949	1956	
LAUREL AND HARDY (LARRY HARMON'S)	TOP SELLERS		1	120	1979	1984	
LAUREL AND HARDY AUTUMN SPECIAL	BYBLOS		1979	1980	1979	1980	
LAUREL AND HARDY EXTRA	TOP SELLERS		1	4	1969	1970	GOLD KEY REPRINTS
LAUREL AND HARDY SPRING SPECIAL	BYBLOS		1980	1980	1980	1980	
LAUREL AND HARDY SUMMER SPECIAL	BYBLOS		1979	1981	1979	1981	
LAUREL AND HARDY WINTER SPECIAL	BYBLOS		1979	1981	1979	1981	
LAUREL AND HARDY, LARRY HARMON'S	GOLD KEY		1	2	1967	1967	
LAW AGAINST CRIME	ESSENKAY PUBLISHING CO.		1	3	1948	1948	
LAW AND CHAOS	FATHER TREE PRESS (WARP GRAPHICS)				1987	1987	
LAWBREAKERS	CHARLTON COMICS		1	9	1951	1952	
LAWBREAKERS ALWAYS LOSE!	MARVEL ENTERTAINMENT GROUP		1	10	1948	1949	
LAWBREAKERS SUSPENSE STORIES	CHARLTON COMICS		10	15	1953	1953	FORMERLY LAWBREAKERS
LAWDOG	MARVEL ENTERTAINMENT GROUP		1	9	1993	NOW	
LAWDOG VS GRIMROD	MARVEL ENTERTAINMENT GROUP		1	1	1993	1993	
LAWMAN	DELL PUBLISHING COMPANY		3	11	1960	1962	

COMIC TITLE	PUBLISHER	Vol No.	Srt No.	End No.	Str. Year	End Year	COMMENTS
LAZARUS CHURCHYARD	TUNDRA		1	1	1992	1992	
LAZARUS CHURCHYARD	TUNDRA		1	3	1992	1992	
LAZARUS CHURCHYARD COLLECTION	ATOMEKA		1	1	1993	1993	
LAZARUS LAMB IN THE RIDDLE OF THE SPHINCTER	PLUTO PRESS		1	1	1983	1983	
LAZIEST SECRETARY IN THE WORLD, THE	DC COMICS INC.				1990	1990	
LEA: THE CONFESSIONS OF JULIUS ANTOINE	ACME PRESS		1	1	1989	1989	
LEADING COMICS	DC COMICS INC.		1	32	1941	1950	1-14 SUPERHERO & ADVENTURE, 15-33 FUNNY ANIMALS
LEADING SCREEN COMICS	DC COMICS INC.		34	77	1950	1955	ISSUES 1-33 TITLED AS LEADING COMICS
LEAGUE OF CHAMPIONS	HEROIC PUBLISHING		1	11	1990	NOW	
LEATHER AND LACE	AIRCEL		1	13	1989	1991	
LEATHER AND LACE SUMMER SPECIAL	AIRCEL		1	1	1990	1990	
LEAVE IT TO BINKY	DC COMICS INC.		1	71	1948	1970	
LEGACY	MAJESTIC ENTERTAINMENT		1	1	1993	NOW	
LEGEND HORROR CLASSICS	HARPDOWN PUBLISHING		1	12	1975	1976	
LEGEND HORROR CLASSICS COLLECTOR'S EDITION	HARPDOWN PUBLISHING		1	1	1976	1976	
LEGEND OF AQUAMAN, THE	DC COMICS INC.		1	1	1989	1989	
LEGEND OF CUSTER, THE	DELL PUBLISHING COMPANY		1	1	1968	1968	
LEGEND OF JESSE JAMES, THE	GOLD KEY		10172602	10172602	1966	1966	
LEGEND OF THE SHIELD ANNUAL, THE	DC COMICS INC.		1	1	1992	1992	
LEGEND OF THE SHIELD, THE	DC COMICS INC.		1	16	1991	1992	
LEGEND OF WONDER WOMAN, THE	DC COMICS INC.		1	4	1986	1986	
LEGEND OF YOUNG DICK TURPIN, THE	GOLD KEY		1	1	1966	1966	
LEGEND OF ZELDA, THE	VALIANT / VOYAGER COMMUNICATIONS	1	1	4	1990	1990	
LEGEND OF ZELDA, THE	VALIANT / VOYAGER COMMUNICATIONS	2	1	5	1991	1991	
LEGENDS	DC COMICS INC.		1	1	1993	1993	
LEGENDS	DC COMICS INC.		1	6	1986	1987	
LEGENDS OF DANIEL BOONE, THE	DC COMICS INC.		1	8	1955	1957	
LEGENDS OF NASCAR	VORTEX		1	11	1990	NOW	
LEGENDS OF THE STARGRAZERS	INNOVATION		1	5	1989	1990	
LEGENDS OF THE WORLD'S FINEST	DC COMICS INC.		1	2	1994	1994	
LEGION	DC COMICS INC.		1	63	1989	NOW	
LEGION ANNUAL	DC COMICS INC.		1	4	1989	NOW	
LEGION OF MONSTERS	MARVEL ENTERTAINMENT GROUP		1	1	1975	1975	
LEGION OF NIGHT, THE	MARVEL ENTERTAINMENT GROUP		1	2	1991	1991	
LEGION OF STUPID HEROES	BLACKTHORNE		1	1	1987	1987	
LEGION OF SUBSTITUTE HEROES SPECIAL	DC COMICS INC.		1	1	1985	1985	
LEGION OF SUPER-HEROES	DC COMICS INC.		1	4	1973	1973	
LEGION OF SUPER-HEROES	DC COMICS INC.	1	259	313	1980	1984	FORMERLY "SUPERBOY AND THE LEGION OF SUPER-HEROES". BECOMES "TALES OF THE LEGION" WITH ISSUE NO.314
LEGION OF SUPER-HEROES	DC COMICS INC.	2	1	63	1984	1989	
LEGION OF SUPER-HEROES	DC COMICS INC.	3	1	54	1989	NOW	
LEGION OF SUPER-HEROES ANNUAL	DC COMICS INC.	1	1	5	1982	1984	
LEGION OF SUPER-HEROES ANNUAL	DC COMICS INC.	2	1	5	1984	1989	
LEGION OF SUPER-HEROES ANNUAL	DC COMICS INC.	3	1	4	1990	NOW	
LEGION OF SUPER-HEROES ARCHIVES	DC COMICS INC.		1	3	1991	NOW	
LEGION OF SUPER-HEROES: GREAT DARKNESS SAGA	DC COMICS INC.		1	1	1989	1989	
LEGION X-1	GREATER MERCURY COMICS	1	1	2	1989	1989	
LEGION X-1	GREATER MERCURY COMICS	2	1	6	1989	1990	
LEGION X-2	GREATER MERCURY COMICS		1	10	1989	1991	
LEGIONNAIRES	DC COMICS INC.		1	11	1993	NOW	
LEGIONNAIRES 3	DC COMICS INC.		1	4	1986	1986	
LEMONADE KID, THE	AC COMICS		1	1	1990	1990	
LENSMAN	ETERNITY		1	6	1990	1990	
LENSMAN: COLLECTOR'S EDITION	ETERNITY		1	1	1990	1990	
LENSMAN: WAR OF THE GALAXIES	ETERNITY		1	7	1990	1991	
LEO THE LION	I.W. ENTERPRISES		1	1	???	???	REPRINT
LEROY	STANDARD COMICS		1	6	1949	1950	
LESTER GIRLS: THE LIZARD'S TRAIL	ETERNITY		1	3	1991	1991	
LET'S PRETEND	D.S. PUBLISHING CO.		1	3	1950	1950	
LET'S READ THE NEWSPAPER	CHARLTON COMICS		1	1	1974	1974	
LET'S TAKE A TRIP	PINES		1	1	1958	1958	
LETHAL FOES OF SPIDER-MAN	MARVEL ENTERTAINMENT GROUP		1	4	1993	1993	
LETHARGIC COMICS	ALPHA PRODUCTIONS		1	5	1994	NOW	
LEX LUTHOR, THE UNAUTHORISED BIOGRAPHY OF	DC COMICS INC.		1	1	1989	1989	
LI'L ABNER	L. MILLER PUBLISHING COMPANY (UK)		1	1	1945	1945	REPRINTS
LI'L ABNER	TOBY PRESS PUBLICATIONS		1	1	1951	1951	
LI'L ABNER	UNITED FEATURES SYNDICATE		1939	1940	1939	1940	
LI'L ABNER & THE CREATURES FROM DROP-OUTER SPACE	HARVEY PUBLICATIONS		1	1	???	???	
LI'L ABNER BY AL CAPP	HARVEY PUBLICATIONS		1	1	1955	1955	
LI'L ABNER JOINS THE NAVY	TOBY PRESS PUBLICATIONS		1	1	1950	1950	
LI'L ABNER, AL CAPP'S	HARVEY PUBLICATIONS		61	95	1947	1955	
LI'L GENIUS	CHARLTON COMICS		1	55	1954	1986	
LI'L GHOST	FAGO PUBLICATIONS	2	1	3	1958	1959	
LI'L GHOST	ST JOHN PUBLISHING	1	1	1	1958	1958	
LI'L GRUSOME	ECLIPSE		1	1	1990	1990	
LI'L JINX	ARCHIE PUBLICATIONS		11	16	1956	1957	FORMERLY GINGER
LI'L JINX GIANT LAUGH-OUT	ARCHIE PUBLICATIONS		33	43	1971	1973	
LI'L MENACE	FAGO PUBLICATIONS		1	3	1958	1959	
LI'L PALS	MARVEL ENTERTAINMENT GROUP		1	5	1972	1973	
LI'L PAN	FOX FEATURES SYNDICATE		6	8	1947	1947	FORMERLY ROCKET KELLY
LI'L RASCAL TWINS	CHARLTON COMICS		6	18	1957	1960	FORMERLY NATURE BOY
LI'L TOMBOY	CHARLTON COMICS		92	107	1956	1960	FORMERLY FAWCETT'S FUNNY ANIMALS
LI'L WILLIE COMICS	MARVEL ENTERTAINMENT GROUP		20	21	1949	1949	FORMERLY WILLIE COMICS
LIBBY ELLIS	MALIBU COMICS ENTERTAINMENT INC.		1	4	1987	1988	
LIBERATOR	MALIBU COMICS ENTERTAINMENT INC.		1	6	1987	1988	
LIBERTY COMICS	GREEN PUBLISHING COMPANY		4	15	1945	1946	
LIBERTY GUARDS	CHICAGO TRIBUNE AND OTHER NEWSPAPERS		1	1	1946	1946	

COMIC TITLE	PUBLISHER	Vol No.	Srt No.	End No.	Str. Year	End Year	COMMENTS
LIBERTY PROJECT	ECLIPSE		1	8	1987	1988	
LIBERTY SCOUTS	CENTAUR PUBLICATIONS		2	3	1941	1941	
LIBRA	ETERNITY		1	1	1987	1987	
LIDSVILLE	GOLD KEY		1	5	1972	1973	
LIEUTENANT BLUEBERRY	MARVEL ENTERTAINMENT GROUP		1	3	1991	1991	
LIEUTENANT BLUEBERRY	METHUEN & CO LTD		1	4	1977	1978	
LIEUTENANT, THE	DELL PUBLISHING COMPANY		1	1	1964	1964	
LIFE AND TIMES OF THE SCHMOO	CONVOY		1	1	1949	1949	REPRINTS
LIFE IS ONE BIG BED OF NAILS	PAPAS		1	1	1968	1968	
LIFE OF CAPTAIN MARVEL, THE	MARVEL ENTERTAINMENT GROUP		1	1	1990	1990	
LIFE OF CAPTAIN MARVEL, THE	MARVEL ENTERTAINMENT GROUP		1	5	1985	1985	
LIFE OF CHRIST	DARTON LONGMAN & TODD		1	1	1977	1977	
LIFE OF CHRIST VISUALISED	STANDARD PUBLICATIONS		1	1	1946	1946	
LIFE OF CHRIST VISUALISED	STANDARD PUBLICATIONS			3	1942	1943	
LIFE OF CHRIST, THE	CAETECHETICAL EDUCATIONAL SOCIETY		301	301	1949	1949	
LIFE OF CHRIST, THE	MARVEL ENTERTAINMENT GROUP		1	1	1992	1992	
LIFE OF ESTHER VISUALISED	STANDARD PUBLICATIONS		2062	2062	1947	1947	
LIFE OF GROO	MARVEL ENTERTAINMENT GROUP		1	1	1993	1993	
LIFE OF JOSEPH VISUALISED	STANDARD PUBLICATIONS		1054	1054	1946	1946	
LIFE OF POPE JOHN PAUL II, THE	MARVEL ENTERTAINMENT GROUP		1	1	1983	1983	
LIFE OF THE BLESSED VIRGIN	CAETECHETICAL EDUCATIONAL SOCIETY		1	1	1950	1950	
LIFE STORY	FAWCETT PUBLICATIONS		1	47	1949	1953	
LIFE STORY	L. MILLER PUBLISHING COMPANY (UK)		1	24	1959	1959	FAWCETT REPRINTS
LIFE WITH ARCHIE	ARCHIE PUBLICATIONS		1	286	1958	1991	
LIFE WITH MILLIE	MARVEL ENTERTAINMENT GROUP		8	20	1960	1962	FORMERLY A DATE WITH MILLIE
LIFE WITH SNARKY PARKER	FOX FEATURES SYNDICATE		1	1	1950	1950	
LIFE'S LIKE THAT	CROYDON PUBLISHERS		1	1	1945	1945	
LIFE'S LITTLE JOKES	M.S. PUBLISHING		1	1	1924	1924	
LIGHT AND DARKNESS WAR, THE	MARVEL ENTERTAINMENT GROUP		1	6	1988	1989	
LIGHT FANTASTIC, TERRY PRATCHETT'S	CORGI		1	1	1993	1993	
LIGHT FANTASTIC, THE	CORGI		1	1	1993	1993	
LIGHT FANTASTIC, THE	INNOVATION		1	4	1992	1992	
LIGHTNING COMICS	ACE PUBLISHING		4	13	1940	1942	FORMERLY SURE-FIRE
LIGHTNING COMICS, THE	KANGEROO		1	1	1946	1946	
LILLIPUT	HULTON PRESS LTD		206	210	40'S	50'S	MAGAZINE FROM THE 40'S AND 50'S
LILY OF THE ALLEY IN THE FUNNIES	WHITMAN		936	936	20'S	20'S	1920'S
LIMITED COLLECTOR'S EDITION	DC COMICS INC.		21	59	1973	1978	
LINDA	AJAX		1	4	1954	1954	
LINDA CARTER, STUDENT NURSE	ATLAS		1	9	1961	1963	
LINDA LARK	DELL PUBLISHING COMPANY		1	8	1961	1963	
LINUS	MILANO LIBRARY		1	1	1970	1970	
LINUS, THE LIONHEARTED	GOLD KEY		1	1	1965	1965	
LION	IPC		1	1136	1952	1974	
LION ANNUAL	FLEETWAY		1954	1983	1954	1983	
LION BOOK OF GREAT CONQUERORS	FLEETWAY		1	1	1970	1970	
LION BOOK OF HOW IT WORKS	FLEETWAY		1	1	1968	1968	
LION BOOK OF MOTOR RACING	FLEETWAY		1	1	1970	1970	
LION BOOK OF SPEED	FLEETWAY		1	1	1963	1963	
LION BOOK OF WAR ADVENTURES	FLEETWAY		1	1	1962	1962	
LION HOLIDAY SPECIAL	IPC		1974	1980	1974	1980	
LION PICTURE LIBRARY	FLEETWAY		1	136	1963	1969	
LION SUMMER SPECIAL	FLEETWAY		1968	1980	1968	1980	
LION SUMMER SPECTACULAR: EPIC	FLEETWAY		1	1	1967	1967	
LIPPY THE LION AND HARDY HAR HAR	GOLD KEY		1	1	1963	1963	
LITA FORD	ROCK-IT COMIX		1	1	1993	1993	
LITTLE AL OF THE F.B.I.	ZIFF-DAVIS PUBLISHING COMPANY		10	11	1950	1951	
LITTLE AL OF THE SECRET SERVICE	ZIFF-DAVIS PUBLISHING COMPANY		1	3	1951	1951	
LITTLE ALONZO	MACY'S DEPARTMENT STORE		1	1	1938	1938	
LITTLE AMBROSE	ARCHIE PUBLICATIONS		1	1	1958	1958	
LITTLE ANGEL	PINES		5	16	1954	1959	
LITTLE ANNIE ROONEY	DAVID MCKAY PUBLICATIONS		1	1	1935	1935	
LITTLE ANNIE ROONEY	DAVID MCKAY PUBLICATIONS		1	1	1938	1938	
LITTLE ANNIE ROONEY	ST JOHN PUBLISHING		1	3	1948	1948	
LITTLE ARCHIE	ARCHIE PUBLICATIONS		1	1	1991	1991	
LITTLE ARCHIE	ARCHIE PUBLICATIONS	1	1	180	1956	1983	
LITTLE ARCHIE	ARCHIE PUBLICATIONS	2	1	1	1991	1991	
LITTLE ARCHIE COMICS DIGEST ANNUAL	ARCHIE PUBLICATIONS	1	1	48	1977	1991	
LITTLE ARCHIE DIGEST MAGAZINE	ARCHIE PUBLICATIONS	1	1	48	1977	1991	
LITTLE ARCHIE DIGEST MAGAZINE	ARCHIE PUBLICATIONS	2	1	9	1991	NOW	
LITTLE ARCHIE IN ANIMAL LAND	ARCHIE PUBLICATIONS		1	19	1957	1958	
LITTLE ARCHIE MYSTERY	ARCHIE PUBLICATIONS		1	2	1963	1963	
LITTLE ARCHIE MYSTERY COMICS	ARCHIE PUBLICATIONS		1	2	1963	1963	
LITTLE ASPIRIN	MARVEL ENTERTAINMENT GROUP		1	3	1949	1949	
LITTLE ASPIRIN	UNITED-ANGLO PRODUCTIONS		1	1	1950	1950	ATLAS REPRINTS
LITTLE AUDREY	HARVEY PUBLICATIONS	2	25	53	1952	1957	
LITTLE AUDREY	HARVEY PUBLICATIONS	3	1	7	1992	NOW	
LITTLE AUDREY	ST JOHN PUBLISHING		1	24	1948	1952	
LITTLE AUDREY	ST JOHN PUBLISHING	1	1	24	1948	1952	
LITTLE AUDREY AND MELVIN	HARVEY PUBLICATIONS		1	61	1962	1973	
LITTLE AUDREY TV FUNTIME	HARVEY PUBLICATIONS		1	33	1962	1971	
LITTLE AUDREY YEARBOOK	ST JOHN PUBLISHING		1	1	1950	1950	
LITTLE BIT	ST JOHN PUBLISHING		1	2	1949	1949	
LITTLE DOT	HARVEY PUBLICATIONS	1	1	164	1953	1976	
LITTLE DOT	HARVEY PUBLICATIONS	2	1	6	1992	NOW	
LITTLE DOT DOTLAND	HARVEY PUBLICATIONS		1	61	1962	1973	
LITTLE DOT UNCLE & AUNTS	HARVEY PUBLICATIONS		1	52	1961	1974	
LITTLE DRACULA	HARVEY PUBLICATIONS		1	3	1992	1992	
LITTLE EGO	CATALAN COMMUNICATIONS				1989	1989	
LITTLE EVA	I.W. ENTERPRISES		1	18	1963	1964	REPRINTS
LITTLE EVA	ST JOHN PUBLISHING		1	31	1952	1956	

COMIC TITLE	PUBLISHER	Vol No.	Srt No.	End No.	Str. Year	End Year	COMMENTS
LITTLE EVA 3-D	ST JOHN PUBLISHING		1	2	1953	1953	
LITTLE FIR TREE, THE	W.T. GRANT COMPANY		1	1	1942	1942	
LITTLE GIANT DETECTIVE FUNNIES	CENTAUR PUBLICATIONS		1	4	1938	1939	
LITTLE GIANT MOVIE FUNNIES	CENTAUR PUBLICATIONS		1	2	1938	1938	
LITTLE IKE	ST JOHN PUBLISHING		1	4	1953	1953	
LITTLE IODINE	DELL PUBLISHING COMPANY		1	56	1950	1962	
LITTLE JACK FROST	AVON BOOKS		1	1	1951	1951	
LITTLE JOE	ST JOHN PUBLISHING		1	1	1953	1953	
LITTLE JOHNNY AND THE TEDDY BEARS	REILLY AND BRITTON CO.		1	1	1907	1907	
LITTLE KLINKER	MONTGOMERY WARD		1	1	1960	1960	
LITTLE LANA	MARVEL ENTERTAINMENT GROUP		8	9	1949	1950	FORMERLY LANA
LITTLE LENNY	MARVEL ENTERTAINMENT GROUP		1	3	1949	1949	
LITTLE LENNY	UNITED-ANGLO PRODUCTIONS		1	1	1950	1950	ATLAS REPRINTS
LITTLE LIZZIE	ATLAS	2	1	3	1953	1954	
LITTLE LIZZIE	MARVEL ENTERTAINMENT GROUP	1	1	5	1949	1950	
LITTLE LOTTA	HARVEY PUBLICATIONS	1	1	121	1955	1976	
LITTLE LOTTA	HARVEY PUBLICATIONS	2	1	4	1992	NOW	
LITTLE LOTTA FOODLAND	HARVEY PUBLICATIONS		1	29	1963	1972	
LITTLE LULU	GOLD KEY		165	257	1972	1984	FORMERLY MARGE'S LITTLE LULU
LITTLE LULU	WHITMAN		258	268	1983	1984	
LITTLE LULU	WORLD DISTRIBUTORS LTD		1	3	1955	1955	DELL REPRINTS
LITTLE MARVEL COMIC	R. & L. LOCKER		1	1	1946	1946	
LITTLE MAX COMICS	HARVEY PUBLICATIONS		1	73	1949	1961	
LITTLE MAX COMICS	UNITED-ANGLO PRODUCTIONS		1	4	1953	1953	HARVEY REPRINTS
LITTLE MERMAID MOVIE ADAPTATION	WALT DISNEY		1	1	1990	1990	
LITTLE MERMAID, THE	WALT DISNEY		1	4	1992	1992	
LITTLE MERMAID: UNDER THE SEA	WALT DISNEY		1	1	1992	1992	
LITTLE MISS MUFFET	KING FEATURES		11	13	1948	1949	
LITTLE MISS SUNBEAM ADVENTURES IN SPACE	MAGAZINE ENTERPRISES		1	1	1955	1955	
LITTLE MISS SUNBEAM BREAD GIVEAWAYS	QUALITY BAKERS OF AMERICA		1	4	1949	1950	
LITTLE MISS SUNBEAM BREAD GIVEAWAYS	QUALITY BAKERS OF AMERICA	2	1	2	1957	1961	
LITTLE MISS SUNBEAM COMICS	MAGAZINE ENTERPRISES		1	4	1950	1951	
LITTLE MONSTERS, THE	GOLD KEY		1	44	1964	1978	
LITTLE NEMO IN SLUMBERLAND	CUPPLES AND LEON CO.		1909	1909	1909	1909	
LITTLE NEMO IN SLUMBERLAND	DOFFIELD AND CO.		1906	1906	1906	1906	
LITTLE NEMO IN SLUMBERLAND	MCKAY FEATURES		1905	1911	1905	1911	
LITTLE NEMO IN SLUMBERLAND	NOSTALGIA PRESS		1969	1970	1969	1970	
LITTLE NEMO IN SLUMBERLAND IN 3-D	BLACKTHORNE		1	1	1987	1987	
LITTLE ORPHAN	DELL PUBLISHING COMPANY		1	3	1948	1948	
LITTLE ORPHAN ANNIE	CUPPLES AND LEON CO.		1	9	1926	1934	
LITTLE ORPHAN ANNIE JUNIOR COMMANDOS GIVEAWAY	DELL PUBLISHING COMPANY		1	1	1947	1947	
LITTLE ORPHAN ANNIE POPPED WHEAT GIVEAWAY	DELL PUBLISHING COMPANY		1	1	1947	1947	
LITTLE ORPHAN ANNIE QUAKER SPARKIES GIVEAWAY	DELL PUBLISHING COMPANY		1	3	1940	1942	
LITTLE ROQUEFORT COMICS	ST JOHN PUBLISHING		1	10	1952	1958	
LITTLE SAD SACK	HARVEY PUBLICATIONS		1	19	1964	1967	
LITTLE SAMMY SNEEZE	N.Y. HERALD		1	1	1905	1905	
LITTLE SCOUTS	DELL PUBLISHING COMPANY		2	6	1951	1952	
LITTLE SHERIFF WESTERN COMIC	DONALD PETERS		1	96	1951	1958	
LITTLE SHOP OF HORRORS	DC COMICS INC.		1	1	1987	1987	
LITTLE SPARKS	AMALGAMATED PRESS	1	328	331	1920	1920	FORMERLY SPARKS
LITTLE SPARKS	AMALGAMATED PRESS	2	1	124	1920	1922	
LITTLE SPUNKY	I.W. ENTERPRISES		1	1	60'S	60'S	REPRINT; NO DATE
LITTLE STOOGES, THE	GOLD KEY		1	7	1972	1974	
LITTLE TREE THAT WASN'T WANTED, THE	W.T. GRANT COMPANY		1	1	1960	1960	
LITTLE WONDER COMIC	R. & L. LOCKER		1	1	1946	1946	
LIVING BIBLE, THE	LIVING BIBLE CO.		1	3	1945	1946	
LIVINGSTONE MOUNTAIN	ADVENTURE COMICS		1	4	1991	1991	
LIZARD LADY	AIRCEL		1	4	1991	1991	
LLOYD LLEWELLYN	FANTAGRAPHICS		1	6	1986	1988	
LLOYD LLEWELLYN SPECIAL	FANTAGRAPHICS		1	1	1988	1988	
LLOYD LLEWELYN	FANTAGRAPHICS				1990	1990	
LOAD O' FUN	HOLLAND PRESS		1	1	1947	1947	
LOAD RUNNER	EEC PUBLICATIONS		1	13	1983	1983	
LOBO	DC COMICS INC.		1	2	1993	NOW	
LOBO	DC COMICS INC.		1	4	1990	1991	
LOBO	DELL PUBLISHING COMPANY		1	2	1965	1966	
LOBO ANNUAL	DC COMICS INC.		1	1	1993	NOW	
LOBO CONVENTION SPECIAL	DC COMICS INC.		1	1	1993	1993	
LOBO PARAMILITARY CHRISTMAS SPECIAL	DC COMICS INC.		1	1	1991	1991	
LOBO'S BACK	DC COMICS INC.		1	1	1993	1993	
LOBO'S BACK	DC COMICS INC.		1	4	1992	1992	
LOBO'S GREATEST HITS	DC COMICS INC.		1	1	1992	1992	
LOBO: A CONTRACT ON GAWD	DC COMICS INC.		1	4	1994	1994	
LOBO: BLAZING CHAINS OF LOVE	DC COMICS INC.		1	1	1992	1992	
LOBO: INFANTICIDE	DC COMICS INC.		1	4	1992	1993	
LOBO: PORTRAIT OF A VICTIM	DC COMICS INC.		1	1	1993	1993	
LOBO: THE LAST CZARNIAN	DC COMICS INC.		1	1	1992	1992	
LOBO: UNAMERICAN GLADIATORS	DC COMICS INC.		1	4	1993	1993	
LOBOCOP	DC COMICS INC.		1	1	1993	1993	
LOC	NEW MEDIA PUBLISHING INC		1	6	1982	1983	
LOCO	SATIRE PUBLICATIONS		1	3	1958	1959	
LOCO VS PULVERINE	ECLIPSE		1	1	1992	1992	
LOGAN'S RUN	ADVENTURE COMICS		1	6	1990	1991	
LOGAN'S RUN	MARVEL ENTERTAINMENT GROUP		1	7	1977	1977	
LOGAN'S RUN ANNUAL	BROWN WATSON		1978	1978	1978	1978	
LOGAN'S WORLD	ADVENTURE COMICS		1	6	1991	1991	
LOIS LANE	DC COMICS INC.		1	2	1986	1986	
LOIS LANE - SEE ALSO SUPERMAN'S GIRL FRIEND							
LOLLIPOPS COMIC	PHILIMAR		1	3	1949	1949	

COMIC TITLE	PUBLISHER	Vol No.	Srt No.	End No.	Str. Year	End Year	COMMENTS
LONDON EXPLORER	ASSOCIATED NEWSPAPERS		1	1	1952	1952	
LONDON IS STRANGER THAN FICTION	ASSOCIATED NEWSPAPERS		1	1	1951	1951	
LONDON'S DARK	TITAN BOOKS		1	1	1989	1989	
LONE EAGLE	AJAX		1	4	1954	1954	
LONE EAGLE	L. MILLER PUBLISHING COMPANY (UK)		1	1	1956	1956	FARRELL REPRINTS
LONE GROOVER EXPRESS	BENYON/EEL PIE		1	1	1976	1976	
LONE GROOVER'S LITTLE READ BOOK	BENYON/EEL PIE		1	1	1981	1981	
LONE RANGER	METHUEN & CO LTD		1	2	1977	1977	DELL REPRINTS
LONE RANGER	TOP SELLERS		1	2	1970	???	DELL REPRINTS
LONE RANGER	WORLD DISTRIBUTORS LTD		1	66	1953	1958	DELL REPRINTS
LONE RANGER ADVENTURE STORIES	ADPRINT	1957	1960	1957	1960		
LONE RANGER ALBUM, THE	WORLD DISTRIBUTORS LTD		1	1	1957	1957	
LONE RANGER CHEERIOS GIVEAWAYS, THE	DELL PUBLISHING COMPANY		1	1	1954	1954	
LONE RANGER COMIC ALBUM, THE	WORLD DISTRIBUTORS LTD		1	5	1950	1954	
LONE RANGER COMICS, THE	LONE RANGER, INC.		1	1	1939	1939	
LONE RANGER DOLL GIVEAWAYS, THE	DELL PUBLISHING COMPANY		1	1	1973	1973	
LONE RANGER FEATURE BOOK, THE	DELL PUBLISHING COMPANY		21	24	1940	1941	
LONE RANGER WESTERN TREASURY	DELL PUBLISHING COMPANY		3	3	1955	1955	FORMERLY LONE RANGER WESTERN TREASURY
LONE RANGER IN "MILK FOR BIG MIKE", THE	DELL PUBLISHING COMPANY		1	1	1955	1955	
LONE RANGER LARGE FEATURE COMIC, THE	DELL PUBLISHING COMPANY		3	7	1939	1939	
LONE RANGER MERITA BREAD GIVEAWAY, THE	DELL PUBLISHING COMPANY		1	1	1954	1954	
LONE RANGER MOVIE STORY	DELL PUBLISHING COMPANY				1956	1956	
LONE RANGER TELEVISION STORY BOOK, THE	PBS		1963	1967	1963	1967	
LONE RANGER WESTERN TREASURY	DELL PUBLISHING COMPANY		1	2	1953	1954	BECOMES LONE RANGER GOLDEN WESTERN TREASURY
LONE RANGER'S COMPANION TONTO, THE	DELL PUBLISHING COMPANY		2	33	1951	1959	
LONE RANGER'S FAMOUS HORSE HI-YO SILVER, THE	DELL PUBLISHING COMPANY		3	36	1952	1960	
LONE RANGER, THE	BROWN WATSON		1	1	1975	1975	
LONE RANGER, THE	DELL PUBLISHING COMPANY		1	145	1948	1962	
LONE RANGER, THE	GOLD KEY		1	28	1964	1977	
LONE RANGER, THE	WORLD DISTRIBUTORS LTD		1964	1969	1964	1969	
LONE RANGER: HOW THE LONE RANGER CAPTURED SILVER	DELL PUBLISHING COMPANY		1	1	1936	1936	
LONE RIDER	PEMBERTON		1	3	1951	1951	FARRELL REPRINTS
LONE RIDER	SUPERIOR COMICS		1	26	1951	1955	
LONE RIDER PICTURE LIBRARY	FLEETWAY		1	16	1961	1962	
LONE RIDER, THE	FARREL PUBLICATIONS		1	26	1951	1955	
LONE STAR MAGAZINE	ATLAS UK	3	1	99	1952	1953	
LONE WOLF AND CUB	FIRST		1	49	1987	NOW	
LONELY HEART	AJAX	9	14	1955	1956	FORMERLY DEAR LONELY HEARTS	
LONER	FLEETWAY		1	7	1990	1991	
LONG BOW	ATLAS UK		1	31	1960	1964	FICTION HOUSE REPRINTS
LONG BOW, INDIAN BOY	FICTION HOUSE		1	9	1951	1953	
LONG JOHN SILVER	L. MILLER PUBLISHING COMPANY (UK)		1	2	1956	1956	CHARLTON REPRINTS
LONG JOHN SILVER AND THE PIRATES	CHARLTON COMICS		30	32	1956	1957	FORMERLY TERRY AND THE PIRATES
LONGSHOT	MARVEL ENTERTAINMENT GROUP		1	1	1989	1989	
LONGSHOT	MARVEL ENTERTAINMENT GROUP		1	6	1985	1986	
LOOK ALIVE	IPC		1	5	1982	1982	
LOOK AND LAUGH	PHILIMAR		1	2	1949	1949	
LOOK AND LEARN	FLEETWAY		1	1049	1962	1982	
LOOK AND LEARN HOLIDAY SPECIAL	IPC		1	1	1976	1976	
LOOK-IN DANGER MOUSE SPECIAL	INDEPENDENT TELEVISION		1	1	1982	1982	
LOOK-IN FOLLYFOOT SPECIAL	INDEPENDENT TELEVISION		1	1	1973	1973	
LOOK-IN MADABOUT SPECIAL	INDEPENDENT TELEVISION		1	1	1984	1984	
LOOK-IN SUMMER SPECIAL	INDEPENDENT TELEVISION		1	1	1974	1974	
LOONEY SPORTS	3-STRIKES PUBLISHING CO.		1	1	1975	1975	
LOONEY TUNES	DC COMICS INC.		1	3	1994	NOW	
LOONEY TUNES	GOLD KEY		1	37	1975	1983	
LOONEY TUNES	WHITMAN		38	47	1983	1984	
LOONEY TUNES	WORLD DISTRIBUTORS LTD		1	1	1953	1953	DELL REPRINTS
LOONEY TUNES AND MERRIE MELODIES COMICS	DELL PUBLISHING COMPANY		1	246	1941	1962	
LOONEY TUNES MAGAZINE	DC COMICS INC.		1	7	1990	1990	
LOOSE CANNONS	MARVEL ENTERTAINMENT GROUP		1	4	1994	1994	MARVEL UK TITLE
LORD HORROR	SAVOY ADULT GRAPHICS		1	6	1989	1991	
LORDS OF MISRULE	ATOMEKA		1	1	1993	1993	
LORDS OF THE ULTRA REALM	DC COMICS INC.		1	6	1986	1986	
LORDS OF THE ULTRA REALM SPECIAL	DC COMICS INC.		1	1	1987	1987	
LORNA THE JUNGLE GIRL	ATLAS		1	26	1953	1957	
LORNA THE JUNGLE GIRL	L. MILLER PUBLISHING COMPANY (UK)		1	9	1952	1952	ATLAS REPRINTS
LOSERS SPECIAL	DC COMICS INC.		1	1	1985	1985	
LOST CONTINENT, THE	ECLIPSE		1	6	1990	1991	
LOST FRANKENSTEIN PAGES	APPLE COMICS		1	1	1993	1993	
LOST IN SPACE	GOLD KEY		37	59	1973	1982	FORMERLY SPACE FAMILY ROBINSON
LOST IN SPACE	INNOVATION		1	11	1991	1993	
LOST IN SPACE ANNUAL	INNOVATION		1	2	1991	1992	
LOST IN SPACE SPECIAL EDITION	INNOVATION		1	2	1992	1993	
LOST IN SPACE: PROJECT ROBINSON	INNOVATION		1	1	1993	1993	
LOST IN SPACE: STRANGERS	INNOVATION		1	1	1993	1993	
LOST IN SPACE: VOYAGE TO THE BOTTOM OF THE SOUL	INNOVATION		1	6	1993	1994	
LOST PLANET	ECLIPSE		1	6	1987	1989	
LOST WORLD COMICS	CARTOON ART		1	1	1950	1950	FICTION HOUSE REPRINTS
LOST WORLDS	STANDARD COMICS		5	6	1952	1952	
LOT O' FUN	AMALGAMATED PRESS		1	1196	1906	1929	
LOT 'O' FUN COMICS	ROBERT ALLEN		1	1	1940	1940	
LOVE ADVENTURES	MARVEL ENTERTAINMENT GROUP		1	12	1949	1952	
LOVE AFFAIR	L. MILLER PUBLISHING COMPANY (UK)		1	3	50'S	50'S	FAWCETT REPRINTS
LOVE AND MARRIAGE	I.W. ENTERPRISES	2	1	17	1963	1964	REPRINTS
LOVE AND MARRIAGE	SUPERIOR COMICS	1	1	16	1952	1954	

COMIC TITLE	PUBLISHER	Vol No.	Srt No.	End No.	Str. Year	End Year	COMMENTS
LOVE AND ROCKETS	FANTAGRAPHICS		1	43	1982	NOW	
LOVE AND ROMANCE	CHARLTON COMICS		1	24	1971	1975	
LOVE AT FIRST SIGHT	ACE MAGAZINES		1	42	1949	1956	
LOVE CLASSICS	MARVEL ENTERTAINMENT GROUP		1	2	1949	1950	
LOVE CONFESSIONS	QUALITY COMICS		1	54	1949	1956	
LOVE DIARY	CHARLTON COMICS		1	102	1958	1976	
LOVE DIARY	OUR PUBLISHING/TOYTOWN/PATCHES		1	48	1949	1955	
LOVE DIARY	QUALITY COMICS		1	1	1949	1949	
LOVE DRAMAS	MARVEL ENTERTAINMENT GROUP		1	2	1949	1950	
LOVE EXPERIENCES	ACE PERIODICALS		1	38	1949	1956	
LOVE JOURNAL	OUR PUBLISHING/TOYTOWN/PATCHES		10	25	1951	1954	
LOVE LESSONS	HARVEY PUBLICATIONS		1	5	1949	1950	
LOVE LETTERS	QUALITY COMICS		1	51	1949	1956	
LOVE LIFE	PL PUBLISHING		1	1	1951	1951	
LOVE MACHINE	CATALAN COMMUNCATIONS				1991	1991	
LOVE MEMORIES	FAWCETT PUBLICATIONS		1	4	1949	1950	
LOVE MYSTERY	FAWCETT PUBLICATIONS		1	3	1950	1950	
LOVE PROBLEMS AND ADVICE ILLUSTRATED	HARVEY PUBLICATIONS		1	44	1949	1957	
LOVE ROMANCE	AMALGAMATED PRESS		1	2	1950	1950	
LOVE ROMANCES	TIMELY COMICS		6	106	1949	1963	FORMERLY IDEAL LOVE ROMANCES
LOVE SCANDALS	QUALITY COMICS		1	5	1950	1950	
LOVE SECRETS	MARVEL ENTERTAINMENT GROUP		1	2	1949	1950	
LOVE SECRETS	QUALITY COMICS		32	56	1953	1956	FORMERLY LOVE LETTERS
LOVE STORIES	DC COMICS INC.		147	152	1972	1973	FORMERLY HEART THROBS
LOVE STORIES	FOX FEATURES SYNDICATE		6	12	1950	1951	FORMERLY MY LOVE AFFAIR
LOVE STORIES OF MARY WORTH	HARVEY PUBLICATIONS		1	5	1949	1950	
LOVE STORY OF CHARLES AND DIANA	IPC		1	1	1982	1982	
LOVE STORY PICTURE LIBRARY	IPC		1	2	1952	???	
LOVE STORY PICTURE LIBRARY HOLIDAY SPECIAL	IPC		1	1	1972	1972	
LOVE TALES	MARVEL ENTERTAINMENT GROUP		36	75	1949	1957	FORMERLY THE HUMAN TORCH
LOVE TRAILS	MARVEL ENTERTAINMENT GROUP		1	2	1949	1950	
LOVECRAFT	ADVENTURE COMICS		1	4	1991	1992	
LOVELAND	MARVEL ENTERTAINMENT GROUP		1	2	1949	1950	
LOVELORN	AMERICAN COMIC GROUP		1	51	1949	1954	
LOVERS	L. MILLER PUBLISHING COMPANY (UK)		1	12	1956	1956	MARVEL REPRINTS
LOVERS	MARVEL ENTERTAINMENT GROUP		23	86	1949	1957	FORMERLY BLONDE PHANTOM
LOVERS' LANE	LEV GLEASON PUBLICATIONS		1	41	1949	1954	
LOWLIFE	CALIBER PRESS		1	3	1991	NOW	
LUCIFER	HARRIER		1	4	1990	1990	
LUCIFER	TRIDENT		1	3	1990	1990	
LUCIFER'S HAMMER	INNOVATION		1	2	1993	NOW	
LUCK IN THE HEAD	DARK HORSE COMICS		1	1	1993	1993	
LUCKY '7' COMICS	HOWARD PUBLISHERS		1	1	1944	1944	
LUCKY CHARM	D.C. THOMSON		1	20	1979	1984	
LUCKY COMIC, THE	MARTIN & REID		1	1	1948	1948	
LUCKY COMICS	CONSOLIDATED MAGAZINES		1	5	1944	1946	
LUCKY DICE COMIC	FUNNIBOOK CO.		1	1	1946	1946	
LUCKY DIP	CHILDREN'S PRESS		1	1	1948	1948	
LUCKY DIP COMIC	PHILIMAR		1	1	1948	1948	
LUCKY DUCK	STANDARD COMICS		5	8	1953	1953	
LUCKY FIGHTS IT THROUGH	EC COMICS		1	1	1949	1949	V.D. PREVENTION BY HARVEY KURTZMAN
LUCKY LUKE: JESSE JAMES	BROCKHAMPTON PRESS		1	1	1970	1970	EUROPEAN REPRINTS
LUCKY STAR	NATIONWIDE PUBLISHERS		1	14	1950	1955	
LUCKY STAR GIVEAWAY	NATIONWIDE PUBLISHERS		1	1	1955	1955	
LUCY SHOW, THE	ST JOHN PUBLISHING		1	4	1963	1964	
LUCY, THE REAL GONE GAL	ST JOHN PUBLISHING		1	4	1953	1953	
LUDWIG VON DRAKE	DELL PUBLISHING COMPANY		1	4	1961	1962	
LUDWIG VON DRAKE: FISH STAMPEDE	DELL PUBLISHING COMPANY		1	1	1962	1962	
LUGER	ECLIPSE		1	3	1986	1987	
LUKE CAGE, POWER MAN	MARVEL ENTERTAINMENT GROUP		17	47	1974	1977	FORMERLY HERO FOR HIRE, LUKE CAGE
LUM	VIZ		1	8	1989	1990	
LUNATICKLE	WHITESTONE PUBLICATIONS		1	2	1956	1956	
LUST OF THE NAZI WEASEL WOMEN	FANTAGRAPHICS		1	5	1990	NOW	
LUTHER ARKWRIGHT, THE ADVENTURES OF	DARK HORSE COMICS		1	9	1990	1991	
LUTHER ARKWRIGHT, THE ADVENTURES OF	NEVER LIMITED	1	1	1	1982	1982	
LUTHER ARKWRIGHT, THE ADVENTURES OF	VALKYRIE		1	10	1987	1989	
LUTHER ARKWRIGHT, THE ADVENTURES OF	VALKYRIE	2	1	3	1989	1989	
LUX & ALBY	ACME PRESS		1	2	1993	NOW	
LUX & ALBY	DARK HORSE COMICS		1	6	1993	NOW	
LYCANTHROPE LEO	VIZ		1	7	1994	1994	
LYCRA-WOMAN & SPANDEX-GIRL TIME TRAVEL SPECIAL	COMIC ZONE PRODUCTIONS	1	1	1	1993	1993	
LYNDON B. JOHNSON	DELL PUBLISHING COMPANY		12445503	12445503	1965	1965	

M

M	ECLIPSE		1	4	1990	1992	
M.A.C.H.1	FLEETWAY		1	9	1990	1991	
M.A.R.S. PATROL TOTAL WAR	GOLD KEY		3	10	1966	1969	FORMERLY TOTAL WAR
M.A.X. YEARBOOK	MARVEL ENTERTAINMENT GROUP		1	1	1993	1993	
M.I.C.R.A.	COMICS INTERVIEW		1	7	1986	NOW	
MACABRE STORIES	JOHN SPENCER		1	6	1967	1967	
MACHINE MAN	MARVEL ENTERTAINMENT GROUP		1	1	1985	1985	
MACHINE MAN	MARVEL ENTERTAINMENT GROUP		1	19	1978	1981	
MACHINE MAN	MARVEL ENTERTAINMENT GROUP		1	4	1984	1985	
MACK BOLAN: THE EXECUTIONER	INNOVATION		1	3	1993	NOW	

COMIC TITLE	PUBLISHER	Vol No.	Srt No.	End No.	Str. Year	End Year	COMMENTS
MACO TOY'S COMIC	CHARLTON COMICS		I	I	1959	1959	
MACROSS	COMICO		I	I	1984	1984	
MACROSS II	VIZ		I	10	1992	1993	
MAD	EC COMICS		I	320	1952	NOW	FULL TITLE ON EARLY ISSUES, "TALES CALCULATED TO DRIVE YOU MAD"
MAD 84	EC COMICS		I	I	1984	1984	
MAD ABOUT MILLIE	MARVEL ENTERTAINMENT GROUP		I	17	1969	1970	
MAD ABOUT MILLIE ANNUAL	MARVEL ENTERTAINMENT GROUP		I	I	1971	1971	
MAD ANNUAL, MORE TRASH FROM	EC COMICS		I	12	1958	1969	
MAD ANNUAL, WORST FROM	EC COMICS		I	12	1958	1969	
MAD DISCO	EC COMICS		I	I	1980	1980	
MAD DOG	MARVEL ENTERTAINMENT GROUP		I	6	1993	1993	
MAD DOG MAGAZINE	BLACKTHORNE		I	3	1986	1987	
MAD DOGS	ECLIPSE		I	3	1992	1992	
MAD HATTER, THE	O.W. COMICS		I	2	1946	1946	
MAD HOUSE	ARCHIE PUBLICATIONS		95	130	1974	1982	FORMERLY MADHOUSE GLADS
MAD HOUSE ANNUAL	ARCHIE PUBLICATIONS		8	12	1970	1975	
MAD HOUSE COMICS DIGEST	ARCHIE PUBLICATIONS		I	8	1975	1982	
MAD MAGAZINE	MAD COMICS		304	325	1967	NOW	
MAD SUPER SPECIAL	EC COMICS		93	93	1970	NOW	
MAD SUPER SPECIAL	MAD COMICS		94	94	1968	NOW	
MADAME XANADU	DC COMICS INC.		I	I	1981	1981	
MADBALLS	MARVEL ENTERTAINMENT GROUP		I	10	1986	1988	
MADHOUSE	AJAX	I	I	4	1954	1954	
MADHOUSE	FARREL PUBLICATIONS	2	I	4	1957	1957	
MADHOUSE GLADS	ARCHIE PUBLICATIONS		73	94	1970	1974	FORMERLY MADHOUSE GLADS MA-AD
MADHOUSE MA-AD	ARCHIE PUBLICATIONS		67	72	1969	1970	FORMERLY MADHOUSE MA-AD JOKES
MADMAN	TUNDRA		I	3	1992	1992	
MADMAN ADVENTURES	TUNDRA		I	3	1993	1993	
MAELSTROM	AIRCEL		I	13	1987	1988	
MAGE: CHANTRY BOOK	WHITE WOLF PUBLISHING		I	I	1993	1993	
MAGE: THE HERO DISCOVERED	COMICO		I	15	1984	1986	
MAGGOTS	HAMILTON COMICS		I	4	1991	1992	
MAGGOTS IN COLOUR	HAMILTON COMICS		I	I	1992	1992	
MAGIC	D.C. THOMSON		I	161	1976	1979	
MAGIC AGENT	AMERICAN COMIC GROUP		I	3	1962	1962	
MAGIC AGENT: JOHN FORCE	AMERICAN COMIC GROUP		I	3	1961	1961	
MAGIC COMIC	MARTIN & REID		I	I	1948	1948	
MAGIC COMIC, THE	D.C. THOMSON		I	80	1939	1941	
MAGIC COMICS	DAVID MCKAY PUBLICATIONS		I	123	1939	1949	
MAGIC FLUTE, THE	ECLIPSE		I	I	1991	1991	
MAGIC FLUTE, THE	ECLIPSE		I	3	1990	1990	
MAGIC FUN BOOK	D.C. THOMSON	1940	1941	1940	1941		
MAGIC MONKEY	DR. LEUNG'S		I	I	1992	1992	
MAGIC OF CHRISTMAS AT NEWBERRYS, THE	E.S.LONDON		I	I	1967	1967	
MAGIC-BEANO BOOK, THE	D.C. THOMSON				1943	1950	FORMERLY THE BEANO BOOK, WHICH IT BECAME AGAIN FROM 1951
MAGIK	MARVEL ENTERTAINMENT GROUP		I	4	1983	1984	
MAGILLA GORILLA	CHARLTON COMICS	2	I	5	1970	1971	
MAGILLA GORILLA	GOLD KEY	I	I	10	1964	1968	
MAGNA-MAN THE LAST SUPERHERO	COMICS INTERVIEW		I	3	1988	1989	
MAGNESIUM ARC	CALIBER PRESS		I	I	1993	1993	
MAGNETS: ROBOT DISMANTLER	PARODY PRESS		I	I	1993	1993	
MAGNO COMIC	INTERNATIONAL		I	I	1946	1946	
MAGNUS ROBOT FIGHTER	GOLD KEY		I	46	1963	1977	
MAGNUS ROBOT FIGHTER	VALIANT / VOYAGER COMMUNICATIONS		I	34	1991	NOW	ISSUE 0 WAS PUBLISHED BETWEEN ISSUES 8 AND 9.
MAGNUS ROBOT FIGHTER, VINTAGE	VALIANT / VOYAGER COMMUNICATIONS		I	4	1991	1992	
MAGNUS ROBOT FIGHTER/NEXUS	VALIANT / VOYAGER COMMUNICATIONS		I	I	1993	1994	
MAI THE PSYCHIC GIRL	ECLIPSE		I	28	1987	1988	
MAISON IKKOKU	VIZ		I	7	1993	1993	
MAISON IKKOKU	VIZ	2	I	6	1994	1994	
MAJOR HOOPLE COMICS	NEDOR (BETTER PUBLICATIONS)		I	I	1943	1943	
MAJOR INAPAK THE SPACE ACE	MAGAZINE ENTERPRISES		I	I	1951	1951	INAPAK (CHOCOLATE DRINK) GIVE AWAY
MAJOR VICTORY COMICS	HARRY A CHESLER		I	3	1944	1945	
MAKABRE	APOCALYPSE		I	I	1991	1991	
MALIBU SIGNATURE SERIES	MALIBU COMICS ENTERTAINMENT INC.		I	I	1993	1993	
MALIBU SUN PREVIEW	MALIBU COMICS ENTERTAINMENT INC.		I	I	1993	NOW	
MALU IN THE LAND OF ADVENTURE	I.W. ENTERPRISES		I	I	1964	1964	
MAMMOTH COMICS	WHITMAN		I	I	1938	1938	
MAMMY YOKUM & THE GREAT DOGPATCH MYSTERY	TOBY PRESS PUBLICATIONS		I	I	1951	1951	FEATURES L'IL ABNER
MAN COMICS	ATLAS		I	28	1949	1953	
MAN COMICS	MARVEL ENTERTAINMENT GROUP		I	28	1949	1953	
MAN EATING COW	NEW ENGLAND COMICS		I	3	1992	NOW	
MAN FROG	MAD DOG		I	2	1987	1987	
MAN FROM ATLANTIS	MARVEL ENTERTAINMENT GROUP		I	7	1978	1978	
MAN FROM U.N.C.L.E. ALL COLOUR COMIC ALBUM, THE	WORLD DISTRIBUTORS LTD		I	I	1966	1966	
MAN FROM U.N.C.L.E. ANNUAL, THE	WORLD DISTRIBUTORS LTD	1966	1969	1966	1969		
MAN FROM U.N.C.L.E. TELEVISION STORYBOOK, THE	PBS	1967	1968	1967	1968		
MAN FROM U.N.C.L.E. WORLD ADVENTURE LIBRARY, THE	WORLD DISTRIBUTORS LTD		I	14	1966	1966	DELL REPRINTS
MAN FROM U.N.C.L.E.: BIRDS OF PREY AFFAIR	MILLENIUM		I	2	1993	1993	
MAN FROM U.N.C.L.E.:END OF WORLD AFFAIR	MILLENIUM		I	I	1993	1993	
MAN FROM UNCLE	GOLD KEY		I	22	1965	1969	
MAN IN BLACK	HARVEY PUBLICATIONS		I	4	1957	1958	
MAN O' WARS	FICTION HOUSE		I	I	1953	1953	
MAN O' WARS	I.W. ENTERPRISES		I	I	1964	1964	REPRINT
MAN OF PEACE, POPE PIUS XII	CAETECHETICAL EDUCATIONAL SOCIETY		I	I	1950	1950	
MAN OF RUST	BLACKTHORNE		I	I	1986	1986	

COMIC TITLE	PUBLISHER	Vol No.	Srt No.	End No.	Str. Year	End Year	COMMENTS
MAN OF STEEL	DC COMICS INC.		1	1	1987	1987	
MAN OF STEEL, THE	DC COMICS INC.		1	6	1986	1986	
MAN OF WAR	CENTAUR PUBLICATIONS		1	2	1941	1942	
MAN OF WAR	ECLIPSE		1	3	1987	1988	
MAN OF WAR	MALIBU COMICS ENTERTAINMENT INC.		1	7	1993	NOW	
MAN THING	MARVEL ENTERTAINMENT GROUP	1	1	22	1974	1975	
MAN THING	MARVEL ENTERTAINMENT GROUP	2	1	11	1979	1981	
MAN THING GIANT SIZE	MARVEL ENTERTAINMENT GROUP	1	1	5	1974	1975	
MAN-BAT	DC COMICS INC.		1	2	1975	1976	
MAN-BAT VERSUS BATMAN	DC COMICS INC.		1	1	1984	1984	
MANDRAKE THE MAGICIAN	KING FEATURES		1	10	1966	1967	
MANDRAKE THE MAGICIAN	L. MILLER PUBLISHING COMPANY (UK)		1	1	1967	1967	
MANDRAKE THE MAGICIAN WORLD ADVENTURE LIBRARY	WORLD DISTRIBUTORS LTD		1	8	1967	1967	
MANDY	D.C. THOMSON		1	2	1967	1991	
MANDY PICTURE STORY LIBRARY	D.C. THOMSON		1	2	1978	NOW	
MANGA MANIA	DARK HORSE COMICS		1	8	1993	NOW	
MANGA MONTHLY	FATHOM PRESS		0	2	1991	NOW	
MANGAZINE	AMBITION	2	1	16	1991	NOW	
MANHUNT	STREAMLINE		1	4	1951	1951	
MANHUNT!	MAGAZINE ENTERPRISES		1	14	1947	1953	
MANHUNTER	DC COMICS INC.		1	1	1984	1984	
MANHUNTER	DC COMICS INC.		1	24	1988	1990	
MANHUNTER	L. MILLER PUBLISHING COMPANY (UK)		50	50	50'S	50'S	US REPRINT
MANIMAL	RENEGADE PRESS		1	1	1986	1986	
MANTECH ROBOT WARRIORS	ARCHIE PUBLICATIONS		1	6	1984	1985	
MANTRA	MALIBU COMICS ENTERTAINMENT INC.		1	6	1993	NOW	
MANTUS FILES, THE	ETERNITY		1	4	1991	1991	
MANY GHOSTS OF DR. GRAVES, THE	CHARLTON COMICS		1	75	1967	1982	
MANY LOVES OF DOBIE GILLIS	DC COMICS INC.		1	26	1960	1964	
MARADA THE SHE-WOLF	MARVEL ENTERTAINMENT GROUP				1986	1986	
MARAUDER	CALIBER PRESS		1	1	1992	1993	
MARCH OF COMICS	K.K. PUBLICATIONS		1	488	1946	1982	
MARCH OF CRIME	FOX FEATURES SYNDICATE		1	3	1950	1951	FORMERLY MY LOVE AFFAIR
MARCO POLO	CHARLTON COMICS		1	1	1962	1962	
MARGE'S LITTLE LULU	DELL PUBLISHING COMPANY		1	164	1948	1972	
MARGE'S LITTLE LULU & ALVIN STORY TELLING TIME	DELL PUBLISHING COMPANY		1	1	1959	1959	
MARGE'S LITTLE LULU & HER FRIENDS	DELL PUBLISHING COMPANY		4	4	1956	1956	
MARGE'S LITTLE LULU & HER SPECIAL FRIENDS	DELL PUBLISHING COMPANY		3	3	1955	1955	
MARGE'S LITTLE LULU & TUBBY ANNUAL	DELL PUBLISHING COMPANY		1	2	1953	1954	
MARGE'S LITTLE LULU & TUBBY AT SUMMER CAMP	DELL PUBLISHING COMPANY		5	2	1957	1958	TWO ISSUES ONLY, ISSUE 5 PUBLISHED FIRST
MARGE'S LITTLE LULU & TUBBY HALLOWEEN FUN	DELL PUBLISHING COMPANY		6	2	1957	1958	TWO ISSUES ONLY, ISSUE 6 PUBLISHED FIRST
MARGE'S LITTLE LULU & TUBBY IN ALASKA	DELL PUBLISHING COMPANY		1	1	1959	1959	
MARGE'S LITTLE LULU & TUBBY IN JAPAN	DELL PUBLISHING COMPANY		1	1	1962	1962	
MARGE'S LITTLE LULU ON VACATION	DELL PUBLISHING COMPANY		1	1	1954	1954	
MARGE'S LITTLE LULU SUMMER CAMP	GOLD KEY		1	1	1967	1967	
MARGE'S LITTLE LULU TRICK N' TREAT	GOLD KEY		1	1	1962	1962	
MARGE'S TUBBY	DELL PUBLISHING COMPANY		5	49	1952	1962	
MARGE'S TUBBY & HIS CLUBHOUSE PETS	DELL PUBLISHING COMPANY		1	1	1956	1956	
MARGIE COMICS	MARVEL ENTERTAINMENT GROUP		35	49	1946	1949	FORMERLY COMEDY COMICS
MARGOT IN BAD TOWN	TUNDRA		1	1	1992	1992	
MARILYN	AMALGAMATED PRESS		1	547	1955	1965	
MARINE WAR HEROES	CHARLTON COMICS		1	18	1964	1967	
MARINES AT WAR	ATLAS		5	7	1957	1957	FORMERLY TALES OF THE MARINES
MARINES ATTACK	CHARLTON COMICS		1	9	1964	1966	
MARINES IN ACTION	ATLAS		1	14	1955	1957	
MARINES IN ACTION	STREAMLINE		1	1	1955	1955	ATLAS REPRINTS
MARINES IN BATTLE	ATLAS		1	25	1954	1958	
MARINES IN BATTLE	STREAMLINE		1	1	1955	1955	ATLAS
MARK CONWAY	L. MILLER PUBLISHING COMPANY (UK)		1	1	1959	1959	
MARK HAZZARD: MERC	MARVEL ENTERTAINMENT GROUP		1	12	1986	1987	
MARK HAZZARD: MERC ANNUAL	MARVEL ENTERTAINMENT GROUP		1	1	1987	1987	
MARK STEEL	AMERICAN IRON & STEEL CORP.	1967	1972	1967	1972		
MARK TRAIL	STANDARD COMICS		1	5	1955	1959	
MARK TRAIL ADVENTURE BOOK OF NATURE	FAWCETT PUBLICATIONS		1	1	1958	1958	
MARK TYNE	JOHN SPENCER		1	2	1967	1967	
MARK, THE	DARK HORSE COMICS		1	1	1993	1994	
MARK, THE	DARK HORSE COMICS		1	6	1987	1988	
MARKED FOR MURDER	TOP SELLERS		1	2	60'S	60'S	FOREIGN REPRINTS
MARKSMAN	HEROIC PUBLISHING		1	5	1987	1988	
MARKSMAN ANNUAL	HEROIC PUBLISHING		1	1	1988	1988	
MARMADUKE MONK	I.W. ENTERPRISES		1	1	1963	1963	
MARMADUKE MONK	SUPER COMICS		1	14	1963	1963	
MARMADUKE MOUSE	QUALITY COMICS		1	1	1963	1963	REPRINT
MARMADUKE MOUSE	QUALITY COMICS		1	65	1946	1956	
MARMADUKE'S GREAT DAY	BROCKHAMPTON PRESS		1	1	1962	1962	
MARMADUKE, A WEEK WITH	BROCKHAMPTON PRESS		1	1	1964	1964	
MARRIED BLISS	MARTIN & REID		1	1	1946	1946	
MARRIED WITH CHILDREN 3-D	NOW		1	1	1993	1993	
MARRIED WITH CHILDREN ANNUAL	NOW		1	1	1993	NOW	
MARRIED WITH CHILDREN: LOTTO FEVER	NOW		1	3	1994	1994	
MARRIED...WITH CHILDREN	NOW	1	1	11	1990	1991	
MARRIED...WITH CHILDREN	NOW	2	1	12	1991	NOW	
MARRIED...WITH CHILDREN 2099	NOW		1	3	1993	1993	
MARRIED...WITH CHILDREN FLASHBACK SPECIAL	NOW		1	1	1993	1993	
MARRIED...WITH CHILDREN: KELLY BUNDY SPECIAL	NOW		1	1	1992	1992	
MARRIED...WITH CHILDREN: OFF BROADWAY	NOW		1	1	1993	1993	
MARRIED...WITH CHILDREN: QUANTUM QUARTET	NOW		1	2	1993	1993	
MARS	FIRST		1	12	1984	1985	
MARS COMICS	STREAMLINE		1	1	1950	1950	FICTION HOUSE REPRINTS

INDEX OF COMIC TITLES AND THEIR PUBLISHERS

COMIC TITLE	PUBLISHER	Vol No.	Srt No.	End No.	Str. Year	End Year	COMMENTS
MARS ON EARTH	DC COMICS INC.		1	1	1992	1992	
MARSHAL BLUEBERRY	MARVEL ENTERTAINMENT GROUP		1	1	1991	1991	
MARSHAL LAW	MARVEL ENTERTAINMENT GROUP		1	6	1987	1989	
MARSHAL LAW TAKES MANHATTAN	APOCALYPSE		1	1	1991	1991	
MARSHAL LAW TAKES MANHATTAN (CRIME & PUNISHMENT)	MARVEL ENTERTAINMENT GROUP		1	1	1989	1989	
MARSHAL LAW: BLOOD, SWEAT & TEARS	DARK HORSE COMICS		1	1	1993	1993	
MARSHAL LAW: CAPE FEAR	DARK HORSE COMICS		1	1	1993	1993	
MARSHAL LAW: FEAR & LOATHING	MARVEL ENTERTAINMENT GROUP		1	1	1990	1990	
MARSHAL LAW: KINGDOM OF THE BLIND	APOCALYPSE		1	1	1990	1990	
MARSHAL LAW: SUPER BABYLON	DARK HORSE COMICS		1	1	1992	1992	
MARSHAL LAW: THE HATEFUL DEAD	MARVEL ENTERTAINMENT GROUP		1	1	1991	1991	
MARSMAN COMICS	CARTOON ART		1	1	1948	1948	
MARTIAL AWE	JOHN W. FISHER		1	1	1946	1946	
MARTIAN MANHUNTER	DC COMICS INC.		1	4	1988	1988	
MARTIAN MANHUNTER: AMERICAN SECRETS	DC COMICS INC.		1	3	1992	1992	
MARTIN KANE	FOX FEATURES SYNDICATE		1	2	1950	1950	FORMERLY MY SECRET AFFAIR
MARTY MOUSE	I.W. ENTERPRISES		1	1	1958	1958	REPRINT
MARVEL 1993 HOLIDAY SPECIAL	MARVEL ENTERTAINMENT GROUP		1	1	1993	1993	
MARVEL ACTION	MARVEL ENTERTAINMENT GROUP		1	15	1981	1981	
MARVEL ACTION UNIVERSE	MARVEL ENTERTAINMENT GROUP		1	1	1989	1989	
MARVEL ADVENTURE	MARVEL ENTERTAINMENT GROUP		1	6	1975	1976	
MARVEL AGE	MARVEL ENTERTAINMENT GROUP		1	133	1982	NOW	
MARVEL AGE ANNUAL	MARVEL ENTERTAINMENT GROUP		1	4	1986	NOW	
MARVEL AGE PREVIEW	MARVEL ENTERTAINMENT GROUP		1	2	1990	NOW	
MARVEL AND DC PRESENT	MARVEL ENTERTAINMENT GROUP/DC COMICS INC.		1	1	1982	1982	X-MEN AND TEEN TITANS TEEM-UP
MARVEL BOY	MAGAZINE ENTERPRISES		1	2	1950	1951	
MARVEL CHILLERS	MARVEL ENTERTAINMENT GROUP		1	7	1975	1976	
MARVEL CLASSICS COMICS	MARVEL ENTERTAINMENT GROUP		1	12	1981	1982	
MARVEL CLASSICS COMICS SERIES FEATURING...	MARVEL ENTERTAINMENT GROUP		1	36	1976	1978	
MARVEL COLLECTOR'S EDITION: X-MEN	MARVEL ENTERTAINMENT GROUP		1	1	1993	1993	STRIDEX EDITION
MARVEL COLLECTOR'S EDITION: X-MEN	MARVEL ENTERTAINMENT GROUP		1	4	1993	NOW	PIZZA HUT EDITION
MARVEL COLLECTORS EDITION: WOLVERINE AND SPIDER-MAN	MARVEL ENTERTAINMENT GROUP		1	1	1993	1993	
MARVEL COLLECTORS ITEM CLASSICS	MARVEL ENTERTAINMENT GROUP		1	22	1965	1969	
MARVEL COMIC	MARVEL ENTERTAINMENT GROUP		330	352	1979	1979	PREVIOUSLY MIGHTY WORLD OF MARVEL
MARVEL COMICS	TIMELY COMICS		1	1	1939	1939	
MARVEL COMICS PRESENTS	MARVEL ENTERTAINMENT GROUP		1	149	1988	NOW	
MARVEL COMICS SUPER SPECIAL	MARVEL ENTERTAINMENT GROUP		1	41	1977	1986	
MARVEL COMICS TRY OUT BOOK	MARVEL ENTERTAINMENT GROUP		1	1	1986	1986	
MARVEL COMICS: THE FIRST EVER	MARVEL ENTERTAINMENT GROUP		1	1	1990	1990	
MARVEL DOUBLE FEATURE	MARVEL ENTERTAINMENT GROUP		1	21	1973	1977	
MARVEL FAMILY	FAWCETT PUBLICATIONS		1	89	1945	1954	
MARVEL FAMILY, THE	L. MILLER PUBLISHING COMPANY (UK)	1	1	3	1949	1949	
MARVEL FAMILY, THE	L. MILLER PUBLISHING COMPANY (UK)	2	1	30	1950	1953	
MARVEL FANFARE	MARVEL ENTERTAINMENT GROUP		1	60	1982	1992	
MARVEL FEATURE	MARVEL ENTERTAINMENT GROUP	1	1	12	1971	1973	
MARVEL FEATURE	MARVEL ENTERTAINMENT GROUP	2	1	7	1975	1976	
MARVEL FIVE FABULOUS DECADES	MARVEL ENTERTAINMENT GROUP		1	1	1992	1992	
MARVEL FRONTIER COMICS UNLIMITED	MARVEL ENTERTAINMENT GROUP		1	1	1993	NOW	MARVEL UK TITLE
MARVEL FUMETTI BOOK	MARVEL ENTERTAINMENT GROUP		1	1	1984	1984	
MARVEL GRAPHIC NOVEL	MARVEL ENTERTAINMENT GROUP		1	20	1982	NOW	NO.1 WAS DEATH OF CAPTAIN MARVEL
MARVEL GREATEST COMICS	MARVEL ENTERTAINMENT GROUP		23	96	1969	1981	FORMERLY MARVEL COLLECTORS ITEM CLASSICS
MARVEL HOLIDAY SPECIAL	MARVEL ENTERTAINMENT GROUP		1	1	1991	1991	
MARVEL ILLUSTRATED BOOKS	MARVEL ENTERTAINMENT GROUP		1	1	1992	1992	
MARVEL ILLUSTRATED: SWIMSUIT ISSUE	MARVEL ENTERTAINMENT GROUP		1	2	1991	1991	
MARVEL MADHOUSE	MARVEL ENTERTAINMENT GROUP		1	17	1981	1982	
MARVEL MASTERPIECES COLLECTION	MARVEL ENTERTAINMENT GROUP		1	4	1993	1993	
MARVEL MASTERWORKS	MARVEL ENTERTAINMENT GROUP		1	1	1992	1992	
MARVEL MASTERWORKS	MARVEL ENTERTAINMENT GROUP		1	25	1987	NOW	
MARVEL MINI-BOOKS	MARVEL ENTERTAINMENT GROUP		1	6	1966	1966	
MARVEL MOVIE PREMIERE	MARVEL ENTERTAINMENT GROUP		1	1	1975	1975	
MARVEL MOVIE SHOWCASE FEATURING STAR WARS	MARVEL ENTERTAINMENT GROUP		1	2	1982	1982	
MARVEL MOVIE SPOTLIGHT FEATURING RAIDERS/LOST ARK	MARVEL ENTERTAINMENT GROUP		1	1	1982	1982	
MARVEL MYSTERY COMICS	MARVEL ENTERTAINMENT GROUP		2	92	1939	1949	FORMERLY MARVEL COMICS
MARVEL NO-PRIZE BOOK, THE	MARVEL ENTERTAINMENT GROUP		1	1	1983	1983	
MARVEL POSTER BOOK	MARVEL ENTERTAINMENT GROUP		1	1	1991	1991	
MARVEL PREMIERE	MARVEL ENTERTAINMENT GROUP		1	61	1972	1981	
MARVEL PRESENTS	MARVEL ENTERTAINMENT GROUP		1	12	1975	1977	
MARVEL PREVIEW	MARVEL ENTERTAINMENT GROUP		1	24	1975	1980	
MARVEL PREVIEW	MARVEL ENTERTAINMENT GROUP	2	1	1	1993	NOW	
MARVEL SAGA, THE	MARVEL ENTERTAINMENT GROUP		1	25	1985	1987	
MARVEL SPECIAL EDITION FEATURING...	MARVEL ENTERTAINMENT GROUP	1	1	3	1975	1978	
MARVEL SPECIAL EDITION FEATURING...	MARVEL ENTERTAINMENT GROUP	2	1	1	1980	1980	
MARVEL SPECTACULAR	MARVEL ENTERTAINMENT GROUP		1	19	1973	1975	
MARVEL SPOTLIGHT	MARVEL ENTERTAINMENT GROUP	1	1	33	1971	1977	
MARVEL SPOTLIGHT	MARVEL ENTERTAINMENT GROUP	2	1	11	1979	1981	
MARVEL SUPER ACTION	MARVEL ENTERTAINMENT GROUP		1	1	1976	1976	
MARVEL SUPER ACTION	MARVEL ENTERTAINMENT GROUP		1	38	1977	1981	
MARVEL SUPER ADVENTURE	MARVEL ENTERTAINMENT GROUP		1	26	1981	1981	
MARVEL SUPER ADVENTURE WINTER SPECIAL	MARVEL ENTERTAINMENT GROUP		1	1	1980	1980	
MARVEL SUPER HEROES	MARVEL ENTERTAINMENT GROUP		1	1	1966	1966	
MARVEL SUPER HEROES	MARVEL ENTERTAINMENT GROUP		353	397	1979	1983	FORMERLY MARVEL COMIC
MARVEL SUPER HEROES AND THE OCCULT	MARVEL ENTERTAINMENT GROUP		1	1	1980	1980	
MARVEL SUPER HEROES SECRET WARS	MARVEL ENTERTAINMENT GROUP		1	12	1984	1985	
MARVEL SUPER HEROES SUMMER SPECIAL	MARVEL ENTERTAINMENT GROUP		1	1	1979	1979	
MARVEL SUPER SPECIAL	MARVEL ENTERTAINMENT GROUP		1	41	1977	1986	
MARVEL SUPERHEROES	MARVEL ENTERTAINMENT GROUP	1	12	106	1967	1982	FORMERLY FANTASY MASTERPIECES

COMIC TITLE	PUBLISHER	Vol No.	Srt No.	End No.	Str. Year	End Year	COMMENTS
MARVEL SUPERHEROES	MARVEL ENTERTAINMENT GROUP	2	I	15	1990	NOW	
MARVEL SUPERHEROES ANNUAL	GRAND DREAMS		1980	1980	1980	1980	
MARVEL SUPERHEROES OMNIBUS	MARVEL ENTERTAINMENT GROUP		I	I	1986	1986	
MARVEL SWIMSUIT SPECIAL	MARVEL ENTERTAINMENT GROUP		1992	1993	1992	1993	
MARVEL TAILS: PETER PORKER SPECTACULAR SPIDERHAM	MARVEL ENTERTAINMENT GROUP		I	I	1983	1983	
MARVEL TALES	ATLAS		93	159	1949	1957	FORMERLY MARVEL MYSTERY TALES
MARVEL TALES	MARVEL ENTERTAINMENT GROUP		I	282	1964	NOW	
MARVEL TEAM UP	MARVEL ENTERTAINMENT GROUP		I	150	1972	1985	
MARVEL TEAM UP ANNUAL	MARVEL ENTERTAINMENT GROUP		I	7	1976	1984	
MARVEL TEAM UP, THE OFFICIAL MARVEL INDEX TO	MARVEL ENTERTAINMENT GROUP		I	6	1986	1987	
MARVEL TEAM-UP	MARVEL ENTERTAINMENT GROUP		I	25	1980	1981	
MARVEL TEAM-UP WINTER SPECIAL	MARVEL ENTERTAINMENT GROUP		I	I	1980	1980	
MARVEL TREASURY EDITION	MARVEL ENTERTAINMENT GROUP		I	28	1974	1981	
MARVEL TREASURY OF OZ: THE MARVELLOUS LAND OF OZ	MARVEL ENTERTAINMENT GROUP		I	I	1975	1975	
MARVEL TREASURY SPECIAL	MARVEL ENTERTAINMENT GROUP		I	II	1974	1976	
MARVEL TRIPLE ACTION	MARVEL ENTERTAINMENT GROUP		I	47	1972	1979	
MARVEL TRIPLE ACTION GIANT SIZE	MARVEL ENTERTAINMENT GROUP		I	2	1975	1975	
MARVEL TWO IN ONE	MARVEL ENTERTAINMENT GROUP		I	100	1974	1983	
MARVEL TWO IN ONE ANNUAL	MARVEL ENTERTAINMENT GROUP		I	7	1976	1982	
MARVEL UNIVERSE DELUXE, OFFICIAL HANDBOOK OF THE	MARVEL ENTERTAINMENT GROUP	2	I	20	1985	1988	
MARVEL UNIVERSE MASTER EDITION, OFFICIAL HANDBOOK	MARVEL ENTERTAINMENT GROUP		I	36	1991	1993	
MARVEL UNIVERSE UPDATE, OFFICIAL HANDBOOK OF THE	MARVEL ENTERTAINMENT GROUP		I	8	1989	1990	
MARVEL UNIVERSE, OFFICIAL HANDBOOK OF THE	MARVEL ENTERTAINMENT GROUP		I	10	1987	1988	
MARVEL UNIVERSE, OFFICIAL HANDBOOK OF THE	MARVEL ENTERTAINMENT GROUP	I	I	15	1983	1984	
MARVEL X-MEN COLLECTION	MARVEL ENTERTAINMENT GROUP		I	2	1993	1994	
MARVEL YEAR IN REVIEW	MARVEL ENTERTAINMENT GROUP		1989	1993	1989	1993	
MARVELMAN	L. MILLER PUBLISHING COMPANY (UK)	25	370	1954	1963	PREVIOUSLY CAPTAIN MARVEL	
MARVELMAN ANNUAL	L. MILLER PUBLISHING COMPANY (UK)		1954	1963	1954	1963	
MARVELMAN FAMILY	L. MILLER PUBLISHING COMPANY (UK)		I	30	1956	1959	
MARVELMAN FAMILY ANNUAL	L. MILLER PUBLISHING COMPANY (UK)		I	I	1963	1963	
MARVELMAN JNR. ANNUAL	L. MILLER PUBLISHING COMPANY (UK)		I	I	1963	1963	
MARVELMAN SPECIAL	QUALITY (FLEETWAY)		I	I	1984	1984	
MARVELS	MARVEL ENTERTAINMENT GROUP		I	4	1994	1994	
MARVELS OF SCIENCE	CHARLTON COMICS		I	4	1946	1946	
MARVIN MOUSE	ATLAS		I	I	1957	1957	
MARY MARVEL	L. MILLER PUBLISHING COMPANY (UK)		I	I	1947	1947	FAWCETT REPRINTS
MARY MARVEL COMICS	FAWCETT PUBLICATIONS		I	28	1945	1948	
MARY MOUSE	BROCKHAMPTON PRESS		I	22	1942	1964	
MARY WORTH	ARGO PUBLISHING		I	I	1956	1956	
MARY'S GREATEST APOSTLE	CAETECHETICAL EDUCATIONAL SOCIETY		I	I	???	???	NO DATE
MASK	DC COMICS INC.		I	I	1993	1993	
MASK	DC COMICS INC.	I	I	4	1985	1985	
MASK	DC COMICS INC.	2	I	9	1987	1987	
MASK COMICS	RURAL HOME PUBLISHING COMPANY		I	2	1945	1945	
MASK OF FU MANCHU, THE	AVON BOOKS		I	I	1951	1951	
MASK RETURNS, THE	DARK HORSE COMICS		I	4	1992	1992	
MASK, THE	DARK HORSE COMICS	0	4	1991	1991		
MASKED BANDIT, THE	AVON BOOKS		I	I	1952	1952	
MASKED MAN	ECLIPSE		I	12	1985	1988	
MASKED MARVEL	CENTAUR PUBLICATIONS		I	3	1940	1940	
MASKED RAIDER	L. MILLER PUBLISHING COMPANY (UK)	50	66	1957	1958	CHARLTON REPRINTS	
MASKED RAIDER	WORLD DISTRIBUTORS LTD		I	4	1955	1955	CHARLTON REPRINTS
MASKED RAIDER, THE	CHARLTON COMICS		I	30	1955	1961	
MASKED RAIDERS OF THE RANGE	CARTOON ART		I	I	1952	1952	MAGAZINE ENTERPRISES REPRINTS
MASKED RANGER	PREMIER MAGAZINES		I	9	1954	1955	
MASQUES	INNOVATION		I	2	1992	1992	
MASTER COMICS	FAWCETT PUBLICATIONS		I	6	1940	1940	
MASTER COMICS	L. MILLER PUBLISHING COMPANY (UK)		I	96	1945	1958	
MASTER COMICS WITH SLAM BANG COMICS	FAWCETT PUBLICATIONS	7	133	1940	1953		
MASTER DETECTIVE	SUPER COMICS	10	18	1964	1964	REPRINTS	
MASTER OF KUNG FU	MARVEL ENTERTAINMENT GROUP	17	125	1974	1983	FORMERLY MARVEL SPECIAL EDITION	
MASTER OF KUNG FU ANNUAL	MARVEL ENTERTAINMENT GROUP		I	I	1976	1976	
MASTER OF KUNG FU GIANT SIZE	MARVEL ENTERTAINMENT GROUP		I	4	1974	1975	
MASTER OF KUNG FU: BLEEDING BLACK	MARVEL ENTERTAINMENT GROUP		I	I	1991	1991	
MASTER OF RAMPLING GATE	INNOVATION		I	I	1991	1991	
MASTER OF THE VOID	IRON HAMMER GRAPHICS		I	I	1993	NOW	
MASTERMAN COMICS	STREAMLINE		I	10	1952	1953	
MASTERS OF TERROR	MARVEL ENTERTAINMENT GROUP		I	2	1975	1975	
MASTERS OF THE UNIVERSE	DC COMICS INC.		I	3	1983	1983	
MASTERS OF THE UNIVERSE	MARVEL ENTERTAINMENT GROUP		I	9	1986	1988	
MASTERS OF THE UNIVERSE COMIC ALBUM	WESTERN PUBLISHING COMPANY		I	I	1984	1984	
MASTERWORK SERIES OF GREAT COMIC BOOK ARTISTS	DC COMICS INC.		I	3	1983	1983	
MATT BLACK	WILLYPRODS		I	6	1986	1987	
MATT SLADE GUNFIGHTER	ATLAS		I	4	1956	1956	
MATT SLADE GUNFIGHTER	STRATO		I	5	1957	1957	ATLAS/DC REPRINTS
MAUD	FREDERICK A. STOKES		I	I	1906	1906	
MAURETANIA	PENGUIN BOOKS				1990	1990	
MAUS II	PANTHEON		I	I	1992	1992	
MAUS II	PENGUIN BOOKS		I	I	1992	1992	
MAVERICK	DELL PUBLISHING COMPANY	7	19	1959	1962		
MAVERICK MARSHAL	CHARLTON COMICS		I	7	1958	1960	
MAVERICK MARSHAL	L. MILLER PUBLISHING COMPANY (UK)	50	52	1959	1959	CHARLTON REPRINTS	
MAVERICKS	DAGGER ENTERPRISES		I	I	1993	NOW	
MAX BREWSTER: THE UNIVERSAL SOLDIER	FLEETWAY		I	4	1993	NOW	
MAX OVERLOAD	DARK HORSE COMICS		I	3	1994	NOW	

COMIC TITLE	PUBLISHER	Vol No.	Srt No.	End No.	Str. Year	End Year	COMMENTS
MAXIMORTAL	TUNDRA		1	6	1993	NOW	
MAXWELL MOUSE FOLLIES	RENEGADE PRESS		1	6	1986	1986	
MAXWELL THE MAGIC CAT	ACME PRESS		1	4	1986	1987	
MAXX	IMAGE COMICS		1	6	1993	NOW	ISSUE NUMBERED .5, WAS A "SEND-A-WAY"
MAXX 1/2	IMAGE COMICS		1	1	1993	1993	
MAXX ADVENTURE SUPPLEMENT	IMAGE COMICS		1	1	1993	1993	
MAYA	GOLD KEY		1	1	1968	1968	
MAYHEM	DARK HORSE COMICS		1	4	1989	1989	
MAZE AGENCY	COMICO		1	7	1988	1989	
MAZE AGENCY	INNOVATION		1	23	1989	NOW	
MAZE AGENCY ANNUAL	INNOVATION		1	1	1990	1990	
MAZE AGENCY CHRISTMAS SPECIAL, THE	INNOVATION		1	1	1992	1992	
MAZE BOOK: THE MAZE AGENCY COLLECTION	INNOVATION		1	1	1993	1993	
MAZIE	NATIONWIDE PUBLISHERS		1	7	1950	1951	
MAZIE & HER FRIENDS	HARVEY PUBLICATIONS		1	28	1953	1958	
MAZING MAN	DC COMICS INC.		1	13	1986	1986	
MAZING MAN SPECIAL	DC COMICS INC.		1	3	1988	1990	
MAZINGER	FIRST		1	1	1990	1990	
MCCRORY'S CHRISTMAS BOOK	WESTERN PUBLISHING COMPANY	·	1	1	1956	1956	
MCCRORY'S WONDERFUL CHRISTMAS	PROMOTIONAL PUBLICATIONS COMPANY		1	1	1954	1954	
MCHALE'S NAVY	DELL PUBLISHING COMPANY		1	3	1963	1964	
MCKEEVER & THE COLONEL	DELL PUBLISHING COMPANY		1	3	1963	1963	
MCKEEVER AND THE COLONEL	DELL PUBLISHING COMPANY		1	3	1963	1963	
MD	EC COMICS		1	5	1955	1956	
MEADOWLARK	PARODY PRESS		1	1	1992	1992	
MEAN MACHINE: TRAVELS WITH MY SHRINK	FLEETWAY		1	1	1993	NOW	
MEAN STREAK	CONTENDER COMICS		1	1	1993	NOW	
MECHA	DARK HORSE COMICS		1	6	1987	1989	
MECHANIC GEMINI	SUN COMICS PUBLISHING		1	1	1992	NOW	
MECHANICS	FANTAGRAPHICS		1	3	1985	1985	
MECHANISMO	FLEETWAY	1	1	1	1992	1992	
MECHANOIDS, THE	CALIBER PRESS		1	5	1990	NOW	
MECHTHINGS	RENEGADE PRESS		1	4	1987	1988	
MEDAL FOR BOWZER, A	WILL EISNER		1	1	1948	1950	
MEDAL OF HONOR COMICS	A.S. CURTIS		1	1	1946	1946	
MEET ANGEL	DC COMICS INC.	7	7	7	1969	1969	FORMERLY ANGEL AND THE APE
MEET CORLISS ARCHER	FOX FEATURES SYNDICATE		1	3	1948	1948	
MEET HIYA A FRIEND OF SANTA CLAUS	JULIAN PROSKAUER/SUNDIAL SHOE STORES		1	1	1949	1949	
MEET MERTON	I.W. SUPER	9	18	18	1963	1963	
MEET MERTON	TOBY PRESS PUBLICATIONS		1	4	1953	1954	
MEET MISS BLISS	ATLAS		1	4	1955	1955	
MEET MISS PEPPER	ST JOHN PUBLISHING	5	5	6	1954	1954	FORMERLY LUCY, THE REAL GONE GAL
MEGADETH	ROCK-IT COMIX		1	1	1994	1994	
MEGALITH	CONTINUITY COMICS		1	10	1993	1994	
MEGALITH	CONTINUITY COMICS		1	2	1985	1985	
MEGALITH	CONTINUITY COMICS	1	1	13	1989	1993	
MEGALITH	CONTINUITY COMICS	2	0	6	1993	NOW	
MEGALITH/HYBRIDS	CONTINUITY COMICS	0	0	0	1993	1993	
MEGATON	MEGATON COMICS	1	1	8	1983	1985	
MEGATON	MEGATON COMICS	2	1	3	1987	1987	
MEGATON CHRISTMAS SPECIAL	MEGATON COMICS		1	1	1987	1987	
MEGATON EXPLOSION	MEGATON COMICS		1	1	1987	1987	
MEGATON MAN	KITCHEN SINK		1	10	1984	1986	
MEGATON MAN MEETS THE UNCATEGORIZABLE X-THEMS	KITCHEN SINK		1	1	1989	1989	
MEGATON SPECIAL	MEGATON COMICS		1	1	1987	1987	
MEGATON X-MAS SPECIAL	EXPRESS PUBLICATIONS		1	1	1993	1993	
MEK MEMOIRS	KEVIN O'NEILL		1	1	1976	1976	
MEL ALLEN SPORTS COMICS	STANDARD COMICS	5	5	6	1949	1950	
MELODY	KITCHEN SINK		1	6	1988	1990	
MELTDOWN	MARVEL ENTERTAINMENT GROUP		1	6	1991	1992	
MELTDOWN: HAVOK & WOLVERINE	MARVEL ENTERTAINMENT GROUP		1	1	1991	1991	
MELTDOWN: HAVOK AND WOLVERINE	MARVEL ENTERTAINMENT GROUP		1	4	1988	1989	
MELTING POT	KITCHEN SINK		1	1	1993	1994	SIMON BISLEY ART
MELVIN MONSTER	DELL PUBLISHING COMPANY		1	10	1965	1969	
MELVIN THE MONSTER	ATLAS		1	6	1956	1957	
MEMORIES	MARVEL ENTERTAINMENT GROUP		1	1	1992	1992	
MEN AGAINST CRIME	ACE MAGAZINES	3	3	7	1951	1951	FORMERLY MR. RISK
MEN IN ACTION	AJAX	2	1	9	1957	1958	
MEN IN ACTION	ATLAS	1	1	9	1952	1952	
MEN IN BLACK, THE	AIRCEL	1	1	4	1991	1991	
MEN IN BLACK, THE	AIRCEL	2	1	3	1992	1992	
MEN OF BATTLE	CAETECHETICAL EDUCATIONAL SOCIETY		1	1	1943	1943	
MEN OF COURAGE	CAETECHETICAL EDUCATIONAL SOCIETY	2	2	20	1949	1949	
MEN OF WAR	DC COMICS INC.		1	26	1977	1990	
MEN'S ADVENTURES	MARVEL ENTERTAINMENT GROUP	4	4	28	1950	1954	FORMERLY TRUE ADVENTURES
MENACE	ATLAS		1	11	1953	1954	
MENG & ECKER	SAVOY ADULT GRAPHICS		1	5	1989	NOW	
MEPHISTO VERSUS FOUR HEROES	MARVEL ENTERTAINMENT GROUP		1	4	1987	1987	
MERCY	DC COMICS INC.		1	1	1993	1993	
MERLIN	ADVENTURE COMICS	1	1	6	1990	1991	
MERLIN	ADVENTURE COMICS	2	1	2	1992	1993	
MERLIN AND EXCALIBUR IN QUEST OF THE KING	MARVEL ENTERTAINMENT GROUP		1	1	1981	1981	
MERLINREALM IN 3-D	BLACKTHORNE		1	1	1985	1985	
MERMAID FOREST	VIZ		1	1	1993	1994	
MERRY AND BRIGHT	AMALGAMATED PRESS		1	928	1910	1935	
MERRY AND BRIGHT	HAMILTON COMICS		1	1	1947	1947	
MERRY CHRISTMAS FROM SEARS TOYLAND	SEARS AND ROEBUCK COMPANY		1	1	1939	1939	
MERRY CHRISTMAS, A	K.K. PUBLICATIONS		1948	1956	1948	1956	
MERRY COMICS	CARLTON PUBLISHING CO.		1	1	1945	1945	

COMIC TITLE	PUBLISHER	Vol No.	Srt No.	End No.	Str. Year	End Year	COMMENTS
MERRY COMICS	FOUR STAR COMICS CORP/SUPERIOR COMICS LTD		1	1	1947	1947	
MERRY COMICS	P.M. PRODUCTIONS		1	1	1944	1944	
MERRY FROM MICKEY MOUSE	K.K. PUBLICATIONS		1	1	1939	1939	
MERRY GO ROUND	SWINNERTONS		1	1	1946	1946	
MERRY MADCAP COMIC	PHILIMAR		1	1	1947	1947	
MERRY MAKER	JOHN MATTHEW		1	10	1946	1948	
MERRY MAKER COMIC, THE	ALGAR/L. BURN		1	11	1946	1947	
MERRY MARVEL COMIC	PHILIMAR		1	1	1947	1947	
MERRY MASCOT	JOHN MATTHEW		1	2	1947	1947	
MERRY MAYPOLE COMIC	P.L. PUBLISHING		1	1	1949	1949	
MERRY MIDGET	PROVINCIAL COMICS		1	20	1931	1932	
MERRY MIRTHQUAKE COMIC, THE	PHILIMAR		1	1	1949	1949	
MERRY MOMENTS	C.A. RANSOM		1	28	1928	1929	
MERRY MOMENTS	GEORGE NEWNES		1	194	1919	1922	
MERRY MOMENTS	MARTIN & REID		1	4	1946	1948	
MERRY MOUSE	AVON BOOKS		1	4	1953	1954	
MERRY PLAY	P.M. PRODUCTIONS		1	1	1949	1949	
MERRY PLAY COMIC	PHILIMAR		1	1	1947	1947	
MERRY TALES	TOP SELLERS		1	4	1970	1970	
MERRY-GO-ROUND	J.B. ALLEN		1	4	1949	1949	
MERRY-GO-ROUND	MARTIN & REID		1	14	1946	1949	
MERRY-GO-ROUND COMIC	FOLDES PRESS		1	1	1947	1947	
MERRYMAKER, THE	NATIONAL SPORT PUBLICATIONS		1	1	1947	1947	
META 4	FIRST		1	3	1991	1991	
METACOPS!	MONSTER COMICS		1	3	1991	NOW	
METAL BIKINI	ETERNITY		1	6	1990	1991	
METAL MEN	DC COMICS INC.		1	4	1993	1993	
METAL MEN	DC COMICS INC.		1	56	1963	1978	
METALLICA	ROCK-IT COMIX		1	1	1993	1994	
METAMORPHO	DC COMICS INC.		1	2	1965	1967	
METAMORPHO	DC COMICS INC.		1	4	1993	1993	
METAPHISIQUE	ECLIPSE		1	2	1992	1992	
METEOR COMICS	L.L. BAIRD		1	1	1945	1945	
METEOR MAN	MARVEL ENTERTAINMENT GROUP		1	6	1993	NOW	
METEOR MAN MOVIE ADAPTATION	MARVEL ENTERTAINMENT GROUP		1	1	1993	1993	
METEOR, THE	CHILDREN'S PRESS		1	1	1948	1948	
METEOR, THE	PAGET	1	1	5	1948	1948	
METEOR, THE	PAGET	2	1	1	1948	1948	
METROPOL	MARVEL ENTERTAINMENT GROUP		1	12	1991	1992	
METROPOL A.D.	MARVEL ENTERTAINMENT GROUP		1	3	1992	1992	
MGM'S LASSIE	DELL PUBLISHING COMPANY		1	36	1950	1957	
MGM'S MARVEL WIZARD OF OZ	MARVEL ENTERTAINMENT GROUP		1	1	1975	1975	
MGM'S MOUSE MUSKETEERS	DELL PUBLISHING COMPANY		8	21	1956	1962	
MGM'S SPIKE AND TYKE	DELL PUBLISHING COMPANY		4	24	1955	1962	
MICHAEL MAUSER, THE NEW CRIME FILES OF	APPLE COMICS		1	1	1991	NOW	
MICHAELANGELO CHRISTMAS SPECIAL	MIRAGE STUDIOS		1	1	1991	1991	
MICK MARTIN	MARTIN & REID		1	1	1949	1949	
MICKEY AND DONALD	GLADSTONE		1	18	1988	1990	
MICKEY FINN	EASTERN COLOR PRINTING COMPANY		1	15	1942	1949	
MICKEY FINN	EASTERN COLOR PRINTING COMPANY	3	1	2	1952	1952	
MICKEY MOUSE	DELL PUBLISHING COMPANY		28	84	1952	1962	
MICKEY MOUSE	GLADSTONE		1	256	1986	1990	
MICKEY MOUSE	GOLD KEY		85	204	1962	1985	
MICKEY MOUSE	WHITMAN		205	218	1984	1986	
MICKEY MOUSE	WHITMAN		948	948	1933	1933	
MICKEY MOUSE ADVENTURES	WALT DISNEY		1	18	1990	1991	
MICKEY MOUSE ALMANAC	DELL PUBLISHING COMPANY		1	1	1957	1957	
MICKEY MOUSE ANNUAL	DAVID MCKAY PUBLICATIONS		1	4	1931	1934	
MICKEY MOUSE ANNUAL	DEAN & SON		1931	1965	1931	1965	
MICKEY MOUSE BIRTHDAY PARADE	DELL PUBLISHING COMPANY		1	1	1953	1953	
MICKEY MOUSE BIRTHDAY PARTY	DELL PUBLISHING COMPANY		1	1	1953	1953	
MICKEY MOUSE COMICS DIGEST	GLADSTONE		1	5	1986	1987	
MICKEY MOUSE HOLIDAY SPECIAL	WILLBANK PUBLISHING L		1936	1938	1936	1938	
MICKEY MOUSE IN FANTASY LAND	DELL PUBLISHING COMPANY		1	1	1957	1957	
MICKEY MOUSE IN FRONTIER LAND	DELL PUBLISHING COMPANY		1	1	1956	1956	
MICKEY MOUSE MAGAZINE	K.K. PUBLICATIONS	1	1	12	1935	1936	
MICKEY MOUSE MAGAZINE	K.K. PUBLICATIONS	2	1	13	1936	1937	
MICKEY MOUSE MAGAZINE	K.K. PUBLICATIONS	3	1	12	1937	1938	
MICKEY MOUSE MAGAZINE	K.K. PUBLICATIONS	4	1	12	1938	1939	
MICKEY MOUSE MAGAZINE	K.K. PUBLICATIONS	5	1	12	1939	1940	
MICKEY MOUSE MAGAZINE	KAY KAMEN INC.	1	1	9	1933	1933	
MICKEY MOUSE MAGAZINE	WALT DISNEY	1	1	12	1933	1934	
MICKEY MOUSE MAGAZINE	WALT DISNEY	2	1	12	1934	1935	
MICKEY MOUSE MARCH OF COMICS ANNUAL	K.K. PUBLICATIONS		1947	1951	1947	1951	
MICKEY MOUSE SUMMER FUN	DELL PUBLISHING COMPANY		1	1	1958	1958	BECOMES SUMMER FUN
MICKEY MOUSE WEEKLY	WILLBANK PUBLISHING L		1	920	1936	1957	
MICKEY MOUSE XMAS SPECIAL	WILLBANK PUBLISHING L		1	1	1939	1939	
MICROBOTS, THE	GOLD KEY		1	1	1971	1971	
MICRONAUTS	MARVEL ENTERTAINMENT GROUP	1	1	59	1979	1984	
MICRONAUTS	MARVEL ENTERTAINMENT GROUP	2	1	20	1984	1986	
MICRONAUTS ANNUAL	MARVEL ENTERTAINMENT GROUP	1	1	2	1979	1980	
MICRONAUTS SPECIAL EDITION	MARVEL ENTERTAINMENT GROUP		1	5	1983	1984	
MIDGET COMIC, THE	D.C. THOMSON		1	1	1937	1937	
MIDGET COMIC, THE	D.C. THOMSON		1	4	1930	1930	
MIDGET COMIC, THE	R. & L. LOCKER		1	1	1946	1946	
MIDGET COMICS	P.M. PRODUCTIONS		1	1	1944	1944	
MIDGET COMICS	ST JOHN PUBLISHING		1	2	1950	1950	
MIDGET, THE	PROVINCIAL COMICS		1	13	1931	1931	
MIDNIGHT	AJAX		1	6	1957	1958	

COMIC TITLE	PUBLISHER	Vol No.	Srt No.	End No.	Str. Year	End Year	COMMENTS
MIDNIGHT EYE : GOKU, MOONLIGHT SCOPE	VIZ		1	1	1992	1992	
MIDNIGHT EYE : GOKU, P.I.	VIZ		1	6	1991	1992	
MIDNIGHT MEN	MARVEL ENTERTAINMENT GROUP		1	4	1993	1993	
MIDNIGHT MYSTERY	AMERICAN COMIC GROUP		1	7	1961	1961	
MIDNIGHT SONS UNLIMITED	MARVEL ENTERTAINMENT GROUP		1	4	1993	NOW	
MIDNIGHT SURFER SPECIAL	QUALITY (FLEETWAY)		1	2	1986	1986	
MIDNIGHT SURFER SPECIAL	QUALITY (FLEETWAY)		2	2	1986	1986	PREVIOUSLY STRONTIUM DOG SPECIAL
MIDNIGHT TALES	CHARLTON COMICS		1	18	1972	1976	
MIDNITE, THE REBEL SKUNK	BLACKTHORNE		1	3	1986	1987	
MIGHTY ATOM, THE	DENLEE PUBLISHING CO.		1	1	1948	1948	
MIGHTY ATOM, THE	I.W. ENTERPRISES		1	1	???	???	
MIGHTY ATOM, THE	MAGAZINE ENTERPRISES	1	6	6	1949	1949	FORMERLY MIGHTY ATOM AND THE PIXIES, THE
MIGHTY ATOM, THE	MAGAZINE ENTERPRISES	2	1	6	1957	1958	
MIGHTY BEAR	AJAX	2	1	3	1957	1958	
MIGHTY BEAR	STAR PUBLICATIONS	1	13	14	1954	1954	FORMERLY FUN COMICS
MIGHTY BOMBSHELLS	ANTARTIC PRESS		1	1	1993	NOW	
MIGHTY COMIC	PHILLIP MARX		1	1	1945	1945	
MIGHTY COMIC ANNUAL	GERALD SWAN		1	1	1952	1952	
MIGHTY COMICS PRESENTS	ARCHIE PUBLICATIONS		40	50	1966	1967	FORMERLY FLYMAN
MIGHTY CRUSADERS, THE	MIGHTY COMICS		1	7	1965	1966	
MIGHTY CRUSADERS, THE	RED CIRCLE		1	13	1983	1985	
MIGHTY GHOST	AJAX	4	4	4	1958	1958	FORMERLY MIGHTY BEAR
MIGHTY HERCULES, THE	GOLD KEY		1	2	1963	1963	
MIGHTY HEROES, THE	DELL PUBLISHING COMPANY		1	4	1967	1967	
MIGHTY MAGNOR	MALIBU COMICS ENTERTAINMENT INC.		1	5	1993	NOW	
MIGHTY MARVEL WESTERN, THE	MARVEL ENTERTAINMENT GROUP		1	46	1968	1976	
MIGHTY MIDGET COMICS, THE	SAMUEL LOWE COMPANY				1942	1943	MINIATURE COMICS FEATURING VARIOUS CHARACTERS
MIGHTY MITES, THE	ETERNITY		1	3	1986	1986	
MIGHTY MOUSE	DELL PUBLISHING COMPANY		166	172	1966	1968	
MIGHTY MOUSE	GOLD KEY		161	172	1964	1980	161-165 CALLED MIGHTY MOUSE, 14 YEAR GAP 165-166
MIGHTY MOUSE	MARVEL ENTERTAINMENT GROUP		1	10	1990	1991	
MIGHTY MOUSE	ST JOHN PUBLISHING	2	5	83	1947	1959	
MIGHTY MOUSE	TIMELY COMICS	1	1	4	1946	1947	
MIGHTY MOUSE ADVENTURE STORIES	ST JOHN PUBLISHING		1	1	1953	1953	
MIGHTY MOUSE ADVENTURES	ST JOHN PUBLISHING		1	1	1951	1951	
MIGHTY MOUSE ALBUM	ST JOHN PUBLISHING		1	2	1952	1952	
MIGHTY MOUSE FUN CLUB MAGAZINE	PINES		1	6	1957	1958	
MIGHTY MUTANIMALS	ARCHIE PUBLICATIONS		1	3	1991	1991	
MIGHTY MUTANIMALS	ARCHIE PUBLICATIONS	2	1	9	1992	1993	
MIGHTY MUTANIMALS SPECIAL	ARCHIE PUBLICATIONS		1	1	1992	1992	
MIGHTY SAMSON	GOLD KEY		1	32	1964	1982	
MIGHTY WORLD OF MARVEL	MARVEL ENTERTAINMENT GROUP	1	1	329	1972	1979	
MIGHTY WORLD OF MARVEL	MARVEL ENTERTAINMENT GROUP	2	1	17	1983	1984	
MIGHTY WORLD OF MARVEL SUMMER SPECIAL	MARVEL ENTERTAINMENT GROUP		1	1	1983	1983	
MIKE BARNETT MAN AGAINST CRIME	L. MILLER PUBLISHING COMPANY (UK)		50	54	1952	1952	FAWCETT REPRINTS
MIKE BARNETT, MAN AGAINST CRIME	FAWCETT PUBLICATIONS		1	6	1951	1952	
MIKE DONOVAN DETECTIVE COMIC	ARNOLD BOOK CO..		1	1	1951	1951	
MIKE SHAYNE PRIVATE EYE	TOP SELLERS		1	1	1962	1962	DELL REPRINTS
MILESTONE MAGAZINE FOR KIDS	WELSH PUBLICATIONS		1	1	1994	1994	
MILITARY COMICS	QUALITY COMICS		1	43	1941	1945	
MILITARY WILLY	J.I. AUSTEN CO.		1	1	1907	1907	
MILLENNIUM	DC COMICS INC.		1	8	1988	1988	
MILLENNIUM INDEX	ICG & ECLIPSE		1	2	1988	1988	
MILLIE THE MODEL	MARVEL ENTERTAINMENT GROUP		1	207	1945	1973	
MILLIE THE MODEL ANNUAL	MARVEL ENTERTAINMENT GROUP		1	12	1962	1971	
MILLIE, THE LOVABLE MONSTER	DELL PUBLISHING COMPANY	12		4	1962	1973	
MILLION DOLLAR DIGEST, RICHIE RICH'S	HARVEY PUBLICATIONS		1	30	1986	1992	
MILT GROSS FUNNIES	MILT GROSS INC.		1	2	1947	1947	
MILTON THE MONSTER & FEARLESS FLY	GOLD KEY		1	1	1966	1966	
MINIATURE COMIC, THE	P.M. PRODUCTIONS		1	2	1944	1944	
MINOTAUR'S TALE, THE	VICTOR GOLLANCZ		1	1	1992	1992	
MINOTAURS TALE, THE	DARK HORSE COMICS		1	1	1992	1992	
MINUTE MAN	FAWCETT PUBLICATIONS		1	3	1941	1942	
MINUTE MAN	SOVEREIGN SERVICE STATION		1	1	???	???	PETROL SERVICE GIVE AWAY
MINUTE MAN ANSWERS THE CALL, THE	M.C. GAINES		1	1	1942	1942	
MIRACLE COMICS	HILLMAN PERIODICALS		1	4	1940	1941	
MIRACLE MAN	TOP SELLERS		1	13	1965	1965	
MIRACLE SQUAD	UPSHOT		1	4	1986	1987	
MIRACLE SQUAD: BLOOD AND DUST	APPLE COMICS		1	4	1989	1989	
MIRACLEMAN	ECLIPSE		1	24	1985	NOW	
MIRACLEMAN 3-D SPECIAL	ECLIPSE		1	1	1985	1985	
MIRACLEMAN FAMILY	ECLIPSE		1	2	1988	1988	
MIRACLEMAN: APOCRYPHA	ECLIPSE		1	1	1993	1993	
MIRACLEMAN: THE APOCRYPHA	ECLIPSE		1	3	1991	1992	
MIRACULOUS CIRCUMSTANCES	LUDDITE ENTERPRISES		1	2	1982	1982	
MIRROR MAN COMIC, THE	DONALD PETERS		21	21	1950	1950	
MIRROR WALKER	NOW		1	2	1989	1989	
MIRTH COMIC, THE	PHILIMAR		1	1	1948	1948	
MISCHIEVOUS MONKS OF CROCODILE ISLE, THE	J.I. AUSTEN CO.		1	1	1908	1908	
MISS AMERICA COMICS	MARVEL ENTERTAINMENT GROUP		1	1	1944	1944	
MISS AMERICA MAGAZINE	MARVEL ENTERTAINMENT GROUP		1	93	1944	1958	FORMERLY MISS AMERICA
MISS BEVERLY HILLS OF HOLLYWOOD	DC COMICS INC.		1	9	1949	1950	
MISS CAIRO JONES	CROYDON PUBLISHERS		1	1	1945	1945	
MISS FURY	ADVENTURE COMICS		1	4	1991	1991	
MISS FURY COMICS	TIMELY COMICS		1	8	1942	1946	NEWSPAPER STRIP REPRINTS
MISS FURY QUARTERLY	A PLUS COMICS		1	1	1992	NOW	
MISS LIBERTY	BURTEN PUBLISHING CO.		1	1	1945	1945	

COMIC TITLE	PUBLISHER	Vol No.	Srt No.	End No.	Str. Year	End Year	COMMENTS
MISS MELODY LANE OF BROADWAY	DC COMICS INC.		1	3	1950	1950	
MISS PEACH	DELL PUBLISHING COMPANY		1	1	1963	1963	
MISSING MARTIAN	ETERNITY		1	2	1990	1990	
MISSION IMPOSSIBLE	DELL PUBLISHING COMPANY		1	5	1967	1968	
MISTER E	DC COMICS INC.		1	4	1991	1991	
MISTER ED, THE TALKING HORSE	GOLD KEY		1	4	1962	1964	
MISTER FIXITT	HEROIC PUBLISHING		1	1	1993	NOW	
MISTER MIRACLE	DC COMICS INC.	1	1	25	1971	1978	
MISTER MIRACLE	DC COMICS INC.	2	1	28	1989	1991	
MISTER MIRACLE SPECIAL	DC COMICS INC.		1	1	1987	1987	
MISTER MYSTERY	MEDIA ARTS PUBLISHING		1	18	1951	1954	
MISTER UNIVERSE, PROFESSIONAL WRESTLER	STANMORE PUBLICATIONS		1	5	1951	1952	
MISTER X	VORTEX	1	1	14	1984	1988	
MISTER X	VORTEX	2	1	12	1989	1990	
MISTY	IPC		1	102	1978	1979	
MITZI COMICS	TIMELY COMICS		1	1	1948	1948	
MITZI'S BOY FRIEND	MARVEL ENTERTAINMENT GROUP		2	7	1948	1949	FORMERLY MITZI
MITZI'S ROMANCES	MARVEL ENTERTAINMENT GROUP		8	10	1949	1949	FORMERLY MITZI'S BOY FRIEND
MOBILE SUIT GUNDAM 0083	VIZ		1	2	1993	NOW	
MOBY DICK	UNITED-ANGLO PRODUCTIONS		1	2	1951	1951	
MOBY DUCK	GOLD KEY		1	30	1967	1978	
MOD	KITCHEN SINK		1	1	1981	1981	
MOD LOVE	WESTERN PUBLISHING COMPANY		1	1	1967	1967	
MOD SQUAD	DELL PUBLISHING COMPANY		1	10	1969	1971	
MOD WHEELS	GOLD KEY		1	19	1971	1976	
MODEL FUN	HARIE PUBLICATIONS		3	5	1954	1955	
MODELLING WITH MILLIE	MARVEL ENTERTAINMENT GROUP		21	54	1963	1967	FORMERLY LIFE WITH MILLIE
MODERN CLASSICS: FREAKS AMOUR	DARK HORSE COMICS		1	3	1992	1993	
MODERN COMICS	MODERM FICTION		1	1	1949	1949	
MODERN COMICS	QUALITY COMICS		44	102	1945	1950	FORMERLY MILITARY COMICS
MODERN LOVE	EC COMICS		1	8	1949	1950	
MODESTY BLAISE	DC COMICS INC.		1	2	1993	1993	
MODNIKS, THE	GOLD KEY		1	2	1967	1970	
MOE & SHMOE COMICS	O.S. PUBLISHING CO.		1	2	1948	1948	
MOEBIUS	MARVEL ENTERTAINMENT GROUP		1	8	1987	NOW	
MOEBIUS: CHAOS	MARVEL ENTERTAINMENT GROUP		1	1	1991	1991	
MOLLY MANTON'S ROMANCES	MARVEL ENTERTAINMENT GROUP		1	2	1949	1949	
MOLLY O'DAY	AVON BOOKS		1	1	1945	1945	
MONKEES, THE	DELL PUBLISHING COMPANY		1	17	1967	1969	
MONKEY & THE BEAR, THE	ATLAS		1	3	1953	1954	
MONKEY BUSINESS	PARODY PRESS		1	3	1993	NOW	
MONKEY SHINES OF MARSALEEN	CUPPLES AND LEON CO.		1	1	1909	1909	
MONKEYSHINES COMICS	ACE PUBLISHING		1	27	1944	1949	
MONOLITH	COMICO		1	4	1991	1991	
MONOSHOCK	SAVOY ADULT GRAPHICS		1	1	1992	1992	
MONROES, THE	DELL PUBLISHING COMPANY		1	1	1967	1967	
MONSTER	FICTION HOUSE		1	2	1953	1953	
MONSTER ID COMIC, THE	FLEETWAY		1	383	1930	1932	
MONSTER BOY	MONSTER COMICS		1	1	1991	1991	
MONSTER CLUB	PIONEER		1	1	1980	1980	
MONSTER COMIC	PHILLIP MARX		1	1	1945	1945	
MONSTER COMIC, THE	C.A. PEARSON		1	2	1939	1939	
MONSTER CRIME COMICS	HILLMAN PERIODICALS		1	1	1952	1952	
MONSTER HOWLS	HUMOR-VISION		1	1	1966	1966	
MONSTER HUNTERS	CHARLTON COMICS		1	19	1975	1979	
MONSTER IN MY POCKET	HARVEY PUBLICATIONS		1	4	1991	1991	
MONSTER IN MY POCKET ANNUAL	HARVEY PUBLICATIONS		1	1	1991	1991	
MONSTER MASSACRE	ATOMEKA		1	1	1993	1993	
MONSTER MASSACRE	BLACK BALL COMICS		1	1	1993	NOW	
MONSTER MASSACRE: CARNOSAUR CARNAGE	ATOMEKA		1	1	1993	1993	
MONSTER MASTERWORKS	MARVEL ENTERTAINMENT GROUP		1	1	1990	1990	
MONSTER MENACE	MARVEL ENTERTAINMENT GROUP		1	4	1993	1994	
MONSTER MONTHLY	MARVEL ENTERTAINMENT GROUP		1	4	1982	1983	
MONSTER POSSE	ADVENTURE COMICS		1	3	1992	1992	
MONSTER TIMES, THE	MONSTER TIMES PUBLISHING COMPANY		1	4	1972	1973	NEWSPAPER FORMAT
MONSTERS FROM OUTER SPACE	ADVENTURE COMICS		1	2	1993	1994	
MONSTERS ON THE PROWL	MARVEL ENTERTAINMENT GROUP		9	30	1971	1974	FORMERLY CHAMBER OF DARKNESS
MONSTERS UNLEASHED	MARVEL ENTERTAINMENT GROUP		1	11	1973	1975	
MONSTERS UNLEASHED ANNUAL	MARVEL ENTERTAINMENT GROUP		1	1	1975	1975	
MONTE HALE WESTERN	FAWCETT PUBLICATIONS		29	88	1948	1956	FORMERLY MARY MARVEL COMICS
MONTE HALE WESTERN	L. MILLER PUBLISHING COMPANY (UK)	1	1	1	1950	1950	FAWCETT REPRINTS
MONTE HALE WESTERN	L. MILLER PUBLISHING COMPANY (UK)	2	50	118	1951	1959	
MONTY HALL OF THE U.S. MARINES	TOBY PRESS PUBLICATIONS		1	11	1951	1953	
MOON COMICS	A. HALLE		1	1	1948	1948	
MOON COMIX	BIRMINGHAM ARTS LAB		1	2	1977	1977	
MOON GIRL AND THE PRINCE	EC COMICS		1	8	1947	1949	
MOON KNIGHT	MARVEL ENTERTAINMENT GROUP	1	1	38	1980	1984	
MOON KNIGHT SPECIAL	MARVEL ENTERTAINMENT GROUP		1	1	1992	1992	
MOON KNIGHT SPECIAL EDITION	MARVEL ENTERTAINMENT GROUP		1	3	1992	1992	
MOON KNIGHT: DIVIDED WE FALL	MARVEL ENTERTAINMENT GROUP		1	1	1992	1992	
MOON KNIGHT: FIST OF KHONSHU	MARVEL ENTERTAINMENT GROUP	2	1	6	1985	1985	
MOON KNIGHT: MARC SPECTOR	MARVEL ENTERTAINMENT GROUP	3	1	58	1989	1994	
MOON MULLINS	AMERICAN COMIC GROUP		1	8	1947	1949	
MOON MULLINS	CUPPLES AND LEON CO.		1	7	1927	1933	
MOON MULLINS BIG BOOK	CUPPLES AND LEON CO.		1	1	1930	1930	
MOON, A GIRL...ROMANCE	EC COMICS		9	12	1949	1950	FORMERLY MOON GIRL
MOONSHADOW	MARVEL ENTERTAINMENT GROUP		1	1	1987	1987	
MOONSHADOW	MARVEL ENTERTAINMENT GROUP		1	12	1985	1987	
MOONSHADOW LIMITED HARDCOVER	MARVEL ENTERTAINMENT GROUP		1	1	1987	1987	
MOPSY	ST JOHN PUBLISHING		1	19	1948	1953	

COMIC TITLE	PUBLISHER	Vol No.	Srt No.	End No.	Str. Year	End Year	COMMENTS
MORBIUS REVISITED	MARVEL ENTERTAINMENT GROUP		I	5	1993	NOW	
MORBIUS: THE LIVING VAMPIRE	MARVEL ENTERTAINMENT GROUP		I	18	1992	NOW	
MORE FUN COMICS	DC COMICS INC.		7	127	1936	1947	
MORE SEYMOUR	ARCHIE PUBLICATIONS		I	I	1963	1963	
MORGANA X	SKY COMICS		I	6	1994	1994	
MORLOCK 2001	ATLAS		I	3	1975	1975	
MORNINGSTAR BOOK ONE: BLACK DOG	TRIDENT		I	I	1990	1990	
MORNINGSTAR SPECIAL	COMICO		I	I	1990	1990	
MORT THE DEAD TEENAGER	MARVEL ENTERTAINMENT GROUP		I	I	1993	1994	
MORTIE: MAZIE'S FRIEND	MAGAZINE PUBLISHERS		I	4	1952	1953	
MOSES & THE TEN COMMANDMENTS	DELL PUBLISHING COMPANY		I	I	1957	1957	
MOTHER OF US ALL	CAETECHETICAL EDUCATIONAL SOCIETY		I	I	1950	1950	
MOTHER TERESA OF CALCUTTA	MARVEL ENTERTAINMENT GROUP		I	I	1984	1984	
MOTION PICTURE COMICS	FAWCETT PUBLICATIONS		101	114	1950	1953	
MOTION PICTURE COMICS	L. MILLER PUBLISHING COMPANY (UK)		50	59	1951	1952	FAWCETT REPRINTS
MOTION PICTURE FUNNIES WEEKLY	FIRST FUNNIES		I	I	1939	1939	
MOTORHEAD SPECIAL	DARK HORSE COMICS		I	I	1994	1994	
MOTORMOUTH	MARVEL ENTERTAINMENT GROUP		I	12	1992	1993	
MOTORMOUTH: RE-MIX	MARVEL ENTERTAINMENT GROUP		I	4	1994	1994	MARVEL UK TITLE
MOVIE CLASSICS	DELL PUBLISHING COMPANY		112506	922308	1963	1969	
MOVIE CLASSICS	WORLD DISTRIBUTORS LTD		I	88	1955	1960	DELL REPRINTS
MOVIE COMICS	GOLD KEY		10042	30032	1962	1972	
MOVIE THRILLERS	MAGAZINE ENTERPRISES		I	I	1949	1949	
MOVIE TOWN ANIMAL ANTICS	DC COMICS INC.		24	51	1950	1954	FORMERLY ANIMAL ANTICS
MOVIE TUNES COMICS	MARVEL ENTERTAINMENT GROUP		3	3	1946	1946	FORMERLY ANIMATED MOVIE TUNES COMICS
MR MONSTER VS NAZIS FROM MARS	ATOMEKA		I	I	1993	1993	
MR T AND THE T-FORCE	NOW		I	4	1993	NOW	
MR. & MRS.	WHITMAN		I	2	1922	1922	
MR. & MRS. J.EVIL SCIENTIST	GOLD KEY		I	4	1963	1966	
MR. ANTHONY'S LOVE CLINIC	HILLMAN PERIODICALS		I	5	1949	1950	
MR. BUG GOES TO TOWN	K.K. PUBLICATIONS		I	I	1941	1941	
MR. DISTRICT ATTORNEY	DC COMICS INC.		I	67	1948	1959	
MR. DISTRICT ATTORNEY	THORPE & PORTER		I	23	1953	1953	DC REPRINTS
MR. LIZARD SPECIAL	NOW		I	I	1992	1992	
MR. MAGOO, THE NEARSIGHTED	DELL PUBLISHING COMPANY		I	5	1962	1963	
MR. MONSTER	DARK HORSE COMICS		I	8	1988	1988	
MR. MONSTER	ECLIPSE		I	10	1985	1987	
MR. MONSTER'S SUPER-DUPER SPECIALS	ECLIPSE		I	8	1986	1987	
MR. RISK	ACE PUBLISHING		7	2	1950	1950	FORMERLY ALL ROMANCES
MRS WEBER'S DIARY	FONTANA		I	I	1982	1982	
MS MYSTIC	CONTINUITY COMICS	I	I	9	1987	NOW	
MS MYSTIC	CONTINUITY COMICS	2	I	3	1993	NOW	
MS MYSTIC	CONTINUITY COMICS	3	I	3	1993	NOW	
MS MYSTIC	PACIFIC COMICS		I	2	1982	1984	
MS. MARVEL	MARVEL ENTERTAINMENT GROUP		I	23	1977	1979	
MS. TREE	AARDVARK PUBLICATIONS		10	18	1984	1985	CONTINUED FROM ECLIPSE SERIES
MS. TREE	ECLIPSE		I	9	1983	1984	
MS. TREE	RENEGADE PRESS		I	50	1985	1989	CONTINUED FROM AARDVARK SERIES
MS. TREE 3-D	RENEGADE PRESS		I	I	1985	1985	
MS. TREE QUARTERLY	DC COMICS INC.		I	10	1990	NOW	
MS. TREE'S 1950'S THREE DIMENSIONAL CRIME	RENEGADE PRESS		I	I	1987	1987	
MS. VICTORY GOLDEN ANNIVERSARY SPECIAL	AC COMICS		I	I	1991	1991	
MUGGSY MOUSE	I.W. ENTERPRISES		I	2	1964	1964	
MUGGSY MOUSE	MAGAZINE ENTERPRISES		I	5	1951	1954	
MUGGSY MOUSE	SUPER COMICS		14	14	1963	1963	
MUGGY-DOO, BOY CAT	STANHALL		I	4	1953	1954	
MUGGY-DOO, BOY CAT	SUPER COMICS		12	16	1963	1964	
MUMMY ARCHIVES, THE	MILLENIUM		I	I	1992	1992	
MUMMY OR RAMSES THE DAMNED, ANNE RICE'S	MILLENIUM		I	12	1990	1991	
MUMMY'S CURSE, THE	AIRCEL		I	4	1990	1991	
MUMMY, THE	MONSTER COMICS		I	4	1991	1991	
MUMMY, THE	TOP SELLERS		I	I	1963	1963	DELL REPRINTS
MUNDEN'S BAR ANNUAL	FIRST		I	2	1988	1991	
MUNSTERS, THE	GOLD KEY		I	16	1965	1968	
MUPPET BABIES ADVENTURES	HARVEY PUBLICATIONS		I	4	1993	NOW	
MUPPET BABIES BIG BOOK	HARVEY PUBLICATIONS		I	I	1992	NOW	
MUPPET BABIES, THE	MARVEL ENTERTAINMENT GROUP		I	5	1985	1989	
MUPPETS TAKE MANHATTAN, THE	MARVEL ENTERTAINMENT GROUP		I	3	1984	1985	
MURCIELAGA SHE BAT	HEROIC PUBLISHING		I	6	1993	1993	
MURDER	RENEGADE PRESS		I	5	1986	1986	
MURDER BAG	PEARSON		I	3	1959	1959	
MURDER TALES	WORLD FAMOUS PUBLICATIONS		10	11	1970	1971	
MURDER, INCORPORATED	FOX FEATURES SYNDICATE	I	I	15	1948	1949	
MURDER, INCORPORATED	FOX FEATURES SYNDICATE	2	I	3	1950	1951	
MURDEROUS GANGSTERS	AVON BOOKS		I	4	1951	1952	
MURDEROUS GANGSTERS	AVON PERIODICALS		I	4	1951	1952	
MUSHMOUSE AND PUNKIN PUSS	GOLD KEY		I	I	1965	1965	
MUTANT ZONE	AIRCEL		I	3	1991	1991	
MUTATIS	MARVEL ENTERTAINMENT GROUP		I	3	1992	1992	
MUTINY	ARAGON MAGAZINES		I	3	1954	1955	
MUTT AND JEFF	CUPPLES AND LEON CO.		I	3	1926	1929	
MUTT AND JEFF	CUPPLES AND LEON CO.		6	22	1916	1933	
MUTT AND JEFF	DC COMICS INC.		I	103	1939	1958	
MUTT AND JEFF	DELL PUBLISHING COMPANY		104	115	1958	1959	
MUTT AND JEFF	EMBEE DISTRIBUTION CO.		I	I	1921	1921	
MUTT AND JEFF	HARVEY PUBLICATIONS		116	148	1960	1965	

COMIC TITLE	PUBLISHER	Vol No.	Srt No.	End No.	Str. Year	End Year	COMMENTS
MUTT AND JEFF CARTOON, THE	BALL PUBLICATIONS		1	5	1910	1916	
MUTT AND JEFF JOKES	HARVEY PUBLICATIONS		1	3	1960	1961	
MUTT AND JEFF NEW JOKES	HARVEY PUBLICATIONS		1	4	1963	1965	
MY CONFESSIONS	FOX FEATURES SYNDICATE		7	10	1949	1950	FORMERLY WESTERN TRUE CRIME
MY DATE COMICS	HILLMAN PERIODICALS		1	4	1947	1948	
MY DESIRE	FOX FEATURES SYNDICATE		30	32	1949	1950	FORMERLY JO-JO COMICS
MY DIARY	MARVEL ENTERTAINMENT GROUP		1	2	1949	1950	
MY DOG TIGE	BUSTER BROWN SHOES		1	1	1957	1957	
MY EXPERIENCE	FOX FEATURES SYNDICATE		19	22	1949	1950	FORMERLY ALL TOP
MY FAVOURITE	AMALGAMATED PRESS		1	351	1928	1934	FORMERLY COMIC LIFE
MY FAVOURITE MARTIAN	GOLD KEY		1	9	1964	1966	
MY FRIEND IRMA	MARVEL ENTERTAINMENT GROUP		3	48	1950	1955	FORMERLY MY DIARY
MY GIRL PEARL	ATLAS		1	11	1955	1961	
MY GREAT LOVE	FOX FEATURES SYNDICATE		1	4	1949	1950	
MY GREATEST ADVENTURE	DC COMICS INC.		1	85	1955	1964	
MY GREATEST THRILLS IN BASEBALL	MISSION OF CALIFORNIA		1	???	???	???	
MY INTIMATE AFFAIR	FOX FEATURES SYNDICATE		1	2	1950	1950	
MY LIFE	FOX FEATURES SYNDICATE		4	15	1948	1950	FORMERLY MEET CORLISS ARCHER
MY LITTLE MARGIE	CHARLTON COMICS		1	54	1954	1964	
MY LITTLE MARGIE'S BOY FRIENDS	CHARLTON COMICS		1	11	1955	1958	
MY LITTLE MARGIE'S FASHIONS	CHARLTON COMICS		1	5	1959	1959	
MY LOVE	MARVEL ENTERTAINMENT GROUP	1	1	4	1949	1950	
MY LOVE	MARVEL ENTERTAINMENT GROUP	2	1	39	1969	1976	
MY LOVE AFFAIR	FOX FEATURES SYNDICATE		1	6	1949	1950	
MY LOVE LIFE	FOX FEATURES SYNDICATE		6	13	1949	1951	FORMERLY ZEGRA
MY LOVE MEMOIRS	FOX FEATURES SYNDICATE		9	12	1949	1950	FORMERLY OUTLAW WOMEN
MY LOVE SECRET	FOX FEATURES SYNDICATE		24	53	1949	1954	FORMERLY PHANTOM LADY
MY LOVE STORY	FOX FEATURES SYNDICATE		1	9	1956	1957	
MY NAME IS CHAOS	DC COMICS INC.		1	4	1992	1992	
MY ONLY LOVE	CHARLTON COMICS		1	9	1975	1976	
MY OWN ROMANCE	ATLAS		60	75	1958	1960	
MY OWN ROMANCE	MARVEL ENTERTAINMENT GROUP		4	76	1949	1960	
MY PAST CONFESSIONS	FOX FEATURES SYNDICATE		7	11	1949	1950	FORMERLY WESTERN THRILLERS
MY PERSONAL PROBLEM	AJAX	1	1	4	1955	1956	
MY PERSONAL PROBLEM	STEINWAY/AMERICA'S BEST	2	1	3	1957	1958	
MY PRIVATE LIFE	FOX FEATURES SYNDICATE		16	17	1950	1950	FORMERLY MURDER, INC
MY REAL LOVE	STANDARD COMICS		5	5	1952	1952	
MY ROMANCE	MARVEL ENTERTAINMENT GROUP		1	3	1948	1949	
MY ROMANTIC ADVENTURES	AMERICAN COMIC GROUP		68	138	1956	1964	FORMERLY ROMANTIC ADVENTURES
MY SECRET	SUPERIOR COMICS		1	3	1949	1949	
MY SECRET AFFAIR	FOX FEATURES SYNDICATE		1	3	1949	1950	
MY SECRET CONFESSION	STERLING COMICS		1	1	1955	1955	
MY SECRET LIFE	CHARLTON COMICS		19	47	1957	1962	FORMERLY YOUNG LOVERS
MY SECRET LIFE	FOX FEATURES SYNDICATE		22	27	1949	1950	FORMERLY WESTERN OUTLAWS
MY SECRET MARRIAGE	I.W. SUPER		9	9	60'S	60'S	
MY SECRET MARRIAGE	SUPERIOR COMICS		1	24	1953	1956	
MY SECRET ROMANCE	FOX FEATURES SYNDICATE		1	2	1950	1950	
MY SECRET STORY	FOX FEATURES SYNDICATE		26	29	1949	1950	FORMERLY CAPTAIN KIDD
MY STORY	FOX FEATURES SYNDICATE		5	12	1949	1950	FORMERLY ZAGO
MY TRUE LOVE	FOX FEATURES SYNDICATE		65	69	1949	1950	FORMERLY WESTERN KILLERS
MYRA	MYRA HANCOCK		1	9	1982	NOW	
MYS-TECH WARS	MARVEL ENTERTAINMENT GROUP		1	4	1993	1993	
MYSTERIES OF SCOTLAND YARD	CARTOON ART		1	1	1955	1955	MAGAZINE ENTERPRISES REPRINTS
MYSTERIES OF THE UNEXPLORED	G.T. LIMITED		1	1	1959	1959	
MYSTERIES OF UNEXPLORED WORLDS	L. MILLER PUBLISHING COMPANY (UK)		1	1	1956	1956	CHARLTON REPRINTS
MYSTERIES OF UNEXPLORED WORLDS	CHARLTON COMICS		1	48	1956	1965	
MYSTERIES WEIRD AND STRANGE	SUPERIOR COMICS		1	11	1953	1955	
MYSTERIOUS ADVENTURES	STORY COMICS		1	25	1951	1955	
MYSTERIOUS ISLE	DELL PUBLISHING COMPANY		1	1	1963	1964	
MYSTERIOUS STORIES	PREMIER MAGAZINES		2	7	1954	1955	FORMERLY HORROR FROM THE TOMB
MYSTERIOUS SUSPENSE	CHARLTON COMICS		1	1	1968	1968	
MYSTERIOUS TRAVELER COMICS	TRANS-WORLD PUBLICATIONS		1	1	1948	1948	
MYSTERY COMICS	T.V. BOARDMAN		7	11	1940	1941	
MYSTERY COMICS	WILLIAM H. WISE		1	4	1944	1944	
MYSTERY COMICS DIGEST	GOLD KEY		1	26	1972	1975	
MYSTERY IN SPACE	DC COMICS INC.		1	117	1951	1981	
MYSTERY IN SPACE	L. MILLER PUBLISHING COMPANY (UK)		1	9	1952	1954	DC REPRINTS
MYSTERY IN SPACE	STRATO		1	13	1954	1955	DC REPRINTS
MYSTERY MEN COMICS	FOX FEATURES SYNDICATE		1	31	1939	1942	
MYSTERY TALES	ATLAS		1	54	1952	1957	
MYSTERY TALES	SUPER COMICS		16	18	1964	1964	
MYSTIC	ATLAS		1	61	1951	1957	
MYSTIC	L. MILLER PUBLISHING COMPANY (UK)		1	66	1961	1966	ATLAS AND MARVEL REPRINTS
MYSTIC COMICS	TIMELY COMICS	1	1	10	1940	1942	
MYSTIC COMICS	TIMELY COMICS	2	1	4	1944	1945	
MYSTICAL TALES	ATLAS		1	8	1956	1957	
MYTH CONCEPTIONS	APPLE COMICS		1	7	1987	1988	
MYTHADVENTURES	WARP GRAPHICS		1	12	1984	1986	
MYTHFITS	HEROIC PUBLISHING		1	1	1993	NOW	
MYTHOLOGY OF AN ABANDONED CITY	TUNDRA		1	1	1993	1993	

N

NAM, THE	MARVEL ENTERTAINMENT GROUP		1	1	1991	1991	
NAM, THE	MARVEL ENTERTAINMENT GROUP		1	84	1986	1993	
NAMOR THE SUB-MARINER	MARVEL ENTERTAINMENT GROUP		1	47	1990	NOW	
NAMOR THE SUB-MARINER ANNUAL	MARVEL ENTERTAINMENT GROUP		1	3	1991	NOW	
NAMORA	MARVEL ENTERTAINMENT GROUP		1	3	1948	1948	

COMIC TITLE	PUBLISHER	Vol No.	Srt No.	End No.	Str. Year	End Year	COMMENTS
NANCY AND SLUGGO	DELL PUBLISHING COMPANY	2	146	187	1957	1962	
NANCY AND SLUGGO	GOLD KEY	2	188	192	1962	1963	
NANCY AND SLUGGO	ST JOHN PUBLISHING	2	121	145	1955	1957	FORMERLY SPARKLER COMICS
NANCY AND SLUGGO	UNITED FEATURES SYNDICATE		16	23	1949	1954	
NANCY AND SLUGGO	UNITED FEATURES SYNDICATE	1	16	23	1949	1954	
NANCY AND SLUGGO TRAVEL TIME	DELL PUBLISHING COMPANY		1	1	1958	1958	
NANNY AND THE PROFESSOR	DELL PUBLISHING COMPANY		1	2	1970	1970	
NAPALM KISS	BIRMINGHAM ARTS LAB		1	1	1977	1977	
NAPOLEON AND UNCLE ELBY	EASTERN COLOR PRINTING COMPANY		1	1	1942	1942	
NAPOLEON AND UNCLE ELBY	EASTERN COLOR PRINTING COMPANY		1	1	1945	1945	
NASTY TALES	BLOOM PUBLICATIONS		1	7	1971	1972	
NATHANIEL DUSK	DC COMICS INC.	1	1	4	1984	1984	
NATHANIEL DUSK	DC COMICS INC.	2	1	4	1985	1986	
NATION OF SNITCHES	DC COMICS INC.		1	1	1990	1990	
NATIONAL COMICS	QUALITY COMICS		1	75	1940	1949	
NATIONAL CRUMB, THE	MAYFAIR PUBLICATIONS		1	1	1975	1975	
NATIONAL VELVET	GOLD KEY		1	2	1962	1963	
NATURE BOY	CHARLTON COMICS		3	5	1956	1957	FORMERLY DANNY BLAZE
NATURE BOY	L. MILLER PUBLISHING COMPANY (UK)		1	2	1957	1957	CHARLTON REPRINTS
NATURE OF THE BEAST	CALIBER PRESS		1	3	1991	1992	
NAUSIATING MYSTERY COMIX	NAUSEATING COMIX GROUP		1	1	1971	1971	
NAUSICAA OF THE VALLEY OF WIND	VIZ	1	1	7	1987	1989	
NAUSICAA OF THE VALLEY OF WIND	VIZ	2	1	4	1989	1990	
NAUSICAA OF THE VALLEY OF WIND	VIZ	3	1	3	1992	1992	
NAVY ACTION	ATLAS		1	18	1954	1957	
NAVY COMBAT	ATLAS		1	20	1955	1958	
NAVY HEROES	ALMANAC PUBLISHING CO.		1	1	1945	1945	
NAVY PATROL	KEY PUBLICATIONS		1	4	1955	1955	
NAVY PATROL	STREAMLINE		1	1	1955	1955	KEY PUBLICATIONS REPRINTS
NAVY TALES	ATLAS		1	4	1957	1957	
NAVY TASK FORCE	STANMORE PUBLICATIONS		1	8	1954	1956	
NAVY TASK FORCE	STREAMLINE		1	1	1955	1955	STANMORE REPRINTS
NAVY WAR HEROES	CHARLTON COMICS		1	7	1964	1965	
NAZA: STONE AGE WARRIOR	DELL PUBLISHING COMPANY		1	9	1963	1966	
NAZZ, THE	DC COMICS INC.		1	4	1990	1991	
NEAR MINT	AL DELLINGES PUBLICATIONS		1	3	1980	1980	
NEAR MYTHS	GALAXY MEDIA		1	5	1978	1980	
NEAR MYTHS	GALAXY MEDIA DISTRIBUTION		1	2	1978	1980	
NEAR MYTHS	RIP OFF PRESS		1	6	1990	NOW	
NEBBS, THE	CROYDON PUBLISHERS		1	1	1945	1945	
NEBBS, THE	CUPPLES AND LEON CO.		1	1	1928	1928	
NECROMANCER	CITADEL COMICS		1	4	1992	1993	
NECROMANCER: SEASON OF THE WITCH	INNOVATION		1	3	1991	1991	
NECROPOLIS	FLEETWAY		1	9	1992	1993	
NECROSCOPE	MALIBU COMICS ENTERTAINMENT INC.		1	5	1992	1993	
NECROSCOPE BOOK II: WAMPHYRI	MALIBU COMICS ENTERTAINMENT INC.		1	2	1993	1994	
NEGATIVE BURN: AN ANTHOLOGY	CALIBER PRESS		1	5	1993	NOW	
NEGRO HEROES	PARENTS MAGAZINE INSTITUTE		1	2	1947	1948	
NEGRO ROMANCE	FAWCETT PUBLICATIONS		1	3	1950	1950	
NEGRO ROMANCES	CHARLTON COMICS	4	4	4	1955	1955	FORMERLY NEGRO ROMANCE
NEIL THE HORSE COMICS AND STORIES	AARDVARK-VANAHEIM		1	15	1983	1985	
NELLIE THE NURSE	ATLAS		1	1	1957	1957	
NELLIE THE NURSE	MARVEL ENTERTAINMENT GROUP		1	36	1945	1952	
NEMESIS	TITAN BOOKS		1	9	1984	1989	
NEMESIS THE BEGINNING	TITAN BOOKS		1	9	1992	1992	
NEMESIS THE WARLOCK	EAGLE		1	7	1984	1985	
NEMESIS THE WARLOCK	FLEETWAY		1	22	1989	1991	
NEON CITY	INNOVATION		1	1	1991	1991	
NEON CITY : AFTER THE FALL	INNOVATION		1	1	1992	NOW	
NEUROMANCER: THE GRAPHIC NOVEL	MARVEL ENTERTAINMENT GROUP		1	1	1989	1989	
NEUTRO	DELL PUBLISHING COMPANY		1	1	1967	1967	
NEVER AGAIN	CHARLTON COMICS		1	2	1955	1956	
NEVERWHERE	ARIEL BOOKS INC		1	1	1978	1978	
NEW ADVENTURE COMICS	DC COMICS INC.		12	31	1937	1938	FORMERLY NEW COMICS
NEW ADVENTURES OF BARBARELLA	VIRGIN		1	4	1981	1981	
NEW ADVENTURES OF CHARLIE CHAN, THE	DC COMICS INC.		1	6	1958	1959	
NEW ADVENTURES OF DON JUAN, THE	PETT		1	1	1948	1948	
NEW ADVENTURES OF HUCK FINN, THE	GOLD KEY		1	1	1968	1968	
NEW ADVENTURES OF PETER PAN, THE	WESTERN PUBLISHING COMPANY		1	1	1953	1953	
NEW ADVENTURES OF PINOCCHIO, THE	DELL PUBLISHING COMPANY		1	3	1962	1963	
NEW AMERICA	ECLIPSE		1	4	1987	1988	
NEW ARCHIES DIGEST	ARCHIE PUBLICATIONS		1	14	1988	1991	
NEW ARCHIES DIGEST MAGAZINE	ARCHIE PUBLICATIONS		1	14	1988	1991	
NEW ARCHIES, THE	ARCHIE PUBLICATIONS		1	28	1987	1990	
NEW AVENGERS ANNUAL	BROWN WATSON		1977	1978	1977	1978	
NEW BOOK OF COMICS	DC COMICS INC.		1	2	1937	1938	
NEW BREED	CALIBER PRESS		1	1	1993	NOW	
NEW COMICS	DC COMICS INC.		1	11	1935	1936	
NEW COMICS, THE	PHILLIP MARX		1	2	1942	1942	
NEW FRONTIER	DARK HORSE COMICS		1	3	1992	1992	
NEW FUN COMICS	DC COMICS INC.		1	6	1935	1935	
NEW FUNNIES	DELL PUBLISHING COMPANY		65	288	1942	1962	WALTER LANTZ NEW FUNNIES FROM 109
NEW FUNNIES	GERALD SWAN		1	42	1940	1951	
NEW FUNNIES AUTUMN SPECIAL	GERALD SWAN		1941	1941	1941	1941	
NEW FUNNIES BUMPER	GERALD SWAN		1	1	1950	1950	
NEW FUNNIES SPRING SPECIAL	GERALD SWAN		1941	1943	1941	1943	
NEW FUNNIES WINTER SPECIAL	GERALD SWAN		1941	1944	1941	1944	
NEW GODS CLASSICS	DC COMICS INC.		1	6	1984	1984	
NEW GODS, THE	DC COMICS INC.	1	1	11	1971	1978	
NEW GODS, THE	DC COMICS INC.	2	1	29	1989	1991	

COMIC TITLE	PUBLISHER	Vol No.	Srt No.	End No.	Str. Year	End Year	COMMENTS
NEW GUARDIANS	DC COMICS INC.		I	12	1988	1989	
NEW HEROIC COMICS	FAMOUS FUNNIES PUBLICATIONS		41	97	1940	1955	
NEW HUMANS	ETERNITY		I	15	1987	1989	
NEW HUMANS ANNUAL	ETERNITY		I	I	1989	1989	
NEW JUNGLE COMICS	CARTOON ART		I	I	1950	1950	
NEW KIDS ON THE BLOCK	HARVEY PUBLICATIONS		I	9	1990	1991	
NEW KIDS ON THE BLOCK BACKSTAGE PASS	HARVEY PUBLICATIONS		I	7	1991	1991	
NEW KIDS ON THE BLOCK CHILLIN	HARVEY PUBLICATIONS		I	7	1990	1991	
NEW KIDS ON THE BLOCK COMICS TOUR	HARVEY PUBLICATIONS		I	7	1990	1991	
NEW KIDS ON THE BLOCK MAGIC SUMMER TOUR	HARVEY PUBLICATIONS		I	I	1990	1990	
NEW MEN IN BATTLE	CAETECHETICAL EDUCATIONAL SOCIETY		I	2	1949	1949	
NEW MUTANTS ANNUAL, THE	MARVEL ENTERTAINMENT GROUP		I	7	1984	1991	
NEW MUTANTS SPECIAL EDITION, THE	MARVEL ENTERTAINMENT GROUP		I	I	1985	1985	
NEW MUTANTS SUMMER SPECIAL, THE	MARVEL ENTERTAINMENT GROUP		I	I	1990	1990	
NEW MUTANTS, THE	MARVEL ENTERTAINMENT GROUP		I	100	1983	1991	
NEW MUTANTS: THE DEMON BEAR SAGA	MARVEL ENTERTAINMENT GROUP				1991	1991	
NEW PEOPLE, THE	DELL PUBLISHING COMPANY		I	2	1970	1970	
NEW ROMANCES	STANDARD COMICS		I	21	1951	1954	
NEW STATESMEN	FLEETWAY		I	6	1989	1990	
NEW STATESMEN, THE COMPLETE	FLEETWAY		I	I	1990	1990	
NEW TALENT SHOWCASE	DC COMICS INC.		I	19	1984	1985	
NEW TEEN TITANS (TALES OF THE TEEN TITANS)	DC COMICS INC.	I	I	91	1980	1984	
NEW TEEN TITANS ANNUAL, THE	DC COMICS INC.	I	I	2	1982	1983	
NEW TEEN TITANS ANNUAL, THE	DC COMICS INC.	2	I	4	1985	1988	
NEW TEEN TITANS GIVEAWAY (DRUG AWARENESS)	DC COMICS INC.		I	3	1983	1983	
NEW TEEN TITANS, THE	DC COMICS INC.		I	4	1980	1980	
NEW TEEN TITANS, THE	DC COMICS INC.	2	I	49	1984	1988	
NEW TEEN TITANS: JUDAS CONTRACT	DC COMICS INC.		I	I	1988	1988	
NEW TERRYTOONS	DELL PUBLISHING COMPANY		I	8	1960	1962	
NEW TERRYTOONS	DELL PUBLISHING COMPANY	I	I	8	1960	1962	
NEW TERRYTOONS	GOLD KEY		I	54	1962	1979	
NEW TERRYTOONS	GOLD KEY	2	I	54	1962	1979	
NEW TESTAMENT STORIES VISUALISED	STANDARD COMICS		I	2	1946	1947	
NEW TICK	NEW ENGLAND COMICS		I	I	1993	NOW	
NEW TITANS ANNUAL, THE	DC COMICS INC.	5	9	1989	NOW		
NEW TITANS, THE	DC COMICS INC.	50	107	1988	NOW		FORMERLY NEW TEEN TITANS, THE
NEW TWO FISTED TALES	DARK HORSE COMICS		I	I	1993	NOW	
NEW VISIONS: THE ART OF THE STAR WARS GALAXY	TOPPS		I	I	1993	1993	
NEW WARRIORS ANNUAL, THE	MARVEL ENTERTAINMENT GROUP		I	3	1991	NOW	
NEW WARRIORS, THE	MARVEL ENTERTAINMENT GROUP		I	I	1992	1992	
NEW WARRIORS, THE	MARVEL ENTERTAINMENT GROUP		I	44	1990	NOW	
NEW WAVE	ECLIPSE		I	14	1986	1987	
NEW WAVE VS THE VOLUNTEERS 3-D	ECLIPSE		I	2	1987	1987	
NEW WORLDS COMIC	CARDAL/W. DALY		I	I	1947	1947	
NEW YORK NEW YORK	FANTAGRAPHICS				1988	1988	
NEW YORK WORLD'S FAIR	DC COMICS INC.		1939	1940	1939	1940	
NEW YORK: YEAR ZERO	ECLIPSE		I	4	1988	1988	
NEWLYWEDS AND THEIR BABY	SAALFIELD PUBLISHING COMPANY		I	I	1907	1907	
NEWLYWEDS AND THEIR BABY'S COMIC PICTURES, THE	SAALFIELD PUBLISHING COMPANY		I	I	1917	1917	
NEWSTIME: LIFE & DEATH O/T MAN OF STEEL	DC COMICS INC.		I	I	1993	1993	
NEWSTRALIA	INNOVATION		I	I	1989	1989	
NEXT MAN	COMICO		I	5	1985	1985	
NEXT NEXUS	FIRST		I	4	1989	1989	
NEXUS	FIRST		I	2	1993	1993	
NEXUS	FIRST	2	I	82	1983	1991	
NEXUS LEGENDS	FIRST		I	23	1988	1991	
NEXUS MAGAZINE	CAPITAL COMICS	I	I	3	1981	1984	
NEXUS: ALIEN JUSTICE	DARK HORSE COMICS		I	2	1993	1994	
NEXUS: THE LIBERATOR	DARK HORSE COMICS		I	4	1992	1993	
NEXUS: THE ORIGIN	DARK HORSE COMICS		I	I	1993	1993	
NFL PRO ACTION	MARVEL ENTERTAINMENT GROUP		I	I	1993	1993	
NFL SUPERPRO	MARVEL ENTERTAINMENT GROUP		I	I	1991	1991	
NFL SUPERPRO	MARVEL ENTERTAINMENT GROUP		I	11	1991	1992	
NFL SUPERPRO SPECIAL	MARVEL ENTERTAINMENT GROUP		I	I	1991	1991	
NICK FURY VS S.H.I.E.L.D.	MARVEL ENTERTAINMENT GROUP		I	I	1989	1989	
NICK FURY VS S.H.I.E.L.D.	MARVEL ENTERTAINMENT GROUP		I	6	1988	1988	
NICK FURY, AGENT OF SHIELD	MARVEL ENTERTAINMENT GROUP	I	I	18	1968	1971	
NICK FURY, AGENT OF SHIELD	MARVEL ENTERTAINMENT GROUP	2	I	46	1989	1993	
NICK FURY, AGENT OF SHIELD CLASSICS	MARVEL ENTERTAINMENT GROUP		I	5	1973	1973	
NICK FURY, AGENT OF SHIELD SPECIAL EDITION	MARVEL ENTERTAINMENT GROUP		I	2	1983	1984	
NICK HALIDAY	ARGO PUBLISHING		I	I	1956	1956	
NICK HAZARD	HARRIER		I	I	1988	1988	
NICKEL COMICS	DELL PUBLISHING COMPANY		I	I	1938	1938	
NICKEL COMICS	FAWCETT PUBLICATIONS		I	8	1940	1940	
NIGHT AND THE ENEMY	COMICO		I	I	1988	1988	
NIGHT FORCE	DC COMICS INC.		I	14	1982	1983	
NIGHT GLIDER	TOPPS		I	I	1993	1993	
NIGHT MAN, THE	MALIBU COMICS ENTERTAINMENT INC.		I	3	1993	NOW	
NIGHT MUSIC	ECLIPSE		I	7	1984	1988	
NIGHT NURSE	MARVEL ENTERTAINMENT GROUP		I	4	1972	1973	
NIGHT OF MYSTERY	AVON BOOKS		I	I	1953	1953	
NIGHT OF THE LIVING DEAD	FANTACO		0	3	1990	1991	
NIGHT OF THE LIVING DEAD	FANTACO	2	I	I	1994	1994	
NIGHT OF THE LIVING DEAD PRELUDE	FANTACO		I	I	1992	1992	
NIGHT OF THE LIVING DEAD: AFTERMATH	FANTACO		I	I	1992	1992	
NIGHT OF THE LIVING DEAD: LONDON	FANTACO		I	4	1993	1993	
NIGHT RIDER	MARVEL ENTERTAINMENT GROUP		I	6	1974	1975	
NIGHT THRASHER	MARVEL ENTERTAINMENT GROUP		I	8	1993	NOW	
NIGHT THRASHER: FOUR CONTROL	MARVEL ENTERTAINMENT GROUP		I	4	1992	1993	

INDEX OF COMIC TITLES AND THEIR PUBLISHERS

COMIC TITLE	PUBLISHER	Vol No.	Srt No.	End No.	Str. Year	End Year	COMMENTS
NIGHT WALKER	FLEETWAY		I	2	1993	1994	
NIGHT ZERO	FLEETWAY		I	6	1990	1990	
NIGHT'S CHILDREN	FANTACO		I	4	1991	1991	
NIGHTBIRD	HARRIER		I	2	1988	1988	
NIGHTBREED	MARVEL ENTERTAINMENT GROUP		I	I	1991	1991	
NIGHTBREED	MARVEL ENTERTAINMENT GROUP		I	25	1990	NOW	
NIGHTBREED CHRONICLES	MARVEL ENTERTAINMENT GROUP		I	I	1990	1990	
NIGHTCAT	MARVEL ENTERTAINMENT GROUP		I	I	1991	1991	
NIGHTCRAWLER	MARVEL ENTERTAINMENT GROUP		I	4	1985	1986	
NIGHTINGALE, THE	HENRY A. STANSBURY ONCE-UPON-A-TIME PRESS		I	I	1948	1948	
NIGHTMARE	ST JOHN PUBLISHING		10	13	1953	1954	FORMERLY WEIRD HORRORS
NIGHTMARE	TOP SELLERS		I	3	1972	1972	
NIGHTMARE	ZIFF-DAVIS PUBLISHING COMPANY		I	4	1952	1953	
NIGHTMARE AND CASPER	HARVEY PUBLICATIONS		I	5	1963	1964	
NIGHTMARE MAGAZINE	SKYWALD PUBLISHING		I	21	1970	1975	
NIGHTMARE ON ELM STREET, A	INNOVATION		I	6	1991	1992	
NIGHTMARE ON ELM STREET, FREDDY FRUEGERS	MARVEL ENTERTAINMENT GROUP		I	2	1989	1989	
NIGHTMARE ON ELM STREET: THE BEGINNING	INNOVATION		I	2	1992	1992	
NIGHTMARE SUSPENSE PICTURE STORIES	M.V. FEATURES		I	14	1966	1967	
NIGHTMARE, ALEX NINO'S	INNOVATION		I	I	1989	1989	
NIGHTMARES	ECLIPSE		I	2	1985	1985	
NIGHTMASK	MARVEL ENTERTAINMENT GROUP		I	12	1986	1987	
NIGHTRAVEN: COLLECTED STORIES	MARVEL ENTERTAINMENT GROUP		I	I	1990	1990	
NIGHTRAVEN: HOUSE OF CARDS	MARVEL ENTERTAINMENT GROUP		I	I	1991	1991	
NIGHTRIDER	MARVEL ENTERTAINMENT GROUP		I	6	1974	1975	
NIGHTS CHILDREN: DOUBLE INDEMNITY	FANTACO		I	I	1991	1991	
NIGHTS CHILDREN: FOREPLAY	FANTACO		I	I	1992	1992	
NIGHTSLINGER	CALIBER PRESS		I	I	1993	NOW	
NIGHTSTALKERS	MARVEL ENTERTAINMENT GROUP		I	17	1992	NOW	
NIGHTSTREETS	ARROW COMICS		I	2	1991	1991	
NIGHTSTREETS	ARROW COMICS		I	5	1985	1987	
NIGHTVEIL	AC COMICS		I	7	1984	1987	
NIGHTVEIL CAULDRON HORROR	AC COMICS		I	3	1989	1991	
NIGHTVEIL SPECIAL	AC COMICS		I	I	1987	1987	
NIGHTVISION	REBEL STUDIOS		I	3	1991	NOW	
NIGHTWATCH	MARVEL ENTERTAINMENT GROUP		I	3	1994	NOW	
NINA'S ALL TIME COLLECTOR CLASSIC COMICS	DARK HORSE COMICS		I	I	1993	1993	
NINJA	ETERNITY		I	13	1986	1987	
NINJA ELITE	ADVENTURE COMICS		I	7	1987	1988	
NINJA FUNNIES	ETERNITY		I	5	1987	1987	
NINJA HIGH SCHOOL	ETERNITY		I	39	1991	NOW	
NINJA HIGH SCHOOL	MALIBU COMICS ENTERTAINMENT INC.		I	2	1990	1990	
NINJA HIGH SCHOOL ANNUAL	ETERNITY		I	I	1993	NOW	
NINJA HIGH SCHOOL IN COLOUR	ETERNITY		I	13	1992	NOW	
NINJA HIGH SCHOOL YEAR BOOK	ANTARTIC PRESS		I	3	1989	NOW	
NINJA HIGH SCHOOL/SPEED RACER	ETERNITY		I	2	1993	NOW	
NINJAK	VALIANT / VOYAGER COMMUNICATIONS		I	2	1993	NOW	
NINJUTSU, ART OF THE NINJA	SOLSON		I	3	1986	1986	
NINNY'S POP	SAALFIELD PUBLISHING COMPANY		I	I	1917	1917	
NINTENDO COMICS SYSTEM	VALIANT / VOYAGER COMMUNICATIONS	I	I	2	1990	1990	
NINTENDO COMICS SYSTEM	VALIANT / VOYAGER COMMUNICATIONS	2	I	12	1991	1991	
NIPPER ANNUAL	ASSOCIATED NEWSPAPERS		1935	1941	1935	1941	
NIPPER CARTOON: 100 OF THE BEST	B. & H. WHITE		I	I	1946	1946	
NIPPER OMNIBUS OF COMIC STRIPS	B. & H. WHITE		I	I	1948	1948	
NIPPER, THE	BRIAN WHITE		I	I	1944	1944	
NO GUTS OR GLORY	FANTAGRAPHICS		I	I	1991	1991	
NO HIDING PLACE ANNUAL	WORLD DISTRIBUTORS LTD		I	I	1966	1966	
NO TIME FOR SERGEANTS	DELL PUBLISHING COMPANY		I	3	1965	1965	
NO. 10	BEAVERBROOK		I	I	1973	1973	
NOCTURNE	AIRCEL		I	3	1991	1991	
NODDY AND HIS FRIENDS	HUDVALE		I	49	1974	1975	
NOMAD	MARVEL ENTERTAINMENT GROUP		I	22	1992	1994	
NOMAD	MARVEL ENTERTAINMENT GROUP		I	4	1990	1991	
NOMAN	TOWER COMICS		I	2	1966	1967	
NON SPORT UPDATE	BECKETT PUBLISHING	5			1994	1994	
NOODNIK 3-D	COMIC MEDIA/ALAN HARDY ASSOCIATE		I	I	1953	1953	
NOOKNIK COMICS	COMIC MEDIA/ALAN HARDY ASSOCIATE		2	5	1953	1954	
NORMALMAN 3-D ANNUAL	RENEGADE PRESS		I	I	1987	1987	
NORTHSTAR	MARVEL ENTERTAINMENT GROUP		I	4	1994	1994	
NORTHWEST MOUNTIES	ST JOHN PUBLISHING		I	4	1948	1949	
NOSEY PARKER'S HOLIDAY SPECIAL	D.C. THOMSON		I	I	1938	1938	
NOSEY PARKER'S MIDGET COMIC	D.C. THOMSON		I	I	1935	1935	
NOSFERATU	DARK HORSE COMICS		I	I	1991	1991	
NOSFERATU	TOME PRESS		I	2	1991	1991	
NOSFERATU: PLAGUE OF TERROR	MILLENIUM		I	4	1991	1991	
NOT BRAND ECHH	MARVEL ENTERTAINMENT GROUP		I	13	1967	1969	
NOVA	MARVEL ENTERTAINMENT GROUP	2	I	3	1993	NOW	
NOVA, THE MAN CALLED	MARVEL ENTERTAINMENT GROUP	I	I	25	1976	1979	
NOW WHAT	NOW		I	11	1989	1990	
NTH MAN, THE ULTIMATE NINJA	MARVEL ENTERTAINMENT GROUP		I	16	1989	1990	
NUCLEUS	HERO GRAPHICS		I	I	1979	1979	
NUKLA	DELL PUBLISHING COMPANY		I	4	1965	1966	
NURSE BETSY CRANE	CHARLTON COMICS		12	27	1961	1964	FORMERLY TEEN SECRET DIARY
NURSE LINDA LARK	TOP SELLERS		I	I	1965	1965	DELL REPRINTS
NURSERY RHYMES	ZIFF-DAVIS PUBLISHING COMPANY		2	10	1950	1951	
NURSES, THE	GOLD KEY		I	3	1963	1963	
NUTS!	PREMIER MAGAZINES		I	2	1958	1958	
NUTSY SQUIRREL	DC COMICS INC.		61	72	1954	1957	FORMERLY HOLLYWOOD FUNNY FOLKS
NUTTY COMICS	FAWCETT PUBLICATIONS		I	I	1946	1946	

INDEX OF COMIC TITLES AND THEIR PUBLISHERS

COMIC TITLE	PUBLISHER	Vol No.	Srt No.	End No.	Str. Year	End Year	COMMENTS
NUTTY COMICS	HARVEY PUBLICATIONS		1	8	1945	1947	
NUTTY LIFE	FOX FEATURES SYNDICATE		2	2	1946	1946	FORMERLY KRAZY LIFE
NYOKA THE JUNGLE GIRL	FAWCETT PUBLICATIONS		2	77	1945	1953	
NYOKA THE JUNGLE GIRL	L. MILLER PUBLISHING COMPANY (UK)		50	117	1951	1959	
NYOKA THE JUNGLE GIRL	L. MILLER PUBLISHING COMPANY (UK)	1	1	1	1950	1950	FAWCETT REPRINTS
NYOKA, THE JUNGLE GIRL	CHARLTON COMICS	2	14	22	1955	1957	FORMERLY ZOO FUNNIES
NYOKA, THE JUNGLE GIRL	FAWCETT PUBLICATIONS	1	2	77	1945	1953	FORMERLY JUNGLE GIRL

COMIC TITLE	PUBLISHER	Vol No.	Srt No.	End No.	Str. Year	End Year	COMMENTS
O'MALLEY AND THE ALLEY CATS	GOLD KEY		1	9	1971	1974	
O.G. WHIZ	GOLD KEY		1	11	1971	1979	
O.S.S.	PEARSON		1	9	1958	1959	
OAKLAND PRESS FUNNYBOOK, THE	OAKLAND PRESS				1978	1980	NO NUMBERS, DATES ONLY
OAKY DOAKS	EASTERN COLOR PRINTING COMPANY		1	1	1942	1942	
OBIE	STORE COMICS		1	1	1953	1953	
OBNOXIO THE CLOWN VS THE X-MEN	MARVEL ENTERTAINMENT GROUP		1	1	1983	1983	
OCCULT FILES OF DOCTOR SPEKTOR, THE	GOLD KEY		1	24	1973	1977	
OCCULT FILES OF DOCTOR SPEKTOR, THE	WHITMAN		25	25	1982	1982	
OCCULT FILES OF DR. SPEKTOR, THE	GOLD KEY		1	25	1973	1977	
OCCULT FILES OF DR. SPEKTOR, THE	MODERN COMICS		9	9	1977	1977	
OF SUCH IS THE KINGDOM	GEORGE PFLAUM		1	1	1955	1955	
OFFCASTES	MARVEL ENTERTAINMENT GROUP		1	3	1993	NOW	
OFFICE HOURS CARTOONS, THE DAILY EXPRESS	LANE PUBLICATIONS		1	1	1931	1931	
OFFICIAL BUZ SAWYER	PIONEER		1	5	1988	1989	
OFFICIAL CRISIS ON INFINITE EARTHS CROSSOVER INDEX	ICG & ECLIPSE		1	1	1986	1986	
OFFICIAL CRISIS ON INFINITE EARTHS INDEX, THE	ICG & ECLIPSE		1	1	1986	1986	
OFFICIAL DOOM PATROL INDEX, THE	ICG & ECLIPSE		1	2	1986	1986	
OFFICIAL HAWKMAN INDEX, THE	ICG & ECLIPSE		1	2	1986	1986	
OFFICIAL JOHNNY HAZARD	PIONEER		1	5	1988	1989	
OFFICIAL JUNGLE JIM	PIONEER		1	16	1988	1989	
OFFICIAL JUNGLE JIM ANNUAL	PIONEER		1	1	1989	1989	
OFFICIAL JUSTICE LEAGUE OF AMERICA INDEX, THE	ICG & ECLIPSE		1	8	1986	1987	
OFFICIAL LEGION OF SUPER-HEROES INDEX	ICG & ECLIPSE		1	5	1985	1987	
OFFICIAL MANDRAKE	PIONEER		1	15	1988	1989	
OFFICIAL MODESTY BLAISE	PIONEER		1	8	1988	1989	
OFFICIAL MODESTY BLAISE COLLECTION	PIONEER				1989	1989	
OFFICIAL PRINCE VALIANT	PIONEER		1	1	1989	1989	
OFFICIAL PRINCE VALIANT	PIONEER		1	18	1988	1989	
OFFICIAL PRINCE VALIANT ANNUAL	PIONEER		1	1	1988	1988	
OFFICIAL PRINCE VALIANT MONTHLY	PIONEER		1	1	1989	1989	
OFFICIAL RIP KIRBY	PIONEER		1	5	1988	1989	
OFFICIAL SECRET AGENT	PIONEER		1	7	1988	1989	
OFFICIAL SUPERMAN IV POSTER MAGAZINE	O'QUINN STUDIOS		1	1	1987	1987	
OFFICIAL TEEN TITANS INDEX	ICG & ECLIPSE		1	5	1985	1985	
OFFICIAL ZEN INTERGALACTIC NINJA SOURCEBOOK	PARODY PRESS		1	1	1993	1993	
OGOTH AND UGLY BOOT	H. BUNCH ASSOCIATES		1	1	1973	1973	
OH BOY! COMICS	PAGET		1	24	1948	1951	
OH SKIN-NAY!	P.F. VOLLAND & CO.		1	1	1913	1913	
OH! WICKED WANDA	PENTHOUSE		1	1	1976	1976	
OH, BROTHER!	STANHALL		1	5	1953	1953	
OINK!	IPC		1	50	1986	1990	
OINK! HOLIDAY SPECIAL	IPC		1	1	1988	1988	
OKAY COMIC	INTERNATIONAL		1	4	1947	1949	
OKAY COMICS	UNITED FEATURES SYNDICATE		1	1	1940	1940	
OKAY COMICS WEEKLY	T.V. BOARDMAN		1	20	1937	1938	
OKLAHOMA KID	AJAX		1	4	1957	1958	
OKLAHOMA KID	L. MILLER PUBLISHING COMPANY (UK)		1	1	1957	1957	AJAX REPRINTS
OKTOBERFEST COMICS	NOW AND THEN COMICS		1	1	1986	1986	
OLD GLORY COMICS	CHESAPEAKE & OHIO RAILWAY		1	1	1944	1944	
OLYMPIANS, THE	MARVEL ENTERTAINMENT GROUP		1	2	1991	1992	
OMAC, ONE MAN ARMY CORPS	DC COMICS INC.		1	4	1991	1991	
OMAC, ONE MAN ARMY CORPS	DC COMICS INC.		1	8	1974	1975	
OMAHA THE CAT DANCER	KITCHEN SINK		0	15	1984	1992	
OMAHA THE CAT DANCER	STEEL DRAGON		1	2	1984	1984	
OMEGA	REBEL STUDIOS		1	2	1987	1987	
OMEGA MEN ANNUAL, THE	DC COMICS INC.		1	2	1984	1985	
OMEGA MEN, THE	DC COMICS INC.		1	38	1982	1986	
OMEGA THE UNKNOWN	MARVEL ENTERTAINMENT GROUP		1	12	1976	1977	
OMEN	NORTHSTAR		1	3	1989	1989	
ON A PALE HORSE	INNOVATION		1	4	1993	1994	
ON THE AIR	NBC NETWORK COMICS		1	1	1947	1947	
ON THE LINE	KAYE & WARD		1	1	1969	1969	
ON THE LINKS	ASSOCIATED FEATURE SERVICES		1	1	1926	1926	
ON THE SCENE PRESENTS	WARREN PUBLISHING CO		1966	1980	1966	1980	
ON THE SPOT, PRETTY BOY FLOYD	FAWCETT PUBLICATIONS		1	1	1948	1948	
ONE MILE UP	ECLIPSE		1	2	1992	1992	
ONE MILLION YEARS AGO	ST JOHN PUBLISHING		1	1	1953	1953	
ONE SHOT WESTERN	CALIBER PRESS		1	1	1992	1992	
ONE, THE	MARVEL ENTERTAINMENT GROUP		1	6	1985	1986	
ONYX OVERLORD	MARVEL ENTERTAINMENT GROUP		1	4	1992	1993	
OOJAH SKETCH, THE	LONDON PUBLISHING		1	422	1921	1929	
OOR WULLIE ANNUAL	D.C. THOMSON		1941	1993	1941	1993	
OOR WULLIE SUMMER FUN SPECIAL	D.C. THOMSON		1980	1981	1980	1981	
OPEN SEASON	RENEGADE PRESS		1	6	1987	1987	

COMIC TITLE	PUBLISHER	Vol No.	Srt No.	End No.	Str. Year	End Year	COMMENTS
OPEN SPACE	MARVEL ENTERTAINMENT GROUP		I	4	1989	1990	
OPERA	ECLIPSE		I	I	1991	1991	
OPERATION PERIL	AMERICAN COMIC GROUP		I	16	1950	1953	LAST 4 ISSUES ALL WAR STORIES
OPIUM	KNOCKABOUT		I	I	1986	1986	
OPTIMIST	COMIC COLLECTIVE		I	I	1976	1976	
ORAL ROBERTS TRUE STORIES	TELEPIX PUBLICATION		I	119	1956	1959	
ORANGE BIRD AND THE NUTRITION KNOW HOW REVUE, THE	WALT DISNEY		I	I	1983	1983	
ORANGE BIRD IN NUTRITION ADVENTURES, THE	WALT DISNEY		I	I	1980	1980	
ORANGE BIRD, THE	WALT DISNEY		I	I	1980	1983	
ORANGE HAND	ORANGE HAND		I	I	1974	1974	
ORBIT	ECLIPSE		I	3	1990	1990	
ORIENTAL HEROES	JADEMAN COMICS		I	55	1988	1992	
ORIGINAL ADVENTURES OF CHOLLY AND FLYTRAP, THE	MARVEL ENTERTAINMENT GROUP				1991	1991	
ORIGINAL BLACK CAT, THE	LORNE HARVEY PUBLICATIONS		I	8	1992	NOW	
ORIGINAL DICK TRACY, THE	GLADSTONE		I	5	1990	NOW	
ORIGINAL E-MAN, THE	FIRST		I	7	1985	1986	
ORIGINAL GHOST RIDER RIDES AGAIN, THE	MARVEL ENTERTAINMENT GROUP		I	7	1991	1992	
ORIGINAL GHOST RIDER, THE	MARVEL ENTERTAINMENT GROUP		I	20	1992	1993	
ORIGINAL MAN	ANIA PUBLISHING		I	I	1993	NOW	
ORIGINAL SHIELD, THE	ARCHIE PUBLICATIONS		I	2	1984	1984	
ORIGINAL X-MEN	MARVEL ENTERTAINMENT GROUP		I	17	1983	1983	
ORIGINAL ZOY!, THE	ECLIPSE		I	I	1990	1990	
ORION	DARK HORSE COMICS		I	6	1993	1994	
ORLAK: FLESH & STEEL	CALIBER PRESS		I	I	1992	1992	
ORLAK: REDUX	CALIBER PRESS		I	I	1991	1991	
ORPHEUS	STEVE MOORE		I	2	1971	1973	
OSCAR COMICS	MARVEL ENTERTAINMENT GROUP		I	13	1947	1949	FORMERLY FUNNY TUNES
OTHELLO	CALIBER PRESS		I	I	1993	1993	
OTHER WORLDS ALBUM	G.T. LIMITED		I	I	1959	1959	
OUR ARMY AT WAR	DC COMICS INC.		I	301	1952	1977	
OUR FIGHTING FORCES	DC COMICS INC.		I	181	1954	1978	
OUR FLAG COMICS	ACE MAGAZINES			5	1941	1942	
OUR GANG COMICS	DELL PUBLISHING COMPANY		I	59	1942	1949	
OUR LADY OF FATIMA	CAETECHETICAL EDUCATIONAL SOCIETY		395	395	1955	1955	
OUR LOVE	MARVEL ENTERTAINMENT GROUP		I	2	1949	1950	
OUR LOVE STORY	MARVEL ENTERTAINMENT GROUP		I	38	1969	1976	
OUR SECRET	SUPERIOR COMICS		4	8	1949	1950	FORMERLY MY SECRET
OUT OF THE NIGHT	AMERICOMICS		I	17	1952	1954	
OUT OF THE PAST A CLUE TO THE FUTURE	EC COMICS		I	I	1946	1946	
OUT OF THE SHADOWS	STANDARD COMICS		5	14	1952	1954	
OUT OF THE VORTEX	DARK HORSE COMICS		I	4	1993	1994	
OUT OF THIS WORLD	ALAN CLASS AND CO LTD	I			60'S	70'S	CHARLTON REPRINTS
OUT OF THIS WORLD	ALAN CLASS AND CO LTD	2			70'S	70'S	CHARLTON REPRINTS
OUT OF THIS WORLD	AVON BOOKS		I	I	1950	1950	
OUT OF THIS WORLD	CHARLTON COMICS		I	16	1956	1959	
OUT OF THIS WORLD	STRATO		I	22	1951	1953	
OUT-AND-OUT SMASHER COMIC, THE	P.J. PRESS		I	I	1947	1947	
OUTBURST OF EVERETT TRUE	SAALFIELD PUBLISHING COMPANY		I	I	1907	1907	
OUTCASTS	DC COMICS INC.		I	12	1987	1988	
OUTER LIMITS, THE	DELL PUBLISHING COMPANY		I	18	1964	1969	
OUTER SPACE	ALAN CLASS AND CO LTD		I	9	1961	1961	CHARLTON REPRINTS
OUTER SPACE	CHARLTON COMICS	I	17	25	1958	1959	
OUTER SPACE	CHARLTON COMICS	2	I	I	1968	1968	
OUTER SPACE	G.T. LIMITED		I	I	1959	1959	
OUTER SPACE	L. MILLER PUBLISHING COMPANY (UK)		I	I	1958	1958	CHARLTON REPRINTS
OUTLANDER	ETERNITY		I	7	1987	1988	
OUTLANDERS	DARK HORSE COMICS		0	33	1989	1992	
OUTLANDERS COLLECTION	DARK HORSE COMICS				1994	1994	
OUTLANDERS EPILOGUE	DARK HORSE COMICS		I	I	1994	1994	
OUTLANDERS SPECIAL	DARK HORSE COMICS		I	I	1993	1993	
OUTLAW FIGHTERS	ATLAS		I	5	1954	1955	
OUTLAW KID, THE	MARVEL ENTERTAINMENT GROUP	I	I	19	1954	1957	
OUTLAW KID, THE	MARVEL ENTERTAINMENT GROUP	2	I	30	1970	1975	
OUTLAWS	DC COMICS INC.		I	8	1992	1993	
OUTLAWS	STREAMLINE		I	I	1955	1955	
OUTLAWS OF THE WEST	CHARLTON COMICS		11	88	1957	1980	FORMERLY CODY OF THE PONY EXPRESS
OUTLAWS OF THE WEST	L. MILLER PUBLISHING COMPANY (UK)		I	7	1958	1959	CHARLTON REPRINTS
OUTLAWS OF THE WILD WEST	AVON BOOKS		I	I	1952	1952	
OUTLAWS PICTURE AND STORY ALBUM	MELLIFONT		4	4	50'S	50'S	
OUTLAWS WESTERN STORIES	STREAMLINE		I	2	1954	1954	US REPRINTS
OUTLAWS, THE	STAR PUBLICATIONS		10	14	1952	1954	FORMERLY WESTERN CRIME CASES
OUTPOST ADVENTURE COMIC, THE	MARTIN & REID		I	I	1950	1950	
OUTRAGEOUS TALES FROM THE OLD TESTAMENT	KNOCKABOUT		I	I	1987	1987	
OUTSIDERS THE, ANNUAL	DC COMICS INC.		I	I	1986	1986	
OUTSIDERS THE, SPECIAL	DC COMICS INC.		I	I	1987	1987	
OUTSIDERS, THE	DC COMICS INC.	I	I	28	1985	1988	
OUTSIDERS, THE	DC COMICS INC.	2	I	3	1993	NOW	
OUTSTANDING AMERICAN WAR HEROES	PARENTS MAGAZINE INSTITUTE		I	I	1944	1944	
OVERKILL	MARVEL ENTERTAINMENT GROUP	I	I	42	1992	NOW	
OVERSEAS COMICS	U.S. ARMED FORCES		23	65	1944	1944	
OVERSTREET COMIC BOOK MARKETPLACE	OVERSTREET PUBLICATIONS		I	12	1992	NOW	
OVERSTREET COMICS & CARDS PRICE GUIDE ANNUAL	AVON BOOKS		I	I	1992	1992	
OVERSTREET'S ADVANCED COMIC COLLECTOR	OVERSTREET PUBLICATIONS		I	2	1993	NOW	
OWL, THE	GOLD KEY		I	2	1967	1968	
OXYDOL-DREFT	OXYDOL-DREFT		I	6	1950	1950	
OZARK IKE	STANDARD COMICS		11	25	1948	1952	
OZZIE & BABS	FAWCETT PUBLICATIONS		I	13	1947	1949	
OZZY OSBOURNE	ROCK-IT COMIX		I	I	1993	1993	

COMIC TITLE	PUBLISHER	Vol No.	Srt No.	End No.	Str. Year	End Year	COMMENTS

P

COMIC TITLE	PUBLISHER	Vol No.	Srt No.	End No.	Str. Year	End Year	COMMENTS
P.C.49	HAWK BOOKS			1	1	1990	1990	
P.C.49 ANNUAL	DAKERS		1956	1956	1956	1956	
P.C.49 ANNUAL	JUVENILE PRODUCTIONS		1951	1953	1951	1953	
P.C.49 ANNUAL	PREVIEW		1953	1954	1953	1954	
P.I.'S: MICHAEL MAUSER AND MS. TREE	FIRST		1	3	1983	1985	
P.J. WARLOCK	ECLIPSE		1	3	1986	1987	
PACIFIC PRESENTS	PACIFIC COMICS		1	4	1982	1984	
PACT, THE	IMAGE COMICS		1	2	1994	NOW	
PADRE OF THE POOR	CAETECHETICAL EDUCATIONAL SOCIETY		1	1	???	???	
PAGEANT OF COMICS	ST JOHN PUBLISHING		1	2	1947	1947	
PAGET COMIC, THE	PAGET		1	24	1948	1949	VARIOUS INDIVIDUAL COMICS
PAGET'S BUMPER TOTS COMIC	PAGET		1	1	1950	1950	
PAGET'S FUNNY CUTS COMIC	PAGET		1	8	1949	1949	
PAGET'S SUPER DUPER COMIC	PAGET		1	1	1950	1950	
PAGET'S TUPNEY	PAGET		1	10	1949	1949	
PAGETS COMIC	PAGET		1	10	1948	1949	VARIOUS ONE-OFF ISSUES
PALE HORSES	ATOMEKA		1	4	1993	1993	
PANCHO VILLA	AVON BOOKS		1	1	1950	1950	
PANCHO VILLA WESTERN COMIC	L. MILLER PUBLISHING COMPANY (UK)		1	63	1954	1959	
PANDA COMICS	B.B. LIMITED		701	701	1949	1949	
PANDA KHAN, CHRONICLES OF	ABACUS		1	1	1990	1990	
PANDA KHAN, CHRONICLES OF	ABACUS		1	4	1990	1990	
PANGO	MUNDIAL PRESS		50	85	1953	1956	
PANHANDLE PETE AND JENNIFER	J. CHARLES LARUE		1	3	1951	1951	
PANIC	EC COMICS		1	12	1954	1956	
PANIC	PANIC PUBLICATIONS		1	12	1958	1966	
PANTO PLAYTIME	HOTSPUR PUBLISHING CO.		1	1	1948	1948	
PANTO PRANKS	HOTSPUR PUBLISHING CO.		1	1	1949	1949	
PARADE COMICS	AJAX		1	1	1957	1957	
PARADE OF PLEASURE	DERRIC VERSCHOYLE LTD.		1	1	1954	1954	ENGLISH EQUIVALENT OF SEDUCTION OF THE INNOCENT
PARADIGM	GAUNTLET COMICS		1	1	1993	NOW	
PARADOID TALES OF NEUROSIS	PARANOID TALES OF NEUROSIS		1	1	1993	1993	
PARAGON: DARK APOCALYPSE	AIRCEL		1	4	1993	1994	
PARAMOUNT ANIMATED COMICS	HARVEY PUBLICATIONS		1	22	1953	1956	
PARAMOUNT COMIC	R. & L. LOCKER		1	1	1945	1945	
PARANOIA	ADVENTURE COMICS		1	6	1992	1992	
PARIS THE MAN OF PLASTER	ECLIPSE		1	6	1986	1987	
PARODY	ARMOUR PUBLISHING		1	1	1977	1977	
PARSIFAL	STAR REACH		1	1	1978	1978	
PARTICLE DREAMS	FANTAGRAPHICS		1	6	1986	1987	
PARTNERS IN PANDEMONIUM	CALIBER PRESS		1	3	1991	1992	
PARTRIDGE FAMILY, THE	CHARLTON COMICS		1	21	1971	1973	
PARTS UNKNOWN	ECLIPSE		1	4	1992	1992	
PARTS UNKNOWN II: THE NEXT INVASION	ECLIPSE		1	1	1993	1994	
PASSION, THE	CAETECHETICAL EDUCATIONAL SOCIETY		394	394	1955	1955	
PAT BOONE	DC COMICS INC.		1	5	1959	1960	
PAT SAVAGE : WOMAN OF BRONZE SPECIAL	MILLENIUM		1	1	1992	1992	
PAT THE BRAT	ARCHIE PUBLICATIONS			33	1953	1959	NO NUMBERS PUBLISHED IN 1953, NO. 1 FOLLOWED IN 1955
PAT THE BRAT	ARCHIE PUBLICATIONS		1	1	1953	1953	
PAT THE BRAT COMICS DIGEST MAGAZINE	ARCHIE PUBLICATIONS		1	1	1980	1980	
PATCHES	RURAL HOME PUBLISHING COMPANY		1	11	1945	1947	
PATHWAYS TO FANTASY	PACIFIC COMICS		1	1	1984	1984	
PATSY AND HEDY	MARVEL ENTERTAINMENT GROUP		1	110	1952	1967	
PATSY AND HEDY ANNUAL	MARVEL ENTERTAINMENT GROUP		1	1	1963	1963	
PATSY AND HER PALS	MARVEL ENTERTAINMENT GROUP		1	29	1953	1957	
PATSY WALKER	MARVEL ENTERTAINMENT GROUP		1	124	1945	1965	
PATSY WALKER FASHION PARADE	MARVEL ENTERTAINMENT GROUP		1	1	1966	1966	
PATSY'S CHRISTMAS REFLECTIONS	MIRROR PRESS PUBLICATIONS		1	1	1948	1948	
PATTY POWERS	ATLAS		4	7	1955	1956	FORMERLY DELLA VISION
PAUL TEMPLE ANNUAL	R. & L. LOCKER		1	1	1948	1948	
PAUL TEMPLE LIBRARY	MICRON/SMITH		1	1	1948	1948	
PAUL TERRY'S COMICS	ST JOHN PUBLISHING		85	125	1951	1955	FORMERLY TERRY-TOON COMICS
PAUL TERRY'S HOW TO DRAW FUNNY CARTOONS	TERRYTOONS, INC.		1	1	1940	1940	
PAUL THE SAMURAI	NEW ENGLAND COMICS	1	1	4	1991	1991	
PAUL THE SAMURAI	NEW ENGLAND COMICS	2	1	8	1993	NOW	
PAWNEE BILL	YOUTHFUL MAGAZINES		1	3	1951	1951	
PAY-OFF	D.S. PUBLISHING CO.		1	5	1948	1949	
PEACEMAKER	CHARLTON COMICS	1	1	5	1967	1967	
PEACEMAKER	DC COMICS INC.		1	4	1988	1988	
PEACEMAKER	MODERN COMICS	2	1	2	1978	1978	
PEANUTS	DELL PUBLISHING COMPANY		4	13	1960	1962	
PEANUTS	GOLD KEY		1	4	1963	1964	
PEANUTS JUBILEE	PENGUIN BOOKS				1976	1976	
PEBBLES & BAMM BAMM	CHARLTON COMICS		1	36	1972	1976	
PEBBLES & BAMM BAMM	HARVEY PUBLICATIONS		1	3	1993	NOW	
PEBBLES AND BAMM-BAMM GIANT SIZE	HARVEY PUBLICATIONS		1	1	1993	NOW	
PEBBLES FLINTSTONE	GOLD KEY		1	1	1963	1963	
PECOS BILL	TOP SELLERS		1		1971	1973	
PECOS BILL	WESTWORLD PUBLICATIONS		1	91	1951	1959	
PECOS BILL PICTURE LIBRARY	FAME PRESS		1	28	1962	1964	
PEDRO	FOX FEATURES SYNDICATE		1	2	1950	1950	FORMERLY MY PRIVATE LIFE
PELLEAS AND MELISANDE	ECLIPSE		1	2	1986	1986	
PENDRAGON	AIRCEL		1	2	1990	1990	
PENDULUM	ADVENTURE COMICS		1	4	1993	1993	
PENDULUM ILLUSTRATED BIOGRAPHIES	PENDULUM PRESS				1979	1979	

COMIC TITLE	PUBLISHER	Vol No.	Srt No.	End No.	Str. Year	End Year	COMMENTS
PENDULUM ILLUSTRATED CLASSICS	PENDULUM PRESS		1	6	1973	1978	
PENDULUM ILLUSTRATED ORIGINALS	PENDULUM PRESS		944254	944254	1979	1979	
PENDULUM'S ILLUSTRATED STORIES	PENDULUM PRESS		1	72	1990	1990	
PENNY	AVON BOOKS		1	6	1947	1949	
PENNY COMIC, THE	P.M. PRODUCTIONS		1	1	1946	1946	
PENNY COMICS OF THE THIRTIES	NEW ENGLISH LIBRARY		1	1	1975	1975	
PENTACLE: SIGN OF THE FIVE	ETERNITY		1	4	1991	1991	
PEP COMICS	ARCHIE PUBLICATIONS		1	415	1940	1987	
PERCIE AND FERDIE	CUPPLES AND LEON CO.		1	1	1921	1921	
PERFECT CRIME	PEMBERTON		1	2	1951	1951	CROSS REPRINTS
PERFECT CRIME, THE	CROSS PUBLICATIONS		1	33	1949	1953	
PERFECT LOVE	ZIFF-DAVIS PUBLISHING COMPANY		1	10	1951	1953	
PERG	LIGHTNING COMICS		1	1	1993	NOW	
PERISHERS ANNUAL, THE	WORLD DISTRIBUTORS LTD	1979	1980	1979	1980	
PERISHERS OMNIBUS, THE	MIRROR PRESS PUBLICATIONS		1	3	1974	1976	
PERISHERS OMNIBUS, THE	MIRROR PRESS PUBLICATIONS		28	35	1981	NOW	FORMERLY PERISHERS, THE
PERISHERS RATHER BIG FOR ITS SIZE BOOK, THE	MIRROR PRESS PUBLICATIONS		1	1	1979	1979	
PERISHERS RATHER BIG LITTLE BOOKS, THE	MIRROR PRESS PUBLICATIONS		1	1	1979	1979	
PERISHERS SPECTACOLOUR, THE	MIRROR PRESS PUBLICATIONS		1	1	1979	1979	
PERISHERS, HERE COME THE	MIRROR PRESS PUBLICATIONS		1	1	1979	1979	
PERISHERS, THE	MIRROR PRESS PUBLICATIONS		1	27	1963	1981	
PERISHERS: THE TALE OF A TAIL	MIRROR PRESS PUBLICATIONS		1	1	1981	1981	
PERRY MASON MYSTERY MAGAZINE	DELL PUBLISHING COMPANY		1	2	1964	1964	
PERSONAL LOVE	DELL PUBLISHING COMPANY		1	33	1950	1953	
PERSONAL LOVE	PRIZE/HEADLINE/FEATURE		1	14	1957	1959	
PERSUADERS HOLIDAY SPECIAL	POLYSTYLE		1	1	1972	1972	
PETE & MOE VISIT PROFESSOR SWIZZLE'S ROBOTS	DARK HORSE COMICS		1	1	1993	1993	
PETE MANGAN OF THE SPACE PATROL	L. MILLER PUBLISHING COMPANY (UK)		50	55	1953	1953	
PETE THE PANIC	STANMORE PUBLICATIONS		1	1	1955	1955	
PETER CANNON: THUNDERBOLT	DC COMICS INC.		1	12	1992	1993	
PETER COTTONTAIL	KEY PUBLICATIONS		1	1	1954	1954	3-D
PETER COTTONTAIL	KEY PUBLICATIONS		1	2	1954	1954	
PETER DAVID'S "BUT I DIGRESS"	KRAUSE PUBLICATIONS				1994	1994	
PETER PAN MOVIE ADAPTATION	WALT DISNEY		1	1	1991	1991	
PETER PAN TREASURE CHEST	DELL PUBLISHING COMPANY		1	1	1953	1953	
PETER PAN: RETURN TO NEVER NEVER LAND	ADVENTURE COMICS		1	2	1991	1991	
PETER PANDA	DC COMICS INC.		1	31	1953	1958	
PETER PARKER - SEE SPECTACULAR SPIDER-MAN							
PETER PAUL AND PERCY, THE AMAZING ADVENTURES OF	FABER & FABER		1	1	1942	1942	
PETER PAUL AND PERCY, THE PRANKS OF	FABER & FABER		1	1	1945	1945	
PETER PAUL'S 4 IN 1 JUMBO COMIC BOOK	CAPITOL STORIES		1	1	1953	1953	
PETER PENNY AND HIS MAGIC DOLLAR	AMERICAN BANKERS		1	1	1947	1947	
PETER PIG	STANDARD COMICS		5	6	1953	1953	
PETER PORKCHOPS	DC COMICS INC.		1	62	1949	1960	
PETER PORKER, THE SPECTACULAR SPIDERHAM	MARVEL ENTERTAINMENT GROUP		1	17	1985	1987	
PETER POTAMUS	GOLD KEY		1	1	1965	1965	
PETER RABBIT	FAGO PUBLICATIONS		1	1	1958	1958	
PETER RABBIT	JOHN H. EGGERS CO.		1	4	1922	1923	
PETER RABBIT 3-D	ETERNITY		1	1	1990	1990	
PETER RABBIT'S EASTER PARADE	AVON BOOKS		1	1	1952	1952	
PETER RABBIT'S JUMBO BOOK	AVON BOOKS		1	1	1954	1954	
PETER RABBIT, THE ADVENTURES OF	AVON BOOKS		1	34	1947	1956	
PETER WHEAT ARTIST'S WORKBOOK	BAKERS ASSOCIATES		1	1	1954	1954	
PETER WHEAT FOUR IN ONE FUN PACK	BAKERS ASSOCIATES		1	1	1954	1954	
PETER WHEAT FUN BOOK	BAKERS ASSOCIATES		1	1	1952	1952	
PETER WHEAT NEWS	BAKERS ASSOCIATES		1	30	1948	1950	
PETER WHEAT, THE ADVENTURES OF	BAKERS ASSOCIATES	1	1	1	1948	1948	
PETER WHEAT, THE ADVENTURES OF	BAKERS ASSOCIATES	2	1	66	1948	1956	
PETER, THE LITTLE PEST	MARVEL ENTERTAINMENT GROUP		1	4	1969	1970	
PETS PLAYTIME COMIC	PHILIMAR		1	1	1949	1949	
PETTICOAT JUNCTION	DELL PUBLISHING COMPANY		1	5	1964	1965	
PETWORKS VS WILDK.A.T.S.	PARODY PRESS		1	1	1993	1993	
PHANTOM BLOT, THE	GOLD KEY		1	7	1964	1966	
PHANTOM FORCE	GENESIS WEST		1	3	1994	1994	
PHANTOM FORCE	IMAGE COMICS		1	1	1993	1994	
PHANTOM LADY	AJAX	2	1	4	1954	1955	
PHANTOM LADY	FOX FEATURES SYNDICATE		13	23	1947	1949	
PHANTOM LADY	FOX FEATURES SYNDICATE	1	13	23	1947	1949	
PHANTOM OF FEAR CITY	ECLIPSE		1	4	1993	NOW	
PHANTOM OF THE OPERA, THE	ETERNITY		1	1	1988	1988	
PHANTOM RANGER COMICS, THE	WORLD DISTRIBUTORS LTD		1	18	1955	1955	
PHANTOM STRANGER, THE	DC COMICS INC.		1	4	1987	1988	
PHANTOM STRANGER, THE	DC COMICS INC.	1	1	6	1952	1953	
PHANTOM STRANGER, THE	DC COMICS INC.	2	1	41	1969	1976	
PHANTOM WITCH DOCTOR	AVON BOOKS		1	1	1952	1952	
PHANTOM WORLD ADVENTURE LIBRARY, THE	WORLD DISTRIBUTORS LTD		1	8	1967	1967	
PHANTOM ZONE, THE	DC COMICS INC.		1	4	1982	1982	
PHANTOM, THE	CHARLTON COMICS		30	74	1969	1977	
PHANTOM, THE	DC COMICS INC.		1	13	1989	1990	
PHANTOM, THE	DC COMICS INC.		1	4	1988	1988	
PHANTOM, THE	GOLD KEY		1	29	1962	1966	
PHANTOM, THE	KING FEATURES	18		28	1966	1967	
PHANTOM, THE	L. MILLER PUBLISHING COMPANY (UK)		1	18	1959	1961	
PHANTOM, THE	WOLF PUBLISHING		1	8	1992	1993	
PHAZE	ECLIPSE		1	2	1988	1988	
PHIL RIZZUTO	FAWCETT PUBLICATIONS		1	1	1951	1951	
PHILBERT DESANEX 100,000TH DREAM	HASSLE FREE PRESS		1	1	1979	1979	
PHOENIX	ATLAS		1	4	1975	1975	
PHOENIX: THE UNTOLD STORY	MARVEL ENTERTAINMENT GROUP		1	1	1984	1984	

INDEX OF COMIC TITLES AND THEIR PUBLISHERS

COMIC TITLE	PUBLISHER	Vol No.	Srt No.	End No.	Str. Year	End Year	COMMENTS
PHONEY PAGES, THE	RENEGADE PRESS		1	2	1986	1986	
PICNIC PARADE	DELL PUBLISHING COMPANY		6	8	1955	1957	FORMERLY VACATION PARADE
PICTORIAL CONFESSIONS	ST JOHN PUBLISHING		1	3	1949	1949	
PICTORIAL LOVE STORIES	CHARLTON COMICS		22	26	1949	1950	FORMERLY TIM MCCOY
PICTORIAL LOVE STORIES	ST JOHN PUBLISHING		1	1	1952	1952	
PICTORIAL ROMANCES	ST JOHN PUBLISHING		4	24	1950	1954	FORMERLY PICTORIAL CONFESSIONS
PICTURE CLASSICS	WATTS		1	1	1980	1980	
PICTURE EPICS	GERALD SWAN		1	4	1952	1952	
PICTURE NEWS	LAFAYETTE STREET CORP.		1	10	1946	1947	
PICTURE PARADE	GILBERTON PUBLICATIONS		1	3	1953	1953	
PICTURE PRANKS COMIC	MARTIN & REID		1	1	1944	1944	
PICTURE PROGRESS	GILBERTON PUBLICATIONS		5	17	1954	1955	FORMERLY PICTURE PARADE
PICTURE STORIES FROM AMERICAN HISTORY	EC COMICS		1	4	1945	1947	
PICTURE STORIES FROM SCIENCE	EC COMICS		1	2	1947	1947	
PICTURE STORIES FROM THE BIBLE	EC COMICS	1	1	4	1942	1943	
PICTURE STORIES FROM THE BIBLE	EC COMICS	2	1	4	1947	1947	
PICTURE STORIES FROM THE BIBLE: LIFE OF CHRIST ED.	DC COMICS INC.		1	1	1945	1945	
PICTURE STORIES FROM THE BIBLE: NEW TESTAMENT	EC COMICS		1	1	1946	1946	
PICTURE STORIES FROM THE BIBLE: NEW TESTAMENT	EC COMICS	1	1	3	1946	1946	
PICTURE STORIES FROM THE BIBLE: OLD TESTAMENT	EC COMICS		1	1	1945	1945	
PICTURE STORIES FROM WORLD HISTORY	EC COMICS		1	2	1947	1947	
PICTURE STORIES OF WORLD WAR TWO	C.A. PEARSON		1	56	1960	1962	
PICTURE STORY POCKET WESTERN	WORLD DISTRIBUTORS LTD		1	24	1958	1959	
PICTURE STORY READERS	JOHN MURRAY		1	8	1956	1956	
PICTURE STRIP BOOK	COLLINS		1	3	1955	1955	
PIGMY COMIC, THE	P.M. PRODUCTIONS		1	1	1944	1944	
PILGRIM'S PROGRESS, THE	MARVEL ENTERTAINMENT GROUP		1	1	1993	1993	
PILLAR BOX COMIC, THE	REYNARD PRESS		1	1	1947	1947	
PILOT, THE	AMALGAMATED PRESS		1	131	1935	1938	
PIN-UP PETE	TOBY PRESS PUBLICATIONS		1	1	1952	1952	
PINEAPPLE ARMY	VIZ		1	10	1988	1989	
PINHEAD	MARVEL ENTERTAINMENT GROUP		1	4	1993	NOW	EPIC TITLE
PINHEAD AND FOODINI	FAWCETT PUBLICATIONS		1	4	1951	1952	
PINHEAD/MARSHALL LAW: LAW IN HELL	MARVEL ENTERTAINMENT GROUP		1	2	1993	1993	
PINK FLOYD EXPERIENCE, THE	REVOLUTIONARY COMICS		1	5	1991	1992	
PINK LAFFIN	WHITMAN		1	1	1922	1922	
PINK PANTHER GIANT SIZE, THE	HARVEY PUBLICATIONS		1	1	1993	1993	
PINK PANTHER MINI COMIC, THE	GOLD KEY		1	1	1976	1976	
PINK PANTHER, THE	GOLD KEY		1	87	1971	1984	
PINK PANTHER, THE	HARVEY PUBLICATIONS		2	6	1993	NOW	
PINOCCHIO	MONTGOMERY WARD		1	1	1940	1940	
PINOCCHIO AND THE EMPEROR OF THE NIGHT	MARVEL ENTERTAINMENT GROUP		1	1	1986	1986	
PINOCCHIO, ADVENTURES OF	WHITMAN		3	3	1982	1982	
PINWHEEL, THE	MCKENZIE/VINCENT		1	1	1948	1948	
PIONEER PICTURE STORIES	STREET AND SMITH PUBLICATIONS		1	9	1941	1943	
PIONEER WESTERN COMIC, THE	WYNDHAM HOUSE		1	2	1950	1950	
PIP AND SQUEAK	MIRROR PRESS PUBLICATIONS				1921	1925	
PIP POP COMIC	PHILIMAR		1	1	1949	1949	
PIPPIN	TV		1	459	1966	1975	
PIRACY	EC COMICS		1	7	1954	1955	
PIRATES COMICS	HILLMAN PERIODICALS		1	4	1950	1950	
PIRATES COMICS	STREAMLINE		1	7	1951	1952	REPRINTS VARIOUS US MATERIAL
PIRATES OF DARK WATER	MARVEL ENTERTAINMENT GROUP		1	9	1991	1992	
PITT	IMAGE COMICS		1	2	1993	NOW	
PITT, THE	MARVEL ENTERTAINMENT GROUP		1	1	1988	1988	
PITTS	PARODY PRESS		1	1	1992	1992	
PIUS XII MAN OF PEACE	CAETECHETICAL EDUCATIONAL SOCIETY		1	???	???	???	
PIXIE AND DIXIE AND MR. JINKS	GOLD KEY		1	1	1963	1963	
PIXIE PUZZLE ROCKET TO ADVENTURELAND	AVON BOOKS		1	1	1952	1952	
PIXIES, THE	MAGAZINE ENTERPRISES		1	5	1946	1948	
PIXY JUNKET	VIZ		1	6	1993	NOW	
PLAN 9 FROM OUTER SPACE	ETERNITY		1	4	1990	1991	
PLANET 29	CALIBER PRESS		1	3	1991	1992	
PLANET COMICS	BLACKTHORNE		1	3	1988	1988	
PLANET COMICS	CARTOON ART		1	1	1950	1950	FICTION HOUSE REPRINTS
PLANET COMICS	FICTION HOUSE		1	73	1940	1954	
PLANET COMICS	R. & L. LOCKER		1	5	1951	1951	FICTION HOUSE REPRINTS
PLANET OF THE APES	ADVENTURE COMICS		1	24	1990	1992	
PLANET OF THE APES	MARVEL ENTERTAINMENT GROUP		1	29	1974	1977	
PLANET OF THE APES (U.K.)	MARVEL ENTERTAINMENT GROUP		1	123	1974	1977	
PLANET OF THE APES ANNUAL	ADVENTURE COMICS		1	1	1991	1991	
PLANET OF THE APES, TERROR ON THE	ADVENTURE COMICS		1	4	1991	1991	
PLANET OF THE APES: BLOOD OF THE APES	ADVENTURE COMICS		1	4	1992	1992	
PLANET OF THE APES: FORBIDDEN ZONE	ADVENTURE COMICS		1	4	1992	1993	
PLANET OF THE APES: SINS OF THE FATHERS	ADVENTURE COMICS		1	1	1992	1992	
PLANET OF THE APES: URCHAK'S FOLLY	ADVENTURE COMICS		1	4	1991	1991	
PLANET OF VAMPIRES	ATLAS		1	3	1975	1975	
PLANET PATROL	ARCOMICS		1	1	1993	NOW	
PLANET STORIES	ATLAS UK		1	1	1961	1961	FICTION HOUSE REPRINTS
PLANET TERRY	MARVEL ENTERTAINMENT GROUP		1	9	1985	1986	
PLANET X	ETERNITY		1	1	1991	1991	
PLANET, THE	J.B. ALLEN		1	2	1949	1949	
PLASM	DEFIANT		0	0	1993	1993	PREQUEL TO WARRIORS OF PLASM, 150 TRADING CARDS MAKE UP THE STORY.
PLASMA BABY	CALIBER PRESS		1	3	1992	1993	
PLASMER	MARVEL ENTERTAINMENT GROUP		1	4	1993	1993	
PLASTIC FORKS	MARVEL ENTERTAINMENT GROUP		1	5	1990	1990	
PLASTIC MAN	DC COMICS INC.		1	20	1966	1977	
PLASTIC MAN	DC COMICS INC.		1	4	1988	1989	
PLASTIC MAN	POPULAR		5	60	1951	1951	QUALITY REPRINTS

COMIC TITLE	PUBLISHER	Vol No.	Srt No.	End No.	Str. Year	End Year	COMMENTS
PLASTIC MAN	QUALITY COMICS		1	64	1943	1956	
PLASTRON CAFE	MIRAGE STUDIOS		1	1	1992	NOW	
PLAYFUL LITTLE AUDREY	HARVEY PUBLICATIONS		1	121	1957	1976	
PLAYGROUND	CALIBER PRESS		1	1	1990	1990	
PLAYHOUR	AMALGAMATED PRESS				1955	1990	NO NUMBERS, DATES ONLY
PLOP!	DC COMICS INC.		1	24	1973	1976	
POCAHONTAS	POCAHONTAS FUEL CO.		1	2	1941	1942	
POCKET CHILLER LIBRARY	TOP SELLERS		1	2	1971	???	
POCKET COMIC	P.M. PRODUCTIONS		1	1	1944	1944	
POCKET COMICS	HARVEY PUBLICATIONS		1	4	1941	1942	
POCKET DETECTIVE LIBRARY	TOP SELLERS		1	2	1971	???	
POCKET ROMANCE LIBRARY	TOP SELLERS		1	2	1971	???	
POCKET WAR LIBRARY	TOP SELLERS		1	2	1971	???	
POCKET WESTERN LIBRARY	TOP SELLERS		1	2	1971	???	
POGO PARADE	DELL PUBLISHING COMPANY		1	1	1953	1953	
POGO POSSUM	DELL PUBLISHING COMPANY		1	16	1949	1954	
POLICE ACADEMY	MARVEL ENTERTAINMENT GROUP		1	9	1989	1990	
POLICE ACTION	ATLAS	1	1	7	1954	1954	
POLICE ACTION	ATLAS	2	1	3	1975	1975	
POLICE AGAINST CRIME	PREMIER MAGAZINES		1	9	1954	1955	
POLICE BADGE #479	ATLAS	5	5	5	1955	1955	FORMERLY SPY THRILLERS
POLICE COMIC	ARCHER/KING COMICS		1	6	1953	1953	QUALITY REPRINTS
POLICE COMICS	QUALITY COMICS		1	127	1941	1953	
POLICE LINE-UP	REALISTIC PUBLICATIONS		1	4	1951	1952	
POLICE THRILLS	AJAX		1	1	1954	1954	
POLICE TRAP	MAINLINE		1	6	1954	1955	
POLICE TRAP	SUPER COMICS		11	18	1963	1964	
POLL PARROT	K.K. PUBLICATIONS	1	1	4	1950	1951	
POLL PARROT	K.K. PUBLICATIONS	2	1	16	1959	1962	
POLLY PIGTAILS	PARENTS MAGAZINE INSTITUTE		1	43	1946	1949	
PONYTAIL	CHARLTON COMICS		13	20	1962	1971	
PONYTAIL	DELL PUBLISHING COMPANY		1	12	1962	1965	
POP COMICS	MODERN STORE PUBLISHING		1	1	1955	1955	
POP PICTURE LIBRARY	MICRON/SMITH		1	2	1965	???	
POP SHOTS	JOHN W. FISHER		1	1	1946	1946	
POP-POP COMICS	R.B. LEFFINGWELL & CO.		1	1	1945	1945	
POPEYE	CHARLTON COMICS		1	15	1972	1974	
POPEYE	DAVID MCKAY PUBLICATIONS		1	2	1935	1935	
POPEYE	HARVEY PUBLICATIONS		1	3	1993	NOW	
POPEYE	L. MILLER PUBLISHING COMPANY (UK)		1	30	1959	1963	
POPEYE	PEMBERTON		1	19	1950	1951	
POPEYE	WORLD DISTRIBUTORS LTD		1	7	1957	1957	WESTERN PRINTING REPRINTS
POPEYE CARTOON BOOK	SAALFIELD PUBLISHING COMPANY		1	1	1934	1934	
POPEYE FEATURE BOOKS	DAVID MCKAY PUBLICATIONS		1	14	1937	1939	
POPEYE GIANT SIZE	HARVEY PUBLICATIONS		1	1	1993	NOW	
POPEYE SPECIAL	OCEAN COMICS		1	2	1987	1988	
POPEYE THE SAILOR	CHARLTON COMICS		94	138	1969	1977	
POPEYE THE SAILOR	CHARLTON COMICS		94	94	1969	1969	BOLD DETERGENT GIVE AWAY
POPEYE THE SAILOR	DELL PUBLISHING COMPANY		1	171	1948	1962	
POPEYE THE SAILOR	GOLD KEY		66	80	1962	1966	
POPEYE THE SAILOR	KING FEATURES		81	92	1966	1967	
POPEYE THE SAILOR	WHITMAN		139	171	1978	1984	
POPPO OF THE POPCORN THEATRE	FULLER PUBLISHING		1	13	1955	1956	WEEKLY
POPSICLE PETE FUN BOOK	JOE LOWE CO/PICTORIAL NEWS		1	2	1947	1948	
POPULAR COMICS	DELL PUBLISHING COMPANY		1	145	1936	1948	
POPULAR ROMANCE	BETTER STANDARD PUBLICATIONS/VISUAL EDITIONS		5	27	1949	1954	
POPULAR TEEN-AGERS	STAR PUBLICATIONS		5	23	1950	1954	FORMERLY SCHOOL DAY ROMANCES
PORE L'IL MOSE	CUPPLES AND LEON CO.		1	1	1902	1902	
PORKY PIG	DELL PUBLISHING COMPANY		25	81	1952	1962	
PORKY PIG	GOLD KEY		1	93	1965	1984	
PORKY PIG	GOLD KEY	2	1	93	1965	1983	
PORKY PIG	WHITMAN		94	109	1982	1984	
PORKY PIG	WHITMAN	2	94	109	1983	1984	
PORKY'S BOOK OF TRICKS	K.K. PUBLICATIONS		1	1	1942	1942	
PORTIA PRINZ OF THE GLAMAZONS	ECLIPSE		1	6	1986	1987	
POW MAGAZINE	HUMOR-VISION		1	2	1966	1967	
POW!	ODHAMS		1	86	1967	1968	
POW! ANNUAL	ODHAMS		1968	1972	1968	1972	
POWER & GLORY	MALIBU COMICS ENTERTAINMENT INC.		1	4	1993	1994	
POWER COMIC	MARTIN & REID		1	1	1950	1950	
POWER COMICS	ECLIPSE		1	4	1988	1988	
POWER COMICS	HOLYOKE PUBLISHING COMPANY		1	4	1944	1945	
POWER COMICS	POWER COMICS		1	5	1977	1977	
POWER FACTOR	INNOVATION		1	3	1990	NOW	
POWER FACTOR SPECIAL	INNOVATION		1	1	1990	1990	
POWER GIRL	DC COMICS INC.		1	4	1988	1988	
POWER LORDS	DC COMICS INC.		1	3	1983	1984	
POWER MAN	MARVEL ENTERTAINMENT GROUP		48	49	1977	1977	FORMERLY LUKE CAGE POWER MAN
POWER MAN AND IRON FIST	MARVEL ENTERTAINMENT GROUP		50	125	1977	1986	FORMERLY POWER MAN
POWER MAN ANNUAL	MARVEL ENTERTAINMENT GROUP		1	1	1976	1976	
POWER MAN GIANT SIZE	MARVEL ENTERTAINMENT GROUP		1	1	1975	1975	
POWER OF THE ATOM, THE	DC COMICS INC.		1	18	1988	1989	
POWER P.E.T.S., TALES	A PLUS COMICS		1	1	1992	1992	
POWER PACHYDERMS	MARVEL ENTERTAINMENT GROUP		1	1	1989	1989	
POWER PACK	MARVEL ENTERTAINMENT GROUP		1	62	1984	1991	
POWER PACK & CLOAK AND DAGGER	MARVEL ENTERTAINMENT GROUP		1	1	1989	1989	
POWER PACK HOLIDAY SPECIAL	MARVEL ENTERTAINMENT GROUP		1	1	1992	1992	
POWER PACK: ORIGIN ALBUM	MARVEL ENTERTAINMENT GROUP				1988	1988	
POWER RECORD COMICS	MARVEL ENTERTAINMENT GROUP				1974	1978	

INDEX OF COMIC TITLES AND THEIR PUBLISHERS

COMIC TITLE	PUBLISHER	Vol No.	Srt No.	End No.	Str. Year	End Year	COMMENTS
POWERHOUSE PEPPER COMICS	MARVEL ENTERTAINMENT GROUP		1	5	1943	1948	
POWERLINE	MARVEL ENTERTAINMENT GROUP		1	8	1988	1989	
PRAIRIE MOON AND OTHER STORIES	DARK HORSE COMICS		1	1	1992	1992	
PRAIRIE! WESTERN	SCION		1	2	1952	1952	
PRANG COMIC	HOTSPUR PUBLISHING CO.		1	1	1948	1948	
PREDATOR	DARK HORSE COMICS	1	1	4	1989	1990	
PREDATOR II MOVIE ADAPTATION	DARK HORSE COMICS		1	2	1991	1991	
PREDATOR VS MAGNUS ROBOT FIGHTER	DARK HORSE COMICS		1	2	1992	1992	
PREDATOR: BAD BLOOD	DARK HORSE COMICS		1	1	1993	1994	
PREDATOR: BIG GAME	DARK HORSE COMICS		1	1	1993	1993	
PREDATOR: BIG GAME	DARK HORSE COMICS		1	4	1991	1991	
PREDATOR: BLOODY SANDS OF TIME	DARK HORSE COMICS		1	2	1992	1992	
PREDATOR: COLD WAR	DARK HORSE COMICS		1	1	1993	1993	
PREDATOR: COLD WAR	DARK HORSE COMICS		1	4	1991	1991	
PREDATOR: RACE WAR	DARK HORSE COMICS	0	4	1993	1993		
PREMIER, THE	PAGET		1	7	1948	1948	
PRETEEN DIRTY GENE KUNG-FU KANGAROOS	BLACKTHORNE		1	3	1986	1986	
PRETTY SOLDIER PAPERMOON	JAPAN PUBLICATIONS LIBRARY				1994	1994	JAPANESE TEXT
PREZ	DC COMICS INC.		1	4	1973	1974	
PRICE, THE	ECLIPSE		1	1	1981	1981	
PRIDE OF THE YANKEES, THE	MAGAZINE ENTERPRISES		1	1	1949	1949	
PRIMAL	DARK HORSE COMICS		1	2	1992	1993	
PRIME	MALIBU COMICS ENTERTAINMENT INC.		1	8	1993	NOW	
PRIME SLIME TALES	NOW		1	4	1986	1987	
PRIMUS	CHARLTON COMICS		1	7	1972	1972	
PRINCE AND THE PAUPER MOVIE ADAPTATION	WALT DISNEY		1	1	1990	1990	
PRINCE COMIC, THE	ENSIGN/W. FORSHAW		1	2	1947	1947	
PRINCE VALIANT	PIONEER		1	1	1990	1990	
PRINCE VANDAL	TRIUMPHANT COMICS		1	2	1993	NOW	
PRINCE: ALTER EGO	DC COMICS INC.		1	1	1992	1992	
PRINCESS	AMALGAMATED PRESS		1	346	1960	1967	
PRINCESS PICTURE LIBRARY	FLEETWAY		1	120	1961	1966	
PRINCESS TINA	IPC				1967	1973	
PRISON BREAK!	AVON BOOKS		1	5	1951	1952	
PRISON RIOT	AVON BOOKS		1	1	1952	1952	
PRISON TO PRAISE	LOGOS INTERNATIONAL		1	1	1974	1974	
PRISONER, THE	DC COMICS INC.		1	1	1990	1990	
PRISONER, THE	DC COMICS INC.		1	4	1988	1989	
PRIVATE EYE	ATLAS		1	8	1951	1952	
PRIVATE EYE PICTURE LIBRARY	C.A. PEARSON		1	2	1963	???	
PRIVATE LIVES ROMANCES	L. MILLER PUBLISHING COMPANY (UK)		1	9	1959	1959	STANDARD REPRINTS
PRIVATE SECRETARY	DELL PUBLISHING COMPANY		1	2	1962	1963	
PRIZE COMICS	PRIZE PUBLICATIONS		1	68	1940	1948	
PRIZE COMICS WESTERN	PRIZE PUBLICATIONS	69	119	1948	1956		FORMERLY PRIZE COMICS
PRIZE COMICS WESTERN	STREAMLINE		1	9	1950	1950	PRIZE REPRINTS
PRIZE MYSTERY	KEY PUBLICATIONS		1	3	1955	1955	
PROFESSIONAL: GOLGO 13	VIZ		1	4	1991	1991	
PROFESSOR COFFIN	CHARLTON COMICS	19	21	1985	1986		
PROFESSOR OM	INNOVATION		1	1	1990	1990	
PROJECT A-KO	MALIBU COMICS ENTERTAINMENT INC.		1	4	1994	NOW	
PROJECT SWORD	CITY		1	1	1968	1968	
PROJECT X: THUMP'N GUTS	KITCHEN SINK		1	1	1994	1994	
PROPELLERMAN	DARK HORSE COMICS		1	7	1993	1994	
PROPHET	IMAGE COMICS		1	3	1993	NOW	
PROPOGANDA COMICS	A PLUS COMICS		1	1	1992	NOW	
PROTECTORS HANDBOOK, THE	MALIBU COMICS ENTERTAINMENT INC.		1	1	1992	1992	
PROTECTORS, THE	MALIBU COMICS ENTERTAINMENT INC.		1	16	1992	NOW	
PROTECTORS/EX-MUTANTS ADVENTURE SUPPLEMENT	MALIBU COMICS ENTERTAINMENT INC.		1	1	1993	1993	
PROTOCULTURE ADDICTS	IANUS PUBLICATIONS		1	15	1990	NOW	
PROTOTYPE	MALIBU COMICS ENTERTAINMENT INC.		1	6	1993	NOW	
PROWLER	ECLIPSE		1	4	1987	1987	
PSI FORCE	MARVEL ENTERTAINMENT GROUP		1	32	1986	1989	
PSI FORCE ANNUAL	MARVEL ENTERTAINMENT GROUP		1	1	1987	1987	
PSI JUDGE ANDERSON	FLEETWAY		1	18	1991	NOW	
PSI JUDGE ANDERSON	TITAN BOOKS		1	5	1987	1990	
PSI-JUDGE ANDERSON: ENGRAMS	FLEETWAY		1	2	1993	NOW	
PSI-JUDGE ANDERSON: PSI-FILES	FLEETWAY		1	1	1993	NOW	
PSSST!	ART POOL PRODUCTIONS		1	10	1982	1982	
PSYCHO	DC COMICS INC.		1	3	1991	1991	
PSYCHO	SKYWALD PUBLISHING		1	24	1971	1975	
PSYCHO	TOP SELLERS		1	2	1972	???	SKYWALD REPRINTS
PSYCHO ANNUAL	SKYWALD PUBLISHING	1972	1990	1972	1972		
PSYCHO FALL SPECIAL	SKYWALD PUBLISHING		1	1	1974	1974	
PSYCHO KILLERS	COMIC ZONE PRODUCTIONS		1	3	1992	NOW	
PSYCHO YEARBOOK	SKYWALD PUBLISHING		1	1	1974	1974	
PSYCHO, ALFRED HITCHCOCK	INNOVATION		1	3	1991	1992	
PSYCHOANALYSIS	EC COMICS		1	4	1955	1955	
PSYCHOBLAST	FIRST		1	9	1987	1988	
PSYCHONAUTS	MARVEL ENTERTAINMENT GROUP		1	4	1993	NOW	
PTERANO-MAN	KITCHEN SINK		1	1	1990	1990	
PUB DOG	DAILY EXPRESS/BEAVERBROOK		1	1	1984	1984	
PUBLIC DEFENDER IN ACTION	CHARLTON COMICS	7	12	1956	1957		FORMERLY POLICE TRAP
PUBLIC ENEMIES	D.S. PUBLISHING CO.		1	9	1948	1949	
PUBLIC ENEMIES	R. & L. LOCKER		1	8	1949	1949	D.S. PUBLISHING REPRINTS
PUCK	AMALGAMATED PRESS		1	1867	1904	1940	
PUDGY PIG	CHARLTON COMICS		1	2	1958	1958	
PUMMELER	PARODY PRESS		1	1	1992	1992	
PUMMELER $2099	PARODY PRESS		1	1	1993	1993	
PUMPKINHEAD	DARK HORSE COMICS		1	2	1993	1994	

COMIC TITLE	PUBLISHER	Vol No.	Srt No.	End No.	Str. Year	End Year	COMMENTS
PUNCH AND JUDY COMIC	MARTIN & REID		1	1	1949	1949	
PUNCH AND JUDY COMICS	HILLMAN PERIODICALS		1	43	1944	1951	
PUNCH COMICS	HARRY A CHESLER		1	23	1941	1948	
PUNCHY AND THE BLACK WIDOW	CHARLTON COMICS	10		12	1985	1986	
PUNISHER	MARVEL ENTERTAINMENT GROUP		1	5	1986	1986	
PUNISHER	MARVEL ENTERTAINMENT GROUP		1	86	1987	NOW	
PUNISHER (MAGAZINE)	MARVEL ENTERTAINMENT GROUP		1	16	1989	1990	
PUNISHER 2099	MARVEL ENTERTAINMENT GROUP		1	13	1993	NOW	
PUNISHER AND CAPTAIN AMERICA: BLOOD & GLORY	MARVEL ENTERTAINMENT GROUP		1	3	1992	1992	
PUNISHER AND WOLVERINE: AFRICAN SAGA	MARVEL ENTERTAINMENT GROUP		1	1	1989	1989	
PUNISHER ANNIVERSARY MAGAZINE	MARVEL ENTERTAINMENT GROUP				1993	1993	
PUNISHER ANNUAL	MARVEL ENTERTAINMENT GROUP		1	6	1988	NOW	
PUNISHER ARMORY	MARVEL ENTERTAINMENT GROUP		1	8	1990	NOW	
PUNISHER AUTUMN SPECIAL, THE	MARVEL ENTERTAINMENT GROUP		1	1	1992	1992	
PUNISHER CLASSICS	MARVEL ENTERTAINMENT GROUP		1	1	1989	1989	
PUNISHER HOLIDAY SPECIAL	MARVEL ENTERTAINMENT GROUP		1	2	1992	1992	
PUNISHER MOVIE SPECIAL	MARVEL ENTERTAINMENT GROUP		1	1	1989	1989	
PUNISHER SUMMER SPECIAL	MARVEL ENTERTAINMENT GROUP		1	2	1991	1992	
PUNISHER VS WOLVERINE: THE AFRICAN SAGA	MARVEL ENTERTAINMENT GROUP		1	1	1990	1990	
PUNISHER WAR JOURNAL	MARVEL ENTERTAINMENT GROUP		1	62	1988	NOW	
PUNISHER WAR ZONE	MARVEL ENTERTAINMENT GROUP		1	23	1992	NOW	
PUNISHER WAR ZONE ANNUAL	MARVEL ENTERTAINMENT GROUP		1	1	1993	1993	
PUNISHER, THE (BRITISH)	MARVEL ENTERTAINMENT GROUP		1	30	1989	1990	
PUNISHER/WIDOW: SPINNING DOOMSDAYS WEB	MARVEL ENTERTAINMENT GROUP		1	1	1993	1993	
PUNISHER: ASSASSIN'S GUILD	MARVEL ENTERTAINMENT GROUP		1	1	1993	1993	
PUNISHER: BACK TO SCHOOL SPECIAL	MARVEL ENTERTAINMENT GROUP		1	1	1992	1992	
PUNISHER: BLOOD ON THE MOORS	MARVEL ENTERTAINMENT GROUP		1	1	1992	1992	
PUNISHER: BLOODLINES	MARVEL ENTERTAINMENT GROUP		1	1	1991	1991	
PUNISHER: CIRCLE OF BLOOD	MARVEL ENTERTAINMENT GROUP		1	1	1988	1988	
PUNISHER: DIE HARD IN THE BIG EASY	MARVEL ENTERTAINMENT GROUP		1	1	1992	1992	
PUNISHER: EYE FOR AN EYE	MARVEL ENTERTAINMENT GROUP		1	1	1991	1991	
PUNISHER: G-FORCE	MARVEL ENTERTAINMENT GROUP		1	1	1992	1992	
PUNISHER: GHOSTS OF INNOCENTS	MARVEL ENTERTAINMENT GROUP		1	2	1993	1993	
PUNISHER: INTRUDER	MARVEL ENTERTAINMENT GROUP		1	1	1990	1990	
PUNISHER: INTRUDER	MARVEL ENTERTAINMENT GROUP		1	1	1991	1991	
PUNISHER: KINGDOM GONE	MARVEL ENTERTAINMENT GROUP		1	1	1993	1993	
PUNISHER: NO ESCAPE	MARVEL ENTERTAINMENT GROUP		1	1	1990	1990	
PUNISHER: ORIGIN OF MICRO CHIP	MARVEL ENTERTAINMENT GROUP		1	2	1993	1993	
PUNISHER: P.O.V.	MARVEL ENTERTAINMENT GROUP		1	4	1991	1991	
PUNISHER: RETURN TO BIG NOTHING	MARVEL ENTERTAINMENT GROUP		1	1	1989	1989	
PUNISHER: THE GHOSTS OF INNOCENTS	MARVEL ENTERTAINMENT GROUP		1	1	1946	1946	
PUNISHER: THE PRIZE	MARVEL ENTERTAINMENT GROUP		1	1	1990	1990	
PUPPET MASTER	ETERNITY		1	4	1991	1991	
PUPPET MASTER: CHILDREN OF THE PUPPET MASTER	ETERNITY		1	2	1991	1991	
PUPPETOONS, GEORGE PAL'S	L. MILLER PUBLISHING COMPANY (UK)		1	2	1951	1951	FAWCETT REPRINTS
PURE IMAGES	PURE IMAGINATION		1	6	1990	NOW	
PURE OIL COMICS	PURE OIL GIVEAWAYS		1	1	30'S	30'S	2 1930'S GIVEAWAYS
PURGE	ANIA PUBLISHING		1	1	1993	1993	
PURPLE HOOD	JOHN SPENCER		1	2	1967	1967	
PUSSYCAT	MARVEL ENTERTAINMENT GROUP		1	1	1968	1968	
PUZZLE FUN COMICS	GEORGE R. DOUGHERTY		1	2	1946	1946	

Q

COMIC TITLE	PUBLISHER	Vol No.	Srt No.	End No.	Str. Year	End Year	COMMENTS
Q-UNIT	HARRIS COMICS		1	1	1993	1993	
QUACK	STAR REACH		1	6	1976	1977	
QUADRANT	QUADRANT PUBLICATIONS		1	7	1983	1986	
QUAGMIRE U.S.A.	ANTARTIC PRESS		1	1	1994	NOW	
QUAKER OATS	QUAKER OATS GIVEAWAYS		1	4	1965	1965	4 VERSIONS
QUANTUM CREEP	PARODY PRESS		1	1	1993	1993	
QUANTUM LEAP	INNOVATION		1	12	1991	1993	
QUANTUM LEAP ANNUAL	INNOVATION		1	1	1993	1993	
QUANTUM LEAP BOOK	BOXTREE		1	1	1992	1992	
QUANTUM LEAP SPECIAL EDITION	INNOVATION		1	1	1992	1992	
QUANTUM LEAP TIME & SPACE SPECIAL	INNOVATION		1	1	1993	NOW	
QUANTUM LEAP: SECOND CHILDHOOD	INNOVATION		1	3	1994	1994	
QUASAR	MARVEL ENTERTAINMENT GROUP		1	3	1992	1992	
QUASAR	MARVEL ENTERTAINMENT GROUP		1	55	1989	NOW	
QUEEN OF THE DAMNED, ANNE RICE'S	INNOVATION		1	11	1992	1994	
QUEEN OF THE WEST, DALE EVANS	DELL PUBLISHING COMPANY	3		22	1954	1959	
QUEST FOR DREAMS LOST	LITERARY VOLUNTEERS OF CHICAGO		1	1	1987	1987	
QUESTAR ILLUSTRATED SCIENCE FICTION CLASSICS	GOLDEN PRESS		1	1	1977	1977	
QUESTION ANNUAL, THE	DC COMICS INC.		1	2	1988	1988	
QUESTION QUARTERLY, THE	DC COMICS INC.		1	5	1990	1992	
QUESTION, THE	DC COMICS INC.		1	36	1987	1990	
QUESTION: THUNDER OVER THE ABYSS	DC COMICS INC.		1	1	1992	1992	
QUESTPROBE	MARVEL ENTERTAINMENT GROUP		1	3	1984	1985	
QUICK TRIGGER WESTERN	L. MILLER PUBLISHING COMPANY (UK)		1	8	1967	1967	ATLAS/MARVEL REPRINTS
QUICK-DRAW MCGRAW	CHARLTON COMICS	2		8	1970	1972	
QUICK-DRAW MCGRAW	DELL PUBLISHING COMPANY	1	2	11	1960	1962	
QUICK-DRAW MCGRAW	GOLD KEY	1	12	15	1962	1969	
QUICK-TRIGGER WESTERN	ATLAS		12	19	1956	1957	FORMERLY QUICK-TRIGGER WESTERN ACTION

COMIC TITLE	PUBLISHER	Vol No.	Srt No.	End No.	Str. Year	End Year	COMMENTS

R

COMIC TITLE	PUBLISHER	Vol No.	Srt No.	End No.	Str. Year	End Year	COMMENTS
R CRUMB CHECKLIST	BOATNER NORTON PRESS				1981	1981	
R.D.H. COMIX	R.D. HARWOOD		1	1	1971	1971	
R.O.B.O.T. BATTALION 2050	ECLIPSE		1	1	1988	1988	
RACCOON KIDS, THE	DC COMICS INC.		52	64	1954	1957	FORMERLY MOVIETOWN ANIMAL ANTICS
RACE FOR THE MOON	ALAN CLASS AND CO LTD		1	1	1959	1959	HARVEY REPRINTS
RACE FOR THE MOON	HARVEY PUBLICATIONS		1	3	1958	1958	
RACE FOR THE MOON	STRATO		1	23	1959	1960	HARVEY REPRINTS
RACE INTO SPACE	ALAN CLASS AND CO LTD		1	1	1961	1961	US REPRINTS
RACE OF SCORPIONS	DARK HORSE COMICS		1	4	1991	1991	
RACER X	NOW		1	11	1988	1989	
RACK AND PAIN	DARK HORSE COMICS		1	4	1994	1994	
RACKET SQUAD IN ACTION	CAPITOL STORIES		1	29	1952	1958	
RADAR THE MAN FROM THE UNKNOWN	FAME PRESS		1	16	1961	1961	
RADIANT COMICS	P.M. PRODUCTIONS		1	1	1943	1943	
RADIANT LOVE	GILLMOR MAGAZINES		2	6	1953	1954	FORMERLY DARING LOVE
RADIO BOY	ECLIPSE		1	1	1987	1987	
RADIO FUN	AMALGAMATED PRESS		1	1167	1938	1961	
RADIO FUN ANNUAL	AMALGAMATED PRESS		1940	1960	1940	1960	
RADIOACTIVE MAN	BONGO COMICS		1	1	1993	NOW	
RAGAMUFFINS	ECLIPSE		1	1	1985	1985	
RAGGEDY ANN AND ANDY	DELL PUBLISHING COMPANY		1	1	1955	1955	
RAGGEDY ANN AND ANDY	DELL PUBLISHING COMPANY	1	1	39	1946	1949	
RAGGEDY ANN AND ANDY	DELL PUBLISHING COMPANY	2	1	4	1964	1966	
RAGGEDY ANN AND ANDY	GOLD KEY	3	1	6	1971	1973	
RAGMAN	DC COMICS INC.		1	5	1976	1977	
RAGMAN	DC COMICS INC.		1	8	1991	1992	
RAGMAN: CRY OF THE DEAD	DC COMICS INC.		1	6	1993	1993	
RAGNAROK GUY	SUN COMICS PUBLISHING		1	1	1992	NOW	
RAGS RABBIT	HARVEY PUBLICATIONS		11	18	1951	1954	
RAI	VALIANT / VOYAGER COMMUNICATIONS		1	1	1993	1993	
RAI	VALIANT / VOYAGER COMMUNICATIONS		1	8	1991	1992	ISSUE 0 WAS PUBLISHED BETWEEN ISSUE 8 AND 9 IN NOVEMBER 1992.
RAI AND THE FUTURE FORCE	VALIANT / VOYAGER COMMUNICATIONS		9	19	1993	NOW	FORMERLY RAI
RAIDER 3000	CALIBER PRESS		1	1	1992	NOW	
RAIDERS OF THE LOST ARK	MARVEL ENTERTAINMENT GROUP		1	3	1981	1981	
RAIKA	SUN COMICS PUBLISHING		1	20	1992	NOW	
RAIN	TUNDRA		1	5	1991	1992	
RAINBOW BRITE AND THE STAR-STEALER	DC COMICS INC.		1	1	1985	1985	
RAINBOW, THE	AMALGAMATED PRESS		1	1898	1914	1956	
RALPH KINER, HOME RUN KING	FAWCETT PUBLICATIONS		1	1	1950	1950	
RALPH SNART ADVENTURES	NOW	1	1	3	1986	1986	
RALPH SNART ADVENTURES	NOW	2	1	9	1986	1987	
RALPH SNART ADVENTURES	NOW	3	1	31	1988	1992	
RALPH SNART ADVENTURES	NOW	4	1	3	1992	1992	
RALPH SNART ADVENTURES 3-D SPECIAL	NOW		1	1	1992	1992	
RAMAR OF THE JUNGLE	CHARLTON COMICS		2	5	1955	1956	
RAMAR OF THE JUNGLE	L. MILLER PUBLISHING COMPANY (UK)		1	4	1959	1959	CHARLTON REPRINTS
RAMAR OF THE JUNGLE	TOBY PRESS PUBLICATIONS		1	1	1954	1954	
RAMNA 1/2	VIZ	3	1	1	1993	1995	
RAMPAGE	MARVEL ENTERTAINMENT GROUP	1	1	77	1977	1978	
RAMPAGE MONTHLY	MARVEL ENTERTAINMENT GROUP		1	54	1978	1982	FORMERLY RAMPAGE
RAMPAGING HULK, THE	MARVEL ENTERTAINMENT GROUP		1	9	1977	1978	
RANCH PICTURE AND STORY ALBUM	MELLIFONT		6	6	50'S	50'S	
RANCHER, THE	MARTIN & REID		1	1	1949	1949	
RANGE BUSTERS	CHARLTON COMICS	2	8	10	1955	1955	FORMERLY COWBOY LOVE
RANGE BUSTERS	FOX FEATURES SYNDICATE	1	1	8	1950	1951	
RANGE BUSTERS	UNITED-ANGLO PRODUCTIONS		1	1	1951	1951	FOX FEATURES REPRINTS
RANGE ROMANCES	QUALITY COMICS		1	5	1949	1950	
RANGELAND LOVE	ATLAS		1	2	1949	1950	
RANGELAND WESTERN	MARTIN & REID		1	1	1949	1949	
RANGER	FLEETWAY		1	40	1965	1966	
RANGER WESTERN COMIC, THE	DONALD PETERS		1	6	1955	1956	
RANGERS COMICS	CARTOON ART	1	1	1	1950	1950	FICTION HOUSE REPRINTS
RANGERS COMICS	FICTION HOUSE		1	69	1941	1953	
RANGERS COMICS	THORPE & PORTER		1	2	1952	???	FICTION HOUSE REPRINTS
RANGO	DELL PUBLISHING COMPANY		1	1	1967	1967	
RANK & STINKY	PARODY PRESS		1	1	1993	1993	
RANMA 1/2	VIZ	1	1	7	1992	1993	
RANMA 1/2	VIZ	2	1	11	1993	NOW	
RANMA 1/2	VIZ	3	1	1	1993	NOW	
RANXEROX 2: HAPPY BIRTHDAY, LUBNA	CATALAN COMMUNICATIONS		1	1	1987	1987	
RANXEROX IN NEW YORK	CATALAN COMMUNICATIONS		1	1	1984	1984	
RAPID REFLEXES	KNOCKABOUT		1	1	1990	1990	
RAT PATROL, THE	DELL PUBLISHING COMPANY		1	6	1967	1969	
RATFINK	CANROM, INC.		1	1	1964	1964	
RATMAN	COMICO		1	2	1992	1992	
RATMAN: DARK CIRCLE	COMICO		1	4	1993	1993	
RATTLER	TARGET PUBLICATIONS		1	269	1933	1938	
RATTLER AND CHUCKLER	TARGET PUBLICATIONS		1	25	1938	1939	FORMERLY RATTLER AND CHUCKLER
RAVAGE	FATHOM PRESS		1	1	1992	NOW	
RAVAGE 2099	MARVEL ENTERTAINMENT GROUP		1	16	1992	NOW	
RAVENS & RAINBOWS	PACIFIC COMICS		1	1	1983	1983	
RAVER	MALIBU COMICS ENTERTAINMENT INC.		1	3	1993	NOW	
RAW PURPLE	BEYOND THE EDGE		1	1	1977	1977	
RAWHEAD REX	ECLIPSE		1	1	1993	1993	MATURE READERS
RAWHIDE	GOLD KEY		1	2	1963	1964	
RAWHIDE KID	MARVEL ENTERTAINMENT GROUP		1	151	1955	1979	

COMIC TITLE	PUBLISHER	Vol No.	Srt No.	End No.	Str. Year	End Year	COMMENTS
RAWHIDE KID	MARVEL ENTERTAINMENT GROUP		1	4	1985	1985	
RAWHIDE KID SPECIAL	MARVEL ENTERTAINMENT GROUP		1	1	1971	1971	
RAY BRADBURY COMICS	TOPPS		1	5	1993	NOW	
RAY REAGAN	MODERM FICTION		1	1	1949	1949	
RAY, THE	DC COMICS INC.		1	2	1994	NOW	
RAY, THE	DC COMICS INC.		1	6	1992	1992	
RAY: IN A BLAZE OF POWER, THE	DC COMICS INC.		1	1	1994	1994	
RAZOR	LONDON NIGHT STUDIO		0	0	1992	NOW	
RAZOR ANNUAL	LONDON NIGHT STUDIO		1	1	1993	1993	
RAZORGUTS	MONSTER COMICS		1	4	1991	1991	
RAZORLINE: THE FIRST CUT	MARVEL ENTERTAINMENT GROUP		1	1	1993	1993	
RAZZLE DAZZLE	CARTOON ART		1	2	1946	1947	
RE-ANIMATOR	ADVENTURE COMICS		1	3	1991	1992	
RE-ANIMATOR, DAWN OF THE	ADVENTURE COMICS		1	4	1992	1992	
RE-ANIMATOR: TALES OF HERBERT WEST	ADVENTURE COMICS		1	1	1991	1991	
REAGAN'S RAIDERS	SOLSON		1	3	1986	1986	
REAL ADVENTURE COMICS	GILLMOR MAGAZINES		1	1	1955	1955	
REAL CLUE CRIME STORIES	HILLMAN PERIODICALS		1	78	1947	1953	FORMERLY CLUE COMICS
REAL CLUE CRIME STORIES	STREAMLINE		1	2	1951	1951	HILLMAN REPRINTS
REAL EXPERIENCES	ATLAS		25	25	1950	1950	FORMERLY TINY TESSIE
REAL FACT COMICS	DC COMICS INC.		1	21	1946	1949	
REAL FUN OF DRIVING!, THE	CHRYSLER CORP.		1	2	1965	1967	
REAL FUNNIES	NEDOR (BETTER PUBLICATIONS)		1	3	1943	1943	
REAL GHOSTBUSTERS ANNUAL, THE	NOW	1	1	1	1991	1991	
REAL GHOSTBUSTERS SUPER 3-D SPECIAL, THE	NOW		1	1	1991	1991	
REAL GHOSTBUSTERS, THE	NOW	1	1	28	1988	1990	
REAL GHOSTBUSTERS, THE	NOW	2	1	8	1991	NOW	
REAL GIRL	FANTAGRAPHICS		1	4	1991	1992	
REAL HEROES COMICS	PARENTS MAGAZINE INSTITUTE		1	16	1941	1946	
REAL HIT	FOX FEATURES SYNDICATE		1	1	1944	1944	
REAL LIFE COMICS	NEDOR (BETTER PUBLICATIONS)		1	59	1941	1952	
REAL LIFE SECRETS	ACE PERIODICALS		1	1	1949	1949	
REAL LIFE STORIES	CARTOON ART		1	1	1955	1955	MAGAZINE ENTERPRISES REPRINTS
REAL LIFE STORY OF FESS PARKER	DELL PUBLISHING COMPANY		1	1	1955	1955	
REAL LOVE	ACE PERIODICALS		25	76	1949	1956	FORMERLY HAP HAZARD
REAL SCREEN COMICS	DC COMICS INC.		2	128	1945	1959	FORMERLY REAL SCREEN FUNNIES
REAL SCREEN FUNNIES	DC COMICS INC.		1	1	1945	1945	TITLE CHANGED TO REAL SCREEN COMICS #2 ONWARDS
REAL SECRETS	ACE PERIODICALS		2	5	1950	1950	FORMERLY REAL LIFE SECRETS
REAL SPORTS COMICS	HILLMAN PERIODICALS		1	1	1948	1948	
REAL WAR STORIES	ECLIPSE		1	2	1987	1991	
REAL WEST ROMANCES	CRESTWOOD PUBLISHING		1	7	1949	1950	
REAL WESTERN HERO	ARNOLD BOOK CO.		70	70	1949	1949	FAWCETT REPRINTS
REAL WESTERN HERO	FAWCETT PUBLICATIONS		70	75	1948	1949	FORMERLY WOW
REALISTIC ROMANCES	REALISTIC PUBLICATIONS		1	17	1951	1954	
REALM HANDBOOK, THE	CALIBER PRESS		1	1	1993	1993	
REALM OF THE DEAD	CALIBER PRESS		1	2	1993	NOW	
REALM, THE	CALIBER PRESS		1	4	1986	NOW	
REALM, THE	CALIBER PRESS		1	5	1988	NOW	
REALM, THE	CALIBER PRESS	2	1	1	1992	NOW	
RECORD BOOK OF FAMOUS POLICE CASES	ST JOHN PUBLISHING		1	1	1949	1949	
RED ARROW	P.L. PUBLISHING		1	3	1951	1951	
RED ARROW COMICS	CARTOON ART		1	1	1948	1948	
RED BALL COMIC BOOK	PARENTS MAGAZINE INSTITUTE		1	1	1947	1947	
RED BAND COMICS	ENWIL ASSOCIATES		1	4	1945	1945	
RED CIRCLE COMICS	RURAL HOME PUBLISHING COMPANY		1	4	1945	1945	
RED CIRCLE SORCERY	RED CIRCLE		6	11	1974	1975	
RED COMET INTERPLANETARY ADVENTURES	ATLAS UK		1	1	1961	1961	FICTION HOUSE REPRINTS
RED DAGGER	D.C. THOMSON		1	30	1979	1984	
RED DOG	ECLIPSE		1	4	1988	NOW	
RED DRAGON COMICS	STREET AND SMITH PUBLICATIONS	1	5	9	1943	1944	FORMERLY TRAIL BLAZERS
RED DRAGON COMICS	STREET AND SMITH PUBLICATIONS	2	1	7	1947	1949	
RED DWARF	FLEETWAY	2	1	3	1993	NOW	
RED DWARF MAGAZINE	FLEETWAY	1	1	14	1992	1993	
RED DWARF MAGAZINE	FLEETWAY	2	1	14	1993	NOW	
RED FLASH COMIC	PHILMAR		1	2	1948	1949	
RED FOX	MAGAZINE ENTERPRISES		15	15	1954	1954	FORMERLY MANHUNT!
RED HAWK	CARTOON ART		1	1	1953	1953	MAGAZINE ENTERPRISES REPRINTS
RED ICEBERG, THE	CAETECHETICAL EDUCATIONAL SOCIETY		1	2	1960	1960	
RED MASK	MAGAZINE ENTERPRISES		42	54	1954	1957	FORMERLY TIM HOLT
RED MOUNTAIN FEATURING QUANTRELL'S RAIDERS	AVON BOOKS		1	1	1952	1952	
RED RABBIT COMICS	DEARFIELD PUBLISHING		1	22	1947	1951	
RED RANGER, THE	MODERM FICTION		1	1	1949	1949	
RED RAVEN COMICS	TIMELY COMICS		1	1	1940	1940	
RED RAZORS	FLEETWAY		1	3	1993	1993	
RED RYDER COMICS	HAWLEY/DELL PUBLISHING COMPANY		1	151	1940	1957	HAWLEY PUBLISHED ISSUES NOS.1-5, DELL PUBLISHED FROM NO.6 ON
RED RYDER COMICS	WORLD DISTRIBUTORS LTD		1	60	1954	1959	DELL REPRINTS
RED RYDER PAINT BOOK	WHITMAN		1	1	1941	1941	
RED SEAL COMICS	SUPERIOR COMICS		14	22	1945	1947	FORMERLY CARNIVAL COMICS
RED SONJA	MARVEL ENTERTAINMENT GROUP	1	1	15	1977	1979	
RED SONJA	MARVEL ENTERTAINMENT GROUP	2	1	2	1983	1983	
RED SONJA	MARVEL ENTERTAINMENT GROUP	3	1	13	1983	1986	
RED SONJA MOVIE ADAPTATION	MARVEL ENTERTAINMENT GROUP		1	2	1985	1985	
RED SPOT COMIC, THE	MARTIN & REID		1	1	1944	1944	
RED TORNADO	DC COMICS INC.		1	4	1984	1985	
RED WARRIOR	MARVEL ENTERTAINMENT GROUP		1	6	1951	1951	
RED WOLF	MARVEL ENTERTAINMENT GROUP		1	9	1972	1973	
REDBLADE	DARK HORSE COMICS		1	3	1993	NOW	
REDDY GOOSE	INTERNATIONAL SHOE CO.		1	16	1958	1962	

INDEX OF COMIC TITLES AND THEIR PUBLISHERS

COMIC TITLE	PUBLISHER	Vol No.	Srt No.	End No.	Str. Year	End Year	COMMENTS
REDDY KILOWATT	EC COMICS		1946	1960	1946	1960	
REDDY MADE MAGIC	EC COMICS		1956	1958	1956	1958	
REDFOX	HARRIER		1	20	1986	1989	
REDFOX, THE BOOK OF	HARRIER		1	2	1986	1989	
REDSKIN	STREAMLINE		1	2	50'S	50'S	YOUTHFUL MAGAZINE CENSORED REPRINTS
REDSKIN	YOUTHFUL MAGAZINES		1	12	1950	1952	
REEL COMICS	R. & L. LOCKER		1	1	1944	1944	
REESE'S PIECES	ECLIPSE		1	2	1985	1985	
REFLECTIONS FOR CHILDREN	MIRROR PRESS PUBLICATIONS		1	1	1947	1947	
REFORM SCHOOL GIRL!	REALISTIC PUBLICATIONS		1	1	1951	1951	
REG'LAR FELLERS	CUPPLES AND LEON CO.		1	1	1929	1929	
REG'LAR FELLERS	CUPPLES AND LEON CO.		1	2	1921	1925	
REG'LAR FELLERS	STANDARD COMICS		5	6	1947	1948	
REGAL COMIC	L. MILLER PUBLISHING COMPANY (UK)		1	1	50'S	50'S	FAWCETT REPRINTS
REGENTS ILLUSTRATED COMICS	PRENTICE HALL REGENTS TEACHING MANUAL		1	1	1981	1981	
REGGIE	ARCHIE PUBLICATIONS		15	18	1963	1965	FORMERLY ARCHIE'S RIVAL, REGGIE
REGGIE AND ME	ARCHIE PUBLICATIONS		19	126	1966	1980	FORMERLY REGGIE
REGGIE'S REVENGE	ARCHIE PUBLICATIONS		1	1	1994	NOW	
REGGIE'S WISE GUY JOKES	ARCHIE PUBLICATIONS		1	60	1968	1982	
REGISTERED NURSE	CHARLTON COMICS		1	1	1963	1963	
REID FLEMING, WORLD'S TOUGHEST MILKMAN	ECLIPSE	1	1	1	1980	1980	
REID FLEMING, WORLD'S TOUGHEST MILKMAN	ECLIPSE	2	1	5	1986	1986	
REIGN OF THE DRAGONLORD	ETERNITY		1	2	1986	1986	
REIKI WARRIORS	HEROIC PUBLISHING		1	1	1993	NOW	
REMEMBER PEARL HARBOR	STREET AND SMITH PUBLICATIONS		1	1	1942	1942	
REN & STIMPY: DON'T TRY THIS AT HOME	MARVEL ENTERTAINMENT GROUP		1	1	1994	1994	
REN & STIMPY: RUNNING JOKE	MARVEL ENTERTAINMENT GROUP		1	1	1993	1993	
REN AND STIMPY SHOW, THE	MARVEL ENTERTAINMENT GROUP		1	16	1992	NOW	
REN AND STIMPY: POWDERED TOAST MAN	MARVEL ENTERTAINMENT GROUP		1	1	1994	1994	
RENEGADE ROMANCE	RENEGADE PRESS		1	2	1987	1988	
RENO BROWNE, HOLLYWOOD'S GREATEST COWGIRL	MARVEL ENTERTAINMENT GROUP		50	52	1950	1950	FORMERLY MARGIE COMICS
REPTILICUS	CHARLTON COMICS		1	2	1961	1961	
REPTISAURUS	CHARLTON COMICS		3	8	1963	1968	FORMERLY REPTILICUS
REPTISAURUS SPECIAL EDITION	CHARLTON COMICS		1	1	1963	1963	
REQUIEM FOR DRACULA	MARVEL ENTERTAINMENT GROUP		1	1	1993	1993	
RESCUERS DOWN UNDER MOVIE ADAPTATION	WALT DISNEY		1	1	1990	1990	
RESIDENTS: FREAK SHOW	DARK HORSE COMICS		1	1	1992	1992	
RETALIATOR, THE	ECLIPSE		1	4	1992	1992	
RETIEF	ADVENTURE COMICS		1	6	1987	1988	
RETIEF	MAD DOG		1	6	1987	1988	
RETIEF OF THE C.D.T	MAD DOG		1	1	1988	1988	
RETIEF: DIPLOMATIC IMMUNITY	ADVENTURE COMICS		1	6	1991	1991	
RETIEF: GIANT KILLER	ADVENTURE COMICS		1	1	1991	1991	
RETIEF: GRIME AND PUNISHMENT	ADVENTURE COMICS		1	1	1991	1991	
RETIEF: THE GARBAGE INVASION	ADVENTURE COMICS		1	1	1991	1991	
RETURN OF GORGO, THE	CHARLTON COMICS		2	3	1963	1964	FORMERLY GORGO'S REVENGE
RETURN OF MEGATON MAN	KITCHEN SINK		1	3	1988	1988	
RETURN OF THE NEW GODS	DC COMICS INC.		12	19	1977	1978	CONTINUED FROM NEW GODS V1
RETURN OF THE OUTLAW	TOBY PRESS PUBLICATIONS		1	11	1953	1955	
RETURN TO KONGA, THE	CHARLTON COMICS		1	1	1962	1962	
REVEALING ROMANCES	ACE MAGAZINES		1	6	1949	1950	
REVENGE OF THE PROWLER	ECLIPSE		1	4	1988	1988	
REVENGERS	CONTINUITY COMICS	1		1	1985	1985	
REVENGERS	CONTINUITY COMICS		1	8	1987	1987	
REVENGERS FEATURING ARMOR AND SILVER STREAK	CONTINUITY COMICS		1	6	1985	1985	
REVENGERS FEATURING MEGALITH	CONTINUITY COMICS	1	1	2	1985	1985	
REVENGERS FEATURING MEGALITH	CONTINUITY COMICS	2	1	6	1987	NOW	
REVENGERS SPECIAL	CONTINUITY COMICS		1	1	1992	NOW	
REVOLVER	FLEETWAY		1	2	1990	1991	
REVOLVER	RENEGADE PRESS		1	12	1985	1986	
REVOLVER ANNUAL	RENEGADE PRESS		1	1	1986	1986	
REVOLVER HORROR SPECIAL	FLEETWAY		1	1	1990	1990	
REVOLVER ROMANCE SPECIAL	FLEETWAY		1	1	1991	1991	
REVOLVING DOORS	BLACKTHORNE		1	3	1986	1987	
REX ALLEN	WORLD DISTRIBUTORS LTD		1	16	1953	1954	WESTERN PUBLISHING REPRINTS
REX ALLEN COMICS	DELL PUBLISHING COMPANY		2	31	1951	1959	
REX DEXTER OF MARS	FOX FEATURES SYNDICATE		1	1	1940	1940	
REX HART	TIMELY COMICS		6	8	1949	1950	FORMERLY BLAZE CARSON
REX MORGAN, M.D.	ARGO PUBLISHING		1	3	1955	1956	
RIBIT!	COMICO		1	4	1989	1989	
RIBTICKLER	FOX FEATURES SYNDICATE	1	1	9	1945	1947	
RIBTICKLER	GREEN PUBLISHING COMPANY	2	3	8	1957	1957	
RIBTICKLER	NORLEN MAGAZINES	3	3	8	1959	1959	
RICHARD SHAFFER CODENAME SCORPIO	QUASAR		1	1	1975	1975	
RICHIE RICH	HARVEY PUBLICATIONS	1	1	254	1960	1991	
RICHIE RICH	HARVEY PUBLICATIONS	2	1	21	1992	NOW	
RICHIE RICH ADVENTURE DIGEST MAGAZINE	HARVEY PUBLICATIONS		1	4	1992	NOW	
RICHIE RICH AND BELLYHOPS	HARVEY PUBLICATIONS		1	1	1977	1977	
RICHIE RICH AND CADBURY	HARVEY PUBLICATIONS		1	29	1977	1991	
RICHIE RICH AND CASPER	HARVEY PUBLICATIONS		1	45	1974	1982	
RICHIE RICH AND DOLLAR THE DOG	HARVEY PUBLICATIONS		1	24	1977	1982	
RICHIE RICH AND DOT	HARVEY PUBLICATIONS		1	1	1974	1974	
RICHIE RICH AND GLORIA	HARVEY PUBLICATIONS		1	25	1977	1982	
RICHIE RICH AND HIS GIRLFRIENDS	HARVEY PUBLICATIONS		1	16	1979	1982	
RICHIE RICH AND HIS MEAN COUSIN REGGIE	HARVEY PUBLICATIONS		1	3	1979	1980	
RICHIE RICH AND JACKIE JOKERS	HARVEY PUBLICATIONS		1	48	1973	1982	
RICHIE RICH AND PROFESSOR KEANBEAN	HARVEY PUBLICATIONS		1	2	1990	1990	

COMIC TITLE	PUBLISHER	Vol No.	Srt No.	End No.	Str. Year	End Year	COMMENTS
RICHIE RICH AND TIMMY TIME	HARVEY PUBLICATIONS		1	1	1977	1977	
RICHIE RICH BANK BOOKS	HARVEY PUBLICATIONS		1	59	1972	1982	
RICHIE RICH BEST OF THE YEARS	HARVEY PUBLICATIONS		1	6	1977	1980	
RICHIE RICH BIG BOOK	HARVEY PUBLICATIONS		1	2	1992	NOW	
RICHIE RICH BIG BUCKS	HARVEY PUBLICATIONS		1	8	1991	1992	
RICHIE RICH BILLIONS	HARVEY PUBLICATIONS		1	48	1974	1982	
RICHIE RICH CASH	HARVEY PUBLICATIONS		1	47	1974	1982	
RICHIE RICH CASH MONEY	HARVEY PUBLICATIONS		1	2	1992	1992	
RICHIE RICH DIAMONDS	HARVEY PUBLICATIONS		1	59	1972	1982	
RICHIE RICH DIGEST	HARVEY PUBLICATIONS	24	39		1990	NOW	
RICHIE RICH DOLLARS AND CENTS	HARVEY PUBLICATIONS		1	109	1963	1982	
RICHIE RICH FORTUNES	HARVEY PUBLICATIONS		1	63	1971	1982	
RICHIE RICH GEMS	HARVEY PUBLICATIONS		1	43	1974	1982	
RICHIE RICH GIANT SIZE	HARVEY PUBLICATIONS		1	3	1992	NOW	
RICHIE RICH GOLD AND SILVER	HARVEY PUBLICATIONS		1	42	1975	1982	
RICHIE RICH GOLD NUGGETS DIGEST MAGAZINE	HARVEY PUBLICATIONS		1	4	1990	NOW	
RICHIE RICH HOLIDAY DIGEST MAGAZINE ANNUAL	HARVEY PUBLICATIONS		1	5	1980	1989	
RICHIE RICH INVENTIONS	HARVEY PUBLICATIONS		1	26	1977	1982	
RICHIE RICH JACKPOTS	HARVEY PUBLICATIONS		1	58	1972	1982	
RICHIE RICH MILLION DOLLAR DIGEST MAGAZINE	HARVEY PUBLICATIONS		1	32	1980	NOW	
RICHIE RICH MILLIONS	HARVEY PUBLICATIONS		1	113	1961	1982	
RICHIE RICH MONEY WORLD	HARVEY PUBLICATIONS		1	59	1972	1982	
RICHIE RICH MONEY WORLD DIGEST	HARVEY PUBLICATIONS		1	8	1991	NOW	
RICHIE RICH PROFITS	HARVEY PUBLICATIONS		1	47	1974	1982	
RICHIE RICH RELICS	HARVEY PUBLICATIONS		1	6	1988	1989	
RICHIE RICH RICHES	HARVEY PUBLICATIONS		1	59	1972	1982	
RICHIE RICH SUCCESS STORY	HARVEY PUBLICATIONS		1	105	1964	1982	
RICHIE RICH TREASURE CHEST DIGEST	HARVEY PUBLICATIONS		1	1	1982	1982	
RICHIE RICH VACATION DIGEST	HARVEY PUBLICATIONS		1	1	1992	1992	
RICHIE RICH VACATION DIGEST MAGAZINE	HARVEY PUBLICATIONS		1	1	1991	1991	
RICHIE RICH VACATIONS DIGEST	HARVEY PUBLICATIONS		1	8	1977	1982	
RICHIE RICH VAULT OF MYSTERY	HARVEY PUBLICATIONS		1	47	1974	1982	
RICHIE RICH ZILLIONZ	HARVEY PUBLICATIONS		1	33	1976	1982	
RICHIE RICH, CASPER & WENDY NATIONAL LEAGUE	HARVEY PUBLICATIONS		1	2	1976	1976	
RICKY	STANDARD COMICS	5	5		1953	1953	
RIDER, THE	AJAX		1	5	1957	1958	
RIDER, THE	L. MILLER PUBLISHING COMPANY (UK)		1	2	1957	1957	AJAX REPRINTS
RIDERS OF THE RANGE	HAWK BOOKS		1	1	1990	1990	REPRINTS FROM EAGLE
RIFLEMAN, THE	DELL PUBLISHING COMPANY	2	20		1960	1964	
RIMA THE JUNGLE GIRL	DC COMICS INC.		1	7	1974	1975	
RIME OF THE ANCIENT MARINER	KNOCKABOUT		1	1	1990	1990	
RIN TIN TIN	DELL PUBLISHING COMPANY	10	38		1954	1963	
RIN TIN TIN	TOP SELLERS		1	2	1972	1974	
RIN TIN TIN	WORLD DISTRIBUTORS LTD		1	13	1955	1956	DELL
RING OF ROSES	DARK HORSE COMICS		1	4	1992	1992	
RING OF THE NIBELUNG, THE	DC COMICS INC.				1991	1991	
RING, THE	DC COMICS INC.		1	4	1990	1990	
RINGO KID WESTERN	L. MILLER PUBLISHING COMPANY (UK)		1	17	1955	1956	ATLAS REPRINTS
RINGO KID WESTERN, THE	ATLAS		1	21	1954	1957	
RINGO KID, THE	MARVEL ENTERTAINMENT GROUP	2	1	30	1970	1976	
RIO AT BAY	DARK HORSE COMICS		1	1	1993	1993	
RIO AT BAY	DARK HORSE COMICS		1	2	1992	1992	
RIO KID	ETERNITY		1	2	1991	1991	
RIOT	ATLAS		1	6	1954	1956	
RIOT GEAR	TRIUMPHANT COMICS		1	4	1993	NOW	
RIOT GEAR: VIOLENT PAST	TRIUMPHANT COMICS		1	2	1994	1994	
RIP CARSON	CARTOON ART		1	1	1950	1950	FICTION HOUSE REPRINTS
RIP CARSON	UNITED-ANGLO PRODUCTIONS		1	1	1951	1951	FICTION HOUSE REPRINTS
RIP HUNTER TIME MASTER	DC COMICS INC.		1	29	1961	1965	
RIP IN TIME	FANTAGOR				1990	1990	
RIP IN TIME	FANTAGOR		1	5	1986	1987	
RIP KIRBY: MORAY'S LAST GAMBLE	ASSOCIATED NEWSPAPERS		1	1	50'S	50'S	
RIP KIRBY: POISON AND PARADISE	ASSOCIATED NEWSPAPERS		1	1	1950	1950	
RIP KIRBY: THE BEAUMONT CASE/FARADAY MURDER	ASSOCIATED NEWSPAPERS		1	1	1956	1956	
RIP KIRBY: THE MAN WHO STOLE A MILLION	ASSOCIATED NEWSPAPERS		1	1	50'S	50'S	
RIP KIRBY: THE MENACE OF THE MANGLER	ASSOCIATED NEWSPAPERS		1	1	1948	1948	
RIPLEY'S BELIEVE IT OR NOT STORY DIGEST MAGAZINE	GOLD KEY		1	4	1970	1970	
RIPLEY'S BELIEVE IT OR NOT TRUE GHOST STORIES	GOLD KEY		1	2	1965	1966	
RIPLEY'S BELIEVE IT OR NOT TRUE WAR STORIES	GOLD KEY	3	3		1966	1966	FORMERLY RIPLEY'S...TRUE GHOST STORIES
RIPLEY'S BELIEVE IT OR NOT! TRUE WEIRD	RIPLEY ENTERPRISES		1	2	1966	1966	
RIPLEY'S BELIEVE IT OR NOT: ANIMAL ODDITIES	RIPLEY'S & SUN COMICS (SCHANES PRODUCTIONS)		1	1	1993	NOW	
RIPLEY'S BELIEVE IT OR NOT: BEAUTY	SUN COMICS PUBLISHING		1	1	1993	1993	
RIPLEY'S BELIEVE IT OR NOT: COINCIDENCES	RIPLEY'S & SUN COMICS (SCHANES PRODUCTIONS)		1	1	1993	NOW	
RIPLEY'S BELIEVE IT OR NOT: CRIME AND MURDER	RIPLEY'S & SUN COMICS (SCHANES PRODUCTIONS)		1	3	1993	NOW	
RIPLEY'S BELIEVE IT OR NOT: CRUELTY	RIPLEY'S & SUN COMICS (SCHANES PRODUCTIONS)		1	1	1993	NOW	
RIPLEY'S BELIEVE IT OR NOT: DEATH	SUN COMICS PUBLISHING		1	1	1993	1993	
RIPLEY'S BELIEVE IT OR NOT: FAIRY TALES	RIPLEY'S & SUN COMICS (SCHANES PRODUCTIONS)		1	2	1993	NOW	
RIPLEY'S BELIEVE IT OR NOT: FEATS	RIPLEY'S & SUN COMICS (SCHANES PRODUCTIONS)		1	1	1993	NOW	
RIPLEY'S BELIEVE IT OR NOT: FOOTBALL	RIPLEY'S & SUN COMICS (SCHANES PRODUCTIONS)		1	1	1993	NOW	
RIPLEY'S BELIEVE IT OR NOT: GOLF	RIPLEY'S & SUN COMICS (SCHANES PRODUCTIONS)		1	1	1993	NOW	
RIPLEY'S BELIEVE IT OR NOT: HYGIENE	SUN COMICS PUBLISHING		1	1	1993	1993	
RIPLEY'S BELIEVE IT OR NOT: INVENTIONS	RIPLEY'S & SUN COMICS (SCHANES PRODUCTIONS)		1	1	1993	NOW	

COMIC TITLE	PUBLISHER	Vol No.	Srt No.	End No.	Str. Year	End Year	COMMENTS
RIPLEY'S BELIEVE IT OR NOT: MODERN WONDERS	RIPLEY'S & SUN COMICS (SCHANES PRODUCTIONS)		I	I	1993	NOW	
RIPLEY'S BELIEVE IT OR NOT: MURDERS	RIPLEY'S & SUN COMICS (SCHANES PRODUCTIONS)		I	I	1993	NOW	
RIPLEY'S BELIEVE IT OR NOT: ODD PLACES	RIPLEY'S & SUN COMICS (SCHANES PRODUCTIONS)		I	I	1993	NOW	
RIPLEY'S BELIEVE IT OR NOT: ORIENT	RIPLEY'S & SUN COMICS (SCHANES PRODUCTIONS)		I	I	1993	NOW	
RIPLEY'S BELIEVE IT OR NOT: PRODIGIES	RIPLEY'S & SUN COMICS (SCHANES PRODUCTIONS)		I	2	1993	NOW	
RIPLEY'S BELIEVE IT OR NOT: RECORDS	RIPLEY'S & SUN COMICS (SCHANES PRODUCTIONS)		I	I	1993	NOW	
RIPLEYS BELIEVE IT OR NOT: RELIGION	RIPLEY'S & SUN COMICS (SCHANES PRODUCTIONS)		I	I	1993	NOW	
RIPLEY'S BELIEVE IT OR NOT: SPORT RECORDS	SUN COMICS PUBLISHING		I	I	1993	1993	
RIPLEY'S BELIEVE IT OR NOT: SPORTS FEATS	RIPLEY'S & SUN COMICS (SCHANES PRODUCTIONS)		I	I	1993	NOW	
RIPLEY'S BELIEVE IT OR NOT: STRANGE PEOPLE	RIPLEY'S & SUN COMICS (SCHANES PRODUCTIONS)		I	I	1993	NOW	
RIPLEY'S BELIEVE IT OR NOT: SUPERSTITIONS	RIPLEY'S & SUN COMICS (SCHANES PRODUCTIONS)		I	I	1993	NOW	
RIPLEY'S BELIEVE IT OR NOT: THE MACABRE	RIPLEY'S & SUN COMICS (SCHANES PRODUCTIONS)		I	I	1993	NOW	
RIPLEY'S BELIEVE IT OR NOT: UNUSUAL DEATH	SUN COMICS PUBLISHING		I	I	1993	1993	
RIPLEY'S BELIEVE IT OR NOT: WILD ANIMALS	SUN COMICS PUBLISHING		I	I	1993	1993	
RIPLEYS BELIEVE IT OR NOT	GOLD KEY		I	94	1967	1980	FORMERLY RIPLEY'S TRUE WAR STORIES
RIPLEYS BELIEVE IT OR NOT	HARVEY PUBLICATIONS		I	4	1953	1954	
RIPPER	AIRCEL		I	6	1989	1990	
RIPPING COMIC, THE	J.T. COMICS		I	I	1948	1948	
RIVERDALE HIGH	ARCHIE PUBLICATIONS		I	10	1990	1991	
RIVETS	ARGO PUBLISHING		I	3	1956	1956	
RO-BUSTERS	TITAN BOOKS		I	2	1983	1983	
ROACHMILL	BLACKTHORNE		I	6	1986	1987	
ROACHMILL	DARK HORSE COMICS		I	10	1988	1990	
ROADKILL: DEADWORLD CHRONICLES	CALIBER PRESS		I	I	1993	1993	
ROADKILL: DEADWORLD CHRONICLES	CALIBER PRESS		I	I	1993	NOW	
ROARING WESTERN	STREAMLINE		I	I	1952	1952	US REPRINTS
ROBBIN' $3000	PARODY PRESS		I	I	1993	1993	
ROBIN	DC COMICS INC.		I	3	1993	NOW	
ROBIN	DC COMICS INC.	I	I	5	1991	1991	
ROBIN	IPC		I	830	1953	1969	
ROBIN 3000	DC COMICS INC.		I	2	1993	1993	
ROBIN ANNUAL	DC COMICS INC.		I	2	1992	NOW	
ROBIN HOOD	DELL PUBLISHING COMPANY		I	I	1963	1963	
ROBIN HOOD	ECLIPSE		I	3	1991	1991	
ROBIN HOOD	L. MILLER PUBLISHING COMPANY (UK)		I	34	1957	1959	
ROBIN HOOD	WESTERN PUBLISHING COMPANY		I	I	1973	1973	
ROBIN HOOD	WORLD DISTRIBUTORS LTD		I	4	1955	1955	US REPRINTS
ROBIN HOOD AND HIS MERRY MEN	CHARLTON COMICS		28	38	1956	1958	FORMERLY DANGER AND ADVENTURE
ROBIN HOOD AND HIS MERRY MEN	STREAMLINE		I	2	1956	1956	CHARLTON REPRINTS
ROBIN HOOD ANNUAL	AMALGAMATED PRESS		1957	1960	1957	1960	
ROBIN HOOD TALES	DC COMICS INC.		I	14	1957	1958	
ROBIN HOOD TALES	QUALITY COMICS		I	6	1956	1956	
ROBIN HOOD'S FRONTIER DAYS	SHOE STORE GIVEAWAYS		I	I	1955	1955	7 VERSIONS
ROBIN HOOD, THE ADVENTURES OF	MAGAZINE ENTERPRISES		I	6	1955	1957	
ROBIN HOOD, THE NEW ADVENTURES OF	WALT DISNEY		I	I	1952	1952	4 VERSIONS
ROBIN II: JOKER'S WILD	DC COMICS INC.	2	I	4	1991	1992	
ROBIN II: JOKERS WILD MULTI PACK	DC COMICS INC.		I	I	1991	1991	
ROBIN III: CRY OF THE HUNTRESS	DC COMICS INC.	3	I	6	1992	1993	
ROBIN MINI MULTI PACK	DC COMICS INC.		I	I	1991	1991	
ROBIN SPECIAL	FLEETWAY		I	I	1992	1992	DC REPRINTS
ROBIN: A HERO REBORN	DC COMICS INC.		I	I	1991	1991	
ROBIN: TRAGEDY AND TRIUMPH	DC COMICS INC.		I	I	1993	1993	
ROBINSON CRUSOE	DELL PUBLISHING COMPANY		I	I	1963	1964	
ROBOCOP	MARVEL ENTERTAINMENT GROUP		I	23	1990	1992	
ROBOCOP 1 MOVIE ADAPTATION	MARVEL ENTERTAINMENT GROUP		I	I	1987	1987	
ROBOCOP 2 MOVIE ADAPTATION	MARVEL ENTERTAINMENT GROUP		I	I	1990	1990	
ROBOCOP 2 MOVIE ADAPTATION	MARVEL ENTERTAINMENT GROUP		I	3	1990	1990	
ROBOCOP 3 MOVIE ADAPTATION	DARK HORSE COMICS		I	3	1993	1993	
ROBOCOP MOVIE SPECIAL	MARVEL ENTERTAINMENT GROUP		I	I	1988	1988	
ROBOCOP VERSUS TERMINATOR COMPILATION	DIAMOND PUBLICATIONS		I	I	1993	1993	STAR SYSTEM EDITION
ROBOCOP VS TERMINATOR	DARK HORSE COMICS		I	4	1992	1992	
ROBOCOP: MORTAL COILS	DARK HORSE COMICS		I	4	1993	1994	
ROBOCOP: PRIME SUSPECT	DARK HORSE COMICS		I	I	1993	1993	
ROBOCOP: PRIME SUSPECT	DARK HORSE COMICS		I	4	1992	1993	
ROBOCOP: ROULETTE	DARK HORSE COMICS		I	I	1994	1994	
ROBOHUNTER	EAGLE		I	5	1984	1985	
ROBOHUNTER	TITAN BOOKS		I	4	1982	1985	
ROBOHUNTER, SAM SLADE	FLEETWAY		I	33	1984	1987	
ROBOT COMICS	RENEGADE PRESS		0	0	1987	1987	
ROBOT REBELLION	STREAMLINE		I	I	1951	1951	US REPRINTS
ROBOTECH DEFENDERS	DC COMICS INC.		I	2	1985	1985	
ROBOTECH II: THE SENTINELS	ETERNITY	I	I	16	1988	1990	
ROBOTECH II: THE SENTINELS	ETERNITY	2	I	21	1990	NOW	
ROBOTECH II: THE SENTINELS	ETERNITY	3	I	5	1993	NOW	
ROBOTECH II: THE SENTINELS-CYBER PIRATES	ETERNITY		I	4	1991	1991	
ROBOTECH II: THE SENTINELS-HANDBOOK	ETERNITY		I	3	1991	1991	
ROBOTECH II: THE SENTINELS-MALCONTENT UPRISINGS	ETERNITY		I	I	1993	1995	
ROBOTECH II: THE SENTINELS-SWIMSUIT SPECTACULAR	ETERNITY		I	I	1992	1992	
ROBOTECH IN 3-D	COMICO		I	I	1987	1987	

COMIC TITLE	PUBLISHER	Vol No.	Srt No.	End No.	Str. Year	End Year	COMMENTS
ROBOTECH MASTERS	COMICO		I	23	1985	1988	
ROBOTECH SPECIAL	COMICO		I	I	1988	1988	
ROBOTECH: FIREWALKERS	ETERNITY		I	I	1992	1992	
ROBOTECH: GENESIS	ETERNITY		I	I	1993	1993	
ROBOTECH: GENESIS	ETERNITY		I	6	1992	1993	
ROBOTECH: INVID WAR	ETERNITY		I	18	1992	NOW	
ROBOTECH: INVID WAR AFTERMATH	ETERNITY		I	I	1993	NOW	
ROBOTECH: RETURN TO MACROSS	ETERNITY		I	9	1993	NOW	
ROBOTECH: THE MACROSS SAGA	COMICO		I	36	1985	1989	FORMERLY MACROSS
ROBOTECH: THE NEW GENERATION	COMICO		I	25	1985	1988	
ROBOTIX	MARVEL ENTERTAINMENT GROUP		I	4	1986	1986	
ROBOTMEN OF THE LOST PLANET	AVON BOOKS		I	I	1952	1952	
ROCK 'N' ROLL MADNESS FUNNIES	H. BUNCH ASSOCIATES		I	2	1973	1974	
ROCK AND ROLLO	CHARLTON COMICS	14		19	1957	1958	FORMERLY TV TEENS
ROCK FANTASY COMICS	ROCK FANTASY		I	12	1989	1991	
ROCK HAPPENING	HARVEY PUBLICATIONS		I	2	1969	1969	
ROCK N ROLL COMICS	REVOLUTIONARY COMICS		I	47	1989	1992	
ROCKET	NEWS OF THE WORLD/ERIC BEMROSE		I	33	1956	1956	
ROCKET	TARGET PUBLICATIONS		I	157	1935	1938	
ROCKET COMIC, THE	HOTSPUR PUBLISHING CO.		I	I	1948	1948	
ROCKET COMIC, THE	P.M. PRODUCTIONS		I	2	1949	1949	
ROCKET COMICS	HILLMAN PERIODICALS		I	3	1940	1940	
ROCKET KELLY	FOX FEATURES SYNDICATE		I	5	1944	1946	
ROCKET RACOON	MARVEL ENTERTAINMENT GROUP		I	4	1985	1985	
ROCKET RANGER	ADVENTURE COMICS		I	5	1991	1991	
ROCKET SHIP X	FOX FEATURES SYNDICATE		I	2	1951	1952	
ROCKET TO THE MOON	AVON BOOKS		I	I	1951	1951	
ROCKETEER ADVENTURE MAGAZINE, THE	COMICO		I	2	1988	1989	
ROCKETEER MOVIE ADAPTATION	WALT DISNEY		I	I	1992	1992	
ROCKETEER MOVIE MAGAZINE	TOPPS		I	I	1992	1992	
ROCKETEER SPECIAL EDITION, THE	ECLIPSE		I	I	1984	1984	
ROCKETMAN	AJAX		I	I	1952	1952	
ROCKETMAN: KING OF THE ROCKET MEN	INNOVATION		I	4	1991	1991	
ROCKETS - A WAY OF LIFE	ASSORTED IMAGES LTD.		I	I	1988	1988	
ROCKETS AND RANGE RIDERS	RICHFIELD OIL CORP.		I	I	1957	1957	
ROCKETSHIP X	UNITED-ANGLO PRODUCTIONS		I	I	1951	1951	FOX FEATURES REPRINTS
ROCKMEEZ	JZINK COMICS		I	4	1992	NOW	
ROCKOLA GREATEST HITS	MIRAGE STUDIOS		I	I	1987	1987	
ROCKY AND HIS FIENDISH FRIENDS	GOLD KEY		I	5	1962	1963	
ROCKY HORROR PICTURE SHOW COMIC BOOK, THE	CALIBER PRESS		I	3	1990	1990	
ROCKY LANE WESTERN	CHARLTON COMICS	56		87	1954	1959	
ROCKY LANE WESTERN	FAWCETT PUBLICATIONS		I	55	1949	1954	
ROCKY LANE WESTERN	L. MILLER PUBLISHING COMPANY (UK)	50		139	1950	1959	FAWCETT REPRINTS
ROCKY MOUNTAIN KING WESTERN COMIC	L. MILLER PUBLISHING COMPANY (UK)		I	65	1955	1959	
ROD CAMERON WESTERN	FAWCETT PUBLICATIONS		I	20	1950	1953	
ROD CAMERON WESTERN	L. MILLER PUBLISHING COMPANY (UK)		I	64	1950	1960	FAWCETT REPRINTS
ROG 2000, THE COMPLETE	PACIFIC COMICS				1982	1982	
ROGAN GOSH	DC COMICS INC.		I	I	1994	1994	
ROGER BEAN, R.G.	INDIANA NEWS CO.		I	5	1915	1917	
ROGER DODGER	STANDARD COMICS	5		5	1952	1952	
ROGER RABBIT	WALT DISNEY		I	18	1990	1991	
ROGER RABBIT'S TOONTOWN	WALT DISNEY		I	6	1991	1991	
ROGER RABBIT: THE OFFICIAL COMICS ADAPTATION	MARVEL ENTERTAINMENT GROUP				1989	1989	
ROGER RABBIT: THE RESURRECTION OF DOOM	MARVEL ENTERTAINMENT GROUP				1990	1990	
ROGER RABBIT: TUMMY TROUBLE	WALT DISNEY		I	I	1992	1992	
ROGER WILCO	ADVENTURE COMICS		I	3	1992	1992	
ROGUE TROOPER	FLEETWAY		I	3	1984	1987	
ROGUE TROOPER	FLEETWAY		I	49	1986	1990	
ROGUE TROOPER ANNUAL	FLEETWAY	1991		1991	1991	1991	
ROGUE TROOPER'S FUTURE WARS	FLEETWAY		I	I	1988	1988	
ROGUE TROOPER: WAR MACHINE	TUNDRA		I	I	1993	1993	
ROGUE TROOPER: WARRIOR	FLEETWAY		I	9	1991	1992	
ROIDRAGE	MARVEL ENTERTAINMENT GROUP		I	I	1993	NOW	MARVEL UK TITLE
ROLY POLY COMIC BOOK	GREEN PUBLISHING COMPANY		I	15	1944	1946	
ROM	MARVEL ENTERTAINMENT GROUP		I	75	1979	1986	
ROM ANNUAL	MARVEL ENTERTAINMENT GROUP		I	4	1982	1985	
ROMAN HOLIDAYS, THE	GOLD KEY		I	4	1973	1973	
ROMANCE AND CONFESSION STORIES	ST JOHN PUBLISHING		I	I	1949	1949	
ROMANCE DIARY	MARVEL ENTERTAINMENT GROUP		I	2	1949	1950	
ROMANCE STORIES OF TRUE LOVE	HARVEY PUBLICATIONS	45		52	1957	1958	FORMERLY LOVE PROBLEMS AND ADVICE
ROMANCE TALES	MARVEL ENTERTAINMENT GROUP	7		9	1949	1950	FORMERLY WESTERN WINNERS
ROMANCE TRAIL	DC COMICS INC.		I	6	1949	1950	
ROMANCES OF NURSE HELEN GRANT, THE	ATLAS		I	I	1957	1957	
ROMANCES OF THE WEST	MARVEL ENTERTAINMENT GROUP		I	2	1949	1950	
ROMANTIC ADVENTURES	AMERICOMICS		I	67	1949	1956	
ROMANTIC AFFAIRS	MARVEL ENTERTAINMENT GROUP	3		3	1950	1950	FORMERLY MOLLY MANTON'S ROMANCES
ROMANTIC CONFESSIONS	HILLMAN PERIODICALS		I	25	1949	1953	
ROMANTIC HEARTS	MERIT PUBLISHING	2		12	1953	1955	
ROMANTIC HEARTS	STORY COMICS	1		10	1951	1952	
ROMANTIC LOVE	AVON BOOKS		I	23	1949	1954	
ROMANTIC LOVE	QUALITY COMICS	4		4	1950	1950	
ROMANTIC MARRIAGE	ST JOHN PUBLISHING	18		24	1953	1954	
ROMANTIC MARRIAGE	ZIFF-DAVIS PUBLISHING COMPANY		I	17	1950	1952	
ROMANTIC PICTURE NOVELETTES	MAGAZINE ENTERPRISES		I	I	1946	1946	
ROMANTIC SECRETS	CHARLTON COMICS	2	5	52	1955	1964	
ROMANTIC SECRETS	FAWCETT PUBLICATIONS	1	I	39	1949	1953	
ROMANTIC STORY	CHARLTON COMICS	23		130	1954	1973	
ROMANTIC STORY	FAWCETT PUBLICATIONS		I	22	1949	1953	
ROMANTIC WESTERN	FAWCETT PUBLICATIONS		I	3	1949	1950	

COMIC TITLE	PUBLISHER	Vol. No.	Srt No.	End No.	Str. Year	End Year	COMMENTS
ROMEO BROWN (DAILY STRIPS)	JOHN DAKIN		2	6	1979	1960	
ROMEO TUBBS	FOX FEATURES SYNDICATE		26	28	1950	1952	FORMERLY MY SECRET LIFE
ROMEO TUBBS	UNITED-ANGLO PRODUCTIONS		1	1	1951	1951	FOX FEATURES REPRINTS
RONALD MCDONALD	CHARLTON COMICS		1	4	1970	1971	
RONIN	DC COMICS INC.		1	1	1987	1987	
RONIN	DC COMICS INC.		1	6	1983	1984	
ROOK	WARREN PUBLISHING CO		1	14	1979	1982	
ROOKIE COP	CHARLTON COMICS		27	33	1955	1957	FORMERLY CRIME AND JUSTICE
ROOKIE COP	L. MILLER PUBLISHING COMPANY (UK)		1	?	1956	???	CHARLTON REPRINTS
ROOM 222	DELL PUBLISHING COMPANY		1	4	1970	1971	
ROOTIE KAZOOTIE	DELL PUBLISHING COMPANY		1	4	1952	1954	
ROSE	HEROIC PUBLISHING		1	1	1992	NOW	
ROSE OF BAGDAD, THE	GAYWOOD PRESS		1	1	1952	1952	
ROUGH RAIDERS	BLUE COMET		1	3	1990	NOW	
ROUGH RAIDERS ANNUAL	BLUE COMET		1	1	1990	1990	
ROUNDUP	D.S. PUBLISHING CO.		1	5	1948	1949	
ROUNDUP BUDGET OF FUN AND ADVENTURE, THE	CHILDREN'S PRESS		1	1	1948	1948	
ROVER MIDGET COMIC, THE	D.C. THOMSON		1	1	1933	1933	
ROVER SUMMER FUN BOOK, THE	D.C. THOMSON		1	1	1936	1936	
ROVERS	MALIBU COMICS ENTERTAINMENT INC.		1	5	1987	1988	
ROY CAMPANELLA, BASEBALL HERO	FAWCETT PUBLICATIONS		1	1	1950	1950	
ROY CARSON	BOARDMAN		1	8	1948	1951	ISSUES UNNUMBERED
ROY CARSON COMIC ANNUAL	POPULAR		1953	1954	1953	1954	
ROY OF THE ROVERS	IPC				1976	1993	NO NUMBERS, DATES ONLY
ROY ROGERS AND TRIGGER	DELL PUBLISHING COMPANY		92	145	1955	1961	
ROY ROGERS AND TRIGGER	GOLD KEY		1	1	1967	1967	
ROY ROGERS COMICS	DELL PUBLISHING COMPANY		1	91	1948	1955	
ROY ROGERS COMICS	PEMBERTON		1	100	1951	1959	DELL REPRINTS
ROY ROGERS' TRIGGER	DELL PUBLISHING COMPANY		2	17	1951	1955	
ROY ROGERS' TRIGGER	PEMBERTON		1	14	1952	1953	DELL REPRINTS
ROYAL ROY	MARVEL ENTERTAINMENT GROUP		1	5	1985	1986	
RUDOLPH THE RED-NOSED REINDEER	DC COMICS INC.		1950	1962	1950	1962	
RUFF & REDDY	DELL PUBLISHING COMPANY		4	12	1958	1962	
RUGGED ACTION	ATLAS		1	4	1954	1955	
RULAH JUNGLE GODDESS	FOX FEATURES SYNDICATE		17	27	1948	1949	FORMERLY ZOOT
RUMMAGE $2099	PARODY PRESS		1	1	1993	1993	
RUN, BUDDY, RUN	GOLD KEY		1	1	1967	1967	
RUNE	MALIBU COMICS ENTERTAINMENT INC.		1	4	1994	NOW	
RUPERT ACTIVITY BOOK	OLDBOURNE BOOK CO.		1	2	1959	1959	
RUPERT ADVENTURE SERIES	EXPRESS PUBLICATIONS		1	50	1948	1963	
RUPERT AND HIS FRIEND MARGOT	SAMPSON LOW MARSTON		1	1	1949	1949	
RUPERT AND HIS WONDERFUL BOOTS	SAMPSON LOW MARSTON		1	1	1946	1946	
RUPERT AND THE BLUE MIST	STANFIELD		1	1	1975	1975	
RUPERT AND THE MAGICIAN'S HAT	STANFIELD		1	1	1975	1975	
RUPERT AND THE PINK LETTER	OLDBOURNE BOOK CO.		1	1	1960	1960	
RUPERT AND THE POSTMAN	STANFIELD		1	1	1975	1975	
RUPERT ANNUAL	EXPRESS PUBLICATIONS		1936	1990	1936	1990	
RUPERT ANNUAL FACSIMILE	EXPRESS PUBLICATIONS		1936	1938	1936	1938	
RUPERT AT ROCKY BAY	OLDBOURNE BOOK CO.		1	1	1960	1960	
RUPERT COLOUR LIBRARY	PURNELL		1	1	1976	1976	
RUPERT FORTNIGHTLY	CELEBRITY COMICS		1	20	1989	1990	
RUPERT GOES TO THE MOON	STANFIELD		1	1	1975	1975	
RUPERT HOLIDAY SPECIAL	POLYSTYLE		1979	1981	1979	1981	
RUPERT SUMMER SPECIAL	MARVEL ENTERTAINMENT GROUP		1	1	1983	1983	
RUPERT THE KNIGHT AND THE LADY	SAMPSON LOW MARSTON		1	1	1949	1949	
RUPERT TV STORYBOOKS	STANFIELD		1	6	1978	1978	
RUPERT WEEKLY	MARVEL ENTERTAINMENT GROUP		1	100	1982	1984	
RUST	ADVENTURE COMICS		1	4	1992	1992	
RUST	NOW	1	1	13	1987	1989	
RUST	NOW	2	1	7	1988	1989	
RUSTY COMICS	MARVEL ENTERTAINMENT GROUP		12	22	1947	1949	FORMERLY KID MOVIE COMICS
RUSTY, BOY DETECTIVE	LEV GLEASON PUBLICATIONS		1	5	1955	1955	

S

COMIC TITLE	PUBLISHER	Vol. No.	Srt No.	End No.	Str. Year	End Year	COMMENTS
S'MATTER POP?	SAALFIELD PUBLISHING COMPANY		1	1	1917	1917	
S.O.F.T. CORPS	PERSONALITY COMICS		1	1	1992	1992	
S.T.A.R. CORPS	DC COMICS INC.		1	4	1993	NOW	
S.T.A.T.	MAJESTIC ENTERTAINMENT		1	1	1993	NOW	
SAARI, THE JUNGLE GODDESS	P.L. PUBLISHING		1	1	1951	1951	
SABER TIGER	VIZ				1991	1991	
SABLE	FIRST		1	27	1988	1990	
SABRE	ECLIPSE		1	14	1982	1985	
SABRE ROMANTIC STORIES IN PICTURES	SABRE		1	2	1971	???	
SABRE THRILLER PICTURE LIBRARY	SABRE		1	2	1971	???	
SABRE WAR PICTURE LIBRARY	SABRE		1	2	1971	???	
SABRE WESTERN STORIES IN PICTURES	SABRE		1	2	1971	???	
SABRETOOTH	MARVEL ENTERTAINMENT GROUP		1	4	1993	1993	
SABRETOOTH CLASSICS	MARVEL ENTERTAINMENT GROUP		1	2	1994	NOW	
SABRINA'S HALLOWEEN SPOOKTACULAR	ARCHIE PUBLICATIONS		1	1	1993	1993	
SABRINA, THE TEENAGE WITCH	ARCHIE PUBLICATIONS		1	77	1971	1983	
SABU	UNITED-ANGLO PRODUCTIONS		1	4	1951	1951	FOX FEATURES REPRINTS
SABU, "ELEPHANT BOY"	FOX FEATURES SYNDICATE		1	2	1950	1950	FORMERLY MY SECRET STORY
SACHS & VIOLENS	MARVEL ENTERTAINMENT GROUP		1	1	1993	1994	
SACRAMENTS, THE	CAETECHETICAL EDUCATIONAL SOCIETY		304	304	1955	1955	
SAD CASE OF WAITING ROOM WILLIE, THE	AMERICAN VISUALS CORPORATION		1	1	1950	1950	

COMIC TITLE	PUBLISHER	Vol No.	Srt No.	End No.	Str. Year	End Year	COMMENTS
SAD SACK	TOP SELLERS		1	?	1973	???	HARVEY REPRINTS
SAD SACK AND THE SARGE	HARVEY PUBLICATIONS		1	155	1957	1982	
SAD SACK ARMY LIFE	HARVEY PUBLICATIONS		58	61	1963	1976	
SAD SACK COMICS	HARVEY PUBLICATIONS		1	289	1949	NOW	
SAD SACK FUN AROUND THE WORLD	HARVEY PUBLICATIONS		1	1	1974	1974	
SAD SACK GOES HOME	HARVEY PUBLICATIONS				1951	1951	
SAD SACK LAUGH SPECIAL	HARVEY PUBLICATIONS		1	93	1958	1977	
SAD SACK NAVY GOBS 'N' GALS	HARVEY PUBLICATIONS		1	8	1972	1973	
SAD SACK USA	HARVEY PUBLICATIONS		1	8	1972	1974	
SAD SACK USA VACATION	HARVEY PUBLICATIONS		1	8	1972	1973	
SAD SACK WITH SARGE & SADIE	HARVEY PUBLICATIONS		1	8	1972	1973	
SAD SACK WITH SARGE AND SADIE	HARVEY PUBLICATIONS		1	8	1972	1973	
SAD SACK'S ARMY LIFE PARADE	HARVEY PUBLICATIONS		1	57	1963	1975	
SAD SACK, THE ORIGINAL	HARVEY PUBLICATIONS		1	1	1992	1992	
SAD SACK: THE NEWSPAPER STRIP	HARVEY PUBLICATIONS		1	1	1993	1993	
SAD SACKS FUNNY FRIENDS	HARVEY PUBLICATIONS		1	75	1955	1969	
SAD SAD SACK WORLD	HARVEY PUBLICATIONS		1	46	1964	1973	
SADDLE JUSTICE	EC COMICS		3	8	1948	1949	FORMERLY HAPPY HOULIHANS
SADDLE ROMANCES	EC COMICS		9	11	1949	1950	FORMERLY SADDLE JUSTICE
SAFEST PLACE	DARK HORSE COMICS		1	1	1993	1993	
SAFETY BELT MAN	CRY FOR DAWN PUBLICATIONS		1	1	1993	1993	
SAGA OF BIG RED, THE	OMAHA-WORLD HERALD		1	1	1976	1976	
SAGA OF RA'S AL GHUL	DC COMICS INC.		1	1	1991	1991	
SAGA OF RA'S AL GHUL	DC COMICS INC.		1	4	1988	1988	
SAGA OF THE HUMAN TORCH	MARVEL ENTERTAINMENT GROUP		1	4	1990	1990	
SAGA OF THE MAN-ELF, THE	TRIDENT		1	5	1989	1990	
SAGA OF THE REALM	CALIBER PRESS		1	3	1992	NOW	
SAGA OF THE SUB-MARINER	MARVEL ENTERTAINMENT GROUP		1	12	1988	1989	
SAIGON CHRONICLES	A PLUS COMICS		1	2	1991	NOW	
SAILOR SWEENEY	ATLAS		12	14	1956	1956	FORMERLY NAVY ACTION
SAILOR'S STORY	MARVEL ENTERTAINMENT GROUP		1	1	1987	1987	
SAINT ANNUAL, THE	PBS		1	1	1973	1973	
SAINT ANNUAL, THE	WORLD DISTRIBUTORS LTD		1968	1970	1968	1970	
SAINT ANNUAL, THE RETURN OF THE	STAFFORD PEMBERTON		1979	1980	1979	1980	
SAINT DETECTIVE CASES, THE	THORPE & PORTER		1	4	1951	1952	AVON REPRINTS
SAINT SINNER	MARVEL ENTERTAINMENT GROUP		1	6	1993	NOW	
SAINT TELEVISION STORY BOOK, THE	PBS		1	1	1971	1971	
SAINT, THE	AVON BOOKS		1	12	1947	1952	
SAINT, THE	TOP SELLERS		1	5	1966	1966	
SALOME	ECLIPSE		1	1	1987	1987	
SAM AND MAX FREELANCE POLICE COLOUR COLLECTION	MARVEL ENTERTAINMENT GROUP		1	1	1992	1992	
SAM AND MAX FREELANCE POLICE SPECIAL	COMICO		1	1	1989	1989	
SAM AND MAX GO TO THE MOON DIRT BAG SPECIAL	MARVEL ENTERTAINMENT GROUP		1	1	1992	1992	
SAM AND MAX SHOW	MARVEL ENTERTAINMENT GROUP		1	3	1993	1993	
SAM BRONX AND THE ROBOTS	ACME PRESS		1	1	1990	1990	
SAM HILL PRIVATE EYE	ARCHIE PUBLICATIONS		1	7	1950	1951	
SAM HILL PRIVATE EYE COMICS	THORPE & PORTER		1	5	1952	1952	CLOSEUP INC. REPRINTS
SAMSON	AJAX	2	12	14	1955	1955	FORMERLY FANTASTIC COMICS
SAMSON	FOX FEATURES SYNDICATE	1	1	6	1940	1941	
SAMSON	L. MILLER PUBLISHING COMPANY (UK)		1	3	1955	1955	AJAX REPRINTS
SAMSON AND DELILAH	STREAMLINE		1	1	1950	1950	FOX FEATURES REPRINTS
SAMURAI	AIRCEL	1	1	23	1985	1987	
SAMURAI	AIRCEL	2	1	3	1988	1988	
SAMURAI	AIRCEL	3	1	7	1989	NOW	
SAMURAI CAT	MARVEL ENTERTAINMENT GROUP		1	3	1991	1991	
SAMURAI FUNNIES	SOLSON		1	2	1987	1987	
SAMURAI SANTA	SOLSON		1	1	1987	1987	
SAMURAI SEVEN	CALIBER PRESS		1	4	1992	1993	
SAMURAI, SON OF DEATH	ECLIPSE		1	1	1987	1987	
SAMURAI: DEATH OF A LEGEND	NIGHT WYND ENTERPRISES		1	4	1993	1993	
SAMURAI: DEMON SWORD	NIGHT WYND ENTERPRISES		1	4	1993	1993	
SAMURAI: MYSTIC CULT	NIGHT WYND ENTERPRISES		1	4	1992	1993	
SAMURAI: VAMPIRE'S HUNT	NIGHT WYND ENTERPRISES		1	4	1992	1992	
SAMURAI: YAKUZAS REVENGE	NIGHT WYND ENTERPRISES		1	4	1993	1993	
SAMUREE	CONTINUITY COMICS		1	3	1993	NOW	
SAMUREE	CONTINUITY COMICS	2	1	7	1993	1994	
SAMUREE	CONTINUITY COMICS	2	2	2	1993	NOW	
SANCTUARY	VIZ		1	9	1992	1993	
SANCTUARY	VIZ	1	1	2	1993	NOW	
SANCTUARY II	VIZ		1	8	1993	NOW	
SANCTUM	KITCHEN SINK		1	1	1992	1992	
SANDMAN MYSTERY THEATRE	DC COMICS INC.		1	11	1993	NOW	
SANDMAN SPECIAL	DC COMICS INC.	2	1	1	1991	1991	
SANDMAN, THE	DC COMICS INC.	1	1	6	1974	1976	
SANDMAN, THE	DC COMICS INC.	2	1	57	1989	NOW	
SANDMAN: A GAME OF YOU	DC COMICS INC.		1	1	1992	1992	
SANDMAN: A GAME OF YOU	DC COMICS INC.		1	1	1993	1993	
SANDMAN: BRIEF LIVES	TITAN BOOKS		1	1	1994	1994	
SANDMAN: DOLLS HOUSE	DC COMICS INC.		1	1	1990	1990	
SANDMAN: DREAM COUNTRY	DC COMICS INC.		1	1	1991	1991	
SANDMAN: FABLES AND REFLECTIONS	DC COMICS INC.		1	1	1993	1993	
SANDMAN: FABLES AND REFLECTIONS	TITAN BOOKS		1	1	1993	1993	
SANDMAN: PRELUDES & NOCTURNES	DC COMICS INC.		1	1	1990	1990	
SANDMAN: SEASONS OF THE MIST	DC COMICS INC.		1	1	1991	1991	
SANDMAN: SEASONS OF THE MIST	DC COMICS INC.		1	1	1992	1992	
SANDS OF THE SOUTH PACIFIC	TOBY PRESS PUBLICATIONS		1	1	1953	1953	
SANTA AND POLYANNA PLAY THE GLAD GAME	WALT DISNEY		1	1	1960	1960	
SANTA AND THE BUCCANEERS	PROMOTIONAL PUBLICATIONS COMPANY		1	1	1959	1959	
SANTA AND THE CHRISTMAS CHICKADEE	MURPHY'S		1	1	1974	1974	

INDEX OF COMIC TITLES AND THEIR PUBLISHERS

COMIC TITLE	PUBLISHER	Vol No.	Srt No.	End No.	Str. Year	End Year	COMMENTS
SANTA AND THE PIRATES	PROMOTIONAL PUBLICATIONS COMPANY		I	I	1952	1952	
SANTA CLAUS FUNNIES	DELL PUBLISHING COMPANY		I	I	1952	1952	
SANTA CLAUS FUNNIES	DELL PUBLISHING COMPANY		I	2	1942	1943	
SANTA CLAUS FUNNIES	WHITMAN		I	I	1940	1940	
SANTA CLAUS PARADE	ZIFF-DAVIS PUBLISHING COMPANY		I	3	1951	1955	
SANTA CLAWS	ETERNITY		I	I	1991	1991	
SANTA ON THE JOLLY ROGER	PROMOTIONAL PUBLICATIONS COMPANY		I	I	1965	1965	
SANTA! SANTA!	MONTGOMERY WARD		I	I	1974	1974	
SANTA'S CHRISTMAS COMIC VARIETY SHOW	SEARS AND ROEBUCK COMPANY		I	I	1943	1943	
SANTA'S CHRISTMAS COMICS	STANDARD COMICS		I	I	1952	1952	
SANTA'S CHRISTMAS TIME STORIES	PREMIUM SALES INC.		I	I	1940	1940	
SANTA'S CIRCUS	PROMOTIONAL PUBLICATIONS COMPANY		I	I	1964	1964	
SANTA'S NEW STORY BOOK	WALLACE HAMILTON CAMPBELL		I	I	1949	1949	
SANTA'S REAL STORY BOOK	WALLACE HAMILTON CAMPBELL		I	I	1949	1952	
SANTA'S RIDE	W.T. GRANT COMPANY		I	I	1959	1959	
SANTA'S RODEO	PROMOTIONAL PUBLICATIONS COMPANY		I	I	1964	1964	
SANTA'S SECRETS	SAM. B. ANSON		I	I	1951	1952	
SANTA'S STORIES	K.K. PUBLICATIONS		I	I	1953	1953	
SANTA'S SURPRISE	K.K. PUBLICATIONS		I	I	1947	1947	
SANTA'S TOYTOWN FUN BOOK	PROMOTIONAL PUBLICATIONS COMPANY		I	2	1952	1953	
SAPPHIRE	AIRCEL		I	10	1990	NOW	
SARGE SNORKEL	CHARLTON COMICS		I	17	1973	1976	
SARGE STEEL	CHARLTON COMICS		I	8	1964	1966	
SATANS SIX	TOPPS		I	4	1993	1994	
SAVAGE ACTION	MARVEL ENTERTAINMENT GROUP		I	15	1979	1982	
SAVAGE COMBAT TALES	ATLAS		I	3	1975	1975	
SAVAGE DRAGON	IMAGE COMICS		I	I	1993	1993	
SAVAGE DRAGON	IMAGE COMICS		I	3	1992	1992	
SAVAGE DRAGON	IMAGE COMICS		I	6	1993	NOW	
SAVAGE DRAGON LIMITED EDITION	IMAGE COMICS		I	I	1993	1993	
SAVAGE DRAGON VS SAVAGE MEGATON MAN	IMAGE COMICS		I	I	1993	1993	
SAVAGE RETURN OF DRACULA	MARVEL ENTERTAINMENT GROUP		I	I	1992	1992	
SAVAGE SWORD OF CONAN (BRITISH)	MARVEL ENTERTAINMENT GROUP	I	I	18	1975	1975	
SAVAGE SWORD OF CONAN (BRITISH)	MARVEL ENTERTAINMENT GROUP	2	I	93	1977	1985	
SAVAGE SWORD OF CONAN (US)	MARVEL ENTERTAINMENT GROUP		I	218	1974	NOW	
SAVAGE SWORD OF CONAN ANNUAL	MARVEL ENTERTAINMENT GROUP		I	I	1975	1975	
SAVAGE TALES	MARVEL ENTERTAINMENT GROUP	I	I	11	1971	1975	
SAVAGE TALES	MARVEL ENTERTAINMENT GROUP	2	I	9	1985	1987	
SAVAGE TALES ANNUAL	MARVEL ENTERTAINMENT GROUP		I	I	1975	1975	
SAVED BY THE BELL	HARVEY PUBLICATIONS	I	I	4	1992	1992	
SAVED BY THE BELL	HARVEY PUBLICATIONS	2	I	5	1992	1992	
SAVED BY THE BELL SPECIAL	HARVEY PUBLICATIONS		I	I	1992	1992	
SAVED BY THE BELL SUMMER SPECIAL	HARVEY PUBLICATIONS		I	I	1992	1992	
SAVIOUR	TRIDENT		I	I	1990	1990	
SAVIOUR	TRIDENT		I	6	1989	1990	
SCAB	FANTACO		I	I	1992	1992	
SCAMP	DELL PUBLISHING COMPANY	5	I	16	1958	1961	
SCAMP	GOLD KEY		I	45	1967	1979	
SCARAB	DC COMICS INC.		I	3	1993	NOW	
SCARAMOUCH	INNOVATION		I	2	1990	1990	
SCARECROW OF ROMNEY MARSH, THE	GOLD KEY		I	3	1964	1965	
SCARLET IN GASLIGHT	ETERNITY		I	8	1987	1989	
SCARLET WITCH	MARVEL ENTERTAINMENT GROUP		I	3	1993	NOW	
SCARLETT	DC COMICS INC.		I	13	1992	NOW	
SCARY BOOK, THE	CALIBER PRESS		I	4	1992	NOW	
SCARY TALES	CHARLTON COMICS		I	46	1975	1984	
SCARY TALES	MODERN COMICS		I	I	1977	1977	REPRINTS
SCAVENGERS	FLEETWAY		I	26	1986	1988	
SCAVENGERS	TRIUMPHANT COMICS		I	6	1993	NOW	
SCHOOL DAY ROMANCES	STAR PUBLICATIONS		I	4	1949	1950	
SCHOOL FRIEND PICTURE LIBRARY	AMALGAMATED PRESS		I	88	1962	1965	
SCHOOL FRIENDS	AMALGAMATED PRESS		I	766	1950	1965	
SCHOOLGIRL	GERALD SWAN		I	I	1951	1951	ARCHIE REPRINTS
SCHOOLGIRLS' PICTURE LIBRARY	AMALGAMATED PRESS		I	327	1957	1965	
SCHWINN BICYCLE BOOK ANNUAL	SCHWINN BICYCLE CO.		1949	1959	1949	1959	
SCIENCE COMICS	ACE MAGAZINES	2	I	5	1946	1946	
SCIENCE COMICS	EXPORT PUBLICATIONS ENTERTAINMENT INC.		I	I	1951	1951	
SCIENCE COMICS	FOX FEATURES SYNDICATE		I	8	1940	1940	
SCIENCE COMICS	FOX FEATURES SYNDICATE	I	I	8	1940	1940	
SCIENCE COMICS	ZIFF-DAVIS PUBLISHING COMPANY		I	I	1947	1947	
SCIENCE SERVICE, THE	ATOMIC COMICS		I	I	1989	1989	
SCIMIDAR	ETERNITY	3	I	4	1990	1990	
SCIMIDAR: FEAST AND FAMINE	ETERNITY	2	I	4	1989	1989	
SCIMIDAR: LIVING COLOUR	ETERNITY	5	I	4	1991	1991	
SCIMIDAR: PIN UP BOOK	ETERNITY		I	I	1991	1991	
SCIMIDAR: PLEASURE AND PAIN	ETERNITY	I	I	4	1988	1989	
SCIMIDAR: SLASHDANCE	AIRCEL	6	I	4	1992	1993	
SCIMIDAR: WILD THING	ETERNITY	4	I	4	1990	1991	
SCOOBY DOO	CHARLTON COMICS		I	11	1975	1976	
SCOOBY DOO	HARVEY PUBLICATIONS		I	3	1992	NOW	
SCOOBY DOO	MARVEL ENTERTAINMENT GROUP		I	9	1977	1979	
SCOOBY DOO BIG BOOK	HARVEY PUBLICATIONS		I	2	1992	NOW	
SCOOBY DOO GIANT SIZE	HARVEY PUBLICATIONS		I	2	1992	NOW	
SCOOBY DOO WHERE ARE YOU?	GOLD KEY		I	30	1970	1975	
SCOOP	D.C. THOMSON		I	194	1978	1981	
SCOOP COMICS	HARRY A CHESLER		I	8	1941	1944	
SCOOP WESTERN, THE	MARTIN & REID		I	I	1950	1950	
SCOOPS COMIC	HOTSPUR PUBLISHING CO.		I	I	1948	1948	
SCOOTER COMICS	RUCKER PUBL. CO.		I	I	1946	1946	

COMIC TITLE	PUBLISHER	Vol No.	Srt No.	End No.	Str. Year	End Year	COMMENTS
SCORCHED EARTH	TUNDRA		1	4	1991	1991	
SCORCHER	IPC		1	70	1970	1971	
SCORCHER AND SCORE	IPC		1	167	1971	1974	
SCORCHY	GOLD STAR PUBLICATIONS LTD		1	1	1972	1972	US REPRINTS
SCORE 'N' ROAR	IPC		1	41	1970	1971	
SCORE, THE	DC COMICS INC.		1	4	1989	1989	
SCORPIO ROSE	ECLIPSE		1	2	1983	1983	
SCORPION	ATLAS		1	3	1975	1975	
SCORPION CORPS	DAGGER ENTERPRISES		2	2	1993	NOW	
SCOTLAND YARD	FAME PRESS		1	2	1965	1965	
SCOTLAND YARD, INSPECTOR FARNSWORTH OF	CHARLTON COMICS		1	4	1955	1956	
SCOTT MUSGROVE'S FAT DOG MENDOZA	DARK HORSE COMICS		1	1	1993	1993	
SCOUT	ECLIPSE		1	24	1985	1987	
SCOUT : HANDBOOK	ECLIPSE		1	1	1987	1987	
SCOUT : WAR SHAMAN	ECLIPSE		1	16	1988	1989	
SCREAM	IPC		1	15	1984	1984	
SCREAM	SKYWALD PUBLISHING		1	11	1973	1975	
SCREAM COMICS	ACE MAGAZINES		1	19	1944	1948	
SCREAM PLAY	AIRCEL		1	2	1992	1992	
SCREAM!	IPC		1	15	1984	1984	
SCREWTAPE LETTERS	MARVEL ENTERTAINMENT GROUP		1	1	1993	1993	
SCRIBBLY	DC COMICS INC.		1	15	1948	1952	
SCUM OF THE EARTH	AIRCEL		1	3	1990	1991	
SEA DEVIL, THE	SCION		1	1	1952	1952	
SEA DEVILS	DC COMICS INC.		1	35	1961	1967	
SEA HERO	SCION		1	1	1952	1952	
SEA HOUND, THE	AVON BOOKS		1	4	1945	1946	
SEA HOUND, THE	CAPTAIN SILVER SYNDICATE		3	4	1949	1949	
SEA HUNT	DELL PUBLISHING COMPANY		4	13	1960	1962	
SEAQUEST DSV	NEMESIS COMICS		1	1	1993	1993	
SEARCH FOR LOVE	AMERICOMICS		1	3	1950	1950	
SEASIDE COMIC	C.A. PEARSON		1930	1939	1930	1939	
SEBASTIAN	WALT DISNEY		1	2	1992	1992	
SEBASTIAN O	DC COMICS INC.		1	3	1993	1993	
SEBASTIAN: TRAVELS THE WORLD	WALT DISNEY		1	1	1992	1992	
SECOND CITY	HARRIER		1	4	1986	1987	
SECOND LIFE OF DOCTOR MIRAGE	VALIANT / VOYAGER COMMUNICATIONS		1	5	1993	NOW	
SECRET AGENT	CHARLTON COMICS	2	9	10	1966	1967	FORMERLY SARGE STEEL
SECRET AGENT	FLEETWAY		1	26	1967	1968	
SECRET AGENT	GOLD KEY		1	2	1966	1968	
SECRET AGENT PICTURE LIBRARY	C.A. PEARSON		1	2	1961	1962	
SECRET AGENT PICTURE LIBRARY HOLIDAY SPECIAL	FLEETWAY		1967	1970	1967	1970	
SECRET AGENT X-9	DAVID MCKAY PUBLICATIONS		1	2	1934	1934	
SECRET CITY SAGA	TOPPS		0	4	1993	1994	
SECRET DEFENDERS	MARVEL ENTERTAINMENT GROUP		1	12	1993	NOW	
SECRET DIARY OF EERIE ADVENTURES	AVON BOOKS		1	1	1953	1953	
SECRET HEARTS	DC COMICS INC.		1	153	1949	1971	
SECRET LOVE	AJAX	1	1	3	1955	1956	
SECRET LOVE	AJAX	2	1	6	1957	1958	
SECRET LOVES	QUALITY COMICS		1	6	1949	1950	
SECRET MISSIONS	ST JOHN PUBLISHING		1	1	1950	1950	
SECRET MISSIONS	STREAMLINE		1	1	1951	1951	FOX FEATURES REPRINTS
SECRET MYSTERIES	RIBAGE PUBLISHING CO.		16	19	1954	1955	FORMERLY CRIME MYSTERIES & CRIME SMASHERS
SECRET OF THE DWARFS	COMICO		1	1	1992	1992	
SECRET OF THE SALAMANDER, THE	DARK HORSE COMICS		1	1	1992	1992	
SECRET ORIGINS	DC COMICS INC.		1	7	1973	1974	
SECRET ORIGINS	DC COMICS INC.	2	1	1	1990	1990	
SECRET ORIGINS	DC COMICS INC.	2	1	50	1986	1990	
SECRET ORIGINS ANNUAL	DC COMICS INC.	1	1	1	1961	1961	
SECRET ORIGINS ANNUAL	DC COMICS INC.	2	1	3	1987	1989	
SECRET ORIGINS SPECIAL	DC COMICS INC.	2	1	1	1989	1989	
SECRET ROMANCE	CHARLTON COMICS		1	48	1968	1980	
SECRET ROMANCES	SUPERIOR COMICS		1	27	1951	1955	
SECRET SERVICE	STREAMLINE		1	1	1951	1951	US REPRINTS
SECRET SERVICE PICTURE LIBRARY	M.V. FEATURES		1	18	1965	1966	
SECRET SIX	DC COMICS INC.		1	7	1968	1969	
SECRET SOCIETY OF SUPER-VILLAINS	DC COMICS INC.		1	15	1976	1978	
SECRET SQUIRREL	GOLD KEY		1	1	1966	1966	
SECRET STORY ROMANCES	ATLAS		1	21	1953	1956	
SECRET WARS	MARVEL ENTERTAINMENT GROUP		1	1	1993	1993	
SECRET WARS	MARVEL ENTERTAINMENT GROUP		1	80	1985	1987	
SECRET WARS II	MARVEL ENTERTAINMENT GROUP		1	9	1985	1986	
SECRET WARS II SPECIAL	MARVEL ENTERTAINMENT GROUP		1	1	1986	1986	
SECRET WARS WINTER SPECIAL	MARVEL ENTERTAINMENT GROUP		1	1	1985	1985	
SECRET WEAPONS	VALIANT / VOYAGER COMMUNICATIONS		1	11	1993	NOW	
SECRETS OF LOVE	GERALD SWAN		1	2	1954	???	STAR REPRINTS
SECRETS OF LOVE AND MARRIAGE	CHARLTON COMICS		1	25	1956	1961	
SECRETS OF SINISTER HOUSE	DC COMICS INC.		5	18	1972	1974	FORMERLY SINISTER HOUSE OF SECRET LOVE
SECRETS OF THE HAUNTED HOUSE	DC COMICS INC.		1	46	1975	1982	
SECRETS OF THE LEGION OF SUPER-HEROES	DC COMICS INC.		1	3	1981	1981	
SECRETS OF THE UNKNOWN	ALAN CLASS AND CO LTD		1	249	1962	1989	
SECRETS OF TRUE LOVE	ST JOHN PUBLISHING		1	1	1958	1958	
SECRETS OF YOUNG BRIDES	CHARLTON COMICS	1	5	44	1957	1964	
SECRETS OF YOUNG BRIDES	CHARLTON COMICS	2	1	9	1975	1976	
SECTAURS	MARVEL ENTERTAINMENT GROUP		1	8	1985	1986	
SEDUCTION OF THE INNOCENT	ECLIPSE		1	6	1985	1986	
SEDUCTION OF THE INNOCENT	RINEHART & CO.		1	3	1953	1954	THREE PRINTINGS: WRITTEN BY FREDERIC WERTHAM

COMIC TITLE	PUBLISHER	Vol No.	Srt No.	End No.	Str. Year	End Year	COMMENTS
SEEKER	SKY COMICS		1	3	1994	NOW	
SEEKER: VENGEANCE	SKY COMICS		1	1	1993	NOW	
SELECT DETECTIVE	D.S. PUBLISHING CO.		1	3	1948	1949	
SEMPER-FI	MARVEL ENTERTAINMENT GROUP		1	10	1988	1989	
SENORITA KID	CARTOON ART		1	1	1950	1950	FICTION HOUSE REPRINTS
SENSATION COMICS	DC COMICS INC.		1	109	1942	1952	
SENSATION MYSTERY	DC COMICS INC.		110	116	1952	1953	FORMERLY SENSATION COMICS
SENSATIONAL POLICE CASES	AVON BOOKS	1	1	1	1952	1952	
SENSATIONAL POLICE CASES	AVON BOOKS	2	1	4	1954	1954	
SENSATIONAL POLICE CASES	I.W. ENTERPRISES		5	5	1963	1963	REPRINTS
SENSATIONAL SPIDER-MAN, THE	MARVEL ENTERTAINMENT GROUP				1989	1989	
SENSATIONAL SPIDER-MAN:NOTHING CAN STOP JUGGERNAUT	MARVEL ENTERTAINMENT GROUP				1989	1989	
SENSEI	FIRST		1	4	1989	1989	
SENTINEL	HARRIER		1	4	1987	1987	
SENTINELS OF JUSTICE	AC COMICS		1	5	1985	1986	
SENTRY SPECIAL	INNOVATION		1	41	1991	1991	
SERAPHIM	INNOVATION		1	2	1990	1990	
SERGEANT BARNEY PARKER	ATLAS		1	3	1956	1956	
SERGEANT O'BRIEN	S.N.P.J./MUNDIAL		50	91	1952	1954	REPRINTS FRENCH STRIP
SERGEANT PAT OF RADIO PATROL	MODERM FICTION		1	1	1948	1948	
SERGEANT PRESTON OF THE YUKON	DELL PUBLISHING COMPANY		1	4	1956	1956	4 VERSIONS
SERGEANT PRESTON OF THE YUKON	DELL PUBLISHING COMPANY		5	29	1952	1959	
SERGEANT PRESTON OF THE YUKON	WORLD DISTRIBUTORS LTD		1	16	1953	1954	WESTERN PUBLISHING REPRINTS
SERIOUS COMICS	H. BUNCH ASSOCIATES		1	1	1975	1975	
SERPENT RISING	CALIBER PRESS		1	1	1992	NOW	
SERPENTYNE	NIGHT WYND ENTERPRISES		1	3	1992	1992	
SEVEN AGES OF WOMAN	KNOCKABOUT		1	1	1989	1989	
SEVEN BLOCK	MARVEL ENTERTAINMENT GROUP		1	1	1990	1990	
SEVEN DEADLY SINS	KNOCKABOUT		1	1	1989	1989	
SEVEN SEAS COMICS	UNITED FEATURES SYNDICATE		1	6	1946	1947	
SEWAGE DRAGOON	PARODY PRESS		1	1	1993	1993	
SEX WARRIOR	APOCALYPSE		1	1	1991	1991	
SEX WARRIOR	DARK HORSE COMICS		1	2	1993	1993	
SEXY TALES	TOP SELLERS		1	3	1974	1974	
SEYMOUR, MY SON	ARCHIE PUBLICATIONS		1	1	1963	1963	
SGT. BILKO	DC COMICS INC.		1	18	1957	1960	
SGT. BILKO'S PVT. DOBERMAN	DC COMICS INC.		1	11	1958	1960	
SGT. FURY AND HIS HOWLING COMMANDOS	MARVEL ENTERTAINMENT GROUP		1	167	1963	1981	
SGT. FURY ANNUAL	MARVEL ENTERTAINMENT GROUP		1	7	1965	1971	
SGT. ROCK	DC COMICS INC.	1	302	422	1977	1988	FORMERLY OUR ARMY AT WAR
SGT. ROCK ANNUAL	DC COMICS INC.		2	4	1982	1984	FORMERLY SGT. ROCK'S PRIZE BATTLE TALES
SGT. ROCK PRIZE BATTLE TALES	DC COMICS INC.		1	1	1964	1964	
SGT. ROCK SPECIAL	DC COMICS INC.		1	1	1992	1992	
SGT. ROCK SPECIAL	DC COMICS INC.	2	1	21	1988	1992	
SHADE THE CHANGING MAN	DC COMICS INC.	1	1	8	1977	1978	
SHADE THE CHANGING MAN	DC COMICS INC.	2	1	44	1990	NOW	
SHADO SONG OF THE DRAGON	DC COMICS INC.		1	4	1992	1992	
SHADOW CABINET	DC COMICS INC.		0	0	1993	NOW	
SHADOW COMICS	STREET AND SMITH PUBLICATIONS	1	1	12	1940	1941	
SHADOW COMICS	STREET AND SMITH PUBLICATIONS	2	1	12	1941	1942	
SHADOW COMICS	STREET AND SMITH PUBLICATIONS	3	1	12	1942	1943	
SHADOW COMICS	STREET AND SMITH PUBLICATIONS	4	1	12	1943	1944	
SHADOW COMICS	STREET AND SMITH PUBLICATIONS	5	1	12	1944	1945	
SHADOW COMICS	STREET AND SMITH PUBLICATIONS	6	1	12	1945	1946	
SHADOW COMICS	STREET AND SMITH PUBLICATIONS	7	1	12	1946	1947	
SHADOW COMICS	STREET AND SMITH PUBLICATIONS	8	1	12	1947	1948	
SHADOW COMICS	STREET AND SMITH PUBLICATIONS	9	1	5	1948	1949	
SHADOW OF THE BATMAN	DC COMICS INC.		1	5	1985	1986	
SHADOW OF THE TORTURER, THE	INNOVATION		1	6	1991	1991	
SHADOW RIDERS	MARVEL ENTERTAINMENT GROUP		1	4	1993	1993	
SHADOW STRIKES ANNUAL, THE	DC COMICS INC.		1	1	1989	1989	
SHADOW STRIKES, THE	DC COMICS INC.		1	31	1989	1992	
SHADOW WAR OF HAWKMAN	DC COMICS INC.		1	4	1985	1985	
SHADOW, PRIVATE FILES OF THE	DC COMICS INC.		1	1	1989	1989	
SHADOW, THE	ARCHIE PUBLICATIONS		1	8	1964	1965	
SHADOW, THE	DC COMICS INC.		1	1	1987	1987	
SHADOW, THE	DC COMICS INC.		1	4	1986	1986	
SHADOW, THE	DC COMICS INC.	1	1	12	1973	1974	
SHADOW, THE	DC COMICS INC.	2	1	19	1987	1989	
SHADOW, THE ANNUAL	DC COMICS INC.	2	1	2	1987	1988	
SHADOW: BLOOD & JUDGEMENT	DC COMICS INC.				1987	1987	
SHADOW: IN THE COILS OF THE LEVIATHAN	DARK HORSE COMICS		1	2	1993	1994	
SHADOWALKER	AIRCEL		1	3	1988	1991	
SHADOWALKER CHRONICLES, THE	GROUND ZERO GRAPHICS		1	5	1991	1992	
SHADOWHAWK	IMAGE COMICS		1	4	1992	1992	
SHADOWHAWK II, THE SECRET REVEALED	IMAGE COMICS		1	3	1993	1993	
SHADOWHAWK III	IMAGE COMICS		1	2	1993	1994	
SHADOWHAWK LIMITED EDITION	IMAGE COMICS		1	1	1993	1993	
SHADOWHAWK SECRET REVEALED FACTFILE	IMAGE COMICS		1	1	1993	1993	
SHADOWHAWK: OUT OF THE SHADOWS	IMAGE COMICS		1	1	1993	1993	
SHADOWMAN	VALIANT / VOYAGER COMMUNICATIONS				1994	1994	POLYBAGGED WITH DARQUE PASSAGES COMIC
SHADOWMAN	VALIANT / VOYAGER COMMUNICATIONS		1	24	1992	NOW	
SHADOWMASTERS	MARVEL ENTERTAINMENT GROUP		1	4	1989	1990	
SHADOWMEN, THE	TRIDENT		1	2	1990	1990	
SHADOWS FROM BEYOND	CHARLTON COMICS	2	50	50	1966	1966	FORMERLY UNUSUAL TALES
SHADOWS FROM THE GRAVE	RENEGADE PRESS		1	2	1987	1988	
SHAMAN	CONTINUITY COMICS		1	1	1993	1993	
SHAMAN	CONTINUITY COMICS		1	1	1993	1994	

COMIC TITLE	PUBLISHER	Vol No.	Srt No.	End No.	Str. Year	End Year	COMMENTS
SHAMAN'S TEARS	IMAGE COMICS		1	2	1993	NOW	
SHAMBALLA	MARVEL ENTERTAINMENT GROUP		1	1	1991	1991	
SHANGHAIED	ETERNITY		1	3	1987	1987	
SHANNA THE SHE-DEVIL	MARVEL ENTERTAINMENT GROUP		1	5	1972	1973	
SHARP COMICS	H.C. BLACKERBY		1	2	1945	1946	
SHARP-SHOOTER WESTERN ALBUM	G.T. LIMITED		1	1	1959	1959	
SHATTER	FIRST		1	14	1985	1988	
SHATTER SPECIAL	FIRST		1	1	1985	1985	
SHATTERED EARTH	ETERNITY		1	9	1988	1989	
SHATTERPOINT	ETERNITY		1	4	1990	1991	
SHAZAM ARCHIVES	DC COMICS INC.		1	1	1993	1993	
SHAZAM!	DC COMICS INC.		1	35	1973	1978	
SHAZAM, THE POWER OF	DC COMICS INC.		1	1	1994	1994	
SHAZAM: THE NEW BEGINNING	DC COMICS INC.		1	4	1987	1987	
SHE BAT	HEROIC PUBLISHING		1	2	1992	NOW	
SHE BUCCANEER	MONSTER COMICS		1	2	1992	1992	
SHE HULK	MARVEL ENTERTAINMENT GROUP		1	1	1992	1992	
SHE HULK IN CEREMONY	MARVEL ENTERTAINMENT GROUP		1	2	1990	1990	
SHE HULK, THE SAVAGE	MARVEL ENTERTAINMENT GROUP	1	1	25	1980	1982	
SHE HULK, THE SENSATIONAL	MARVEL ENTERTAINMENT GROUP	2	1	60	1989	1994	
SHE-CAT	AC COMICS		1	4	1990	1991	
SHEENA	MARVEL ENTERTAINMENT GROUP		1	2	1984	1985	
SHEENA 3D	ECLIPSE		1	1	1985	1985	
SHEENA, QUEEN OF THE JUNGLE	FICTION HOUSE		1	18	1942	1953	
SHELL SHOCK	MIRAGE STUDIOS		1	1	1989	1989	
SHERIFF AND ELMOS'S OWN, THE	SCREEN STORIES		1	5	1949	1950	FORMERLY SHERIFF, THE
SHERIFF BOB DIXON'S CHUCK WAGON	AVON BOOKS		1	1	1950	1950	
SHERIFF OF COCHISE	C.A. PEARSON		1	3	1959	1959	
SHERIFF OF COCHISE, THE	MOBIL GIVEAWAY		1	1	1957	1957	
SHERIFF OF TOMBSTONE	CHARLTON COMICS	1	17	1958	1961		
SHERIFF OF TOMBSTONE	L. MILLER PUBLISHING COMPANY (UK)	50	55	1959	1959		CHARLTON REPRINTS
SHERIFF, THE	SCREEN STORIES		1	4	1948	1949	
SHERLOCK HOLMES	CHARLTON COMICS		1	2	1955	1956	
SHERLOCK HOLMES	DC COMICS INC.		1	1	1975	1975	
SHERLOCK HOLMES	ETERNITY		1	23	1988	NOW	
SHERLOCK HOLMES	MALIBU COMICS ENTERTAINMENT INC.		1	4	1989	1989	CLASSIC COMIC STRIPS
SHERLOCK HOLMES: ADVENTURE OF THE NAVAL TREATY	TOME PRESS		1	1	1991	1991	
SHERLOCK HOLMES: CHRONICLES OF CRIME AND MYSTERY	NORTHSTAR		1	3	1992	1992	
SHERLOCK HOLMES: CURIOUS CASE OF VANISHING VILLAIN	TUNDRA		1	1	1991	1991	
SHERLOCK HOLMES: HOUND OF THE BASKERVILLES	INNOVATION		1	1	1992	1992	
SHERLOCK HOLMES: RETURN OF THE DEVIL	ADVENTURE COMICS		1	2	1992	1992	
SHERLOCK HOLMES: THE HOUND OF THE BASKERVILLES	COLLINS		1	1	1991	1991	
SHERLOCK HOLMES: THE MUSGRAVE RITUAL	TOME PRESS		1	1	1991	1991	
SHERLOCK HOLMES: THE SPECKLED BAND/BLUE CARBUNCLE	COLLINS		1	1	1991	1991	
SHERRY THE SHOWGIRL	ATLAS		1	7	1956	1957	
SHI: THE WAY OF THE WARRIOR	EMPIRE PUBLICATIONS		1	1	1994	NOW	
SHIELD WIZARD COMICS	M.L.J. MAGAZINES		1	13	1940	1944	
SHIELD, THE	RED CIRCLE	1	3	1983	1983		
SHIELD-STEEL STERLING	ARCHIE PUBLICATIONS	3	3	1983	1983		FORMERLY SHIELD, THE
SHIP AHOY	SPOTLIGHT COMICS		1	1	1944	1944	
SHIPWRECKED	WALT DISNEY		1	1	1990	1990	
SHIVER AND SHAKE	IPC		1	83	1973	1974	
SHOCK	PORTMAN		1	4	1979	1980	US REPRINTS
SHOCK	STANLEY PUBLICATIONS	1	1	8	1969	1970	
SHOCK	STANLEY PUBLICATIONS	2	1	6	1970	1971	
SHOCK	STANLEY PUBLICATIONS	3	1	4	1971	1971	
SHOCK DETECTIVE STORIES	STAR PUBLICATIONS		20	21	1952	1952	FORMERLY CRIME FIGHTING DETECTIVE
SHOCK ILLUSTRATED	EC COMICS		1	3	1955	1956	
SHOCK SUSPENSTORIES	EC COMICS	1	1	18	1952	1955	
SHOCK SUSPENSTORIES	RUSS COCHRAN		1	6	1992	NOW	
SHOCK THERAPY	HARRIER		1	7	1986	1987	
SHOCKING MYSTERY CASES	STAR PUBLICATIONS		50	60	1952	1954	FORMERLY THRILLING CRIME CASES
SHOCKING TALES DIGEST MAGAZINE	HARVEY PUBLICATIONS		1	1	1981	1981	
SHOCKWAVE	LONDON EDITIONS MAGAZINES		1	4	1991	1991	DC REPRINTS
SHOGUN WARRIORS	MARVEL ENTERTAINMENT GROUP		1	20	1979	1980	
SHOOK UP	DODSWORTH PUBL. CO.		1	1	1958	1958	
SHOOTING STAR COMIC	SCION		1	1	1948	1948	
SHORTY SHINER	DANDY MAGAZINES/CHARLES BIRO		1	3	1956	1956	
SHOTS FROM THE FILMS	D. MCKENZIE		1	1	1948	1948	
SHOWBOAT COMIC, THE	PICTORIAL ART		1	1	1948	1948	
SHOWCASE	DC COMICS INC.		1	104	1956	1978	
SHOWCASE '93	DC COMICS INC.		1	12	1992	1993	
SHOWCASE '94	DC COMICS INC.		1	1	1993	1994	
SHOWGIRLS	ATLAS	4	2	1957	1957		FORMERLY SHERRY THE SHOWGIRL
SHRIEK	FANTACO		1	4	1989	1990	
SHRIEK SPECIAL	FANTACO		1	1	1992	1992	
SHROUD, THE	MARVEL ENTERTAINMENT GROUP		1	1	1994	1994	
SHURIKEN	ETERNITY		1	6	1991	1992	
SHURIKEN TEAM UP	ETERNITY		1	3	1992	NOW	
SHURIKEN: COLD STEEL	ETERNITY		1	6	1987	1987	
SICK	CHARLTON COMICS		109	131	1976	1980	
SICK	FEATURE PUBLICATIONS		1	131	1960	1980	
SICK 7TH ANNUAL YEARBOOK	FEATURE PUBLICATIONS		1	1	1967	1967	
SICK ANNUAL	CHARLTON COMICS		2	4	1980	1980	
SICK ANNUAL	FEATURE PUBLICATIONS		1969	1971	1969	1971	
SICK ANNUAL	FEATURE PUBLICATIONS	2	2	4	1980	1980	

COMIC TITLE	PUBLISHER	Vol No.	Srt No.	End No.	Str. Year	End Year	COMMENTS
SICK BIG SICK LAFF-IN	FEATURE PUBLICATIONS			I	I	1968	1968	
SICK BIRTHDAY ANNUAL	FEATURE PUBLICATIONS			I	I	1968	1968	
SICK SPECIAL	FEATURE PUBLICATIONS			2	2	1978	1978	
SICK YEARBOOK	FEATURE PUBLICATIONS			14	15	1974	1975	
SIDESHOW	AVON BOOKS			I	I	1949	1949	
SIDESHOW COMICS	PAN GRAPHICS			I	8	1988	NOW	
SIEGEL & SHUSTER: DATELINE 1930'S	ECLIPSE			I	2	1984	1985	
SIGNAL TO NOISE	VICTOR GOLLANCZ			I	I	1992	1992	
SILBUSTER	ANTARTIC PRESS			I	4	1994	NOW	
SILENCERS COMPILATION	CALIBER PRESS			I	I	1992	1992	
SILENCERS, THE	CALIBER PRESS			I	4	1991	1991	
SILENT INVASION	RENEGADE PRESS			I	12	1988	1988	
SILENT INVASION, THE	NBM PUBLISHING			I	4	1988	1989	
SILENT MOBIUS	VIZ	I		I	6	1991	1992	
SILENT MOBIUS	VIZ	2		I	5	1992	1992	
SILENT MOBIUS	VIZ	3		I	5	1992	1993	
SILENT MOBIUS	VIZ	4		I	5	1993	1994	
SILENT MOBIUS	VIZ	5		I	I	1993	1994	
SILLY SYMPHONIES	DELL PUBLISHING COMPANY			I	9	1952	1959	
SILLY TUNES	TIMELY COMICS			I	7	1945	1947	
SILVER KID WESTERN	STANMORE PUBLICATIONS			I	5	1954	1955	
SILVER KID WESTERN	STREAMLINE			I	2	1955	1955	STANMORE REPRINTS
SILVER KING, THE	P.M. PRODUCTIONS			I	I	1946	1946	
SILVER SABLE	MARVEL ENTERTAINMENT GROUP			I	22	1992	NOW	
SILVER SPARKS COMIC	PHILLIP MARX			I	I	1946	1946	
SILVER STAR	PACIFIC COMICS			I	6	1983	1983	
SILVER STAR	TOPPS			I	I	1993	1994	
SILVER STAR FUN COMIC, THE	P.M. PRODUCTIONS			I	I	1946	1946	
SILVER STREAK COMICS	YOUR GUIDE PUBLISHING			I	7	1939	1940	
SILVER STREAK COMICS	YOUR GUIDE/NEW FRIDAY/COMIC HOUSE/NEWSBROOK PUBL.			I	24	1939	1946	BECOMES "CRIME DOES NOT PAY" WITH ISSUE NO.22 (JULY 1942). ISSUE NOS.22-24 WERE REPRINTS, PUBLISHED IN 1946.
SILVER SURFER	MARVEL ENTERTAINMENT GROUP			I	2	1988	1989	
SILVER SURFER	MARVEL ENTERTAINMENT GROUP	I		I	18	1968	1982	
SILVER SURFER	MARVEL ENTERTAINMENT GROUP	2		I	I	1982	1982	
SILVER SURFER	MARVEL ENTERTAINMENT GROUP	3		I	89	1987	NOW	
SILVER SURFER ANNUAL	MARVEL ENTERTAINMENT GROUP	3		I	6	1988	NOW	
SILVER SURFER ULTIMATE COSMIC EXPERIENCE	SIMON AND SCHUSTER			I	I	1978	1978	
SILVER SURFER VS DRACULA	MARVEL ENTERTAINMENT GROUP			I	I	1993	1993	
SILVER SURFER WINTER SPECIAL	MARVEL ENTERTAINMENT GROUP			I	I	1982	1982	
SILVER SURFER/WARLOCK: RESURRECTION	MARVEL ENTERTAINMENT GROUP			I	I	1993	1993	
SILVER SURFER: FIRST COMING OF GALACTUS	MARVEL ENTERTAINMENT GROUP			I	I	1993	1993	
SILVER SURFER: HOMECOMING	MARVEL ENTERTAINMENT GROUP			I	I	1991	1991	
SILVER SURFER: JUDGEMENT DAY	MARVEL ENTERTAINMENT GROUP			I	I	1988	1988	
SILVER SURFER: JUDGEMENT DAY	MARVEL ENTERTAINMENT GROUP			I	I	1989	1989	
SILVER SURFER: PARABLE	MARVEL ENTERTAINMENT GROUP			I	I	1989	1989	
SILVER SURFER: PARABLE	MARVEL ENTERTAINMENT GROUP			I	I	1991	1991	
SILVER SURFER: REBIRTH OF THANOS	MARVEL ENTERTAINMENT GROUP			I	I	1993	1993	
SILVER SURFER: THE ENSLAVERS	MARVEL ENTERTAINMENT GROUP			I	I	1993	1993	
SILVERBACK	COMICO			I	3	1989	1989	
SILVERBLADE	DC COMICS INC.			I	12	1987	1988	
SILVERHAWKS	MARVEL ENTERTAINMENT GROUP			I	6	1987	1988	
SILVERHEELS	PACIFIC COMICS			I	3	1983	1984	
SILVERSTORM	AIRCEL			I	4	1990	1991	
SIMPSONS COMICS	BONGO COMICS			I	I	1993	NOW	
SIMPSONS COMICS AND STORIES	WELSH PUBLICATIONS			I	I	1993	1993	
SIMPSONS ILLUSTRATED	WELSH PUBLICATIONS			I	4	1992	NOW	
SIMPSONS ILLUSTRATED 3-D	MARVEL ENTERTAINMENT GROUP			I	I	1991	1991	
SIN CITY	DARK HORSE COMICS			I	I	1993	1993	
SIN CITY COLLECTION	DIAMOND PUBLICATIONS			I	I	1993	1993	STAR SYSTEM EDITION
SIN CITY LIMITED EDITION	DARK HORSE COMICS			I	I	1993	1993	
SIN CITY: A DAME TO KILL FOR	DARK HORSE COMICS			I	2	1993	1994	
SINBAD AND THE EYE OF THE TIGER	GENERAL BOOK DISTRIB			I	I	1977	1977	
SINBAD JR	DELL PUBLISHING COMPANY			I	3	1965	1966	
SINBAD THE SAILOR	CHILDREN'S PRESS			I	I	1948	1948	
SINBAD, JR	DELL PUBLISHING COMPANY			I	3	1965	1966	
SINBAD: THE FOUR TRIALS	ADVENTURE COMICS			I	4	1990	1990	
SINBAD: THE HOUSE OF GOD	ADVENTURE COMICS			I	4	1991	1991	
SINERGY	CALIBER PRESS			I	I	1992	1993	
SINGLE SERIES	UNITED FEATURES SYNDICATE			I	28	1938	1942	
SINISTER HOUSE OF SECRET LOVE, THE	DC COMICS INC.			I	4	1971	1972	
SINISTER LEGENDS	SAVOY ADULT GRAPHICS			I	I	1988	1988	
SINISTER TALES	ALAN CLASS AND CO LTD			I	227	1964	1989	
SINKING	MARVEL ENTERTAINMENT GROUP			I	I	1992	1992	
SINNER	FANTAGRAPHICS			I	7	1987	NOW	
SINNERS	DC COMICS INC.			I	I	1993	1993	
SIRENS	CALIBER PRESS			I	I	1993	1994	
SISTERHOOD OF STEEL, THE	MARVEL ENTERTAINMENT GROUP			I	8	1984	1986	
SIX COMICS OF WORLD WAR ONE	PETER WAY			I	I	1972	1972	
SIX FROM SIRIUS	MARVEL ENTERTAINMENT GROUP	I		I	I	1988	1988	
SIX FROM SIRIUS	MARVEL ENTERTAINMENT GROUP	I		I	4	1984	1984	
SIX FROM SIRIUS	MARVEL ENTERTAINMENT GROUP	2		I	4	1986	1986	
SIX MILLION DOLLAR MAN ANNUAL	CHARLTON COMICS			I	I	1976	1976	
SIX MILLION DOLLAR MAN MAGAZINE, THE	CHARLTON COMICS			I	7	1976	1977	
SIX MILLION DOLLAR MAN, THE	CHARLTON COMICS			I	9	1976	1978	
SIX-GUN HEROES	A PLUS COMICS			I	I	1991	1991	REPRINTS
SIX-GUN HEROES	CHARLTON COMICS			24	83	1954	1965	FORMERLY PUBLISHED BY FAWCETT
SIX-GUN HEROES	FAWCETT PUBLICATIONS			I	23	1950	1953	
SIX-GUN HEROES	L. MILLER PUBLISHING COMPANY (UK)	I		I	114	1950	1959	FAWCETT REPRINTS
SIX-GUN HEROES WESTERN COMIC ANNUAL	L. MILLER PUBLISHING COMPANY (UK)			I	I	1961	1961	

COMIC TITLE	PUBLISHER	Vol No.	Srt No.	End No.	Str. Year	End Year	COMMENTS
SIX-GUN WESTERN	ATLAS		1	4	1957	1957	
SIX-GUN WESTERN	L. MILLER PUBLISHING COMPANY (UK)		1	9	1957	1957	ATLAS REPRINTS
SKATEMAN	PACIFIC COMICS		1	1	1983	1983	
SKEEZIZ AND HIS UNCLE WALT	REILLY AND LEE PUBLISHERS		1	1	1924	1924	
SKEEZIZ AND PAL	REILLY AND LEE PUBLISHERS		1	1	1925	1925	
SKEEZIZ AND UNCLE WALT	REILLY AND LEE PUBLISHERS	1	1	1	1924	1924	
SKEEZIZ AND UNCLE WALT	REILLY AND LEE PUBLISHERS	2	1	1	1927	1927	
SKEEZIZ AT THE CIRCUS	REILLY AND LEE PUBLISHERS		1	1	1926	1926	
SKEEZIZ OUT WEST	REILLY AND LEE PUBLISHERS		1	1	1928	1928	
SKELETON HAND	AMERICOMICS		1	6	1952	1953	
SKIDMARKS	TUNDRA		1	3	1992	1992	
SKIN	TUNDRA		1	1	1992	1992	
SKIN GRAFT	DC COMICS INC.		1	4	1993	1993	
SKIPPER MIDGET COMIC, THE	D.C. THOMSON		1	1	1934	1934	
SKIZZ	TITAN BOOKS		1	1	1989	1989	
SKIZZ: FIRST ENCOUNTER	FLEETWAY		1	3	1993	NOW	
SKREEMER	DC COMICS INC.		1	6	1989	1989	
SKROG	COMICO		1	1	1984	1984	
SKROG (YIP YIP YAY) SPECIAL	CRYSTAL PUBLICATIONS		1	1	1987	1987	
SKULL AND BONES	DC COMICS INC.		1	3	1992	1992	
SKULL THE SLAYER	MARVEL ENTERTAINMENT GROUP		1	8	1975	1976	
SKY BLAZERS	HAWLEY		1	2	1940	1940	
SKY GAL	AC COMICS		1	1	1993	NOW	
SKY HERO COMIC	SCION		1	1	1952	1952	
SKY HIGH COMIC	P.M. PRODUCTIONS		1	1	1949	1949	
SKY KING "RUNAWAY TRAIN"	NATIONAL BISCUIT CO.		1	1	1964	1964	
SKY PILOT	ZIFF-DAVIS PUBLISHING COMPANY	10	11	11	1950	1951	
SKY POLICE COMICS	SCION		1	1	1949	1949	FICTION HOUSE REPRINTS
SKY SHERIFF	D.S. PUBLISHING CO.		1	1	1948	1948	
SKY SHERIFF	PEMBERTON		1	1	1951	1951	
SKY WOLF	ECLIPSE		1	3	1988	1988	
SKYLINE COMIC	SCION		1	1	1952	1952	
SKYMAN	COLUMBIA COMICS GROUP		1	4	1941	1948	
SKYROCKET	HARRY A CHESLER		1	1	1944	1944	
SLAINE BOOK ONE	TITAN BOOKS		1	1	1985	1985	
SLAINE GAMING BOOK	TITAN BOOKS		1	1	1986	1986	
SLAINE POSTER MAGAZINE	FLEETWAY		1	1	1994	1994	
SLAINE THE BERSERKER	FLEETWAY		1	28	1986	1988	
SLAINE THE HORNED GOD	FLEETWAY		1	6	1993	1994	
SLAINE THE HORNED GOD, THE COLLECTED	FLEETWAY		1	1	1993	1993	
SLAINE THE HORNED GOD: THE COMPLETE STORY	MANDARIN (2000 AD BOOKS)		1	1	1993	1993	
SLAINE THE KING	TITAN BOOKS		1	1	1987	1987	
SLAINE THE KING SPECIAL EDITION	TITAN BOOKS		1	1	1990	1990	
SLAINE, THE COLLECTED	FLEETWAY		1	1	1993	1993	
SLAINE: THE HORNED GOD	FLEETWAY		1	3	1989	1991	
SLAM BANG COMICS	FAWCETT PUBLICATIONS		1	7	1940	1940	
SLAM BANG COMICS	L. MILLER PUBLISHING COMPANY (UK)		1	8	1954	1954	FAWCETT REPRINTS
SLAM BANG COMICS	POST CEREAL GIVEAWAYS	9	9	9	???	???	
SLAPSTICK	MARVEL ENTERTAINMENT GROUP		1	4	1992	1993	
SLAPSTICK COMICS	COMICS MAGAZINE CO.		1	1	1946	1946	
SLASH	NORTHSTAR		1	2	1992	NOW	
SLASH MARAUD	DC COMICS INC.		1	6	1987	1988	
SLASH-D DOUBLECROSS	ST JOHN PUBLISHING		1	1	1950	1950	
SLAUGHTERMAN	COMICO		1	2	1983	1983	
SLAVE GIRL COMICS	AVON BOOKS	2	1	2	1949	1949	
SLAVE GIRL COMICS	ETERNITY	2	1	1	1989	1989	
SLEDGE HAMMER	MARVEL ENTERTAINMENT GROUP		1	4	1988	1988	
SLEEPING BEAUTY	DELL PUBLISHING COMPANY		1	1	1959	1959	
SLEEPWALKER	MARVEL ENTERTAINMENT GROUP		1	33	1991	1994	
SLEEPWALKER HOLIDAY SPECIAL	MARVEL ENTERTAINMENT GROUP		1	1	1993	1993	
SLEEZE BROTHERS	MARVEL ENTERTAINMENT GROUP		1	6	1989	1990	
SLEEZE BROTHERS FILE	MARVEL ENTERTAINMENT GROUP		1	1	1990	1990	
SLEEZE BROTHERS SPECIAL	MARVEL ENTERTAINMENT GROUP		1	1	1991	1991	
SLICK CHICK COMICS	LEADER ENTERPRISES		1	3	1947	1947	
SLICK FUN	GERALD SWAN		1	19	1940	1945	
SLICK FUN SPRING SPECIAL	GERALD SWAN		1	1	1942	1942	
SLICK FUN WINTER SPECIAL	GERALD SWAN		1	1	1942	1942	
SLOW DANCE WITH DEATH	COMICO		1	1	1992	1992	
SLUDGE	MALIBU COMICS ENTERTAINMENT INC.		1	3	1993	NOW	
SLUGGER	LEV GLEASON PUBLICATIONS		1	1	1956	1956	
SLY SINISTER SCURVY ADVS. OF CPT. REILLY-FFOULL	MIRROR PRESS PUBLICATIONS		1	1	1940	1940	
SMALL KILLING, A	VICTOR GOLLANCZ		1	1	1991	1991	
SMASH COMICS	QUALITY (FLEETWAY)		1	85	1939	1949	
SMASH COMICS	T.V. BOARDMAN		7	11	1940	1941	QUALITY REPRINTS
SMASH HIT SPORTS COMICS	ESSENKAY PUBLISHING CO.	2	1	1	1949	1949	
SMASH!	ODHAMS		1	257	1966	1971	
SMASH! ANNUAL	ODHAMS	1967	1976	1967	1976		
SMASH! HOLIDAY SPECIAL	IPC	1969	1970	1969	1970		
SMASHER COMIC	CAS LIMITED		1	1	1947	1947	
SMASHER COMICS	TONGARD PUBLISHING		1	1	1947	1947	
SMILE COMICS	MODERN STORE PUBLISHING		1	1	1955	1955	
SMILEY BURNETTE WESTERN	FAWCETT PUBLICATIONS		1	4	1950	1950	
SMILIN' JACK	DELL PUBLISHING COMPANY		1	8	1948	1949	
SMILIN' JACK SHOE STORE GIVEAWAY	DELL PUBLISHING COMPANY		1	1	1938	1938	
SMILIN' JACK SPARKED WHEAT GIVEAWAY	DELL PUBLISHING COMPANY		1	1	1942	1942	
SMILIN'JACK POPPED WHEAT GIVEAWAY	DELL PUBLISHING COMPANY		1	1	1947	1947	
SMILING BURNETTE WESTERN	L. MILLER PUBLISHING COMPANY (UK)		1	4	1950	1950	FAWCETT REPRINTS
SMITTY	DELL PUBLISHING COMPANY		1	7	1947	1949	
SMITTY ANNUAL	CUPPLES AND LEON CO.	1928	1933	1928	1933		
SMITTY HARDCOVER EDITIONS	CUPPLES AND LEON CO.	1928	1933	1928	1933		

COMIC TITLE	PUBLISHER	Vol No.	Srt No.	End No.	Str. Year	End Year	COMMENTS
SMOKEY BEAR	GOLD KEY		1	13	1970	1973	
SMOKEY STOVER GENERAL MOTORS GIVEAWAY	DELL PUBLISHING COMPANY		1	1	1953	1953	
SMOKEY STOVER NATIONAL FIRE PROTECTION GIVEAWAY	DELL PUBLISHING COMPANY		1	1	1953	1954	
SMOKEY THE BEAR, THE TRUE STORY OF	DELL PUBLISHING COMPANY		1	1	1959	1959	
SMOKING GUNS WESTERN	SCION		1	1	1952	1952	
SMUGGLER'S CREEK	HOTSPUR PUBLISHING CO.		1	1	1949	1949	
SMURFS	MARVEL ENTERTAINMENT GROUP		1	3	1982	1983	
SNAFU	ATLAS		1	2	1955	1956	
SNAGGLEPUSS	GOLD KEY		1	4	1962	1963	
SNAKE EYES	FANTAGRAPHICS		1	1	1991	1991	
SNAP	HARRY A CHESLER		9	9	1944	1944	FORMERLY SCOOP
SNAPPY COMICS	CIMA PUBL. CO.		1	1	1945	1945	
SNARF	KITCHEN SINK		1	25	1989	1991	
SNIFFY THE PUP	STANDARD COMICS		5	18	1949	1953	
SNOOPER AND BLABBER DETECTIVES	GOLD KEY		1	3	1962	1963	
SNOOZY DIVES IN	BROCKHAMPTON PRESS		1	1	1960	1960	
SNOOZY THE SEA LION	BROCKHAMPTON PRESS		1	1	1959	1959	
SNOW FOR CHRISTMAS	W.T. GRANT COMPANY		1	1	1957	1957	
SNOW WHITE	TOP SELLERS		1	1	1974	1974	
SNOW WHITE AND THE SEVEN DWARFS	BENDIX WASHING MACHINES		1	1	1952	1952	
SNOW WHITE AND THE SEVEN DWARFS	PROMOTIONAL PUBLICATIONS COMPANY		1	1	1957	1957	
SNOW WHITE AND THE SEVEN DWARFS	WESTERN PUBLISHING COMPANY		1	1	1958	1958	
SNOW WHITE AND THE SEVEN DWARFS GOLDEN ANNIVERSARY	GLADSTONE		1	1	1987	1987	
SNOW WHITE AND THE SEVEN DWARFS IN "MILKY WAY"	AMERICAN DAIRY ASSOCIATION		1	1	1955	1955	
SOAP OPERA LOVE	CHARLTON COMICS		1	3	1983	1983	
SOAP OPERA ROMANCES	CHARLTON COMICS		1	5	1982	1983	
SOJOURN	WHITE CLIFFS PUBLISHING CO INC		1	2	1977	1978	
SOLAR MAN OF THE ATOM	VALIANT / VOYAGER COMMUNICATIONS		1	31	1991	NOW	
SOLAR, MAN OF THE ATOM	VALIANT / VOYAGER COMMUNICATIONS		1	1	1994	1994	
SOLAR WIND	PAPER TIGER/DRAGON'S WORLD LTD				1980	1980	
SOLARMAN	MARVEL ENTERTAINMENT GROUP		1	2	1989	1989	
SOLDIER & MARINE COMICS	CHARLTON COMICS	1	11	12	1954	1955	
SOLDIER & MARINE COMICS	CHARLTON COMICS	2	9	9	1956	1956	FORMERLY NEVER AGAIN
SOLDIER COMICS	FAWCETT PUBLICATIONS		1	11	1952	1953	
SOLDIER COMICS	L. MILLER PUBLISHING COMPANY (UK)		1	6	1952	1952	FAWCETT REPRINTS
SOLDIERS OF FORTUNE	AMERICOMICS		1	13	1951	1953	
SOLICITATIONS	INNOVATION		1	1	1989	1989	
SOLITAIRE	MALIBU COMICS ENTERTAINMENT INC.		1	1	1993	NOW	ULTRAVERSE TITLE
SOLO	CITY		1	31	1967	1967	
SOLO EX-MUTANTS	ETERNITY		1	6	1988	1989	
SOLOMON KANE IN 3-D	BLACKTHORNE		1	1	1988	1988	
SOLOMON KANE, THE SWORD OF	MARVEL ENTERTAINMENT GROUP		1	6	1985	1986	
SOLSON CHRISTMAS SPECIAL: SAMURAI SANTA	SOLSON		1	1	1986	1986	
SOLTHENIS, THE	ROGUE'S GALLERY, THE		1	1	1987	1987	
SOLUTION, THE	MALIBU COMICS ENTERTAINMENT INC.		1	3	1993	NOW	
SOMERSET HOLMES	PACIFIC COMICS		1	6	1983	1984	
SOMETIME STORIES	HOURGLASS COMICS		1	1	1977	1977	
SON OF AMBUSH BUG	DC COMICS INC.		1	6	1986	1986	
SON OF CELLULOID	ECLIPSE		1	1	1991	1991	
SON OF MUTANT WORLD	FANTAGOR		1	5	1990	1991	
SON OF SATAN	MARVEL ENTERTAINMENT GROUP		1	8	1975	1977	
SON OF SINBAD	ST JOHN PUBLISHING		1	1	1950	1950	
SON OF TOMAHAWK	DC COMICS INC.		131	140	1971	1972	CONTINUED FROM TOMAHAWK SERIES
SON OF VULCAN	CHARLTON COMICS		49	50	1965	1966	FORMERLY MYSTERIES OF UNEXPLORED WORLDS
SON OF YUPPIES FROM HELL	MARVEL ENTERTAINMENT GROUP		1	1	1990	1990	
SONIC DESERTER	SUN COMICS PUBLISHING		1	1	1992	NOW	
SONIC DISRUPTORS	DC COMICS INC.		1	7	1987	1988	
SONIC THE HEDGEHOG	ARCHIE PUBLICATIONS		0	3	1993	1993	
SONIC THE HEDGEHOG	ARCHIE PUBLICATIONS		1	8	1993	NOW	
SORORITY SECRETS	TOBY PRESS PUBLICATIONS		1	1	1954	1954	
SOULQUEST	INNOVATION		1	1	1989	1989	
SOULSEARCHERS AND COMPANY	ECLIPSE		1	4	1993	1994	
SOUPY SALES COMIC BOOK	ARCHIE PUBLICATIONS		1	1	1965	1965	
SOUTHERN KNIGHTS	COMICS INTERVIEW		2	36	1983	NOW	
SOUTHERN KNIGHTS SPECIAL	COMICS INTERVIEW		1	1	1989	1989	
SOUTHERN SQUADRON	AIRCEL		1	4	1990	1991	
SOUTHERN SQUADRON: FREEDOM OF INFORMATION ACT	ETERNITY		1	4	1992	1992	
SOVIET SUPER SOLDIERS	MARVEL ENTERTAINMENT GROUP		1	1	1992	1992	
SPACE ACE	ATLAS UK		1	32	1960	1963	
SPACE ACTION	ACE MAGAZINES		1	3	1952	1952	
SPACE ADVENTURES	CHARLTON COMICS	1	1	59	1952	1964	
SPACE ADVENTURES	CHARLTON COMICS	3	2	60	1967	1979	
SPACE ADVENTURES	L. MILLER PUBLISHING COMPANY (UK)		1	2	1950	???	CHARLTON REPRINTS
SPACE ADVENTURES	L. MILLER PUBLISHING COMPANY (UK)	2	50	50	1953	???	CHARLTON REPRINTS
SPACE ADVENTURES PRESENTS SPACE TRIP TO THE MOON	ALAN CLASS AND CO LTD		1	1	1961	1961	CHARLTON REPRINTS
SPACE AND ADVENTURE COMICS	L. MILLER PUBLISHING COMPANY (UK)		1	2	1961	1961	
SPACE ARK	APPLE COMICS		1	5	1985	1988	
SPACE BEAVER	TEN BUCKS COMICS		1	11	1986	1988	
SPACE BUSTERS	ZIFF-DAVIS PUBLISHING COMPANY		1	3	1952	1952	
SPACE COMICS	ARNOLD BOOK CO.		50	81	1953	1954	
SPACE COMICS	AVON BOOKS		4	5	1954	1954	FORMERLY FUNNY TUNES
SPACE COMICS OMNIBUS	ARNOLD BOOK CO.		1	1	1954	1954	
SPACE COMMANDER KERRY	L. MILLER PUBLISHING COMPANY (UK)		50	55	1953	1954	
SPACE COMMANDO COMICS	L. MILLER PUBLISHING COMPANY (UK)		50	59	1953	1954	
SPACE DETECTIVE	AVON BOOKS		1	4	1951	1952	

COMIC TITLE	PUBLISHER	Vol No.	Srt No.	End No.	Str. Year	End Year	COMMENTS
SPACE FAMILY ROBINSON	GOLD KEY		1	36	1962	1969	
SPACE GHOST	COMICO		1	1	1987	1987	
SPACE GHOST	GOLD KEY		1	1	1967	1967	
SPACE GIANTS, THE	FBN PUBLICATIONS		1	1	1979	1979	
SPACE HERO COMIC	SCION		1	2	1952	1952	
SPACE KAT-ETS IN 3-D	POWER COMICS		1	1	1953	1953	
SPACE MAN	DELL PUBLISHING COMPANY		2	10	1962	1972	
SPACE MOUSE	AVON BOOKS	1	1	5	1953	1954	
SPACE MOUSE	GOLD KEY	2	1	5	1962	1963	
SPACE MYSTERIES	I.W. ENTERPRISES		1	8	1964	1964	REPRINTS
SPACE PATROL	ADVENTURE COMICS		1	3	1992	1992	
SPACE PATROL	YOUNG WORLD	12		24	1964	1964	
SPACE PATROL	ZIFF-DAVIS PUBLISHING COMPANY		1	2	1952	1952	
SPACE PATROL'S SPECIAL MISSION	ZIFF-DAVIS PUBLISHING COMPANY		1	1	1952	1952	
SPACE PICTURE LIBRARY HOLIDAY SPECIAL	IPC	1977	1981	1977	1981		
SPACE SQUADRON	MARVEL ENTERTAINMENT GROUP		1	5	1951	1952	
SPACE SQUADRON	STREAMLINE		1	2	1951	1951	ATLAS REPRINTS
SPACE THILLERS	AVON BOOKS		1	1	1954	1954	
SPACE TRAVELLERS	DONALD PETERS		1	10	1950	1950	
SPACE USAGI	MIRAGE STUDIOS		1	3	1992	1992	
SPACE USAGI II: WHITE STAR RISING	MIRAGE STUDIOS		1	1	1993	1994	
SPACE WAR	CHARLTON COMICS		1	34	1959	1979	
SPACE WESTERN	CHARLTON COMICS		40	45	1952	1953	FORMERLY COWBOY WESTERN COMICS
SPACE WORLDS	ATLAS		6	6	1952	1952	FORMERLY SPACE SQUADRON
SPACE: 1999	CHARLTON COMICS	1	1	7	1975	1976	
SPACE: 1999	CHARLTON COMICS	2	1	8	1975	1976	
SPACE: 1999 ANNUAL	WORLD DISTRIBUTORS LTD	1975	1979	1975	1979		
SPACED	ECLIPSE		1	13	1982	1988	
SPACED SPECIAL EDITION	ECLIPSE		1	1	1983	1983	
SPACEHAWK	DARK HORSE COMICS		1	5	1992	NOW	
SPACEMAN	ATLAS		1	6	1953	1954	
SPACEMAN	GOULD-LIGHT		1	15	1953	1954	
SPACEMAN COMICS	CARTOON ART		1	1	1950	1950	FICTION HOUSE REPRINTS
SPACEMEN YEARBOOK	WARREN PUBLISHING CO	1960	1975	1960	1975		
SPACEWAYS COMIC ANNUAL	MORING	1953	1955	1953	1955		
SPANNERS GALAXY	DC COMICS INC.		1	6	1984	1985	
SPARK MAN	DONALD PETERS	19		19	1950	1950	
SPARK MAN	FRANCIS M. MCQUEENY		1	1	1945	1945	
SPARKIE, RADIO PIXIE	ZIFF-DAVIS PUBLISHING COMPANY		1	3	1951	1952	
SPARKLE COMICS	UNITED FEATURES SYNDICATE		1	33	1948	1954	
SPARKLER	AMALGAMATED PRESS		1	251	1934	1939	FORMERLY MY FAVOURITE
SPARKLER	PROVINCIAL COMICS		1	20	1931	1932	
SPARKLER COMICS	UNITED FEATURES SYNDICATE	1	1	2	1940	1940	
SPARKLER COMICS	UNITED FEATURES SYNDICATE	2	1	120	1941	1955	
SPARKLET COMICS	PHILIMAR		1	2	1948	1948	
SPARKLING COMIC	INTERNATIONAL		1	1	1945	1945	3 VERSIONS
SPARKLING COMIC, THE	PHILLIP MARX		1	1	1945	1945	
SPARKLING LOVE	AVON BOOKS	1	1	1	1950	1950	
SPARKLING LOVE	AVON BOOKS	2	1	1	1953	1953	REPRINT
SPARKLING STARS	HOLYOKE PUBLISHING COMPANY		1	33	1944	1948	
SPARKPLUG	HEROIC PUBLISHING		1	1	1993	1993	
SPARKS	JAMES HENDERSON	1	1	198	1914	1917	
SPARKS	JAMES HENDERSON	2	277	327	1919	1920	PREVIOUSLY SPARKS AND THE BIG COMIC
SPARKS AND THE BIG COMIC	JAMES HENDERSON		247	276	1918	1919	PREVIOUSLY SPARKS AND THE BIG COMIC
SPARKY	D.C. THOMSON		1	652	1965	1977	
SPARKY WATTS	UNITED-ANGLO PRODUCTIONS		1	2	1949	1949	COLUMBIA PUBLICATIONS REPRINTS
SPARKY WATTS ANNUAL	COLUMBIA COMICS GROUP		1	10	1942	1949	
SPARROW	DC COMICS INC.		1	1	1990	1990	
SPAWN	IMAGE COMICS		1	21	1992	NOW	
SPAWN/BATMAN	IMAGE COMICS		1	1	1994	1994	
SPECIAL AGENT	PARENTS MAGAZINE INSTITUTE		1	8	1947	1949	
SPECIAL COLLECTOR'S EDITION	MARVEL ENTERTAINMENT GROUP		1	1	1975	1975	
SPECIAL COMICS	M.L.J. MAGAZINES		1	1	1941	1942	
SPECIAL DELIVERY	POST HALL SYNDICATE		1	1	1951	1951	
SPECIAL EDITION COMICS	FAWCETT PUBLICATIONS		1	1	1940	1940	
SPECIAL EDITION U.S NAVY GIVEAWAYS	DC COMICS INC.		1	6	1944	1945	
SPECIAL MARVEL EDITION	MARVEL ENTERTAINMENT GROUP		1	16	1971	1974	
SPECIAL WAR SERIES	CHARLTON COMICS	4	1	4	1965	1965	
SPECTACULAR ADVENTURES	ST JOHN PUBLISHING		2	2	1950	1950	FORMERLY ADVENTURES
SPECTACULAR COLOUR COMIC	SCION		1	2	1951	1951	
SPECTACULAR CRIMES	STREAMLINE		1	2	1951	1951	FOX FEATURES REPRINTS
SPECTACULAR FEATURE MAGAZINE, A	FOX FEATURES SYNDICATE		11	11	1950	1950	FORMERLY MY CONFESSIONS
SPECTACULAR FEATURES	STREAMLINE		1	1	1951	1951	FOX FEATURES REPRINTS
SPECTACULAR FEATURES MAGAZINE	FOX FEATURES SYNDICATE		12	3	1950	1950	FORMERLY SPECTACULAR FEATURE MAGAZINE, A
SPECTACULAR SPIDER-MAN	MARVEL ENTERTAINMENT GROUP		1	209	1976	NOW	
SPECTACULAR SPIDER-MAN ANNUAL	MARVEL ENTERTAINMENT GROUP		1	13	1979	NOW	
SPECTACULAR SPIDER-MAN, PETER PARKER	MARVEL ENTERTAINMENT GROUP		1	2	1968	1968	
SPECTACULAR STORIES MAGAZINE	FOX FEATURES SYNDICATE		4	3	1950	1950	FORMERLY A STAR PRESENTATION
SPECTRE STORIES	JOHN SPENCER		1	6	1967	1967	
SPECTRE THE, ANNUAL	DC COMICS INC.	2	1	1	1988	1988	
SPECTRE, THE	DC COMICS INC.	1	1	10	1967	1969	
SPECTRE, THE	DC COMICS INC.	2	1	31	1987	1989	
SPECTRE, THE	DC COMICS INC.	3	1	15	1992	NOW	
SPECTRE, THE WRATH OF	DC COMICS INC.		1	4	1988	1988	
SPECTRE: CRIMES & PUNISHMENTS	DC COMICS INC.		1	1	1993	1993	
SPEED	IPC		1	31	1980	1980	
SPEED BUGGY	CHARLTON COMICS		1	9	1975	1976	
SPEED COMICS	HARVEY PUBLICATIONS		14	44	1941	1947	
SPEED COMICS	SPEED PUBLICATIONS		1	13	1939	1941	

COMIC TITLE	PUBLISHER	Vol No.	Srt No.	End No.	Str. Year	End Year	COMMENTS
SPEED DEMONS	CHARLTON COMICS		5	10	1957	1958	FORMERLY FRANK MERRIWELL AT YALE
SPEED GALE COMICS	CARTOON ART		1	1	1947	1947	
SPEED KINGS COMIC	MANS WORLD		12	17	1953	1964	
SPEED RACER	NOW	1	1	42	1987	1992	
SPEED RACER	NOW	2	1	3	1992	1992	
SPEED RACER 3-D SPECIAL	NOW		1	1	1993	NOW	
SPEED RACER CLASSICS	NOW		1	2	1992	1992	
SPEED RACER FEATURING NINJA HIGH SCHOOL	NOW		1	4	1993	1993	
SPEED RACER SPECIAL	NOW		1	2	1987	NOW	
SPEED RACER, NEW ADVENTURES OF	NOW		1	1	1993	NOW	
SPEED SMITH THE HOT ROD KING	ZIFF-DAVIS PUBLISHING COMPANY		1	1	1952	1952	
SPEEDBALL	MARVEL ENTERTAINMENT GROUP		1	11	1988	1989	
SPELLBINDERS/SCAVENGERS	FLEETWAY		1	26	1986	1989	
SPELLBOUND	ATLAS		1	34	1952	1957	
SPELLBOUND	L. MILLER PUBLISHING COMPANY (UK)		1	66	1961	1966	ATLAS REPRINTS
SPELLBOUND	MARVEL ENTERTAINMENT GROUP		1	6	1988	1988	
SPELLBOUND MAGAZINE	CARTOON ART		1	1	1952	1952	MAGAZINE ENTERPRISES REPRINTS
SPELLJAMMER COMICS	DC COMICS INC.		1	15	1990	1992	
SPENCER SPOOK	AMERICOMICS	100	101	1955	1955	FORMERLY GIGGLE BOOKS
SPICY HORROR STORIES	MALIBU COMICS ENTERTAINMENT INC.				1990	1990	
SPICY TALES	ETERNITY		1	20	1989	NOW	
SPIDER, THE	ECLIPSE		1	3	1991	1991	
SPIDER-MAN	MARVEL ENTERTAINMENT GROUP		1	43	1990	NOW	
SPIDER-MAN 2099	MARVEL ENTERTAINMENT GROUP		1	17	1992	NOW	
SPIDER-MAN 30TH ANNIVERSARY POSTER MAGAZINE	MARVEL ENTERTAINMENT GROUP		1	1	1992	1992	
SPIDER-MAN AND DAREDEVIL: SPECIAL EDITION	MARVEL ENTERTAINMENT GROUP		1	1	1984	1984	
SPIDER-MAN AND HIS AMAZING FRIENDS	MARVEL ENTERTAINMENT GROUP		1	4	1981	1981	
SPIDER-MAN AND HULK SPECIAL	MARVEL ENTERTAINMENT GROUP		1	3	1979	1981	
SPIDER-MAN AND POWER PACK (GIVEAWAY)	MARVEL ENTERTAINMENT GROUP		1	1	1984	1984	
SPIDER-MAN AND ZOIDS	MARVEL ENTERTAINMENT GROUP		1	51	1986	1987	
SPIDER-MAN ANNUAL	WORLD DISTRIBUTORS LTD	1978	1984	1978	1984		
SPIDER-MAN CHRONICLES	FANTACO		1	1	1982	1982	
SPIDER-MAN CLASSICS	MARVEL ENTERTAINMENT GROUP		1	12	1993	NOW	
SPIDER-MAN COMIC WEEKLY	MARVEL ENTERTAINMENT GROUP		1	666	1973	1985	
SPIDER-MAN COMICS MAGAZINE	MARVEL ENTERTAINMENT GROUP		1	13	1987	1988	DIGEST SIZE REPRINTS
SPIDER-MAN COMICS WEEKLY (UK)	MARVEL ENTERTAINMENT GROUP		1	666	1973	1985	
SPIDER-MAN HOLIDAY SPECIAL	MARVEL ENTERTAINMENT GROUP	1992	1992	1992	1992		
SPIDER-MAN MAGAZINE	MARVEL ENTERTAINMENT GROUP		1	1	1994	NOW	
SPIDER-MAN POCKET BOOK	MARVEL ENTERTAINMENT GROUP		1	28	1980	1982	
SPIDER-MAN SAGA	MARVEL ENTERTAINMENT GROUP		1	4	1991	1991	
SPIDER-MAN SUMMER SPECIAL	MARVEL ENTERTAINMENT GROUP	1979	1987	1979	1987		
SPIDER-MAN SUMMER SPECIAL (UK)	MARVEL ENTERTAINMENT GROUP	1979	1985	1979	1987		
SPIDER-MAN UNLIMITED	MARVEL ENTERTAINMENT GROUP		1	4	1993	NOW	
SPIDER-MAN VS DRACULA	MARVEL ENTERTAINMENT GROUP		1	1	1993	1993	
SPIDER-MAN VS VENOM	MARVEL ENTERTAINMENT GROUP		1	1	1990	1990	
SPIDER-MAN VS WOLVERINE	MARVEL ENTERTAINMENT GROUP	1	1	1	1987	1987	
SPIDER-MAN VS WOLVERINE	MARVEL ENTERTAINMENT GROUP	2	1	1	1990	1990	REPRINTS
SPIDER-MAN WINTER SPECIAL	MARVEL ENTERTAINMENT GROUP	1979	1985	1979	1985		
SPIDER-MAN, STORM AND POWER MAN (GIVEAWAY)	MARVEL ENTERTAINMENT GROUP		1	1	1982	1982	
SPIDER-MAN/DR. STRANGE: WAY TO DUSTY DEATH	MARVEL ENTERTAINMENT GROUP		1	1	1993	1993	
SPIDER-MAN/PUNISHER: DESIGNER GENES	MARVEL ENTERTAINMENT GROUP		1	1	1993	1993	
SPIDER-MAN/X-FACTOR: SHADOWGATES	MARVEL ENTERTAINMENT GROUP		1	2	1994	1994	
SPIDER-MAN: CARNAGE	MARVEL ENTERTAINMENT GROUP		1	1	1993	1993	
SPIDER-MAN: COSMIC ADVENTURES	MARVEL ENTERTAINMENT GROUP		1	1	1993	1993	
SPIDER-MAN: MUTANT AGENDA	MARVEL ENTERTAINMENT GROUP		0	0	1993	1993	
SPIDER-MAN: MUTANT AGENDA	MARVEL ENTERTAINMENT GROUP		1	1	1994	1994	
SPIDER-MAN: ORIGIN OF THE HOBGOBLIN	MARVEL ENTERTAINMENT GROUP		1	1	1993	1993	
SPIDER-MAN: TORMENT	MARVEL ENTERTAINMENT GROUP				1992	1992	REPRINTS SPIDER-MAN NOS. 1–5
SPIDER-MAN: VENOM RETURNS	MARVEL ENTERTAINMENT GROUP		1	1	1993	1993	
SPIDER: REIGN OF THE VAMPIRE KING, THE	ECLIPSE		1	3	1992	1992	
SPIDERFEMME VS. DENIM	PERSONALITY COMICS		1	1	1992	1992	
SPIDERWOMAN	MARVEL ENTERTAINMENT GROUP		1	4	1993	1993	
SPIDERWOMAN	MARVEL ENTERTAINMENT GROUP		1	50	1978	1983	
SPIDEY "ALL" (GIVEAWAY)	MARVEL ENTERTAINMENT GROUP		1	4	1980	1983	
SPIDEY SUPER STORIES	MARVEL ENTERTAINMENT GROUP		1	57	1974	1982	
SPIKE	D.C. THOMSON		1	67	1983	1984	
SPINE-TINGLING TALES	GOLD KEY		1	4	1975	1976	
SPINELESS MAN $2099	PARODY PRESS		1	1	1993	1993	
SPIRAL CAGE, THE	TITAN BOOKS		1	1	1990	1990	
SPIRAL PATH	ECLIPSE		1	2	1986	1986	
SPIRAL ZONE	DC COMICS INC.		1	4	1988	1988	
SPIRIT	T.V. BOARDMAN		12	17	1949	1949	REPRINTS EISNER MATERIAL
SPIRIT MAGAZINE, THE	WARREN PUBLISHING CO		1	41	1974	1983	
SPIRIT SPECIAL, THE	WARREN PUBLISHING CO		1	1	1975	1975	
SPIRIT WORLD	DC COMICS INC.		1	1	1971	1971	
SPIRIT, THE	FICTION HOUSE	2	1	5	1952	1954	
SPIRIT, THE	HARVEY PUBLICATIONS		1	2	1966	1967	
SPIRIT, THE	I.W. SUPER	11	12	1963	1964		
SPIRIT, THE	KITCHEN SINK		1	87	1983	1992	
SPIRIT, THE	NEWSPAPER DISTRIBUTIONS	31140	31140	1940	1952		WEEKLY STRIP
SPIRIT, THE	QUALITY COMICS		1	22	1944	1950	
SPIRIT, THE OUTER SPACE	KITCHEN SINK				1994	1994	
SPIRIT: THE DAILIES	KEN PIERCE		1	4	1980	1980	
SPIRIT: THE ORIGIN YEARS, THE	KITCHEN SINK		1	9	1992	NOW	
SPITFIRE AND THE TROUBLESHOOTERS	MARVEL ENTERTAINMENT GROUP		1	13	1986	1987	"CODENAME: SPITFIRE" FROM ISSUE #10
SPITFIRE COMICS	HARVEY PUBLICATIONS		1	2	1941	1941	
SPITFIRE, UNDERCOVER AGENT	MALVERNE HERALD	132	133	1944	1945		
SPLAT	MAD DOG		1	3	1987	1987	
SPLATTER	NORTHSTAR		1	7	1991	NOW	
SPLATTER ANNUAL	NORTHSTAR		1	1	1993	NOW	

COMIC TITLE	PUBLISHER	Vol No.	Srt No.	End No.	Str. Year	End Year	COMMENTS
SPLITTING IMAGE	IMAGE COMICS		1	2	1993	NOW	
SPOOF	MARVEL ENTERTAINMENT GROUP		1	5	1970	1973	
SPOOF COMICS	PERSONALITY COMICS		1	17	1992	NOW	
SPOOK	STAR PUBLICATIONS		22	30	1953	1954	FORMERLY SHOCK DETECTIVE CASES
SPOOK COMICS	STAR PUBLICATIONS		1	1	1946	1946	
SPOOKY	HARVEY PUBLICATIONS		1	4	1991	1992	
SPOOKY DIGEST	HARVEY PUBLICATIONS		1	1	1992	NOW	
SPOOKY HAUNTED HOUSE	HARVEY PUBLICATIONS		1	15	1972	1975	
SPOOKY MYSTERIES	HARVEY PUBLICATIONS		1	1	1946	1946	
SPOOKY SPOOKTOWN	HARVEY PUBLICATIONS		1	66	1961	1976	
SPOOKY THE TUFF LITTLE GHOST	HARVEY PUBLICATIONS	1	1	161	1955	1980	
SPOON VS BATBABE	PARODY PRESS		1	1	1993	1993	
SPORT COMICS	STREET AND SMITH PUBLICATIONS		1	4	1940	1941	
SPORT KOMIC, THE	MERSEY LEISURE PUBLISHING		1	1	1948	1948	
SPORT STARS	PARENTS MAGAZINE INSTITUTE		1	4	1946	1946	
SPORT THRILLS	STAR PUBLICATIONS		11	15	1950	1951	FORMERLY DICK COLE
SPORT THRILLS REPRINT	STAR PUBLICATIONS		11	12	1951	1951	
SPORTING SAM	EXPRESS PUBLICATIONS		1	1	1979	1979	
SPORTS ACTION	MARVEL ENTERTAINMENT GROUP		2	14	1950	1952	FORMERLY SPORT STARS
SPORTS PARADE	MIRROR PRESS PUBLICATIONS		1	1	1947	1947	
SPORTS STARS	MARVEL ENTERTAINMENT GROUP		1	1	1949	1949	
SPOTLIGHT	MARVEL ENTERTAINMENT GROUP		1	4	1978	1979	
SPOTLIGHT COMICS	HARRY A CHESLER		1	3	1944	1945	
SPOTTY THE PUP	AVON BOOKS	1	2	3	1953	1954	
SPOTTY THE PUP	REALISTIC PUBLICATIONS	2	1	1	1953	1953	
SPRING COMIC, THE	C.A. PEARSON		1	3	1932	1934	
SPRING HEEL JACK: REVENGE OF THE RIPPER	REBEL STUDIOS	3	3	3	1993	1994	
SPUNKY THE SMILING SPOOK	AJAX		1	4	1957	1958	
SPUNKY, JUNIOR COWBOY	STANDARD COMICS		1	7	1949	1951	
SPY 13 PICTURE LIBRARY SUMMER SPECIAL	FLEETWAY		1	1	1966	1966	
SPY AND COUNTERSPY	AMERICOMICS		1	2	1949	1949	
SPY CASES	ATLAS		1	19	1950	1953	FORMERLY THE KELLYS
SPY FIGHTERS	MARVEL ENTERTAINMENT GROUP		1	15	1951	1953	
SPY SMASHER	FAWCETT PUBLICATIONS		1	11	1941	1943	
SPY SMASHER	L. MILLER PUBLISHING COMPANY (UK)		1	4	1953	1953	FAWCETT REPRINTS
SPY THRILLERS	ATLAS		1	4	1954	1955	
SPYKE	MARVEL ENTERTAINMENT GROUP		1	4	1993	1993	
SPYMAN	HARVEY PUBLICATIONS		1	3	1966	1967	
SPYMASTER COMICS	SCION		1	3	1951	1952	
SQUADRON SUPREME	MARVEL ENTERTAINMENT GROUP		1	1	1989	1989	
SQUADRON SUPREME	MARVEL ENTERTAINMENT GROUP		1	12	1985	1986	
SQUALOR	FIRST		1	4	1989	1990	
SQUEEKS	LEV GLEASON PUBLICATIONS		1	5	1953	1954	
SQUIBS FUN COMIC	MARTIN & REID		1	1	1949	1949	
ST. GEORGE	MARVEL ENTERTAINMENT GROUP		1	8	1988	1989	
ST. SWITHINS DAY	TRIDENT		1	1	1990	1990	
STAINLESS STEEL RAT, THE	EAGLE		1	6	1985	1986	
STALKER	DC COMICS INC.		1	4	1975	1976	
STALKERS	MARVEL ENTERTAINMENT GROUP		1	12	1990	1991	
STAMP COMICS	YOUTHFUL MAGAZINES		1	7	1951	1952	
STAMPEDE PICTURE AND STORY ALBUM	MELLIFONT		1	1	1950	1950	
STAN SHAW'S BEAUTY & THE BEAST	DARK HORSE COMICS		1	1	1993	1993	
STANLEY AND HIS MONSTER	DC COMICS INC.		1	4	1993	1993	
STAR BLECCH	PARODY PRESS		1	1	1993	NOW	
STAR BRAND, THE	MARVEL ENTERTAINMENT GROUP		1	19	1986	1989	
STAR BRAND, THE ANNUAL	MARVEL ENTERTAINMENT GROUP		1	1	1987	1987	
STAR COMICS	CENTAUR PUBLICATIONS	2	1	7	1939	1939	
STAR COMICS	DONALD PETERS		1	2	1954	1954	
STAR COMICS	HARRY A CHESLER	1	1	16	1937	1938	
STAR COMICS	P.M. PRODUCTIONS		1	2	1943	1943	
STAR FLASH COMIC	P.M. PRODUCTIONS		1	2	1948	1948	
STAR GATE, THE	MILLENIUM		1	2	1994	1994	
STAR HEROES	MARVEL ENTERTAINMENT GROUP		1	1	1979	1979	
STAR HEROES POCKET BOOK	MARVEL ENTERTAINMENT GROUP		1	10	1980	1981	
STAR HUNTERS	DC COMICS INC.		1	7	1977	1978	
STAR PIRATE COMICS	CARTOON ART		1	1	1950	1950	FICTION HOUSE REPRINTS
STAR PRESENTATION, A	FOX FEATURES SYNDICATE		3	3	1950	1950	FORMERLY MY SECRET ROMANCE
STAR QUEST COMIX	WARREN PUBLISHING CO		1	1	1978	1978	
STAR RANGER	ULTEM PUBLICATIONS		1	12	1937	1938	
STAR RANGER FUNNIES	CENTAUR PUBLICATIONS	1	15	15	1938	1938	FORMERLY COWBOY COMICS
STAR RANGER FUNNIES	CENTAUR PUBLICATIONS	2	1	5	1939	1939	
STAR RANGERS	ADVENTURE COMICS		1	3	1987	1988	
STAR REACH CLASSICS	ECLIPSE		1	8	1984	1984	
STAR ROCKET	MORING		1	4	1953	1953	
STAR SPANGLED COMICS	DC COMICS INC.		1	130	1941	1952	
STAR SPANGLED WAR STORIES	DC COMICS INC.		131	204	1952	1977	FORMERLY STAR SPANGLED COMICS
STAR STREAMLINE COMIC	STREAMLINE		1	1	1950	1950	US REPRINTS
STAR STUDDED	SUPERIOR COMICS		1	2	1945	1945	
STAR TEAM	MARVEL ENTERTAINMENT GROUP		1	1	1977	1977	
STAR TREK	DC COMICS INC.	1	1	58	1984	1988	
STAR TREK	DC COMICS INC.	2	1	57	1989	NOW	
STAR TREK	GOLD KEY		1	61	1967	1979	
STAR TREK	MARVEL ENTERTAINMENT GROUP		1	18	1980	1982	
STAR TREK	TRIDENT		1	4	1992	NOW	DC REPRINTS
STAR TREK ANNUAL	DC COMICS INC.	1	1	3	1985	1988	
STAR TREK ANNUAL	DC COMICS INC.	2	1	4	1990	NOW	
STAR TREK CHRONOLOGY	POCKET BOOKS		1	1	1994	1994	
STAR TREK ENCYCLOPEDIA	POCKET BOOKS				1994	1994	
STAR TREK FAN CLUB MAGAZINE	STAR TREK FAN CLUB		17	94	1985	NOW	

COMIC TITLE	PUBLISHER	Vol No.	Srt No.	End No.	Str. Year	End Year	COMMENTS
STAR TREK FAN CLUB OF THE UK MAGAZINE, THE OFFICIAL	AFM		1	3	1993	NOW	
STAR TREK MOVIE ADAPTATION	DC COMICS INC.		1	6	1984	1992	
STAR TREK NEXT GEN. FX MAKEUP SPECIAL	STARLOG		1	1	1993	1993	
STAR TREK NEXT GENERATION	DC COMICS INC.		1	55	1989	NOW	
STAR TREK NEXT GENERATION	DC COMICS INC.		1	6	1991	1991	
STAR TREK NEXT GENERATION ANNUAL	DC COMICS INC.		1	4	1990	NOW	
STAR TREK NEXT GENERATION COMPANION	POCKET BOOKS		1	1	1992	1992	
STAR TREK NEXT GENERATION MAGAZINE	STARLOG		1	26	1987	NOW	
STAR TREK NEXT GENERATION SPECIAL	DC COMICS INC.		1	1	1993	1993	
STAR TREK NEXT GENERATION TECHNICAL JOURNAL	STARLOG		1	1	1992	1992	
STAR TREK NEXT GENERATION: CHRONOLOGY	SIMON AND SCHUSTER		1	1	1993	1993	
STAR TREK NEXT GENERATION: STAR LOST	SIMON AND SCHUSTER		1	1	1993	1993	
STAR TREK NEXT GENERATION: TECHNICAL MANUAL	BOXTREE		1	1	1992	1992	
STAR TREK NEXT GENERATION: TECHNICAL MANUAL	SIMON AND SCHUSTER		1	1	1992	1992	
STAR TREK NEXT GENERATION: THE MODALA IMPERATIVE	DC COMICS INC.		1	4	1991	1991	
STAR TREK SPECIAL	DC COMICS INC.		1	1	1994	1994	
STAR TREK SPECIAL	IPC		1	1	1978	1978	
STAR TREK SUMMER SPECIAL	MARVEL ENTERTAINMENT GROUP		1	1	1981	1981	
STAR TREK WINTER SPECIAL	MARVEL ENTERTAINMENT GROUP		1	1	1982	1982	
STAR TREK WINTER SPECIAL	POLYSTYLE		1	1	1975	1975	
STAR TREK: CAPTAIN'S LOGS	BOXTREE		1	1	1993	1993	
STAR TREK: CHRONOLOGY	POCKET BOOKS				1993	1993	
STAR TREK: DEBT OF HONOUR	DC COMICS INC.		1	1	1992	1992	
STAR TREK: DEEP SPACE NINE	MALIBU COMICS ENTERTAINMENT INC.		1	5	1993	NOW	
STAR TREK: DEEP SPACE NINE	STARLOG		1	3	1992	NOW	
STAR TREK: DEEP SPACE NINE LIMITED EDITION PREVIEW	MALIBU COMICS ENTERTAINMENT INC.		1	2	1993	1993	
STAR TREK: MIRROR UNIVERSE SAGA	DC COMICS INC.		1	1	1991	1991	
STAR TREK: SAREK	POCKET BOOKS				1994	1994	
STAR TREK: THE BEST OF	DC COMICS INC.		1	1	1991	1991	
STAR TREK: THE MODALA IMPERATIVE	DC COMICS INC.		1	1	1992	1992	
STAR TREK: THE MODALA IMPERATIVE	DC COMICS INC.		1	4	1991	1991	
STAR TREK: THE MODALA IMPERATIVE	TITAN BOOKS		1	1	1992	1992	
STAR TREK: WHO KILLED CAPTAIN KIRK?	DC COMICS INC.		1	1	1993	1993	
STAR TREK: WORLDS OF THE FEDERATION	TITAN BOOKS				1992	1992	
STAR WARS	MARVEL ENTERTAINMENT GROUP		1	107	1977	1986	
STAR WARS ANNUAL	MARVEL ENTERTAINMENT GROUP		1	3	1979	1983	
STAR WARS SUMMER SPECIAL	MARVEL ENTERTAINMENT GROUP		1983	1985	1983	1985	
STAR WARS TECHNICAL JOURNAL	STARLOG		1	1	1993	NOW	
STAR WARS UK	DARK HORSE COMICS		1	10	1993	NOW	
STAR WARS WEEKLY	MARVEL ENTERTAINMENT GROUP		1	171	1978	1983	
STAR WARS WINTER SPECIAL	MARVEL ENTERTAINMENT GROUP		1983	1984	1983	1984	
STAR WARS, CLASSIC	DARK HORSE COMICS		1	15	1992	NOW	
STAR WARS: DARK EMPIRE	DARK HORSE COMICS		1	1	1993	1993	
STAR WARS: DARK EMPIRE	DARK HORSE COMICS		1	6	1992	1992	
STAR WARS: RETURN OF THE JEDI	MARVEL ENTERTAINMENT GROUP		1	155	1983	1986	
STAR WARS: RETURN OF THE JEDI	MARVEL ENTERTAINMENT GROUP		1	4	1983	1984	
STAR WARS: TALES OF THE JEDI	DARK HORSE COMICS		1	3	1993	1994	
STAR WARS: THE LAST COMMAND	BANTUM PUBLISHING				1993	1993	
STARBLAST	MARVEL ENTERTAINMENT GROUP		1	1	1993	1994	
STARBLAZER	D.C. THOMSON		1	281	1979	1991	
STARBLAZERS	COMICO	1	1	1	1991	1991	
STARBLAZERS	COMICO	1	1	4	1987	1987	
STARBLAZERS	COMICO	2	1	5	1989	1989	
STARBURST	VISUAL IMAGINATION		1	176	1978	NOW	
STARCHILD	TALIESIN PRESS		1	1	1992	NOW	
STARDUSTERS	NIGHT WYND ENTERPRISES		1	4	1991	1992	
STARFIRE	DC COMICS INC.		1	8	1976	1977	
STARK TERROR	PORTMAN		1	4	1979	1980	STANMORE REPRINTS
STARK TERROR	STANLEY PUBLICATIONS		1	5	1970	1971	
STARK: FUTURE	AIRCEL		1	17	1986	1987	
STARLET O'HARA IN HOLLYWOOD	STANDARD COMICS		1	4	1948	1949	
STARLIGHT COMICS, THE	BEAR HUDSON		1	1	1947	1947	
STARLOG	STARLOG		1	199	1976	NOW	
STARLOG PHOTO GUIDEBOOK: FANTASTIC 3-D	STARLOG				1982	1982	
STARLORD	IPC		1	22	1978	1978	
STARLORD ANNUAL	FLEETWAY		1980	1982	1980	1982	
STARLORD SPECIAL EDITION	MARVEL ENTERTAINMENT GROUP		1	1	1982	1982	
STARLORD SUMMER SPECIAL	IPC		1	1	1978	1978	
STARMAN	DC COMICS INC.		1	45	1988	1992	
STARRIORS	MARVEL ENTERTAINMENT GROUP		1	4	1984	1985	
STARRY SPANGLES COMIC	PHILIMAR		1	1	1948	1948	
STARS AND STRIPES COMICS	CENTAUR PUBLICATIONS		2	6	1941	1941	
STARS MY DESTINATION, THE	MARVEL ENTERTAINMENT GROUP		1	1	1992	1992	
STARSLAYER	FIRST		1	34	1982	1985	
STARSTONE	AIRCEL		1	3	1991	1991	
STARSTRUCK	MARVEL ENTERTAINMENT GROUP		1	6	1985	1986	
STARSTRUCK THE EXPANDING UNIVERSE	DARK HORSE COMICS		1	4	1990	1991	
STARTLING COMICS	NEDOR (BETTER PUBLICATIONS)		1	1	1940	1948	
STARTLING DETECTIVE	STREAMLINE		1	1	1951	1951	FOX FEATURES REPRINTS
STARTLING TERROR TALES	ARNOLD BOOK CO.		1	1	1954	1954	STAR REPRINTS
STARTLING TERROR TALES	STAR PUBLICATIONS	1	10	13	1952	1953	
STARTLING TERROR TALES	STAR PUBLICATIONS	2	4	11	1953	1954	
STATIC	DC COMICS INC.		1	9	1993	NOW	
STATIC, CHARLTON ACTION FEATURING	CHARLTON COMICS		11	12	1985	1985	
STEALTH FORCE	ETERNITY		1	8	1987	1988	
STEED AND MRS PEEL	ECLIPSE		1	3	1990	1991	
STEEL	DC COMICS INC.		1	1	1993	NOW	

COMIC TITLE	PUBLISHER	Vol No.	Srt No.	End No.	Str. Year	End Year	COMMENTS
STEEL ANGEL	CALIBER PRESS		1	3	1992	1993	
STEEL CLAW	FLEETWAY		1	4	1986	1987	
STEEL STERLING	ARCHIE PUBLICATIONS		4	7	1984	1984	FORMERLY SHIELD-STEEL STERLING
STEEL, THE INDESTRUCTIBLE MAN	DC COMICS INC.		1	5	1978	1978	
STEELGRIP STARKEY	MARVEL ENTERTAINMENT GROUP		1	6	1986	1987	
STEELTOWN ROCKERS	MARVEL ENTERTAINMENT GROUP		1	10	1990	1990	
STERANKOS HISTORY OF COMICS	SUPER GRAPHICS		1	2	1970	1970	
STEVE CANYON	GROSSET & DUNLOP		100100	100100	1959	1959	
STEVE CANYON 3-D	KITCHEN SINK		1	1	1986	1986	
STEVE CANYON COMICS	HARVEY PUBLICATIONS		1	6	1948	1948	REPRINTS
STEVE CANYON DEPARTMENT STORE GIVEAWAY	HARVEY PUBLICATIONS		1	1	1948	1948	
STEVE CANYON MAGAZINE	KITCHEN SINK		1	24	1986	NOW	
STEVE CANYON'S SECRET MISSION	HARVEY PUBLICATIONS		1	1	1951	1951	
STEVE CANYON: STRICTLY FOR THE SMART BIRDS	HARVEY PUBLICATIONS		1	1	1951	1951	
STEVE ROPER	HARVEY PUBLICATIONS		1	5	1948	1948	
STEVE SAMPSON	L. MILLER PUBLISHING COMPANY (UK)		1	40	1953	1955	
STEVE ZODIAC AND THE FIREBALL XL-5	GOLD KEY		1	1	1964	1964	
STEVIE	MAGAZINE PUBLISHERS		1	6	1952	1954	
STING OF THE GREEN HORNET	NOW		1	1	1993	1993	
STING OF THE GREEN HORNET	NOW		1	4	1992	1992	
STINGRAY	BOXTREE				1993	1993	
STINGRAY ANNUAL	CITY		1965	1966	1965	1966	
STINGRAY ANNUAL	FLEETWAY		1992	1993	1992	1993	
STINGRAY SUMMER SPECIAL	POLYSTYLE		1	1	1983	1983	
STINGRAY TELEVISION STORYBOOK	PBS		1	1	1965	1965	
STINGRAY: BATTLE STATIONS	RAVETTE BOOKS		1	1	1992	1992	TV CENTURY 21 REPRINTS
STINGRAY: STAND BY FOR ACTION	RAVETTE BOOKS		1	1	1992	1992	TV CENTURY 21 REPRINTS
STINGRAY: THE COMIC	FLEETWAY		1	10	1992	NOW	
STIRRING WESTERN	STREAMLINE		1	12	50'S	50'S	
STONE PROTECTORS	HARVEY PUBLICATIONS		1	2	1994	NOW	
STONEY BURKE	DELL PUBLISHING COMPANY		1	2	1963	1963	
STONY CRAIG	PENTAGON PUBLISHING CO.		1	1	1946	1946	REPRINTS
STORIES BY FAMOUS AUTHORS ILLUSTRATED	SEABOARD PUBLISHING/FAMOUS AUTHORS		1	13	1950	1951	
STORIES OF BILLY THE BEE	BEAVERBROOK		1	1	1950	1950	
STORIES OF CHRISTMAS	K.K. PUBLICATIONS		1	1	1942	1942	
STORIES OF ROMANCE	ATLAS		5	13	1956	1957	FORMERLY MEET MISS BLISS
STORM: THE DEEP WORLD	BEAP/OBERON		1	1	1982	1982	
STORM: THE LAST FIGHTER	TITAN BOOKS		1	1	1987	1987	
STORM: THE PIRATES OF PENDARVE	TITAN BOOKS		1	1	1989	1989	
STORMBRINGER	SAVOY ADULT GRAPHICS		1	1	1980	1980	
STORMWATCH	IMAGE COMICS		0	6	1993	NOW	
STORMWATCH SOURCEBOOK	IMAGE COMICS		1	1	1994	1994	
STORMWATCH YEARBOOK	IMAGE COMICS		1	1	1994	1994	
STORMWATCHER	ECLIPSE		1	4	1989	1989	
STORY HOUR SERIES	WHITMAN		1	2	1948	1949	
STORY HOUR SERIES	WHITMAN	1	1	3	1948	1948	GIVEN AWAY WITH SUBSCRIPTION
STORY HOUR SERIES	WHITMAN	2	1	2	1949	1949	GIVEN AWAY WITH SUBSCRIPTION
STORY HOUR SERIES	WHITMAN	3	800	808	1951	1953	GIVEN AWAY WITH SUBSCRIPTION
STORY OF EDISON, THE	EC COMICS		1	1	1956	1956	
STORY OF HARRY S. TRUMAN, THE	DEMOCRATIC NATIONAL COMMITTEE		1	1	1948	1948	
STORY OF MARTHA WAYNE, THE	ARGO PUBLISHING		1	1	1956	1956	
STORY OF THE COMMANDOS, THE	GILBERTON PUBLICATIONS		1	1	1943	1943	
STRAIGHT ARROW	CARTOON ART		1	1	1952	1952	MAGAZINE ENTERPRISES REPRINTS
STRAIGHT ARROW	MAGAZINE ENTERPRISES		1	55	1950	1956	
STRANGE	AJAX		1	6	1957	1958	
STRANGE ADVENTURES	DC COMICS INC.		1	244	1950	1973	
STRANGE AND BIZARRE ORIGIN OF HERBERT WEST, THE	MILLENIUM		1	1	1993	1993	
STRANGE AS IT SEEMS	BLUE STAR PUBLISHING CO.		1	1	1932	1932	
STRANGE AS IT SEEMS	UNITED FEATURES SYNDICATE		1	2	1939	1939	SINGLE SERIES 9
STRANGE COMBAT TALES	MARVEL ENTERTAINMENT GROUP		1	4	1993	1993	
STRANGE CONFESSIONS	ZIFF-DAVIS PUBLISHING COMPANY		1	4	1952	1952	
STRANGE DAYS	ECLIPSE		1	3	1984	1985	
STRANGE EMBRACE	ATOMEKA		1	4	1993	1993	
STRANGE FANTASY	AJAX		1	14	1952	1954	FORMERLY ROCKETMAN
STRANGE GALAXY	EERIE PUBLICATIONS	1	8	11	1971	1971	
STRANGE JOURNEY	AJAX		1	4	1957	1958	
STRANGE MYSTERIES	I.W. ENTERPRISES		9	9	1963	1963	REPRINTS
STRANGE MYSTERIES	SUPERIOR COMICS		1	21	1951	1955	
STRANGE MYSTERIES SUPER REPRINTS	SUPER COMICS		10	18	1963	1964	
STRANGE PLANETS	I.W. SUPER		1	18	1963	1964	
STRANGE SPORTS STORIES	ADVENTURE COMICS		1	3	1973	1974	
STRANGE STORIES	JOHN SPENCER		1	6	1967	1967	
STRANGE STORIES FROM ANOTHER WORLD	FAWCETT PUBLICATIONS		1	6	1952	1953	FORMERLY UNKNOWN WORLD
STRANGE STORIES OF SUSPENSE	ATLAS		5	16	1955	1957	FORMERLY RUGGED ACTION
STRANGE SUSPENSE STORIES	CHARLTON COMICS	1	1	77	1954	1965	CONTINUES FAWCETT SERIES
STRANGE SUSPENSE STORIES	CHARLTON COMICS	2	2	9	1969	1969	
STRANGE SUSPENSE STORIES	CHARLTON COMICS	3	1	4	1967	1967	
STRANGE SUSPENSE STORIES	G.T. LIMITED		1	1	1959	1959	
STRANGE TALES	MARVEL ENTERTAINMENT GROUP	1	1	188	1951	1976	
STRANGE TALES	MARVEL ENTERTAINMENT GROUP	2	1	19	1987	1988	
STRANGE TALES ANNUAL	MARVEL ENTERTAINMENT GROUP	1	1	2	1962	1963	
STRANGE TALES OF THE UNUSUAL	ATLAS		1	11	1955	1957	
STRANGE TERRORS	ST JOHN PUBLISHING		1	7	1952	1953	
STRANGE WORLDS	AVON BOOKS		1	22	1950	1955	ISSUES #18 CONTINUES FROM EERIE #17
STRANGE WORLDS	I.W. ENTERPRISES		5	5	???	???	REPRINTS
STRANGE WORLDS	MANS WORLD		12	17	1953	1954	
STRANGE WORLDS	MARVEL ENTERTAINMENT GROUP		1	5	1958	1959	
STRANGE WORLDS	THORPE & PORTER		1	2	1951	???	AVON REPRINTS
STRANGE WORLDS OF YOUR DREAMS	PRIZE PUBLICATIONS		1	4	1952	1953	

COMIC TITLE	PUBLISHER	Vol No.	Srt No.	End No.	Str. Year	End Year	COMMENTS
STRANGERS, THE	MALIBU COMICS ENTERTAINMENT INC.		1	7	1993	NOW	
STRATA	RENEGADE PRESS		1	6	1986	1987	
STRATONAUT	NIGHT WYND ENTERPRISES		1	4	1992	1992	
STRATOSFEAR	CALIBER PRESS		1	1	1993	1994	
STRAWBERRY SHORTCAKE	MARVEL ENTERTAINMENT GROUP		1	7	1985	1986	
STRAY TOASTERS	MARVEL ENTERTAINMENT GROUP		1	4	1988	1989	
STREAMLINE COMICS	CARDAL/W. DALY		1	4	1947	1947	
STREAMLINE PICTORIAL ROMANCE	STREAMLINE		1	7	1950	1950	
STREET COMIX	ARTS LAB PRESS		1	5	1976	1978	
STREET COMIX	KING FEATURES		1	2	1973	1973	
STREET FIGHTER	MALIBU COMICS ENTERTAINMENT INC.		1	3	1993	1993	
STREET HEROES 2005	ETERNITY		1	3	1990	1990	
STREET MUSIC	FANTAGRAPHICS		1	6	1986	NOW	
STREET POET RAY	MARVEL ENTERTAINMENT GROUP		1	5	1990	1990	
STREET SHADOWS	CALIBER PRESS		1	2	1992	1993	
STREET WOLF	BLACKTHORNE		1	3	1986	1986	
STREETS	DC COMICS INC.		1	3	1992	NOW	
STRICTLY PRIVATE	EASTERN COLOR PRINTING COMPANY		1	2	1942	1942	
STRIKE	ECLIPSE		1	6	1987	1988	
STRIKE FORCE AMERICA	COMICO		1	1	1992	NOW	
STRIKE FORCE AMERICA SPECIAL EDITION	COMICO		1	1	1993	NOW	
STRIKE FORCE AMERICA SPECIAL EDITION A	COMICO		1	1	1993	NOW	
STRIKE FORCE AMERICA SPECIAL EDITION B	COMICO		1	1	1993	NOW	
STRIKE VS SGT. STRIKE SPECIAL	ECLIPSE		1	1	1988	1988	
STRIKEFORCE MORITURI	MARVEL ENTERTAINMENT GROUP		1	32	1986	1989	
STRIKER THE ARMORED WARRIOR	VIZ		1	1	1993	1993	
STRIKER THE ARMORED WARRIOR	VIZ		1	4	1992	1992	
STRIP	MARVEL ENTERTAINMENT GROUP		1	20	1990	1990	
STRIP COMICS	FAIRYLITE		1	1	1944	1944	
STRIP SEARCH	ESCAPE		1	1	1989	1989	
STRIP SEARCH 2	ESCAPE		1	1	1991	1991	
STRONG MAN	MAGAZINE ENTERPRISES		1	4	1955	1955	
STRONTIUM BITCH	FLEETWAY		1	2	1993	1993	
STRONTIUM DOG	EAGLE		1	4	1985	1986	
STRONTIUM DOG	QUALITY (FLEETWAY)		1	29	1987	1989	
STRONTIUM DOG	TITAN BOOKS		1	1	1985	1985	
STRONTIUM DOG SPECIAL	QUALITY (FLEETWAY)		1	1	1986	1986	
STRYFE'S STRIKE FILE	MARVEL ENTERTAINMENT GROUP		1	1	1993	1993	
STUDS KIRBY: THE VOICE OF AMERICA	FANTAGRAPHICS				1989	1989	
STUMBO TINYTOWN	HARVEY PUBLICATIONS		1	13	1963	1966	
STUNT DAWGS	HARVEY PUBLICATIONS		1	1	1993	1993	
STUNTMAN COMICS	HARVEY PUBLICATIONS		1	3	1946	1946	
STUPID	IMAGE COMICS		1	1	1993	1993	
STUPID HEROES	MIRAGE STUDIOS		1	1	1993	NOW	
SUB-MARINER	MARVEL ENTERTAINMENT GROUP		1	4	1984	1984	
SUB-MARINER ANNUAL	MARVEL ENTERTAINMENT GROUP		1	2	1971	1972	
SUB-MARINER COMICS	TIMELY COMICS		1	42	1941	1955	
SUB-MARINER, THE	MARVEL ENTERTAINMENT GROUP	2	1	72	1968	1974	
SUBMARINE ATTACK	CHARLTON COMICS		11	54	1958	1966	FORMERLY SPEED DEMONS
SUBSPECIES	ETERNITY		1	4	1991	1991	
SUBURBAN HIGH LIFE	SLAVE LABOR		1	4	1987	1988	
SUBURBAN NIGHTMARES	RENEGADE PRESS		1	4	1988	1988	
SUBURBAN NINJA SHE-DEVILS, THE	MARVEL ENTERTAINMENT GROUP		1	1	1992	1992	
SUDDENLY AT TWO O'CLOCK IN THE MORNING	LAST MINUTE PRODUCTIONS		1	1	1974	1974	
SUE & SALLY SMITH	CHARLTON COMICS	2	48	54	1962	1963	FORMERLY MY SECRET LIFE
SUGAR AND SPIKE	DC COMICS INC.		1	99	1956	1971	
SUGAR BEAR	POST CEREAL GIVEAWAYS		1	1	1975	1975	
SUGAR BOWL COMICS	POST CEREAL GIVEAWAYS		1	5	1948	1949	
SUICIDE SQUAD	DC COMICS INC.		1	66	1987	1992	
SUICIDE SQUAD ANNUAL	DC COMICS INC.		1	1	1988	1988	
SULTRY TEENAGE SUPER-FOXES	SOLSON		1	1	1987	1987	
SUMMER COMIC ANNUAL, THE	C.A. PEARSON		1932	1938	1932	1938	
SUMMER FUN	CHARLTON COMICS		54	54	1966	1966	FORMERLY L'IL GENIUS
SUMMER FUN	DELL PUBLISHING COMPANY		2	2	1959	1959	FORMERLY MICKEY MOUSE SUMMER FUN
SUMMER HOLIDAY COMIC, THE	C.A. PEARSON		1	1	1935	1935	
SUMMER LOVE	CHARLTON COMICS	2	46	48	1965	1968	FORMERLY BRIDES IN LOVE
SUN	AMALGAMATED PRESS		1	537	1947	1959	
SUN DEVILS	DC COMICS INC.		1	12	1984	1985	
SUN FUN KOMICS	SUN COMICS PUBLISHING		1	1	1939	1939	
SUN GIRL	MARVEL ENTERTAINMENT GROUP		1	3	1948	1948	
SUN RUNNERS	ECLIPSE		1	7	1984	1985	
SUN RUNNERS CHRISTMAS SPECIAL	AMAZING COMICS		1	1	1987	1987	
SUNBEAM, THE	AMALGAMATED PRESS	1	1	173	1922	1926	FORMERLY LITTLE SPARKS
SUNBEAM, THE	AMALGAMATED PRESS	2	1	747	1926	1940	
SUNDANCE KID	SKYWALD PUBLISHING		1	1	1971	1971	
SUNDANCE WESTERN	WORLD DISTRIBUTORS LTD		50	51	1970	???	
SUNDAY EXTRA	SUNDAY CITIZEN		1	110	1965	1967	
SUNDAY FUNNIES	HARVEY PUBLICATIONS		1	1	1950	1950	
SUNDAY POST FUN SECTION	D.C. THOMSON				1936	NOW	PULLOUT FROM NEWSPAPER
SUNNY COMIC	INTERNATIONAL		1	1	1945	1945	
SUNNY COMIC	P.M. PRODUCTIONS		1	1	1945	1945	
SUNNY FUN COMIC	PHILIMAR		1	1	1948	1948	
SUNNY SANDS	C.A. PEARSON		1	1	1939	1939	
SUNNY, AMERICA'S SWEETHEART	FOX FEATURES SYNDICATE		11	14	1947	1948	FORMERLY COSMO CAT
SUNNYTIMES COMIC	RAYBURN PRODUCTIONS		1	1	1948	1948	
SUNRISE	HARRIER		1	2	1987	1987	
SUNSET CARSON	CHARLTON COMICS		1	4	1951	1951	
SUNSHINE	TARGET PUBLICATIONS		1	39	1938	1939	
SUPER ADVENTURE	ALEX WHITE		1	36	1968	1969	
SUPER ADVENTURES	JOHN MATTHEW		1	1	1946	1946	

COMIC TITLE	PUBLISHER	Vol No.	Srt No.	End No.	Str. Year	End Year	COMMENTS
SUPER ALBUM, THE	MORING		1	1	1956	1956	
SUPER ANIMALS PRESENTS PIDGY & THE MAGIC GLASSES	STAR PUBLICATIONS		1	1	1953	1953	3-D
SUPER BOOK OF COMICS	WESTERN PUBLISHING COMPANY	1	1	10	1943	1943	
SUPER BOOK OF COMICS	WESTERN PUBLISHING COMPANY	2	1	8	1943	1943	
SUPER BRAT	I.W. ENTERPRISES		1	10	1958	1963	REPRINTS
SUPER BRAT	TOBY PRESS PUBLICATIONS		1	4	1954	1954	
SUPER CAT	AJAX	2	1	4	1957	1958	
SUPER CAT	STAR PUBLICATIONS	1	56	58	1953	1954	FORMERLY FRISKIE ANIMALS
SUPER CIRCUS	CROSS PUBLICATIONS		1	5	1951	1951	
SUPER COMIC STRIPS	MARTIN & REID		1	1	1949	1949	
SUPER COMICS	DELL PUBLISHING COMPANY		1	121	1938	1949	
SUPER COMICS	P.M. PRODUCTIONS		1	1	1943	1943	
SUPER COMICS REPRINTS	P.M. PRODUCTIONS		1	1	1946	1946	REPRINTS
SUPER DC	DC COMICS INC.		1	14	1976	1976	
SUPER DC BUMPER BOOK	TOP SELLERS		1	1	1970	1970	
SUPER DC GIANT	DC COMICS INC.		13	27	1970	1976	
SUPER DUCK COMICS	ARCHIE PUBLICATIONS		5	94	1945	1960	CONTINUES MLJ SERIES
SUPER DUCK COMICS	M.L.J. MAGAZINES		1	4	1944	1945	
SUPER DUPER	HARVEY PUBLICATIONS		5	11	1941	1941	
SUPER DUPER COMICS	F.E. HOWARD		3	3	1947	1947	FORMERLY LATEST COMICS
SUPER FRIENDS SPECIAL, THE	DC COMICS INC.		1	1	1981	1981	
SUPER FRIENDS, THE	DC COMICS INC.		1	47	1976	1981	
SUPER FUN	GILLMOR MAGAZINES		1	1	1956	1956	
SUPER FUNNIES	SUPERIOR COMICS		1	4	1953	1954	
SUPER FUNNIES	T.V. BOARDMAN		29	33	1940	1941	QUALITY REPRINTS
SUPER GOOF	GOLD KEY		1	57	1965	1980	
SUPER GOOF	WHITMAN		58	74	1980	1982	
SUPER GREEN BERET	LIGHTNING COMICS		1	2	1967	1967	
SUPER HEROES	DELL PUBLISHING COMPANY		1	4	1967	1967	
SUPER JOLLY ROGER	MARTIN & REID		12	12	1949	1949	PREVIOUSLY JOLLY CHUCKLES
SUPER MAG	YOUNG WORLD		1	28	1964	1965	GOLD KEY REPRINTS
SUPER MAGIC	STREET AND SMITH PUBLICATIONS		1	1	1941	1941	
SUPER MAGICIAN COMICS	STREET AND SMITH PUBLICATIONS	1	2	8	1941	1942	FORMERLY SUPER MAGIC
SUPER MAGICIAN COMICS	STREET AND SMITH PUBLICATIONS	2	1	12	1942	1943	
SUPER MAGICIAN COMICS	STREET AND SMITH PUBLICATIONS	3	1	12	1943	1944	
SUPER MAGICIAN COMICS	STREET AND SMITH PUBLICATIONS	4	1	12	1945	1946	
SUPER MAGICIAN COMICS	STREET AND SMITH PUBLICATIONS	5	1	8	1946	1947	
SUPER MARIO BROS., THE ADVENTURES OF	VALIANT / VOYAGER COMMUNICATIONS	1	1	5	1990	1991	
SUPER MARIO BROS., THE ADVENTURES OF	VALIANT / VOYAGER COMMUNICATIONS	2	1	5	1991	1991	
SUPER MARIO BROTHERS SPECIAL EDITION	VALIANT / VOYAGER COMMUNICATIONS		1	1	1990	1990	
SUPER MOUSE	ALAN CLASS AND CO LTD		1	1	1950	1950	CHARLTON REPRINTS
SUPER PICTURE SPECIAL	IPC		1	1	1969	1969	
SUPER POWERS	DC COMICS INC.	1	1	5	1984	1984	
SUPER POWERS	DC COMICS INC.	2	1	6	1985	1986	
SUPER POWERS	DC COMICS INC.	3	1	4	1986	1986	
SUPER PUP	AVON BOOKS		4	5	1954	1954	FORMERLY SPOTTY THE PUP
SUPER RABBIT	TIMELY COMICS		1	14	1944	1948	
SUPER RICHIE	HARVEY PUBLICATIONS		1	4	1975	1976	
SUPER SCIENCE THRILLS	INTERNATIONAL		1	1	1945	1945	
SUPER SMASHER COMIC	CO-ORDINATION PRESS		1	1	1947	1947	
SUPER SOLDIERS	MARVEL ENTERTAINMENT GROUP		1	8	1993	NOW	
SUPER SPY	CENTAUR PUBLICATIONS		1	2	1940	1940	
SUPER STAR	BERKELEY THOMSON/FORDWYCH		1	4	1949	1949	
SUPER STREAMLINE COMICS	STREAMLINE		1	1	1952	1952	US REPRINTS
SUPER TEAM FAMILY	DC COMICS INC.		1	15	1975	1978	
SUPER THRILL ALBUM	G.T. LIMITED		1	1	1959	1959	
SUPER VILLAINS: THE BADDEST OF THE BAD	WARRIOR PUBLISHING				1994	1994	
SUPER WESTERN COMICS	STREAMLINE		1	2	1951	1951	YOUTHFUL REPRINTS
SUPER WESTERN COMICS	YOUTHFUL MAGAZINES		1	4	1950	1951	
SUPER-BOOK OF COMICS	WESTERN PUBLISHING COMPANY	1	1	30	1944	1947	
SUPER-BOOK OF COMICS	WESTERN PUBLISHING COMPANY	2	1	30	1947	1948	
SUPER-BUMPER COMIC, THE	VALENTINE & SON		1	1	1948	1948	
SUPER-DOOPER COMICS	ABLE MANUFACTURING CO.		1	8	1946	1946	
SUPER-DUPER COMICS	CARTOON ART		1	20	1946	1950	
SUPER-HEROES BATTLE SUPER-GORILLAS	DC COMICS INC.		1	1	1976	1976	
SUPER-HEROES MONTHLY	LONDON EDITIONS MAGAZINES		1	19	1980	1982	
SUPER-HEROES PUZZLES AND GAMES	MARVEL ENTERTAINMENT GROUP		1	1	1979	1979	
SUPER-HEROES, THE	MARVEL ENTERTAINMENT GROUP		1	50	1975	1976	
SUPER-MYSTERY COMICS	ACE MAGAZINES	1	1	6	1940	1941	
SUPER-MYSTERY COMICS	ACE MAGAZINES	2	1	6	1941	1942	
SUPER-MYSTERY COMICS	ACE MAGAZINES	3	1	6	1942	1943	
SUPER-MYSTERY COMICS	ACE MAGAZINES	4	1	6	1944	1945	
SUPER-MYSTERY COMICS	ACE MAGAZINES	5	1	6	1945	1946	
SUPER-MYSTERY COMICS	ACE MAGAZINES	6	1	6	1946	1947	
SUPER-MYSTERY COMICS	ACE MAGAZINES	7	1	6	1947	1948	
SUPER-MYSTERY COMICS	ACE MAGAZINES	8	1	6	1948	1949	
SUPER-SONIC THE SUPER COMIC	MANS WORLD		12	17	1953	1954	
SUPERBABE	PERSONALITY COMICS		1	1	1992	1992	
SUPERBOY	DC COMICS INC.	1	1	258	1949	1979	"SUPERBOY & THE LEGION OF SUPER-HEROES" ISSUES NOS.231-258. BECOMES "LEGION OF SUPER-HEROES" WITH ISSUE NO.259 (JANUARY 1980)
SUPERBOY	DC COMICS INC.	2	1	2	1993	NOW	
SUPERBOY ANNUAL	DC COMICS INC.	1	1	1	1964	1964	
SUPERBOY SPECIAL	DC COMICS INC.		1	1	1992	1992	
SUPERBOY SPECTACULAR	DC COMICS INC.		1	1	1980	1980	
SUPERBOY THE COMIC BOOK	DC COMICS INC.		1	22	1990	1991	
SUPERBOY, THE NEW ADVENTURES OF	DC COMICS INC.		1	54	1980	1984	
SUPERCAR	GOLD KEY		1	4	1962	1963	

COMIC TITLE	PUBLISHER	Vol No.	Srt No.	End No.	Str. Year	End Year	COMMENTS
SUPERCAR (A LITTLE GOLDEN BOOK)	GOLDEN PRESS		1	1	1962	1962	
SUPERCAR ANNUAL	COLLINS		1961	1963	1961	1963	
SUPERCOLOURED COMIC ANNUAL, THE	T.V. BOARDMAN		1949	1951	1949	1951	
SUPERCOPS	NOW		1	8	1990	NOW	
SUPERFIRE COMIC	PHILIMAR		1	2	1949	1949	
SUPERGEAR COMICS	JACOBS CORP.		1	1	1976	1976	
SUPERGIRL	DC COMICS INC.		1	1	1993	1994	
SUPERGIRL	DC COMICS INC.	1	1	10	1972	1974	
SUPERGIRL	HIPPO BOOKS, DIVISION OF SCHOLASTIC BOOK SERVICES				1984	1984	
SUPERGIRL GIVEAWAY	DC COMICS INC.		1	1	1984	1986	
SUPERGIRL MOVIE ADAPTATION	DC COMICS INC.		1	1	1985	1985	
SUPERGIRL, THE DARING NEW ADVENTURES OF	DC COMICS INC.	2	1	23	1982	1983	
SUPERGIRL/TEAM LUTHOR SPECIAL	DC COMICS INC.		1	1	1992	1992	
SUPERHEROES ANNUAL	BROWN WATSON		1	1	1978	1978	
SUPERHEROES ANNUAL, THE	EGMONT		1	1	1982	1982	
SUPERHEROES GIANT SIZE	MARVEL ENTERTAINMENT GROUP		1	1	1974	1974	
SUPERHEROES VERSUS SUPERVILLAINS	ARCHIE PUBLICATIONS		1	1	1966	1966	
SUPERIOR STORIES	NESBIT PUBLISHING CO.		1	4	1955	1955	
SUPERMAN	DC COMICS INC.	1	1	423	1939	1986	
SUPERMAN	DC COMICS INC.	2	1	86	1987	NOW	
SUPERMAN	LONDON EDITIONS MAGAZINES		1	56	1988	NOW	
SUPERMAN & BATMAN MAGAZINE	DC COMICS INC.		1	3	1993	NOW	
SUPERMAN (UK)	LONDON EDITIONS MAGAZINES		1	56	1988	NOW	
SUPERMAN AND SPIDER-MAN	MARVEL ENTERTAINMENT GROUP		1	1	1982	1982	REPRINTS
SUPERMAN ANNUAL	DC COMICS INC.	1	1	13	1960	1986	
SUPERMAN ANNUAL	DC COMICS INC.	2	1	5	1987	NOW	
SUPERMAN ANNUAL	WORLD DISTRIBUTORS LTD		1951	1993	1951	NOW	
SUPERMAN ANTI-SMOKING BOOK	HEALTH EDUCATION COUNCIL		1	2	1981	1982	
SUPERMAN ARCHIVES	DC COMICS INC.		1	3	1989	NOW	
SUPERMAN FAMILY, THE	DC COMICS INC.		164	222	1974	1982	FORMERLY SUPERMAN'S PAL JIMMY OLSEN
SUPERMAN FOR EARTH	DC COMICS INC.		1	1	1991	1991	
SUPERMAN GALLERY	DC COMICS INC.		1	1	1993	1993	
SUPERMAN KELLOGGS GIVEAWAY	DC COMICS INC.		1	1	1954	1954	
SUPERMAN MEETS THE QUIK BUNNY	DC COMICS INC.		1	1	1987	1987	
SUPERMAN METROPOLIS EDITION, THE AMAZING WORLD OF	DC COMICS INC.		1	1	1973	1973	
SUPERMAN MINIATURE	DC COMICS INC.		1	3	1955	1955	
SUPERMAN MOVIE ADAPTATION	DC COMICS INC.		3	4	1983	1987	
SUPERMAN PIZZA HUT PREMIUM	DC COMICS INC.		1	1	1977	1977	
SUPERMAN POCKETBOOK	EGMONT		1	2	1978	???	
SUPERMAN PY-CO-PAY TOOTH POWDER GIVEAWAY	DC COMICS INC.		1	1	1942	1942	
SUPERMAN RADIO SHACK GIVEAWAYS	DC COMICS INC.		1	3	1980	1982	
SUPERMAN RECORD COMIC	DC COMICS INC.		1	1	1966	1966	
SUPERMAN SPECIAL	DC COMICS INC.	1	1	3	1983	1985	
SUPERMAN SPECIAL	DC COMICS INC.	2	1	1	1993	1993	
SUPERMAN SPECTACULAR	DC COMICS INC.		1	1	1982	1982	
SUPERMAN SPECTACULAR	LONDON EDITIONS MAGAZINES		1	1	1982	1982	DC SUPERHEROES PRESENTS
SUPERMAN VERSUS THE AMAZING SPIDER-MAN	DC COMICS INC.		1	2	1976	1976	
SUPERMAN WORKBOOK	DC COMICS INC.		1	1	1945	1945	
SUPERMAN'S BUDDY	DC COMICS INC.	1	1	1	1954	1954	WITH BOX AND COSTUME
SUPERMAN'S BUDDY	DC COMICS INC.	2	1	1	1954	1954	WITHOUT BOX AND COSTUME
SUPERMAN'S CHRISTMAS ADVENTURE	DC COMICS INC.		1940	1944	1940	1944	
SUPERMAN'S GIRL FRIEND LOIS LANE	DC COMICS INC.		1	137	1958	1974	
SUPERMAN'S GIRL FRIEND LOIS LANE ANNUAL	DC COMICS INC.		1	2	1962	1963	
SUPERMAN'S PAL JIMMY OLSEN	DC COMICS INC.		1	163	1954	1974	
SUPERMAN, DEATH OF	DC COMICS INC.		1	1	1993	1993	
SUPERMAN, LEGACY OF	DC COMICS INC.		1	1	1993	1993	
SUPERMAN, RETURN OF	DC COMICS INC.		1	1	1993	1993	
SUPERMAN, RETURN OF	TITAN BOOKS		1	1	1993	1993	
SUPERMAN, THE DEATH AND LIFE OF	BANTUM PUBLISHING		1	1	1993	1993	
SUPERMAN, WORLD WITHOUT	DC COMICS INC.		1	1	1993	1993	
SUPERMAN-TIM	DC COMICS INC.		1942	1950	1942	1950	
SUPERMAN/DOOMSDAY: HUNTER/PREY	DC COMICS INC.		1	3	1994	1994	
SUPERMAN: PANIC IN THE SKY	DC COMICS INC.		1	1	1993	1993	
SUPERMAN: SPEEDING BULLETS	DC COMICS INC.		1	1	1993	1993	
SUPERMAN: THE EARTH STEALERS	DC COMICS INC.		1	1	1988	1988	
SUPERMAN: THE MAN OF STEEL	DC COMICS INC.		1	30	1991	NOW	
SUPERMAN: THE MAN OF STEEL ANNUAL	DC COMICS INC.		1	2	1992	NOW	
SUPERMAN: THE SECRET YEARS	DC COMICS INC.		1	4	1985	1985	
SUPERMAN: UNDER A YELLOW SUN	DC COMICS INC.		1	1	1994	1994	
SUPERMOUSE	PINES		35	45	1956	1958	CONTINUED FROM STANDARD SERIES
SUPERMOUSE	STANDARD COMICS		1	34	1948	1955	
SUPERMOUSE GIANT SUMMER ISSUE	PINES		1	1	1958	1958	
SUPERMOUSE SUMMER HOLIDAY ISSUE	PINES		1	1	1957	1957	
SUPERNATURAL THRILLERS	MARVEL ENTERTAINMENT GROUP		1	15	1972	1975	
SUPERPATRIOT	IMAGE COMICS		1	4	1993	NOW	
SUPERRICHIE	HARVEY PUBLICATIONS		5	18	1976	1979	FORMERLY SUPER RICHIE
SUPERSNIPE COMICS	STREET AND SMITH PUBLICATIONS	1	6	12	1942	1943	FORMERLY ARMY AND NAVY
SUPERSNIPE COMICS	STREET AND SMITH PUBLICATIONS	2	1	12	1944	1945	
SUPERSNIPE COMICS	STREET AND SMITH PUBLICATIONS	3	1	12	1945	1946	
SUPERSNIPE COMICS	STREET AND SMITH PUBLICATIONS	4	1	12	1947	1948	
SUPERSNIPE COMICS	STREET AND SMITH PUBLICATIONS	5	1	1	1949	1949	
SUPERSPOOK	AJAX		4	4	1958	1958	FORMERLY FRISKY ANIMALS ON PARADE
SUPERSTARS GIANT SIZE	MARVEL ENTERTAINMENT GROUP		1	1	1974	1974	
SUPERTEAM FAMILY	DC COMICS INC.		1	15	1975	1978	
SUPERTHRILLER/SUPER THRILLER COMIC	WORLD DISTRIBUTORS LTD		5	33	1948	???	PREVIOUSLY THE THRILLER
SUPERVILLAIN CLASSICS	MARVEL ENTERTAINMENT GROUP		1	1	1983	1983	
SUPERVILLAIN TEAM UP	MARVEL ENTERTAINMENT GROUP		1	17	1975	1980	

COMIC TITLE	PUBLISHER	Vol No.	Srt No.	End No.	Str. Year	End Year	COMMENTS
SUPERVILLAIN TEAM UP GIANT SIZE	MARVEL ENTERTAINMENT GROUP		1	2	1975	1975	
SUPERWORLD COMICS	HUGO GERNSBACK		1	3	1940	1940	
SUPREME	IMAGE COMICS		1	9	1992	NOW	
SUPREMIE	PARODY PRESS		1	1	1992	1992	
SUPRISING ADVENTURES OF CLUMSY BOY CRUSOE	GRIFFIN & FARRON		1	1	1877	1877	
SURE-FIRE COMICS	ACE MAGAZINES		1	4	1940	1940	
SURF N' WHEELS	CHARLTON COMICS		1	6	1969	1969	
SURGE	ECLIPSE		1	4	1984	1985	
SURPRISE ADVENTURES	STERLING COMICS		3	5	1955	1955	FORMERLY TORMENTED
SURPRISE COMIC	PAGET		1	5	1948	1948	
SURVIVE	APPLE COMICS		1	1	1991	1991	
SURVIVORS, THE	PRELUDE		1	3	1986	1987	
SUSIE OF THE SUNDAY DESPATCH	ASSOCIATED NEWSPAPERS		1	1	1956	1956	
SUSPENSE	ATLAS		1	29	1949	1953	
SUSPENSE COMICS	CONTINENTAL PUBLICATIONS		1	12	1943	1946	
SUSPENSE DETECTIVE	FAWCETT PUBLICATIONS		1	5	1952	1953	
SUSPENSE MAGAZINE	CARTOON ART		1	1	1952	1952	MAGAZINE ENTERPRISES REPRINTS
SUSPENSE PICTURE LIBRARY HOLIDAY SPECIAL	IPC		1977	1981	1977	1981	
SUSPENSE STORIES	ALAN CLASS AND CO LTD		1	241	1963	1989	
SUZIE AND JONNIE, THE LAID BACK ADVENTURES OF	ANTONIO GURU		1	1	1981	1981	
SUZIE COMICS	ARCHIE PUBLICATIONS		49	100	1945	1954	FORMERLY LAUGH COMIX
SWAMP FOX, THE	WALT DISNEY		1	3	1960	1960	
SWAMP THING	DC COMICS INC.	1	1	24	1972	1976	
SWAMP THING ANNUAL	DC COMICS INC.	2	1	7	1982	NOW	
SWAMP THING, ROOTS OF THE	DC COMICS INC.		1	5	1986	1986	
SWAMP THING, THE SAGA OF	DC COMICS INC.	2	1	139	1982	NOW	
SWAMP THING: DARK GENESIS	DC COMICS INC.		1	1	1992	1992	
SWAMP THING: LOVE AFTER DEATH	DC COMICS INC.		1	1	1990	1990	
SWAMP THING: SAGA OF THE	DC COMICS INC.		1	1	1987	1989	
SWAT MALONE	SWAT MALONE ENTERPRISES		1	1	1955	1955	
SWEENEY	STANDARD COMICS		4	10	1949	1949	FORMERLY BUZ SAWYER
SWEET LOVE	HARVEY PUBLICATIONS		1	5	1949	1950	
SWEET ROMANCE	CHARLTON COMICS		1	1	1968	1968	
SWEET SIXTEEN	MARVEL ENTERTAINMENT GROUP		1	6	1991	1991	
SWEET SIXTEEN	PARENTS MAGAZINE INSTITUTE		1	13	1946	1948	
SWEET SIXTEEN BACK TO SCHOOL SPECIAL	MARVEL ENTERTAINMENT GROUP		1	1	1992	1992	
SWEETHEART DIARY	CHARLTON COMICS		32	65	1955	1962	CONTINUES FAWCETT SERIES
SWEETHEART DIARY	FAWCETT PUBLICATIONS		1	32	1949	1953	
SWEETHEARTS	CHARLTON COMICS		23	137	1954	1973	CONTINUED FROM FAWCETT SERIES
SWEETHEARTS	FAWCETT PUBLICATIONS		68	122	1948	1954	FORMERLY CAPTAIN MIDNIGHT
SWEETIE PIE	AJAX		1	15	1955	1957	
SWELL COMIC	P.M. PRODUCTIONS		1	2	1948	1949	
SWIFT	HULTON PRESS LTD		1	462	1954	1963	
SWIFT ANNUAL	HULTON PRESS LTD		1955	1963	1955	1963	
SWIFT ARROW	AJAX	1	1	5	1954	1954	
SWIFT ARROW	AJAX	2	1	3	1957	1957	
SWIFT ARROW	L. MILLER PUBLISHING COMPANY (UK)		1	4	1957	1957	AJAX REPRINTS
SWIFT ARROW'S GUNFIGHTERS	AJAX		4	4	1957	1957	FORMERLY SWIFT ARROW
SWIFT MORGAN	T.V. BOARDMAN		1	7	1948	1951	
SWIFT MORGAN SPACE COMIC	POPULAR		50	52	1953	1953	
SWIFTSURE	HARRIER		1	18	1985	1987	
SWING WITH SCOOTER	DC COMICS INC.		1	36	1966	1972	
SWORD OF FREEDOM	PEARSON		1	4	1959	1959	
SWORD OF SORCERY	DC COMICS INC.		1	5	1973	1973	
SWORD OF THE ATOM	DC COMICS INC.		1	4	1983	1983	
SWORD OF THE ATOM SPECIAL	DC COMICS INC.		1	3	1984	1988	
SWORDS OF HEAVEN, FLOWERS OF HELL	STAR PUBLICATIONS		1	1	1979	1979	HEAVY METAL REPRINTS
SWORDS OF SHAR-PEI	CALIBER PRESS		1	3	1991	1991	
SWORDS OF TEXAS	ECLIPSE		1	4	1987	1988	
SWORDS OF THE SWASHBUCKLERS	MARVEL ENTERTAINMENT GROUP		1	12	1985	1987	
SYPHONS	NOW		1	3	1994	1994	
SYPHONS	NOW		1	7	1986	1987	

T

COMIC TITLE	PUBLISHER	Vol No.	Srt No.	End No.	Str. Year	End Year	COMMENTS
T MINUS 1	RENEGADE PRESS		1	2	1988	1988	
T-MAN	QUALITY COMICS		1	38	1951	1956	
T-MAN FIGHTER OF CRIME	ARCHER/KING COMICS		1	6	1953	1953	QUALITY REPRINTS
T.H.E. CAT	DELL PUBLISHING COMPANY		1	4	1967	1967	
T.H.U.N.D.E.R. AGENTS	JC COMICS		1	2	1983	1984	
T.H.U.N.D.E.R. AGENTS	TOWER COMICS		1	20	1965	1969	
TAFFY COMICS	RURAL HOME PUBLISHING COMPANY		1	12	1945	1948	
TAILGUNNER JO	DC COMICS INC.		1	6	1988	1989	
TAILSPIN	SPOTLIGHT COMICS		1	1	1944	1944	
TAILSPIN TOMMY	CUPPLES AND LEON CO.		1	1	1932	1932	
TAILSPIN TOMMY	SERVICE PUBL. CO.		1	1	1946	1946	
TAILSPIN TOMMY	UNITED FEATURES SYNDICATE		23	23	1940	1940	
TAILSPIN TOMMY STORY & PICTURE BOOK	MCLOUGHLIN BROS.		266	266	1931	1931	
TAKEN UNDER	CALIBER PRESS		1	1	1992	1992	
TAKEN UNDER SPECIAL	CALIBER PRESS		1	1	1992	1992	
TALES CALCULATED TO DRIVE YOU BATS	ARCHIE PUBLICATIONS	1	1	7	1961	1966	
TALES CALCULATED TO DRIVE YOU BATS	ARCHIE PUBLICATIONS	2	1	1	1966	1966	
TALES FROM THE CRYPT	ARNOLD BOOK CO.		1	2	1952	1952	EC REPRINTS
TALES FROM THE CRYPT	EC COMICS	1	20	46	1950	1955	FORMERLY THE CRYPT OF TERROR
TALES FROM THE CRYPT	EERIE PUBLICATIONS		1	6	1968	1968	
TALES FROM THE CRYPT	GLADSTONE		1	7	1990	1991	
TALES FROM THE CRYPT	RUSS COCHRAN		1	4	1992	1992	

COMIC TITLE	PUBLISHER	Vol No.	Srt No.	End No.	Str. Year	End Year	COMMENTS
TALES FROM THE CRYPT: THE HAUNT OF FEAR	RUSS COCHRAN		1	5	1992	1992	
TALES FROM THE CRYPT: VAULT OF HORROR	RUSS COCHRAN		1	5	1992	1992	
TALES FROM THE EDGE	VANGUARD COMICS		1	1	1993	NOW	MATURE READERS
TALES FROM THE FRIDGE	H. BUNCH ASSOCIATES		1	1	1974	1974	KITCHEN SINK REPRINTS
TALES FROM THE GREAT BOOK	H. BUNCH ASSOCIATES		1	4	1955	1956	
TALES FROM THE HEART OF AFRICA - TEMPORARY NATIVES	MARVEL ENTERTAINMENT GROUP		1	1	1990	1990	
TALES FROM THE TOMB	DELL PUBLISHING COMPANY		1	1	1962	1962	
TALES FROM THE TOMB	EERIE PUBLICATIONS		1	33	1969	1975	
TALES FROM TROMAVILLE	WELSH PUBLICATIONS		1	1	1993	NOW	
TALES OF ACTION	ALAN CLASS AND CO LTD		1	2	50'S	50'S	US REPRINTS
TALES OF ASGARD	MARVEL ENTERTAINMENT GROUP	1	1	1	1968	1968	
TALES OF ASGARD	MARVEL ENTERTAINMENT GROUP	2	1	1	1984	1984	
TALES OF DEMON DICK & BUNKER BILL	WHITMAN		793	793	1934	1934	
TALES OF DREAD ALBUM	G.T. LIMITED		1	1	1959	1959	
TALES OF EVIL	ATLAS		1	3	1975	1975	
TALES OF G.I. JOE	MARVEL ENTERTAINMENT GROUP		1	15	1988	1989	
TALES OF HORROR	TOBY PRESS PUBLICATIONS		1	13	1952	1954	
TALES OF JUSTICE	ATLAS		53	67	1955	1957	
TALES OF LETHARGY	ALPHA PRODUCTIONS		3	3	1993	1993	
TALES OF ORDINARY MADNESS	DARK HORSE COMICS		1	4	1992	1992	
TALES OF SKITTLE-SHARPERS AND THIMBLE-RIGGERS	TO YIELD PRESS		1	3	1991	NOW	
TALES OF SUSPENSE	MARVEL ENTERTAINMENT GROUP		1	99	1959	1968	BECOMES CAPTAIN AMERICA #100
TALES OF TERROR	ECLIPSE		1	13	1985	1987	
TALES OF TERROR	EERIE PUBLICATIONS		1	1	1964	1964	
TALES OF TERROR	PORTMAN		1	3	1978	???	MARVEL REPRINTS
TALES OF TERROR	TOBY PRESS PUBLICATIONS		1	1	1952	1952	
TALES OF TERROR ANNUAL	EC COMICS		1	3	1951	1953	
TALES OF TERROR PICTURE LIBRARY	FAME PRESS		1	2	1966	???	
TALES OF THE BEANWORLD	ECLIPSE		1	20	1985	1991	
TALES OF THE GHOST CASTLE	DC COMICS INC.		1	3	1975	1975	
TALES OF THE GREEN BERET	DELL PUBLISHING COMPANY		1	5	1967	1969	
TALES OF THE GREEN HORNET	NOW	1	1	2	1991	1991	
TALES OF THE GREEN HORNET	NOW	2	1	8	1992	1992	
TALES OF THE GREEN HORNET	NOW	3	1	3	1992	1993	
TALES OF THE GREEN LANTERN CORPS, THE	DC COMICS INC.		1	3	1981	1981	
TALES OF THE KILLERS	WORLD FAMOUS PUBLICATIONS	1	10	11	1970	1971	
TALES OF THE LEGION OF SUPER-HEROES	DC COMICS INC.		314	354	1984	1987	FORMERLY "THE LEGION OF SUPER-HEROES"
TALES OF THE MARINES	ATLAS		4	4	1957	1957	FORMERLY DEVIL-DOG DUGAN
TALES OF THE MYSTERIOUS TRAVELER	CHARLTON COMICS	1	1	13	1956	1959	
TALES OF THE MYSTERIOUS TRAVELER	CHARLTON COMICS	2	14	15	1985	1985	
TALES OF THE MYSTERIOUS TRAVELLER	G.T. LIMITED		1	1	1959	1959	
TALES OF THE SUN RUNNERS	SIRIUS COMICS		1	3	1986	1987	
TALES OF THE SUPERNATURAL	ALAN CLASS AND CO LTD		1	1	1960	1960	US REPRINTS
TALES OF THE UNDERWORLD	ALAN CLASS AND CO LTD		1	5	1960	1960	CHARLTON REPRINTS
TALES OF THE UNEXPECTED	DC COMICS INC.		1	104	1956	1968	
TALES OF THE ZOMBIE	MARVEL ENTERTAINMENT GROUP	1	1	10	1973	1973	
TALES OF THE ZOMBIE	MARVEL ENTERTAINMENT GROUP	2	1	1	1974	1975	
TALES OF THE ZOMBIE ANNUAL	MARVEL ENTERTAINMENT GROUP		1	1	1975	1975	
TALES OF VOODOO	EERIE PUBLICATIONS	1	1	11	1968	1968	
TALES OF VOODOO	EERIE PUBLICATIONS	2	1	4	1969	1969	
TALES OF VOODOO	EERIE PUBLICATIONS	3	1	6	1970	1970	
TALES OF VOODOO	EERIE PUBLICATIONS	4	1	6	1971	1971	
TALES OF VOODOO	EERIE PUBLICATIONS	5	1	6	1972	1972	
TALES OF VOODOO	EERIE PUBLICATIONS	6	1	6	1973	1973	
TALES OF VOODOO	EERIE PUBLICATIONS	7	1	6	1974	1974	
TALES OF VOODOO ANNUAL	EERIE PUBLICATIONS		1	1	1970	1970	
TALES TO ASTONISH	MARVEL ENTERTAINMENT GROUP	1	1	101	1959	1968	BECOMES INCREDIBLE HULK #102
TALES TO ASTONISH	MARVEL ENTERTAINMENT GROUP	2	1	14	1979	1981	
TALES TOO TERRIBLE TO TELL	NEW ENGLAND COMICS		1	7	1990	NOW	
TALESPIN	WALT DISNEY		1	7	1992	1992	
TALESPIN, DISNEY'S	WALT DISNEY		1	4	1991	1991	
TALESPIN: SURPRISE IN THE SKIES	WALT DISNEY		1	1	1992	1992	
TALKING KOMICS	BELDA RECORD & PUBL. CO.		1	1	1947	1947	
TALKING TURKEY	GALAXY PUBLICATIONS		1	8	1991	1992	
TALLY-HO COMICS	SWAPPERS QUARTERLY		1	1	1944	1944	
TALOS OF THE WILDERNESS SEA	DC COMICS INC.		1	1	1987	1987	
TAMMY	IPC				1971	1984	
TANK GIRL	DARK HORSE COMICS		1	1	1992	1992	
TANK GIRL	DARK HORSE COMICS	1	1	4	1991	1991	
TANK GIRL	DARK HORSE COMICS	2	1	4	1993	1993	
TANK GIRL	PENGUIN BOOKS		1	1	1990	1990	
TANK GIRL II	DARK HORSE COMICS		1	1	1993	1993	
TAPPING THE VEIN	ECLIPSE		1	6	1990	NOW	
TARA: TEAM TARAGONIA	AC COMICS		1	1	1993	1993	
TARGET	TARGET PUBLICATIONS		1	176	1935	1938	
TARGET AND ROCKET	TARGET PUBLICATIONS		1	24	1938	1939	FORMERLY TARGET AND ROCKET
TARGET COMICS	L. MILLER PUBLISHING COMPANY (UK)		1	6	1952	1952	STAR REPRINTS
TARGET COMICS	STAR PUBLICATIONS		1	105	1940	1949	
TARGET WESTERN ROMANCES	STAR PUBLICATIONS		106	107	1949	1950	FORMERLY TARGET COMICS
TARGET: AIRBOY	ECLIPSE		1	1	1988	1988	
TARGET: THE CORRUPTORS	DELL PUBLISHING COMPANY		1	3	1962	1962	
TARGITT: MAN-STALKER	ATLAS		1	3	1975	1975	
TARZAN	DC COMICS INC.		207	258	1972	1977	CONTINUES GOLD KEY SERIES
TARZAN	DELL PUBLISHING COMPANY		1	131	1948	1962	
TARZAN	GOLD KEY		132	206	1962	1972	
TARZAN	MARVEL ENTERTAINMENT GROUP		1	29	1977	1979	
TARZAN ADVENTURES	WESTWORLD PUBLICATIONS		1	342	1951	1959	
TARZAN ANNUAL	DELL PUBLISHING COMPANY		2	7	1953	1958	FORMERLY TARZAN'S JUNGLE ANNUAL
TARZAN ANNUAL	MARVEL ENTERTAINMENT GROUP		1	3	1977	1979	

INDEX OF COMIC TITLES AND THEIR PUBLISHERS

COMIC TITLE	PUBLISHER	Vol No.	Srt No.	End No.	Str. Year	End Year	COMMENTS
TARZAN AUTUMN SPECIAL	BYBLOS		1979	1980	1979	1980	
TARZAN BOOK, THE ILLUSTRATED	GROSSET & DUNLOP		1	1	1929	1934	2 PRINTINGS
TARZAN BOOK, THE ILLUSTRATED	HOUSE OF GREYSTOKE		1	1	1967	1967	2 EDITIONS
TARZAN COMIC	DONALD PETERS		1	19	1950	1951	
TARZAN DIGEST	DC COMICS INC.		1	1	1972	1972	
TARZAN FAMILY, THE	DC COMICS INC.		60	66	1975	1976	FORMERLY KORAK, SON OF TARZAN
TARZAN LARGE FEATURE COMIC	UNITED FEATURES SYNDICATE		5	5	1939	1939	
TARZAN LORD OF THE JUNGLE	GOLD KEY		1	1	1965	1965	
TARZAN OF THE APES	METROPOLITAN PRINTING CO.		1	1	1934	1934	
TARZAN OF THE APES	TOP SELLERS	1	1	?	1970	1971	WESTERN PUBLISHING REPRINTS
TARZAN OF THE APES	TOP SELLERS	2	1	100	1971	1975	WESTERN PUBLISHING REPRINTS
TARZAN OF THE APES MOVIE ADAPTATION	MARVEL ENTERTAINMENT GROUP		1	2	1984	1984	
TARZAN OF THE APES SPECIAL SUPER ADVENTURE	WILLIAMS PUBLISHING		1	2	1972	1972	DELL REPRINTS
TARZAN OF THE APES TO COLOR	SAALFIELD PUBLISHING COMPANY		988	988	1933	1933	
TARZAN SPRING SPECIAL	BYBLOS		1980	1980	1980	1980	
TARZAN SUMMER SPECIAL	BYBLOS		1978	1981	1978	1981	
TARZAN WEEKLY	BYBLOS				1977	1977	NO NUMBERS, DATES ONLY RAN WEEKLY FOR 15 ISSUES
TARZAN WINTER SPECIAL	BYBLOS		1979	1981	1979	1981	
TARZAN WORLD ADVENTURE LIBRARY	WORLD DISTRIBUTORS LTD		1	4	1967	1967	WESTERN PUBLISHING REPRINTS
TARZAN: LOVES, LIES AND THE LOST CITY	MALIBU COMICS ENTERTAINMENT INC.		1	3	1992	1992	
TARZAN: THE BECKONING	MALIBU COMICS ENTERTAINMENT INC.		1	7	1992	1993	
TARZAN: THE WARRIOR	MALIBU COMICS ENTERTAINMENT INC.		1	5	1992	1992	
TARZAN'S JUNGLE ANNUAL	DELL PUBLISHING COMPANY		1	1	1952	1952	BECOMES TARZAN ANNUAL
TASMANIAN DEVIL & HIS TASTY FRIENDS	GOLD KEY		1	1	1962	1962	
TASTEE-FREEZ COMICS	HARVEY PUBLICATIONS		1	6	1957	1957	
TEAM AMERICA	MARVEL ENTERTAINMENT GROUP		1	12	1982	1983	
TEAM ANARCHY	DAGGER ENTERPRISES		1	3	1993	NOW	
TEAM HELIX	MARVEL ENTERTAINMENT GROUP		1	1	1983	1983	
TEAM TITANS	DC COMICS INC.		1	17	1992	NOW	
TEAM TITANS ANNUAL	DC COMICS INC.		1	1	1993	NOW	
TEAM YANKEE	FIRST		1	6	1989	1989	
TEAM YOUNGBLOOD	IMAGE COMICS		1	4	1993	NOW	
TECUMSEH!	ECLIPSE				1992	1992	
TEDDY ROOSEVELT & HIS ROUGH RIDERS	AVON BOOKS		1	1	1950	1950	
TEDDY TAIL AND THE CAVE MEN	ASSOCIATED NEWSPAPERS		1	1	1952	1952	
TEDDY TAIL AND THE GNOMES	ASSOCIATED NEWSPAPERS		1	1	1952	1952	
TEDDY TAIL AND THE MAGIC DRINK	ASSOCIATED NEWSPAPERS		1	1	1950	1950	
TEDDY TAIL AND THE PEARL THIEF	ASSOCIATED NEWSPAPERS		1	1	1950	1950	
TEDDY TAIL AT THE SEASIDE	A & C BLACK		1	1	1920	1920	
TEDDY TAIL GOES WEST	ASSOCIATED NEWSPAPERS		1	1	1951	1951	
TEDDY TAIL IN FAIRYLAND	A & C BLACK		1	1	1916	1916	
TEDDY TAIL IN HISTORYLAND	A & C BLACK		1	1	1917	1917	
TEDDY TAIL IN NURSERY RHYME LAND	A & C BLACK		1	1	1915	1915	
TEDDY TAIL IN TOYLAND	A & C BLACK		1	1	1922	1922	
TEDDY TAIL'S ADVENTURES IN THE A.B. SEA	A & C BLACK		1	1	1926	1926	
TEDDY TAIL'S ALPHABET	A & C BLACK		1	1	1921	1921	
TEDDY TAIL'S FAIRY TALE	A & C BLACK		1	1	1919	1919	
TEDDY TAIL'S FAIRY TALE AND IN BABYLAND	A & C BLACK		1	1	1921	1921	
TEDDY TAIL, ADVENTURES OF	A & C BLACK		1	1	1915	1915	
TEDDY TAIL: THE WILLOW PATTERN STORY	ASSOCIATED NEWSPAPERS		1	1	1951	1951	
TEE AND VEE CROSLEY IN TELEVISION LAND COMICS	CROSLEY DIVISION		1	1	1951	1951	
TEEN BEAM	DC COMICS INC.		2	2	1968	1968	FORMERLY TEEN BEAT
TEEN BEAT	DC COMICS INC.		1	1	1967	1967	
TEEN COMICS	MARVEL ENTERTAINMENT GROUP		21	35	1947	1950	FORMERLY ALL TEEN
TEEN CONFESSIONS	CHARLTON COMICS		1	97	1959	1976	
TEEN LIFE	QUALITY COMICS		3	5	1945	1945	FORMERLY YOUNG LIFE
TEEN ROMANCES	SUPER COMICS		10	17	1964	1964	REPRINTS
TEEN SECRET DIARY	CHARLTON COMICS	1	1	11	1959	1961	
TEEN SECRET DIARY	CHARLTON COMICS	2	1	1	1972	1972	
TEEN TITANS	DC COMICS INC.		1	53	1966	1978	
TEEN TITANS AND X-MEN - SEE MARVEL AND DC PRESENT							
TEEN TITANS ANNUAL, TALES OF THE	DC COMICS INC.	1	3	5	1984	1987	
TEEN TITANS SPOTLIGHT	DC COMICS INC.		1	21	1986	1988	
TEEN-AGE BRIDES	HARVEY PUBLICATIONS		1	7	1953	1954	
TEEN-AGE CONFIDENTIAL CONFESSIONS	CHARLTON COMICS		1	22	1960	1964	
TEEN-AGE DIARY SECRETS	ST JOHN PUBLISHING		4	9	1949	1950	FORMERLY BLUE RIBBON COMICS
TEEN-AGE LOVE	CHARLTON COMICS	2	4	96	1958	1973	FORMERLY INTIMATE
TEEN-AGE ROMANCE	MARVEL ENTERTAINMENT GROUP		77	86	1960	1962	
TEEN-AGE ROMANCES	ST JOHN PUBLISHING		1	45	1949	1955	
TEEN-AGE TALK	I.W. ENTERPRISES		1	9	1964	1964	REPRINTS
TEEN-AGE TEMPTATIONS	ST JOHN PUBLISHING		1	9	1952	1954	
TEEN-IN	TOWER COMICS		1	4	1968	1969	
TEENA	MAGAZINE ENTERPRISES		11	15	1948	1948	
TEENA	STANDARD COMICS		20	22	1949	1950	
TEENAGE HOTRODDERS	CHARLTON COMICS		1	24	1963	1967	
TEENAGE MUTANT N.T.: MARTIAL ARTS TRAINING MANUAL	SOLSON		1	4	1986	1986	
TEENAGE MUTANT NINJA TURTLES	ARCHIE PUBLICATIONS		1	54	1989	NOW	
TEENAGE MUTANT NINJA TURTLES	MIRAGE STUDIOS		1	62	1984	NOW	
TEENAGE MUTANT NINJA TURTLES	MIRAGE STUDIOS	2	1	2	1993	NOW'	
TEENAGE MUTANT NINJA TURTLES ADVENTURES	ARCHIE PUBLICATIONS		1	3	1988	1988	
TEENAGE MUTANT NINJA TURTLES ADVENTURES	NESPRAY		1	3	1988	1988	
TEENAGE MUTANT NINJA TURTLES ADVENTURES SPECIAL	ARCHIE PUBLICATIONS		1	4	1992	1992	
TEENAGE MUTANT NINJA TURTLES CHRISTMAS SPECIAL	MIRAGE STUDIOS		1	1	1990	1990	
TEENAGE MUTANT NINJA TURTLES CLASSICS DIGEST	ARCHIE PUBLICATIONS		1	4	1993	NOW	
TEENAGE MUTANT NINJA TURTLES I: MOVIE ADAPTATION	MIRAGE STUDIOS		1	1	1990	1990	

COMIC TITLE	PUBLISHER	Vol No.	Srt No.	End No.	Str. Year	End Year	COMMENTS
TEENAGE MUTANT NINJA TURTLES II: SECRET OF OOZE	ARCHIE PUBLICATIONS		1	1	1991	1991	
TEENAGE MUTANT NINJA TURTLES III: BACK IN TIME	ARCHIE PUBLICATIONS		1	1	1993	1993	
TEENAGE MUTANT NINJA TURTLES MEET ARCHIE	ARCHIE PUBLICATIONS		1	1	1991	1991	
TEENAGE MUTANT NINJA TURTLES MOVIE PARODY	MIRAGE STUDIOS				1990	1990	
TEENAGE MUTANT NINJA TURTLES PRESENTS APRIL O'NEIL	ARCHIE PUBLICATIONS		1	3	1993	1993	
TEENAGE MUTANT NINJA TURTLES SOURCEBOOK	ARCHIE PUBLICATIONS		1	2	1993	1993	
TEENAGE MUTANT NINJA TURTLES WINTER SPECIAL	ARCHIE PUBLICATIONS		1	1	1991	1991	
TEENAGE MUTANT NINJA TURTLES, HOW TO DRAW	SOLSON		1	1	1986	1986	
TEENAGE MUTANT NINJA TURTLES, TALES OF THE	MIRAGE STUDIOS		1	7	1987	1989	
TEENAGE MUTANT NINJA TURTLES/SAVAGE DRAGON	MIRAGE STUDIOS		1	1	1993	1993	
TEENAGE MUTANT NINJA TURTLES: DONATELLO	MIRAGE STUDIOS		1	1	1986	1986	
TEENAGE MUTANT NINJA TURTLES: HAUNTED PIZZA	MIRAGE STUDIOS		1	1	1992	1992	
TEENAGE MUTANT NINJA TURTLES: LEONARDO	MIRAGE STUDIOS		1	1	1986	1986	
TEENAGE MUTANT NINJA TURTLES: MERDUDE	ARCHIE PUBLICATIONS		1	2	1992	1992	
TEENAGE MUTANT NINJA TURTLES: MICHAELANGELO	MIRAGE STUDIOS		1	1	1986	1986	
TEENAGE MUTANT NINJA TURTLES: RAPHAEL	MIRAGE STUDIOS		1	1	1985	1985	
TEENAGE MUTANT NINJA TURTLES: THE MALTESE TURTLE	MIRAGE STUDIOS		1	1	1993	1993	
TEENAGE MUTANT NINJA TURTLES/CONSERVATION CORPS	ARCHIE PUBLICATIONS		1	1	1992	1992	
TEENAGENTS	TOPPS		1	3	1993	NOW	
TEENIE WEENIES, THE	ZIFF-DAVIS PUBLISHING COMPANY		10	11	1950	1951	
TEEPEE TIM	AMERICAN COMIC GROUP		100	102	1955	1955	FORMERLY HA-HA COMICS
TEGRA JUNGLE EMPRESS	FOX FEATURES SYNDICATE		1	1	1948	1948	
TEKQ	CALIBER PRESS		1	4	1992	1993	
TEKWORLD, WILLIAM SHATNER'S	MARVEL ENTERTAINMENT GROUP		1	18	1992	NOW	
TELEVISION COMICS	STANDARD COMICS		5	8	1950	1950	
TELEVISION FAVOURITES COMIC	WORLD DISTRIBUTORS LTD		1	18	1958	1959	DELL REPRINTS
TELEVISION PUPPET SHOW	AVON BOOKS		1	2	1950	1950	
TELL IT TO THE MARINES	I.W. ENTERPRISES		1	9	1955	1955	REPRINTS
TELL IT TO THE MARINES	TOBY PRESS PUBLICATIONS		1	15	1952	1955	
TELL ME DARK	DC COMICS INC.		1	1	1993	1993	
TEMPERED STEELE SPECTACULAR	SKY COMICS		1	1	1994	1994	
TEMPUS FUGITIVE	DC COMICS INC.		1	4	1990	1991	
TEN STORY LOVE	ACE PERIODICALS		177	209	1951	1956	FORMERLY TEN STORY LOVE MAGAZINE
TEN YEARS OF LOVE AND ROCKETS	FANTAGRAPHICS		1	1	1993	1993	
TENDER LOVE STORIES	SKYWALD PUBLISHING		1	4	1971	1971	
TENDER ROMANCE	KEY PUBLICATIONS		1	2	1953	1954	
TENNESSEE JED	FOX FEATURES SYNDICATE		1	1	1945	1945	
TENNIS FOR SPEED, STAMINA, STRENGTH, SKILL	TENNIS EDUCATIONAL FOUNDATION		1	1	1956	1956	
TENSE SUSPENSE	FAGO PUBLICATIONS		1	2	1958	1959	
TERMINAL DRIFT	NEOTEK ICONOGRAPHY		1	3	1993	1993	
TERMINAL POINT	DARK HORSE COMICS		1	3	1992	1993	
TERMINATOR	NOW		1	17	1988	1989	
TERMINATOR 2	MARVEL ENTERTAINMENT GROUP		1	1	1991	1991	
TERMINATOR 2	MARVEL ENTERTAINMENT GROUP		1	3	1991	1991	
TERMINATOR, THE	DARK HORSE COMICS		1	1	1991	1991	
TERMINATOR, THE	DARK HORSE COMICS		1	17	1991	1993	
TERMINATOR, THE	TRIDENT		1	10	1991	1992	
TERMINATOR: ALL MY FUTURES PAST, THE	NOW		1	2	1990	1990	
TERMINATOR: ENDGAME	DARK HORSE COMICS		1	1	1993	1993	
TERMINATOR: ENDGAME, THE	DARK HORSE COMICS		1	3	1992	1992	
TERMINATOR: HUNTERS AND KILLERS	DIAMOND PUBLICATIONS		1	1	1993	1993	STAR SYSTEM EDITION
TERMINATOR: HUNTERS AND KILLERS, THE	DARK HORSE COMICS		1	3	1992	1992	
TERMINATOR: SECONDARY OBJECTIVES, THE	DARK HORSE COMICS		1	1	1992	1992	
TERMINATOR: SECONDARY OBJECTIVES, THE	DARK HORSE COMICS		1	4	1991	1991	
TERMINATOR: TEMPEST, THE	DARK HORSE COMICS		1	1	1991	1991	
TERMINATOR: TEMPEST, THE	DARK HORSE COMICS		1	4	1990	1990	
TERMINATOR: THE BURNING EARTH, THE	NOW		1	1	1990	1990	
TERMINATOR: THE BURNING EARTH, THE	NOW		1	5	1990	1990	
TERMINATOR: THE ENEMY WITHIN, THE	DARK HORSE COMICS		1	1	1992	1992	
TERMINATOR: THE ENEMY WITHIN, THE	DARK HORSE COMICS		1	4	1991	1992	
TERRARISTS	MARVEL ENTERTAINMENT GROUP		1	4	1993	1993	
TERRIBLE TEN, THE	YOUNG WORLD		11	23	1964	1964	
TERRIFIC	ODHAMS		1	43	1967	1968	MARVEL REPRINTS
TERRIFIC ANNUAL	ODHAMS		1	1	1969	1969	
TERRIFIC COMICS	COMIC MEDIA/ALAN HARDY ASSOCIATE		14	16	1954	1955	FORMERLY HORRIFIC
TERRIFIC COMICS	CONTINENTAL PUBLICATIONS		1	6	1944	1944	
TERRIFYING TALES	STAR PUBLICATIONS		11	15	1953	1954	FORMERLY STARTLING TERROR TALES
TERROR ILLUSTRATED	EC COMICS		1	2	1955	1956	
TERROR INC.	MARVEL ENTERTAINMENT GROUP		1	13	1992	1993	
TERROR TALES	EERIE PUBLICATIONS	1	7	11	1969	1969	
TERROR TALES	EERIE PUBLICATIONS	2	1	6	1970	1970	
TERROR TALES	EERIE PUBLICATIONS	3	1	6	1971	1971	
TERROR TALES	EERIE PUBLICATIONS	4	1	7	1972	1972	
TERROR TALES	EERIE PUBLICATIONS	5	1	6	1973	1973	
TERROR TALES	EERIE PUBLICATIONS	6	1	6	1974	1974	
TERROR TALES	EERIE PUBLICATIONS	7	1	4	1976	1976	
TERROR TALES	EERIE PUBLICATIONS	8	1	3	1977	1977	
TERRORS OF THE JUNGLE	STAR PUBLICATIONS	1	17	21	1952	1954	FORMERLY JUNGLE THRILLS
TERRORS OF THE JUNGLE	STAR PUBLICATIONS	2	4	10	1953	1954	
TERRY AND THE PIRATES	CHARLTON COMICS		26	28	1955	1955	
TERRY AND THE PIRATES	HARVEY PUBLICATIONS		3	26	1947	1951	
TERRY BEARS COMICS	ST JOHN PUBLISHING		1	3	1952	1952	
TERRY-TOON GIANT SUMMER FUN BOOK ANNUAL	PINES		101	102	1957	1958	
TERRY-TOONS COMICS	ST JOHN PUBLISHING	1	60	86	1947	1951	FORMERLY BEST WESTERN
TERRY-TOONS COMICS	ST JOHN PUBLISHING	2	1	9	1952	1953	
TERRY-TOONS COMICS	TIMELY COMICS		1	86	1942	1947	
TERRYTOONS, THE TERRY BEARS	PINES		4	4	1958	1958	FORMERLY TERRY BEARS

COMIC TITLE	PUBLISHER	Vol No.	Srt No.	End No.	Str. Year	End Year	COMMENTS
TESSIE THE TYPIST	TIMELY COMICS		1	23	1944	1949	
TEX AUSTIN	L. MILLER PUBLISHING COMPANY (UK)		1	3	1959	1959	US REPRINTS
TEX DAWSON, GUN-SLINGER	MARVEL ENTERTAINMENT GROUP		1	1	1973	1973	
TEX FARRELL	D.S. PUBLISHING CO.		1	1	1948	1948	
TEX GRANGER	PARENTS MAGAZINE INSTITUTE		18	24	1948	1949	FORMERLY CALLING ALL BOYS
TEX MORGAN	MARVEL ENTERTAINMENT GROUP		1	9	1948	1950	
TEX RITTER WESTERN	CHARLTON COMICS		21	46	1954	1959	
TEX RITTER WESTERN	FAWCETT PUBLICATIONS		1	20	1950	1954	
TEX RITTER WESTERN	L. MILLER PUBLISHING COMPANY (UK)		50	99	1951	1959	FAWCETT REPRINTS
TEX TAYLOR	MARVEL ENTERTAINMENT GROUP		1	9	1948	1950	
TEX WILLER	TOP SELLERS		1	2	1971	???	
TEXAN, THE	PEMBERTON		1	8	1951	1951	ST. JOHN REPRINTS
TEXAN, THE	ST JOHN PUBLISHING		1	10	1948	1951	
TEXAS CHAINSAW MASSACRE	NORTHSTAR		1	3	1992	1992	
TEXAS KID	ATLAS		1	10	1951	1952	
TEXAS KID COMICS	THORPE & PORTER		1	2	1952	1952	ATLAS REPRINTS
TEXAS RANGERS IN ACTION	CHARLTON COMICS		5	79	1956	1970	FORMERLY CAPTAIN GALLANT
TEXAS RANGERS IN ACTION	L. MILLER PUBLISHING COMPANY (UK)		1	16	1959	1959	CHARLTON REPRINTS
THANE OF BAGARTH	CHARLTON COMICS		24	25	1985	1985	
THANOS QUEST, THE	MARVEL ENTERTAINMENT GROUP		1	2	1990	1990	
THARG THE MIGHTY'S DATABASE	FLEETWAY		1	1	1991	1991	
THAT THE WORLD MAY BELIEVE	CAETECHETICAL EDUCATIONAL SOCIETY				???	???	
THAT WILKIN BOY	ARCHIE PUBLICATIONS		1	52	1969	1982	
THAT'S MY POP! GOES NUTS FOR FAIR	BYSTANDER PRESS		1	1	1939	1939	
THEO DRAK DETECTIVE	L. MILLER PUBLISHING COMPANY (UK)		1	1	1959	1959	
THEY RING THE BELL	FOX FEATURES SYNDICATE		1	1	1946	1946	
THIMBLE THEATRE STARRING POPEYE	SONNET PUBLISHING CO.		1	2	1931	1932	
THIMK	COUNTERPOINT		1	6	1958	1959	
THING FROM ANOTHER WORLD, THE	DARK HORSE COMICS		1	2	1991	1992	
THING FROM ANOTHER WORLD: CLIMATE OF FEAR, THE	DARK HORSE COMICS		1	1	1993	1993	
THING FROM ANOTHER WORLD: CLIMATE OF FEAR, THE	DARK HORSE COMICS		1	4	1992	1992	
THING FROM ANOTHER WORLD: ETERNAL VOWS	DARK HORSE COMICS		1	3	1993	1994	
THING IS BIG BEN, THE	MARVEL ENTERTAINMENT GROUP		1	18	1984	1984	
THING!, THE	CHARLTON COMICS		1	18	1952	1954	
THING, THE	MARVEL ENTERTAINMENT GROUP		1	36	1983	1986	
THING, THE: PROJECT PEGASUS SAGA	MARVEL ENTERTAINMENT GROUP		1	1	1989	1989	
THIRD WORLD WAR	FLEETWAY		1	6	1990	1991	
THIRTEEN (GOING ON EIGHTEEN)	DELL PUBLISHING COMPANY		1	29	1961	1971	
THIRTEEN GOING ON 18	DELL PUBLISHING COMPANY		1	29	1962	1971	
THIRTEEN O'CLOCK	DARK HORSE COMICS		1	1	1992	1992	
THIRTY SECONDS OVER TOYKO	DAVID MCKAY PUBLICATIONS		1	1	1943	1943	
THIS IS SUSPENSE!	CHARLTON COMICS		23	26	1955	1955	FORMERLY STRANGE SUSPENSE STORIES
THIS IS WAR	STANDARD COMICS		5	9	1952	1953	
THIS MAGAZINE IS CRAZY	CHARLTON COMICS		2	8	1957	1959	
THIS MAGAZINE IS HAUNTED	CHARLTON COMICS	1	15	21	1954	1954	
THIS MAGAZINE IS HAUNTED	CHARLTON COMICS	2	12	16	1957	1958	FORMERLY ZAZA THE MYSTIC
THIS MAGAZINE IS HAUNTED	FAWCETT PUBLICATIONS	1	1	14	1951	1953	
THOR BALLAD OF BETA RAY BILL, THE	MARVEL ENTERTAINMENT GROUP		1	1	1993	1993	
THOR CORPS	MARVEL ENTERTAINMENT GROUP		1	4	1993	1993	
THOR, THE MIGHTY	MARVEL ENTERTAINMENT GROUP		126	471	1966	NOW	FORMERLY JOURNEY INTO MYSTERY
THOR, THE MIGHTY ANNUAL	MARVEL ENTERTAINMENT GROUP		2	18	1966	NOW	FORMERLY JOURNEY INTO MYSTERY ANNUAL
THOR, THE MIGHTY GIANT SIZE	MARVEL ENTERTAINMENT GROUP		1	1	1975	1975	
THOR: ALONE AGAINST THE CELESTIALS	MARVEL ENTERTAINMENT GROUP		1	1	1992	1992	
THOR: I, WHOM THE GODS WOULD DESTROY	MARVEL ENTERTAINMENT GROUP		1	1	1987	1987	
THORR-SVERD SWORD OF THOR	VINCENT		1	3	1987	1987	
THREAT	FANTAGRAPHICS		1	10	1985	1987	
THREE CHEERS COMIC	LEWIS-KING PUBLICATIONS		1	1	1946	1946	
THREE COMICS	PENNY KING CO.		1	4	1944	1944	
THREE DIMENSION COMICS	MONTHLY MAGAZINES		1	2	1953	1953	ST. JOHN REPRINTS OLD MIGHTY MOUSE STORIES IN 3-D
THREE DIMENSION COMICS STARRING THE THREE STOOGES	ST JOHN PUBLISHING		2	3	1953	1953	3-D
THREE DIMENSIONAL ALIEN WORLDS	PACIFIC COMICS		1	1	1984	1984	
THREE DIMENSIONAL DNAGENTS	ECLIPSE		1	1	1986	1986	
THREE DIMENSIONAL EC CLASSICS	EC COMICS		1	1	1954	1954	
THREE DIMENSIONAL SEDUCTION OF THE INNOCENT	ECLIPSE		1	2	1985	1986	
THREE DIMENSIONAL TALES FROM THE CRYPT OF TERROR	EC COMICS		1	1	1954	1954	
THREE MOUSKETEERS, THE	DC COMICS INC.	1	1	26	1956	1960	
THREE MOUSKETEERS, THE	DC COMICS INC.	2	1	7	1970	1971	
THREE MUSKETEERS	MARVEL ENTERTAINMENT GROUP		1	2	1993	1993	
THREE NURSES	CHARLTON COMICS		18	23	1963	1964	FORMERLY CONFIDENTIAL DIARY
THREE RASCALS	I.W. ENTERPRISES		1	10	1958	1963	REPRINTS
THREE RING COMICS	SPOTLIGHT COMICS		1	1	1945	1945	
THREE STOOGES	DELL PUBLISHING COMPANY		6	55	1961	1962	
THREE STOOGES	GOLD KEY		10	55	1962	1972	
THREE STOOGES IN 3-D	ECLIPSE		1	3	1986	1987	
THREE STOOGES IN COLOUR	HELNIT PUBLISHING COMPANIES		1	1	1992	1992	
THREE STOOGES, THE	MALIBU COMICS ENTERTAINMENT INC.		1	1	1991	1991	
THREE WESTERNERS	CARTOON ART		1	4	1951	1951	US REPRINTS
THREE-DIMENSION ADVENTURES (SUPERMAN)	DC COMICS INC.				1953	1953	
THRILL COMICS	GERALD SWAN		1	35	1940	1950	
THRILL COMICS SPECIAL	GERALD SWAN		1943	1943	1943	1943	
THRILL COMICS SPRING SPECIAL	GERALD SWAN		1942	1942	1942	1942	
THRILL COMICS SUMMER SPECIAL	GERALD SWAN		1941	1941	1941	1941	
THRILL-O-RAMA	HARVEY PUBLICATIONS		1	3	1965	1966	
THRILLER	DC COMICS INC.		1	12	1983	1984	

COMIC TITLE	PUBLISHER	Vol No.	Srt No.	End No.	Str. Year	End Year	COMMENTS
THRILLER	WORLD DISTRIBUTORS LTD		1	2	1970	???	
THRILLER COMICS	AMALGAMATED PRESS		1	162	1951	???	
THRILLER PICTURE LIBRARY	FLEETWAY		163	45	???	1963	FORMERLY THRILLER COMICS
THRILLER, THE	FOLDES PRESS		1	4	1946	1947	
THRILLING ADVENTURE STORIES	ATLAS		1	2	1975	1975	
THRILLING ADVENTURES IN STAMPS COMICS	STAMP COMICS		8	8	1953	1953	FORMERLY STAMP COMICS
THRILLING COMICS	STANDARD COMICS		1	80	1940	1951	
THRILLING CRIME CASES	STAR PUBLICATIONS		41	49	1950	1952	FORMERLY 4MOST
THRILLING HERO	MANS WORLD		16	19	1953	1953	
THRILLING ROMANCES	STANDARD COMICS		5	26	1949	1954	
THRILLING TRUE STORY OF THE BASEBALL	FAWCETT PUBLICATIONS		1	1	1952	1952	
THRILLOGY	PACIFIC COMICS		1	1	1984	1984	
THRILLS	R.C. PATE		1	1	1945	1945	
THRILLS AND FUN COMIC	MARTIN & REID		1	1	1944	1944	
THRILLS OF TOMORROW	HARVEY PUBLICATIONS		17	20	1954	1955	FORMERLY TOMB OF TERROR
THRRP!	KNOCKABOUT		1	1	1987	1987	
THUMBSCREWS	CALIBER PRESS		1	3	1992	1993	
THUN'DA KING OF THE CONGO	MAGAZINE ENTERPRISES		1	1	1952	1953	
THUN'DA TALES	FANTAGRAPHICS		1	1	1987	1987	
THUNDER	IPC		1	22	1970	1971	
THUNDER ACTION	SAVOY ADULT GRAPHICS		1	4	1986	1987	
THUNDER COMICS	STREAMLINE		1	1	1951	1951	FICTION HOUSE REPRINTS
THUNDERBIRDS ANNUAL	CITY		1966	1970	1966	1970	
THUNDERBIRDS ANNUAL	GRAND DREAMS		1992	1994	1992	1994	
THUNDERBIRDS ANNUAL	PURNELL		1972	1972	1972	1972	
THUNDERBIRDS ARE GO	FLEETWAY		1	1	1992	1992	
THUNDERBIRDS EXTRA	CITY		1	1	1966	1966	
THUNDERBIRDS HOLIDAY SPECIAL	FLEETWAY		1992	1992	1992	1992	
THUNDERBIRDS IN SPACE	RAVETTE BOOKS		1	1	1992	1992	
THUNDERBIRDS POSTER MAGAZINE	FLEETWAY		1	5	1992	1992	
THUNDERBIRDS SPECIAL	POLYSTYLE		1971	1984	1971	1984	
THUNDERBIRDS TELEVISION STORYBOOK	PBS		1	1	1966	1966	
THUNDERBIRDS THE COLLECTION	FLEETWAY		1	1	1992	1992	
THUNDERBIRDS THE COMIC	FLEETWAY		1	59	1991	NOW	
THUNDERBIRDS TO THE RESCUE	RAVETTE BOOKS		1	1	1992	1992	
THUNDERBIRDS: DANGER ZONE	RAVETTE BOOKS		1	1	1992	1992	
THUNDERBOLT	CHARLTON COMICS		1	60	1966	1967	
THUNDERBOLT	MODERN COMICS		57	58	1977	1977	REPRINTS
THUNDERBUNNY	RED CIRCLE		1	1	1984	1984	
THUNDERBUNNY	WARP GRAPHICS		1	2	1985	1985	
THUNDERCATS	MARVEL ENTERTAINMENT GROUP		1	24	1985	1988	
THUNDERCATS (U.K.)	MARVEL ENTERTAINMENT GROUP		1	129	1989	1991	
THUNDERSAUR	INNOVATION		1	1	1991	1991	
THUNDERSTRIKE	MARVEL ENTERTAINMENT GROUP		1	5	1993	NOW	
TIC TAC TOE COMICS	PEMBERTON		1	1	1951	1951	
TICK SPECIAL EDITION, THE	NEW ENGLAND COMICS		1	2	1988	1988	
TICK TOCK COMICS	MAGAZINE ENTERPRISES		1	33	1946	1951	
TICK'S GIANT CIRCUS OF THE MIGHTY, THE	NEW ENGLAND COMICS		1	2	1992	1992	
TICK, THE	NEW ENGLAND COMICS		1	12	1988	NOW	
TICKLE COMICS	MODERN STORE PUBLISHING		1	1	1955	1955	
TIGER	CHARLTON COMICS		1	6	1970	1971	
TIGER	IPC		1	1565	1954	1985	
TIGER ANNUAL	FLEETWAY		1957	1987	1957	1987	
TIGER GIRL	CARTOON ART		1	1	1950	1950	FICTION HOUSE REPRINTS
TIGER GIRL	GOLD KEY		1	1	1968	1968	
TIGER HOLIDAY SPECIAL	IPC		1971	1976	1971	1976	
TIGER SPORTS LIBRARY	FLEETWAY		1	12	1961	1961	
TIGER TIM'S TALES	AMALGAMATED PRESS		1	28	1919	1920	
TIGER TIM'S WEEKLY	AMALGAMATED PRESS	1	1	94	1920	1921	FORMERLY TIGER TIM'S TALES
TIGER TIM'S WEEKLY	AMALGAMATED PRESS	2	1	965	1921	1940	
TIGER-X	ETERNITY	1	1	3	1988	1989	
TIGER-X	ETERNITY	2	1	4	1989	1990	
TIGERMAN	ATLAS		1	3	1975	1975	
TIGRESS	HEROIC PUBLISHING		1	5	1992	NOW	
TILLIE THE TOILER ANNUAL	CUPPLES AND LEON CO.		1	8	1925	1933	
TILLY AND TED TINKERTOTLAND	W.T. GRANT COMPANY		1	1	1945	1945	
TIM	TIM STORES		1	4	1950	1950	FORMERLY SUPERMAN-TIM
TIM HOLT	CARTOON ART		1	4	1952	1952	MAGAZINE ENTERPRISE REPRINTS
TIM HOLT	MAGAZINE ENTERPRISES		1	41	1948	1954	
TIM HOLT	UNITED-ANGLO PRODUCTIONS		1	4	1953	1953	MAGAZINE ENTERPRISES REPRINTS
TIM HOLT	WORLD DISTRIBUTORS LTD		1	24	1953	1954	MAGAZINE ENTERPRISES REPRINTS
TIM HOLT WESTERN ANNUAL	AC COMICS		1	1	1992	1992	
TIM IN SPACE	TIM STORES		1	1	1950	1950	FORMERLY GENE AUTRY TIM
TIM MCCOY	CHARLTON COMICS		16	21	1948	1949	FORMERLY ZOO FUNNIES
TIM MCCOY, POLICE CAR 17	WHITMAN		674	674	1934	1934	
TIM TOMORROW	TIM STORES		1	1	1951	1951	FORMERLY TIM IN SPACE
TIM TYLER	BETTER PUBLICATIONS		1	1	1942	1942	
TIM TYLER COWBOY	STANDARD COMICS		11	18	1948	1950	
TIMBER WOLF	DC COMICS INC.		1	5	1992	1993	
TIME 2: THE EPIPHANY	FIRST				1986	1986	
TIME 2: THE SATISFACTION OF BLACK MARIAH	FIRST				1987	1987	
TIME BANDITS	MARVEL ENTERTAINMENT GROUP		1	1	1992	1992	
TIME BEAVERS	FIRST		1	1	1985	1985	
TIME FOR LOVE	CHARLTON COMICS		1	47	1967	1976	
TIME FOR LOVE	CHARLTON COMICS	2	53	53	1966	1966	FORMERLY ROMANTIC SECRETS
TIME GATES	DOUBLE EDGE PUBLISHING		1	4	1991	1991	
TIME JUMP WAR, THE	APPLE COMICS		1	3	1991	1991	
TIME KILLERS	FLEETWAY		1	7	1993	NOW	
TIME MACHINE, THE	ETERNITY		1	3	1990	1990	
TIME MASTER	CONTINUITY COMICS		1	1	1993	NOW	

INDEX OF COMIC TITLES AND THEIR PUBLISHERS

COMIC TITLE	PUBLISHER	Vol No.	Srt No.	End No.	Str. Year	End Year	COMMENTS
TIME MASTERS	DC COMICS INC.		1	8	1990	1990	
TIME TUNNEL, THE	GOLD KEY		1	2	1967	1967	
TIME TWISTERS	FLEETWAY		1	21	1987	1989	
TIME WARP	DC COMICS INC.		1	5	1979	1980	
TIMEDRIFTER	INNOVATION		1	3	1990	1990	
TIMESPIRITS	MARVEL ENTERTAINMENT GROUP		1	8	1985	1986	
TIMESTRYKE	MARVEL ENTERTAINMENT GROUP		1	1	1993	1994	MARVEL UK TITLE
TIMMY THE TIMID GHOST	CHARLTON COMICS	1	3	45	1956	1966	FORMERLY WIN-A-PRIZE
TIMMY THE TIMID GHOST	CHARLTON COMICS	2	1	26	1967	1986	
TINA	FLEETWAY		1	30	1967	1967	
TINTIN AND THE BLUE ORANGES	METHUEN & CO LTD		1	1	1967	1967	
TINTIN AND THE GOLDEN FLEECE	METHUEN & CO LTD		1	1	1965	1965	
TINTIN IN THE LAND OF THE SOVIETS	METHUEN & CO LTD		1	1	1989	1989	
TINTIN IN TIBET	METHUEN & CO LTD		1	1	1962	1962	
TINTIN, THE MAKING OF	METHUEN & CO LTD		1	2	1983	1985	
TINTIN: CIGARS OF THE PHARAOH	MAMMOTH				1971	1971	
TINTIN: FLIGHT 714	MAMMOTH				1968	1968	
TINTIN: IN AMERICA	MAMMOTH				1978	1978	
TINTIN: KING OTTOKAR'S SCEPTRE	MAMMOTH				1958	1958	
TINTIN: LAND OF THE BLACK GOLD	MAMMOTH				1972	1972	
TINTIN: PRISONERS OF THE SUN	METHUEN & CO LTD		1	1	1962	1962	
TINTIN: RED RACKHAM'S TREASURE	MAMMOTH				1959	1959	
TINTIN: RED SEA SHARKS AFFAIR	MAMMOTH				1960	1960	
TINTIN: SECRET OF THE UNICORN	MAMMOTH				1959	1959	
TINTIN: THE BLACK ISLAND	METHUEN & CO LTD		1	1	1966	1966	
TINTIN: THE BLUE LOTUS	METHUEN & CO LTD		1	1	1983	1983	
TINTIN: THE BROKEN EAR	MAMMOTH				1975	1975	
TINTIN: THE CALCULUS	MAMMOTH				1960	1960	
TINTIN: THE CASTAFIORE EMERALD	METHUEN & CO LTD		1	1	1963	1963	
TINTIN: THE CRAB WITH THE GOLDEN CLAWS	MAMMOTH				1958	1958	
TINTIN: THE CRAB WITH THE GOLDEN CLAWS	METHUEN & CO LTD		1	1	1959	1959	
TINTIN: THE LAKE OF SHARKS	MAMMOTH				1973	1973	
TINTIN: THE PICARDS	MAMMOTH				1976	1976	
TINTIN: THE SEVEN CRYSTAL BALLS	MAMMOTH				1959	1959	
TINTIN: THE SEVEN CRYSTAL BALLS	METHUEN & CO LTD		1	1	1962	1962	
TINTIN: THE SHOOTING STAR	MAMMOTH				1961	1961	
TINY COMIC	P.M. PRODUCTIONS		1	1	1945	1945	
TINY TESSIE	MARVEL ENTERTAINMENT GROUP		24	24	1949	1949	FORMERLY TESSIE
TINY TOON ADVENTURES	DC COMICS INC.		1	5	1990	1991	
TINY TOT COMICS	EC COMICS		1	10	1946	1947	
TINY TOT FUNNIES	HARVEY PUBLICATIONS		9	9	1951	1951	FORMERLY FAMILY FUNNIES
TINY TOTS	AMALGAMATED PRESS		1	1334	1927	1959	
TINY TOTS COMICS	DELL PUBLISHING COMPANY		1	2	1943	1943	
TIP TOP	AMALGAMATED PRESS		1	727	1934	1954	
TIP TOP COMICS	DELL PUBLISHING COMPANY		211	225	1957	1961	
TIP TOP COMICS	L. MILLER PUBLISHING COMPANY (UK)		1	2	1940	1941	UNITED FEATURES REPRINTS
TIP TOP COMICS	ST JOHN PUBLISHING		188	210	1954	1957	
TIP TOP COMICS	UNITED FEATURES SYNDICATE		1	187	1936	1957	
TIP TOPPER COMICS	UNITED FEATURES SYNDICATE		1	28	1949	1954	
TIPPY TEEN	TOWER COMICS		1	27	1965	1970	
TIPPY TEEN SPECIAL COLLECTORS EDITION	TOWER COMICS		1	1	1969	1969	
TIPPY TERRY	I.W. ENTERPRISES		1	1	1963	1963	REPRINTS
TIPPY'S FRIENDS GO-GO & ANIMAL	TOWER COMICS		1	15	1966	1969	
TITANS	MARVEL ENTERTAINMENT GROUP		1	58	1975	1976	
TITANS POCKET BOOK	MARVEL ENTERTAINMENT GROUP		1	13	1980	1981	
TITANS SELL OUT SPECIAL, THE	DC COMICS INC.		1	1	1992	1992	
TITBITS SCIENCE FICTION COMIC	PEARSON		1	6	1953	1954	
TITBITS WILD WEST COMICS	PEARSON		1	6	1953	1954	
TMNT/FLAMING CARROT CROSSOVER: LAND OF GREEN FIRE	MIRAGE STUDIOS		1	1	1993	1993	
TNT COMICS	CHARLES PUBLICATIONS CO.		1	1	1946	1946	
TO RIVERDALE AND BACK AGAIN	ARCHIE PUBLICATIONS		1	1	1990	1990	
TODAY'S BRIDES	AJAX		1	4	1955	1956	
TODAY'S ROMANCE	STANDARD COMICS		5	8	1952	1952	
TODAYS COLLECTOR	KRAUSE PUBLICATIONS		1	9	1992	NOW	
TOKA, JUNGLE KING	DELL PUBLISHING COMPANY		1	10	1964	1967	
TOM AND JERRY	GOLD KEY		213	327	1962	1980	
TOM AND JERRY	HARVEY PUBLICATIONS		1	14	1992	NOW	
TOM AND JERRY	THORPE & PORTER		1	4	1953	1953	DELL REPRINTS
TOM AND JERRY	WHITMAN		328	344	1980	1982	
TOM AND JERRY ADVENTURES	HARVEY PUBLICATIONS		1	1	1992	NOW	
TOM AND JERRY AND FRIENDS	HARVEY PUBLICATIONS		1	4	1992	NOW	
TOM AND JERRY BACK TO SCHOOL	DELL PUBLISHING COMPANY		1	1	1956	1956	
TOM AND JERRY BIG BOOK	HARVEY PUBLICATIONS		1	2	1992	NOW	
TOM AND JERRY COMICS	DELL PUBLISHING COMPANY		60	212	1949	1962	FORMERLY OUR GANG
TOM AND JERRY DIGEST	HARVEY PUBLICATIONS		1	1	1992	NOW	
TOM AND JERRY GIANT SIZE	HARVEY PUBLICATIONS		1	2	1993	NOW	
TOM AND JERRY HOLIDAY SPECIAL	POLYSTYLE		1975	1984	1975	1984	
TOM AND JERRY MOUSE FROM T.R.A.P.	GOLD KEY		1	1	1966	1966	
TOM AND JERRY PICNIC TIME	DELL PUBLISHING COMPANY		1	1	1958	1958	
TOM AND JERRY SPECIAL	HARVEY PUBLICATIONS		1	1	1991	1991	
TOM AND JERRY SUMMER FUN	DELL PUBLISHING COMPANY		1	4	1954	1957	
TOM AND JERRY SUMMER FUN	GOLD KEY		1	1	1967	1967	
TOM AND JERRY SUMMER SPECIAL	POLYSTYLE		1973	1974	1973	1974	
TOM AND JERRY TOY FAIR	DELL PUBLISHING COMPANY		1	1	1958	1958	
TOM AND JERRY WEEKLY	SPOTLIGHT COMICS		1	43	1973	1974	DELL REPRINTS
TOM AND JERRY WINTER CARNIVAL	DELL PUBLISHING COMPANY		1	2	1952	1953	BECOMES TOM AND JERRY WINTER FUN
TOM AND JERRY WINTER FUN	DELL PUBLISHING COMPANY		3	7	1954	1958	FORMERLY TOM AND JERRY WINTER CARNIVAL
TOM AND JERRY WINTER SPECIAL	POLYSTYLE		1976	1979	1976	1979	
TOM CAT	CHARLTON COMICS		4	8	1956	1957	FORMERLY BO

319

COMIC TITLE	PUBLISHER	Vol No.	Srt No.	End No.	Str. Year	End Year	COMMENTS
TOM CORBETT	ETERNITY	1	1	4	1990	1990	
TOM CORBETT	ETERNITY	2	1	4	1990	1991	
TOM CORBETT SPACE CADET	WORLD DISTRIBUTORS LTD		1	9	1953	1953	DELL REPRINTS
TOM CORBETT, SPACE CADET	DELL PUBLISHING COMPANY	1	4	11	1952	1954	
TOM CORBETT, SPACE CADET	PRIZE PUBLICATIONS	2	1	3	1955	1955	
TOM CORBETT, THE ORIGINAL	ETERNITY		1	5	1990	1991	
TOM MIX COMICS	RALSTON PURINA CO.		1	12	1940	1942	
TOM MIX WESTERN	AC COMICS		1	2	1988	1988	
TOM MIX WESTERN	FAWCETT PUBLICATIONS		1	61	1948	1953	
TOM MIX WESTERN COMICS	L. MILLER PUBLISHING COMPANY (UK)	1	1	3	1951	1951	FAWCETT REPRINTS
TOM MIX WESTERN COMICS	L. MILLER PUBLISHING COMPANY (UK)	2	50	134	1951	1959	
TOM MIX WESTERN HOLIDAY ALBUM	AC COMICS		1	1	1990	1990	
TOM PUSS COMICS	B.B. LIMITED		700	700	1949	1949	
TOM SAWYER & HUCK FINN	STOLL AND EDWARDS		1	1	1925	1925	
TOM TERRIFIC!	PINES		1	6	1957	1958	
TOM-TOM & ITCHI THE MONK	MAGAZINE ENTERPRISES		1	1	1957	1958	
TOM-TOM, THE JUNGLE BOY	I.W. ENTERPRISES		1	10	1957	1958	REPRINTS
TOM-TOM, THE JUNGLE BOY	MAGAZINE ENTERPRISES		1	3	1947	1947	
TOMAHAWK	DC COMICS INC.		1	130	1950	1971	SERIES CONTINUED AS SON OF TOMAHAWK FROM #131
TOMAHAWK	STRATO		1	40	1954	1957	DC REPRINTS
TOMB OF DARKNESS	MARVEL ENTERTAINMENT GROUP		9	23	1974	1976	FORMERLY BEWARE
TOMB OF DRACULA	MARVEL ENTERTAINMENT GROUP		1	4	1991	1992	
TOMB OF DRACULA	MARVEL ENTERTAINMENT GROUP		1	6	1979	1980	
TOMB OF DRACULA	MARVEL ENTERTAINMENT GROUP		1	70	1972	1979	
TOMB OF DRACULA GIANT SIZE	MARVEL ENTERTAINMENT GROUP		2	5	1974	1975	
TOMB OF TERROR	HARVEY PUBLICATIONS		1	16	1952	1954	
TOMMY OF THE BIG TOP	KING FEATURES		10	12	1948	1949	
TOMORROW KNIGHTS	MARVEL ENTERTAINMENT GROUP		1	8	1990	1991	
TONS O' FUN COMIC	PHILIMAR		1	1	1948	1948	
TONTO	WORLD DISTRIBUTORS LTD		1	32	1953	1955	DELL REPRINTS
TONY TRENT	COLUMBIA COMICS GROUP	3	4		1948	1949	
TONY TRENT COMICS	STREAMLINE		1	1	1951	1951	COLUMBIA PUBLICATIONS REPRINTS
TOODLE TWINS, THE	ARGO PUBLISHING		1	1	1956	1956	
TOODLE TWINS, THE	ZIFF-DAVIS PUBLISHING COMPANY		1	10	1951	1951	
TOON MAGAZINE	BLACK BEAR PRESS		1	1	1993	NOW	
TOONERVILLE TROLLEY	CUPPLES AND LEON CO.		1	1	1921	1921	
TOP CAT	CHARLTON COMICS		1	20	1970	1973	
TOP CAT	DELL PUBLISHING COMPANY		1	3	1961	1962	
TOP CAT	GOLD KEY		4	31	1962	1970	CONTINUES DELL SERIES
TOP COMICS	GOLD KEY	2	1	4	1967	1967	ALL REPRINTS; COMPANION TO K.K SERIES
TOP COMICS	K.K. PUBLICATIONS	1	1	4	1967	1967	ALL REPRINTS
TOP DETECTIVE COMICS	I.W. ENTERPRISES		9	9	1964	1964	REPRINTS
TOP DOG	MARVEL ENTERTAINMENT GROUP		1	10	1985	1987	
TOP ELIMINATOR	CHARLTON COMICS		25	29	1967	1968	FORMERLY TEENAGE HOTRODDERS
TOP FLIGHT COMICS	FOUR STAR COMICS CORP/SUPERIOR COMICS LTD	1	1	1	1947	1947	
TOP FLIGHT COMICS	ST JOHN PUBLISHING	2	1	1	1949	1949	
TOP JUNGLE COMICS	I.W. SUPER		1	1	1964	1964	REPRINTS
TOP LOVE STORIES	STAR PUBLICATIONS	3	19		1951	1954	FORMERLY GASOLINE ALLEY
TOP MARK ADVENTURES	FOLDES PRESS		1	1	1947	1947	
TOP SECRET	HILLMAN PERIODICALS		1	1	1952	1952	
TOP SECRET PICTURE LIBRARY	IPC		1	40	1974	1976	
TOP SECRETS OF THE F.B.I.	STREET AND SMITH PUBLICATIONS		1	10	1947	1949	
TOP SPOT	AMALGAMATED PRESS		1	58	1958	1960	
TOP THREE	FAME PRESS		1	124	1961	1966	
TOP-HOLE COMICS	P.M. PRODUCTIONS		1	1	1943	1943	
TOP-NOTCH COMIC, THE	SAWARD & CO.		1	1	1947	1947	
TOP-NOTCH COMICS	M.L.J. MAGAZINES		1	45	1939	1944	
TOPICAL FUNNIES	GERALD SWAN		1	36	1940	1951	
TOPICAL FUNNIES AUTUMN SPECIAL	GERALD SWAN		1	1	1941	1941	
TOPICAL FUNNIES DOUBLE SPECIAL	GERALD SWAN		1	1	1946	1946	
TOPICAL FUNNIES SPECIAL	GERALD SWAN		1	1	1943	1943	
TOPICAL FUNNIES SPRING SPECIAL	GERALD SWAN		1	1	1941	1941	
TOPICAL FUNNIES SUMMER SPECIAL	GERALD SWAN		1	1	1942	1942	
TOPICAL FUNNIES WINTER SPECIAL	GERALD SWAN		1	1	1941	1941	
TOPIX	CAETECHETICAL EDUCATIONAL SOCIETY	9	1	30	1950	1951	
TOPIX	GRAFTON		1	4	1950	1950	CAETECHETICAL REPRINTS
TOPIX COMICS	CAETECHETICAL EDUCATIONAL SOCIETY	1	1	4	1942	1942	WEEKLY
TOPIX COMICS	CAETECHETICAL EDUCATIONAL SOCIETY	2	1	10	1943	1943	WEEKLY
TOPIX COMICS	CAETECHETICAL EDUCATIONAL SOCIETY	3	1	10	1944	1944	WEEKLY
TOPIX COMICS	CAETECHETICAL EDUCATIONAL SOCIETY	4	1	10	1945	1945	WEEKLY
TOPIX COMICS	CAETECHETICAL EDUCATIONAL SOCIETY	5	1	15	1946	1946	WEEKLY
TOPIX COMICS	CAETECHETICAL EDUCATIONAL SOCIETY	6	1	14	1947	1947	WEEKLY
TOPIX COMICS	CAETECHETICAL EDUCATIONAL SOCIETY	7	1	20	1948	1948	WEEKLY
TOPIX COMICS	CAETECHETICAL EDUCATIONAL SOCIETY	8	1	30	1949	1949	WEEKLY
TOPIX COMICS	CAETECHETICAL EDUCATIONAL SOCIETY	9	1	30	1950	1951	WEEKLY
TOPIX COMICS	CAETECHETICAL EDUCATIONAL SOCIETY	10	1	15	1952	1952	WEEKLY
TOPPER	D.C. THOMSON		1	1963	1953	1990	
TOPPER BOOK ANNUAL	D.C. THOMSON		1955	1993	1955	NOW	
TOPPER PICTURE BOOK	D.C. THOMSON		1	1	1954	1954	
TOPPER SUMMER SPECIAL	D.C. THOMSON		1983	1992	1983	1992	
TOPPS COMICS	FOUR STAR COMICS CORP/SUPERIOR COMICS LTD		1	1	1947	1947	
TOPPS COMICS PRESENTS	TOPPS		0	0	1993	1993	
TOPS	LEV GLEASON PUBLICATIONS		1	2	1949	1949	RARE
TOPS COMICS	CONSOLIDATED MAGAZINES		1	1	1944	1944	
. TOPS COMICS	LEV GLEASON PUBLICATIONS		2001	2003	1944	1944	
TOPS IN ADVENTURE	ZIFF-DAVIS PUBLISHING COMPANY		1	1	1952	1952	
TOPS IN HUMOUR	LEV GLEASON PUBLICATIONS		1	2	1944	1944	

COMIC TITLE	PUBLISHER	Vol No.	Srt No.	End No.	Str. Year	End Year	COMMENTS
TOPS SPOT COMICS	TOP SPOT PUBL. CO.		1	1	1945	1945	
TOPSY-TURVY	R.B. LEFFINGWELL & CO.		1	1	1945	1945	
TOR	DC COMICS INC.		1	6	1975	1976	
TOR	ST JOHN PUBLISHING		3	5	1953	1954	FORMERLY ONE MILLION YEARS AGO
TOR 3-D	ECLIPSE		1	2	1986	1986	
TOR 3-D	ST JOHN PUBLISHING		1	3	1953	1953	
TOR JOHNSON: HOLLYWOOD	MONSTER COMICS		1	1	1991	1991	
TORCHY	INNOVATION		1	4	1992	1992	
TORCHY	QUALITY COMICS		1	6	1949	1950	
TORCHY GIFTBOOK	MIRROR PRESS PUBLICATIONS		1960	1964	1960	1964	
TORCHY SUMMER FUN SPECIAL	INNOVATION		1	1	1992	1992	
TORG: REALITY STORM	ADVENTURE COMICS		1	4	1991	1991	
TORMENTED, THE	STERLING COMICS		1	2	1954	1954	
TORNADO	IPC		1	22	1979	1979	
TORNADO SUMMER SPECIAL	IPC		1	1	1979	1979	
TORPEDO 1936	CATALAN COMMUNICATIONS		1	6	1984	1984	
TORRID	GOLD STAR PUBLICATIONS LTD		1	12	1979	1982	
TORTURE GARDENS	RE/SEARCH PUBLICATIONS				1989	1989	
TOTAL CARNAGE	DARK HORSE COMICS		1	2	1993	NOW	
TOTAL ECLIPSE	ECLIPSE		1	5	1988	1989	
TOTAL ECLIPSE: THE SERAPHIM OBJECTIVE	ECLIPSE		1	1	1988	1988	
TOTAL RECALL MOVIE ADAPTATION	DC COMICS INC.		1	1	1990	1990	
TOTAL WAR	GOLD KEY		1	2	1965	1965	
TOTEM PICTURE LIBRARY IN COLOUR	FAME PRESS		1	102	1961	1967	
TOUGH KID SQUAD COMICS	TIMELY COMICS		1	1	1942	1942	
TOWER OF SHADOWS	MARVEL ENTERTAINMENT GROUP		1	9	1969	1971	
TOWER OF SHADOWS ANNUAL	MARVEL ENTERTAINMENT GROUP		1	1	1971	1971	
TOWN THAT SANTA FORGOT, THE	W.T. GRANT COMPANY		1	1	1961	1961	
TOXIC	APOCALYPSE		1	14	1991	1991	
TOXIC AVENGER	MARVEL ENTERTAINMENT GROUP		1	11	1991	1992	
TOXIC CRUSADERS	MARVEL ENTERTAINMENT GROUP		1	8	1992	1993	
TOXIC CRUSADERS	MARVEL ENTERTAINMENT GROUP	2	1	4	1993	1993	
TOY TOWN COMICS	TOYTOWN PUBLICATIONS		1	7	1945	1947	
TOYBOY	CONTINUITY COMICS		1	8	1986	NOW	
TOYLAND COMICS	FICTION HOUSE		1	4	1947	1947	
TRACKER: MEAGRE MILLIONS	BLACKTHORNE		1	4	1988	1988	
TRAGG AND THE SKY GODS	GOLD KEY		1	8	1975	1977	
TRAGG AND THE SKY GODS	WHITMAN	9	9	9	1982	1982	CONTINUES GOLD KEY SERIES
TRAIL BLAZERS	STREET AND SMITH PUBLICATIONS		1	4	1941	1942	
TRAIL COLT	MAGAZINE ENTERPRISES		1	2	1949	1949	
TRAMPS IN THE KINGDOM	HODDER AND STOUGHTON/DARGUAD		1	1	1979	1979	
TRANCERS	ETERNITY		1	2	1991	1991	
TRANCERS, ADVENTURES JD	ETERNITY		1	1	1991	1991	
TRANSFORMERS	MARVEL ENTERTAINMENT GROUP		1	80	1984	1991	
TRANSFORMERS MOVIE ADAPTION	MARVEL ENTERTAINMENT GROUP		1	3	1986	1987	
TRANSFORMERS SUMMER SPECIAL	MARVEL ENTERTAINMENT GROUP		1983	1990	1983	1990	
TRANSFORMERS UNIVERSE	MARVEL ENTERTAINMENT GROUP		1	4	1986	1987	
TRANSFORMERS WEEKLY	MARVEL ENTERTAINMENT GROUP		1	332	1984	1991	
TRANSFORMERS: GENERATION 2	MARVEL ENTERTAINMENT GROUP		1	5	1993	NOW	
TRANSFORMERS: THE HEADMASTERS	MARVEL ENTERTAINMENT GROUP		1	4	1987	1987	
TRANSIT	VORTEX		1	5	1987	1989	
TRANSMUTATION OF IKE GARUDA	MARVEL ENTERTAINMENT GROUP		1	2	1991	1992	
TRANSYLVANIA SPECIAL	CONTINUITY COMICS		1	1	1991	1991	
TRAPPED	HARVEY PUBLICATIONS		1	1	1951	1951	
TRAPPED!	ACE PERIODICALS		1	5	1954	1955	
TRASH	FLEETWAY		1	2	1993	NOW	
TRASHMAN LIVES!	FANTAGRAPHICS				1989	1989	
TRAVELS OF HAPPY HOOLIGAN, THE	FREDRICK A. STOKES CO.		1	1	1906	1906	
TRAVELS OF JAIMIE MCPHEETERS, THE	GOLD KEY		1	1	1963	1963	
TREASURARY OF DOGS	DELL PUBLISHING COMPANY		1	1	1956	1956	
TREASURARY OF HORSES	DELL PUBLISHING COMPANY		1	1	1955	1955	
TREASURE CHEST	CAETECHETICAL EDUCATIONAL SOCIETY	1	1	6	1946	1946	
TREASURE CHEST	CAETECHETICAL EDUCATIONAL SOCIETY	2	1	20	1946	1947	
TREASURE CHEST	CAETECHETICAL EDUCATIONAL SOCIETY	3	1	20	1947	1948	
TREASURE CHEST	CAETECHETICAL EDUCATIONAL SOCIETY	4	1	20	1948	1949	
TREASURE CHEST	CAETECHETICAL EDUCATIONAL SOCIETY	5	1	20	1949	1950	
TREASURE CHEST	CAETECHETICAL EDUCATIONAL SOCIETY	6	1	20	1950	1951	
TREASURE CHEST	CAETECHETICAL EDUCATIONAL SOCIETY	7	1	20	1951	1952	
TREASURE CHEST	CAETECHETICAL EDUCATIONAL SOCIETY	8	1	20	1952	1953	
TREASURE CHEST	CAETECHETICAL EDUCATIONAL SOCIETY	9	1	20	1953	1954	
TREASURE CHEST	CAETECHETICAL EDUCATIONAL SOCIETY	10	1	20	1954	1955	
TREASURE CHEST	CAETECHETICAL EDUCATIONAL SOCIETY	11	1	10	1955	1956	
TREASURE CHEST	CAETECHETICAL EDUCATIONAL SOCIETY	12	1	20	1956	1957	
TREASURE CHEST	CAETECHETICAL EDUCATIONAL SOCIETY	13	1	20	1957	1958	
TREASURE CHEST	CAETECHETICAL EDUCATIONAL SOCIETY	14	1	20	1958	1959	
TREASURE CHEST	CAETECHETICAL EDUCATIONAL SOCIETY	15	1	20	1959	1960	
TREASURE CHEST	CAETECHETICAL EDUCATIONAL SOCIETY	16	1	20	1960	1961	
TREASURE CHEST	CAETECHETICAL EDUCATIONAL SOCIETY	17	1	20	1961	1963	
TREASURE CHEST	CAETECHETICAL EDUCATIONAL SOCIETY	18	1	20	1963	1963	
TREASURE CHEST	CAETECHETICAL EDUCATIONAL SOCIETY	19	1	20	1964	1964	
TREASURE CHEST	CAETECHETICAL EDUCATIONAL SOCIETY	20	1	20	1964	1965	
TREASURE CHEST	CAETECHETICAL EDUCATIONAL SOCIETY	21	1	20	1965	1965	
TREASURE CHEST	CAETECHETICAL EDUCATIONAL SOCIETY	22	1	20	1966	1966	
TREASURE CHEST	CAETECHETICAL EDUCATIONAL SOCIETY	23	1	20	1967	1967	
TREASURE CHEST	CAETECHETICAL EDUCATIONAL SOCIETY	24	1	20	1968	1968	
TREASURE CHEST	CAETECHETICAL EDUCATIONAL SOCIETY	25	1	20	1969	1970	
TREASURE CHEST	CAETECHETICAL EDUCATIONAL SOCIETY	26	1	20	1971	1971	
TREASURE CHEST	CAETECHETICAL EDUCATIONAL SOCIETY	27	1	8	1971	1972	
TREASURE CHEST OF THE WORLD'S BEST COMICS	SUPERIOR COMICS		1	1	1945	1945	
TREASURE CHEST SUMMER EDITION	CAETECHETICAL EDUCATIONAL SOCIETY	1	1	6	1966	1966	

COMIC TITLE	PUBLISHER	Vol No.	Srt No.	End No.	Str. Year	End Year	COMMENTS
TREASURE CHEST SUMMER EDITION	CAETECHETICAL EDUCATIONAL SOCIETY	2	1	6	1967	1967	
TREASURE COMIC	MARTIN & REID		1	1	1949	1949	
TREASURE COMICS	PRIZE PUBLICATIONS		1	12	1945	1947	
TREASURY OF COMICS	ST JOHN PUBLISHING	1	1	5	1947	1948	
TREASURY OF COMICS	ST JOHN PUBLISHING	2	1	5	1948	1948	
TREASURY OF COMICS YEARBOOK	ST JOHN PUBLISHING	2	1948	1950	1948	1950	
TREKKER	DARK HORSE COMICS		1	9	1987	NOW	
TREKKER COLOUR SPECIAL	DARK HORSE COMICS		1	1	1989	1989	
TRENCHER	IMAGE COMICS		1	4	1993	NOW	
TRENCHER X-MAS BITES HOLIDAY BLOW-OUT	BLACK BALL COMICS		1	1	1993	1993	
TRIAL OF VENOM	MARVEL ENTERTAINMENT GROUP		1	1	1993	1993	
TRIAL RUN	MILLER PUBLISHING (US)		1	2	1990	1990	
TRIALS OF LULU AND LEANDER, THE	STOKES & CO.		1	1	1906	1906	
TRIALS OF NASTY TALES, THE	H. BUNCH ASSOCIATES		1	1	1973	1973	
TRIARCH	CALIBER PRESS		1	4	1991	NOW	
TRIBE	AXIS	2	2	2	1993	NOW	FORMERLY PUBLISHED BY IMAGE
TRIBE	IMAGE COMICS		1	1	1993	1993	SERIES CONTINUED BY AXIS
TRIBE - THE BOOK	AXIS				1994	1994	
TRICKSTER KING MONKEY	EASTERN COLOR PRINTING COMPANY		1	2	1988	1988	
TRICKY DICKY: TEN YEARS ON	ANN SUMMERS PUBLISHING				1988	1988	
TRIDENT	TRIDENT		1	8	1989	1990	
TRIFFIK!	COMMUNICATIONS INNOVATIONS		1	6	1992	1992	
TRIGAN EMPIRE, LOOK AND LEARN BOOK OF THE	FLEETWAY		1	1	1973	1973	
TRIGAN EMPIRE, TALES FROM THE	HAWK BOOKS		1	1	1989	1989	
TRIGAN EMPIRE, THE	HAMLYN PUBLISHING GROUP LTD		1	1	1978	1978	
TRIGGER TWINS	DC COMICS INC.		1	1	1973	1973	
TRIGGER WESTERN ALBUM	G.T. LIMITED		1	1	1959	1959	
TRIPLE TERROR, THE	DONALD PETERS	20		20	1949	1949	UNITED FEATURES REPRINTS
TRIPLE THREAT	HOLYOKE PUBLISHING COMPANY		1	1	1945	1945	
TRITON: COMIC CARDS & COLLECTIBLES	ATTIC BOOKS		1	1	1993	NOW	
TRIUMPH	AMALGAMATED PRESS		1	814	1924	1940	
TRIUMPHANT UNLEASHED	TRIUMPHANT COMICS		1	1	1993	NOW	
TROLL	IMAGE COMICS		1	1	1993	NOW	
TROLLORDS	COMICO		1	5	1988	1989	
TROLLORDS: DEATH AND KISSES	APPLE COMICS		1	6	1989	1990	
TROMBONE	KNOCKABOUT		1	1	1990	1990	
TROUBLE WITH GIRLS	COMICO		1	23	1989	NOW	
TROUBLE WITH GIRLS	ETERNITY		1	14	1987	1989	
TROUBLE WITH GIRLS	MARVEL ENTERTAINMENT GROUP		1	4	1993	1993	
TROUBLE WITH GIRLS ANNUAL	ETERNITY		1	1	1988	1988	
TROUBLE WITH GIRLS CHRISTMAS SPECIAL	ETERNITY		1	1	1992	1992	
TROUBLED SOULS	FLEETWAY				1990	1990	
TRUE 3-D	HARVEY PUBLICATIONS		1	2	1953	1954	
TRUE 3-D	UNITED-ANGLO PRODUCTIONS		1	1	1954	1954	HARVEY REPRINTS
TRUE ADVENTURES	MARVEL ENTERTAINMENT GROUP	3		3	1950	1950	FORMERLY TRUE WESTERN
TRUE ANIMAL PICTURE STORIES	TRUE COMICS PRESS		1	2	1947	1947	
TRUE AVIATION PICTURE STORIES	PARENTS MAGAZINE INSTITUTE		1	15	1942	1946	
TRUE BRIDE'S EXPERIENCES	HARVEY PUBLICATIONS		1	16	1954	1956	
TRUE BRIDE-TO-BE ROMANCES	HARVEY PUBLICATIONS	17		30	1956	1958	FORMERLY TRUE BRIDE'S EXPERIENCES
TRUE COMICS	PARENTS MAGAZINE INSTITUTE		1	84	1941	1950	
TRUE COMICS AND ADVENTURE STORIES	PARENTS MAGAZINE INSTITUTE		1	2	1965	1965	
TRUE COMPLETE MYSTERY	MARVEL ENTERTAINMENT GROUP	5		8	1949	1949	FORMERLY COMPLETE MYSTERY
TRUE COMPLETE MYSTERY	STREAMLINE		1	1	1950	1950	ATLAS REPRINTS
TRUE CONFIDENCES	FAWCETT PUBLICATIONS		1	4	1949	1950	
TRUE CRIME CASE, OFFICIAL	MARVEL ENTERTAINMENT GROUP	24		25	1947	1948	FORMERLY SUB-MARINER
TRUE CRIME CASES	ST JOHN PUBLISHING		1	1	1944	1944	
TRUE CRIME COMICS	ECLIPSE	2		2	1993	NOW	
TRUE CRIME COMICS	MAGAZINE VILLAGE	1	2	6	1947	1949	
TRUE CRIME COMICS	MAGAZINE VILLAGE	2	1	1	1949	1949	
TRUE CRIME COMICS SPECIAL	ECLIPSE		1	1	1993	NOW	
TRUE FAITH	FLEETWAY		1	1	1990	1990	
TRUE LIFE ADVENTURES	MANS WORLD	12		17	1953	1954	
TRUE LIFE ROMANCES	AJAX		1	3	1955	1956	
TRUE LIFE SECRETS	L. MILLER PUBLISHING COMPANY (UK)		1	20	1952	1952	CHARLTON REPRINTS
TRUE LIFE SPORTS	SPORTS CARTOON		1	1	1953	1953	
TRUE LIFE TALES	MARVEL ENTERTAINMENT GROUP	8		2	1949	1950	FORMERLY MITZI'S ROMANCES
TRUE LOVE	ECLIPSE		1	2	1986	1986	
TRUE LOVE CONFESSIONS	CARTOON ART		1	1	1954	1954	
TRUE LOVE CONFESSIONS	PREMIER MAGAZINES		1	11	1954	1956	
TRUE LOVE CONFESSIONS	TRENT		1	12	1953	1953	
TRUE LOVE PICTORIAL	ST JOHN PUBLISHING		1	11	1952	1954	
TRUE LOVE ROMANCES	TRENT		1	12	1953	1953	
TRUE MOVIE AND TELEVISION	TOBY PRESS PUBLICATIONS		1	4	1950	1951	
TRUE MYSTERY	STREAMLINE		1	1	1953	1953	FOX FEATURES REPRINTS
TRUE POLICE COMICS	CARTOON ART		1	1	1950	1950	
TRUE SECRETS	ATLAS	4		40	1951	1956	CONTINUES MARVEL SERIES
TRUE SECRETS	L. MILLER PUBLISHING COMPANY (UK)		1	2	1955	???	ATLAS REPRINTS
TRUE SECRETS	MARVEL ENTERTAINMENT GROUP	3		3	1950	1950	FORMERLY OUR LOVE
TRUE SPORT PICTURE STORIES	STREET AND SMITH PUBLICATIONS	1	5	12	1942	1943	FORMERLY SPORT COMICS
TRUE SPORT PICTURE STORIES	STREET AND SMITH PUBLICATIONS	2	1	12	1944	1945	
TRUE SPORT PICTURE STORIES	STREET AND SMITH PUBLICATIONS	3	1	12	1946	1947	
TRUE SPORT PICTURE STORIES	STREET AND SMITH PUBLICATIONS	4	1	12	1948	1949	
TRUE SPORT PICTURE STORIES	STREET AND SMITH PUBLICATIONS	5	1	2	1949	1949	
TRUE STORIES OF ROMANCE	FAWCETT PUBLICATIONS		1	3	1950	1950	
TRUE SWEETHEART SECRETS	FAWCETT PUBLICATIONS		1	44	1950	1953	
TRUE TALES OF LOVE	ATLAS	22		31	1956	1957	FORMERLY SECRET STORY ROMANCES
TRUE TALES OF ROMANCE	FAWCETT PUBLICATIONS	4		4	1950	1950	
TRUE TO LIFE ROMANCES	GERALD SWAN		1	16	1954	1955	STAR REPRINTS
TRUE WAR	IPC		1	3	1978	1978	
TRUE WAR EXPERIENCES	HARVEY PUBLICATIONS		1	4	1952	1952	

INDEX OF COMIC TITLES AND THEIR PUBLISHERS

COMIC TITLE	PUBLISHER	Vol No.	Srt No.	End No.	Str. Year	End Year	COMMENTS
TRUE WAR EXPERIENCES	UNITED-ANGLO PRODUCTIONS		1	1	1953	1953	HARVEY REPRINTS
TRUE WAR ROMANCES	QUALITY COMICS		1	21	1952	1955	
TRUE WEST ROMANCE	QUALITY COMICS		21	21	1952	1952	
TRUE WESTERN	MARVEL ENTERTAINMENT GROUP		1	2	1949	1950	
TRUE WESTERN	THORPE & PORTER		1	1	50'S	50'S	MARVEL REPRINTS
TRUE-TO-LIFE ROMANCES	STAR PUBLICATIONS		1	23	1949	1954	FORMERLY GUNS AGAINST GANGSTERS
TRUELY AMAZING LOVE STORIES	ANTONIO GURU		1	1	1977	1977	
TRUMP	HMH PUBLISHING CO.		1	2	1957	1957	
TRUTHFUL LOVE	YOUTHFUL MAGAZINES		2	2	1950	1950	FORMERLY YOUTHFUL LOVE
TUFF GHOSTS STARRING SPOOKY	HARVEY PUBLICATIONS		1	43	1962	1972	
TUFFY	STANDARD COMICS		5	9	1949	1950	
TUROK SON OF STONE	GOLD KEY		30	125	1962	1974	
TUROK SON OF STONE	WHITMAN		126	130	1974	1982	
TUROK, SON OF STONE	DELL PUBLISHING COMPANY		3	29	1956	1962	
TUROK, SON OF STONE	GOLD KEY		30	89	1962	1974	
TUROK, SON OF STONE	WHITMAN		90	130	1974	1981	
TUROK, SON OF STONE GIANT	GOLD KEY		1	1	1966	1966	
TUROK: DINOSAUR HUNTER	VALIANT / VOYAGER COMMUNICATIONS		1	10	1993	NOW	
TURTLE SOUP	MIRAGE STUDIOS		1	1	1987	1987	
TURTLE SOUP	MIRAGE STUDIOS		1	4	1991	1992	
TV 21	IPC		1	105	1969	1971	
TV 21 ANNUAL	FLEETWAY		1969	1973	1969	1973	
TV 21 SPRING EXTRA: THUNDERBIRDS	CITY		1	1	1967	1967	
TV ACTION	POLYSTYLE		59	132	1972	1973	PREVIOUSLY COUNTDOWN
TV ACTION & COUNTDOWN HOLIDAY SPECIAL	POLYSTYLE		1	1	1972	1972	
TV ACTION ANNUAL	POLYSTYLE		1973	1974	1973	1974	
TV ACTION HOLIDAY SPECIAL	POLYSTYLE		1	1	1973	1973	
TV CASPER AND COMPANY	HARVEY PUBLICATIONS		1	46	1963	1974	
TV CENTURY 21	CITY		1	242	1965	1969	
TV CENTURY 21 ANNUAL	CITY		1965	1968	1965	1968	
TV CENTURY 21 INTERNATIONAL EXTRA	CITY		1	1	1965	1965	
TV CENTURY 21 STINGRAY SPECIAL	CITY		1	1	1965	1965	
TV CENTURY 21 SUMMER EXTRA	CITY		1965	1966	1965	1966	
TV COMEDY SCENE	ITV BOOKS LIMITED		1	1	1976	1976	
TV COMIC	POLYSTYLE		1	1697	1951	1984	
TV COMIC ANNUAL	POLYSTYLE		1954	1985	1954	1985	
TV COMIC HOLIDAY SPECIAL	POLYSTYLE		1963	1984	1963	1984	
TV COMIC SUMMER SPECIAL	TV		1	1	1962	1962	
TV CRIMEBUSTERS	TV		1	1	1962	1962	
TV EXPRESS	TV		286	375	1960	1962	PREVIOUSLY EXPRESS WEEKLY
TV EXPRESS ANNUAL	TV		1961	1962	1961	1962	PREVIOUSLY EXPRESS ANNUAL
TV FAN	FLEETWAY		313	333	1959	1960	FORMERLY TV FUN
TV FEATURES	MICK ANGLO/ATLAS		1	8	1960	1961	
TV FUN	AMALGAMATED PRESS		1	312	1953	1959	
TV FUN ANNUAL	AMALGAMATED PRESS		1957	1960	1957	1960	
TV HEROES	L. MILLER PUBLISHING COMPANY (UK)		1	26	1958	1960	
TV LAND	TV		1	68	1960	1962	
TV PHOT SERIES	PEARSON		1	4	1960	1960	
TV SCREEN CARTOONS	DC COMICS INC.		129	138	1959	1961	FORMERLY REAL SCREEN
TV STARS	MARVEL ENTERTAINMENT GROUP		1	4	1978	1979	
TV TEENS	CHARLTON COMICS	1	14	15	1954	1954	FORMERLY OZZIE & BABS
TV TEENS	CHARLTON COMICS	2	3	13	1954	1955	
TV TIMES SOUVENIR EXTRA: THE NEW AVENGERS	ITV BOOKS LIMITED				1976	1976	
TV TORNADO	CITY		1	88	1967	1968	
TV TORNADO ANNUAL	CITY		1967	1970	1967	1970	
TV TOYLAND	CITY		1	92	1966	1968	
TV ZONE	VISUAL IMAGINATION		1	28	1989	NOW	
TWEETY AND SYLVESTER	DELL PUBLISHING COMPANY		4	37	1952	1962	
TWEETY AND SYLVESTER	DELL PUBLISHING COMPANY	1	4	37	1954	1962	
TWEETY AND SYLVESTER	GOLD KEY		1	121	1963	1982	
TWEETY AND SYLVESTER	WHITMAN		103	119	1982	1984	
TWEETY AND SYLVESTER	WHITMAN	2	104	121	1984	1984	
TWEETY AND SYLVESTER MINI COMIC	GOLD KEY		1	1	1976	1976	
TWICE TOLD TALES OF UNSUPERVISED EXISTENCE	RIP OFF PRESS		1	1	1991	1991	
TWILIGHT	DC COMICS INC.		1	3	1991	1991	
TWILIGHT AVENGER	ETERNITY		1	8	1988	1989	
TWILIGHT MAN	FIRST		1	4	1989	1989	
TWILIGHT PEOPLE	CALIBER PRESS		1	2	1993	NOW	
TWILIGHT ZONE	GOLD KEY		1	92	1961	1979	
TWILIGHT ZONE	NOW	1	1	4	1991	1992	
TWILIGHT ZONE	WHITMAN		92	92	1982	1982	CONTINUES GOLD KEY SERIES
TWILIGHT ZONE 3D WINTER SPECIAL	NOW		1	1	1993	1993	
TWILIGHT ZONE ANNUAL	NOW	2	1	1	1992	NOW	
TWILIGHT ZONE COMPUTER SPECIAL	NOW		1	1	1993	1993	
TWILIGHT ZONE MINI COMIC	GOLD KEY		1	1	1976	1976	
TWILIGHT ZONE SCI-FI SPECIAL	NOW		1	1	1993	1993	
TWILIGHT ZONE, THE	NOW		1	1	1990	1990	
TWIN EARTHS	R. SUSOR PUBLICATIONS		1	7	1990	1991	
TWINKLE COMICS	SPOTLIGHT COMICS		1	1	1945	1945	
TWIST	KITCHEN SINK		1	1	1987	1987	
TWIST, THE	DELL PUBLISHING COMPANY		1	864209	1962	1962	
TWISTED TALES	PACIFIC COMICS		1	10	1982	1984	
TWISTED TALES OF BRUCE JONES	ECLIPSE		1	4	1986	1986	
TWISTER	HARRIS COMICS		1	1	1992	1992	
TWIZZLE ADVENTURE STORIES ANNUAL	BIRN BROTHERS LTD.		1959	1960	1959	1960	
TWIZZLE STORY BOOK	BIRN BROTHERS LTD.		1	1	1960	1960	
TWO BIT THE WACKY WOODPECKER	TOBY PRESS PUBLICATIONS		1	3	1951	1953	
TWO FISTED TALES	CARTOON ART		1	1	1951	1951	EC REPRINTS
TWO FISTED TALES	EC COMICS	1	18	41	1950	1955	
TWO FISTED TALES	RUSS COCHRAN		1	6	1993	NOW	

COMIC TITLE	PUBLISHER	Vol No.	Srt No.	End No.	Str. Year	End Year	COMMENTS
TWO FISTED TALES ANNUAL	EC COMICS		1952	1953	1952	1953	
TWO GUN KID	L. MILLER PUBLISHING COMPANY (UK)		1	38	1955	1959	ATLAS REPRINTS
TWO GUN KID	MARVEL ENTERTAINMENT GROUP		1	136	1948	1977	
TWO GUN KID	WORLD DISTRIBUTORS LTD		1	1	1950	1950	ATLAS REPRINTS
TWO GUN WESTERN	ARNOLD BOOK CO.		1	1	1952	1952	ATLAS REPRINTS
TWO GUN WESTERN	ATLAS	2	5	12	1956	1957	FORMERLY 2-GUN WESTERN
TWO GUN WESTERN	MARVEL ENTERTAINMENT GROUP	1	5	14	1950	1952	FORMERLY CASEY CRIME PHOTOGRAPHER
TWO GUN WESTERN	UNITED-ANGLO PRODUCTIONS		1	9	1951	???	ATLAS REPRINTS
TYRANNOSAURUS REX	MONSTER COMICS		1	3	1991	NOW	

U

COMIC TITLE	PUBLISHER	Vol No.	Srt No.	End No.	Str. Year	End Year	COMMENTS
U.N. FORCE	CALIBER PRESS		1	5	1993	NOW	
U.N. FORCE FILES	CALIBER PRESS		1	1	1993	NOW	
U.S. AGENT	MARVEL ENTERTAINMENT GROUP		1	4	1993	1993	
U.S. AIR FORCE COMICS	CHARLTON COMICS		1	37	1958	1965	
U.S. FIGHTING AIR FORCE	I.W. ENTERPRISES		1	1	60'S	60'S	REPRINTS
U.S. FIGHTING AIR FORCE	I.W. SUPER		9	9	60'S	60'S	
U.S. FIGHTING MEN	SUPER COMICS		10	18	1963	1964	REPRINTS
U.S. JONES	FOX FEATURES SYNDICATE		1	2	1941	1942	
U.S. MARINES	CHARLTON COMICS		1	1	1964	1964	
U.S. MARINES IN ACTION	AVON BOOKS		1	3	1952	1952	
U.S. PARATROOPS	I.W. ENTERPRISES		1	8	1964	1964	
U.S. TANK COMMANDOS	AVON BOOKS		1	4	1952	1953	
U.S. TANK COMMANDOS	I.W. ENTERPRISES		1	8	1953	1953	REPRINTS
UFO AND ALIEN COMIX	WARREN PUBLISHING CO		1	1	1978	1978	
UFO AND OUTER SPACE	GOLD KEY		14	25	1978	1980	FORMERLY UFO FLYING SAUCERS
UFO ANNUAL	POLYSTYLE		1	1	1971	1971	
UFO ENCOUNTERS	WESTERN PUBLISHING COMPANY		11192	11404	1978	1978	228-PAGES
UFO FLYING SAUCERS	GOLD KEY		1	13	1968	1977	
UFO MYSTERIES	WESTERN PUBLISHING COMPANY		11400	11404	1978	1978	
ULTIMATE WARRIORS WORKOUT	VALIANT / VOYAGER COMMUNICATIONS		1	1	1991	1991	
ULTRA KLUTZ	ONWARD		1	31	1986	NOW	
ULTRA KLUTZ: ORIGINS, OLD & NEW	PARODY PRESS		1	1	1993	1993	
ULTRA KLUTZ: PLACED IN SPACE	PARODY PRESS		1	1	1993	1993	
ULTRA MONTHLY MAGAZINE	MALIBU COMICS ENTERTAINMENT INC.		1	6	1993	NOW	
ULTRAMAN	HARVEY PUBLICATIONS		1	3	1993	NOW	
ULTRAMAN	NEMESIS COMICS		1	1	1993	NOW	
ULTRAMAN	NEMESIS COMICS	2	1	1	1993	NOW	
ULTRAMAN 3D SPECIAL	NOW		1	1	1993	1993	
ULTRAMAN CLASSIC: BATTLE OF THE ULTRA-BROTHERS	VIZ		1	5	1994	1994	
UNCANNY TALES	ALAN CLASS AND CO LTD		1	2	1963	???	ATLAS, FAWCETT, MARVEL REPRINTS
UNCANNY TALES	ATLAS		1	56	1952	1957	
UNCANNY TALES	MARVEL ENTERTAINMENT GROUP		1	12	1973	1975	
UNCENSORED LOVE	ALAN CLASS AND CO LTD		1	1	1960	1960	US REPRINTS
UNCENSORED MOUSE, THE	ETERNITY		1	2	1989	1989	
UNCLE CHARLIE'S FABLES	LEV GLEASON PUBLICATIONS		1	5	1952	1952	
UNCLE JOE'S FUNNIES	CENTAUR PUBLICATIONS		1	1	1938	1938	
UNCLE MILTY	VICTORIA PUBLICATIONS		1	4	1950	1951	
UNCLE SAM QUARTERLY	QUALITY COMICS		1	8	1941	1943	
UNCLE SAM'S CHRISTMAS STORY	PROMOTIONAL PUBLICATIONS COMPANY		1	1	1958	1958	
UNCLE SCROOGE	DELL PUBLISHING COMPANY		4	39	1953	1962	
UNCLE SCROOGE	GLADSTONE		210	242	1986	1990	
UNCLE SCROOGE	GOLD KEY		40	173	1962	1981	
UNCLE SCROOGE	WALT DISNEY		243	282	1990	NOW	
UNCLE SCROOGE	WHITMAN		174	209	1981	1984	
UNCLE SCROOGE ADVENTURES	GLADSTONE		1	21	1987	1990	
UNCLE SCROOGE AND DONALD DUCK	GOLD KEY		1	1	1965	1965	
UNCLE SCROOGE AND MONEY	GOLD KEY		1	1	1967	1967	
UNCLE SCROOGE COMICS DIGEST	GLADSTONE		1	5	1986	1987	
UNCLE SCROOGE DIGEST	GLADSTONE		1	5	1985	1987	
UNCLE SCROOGE GOES TO DISNEYLAND	DELL PUBLISHING COMPANY		1	1	1957	1957	
UNCLE SCROOGE GOES TO DISNEYLAND	GLADSTONE		1	1	1985	1985	
UNCLE SCROOGE GOES TO DISNEYLAND DIGEST	GLADSTONE		1	1	1985	1985	
UNCLE SCROOGE MINI COMIC	WHITMAN		1	1	1976	1976	
UNCLE SCROOGE: BLAST TO THE PAST	WALT DISNEY		1	1	1992	1992	CARTOON TALES
UNDERCOVER	FAME PRESS		1	96	1964	1969	
UNDERCOVER GIRL	UNITED-ANGLO PRODUCTIONS		1	1	1951	1951	MAGAZINE ENTERPRISES REPRINTS
UNDERCOVER GIRL ANNUAL	MAGAZINE ENTERPRISES		5	7	1952	1954	
UNDERDOG	CHARLTON COMICS	1	1	10	1970	1972	
UNDERDOG	GOLD KEY	2	1	23	1975	1979	
UNDERDOG	HARVEY PUBLICATIONS		1	3	1993	NOW	
UNDERDOG GIANT SIZE	HARVEY PUBLICATIONS		1	1	1993	NOW	
UNDERSEA AGENT	TOWER COMICS		1	6	1966	1967	
UNDERSEA FIGHTING COMMANDOS	AVON BOOKS		1	5	1952	1953	
UNDERSEA FIGHTING COMMANDOS	I.W. ENTERPRISES		1	2	1964	1964	REPRINT
UNDERSTANDING COMICS	TUNDRA		1	1	1993	1993	
UNDERWORLD	D.S. PUBLISHING CO.		1	9	1948	1949	
UNDERWORLD	DC COMICS INC.		1	4	1987	1988	
UNDERWORLD	R. & L. LOCKER		1	1	1951	1951	D.S. PUBLISHING REPRINTS
UNDERWORLD CRIME	FAWCETT PUBLICATIONS		1	9	1952	1953	
UNDERWORLD STORY, THE	AVON BOOKS		1	1	1950	1950	
UNEARTHLY SPECTACULARS	HARVEY PUBLICATIONS		1	3	1965	1967	
UNEXPECTED, THE	DC COMICS INC.		105	222	1968	1982	FORMERLY TALES OF THE UNEXPECTED
UNICORN ISLE	APPLE COMICS		1	5	1985	1988	

COMIC TITLE	PUBLISHER	Vol No.	Srt No.	End No.	Str. Year	End Year	COMMENTS
UNION	IMAGE COMICS		1	3	1993	NOW	
UNITED COMICS	UNITED FEATURES SYNDICATE		1	26	1940	1953	FORMERLY FRITZI RITZI
UNITED STATES AIR FORCE PRESENTS: THE HIDDEN CREW	U.S. AIR FORCE		1	1	1964	1964	
UNITED STATES FIGHTING AIR FORCE	SUPERIOR COMICS		1	29	1952	1956	
UNITED STATES MARINES	MAGAZINE ENTERPRISES	5		8	1952	1952	
UNITED STATES MARINES	TOBY PRESS PUBLICATIONS	9		11	1953	1953	
UNITED STATES MARINES	WILLIAM H. WISE	1		4	1943	1944	
UNITY	VALIANT / VOYAGER COMMUNICATIONS	0		1	1992	1992	
UNIVERSAL INTERGALACTIC DISCOVERY CO.	COMICO		1	1	1992	1992	
UNIVERSAL MONSTERS: CREATURE FROM THE BLACK LAGOON	DARK HORSE COMICS		1	1	1993	1993	
UNIVERSAL MONSTERS: DRACULA	DARK HORSE COMICS		1	1	1993	1993	
UNIVERSAL MONSTERS: FRANKENSTEIN	DARK HORSE COMICS		1	1	1993	1993	
UNIVERSAL MONSTERS: THE MUMMY	DARK HORSE COMICS		1	1	1993	1993	
UNIVERSAL PRESENTS DRACULA, THE MUMMY, AND OTHER STORIES	DELL PUBLISHING COMPANY		1	1	1963	1963	
UNIVERSAL SOLDIER	NOW		1	3	1992	1992	
UNKEPT PROMISE	LEGION OF TRUTH		1	1	1949	1949	
UNKNOWN MAN, THE	AVON BOOKS		1	1	1951	1951	
UNKNOWN SOLDIER	DC COMICS INC.		1	12	1988	1989	
UNKNOWN SOLDIER	DC COMICS INC.		205	268	1977	1982	FORMERLY STAR SPANGLED WAR STORIES
UNKNOWN WORLD	FAWCETT PUBLICATIONS		1	1	1952	1952	
UNKNOWN WORLDS	AMERICAN COMIC GROUP		1	57	1960	1967	
UNKNOWN WORLDS OF FRANK BRUNNER	PACIFIC COMICS		1	2	1985	1985	
UNKNOWN WORLDS OF SCIENCE FICTION	MARVEL ENTERTAINMENT GROUP		1	6	1975	1975	
UNKNOWN WORLDS OF SCIENCE FICTION SPECIAL	MARVEL ENTERTAINMENT GROUP		1	1	1976	1976	
UNSANE	STAR PUBLICATIONS	15		15	1954	1954	FORMERLY MIGHTY BEAR AND THE OUTLAWS
UNSEEN	CARTOON ART		1	1	1955	1955	STANDARD COMICS REPRINTS
UNSEEN, THE	STANDARD COMICS	5		15	1952	1954	
UNSUPERVISED EXISTENCE	FANTAGRAPHICS		1	7	1990	NOW	
UNTAMED	MARVEL ENTERTAINMENT GROUP		1	3	1993	1993	
UNTAMED LOVE	FANTAGRAPHICS		1	1	1987	1987	
UNTAMED LOVE	QUALITY (FLEETWAY)		1	5	1950	1950	
UNTOLD LEGEND OF BATMAN, THE	DC COMICS INC.		1	3	1980	1980	
UNTOLD LEGEND OF THE BATMAN, THE	DC COMICS INC.		1	3	1980	1980	CEREAL GIVEAWAYS
UNTOLD ORIGIN OF THE FEM FORCE, THE	AC COMICS		1	1	1992	1992	
UNTOUCHABLES, THE	EASTERN COLOR PRINTING COMPANY		1	20	1988	1988	
UNUSUAL TALES	ALAN CLASS AND CO LTD		1	2	1963	1963	CHARLTON REPRINTS
UNUSUAL TALES	CHARLTON COMICS		1	49	1955	1965	
UNUSUAL TALES	MORING		1	1	1959	1959	CHARLTON REPRINTS
UP YOUR NOSE AND OUT YOUR EAR	KLEVART ENTERPRISES		1	2	1972	1972	
UP-TO-DATE COMICS	KING FEATURES		1	1	1938	1938	
URBAN DECAY	ANUBIS PRESS		1	1	1993	1993	
URBAN LEGENDS	DARK HORSE COMICS		1	1	1993	1993	
URTH 4	CONTINUITY COMICS	1	1	7	1990	1991	
URTH 4	CONTINUITY COMICS	2	1	3	1992	1992	
US 1	MARVEL ENTERTAINMENT GROUP		1	12	1983	1984	
USA COMICS	TIMELY COMICS		1	17	1941	1945	
USA IS READY	DELL PUBLISHING COMPANY		1	1	1941	1941	
USAGI YOJIMBO	FANTAGRAPHICS		1	38	1987	1992	
USAGI YOJIMBO	MIRAGE STUDIOS	2	1	4	1992	1992	
USAGI YOJIMBO COLOR SPECIAL	FANTAGRAPHICS		1	1	1989	1989	
USAGI YOJIMBO SUMMER SPECIAL	FANTAGRAPHICS		1	1	1986	1986	

V

COMIC TITLE	PUBLISHER	Vol No.	Srt No.	End No.	Str. Year	End Year	COMMENTS
V	DC COMICS INC.		1	18	1985	1986	
V FOR VENDETTA	DC COMICS INC.		1	1	1990	1990	
V FOR VENDETTA	DC COMICS INC.		1	10	1988	1989	
V...-COMICS	FOX FEATURES SYNDICATE		1	2	1942	1942	
VACATION IN DISNEYLAND	DELL PUBLISHING COMPANY		1	1	1958	1958	
VACATION IN DISNEYLAND	GOLD KEY		1	1	1965	1965	
VACATION PARADE	DELL PUBLISHING COMPANY		1	5	1950	1954	
VALENTINO	RENEGADE PRESS		1	1	1985	1985	
VALERIA THE SHE BAT	CONTINUITY COMICS		1	5	1993	NOW	
VALIANT	FLEETWAY		1	714	1962	1976	
VALIANT ANNUAL	FLEETWAY		1964	1984	1964	1984	
VALIANT BOOK OF CONQUEST OF THE AIR	FLEETWAY		1	1	1972	1972	
VALIANT BOOK OF MAGIC AND MYSTERY	FLEETWAY		1	1	1976	1976	
VALIANT BOOK OF PIRATES	FLEETWAY		1	1	1967	1967	
VALIANT BOOK OF SPORTS	FLEETWAY		1	1	1973	1973	
VALIANT BOOK OF TV'S SEXTON BLAKE	FLEETWAY		1	1	1969	1969	
VALIANT BOOK OF WEAPONS AND WAR	FLEETWAY		1	1	1976	1976	
VALIANT EFFORTS	VALIANT PRESS		1	2	1991	NOW	
VALIANT ERA	VALIANT / VOYAGER COMMUNICATIONS		1	1	1993	1993	
VALIANT PICTURE LIBRARY	FLEETWAY		1	144	1963	1969	
VALIANT READER GUIDE/VALIANT UNIVERSE	VALIANT / VOYAGER COMMUNICATIONS		1	1	1993	1993	
VALIANT SPACE SPECIAL	FLEETWAY		1967	1968	1967	1968	
VALIANT STORY OF THE WEST	FLEETWAY		1	2	1966	1966	
VALIANT SUMMER SPECIAL	FLEETWAY		1966	1980	1966	1980	
VALIANT VISION STARTER KIT	VALIANT / VOYAGER COMMUNICATIONS		1	1	1993	1993	
VALKYRIE	ECLIPSE	1	1	3	1987	1987	
VALKYRIE	ECLIPSE	2	1	3	1988	1988	
VALLEY OF THE DINOSAURS	CHARLTON COMICS		1	11	1975	1976	
VALOR	DC COMICS INC.		1	16	1982	NOW	
VALOR	EC COMICS		1	5	1955	1955	

INDEX OF COMIC TITLES AND THEIR PUBLISHERS

COMIC TITLE	PUBLISHER	Vol No.	Srt No.	End No.	Str. Year	End Year	COMMENTS
VALOUR	MARVEL ENTERTAINMENT GROUP		1	19	1980	1981	
VALOUR WINTER SPECIAL	MARVEL ENTERTAINMENT GROUP		1	1	1980	1980	
VAMPEROTICA	BRAINSTORM COMICS		1	1	1993	NOW	
VAMPIRE COMPANION, THE	INNOVATION		1	3	1990	1991	
VAMPIRE LESTAT SIGNED, THE	INNOVATION		1	1	1992	1992	
VAMPIRE LESTAT, THE	INNOVATION		1	1	1991	1991	
VAMPIRE LESTAT, THE	INNOVATION		1	12	1990	1991	
VAMPIRE TALES	MARVEL ENTERTAINMENT GROUP		1	11	1973	1975	
VAMPIRE TALES ANNUAL	MARVEL ENTERTAINMENT GROUP		1	1	1975	1975	
VAMPIRE WORLD	ACID RAIN STUDIOS		1	1	1993	NOW	
VAMPIRE: DIABLERIE ENGLAND	WHITE WOLF PUBLISHING		1	1	1993	1993	
VAMPIRE: THE MASQUERADE	WHITE WOLF PUBLISHING		1	1	1991	1991	
VAMPIRELLA	DARK HORSE COMICS		1	4	1991	1992	
VAMPIRELLA	HARRIS COMICS		1	1	1992	1992	
VAMPIRELLA	HARRIS COMICS		1	5	1992	NOW	
VAMPIRELLA	IPC		1	10	1975	1976	WARREN REPRINTS
VAMPIRELLA	WARREN PUBLISHING CO		1	113	1969	1988	
VAMPIRELLA ANNUAL	WARREN PUBLISHING CO		1	1	1972	1972	
VAMPIRELLA SPECIAL	WARREN PUBLISHING CO		1	1	1977	1977	
VAMPIRELLA VS THE CULT OF CHAOS	DARK HORSE COMICS		1	1	1992	1992	
VAMPIRELLA'S SUMMER NIGHTS	DARK HORSE COMICS		1	1	1992	1992	
VAMPIRELLA: A SCARLET THIRST	HARRIS COMICS		1	1	1993	1993	
VAMPIRIC JIHAD	APPLE COMICS		1	1	1991	1991	
VAMPYRE'S KISS	AIRCEL	1	1	4	1990	1990	
VAMPYRES	ETERNITY		1	4	1988	1989	
VANGUARD	IMAGE COMICS	2	1	3	1993	NOW	
VANGUARD	MEGATON COMICS	1	1	1	1987	1987	
VANGUARD ILLUSTRATED	PACIFIC COMICS		1	7	1983	1984	
VANITY	PACIFIC COMICS		1	2	1984	1984	
VANTAGE	VANTAGE		1	7	1993	NOW	
VANTAGE PRESS RELEASE REVIEW	VANTAGE		1	3	1994	NOW	
VAPOR LOCH	SKY COMICS		1	1	1993	NOW	
VARIETY COMICS	RURAL HOME PUBLISHING COMPANY		1	5	1944	1946	
VARSITY	PARENTS MAGAZINE INSTITUTE		1	1	1945	1945	
VAUDEVILLE AND OTHER THINGS	ISAAC H. BLANDIARD LTD.		1	1	1900	1900	
VAULT OF EVIL	MARVEL ENTERTAINMENT GROUP		1	23	1973	1975	
VAULT OF HORROR	ARNOLD BOOK CO.		1	1	1954	1954	EC REPRINTS
VAULT OF HORROR	EC COMICS	1	12	40	1950	1955	FORMERLY WAR AGAINST CRIME
VAULT OF HORROR, THE	GLADSTONE		1	6	1991	1991	
VAULT OF HORROR, THE	RUSS COCHRAN		1	6	1990	1991	
VC'S, THE	FLEETWAY		1	5	1991	1991	
VC'S, THE	TITAN BOOKS		1	2	1987	1987	
VECTOR	NOW		1	3	1986	1986	
VEGAS KNIGHTS	PIONEER		1	1	1989	1989	
VELOCITY	ECLIPSE		1	5	1991	NOW	
VELOCITY	WARREN & GARRY PLEECE		1	5	1988	NOW	
VELVET	ADVENTURE COMICS		1	4	1992	1993	
VENGEANCE SQUAD	CHARLTON COMICS		1	6	1975	1976	
VENGER ROBO	VIZ		1	2	1993	1994	
VENOM: DEATHTRAP THE VAULT	MARVEL ENTERTAINMENT GROUP		1	1	1993	1993	
VENOM: FUNERAL PYRE	MARVEL ENTERTAINMENT GROUP		1	3	1993	1993	
VENOM: LETHAL PROTECTOR	MARVEL ENTERTAINMENT GROUP		1	1	1993	1993	
VENOM: THE ENEMY WITHIN	MARVEL ENTERTAINMENT GROUP		1	1	1993	1994	
VENOM: THE MACE	MARVEL ENTERTAINMENT GROUP		1	3	1994	1994	
VENOM: THE MADNESS	MARVEL ENTERTAINMENT GROUP		1	3	1993	1993	
VENTURE	AC COMICS		1	3	1986	1987	
VENTURE COMIC	P.M. PRODUCTIONS		1	1	1948	1948	
VENUMB	PARODY PRESS		1	1	1992	1992	
VENUS	MARVEL ENTERTAINMENT GROUP		1	19	1948	1952	
VENUS WARS	DARK HORSE COMICS		1	1	1993	1993	
VENUS WARS II, THE	DARK HORSE COMICS		1	15	1992	NOW	
VENUS WARS, THE	DARK HORSE COMICS		1	14	1991	1992	
VERDICT : THE ACOLYTE	CALIBER PRESS		1	1	1992	1992	
VERI BEST SURE FIRE COMICS	HOLYOKE PUBLISHING COMPANY		1	1	1945	1945	REPRINTS
VERONICA	ARCHIE PUBLICATIONS		1	33	1989	NOW	
VERONICA'S PASSPORT DIGEST MAGAZINE	ARCHIE PUBLICATIONS		1	2	1992	NOW	
VERSION	DARK HORSE COMICS	1.1	2.6		1993	NOW	
VERTIGO JAM	DC COMICS INC.		1	1	1993	NOW	
VERTIGO PREVIEW	DC COMICS INC.		1	1	1993	NOW	
VERTIGO VISIONS: PHANTOM STRANGER	DC COMICS INC.		1	1	1993	1993	
VERTIGO VISIONS: THE GEEK	DC COMICS INC.		1	1	1993	1993	
VERY BEST OF MARVEL TRADE PAPERBACK, THE	MARVEL ENTERTAINMENT GROUP		1	1	1991	1991	
VERY BEST SURE SHOT COMICS	HOLYOKE PUBLISHING COMPANY		1	1	1945	1945	REPRINTS
VERY VICKY	CALIBER PRESS		1	1	1992	1992	
VIC AND BLOOD	MAD DOG		1	2	1987	1988	
VIC FLINT	L. MILLER PUBLISHING COMPANY (UK)		1	1	1955	1955	
VIC FLINT, CRIME BUSTER	ST JOHN PUBLISHING		1	5	1948	1949	
VIC JORDAN	ARGO PUBLISHING		1	2	1956	1956	
VIC JORDAN	CIVIL SERVICE PUBLICATION/PENTAGON PUBLISHING CO.		1	1	1945	1945	
VIC TORRY AND HIS FLYING SAUCER	FAWCETT PUBLICATIONS		1	1	1950	1950	
VIC TORRY AND HIS FLYING SAUCER	L. MILLER PUBLISHING COMPANY (UK)		1	1	1950	1950	FAWCETT REPRINTS
VIC VERITY MAGAZINE	VIC VERITY PUBLICATIONS		1	7	1945	1946	
VICIOUS	BRAINSTORM COMICS		1	1	1993	NOW	
VICKI	ATLAS		1	4	1975	1975	
VICKI VALENTINE	RENEGADE PRESS		1	4	1985	1986	
VICKS COMICS	EASTERN COLOR PRINTING COMPANY		1	2	1938	1938	
VICTIMS	ETERNITY		1	6	1988	1989	
VICTOR	D.C. THOMSON		1	1657	1961	1992	
VICTOR FOR BOYS SUMMER SPECIAL	D.C. THOMSON		1967	1993	1967	NOW	

326

COMIC TITLE	PUBLISHER	Vol No.	Srt No.	End No.	Str. Year	End Year	COMMENTS
VICTORY COMICS	HILLMAN PERIODICALS		1	4	1941	1941	
VICTORY FUNNIES	FULTON PUBLISHING CO,		1	1	1944	1944	
VIDEO JACK	MARVEL ENTERTAINMENT GROUP		1	6	1987	1988	
VIETNAM JOURNAL	APPLE COMICS		1	15	1987	1989	
VIETNAM JOURNAL TET '68	APPLE COMICS		1	6	1991	1993	
VIETNAM JOURNAL: INDIAN COUNTRY	APPLE COMICS				1990	1990	
VIETNAM JOURNAL: VALLEY OF DEATH	APPLE COMICS		1	4	1994	1994	
VIEW FROM THE VOID	H. BUNCH ASSOCIATES		1	1	1973	1973	
VIGIL: FALL FROM GRACE	INNOVATION		1	2	1991	1992	
VIGIL: KUKULCAN	INNOVATION		1	1	1993	NOW	
VIGIL: RETURN FROM GRACE	INNOVATION		1	1	1992	NOW	
VIGIL: THE GOLDEN PARTS	INNOVATION		1	1	1992	1992	
VIGILANTE THE, ANNUAL	DC COMICS INC.		1	2	1985	1986	
VIGILANTE, THE	DC COMICS INC.		1	50	1983	1988	
VIKING PRINCE: THE VIKINGS GLORY	DC COMICS INC.		1	1	1991	1991	
VILLAIN & HERO	CRY FOR DAWN PUBLICATIONS		1	1	1993	1993	
VILLAINS AND VIGILANTES	ECLIPSE		1	4	1986	1987	
VINTAGE PACK	MARVEL ENTERTAINMENT GROUP		1	1	1993	1993	
VIOLENT CASES	ESCAPE		1	1	1987	1987	
VIRGINIAN, THE	GOLD KEY		1	1	1963	1963	
VIRUS	DARK HORSE COMICS		1	4	1993	1993	
VISION AND SCARLET WITCH	MARVEL ENTERTAINMENT GROUP	1	1	4	1982	1983	
VISION AND SCARLET WITCH	MARVEL ENTERTAINMENT GROUP	2	1	12	1985	1986	
VISIONARIES	MARVEL ENTERTAINMENT GROUP		1	6	1987	1988	
VISIONS	VISION PUBLICATIONS		1	5	1979	1983	
VIZ COMIC	JOHN BROWN PUBLISHING		1	53	1979	NOW	
VIZ HOLIDAY SPECIAL	JOHN BROWN PUBLISHING		1	1	1988	1988	
VIZ MONSTER SEX REMIX	JOHN BROWN PUBLISHING		5	6	1985	1985	FORMERLY THE BEST OF VIZ
VIZ PRESENTS THE PATHETIC SHARKS BUMPER SPECIAL	JOHN BROWN PUBLISHING		1	1	1991	1991	
VIZ, THE BEST OF	JOHN BROWN PUBLISHING		1	4	1983	1983	
VIZ: BILLY THE FISH FOOTBALL YEARBOOK	JOHN BROWN PUBLISHING		1	1	1990	1990	
VIZ: THE BIG HARD ONE	JOHN BROWN PUBLISHING		1	1	1986	1986	
VIZ: THE BIG HARD ONE NUMBER TWO	JOHN BROWN PUBLISHING		1	1	1987	1987	
VIZ: THE BIG PINK STIFF ONE	JOHN BROWN PUBLISHING		1	1	1988	1988	
VIZ: THE DOG'S BOLLOCKS	JOHN BROWN PUBLISHING		1	1	1989	1989	
VIZ: THE SAUSAGE SANDWICH	JOHN BROWN PUBLISHING		1	1	1991	1991	
VIZ: THE SPUNKY PARTS	JOHN BROWN PUBLISHING				1990	1990	
VOID INDIGO	MARVEL ENTERTAINMENT GROUP		1	2	1984	1985	
VOLTAR	A PLUS COMICS		1	1	1992	NOW	
VOLTRON DEFENDER OF THE UNIVERSE	MODERN COMICS		1	3	1984	1984	
VOODA, JUNGLE PRINCESS	AJAX	20	22		1955	1955	FORMERLY VOODOO
VOODOO	AJAX		1	19	1952	1955	
VOODOO	L. MILLER PUBLISHING COMPANY (UK)		1	8	1961	1961	ATLAS REPRINTS
VOODOO ANNUAL	AJAX		1	1	1952	1952	
VORTEX	COMICO	1	1	4	1991	1992	
VORTEX	COMICO	2	1	4	1993	1993	
VORTEX	VORTEX		1	15	1982	1988	
VOYAGE TO THE BOTTOM OF THE SEA	DELL PUBLISHING COMPANY		1	16	1964	1970	
VOYAGE TO THE DEEP	DELL PUBLISHING COMPANY		1	4	1962	1964	
VOYUESE - WOMEN VIEW SEX	KNOCKABOUT		1	1	1991	1991	
VULCAN (NATIONAL EDITION)	IPC		1	28	1975	1976	
VULCAN (SCOTTISH EDITION)	IPC		1	30	1975	1975	
VULCAN ANNUAL	FLEETWAY		1	1	1977	1977	
VULCAN HOLIDAY SPECIAL	IPC		1	1	1976	1976	
VULCAN MINI-COMIC	IPC		1	3	1976	1976	SUPPLEMENT TO VALIANT

W

COMIC TITLE	PUBLISHER	Vol No.	Srt No.	End No.	Str. Year	End Year	COMMENTS
WACKO	IDEAL PUBLICATIONS		1	3	1980	1981	
WACKY ADVENTURES OF CRACKY	GOLD KEY		1	12	1972	1975	
WACKY DUCK	I.W. ENTERPRISES		1	7	1958	1958	REPRINTS
WACKY DUCK	MARVEL ENTERTAINMENT GROUP	1	3	6	1946	1947	FORMERLY DOPEY DUCK
WACKY DUCK	MARVEL ENTERTAINMENT GROUP	2	1	2	1948	1948	
WACKY RACES	GOLD KEY		1	7	1969	1972	
WACKY SQUIRREL	DARK HORSE COMICS		1	4	1987	1988	
WACKY SQUIRREL SUMMER FUN SPECIAL	DARK HORSE COMICS		1	1	1988	1988	
WACKY SQUIRREL'S HALOWEEN ADVENTURE SPECIAL	DARK HORSE COMICS		1	1	1987	1987	
WACKY WITCH	GOLD KEY		1	21	1971	1975	
WACKY WOODPECKER	I.W. ENTERPRISES		1	7	1958	1958	REPRINTS
WAGON TRAIN	DELL PUBLISHING COMPANY	1	4	13	1958	1962	
WAGON TRAIN	GOLD KEY	2	1	4	1964	1964	
WAGONS, ROLL! WESTERN	G.T. LIMITED		1	1	1959	1959	
WAGS	T.V. BOARDMAN		1	88	1937	1938	
WAGS SPECIAL	T.V. BOARDMAN		1	1	1938	1938	
WALLENSTEIN THE MONSTER	TOP SELLERS		1	1	1974	1974	
WALLY	GOLD KEY		1	4	1962	1963	
WALLY THE WIZARD	MARVEL ENTERTAINMENT GROUP		1	12	1985	1986	
WALLY WOOD'S T.H.U.N.D.E.R. AGENTS	DELUXE COMICS		1	5	1984	1986	
WALT DISNEY CHRISTMAS PARADE	WHITMAN		11191	11191	1977	1977	
WALT DISNEY COMICS DIGEST	GOLD KEY		1	57	1968	1976	
WALT DISNEY PRESENTS	DELL PUBLISHING COMPANY	2	6		1959	1961	
WALT DISNEY SERIES	WORLD DISTRIBUTORS LTD		1	52	1956	1957	DELL SERIES
WALT DISNEY SHOWCASE	GOLD KEY		1	54	1970	1980	
WALT DISNEY'S AUTUMN ADVENTURES	WALT DISNEY		1	2	1990	1991	
WALT DISNEY'S CHRISTMAS PARADE	GLADSTONE		1	2	1988	1989	
WALT DISNEY'S CHRISTMAS PARADE	GLADSTONE		1	1	1988	1988	

INDEX OF COMIC TITLES AND THEIR PUBLISHERS

COMIC TITLE	PUBLISHER	Vol No.	Srt No.	End No.	Str. Year	End Year	COMMENTS
WALT DISNEY'S CHRISTMAS PARADE	GOLD KEY		I	9	1963	1972	
WALT DISNEY'S COMICS AND STORIES	DELL PUBLISHING COMPANY		I	587	1940	1962	
WALT DISNEY'S COMICS AND STORIES	DELL PUBLISHING COMPANY		1945	1952	1945	1952	
WALT DISNEY'S COMICS AND STORIES	GLADSTONE		511	588	1986	NOW	
WALT DISNEY'S COMICS AND STORIES	GOLD KEY		264	473	1962	1982	
WALT DISNEY'S COMICS AND STORIES	WALT DISNEY		I	I	1943	1943	
WALT DISNEY'S COMICS AND STORIES	WALT DISNEY		548	586	1990	NOW	
WALT DISNEY'S COMICS AND STORIES	WHITMAN		474	510	1982	1984	
WALT DISNEY'S COMICS DIGEST	GLADSTONE		I	7	1986	1987	
WALT DISNEY'S HOLIDAY PARADE	WALT DISNEY		I	2	1990	1991	
WALT DISNEY'S MAGAZINE	WESTERN PUBLISHING COMPANY		4	18	1957	1959	FORMERLY WALT DISNEY'S MICKEY MOUSE CLUB
WALT DISNEY'S MICKEY MOUSE	WALT DISNEY		I	56	1958	1959	
WALT DISNEY'S MICKEY MOUSE CLUB MAGAZINE	WESTERN PUBLISHING COMPANY		I	7	1956	1957	
WALT DISNEY'S MICKEY MOUSE CLUB MAGAZINE ANNUAL	WESTERN PUBLISHING COMPANY		I	2	1956	1957	
WALT DISNEY'S PICTURE TREASURY	IPC		1972	1976	1972	1976	
WALT DISNEY'S PINOCCHIO SPECIAL	GLADSTONE		I	I	1990	1990	
WALT DISNEY'S SPRING FEVER	WALT DISNEY		I	I	1991	1991	
WALT DISNEY'S UNCLE REMUS AND BREER RABBIT	COLLINS		I	I	1947	1947	DELL REPRINTS
WALT DISNEY'S WEEKLY	WALT DISNEY		I	118	1959	1961	
WALT KELLY'S CHRISTMAS CLASSICS	ECLIPSE		I	I	1987	1987	
WALT KELLY'S SANTA CLAUS ADVENTURES	INNOVATION		I	I	1991	1991	
WALT KELLY'S SPRINGTIME TALES	ECLIPSE		I	I	1988	1988	
WALTER LANTZ ANDY PANDA	GOLD KEY		I	23	1973	1978	
WAMBI JUNGLE BOY	R. & L. LOCKER		I	I	1951	1951	FICTION HOUSE REPRINTS
WAMBI, JUNGLE BOY	FICTION HOUSE		I	18	1942	1953	
WAMBI, JUNGLE BOY	I.W. ENTERPRISES		8	8	1964	1964	REPRINTS
WANDERERS, THE	DC COMICS INC.		I	13	1988	1989	
WANDERING STARS	FANTAGRAPHICS		I	I	1987	1987	
WANTED COMICS	ARNOLD BOOK CO.		I	3	1948	1948	ORBIT REPRINTS
WANTED COMICS	TOYTOWN PUBLICATIONS		9	53	1947	1953	
WANTED, THE WORLD'S MOST DANGEROUS VILLAINS	DC COMICS INC.		I	9	1972	1973	
WAR	CHARLTON COMICS		I	49	1975	1978	
WAR	L. MILLER PUBLISHING COMPANY (UK)		I	II	1961	1962	ATLAS REPRINTS
WAR	MODERN COMICS		7	9	1977	1977	REPRINTS
WAR ACTION	ATLAS		I	14	1952	1953	
WAR ADVENTURES	ATLAS		I	13	1952	1953	
WAR ADVENTURES ON THE BATTLEFIELD	ATLAS		I	II	1952	1953	
WAR AGAINST CRIME!	EC COMICS		I	II	1948	1950	
WAR AND ATTACK	CHARLTON COMICS	I	I	I	1964	1964	
WAR AND ATTACK	CHARLTON COMICS	2	54	63	1966	1967	FORMERLY FIGHTIN' AIR FORCE
WAR AT SEA	CHARLTON COMICS		22	42	1957	1961	FORMERLY SPACE ADVENTURE
WAR AT SEA	L. MILLER PUBLISHING COMPANY (UK)		I	I	1958	1958	CHARLTON REPRINTS
WAR AT SEA PICTURE LIBRARY	FLEETWAY		I	36	1962	1963	
WAR BATTLES	HARVEY PUBLICATIONS		I	9	1952	1953	
WAR BIRDS	FICTION HOUSE		I	3	1952	1953	
WAR COMBAT	ATLAS		I	5	1952	1952	
WAR COMICS	DELL PUBLISHING COMPANY		I	4	1940	1941	
WAR COMICS	GERALD SWAN		I	20	1940	1943	
WAR COMICS	MARVEL ENTERTAINMENT GROUP		I	49	1950	1957	
WAR COMICS	STREAMLINE		I	3	1951	1951	ATLAS REPRINTS
WAR COMICS SPRING SPECIAL	GERALD SWAN		1943	1943	1943	1943	
WAR COMICS SUMMER SPECIAL	GERALD SWAN		1941	1942	1941	1942	
WAR COMICS WINTER SPECIAL	GERALD SWAN		1941	1941	1941	1941	
WAR DANCER	DEFIANT		I	3	1994	NOW	
WAR DOGS OF THE U.S. ARMY	AVON BOOKS		I	I	1952	1952	
WAR FURY	COMIC MEDIA/ALAN HARDY ASSOCIATE		I	4	1952	1953	
WAR HERO	WORLD DISTRIBUTORS LTD		50	51	1970	???	
WAR HEROES	ACE MAGAZINES	2	I	8	1952	1953	
WAR HEROES	CHARLTON COMICS		I	27	1963	1967	
WAR HEROES	DELL PUBLISHING COMPANY	I	I	II	1942	1945	
WAR IS HELL	MARVEL ENTERTAINMENT GROUP		I	15	1973	1975	
WAR MACHINE	MARVEL ENTERTAINMENT GROUP		I	3	1994	NOW	
WAR MAN	MARVEL ENTERTAINMENT GROUP		I	2	1993	1993	
WAR OF THE GODS	DC COMICS INC.		I	4	1991	1992	
WAR OF THE WORLDS	ETERNITY		I	6	1988	1990	
WAR PICTURE LIBRARY	FLEETWAY		I	2103	1958	1984	
WAR PICTURE LIBRARY HOLIDAY SPECIAL	IPC		1963	1993	1963	NOW	
WAR REPORT	AJAX		I	5	1952	1953	
WAR SHIPS	DELL PUBLISHING COMPANY		I	I	1942	1942	
WAR SIRENS LIBERTY BELLES	HARVEY PUBLICATIONS		I	I	1991	1991	
WAR STORIES	DELL PUBLISHING COMPANY	5	8	1942	1943		FORMERLY WAR COMICS
WAR STORIES (KOREA)	AJAX		I	5	1952	1953	
WAR VICTORY ADVENTURES	HARVEY PUBLICATIONS		I	3	1942	1944	
WAR WINGS	CHARLTON COMICS		I	I	1968	1968	
WAR, THE	MARVEL ENTERTAINMENT GROUP		I	4	1989	1989	
WAR-PATH! PICTURE AND STORY ALBUM	MELLIFONT		I	I	50'S	50'S	
WARFRONT	HARVEY PUBLICATIONS		I	39	1951	1967	
WARHEADS	MARVEL ENTERTAINMENT GROUP		I	14	1992	1993	
WARHEADS: BLACK DAWN	MARVEL ENTERTAINMENT GROUP		I	2	1993	1993	
WARHIDE	MARVEL ENTERTAINMENT GROUP		I	4	1994	1994	MARVEL UK TITLE
WARLOCK & THE INFINITY WATCH	MARVEL ENTERTAINMENT GROUP		I	26	1992	NOW	
WARLOCK (SPECIAL EDITION)	MARVEL ENTERTAINMENT GROUP		I	6	1982	1983	1ST REPRINT SERIES
WARLOCK 5	AIRCEL	2	I	7	1989	NOW	
WARLOCK 5 BOOK I	AIRCEL		I	22	1986	1989	
WARLOCK 5: THE GATHERING	NIGHT WYND ENTERPRISES		I	I	1993	NOW	
WARLOCK CHRONICLES	MARVEL ENTERTAINMENT GROUP		I	8	1993	NOW	
WARLOCK REPRINTS	MARVEL ENTERTAINMENT GROUP	2	I	6	1992	1992	2ND REPRINT SERIES

COMIC TITLE	PUBLISHER	Vol No.	Srt No.	End No.	Str. Year	End Year	COMMENTS
WARLOCK, THE POWER OF	MARVEL ENTERTAINMENT GROUP		1	15	1972	1976	
WARLOCKS	AIRCEL		1	12	1988	NOW	
WARLOCKS SPECIAL EDITION	AIRCEL		1	1	1983	1983	
WARLORD	D.C. THOMSON		1	627	1974	1986	
WARLORD	DC COMICS INC.		1	133	1976	1988	
WARLORD	DC COMICS INC.		1	6	1992	1992	
WARLORD ANNUAL	DC COMICS INC.		1	6	1982	1987	
WARLORD PETER FLINT SPECIAL	D.C. THOMSON		1	1	1976	1976	
WARLORD SUMMER SPECIAL	D.C. THOMSON		1975	1980	1975	1980	
WARLORD: SAVAGE EMPIRE	DC COMICS INC.		1	1	1992	1992	
WARP	FIRST		1	19	1983	1985	
WARP GRAPHICS ANNUAL	WARP GRAPHICS		1	1	1986	1986	
WARP SPECIAL	FIRST		1	3	1983	1984	
WARPATH	KEY PUBLICATIONS		1	3	1954	1955	
WARPATH/INDIANS ON THE WARPATH	STREAMLINE		1	3	1955	1955	
WARPWALKING	CALIBER PRESS		1	4	1992	1993	
WARREN PRESENTS	WARREN PUBLISHING CO		1	14	1979	1981	
WARREN PRESENTS: THE ROOK	WARREN PUBLISHING CO		1	1	1979	1979	
WARRIOR	PENWITH/DEREK G. SKINN	1	1	6	1974	1975	
WARRIOR	QUALITY (FLEETWAY)		1	26	1982	1985	
WARRIOR COMICS	H.C. BLACKERBY		1	1	1945	1945	
WARRIOR SUMMER SPECIAL	QUALITY (FLEETWAY)		1982	1982	1982	1982	
WARRIOR WOMEN	MARVEL ENTERTAINMENT GROUP		1	1	1980	1980	
WARRIORS	ADVENTURE COMICS		1	7	1987	NOW	
WARRIORS OF PLASM	DEFIANT		1	6	1993	NOW	
WARRIORS OF PLASM TP	DEFIANT		1	1	1994	1994	
WARRIORS OF PLASM: HOME FOR THE HOLIDAYS	DEFIANT		1	1	1993	1993	
WART AND THE WIZARD	GOLD KEY		1	1	1964	1964	
WARTIME ROMANCES	ST JOHN PUBLISHING		1	18	1951	1953	
WARTS AND ALL	PENGUIN BOOKS				1990	1990	
WARWORLD	DARK HORSE COMICS		1	1	1989	1989	
WASHABLE JONES AND SHMOO	HARVEY PUBLICATIONS		1	1	1953	1953	
WASTELAND	DC COMICS INC.		1	18	1987	1989	
WATCH, THE BEST OF	VANGUARD COMICS		1	1	1993	1993	
WATCHCATS	HARRIER		1	1	1987	1987	
WATCHMEN	DC COMICS INC.		1	1	1988	1988	
WATCHMEN	DC COMICS INC.		1	12	1986	1987	
WAVEMAKERS	BLIND BAT PRESS		1	1	1990	NOW	
WCW WORLD CHAMPIONSHIP WRESTLING	MARVEL ENTERTAINMENT GROUP		1	12	1992	1993	
WEATHER-BIRD	WESTERN PUBLISHING COMPANY		1	16	1958	1962	
WEATHER-BIRD COMICS	WEATHER BIRD SHOES		1	1	1957	1957	SEVERAL VERSIONS
WEAVEWORLD	MARVEL ENTERTAINMENT GROUP		1	3	1991	1992	
WEB OF EVIL	QUALITY COMICS		1	21	1952	1954	
WEB OF HORROR	MAJOR MAGAZINES INC		1	3	1969	1970	
WEB OF SPIDER-MAN	MARVEL ENTERTAINMENT GROUP		1	110	1985	NOW	
WEB OF SPIDER-MAN ANNUAL	MARVEL ENTERTAINMENT GROUP		1	9	1985	NOW	
WEB, THE	DC COMICS INC.		1	14	1991	1992	IMPACT TITLE
WEB, THE ANNUAL	DC COMICS INC.		1	1	1992	1992	IMPACT TITLE
WEDDING BELLS	QUALITY COMICS		1	19	1954	1956	
WEDDING OF DRACULA	MARVEL ENTERTAINMENT GROUP		1	1	1992	1992	
WEE CHUMS COMIC	PHILIMAR		1	1	1949	1949	
WEEKEND MAIL COMIC	ASSOCIATED NEWSPAPERS				1955	1955	
WEEKENDER, THE	RUCKER PUBL. CO.	1	4	4	1945	1945	
WEEKENDER, THE	RUCKER PUBL. CO.	2	1	1	1946	1946	
WEEKLY COMIC MAGAZINE	FOX FEATURES SYNDICATE		1	2	1940	1940	SEVERAL VERSIONS
WEIRD	EERIE PUBLICATIONS		1	2	1966	1977	
WEIRD ADVENTURES	P.L. PUBLISHING		1	3	1951	1951	
WEIRD ADVENTURES	ZIFF-DAVIS PUBLISHING COMPANY		10	10	1951	1951	
WEIRD CHILLS	KEY PUBLICATIONS		1	3	1954	1954	
WEIRD COMICS	FOX FEATURES SYNDICATE		1	20	1940	1942	
WEIRD FANTASY	EC COMICS	1	13	17	1950	1953	FORMERLY A MOON, A GIRL, ROMANCE
WEIRD FANTASY	EC COMICS	3	1	6	1993	NOW	
WEIRD FANTASY	RUSS COCHRAN	2	6	22	1992	1992	
WEIRD HORRORS	ST JOHN PUBLISHING		1	9	1952	1953	
WEIRD MYSTERIES	GILLMOR MAGAZINES		1	12	1952	1954	
WEIRD MYSTERIES	PASTIME PUBLICATIONS		1	1	1959	1959	
WEIRD MYSTERY TALES	DC COMICS INC.		1	24	1972	1975	
WEIRD PLANETS	ALAN CLASS AND CO LTD		1	21	1962	1963	ATLAS, CHARLTON REPRINTS
WEIRD SCIENCE	EC COMICS	1	12	22	1950	1953	FORMERLY SADDLE ROMANCE
WEIRD SCIENCE	GLADSTONE		1	4	1992	1992	
WEIRD SCIENCE	RUSS COCHRAN		1	6	1990	1991	
WEIRD SCIENCE ILLUSTORIES	CARTOON ART		1	1	1956	1956	MAGAZINE ENTERPRISES REPRINTS
WEIRD SCIENCE-FANTASY	EC COMICS		1	6	1954	1955	FORMERLY WEIRD SCIENCE & WEIRD FANTASY
WEIRD SCIENCE-FANTASY	RUSS COCHRAN	2	1	2	1992	NOW	
WEIRD SCIENCE-FANTASY ANNUAL	EC COMICS		1	2	1952	1953	
WEIRD SUSPENSE	ATLAS		1	3	1975	1975	
WEIRD TALES ILLUSTRATED	MILLENIUM		1	2	1992	NOW	
WEIRD TALES OF THE FUTURE	ARAGON MAGAZINES		1	8	1952	1953	
WEIRD TALES OF THE MACABRE	ATLAS		1	2	1975	1975	
WEIRD TERROR	COMIC MEDIA/ALAN HARDY ASSOCIATE		1	13	1952	1954	
WEIRD THRILLERS	ZIFF-DAVIS PUBLISHING COMPANY		1	5	1951	1952	
WEIRD WAR TALES	DC COMICS INC.		1	124	1971	1983	
WEIRD WESTERN TALES	DC COMICS INC.		12	70	1972	1980	FORMERLY ALL-STAR WESTERN
WEIRD WONDER TALES	MARVEL ENTERTAINMENT GROUP		1	28	1973	1977	
WEIRD WORLDS	DC COMICS INC.		1	10	1972	1974	
WEIRD WORLDS	EERIE PUBLICATIONS		1	14	1970	1971	
WEIRD WORLDS	THORPE & PORTER		1	2	1953	???	ATLAS REPRINTS
WEIRD, THE	DC COMICS INC.		1	4	1988	1988	
WELCOME BACK KOTTER	DC COMICS INC.		1	10	1976	1978	

INDEX OF COMIC TITLES AND THEIR PUBLISHERS

COMIC TITLE	PUBLISHER	Vol No.	Srt No.	End No.	Str. Year	End Year	COMMENTS
WENDIGO	CALIBER PRESS		I	I	1991	1991	
WENDY PARKER COMICS	ATLAS		I	8	1953	1954	
WENDY WITCH DIGEST	HARVEY PUBLICATIONS		I	5	1991	NOW	
WENDY WITCH WORLD	HARVEY PUBLICATIONS		I	93	1961	1974	
WENDY, THE GOOD LITTLE WITCH	HARVEY PUBLICATIONS	I	I	99	1960	1990	
WENDY, THE GOOD LITTLE WITCH	HARVEY PUBLICATIONS	2	I	13	1991	NOW	
WEREWOLF	DELL PUBLISHING COMPANY		I	3	1966	1967	
WEREWOLF	MARVEL ENTERTAINMENT GROUP		I	I	1981	1981	
WEREWOLF BY NIGHT	MARVEL ENTERTAINMENT GROUP		I	43	1972	1977	
WEREWOLF BY NIGHT GIANT SIZE	MARVEL ENTERTAINMENT GROUP		2	5	1974	1975	
WEREWOLVES & VAMPIRES	CHARLTON COMICS		I	I	1962	1962	
WES SLADE	EXPRESS PUBLICATIONS		I	I	1979	1979	
WESTERN ACTION	ATLAS		I	I	1975	1975	
WESTERN ACTION	I.W. ENTERPRISES		7	7	1964	1964	REPRINTS
WESTERN ACTION THRILLERS	DELL PUBLISHING COMPANY		I	I	1937	1937	
WESTERN ADVENTURE LIBRARY	MICRON/SMITH		I	2	1963	???	
WESTERN ADVENTURES COMICS	ACE MAGAZINES		I	6	1948	1949	
WESTERN BANDIT TRAILS	ST JOHN PUBLISHING		I	3	1949	1949	
WESTERN BANDITS	AVON BOOKS		I	I	1952	1952	
WESTERN BUMPER ALBUM	TOP SELLERS		I	3	1972	1972	
WESTERN CLASSICS	TOP SELLERS		I	2	1972	1972	DELL REPRINTS
WESTERN CLASSICS	WORLD DISTRIBUTORS LTD		I	40	1958	1960	
WESTERN COMICS	DC COMICS INC.		I	85	1948	1961	
WESTERN CRIME BUSTERS	TROJAN MAGAZINES		I	10	1950	1952	
WESTERN CRIME CASES	STAR PUBLICATIONS		9	9	1951	1951	FORMERLY INDIAN WARRIORS
WESTERN DAYS	SCION		I	I	1952	1952	
WESTERN DESPERADO COMICS	FAWCETT PUBLICATIONS		8	8	1940	1940	FORMERLY SLAM BANG COMICS
WESTERN FIGHTERS	CARTOON ART		I	2	1951	1951	HILLMAN REPRINTS
WESTERN FIGHTERS	HILLMAN PERIODICALS		I	43	1948	1953	
WESTERN FIGHTERS	HILLMAN PERIODICALS	I	I	12	1948	1949	
WESTERN FIGHTERS	HILLMAN PERIODICALS	2	I	12	1949	1950	
WESTERN FIGHTERS	HILLMAN PERIODICALS	3	I	12	1950	1951	
WESTERN FIGHTERS	HILLMAN PERIODICALS	4	I	7	1952	1953	
WESTERN FIGHTERS	STREAMLINE		I	4	1951	1954	HILLMAN REPRINTS
WESTERN FIGHTERS 3-D	STAR PUBLICATIONS		I	I	1953	1953	
WESTERN FRONTIER	P.L. PUBLISHING		I	7	1951	1952	
WESTERN FUN COMIC	GERALD SWAN		8	13	1953	1954	PREVIOUSLY WESTERN WAR COMIC
WESTERN GUNFIGHTERS	ATLAS	I	20	27	1956	1957	FORMERLY APACHE KID
WESTERN GUNFIGHTERS	MARVEL ENTERTAINMENT GROUP	2	I	33	1970	1975	
WESTERN GUNFIGHTERS SUMMER SPECIAL	MARVEL ENTERTAINMENT GROUP		1980	1981	1980	1981	
WESTERN GUNFIGHTERS WINTER SPECIAL	MARVEL ENTERTAINMENT GROUP		1981	1981	1981	1981	
WESTERN HEARTS	STANDARD COMICS		I	10	1949	1952	
WESTERN HERO	FAWCETT PUBLICATIONS		76	112	1949	1952	FORMERLY WOW COMICS & REAL WESTERN HERO
WESTERN HERO	L. MILLER PUBLISHING COMPANY (UK)		50	149	1949	1950	FAWCETT REPRINTS
WESTERN KID	ATLAS	I	I	17	1954	1957	
WESTERN KID	L. MILLER PUBLISHING COMPANY (UK)		I	12	1955	1955	ATLAS REPRINTS
WESTERN KID	MARVEL ENTERTAINMENT GROUP	2	I	5	1971	1972	
WESTERN KILLERS	FOX FEATURES SYNDICATE		60	64	1948	1949	
WESTERN KILLERS	STREAMLINE		I	I	50'S	50'S	
WESTERN LIFE ROMANCES	MARVEL ENTERTAINMENT GROUP		I	2	1949	1950	
WESTERN LOVE	PRIZE PUBLICATIONS		I	5	1949	1950	
WESTERN LOVE TRAILS	ACE MAGAZINES		7	9	1949	1950	FORMERLY WESTERN ADVENTURES
WESTERN OUTLAWS	ATLAS		I	21	1954	1957	
WESTERN OUTLAWS	FOX FEATURES SYNDICATE		17	21	1948	1949	FORMERLY JUNIOR COMICS
WESTERN OUTLAWS	GERALD SWAN		I	8	1954	1954	PRIZE REPRINTS
WESTERN OUTLAWS	L. MILLER PUBLISHING COMPANY (UK)		I	2	1954	1954	MARVEL REPRINTS
WESTERN OUTLAWS	STREAMLINE		I	2	1955	1955	
WESTERN OUTLAWS AND SHERIFFS	MARVEL ENTERTAINMENT GROUP		60	73	1949	1952	FORMERLY BEST WESTERN
WESTERN PICTURE LIBRARY	C.A. PEARSON		I	20	1958	1959	
WESTERN PICTURE LIBRARY	G.M. SMITH		501	828	1979	1985	
WESTERN PICTURE STORIES	COMICS MAGAZINE CO.		I	3	1937	1937	
WESTERN ROUGH RIDERS	GILLMOR MAGAZINES		I	4	1954	1955	
WESTERN ROUGH RIDERS	STREAMLINE		I	2	1955	1955	STANMORE REPRINTS
WESTERN ROUNDUP (DELL GIANT COMICS)	DELL PUBLISHING COMPANY		I	25	1952	1959	
WESTERN ROUNDUP COMIC	WORLD DISTRIBUTORS LTD		I	398	1955	1958	DELL REPRINTS
WESTERN STAR PICTURE LIBRARY	M.V. FEATURES		I	2	1965	???	
WESTERN STARS COMIC	L. MILLER PUBLISHING COMPANY (UK)		I	17	1952	1958	FAWCETT REPRINTS
WESTERN SUPER THRILLER COMICS	WORLD DISTRIBUTORS LTD		34	82	50'S	50'S	PREVIOUSLY SUPER THRILLER
WESTERN TALES	BRUGEDITOR		I	2	1962	???	
WESTERN TALES	HARVEY PUBLICATIONS		31	33	1955	1956	FORMERLY WITCHES' WESTERN TALES
WESTERN TALES	UNITED-ANGLO PRODUCTIONS		I	2	1956	1956	HARVEY REPRINTS
WESTERN TALES	WORLD DISTRIBUTORS LTD		I	I	1955	1955	HARVEY REPRINTS
WESTERN TALES OF BLACK RIDER	ATLAS		28	31	1955	1955	FORMERLY BLACK RIDER
WESTERN TEAM UP	MARVEL ENTERTAINMENT GROUP		I	I	1973	1973	
WESTERN THRILLER	STREAMLINE		I	I	1955	1955	PRIZE, FICTION HOUSE REPRINTS
WESTERN THRILLERS	ATLAS		I	4	1954	1955	
WESTERN THRILLERS	FOX FEATURES SYNDICATE		I	6	1948	1949	
WESTERN THRILLERS	M.S. PUBLISHING		52	52	1954	1954	REPRINTS
WESTERN THRILLERS	STREAMLINE		I	I	1950	1950	FOX FEATURES REPRINTS
WESTERN TRAIL PICTURE LIBRARY	FAME PRESS		I	2	1966	???	
WESTERN TRAILS	ATLAS		I	2	1957	1957	
WESTERN TRAILS	L. MILLER PUBLISHING COMPANY (UK)		I	5	1957	1957	ATLAS REPRINTS
WESTERN TRAILS	STREAMLINE		I	I	50'S	50'S	
WESTERN TRUE CRIME	FOX FEATURES SYNDICATE		I	6	1948	1949	
WESTERN WAR COMIC	GERALD SWAN	I	I	5	1949	1950	
WESTERN WAR COMIC	GERALD SWAN	2	I	6	1952	1953	
WESTERN WINNERS	MARVEL ENTERTAINMENT GROUP		5	7	1949	1949	FORMERLY ALL-WESTERN WINNERS
WESTERNER, THE	I.W. SUPER		14	41	1948	1951	
WESTERNER, THE	SUPER COMICS		15	17	1964	1964	REPRINTS

INDEX OF COMIC TITLES AND THEIR PUBLISHERS

COMIC TITLE	PUBLISHER	Vol No.	Srt No.	End No.	Str. Year	End Year	COMMENTS
WESTWORLD FOURSOME COMIC	WESTWORLD PUBLICATIONS		1	14	50'S	50'S	
WETWORKS	IMAGE COMICS		1	1	1994	1994	
WHACK	ST JOHN PUBLISHING		1	3	1953	1954	ISSUE NO. WAS 3-D
WHACKY RODEO	FUNNIBOOK CO.		1	2	1947	1947	
WHAM COMICS	CENTAUR PUBLICATIONS		1	2	1940	1940	
WHAM!	ODHAMS		1	187	1964	1968	
WHAM! ANNUAL	ODHAMS	1966	1974	1966	1974		
WHAM-O GIANT COMICS	WHAM-O MFG CO.		1	1	1967	1967	
WHAT IF?	MARVEL ENTERTAINMENT GROUP	1	1	47	1977	1984	
WHAT IF?	MARVEL ENTERTAINMENT GROUP	2	1	59	1989	NOW	
WHAT IF? SPECIAL	MARVEL ENTERTAINMENT GROUP		1	1	1988	1988	
WHAT THE? FALL SPECIAL	MARVEL ENTERTAINMENT GROUP		1	1	1993	1993	
WHAT THE? SUMMER SPECIAL	MARVEL ENTERTAINMENT GROUP		1	1	1993	1993	
WHAT THE?!	MARVEL ENTERTAINMENT GROUP		1	25	1988	NOW	
WHAT'S BEHIND THESE HEADLINES?	WILLIAM C. POPPER		1	1	1948	1948	
WHAT'S NEW? THE COLLECTED ADV. OF PHIL & DIXIE	PALLIARD PRESS		1	2	1991	1991	
WHEATIES	WALT DISNEY		1	4	1950	1951	
WHEE COMICS	MODERN STORE PUBLISHING		1	1	1955	1955	
WHEELIE AND THE CHOPPER BUNCH	CHARLTON COMICS		1	7	1975	1976	
WHEELS	BYBLOS		1	2	1978	1978	
WHERE CREATURES ROAM	MARVEL ENTERTAINMENT GROUP		1	8	1970	1971	
WHERE MONSTERS DWELL	MARVEL ENTERTAINMENT GROUP		1	38	1970	1975	
WHERE'S HUDDLES?	GOLD KEY		1	3	1971	1971	
WHIP WILSON	MARVEL ENTERTAINMENT GROUP	9	11	1950	1950		FORMERLY REX HART
WHIRLWIND COMICS	NITA PUBLICATIONS		1	3	1940	1940	
WHISPER	CAPITAL COMICS		1	2	1983	1984	
WHISPER	FIRST		1	37	1986	1990	
WHISPER SPECIAL	FIRST		1	1	1985	1985	
WHITE CHIEF OF THE PAWNEE INDIANS	AVON BOOKS		1	1	1951	1951	
WHITE DEVIL	ETERNITY		1	6	1990	1991	
WHITE FANG	WALT DISNEY		1	1	1991	1991	
WHITE INDIAN	MAGAZINE ENTERPRISES	11	15	1953	1954		
WHITE PRINCESS OF THE JUNGLE	AVON BOOKS		1	5	1951	1952	
WHITE RIDER AND THE SUPER HORSE	STAR PUBLICATIONS		1	6	1950	1951	FORMERLY HUMDINGER
WHITE TRASH	TUNDRA		1	3	1992	1992	
WHITMAN COMICS BOOKS	WHITMAN		1	8	1962	1962	
WHIZ COMICS	FAWCETT PUBLICATIONS		1	155	1940	1953	
WHIZ COMICS	L. MILLER PUBLISHING COMPANY (UK)	60	128	1950	1959		FAWCETT REPRINTS
WHIZZBANG COMIC	PHILIMAR		1	1	1948	1948	
WHIZZER AND CHIPS	IPC				1969	1990	NO NUMBERS, DATES ONLY
WHIZZER AND CHIPS HOLIDAY SPECIAL	IPC	1970	1991	1970	1991		
WHIZZER COMICS	CARTOON ART		1	5	1947	1948	
WHO FRAMED ROGER RABBIT	LONDON NIGHT STUDIO		1	1	1990	1990	
WHO IS NEXT?	STANDARD COMICS	5	5	1953	1953		
WHO'S WHO	DC COMICS INC.		1	26	1984	1987	
WHO'S WHO DELUXE	DC COMICS INC.		1	16	1990	1992	
WHO'S WHO IN STAR TREK	DC COMICS INC.		1	2	1987	1987	
WHO'S WHO IN THE LEGION	DC COMICS INC.		1	7	1988	1988	
WHO'S WHO UPDATE (1987)	DC COMICS INC.		1	5	1987	1987	
WHO'S WHO UPDATE (1988)	DC COMICS INC.		1	4	1988	1988	
WHO'S WHO UPDATE (1993)	DC COMICS INC.		1	1	1993	1993	
WHODUNIT	D.S. PUBLISHING CO.		1	3	1948	1949	
WHODUNNIT?	ECLIPSE		1	3	1986	1987	
WHOOPEE COMIC	PHILIMAR		1	1	1949	1949	
WHOOPEE!	IPC				1974	1985	NO NUMBERS, DATES ONLY
WHOPPING COMIC	INTERNATIONAL		1	1	1945	1945	
WHY I HATE SATURN	DC COMICS INC.				1991	1991	
WILBUR COMICS	ARCHIE PUBLICATIONS		1	90	1944	1965	
WILBUR COMICS	GERALD SWAN		1	2	1950	???	ARCHIE REPRINTS
WILD	ATLAS		1	5	1954	1954	
WILD ANGELS	MARVEL ENTERTAINMENT GROUP		1	4	1993	1994	MARVEL UK TITLE
WILD ANIMALS	PACIFIC COMICS		1	1	1982	1982	
WILD BILL ELLIOTT COMICS	WORLD DISTRIBUTORS LTD		1	18	1954	1955	DELL REPRINTS
WILD BILL HICKOK	AVON BOOKS		1	28	1949	1956	
WILD BILL HICKOK	I.W. ENTERPRISES		1		60'S	60'S	REPRINTS
WILD BILL HICKOK	SUPER COMICS	10	12	60'S	60'S		
WILD BILL HICKOK AND JINGLES	CHARLTON COMICS	68	75	1958	1959		FORMERLY COWBOY WESTERN
WILD BILL HICKOK AND JINGLES	L. MILLER PUBLISHING COMPANY (UK)		1	16	1959	1960	DELL REPRINTS
WILD BILL HICKOK COMICS	THORPE & PORTER		1	14	1952	1954	AVON REPRINTS
WILD BILL PECOS THE WESTERNER	PEMBERTON		1	63	1953	1958	WANTED COMICS REPRINTS
WILD BOY OF THE CONGO	ST JOHN PUBLISHING	4	7	1951	1955		
WILD BOY OF THE CONGO	ZIFF-DAVIS PUBLISHING COMPANY	10	12	1951	1951		
WILD CARDS	MARVEL ENTERTAINMENT GROUP		1	1	1991	1991	
WILD CARDS	MARVEL ENTERTAINMENT GROUP		1	4	1990	1990	
WILD DOG	DC COMICS INC.		1	4	1987	1987	
WILD DOG SPECIAL	DC COMICS INC.		1	1	1989	1989	
WILD FRONTIER	CHARLTON COMICS		1	7	1955	1957	
WILD FRONTIER	L. MILLER PUBLISHING COMPANY (UK)		1	2	1955	1956	CHARLTON REPRINTS
WILD KINGDOM	WESTERN PUBLISHING COMPANY		1	1	1965	1965	
WILD KNIGHTS	ETERNITY		1	10	1988	1989	
WILD THING	MARVEL ENTERTAINMENT GROUP		1	6	1993	NOW	MARVEL UK TITLE
WILD WEST	CHARLTON COMICS	2	58	58	1966	1966	FORMERLY BLACK FURY
WILD WEST	MARVEL ENTERTAINMENT GROUP	1	1	2	1948	1948	
WILD WEST C.O.W. BOYS OF MOO MOO MESA	ARCHIE PUBLICATIONS	1	1	3	1992	1993	
WILD WEST C.O.W. BOYS OF MOO MOO MESA	ARCHIE PUBLICATIONS	2	1	3	1993	1993	
WILD WEST PICTURE LIBRARY	FLEETWAY		1	114	1966	1971	
WILD WEST PICTURE LIBRARY HOLIDAY SPECIAL	IPC	1973	1974	1973	1974		
WILD WEST PICTURE STORIES	C.A. PEARSON		1	2	1960	???	
WILD WEST RODEO	STAR PUBLICATIONS		1	1	1953	1953	
WILD WESTERN	L. MILLER PUBLISHING COMPANY (UK)		1	9	1955	1955	ATLAS/MARVEL REPRINTS

COMIC TITLE	PUBLISHER	Vol No.	Srt No.	End No.	Str. Year	End Year	COMMENTS
WILD WESTERN	MARVEL ENTERTAINMENT GROUP		3	57	1948	1957	FORMERLY WILD WEST
WILD WESTERN	STREAMLINE		1	1	1951	1951	PRIZE REPRINTS
WILD WESTERN ACTION	SKYWALD PUBLISHING		1	2	1971	1971	
WILD WESTERN ROUNDUP	DECKER PUBLICATIONS		1	1	1957	1957	
WILD WESTERN ROUNDUP	I.W. ENTERPRISES		1	1	1960	1961	REPRINT
WILD WILD WEST, THE	GOLD KEY		1	7	1966	1969	
WILD WILD WEST, THE	MILLENIUM		1	4	1990	1990	
WILD, THE	EASTERN COLOR PRINTING COMPANY		1	7	1988	1988	
WILD, THIS MAGAZINE IS	DELL PUBLISHING COMPANY		1	3	1968	1968	
WILDBRATS	FANTAGRAPHICS		1	1	1992	1992	
WILDC.A.T.S.	IMAGE COMICS		1	1	1993	1993	
WILDC.A.T.S.	IMAGE COMICS		1	6	1992	NOW	
WILDC.A.T.S. SOURCEBOOK	IMAGE COMICS		1	1	1993	1993	
WILDC.A.T.S. TRILOGY	IMAGE COMICS		1	3	1993	1993	
WILDC.A.T.S. YEARBOOK	IMAGE COMICS		1	1	1993	NOW	
WILDCAT	FLEETWAY		1	4	1988	1988	
WILDSTAR: SKY ZERO	IMAGE COMICS		1	4	1993	1993	
WILDSTEER	PARODY PRESS		1	1	1993	1993	
WILL EISNER'S 3-D CLASSICS FEATURING THE SPIRIT	KITCHEN SINK		1	1	1985	1985	
WILL EISNER'S QUARTERLY	KITCHEN SINK		1	8	1984	1986	
WILL ROGERS WESTERN	FOX FEATURES SYNDICATE		5	5	1950	1950	FORMERLY MY GREAT LOVE
WILL ROGERS WESTERN COMIC	UNITED-ANGLO PRODUCTIONS		1	2	1950	1950	FOX FEATURES REPRINTS
WILLIAM SHATNER'S TEKWORLD	MARVEL ENTERTAINMENT GROUP		1	1	1993	1993	
WILLIAM TELL	PEARSON		1	3	1959	1959	
WILLIE COMICS	MARVEL ENTERTAINMENT GROUP		5	23	1946	1950	FORMERLY IDEAL. NO ISSUES #'S 20 OR 21
WILLIE THE PENGUIN	STANDARD COMICS		1	6	1951	1952	
WILLIE THE WISE-GUY	ATLAS		1	1	1957	1957	
WILLIE WESTINGHOUSE EDISON SMITH THE BOY INVENTOR	WILLIAM A. STOKES		1	1	1906	1906	
WILLOW	MARVEL ENTERTAINMENT GROUP		1	3	1988	1988	
WILLOW MOVIE ADAPTATION	MARVEL ENTERTAINMENT GROUP		1	1	1988	1988	
WILLY THE KID BOOK, THE	DUCKWORTH		1	3	1976	1978	
WIN A PRIZE COMICS	CHARLTON COMICS		1	2	1955	1955	
WINDJAMMER, THE	MARTIN & REID		1	1	1950	1950	
WINDY AND WILLY	DC COMICS INC.		1	4	1969	1969	
WINGS COMICS	CARTOON ART		1	1	1950	1950	FICTION HOUSE REPRINTS
WINGS COMICS	FICTION HOUSE		1	124	1940	1954	
WINGS COMICS	STREAMLINE		1	2	1951	1951	FICTION HOUSE REPRINTS
WINGS COMICS	TRENT		1	3	1953	1953	FICTION HOUSE REPRINTS
WINKY DINK, THE ADVENTURES OF	PINES		75	75	1957	1957	
WINNER COMIC, THE	D.J. BURNSIDE		1	2	1947	1948	
WINNIE THE POOH	GOLD KEY		1	17	1977	1977	
WINNIE THE POOH	WHITMAN		18	33	1978	1984	
WINNIE WINKLE	CUPPLES AND LEON CO.		1	4	1930	1933	
WINNIE WINKLE	DELL PUBLISHING COMPANY		1	7	1948	1949	
WINTER WORLD	ECLIPSE		1	3	1988	1988	
WIREHEADS	FLEETWAY		1	1	1993	1994	
WISCO/KLARER COMIC BOOK	MARVEL ENTERTAINMENT GROUP				1948	1964	MINIATURE COMIC GIVEAWAYS
WISE LITTLE HEN, THE	DAVID MCKAY PUBLICATIONS		1934	1935	1934	1935	
WISE LITTLE HEN, THE	WHITMAN		888	888	1937	1937	
WITCHCRAFT	AVON BOOKS		1	6	1952	1953	
WITCHES TALES	EERIE PUBLICATIONS		1	35	1969	1975	
WITCHES TALES	EERIE PUBLICATIONS	1	7	9	1969	1969	
WITCHES TALES	EERIE PUBLICATIONS	2	1	6	1970	1970	
WITCHES TALES	EERIE PUBLICATIONS	3	1	6	1971	1971	
WITCHES TALES	EERIE PUBLICATIONS	4	1	6	1972	1972	
WITCHES TALES	EERIE PUBLICATIONS	5	1	6	1973	1973	
WITCHES TALES	EERIE PUBLICATIONS	6	1	6	1974	1974	
WITCHES TALES	EERIE PUBLICATIONS	7	1	1	1975	1975	
WITCHES TALES	HARVEY PUBLICATIONS		1	28	1951	1954	
WITCHES' WESTERN TALES	HARVEY PUBLICATIONS		29	30	1955	1955	FORMERLY WITCHES TALES
WITCHING HOUR	DC COMICS INC.		1	85	1969	1978	
WITCHING HOUR, ANNE RICE'S	MILLENIUM		1	4	1993	NOW	
WITH THE MARINES ON THE BATTLEFRONTS OF THE WORLD	TOBY PRESS PUBLICATIONS		1	2	1953	1954	
WITH THE U.S. PARATROOPS BEHIND ENEMY LINES	AVON BOOKS		1	6	1951	1952	
WITHIN OUR REACH	MARVEL ENTERTAINMENT GROUP		1	1	1991	1991	
WITNESS, THE	MARVEL ENTERTAINMENT GROUP		1	1	1948	1948	
WITTY COMICS	IRWIN H. RUBIN		1	7	1945	1945	
WIZARD	D.C. THOMSON		1	435	1970	1978	
WIZARD COLLECTORS LIBRARY SERIES	WIZARD		1	1	1994	NOW	
WIZARD GUIDE TO COMICS	WIZARD		1	30	1991	NOW	
WIZARD MIDGET COMIC	D.C. THOMSON		1	1	1954	1954	
WIZARD OF FOURTH STREET	DARK HORSE COMICS		1	2	1987	1988	
WIZARD SPECIAL EDITION: SUPERMAN'S BACK	WIZARD		1	1	1993	1993	
WIZARD X-MEN SPECIAL EDITION	WIZARD		1	1	1993	1993	
WIZARD: 100 MOST COLLECTABLE COMICS	WIZARD		1	1	1992	1992	
WIZARD: THE BEGINNING OF THE VALIANT ERA SPECIAL	WIZARD				1994	1994	
WIZARDS TALE	ECLIPSE		1	3	1993	1993	
WOLFPACK	MARVEL ENTERTAINMENT GROUP		1	1	1987	1987	
WOLFPACK	MARVEL ENTERTAINMENT GROUP		1	12	1988	1989	
WOLPH	BLACKTHORNE		1	1	1987	1987	
WOLVERINE	MARVEL ENTERTAINMENT GROUP		1	1	1987	1987	
WOLVERINE	MARVEL ENTERTAINMENT GROUP		1	4	1982	1982	
WOLVERINE	MARVEL ENTERTAINMENT GROUP		1	78	1988	NOW	
WOLVERINE & GHOST RIDER: ACTS OF VENGEANCE	MARVEL ENTERTAINMENT GROUP		1	1	1993	1993	
WOLVERINE & NICK FURY: SCORPIO CONNECTION	MARVEL ENTERTAINMENT GROUP		1	1	1993	1993	
WOLVERINE BATTLES THE INCREDIBLE HULK	MARVEL ENTERTAINMENT GROUP		1	1	1986	1991	
WOLVERINE IN GLOBAL JEOPARDY	MARVEL ENTERTAINMENT GROUP		1	1	1993	1993	PRODUCED IN ASSOCIATION WITH WWF

COMIC TITLE	PUBLISHER	Vol No.	Srt No.	End No.	Str. Year	End Year	COMMENTS
WOLVERINE RAHNE OF TERRA	MARVEL ENTERTAINMENT GROUP		I	I	1991	1991	
WOLVERINE SAGA	MARVEL ENTERTAINMENT GROUP		I	4	1989	1989	
WOLVERINE SPECIAL EDITION: THE JUNGLE ADVENTURE	MARVEL ENTERTAINMENT GROUP		I	I	1990	1990	
WOLVERINE/PUNISHER: DAMAGING EVIDENCE	MARVEL ENTERTAINMENT GROUP		I	3	1993	1993	
WOLVERINE: BLOOD HUNGRY	MARVEL ENTERTAINMENT GROUP				1993	1993	
WOLVERINE: BLOODLUST	MARVEL ENTERTAINMENT GROUP		I	I	1991	1991	
WOLVERINE: BLOODY CHOICES	MARVEL ENTERTAINMENT GROUP		I	I	1993	1993	
WOLVERINE: EVILUTION	MARVEL ENTERTAINMENT GROUP		I	I	1992	1992	
WOLVERINE: INNER FURY	MARVEL ENTERTAINMENT GROUP		I	I	1993	1993	
WOLVERINE: KILLING	MARVEL ENTERTAINMENT GROUP		I	I	1993	1993	
WOLVERINE: SAVE THE TIGER	MARVEL ENTERTAINMENT GROUP		I	I	1992	1992	
WOLVERINE: WEAPON X	MARVEL ENTERTAINMENT GROUP		I	I	1992	1992	
WOMAN OF THE PROMISE, THE	CAETECHETICAL EDUCATIONAL SOCIETY		I	I	1950	1950	
WOMEN IN LOVE	FOX FEATURES SYNDICATE		I	4	1949	1950	
WOMEN IN LOVE	ZIFF-DAVIS PUBLISHING COMPANY		I	I	1952	1952	
WOMEN OUTLAWS	FOX FEATURES SYNDICATE		I	8	1948	1949	
WOMEN TO LOVE	AVON BOOKS		I	I	1953	1953	REPRINTS
WONDER	AMALGAMATED PRESS		1444	1760	1942	1953	PREVIOUSLY THE FUNNY WONDER
WONDER BOY	AJAX		17	18	1955	1955	FORMERLY TERRIFIC COMICS
WONDER BOY	L. MILLER PUBLISHING COMPANY (UK)		I	3	1955	1955	ATLAS REPRINTS
WONDER COMICS	FOX FEATURES SYNDICATE	I	I	2	1939	1939	
WONDER COMICS	NEDOR (BETTER PUBLICATIONS)	2	I	20	1944	1948	
WONDER DUCK	MARVEL ENTERTAINMENT GROUP		I	3	1949	1950	
WONDER DUCK	UNITED-ANGLO PRODUCTIONS		I	I	1950	1950	MARVEL REPRINTS
WONDER HEROES	SUNBURST PUBLICATIONS		I	2	1981	1984	
WONDER MAN	MARVEL ENTERTAINMENT GROUP		I	29	1991	NOW	
WONDER MAN ANNUAL	MARVEL ENTERTAINMENT GROUP		I	2	1992	NOW	
WONDER MAN SPECIAL	MARVEL ENTERTAINMENT GROUP		I	I	1986	1986	
WONDER STORY COMIC	NEWTON WICKHAM		I	I	1944	1944	
WONDER WOMAN	DC COMICS INC.	I	I	329	1942	1986	
WONDER WOMAN	DC COMICS INC.	2	I	83	1987	NOW	
WONDER WOMAN ANNUAL	DC COMICS INC.	2	I	3	1988	NOW	
WONDER WOMAN PIZZA HUT GIVEAWAYS	DC COMICS INC.		I	I	1977	1977	
WONDER WOMAN SPECIAL	DC COMICS INC.		I	I	1992	1992	
WONDER WORKER OF PERU	CAETECHETICAL EDUCATIONAL SOCIETY		I	I	???	???	
WONDERFUL WORLD OF DUCKS	COLGATE PALMOLIVE CO.		I	I	1975	1975	
WONDERLAND COMICS	FEATURE PUBLICATIONS		I	9	1945	1947	
WONDERMAN	ALEX WHITE		I	26	1967	1968	
WONDERMAN	PAGET		I	24	1949	1951	
WONDERWORLD COMICS	FOX FEATURES SYNDICATE		3	33	1939	1942	FORMERLY WONDER COMICS
WONDERWORLDS	INNOVATION		I	I	1992	1992	
WOODSY OWL	GOLD KEY		I	10	1973	1976	
WOODY WOODPECKER	DELL PUBLISHING COMPANY		16	72	1952	1962	
WOODY WOODPECKER	GOLD KEY		73	187	1962	1982	
WOODY WOODPECKER	HARVEY PUBLICATIONS		I	11	1992	NOW	
WOODY WOODPECKER	WHITMAN		188	201	1982	1984	
WOODY WOODPECKER, ADVENTURES OF	HARVEY PUBLICATIONS		I	I	1992	NOW	
WOODY WOODPECKER BACK TO SCHOOL	DELL PUBLISHING COMPANY		I	6	1952	1956	NO ISSUE NO.5
WOODY WOODPECKER BIG BOOK	HARVEY PUBLICATIONS		I	I	1993	NOW	
WOODY WOODPECKER COUNTY FAIR	DELL PUBLISHING COMPANY		5	2	1956	1958	TWO ISSUES ONLY, ISSUE 5 PUBLISHED 1st
WOODY WOODPECKER DIGEST	HARVEY PUBLICATIONS		I	I	1991	NOW	
WOODY WOODPECKER FRIENDS	HARVEY PUBLICATIONS		I	4	1992	1992	
WOODY WOODPECKER GIANT SIZE	HARVEY PUBLICATIONS		I	I	1992	NOW	
WOODY WOODPECKER HOLIDAY SPECIAL	HARVEY PUBLICATIONS		I	I	1993	1993	
WOODY WOODPECKER SPECIAL	HARVEY PUBLICATIONS		I	I	1991	1991	
WOOLWORTH'S CHRISTMAS STORY BOOK	WESTERN PUBLISHING COMPANY		1952	1954	1952	1954	
WOOLWORTH'S HAPPY TIME CHRISTMAS BOOK	WHITMAN		I	I	1952	1952	
WORDSMITH	CALIBER PRESS		I	2	1990	1990	
WORDSMITH	RENEGADE PRESS		I	12	1985	1988	
WORKIN KLASS SUPER HERO	JOLLY MARTIAN PUBLICATIONS		I	3	1979	1980	
WORLD ACCORDING TO CRUMB, THE	NATIONAL CENTER FOR COMICS & IMAGES				1992	1992	
WORLD AROUND US, THE	GILBERTON PUBLICATIONS		I	36	1958	1961	
WORLD DOMINATION	ROCK-IT COMIX		I	I	1993	1993	
WORLD FAMOUS HEROES MAGAZINE	CENTAUR PUBLICATIONS		I	4	1941	1942	
WORLD FAMOUS STORIES	CROYDON PUBLISHERS		I	I	1945	1945	
WORLD FUN	MARTIN & REID		I	I	1948	1948	
WORLD ILLUSTRATED	THORPE & PORTER		501	536	1960	1960	
WORLD IS HIS PARISH, THE	GEORGE PFLAUM		I	I	1953	1953	
WORLD OF ADVENTURE	GOLD KEY		I	3	1963	1963	
WORLD OF ARCHIE	ARCHIE PUBLICATIONS		I	8	1992	NOW	
WORLD OF FANTASY	ATLAS		I	19	1956	1959	
WORLD OF KRYPTON, THE	DC COMICS INC.	I	I	3	1979	1979	
WORLD OF KRYPTON, THE	DC COMICS INC.	2	I	4	1987	1988	
WORLD OF METROPOLIS	DC COMICS INC.		I	4	1988	1988	
WORLD OF MYSTERY	ATLAS		I	7	1956	1957	
WORLD OF SMALLVILLE	DC COMICS INC.		I	4	1988	1988	
WORLD OF SUSPENSE	ATLAS		I	8	1956	1958	
WORLD OF WHEELS	CHARLTON COMICS		17	32	1967	1970	FORMERLY DRAGSTRIP HOTRODDERS
WORLD OF WHEELS	MODERN COMICS		23	23	1978	1978	REPRINTS
WORLD OF WOOD	ECLIPSE		I	6	1986	1987	
WORLD WAR III	ACE PERIODICALS		I	2	1953	1953	
WORLD WAR STORIES	DELL PUBLISHING COMPANY		I	3	1965	1965	
WORLD WITHOUT END	DC COMICS INC.		I	6	1990	1991	
WORLD WRESTLING FEDERATION BATTLEMANIA	VALIANT / VOYAGER COMMUNICATIONS		I	5	1991	1991	
WORLD'S BEST COMICS	DC COMICS INC.		I	I	1941	1941	BECOMES WORLD'S FINEST
WORLD'S FINEST	DC COMICS INC.		I	3	1990	1990	
WORLD'S FINEST	DC COMICS INC.		2	323	1941	1986	FORMERLY WORLD'S BEST COMICS
WORLD'S FINEST GIVEAWAYS	DC COMICS INC.		1944	1949	1944	1949	
WORLD'S GREATEST SONGS	ATLAS		I	I	1954	1954	

INDEX OF COMIC TITLES AND THEIR PUBLISHERS

COMIC TITLE	PUBLISHER	Vol No.	Srt No.	End No.	Str. Year	End Year	COMMENTS
WORLD'S GREATEST STORIES	JUBILEE COMICS		1	2	1949	1949	
WORLD'S WORST COMICS AWARDS	KITCHEN SINK		1	2	1991	1991	
WORLDS BEYOND	FAWCETT PUBLICATIONS		1	1	1951	1951	
WORLDS FINEST	DC COMICS INC.		1	1	1993	1993	
WORLDS FINEST	TITAN BOOKS		1	1	1993	1993	
WORLDS OF FEAR	FAWCETT PUBLICATIONS	2		10	1952	1953	FORMERLY WORLDS BEYOND
WORLDS OF H.P. LOVECRAFT	CALIBER PRESS		1	2	1993	1993	
WORLDS UNKNOWN	MARVEL ENTERTAINMENT GROUP		1	8	1973	1974	
WOTALIFE COMICS	FOX FEATURES SYNDICATE	1	3	12	1946	1947	FORMERLY NUTTY LIFE
WOTALIFE COMICS	GREEN PUBLISHING COMPANY	3	1	5	1957	1957	
WOTALIFE COMICS	NORLEN MAGAZINES	2	1	1	1959	1959	
WOW COMICS	FAWCETT PUBLICATIONS	2	1	69	1940	1948	FORMERLY WESTERN HERO
WOW COMICS	HENLE PUBLISHING CO.	1	1	4	1936	1936	
WOW COMICS	L. MILLER PUBLISHING COMPANY (UK)			55	1943	1950	FAWCETT REPRINTS
WRATH	MALIBU COMICS ENTERTAINMENT INC.		1	4	1994	NOW	
WRECKERS, THE	HOTSPUR PUBLISHING CO.		2	2	1948	1948	
WULF THE BARBARIAN	ATLAS		1	4	1975	1975	
WYATT EARP	ATLAS		1	34	1955	1973	
WYATT EARP	L. MILLER PUBLISHING COMPANY (UK)		1	44	1957	1960	CHARLTON REPRINTS
WYATT EARP (HUGH O'BRIAN FAMOUS MARSHAL)	DELL PUBLISHING COMPANY	4		13	1958	1961	
WYATT EARP FRONTIER MARSHAL	CHARLTON COMICS	12		72	1956	1967	FORMERLY RANGE BUSTERS

COMIC TITLE	PUBLISHER	Vol No.	Srt No.	End No.	Str. Year	End Year	COMMENTS
X	DARK HORSE COMICS		1	4	1994	NOW	
X-CON'S, THE UNFUNNY	PARODY PRESS		1	1	1993	1993	
X-FACTOR	MARVEL ENTERTAINMENT GROUP		1	99	1986	NOW	
X-FACTOR ANNUAL	MARVEL ENTERTAINMENT GROUP		1	8	1986	NOW	
X-FACTOR: PRISONER OF LOVE	MARVEL ENTERTAINMENT GROUP		1	1	1990	1990	
X-FARCE	ECLIPSE		1	1	1992	1992	
X-FARCE VERSUS X-CONS: X-TINCTION	PARODY PRESS		1	1.5	1993	1993	
X-FORCE	MARVEL ENTERTAINMENT GROUP		1	31	1991	NOW	
X-FORCE & SPIDER-MAN: SABOTAGE	MARVEL ENTERTAINMENT GROUP		1	1	1993	1993	
X-FORCE ANNUAL	MARVEL ENTERTAINMENT GROUP		1	2	1992	NOW	
X-MEN	MARVEL ENTERTAINMENT GROUP		1	29	1991	NOW	SOMETIMES CALLED 2ND SERIES, WITH "X-MEN, THE UNCANNY" BEING THE 1ST.
X-MEN 2099	MARVEL ENTERTAINMENT GROUP		1	6	1993	NOW	
X-MEN ADVENTURES	MARVEL ENTERTAINMENT GROUP		1	1	1993	1993	
X-MEN ADVENTURES	MARVEL ENTERTAINMENT GROUP	1	1	15	1992	1993	
X-MEN ADVENTURES	MARVEL ENTERTAINMENT GROUP	2	1	5	1994	NOW	
X-MEN AND ALPHA FLIGHT	MARVEL ENTERTAINMENT GROUP		1	2	1985	1985	
X-MEN AND TEEN TITANS - SEE MARVEL AND DC PRESENT							
X-MEN AND THE MICRONAUTS, THE	MARVEL ENTERTAINMENT GROUP		1	4	1984	1984	
X-MEN ANNIVERSARY MAGAZINE	MARVEL ENTERTAINMENT GROUP				1993	1993	
X-MEN ANNUAL	MARVEL ENTERTAINMENT GROUP		1	2	1992	NOW	
X-MEN AT THE TEXAS STATE FAIR, THE UNCANNY	MARVEL ENTERTAINMENT GROUP		1	1	1983	1983	
X-MEN CHRONICLES	FANTACO		1	1	1982	1982	
X-MEN CLASSICS	MARVEL ENTERTAINMENT GROUP		1	3	1983	1984	
X-MEN CLASSICS	MARVEL ENTERTAINMENT GROUP		1	92	1986	NOW	
X-MEN COLLECTOR'S EDITION ANNUAL	GRAND DREAMS	1981	1982	1981	1982		
X-MEN GIANT SIZE	MARVEL ENTERTAINMENT GROUP		1	2	1975	1975	
X-MEN MASTERWORKS	MARVEL ENTERTAINMENT GROUP		1	1	1993	1993	
X-MEN POCKET BOOK	MARVEL ENTERTAINMENT GROUP		14	28	1981	1982	
X-MEN POSTER MAGAZINE	MARVEL ENTERTAINMENT GROUP		2	2	1992	NOW	
X-MEN SPECIAL EDITION	MARVEL ENTERTAINMENT GROUP		1	1	1983	1983	
X-MEN SURVIVAL GUIDE TO THE MANSION	MARVEL ENTERTAINMENT GROUP		1	1	1993	1993	
X-MEN UNLIMITED	MARVEL ENTERTAINMENT GROUP		1	3	1993	NOW	
X-MEN VERSUS THE AVENGERS	MARVEL ENTERTAINMENT GROUP		1	1	1993	1993	
X-MEN VERSUS THE AVENGERS, THE	MARVEL ENTERTAINMENT GROUP		1	4	1987	1987	
X-MEN VS DRACULA	MARVEL ENTERTAINMENT GROUP		1	1	1993	1993	
X-MEN WINTER SPECIAL	MARVEL ENTERTAINMENT GROUP	1981	1982	1981	1982		
X-MEN, THE OFFICIAL MARVEL INDEX TO	MARVEL ENTERTAINMENT GROUP		1	7	1987	1988	
X-MEN, THE UNCANNY	MARVEL ENTERTAINMENT GROUP		1	310	1963	NOW	
X-MEN, THE UNCANNY ANNUAL	MARVEL ENTERTAINMENT GROUP		1	17	1970	NOW	
X-MEN, THE UNCANNY EASTER SPECIAL	MARVEL ENTERTAINMENT GROUP		1	1	1992	1992	
X-MEN, THE UNCANNY: DAYS OF FUTURE PAST	MARVEL ENTERTAINMENT GROUP		1	1	1989	1989	
X-MEN/GHOST RIDER	MARVEL ENTERTAINMENT GROUP		1	1	1993	1993	
X-MEN: ALL-NEW ALL-DIFFERENT MASTERWORKS	MARVEL ENTERTAINMENT GROUP		1	1	1993	NOW	
X-MEN: ANIMATION SPECIAL	MARVEL ENTERTAINMENT GROUP		1	1	1991	1991	
X-MEN: DARK PHOENIX SAGA	MARVEL ENTERTAINMENT GROUP		1	1	1993	1993	
X-MEN: DAYS OF FUTURE PRESENT	MARVEL ENTERTAINMENT GROUP		1	1	1992	1992	
X-MEN: FROM THE ASHES	MARVEL ENTERTAINMENT GROUP		1	1	1991	1991	
X-MEN: SPOTLIGHT ON STARJAMMERS	MARVEL ENTERTAINMENT GROUP		1	2	1990	1990	
X-MEN: THE ASGARDIAN WARS	MARVEL ENTERTAINMENT GROUP		1	1	1989	1989	
X-MEN: THE EARLY YEARS	MARVEL ENTERTAINMENT GROUP		1	2	1994	NOW	
X-MEN: THE MANY LOVES OF SCOTT AND JEAN	MARVEL ENTERTAINMENT GROUP				1994	1994	
X-MEN: X-TINCTION AGENDA	MARVEL ENTERTAINMENT GROUP		1	1	1992	1992	
X-O DATABASE	VALIANT / VOYAGER COMMUNICATIONS		1	1	1993	1993	
X-O MANOWAR	VALIANT / VOYAGER COMMUNICATIONS		1	1	1993	1993	
X-O MANOWAR	VALIANT / VOYAGER COMMUNICATIONS		1	26	1992	NOW	ISSUE 0 WAS PUBLISHED IN JULY 1993
X-TERMINATORS	MARVEL ENTERTAINMENT GROUP		1	4	1988	1989	
XANADU: HELIA'S TALE	ECLIPSE		1	1	1988	1988	
XANTH GRAPHIC NOVEL	FATHER TREE PRESS (WARP GRAPHICS)		1	2	1990	1990	
XENON	ECLIPSE		1	23	1987	1989	
XENOTECH	MIRAGE STUDIOS		1	1	1993	NOW	
XENOZOIC TALES	KITCHEN SINK		1	12	1987	NOW	
XENOZOIC TALES: CADILLACS AND DINOSAURS	KITCHEN SINK				1994	1994	5TH PRINTING
XIMOS: VIOLENT PAST	TRIUMPHANT COMICS		1	2	1994	1994	

COMIC TITLE	PUBLISHER	Vol No.	Srt No.	End No.	Str. Year	End Year	COMMENTS
XMAS COMIC	CRAYBURN NEIL		1	1	1947	1947	
XMAS COMICS ANNUAL	FAWCETT PUBLICATIONS	1	1	7	1941	1947	
XMAS COMICS ANNUAL	FAWCETT PUBLICATIONS	2	4	7	1949	1952	196-PAGES
XMAS FUNNIES	KINNEY SHOES CO.		1	1	???	???	1933 REPRINT
XOMBI	DC COMICS INC.		1	1	1993	NOW	
XPRESSO SPECIAL, THE	FLEETWAY		1	2	1991	1991	
XYR	ECLIPSE				1988	1988	PART OF ECLIPSE GRAPHIC NOVEL SERIES

Y

COMIC TITLE	PUBLISHER	Vol No.	Srt No.	End No.	Str. Year	End Year	COMMENTS
YAKKY DOODLE AND CHOPPER	GOLD KEY		1	1	1962	1962	
YAKUZA	ETERNITY		1	5	1987	1988	
YALTA TO KOREA	M. PHILIP CORP. (REPUBLICAN NATIONAL COMMITTEE)		1	1	1952	1952	
YANG	CHARLTON COMICS		1	17	1973	1986	
YANKEE COMICS	HARRY A CHESLER		1	4	1941	1942	
YANKS IN BATTLE	I.W. ENTERPRISES		1	1	1963	1963	REPRINTS YANKS IN BATTLE #3
YANKS IN BATTLE	QUALITY (FLEETWAY)		1	4	1956	1956	
YARDBIRDS, THE	ZIFF-DAVIS PUBLISHING COMPANY		1	1	1952	1952	
YARN MAN	KITCHEN SINK		1	1	1989	1989	
YARNS OF YELLOWSTONE	WORLD COLOR PRESS		1	1	1972	1972	
YATTERING AND JACK	ECLIPSE		1	1	1992	1992	
YAWN	PARODY PRESS		1	1	1993	1993	
YELLOW CLAW	ATLAS		1	4	1956	1957	
YELLOWJACKET COMICS	CHARLTON COMICS		1	10	1944	1946	
YOGI BEAR	CHARLTON COMICS		1	35	1970	1976	
YOGI BEAR	GOLD KEY	10	42	1962	1970		FORMERLY PART OF FOUR COLOUR SERIES BY DELL
YOGI BEAR	HARVEY PUBLICATIONS		1	6	1992	NOW	
YOGI BEAR	MARVEL ENTERTAINMENT GROUP		1	9	1977	1979	
YOGI BEAR BIG BOOK	HARVEY PUBLICATIONS		1	2	1992	NOW	
YOGI BEAR GIANT SIZE	HARVEY PUBLICATIONS		1	2	1992	NOW	
YOGI BERRA	FAWCETT PUBLICATIONS		1	1	1951	1951	
YOSEMITE SAM	GOLD KEY		1	71	1970	1984	
YOSEMITE SAM	WHITMAN	72	81	1982	1984		
YOUNG ALL STARS	DC COMICS INC.		1	31	1987	1989	
YOUNG ALL STARS ANNUAL	DC COMICS INC.		1	1	1988	1988	
YOUNG ALLIES COMICS	TIMELY COMICS		1	20	1941	1946	
YOUNG BRIDES	ARNOLD BOOK CO.		1	10	1952	1952	PRIZE REPRINTS
YOUNG BRIDES	FEATURE PUBLICATIONS	1	1	6	1952	1953	
YOUNG BRIDES	FEATURE PUBLICATIONS	2	1	12	1953	1954	
YOUNG BRIDES	FEATURE PUBLICATIONS	3	1	5	1954	1955	
YOUNG BRIDES	FEATURE PUBLICATIONS	4	2	6	1955	1956	
YOUNG BRIDES	STRATO		1	38	1953	1955	PRIZE REPRINTS
YOUNG DEATH	FLEETWAY		1	3	1993	1993	
YOUNG DEATH	MANDARIN (2000 AD BOOKS)		1	1	1992	1992	
YOUNG DEATH	MANDARIN (2000 AD BOOKS)		1	1	1993	1993	
YOUNG DOCTORS, THE	CHARLTON COMICS		1	6	1963	1963	
YOUNG DRACULA	CALIBER PRESS		1	3	1993	1993	
YOUNG EAGLE	ARNOLD BOOK CO.		1	5	1951	1952	FAWCETT REPRINTS
YOUNG EAGLE	FAWCETT PUBLICATIONS		1	10	1950	1957	
YOUNG EAGLE	L. MILLER PUBLISHING COMPANY (UK)	50	58	1955	1956		
YOUNG HEARTS	MARVEL ENTERTAINMENT GROUP		1	2	1949	1950	
YOUNG HEARTS IN LOVE	SUPER COMICS	17	18	1964	1964		
YOUNG HERO	AC COMICS		1	1	1993	NOW	
YOUNG HEROES	AMERICAN COMIC GROUP	35	37	1955	1955		FORMERLY FORBIDDEN WORLDS
YOUNG INDIANA JONES CHRONICLES, THE	DARK HORSE COMICS		1	12	1992	1993	
YOUNG INDIANA JONES CHRONICLES, THE	WALT DISNEY		1	3	1992	1992	
YOUNG KING COLE	PREMIUM GROUP	1	1	6	1945	1946	
YOUNG KING COLE	PREMIUM GROUP	2	1	7	1946	1947	
YOUNG KING COLE	PREMIUM GROUP	3	1	12	1947	1948	
YOUNG KING COLE DETECTIVE TALES	L. MILLER PUBLISHING COMPANY (UK)		1	2	1959	1959	STAR REPRINTS
YOUNG LAWYERS, THE	DELL PUBLISHING COMPANY		1	2	1971	1971	
YOUNG LIFE	QUALITY (FLEETWAY)		1	2	1945	1945	
YOUNG LOVE	ARNOLD BOOK CO.		1	10	1952	1952	PRIZE REPRINTS
YOUNG LOVE	DC COMICS INC.	39	126	1963	1977		
YOUNG LOVE	PRIZE PUBLICATIONS	1	1	5	1949	1950	
YOUNG LOVE	PRIZE PUBLICATIONS	2	1	12	1950	1951	
YOUNG LOVE	PRIZE PUBLICATIONS	3	1	12	1951	1952	
YOUNG LOVE	PRIZE PUBLICATIONS	4	1	12	1952	1953	
YOUNG LOVE	PRIZE PUBLICATIONS	5	1	12	1953	1954	
YOUNG LOVE	PRIZE PUBLICATIONS	6	1	12	1954	1955	
YOUNG LOVE	PRIZE PUBLICATIONS	7	1	7	1955	1956	
YOUNG LOVE	STRATO		1	34	1953	1955	PRIZE REPRINTS
YOUNG LOVER ROMANCES	TOBY PRESS PUBLICATIONS	4	5	1952	1952		FORMERLY GREAT LOVER
YOUNG LOVERS	CHARLTON COMICS	16	18	1956	1957		
YOUNG LOVERS	FAME PRESS		1	136	1960	1966	
YOUNG LOVERS' LIBRARY	C.A. PEARSON	1	2	1958	???		
YOUNG MARRIAGE	FAWCETT PUBLICATIONS		1	1	1950	1950	
YOUNG MARVELMAN	L. MILLER PUBLISHING COMPANY (UK)	25	370	1954	1963		
YOUNG MARVELMAN ANNUAL	L. MILLER PUBLISHING COMPANY (UK)	1954	1961	1954	1961		
YOUNG MASTER	NEW COMICS GROUP		1	9	1987	1989	
YOUNG MASTER, WORLD OF THE	NEW COMICS GROUP		1	1	1989	1989	
YOUNG MEN	MARVEL ENTERTAINMENT GROUP	4	28	1950	1954		FORMERLY COWBOY ROMANCES
YOUNG REBELS, THE	DELL PUBLISHING COMPANY		1	1	1971	1971	
YOUNG ROMANCE	STRATO		1	33	1955	1955	PRIZE REPRINTS
YOUNG ROMANCE COMICS	DC COMICS INC.	125	208	1963	1975		FORMERLY PUBLISHED BY PRIZE
YOUNG ROMANCE COMICS	PRIZE PUBLICATIONS	1	1	124	1947	1963	CONTINUES TO BE PUBLISHED BY DC, WITH ISSUE NO.125 (AUG/SEPT 1963)

COMIC TITLE	PUBLISHER	Vol No.	Srt No.	End No.	Str. Year	End Year	COMMENTS
YOUNG YUPPIES FROM HELL	MARVEL ENTERTAINMENT GROUP		1	1	1992	1992	
YOUNG ZEN INTERGALACTIC NINJA	ENTITY EXPRESS BOOKS		1	1	1993	1994	
YOUNGBLOOD	IMAGE COMICS		1	4	1992	1993	ISSUE 0 WAS PUBLISHED IN JULY 1993
YOUNGBLOOD YEARBOOK	IMAGE COMICS		1	1	1993	NOW	
YOUNGBLOOD: BATTLEZONE	IMAGE COMICS		1	1	1993	1993	
YOUNGBLOOD: STRIKEFILE	IMAGE COMICS		1	4	1993	1993	
YOUNGSPUD	PERSONALITY COMICS		1	1	1993	1993	
YOUR FAVOURITE FUNNIES	VALENTINE & SON		1	1	1948	1948	
YOUR TRIP TO NEWSPAPERLAND	HARVEY PUBLICATIONS		1	1	1955	1955	
YOUR UNITED STATES	LLOYD JACQUET STUDIOS		1	1	1946	1946	
YOUTHFUL HEARTS	YOUTHFUL MAGAZINES		3	3	1952	1952	
YOUTHFUL LOVE	PIX PARADE	1	1	18	1949	1953	
YOUTHFUL ROMANCES	RIBAGE PUBLISHING CO.	2	5	8	1953	1954	
YUMMY FUR	VORTEX		1	29	1987	NOW	
YUPPIES FROM HELL	MARVEL ENTERTAINMENT GROUP		1	4	1992	NOW	

Z

COMIC TITLE	PUBLISHER	Vol No.	Srt No.	End No.	Str. Year	End Year	COMMENTS
Z-CARS ANNUAL	WORLD DISTRIBUTORS LTD		1963	1966	1963	1966	
ZAGO, JUNGLE PRINCE	FOX FEATURES SYNDICATE		1	4	1948	1949	
ZAMINDAR	INNOVATION		1	4	1993	1993	
ZANE GREY'S STORIES OF THE WEST	DELL PUBLISHING COMPANY		27	39	1955	1958	
ZANE GREY'S STORIES OF THE WEST	WORLD DISTRIBUTORS LTD		1	31	1953	1955	REPRINTS DELL MATERIAL
ZANY	CANDOR PUBLISHING CO.		1	4	1958	1959	
ZAP COMIX	LAST GASP		1	12	1990	1990	
ZATANNA	DC COMICS INC.		1	4	1993	1993	
ZATANNA SPECIAL	DC COMICS INC.		1	1	1987	1987	
ZAZA THE MYSTIC	L. MILLER PUBLISHING COMPANY (UK)		1	2	1956	1956	REPRINTS CHARLTON MATERIAL
ZAZA, THE MYSTIC	CHARLTON COMICS		10	11	1956	1956	FORMERLY CHARLIE CHAN
ZEGRA, JUNGLE EMPRESS	FOX FEATURES SYNDICATE		2	5	1948	1949	FORMERLY TEGRA
ZELL, SWORDANCER	THOUGHT AND IMAGES		1	1	1986	1986	
ZEN INTERGALACTIC NINJA	ARCHIE PUBLICATIONS		0	0	1992	1992	
ZEN INTERGALACTIC NINJA	ZEN COMICS	1	1	4	1992	1993	
ZEN INTERGALACTIC NINJA	ZEN COMICS	2	1	5	1992	1993	
ZEN INTERGALACTIC NINJA	ZEN COMICS	3	1	3	1993	1993	
ZEN INTERGALACTIC NINJA ALL-NEW COLOR SPECIAL	ENTITY EXPRESS BOOKS		1	0	1993	1993	
ZEN INTERGALACTIC NINJA CHRISTMAS SPECIAL	ZEN COMICS		1	1	1993	1993	
ZEN INTERGALACTIC NINJA: GOLD MILESTONE	ENTITY EXPRESS BOOKS				1994	NOW	
ZEN INTERGALACTIC NINJA: STARQUEST	ENTITY EXPRESS BOOKS				1994	NOW	
ZEN INTERGALACTIC NINJA: THE HUNTED	ENTITY EXPRESS BOOKS		1	1	1993	1994	
ZEN: INTERGALACTIC NINJA	ENTITY EXPRESS BOOKS		0	1	1994	NOW	
ZENITH	TITAN BOOKS		1	5	1988	1990	
ZENITH: PHASE ONE	FLEETWAY		1	3	1993	1993	
ZENITH: PHASE TWO	FLEETWAY		1	2	1993	1993	
ZERO PATROL	CONTINUITY COMICS		1	10	1984	NOW	
ZERO TOLERANCE	FIRST		1	4	1990	1991	
ZETRAMAN	ANTARTIC PRESS		1	3	1991	1992	
ZIGGY PIG-SILLY SEAL COMICS	I.W. ENTERPRISES		1	8	1958	1958	REPRINTS TIMELY SERIES
ZIGGY PIG-SILLY SEAL COMICS	TIMELY COMICS		1	6	1944	1946	
ZILLION	ETERNITY		1	3	1993	NOW	
ZIP COMIC	ENSIGN/W. FORSHAW		1	1	1946	1946	
ZIP COMIC	P.M. PRODUCTIONS		1	1	1948	1948	
ZIP COMICS	H. BUNCH ASSOCIATES		1	1	1973	1973	
ZIP COMICS	M.L.J. MAGAZINES		1	47	1940	1947	
ZIP JET	ST JOHN PUBLISHING		1	2	1953	1953	
ZIP-BANG COMIC	ENSIGN/W. FORSHAW		1	2	1946	1947	
ZIPPER-RIPPER COMICS	CARTOON ART		1	1	1946	1946	
ZIPPY COMICS	CARTOON ART		1	1	1947	1947	
ZIPPY THE CHIMP	PINES		50	51	1957	1957	
ZODY, THE MOD ROB	GOLD KEY		1	1	1970	1970	
ZOMBIE	L. MILLER PUBLISHING COMPANY (UK)		1	8	60'S	60'S	REPRINTS EC MATERIAL
ZOMBIE WAR	FANTACO		1	2	1992	1992	
ZOMBIE WAR: EARTH DESTROYED	FANTACO		1	2	1993	1993	
ZONE	DARK HORSE COMICS		1	1	1990	1990	
ZONE CONTINUUM	CALIBER PRESS		1	1	1994	NOW	
ZONE CONTINUUM	CALIBER PRESS		1	2	1992	1992	
ZONES	LONDON EDITIONS MAGAZINES		1	9	1990	1991	
ZOO ANIMALS	STAR PUBLICATIONS		8	8	1954	1954	
ZOO FUNNIES	CHARLTON COMICS	1	1	15	1945	1947	#1 NUMBERED 101. 1ST CHARLTON COMIC
ZOO FUNNIES	CHARLTON COMICS	2	1	13	1953	1955	
ZOO FUNNIES	CHARLTON COMICS	3	1	1	1984	1984	
ZOOM	CHILDREN'S PRESS		1	1	1947	1947	
ZOOM COMICS	CARLTON PUBLISHING CO.		1	1	1945	1945	
ZOONIVERSE	ECLIPSE		1	6	1986	1987	
ZOOT	FOX FEATURES SYNDICATE		1	16	1946	1948	
ZOOT!	FANTAGRAPHICS		1	5	1993	NOW	
ZORRO	DELL PUBLISHING COMPANY		8	15	1959	1961	
ZORRO	GOLD KEY		1	9	1966	1968	
ZORRO	L. MILLER PUBLISHING COMPANY (UK)		50	87	1952	1955	REPRINTS FRENCH MATERIAL
ZORRO	MARVEL ENTERTAINMENT GROUP		1	12	1990	1991	
ZORRO	TOPPS		0	1	1993	NOW	
ZORRO	WORLD DISTRIBUTORS LTD		1	6	1955	1957	REPRINTS DELL MATERIAL
ZOT IN DIMENSION 10 AND A HALF	NOT AVAILABLE COMICS		1	1	1986	1986	
ZOT!	ECLIPSE		1	2	1989	1990	
ZOT!	ECLIPSE		1	36	1984	NOW	
ZOT!	ECLIPSE		2	2	1990	1990	
ZWANNA SON OF ZULU	ANIA PUBLISHING		1	1	1993	NOW	